PHILIPPINES
HANDBOOK

PHILIPPINES
HANDBOOK

THIRD EDITION

CARL PARKES

MOON
TRAVEL
HANDBOOKS

PHILIPPINES HANDBOOK
THIRD EDITION

Published by
Moon Publications, Inc.
5855 Beaudry St.
Emeryville, California 94608, USA

Printed by
Colorcraft

Please send all comments,
corrections, additions,
amendments, and critiques to:

**PHILIPPINES HANDBOOK
MOON TRAVEL HANDBOOKS
5855 BEAUDRY ST.
EMERYVILLE, CA 94608, USA
e-mail: travel@moon.com
www.moon.com**

Printing History
1st edition—1991
3rd edition—September 1999

5 4 3 2 1 0

ISBN: 1-56691-168-0
Library of Congress Cataloging-In-Publication-Data has been applied for.

Map Editor: Gina Wilson Birtcil
Copy Editor: Deana Corbitt Shields
Production & Design: Karen McKinley, David Hurst
Cartography: Bob Race, Brian Bardwell, and Mike Morgenfeld
Index: Valerie Sellers Blanton

Front cover photo: Richard Maschmeyer/courtesy of Superstock, Inc.

All photos by Carl Parkes unless otherwise noted.
All illustrations by Bob Race unless otherwise noted.

Distributed in the United States and Canada by Publishers Group West

Printed in China

*Dedicated to the warm and wonderful people
of the Philippines
and all my friends in San Francisco.*

CONTENTS

INTRODUCTION . . . . **1~53**
The Land 2
   Geology and Geography; Climate; Flora and Fauna
History 11
   Early History; Spanish Era; Revolution Against Spanish Rule; The
   American Era; World War II; Independence and the Quest for Democracy;
   The Saint, The General, The Actor
Government 29
Economy 32
The People 34
   The Chinese; The Muslims; The Hilltribes; The Negritos; Mestizos
Religion 41
   Catholicism; Other Christian Churches; Islam; Other Faiths
Language 45
Filipino Society 47
   The Family; National Characteristics; Filipino Terms
Conduct and Customs 50

SPECIAL TOPICS

Environmental Issues . . . . *8-9*   *Responsible Tourism* *33*
The Philippine Eagle . . . . *10*   *Faith Healing* *42-43*
The Saga of Magellan . . . . *16*   *Language* *46*
Last Days of the Americans *28*

ON THE ROAD . . . . **54~108**
Recreation 54
   Mountain Climbing and Trekking; Water Sports; Scuba Diving
Arts and Entertainment 61
   Music; Dance
Festivals 62
   January; February; March; Holy Week-March/April; May; June; July;
   August; September; October; November; December
Shopping 71
Accommodations and Food 72
   Where to Stay; Food
Getting There 76
   By Air; From North America; From Europe; From Australia and New
   Zealand; From Asia
Getting Around 86
   By Air; By Sea; By Land
Information and Services 91
   Visas; Information; Money; Measurements and Communications

Health and Safety 98
   Before You Go; Insurance; Common Health Problems; Safety
What to Take 106

SPECIAL TOPICS

Sightseeing Highlights *56-57*
Cockfighting-The National
   Pastime *58-59*
Movies Filmed in the Philippines *61*
Save the Wildlife *70*

Popular Filipino Dishes *74*
Jeepneys~The Heart and
   Soul of Filipino Transportation *89*
Travel Advisories *104-105*

MANILA . . . . 109~147
Attractions 112
   Ermita and Malate; Rizal Park; North of Rizal Park; Intramuros; North of
   the River; Pasay City; Makati; Sights around Manila; South of Manila;
   Corregidor
Accommodations 134
   Ermita and Malate
Food 136
Entertainment 138
Getting There and Getting Around 140
Getting Away 141
   By Air; By Bus; By Train; By Ship

SPECIAL TOPIC

Chinese Cemetery~Only for the Wealthy *125*

SOUTH OF MANILA . . . . 148~177
Cavite Province 148
   Cavite Town; Ternate; Tagaytay City-Views over Taal Lake; Taal Lake and
   Volcano; Talisay-Lakeside at Taal
Batangas Province 154
   Batulao; Nasugbu; Fortune Island; Matabungkay; Calatagan; Lemery; San
   Luis and Ligpo Island; Taal City; Anilao; Batangas City; Tanauan and
   Talaga; Lipa City
Laguna Province 161
   Pakil; Paete; Lumban; Pagsanjan; Vicinity of Pagsanjan; Majayjay; Liliw
   (Lilio); Nagcarlan; San Pablo City; The Seven Lakes of San Pablo;
   Alaminos; Hidden Valley Springs Resort; Villa Escudero; Los Banos;
   Mount Makiling; Calamba
Rizal Province 174
   Cainta; Antipolo; Angono; Cardona; Morong; Tanay; Jalajala

SPECIAL TOPICS

Sacred Mount Banahaw *171*
Worshipping Rizal *173*

LUZON-CENTRAL PLAIN............................**178~209**
  History; Transportation
Bulacan Province..179
  Novaliches; Montalban; The Fertility Festival of Obando; Bocaue; Malolos;
  East of the Expressway; Plaridel; Pulilan; Biak-Na-Bato National Park
Pampanga Province...182
  San Fernando; Apalit; Angeles City; Mount Arayat National Park
Zambales Province..192
  San Marcelino Lake; Olongapo; Barrio Barretto and Subic Bay; Zambales
  Coastline
Bataan Peninsula...198
  Down the Peninsula; Balanga to Mariveles; Mariveles; Mount Samat
Tarlac Province...201
  Capas-The Death March Camp; Tarlac
Pangasinan Province and Hundred Islands.....................202
  Urdaneta; Hundred Islands National Park; Alaminos; Lucap; Bolinao;
  Lingayen; Dagupan City; Vicinity of Dagupan
Nueva Ecija Province...208
  Southern Nueva Ecija; Cabanatuan City; San Jose City

SPECIAL TOPICS

The Fury of Pinatubo ....*190-191*   *Some of the Hundred Islands* *204*
The Bataan Death March.............*200*

LUZON-THE CORDILLERA ....**210~248**
Benguet Province...213
  Baguio City; The Halsema Mountain Highway; The Road to Kabayan;
  Kabayan; Mt. Pulog
Mountain Province..225
  Baguio to Bontoc; Bontoc; Maligcong Rice Terraces; Barlig; Sagada;
  Hiking around Sagada
Ifugao Province..236
  Banaue; Attractions near Banaue; Batad; Vicinity of Batad; Mayoyao;
  South of Banaue
Kalinga-Apayao Province......................................244
  The Chico River Valley; Lubuagan and Vicinity; The Route to Abra; Tabuk;
  Apayao

SPECIAL TOPICS

The People of Benguet ....*217*   *The People of Ifugao*..................*238*
The Benguet Mummies...............*223*   *Dam that Chico River*..................*245*
The Bontoc Igorots ....*226-227*   *The People of Kalinga-Apayao*..*246-247*
End of the Rice Terraces?............*237*

LUZON-NORTHWEST COAST ....**249~274**
La Union Province..252
  Agoo; Bauang; San Fernando; North of San Fernando
Ilocos Sur Province..255
  Tagudin to Cervantes; North to Vigan City; Vigan; Magsingal; San Juan

Abra Province 262
Coastal Highway to Bangued; Bangued; From Bangued
Ilocos Norte Province 264
Ilocos Sur to Laoag City; Laoag City; Vicinity of Laoag; North of Laoag City
Batanes Islands 270
Batan Island; Sabtang; Itbayat

SPECIAL TOPICS . . . .

The Tingguians . . . .*263*   *The Ivatans of Batanes* *271*

NORTHEAST LUZON . . . . **275~286**

Nueva Vizcaya Province 277
The Highway North
Quirino Province 278
Aurora Province 279
Isabela Province 280
North Through the Valley; Palanan
Cagayan Province 282
Tuguegarao; Vicinity of Tuguegarao; North to Aparri; Aparri; To Cape
Engaño; To Claveria; The Babuyan Islands

SPECIAL TOPIC . . . .

The Capture of Aguinaldo *281*

SOUTHERN LUZON . . . . **287~314**

Quezon Province 288
Laguna to Lucena City; Lucena City; The South Coast; Quezon National
Park; The Pacific Coast
Camarines Norte Province 293
Quezon to Daet; Daet and Vicinity
Camarines Sur Province 295
From Camarines Norte to Naga City; Naga City; Takal Beach; East of
Naga City; Iriga City
Albay Province 301
Legaspi City; The Coast: Legaspi through Tiwi; Tabaco; Tiwi; South of
Legaspi; Rapu-Rapu and Batan Islands
Catanduanes Island 309
Virac; Around the Island
Sorsogon Province 312
Sorsogon Town; Bacon; Gubat and Rizal Beach; Lake Bulusan; Irosin;
Bulan; Matnog

SPECIAL TOPICS . . . .

The Penafrancia Festival . . . . *297*   *Mayon-The World's Most*
Legends of Lake Buhi . . . . *300*   *Perfect Volcano* *305*

THE VISAYAS . . . . **315~436**
Routes around the Visayas

Bohol 319
History; Transportation; Scuba Diving; Tagbilaran City; Panglao Island;
Balicasag Island; Baclayon; Pamilacan Island; The Chocolate Hills;
Around Bohol; Jao Island

Boracay 329
Activities; Accommodations; Restaurants; Entertainment; Services and
Information; Transportation

Cebu 335
History; Scuba Diving; Transportation; Cebu City; Mandaue City; Mactan
Island; Diving around Mactan; North of Cebu City; Bantayan Island;
Malapascua Island; South of Cebu City; The Southeast Coast; The
Camotes Islands; The West Coast; The Southwest Coast; Moalboal;
South of Moalboal

Leyte 358
History; Transportation; Tacloban; Vicinity of Tacloban; Tacloban to
Ormoc; Ormoc City; Vicinity of Ormoc; South of Tacloban; Maasin and
Vicinity

Marinduque 370
History; Transportation; Around the Island

Masbate 373
History; Transportation; Masbate Town; Around the Island; Ticao Island;
Burias Island

Mindoro 376
History; Scuba Diving; Transportation; Puerto Galera; Calapan; South of
Calapan; Roxas City; South of Roxas City; San Jose; Islands Near San
Jose; San Jose to Abra de Ilog; Apo Reef; Mamburao; Beyond Mamburao;
The Lubang Islands

Negros 389
History; Transportation; Bacolod City; Vicinity of Bacolod; Bacolod to San
Carlos; San Carlos City; South of Bacolod; Dumaguete City; Vicinity of
Dumaguete; North of Dumaguete; Kanlaon (Canlaon) City; Mount
Kanlaon; South of Dumaguete

Panay 404
History; Transportation; Iloilo City; Vicinity of Iloilo City; West of Iloilo City;
North of Iloilo City; Between North and East; East of Iloilo City; Guimaras;
Islands off Northeast Panay; San Jose de Buenavista; Inland from San
Jose; The Southwest Tip; North of San Jose de Buenavista; Semirara
Islands; Roxas City; Vicinity of Roxas City; The Coast of Capiz; Interior
Capiz; Kalibo; South of Kalibo; Northwest of Kalibo

Romblon and Tablas 424
History; Transportation; Romblon; Tablas; Sibuyan; Other Islands

Samar 428
Transportation; Northern Samar; Eastern Samar; Western Samar

Siquijor 434
History; Transportation; Around the Island

SPECIAL TOPICS

Visayan Highlights 316-317
Paradise Lost? 331
The Guitar Factories of Mactan 350
The Poisonous Snakes of Isla
  de Gato 353
Copper Mines and Environmental
  Destruction 356
The Moriones Festival 372

The Mangyans of Mindoro 378-379
Searching for Tamaraw 386
The Iron Dinosaurs of Negros 395
The Ilonggos of Panay 406
Ati-Atihan Festival of Kalibo 422
Marble? In the Philippines? 426
Witchcraft on Siquijor 434

MINDANAO .... 437~497

Introduction 437
History; The People; Transportation

Northeastern Mindanao 446
Surigao City; Siargao Island; Butuan City; Balingoan

Camiguin Island 451
Mambajao; Inland from Mambajao; The Coast West of Mambajao; White
Island; Southeast of Mambajao; Hibok-Hibok Volcano; Day Trip around
the Island

North-Central Mindanao 456
Cagayan De Oro; Vicinity of Cagayan De Oro; Malaybalay; Iligan City;
Vicinity of Iligan; Marawi City; Lake Lanao

Northwestern Mindanao 465
Ozamiz City; Oroquieta City; Dipolog City; Dapitan City

Southern Mindanao 467
Davao City; Samal Island; Mount Apo

Southwestern Mindanao 474
General Santos City; General Santos City to Lake Sebu; Lake Sebu;
Cotabato City

Western Mindanao 481
Zamboanga; Vicinity of Zamboanga; Pagadian City

The Sulu Archipelago 487
Basilan Island; Jolo Island; Tawi-Tawi

SPECIAL TOPICS

The Kaamulan Festival
  of Malaybalay 459
The Peoples of Marawi and
  Lake Lanao 463
The People of the Davao
  Provinces 468-469

The People of Southwestern
  Mindanao 476-477
The T'boli of Lake Sebu 478-479
The People of the Sulu
  Archipelago 488-490

PALAWAN .... 498~522

Introduction 498
History; Scuba Diving; Transportation

Central Palawan 504
Puerto Princesa; Honda Bay; Iwahig Prison and Penal Farm

Southern Palawan 508
  Aborlan and Tigman; Island Bay; Quezon; Tabon Caves; South of
  Quezon; Balabac Island; Islands of the Sulu Sea
North-Central Palawan 512
  Baheli and Nagtabon Beach; Sabang; The Underground River; Port
  Barton; San Vicente; San Rafael; Roxas; Taytay; Liminancong
Northern Palawan 518
  El Nido
The Calamian Group 520
  Busuanga Island; Linapacan Island; Coron Island; Culion Island; The Cuyo
  Islands; Dumaran Island

SPECIAL TOPIC
The People of Palawan *500*

SUGGESTED READING .... **523~525**

INDEX .... **527~539**

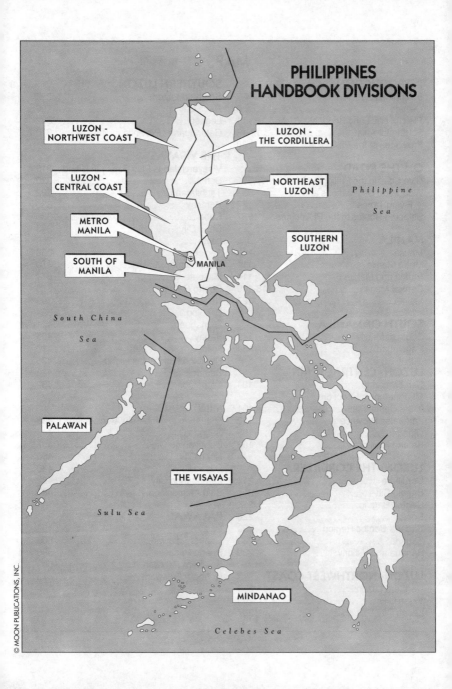

PHILIPPINES HANDBOOK DIVISIONS

LUZON - NORTHWEST COAST

LUZON - THE CORDILLERA

LUZON - CENTRAL COAST

NORTHEAST LUZON

METRO MANILA

SOUTH OF MANILA

SOUTHERN LUZON

MANILA

Philippine Sea

South China Sea

PALAWAN

THE VISAYAS

Sulu Sea

MINDANAO

Celebes Sea

© MOON PUBLICATIONS, INC.

MAPS

INTRODUCTION
Philippines 4-5
Climate 6
Pleistocene Land Bridges 11
Southeast Asia 12-13
Provinces of the Philippines 30

ON THE ROAD
Dive Sites in the Philippine Islands 55
Worldwide Destinations and
   Flying Times 77
Shipping Routes in the Philippines 87

MANILA
Manila 110
Metro Manila 111
Ermita and Malate 114
Central Manila 118-119
Makati 127

SOUTH OF MANILA
South of Manila 149
Pagsanjan 164

LUZON~CENTRAL PLAIN
San Fernando 184
Mt. Pinatubo's Effect on
   the Cental Plain 191
Zambales Province 193
Olongapo 195
Bataan Province 199

LUZON~THE CORDILLERA
Cordillera 211
Baguio City 214
Central Baguio 215
Bontoc 228
Sagada-Bontoc Region 230
Sagada 233
Banaue and Vicinity 239

LUZON~NORTHWEST COAST
Northern Luzon 250
Vigan City 259
Laoag City 267

SOUTHERN LUZON
Southern Luzon 288
Naga City 296
Legaspi 302
Catanduanes Province 310

THE VISAYAS
Visayan Islands Plus Camigan Island . . 318
Bohol 320
Tagbilaran City 322
Boracay 330
Cebu 336
Cebu City 343
Leyte 359
Tacloban 363
Marinduque 370
Masbate 374
Puerto Galera 380
Negros 390
Bacolod 394
Dumaguete 401
Panay 405
Iloilo 410
Romblon and Tablas Islands 425
Samar Island 429
Catbalogan 432

MINDANAO
Mindanao and the Sulu Archipelago . . . 438
Surigao City 447
Cagayan de Oro 457
Iligan City 460
Davao City 470
Zamboanga City 482
Sulu Archipelago 487

PALAWAN
Palawan 499
Central Palawan 505
Puerto Princesa 506
Southern Palawan 509
Northern Palawan 519

MAP SYMBOLS

Symbol	Meaning	Symbol	Meaning	Symbol	Meaning
━━━━	PARKWAY (EXPRESSWAY)	·········	TRAM / CABLE CAR	⚑	WATERFALL
────	MAIN ROAD	──■──	RAILROAD	⌐L	GATE
────	MINOR ROAD	── ──	FERRY	⬡	WATER
─ ─ ─	UNPAVED ROAD	■	SIGHT		
─··─··─	FOOT PATH	●	HOTEL / ACCOMMODATION	✈	AIRPORT
═══	BRIDGE	▲	MOUNTAIN	◉	CITY
┼──┼	TUNNEL			○	TOWN / VILLAGE
────	INTERNATIONAL BORDER	I.	ISLAND	★	POINT OF INTEREST
─··─··─	PROVINCE BORDER	N.P.	NATIONAL PARK		
···──···	OTHER BORDER				

ABBREVIATIONS

d-double

EDSA-East de los Santos
Avenue

GSC-General Santos City

MNLF-Moro National Liberation
Front

NPA-New Peoples Army

PADI-Professional Association
of Diving Instructors

PAL-Philippine Airlines

PLDT-Philippine Long Distance
Telephone Company

PNB-Philippine National Bank

PNR-Philippine National
Railway

pp-per person

s-single

WG&A-Williams, Gothong, and
Aboitz Lines (Superferry)

REQUEST FOR COMMENTS

Travel books are collaborations between authors and readers. While every effort has been made to keep this book accurate and timely, travel conditions change quickly in the Philippines and elsewhere in Southeast Asia. Please let us know about price hikes, new guesthouses, closed restaurants, transportation tips, and anything else that may prove useful to the next traveler. Your information will be checked in the field and then carefully interwoven into the next edition of this book.

A Reader Survey questionnaire in the back of this book will help us find out who you are and your impressions about this guide. Please send your Reader Survey and travel notes to:

Carl Parkes
Philippines Handbook
Moon Travel Handbooks
5855 Beaudry St.
Emeryville, California 94608, USAUSA
e-mail: cparkes@moon.com

ACKNOWLEDGMENTS

Writers write alone, but survive only with generous doses of help and encouragement. Top marks at Moon Publications go to copy editor Deana Corbitt Shields and art director Dave Hurst, all of whom labored well beyond the call of duty. The superb maps are credited to Bob Race, Brian Bardwell, and Mike Morgenfeld. Gratitude is also given to founder Bill Dalton, publisher Bill Newlin, and other Moonbeams who helped realize the book.

Contributions from Readers

I would also like to thank the many readers who wrote to me about their travel adventures:

America: Burt Blackburn (Austin), Susan Brown (New York), Ray Varn Buhler (Wilseyville), Thomas Burns (Ocean Park), Alan Cartledge (AZ), Robert Chiang (San Antonio), Frank Cotter (Mounds View), Pat Crowley (San Diego), Stephen Downes (Marion), Rhys Evans (Grover City), Kathleen Flynn (Los Angeles), Leigh Fox (Guam), Steve Gilman (Norcross), Leslie Hamersly (Index), Stefan Hammond (San Francisco), Dr. Martin Hane (Chicago), Celeste Holmes (Oakland), Harry Hunter (Olympia), Dana Kizlaitis (Oak Lawn), Kate Klein, Irene Malone (San Pablo), Angelo Mercure (San Diego), Dan Moody (Studio City), Jan Morris (Louisville), Michael Newman (Los Angeles), Martin Offenberger (La Habre), James Patterson (Santa Cruz), Mark Peters (Muscatine), John Pierkarski (Huntington Beach), John Pike (Redondo Beach), Rachel Rinaldo (Wilton), William Ring (San Diego), Yancey Rousek (Los Angeles), Priscilla Rowe (San Francisco), Claudia Siegel (Hackensack), Howard Spector (Dallas), Jefferson Swycaffer (San Diego), Michael Triff (Atlanta), Bruce Willis (Glendale), Chantal Yang (Cambridge).

Asia: Philip Drury (China), Bruce Swenson (Japan).

Australia: Gary Deering (True East), Greg Duffy (Burleigh Waters), Martin Ellison (Darlinghurst), Cas Liber (Elizabeth Bay), Kevin Mulrain (Sydney), Morgana Oliver (Wodonga), Catherine Spence (Mona Vale), Keith Stephans (Noose).

Austria: Herber Walland (Graz).

Belgium: Guy Crouna (Tieuen).

Canada: Bob Cadloff (Montreal), Bruce Fraser (Calgary), Melvin Green (Toronto), Pat and Tom Jorginson (Webb), Bruce Moore (Ganges), Lenny

Morgan (Richmond), Scott Pegg (Vancouver), Laura White (Toronto), Tanya Whiteside (Ottawa).

England: Alan Cummings, Jon Bonnin (Sanderfest), Tim Eyre (Nottingham), Linda Grace (Oxford), Mark Gregory (Leeds), David Host (Bulkington), John Maidment (Southbourne), Anthony Maude (Canterbury), C. Miller (London), Peter Moorhouse (Seathwaite), Tim Prentice (Kent), Nick Slade (Flackwell Health), Lois Tadd (Chesham), David Veale (Fishbourne).

Germany: Christiane Moll (Berlin), Ralf Neugebauer (Lubeck), Wolfgang and Mosgit (Brey).

Netherlands: Vander Bel-Kampschuur (Eindhoven), Maarten Camps (Ryswyh), Claantie van der Grinten (Ryswyh), E. Cornelissen (Castricum), Rick Dubbeldam (Sas Van Gert), Jan Valkenbury (Heerlen), Michel van Dam (Den Haag), Erik van Velzen (Zoetermeer), Helle Nielson (Silkeborg), Herbert Walland.

New Zealand: Barry Wells (Wellington).

Spain: Sevvy (Madrid).

Switzerland: Nicolas Chiriotti (Grand Lancy), Rolf Huber (Uitikon-Waldegg), Katharina Hug (Enalinpes).

A Personal Note

Finally, I would like to extend my deepest gratitude and sincerest love to all my friends in San Francisco and throughout the world:

Terra and radio king Nick Marnell, Eric "Phuket Sunset Cruises" & Sue, Roy "Dropzone" Maloney, Norton, Dean (Wolfman) Bowden, Dave, Hai, John Kaeuper, Jimbo & Kelly, Amazing Amos, Linda & Geek, Ellen & artsy Dave, Vince "Dude," Lee & Pam, Ab-Fab Bruce, beam-me-up Scotty & Juiceteen, lovely Rita & Eric, Dara & Rog, Stefan, Joel, Peachy, Deke, Jerome (sans Harley), Ed Samarin, Karen (we'll always have Tahoe), Larsen (you still owe me $40), Zimmie (where's da book?), Stephanie, Hugh, Guru Das, Hazel & Rick, Richard (North Beach '75), Dianne (Aspen '76), Nam Chu (R.I.P.), Doctor Bob & German Ralph, Joe & divine Dyan, Homeless Jim, June, Marty, Ray Jason, Bodewes (Amsterdam), Flynn (Down Under), David Stanley, Joe Biz (R.I.P.), Bob Nilsen (Chico), Marael, Nicole (Paris), Escola Nova de Samba, Lulu and the Atomics, sister Claud, fab Stan, cool Kev & Heather, Mom & Dad.

Puerto Galera

INTRODUCTION

Diego Gutieres, first Pilot who went to the Phillippinas, reports of many strange things: If there bee any Paradise upon earth, it is in that countrey, and addeth, that sitting under a tree, you shal have such sweet smells, with such great content and pleasure, that you shall remember nothing, neither wife, nor children, nor have any kinde of appetite to eate nor drinke.

—*Henry Hawks (1572),* Navigations of English Nations

When I wish to be misinformed about a country, I ask a man who has lived there thirty years.

—*Lord Palmerston,* The Imperial Idea

Three hundred years in the convent and fifty years in Hollywood.

—*Anonymous*

The Philippines is the undiscovered paradise of Southeast Asia. Blessed with over 7,000 sun-drenched islands, this tropical wonderland has just about everything needed for a superb vacation: exquisite white-sand beaches fringed with gently swaying palm trees, unparalleled scuba diving, volcanoes for mountaineers, classic baroque cathedrals, vast expanses of verdant ricefields, outstanding nightlife, and the most enthusiastic festivals in Asia. The Philippines is also an outstanding travel bargain since it offers some of the region's lowest prices for accommodation, food, and transportation—chiefly due to the currency devaluation of 1997.

With all this, you might expect the country to be crowded with visitors and overrun with tour groups. Surprisingly, most of the country remains virtually untouched by mass tourism, giving adventurous travelers the opportunity to easily get off the beaten track.

But what really separates the Philippines from the rest of Asia is the people, whose warmth and enthusiasm are legendary throughout the East. Seldom will you meet such hospitable people—so ready to smile, joke, laugh, and make friends with Western visitors. Perhaps because of their long association with Spain, Filipinos are emotional and passionate about life in a way that seems more Latin than Asian. And because of their American ties, communication is easy since most Filipinos speak English, whether American slang or some homegrown pidgin. They're also a talented race of people. Music fans will be happy to learn that Filipinos, for reasons endlessly debated, are unquestionably Asia's most gifted singers, musicians, dancers, and entertainers.

If you believe that the most important travel experience is to make friends and learn about people, rather than just tour temples and museums, then the Philippines is your country.

THE LAND

The Philippines, 300,439 square km, is roughly the size of Italy, but its fragmented layout gives it an extremely long total coastline of about 18,000 km. It's the world's second-largest archipelago after Indonesia, but it's more compact. The islands stretch nearly 1,850 km in a narrow north-south configuration with the western spurs of Palawan and Sulu extending the archipelago's maximum width to 1,100 km.

The Philippines determines its boundaries by a series of straight lines connecting the external points of its outermost islands, beyond which extends the standard 12-nautical-mile territorial limit. Its marine area is thus over five times larger than its land area; its neighbors are Taiwan (105 km north), Sabah (48 km southwest), and Vietnam (965 km west). Sixty km off its southeast shores lies the 10,057-meter-deep Philippine Trench (Mindanao Deep), the world's deepest spot.

PHILIPPINE MAIN ISLANDS

ISLAND	AREA (SQ. KM)
Luzon	104,688
Mindanao	94,630
Samar	13,429
Negros	13,328
Palawan	11,785
Panay	11,515
Mindoro	10,245
Leyte	9,003
Cebu	5,088
Bohol	4,117
Masbate	4,048

GEOLOGY AND GEOGRAPHY

Formation

The Philippine archipelago began taking shape about 50 million years ago, formed by volcanic eruptions and the buckling of the earth's crust where two tectonic plates collided. It's believed that a southward movement of the Asian landmass formed the shallow China Sea depression and crumpled the edge of the continental shelf. The elongated mountain ranges of the larger Philippine islands are the crests of the folds produced in the submerged ledge. Volcanic activity thrust up cones and spewed lava across the landscape, which has been further modified by coral deposits and the ongoing process of erosion.

During the Ice Age, the sea level was about 50 meters lower than it is today. Exposed land bridges connected the Asian mainland and Borneo to the archipelago, one running through Palawan and Mindoro to Luzon, another through the Sulu Islands to Mindanao. Others linked Celebes with Mindanao, and possibly Taiwan with northern Luzon. When the great ice sheets melted, the land bridges were inundated, leaving the islands exposed in more or less their present configuration.

Topography

The Philippines consists of three main island groupings: Luzon, which includes the islands of Mindoro and Palawan; the Visayan Islands; and Mindanao and the Sulu group. The larger islands have rugged, mountainous interiors, mostly ranges running north to south. The highest summit is Mt. Apo (2,954 meters) on Mindanao.

CARL PARKES

Boracay

Peaks emerge above hills and valleys, which, in turn, rise from the narrow coastal plains, broader interior plains, and major valleys. In some places, especially on the Pacific shores, the mountains drop steeply to the sea. Many islands have extensive coral reefs offshore. The Philippines lies on the volatile Pacific "Ring of Fire," and most of the highest mountains are volcanic in origin. Strong earthquakes have occurred periodically. Various stages of vulcanism are evident, from old, worn-down volcanic stocks to extinct, dormant, and active peaks.

Many of the 7,107 islands are little more than rocks, reefs, or sandbanks. Some 4,600 are named and 1,000 are inhabited. Only 46 are larger than 100 square km, and these represent 98% of the total land area. Just two islands, Luzon and Mindanao, constitute two-thirds of the country, while 11 make up over 92%.

Administratively, the Philippines is divided into 73 provinces plus Metro Manila, which contains Quezon City, the designated capital, and Manila, the de facto capital. Most large cities and seven out of 10 municipalities lie on coastal plains and are no more than 120 km from the sea.

Volcanic Eruptions

The Philippines has had its share of ecological disasters in recent years, but major eruptions at Pinatubo and Mayon brought the Philippines worldwide attention.

On 12 June 1991, after 600 years of lying dormant, Pinatubo, north of Manila, gained notoriety as the most devastating volcanic explosion of this century, killing more than 1,000 people and raining volcanic ash down on the fleeing populace. Flooding ensued and great rivers of volcanic lahar devastated the Central Plain, the Philippine breadbasket. Pinatubo is currently dormant, and the nearby towns of Olongapo and Angeles City have miraculously been revitalized as trade centers.

In February 1993, Mayon in southern Luzon erupted, spewing volcanic debris five km into the air and destroying fertile farmland around Legaspi, killing over 30 people including a group of volcanologists.

CLIMATE

The Philippines is hot and humid year-round with seasons determined by the prevailing winds. Southwest monsoons from June to October bring heavy rains, while modest northeast monsoons from November to February insure a warm and relatively dry season with sporadic rains. The easterly North Pacific tradewinds from March to May guarantee hot, almost unbearable dry weather.

Climate varies by region, but heat and rain can be escaped by moving to higher elevations such as Baguio, the 1,524-meter-high summer

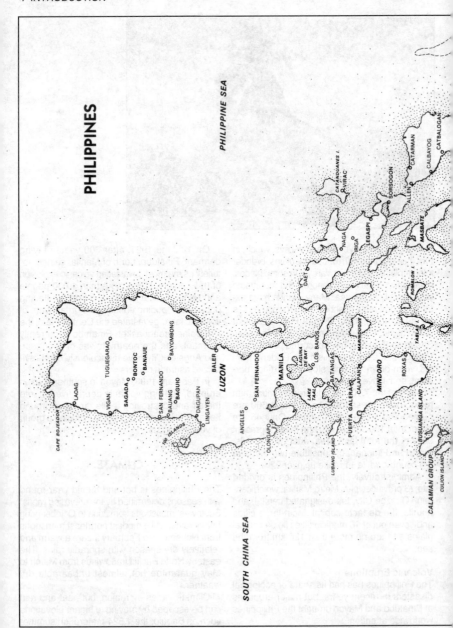

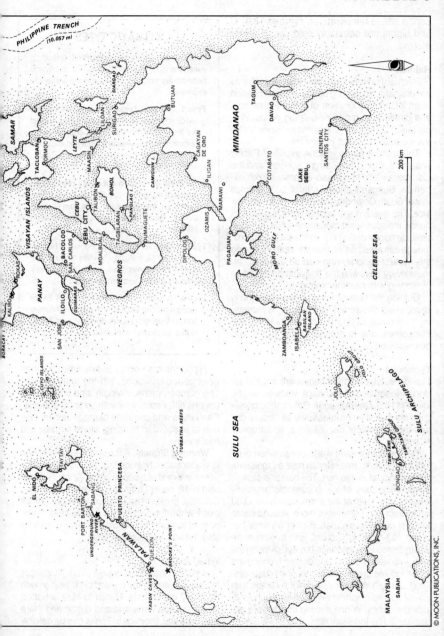

© MOON PUBLICATIONS, INC.

capital where temperatures average 18.3° C and nights are decidedly cold during winter months.

Rainfall

Rainfall is relatively high, but regional contrasts are dramatic, depending on the size and position of an island, the location of mountain ranges, and direction of moisture-bearing winds. Precipitation is highest where these winds strike the mountains, lowest in their lee.

The wettest areas are the exposed Pacific coast (Catanduanes, Samar, Surigao) and the Cordillera while Mindanao embraces both extremes. Surigao's annual rainfall is 38.5 times that of South Cotabato, the country's driest province. The western and central parts receive rain during the southwest monsoons while the eastern side floods during the northeast monsoons, though this area has no true dry season. During the wettest periods, rain can be expected almost every day, with the heaviest precipitation coinciding with passing typhoons.

Outside the rainy season, it tends to come in short, sharp showers. Flash flooding is increasingly common during the rainy season in the Philippines, due to erosion of the topsoil and deforestation.

Typhoons

Typhoons, locally called *bagyo*, are tropical cyclones designated after surface winds exceed 64 knots (118.5 km) per hour. Below this, conditions are classified progressively as tropical disturbances, tropical depressions, and tropical storms.

Typhoons form over warm ocean when clusters of thunderstorms release heat as moisture, which condenses into rain. The center is calm—a cloudless zone of low barometric pressure known as the "eye" of the storm, usually about 30 km in diameter, sometimes more. Around it stirs forceful cyclonic circulation over an area between 100-1,500 km across, with maximum intensity immediately outside the eye. Among the early indications of an approaching typhoon are increased sea swells and pronounced gustiness. Wind strength increases toward the center, with violent squalls reaching over 300 km per hour in extreme cases. Winds circling the eye are accompanied by torrential rain.

CLIMATIC TYPES

Four climatic types are recognized, based on variations in rainfall distribution. These climatic patterns are only guidelines and are subject to anomalies:

Type 1: Two pronounced seasons are May-Oct. (wet) and Nov.-April (dry). July and August are the wettest months, and April and May the hottest. Predominates in Manila and the western Philippines—Mindoro, Palawan, Panay, and Negros.

Type 2: No dry season but a very pronounced period of maximum rainfall May-January. Occurs down the southeast coast from Quezon through Bicol, Samar, and Leyte to eastern Mindanao.

Type 3: Seasons not very pronounced, but relatively dry Nov.-April. Prevails through the central Philippines, from the Cayagan Valley across Cebu to northern Mindanao.

Type 4: More uniformly distributed rainfall. Exists along a broken tract stretching from Batanes and northeastern Luzon, down through Bohol, to include most of central Mindanao.

Typhoons may occur at any time, but their peak period coincides with the rainy season. The number, paths, strength, and timing of typhoons differ each year with up to 30 annually. Casualties and property damage are usually due to associated flooding, storm surges, and tidal waves.

Warning Signals: A three-stage warning system announces typhoons. Signal No. 1 means a possible threat of typhoon within 72 hours, No. 2 within 48 hours, and No. 3 within 36 hours. Schools, businesses, and government offices close when the Signal No. 3 is hoisted. If you hear of a storm approaching, travel quickly or stay put and wait out the storm.

When to Go

The Philippines is best enjoyed from November to February during the dry and clear season with relatively cool nights. March to May is hotter: the landscape turns arid and dusty, and there may be water shortages. Travel can be delight-

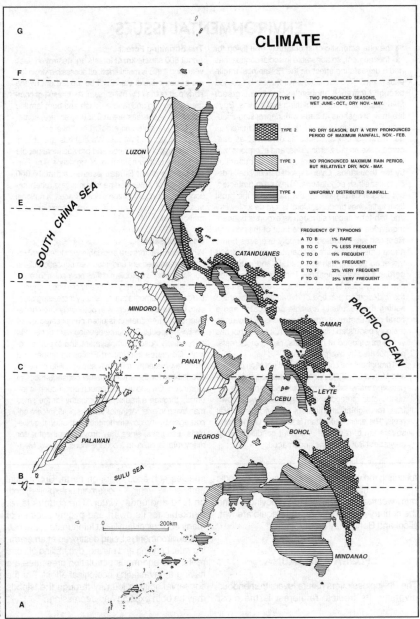

CLIMATE

TYPE 1 — TWO PRONOUNCED SEASONS, WET JUNE - OCT., DRY NOV. - MAY.

TYPE 2 — NO DRY SEASON, BUT A VERY PRONOUNCED PERIOD OF MAXIMUM RAINFALL, NOV. - FEB.

TYPE 3 — NO PRONOUNCED MAXIMUM RAIN PERIOD, BUT RELATIVELY DRY, NOV. - MAY.

TYPE 4 — UNIFORMLY DISTRIBUTED RAINFALL.

FREQUENCY OF TYPHOONS

A TO B	1% RARE
B TO C	7% LESS FREQUENT
C TO D	19% FREQUENT
D TO E	16% FREQUENT
E TO F	32% VERY FREQUENT
F TO G	25% VERY FREQUENT

LUZON

CATANDUANES

SOUTH CHINA SEA

PACIFIC OCEAN

MINDORO

SAMAR

PANAY

LEYTE

CEBU

PALAWAN

NEGROS

BOHOL

SULU SEA

0   200km

MINDANAO

ENVIRONMENTAL ISSUES

The characteristic of spontaneity and living for the moment, so admirable in social context, has had a devastating effect on the Philippines' fragile ecosystems. Too often, the environment is ravaged through ignorance, thoughtlessness, and greed. Many hunters shoot at anything that moves. Boys fire their slingshots at birds with depressing accuracy. Farmers tend to regard wild animals merely as destroyers of crops. Creatures perceived as dangerous, like snakes, crocodiles, and scorpions, are killed on sight. Foreign collectors take butterflies by the thousands. Over-exploitation of shells depletes shellfish populations. Turtles are protected, but people can't pass up the meat and the profit from turtle-shell products. Coral is torn up for jewelry and fish-tank decor; although its export is banned, thousands of kilos are shipped out of the country. Reef fish are gathered to supply overseas home aquariums. Rivers are deliberately poisoned and the dead floating fish scooped up and eaten, regardless of contamination. The one-handed men commonly seen in coastal villages are evidence of the widespread practice of dynamite and cyanide fishing that results in a single good catch and a coral reef destroyed for generations. Palawan is the only populated island in the Philippines that has yet to be stripped of its forests, raped of its reefs, and polluted by overpopulation.

Throughout the country, rampant pollution of rivers and Manila Bay by factories goes uncontrolled. Logging and inadvisable farming practices intensify annual cycles of flood and drought. Silt swept down from the highlands smothers estuaries and coral reefs. The entire ecosystem is affected. Of the 4,000 square km of reef, half is in poor condition, while only about 30% remains undamaged.

The Shrinking Forest

About 800 square km of forests are destroyed each year, and if this is maintained, all accessible virgin forest of commercial value will be logged out by the early part of the new millennium. As a result of commercial logging and random slash-and-burn farming *(kaingin)*, vast areas are afflicted by severe, sometimes irreversible soil erosion and overgrowth by coarse grass and weeds. Watersheds are of critical ecological importance and provide local people with many of their natural resource needs. The Forest Management Bureau estimates that 10,000 square km of watershed need immediate rehabilitation. Even northern Luzon's rice terraces, a national treasure, are threatened. As always, money for reclamation is in short supply.

Complex Issue

While many factors are avoidable with intelligent resource management and improved education of the public, one critical problem defies easy solution: overpopulation. The country is already crowded, and the burgeoning numbers put constantly increasing pressure on the environment with potentially dire consequences. The situation is often complicated by its positive aspects. Resource development generates desperately needed employment and export earnings. Countries that import Philippine timber and other raw materials generally assume little or no responsibility for the environmental consequences of extraction. On a local level, much destruction is tolerated through a traditional sympathy for the small man trying to exist. Activities such as shellcraft are encouraged by the government, even though they deplete resources, since they provide an income for many rural families on a cottage-industry basis. Mon-

---

ful during the wet season since rains are sporadic and the countryside is brilliantly green. Prolonged rainy weather can be avoided by moving around the country—when Manila and Baguio are wet, Bicol and Bohol may be dry.

FLORA AND FAUNA

The Philippines offers nature lovers tremendous diversity. Its tropical rainforest is the most species-rich ecosystem on earth. Substantial parts of the archipelago remain unexplored, both on land and under water. The country is remarkable for its dwarf and pygmy species of many ecological families. Unfortunately, the natural environment is being destroyed at an alarming rate. Logging and mining, dynamiting of coral reefs, and enormous population pressures are having a devastating ecological effect. For the conservationist, a journey through the islands may be both exciting and depressing.

key populations have been reduced as monkeys are caught and sent to the U.S. for the purpose of producing the Salk polio vaccine.

Habitat protection efforts for creatures such as crocodiles often conflict with government priorities for rural economic development. Modern technology developed in temperate countries is applied to the Philippines's tropical conditions with little understanding of long-term consequences. Thus, high-yield crop varieties, chemical fertilizers, and more efficient fishing methods are promoted for the immediate gains in productivity they offer, while the environment's ability to support new input and accelerated rates of extraction over an extended period is largely unknown.

Conservation Efforts

The Philippines realizes that in order to preserve its precious natural heritage, a process of education, combined with the necessary legislation and enforcement of regulations, has to be initiated. Legislation dealing with environmental issues has been introduced. The government has established national parks, recreation areas, and wildlife sanctuaries throughout the country. Conservation programs exist for the Philippine eagle, eastern sarus crane, *tamaraw*, Philippine crocodile, dugong, marine turtles, and some rare deer species. There is a growing consciousness among people of the need to conserve forests and marinelife. A law banning log export has been passed (although logging export continues). In 1992, Palawan was designated a national treasure, because its forests and sealife had not yet been destroyed. A total ban on logging is currently being enforced for all of Palawan.

Various nongovernmental groups such as the World Ecologists have adopted greening and conservation programs. One organization, called Fruitopia, has even gone to the extent of appealing to citizens not to discard the seeds from the fruit they have eaten, but to send them to the organization, which is setting up a fruit seed bank. Fruitopia's goal is to plant fruit trees along public highways, at city parks and plazas, school grounds, and to make fruit available to the public for the picking. There is a reassuring response among the citizens for these programs.

To educate and train Filipino fishermen to conserve marine resources and to solve the illegal fishing practices, the Bantay Dagat ("Guardian of the Seas") program has been launched by the government, with all-out support from the private sector. However, strong resistance is still encountered among businessmen engaged in the export of seaweed, who stand to lose substantial revenue from the export of this commodity, often gathered at the expense of coral reefs. Controversy is also raging on muro-ami fishing and cyanide fishing. Other nongovernmental organizations are also doing their part in protecting the environment. These include the Haribon Foundation, which does excellent work on a slim budget to preserve the country's natural environment, resources, wildlife, and ethnic culture. Haribon organizes field trips to Tubbataha Reefs in the Sulu Sea to observe seabird colonies and enjoy world-class diving, to Mindanao to study Philippine eagles, to Batanes to witness the seasonal hawk migration, and to Kanleon volcano on Negros. Day trips to areas outside Manila occur almost monthly. The foundation has also established a sanctuary at Candaba Swamp in Pampanga for ducks and marsh birds, including many winter migrants from Northeast Asia. For information on meetings or field trips, contact the Haribon Foundation for the Conservation of Natural Resources, Suite 306 Sunrise Condominium, 226 Ortigas Ave., Greenhills, Metro Manila, tel. (02) 721-1693.

Flora

Fertile volcanic soil, abundant rain and sunshine, and the wide range of habitats and elevations give rise to an incredible variety of plantlife in every category, from mosses and lichens (including 1,000 species of fern) to giant trees (about 3,000 species). Plants are mainly of the type found in Indonesia and Malaysia, although Australian (e.g., eucalyptus) and Sino-Himalayan (e.g., rhododendron) types are also found. About 60% of the 10,000 plant species grow only in the archipelago. The Philippines has 54 species of bamboo, a fast-growing woody grass, throughout the islands. It's used for an incredible variety of purposes: houses, bridges, fences, furniture, fish traps, wall-matting, baskets, hats, flutes, and much more.

At sea level, bays and estuaries are fringed by dense mangrove. Nipa palms, commonly used in the construction of native huts, also thrive in brackish water. Coconut palms are generally found below 30 meters, while at 300-1,000 meters dense tropical rainforest contains vines, ferns, orchids, and huge trees with buttressed trunks. The dipterocarp hardwoods, known col-lectively as Philippine mahogany, predominate here. The *molave* group of hardwoods is also important. Above 1,000 meters the trees change from tropical hardwoods to temperate species like the Benguet pine of northern Luzon. Above 5,800 meters trees become progressively stunt-ed and finally give way to scrub and grassy up-land on the highest slopes.

A visit to Manila's markets will introduce you to the wealth of tropical fruits available: bananas, pineapples, papaya, mangoes, durian, and *lan-zones,* to name a few. Flowering plants and trees include hibiscus, frangipani *(kalachuchi),* bougainvillea, and over 1,000 species of orchid. Celebrated varieties include the *waling-waling* of Mindanao, whose blooms measure up to 12.5 cm across and last six weeks, and those of the Cattleya genus.

The national flower is *sampaguita,* a fragrant, star-shaped white blossom commonly sold in leis and given as a gesture of welcome. The na-tional tree, *narra,* has bright yellow flowers, and its durable wood is much favored for furniture and flooring. Filipinos use many different herbs for medicinal and culinary purposes.

Fauna

Although the fossilized remains of elephants have been found, the Philippines today has few large mammals. The absence of major predators means an abundance of small animals.

Philippine fauna forms a distinct subdivision within the Malayan region and provides evidence of the land bridges that once linked the archi-pelago with mainland Asia via Borneo. Palawan is especially rich in wildlife, which is closely re-lated to Borneo's. The wildlife of mainland Min-danao and Sulu also show affinity with Borneo, while northern Luzon has species in common with Taiwan and the Asian mainland.

The burgeoning human population, howev-er, encroaches relentlessly on natural habitats.

THE PHILIPPINE EAGLE

Formerly called the "monkey-eating" eagle, the Philippine eagle is the world's second-largest (after the South American harpy eagle), with a wingspan of over two meters. Although protected by law, it is tragically endangered due to mindless trophy-hunting and the encroach-ment of loggers and *kaingin* farmers on its habi-tat. Only about 50 of these magnificent birds, also known as the haribon, remain today.

Its main bastion is Mindanao; a few also exist in Leyte, Samar, and the Sierra Madre of north-eastern Luzon. It favors dense, primary forest on remote mountainsides where it hunts its prin-cipal food, flying lemurs and flying squirrels. Monkeys, being much harder to catch, make up only a small fraction of its diet. Eagles may live for over 40 years, but their reproduction rate is slow. They produce a single, white, fist-sized egg every two years. Nesting begins late Sep-tember through early December. The nest, which can be three meters wide, is built up to 50 meters above the ground on ferns or orchids growing in the canopies of giant hardwoods found on the lower slopes, usually in ravines.

A captive breeding program near Davao City in Mindanao aims to obtain all the country's cap-tive eagles, breed selected pairs, then free as many as possible. Nesting sites of wild pairs are also carefully monitored. Visitors to the Bara-catan camp on the slopes of Mt. Apo south of Davao City can observe at close range these great brown-and-white birds, with their piercing eyes and majestic crests of long, lanceolated feathers. At present, the Baracatan camp has successfully bred two eagles using the most up-to-date methods of captive breeding.

Deforestation and hunting have caused many species of animals that once ranged broadly to be confined to specific areas. Wild pigs are an exception: they have adapted well to the chang-ing environment.

HISTORY

The Philippines's recorded history began with Magellan's arrival in 1521. Events prior to that are largely a matter of conjecture. Old Chinese and Arab chronicles mention these islands, but textbooks and reference sources often give vastly divergent accounts and dates relating to the pre-Hispanic era. Modern archaeological research provides fragmentary data, but an accurate picture may never emerge.

The long Spanish colonization affected Filipino culture and society profoundly. During the last 100 years, history has accelerated through a dramatic sequence of events: revolution, war against the U.S., American colonization, Japanese occupation, WW II devastation, independence, the imposition of martial law, the rise of "People Power" to overthrow the Marcos regime, and three presidents (Aquino, Ramos, and Estrada).

Filipinos have emerged from their colonial episodes to engage in a confused, sometimes futile search for a unified national identity. They are caught between cultural influences from their indigenous origins, Spanish colonialization, Americanization, dialects, education, and status.

EARLY HISTORY

Elephant, rhinoceros, and stegodon migrated across the ancient land bridges from the Asian mainland via Borneo. Their fossilized bones have been unearthed on Luzon, Panay, and

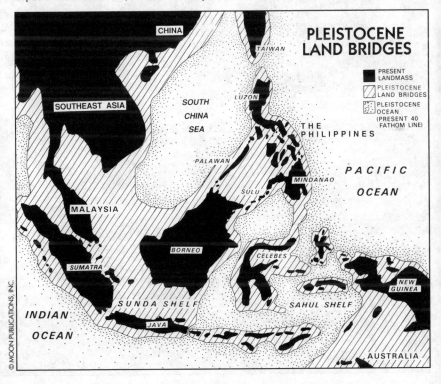

PLEISTOCENE LAND BRIDGES

- ■ PRESENT LANDMASS
- ◨ PLEISTOCENE LAND BRIDGES
- ▩ PLEISTOCENE OCEAN (PRESENT 40 FATHOM LINE)

CHINA · TAIWAN · SOUTHEAST ASIA · SOUTH CHINA SEA · LUZON · THE PHILIPPINES · PALAWAN · MINDANAO · PACIFIC OCEAN · SULU · MALAYSIA · BORNEO · CELEBES · NEW GUINEA · SUMATRA · SUNDA SHELF · SAHUL SHELF · JAVA · INDIAN OCEAN · AUSTRALIA

© MOON PUBLICATIONS, INC.

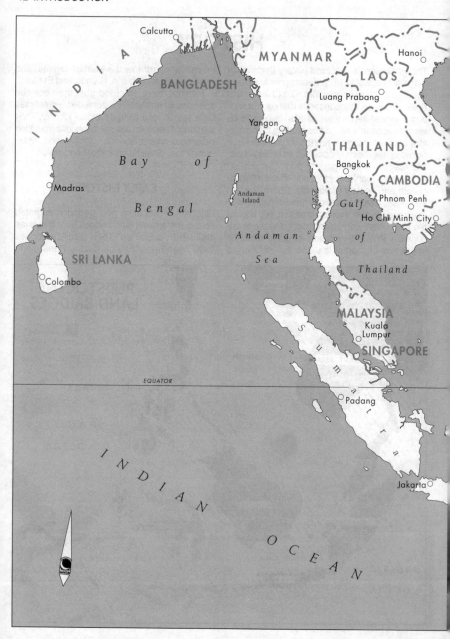

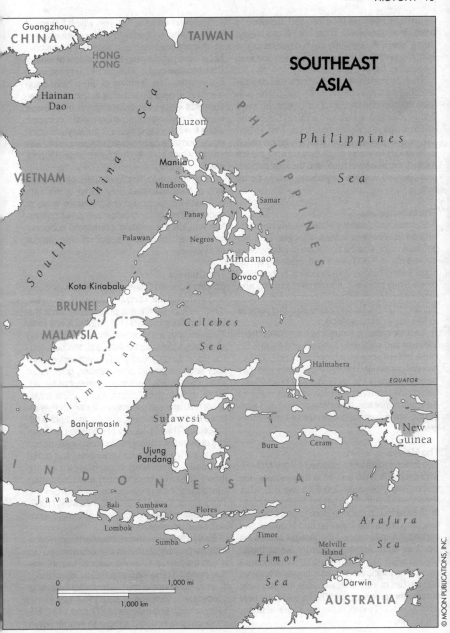

© MOON PUBLICATIONS, INC.

elsewhere. Primitive men followed. Believed to have been Australoid, then later proto-Malay, these Stone Age pygmy cave dwellers came from the jungles of Malaya and Borneo and lived by hunting, fishing, and gathering.

Their descendants, the Negritos, still dwell in remote forests on several islands. Stone artifacts estimated to be over 30,000 years old have been excavated at Palawan's Tabon Caves and in the Cagayan Valley of Luzon. The Tabon Caves also yielded a human skull carbon-dated to 22,000 B.C. About 10,000 years ago, the ice melted, the sea level rose, and the land bridges disappeared. Future migrations had to be by sea.

The Indonesians
Anthropologists debate whether early migrants arrived in waves or a steady trickle. One hypothesis holds that the first wave of Indonesians arrived about 5,000 years ago, crossing in outrigger sailing canoes from Indochina to the Philippines. They practiced nonirrigated farming and brought barkcloth, pottery, woodcarving, tattooing, and a geometric decorative style that persists to this day in tribal artifacts.

Another group is thought to have sailed from Vietnam and southern China around 1500 B.C., while settlers arriving between 800 and 500 B.C. brought copper and bronze implements and may have introduced the techniques of building irrigated rice terraces. It's believed that many of the tribal minorities of northern Luzon and Mindanao are descended from these early immigrants.

The Malays
The Indonesians were followed by the Malays, who may also have arrived in three waves, the first probably between 300 B.C. and A.D. 100. Presumably migrating from the Malay Peninsula, they sailed up through Borneo and Celebes, reaching Luzon via Palawan and Mindoro, and coming to Mindanao and the Visayas across the Celebes Sea. Although headhunters, these Malays were more advanced than the Indonesians. They initiated iron smelting and forging, and the use of iron tools, weapons, utensils, and ornaments spread rapidly. The type of forge they employed is still extant in the mountains of northern Luzon.

The next wave of Malays, which filtered in between the second and 13th centuries, was even more advanced and possessed an alphabet. These people were the ancestors of today's Christian lowlanders. They arrived in boats called *balanghais*. The remains of three have been discovered near Butuan City in Mindanao. Settlements were called *barangays,* after these boats. Significant population growth occurred along the coasts and rivers of the larger islands, made possible by improved means of rice cultivation, which ensured a greater, more dependable food supply.

The final group, the forefathers of the Muslims of Mindanao and Sulu, came in the 14th and 15th centuries. Each successive wave of migrants brought a greater degree of civilization and left pre-existing inhabitants subdued, assimilated, or driven deeper into the interior mountains.

The Chinese
Contact between Chinese and Filipinos probably began during the Tang dynasty (618-987), but didn't reach significant proportions until the Southern Sung dynasty (1127-1279). Amoy (now Xiamen) was a major port from which trading junks' voyages were facilitated by the seasonal monsoon winds. Merchants sought native products such as pearls, coral, amber, gold, turtle shell, civet musk, beeswax, honey, hardwood, gums, resins, dyes, rattan, hemp, Sulu mats, shark fins, and sea cucumbers, for which they offered silk, ivory, mirrors, metals, and above all, porcelain. The superiority of Chinese porcelain jars over native pottery made them highly prized by the early Filipinos for ceremonial and burial purposes. Excavation of old graves such as those at Santa Ana (Manila) and Calatagan (Batangas) has revealed ceramics from the Tang, Sung, Yuan (1279-1368), and Ming (1368-1644) dynasties. Indochinese ceramics have also been uncovered.

Early Chinese writers mention commerce with numerous places in the archipelago, to which they gave Chinese names. Luzon was "Liu sung." Trade was apparently carried out in an atmosphere of mutual trust, honesty, and cooperation. Butuanese sailed to Amoy in the 11th century, and between 1372 and 1424, Filipino envoys brought tribute to emperors in

Peking. Chinese merchants began marrying Filipinas and settled to establish trading centers in the Philippines. One such colony, called Ma-i, comprised what is now Mindoro, Manila, Cavite, Laguna, and southern Quezon. Manila had 150 Chinese residents when the Spanish took it in 1571.

Though trade with China flourished for several hundred years, it reached its zenith in the 18th century and declined somewhat thereafter. If India's cultural influence was primarily spiritual and artistic, that of China tended to be more practical. Its impact, especially great in commerce, crafts, and cooking, is reflected in social customs and the vocabulary of Tagalog and other languages.

The Bornean *Datus*

Legend holds that around 1212, 10 *datus* (patriarchal chiefs) and their retinues fled from a tyrannical sultan in Sabah and landed on Panay Island. Their leader, Datu Puti, bartered with the Ati (Negrito) chief, Marikudo, to acquire the coastal lowlands in exchange for a golden *sadok* (hat), necklace, basin, a *kris* (dagger), and other gifts. The bargain was sealed by a sumptuous feast, with much drinking and dancing, during which the Borneans blackened their faces with soot to resemble the dark-skinned Atis. This event is now celebrated in the Ati-Atihan Festival.

The Atis moved to the interior hills, while seven of the *datus* settled on Panay and three sailed north to Batangas; two stayed there but Datu Puti returned to Borneo. The *datus* brought a relatively advanced culture. Their descendants prospered and dispersed to inhabit other Visayan islands and parts of Southern Luzon.

The Coming of Islam

The first Arab merchants to reach the Philippines were non-Muslims, but it's believed that foreign Muslims had established a trading settlement on Jolo before 1300. Muslim missionaries had come from Arabia to Southeast Asia during the 13th century and were then aided by converted traders and adventurers. By the mid-14th century, Islam had spread from Sumatra to the Malay Peninsula, with the powerful sultanate of Malacca at its heart. A scholar from Mecca known as the Makdum (Arabic for "Master" or "Father") crossed from Malacca to Sulu, where he made converts before his death around 1380. His tomb is on Simunul (Tawi-Tawi).

The Makdum's work was continued by Raja Baguinda, who sailed from Sumatra's Minangkabau region to land at Buansa in 1390. His daughter married Abu Bakr, an Arab missionary-adventurer who arrived in Sulu from Malacca around 1450, declared himself sultan, and ruled with wisdom and strength in accordance with Koranic law. The Sulu sultanate became a powerful independent Islamic state.

Meanwhile, Sharif Mohammed Kabungsuwan reached Cotabato (Mindanao) from Johore in the first quarter of the 16th century. He conquered and converted the tribes of the Cotabato Valley, married a local princess, and established the great Maguindanao sultanate. Islam gave the people of Sulu and Mindanao, who were already skilled sailors and traders, a political and religious structure that in turn provided the impetus for expansion.

Muslim immigrants introduced the concept of territorial states ruled by rajahs or sultans who exercised suzerainty over the *datus*. Marriage alliances were forged between the ruling families of Cotabato, Sulu, and Ternate in the Moluccas. Muslim rulers introduced firearms into the region, and their descendants propagated Islam in other parts of Mindanao, while fortune-seekers from Borneo spread the word northward to Mindoro, southern Luzon, and Manila. Only the Spanish arrival prevented the entire archipelago from becoming an Islamic nation.

SPANISH ERA

Ferdinand Magellan, the great Portuguese explorer and navigator, reached the Philippines in 1521 on his epic voyage around the world, which was financed by Spain. On Easter Sunday, he claimed the land for Spain, paving the way for future colonization. For details of his exploration and subsequent death on Mactan Island, see the special topic **The Saga of Magellan.**

Legazpi and the Rise of Manila

Spain's colonization of the Philippines began in 1565 when Miguel Lopez de Legazpi arrived at Cebu. His four ships were piloted from Mexico by Father Urdaneta, an old navigator-priest who

THE SAGA OF MAGELLAN

The brilliant Portuguese navigator Ferdinand Magellan believed that the Orient could be reached by sailing west. After the Portuguese king rejected his plan, Magellan approached King Charles I of Spain, who agreed to finance an expedition. Five caravels left Spain in 1519 on what was to be one of the greatest single voyages in history. Over a year later, three of the ships navigated the treacherous passage now known as the Strait of Magellan at the tip of South America to emerge into the Pacific. After 14 more weeks of hunger and disease, they reached Guam, where they took on fresh supplies before continuing west.

On 16 March 1521, the Day of Lazarus, Magellan sighted Samar. The following day, he and his Spanish crew landed on Homonhon, an uninhabited island just south of Samar. Friendly natives from nearby Suluan arrived with fish, bananas, coconuts, and *tuba* (palm wine). After an eight-day rest, Magellan weighed anchor for Limasawa, an island south of Leyte. Its ruler, Rajah Kolambu, was being visited by his brother, Rajah Siagu of Butuan, and they welcomed Magellan. The three men sealed their friendship with a blood compact, in which each drank the other's blood mixed with wine.

On Easter Sunday, the first Catholic mass on Philippine soil was celebrated before the Spaniards and natives. Magellan erected a large wooden cross and claimed the land for Spain, naming it the Archipelago of San Lazaro. (A controversy has arisen over whether the mass was actually held near Butuan, which was then called Masawa, a name sufficiently similar to Limasawa to have possibly confused a Spanish chronicler.)

Kolambu piloted Magellan to the flourishing trading port of Zubu (now Cebu). Rajah Humabon—short, fat, tattooed, and adorned with gold—was seated on a palm mat on the ground, eating turtle eggs from porcelain dishes and drinking palm wine through a reed straw. He invited his visitors to join him, and he, too, sealed a blood compact with Magellan. A week later, Humabon, with his family and

800 of his followers, converted to Christianity. Fragments of the wooden cross planted by Magellan still exist in Cebu, as does the small statue of the infant Jesus that he gave to Humabon's wife as a baptismal gift.

Nearby Mactan Island was ruled by Chief Lapu-lapu. It's unclear whether Magellan commanded Lapu-lapu to submit to Spanish sovereignty, or whether he became involved in a petty local dispute, but on 27 April 1521, he waded ashore at Mactan with 60 Spanish soldiers to face Lapu-lapu and 1,000-2,000 defiant natives. A fierce and confused battle ensued, and Magellan fell. Pigafetta, the expedition's chronicler, wrote: "They killed our mirror, our light, our comfort, and our true guide." Lapu-lapu was the first native leader to resist colonizing invaders. Realizing that the visitors weren't invincible, and angry over the repeated violation of their women, the disenchanted Humabon and his men killed another 27 Spaniards in a skirmish. The survivors, greatly reduced in numbers, departed hastily.

After burning one of their own ships off Bohol for lack of crew, the remaining crew and two vessels made for Tidore in the Moluccas. They loaded up with spices, and one set sail for Panama, the other for Spain. Only the latter arrived. The *Victoria* rounded Africa and reached Spain on 6 September 1522, the first ship to circumnavigate the globe.

The expedition had lasted nearly three years. Of the original 264 members, only 18 were left. But the sale of the single cargo of spices more than covered the entire cost of the venture. The *Victoria's* return vindicated Magellan's theory and whetted Spain's appetite for spices and colonies in the Orient. Four more expeditions were dispatched between 1525 and 1542, two of which touched Mindanao without impact. Villalobos, the commander of the fourth party, named Samar and Leyte "Islas Felipinas" in honor of Charles's son, who became King Felipe II in 1556. The name was subsequently extended to the whole archipelago.

had accompanied the 1525 expedition. Owing to Cebuano hostility, Legazpi quickly set off to explore other islands. After visiting Samar, Leyte, Limasawa, Dapitan, and Bohol, where he made a blood compact with chiefs Sikatuna and Sigala, he decided to conquer strategically located Cebu

and make it his base of operations. Superior firepower drove the natives to the hills.

When the undamaged statue of the infant Jesus left by Magellan was discovered in a charred hut, the accompanying friars promptly decided to build a church. Legazpi constructed a fortified settlement that would become Cebu City. At first he had to deal with belligerent natives, lack of food, and mutiny, but he won the co-operation of the Cebuanos after sealing a blood compact with Humabon's son, who agreed to recognize the Spanish government.

Urdaneta had to find the return route to Mexico. He sailed northeast until he found winds that carried him to California, where he turned south. It was a major navigational discovery that paved the way for regular voyages between Acapulco and Manila. Urdaneta dispatched reinforcements, which Legazpi, now appointed governor-general of the new colony, deployed to explore, conquer, and convert other islands. Insufficient food supplies forced Legazpi to move to Panay, where he founded Capiz in 1569.

Meanwhile he heard reports of Manila, with its superb natural harbor and fertile hinterland, and continuing shortages made it imperative that he occupy it. The Spaniards took two attempts to prevail over this prosperous Muslim settlement. In 1570, the young Rajah Sulayman burned his town as he retreated in the face of imminent defeat by Martin de Goiti. The next year, a strong force led by Legazpi himself appeared in Manila Bay. Sulayman's uncle, Lakandula, chief of Tundok (Tondo) across the Pasig River, convinced his nephew of the futility of resistance.

Legazpi took Manila bloodlessly, proclaimed it capital of the Philippines, and began building a Spanish-style walled city. This medieval fortress called Intramuros became Spain's major structure in Asia. The great governor-general died of a heart attack there in 1572.

After the Sword, the Cross

It had taken only 10 years to make the Philippines a Spanish colony. King Felipe II had ordered that a repeat of Spain's bloody conquests in the Americas be avoided, and the general lack of armed resistance facilitated the pacification of the islands with relatively little bloodshed. Then the friars took over. Although the Muslims of Mindanao and Sulu and the pagan hilltribes of the inaccessible interiors were never subdued, the lowlanders of Luzon and the Visayas were converted to Catholicism. Churches were built, often by forced labor.

The country was divided into religious zones of influence. The Augustinians received Batangas, Bulacan, Pampanga, Ilocos, Cebu, and Panay. The Franciscans acquired Bicol and parts of Laguna and Tayabas. The Jesuits operated in Cavite, Marinduque, Samar, Leyte, Bohol, Negros, and spots on Mindanao. The Dominicans took Bataan, Pangasinan, and the Cagayan Valley. The Recollects occupied Romblon and points of northern Palawan, Luzon, and Mindanao. By the end of the 16th century, much of the archipelago was under Spanish control.

The natives were manipulated into docile servants to be used for the glory of church and king.

Magellan's Cross on Cebu Island

CARL PARKES

The friars who replaced local shamans made Catholicism more appealing by adapting many pagan elements to it. Tribal beliefs in a supreme deity and an afterlife were easily transformed; saints' names were given to spirits; belief in magic metamorphosed into faith in miracles; incantations became prayers; and rituals such as propitiation, harvest thanksgiving, and interceding for the sick were replaced by the Mass and Christian rites and fiestas. The simple peasants were impressed with the pageantry, rich ornamentation, luxurious vestments, candlelight vigils, and mystical aspects of the faith. By using a manipulative form of psychology, one priest could control an entire community. Hence, the Spanish needed only a small army of occupation.

The Way of the Cross

Colonial officials only wanted to live away from Spain long enough to make their fortune. The friars, however, were obsessed with their mission and dedicated their lives to it. Ruling with few constraints and invoking God as their ally, they demanded blind acceptance of their word. Anyone who defied their authority was automatically an enemy of order, to be threatened with both physical punishment and divine retribution. To preserve the status quo, the Spaniards distanced themselves from the natives and refused to teach them Spanish. Educational opportunity was long limited to religious studies, taught by the friars in the local dialects. They wanted to make Christians, not citizens. This use of the friars was the principal difference between the Spanish approach, in which economic considerations were secondary to Christian conversion, and that of the other European colonists in Asia. In the early days of their colonial eras, the British and Dutch, for example, governed through trading companies that dealt only with local rulers who, in turn, controlled their own people. This enabled the colonized society to preserve its religion, traditions, and art forms. The Spanish, however, deliberately wiped out most of the indigenous culture, though many aspects of Malay society and outlook have stubbornly survived, and the peasant lifestyle remains basically unchanged.

Spain's lasting legacies are in the areas of religion and government. The Spaniards forged this mass of loosely associated islands and tribes into a nation, with a central government in Manila overseeing a network of regional administrative centers, aided by Catholicism as a major unifying factor. The profound influence of the church endures, together with many fine colonial churches. Replacement of the indigenous communal land ownership with the concept of private property was a very significant change. Spanish influence is also evident in cultural aspects such as personal names, cooking, urban architecture, music, and vocabulary. But the system imposed a severe colonial mentality that has yet to be fully shed.

Spanish Rule

From 1565 to Mexican independence in 1821, the Philippines was administered by the viceroy of New Spain (Mexico), who was subject to the king and the Council of the Indies in Madrid. After 1821, Spain ruled directly. Within the Philippines, the governor-general was the chief executive, and he also served as president of the Royal Audiencia (Supreme Court). The archbishop of Manila, as the ecclesiastical leader, also had tremendous political power. In spite of their being inextricably linked, the relationship between church and state was often one of rivalry and intrigue.

The great autonomy of regional officials was accompanied by rampant graft, corruption, and injustice. Abuses by the encomienderos led to the system's replacement by that of the alcalde mayor (provincial governor), a position that was also eventually abolished due to abuse of power. In reality, Filipinos had very little participation in their own government. Nevertheless, the hierarchical system enabled the hereditary native elite to eventually convert its power into landholding and wealth in the 19th century, thereby forming an oligarchy that still exists.

Spanish hopes of finding a fortune in spices and gold in her only Asian colony were soon disappointed. In addition, they had to finance a series of costly military operations against internal uprisings, the Muslims, and foreign enemies. They therefore devised other ways of extracting wealth from their new colony. These included the payment of tribute, tithes, and numerous taxes; the levy of assessments of rice and other produce on communities; the expropriation of land by the church; the use of press-gang tactics to draft thousands of natives into the army and navy; and various other forms of oppression.

This exploitative colonial policy persisted until the mid-18th century, while economic and agricultural development was ignored. Any native initiative was stifled beneath bureaucratic red tape, while Chinese immigrants assumed an indispensable role in what commerce did exist. This lack of development meant that the archipelago remained a burden on the Mexican treasury until 1782, when the government established a highly profitable tobacco monopoly in northern Luzon.

The Galleon Trade

From 1575 to 1815, the main Spanish economic activity was a lucrative galleon trade between Manila and Acapulco. Each year, one or two huge galleons began their 14,500-km voyage from Manila, laden with Chinese porcelain, silk, textiles, and tea, plus Indian cotton and perfume, Persian carpets, Ceylonese gems, Siamese ivory, Cambodian sandalwood, Moluccan spices, and Japanese lacquerware and cutlery. The total amounts were limited to control the influx of Oriental textiles and other goods into Mexico, since they competed with those supplied by the merchants of Cadiz and Seville, and to stem the corresponding flow of Mexican silver to China in payment.

Though it was a government monopoly, privileged officials illegally sold trading rights to merchants, and some Spaniards, institutions, and Chinese traders made fortunes. Manila acted only as a transshipment port, with no local products being exported, and since it was much more profitable for the wealthy to invest in a galleon voyage than in the economic development of the islands, the latter remained neglected.

The Moro Wars

The Spanish also had problems with the Muslims. Having driven them from the northern islands, the Spaniards attacked them in the south, establishing bases at Zamboanga and in northern Mindanao. The Muslims declared a jihad. Spanish expeditions in Mindanao and Sulu continued intermittently from the 1570s right up until 1895, with occasional treaties never lasting long. Although the Spanish won battles, all attempts to subdue the Muslims failed.

The fervor that Islam inspired, combined with the political centralization inherent in the sultanates, enabled the Muslims to resist Spanish domination, which would have meant the loss, not only of their independence and religion, but also of their economy and lifestyle. Throughout the Spanish era, the Muslim region was regarded as foreign territory, and its inhabitants weren't considered part of Philippine society. The feeling was mutual. Any ties of race and custom that existed between the natives of the northern and southern islands dissolved once the Spanish intervened and labeled them Christianized "Indios" and "Moros," a term relating Muslim Filipinos to the Moors.

Spanish hostility was exacerbated by the fact that their own 800-year occupation by the Moors had ended only in 1492. Spanish colonial policy created an alienation between Christian and Muslim Filipinos that still persists. Christian natives were conscripted for the wars against the Moros, who in turn retaliated against Christian settlements. During the 17th and 18th centuries, Muslim raiders continually forayed along the coasts of the Visayas and Luzon, even raiding Malate, outside Intramuros, in 1769. They burned churches and carried off thousands of captives to be sold in the slave markets of Batavia (Jakarta), Sandakan, and Singapore.

REVOLUTION AGAINST SPANISH RULE

There had been unrest and protest against Spanish abuses since the beginning of the occupation. The first uprising took place in 1574, and by the time the revolution finally came, there had been over 200 sporadic revolts. Most outbreaks were brief and strictly local; the people lacked the resources and organization necessary for prolonged resistance. The Spanish reaction to insurrection was brutal. When thousands of Chinese revolted in 1639, only 150 Spanish families occupied Intramuros. In 1810, 4,000 Spaniards lived amid three million natives.

Spain's defeat by Britain in 1762 persuaded the Filipinos that their oppressors weren't invincible, and unrest continued to simmer and occasionally erupt. But for revolution to ignite, three major catalysts were necessary: a stronger economy, improved communications, and a group of individuals who could articulate the grievances and national aspirations. Expanded trade and external contact brought about these requisite conditions.

Commerce gave rise to a small, prosperous, educated native upper class, which became acquainted with some of the finer aspects of Spanish culture and urban life. In 1863, educational reforms established a public school system and made higher learning available to Filipinos. Children of well-to-do families studied in Manila and, with the opening of the Suez Canal in 1869, in Spain. Once there, they perceived Spain's weakness and became aware of the Latin American revolutions against Spanish rule.

From these youths emerged the *ilustrados* (enlightened ones), who were to form the nucleus of the struggle for independence. Native priests joined them. The term "Filipino" came to mean all inhabitants of the islands, rather than its original definition of Spaniards born in the Philippines. The concept of nationhood, a shared heritage and a common cause, gradually emerged.

The Cavite Mutiny

The first really strong nationalistic sentiment arose in 1872. In Cavite, at the instigation of liberal, educated Filipinos, 200 soldiers mutinied and murdered their Spanish officers. The insurrection was quickly suppressed with wholesale arrests. The government used it as an excuse to liquidate its enemies, which included three native priests—Fathers Gomez, Burgos, and Zamora—who had campaigned for the rights of Filipino clergy. They were implicated in the revolt and garroted. Their execution awakened a powerful, united national consciousness, and demands for reform became more determined. Eventually, revolution was to prevail over moderation.

José Rizal—The Father of the Philippines

The spiritual foundation for independence was laid by reformers such as José Rizal, the Luna brothers, Marcelo H. del Pilar, and Graciano Lopez Jaena. They formed a Propaganda Movement for reform, publishing a nationalist magazine called *La Solidaridad* ("Solidarity") in Spain from 1889 to 1895. Rizal (1861-96) is considered to be among the greatest Malays who ever lived.

He was a genius, a true Renaissance man—a brilliant scholar, eye surgeon, traveler, linguist, painter, sculptor, novelist, dramatist, poet, scientist, historian. The events of 1872 inspired him to write two novels while in Europe: *Noli Me Tangere* ("Touch Me Not") in 1887 and *El Filibusterismo* ("The Subversive") in 1891. They portrayed the authoritarianism and abuses of the friars and government. Officially banned, underground copies stirred the repressed native spirit and aroused aspirations.

Upon Rizal's return to the Philippines in 1892, he founded La Liga Filipina, an organization aiming at peaceful reform. He was promptly exiled as a revolutionary agitator to Dapitan (Mindanao), where he lived with his Irish lover, Josephine Bracken.

Bonifacio and the Katipunan

The night of Rizal's deportation, Andres Bonifacio founded the Katipunan ("Highest and Most Respectable Association of the Sons of the People"), whose objective was independence through revolution. Bonifacio was born in poverty in Tondo (Manila). The Katipunan remained a small, secret society until 1896, when its membership grew rapidly. When the Spanish finally discovered it, they responded with hundreds of arbitrary arrests. A week later, on 26 August, at Balintawak, now in Manila's northern suburbs, Bonifacio tore up his *cedula* (tax certificate) and called for independence, urging his followers to rise in arms. This was the famous "Cry of Balintawak" that signaled the start of the revolution.

The first battle took place four days later. Bonifacio and Emilio Jacinto led 800 Katipuneros in an attack on the Spanish garrison at San Juan del Monte (now in Metro Manila). Simultaneously, eight provinces around Manila rose in defiance of Spain. The revolution spread to other islands. In the following months, Emilio Aguinaldo emerged as a revolutionary leader, winning several battles in his native Cavite province.

Execution of Rizal

After four years in exile, Rizal volunteered as a surgeon with the Spanish army in Cuba. En route to Spain, his ship was intercepted by a cable from Manila ordering his arrest. Although he had opportunity to escape, he allowed himself to be returned to Manila, where he was confined in Fort Santiago. His trial for "rebellion, sedition, and illicit association" was a formality. On 30 December 1896, in what is now Rizal Park, he found himself, at the age of 35, facing a firing squad. This was a major blunder by the Spanish. Rizal was hailed as a hero and martyr, and his execution intensified the revolution.

The Rise of Aguinaldo

An acute rivalry developed between factions loyal to Bonifacio or Aguinaldo. Bonifacio lost popularity due to military failures that contrasted markedly with Aguinaldo's battlefield successes. In March 1897, the Katipunan was replaced by a new revolutionary government with Aguinaldo as president, and in May, Bonifacio was tried and executed for sedition. Aguinaldo had proposed exile, but his advisers persuaded him that Bonifacio's death was in the best interests of the revolution. The unlettered Bonifacio had made enemies among the rebel intelligentsia, and they argued that, if allowed to live, he would foment division in revolutionary ranks.

Perhaps, too, Bonifacio's belief in violent uprising was seen as a long-term threat to the landed elite. Following a series of defeats in Cavite, Aguinaldo established his headquarters at Biakna-Bato (Bulacan), where, upon approval of a constitution, the Biak-na-Bato Republic was founded. The war continued, but the Spanish, in spite of some victories, realized the futility of trying to crush the rebellion. Accordingly, a peace agreement known as the Pact of Biak-na-Bato was negotiated. It involved amnesty for the rebels, payment of an indemnity, and the voluntary exile of Aguinaldo and his colleagues to Hong Kong. They sailed on 27 December, but peace was short-lived, and fighting resumed in several regions. It took the intrusion of international politics to bring matters to a head.

THE AMERICAN ERA

The Philippines fatefully became a pawn in the Spanish-American War, which began over Cuba in April 1898. It became America's first and only colony almost by accident. The U.S. Asiatic squadron was in Hong Kong when its commander, Commodore George Dewey, received a cable ordering him to attack the Spanish navy in the Philippines. On 1 May, he slipped past the batteries of Corregidor, and in the Battle of Manila Bay—one of the most one-sided battles in naval history—he devastated the Spanish fleet off Cavite without losing a man. Having no land forces, he blockaded Manila while awaiting troops from California.

The Spanish governor's belated promise of reforms in exchange for Filipino support fell on deaf ears. Aguinaldo returned and, being assured that the Americans came as liberators, urged the people to rise in their support. A volunteer army routed Spanish forces in the provinces and besieged Manila. On 12 June 1898, Aguinaldo declared Philippine independence from the balcony of his house at Kawit (Cavite), thereby ending 333 years of Spanish colonization.

In the U.S., little was known about the Philippines, but its fate became the subject of intense debate. President McKinley had stated that the U.S. had no plans to annex the islands, but when Dewey cabled "Have captured Philippines; what shall we do with them?" a decision had to be made. McKinley was an isolationist and pacifist, but he was under pressure from more aggressive expansionists like Theodore Roosevelt. After agonizing over his decision, he concluded that colonization was inescapable and justified it by taking a missionary approach. Dewey was instructed to annex them in order to educate, uplift, civilize, and Christianize them. Presumably, McKinley didn't know that the nation had been Catholic for centuries.

Prelude to War

The Americans established a military government. As Filipino disappointment and suspicions grew, tensions mounted. The Aguinaldo government decided that its headquarters at Bacoor (Cavite) was too close to the American lines. It selected Malolos (Bulacan) as the new capital of the Free Philippines and moved there on 10 September. A congress was formed, and it framed the Malolos Constitution, the first democratic constitution drawn up by Asians. The Treaty of Paris, on 10 December 1898, ended the Spanish-American War, ceding the Philippines, Guam, and Puerto Rico to the United States. But the Filipinos, who hadn't been consulted, defied American sovereignty by proclaiming the First Philippine Republic, with Aguinaldo as president, on 23 January 1899.

The Philippine-American War (1899-1901)

Filipino intransigence made this war—also known as the War of Philippine Independence—unavoidable. On 4 February 1899, when an American shot a Filipino soldier on the bridge at San Juan del Monte, Aguinaldo declared war. Battles were fought throughout the islands as the Americans sought to subdue their new colony. The Filipinos won a few, but superior forces and arms achieved an inevitable American victory.

General Arthur MacArthur (father of Douglas) took Malolos, driving the Filipino government north. Aguinaldo disbanded his army and instituted guerrilla warfare. He retreated to Palanan (Isabela), where he hid for 16 months. His capture in 1901 marked the fall of the First Philippine Republic and the end of effective resistance. He was taken to Manila and persuaded to advise Filipinos to accept American rule. The bloody campaign to suppress the rebellion had required two-thirds of the U.S. Army. The tactics used presaged those applied 65 years later in Vietnam. Although President Theodore Roosevelt declared the Philippines "pacified" in 1902, sporadic insurgency continued for several more years.

Early Administration

Partly to appease anti-imperialist critics within the U.S., a colonial policy of "attraction" was conceived, stemming from both the need to placate the Filipinos and a genuine desire to train them in self-government, with a view toward eventual independence. A civil government was established by 1901, and in 1907, the Philippine Assembly, the first elective legislative body in Southeast Asia, was inaugurated to realize the notion of a "partnership in democracy," whereby Filipinos participated in government.

A high degree of autonomy over internal affairs was granted through the Jones Act in 1916. The native social and economic elite that had emerged toward the end of the Spanish era were prominent in the short-lived revolutionary government. Now, as the only Filipinos possessing the prerequisite education, administrative skills, and authority, they cooperated with the Americans to gain appointment to high office and be-

came the mediators between the colonists and the masses.

Toward Independence

Economic policies for the Philippines were based on American commercial and economic needs, but were shaped by compromises between opposing U.S. domestic interests. Colonial development was endorsed by those favoring overseas trade and holdings, while the granting of independence was supported by those desiring to protect U.S. workers from cheap foreign competition. So, ironically, movement toward Philippine independence was more the result of agitation in the U.S. than of internal pressure by Filipinos.

During the Depression, beleaguered American farm and labor groups clamored for colonial independence and the replacement of free-trade agreements with tariff protection. They instigated a law providing for the establishment of a Philippine Commonwealth, with domestic self-government as a 10-year transition to full independence, and in 1935 the fiery Manuel Quezon was inaugurated as president of the Commonwealth government.

The Philippines had a freely elected house and senate, an independent judiciary, and an indigenous civil service. The U.S. remained as observers, with power only over foreign affairs and currency. Quezon introduced a social justice program to quell unrest among the poverty-stricken masses, while simultaneously attempting to reassure the landowners.

WORLD WAR II

In light of Japanese activity in the region, the Philippine armed forces were incorporated into the U.S. Army under General Douglas MacArthur in 1941. They were badly trained and equipped, and incapable of defending their land if war came to the Far East. On 7 December 1941, the Japanese attacked Pearl Harbor in Hawaii and the Pacific war began. The strategically located Philippines lay directly in Japan's line of conquest. MacArthur's faith in 277 U.S. aircraft based at Clark Field in central Luzon was quickly shattered when, the following day, dozens of them were bombed on the tarmac. Japanese landings at Lingayen Gulf on 22 December and Lamon Bay two days later initiated a pincer movement toward Manila. The city was doomed.

The Filipinos convinced MacArthur that the capital and its monuments must be spared, so he forsook its defense and declared it an open city. All he could offer was a desperate contingency plan: withdrawal to the narrow Bataan Peninsula to await American reinforcements. On 2 January 1942, the Philippines found itself subject to yet another imperialist occupation. Before its liberation three years later, tens of thousands of Filipinos and Americans would die in battle, or from disease and malnutrition.

Bataan, Corregidor, and the Death March

Filipino leaders distrusted American promises to defend a territory they were soon scheduled to relinquish. Quezon suggested the granting of immediate independence so that the Philippines could declare neutrality. President Roosevelt rejected this, promising that Americans would defend it to the death. This proved to be the case, as Americans and Filipinos on Bataan fought side by side for four months. Resistance continued far beyond Japanese expectations.

MacArthur crossed to the island of Corregidor, just off Bataan, to direct the slow, fighting retreat down the peninsula. He was ordered by Roosevelt to leave the Philippines and on 11 March departed for Australia, where he made his famous "I shall return" pledge.

On 9 April, 76,000 men squeezed onto the tip of Bataan peninsula were officially surrendered to the Japanese. They were without food or ammunition, and malaria and dysentry were rife. That day, the notorious Death March up the peninsula began. Ten days later, between 7,000 and 10,000, including about 2,600 Americans, had died from exhaustion or sadistic brutality. The suffering survivors were herded into boxcars in San Fernando (Pampanga) and taken to an internment camp at Capas (Tarlac).

By May 1942, four months of saturation bombing had knocked out Corregidor's artillery, and the Japanese landed. The 13,000 remaining Americans and Filipinos retreated into the Malinta Tunnel system and fought for a few more days, but with little water, food, medicine, or ammunition, the commander, General Wainwright, had no option but to surrender.

Japanese Occupation

Japanese military rule was very severe, imposing curtailment of civil liberties, censorship, and conscription of labor. The economy was reoriented toward Japan's war effort with the intention of eventual integration into the Japanese empire. The Filipino elite again acted as mediator between a foreign occupier and the masses. A puppet republic was set up with the collaboration of some of the native leaders, but the populace remained hopeful of liberation.

Corregidor cannon

CARL PARKES

A Philippine government-in-exile was established in Washington, D.C., while in Manila, Dr. Jose P. Laurel, father of Vice President Salvador Laurel, agreed to be president of the crisis government. The occupation was marked by deteriorating economic conditions, critical food shortages, a breakdown of law and order, Japanese brutality, and strong pro-American, anti-Japanese popular sentiment. Guerrilla resistance groups formed and were joined by uncaptured Filipino and American soldiers.

The hunger and hardship were more easily withstood by the downtrodden peasants than the upper classes. A sack of rice could be exchanged for a piece of fine furniture or a bundle of "Mickey Mouse" money—Japanese military notes subject to rampant inflation. Yet through it all, nightclubs and restaurants stayed open for those who could afford them. Their patrons were the ruthless business opportunists who made fortunes by selling war materials to the Japanese military. After the war, this corrupt group would control the distribution of relief supplies, further augmenting its wealth and forming a new bourgeoisie alongside the old landowning families.

MacArthur's Return

The heroic resistance on Bataan and Corregidor proved invaluable, as it tied up the Japanese forces for several months, allowing the Allies to recover from their initial heavy losses in the Pacific theater. The Philippines was destined to become the key battleground in the Pacific war, due to its strategic location. Japan had to retain the islands to protect the shipping lanes for its raw material sources in Southeast Asia and the Dutch East Indies. The U.S. wanted to recapture the archipelago to establish air bases and staging areas for the invasion of Japan.

Eventually, on 20 October 1944, MacArthur was able to make good his promise by returning with an invasion force. The landing, which took place at four spots along a 30-km stretch of coastline on Leyte, involved 700 vessels and 174,000 U.S. servicemen. Once the area was secure, MacArthur and his companions went ashore at Palo. Initially, the Americans met with little resistance, but it took them two months to clear the mountains and plains of Leyte, where Japan's casualties were 20 times those of the United States.

A few days after the Leyte landing, 64 Japanese warships engaged 216 American vessels in the Battle for Leyte Gulf, one of the greatest naval battles in history. Fighting took place simultaneously in three areas: off Cape Engano (Cagayan), off Samar, and in the Surigao Strait (south of Samar). This three-day battle (23-25 October) marked the last use of battle-line formation, in which giant battleships faced and fired on each other at point-blank range, and was also the first time that Japanese pilots employed kamikaze tactics. The Japanese fleet was decimated.

The Liberation of Manila

The Americans commenced their 500-km push from Leyte to Luzon. They were supported by about 250,000 guerrillas who were operating throughout the Philippines. U.S. troops landed at Lingayen Gulf on 9 January 1945 and advanced toward Manila. In February, Corregidor was recaptured after a bloody 11-day battle. It took from 3 to 23 February to liberate Manila. The Americans entered from the north and drove the Japanese across the Pasig River, where they were trapped by U.S. forces advancing from the south.

The desperate Japanese servicemen plunged into an orgy of murder, rape, and destruction in the southern districts of Manila; thousands of Filipinos were killed. The Japanese made their last stand in Intramuros, and the Americans had to fight for it block by block, hand-to-hand. At the end, Manila was the war's second-most devastated city, after Warsaw. The victorious Americans received an ecstatic welcome from the Filipinos. Mopping-up operations continued throughout the archipelago. The last resistance was from General Yamashita, the "Tiger of Malaya," whose forces were entrenched near Kiangan (Ifugao). He formally surrendered at Baguio on 3 September 1945.

INDEPENDENCE AND THE QUEST FOR DEMOCRACY

The war had taken a terrible toll in lives and property, and the economy was a shambles. A million Filipinos had perished. With the capital in ruins, the Commonwealth government resumed office in 1945 and, with U.S. financial aid, undertook the enormous tasks of reconstruction and rehabilitation. Since Quezon had died in 1944, Manuel Roxas was elected the last president of the Commonwealth and, on 4 July 1946, first president of the Philippine Republic. Roxas was strongly pro-U.S.; the lease for the military bases at Angeles and Subic Bay was negotiated during his tenure.

Roxas's presidential successors were Elpidio Quirino, the very popular Ramon Magsaysay (who died in a plane crash), Carlos Garcia, and Diosdado Macapagal. The first two postwar decades were a difficult period. Agrarian unrest caused by failure to reform the feudal landlord-tenant system in central Luzon gave rise to a serious rebellion by the communist Huks (pronounced "hooks"). Having fielded a guerrilla army against the Japanese, the Hukbalahap movement opposed the government after the war. It remained a threat until the mid-'50s and briefly resurged in 1965. With wealth and power controlled by a small, entrenched oligarchy of influential families who were adamantly against reform, discontent was inevitable.

The Marcos Regime
Responsibility for this complex society was inherited by Ferdinand E. Marcos, who was elected president in 1965. He had already led a dramatic life, including successfully defending himself on a murder charge in 1940 and serving as an officer during WW II. Authoritarian and prone to ruling by decree, Marcos proved to be a consummate political tactician and brilliant lawyer. Marcos came to power as a nationalistic social reformer with a broad electoral mandate to deal with the country's chronic problems. Marcos was credited with some positive achievements during his first term of office, notably the initiation of infrastructure programs and increasing rice production. After his fiercely contested re-election in 1969, the economy continued its decline.

A convention called in 1971 to draft a new constitution became the arena for the many conflicting issues that were racking the country. All had supporters and detractors, and the administration faced demonstrations and protests by students and reformist groups of all political persuasions.

During the early '70s, conditions approached anarchy, with riots, street crime, bombings, and assassination attempts. The radical, outlawed Communist Party of the Philippines had formed an armed wing, the New People's Army (NPA); in 1969 and though still a minor force, it began committing acts of terrorism and clashing with government forces. The separatist Moro National Liberation Front (MNLF), representing the dissident Muslims of Mindanao and Sulu, pressed claims for secession by opposing the military in the south, and fighting intensified between Christians and Muslims in Mindanao.

Martial Law
Citing the prevailing economic crisis and threat to national security of insurgency and rapid deterioration in law and order, President Marcos declared martial law in 1972. Its stated objectives were to save the Republic from communism and form a disciplined "New Society." He was constitutionally barred from a third term in office, but under martial law, there would be no elections.

Martial law was at first well-received. It resulted in a dramatic reduction in crime, violence, and the use of guns. Urban streets were safer. The cost was a departure from democratic ideals, involving the detention of opposing politicians and journalists; suspension of Congress, the right of habeas corpus, and freedom of press, speech, and assembly; and the imposition of strict censorship and a midnight-0400 curfew. An estimated 67,000 people were arrested during the early years of martial law.

With his political opponents jailed, exiled, underground, or powerless, and the courts and media under control, Marcos began to rule by decree, unchallenged. He had dismantled his opposition and destroyed the previous system's checks and balances. The New Society, based on "constitutional authoritarianism," claimed peace and order, land reform, economic development, and government reorganization as its aims. A new constitution was ratified by national referendum in 1973, then held in abeyance. It replaced the Congress and Senate with a parliament, the Batasang Pambansa (National Assembly), and set no limit on the number of presidential terms. Referenda approved extension of the presidential term of office and the continuation of martial law.

Martial law ended in 1981. During this period Marcos had restructured the constitution to accommodate his personal rule. The decrees issued under martial law remained in effect, and the dictator retained the authority to rule by decree, use emergency powers, and detain alleged national security violators virtually at will. Marcos was re-elected for six years in 1981 in an election boycotted by his major opponents.

In retrospect, martial law brought increased stability and enabled the attraction of foreign investment to help foster steady economic growth through the '70s, though progress was uneven. While luxury hotels rose in Manila, the government failed to address the root causes of poverty. During this period, too, Marcos developed a powerful political machine, penetrating almost every village in the country, while the might of the Philippine Armed Forces increased dramatically as membership tripled and the influence of its generals expanded.

The Aquino Assassination

The assassination of opposition leader Benigno "Ninoy" Aquino on the Manila International Airport tarmac on 21 August 1983 propelled the Philippines to the forefront of international news coverage and shook the nation. Aquino, who had spent a three-year exile in the U.S. following over seven years of detention under martial law and an official death sentence, was shot in the back of the head within seconds of his arrival.

Somehow the lone "suspect" was immediately killed by security guards. Several thousand supporters had been waiting to greet Aquino, including his sister—bearing a yellow bouquet. (Yellow symbolized a returning prisoner, but it was to become the color of protest.) The assassination and subsequent outrage and protest had a devastating effect on the nation. It galvanized political opposition to the Marcos regime.

The Fall of Marcos

After 20 years in office, the generally positive image that Marcos had nurtured earlier in his tenure had all but eroded. Widespread disillusionment became a pervasive national malaise. As rumors of Marcos's ill health persisted, the eventual presidential succession became the subject of much speculation. With the opposition in disarray, debate focused on the roles, if

any, of the ostentatious and controversial first lady and the military in the nation's political future. In November 1985, growing national and international criticism caused Marcos to call a "snap" presidential election on 7 February 1986 to seek a new mandate. Counting on a disunited opposition, he was confident his well-oiled political machine would deliver the vote as it had so many times before.

Sick and isolated in his palace, Marcos failed to see the moderate forces fomenting around him. These forces needed a figurehead and a reluctant housewife finally came to accept her destiny. Corazon Aquino lacked political experience and a campaign apparatus, but she declared her candidacy. After much bickering, the opposition united at literally the eleventh hour behind "Cory" and her vice-presidential candidate, Salvador Laurel.

Following a bitter and violent election campaign, voting took place amid accusations of wholesale fraud and intimidation. Over 300,000 volunteers—organized by Namfrel, a church-backed citizens' electoral watchdog group—monitored the polls and guarded the ballots. Nevertheless, citizens were disenfranchised by destruction of their registration records, votes bought, paid "flying voters" transported between polling points, threats from Marcos's thugs, and stolen ballot boxes. Both candidates predicted victory.

Early tallies by the Marcos-controlled Commission on Elections (Comelec) and by Namfrel showed Marcos and Aquino ahead, respectively. Returns were delayed as the count dragged on for days. Both candidates claimed victory. Marcos declared that the controversy would be decided by the National Assembly, which he controlled. As expected, the National Assembly declared Marcos the winner on 16 February. Corazon Aquino, addressing almost a million supporters in Rizal Park, refused to concede and announced a peaceful program of civil disobedience, including a boycott of pro-Marcos banks and businesses, and a general strike on the day after Marcos's planned inaugural on 25 February.

For Aquino to take power, however, it was necessary for the military to join her cause. After Marcos announced the retirement of Chief of Staff Gen. Fabian Ver, with Lt. Gen. Fidel Ramos as his replacement, Ver began to make "midnight appointments," replacing Ramos supporters with his own loyalists so that he could retain control of the military even after Ramos had taken over from him. Rumors circulated of an impending declaration of martial law and roundup of Marcos opponents, and on 20 February came the first word of a possible revolt to preempt the martial law by reform movement military officers, who had already denounced the elections as fraudulent.

Four Days in February
The dramatic events of 22-25 February 1986, which saw the downfall of President Marcos after almost 20 years of one-man rule, remain as reminders of "People Power" and the bravery of the Filipino people in risking their lives to preserve freedom and democracy. These events are well documented, reported by the world's media. The defection of General Ramos and Defense Minister Juan Ponce Enrile from the Marcos camp made them heroes. Enrile's abandonment of Marcos was especially significant, since he had served Marcos loyally for 20 years. Enrile and Ramos called on Marcos to resign and turn power over to Aquino.

On Sunday, 23 February, thousands of people amassed outside the two military camps, blocking East de los Santos Ave. (EDSA) and bringing the soldiers food. Ramos told the throng that "what is happening is not a coup d'etat, but a revolution of the people." The term "EDSA Revolution" would subsequently be coined. An armored column dispatched by Ver was prevented from reaching the camps by thousands of people, including women bearing flowers, mothers with infants, and priests and nuns kneeling in prayer. It was a strange, peculiarly Filipino affair—part picnic, part perilous. The troops couldn't advance toward the rebels without killing civilians while the world watched. "People Power," the catch-phrase of the rebellion, had neutralized Marcos's military options, and his indecisiveness during those first 12 hours of the rebellion would cost him his presidency.

On Monday, 24 February, morale was boosted at Camp Crame when helicopters sent by Ver to attack landed instead. Other defectors included air force pilots. After a brief helicopter attack on the palace and on aircraft at Villamor

Air Base, jets under Ramos's control patrolled the sky over the city. Hundreds of thousands of people remained in the streets as a human buffer against attack. Enrile declared the formation of a provisional government under Aquino. The U.S. government, which in its public statements had steadily distanced itself from Marcos, finally called on him to step down, announcing that "attempts to prolong the life of the present regime by violence are futile."

Virtually all media relayed Aquino's inauguration on 25 February at Club Filipino, an exclusive suburban social club, at which she stated, "Sovereignty resides in the people and all government authority emanates from them." The TV coverage of Marcos's own inauguration at Malacanang went off the air. Realizing defeat, Marcos asked Enrile to arrange safe passage from Malacanang, where he was a virtual prisoner. At 2105, four U.S. helicopters took Marcos, Imelda, Ver, their families and aides to Clark Air Force Base. Later, they were whisked away into exile in Hawaii, where Marcos subsequently died in September 1989.

THE SAINT, THE GENERAL, THE ACTOR

Corazon Aquino
After the almost bloodless revolution, the new, inexperienced president faced an awesome task in dealing with the shattered economy and communist insurgency that she had inherited from Marcos. The world press was filled with reports of Marcos's ill-gotten gains, his hidden billions in Swiss bank accounts and real estate holdings, and reports of Imelda's incredible extravagance. The palace doors were thrown open to the public, affording a view of the Marcoses' lavish private lifestyle.

Upon assuming the presidency, Cory Aquino immediately restored the rights of free speech and a free press, and released 500 political prisoners, including communist party leaders. She also dissolved the former constitution and replaced it with a new one, disbanded the discredited National Assembly, replaced the majority of provincial governors and city mayors (who were Marcos loyalists) with her own appointees, and retired over half the country's generals.

In office, President Aquino survived six coup attempts to unseat her, yet economic problems, social inequity, insurgency, political uncertainty, and recurring threats of a military coup persisted throughout her presidency.

Fidel Ramos

Corazon Aquino is credited with restoring democracy to the Philippines, but it was her successor who revitalized the economy and put the country on a firm path for the next millennium. Seven years after the historic "People Power" movement, the Philippines elected a new president, Fidel V. Ramos. The retired general and West Point graduate was ushered into office on 11 May 1992. Also voted in were a new vice president, 24 senators, 200 congressmen, and some 17,000 local officials.

The former military leader received critical endorsement from Corazon Aquino. In accepting President Ramos, Filipinos voted soundly against Marcos crony Eduardo Conjuangco in an obvious vote against authoritarianism. They also voted strongly against Ramon Mitra, in a demonstration against the politics of patronage that dominate Philippine society, but voted in large numbers for antigraft crusader Miriam Santiago as they registered their contempt for corrupt public officials. The litany of losers perhaps told more about contemporary Filipino society than the election of a bespectacled West Point graduate who co-led the February 1986 revolt.

Ramos brought great change to the Philippines by opening the economy to Western investors. Ramos's three-tiered cabinet of military

LAST DAYS OF THE AMERICANS

A prominent and emotionally charged factor in Philippine politics had long been the future of the American bases in the Philippines, namely Clark Field Air Force Base, Subic Bay Naval Base, and four smaller facilities. Clark and Subic were the two largest American military facilities outside the United States. The Military Bases Agreement, made in 1966, expired in September 1991. Discussions between the two countries on the future leases for the bases heated up in May 1990, when the Philippines gave notice to the U.S. that it would terminate the current agreement or nearly double the rent on the bases if any lease were given at all. Contrary to a nationwide referendum that favored the retention of the U.S. bases, which provided over 68,500 jobs for Filipinos and pumped over US$1.4 million a day into the domestic economy, the Philippine Senate and President Aquino voted to deny the Americans access to the bases.

Ironically, Clark Air Force Base in Angeles City closed earlier than expected after the eruption of Mt. Pinatubo in June 1991. Volcanologists predicted the eruption by monitoring activity from Clark Air Force Base, but the U.S. evacuation was not fast enough to save much of the machinery, equipment, hardware, or the businesses around Angeles City. Clark Air Force Base closed for good after Mt. Pinatubo's violent explosion, and looting of the base ensued.

Subic Bay Naval Base, at Olongapo City, was damaged by fallout from Mt. Pinatubo, but the U.S. poured money into cleanup and repairs. The lease on Subic Bay was not up for renewal unless the U.S. was willing to pay millions more. The lease expired in December 1992; to avoid looting, the U.S. Navy removed as much equipment as possible, even taking the kitchen sinks. On 24 November 1992, the American flag was lowered at the Subic Naval Base, officially ending a 93-year-old American military presence in the Philippines. The national anthem was playing when the Pacific Fleet sailed away from Subic Bay; the estimated 10,000 local residents who witnessed the event cried unashamedly.

While the Philippine government boasted of finally having gotten foreigners off their native soil, it could not assuage the bitterness felt by many Filipinos who lost their livelihoods because of their government's nationalism. Many people feel that the government's decision to allow the U.S. bases to close and further devastate the economy was another example of the Philippines shooting itself in the foot.

Currently, there is no U.S. military presence in the Philippines, and Olongapo City and Subic Bay now operate as an international port for trade and recreation. Economically depressed Angeles City has recovered from the Mt. Pinatubo eruption and served as the site of the national independence celebrations in June 1998.

leaders, corporate technocrats, and professional politicians pulled the Philippines out of its economic malaise and returned it to healthy levels not seen since the 1950s.

Today he serves as a senior adviser to the current president, Joseph Estrada.

Joseph Estrada

National elections were most recently held in May 1998; the presidential showdown was between Jose de Venecia—the Speaker of the House and the candidate supported by Ramos—and Joseph Estrada, a one-time B-movie film star and former vice president of the country. The mayor of Manila, a delightful chap named Alfredo Lim (also known as "Dirty Harry" due to his love of guns and law enforcement), also entered the race.

Joseph Estrada easily won the election, which marked yet another turning point in the modern political history of the nation. For decades, Philippine politicians had impressed their electorate with law degrees, tony upbringings, and an elegant vocabulary. Estrada broke all those rules, and more. Although he was actually born into an upper-middle class family in Manila, he always followed the lifestyles of the masses and made a conscious effort to distance himself from the upper echelons of power in Manila. Estrada made no bones about his former drinking habits (to excess) and his love of gambling and fast women. The man publicly acknowledged that he had four mistresses and that he considered the science of economics a bore.

Actually, Estrada proved himself a very clever man, hiding his wit and wisdom behind folkloric babble. The people loved it. They also appreciated the fact that Estrada dropped out of college to become an actor, an actor who faithfully defended the poor and disenfranchised at all costs. He was the leading B-movie actor in the Philippines for almost 20 years, until he threw his cowboy hat into the political ring.

At first, everyone made fun of the man. His legendary ability to mangle English spawned a collection of malapropisms that were published in a book called *ERAPtions: How to Speak English Without Really Trial.* Nobody seemed to care, including Estrada himself.

In interviews with foreign journalists, Estrada would flaunt his anti-intellectualism. He idolized Ronald Reagan, since the former American president was also a retired actor who proved, during his time in office, that all the intellectual snobs were wrong.

He also broke the classic physical mold of traditional Filipino politicians. All had been light-skinned, aristocratic mestizos with plenty of Spanish or Chinese blood. Estrada looked like a real Filipino with his darker skin, bushy mustache, and elevated hairstyle.

And so Estrada easily won the election of 1998. And now he seems to be fulfilling his role as the Ronald Reagan of modern Filipino political life.

GOVERNMENT

The 1987 constitution, approved by plebiscite, reestablished a U.S.-style bicameral legislature, comprising 24 senators elected nationally and 250 congressmen—200 elected to represent districts and 50 appointed for special constituencies. It sharply reduces the power of the president, who is allowed a single six-year presidential term. It bars the military from political activity except voting, restores political freedoms, and expands human rights guarantees. Nepotism and accumulation of personal wealth by a serving president is banned. It is said to be the world's first national constitution to contain the word "love" and calls for social justice based on substantial reforms in labor, land ownership, health, and housing.

Administration

The president is advised by a cabinet comprising appointed ministers. Administratively, the country is divided into a National Capital Region (Metro Manila) and 13 regions, including the Cordillera Autonomous Region and Muslim Mindanao Autonomous Region. These administrative regions comprise 73 provinces, each under the jurisdiction of a governor. Provinces are divided into municipalities (towns); there are 60 chartered cities. Cities and municipalities are headed by a mayor and made up of *barangays,* which are essentially villages or urban districts. The country has more than 43,000 of them.

PROVINCES OF THE PHILIPPINES

0   200km

© MOON PUBLICATIONS, INC.

PROVINCES OF THE PHILIPPINES

1. Batanes
2. Cagayan
3. Ilocos Norte
4. Abra
5. Kalinga-Apayao
6. Ilocos Sur
7. Mountain Province
8. Ifugao
9. Isabela
10. La Union
11. Benguet
12. Nueva Vizcaya
13. Quirino
14. Aurora
15. Pangasinan
16. Zambales
17. Tarlac
18. Nueva Ecija
19. Pampanga
20. Bulacan
21. Bataan
22. Metro Manila
23. Rizal
24. Cavite
25. Laguna

26. Batangas
27. Quezon
28. Camarines Norte
29. Camarines Sur
30. Catanduanes
31. Albay
32. Sorsogon
33. Occidental Mindoro
34. Oriental Mindoro
35. Marinduque
36. Romblon
37. Masbate
38. Northern Samar
39. Western Samar
40. Eastern Samar
41. Palawan
42. Antique
43. Aklan
44. Capiz
45. Iloilo
46. Negros Occidental
47. Negros Oriental
48. Siguijor
49. Cebu
50. Bohol

51. Leyte
52. Southern Leyte
53. Surigao del Norte
54. Camiguin
55. Agusan del Norte
56. Surigao del Sur
57. Misamis Occidental
58. Misamis Oriental
59. Zamboanga del Norte
60. Zamboanga del Sur
61. Lanao del Norte
62. Lanao del Sur
63. Bukidnon
64. Agusan del Sur
65. Maguindanao
66. North Cotabato
67. City of Davao
68. Davao del Norte
69. Davao Oriental
70. Sultan Kudarat
71. South Cotabato
72. Davao del Sur
73. Tawi-Tawi
74. Sulu
75. Basilan

The *barangay* is the basic political unit in the Philippines. It was the term for precolonial communities and derives from the boats on which Malay settlers dispersed through the archipelago. Every citizen is a member of a *barangay* assembly that meets to discuss national and local issues, a system that encourages grassroots participation. Each *barangay* is administered by a *barangay* captain, six councilmen, a treasurer, and a secretary. These elected officials are responsible for law and order and play an intermediary role in linking people to higher authorities. They wield considerable influence and can help determine the outcome of referenda. The government also uses them to consult the people on important questions and the election of mayors, governors, congressmen, senators, even the president. The voting age is 18.

Political Philosophies

Filipinos take a passionate interest in politics. Passing around political gossip is a national pastime. The majority of Filipinos remain deeply committed to democratic ideals, in spite of the social inequality and political corruption they have witnessed. While the Philippines has the longest democratic tradition in Southeast Asia, it's a democracy born of colonial rule, blending elements of Asian hierarchy, Spanish feudalism, and American capitalism.

Filipinos in power tend to be simultaneously authoritarian and paternalistic. Mayors, governors, and other officials have tended to run their areas in near feudal style, dispensing patronage, settling local disputes, and taking a cut from economic activities. The importance of the family in Filipino society is reflected in politics, and campaigns are conducted along family lines. It's a system based on blood ties, reciprocal obligations, and regional identities—factors that intensify the role of patronage and tendency toward graft and corruption.

Elections are vigorously contested at every level, since holding political office yields opportunities for wealth, patronage, and prestige. Voting depends more on personalities and loyalties than on issues and policies. Political rivalries can be intense, and elections have a history of violence, vote-buying, and fraud. Hopes for democracy lie with the emergence of a politically articulate middle class that is independent of the entrenched traditional power centers.

Insurgencies

The Communist Party of the Philippines (CPP) was founded in 1968 as a Maoist breakaway from an older Moscow-oriented party. Its military arm, the New People's Army (NPA), initially operated in northern Luzon, but it expanded under Marcos's misrule. NPA growth has been particularly strong in areas where central government was never solid. For its civilian sympathizers, the attraction has less to do with communist ideology than the reality of being perennially poor and downtrodden. In negotiations with the government, the rebels are represented by the National Democratic Front (NDF), a left-wing political umbrella group.

The task of controlling insurgencies falls on the Armed Forces of the Philippines (AFP), comprising the army, navy, air force, marines, and Philippine Constabulary (PC). They're supplemented by the Integrated National Police and paramilitary Civilian Home Defense Forces (CHDF).

During the Ramos administration, the communist insurgents experienced a decline in power. One reason may be that the popularity of communism has declined all over the world. Another may have been the slight increase in the Philippine standard of living under his administration and his attempts at land reform.

The decline of communist influence in the country has continued under the administration of Joseph Estrada and today presents few political or economic challenges to the state.

ECONOMY

The Philippines is a land of economic contrasts and extremes of personal wealth. Agricultural methods vary from ancient practices to large-scale mechanization; manufacturing processes range from indigenous crafts to advanced technology. In spite of significant industrial growth, the Philippine economy remains basically agrarian. Seventy percent of the people depend on agriculture. The archipelago is rich in natural resources, and, like other Third World countries, its foreign exchange earnings have depended mainly on the sale of primary commodities.

The Philippines's economic growth rate declined during the world recession of the early '80s, aggravated by the assassination of Benigno Aquino in 1983 and the instability of the Marcos regime's final years with its subsequent social unrest. The peso was officially devalued three times from 8.20 pesos to 18 pesos to the U.S. dollar. Since 1986, the peso has been floating freely.

The Southeast Asian currency devaluation crisis of 1997-98 devastated the peso, which fell over 40% in less than six months; it now hovers in the 40-45 pesos-per-dollar range.

Agrarian Reform

Traditionally, land and water were owned by the community and only improvements such as crops, fruit trees, and fish traps were private property. Under the Spanish, land was titled to the state, religious orders, and individuals. Some 70% of the peasants do not own the land they till. An Agrarian Reform Program was introduced in 1972 whereby tenant farmers of rice and corn, often required to give 30-70% of their crop to absentee landlords, were to become eligible to purchase from their landlord a family-size farm of up to three hectares of irrigated land, or five hectares if nonirrigated, with payment spread over 15 years. Tenants producing export crops like sugar and coconuts, and agricultural wage earners, weren't included.

The program proved to be a complex and highly sensitive issue, facing administrative difficulties and the resistance of the entrenched landowners, as it was often used as a weapon against political opponents.

Under the Aquino administration, the Comprehensive Agrarian Reform Law was passed in 1988, covering public and private lands suitable for agriculture. Under this law, the Department of

RESPONSIBLE TOURISM

Responsible Tourism

Tourism, some say, broadens the mind, enriches our lives, spreads prosperity, dissolves political barriers, and promotes international peace. While concurring with most of these sentiments, others feel that mass tourism often destroys what it seeks to discover; it disrupts the economy by funneling dollars into international travel consortiums rather than local enterprise, exploits the people, who find themselves ever more dependent on the tourist dollar, and reinforces cultural stereotypes rather than encouraging authentic dialogue between peoples. Responsible tourism is a movement that attempts to address both the virtues and vices of mass tourism by making each traveler more sensitive to these issues. The fundamental tenet is that travel should benefit *both* the traveler and the host country, and that travelers should travel softly and thoughtfully, with great awareness of their impact on the people and the environment.

Spearheading this movement is the Center for Responsible Tourism (2 Kensington Rd., San Anselmo, CA 94960), a Christian group that holds annual conferences on the impact of mass tourism, publishes a thought-provoking newsletter, and offers workshops on how to lead a responsible tour. Visitors are encouraged to seek out low-impact and locally based travel experiences by patronizing cafés, guesthouses, and pensions owned by indigenous people. Their guidelines:

1. Travel in a spirit of humility, with a genuine desire to meet and talk with the local people.
2. Sensitize yourself to the feelings of your hosts.
3. Cultivate the habit of listening and observing, rather than merely hearing and seeing.
4. Realize that other people's concepts of time and thought patterns may be dramatically different from—not inferior to—your own.
5. Seek out the richness of foreign cultures, not just the escapist lures of tourist posters.

6. Respect and understand local customs.
7. Ask questions and keep a sense of humor.
8. Understand your role as a guest in the country; do not expect special privileges.
9. Spend wisely and bargain with compassion.
10. Fulfill any obligations or promises you make to local people.
11. Reflect on your daily experiences; seek to deepen your understanding of the people, the culture, and the environment.

Selecting a Responsible Tour Operator

Before selecting an adventure travel or tour company, you might want to consider the following guidelines suggested by the Center for Responsible Tourism. If your prospective tour group or travel agent fails the test, investigate alternative travel options or go as an independent traveler.

1. Does the tour organizer demonstrate a cultural and environmental sensitivity? How are local people and culture portrayed in advertising brochures?
2. Who benefits financially from your trip? What percentage of your dollar stays in the country you visit rather than ends up with an international hotel chain, airline, or travel agency?
3. Is a realistic picture of your host country presented, or a sanitized version packaged for tourists?
4. Will you use local accommodations and transportation or be assigned to tourist facilities that prevent a real understanding of the environment?
5. Does your travel itinerary allow adequate time for meeting with local people? If it doesn't, don't go!
6. Has the tour operator or travel agent mentioned anything beyond what's listed in the glossy advertisements? Ask about the social, economic, and political realities of Southeast Asia.

Agrarian Reform (DAR) is charged with acquiring agricultural lands in excess of 50 hectares from each landowner. Landless farmers and farm workers would be given the chance to own a part of the land that they till. Landowners who sold their lands under the Voluntary Offer of Sale (VOS) scheme could receive a five percent cash bonus, in addition to the 25% cash payment from the total value of the land. The balance was to be paid in bonds. If the land was not sold voluntarily within the set period, the DAR's next step was the compulsory acquisition of land.

Loopholes in the land reform law, however, modified the act to the point where most peasants are still landless, and the landowners are fighting reforms in congress. President Ramos attempted to promote land reform, but most of his programs proved ineffectual. President Estrada has also promised to push land reform and help the little man of the Philippines, but time will tell if this vexing problem can ever be resolved.

Tourism

The Philippines puts great faith in tourism as a major component of the economy, providing both employment and foreign exchange. The tourist influx multiplied during the '80s but declined in the '90s due to worldwide recession and signs of instability in the country. Visitors from East Asia (Japan, Hong Kong, Korea, and Taiwan) account for almost 40% of foreign arrivals, followed by visitors from North America, who accounted for more than 23% of arrivals.

Americans, however, topped the list by nationality. Substantial numbers also came from Australia, West Germany, the United Kingdom, Saudi Arabia, Switzerland, and Singapore. Visitors include both the suitcase and backpack varieties.

Manila has an abundance of deluxe hotels, plus an impressive convention center aimed at attracting international functions. Luxury accommodation outside the capital is limited. For budget travelers, inexpensive facilities are readily available.

Return visits by *balikbayan,* Filipinos who are overseas residents, are also encouraged. Many Filipinos work abroad as musicians and entertainers, construction workers, domestic helpers, merchant seamen, etc. These contract workers earn several billion dollars annually, and much of it is repatriated to their relatives at home, forming a major source of foreign exchange.

THE PEOPLE

The Philippine culture is one in which a multiplicity of ethnic groups, each with a distinctive culture, language, and lifestyle, have converged and blended into a unique whole. It has been described as a mixture of "Malay, Madrid, and Madison Avenue." More than 100 ethnological groups are recognized, but nearly 98% of Filipinos (or Pinoys, as they refer to themselves) belong to eight major lowland peoples: the Tagalogs, Ilocanos, Pampanguenos, Pangasinenses, Bicolanos, Warays, Cebuanos, and Ilonggos. Natives have long intermarried with foreigners who came to trade, explore, settle, and colonize.

The country's fragmented island formation has led to a marked regionalism and tribalism united by government, commerce, transport, education, mass media, and common underlying social values and cultural history. The vast majority of Filipinos are Christians, while the major minority groups are Muslims and pagan hilltribes. All three groups are mainly Malay-Indonesian (except for Negritos), but they differ in beliefs, values, laws, historical viewpoint, music, art, and dress. The strength of their social structures, aided by geography,

enabled the Muslims and tribespeople to avoid Spanish and American influences and maintain relative cultural purity, at the expense of education and "progress." The Muslims are oriented more toward the wider Islamic world than to Manila, and the hilltribes dwell on the margin of mainstream society, their traditional lifestyles continually eroded by missionaries, teachers, government officials, and other interest groups.

The majority of Filipinos live in the lowlands with a town center *(poblacion)* growing up around the church, town hall, and market. Roads and trails fan out from the center to *barangays* (villages) or barrios, the Spanish term still in use today. The Spaniards founded the cities of Manila, Cebu, Iloilo, Vigan, and Nueva Caceres (Naga); the Americans designated others, and the rest have developed since independence. Today there are 60 chartered cities. A steady stream of people from the provinces are migrating to Manila and other cities in search of a better life. As they do so, the old folkways are gradually breaking down. Like most major cities today, there are large slum and squatter areas.

Population Explosion

In 1900, there were seven million Filipinos; in 1946, 18 million. Today, the Philippines has around 70 million people. Over half the population resides on the two largest islands of Luzon and Mindanao, and about 95% occupy the 11 major islands. Around 10 million live in Metro Manila. Seventy percent of the people live along the coastal plain, and in major agricultural areas like Luzon's Central Plain. The resulting pressure has affected customs of land inheritance and tenancy.

Family-planning programs run headlong into deeply entrenched obstacles: the powerful influence of the Roman Catholic Church; a child-loving culture; a tradition of large families; and the tendency of parents to view children as "insurance" for their old age. The high fertility rate and a relatively good public health service have meant that more babies survive childbirth and the elderly live longer than in the past. If the birthrate is not restrained, the specter looms of 75 million people by the year 2000, and 115 million by 2020.

Education

The Philippines has one of the highest literacy rates among developing countries, about 89%. In remote villages, diplomas hang on the walls of simple huts, reflecting the high regard throughout the archipelago for education. Education is America's greatest legacy to the Philippines, and although the U.S. colonizers built a public school in nearly every village in the country, many have not been repaired or renovated in almost 50 years. Teachers are low-paid and overworked, so the public school system has some similarities to the schools in the U.S.

Education is patterned after the U.S. system, though a dominant feature here is the prevalence of private schools, sectarian and nonsectarian, at every level. There continues to be a high dropout rate, particularily in rural areas. Many college graduates cannot find decent work, and without a degree there is little hope of landing a good job at all. Nursing schools are very popular, and thousands of Filipinos acquire nursing degrees in hopes of immigrating to the U.S. or Canada for work.

The vast majority of colleges and universities are private institutions. The University of San Carlos (USC) in Cebu City and the University of Santo Tomas (UST) in Manila, dating from 1595 and 1611 respectively, are said to be the oldest universities in Asia. UST is the most highly regarded private tertiary institution, and the University of the Philippines (UP) is the most important state university. Exchange programs with U.S. universities are offered for Americans who want to study in the Philippines. UP's main campus is in Diliman, Quezon City, and it has several branches in the provinces. The Philippines has 1.6 million students, and about 25% of those aged 20-24 are enrolled in higher education—a very high percentage.

THE CHINESE

Ethnic Chinese (defined as those with a degree of Chinese parentage who speak a Chinese dialect and adhere to Chinese customs) number about 2.1 million, four percent of the population. Although this is small compared to other Southeast Asian countries, their influence on the commercial life and food of the Philippines is disproportionate to their numbers. Almost all Chinese immigrants were lower-class males, mostly from Fujian province. The 41,000 Chinese (unofficial estimates tripled this total) recorded in the 1903 census included only 500 China-born women. Many immigrants married Filipinas, and in a successful blending of complementary qualities, their offspring have often achieved social, economic, and political prominence. Chinese Filipinos are found in cities and towns throughout the country, often dominating wholesale and retail trade. Over 50% live in the greater Manila area.

History

Chinese merchants were regularly visiting the archipelago centuries before the Spanish arrived. By the time this lucrative trade peaked in the 16th century, many coastal communities were habitual ports of call for Chinese junks. These brought silk and porcelain for the Spanish galleon trade with Mexico. Attracted by the thriving commerce, Chinese immigrants started flocking to the Philippines. Between 1571 and 1603, the number of immigrants rose from 150 to 30,000. Newcomers were assimilated in the Parian, the original Chinese ghetto in Manila, just outside the walled city of Intramuros. The Spanish enforced segregation by forbidding non-Spaniards from settling "within the walls."

The 17th and 18th centuries were marked by several Chinese uprisings against Spanish taxes, discrimination, and oppression. In spite of massacres and expulsion orders, Chinese immigrants came in a steady flow. They usually adapted to every regime and situation and gained a measure of acceptance by converting to Catholicism and taking native wives. The Spanish were caught in a dilemma, since they regarded the Chinese as a threat to security, yet recognized them as an essential element of the economy. The Chinese controlled rice milling and marketing, money lending, and were skilled artisans who built churches and carved statues. Their presence was profitable for the galleon traders and the friars who baptized them. This situation was demoralizing for Filipinos, who found themselves dominated by the Spanish politically and by the Chinese economically. The Spanish were finally forced to tolerate the Chinese.

With the termination of the galleon trade in 1815, the Spanish liberalized commercial and immigration restrictions and allowed the Chinese to live outside the Parian. But even after segregation ceased to be compulsory, the Chinese stayed close together. With their country-wide trading networks, the Chinese became the middlemen between the native economy and Western merchants. Binondo became the main Chinese neighborhood and commercial district. Upheavals in China in the latter half of the 19th century and opportunities in the Philippines combined to bring Chinese men flocking to Manila, and immigration continued through the U.S. era.

The Chinese Today

Even though many Filipinos have Chinese blood, the ethnic Chinese have never been fully integrated into Philippine society. Their separateness has been sustained by the existence of over 120 Chinese schools. But since immigration from mainland China ceased in 1952, there has been a movement away from the traditional enclave, especially by the young and affluent. In spite of intermarriage, however, a lack of understanding still persists between Chinese and Filipinos. As their traditional customs and values become more diluted, and segregation

less firm, the Chinese are becoming increasingly assimilated into the Philippines's cosmopolitan milieu.

Travelers will come across stores, hotels, and restaurants throughout the country owned by Lims, Ongs, Sins, and Tans. Major cities have Chinese cemeteries and Buddhist and Taoist temples, although many Chinese are Christians. The Chinese cemetery in Manila and the Taoist temple in Cebu City are major tourist attractions. Traditional-style arches announce the entrance to Manila's congested Chinatown. Ongpin, its main thoroughfare, is lined with restaurants, medicine shops, and grocery stores. During the Chinese New Year, the Dragon Dance winds through the streets and open-air Chinese opera is performed. On All Saints Day (1 November), the house-like tombs of Manila's Chinese cemetery are alive with families venerating their ancestors.

The Chinese community has been hit in recent years by a spree of kidnap-for-ransom incidents. Directed at the affluent Chinese, the kidnappers have been successful in terrorizing the Chinese community, but not deterring them from their business. It is not uncommon for wealthy Chinese to have bodyguards, and to be extra cautious when taking children to and from school or community activities. Ramos made strides in cracking down on kidnap-for-ransom gangs, but the threat of kidnappings has forced the Chinese community to boycott, protest, and rattle at the doors of Malacanang Palace to do something to protect them.

THE MUSLIMS

Muslim traders had been visiting the islands for centuries, and Muslim communities ranged from Sulu to Manila. In Sulu and western Mindanao, Islam was sufficiently entrenched to survive Spanish colonization, but it was quickly extinguished in the isolated settlements farther north. Today, about three million Muslims live in Mindanao, mostly in Lanao and Cotabato, and in Sulu and southern Palawan. Manila has a Muslim district in Quiapo. The term "Moro" is commonly used for a Muslim; once considered pejorative, the Muslims themselves now speak of the Bangsa Moro ("Moro Nation"). Islam remains a militant social force, and it has made a resurgence in the south in postwar decades.

Muslim Groups

The Moros comprise 13 distinct cultural-linguistic societies, but 95% fall into four major groups: the Maguindanaos of Cotabato, the Maranaos and closely related Ilanuns of Lanao, and the Tausugs and Samals of Sulu. Muslims have never occupied the whole of Mindanao, and the flood of Christian migrants during this century has decreased their proportion. Their greatest concentrations, both historically and today, are in Cotabato, Lanao, and the Sulu Archipelago where they constitute a majority.

History of Conflict

Alienation between the conservative Muslims and more progressive Christians is a legacy dating back to the Spanish era. The conscription of Christian Filipino soldiers in the war with the Muslims was countered by the latter's slave-grabbing raids on Christian settlements. Tensions have been exacerbated by the huge influx of Christians to Muslim homelands in Mindanao. The feeling of being second-class citizens fed discontent that fueled the idea of secession, for which the Moro National Liberation Front (MNLF) became a rallying point. To address this divisive issue, the Manila government set up a plebiscite in 1989 in which Christians and Muslims voted to say "Yes" or "No" to a Mindanao Autonomous Region. Of the 13 provinces polled, only four voted "Yes." Those four, forming the Muslim Mindanao Autonomous Region, are Lanao del Sur, Maguindanao, Tawi-Tawi, and Sulu.

Social Structure

The major Muslim groups, the Maguindanao, Maranao, and Tausug, live in highly organized societies. The survival of the traditional social and political structure, based on sultans, *datus*, and commoners, and featuring elaborate ceremonies, complements Islam in forging cultural cohesiveness. Sultans, the royalty of the dominant groups, claim descent from the Prophet, and succession is hereditary. There's one Tausug sultan in Sulu, the Maguindanao have three, and the Maranao 15. Although the sultans have lost their formal power, they retain substantial prestige and influence.

Datus provide leadership and protection to their followers. The "datuship" remains a potent political institution, since a *datu's* followers form a voting block if he runs for government office. The Philippine government has incorporated the traditional Muslim leaders into the national political machinery, appealing to them for support. Many young Muslims regard *datus* and sultans as unnecessary in the modern Islamic society they hope to build.

Maratabat

This word derives from Arabic and connotes rank or status and the respect due to it. All Filipinos have a strong sense of pride, and conversely of shame, but among Muslims, and especially the Maranao, it's particularly highly developed. Hence, if a Muslim's dignity is offended, even over a trivial matter, he may demand retribution or exact violent revenge. *Maratabat* is closely linked with family honor, and affronts can lead to generations-long feuds. It's a powerful form of social control, since it governs what Muslims do and what they avoid doing so as not to offend the *maratabat* of others.

The Muslim Orientation

When the Spanish arrived, the social, political, and economic organization of Mindanao and Sulu was more advanced than that of Luzon and the Visayas, and Islam was spreading northward. Spain's failure to prevail over the south left the latter culturally isolated from the rest of the archipelago. The orientation of the Moros has thus been southward and westward toward Indonesia, Malaysia, and Brunei, which contain some of the world's heaviest concentrations of Muslims. The dynastic, political, and commercial links between the Mindanao and Sulu sultanates and these neighboring states are now centuries old. The cultural bond is reflected in their music, dance, arts, crafts, dress, and social customs.

THE HILLTRIBES

The vast majority of the 100-plus ethno-linguistic groups and subgroups are traditionally animist hilltribes, which, together with the Muslims, are classified as National Cultural Minorities. These tribes consist of about 3.5 million members. They inhabit the mountains of Luzon, Mindanao, and a few other islands.

They fall into six broad groups: the Mindanao Lumads (almost two million strong); Bontoc, Ifugao, Ibaloi, Kankanai, Kalinga, Isneg, and Tinggian tribes (760,000), indigenous to the Cordillera Central in northern Luzon; the Caraballo group (130,000), comprising four tribes inhabiting the Caraballo range of east-central Luzon; Mangyan (129,000), the generic name for about 12 groups spread throughout Mindoro; hilltribes in Palawan (90,000); and the Negritos (330,000), the most widely scattered minority group dwelling in secluded forests from Luzon to Mindanao. Some minority people also live in the interior hills of Negros and Panay.

All these groups speak dialects belonging to the Philippine branch of the Malayo-Polynesian language family. They also generally understand the language of the major Christian group adjacent to their territory, since it facilitates trade and communication.

The Winds of Change

The highlanders have existed for centuries in self-sufficient harmony with nature. Although they have traded with neighboring lowlanders since early times, their successful resistance to Spanish colonization enabled them to keep their traditional cultures largely intact until the Americans came in 1898, when the forces of central government and market economy started to undermine their ancient lifestyle. The Americans recognized that successful administration of minority groups required separate policies. U.S. officials attached much importance to anthropological research and won the confidence of hitherto hostile tribes.

The physical and cultural intrusion of outsiders into their homelands, however, has been so rapid and novel that many tribespeople have had difficulty adapting. Numerous well-meaning agencies, foundations, and religious organizations have attempted to "help" the tribespeople adjust to the new reality—with decidedly mixed results.

Many feel that the minorities should be left alone, but unfortunately, it's not that simple. The winds of change have already been unleashed and are fanned by population pressure and cultural expansion. The challenge is to regulate the pace of inevitable change so that the tribespeople can absorb the benefits of progress with a minimum of negative aspects while preserving as much as possible their customs and way of life. The agency responsible for tackling the minorities' special problems while helping them preserve their cultures is the Office of Muslim Affairs and Cultural Communities (OMACC).

The Land Issue

Conflict over the ownership and use of land and its resources is the hilltribes' principal problem. Tribal cultures are deeply rooted in their ancestral lands; losing this territory means severing their link with past generations and losing identity. Many tribespeople feel they *belong* to a territory rather than own it. For them, ownership of land relates to its use and improvement, such as by cultivation, in contrast with Philippine law under which owners can do with their land as they see fit.

The natives complain of oppression, such as discrimination against them in surveys, and the awarding of land rights to influential individuals and corporations. Some tribes have been relocated in an attempt by authorities to protect them, or keep them from involvement in the insurgency that simmers in highland areas. The declaration of tribal territory as forest or mineral reserve without consulting villagers on the disposition of resources has also created much resentment. Over 80% of Luzon's mountain provinces, for example, lie within central Cordillera.

Not only does logging cause soil erosion and deplete the supply of game, food and medicinal plants, fuel and materials for handicraft and construction, but often, natives must obtain a license to hunt and gather in their communal woodland. The Kalingas' stand against the threatened flooding of their land by the Chico River dam project is an example of how, in areas where they predominate, a tribe can successfully resist encroachment. But too often, tribespeople have simply moved on under pressure.

Conflicting Values

The tribespeople used to be ruled by a council of elders. Today, they get their directives from the central government in Manila where bureaucrats may have little knowledge or understanding of the hilltribes. Development projects may fail to consider adequately tribal values. Differences between tribal and Philippine laws can also be

Negritos on Boracay

confusing. For example, divorce is legal under one code, illegal under the other; tribal law allows a Kalinga to avenge a murder, but he'd be guilty under national law.

For internal cases involving such issues as land disputes, theft, and assault, tribespeople prefer customary law, which provides the means of settling conflicts and enforcing sanctions. For serious crimes, the guilty may be punished under both systems, one imposing payment of property to the victim, the other imprisonment.

Movement into Modern Society

The tribespeople have suffered growing pains during their passage into a monetary economy. Their inexperience in handling cash, ignorance of prices, and dependence on middlemen have been exploited by some lowlanders who buy their products at fractional values. An increasing number of tribesmen are leaving their villages to study in cities or work in mining and construction camps. These jobs are often temporary, to earn money to buy land, building materials, animals, or an education for their children.

But for others, especially those with too little land for a comfortable existence, the migration may be more permanent. Unskilled and minimally paid, they usually end up living at subsistence level in substandard housing, exposed to a consumer-oriented lifestyle that they can't afford. The move thus involves a drastic cultural transition from their secure traditional society to a modern, impersonal one.

Visiting Tribespeople

Relatively few highlanders today wear their colorful traditional clothing on a daily basis, and one is fortunate indeed to witness tribal ceremonies featuring music, dancing, and other rituals. The best places for the average traveler to observe tribespeople are Sagada, Bontoc, Banaue, and Batad in northern Luzon. They have accommodations, scenic surroundings, and a fascinating local culture. Visitors should be prepared to contend with irregular transportation and security considerations dictated by dissident activity in highland regions.

THE NEGRITOS

The Negritos are the Philippines's oldest surviving race. Their origin is uncertain, but since they're not seamen, it's believed they migrated over land bridges that once linked mainland Asia to the Philippines via Borneo. Negritos are short (rarely over 1.5 meters) and dark, with kinky hair, thick lips, and flat noses. They're thought to be related to similar peoples found in parts of Indonesia, the Malay Peninsula, New Guinea, and the Andaman Islands. Among the Philippines's cultural minorities, the 330,000 Negritos are the most geographically widespread. They form several groups, whose names vary by region and which differ in some cultural aspects. Their original language is completely lost.

Today, they speak the dialects of the neighboring lowland groups with whom they barter.

Their greatest concentrations are in the forested mountains of Luzon. The Aetas (or Balugas) number 65,000 and are spread through Zambales, Bataan, and the western margins of Pangasinan, Tarlac, and Pampanga. The other groups are: 4,000 Attas (Pugots) in Cagayan, Isabela, and Quirino; 7,000 Dumagats (meaning "Those by the Sea") in Aurora, Quezon, and Rizal; around 30,000 Agtas in the Camarines Provinces; 222,000 Atis in Panay and Negros; 9,000 Mamanwa in Surigao and Agusan del Norte; and about 7,000 Bataks in Palawan.

Traditional Life

Negritos are nomadic hunters, fishermen, and food gatherers, supplementing their subsistence by bartering honey, bananas, *kamote,* and baskets for salt, tobacco, rice, clothing, tools, and metal utensils. They prefer to live in small, self-sufficient bands of up to 10 families (usually related to a common ancestor) and to keep interaction with outsiders to a minimum. Members of these groups are very close and live harmoniously. Leadership rests with the elder men. Marriages are often arranged and a bride price (weapons, cloth, money) is paid. Negritos live in thatched lean-to structures along riverbanks close to the forest. An entire family sleeps, eats, and entertains guests on a grass mat under the shelter, which can be adjusted easily to form a windbreak, or moved from one location to another.

They may stay in one area for a considerable period, planting corn, beans, bananas, cassava, *kamote,* and taro. When the soil is exhausted, they move on. Mobility is aided by the paucity of their belongings. They hunt wild pig, deer, monkeys, lizards, and birds with bows and arrows, spears, traps, and dogs. An unsurpassed knowledge of the creatures and plants of their habitat makes them skilled hunters and proficient in herbal medicine. Their pagan beliefs and rituals confirm a worldview of man's union with nature.

Animist practices invoke a multitude of spirits; prayer, ceremonies, offerings, shamans, trances, talismans, and superstitions all play a role. Noted for their love of music, song, and dance, Negritos are also deft weavers of rattan and abaca and make decorated bamboo combs and lime-holders.

The Negritos Today

The Negritos are the most exploited of all the cultural minorities. For much of their history, they've been forced deeper into the upland forests by incoming migrants. Their isolation has kept them timid and ignorant of lowland ways, which has led to exploitation by merchants who ply them with goods on credit, payable in produce with interest, leading to hopeless debt. They've been subjected to expulsion, relocation, and serfdom. Severing links with their ancestral lands is a severe psychological wrench for them.

Government and religious agencies have established development projects for the Negritos, but nearly all are based on farming, which has little interest for them since it lacks the thrill and challenge of hunting, fishing, and gathering. Also, long exposure to the sun contrasts disagreeably with their cool, shady forest environment. Some find work guiding loggers, or acting as night watchmen in cities like Olongapo. A settled life not only constricts their penchant for space and mobility but imposes unfamiliar social and cultural concepts on them. Not surprisingly, many can't cope with rapid and drastic changes. Alcoholism is a problem, and some have resorted to begging.

MESTIZOS

The mestizo is the offspring of a mixed marriage: between Filipino and Spanish, Filipino and Chinese, etc. Mestizos have been described as the single most important social group in the Philippines. During the 19th century, they acquired land and became involved in agriculture. Wealth and education made them a bourgeois merchant class, the elite of native society.

From their ranks emerged the *ilustrados* who inspired the revolution. José Rizal, for example, was a fifth-generation Chinese mestizo, and former president Corazon Aquino also belongs to this class. The mestizo clans, their scions often U.S.-educated, form a substantial portion of the economic and political oligarchy: around 60 mestizo families control most of the Philippine economy. Representing only about two percent of the population, the mestizos earn 55% of the nation's total personal income.

RELIGION

The Philippines is the only Christian country in Asia. About 90% of Filipinos embrace Christianity; 85% are Roman Catholics. Filipinos are a religious people who turn to faith in times of trouble. But they are not dogmatic; rather, they see religion as a way of life with rituals that provide continuity, communal cohesion, and moral purpose. Most of the world's major religions are represented in Manila. Visitors wishing to attend services should check the telephone directory for addresses of church, synagogue, or temple. To this day, Christian missionaries remain very active in the Philippines—be they Mormons, Jehovah's Witnesses, Mennonites, Catholics, Baptists, or Presbyterians; they're all doing God's work here!

CATHOLICISM

Missionaries accompanying the conquistadors began making converts, and by the 17th century Christianity was firmly established. The task was made easier by the lack of a single, unifying indigenous religion. The friars who replaced the native shamans made Catholicism more attractive by adapting many pagan beliefs and rituals to it, while impressing the people with a combination of ostentation and mysticism. The approach varied according to regional characteristics. In Luzon, where women had long enjoyed social prominence and had been powerful priestesses, the Virgin Mary was emphasized. In the Visayas, where children have always been indulged, the focal point was the Santo Niño ("Holy Infant"). In spite of their many abuses of power and flesh, the friars prevailed. Eventually, a native clergy emerged and became increasingly aware of the need to free their countrymen from the corruption and oppression of the Spanish priests. This element of nationalism in the church was a factor in the growth of revolutionary feeling.

The church deeply pervades the lives of ordinary Filipinos in all but the remotest tribal areas and the staunchly Muslim regions. Personal religious habits vary from genuine piety to an automatic adherence to ritual. Churches, often centuries old, dominate the towns, and the priest is an important figure in every community. Every town holds an annual fiesta in honor of its patron saint, and Holy Week and Christmas have immense significance.

Quiapo Church, Manila—site of the mass for the Feast of the Black Nazarene in January

CARL PARKES

FAITH HEALING

Faith healing is a strange and fascinating aspect of the Philippines, undoubtedly the world's faith-healing center today. Thousands visit the Philippines each year to seek cures for ailments that may have been pronounced incurable by modern medicine. Why the Philippines? This question has aroused much speculation but remains unanswered.

One can note that the rural Filipinos live simply and very close to nature. They're essentially spiritual people, rather than merely religious. Having always believed in *anitos* (spirits), they find it easy to accept the existence of phenomena beyond the comprehension of the five senses. Pre-Hispanic male and female shamans practiced healing, and it's assumed that this survived in the rural villages. Hilltribes still employ traditional healing methods.

It's also claimed that the Philippines lies within a powerful "psychic center of influence," perhaps deriving from a conjectured link between the Philippines (and Pangasinan in particular) and the legendary lost Pacific continent known as Mu or Lemuria, an Atlantis-like land said to have been the home of an ancient civilization with advanced psychic powers.

Mystery and Reality

Psychic surgery, due to its dramatic nature, has attracted the most international attention. It involves the painless insertion of the healer's fingers into the patient's body, removal of tissues, tumors, growths, or foreign matter, and closing the incision without a scar. Psychic surgery occurs to some extent in Brazil, Indonesia, and Central Africa, but only in the Philippines is it so widely practiced.

Strangely, the vast majority of these surgeons come from one province, Pangasinan, although many of them now work in cities such as Manila and Baguio. The world at large became aware of the existence of psychic surgery in the late '50s, when two Americans investigated tales of "miracle cures" in the Philippines. Eleuterio Terte, a healer from San Fabian (Pangasinan), is recognized as the first psychic surgeon. Shortly after WW II, he suddenly discovered that he could open and close bodies with his bare hands. Terte, who never charged his patients, went on to train several of today's renowned psychic surgeons before he died, a poor man, in 1979.

Because it defies all known laws of physics, chemistry, and biology, many conventional scientists assume psychic surgery to be based on trickery, mass hypnosis, magic, or sleight of hand, despite seemingly incontrovertible proof to the contrary. Skeptics claim that healers conceal small razors between their fingers, then extract and discard what are really the bloody organs of pigs and chickens.

The country's major religious festivals provide valuable insight into the Filipino psyche. Many folk touches have been added to harvest and other festivals. Some events are renowned for the intensity of the religious passion they inspire. The vast and fervent throng at Manila's Black Nazarene Procession (9 January) or Good Friday at San Fernando (Pampanga), where volunteers have themselves crucified with nails and flagellantes beat their backs to a raw, bloody mess are unforgettable. The church does not encourage such fanaticism, but one soon realizes that here, Catholicism is practiced with a difference.

The Church and Politics

The church plays a potent political role and was a major factor in the downfall of the Marcos regime. Its head, Jaime Cardinal Sin, is a powerful and respected figure, but he is somewhat at odds with President Estrada, who is also a Catholic. Some priests and nuns have been attracted by liberation theology, a doctrine of social revolution that is at odds with the church's conservative tradition.

Sympathizing with the country's downtrodden peasants, the clergy has been deeply involved in the struggle for social change. Some members advocate radical solutions and have formed ties with the New People's Army. The centrist church hierarchy, led by Cardinal Sin, and the left-leaning liberation theologists have conflicting views on social and political activism. At present, divorce is illegal in the Philippines, and the Catholic Church discourages modern methods of birth control.

However, numerous Western scientists have visited the Philippines to study this phenomenon, and the consensus seems to be that while fakery does occur, and the achievement of cures is somewhat inconsistent and unpredictable, incredible feats of healing have definitely been accomplished. Scientists have seen healers remove clearly visible cysts with their bare hands, extract teeth without anesthesia, and take eyeballs out of their sockets, and many photographs exist of healers' fingers probing beneath incisions they have made.

Not all operations are successful; healers are human and thus imperfect. Their powers fluctuate and occasionally disappear completely. This can be caused by the negative vibrations of those around them, or personal overindulgence in drinking, sex, gambling, etc. Since most healers are from poor backgrounds and have had little schooling, the acquisition of wealth can bring temptation. Thus, directly or indirectly, commercialization can diminish the healer's ability. Yet, prosperous healers also operate effectively, so firm conclusions cannot be made.

It's estimated that psychic surgeons have performed over three million operations during the past 40 years. The constant flow of trusting patients would suggest successful treatment. While an attitude of "faith" would seem to be a prerequisite, the significance of its role in the effectiveness of the cure is uncertain. It's not necessary to be a Christian to be healed; in fact, many patients are Muslims.

The Healers

As many as 15,000 faith healers are found in the Philippines, but only about 80 claim to be psychic surgeons. The others practice several styles of healing, such as magnetic (a laying on of hands) or telepathic healing; some use herbs, saliva, massage, or reflexology; some specialize in a single activity, such as bone-setting. Sometimes the methods are unusual. Healers are generally devout Christians.

Many of those who have resisted commercialization are active members of the Union Espiritista Cristiana de Filipinas ("Christian Spiritists Union of the Philippines"), which believes that the gift of healing should be freely given to those in need. The union has trained most contemporary faith healers, but those who pursue wealth leave the organization and in some cases establish their own churches. Numerous healers ascribe their power to a personal spirit guide. One healer displays a sign in her clinic: "God does the healing. I am just His instrument."

For those wishing to probe further into faith healing, the following books, available in Manila bookstores, are recommended: *The Truth Behind Faith Healing in the Philippines* and *The Magicians of God: The Amazing Stories of Philippine Faith Healers*, both by Jaime T. Licauco, and *Faith Healing and Psychic Surgery in the Philippines*, by Jesus B. Lava and Antonio S. Araneta.

OTHER CHRISTIAN CHURCHES

The Spanish had integrated secular and religious government, but church and state were separated when the U.S. took over, and religious tolerance prevails. Protestant ideas were introduced by American missionaries and schoolteachers, who had the most success among hilltribes and the urban middle class.

Two independent Filipino churches have attracted substantial numbers of adherents, totaling about five percent of the population. Gregorio Aglipay established the Iglesia Filipina Independiente ("Philippine Independent Church") in 1902, a nationalist church that doesn't acknowledge the pope's supremacy. It has signed a covenant with the Episcopal Church. Commonly called the Aglipayan Church, its cathedral in Manila is on Taft Avenue.

The Iglesia ni Kristo ("Church of Christ"), founded in 1914, has grown rapidly since WW II. It's characterized by an authoritarian, evangelical-style, mandatory twice-weekly attendance and tithing, its ministers' high degree of involvement in members' lives, and the temperate lifestyle it demands. Its appeal is partly based on its reputation for taking care of its members and providing jobs and other material benefits. The distinctive large, white churches are landmarks in most towns and cities. Nonmembers are forbidden to attend services.

The country has many other sects, cults, and revivalist movements, usually centered on a charismatic leader offering followers, who are typically poor and underprivileged, a sense of fraternity and promises of a new utopia. Iglesia Watawat ng Lahi ("Flag of the Race") is based on the belief that José Rizal (the Philippines's national hero) was a reincarnation of Christ and will return to redeem the faithful from their life of suffering. Based in Calamba (Laguna), it claims 250,000 believers.

ISLAM

Filipino Muslims are part of the Sunni sect, to which a worldwide majority belongs. Some groups are more orthodox than others, and individual devoutness varies. Formal Koranic doctrine and the practice of Islam here have been somewhat adulterated by ancient animist beliefs and adapted to *adat* (customary law). Pre-Islamic folk beliefs and rituals generally apply to cultivation and the life cycle. Offerings are made to a variety of benign and malign spirits.

Adat embodies the society's unwritten traditional rules of conduct. It governs the course of family life from birth to burial, methods of doing things, and a strict code of honor. It's supplemented by *shari'a* (Islamic law). Larger settlements have an *agama* (religious court) to settle disputes. In rural areas, the local leader will arbitrate according to *adat, shari'a,* or a mixture of both. Questions of religion and custom may be referred to the *ulama* (learned men), composed of imams of mosques, *qadis* (judges), and some of the hajjis (returned pilgrims). Muslim society still retains many feudal elements, and difficulties have arisen in reconciling Islamic and national laws and educational systems. Polygamy and divorce are legal under Islam and illegal under civil law.

A growing number of Muslim students are enrolled in the country's 1,000-plus *madrasas* (religious schools). Usually connected with a mosque, their curriculum includes instruction in Islamic principles and rituals, and reading the Koran in Arabic. Offering courses from kindergarten to second-year college for both males and females, they're not recognized by the government but receive financial assistance from Muslim countries. Muslim institutions of higher learning have also been established in Marawi and elsewhere.

OTHER FAITHS

Buddhism and Taoism

Many Chinese follow Buddhism and Taoism, and cities with large Chinese populations, like Manila and Cebu, have temples. Buddhism in the Philippines has blended to some extent with Catholicism. For example, the temple in Manila's Chinese cemetery contains images of both the Buddha and the Virgin, and the important Feast of the Dead has been moved from its traditional day to coincide with All Saints' Day. Taoism, like Confucianism, is considered a moral and political philosophy rather than a religion.

Indigenous Beliefs

Missionaries have been very active among the cultural minorities. As recent converts, however, the tribespeople maintain many aspects of their traditional religions, including native priests; belief in complex pantheons of both benevolent and malevolent deities and spirits, including those of their ancestors and the elements, usually ruled by a supreme god; carved wooden images; tribal epics; and rituals relating to the life cycle, healing, and planting and harvesting. Much of tribal social life remains based on these rituals, which may involve prayer, incantation, dance, sacrifices, and feasting. About two percent of the country's population is considered animist, but except in the most isolated villages, highlanders practice a combination of animism and Christianity.

The Mystical

The Philippines is a fascinating country for those inclined to search for the mystical. It's the world's foremost place for the practice of faith healing and psychic surgery. Pangasinan, where most of the faith healers come from, has many unexplained mysteries. Mt. Banahaw, sprawling between Laguna and Quezon Provinces, is believed to be a source of mystic power and is held sacred by numerous esoteric sects and hermits that dwell on its slopes. Certain places, such as the islands of Sibuyan and Siquijor, have a reputation for witchcraft and sorcery.

LANGUAGE

Over 100 ethnological groups in the Philippines speak an estimated 70 languages, about 50 of which claim more than 10,000 speakers. Eight major languages, together with their dialects, are the mother tongues of about 90% of the population. Tagalog, spoken in Manila and central Luzon, and Cebuano, spoken in Cebu, Bohol, eastern Negros, and most of Mindanao, are each the first language of about a quarter of the people. Ilocano is the principal language of northern Luzon. Hiligaynon (Ilonggo) is spoken in Panay and western Negros. Bicol predominates in southern Luzon, Waray-Waray in Samar and eastern Leyte, and Pampango and Pangasinan in their respective provinces on Luzon. English and Pilipino, a national language based on Tagalog, are the official languages.

All the indigenous languages derive from a single prototype known as Original Indonesian and belong to the Malayo-Polynesian family of languages. Southeast Asian migrants arrived over an extended period and then spent centuries in isolated settlements. Dialects drifted apart, each to be spoken by a relatively small group. Additional words were acquired from the foreign traders who visited the islands. Tagalog, for example, contains numerous words of Sanskrit, Chinese, Arabic, and Spanish derivation. The early Tagalogs, Pampangos, Ilocanos, Visayans, Hanuno'o (Mangyans), and some other groups developed written alphabets.

Most native languages are mutually incomprehensible, in spite of similarities in grammar and pronunciation. However, some people learn the dialect of a neighboring region. These languages are mainly used in speech, though some newspapers and magazines are published in them.

Spanish

The Philippines is one of the few former colonies of Spain where Spanish hasn't become the national language, despite 333 years of Spanish dominion. Spanish was spoken by the wealthy, land-owning families, and no more than 10% of the population ever spoke it. Instances of its influence on local dialects are seen today through numbers, time, and some culinary terms, particularily in the Chavacano dialect of Zamboanga City, which is as close to Spanish as any Filipino dialect can get.

Spanish was a compulsory subject in some high schools until 1968, but few Filipinos, with the exception of the mestizo class, speak it well. It remains the mother tongue of the Spanish-Filipino mestizos.

English

The Americans established the public school system, with English as the medium of instruction. It has had a profound influence on Philippine life and culture. By 1930, English was entrenched as the language of business, government, and national communication. It has remained so, though the role of Pilipino has strengthened through its expanded use in education and the media. Currently, the Estrada administration wants to make Tagalog the medium of instruction and eliminate English as the first language to learn in school. Although this is probably a sound nationalistic idea, when the rest of Asia is scrambling to learn English and speak it fluently, it seems to be yet another step backward for the Philippines.

Currently, English is much in evidence in the mass media: most TV and radio stations broadcast in both English and Tagalog, and many newspapers and magazines are written in English, with a smattering of Tagalog mixed in. Typically, a newspaper story might be reported in English, but quoted dignitaries or movie stars will have their responses written in Tagalog.

Spoken English can be quaint, with antiquated expressions like "chicks" for girls, brand names used generically, like Colgate for toothpaste and Kodak for camera. Other Filipinos are so bilingual that they jump from English to Tagalog, speaking a mix called Taglish. Try following a conversation as a group of locals yap in their own version of Taglish.

Some native words have made their way into English. "Boondocks" or "boonies," for example,

LANGUAGE

Over 70 dialects and eight major languages are spoken throughout the Philippines. These include Tagalog, based on the Malay language and spoken by over 10 million residents of central Luzon, and the Cebuano language spoken by almost 20 million Visayans. Other languages include Ilocano spoken in northwest Luzon, Bicolano in southern Luzon, Pangasinese in northwestern Luzon, and Hiligaynon in Panay and eastern Negros.

The national language is Pilipino, a variation of Tagalog, although English continues to serve as the lingua franca of the archipelago. This odd situation is a legacy of American rule, when foreign educators established their language as the medium of instruction in all public schools. Today, Pilipino is being promoted over English for reasons of national pride, but most Filipinos continue to speak a heady melange of English, Pilipino, a regional dialect, and Taglish, a bizarre mixture of Tagalog and American slang. The universality of English ensures that basic conversations are possible with almost everybody from college students to loinclothed tribespeople.

Of course, peeling off a few phrases of Tagalog or Pilipino will help to establish your rapport and impress your hosts. It also helps save money. The language is complex in structure but easy to speak since most words are pronounced exactly as spelled. Important exceptions are words spoken with a Spanish inflection (José is pronounced as "ho-zay"), stretched out double consonants (ng is "nang"), double vowels pronounced as two syllables (Lake Taal is "ta-al," maalam is "ma-alam"), and the interchangeability of F and P (as in Pilipino and Filipino). A few useful words and phrases:

Conversation

greetings—*mabuhay*
good morning—*magandang umaga po*
good evening—*magandang gabi po*
goodbye—*paalam na po*
please/thank you—*paki/salamat po*
you're welcome—*wala pong anuman*
yes/no—*oo/hindi*
How are you?—*Kumusta po sila?*
What is your name?—*Anong pangalan mo?*
How old are you?—*Ilang taon ka na?*
Where do you live?—*Saan po kayo nakatira?*
Where are you from?—*Taga saan ka?*
What is your job?—*Anong tarbaho mo?*
How much do you make?—*Magkano ang iyong suweldo?*
Are you married?—*May asawa ka ba?*
How many children?—*Ilan ang anak mo?*
You are beautiful!—*Maganda ka!*
I love you.—*Mahal kita.*
Where are you going?—*Saan ka pupunta?*
I am going to . . . —*upunta ako sa . . .*
no problem—*walang problema*
never mind—*hindi bale*

Bargaining

do you have . . . ?—*meron ba kayong . . . ?*
Where is a cheap hotel?—*Saan may murang hotel?*
How much is this?—*Magkano ito?*
too expensive!—*masyadong mahal!*
anything cheaper?—*mayroon bang mas mura?*
Where is my change?—*Nasaan ang sukli ko?*
It doesn't matter—*Bahalana.*

Numbers

1, 2, 3—*isa, dalawa, tatlo*
4, 5, 6—*apat, lima, anim*
7, 8, 9, 10—*pito, walo, siyam, sampu*
11, 12—*labing isa, labing dalawa*
20, 30—*dalawampu, tatlumpu*
40, 50—*apatnapu, limampu*
100, 1000—*isang daan, isanglibo*

Getting Around

How do I get to . . . ?—*Paano ang pagpunta sa . . . ?*
Where is the bus stop?—*Saan ang hintayan ng bus?*
Which bus is for Manila?—*Aling bus ang papuntang Manila?*
What town is this?—*Anong bayan ito?*
I want to go to Manila.—*Gusto kong pumunta sa Manila.*
I need . . . —*kailangan ko ng . . .*
bathroom—*banyo*
bus station—*istasyon ng bus*
police station—*istasyon ng polise*
village/town/city—*barrio/bayan/lungsod*
hill/mountain—*burol/bundok*

meaning "out in the woods" comes from the Tagalog word *bundok* (mountain). American marines brought the term back to the U.S. after WW II. English is sufficiently understood for the Philippines to claim to be the third-largest English-speaking nation in the world, after the U.S. and the U.K. When speaking to less-educated Filipinos, it is important to speak slowly and distinctly. But be careful not to insult people with pidgin English; many Filipinos understand English a little better than they speak it, and they are sensitive to childlike English when being addressed.

Pilipino

In 1937, President Manuel Quezon suggested the adoption of a national language to unite the multilingual country. Tagalog, the most widely understood native language, was chosen as its basis. In addition to being spoken in and around Manila, it was the language of revolution. The resulting language, known as Pilipino, is highly structured grammatically and has a rich vocabulary, enriched by words from Spanish, English, and other native dialects. Over half the population understands Pilipino, and it is used as a language of business and discussion among different groups of Filipinos.

The Contemporary Philippines

Filipinos are great linguists, and many speak two or three dialects plus English. Cantonese or Fukinese is spoken among the Chinese community, yet they can mix Pilipino and English into their conversation, allowing them to speak three languages at once! Many Muslims understand Arabic, while English has remained the language of the elite; government and business reports and documents are always in English, though the use of Pilipino is increasing as the drive to introduce it into the schools has gained popular support.

People from different areas use English or Pilipino to communicate with each other, while regionally they use the dialect that is their native tongue. Ilocano is used in commerce throughout northern Luzon, Cebuano in much of the Visayas and Mindanao.

FILIPINO SOCIETY

THE FAMILY

Filipino families are much closer than those of the West. The environment is highly personalized. Children are brought up to be polite, cooperative, modest, and religious. Communal feeling is encouraged. Upon marrying, newlyweds usually set up their own home, but family ties remain strong. They often take in a brother or sister to ease the burden on parents and help with chores. The husband is nominally head of the household, but the wife runs the home and manages the finances. They make important decisions together. The fact that divorce is illegal contributes to unity.

Family Obligations

The family defines an orderly world in which each member has a specific place, with obligations and privileges. Dependence and a sense of belonging are fostered. Children are doted on, the elderly respected and cared for. Placing one's parents in an old-folks' home would be considered scandalous. Sharing both good fortune and crisis, the clan operates as disciplinary mechanism, placement agency, and social assistance program. It provides its members with tremendous security, so that to be poor in the Philippines is somewhat different from being poor in the West.

In the absence of a public welfare system, the clan eases the impact of illness or unemployment. When a Filipino needs help, he can depend on his family; likewise, he can be called upon to help others in need. Those with wealth and power, especially, are expected to assist their less fortunate relatives.

Ties are not diminished by distance. Those living away from home contribute to the family budget and are warmly welcomed when they return for fiestas and social occasions. Major decisions are based on consensus, though the advice of elders is given special deference. There's a great deal of sharing. Unlike Westerners, who draw strength from independence,

CARL PARKES

a family portrait

Filipinos like the security of this interdependent existence, with its close bonds bred of mutual responsibility.

Kinship

The family is enlarged through marriage. Filipinos count blood relatives down to fourth cousins, and the relatives of in-laws are considered family. The family is further extended by the *compadrazgo* system, which derives from the Roman Catholic practice of linking the lives of children and their godparents. Godparents act as sponsors at baptism, confirmation, and wedding. In addition to their friends, parents commonly invite their wealthy and powerful acquaintances to become godparents to ensure a child's well-being should they die and to aid the child's social mobility. It's an important relationship in which godparents and their families become the child's family's ritual kin in a public demonstration of reciprocal loyalty that intensifies the personal alliance.

Social Organization

Filipinos place great emphasis on personal loyalty, and the network of allegiance and reciprocal obligation extends to society as a whole. The pre-Hispanic relationship between *datu* and follower has evolved into one between landlords, politicians, doctors, teachers, and businessmen on the one hand, and tenants, workers, etc. on the other. Powerful patrons provide material help, employment, influence, and protection, and are repaid with personal services ranging from specific tasks to political support. Such relationships may be sealed by the *compadrazgo* system.

The Filipina

It has been suggested that Filipino women are "more equal" within their society than Western women are in theirs, a status that predates colonial times. Women in the Philippines maintain a very high profile in public life, from the president down to *barangay* level. They are doctors, lawyers, and bankers, and dominate the fields of education, pharmacy, and dentistry. Women generally acquire more formal education than males at every level; they earn nearly two-thirds of the master's degrees and about 90% of doctorates.

Girls grow up with a strong self-image. While still young, they are given much more responsibility within the family than their brothers. In both urban and farming families, women enjoy equality within the marriage, reinforced by the tracing of kinship through both parents and the system of inheritance. Family property is divided equally among all children, and women retain ownership even after marriage.

Single women are more likely than men to move to a city for study or work. In government offices and corporations, women's exclusion from "macho" expectations of success increases their effectiveness; they can take decision-making risks where men might defer judgment to a higher level to avoid blame for any error. In spite of their demonstrated competence and self-confidence, however, Filipinas still have to contend with life in a man's world. They are paid less than men for equal work.

Husbands and boyfriends often have a double standard when it comes to sexual freedom. Whether waitresses or doctors, many working women are the principal family breadwinners. Yet Filipinas haven't adopted an aggressive feminist or "liberated" stance. They prefer to coexist in a system where men retain the public appearance of power while women often pull the strings.

NATIONAL CHARACTERISTICS

Filipinos by nature dislike doing things alone, whether at work or leisure. Hospital rooms, for example, usually have an extra bed so that a relative can remain with the patient day and night. Loners are considered weird. *Bayanihan* is the communal spirit that enables Filipinos to come together and help each other at a moment's notice in times of need. This group orientation can be seen at many levels: family, clan, and community. Membership gives identity and a sense of belonging to the individual, who responds by conforming to the group's opinions, tastes, and norms. When they move away from home, Filipinos recognize other levels of belonging: their town, city, province, island, region.

Hierarchy

Group structures are hierarchical. From them, most Filipinos derive their strong respect for authority and age, which are equated with wisdom and experience. Individuals are subservient to parents, elders, leaders, and officials, but in turn look to them for support and assistance. It extends to a national level too: strong authoritarian government seems to suit Asians better than Westerners. Filipinos tend to be authoritarian, even dictatorial, when given power, which can stifle initiative on the part of subordinates. At the same time, they may also be paternalistic and benevolent. An employer might, for example, provide his employees with food, medical care, or personal loans. Power is jealously guarded; bureaucrats often don't delegate their signing authority, making petitioners wait during their absence.

Polite forms of address are used toward those of higher social rank, elders, and strangers. In conversation, a Filipino continually shifts from high to low status, depending on whom he's talking to. In Pilipino, it's common for "my poor and insignificant self" to address "your honored and

exalted self." Such expressions of inferiority have evolved from the ancient *datu* system, reinforced by centuries of colonial domination. Awareness of rank and status is reflected in the universal use of titles, e.g., Attorney Santos, Engineer Alvarez, Ex-Mayor Ramos.

Personalized Approach

The Filipino way of doing things is heavily centered on relationships. Trust *(tiwala)* is a key element of camaraderie. Filipinos don't feel comfortable in impersonal situations. In business and politics, this personalized approach too often leads to nepotism, cronyism, and favoritism; ability and merit are often secondary. However, the infusion of a new generation of Western-oriented managers is putting emphasis on competence as criterion. Behavior depends on what others will think, say, or do, whether they'll be pleased or displeased. It's aimed at maintaining "face," smooth interpersonal relationships, group affiliations, and a strong personal alliance network.

Typical Western frankness is considered tactless. Filipinos tend to express truth diplomatically to preserve rapport. In distasteful situations, they avoid confrontation by using respectful language, soft voice, gentle manner, and indirect approaches such as employing intermediaries, euphemisms, allusions, ambiguous expressions, and oblique comments. Such subtlety and indirectness depend on the perceptiveness of the recipient for effectiveness.

FILIPINO TERMS

Bahala Na

Individuals regard their success or failure as due to luck, fate, God, or the spirits, expressed by the phrase *bahala na* ("what will be, will be"). On the positive side, this attitude can sustain a Filipino's morale through hardships; he can smile and make the best of adverse situations. On the negative side, it can breed complacency characterized by a lack of discipline, initiative, or self-confidence. It can make him an escapist, putting problems and tasks off to the indefinite future. It may cause him to embark on irrational courses of action that can lead to danger or debt.

Hiya

Filipinos will go to great lengths to avoid causing others *hiya* (shame). To be criticized as *walang hiya* (shameless, insensitive) is a potent censure. Anxiety about being left without acceptance or approval works as a powerful sanction against improper behavior. It also inhibits self-confidence. A housewife may apologize for the poor quality of her house or food even though the guest is content. It may cause Filipinos to compete to pay a restaurant or bar bill, or to buy things they don't really need so as not to lose face.

Utang Na Loob

A debt of gratitude, honor, or blood, this term literally means "inner debt" or "heart debt." Filipinos live within a network of two-way obligations: requesting and accepting a favor implies a willingness to repay it. They feel indebted when someone makes a loan, finds a relative employment, or smooths a bureaucratic procedure, and will take pains to square such an account. An unpaid *utang na loob* causes *hiya*. But it's accepted that an individual pays according to his means. Thus, a loan may be repaid in small gifts and services rather than cash. Long-term reciprocal relationships may arise, e.g., between landlords and tenants.

Pakikisama

Closely linked with the desire for social acceptance and approval, *pakikisama* (conformity, camaraderie) manifests itself in groups of all kinds and ages regardless of class. To maintain *pakikisama,* Filipinos will yield to group opinion, subjugate ill-feeling beneath a pleasant demeanor, avoid speaking harshly or saying "No" directly, and will only criticize or reprimand very tactfully. *Pakikisama* enriches community spirit and can lead to efficient accomplishment of common goals. But it's also the reason businessmen may tolerate an inefficient staff, particularly in the case of relatives and friends. It can cause people to socialize beyond their means.

Amor Propio

Filipinos are very sensitive to criticism, insults, and hurt feelings, whether real or imagined, and they can become implacable enemies for reasons that Westerners would deem trivial. *Hiya, utang na loob,* and *pakikisama* all affect an individual's *amor proprio* (self-esteem). *Amor propio* demands conformity to approved behavior patterns. It can also lead to showing off, especially in the presence of peers and subordinates. Where there's emotional involvement, there's *amor proprio,* and pricking it may have devastating results.

CONDUCT AND CUSTOMS

Filipinos are among the friendliest, most hospitable people in the world. The widespread understanding of English and familiarity with Western culture make travel and communication far easier than in most Asian lands. But as in any country, an awareness of the local customs and mentality can greatly enhance your visit and help you avoid misunderstandings. Filipinos have a unique outlook on life, as well as their own ways of communicating, coexisting, and accomplishing things. The more a foreigner conforms to these customs, the smoother and more enjoyable a stay will be.

First Impressions

Many visitors are surprised to be addressed openly by strangers in the street. The ubiquitous greeting "Hey Joe" (also "Hey man") derives from the welcome given to liberating U.S. troops in 1945. Today, its use can range from genuine friendliness to slight contempt. Some travelers find it irritating, but there's not much you can do except grin and bear it.

Similarly, when schoolchildren echo, "What's your name?" they don't expect an answer, but will develop a case of the giggles if you respond and ask their name in turn. They always, shyly, tell you their names and the rest of the group chimes in, too. In response to "Where are you going?" a nod and *"Diyan lang"* ("There only") is an appropriate rejoinder.

Filipinos are very polite, but also incredibly curious; with the best of intentions they may ask a range of personal questions. "Why don't you have any children?" or "How come you are still single?" and "Where's your companion?" are common inquiries. Being so group-oriented, Filipinos consider loners abnormal. Thus, if you're invited to a Filipino gathering, it's considered completely natural for you to bring a friend. And if you arrange to meet a Filipino socially, he or she may arrive with several companions, even on a date.

Nicknames are very prevalent; you'll hear them everywhere, from "Cory" Aquino, "Doy" Laurel, and "Bong Bong" Marcos (son of the late president) to "JiJi, JoJo, Benjie, Dodong, Oping, or Recto." Lots of boys and girls are called "Boy" and "Baby," respectively, and many men and women retain those nicknames for life. A favorite of mine belonged to a man whose nickname was "Booboy," but he liked to mock himself by saying, "just call me Boobs."

The strange thing about nicknames is that any dignitary, journalist, politician, or movie star is never quoted without a reference to his or her nickname. For example, a news story will quote a Jose "Boy" Reyes as saying to Isabela "Babes" Fernandez that Ferdinand "Bong Bong" Marcos met with Gloria "G.G." Gomez. It's very distracting and amusing to find new nicknames in the daily papers and magazines.

Filipinos have a strange habit of laughing or giggling to relieve tension in embarrassing or emotional situations; it doesn't mean that an incident is being treated lightly. People don't believe in waiting in line here, so expect to be jostled at post offices, bus stops, etc. When in remote regions, travelers must also get used to being stared at and touched. Curious children stroke beards and the hair on arms and legs.

Touching and holding hands between acquaintances of the same sex, both men and women, is more prevalent than in the West and merely implies close friendship. Yet lovers refrain from being demonstrative in public, and nudity on public beaches is considered offensive. Filipino society is based on reciprocity; you may always ask a favor of a Filipino, and he may not hesitate to ask one in return. Don't lend money if you're really concerned about getting it back. Being able to sing and play guitar or chess are definite social assets for the foreigner.

Time

Filipinos, especially country-dwellers, have a very relaxed attitude toward promptness and punctuality. References to time may be vague at best—"by and by" and "in a little while" are common phrases. However, if a local tells you a bus is due into town "by and by," he probably means within the hour.

Punctuality on social occasions is considered abnormal. Filipinos allow for this by setting appointments ahead of the time intended. If guests are invited for 1900, it's taken for granted that they'll arrive around 2030. A punctual appearance would be met by embarrassed smiles and a general scurrying: it's almost bad manners to behave so formally! As a visitor, it's a good idea to lapse into this time-frame. If you must hurry, don't show petulance at delays or slow service; it will be more effective to quietly explain your situation. Don't, however, depend on transportation departing late.

Women Travelers

Women have high status in Filipino society. A woman traveling alone will find people extremely solicitous of her well-being. In the event a local male makes unwanted advances, a polite but firm word of discouragement usually cools the situation. If a Filipino will not give up, the best defense you have is to ask a Filipina for some help or advice. However, if you have given a Filipino some kind of wrong impression (very easy to do!), he may still persist. Your best recourse is to leave the scene to avoid confrontation.

Photography

Most Filipinos love to be photographed, but it's still good manners to ask before taking someone's photo. The Ifugao of Banaue now pose in native costumes for money, and more remote tribes may require some matches or foodstuff in return. Other villages, such as Bugnay (Kalinga-Apayao), demand a set photography fee, but giving away money for a photo still sets a bad precedent. As in most countries, sensitive subjects such as military installations, slums, Muslim women, etc., should be avoided.

Tipping

Tipping is not a Filipino tradition, but prevails in tourist-oriented situations. Major hotels and upscale restaurants generally add a service charge to the bill; additional tipping is optional. In ordinary restaurants and bars, tipping isn't necessary, though it's certainly appreciated. Porters at airports and hotels, barbers, and hairdressers should be given a small tip.

Funerals

Funerary customs differ somewhat from those in the West. Grief is less private. The family generally holds a wake prior to the burial, and it's not unusual for a passing traveler to be invited. The body lies in state in an open coffin in the house of the deceased or a funeral home. Wakes are well attended, and the mood may be anything but somber. The expression of fond remembrance is accompanied by eating, drinking, card games, and music. Such parties are repeated annually on All Saints Day (1 November), when family and friends meet at the cemetery for an all-night vigil. Processions through the streets of rural towns are common, with family and friends following the hearse while passersby toss money.

Behavior on the Road

As in all polite society, treat sensitive subjects such as sex and religion circumspectly until you know a Filipino well. In most cases, you'll gain little satisfaction in trying to have a friendly debate with a Filipino. You'll often be asked "What can you say about the Philippines?" It's wise to stress the positive aspects and not lecture them. Don't show false sympathy, like asking how much someone earns, then gasping with horror.

Filipinos have a good sense of humor, but don't like jokes relating to their personal life or family, or that embarrass them in front of others. Many new, brief acquaintances made on the road in the Philippines may want to be your "pen pal." The request is common and innocent, although after giving out your address don't be surprised to get letters from Filipinos asking for a girlfriend or husband, textbooks, medicine, money, sponsorship, or advice. Give out your home address at your own risk.

Body Language

Filipinos have a well-developed and commonly used body and sign language. In social situations, they extend their hand and stoop when passing in front of people. The eyebrows are raised in recognition and agreement. People point with pursed lips. When beckoning someone, gesture with the hand turned downward,

never with a crooked forefinger, which is only used for dogs. It's also considered rude to point at somebody. Direct and prolonged eye contact makes them uncomfortable, too.

Ambiguity

Since saving face and maintaining harmonious relationships are so important to Filipinos, they'll generally make an ambiguous statement rather than say "No" to a question, suggestion, invitation, or request. They find it hard to reject or disagree, especially where someone considered superior is involved. When they feel the truth will offend or embarrass, they answer indirectly. A whole code of communication has evolved to ease the situation for both parties. Familiarity with cultural and social conventions enables Filipinos to distinguish between the subtleties of meaning.

They're also very alert to body language. The purpose of an evasive reply is not to deceive, but to please or avoid confrontation. Thus "Yes" could also mean "No," "Maybe," or "I don't know." Foreigners must learn to interpret these ambiguities. For example, if you extend an invitation to Filipinos, or suggest an appointment or rendezvous, their response may stress some condition, such as "If I finish work early." In such cases, there's a strong chance they won't materialize. Tagalog has two expressions for "later": *mamaya* means "later today," and *saka na* means "anytime later, maybe next year."

Asking street directions, or bus or boat schedules, from locals can also be exasperating. If someone appears hesitant, thank them and seek a second opinion. Note, too, that the reply to a negatively phrased question like "Won't there be another bus today?" is usually positive; "Yes" means, "Yes, there won't be another bus today."

Confrontation

Avoid it! Filipinos are very proud and sensitive to criticism, whether of themselves or their country. Never criticize someone in public. If you must make a complaint, do it indirectly: it's the Filipino way. Always request, never demand. Well-mannered people control their emotions in public. Refrain from shouting, insulting, talking down to them, or showing anger, even if provoked. Verbal assault is a crime for which you can be charged in the Philippines.

Filipinos can react excessively to an affront to their honor or dignity, whether real or imagined, particularly among men who've been drinking. In a tense situation, a smile and a soft voice work wonders. Maintaining "face" is vitally important to them, so always give them a way out.

> *I would rather be ashes than dust—*
> *I would rather my spark should burn out in a brilliant blaze*
> *Than it should be stifled in dry rot.*
> *I would rather be a superb meteor,*
> *Every atom of me in magnificent glow,*
> *Than a sleepy and permanent planet.*
> *Man's chief purpose is to live, not to exist:*
> *I shall not waste my days trying to prolong them.*
> *I shall use my time.*
>
> *—Jack London*

> *The use of traveling is to regulate imagination by reality,*
> *and instead of thinking how things may be,*
> *to see them as they are.*
>
> *—Samuel Johnson*

> *If the doors of perception were cleansed*
> *every thing would appear to man as it is, infinite.*
>
> *—William Blake*

M.G.L. DOMENY DE RIENZI

CARL PARKES

ON THE ROAD

Either I am a traveller in ancient times, and faced with a prodigious spectacle which would be almost entirely unintelligible to me and might, indeed, provoke me to mockery or disgust; or I am a traveller of our own day, hastening in search of a vanished reality. In either case I am the loser.

—*Claude Levi-Strauss,*
Tristes Tropiques

Between the Idea and the Reality . . . Falls the Shadow.
—*T.S. Eliot*

RECREATION

MOUNTAIN CLIMBING AND TREKKING

The Philippines is a mountainous country, but many peaks and ridges are covered by dense vegetation, so that the first necessity for scaling them would be a bolo (machete). Trails exist on several of the country's highest mountains, however, and these provide fine hiking. Most are isolated volcanoes, with wonderful views from their summits in clear weather.

Outstanding climbs, each taking two to four days, include Mt. Apo (2,953 meters), the country's highest peak; Mt. Pulog (2,930 meters), the highest on Luzon; Mayon volcano (2,462 meters), currently inadvisable to climb due to volcanic activity; Kanlaon volcano (2,460 meters); and the mystic Mt. Banahaw (2,177 meters). They are approached from Davao, Baguio, Legaspi, Bacolod, and Dolores (Quezon), respectively. In fact, traveling between and climbing these peaks would make an excellent tour of the Philippines in itself. Very pleasant hiking can be enjoyed in the rice terrace area around Sagada, Batad, and Banaue, in national parks, and along quiet rural highways and byways. Increasingly, locally run trekking groups out of Banaue, Baguio, and Sagada are good alternatives to going it alone in the Cordillera range.

The best general time for climbing and trekking, weather-wise, is February through April, though each region has a slightly different climatic pattern. Before starting a climb or trek, check with the relevant regional tourist office. They provide information, have up-to-date reports of any local volcanic or insurgent activity, and can recommend a reliable guide or the name of someone who could assign one. If you are not in an area where a tourism official can help

you, the town mayor or *barangay* captain is your best bet.

Mountaineering clubs in Negros and Davao are not organized for tourists, although they may take a foreigner or two along with them. These groups are particularly good for long-term foreign visitors. Check with the regional tourist office.

WATER SPORTS

Beaches

The Philippines's greatest natural assets are its beaches and its beautiful reefs for divers and snorkelers. They are also a major tourist attraction, since the best weather in the Philippines coincides with the North American, European,

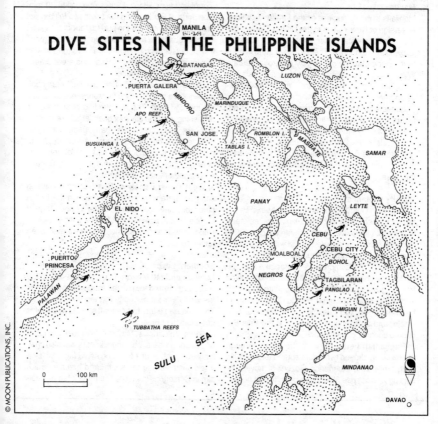

DIVE SITES IN THE PHILIPPINE ISLANDS

SIGHTSEEING HIGHLIGHTS

Rather than a country of monumental ruins or great historical attractions, the Philippines is a country for sunbathing, hiking, nightlife, and relaxation—a welcome relief to travelers burned out on an endless parade of Southeast Asian temples.

First-time visitors with less than a month usually fly into Manila and explore the hilltribe regions of northern Luzon or head directly south to a beach. Travelers with two full months can see the north and then complete an overland loop through the Visayas as described below. Recommended off-the-beaten-track destinations include the beaches of northern Palawan, beautiful Camiguin Island, and remote tribal areas in southern Mindanao.

Manila

Manila is to the Philippines as the famed *New Yorker* version of New York is to the United States—the country's ecopolitical center distorted out of shape by its own self-importance. There's little of great interest here, since Manila was largely destroyed during WW II and the economic growth of recent years has brought with it all the problems of unchecked development.

Sunsets are stunning, and the people are friendly, but major sights are limited to the Malacanang Palace (Marcos's former digs, now open to the public), an elaborate Chinese cemetery, and a heady nightlife scene. The Philippines is best experienced in the countryside and on the beaches rather than in the cities.

Vicinity of Manila

Corregidor: Guarding the entrance to Manila Bay is the rock where American and Filipino forces made their last stand against Japanese forces. Now being restored, the jungle-covered island will intrigue anyone moved by the heroic struggle.

Taal Lake: This impressive crater lake and volcanic cone one hour south of Manila can be viewed from Tagaytay ridge or toured by private boat from Talisay. Visits to Taal often include Cavite's historic bamboo organ, the relaxing seven lakes of San Pablo, and an excellent museum at the Villa Escudero coconut plantation.

Pagsanjan Falls: Running the rapids through the towering canyon two hours southeast of Manila is an exhilarating experience. Dozens of movies, including *Apocalypse Now,* have been filmed here.

Northern Luzon

Circle Route: Aside from along the beaches, perhaps the Philippines's most popular route is a counterclockwise circuit through northern Luzon. This seven- to 14-day journey through spectacular countryside visits the world-famous rice terraces at Banaue, limestone caves near the isolated village of Sagada, and a magnificent highway that winds along the mountain ridges from Bontoc to Baguio. Banaue's ancient manmade rice terraces have justifiably been ranked among the wonders of the world. This is also a great region for hiking, photography, and learning about indigenous hilltribes.

Sagada: One of the Philippines's most peaceful mountain towns sits in a limestone valley 30 minutes north of Bontoc. Sagada takes two full days of travel from Manila, but the superb topography, fine accommodations, and ethnological interests make this an outstanding destination. The rugged all-day bus journey from Bontoc to Baguio is a panoramic experience par excellence.

Baguio: This cool mountain city five hours north of Manila is a popular place for Manileanos to escape the lowland heat. The surrounding countryside is refreshing, and the city has been largely renovated in recent years (new parks, roads, pedestrian overpasses, etc.), but most Western visitors are disappointed with the traffic jams and lack of any compelling sights. Spend your time exploring Banaue and Sagada rather than Baguio.

West Coast Beaches: Beaches near Bauang can't compare with those elsewhere in the Philippines, but their accessibility to Manila and range of facilities will appeal to tourists on a tight schedule. Hundred Islands on Alaminos Bay has largely been ruined by pollution.

Southern Luzon

Legaspi and Mt. Mayon: Legaspi, gateway to the south, is a bustling town in the shadow of Mt. Mayon, the world's most perfectly formed volcanic cone. The area also offers hot thermal springs and a fairly good beach at Rizal.

Other Volcanoes: Mayon is the most famous of all Philippine peaks, but mountaineers can also challenge themselves on Mt. Isarog near Naga, Mt. Iriga a few kilometers to the south, and beautiful Bulusan in Sorsogon Province. The most infamous volcano is Mt. Pinatubo, which erupted in June 1991 and forced the closure of American-run Clark Air Force Base. Climbing this famous peak is one of the newest and most popular outdoor activities in the country.

Other Islands

Bohol: One of the prettiest but least visited islands in the Visayas is known for outstanding Spanish churches, crystalline beaches on nearby Panglao Island, and the eerie geological formations known as the Chocolate Hills. Travel logistics make Bohol an easy side trip from Cebu.

Boracay: The spectacular expanse of crystalline sand, clear waters, and swaying coconut palms have deservedly made Boracay the most famous beach resort in the Philippines. Facilities range from simple nipa-palm bungalows to first-class resorts with air-conditioned chalets, windsurfing, sailing, and entertainment from sunsets to folk music. And after years of unchecked development, the government is finally doing something about the water pollution and lack of sanitation facilities.

Cebu: Cebu City, economic and cultural hub of the Visayan Islands, is a convenient base for exploring the beaches, churches, and diving areas of the central Philippines. Visitors short on time can fly directly to Cebu and make side trips to Bohol, the nearby beaches on Mactan and Moalboal, and then continue west across Negros and Panay to Boracay. Cebu City has good restaurants, great festivals, lively nightlife, and historical attractions connected with the Spanish era.

Mindanao: Travelers not discouraged by the remoteness and political disruptions of Mindanao will discover Muslim townships little changed in generations, some of the country's last remaining stands of tropical forests, and isolated pockets of tribal culture. Camiguin, north of Cagayan de Oro, is a superb island with great beaches and few tourists. Lake Sebu, west of General Santos City in southern Mindanao, is the idyllic homeland of the traditional T'boli people. Islamic lifestyles continue near Marawi City and in the Sulu Archipelago. Davao and "exotic" Zamboanga are modern towns with little of charm or interest.

Mindoro: Puerto Galera on Mindoro Island is an immensely popular beach resort only five hours from Manila. Although haphazard development has ruined some of the region, scuba diving remains outstanding, and the more remote beaches are still inviting.

Negros: Top draws are the ancient steam trains that haul cane on sugar plantations near Bacolod. Train enthusiasts come from all over the world to photograph and ride the rare German and British steamers.

Palawan: Long considered the final frontier of the Philippines, Palawan in recent years has been attracting increasing numbers of travelers who want to get off the beaten track and enjoy some of the best beaches and diving in the country. Highlights include topographic wonders near Puerto Princesa, underground caves near Port Barton, anthropological discoveries at Tabon, and the spectacular scuba diving at El Nido. Travel conditions remain primitive, but accommodations and restaurants are plentiful and cheap.

Palawan is unquestionably the finest destination in the Philippines.

Panay: Spanish churches modified with Filipino designs are the highlights of Iloilo, capital of Panay. Other draws include Sicogon Island and the annual Ati-Atihan festival in Kalibo.

Samar and Leyte: Waterfalls and historical ties to WW II are the main attractions here. Frequent interisland buses and boats connect Samar and Leyte with Luzon and the lower Visayas.

Routes

Visitors with limited time should fly directly from Manila to the beach or island of their choice. Travelers with more time (six to eight weeks) might take a more leisurely approach with an overland journey through northern Luzon and then around the central Visayan Islands. The trip can be done in either direction starting from, and with a return to, Manila, with a combination of boats and public buses.

The clockwise route first visits Legaspi and Mt. Mayon in southern Luzon before continuing south through Samar and Leyte to Cebu. Bohol can be toured between Leyte and Cebu or as an easy backtrack from Cebu. The journey continues west across Negros and Panay to Boracay. Then it's north to Mindoro and the beaches at Puerto Galera before returning to Manila.

Those with less time who want to see the real highlights should fly from Manila to Palawan and then spend a few days or weeks relaxing on the beaches at Sabang, El Nido, or south of Puerto Princesa.

COCKFIGHTING~THE NATIONAL PASTIME

Virtually every town in the Philippines has a cockpit *(galleria* or *sabungan),* and cockfighting takes place every Sunday, on public holidays, and at fiestas. This ancient sport has a fanatical following that cuts across all class barriers. Gambling can be extremely heavy. It's not unusual, in a rural area with few visible sources of substantial income, to see thousands of pesos changing hands. Rural game pits usually consist of a wooden structure with a tin roof, located a short distance out of town. Admission is nominal. The dirt arena is surrounded by banks of wooden benches reaching to the roof, usually jam-packed with noisy aficionados. Urban cockpits are more comfortable and often have a/c sections with padded seats for wealthier enthusiasts. Cockpits in Manila's suburbs include La Loma, Santa Ana, Baclaran, and Pasay City (on Libertad Street).

Good fighting birds are very valuable and get first-class treatment, including high-quality feed and vitamins, plus regular baths and massages. It's common to see an owner strolling around his village caressing a fowl nestled in the crook of his arm. On Sundays, owners meet in a section of the cockpit to match their birds, which are paired by weight, like boxers. Then the gaffer chooses a spur of appropriate length and curve from his selection and, with the owner's approval, ties it at a prescribed angle and height behind the rooster's leg.

The birds are brought into the arena and are held by the tail feathers while they tease each other. The owners place their bets. The spectators scrutinize each bird, which in the case of similar plumage may be distinguished by a colored leg band, before deciding which to back. One handler may put on a hat, so that wagers are placed by calling *"mayroon"* ("with hat") or *"wala"* ("hatless"). Uproar prevails as bettors yell at the *kristos* (bookmakers).

Use of the word *kristo,* Tagalog for Christ, derives from the Christlike extended arm poses they often strike as they move about, shouting the odds, exhorting the gamblers, and acknowledging the bets. Incredibly, they write nothing down, but remember each bet and its odds. Trust works both ways; anyone can place a bet without showing his money. There's a sign language for betting: two fingers raised means P20, horizontal fingers signify hundreds, and fingers pointed downwards represent thousands. If you want to bet, confirm this system with your neighbor at the fight.

The cockfight begins when the leather sheaths of the razor-sharp spurs are removed, the blades examined and wiped with alcohol to remove any poison, and the birds are released to square off. Contests may last from a few seconds to a few minutes. They end when one bird is killed, maimed into submission, or, to the mortification of its owner, runs

---

and Northeast Asian winter. Those making a brief visit to the country may only have time to reach a beach close to Manila; the nearest adequate beach is Matabungkay (Batangas), a three-hour trip, while the beaches of Puerto Galera (Mindoro) are much nicer, but more than a day trip away. The best beach in the country is White Beach on Boracay Island off Panay. There are also good beaches in Palawan, Bohol, and in the central Visayas.

Beach-lovers can choose between developed beach resorts, with first-class accommodations; travelers' beach places, which have reasonably priced cottages; and unspoiled beaches where accommodations are limited or nonexistent. For upscale tourists, the beach clubs and resorts of Cebu, Bohol, and Palawan (El Nido) are good choices. Boracay (also off Panay), Moalboal (Cebu), Port Barton (Palawan), and Camiguin (off northern Mindanao) are all deservedly popular with budget travelers. Around northern Palawan and off Siargao Island (northeast Mindanao) are numerous pristine, deserted beaches.

Surfing

The Philippines is well known for surfing, and surfing magazine reviews have assessed its potential as almost limitless. Its 18,000 km of pioneer coastline territory could keep the inquisitive surfer busy for a while! Most Filipinos aren't familiar with surfing, so it's hard to get useful information. The best-known spot is in Surigao in northeastern Mindanao, where world-class surfing competitions are held each year.

Surfing in the Philippines offers a wide range of waves, including beach breaks, river mouths, point breaks, and some kamikaze reef breaks. In

away. A close fight drives frenzied spectators to a howling crescendo. A losing bird must be picked up and dropped three times to see if it shows any signs of life before it's declared dead. Victory is only confirmed when the dominant cock pecks twice at its victim, even if the latter's dead, in a formal coup de grace.

When the action ceases, the *sentenciador* (he who gives the sentence) grabs both birds by the back neck feathers and brings them together for the decisive pecks. If the winning bird fails to deliver them, by being too badly wounded, for example, it forfeits its victory, and a tie is declared. Sometimes both birds die, but a dead rooster can be declared the winner if he died while on the offensive. The decision of the *sentenciador* is almost never questioned. The betting is then resolved as money is passed between *kristos* and spectators. Trying to renege is not recommended!

The procedure is repeated for each of the many contests that make up a meet, which is often an all-day affair.

Cockfighting can be bloody and is not for the squeamish, but it offers a fascinating glimpse of Filipinos at play (though perhaps they take it rather too seriously for it to be regarded as merely amusement). Few women attend, but there's no problem if Western women do.

CARL PARKES

spite of its exposure to such a wide expanse of ocean, good surf largely depends on local weather conditions. November through May, the Pacific coast faces the prevailing northeast winds. The west side offers good possibilities, but needs a storm in the South China Sea to generate swells; during the typhoon season, June through October, such storms are frequent.

SCUBA DIVING

The Philippines is one of the world's top diving destinations. Thousands of islands with diverse coastlines create an amazing underwater scene where a multitude of coral reefs (covering about 4,000 square km) and sharp drop-offs form a subaquatic world. Much of this underwater world remains unexplored, and it's quite feasible for

determined, experienced divers to locate virgin territory. Visitors who don't do at least some **snorkeling** are missing one of the greatest experiences the Philippines has to offer.

Rewarding dive sites are scattered throughout the archipelago, but the lack of facilities limits options to a few prime areas. The finest, Tubbataha and Apo Reefs, are reached only by dive boat. The best areas for shore-based diving are around the islands between Cebu and Bohol, and dive resorts near El Nido (Palawan) have diving as well. Places with scuba facilities include several spots in Batangas and Cebu; Moalboal is perhaps the cheapest place in the country to dive.

Other popular sites include the Busuanga Island north of Palawan, Dapitan, Davao City, Dumaguete, Iloilo City, Lamon Bay, Nagarao Island, Panglao Island, Puerto Galera, Puerto

Princesa, Salomague Island, Sicogon Island, Sual, Sulu Archipelago, Tagbilaran, and Zamboanga City.

Assuming you're not one of the fortunate few who has his/her own boat with an air compressor, the major considerations in selecting a dive site are accessibility and the refilling of tanks. Small on-site dive shops, which rent all necessary equipment and provide boats and divemasters, have been established in popular travelers' spots such as Moalboal and Puerto Galera. This is certainly the cheapest way to dive. Their prices are extremely reasonable by international standards, making the cost of a day's diving about half what you'd pay elsewhere. Coupled with the availability of inexpensive accommodations and restaurants nearby, these dive shops bring spectacular diving within reach of the budget traveler.

The dive shops in Manila, Cebu, Davao, or Puerto Princesa can make all arrangements for individuals or groups. Their staffs are helpful in incorporating single divers into larger groups, thus enabling the cost of a boat and divemaster to be shared. Those on a budget should always inquire about this possibility, which is most likely on weekends, when local residents are active.

Specialized dive camps located in Anilao (Batangas), Moalboal (Mactan), and Oslob (Cebu) offer full packages, including unlimited diving plus bed and board. Accommodations are generally simple, ranging from tents to rooms and cottages. Some upscale beach resorts and hotels (e.g., in Batangas, Cebu, and on Sicogon) offer scuba service. Catering to a well-heeled clientele, they have first-class facilities, with prices to match.

For those who want to experience the finest diving in the Philippines, and arguably some of the best in the world, *the* way to go is on a dive-boat cruise. These trips cost several hundred dollars per person, but are the only way to reach remote wonder-spots like Apo Reef in the Mindoro Strait and Tubbataha Reef in the Sulu Sea. Also, by sailing to new sites overnight, they enable optimum use of time.

Several companies operate dive boats, with seasonal itineraries. Typically, they might cover Apo Reef and northern Palawan out of San Jose (Mindoro) or Batangas (Jan.-March); Tubbataha and Jessie Beazley reefs out of Puerto Princesa (April-Aug.); and Cebu and Bohol out-islands out of Cebu City (Sept.-Dec.). The dive boats are also available for charter, so interested groups could arrange to dive anywhere in the archipelago.

Information in Manila

An excellent book, *The Diver's Guide to the Philippines* (Unicorn Books Ltd., Hong Kong, 1982), contains detailed information on the major dive areas and is available in Manila bookstores. Since a dive-boat excursion represents a substantial investment, it's worth comparing prices, facilities, and itineraries.

The Department of Tourism has a complete dive map of the Philippines plus brochures and booklets on diving. Remember that if you do not join a dive through a company in Manila, there is ample opportunity to hook up with a certified dive instructor, dive boat, guides and fellow divers in Moalboal, Cebu; Panglao Island, Bohol; Puerto Princesa, Palawan; Puerto Galera, Mindoro and Boracay Island.

Many of the dive resorts now have Web sites; do a search for scuba and the Philippines.

ARTS AND ENTERTAINMENT

MUSIC

The music never stops in the Philippines, emanating from jukeboxes, radios, cassettes, video, laser-disc players, and tuneful voices. Most popular songs are in English or Tagalog, and sometimes other dialects. Mass taste runs the gamut from melodic rock to plaintive Tagalog love and folk songs. There are also some fine native songwriters.

One of the most celebrated is Freddie Aguilar, whose song "Anak" ("Child") has been translated into 40 languages worldwide.

Baguio has several folk houses, frequented by students. Manila and Cebu have a myriad of bars featuring almost every style of contemporary American music, and the island of Boracay has become a mecca for Filipino musicians. The Philippines exports many of its best singers and groups to other Asian capitals.

Manila's Cultural Center has a philharmonic orchestra and concerts by famous international artists, performing everything from rock to classical, while even the Beatles and Bolshoi Ballet have played there. However remote the traveler's destination in the Philippines, he will always be within earshot of music.

Muslim Music

The Muslims have their own musical heritage, heavily influenced by the Islamic and Hindu cultures to the south and west. The major Muslim instrument is the xylophone-like *kulintang,* a horizontal set of eight or 11 knobbed brass or bronze gongs, tonally graded and arranged on an elaborately carved wooden frame.

Among the Maguindanao and Maranao, it's played mostly by women, while in Sulu, it's played by both sexes. It was originally played to appease the spirits causing a person's sickness. Today ensembles perform at weddings

---

MOVIES FILMED IN THE PHILIPPINES

Hollywood has gone to the Philippines many times to use the tropical scenery as the setting for movies based on the era of the Vietnam War.

Too Late the Hero: Cliff Robertson, Michael Caine, and Toshiro Mifune star in this 1970 release shot in Boracay in the late 1960s. A rare chance to see the Philippines' most famous island without all the guesthouses, hotels, condominiums, and golf courses.

Apocalypse Now: The helicopter scenes in Francis Ford Coppola's 1979 masterpiece were filmed at Balera Bay, while the climactic explosion of Kurtz's Cambodian temple was staged on the riverbanks near Pagsanjan Falls. Tribal dance scenes were performed by the Ifugaos of Banaue. Coppola's ex-wife subsequently wrote an intriguing book about their problems with typhoons and clashing personalities.

Platoon: Most of this Academy Award-winning film was filmed in the Philippines.

An Officer and a Gentleman: Richard Gere and Debra Winger star in this 1982 love story whose early parts were filmed in Olongapo.

The Year of Living Dangerously: One of the best films about contemporary politics in the region was filmed in the Philippines in 1983 after Indonesian authorities refused to allow the Australian director to complete the film on location.

Missing in Action: All of the *Missing in Action* films starring Chuck Norris were filmed in the Philippines from 1984 to 1988.

Born on the Fourth of July: Ron Kovic's autobiographical novel was largely filmed in the northern Philippine province of Ilocos Norte. While there in 1989, director Oliver Stone and star Tom Cruise stayed in the Fort Ilocandia Resort Hotel, built by the Marcoses to house guests for the 1983 wedding of their daughter Irene. Stone summed it up: "I have been all over the Far East, and the Philippines has the most natural wonders. The people give their hearts to you; it's like being in the old pirate country in the Carribean."

Fortunes of War: Set in Thailand and Cambodia but actually shot in the Philippines at Subic Bay in 1994 with a cameo appearance by Martin Sheen.

and other festive occasions, and sometimes just for neighborhood entertainment, but it's never played in connection with Islamic rites or during Ramadan or the planting and harvesting seasons.

DANCE

Filipinos dance at festive events and religious ceremonies; they dance to express joy and sorrow, to enact prayer and conflict, to celebrate life and mark death. Filipinos perform everything from ballet to disco with verve and have a wonderful heritage of native dance. Yet the Philippines has never developed a classical dance tradition such as Java, Bali, and Thailand. The islands' cultural fragmentation and the progression of foreign influences have led to a wide range of ethnic dance styles; in general, the form, content, and purpose of dance have changed substantially with time. In the remoter areas, the traveler may observe dance in relatively pure form, performed in actual ritual.

At the other end of the scale are the theatrical revues given by renowned folk dance troupes such as the Bayanihan. There are three main divisions of Filipino folk dance, each reflecting a different culture: indigenous early Malay-, Muslim-, and Spanish-influenced dance. It's possible to see stylized, choreographed folk-dance performances in Manila. Several restaurants offer cultural dance shows with buffets of native dishes. Demonstrations also take place at Nayong Pilipino, near the airport, while the Bayanihan Dance Company performs at Philippine Women's University on Taft Avenue. Folk dance troupes regularly appear at theaters, universities, and hotels in Manila and the provinces.

The Ballet Philippines, founded in 1970 by dancer/choreographer Alice Reyes, has always combined modern ballet with distinctly Filipino themes. One of Reyes's best works is *Tales of the Manuvu,* a modern ballet based on the Manuvu tribes of Mindanao. Other important ballets originating at the Cultural Center are *Sisa,* a dance interpretation of the tragic mother, Sisa, in José Rizal's famous book *Noli Me Tangere; La Lampara,* a ballet based on Rizal's last hours at Fort Santiago before his execution on 30 December 1886; and *Itim-Asu,* a ballet about the death of Governor-General Bustamante, who was assassinated by powerful Spanish friars of the colonial era.

FESTIVALS

Filipinos are fun-loving and reverent, and the fiesta is a perfect occasion to indulge both tendencies. Fiestas are primarily religious, and since every community holds an annual fiesta on the feast day of its patron saint, there's always a fiesta happening somewhere. Most are strictly local affairs, preceded by novenas (nine days of devotion) and announced by colorful street decorations in villages and city districts.

The roots of the Filipino fiesta are ancient. Since the majority of Filipino families live by farming and fishing, they have always felt a need for divine protection from the vagaries of nature. Astute Spanish friars used this dependence to smooth the transition from animism to Catholicism. Thus, Christian festivals often serve the same functions—harvest thanksgiving, prayers for fertility, or a good catch of fish—as their pre-Hispanic counterparts, with the roles of heathen gods assumed by the Santo Niño ("Holy Child"), Virgin Mary, and the saints. About 50 "miraculous" images of these sacred figures are scattered throughout the country, and they form the focal point of many fiestas and pilgrimages.

Fiestas are marked by ritual, music, dancing, and abundant food and drink. The fiesta is also a time when people work together to give the community a face-lift, when hospitality and friendship are expressed, and even the poorest families can indulge in delicacies and break the monotony of their daily lives. At fiesta time, scattered family members return home from other provinces and other lands to renew the bonds of kinship. Most fiestas contain certain indispensable elements, such as high mass, a religious procession (in the streets, on water, or both), ringing church bells, brass band music, fireworks, a cockfight, a beauty contest, or a public dance. There may also be an agricultural fair, cultural presentations, and sports events.

The non-Christian hilltribes also adhere to their traditional ceremonies, which are usually closely aligned with seasonal activities, such as planting and harvesting. There is an exotic blend of mystic, ritual, and joyous dancing, but here too, missionaries sometimes add Christian elements to pagan rites.

Festival Dating

On a much larger scale are the few really major festivals, such as Kalibo's Ati-Atihan and Marinduque's Moriones Festival. Full of color and pageantry, their origin may be grounded in religion, history, folklore, or a combination of these. Fiestas range from the simple to the grandiose, but the occasion is always festive and colorful, and visitors are received with good cheer and hospitality. You could spend a year traveling around the Philippines from fiesta to fiesta, but the amount of eating and drinking involved would strain the toughest stamina.

The main months for fiestas are January, with Ati-Atihan and Sinulog festivals, marked by spirited parades and street dancing; the March/April Lent and Easter period; May, a time of harvest festivals; the June-Sept. rainy season, which is marked by fluvial parades of decorated boats; and the world's longest Christmas celebration in December. Many festivals can be enjoyed as day trips from Manila. For major festivals in the provinces, quality accommodations should be booked as far as possible in advance, or secured through one of the Manila tour companies, though a simple place to sleep can always be found. Transportation will also be crowded.

Note that the dates of many festivals are movable, so check with a tourist office before making a special trip. Newspaper ads of tour companies also indicate the dates of important festivals. Package tours are convenient, but not the cheapest way to go.

The Chinese and Muslim calendars are based on the lunar year, so the days of celebrations vary annually vis-a-vis the Western (Gregorian) calendar. In addition, there are several one-day national holidays, when banks, offices, and museums are closed. If a national holiday of fixed date falls on a Sunday, the following Monday is a legal holiday. And if a public holiday falls close to a weekend, e.g. on a Thursday, the Friday is

often declared a holiday too, making an extra-long weekend.

For additional details on major festivals, check the travel chapters covering the towns where the festivals are held.

JANUARY

1 January: New Year's Day
(national holiday)

The New Year enters to deafening firecrackers and merrymaking. Most Filipinos attend family gatherings and parties. Devout families attend midnight mass.

6 January or 1st Sunday: Three Kings' Day
(nationally celebrated)

Official end of the Christmas season and last day for gift-giving, marked by the Feast of the Three Kings, or Epiphany. Children receive gifts to symbolize the gold, myrrh, and frankincense given to the infant Jesus by the three kings, and the star they followed is represented by star-shaped lanterns hung in windows and doorways. Gasan and Santa Cruz on Marinduque are noted for their Three Kings' Pageant.

9 January: Feast of the Black Nazarene

Quiapo's (Manila) biggest festival. A barefooted man, having made a vow of penance, hauls the life-size Black Nazarene statue on its *carroza* (cart) by two long ropes. The procession inches its way through Quiapo's jam-packed narrow streets, ending with mass at the Quiapo Church. Devotees jostle and push to touch the image with a towel or handkerchief, which they rub over their entire body in a ritual cleansing. They believe that sins will thus be forgiven, and the cloth acquires healing power.

Expect very dense crowds (100,000-plus people). The area's notorious pickpockets claim to be honest for a day. Try to view it from a high building.

The 3rd Weekend: Feast of the Santo Niño
(nationally celebrated)

The feast day of the Holy Infant is widely celebrated with street processions and people taking their own Santo Niño statues to be blessed in the church. Major festivals in Cebu City (Sinulog) and Tondo (Manila).

CARL PARKES

A young woman holds a Santo Niño figure to be blessed.

The 3rd Weekend: Ati-Atihan
(major festival)
The country's most colorful, exuberant festival featuring Mardi Gras-style revelry is worth a special trip from Manila to Kalibo. Experiencing Ati-Atihan ties in well with a visit to Boracay. Ibajay, between Kalibo and Boracay, claims to be the original home of Ati-Atihan and holds its own small festival at the same time as Kalibo.

Similar celebrations are also held at Cebu City (Cebu Sinulog) and Iloilo.

Chinese New Year Celebration
(major festival)
The Chinese New Year begins on the first day of the first new moon after the sun enters Aquarius. The date varies, falling between 21 January and 19 February, because the lunar year may have 12 or 13 moons. The Chinese exchange rice cakes with their friends and celebrate with feasting, firecrackers, open-air Chinese opera, and the

Dragon Dance. Manila's Chinatown and other Chinese communities in Baguio and Cebu also celebrate enthusiastically.

FEBRUARY

6 February: Feast of the Presentation of Our Lord in the Temple
A regional festival, priests bless bundles of *palay* (unhusked rice), which are later mixed with the seeds for the coming season.

14 February: St. Valentine's Day
This day for lovers is widely observed by the romantic and sentimental Filipinos.

MARCH

Saranggolahan
Kite-flying contests with cash prizes are held in many towns during the summer season, March-June. Men and boys fly homemade bamboo-and-paper kites of all sizes, shapes, and colors.

HOLY WEEK—MARCH/APRIL

During Holy Week, Catholic rites are infused with a special fervor. It's a time for street theater and spiritual cleansing, with processions, flagellantes, and passion plays. Holy Week begins on Palm Sunday with the devout bringing palm branches to church to be blessed as symbols of Christ's triumphant entry into Jerusalem. In rural areas, the palms may be dried and ground as a medicinal ingredient. Ceremonies reenacting the washing of the feet of the apostles are held in churches on Holy Wednesday. Holy (or "Maundy") Thursday is marked by a vigil and adoration of the Blessed Sacrament and church visitation (Bisita Iglesia). The devout visit as many as seven churches. Good Friday is a solemn day. In churches, priests expound on Christ's seven last words spoken on the cross. A solemn procession featuring the figure of the dead Christ is held in the late afternoon. Places to see this include Sampaloc (Metro Manila), Kawit (Cavite), Tanay and Talim Island (Rizal), Vigan (Ilocos Sur), and Boac (Marinduque).

In some areas, penitence is performed to fulfill a vow to atone publicly for one's sins. Flagellantes, mostly men, tramp along streets and roads, flogging themselves with bamboo or whips, which are sometimes augmented by leather thongs or glass shards. In coastal areas, penitence may end with a healing dip in the sea. Flagellantes can be seen in Malabon and Navotas (Metro Manila); in Paombong and Bocaue (Bulacan); between Balanga and Bagac (Bataan); in San Fernando, Arayat, and Floridablanca (Pampanga); in Cavite, Nueva Ecija, and Marinduque. In Cainta (Rizal) and elsewhere, barefoot penitents wear thorns on their heads and carry heavy crosses, while being lashed, and even have vinegar applied to the cuts.

In San Fernando (Pampanga) and Orani (Bataan), men volunteer to be actually crucified. They stand on a small wooden platform to prevent the flesh from tearing and are taken down after about five minutes. The wounds, treated with holy water, oils, and the juice of guava leaves, heal within a week or two. Holy Thursday and Good Friday are national holidays.

Easter Sunday

Easter Sunday marks the resurrection of Christ from the dead, and the purple cloth of mourning is removed from the religious images. Church bells peal and alleluias are sung. The *salubong* (meeting) takes place in Pasig, Paranaque, Las Pias, and Marikina (Metro Manila); Cainta and Talim Island (Rizal); and towns of Bulacan, Cavite. After the mass at midnight or dawn, twin processions leave the church by separate doors, led by statues of *Mary the Sorrowful Mother* and the *Resurrected Christ* and followed by women and men, respectively.

As choruses are sung, the images meet beneath an arch adorned with flowers or palm fronds in the church patio or plaza. A little girl dressed as an angel, with wings and a halo, may be lowered from above to remove Mary's black veil. Its removal is connected with superstitions about the harvest (e.g., a smooth unveiling portends a good harvest, a fallen veil drought).

Easter is also marked by many other customs related to growth and renewal: the sick are lifted from their beds to receive new vigor; the short

jump and stretch to gain height; parents toss young children in the air, believing they'll thus thrive; plants are shaken so they'll grow well. The fast of Lent ends with a lavish Easter feast.

Senaculos

In some communities, *senaculos,* dramatizations of the Passion of Christ, are presented. Their origin is probably rooted in religious Auto Sacramentales, which were popular in 16th- and 17th-century Spain, and in Mexican versions of the passion play. *Senaculos* are staged in town plazas and auditoriums, with three crosses set up as the focal point, and may include a procession in which a Christ character carries his cross through the streets. Participation is considered an honor, and the devout amateur actors, who sometimes inherit their roles, wear colorful costumes. Each community has its own interpretation, with verses delivered in the vernacular.

While *senaculos* typically last from three to four hours to two days, one may occasionally continue for weeks during Lent, presenting a

CARL PARKES

Moriones Easter festival, Marinduque

detailed reenactment of Christ's life. The story is often performed in two stages, with the Last Supper and Judas's betrayal depicted on Holy Thursday, and the Crucifixion on Good Friday. The sequence of events may continue with a funeral procession Friday evening and the meeting of the resurrected Christ and his mother on Sunday.

Bulacan (e.g., in Ticay and at the Hiyas complex in Malolos), Pampanga, and Nueva Ecija are noted for impressive *senaculos,* which are also performed at Malabon (Metro Manila); Cainta and Talim Island (Rizal); Samal (Bataan); Iguig (Cagayan); Rapu-Rapu Island (Albay); Barotac Viejo and Jordan, Guimaras Island (Iloilo); Mambajao (Camiguin); and in several parishes of Davao City.

Moriones Festival

Marinduque is a good place to witness many of the Holy Week rites. They lead up to the festival, which begins on Good Friday and climaxes on Easter Sunday, with masked "centurions" chasing one-eyed Longinus, ending with his beheading.

9 April: Bataan Day
(national holiday)
A day of remembrance of the battle and fall of Bataan (1942), which was followed by the Death March up the peninsula. Ceremonies take place at the Mt. Samat shrine (Bataan) and at Capas (Tarlac).

14-16 April: Lami-Lamihan Festival
Colorfully dressed natives participate in a parade, horse races, and more (Basilan).

Turrumba
(major festival)
The festival, held in April or May, as well as on 19 October, pays tribute to Our Lady of Sorrows of Turrumba, widely believed to have miraculous healing powers, whose image was discovered floating in Laguna Lake in 1778. It was originally a procession of the sick and invalid who sought cures for their ailments. The singing and dancing that accompanied those early celebrations are continued to this day (Pakil, Laguna).

MAY

1 May: Labor Day
(national holiday)
There's an afternoon parade in Rizal Park, Manila.

6 May: Araw Ng Kagitingan ("Day of Valor")
(nationally celebrated)
Ceremonies at Mt. Samat's Shrine of Valor (Bataan) and Bessang Pass (Ilocos Sur) honor Filipino and U.S. soldiers who fought in WW II.

14-15 May: Carabao Festival
(major festival)
Carabao (water buffalo) are washed, garlanded, and raced on the streets to the church. In front of the church, they stop and are blessed by the priest. This festival is held in Pulilan (Bulacan), San Isidro (Nueva Ecija), and Angono (Rizal).

15 May: Pahiyas
(major festival)
This harvest festival is celebrated in the municipalities of Lucban, Sariaya, and Tayabas, Quezon.

Flores de Mayo
(major festival)
In the Philippines, the month of May is synonymous with flowers. Young girls dressed in white make daily floral offerings to the Virgin Mary. The festival is climaxed by a religious procession on the last day and may be followed by singing and dancing to string band music beneath lighted bamboo arches in the churchyard.

Santacruzan
(major festival)
The search for the True Cross in the 4th century by Reina Elena ("Queen Helena"), mother of the Roman Emperor Constantine the Great, is widely celebrated. But its religious significance is now secondary to a more earthly display of charm and finery, and its main events are beauty pageants and parades of pretty girls around the towns. The Santacruzan, or Santa Cruz de Mayo ("Holy Cross of May"), is observed as a novena, a nine-day cycle of prayers.

Early evening processions are held in honor of the Virgin Mary. In the pageant, whose main characters are Helena and Constantino, the most beautiful girls of the town become *sagalas*, who are assigned traditional roles and titles as biblical, historical, and mythological heroines. There may be the Queen of Sheba, Reina Fe, Reina Esperanza, and Reina Caridad representing faith, hope, and charity, and others symbolizing justice, liberty, etc. Wearing tiaras and the butterfly-sleeved traditional dresses *(ternos),* they walk beneath floral arches.

The community assigns sponsors for each of the nine nights. They hold open house, prayers, and the procession, in which a cross from the church is passed to the next night's sponsor. It may become an extravagant competition in which each tries to outdo the other in presenting the best refreshments, procession (sometimes even importing movie stars for it), and *bitin* and *palo sebo* games.

The sponsers' own daughters are assured of prominent billing. On 31 May, the festival may culminate in a torchlit parade with brass bands and floral floats bearing local beauties. The Manila suburbs of Las Pinas, Malabon, Navotas, Paranaque, Pasig, and Quezon City are noted for their Santacruzan, as are Antipolo (Rizal), Pagsanjan (Laguna), Igbaras (Iloilo), and the towns of Quezon Province and Marinduque.

Feast of Our Lady of Peace and Good Voyage
This starts on the first of May. The pilgrimage starts the night before when devotees gather in Manila for the long overnight trek to the shrine in Antipolo. Participants come from various walks of life and may be doing it in fulfillment of a vow or as thanksgiving for favors granted. The procession ends with a mass at Our Lady's Shrine. Before WW II, it was not only traditional but fashionable for young men and ladies to go to Antipolo for a picnic by the waterfalls (Antipolo, Rizal).

JUNE

12 June: Independence Day
(national holiday)
The anniversary of the establishment of the First Philippine Republic (1898) is marked throughout the country with parades, speeches, fireworks, concerts, and ringing church bells. In Manila, a huge afternoon civic-military parade is held in Rizal Park.

19 June: Birthday of José Rizal
(nationally celebrated)
The national hero's birthday is marked by civic rites and floral offerings at his memorial in Rizal Park (Manila), at his birthplace in Calamba (Laguna), and elsewhere.

22-25 June: Halaran Festival
(major festival)
This is an Ati-Atihan-type festival (Roxas City).

24 June: Manila Day
The anniversary of Manila's being declared a city (1571) is marked by a parade, film festival, and cultural presentations in Manila.

24 June: Feast of St. John the Baptist
(nationally celebrated)
In places called San Juan, friends, relatives, and passersby "baptize" others by playfully drenching them with water. It matters little how well-dressed the subject is and should be taken in a spirit of fun. In some areas, young men douse local maidens with water made fragrant with *ilang-ilang* blossoms.

Places with notable celebrations include San Juan (Metro Manila), where it's a community fiesta with an afternoon procession; Balayan (Batangas), which holds a Lechon Parade; Punta Taytay, near Bacolod City (Negros Occidental); and Camiguin.

28-30 June: Feast of Saints Peter and Paul
This is a major festival in Apalit, Pampanga.

JULY

The 1st Sunday: Bocaue River Festival
This is a major festival in Bocaue, Bulacan.

4 July: Filipino-American Friendship Day
(national holiday)
Simple rites are observed by the Philippine government and U.S. Embassy to commemorate

the two nations' historical ties. Wreaths are laid at the American Cemetery in Fort Bonifacio, Makati, and there's an evening concert in Rizal Park.

AUGUST

26 August: Cry of Balintawak
(national holiday)
Also called the Cry of Pugad Lawin, this festival commemorates Andres Bonifacio's call for armed struggle, which began the revolution in 1896. Festivities center on the actual site of the incident at Balintawak, on the boundary between Quezon City and Caloocan City, with other rites including one at Monumento (Caloocan).

SEPTEMBER

11 September: Barangay Day
(national holiday)

Kaamulan Festival
This is a major three-day tribal festival in Malaybalay (Bukidnon) on Mindanao.

The 3rd Saturday: Penafrancia Festival
(major festival)
A colorful fluvial procession climaxes this nine-day festival in Naga City, Camarines Sur.

Thanksgiving Day
(national holiday)

29 September: Ang Sinulog
(major festival)
A week of celebration precedes this fiesta in Iligan City.

OCTOBER

The 2nd Sunday: La Naval de Manila
An evening candlelight procession from Santo Domingo Church along Quezon Blvd. honors Our Lady of the Holy Rosary, to whose intercession is attributed a series of Spanish-Filipino naval victories over the Dutch in 1646 (Quezon City and Metro Manila).

Turrumba
See March/April listing (Pakil).

CARL PARKES

decked out for Sinulog

Weekend near the 19th: MassKara Festival
A smiling mask is the symbol of this festival in Bacolod City (Negros Occidental), which was started in 1980 to reflect the people's spirit in spite of hardships caused by the sugar industry's decline. The festival also coincides with the city's charter day on the 19th of October. A spectacular street parade climaxes a weeklong celebration.

10-12 October: Zamboanga Hermosa
Zamboanga City's biggest fiesta commemorates the apparition of the Virgin at Fort Pilar and her miraculous intervention against enemy attacks.

NOVEMBER

1 November: All Saints' Day
(national holiday)
Families throughout the country gather at cemeteries to remember their dead. Graves, which have been whitewashed and cleaned, are decorated with flowers, wreaths, candles, and lights.

A festive atmosphere prevails as people not only pray and meditate, but also eat, drink, sing, play cards and mah-jongg, and hold reunions with relatives. The whole day and night is spent at the cemetery in a 24-hour vigil. The Chinese have particular reverence for their ancestors, placing food on graves and lighting incense as well as candles. This is a good time to visit a Chinese cemetery in Manila or Cebu City.

2 November: All Souls' Day
(nationally celebrated)
Catholics attend mass and visit churches to pray for the souls in purgatory. In several Mindanao towns, food for the dead is offered at the altar.

30 November: National Heroes' Day
(national holiday)
Also called Bonifacio Day. Simple ceremonies honor the country's revolutionary heroes, held on the birthday of Andres Bonifacio. In Manila, wreaths are laid at his monument near the post office.

DECEMBER

8 December: Feast of Our Lady of the Immaculate Conception
(regional festival)
This is celebrated with evening processions, supplemented by cultural presentations, beauty pageants, and fireworks. Special events include: the Malabon Fluvial Parade, a colorful evening procession along the Malabon-Navotas waterway (Metro Manila); the Puerto Princesa (Palawan) city fiesta, preceded by a week of cultural events; the town fiesta of Oton (Iloilo), which features a parade of decorated *carrozas*, followed by a carabao-*carroza* race; and Subayan Keg Subano Festival (major festival), Ozamis City (Misamis Occidental), which combines the city fiesta with a Subanon cultural festival. Fiestas also occur in Pasig (Metro Manila), Antipolo (Rizal), Vigan (Ilocos Sur), Boac (Marinduque), and Roxas City (Panay).

16 December-6 January: Christmas
(nationally celebrated)
The Philippines is said to celebrate the longest Christmas season in the world—22 days! In fact, radios begin to play Christmas tunes in October, and stores hang decorations early. As people get into the Christmas spirit, they too begin decorating their homes and offices, hanging *farols* (star-shaped lanterns) in windows and setting up the *belen* (a model of the nativity scene). An array of *farols* is offered in native markets. Regional styles of *belen* are displayed at Nayong Pilipino, near Manila's international airport. Nativity plays are performed in some Visayan communities.

Christmas traditions are a mixture of native, Spanish, Chinese, and American elements. The result is uniquely Filipino. In the old days, when only one rice crop was sown, Christmas coincided with the harvest. Food was plentiful and there was cause for thanksgiving. The Spanish superimposed the drama and symbolism of the Nativity, the Chinese lent their New Year customs of exploding firecrackers and giving cash gifts to godchildren, and the Americans added "Jingle Bells" and "White Christmas."

Regional customs vary in Bicol—e.g., at Buhi (Camarines Sur), carolers dress as shepherds, and in Negros Occidental, they perform folk dances and comedy skits in addition to singing. In the cities, workers get a Christmas bonus. Even the poorest families try to acquire special food and new clothes.

16-24 December: Simbang Gabi
(nationally celebrated)
Christmas officially begins with a novena of predawn masses, also called Misas de Gallo. Church bells and brass bands summon the faithful at the hour of cockcrow. Participants emerge from church to find stalls serving hot coffee and glutinous rice dishes. The Las Pinas church (Metro Manila) is a good place to attend.

24 December: Christmas Eve
(regional holiday)
Panunuluyan (Tagalog) and *panagbalay* (Visayan) are words meaning "to have a place to stay." Street plays reenact Joseph and Mary's search for shelter prior to Christ's birth. Two people dressed as the couple make a round of the houses, pleading for shelter and receiving a ritual denial. They lead an evening procession featuring saints' images, singing candle-bearers, and a brass band. Finally, they reach the house of the *hermano mayor* (fiesta sponsor) and are invited to enter; refreshments are served. The procession returns to the church for midnight mass.

SAVE THE WILDLIFE

As Asian rainforests are destroyed by man, the first casualties are wildlife. Rainforests are home to 90% of the world's primates, such as monkeys and orangutans; 80% of the world's insects; and half of the world's plants. According to the U.S. Academy of Sciences, a four-square-mile patch of forest will hold 125 different mammals, 400 species of birds, and hundreds of reptiles and amphibians. The region's endangered species include famous animals such as the orangutan, the Asian elephant, the Sumatran rhino, and the Philippine eagle, plus less-well-known animals such as Ridley's leaf-nosed bat, the flat-headed cat, and the violin beetle; an international study lists 166 endangered species in Southeast Asia. The end of the rainforests will bring wildlife destruction comparable only to the mass extinction that wiped out the dinosaurs 65 million years ago.

Spreading the message has largely been the work of rainforest groups, plus the efforts of the World Wildlife Fund and Friends of the Earth. But you, as a traveler, can also help by refusing to purchase animal goods made from protected or endangered species. The United States is the world's largest consumer of wildlife! Travelers often don't realize that seemingly innocuous products made from hides, shells, and feathers—and on sale in public markets in Asia—are often illegal and life-threatening souvenirs. Regulations are complex, but prohibited products include *all* sea-turtle items, Philippine crocodile hides, pangolin (anteater) leather from Thailand and Indonesia, most wild bird feathers, and all ivory products. Just as destructive is the purchase of coral items, since coral collection is directly responsible for the near-complete destruction of sea beds in many Southeast Asian countries. Prohibited items will be seized by customs officials, and you will risk a substantial fine: when in doubt, don't buy!

Places to see this event include Kawit (Cavite), where it's known as Maytinis, and Baliuag (Bulacan). Other events include the Lantern Festival in San Fernando (Pampanga), the Feast of Lanterns in Iloilo City, and a Noise Contest in Bayombong (Nueva Vizcaya).

25 December: Christmas Day
(national holiday)
The midnight mass is known as the Misa de Aguinaldo, or Nativity Mass, or Mass of Gifts. Very early on Christmas morning, families return home for the Noche Buena. This feast of native delicacies is a traditional link with harvest thanksgiving rites. Christmas Eve and Christmas Day are family occasions, with festive lights and music, gift-giving, abundant food and drink, and merrymaking. Children make their rounds of the houses of godparents, relatives, and friends to receive blessings and gifts.

27-30 December: Binirayan Festival
This exuberant festival is a reenactment of the landing of the 10 Bornean *datus* on the island of Panay, and the barter of the island with the Atis. Four days of dancing and revelry fill the streets of San Jose (Antique).

28 December: Holy Innocents' Day
Filipino version of April Fool's Day, with pranks played. Marinduque's towns celebrate Jesus's escape with masked giants and dwarfs roaming the streets, reenacting the Romans' search for the Christ child.

30 December: Rizal Day
(national holiday)
Anniversary commemoration of the 1896 execution of revolutionary hero José Rizal. Ceremonies are held at his memorial in Rizal Park, Manila, and at Calamba (Laguna), his birthplace.

31 December: New Year's Eve
(nationally celebrated)
An evening of family gatherings and partygoing, featuring food, drink, music, and deafening firecrackers. The Binalbal Festival of Tudela (Misamis Occidental) features a noisy parade of people dressed as ghosts and witches to drive away evil spirits.

SHOPPING

The Philippines is not a duty-free haven. Imported items are relatively expensive. Handicrafts are among the best purchases a visitor can make, and discriminating buyers can find some exquisite work. Every region has its own handicraft specialty. Most of them can be bought in Manila, but it's more fun and cheaper to seek out products (and craftspeople) in their native places. Baguio, Cebu, Davao, and Zamboanga are better places to shop than Manila; the towns and villages where the actual handiwork is done are better still. Browse around before buying; don't buy anything of value on your first day, and don't buy handicrafts in Manila until you've come back from the provinces.

Clothes

In addition to skirts, vests, and belts of thick handwoven material, one can make some good buys in light tropical clothing for practical use. The *barong tagalog,* the male national dress, looks good on foreigners too. This translucent, loose-fitting, embroidered, long-sleeved shirt, with cuff links, worn outside the trousers over a plain white T-shirt, serves as both formal and informal wear, but its short-sleeved version, the *polo barong,* is considered casual. A *barong* can be made to order in 24 hours. Prices and quality vary substantially according to the material (*jusi* and *piña* are more expensive than ramie) and whether it's hand- or machine-embroidered. Don't bother with the cheap polyester ones.

The *terno* (female national dress), with its distinctive butterfly sleeves, isn't a practical buy for foreign women, but some lovely *barong*-type kaftans and *jelabas* are available. Manila is also a good place to buy sportswear and conventional clothing, either in stores or made-to-measure (takes one to two days). Large shoe sizes may be hard to find, but custom-made shoes are inexpensive by international standards; try Besa's, 172 Dasmarinas St. in Binondo, or at the Cash 'n Carry Supermarket in Makati.

Antiques

As anywhere, high-quality antiques aren't cheap, but if you know what you're looking for, there are some very good buys: Sung, Yuan, and Ming porcelain, unearthed from numerous old gravesites, jewelry (including some excavated pieces), santos (saints' statuettes of wood, ivory, and bone from the Spanish era), relics of Spanish colonialism and the Japanese occupation, furniture and other family heirlooms, old ethnic ar-

blessed be the Santo Niño

CARL PARKES

tifacts all come onto the market regularly. So do skillfully reproduced fakes, so exercise extreme caution.

Do some research beforehand through the numerous books available on Philippine antiques. Porcelain that has been repaired loses two-thirds of its value. Numerous antique stores are on and around Mabini St., Ermita, in shopping malls in Makati, at the Ayala Museum, and along Tomas Morato in Quezon City. Over the past 20 years, many of the best antique pieces found in the Philippines have been sold abroad, so good pieces are harder to find. Valuable pieces, classified as cultural properties, require an export permit and should bear the registration stamp of the National Museum.

ACCOMMODATIONS AND FOOD

WHERE TO STAY

Overnight accommodations range from budget pensions and tourist inns to economy hotels and luxury hotels. As usual, you get what you pay for. Even within the budget category, standards vary widely. Popular destinations such as Banaue and Boracay offer particularly good value. Here, P150-400 buys a far nicer room than in any big city. Substantial differences also exist between cities. Manila is considerably more expensive than provincial cities: expect to pay anywhere from P350 to P800 for modest accommodations. In the provinces, rooms below P150 generally contain a fan, but not a private bathroom. Above P250, rooms usually have private facilities, and sometimes a/c. As you move into the P500-plus bracket, a/c, sheets, soap, and a towel are expected. If money is no object, excellent five-star facilities are available in Manila, Cebu, Baguio, Davao, and at beach resorts. Checkout time is normally 1200-1300.

Budget Accommodations

Some hotel rates are per person and others are per room. At their worst, cheap hotels can be dirty, windowless, and cater to a mainly "short-time" clientele. An hourly or three-hour rate posted behind the reception desk is a sure sign of the latter. Some of the better family-run guesthouses discourage bringing hospitality girls, although many places don't care; a few may raise the room rate from single to double. Normal precautions regarding valuables and room security should be followed. If you have doubts about a hotel's security, it's better to move to a more expensive one.

The few youth hostels in the Philippines are not particularly good value. Their dormitory accommodations often cost more than a hotel room. Those without a valid International Youth Hostel Card or Student Identification Card pay slightly more than cardholders. Campgrounds, too, are scarce, so carrying a tent is generally not worth the extra weight and hassle of finding campsites.

Upscale Accommodations

The Department of Tourism has classified 18 deluxe hotels, 11 first-class hotels, 18 standard hotels, and 22 economy-class hotels in Metro Manila, plus guesthouses and pensions. There are other luxury hotels scattered about the provinces, particularily in Cebu City, Davao, and Puerto Princesa. Facilities (and prices) in upscale establishments are of international standard.

The historic Manila Hotel is the doyen of Philippine hotels. For a mere US$2,500 a night, you too can occupy the penthouse suite where General Douglas MacArthur lived before WW II. Deluxe hotels have various promotions throughout the year and give good package deals for a low, low price. Ask your travel agent before setting off.

For those not on too tight a budget, a hot bath and swim in the pool are a delightful indulgence after a journey through the provinces. Upscale beach resorts are found in Batangas, Cavite, Cebu, and elsewhere. And between the extremes of budget and five-star is a wide range of one- to four-star establishments. Hotels and lodging houses add a 15% government tax and a 10% service charge to the bill. Tipping above this is optional, but bellboys, porters, and room service attendants are customarily given a small amount, depending on the degree of service.

Extended Stays

Accommodation in any category can usually be negotiated more economically on a weekly or monthly basis. Apartment hotels, or "apartels," are well suited for extended stays, since they usually have large, a/c rooms and cooking facilities, refrigerator, and televisions. The weekend editions of the main Manila newspapers carry ads for regular apartments.

Rents are considerably lower outside Ermita and Makati. At the low end of the scale, families often advertise rooms for "bedspacers." Those planning to live in the Philippines can find useful information in *Living in the Philippines,* published by the American Chamber of Commerce of the Philippines and available at Manila bookstores.

FOOD

Filipino food has great range but admittedly isn't popular with everybody. Critics have charged that native dishes often lack the complexity and refinement of other Southeast Asian cuisines and that sauces tend to be heavy or greasy and unimaginative. On the other hand, many dishes compensate with a freshness and simplicity that accentuate the natural flavors.

An unusual feature of Filipino cooking is the combination of major ingredients, e.g., chicken and shrimp or pork and fish. Soups like *sinigang* and *tinola* are delicious, as is well-prepared *lechon* (roast suckling pig). Sweet morsels are made from glutinous rice, while *halo halo* is a common dessert based on layers of preserved or sweetened fruit, gelatin, custard, and crushed ice. So while Filipino dishes rarely reach sublime heights, it's possible to enjoy satisfying meals, accompanied by the excellent local beer, rum, or coffee.

Origins of Filipino Cuisine

Filipino food is an intriguing blend of Malaysian, Chinese, Spanish, and—most importantly—American cuisines. Regardless of origin, *lechon, lumpia,* and pork *adobo* are now considered national dishes. Regional variations in the fresh ingredients available account for provincial specialties. Centuries of Spanish rule have resulted in about 80% of Filipino dishes being of Spanish derivation.

Interestingly, there was relatively little Mexican influence, despite the ties to a Mexican-based administration and the galleon trade. The Spanish colonialists preferred Iberian dishes, such as *arroz valenciana,* to those of the Mexican Indians. *Adobo* preparation is the only exception, as the tomato, corn, avocado, and potato in *adobo* were all introduced from Mexico.

You'll quickly discover—perhaps to your dismay—that hamburgers, hot dogs, and omelettes are popular throughout the country. You'll also discover that Filipino attempts at Western food have been less than successful. Rather than sticking with poorly prepared Western food, try native dishes such as *adobo* and *kare kare,* served in the smaller cafés, or street food such as *lugaw* and steamed corn.

The most obvious Chinese contribution is noodles, which form the basis of the popular *pancit* dishes. The Chinese also gave the Philippines *lumpia* and chop suey. Some standard dishes, such as the coconut-based *ginataan,* have retained their Malay origin. The Muslims never entered the Spanish sphere, so their cooking has remained heavily Malay. It's spicy, and marked by the use of coconut milk and chilies, the prevalence of cassava as well as rice and seafood, and the absence of pork.

Eating Out

Eating in the Philippines is very inexpensive, though travelers can economize further by patronizing *turo turo* restaurants and the inexpensive street stalls. Also worth seeking out are *kamayan* restaurants, which serve native dishes on banana leaves without the use of silverware. Ordering in most restaurants is easy since menus are printed in English and service personnel speak some English.

Restaurant prices are generally reasonable, though not as cheap as in India, Indonesia, or Thailand. But beer is much cheaper than in those countries. Seafood is a bargain by international standards. Native restaurants abound in Manila, from market stalls and *carinderias* (simple little canteens) to a handful offering gourmet Filipino cuisine. Cafeterias often serve in the *turo turo* (literally "point point") manner rather than by menu; customers select from the range of dishes on display. Also good are the

POPULAR FILIPINO DISHES

Note that many dishes are described simply by their method of cooking: any item stewed in vinegar and garlic is called *adobo*, sour soups are *sinigang*, food sautéed with tomatoes is *pangat*, food cooked in blood is *dinuguan*, and anything raw is *kilawin*. The Philippines also has one of Asia's largest selections of tropical fruits. Be sure to try a *guabano*!

adobo: a distinctive stew made from pork or chicken marinated in vinegar, garlic, soy sauce, and sugar. One of the most popular dishes in the country.

afritada: beef served Spanish style in a rich tomato sauce with olives, green peas, chopped potatoes, and slivered green peppers

asado: meat marinated in *kalamansi* juice and soy sauce, then fried and served with marinade and cubed potatoes, tomatoes, and onions

aso: dog. Popular in northern Luzon among the hilltribes.

baboy: pork

balut: fertilized but unhatched duck eggs incubated 17 days, then boiled and eaten. One of the more bizarre delicacies in the world. Filipinos believe that *baluts* ensure virility and fertility plus have aphrodisiac qualities. Novices should ask for the more mature *balut sa puti*. The proper technique is to pick the top off the shell, suck out the juice, shell completely, add vinegar and salt, and pop the crunchy fellow into your mouth. Several beers make this easier.

bangus: bony but delicious milkfish. Bred locally in fishponds.

bibingka: sweet rice cakes with coconut milk and white cheese

buko: young green coconut

calamares: squid

carne: beef

chicharon: fried pork rinds. Look for the expensive but superb rinds heavily cut with pork meat.

crispy pata: pigs' feet and forelegs fried golden brown, served with soy sauce, garlic, and *kalamansi* juice. Although most Westerners find this dish much too fatty, the crispy skin and accompanying sauce are delicious.

dinuguan: pork and intestines stewed in a rich, dark blood sauce. A mild but surprisingly tasty dish.

ginatan: anything cooked in coconut milk

gulay: vegetables

halo halo: a colorful dessert of shaved ice, colored sweets, white beans, corn, cubed fruits, and evaporated milk

hito: catfish

inihaw: Anything broiled over a charcoal fire is called *inihaw* or *ihaw*.

kare kare: beef, oxtail, or pig knuckles served in a spicy peanut sauce with rice and vegetables

kilawin: raw fish marinated in *kalamansi* juice, vinegar, and onions

lapu-lapu: rock bass

adobong pusit: cuttlefish soup with coconut milk and vinegar

lechon: roast suckling pig served with thick liver sauce. A traditional fiesta specialty.

lumpia: Filipino egg rolls

maise: steamed corn

mami: noodle soup with chicken, beef, or fish

manok: chicken

pancit: noodles prepared in several styles. Canton is egg noodles with meat and vegetables, *guisado* and *malabon* are thin rice noodles, *molo* is Chinese dumplings fried with garlic and meats.

pochero: beef and spicy sausage mixed with vegetables

pusit: cuttlefish

shrimp rebosado: baked shrimp

siopao: Chinese pork buns

sinigang: sour and delicious soup flavored with tamarind, lemon, and *kalamansi*. This Filipino bouillabaisse is made from any kind of meat, fish, or shellfish, with tomatoes, radishes, and *kangkong* leaves added for flavor.

suman: long fingers of sweet rice wrapped in coconut leaves

tabala: raw oysters marinated in *kalamansi* and garlic

tahong: steamed or baked mussels

tapa: a simple breakfast dish of dried beef and onions

ihaw ihaw grills, where pork or chicken is barbecued on sticks. These stalls are all over the country.

Many provincial styles of cooking are available in Manila. One can also find regional Chinese food. Chinese restaurants often also offer inexpensive meals with set courses that are good value. Spanish tastes affected Filipino cooking profoundly, and Manila has some fine Spanish restaurants.

American influence is echoed in a few good steak houses (serving Australian steaks) and many fast-food outlets serving hamburger, pizza, and ice cream. Current trends in tourism are reflected in the numerous German and Japanese restaurants, which often offer good value. The selection of other international cuisines includes French, Italian, Korean, Thai, Pakistani, and Middle Eastern food. Restaurants at popular destinations like Puerto Galera and Boracay cater to Western tastes. In larger regional towns, Filipino food is supplemented by Chinese and fast-food eateries. In remote villages, native food is the rule, which at its worst can consist of dog meat or grilled field rat—so don't forget to B.Y.O.S. (bring your own sardines).

Beverages

Water is generally potable, particularly in urban centers. If in doubt, stick to boiled or bottled liquids. The refreshing water of young coconuts is also available in rural lowland areas. Soft drinks like Coca-Cola and 7-Up are sold everywhere, but aren't always cold out in the villages. Fresh *kalamansi* (citrus) juice is served in most restaurants. Boxed juice and milk are available in most towns, but fresh milk is rarely found outside major cities. The coffee served is usually instant, but native coffee—Batangas *barako*—if you can find it, is excellent. Coffeehouses are a distinctive feature of Muslim towns in Mindanao and Sulu.

Bars are everywhere. Outside strictly Muslim areas in the south, drinking is basic to Filipino social life, and vast quantities of beer, gin, and rum are consumed. Filipino beer is among the finest and cheapest in the East, costing less than 10 pesos per bottle. Longtime leader San Miguel is now being challenged by several new brews such as the lighter Carlsberg and less expensive Manila beer. Five-year-old Tanduay rum and locally produced gins and vodkas are all

first-class spirits. Prices are ridiculously cheap at P20-30 per liter. Filipino wines, on the other hand, are disgustingly sweet and completely unappealing. Fortunately for the wine drinker, good-quality California wines are available at reasonable prices from duty-free shops in Manila.

Residents outside the larger towns often drink home brews such as *tuba* and *tapuey* rather than the more expensive beers or liquors. Both have an alcoholic content of only 12-18 proof but pack a deadly wallop with effects similar to tequila's. *Tuba* is made by extracting the sap from either nipa palms or the tops of young coconut palms. When drunk immediately after gathering, the yellow liquid is slightly sweet and palatable. Overnight fermenting turns the gentle firewater into something bitter and much more potent. Experts claim they can judge the hours of fermentation by the color alone. *Lambanog* is boiled *tuba* distilled in the true Kentucky moonshine manner. *Tapuey* is an alcoholic beverage made from rice or corn popular with the hilltribes of northern Luzon. The Ybanag of the Cagayan Valley make *layaw,* a very strong corn spirit. *Basi,* a homemade wine from Ilocos Norte, is made from crushed sugarcane juice compounded with barks and berries; at its best, it's deliciously smooth.

Hospitality and Etiquette

A stranger passing Filipinos who are eating will automatically be invited to "come and eat." It's polite to say you've already eaten. If people insist, or if there's an abundance of food such as at a wedding or fiesta, then by all means participate. Avoid arriving at a home at meal time unless you're sure of a welcome. Use similar tact if invited to stay at someone's house. Don't accept the first invitation. It's better to point out how inconvenient it would be for the host, or to make a polite excuse, then wait to see if you're pressed further. It's the Filipino way, enabling the visitor to gauge whether an invitation is genuine or not.

When staying with a family, it's important to fit smoothly into the group-oriented social life—privacy may be a scarce commodity. At family gatherings, it's good form to give special attention to the elders. Old men and women may be addressed as *lolo* and *lola,* respectively, and taking their right hand and touching it lightly to your forehead is a traditionally respectful greeting.

Filipinos are very sentimental; they love small gifts, keepsakes, and remembrances, or a postcard expressing thanks for hospitality. Food is always an appropriate gift for a host family. If you travel around, then return to the same family, it's the local custom to bring a gift—*pasalubong*—typically a delicacy of the place you've visited.

Invitations to restaurants and bars are extended and accepted without any obligation to reciprocate. The person who extends the invitation customarily picks up the tab. Never try to "go Dutch" with a Filipino: it's all or nothing. In less-sophisticated establishments, customers attract the attention of the waitperson with a low hiss, then raise fingers to indicate how many beers they want, or draw a rectangle in the air with a finger when they're ready to pay the "chit" (bill). Waitresses are addressed as "Miss or "Excuse me, Miss."

GETTING THERE

BY AIR

Ninoy Aquino International Airport, 12 km from downtown Manila, is served by over 150 flights a week from all major Western and Asian cities. By air, Manila is 90 minutes from Hong Kong, two hours and 40 minutes from Bangkok, three hours from Singapore, seven hours from Sydney, 17 hours from San Francisco, and 19 hours from Europe.

Visitors intending to spend most of the time in the Visayas can avoid Manila by inquiring about direct flights to Cebu. Travelers coming from Borneo or Indonesia should check on air connections from Kota Kinabalu to Zamboanga, and Manado to Davao. The latter is currently served twice weekly by Bouraq.

All travelers are strongly advised to buy roundtrip tickets before arriving in Manila. Discount travel agencies in the Philippines are scarce and price competition between travel agents is minimal. Bucket shops in Tokyo, Hong Kong, Bangkok, and Singapore often beat Manila rates by 25-40% on both one-way and roundtrip tickets.

American travelers will find the latest discount fares listed in the Sunday travel supplements of the *San Francisco Examiner, Los Angeles Times, New York Times,* and other large metropolitan newspapers. Discounted roundtrip fares from the U.S. West Coast to Manila are currently US$725-900.

Fares

All major airlines in North America conform to the price guidelines issued by the International Air Transport Association (IATA). Roundtrip advance-purchase weekday fares from the U.S. West Coast are currently US$1,124 (low season) and US$1,231 (high season). Roundtrip is US$1,440 from New York.

Tickets purchased directly from the airlines cost more than tickets purchased from budget agencies and consolidators, but often carry fewer restrictions and cancellation penalties. Special promotional fares offered by the airlines may even match the discounters, such as roundtrips during the winter months priced US$880-940.

The Philippines can be reached on dozens of airlines with a variety of tickets sold at all possible prices. Read the travel section of your Sunday newspaper for advertised bargains, then call airlines, student travel agencies, and discount wholesalers for their prices and ticket restrictions. Determined travelers can plan itineraries and discover obscure air routes by studying the *Official Airline Guide* at the library.

Ticket prices vary enormously depending on dozens of factors, including type of ticket, season, choice of airline, your flexibility, and experience of the travel agent. It's confusing, but since airfare comprises a major portion of total travel expenses, no amount of time getting it right is wasted. The rule of thumb is that price and restrictions are inversely related; the cheaper the ticket the more hassles such as penalties, odd departure hours, layovers, and risk of last-minute cancellations.

First Class and Business Tickets: First class (coded F) and business class (coded J) are designed for travelers who need maximum flexibility and comfort, and are willing to pay the price.

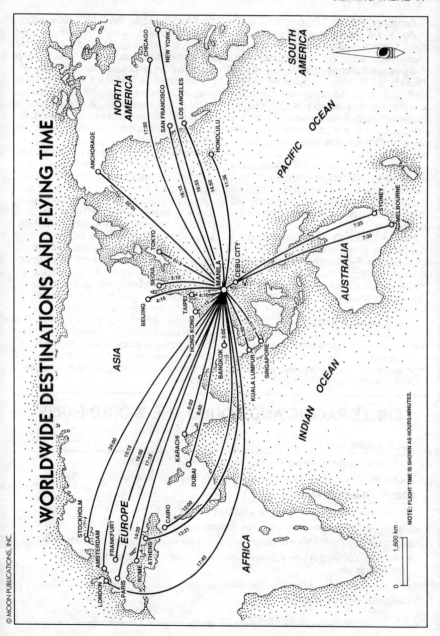

WORLDWIDE DESTINATIONS AND FLYING TIME

NOTE: FLIGHT TIME IS SHOWN AS HOURS:MINUTES.

© MOON PUBLICATIONS, INC.

Economy Tickets: Economy class tickets (coded Y) are cheaper than first and business classes, plus they often lack the advance-purchase requirements and cancellation charges.

Advance-Purchase Excursion (APEX) Tickets: APEX tickets—the airlines' main method for deep discounts—are about 25% less than economy-class tickets but often come loaded with restrictions requiring advance payment, dictating your length of stay, and carrying heavy penalties for cancellations or amendments.

Super-APEX: Super-APEX tickets, somewhat cheaper than regular APEX, are limited in quantity and often sell out quickly. APEX and Super-APEX tickets are recommended for visitors with limited time who need guaranteed air reservations.

Mileage Tickets: These permit the traveler to pay the fare from A to B and make unlimited stops en route. For example, the ticket from San Francisco to Manila costs US$1,361 and permits 9,559 miles. One possible routing is San Francisco-Tokyo-Seoul-Taipei-Hong Kong-Manila. Mileage tickets are generally good for one year, and a mileage surcharge is tacked on for travel beyond the allotted distance. Many airlines have phased out mileage tickets.

Circle-Pacific Tickets: Scheduled on major international airlines, these tickets allow you to circle the North Pacific, Southeast Asia, and the South Pacific for about US$2,400 in economy class. Restrictions are a problem: the ticket limits you to four stopovers, costs US$50 per extra stop, demands 14 days' advance purchase, carries cancellation penalties, has a six-month expiration, and costs US$50 for each reissuance. Worse yet, only those cities served by the principal carrier and partner are possible stopovers. This eliminates most of the smaller but vitally important connections such as Singapore-Jakarta.

Round-the-World Tickets: Another variation of APEX is the RTW ticket sold by several international carriers. Currently, no single carrier offers round-the-world service, but all major U.S. airlines offer round-the-world routes in conjunction with foreign airlines. RTW tickets cost US$2,570 in economy class on the north Pacific route through Tokyo, Seoul, and Hong Kong; and US$3,217 in economy class on the south Pacific route through Australia and New Zealand. Most airlines allow unlimited stopovers, but you can only stop in those cities served by the airlines. Tickets are good for either six months or one year depending on the airline.

The major difference among airlines is ticketing procedure. Some, like Delta, have an open ticket policy—you have to reserve only the first international segment and remaining dates are left unspecified, allowing for last-minute alterations.

CIRCLE-PACIFIC AND ROUND-THE-WORLD FARES

CIRCLE-PACIFIC FARES

U.S.A. (West Coast)-Manila-Hong Kong-Bangkok-Bali-Hawaii-U.S.A.: **US$999**

U.S.A.-Tahiti-Cook Islands-Fiji-New Zealand-Australia-Bali-Bangkok-Hong Kong-U.S.A.: **US$1,699**

ROUND-THE-WORLD FARES

U.S.A.-London-Bangkok-Hong Kong-Manila-U.S.A.: **US$1,399**

U.S.A.-Hawaii-Bali-Bangkok-Kathmandu-Delhi-Amsterdam-U.S.A.: **US$1,599**

U.S.A.-Tahiti-New Zealand-Noumea-Sydney-Jakarta-Singapore-Amman-Vienna-U.S.A.: **US$1,799**

U.S.A.-Tahiti-Cook Islands-Fiji-New Zealand-Australia-Bali-Bangkok-Kathmandu-Delhi-Vienna-U.S.A.: **US$2,199**

U.S.A.-Dublin-Amsterdam-Athens-Cairo-Nairobi-Bombay-Delhi-Kathmandu-Bangkok-Singapore-Jakarta-Bali-Hawaii-U.S.A.: **US$2,299**

One-Way or Roundtrip?

Travelers on a holiday under three weeks should purchase roundtrip tickets from their homeland to ensure reserved seats. Consider a package tour or adventure travel package, which often includes discounted hotels and internal flights to popular destinations.

Travelers with open schedules might consider purchasing a one-way ticket to Manila. All future travel arrangements can then be made in the Philippines, an option that adds flexibility and may save some money. This option also avoids IATA regulations, which dictate that one-way fares priced in U.S. dollars be doubled to arrive at a full-fare roundtrip price.

Low and High Seasons

All airlines and discount agencies price their tickets according to the season.

Airlines in North America and Europe consider the low season the winter months Oct.-April and the high season the summer months May-September. The holiday period Dec.-Jan. is also considered a high season. An intermediate or "shoulder season" is often wedged between the high and low seasons.

The high season for airlines in Australia and New Zealand runs December to 15 January, school holiday periods are shoulder seasons, and the low season is the rest of the year.

Sold-Out Flights

The holiday season Dec.-Jan. can be a difficult time to obtain tickets. Not only are prices about 20% higher, but also the shortage of seats makes confirmed reservations on specific days a real chore.

This exasperating situation was created by the reluctance of the government to allow additional flights into the capital by other international carriers. As with other Asian-based airlines, Philippine Airlines feels it's at an unfair disadvantage against U.S. airlines that have huge domestic networks to feed their transpacific routes. Airlines in the U.S. also benefit from fifth-freedom rights, which allow them to pick up passengers and fly on to a third country in Asia.

Recent problems with Philippine Airlines has also made it difficult to find a seat during the high season. Travelers are advised to make reservations several months in advance to ensure re-

served seats on the most convenient dates. After arrival in Manila, be sure to reconfirm departure dates to avoid losing your reservation.

Passengers are required to reconfirm all flights at least 72 hours prior to departure. **Reconfirmation** is not necessary on the first flight of your itinerary or on flights with a layover of less than 72 hours. Passengers who fail to reconfirm their flights may have their seats automatically canceled and given to other passengers. Some passengers even reconfirm their reconfirmations!

Nonstop, Direct, Connecting?

Airline terminology is almost as confusing as its ticketing policies. Flights are either nonstop, direct, or connecting. A nonstop flight requires no change of planes and makes no stops. A direct flight stops at least once and may involve a change of planes. The flight number remains the same and the second plane must wait for any delayed arrivals. A connecting flight involves different planes and different flight numbers. Connecting planes are not required to wait for delayed flights on the first leg.

Several airlines now fly nonstop from North America to the Philippines, though most require a stop for refueling and possible change of planes in either Tokyo, Seoul, Taipei, or Hong Kong. A stop in Honolulu is often included.

Getting Bumped

Bumping is another problem encountered by an increasing number of passengers heading off to Southeast Asia. The situation has been created by airline executives who routinely overbook flights to maximize their profits and meet yield management goals. Who gets bumped is often based on check-in time: those who checked in last are the first to be bumped. Passengers denied boarding against their will are entitled to compensation, provided they have fulfilled certain requirements, such as confirming their reservation and checking in before the deadline.

Airline managers know that compensation for bumped passengers is a small price to pay to maximize aircraft capacity. The compensation depends on the price of the ticket and the length of delay until the next available flight. Compensation can be free domestic tickets, cash up to US$400, discount coupons for other destinations, or complimentary hotels and meals. Believe it or not, some passengers actually attempt to get bumped to pick up these benefits.

Proof of Onward Passage

Some countries in Asia require incoming travelers to show proof of onward passage. Proof of onward passage can be a plane ticket to some foreign destination or a miscellaneous charge order (MCO). Fortunately, Manila immigration officials rarely check for onward tickets unless they dislike your appearance.

If you're concerned about not having proof of onward passage, you could purchase the cheapest outbound ticket (Manila to Hong Kong for example) and request a refund after you've passed through immigration in Manila. Be sure to buy this ticket with cash or traveler's checks from a major airline carrier. Requesting a refund for an unused ticket with an obscure airline can be a Kafkaesque experience.

Ticket Tips

Bargain tickets sold by major airlines and discount travel agencies often carry heavy restrictions to prevent passengers from changing their minds and thereby saddling the airline with empty seats. Travelers should read the fine print and understand the restrictions, which aren't always spelled out in airline advertisements. Most airlines only give cash refunds in the event of death—not for a sudden change of plans, marriage, birth of a child, traffic delays, or nervous breakdown at the check-in counter. Passengers who need to cancel their flights may, depending on the type of ticket, be able to have the value applied toward the purchase of another nonrefundable ticket for up to one year after the first was issued. Other tickets are partially refundable, but penalties can be 25-75% of the ticket value.

Tickets issued by travel agents will be marked either "OK" or "RQ" (or "on request"). The OK stamp next to the destination indicates the travel agent has checked with the airline and the seat has been reserved in your name. An RQ or "on request" stamp means your seat has not been confirmed by your agent and you are going to be on standby. This is a big problem with many travel agencies in Bangkok, but not so serious in Manila. Be sure your ticket is marked "OK" before payment.

Airline tickets cannot be legally transferred from one passenger to another, despite the advertisements placed in newspapers and on bulletin boards in youth hostels and guesthouses. International departures are usually checked by matching the name on the ticket with the name on the passport.

Tickets purchased from mileage brokers are prohibited by airlines and subject to seizure at the airport. In other words, mileage certificates obtained from frequent flyer programs and sold to the public at steep discounts are nontransferable.

Tour conductor tickets given to travel agents as a reward for selling seats on group tours cannot be legally sold or transferred but may be given away as presents. Always check your bargain ticket to see if it's marked "no fare" or "no miles," two terms given by discount operators to denote budget tickets without fare guarantees or mileage benefits.

For passengers, air travel is getting worse. The number of passengers angry enough to complain to the Department of Transportation has risen to record levels in recent years. A few tips may help reduce the aggravation.

Try to avoid flying on weekends or holidays when airport congestion is bad and flight cancellations and delays are most common. Avoid rush hours in the early mornings and evenings. Request your boarding pass when you make your reservation or take advantage of the new "ticketless" travel options offered by many airlines.

Don't check additional baggage; carry everything possible onto the plane. Ask your travel agent about legal limits and pack accordingly. Remove old airport destination tags and write your permanent business address and phone number at your destination on your luggage tag. File claims for lost baggage before you leave the airport.

Know your legal rights. Contact the U.S. Department of Transportation's Office of Consumer Affairs (tel. 202-366-2220) for a copy of *Fly Rights: A Guide to Air Travel in the U.S.*

Consolidators

The cheapest tickets to Asia are sold by wholesalers who take advantage of special rates for group tours by purchasing large blocks of unsold seats. Once an airline concludes it can't sell all of its seats, consolidators are offered a whopping 20-40% commission to do the job. They then use most of the commission to offer clients reduced ticket prices.

The drawbacks are these companies rarely provide travel counseling, they keep you guessing about which airline you'll fly, tickets often carry penalties, and routings can be slow and byzantine. Try to get the cheapest ticket, on the best airline, with the fewest unnecessary stops. Consolidators sell tickets through student bureaus, independent travel agents, and travel clubs. In fact, you can buy consolidator tickets from almost everyone except the consolidators themselves and the airlines.

Roundtrip prices currently average US$500-600 from the U.S. West Coast cities to Tokyo, US$550/650 low season/high season to Hong Kong, and US$750-950 to Bangkok, Singapore, and Manila. East Coast departures add US$150-200. Current fares are advertised in the Sunday travel sections of major newspapers. Advance planning is essential since the best deals often sell out months in advance.

The following penalties and restrictions may apply to consolidator tickets: Peak fares in effect June-Aug. mean an extra US$50-100; tickets purchased less than 90 days in advance are subject to an additional US$50-150; flight cancellations or changes before the ticket issue usually cost US$50; and cancellations within 30 days of departure or any time after the ticket has been issued cost you up to 25% of the fare.

Couriers

Aside from working as a travel agent or hijacking a plane, the cheapest way to reach Southeast Asia is to carry urgent mail for a courier company. Anyone can do this, and it's perfectly legal—no drugs or guns are carried, just stock certificates and registered mail. However, you're generally limited to carry-on luggage, and length of stay averages two to four weeks.

The best source of accurate information on courier flights is an extremely helpful monthly newsletter from **Travel Unlimited**, P.O. Box 1058, Allston, MA 02134. Editor Tom Lantos charges US$25 for 12 monthly issues—a great deal since you'll save hundreds on your first flight, whether heading to Asia, Europe, or South America.

COURIER COMPANIES

SAN FRANCISCO DEPARTURES

Jupiter Air, tel. (415) 872-0845
UTL Travel, tel. (415) 583-5074
I.B.C., tel. (310) 607-0125

LOS ANGELES DEPARTURES

Jupiter Air, tel. (310) 670-5123
I.B.C., tel. (310) 607-0125
Midnight, tel. 310-330-7096

CANADA DEPARTURES

FB Couriers, tel. (514) 633-0740
Jet Services, tel. (514) 331-7470

LONDON DEPARTURES

Courier Travel, tel. (171) 351-0300
Bridges, tel. (181) 759-5040
BA Travel, tel. (181) 564-7009
Norwood Travel, tel. (181) 674-8214

SYDNEY DEPARTURES

Polo Express, tel. (02) 693-5866
Jupiter, tel. (02) 369-2704

Standby Couriers: Absolutely the cheapest way to reach the Philippines is as a standby courier. Call any of the companies listed in the chart **Courier Companies** and tell them you can replace passengers who cancel their reservations at the last moment. Courier companies welcome standby volunteers. Companies are legally allowed to confiscate the nonrefundable deposit paid by the client, in many cases the full value of the ticket. Standby prices decline as the departure approaches. For example, a flight leaving in five days may be discounted only US$100-150, since the courier company has plenty of time to find a replacement. Flights departing in under two days force the company to offer ridiculous fares, such as US$100 roundtrip to Bangkok.

FROM NORTH AMERICA

Planning Your Route

By now you've studied the historical, geographical, and cultural background of the country, decided where to go and your motivations for travel, decided what activities carry the strongest appeal, determined your allotted time and monetary limits, and formed a general itinerary for your adventure. You've taken care of legal documents, checked your health, surfed the Internet, and packed your bag. You've also learned about types of tickets, pitfalls, and cheaper travel options from couriers and consolidators.

One last task before purchasing a ticket and hopping on a plane is to plan your route. Of course, if time is limited, you can just fly directly to Manila. However, if you have extra time and are flexible about deadlines, you might visit a few other countries, whether starting from the United States, Australia, or Europe.

Americans can reach the Philippines direct from the U.S. West Coast via the northern loop through Japan and Hong Kong, or across the South Pacific.

Northern Loop: The north Pacific loop includes optional stops in Japan, Korea, Taiwan, and Hong Kong before continuing into China or down to Manila. This one-way ticket—often on an airline such as Korean Air or China Air—costs under US$900 from budget travel agencies in San Francisco and Los Angeles.

South Pacific Loop: The southern loop includes stops in the South Pacific, New Zealand, and Australia before arriving in Bali and continuing up to the Philippines. This ticket—often standby on various carriers—costs around US$1,200-1,400 to Bali from student agencies.

Roundtrip: Another popular and relatively inexpensive itinerary begins with the northern Pacific loop, travels through the Philippines and Southeast Asia, routes across the South Pacific, then returns to the United States. This journey covers most of Asia for about US$2,000 in total airfare—a once-in-a-lifetime experience.

Major Airlines in North America
U.S. East Coast travelers can use the North American airlines listed below or a European airline such as Swissair (17 hours, change in Zurich) or Finnair (18 hours, change in Helsinki).

Philippine Airlines: Start with Philippine Airlines, since it often offers promotional fares. PAL's toll-free number, tel. (800) 435-9725 translates to "I FLY PAL." PAL has offices in Chicago,
Dallas, Florida, Honolulu, Los Angeles, New York, San Diego, San Francisco, and Washington, D.C.

A million and a half Filipinos live in the U.S., and cities with large Filipino populations, such as San Francisco, Daly City, and Los Angeles, have Filipino-owned travel agencies that cater specially to the "ethnic" market and should also offer competitive prices

Northwest Airlines (NWA): Northwest Airlines serves Manila with connecting flights from Los Angeles, San Francisco, Seattle, Chicago, Dallas, Detroit, Washington, D.C., and New York. Fares are identical to those of other major airlines. Daily service from Toronto via Detroit or Los Angeles costs US$1,566.

United Airlines (UA): United Airlines flies to Manila from Canada (Toronto and Vancouver) and from major U.S. cities via Tokyo, Taipei, or Seoul. United offers low-priced promotional fares during the winter. Contact United's travel division (tel. 800-328-6877) for information on organized tours.

Canadian Airlines International (CP): Canadian Airlines flies from Toronto and Montreal via Vancouver to Manila. Promotional fares are available during the winter months, but rates on U.S. carriers departing from the United States are generally much lower.

Other Airlines
Singapore Airlines, Malaysian Airlines, Korean Air, China Air, Japan Airlines, Cathay Pacific, and other Asian-based airlines offer Super-APEX flights from U.S. West Coast cities to Manila for US$900-1,100.

Budget Travel Agencies in North America
Some of the best advice on airline ticketing can be found at agencies that specialize in the youth and student markets.

Student Travel Australia: STA serves not only students and youths, but also nonstudents and tour groups. In the United States call (800) 777-0112 for the nearest office.

Hostelling International (HI): The former International Youth Hostel Federation (IYH) and their associated American Youth Hostels (AYH) provide budget travel information and confirmed reservations at any of almost 200 hostels in the U.S. and abroad. Contact HI-AYH, 733 15th St.

AIRLINE TOLL-FREE NUMBERS

British Airways, tel. (800) 247-9297

Cathay Pacific, tel. (800) 233-2742

China Air, tel. (800) 227-5118

Delta Air Lines, tel. (800) 241-4141

Finnair, tel. (800) 950-5000

Garuda, tel. (800) 342-7832

Japan Airlines, tel. (800) 525-3663

KLM, tel. (800) 347-7747

Lufthansa, tel. (800) 645-3880

Malaysian Airlines, tel. (800) 421-8641

Northwest Airlines, tel. (800) 447-4747

Philippine Airlines, tel. (800) 435-9725

Silk Air, tel. (800) 745-5247

Singapore Airlines, tel. (800) 742-3333

Swissair, tel. (800) 221-4750

Thai International, tel. (800) 426-5204

United Airlines, tel. (800) 538-2929

NW, Suite 840, Washington, D.C. 20005, tel. (202) 783-6161.

Air Brokers International: A dependable discount agency with many years of experience in the Asian market, Air Brokers sells discount tickets and can help with circle-Pacific and round-the-world airfares. Contact Air Brokers International, 323 Geary St., Suite 411, San Francisco, CA 94102, tel. (800) 883-3273, fax (415) 397-4767.

Council Travel: This excellent travel organization, a division of the Council on International Educational Exchange, has 37 offices in the U.S. and representatives in Europe and Australia. Prices are low and service reliable since they deal only with reputable airlines to minimize travel problems. Best of all, Council Travel sales agents are experienced travelers who often have firsthand knowledge of Southeast Asia. Council Travel also sells the Youth Hostel Association Card, International Student Identity Card (ISIC), Youth International Educational Exchange Card (for nonstudents under 26), plus travel and health insurance. Larger offices in some major cities include: San Francisco, tel. (415) 421-3473; Los Angeles, tel. (213) 208-3551; Seattle, tel. (206) 632-2448; Chicago, tel. (312) 951-0585; Boston, tel. (617) 266-1926; New York, tel. (212) 661-1450.

FROM EUROPE

Europeans can overland to Bangkok and continue with a flight to Manila, take a direct flight, or make a stop in the Middle East or India. Budget agencies listed below can advise you on routes and prices.

Major Airlines in Europe

British Airways, Qantas, and Thai International offer direct nonstop flights from London to Bangkok that take about 12 hours. Other major airlines on the continent also fly direct to Manila.

Manila can also be reached on the smaller airlines and national airlines associated with each country. These airlines can be useful for stops en route; try Air India, Kuwaiti Airlines, Gulf Air, and Royal Jordanian Airlines. Allow four hours for a change of planes.

Budget Travel Agencies in England

The following agencies sell the lowest-priced tickets from London to the Philippines.

Trailfinders: Travelers in England should contact the nation's largest budget travel agency at 42-48 Earls Court Rd., London W8 7RG, tel. (0171) 938-3366; 194 Kensington High St., London W8 7RG, tel. (0171) 938-3939; 58 Deansgate, Manchester M3, tel. (0161) 839-6969.

Council Travel: Council Travel staffs 10 offices in Europe and one in London, 28a Poland St., London W1, tel. (0171) 437-7767.

Campus Travel: Campus operates several offices in Britain—52 Grosvenor Gardens, London SW1W OAG, tel. (0171) 730-3402; 541 Bristol Rd., Selly Oak, Birmingham B29 6AU, tel. (021) 414-1848; 39 Queen's Rd., Clifton, Bristol BS8 1QE, tel. (0117) 929-2494; 3 Emmananuel St., Cambridge CB1 1NE, tel. (01223) 324283; 53 Forest Rd., Edinburgh EH1 2QP, tel. (031) 225-6111; 13 High St., Oxford OX1 1DD, tel. (01865) 242067.

STA Travel: Many STA offices are located throughout England, including 74 Old Brompton Rd., London SW7 L3H, tel. (0171) 581-4132; 25 Queen's Rd., Bristol BS8 1QE, tel. (0117) 929-2494; 38 Sidney St., Cambridge CB2 3HX, tel. (01223) 66966; 88 Vicar Lane, Leeds LS1 7JH, tel. (0113) 244-9212; 75 Deansgate, Manchester M3 2BW, tel. (0161) 834-0668; 36-38

George St., Oxford OX1 2OJ, tel. (01865) 792800; and universities at Birmingham, Kent, London, and Loughborough.

Budget Travel Agencies in Other European Nations

Council Travel: Council Travel has 10 offices on the continent. Three of the largest: Paris, tel. (1) 4563-1987; Lyons, tel. (7) 7837-0956; and Dusseldorf, tel. (211) 329-088.

Globetrotter Travel: Swiss and German travelers can try Okista, ESSR, Asta, Ontej, Unitra, Artu, Alternativ Tours, Asien-Reisen, or Globetrotter Travel Service. Globetrotter, the largest student travel agency in Germany, also distributes a useful travel magazine entitled *Travel Info*. Globetrotter addresses in Germany: Rennweg 35, 8001 Zurich, tel. (01) 211-7780; Neuengasse 23, 3001 Bern, tel. (031) 211-121; Falknerstrasse 1, 4001 Basel, tel. (061) 257-766; Rutligasse 2, 6003 Luzern, tel. (041) 221-025; Merkurstrasse 4, 9001 St. Gallen, tel. (071) 228-222; Stadthausstrasse 65, 8401 Winterthur, tel. (052) 221-426.

FROM AUSTRALIA AND NEW ZEALAND

Routes from Australia

Travelers heading to the Philippines from Australia can fly directly to Bali, Singapore, or Bangkok and then continue by air across to Manila.

Airlines in Australia

Flights to the Philippines are available from major airlines such as Qantas, Thai International, British Airways, and Lauda Air; and from smaller airlines such as Olympic and Alitalia.

Return fares on major airlines from Sydney, Melbourne, and Brisbane start at A$950 in the low season, A$1,080 during the shoulder periods (school holidays), and A$1,180 during the high season from December to 15 January. Perth runs about A$100-150 cheaper than Sydney or Melbourne.

Secondary airlines such as Olympic and Alitalia sell tickets for A$100-200 less than the major airlines. Tickets for stays under 30 days are A$50-75 cheaper than tickets for excursions over 90 days.

Airlines in New Zealand

Airlines serving the Philippines include Air New Zealand, Thai International, and British Airways.

Return fares from Auckland range NZ$1,509-1,760 depending on the season. Discount tickets must be booked and purchased at least 21 days in advance.

Budget Travel Agencies in Australia and New Zealand

STA: Offices are located at 222-224 Faraday St., Carlton, Melbourne 3053, tel. (03) 347-4711; 1a Lee St., Railway Square, Sydney 2000, tel. (02) 519-9866; 10 High St., Auckland, tel. (09) 309-9723.

Travel Specialists: In Sydney, call (02) 267-9122.

Sydney Flight Centre: In Sydney, call (02) 221-2666.

FROM ASIA

The Philippines can also be reached by air from nearby Asian destinations. Useful flights include Malaysian Airlines from Kuala Lumpur, Cathay Pacific from Hong Kong, and Garuda Indonesia from Bali and Jakarta to Manila. Flights around Southeast Asia are quick, are reasonably priced, and reduce the ordeals of overland travel.

Hong Kong, Bangkok, Penang, and Singapore are major discounting centers due to the lack of government restrictions and intense competition among travel agencies and airlines. Hong Kong probably has the edge. Among the latter three, there may not be many choices; it's usually preferable to buy your ticket in the city from which you'll fly. You can find some good fares to the U.S. via Manila.

From Bangkok

Bangkok has many discount travel agencies. Several are in the Soi Ngam Duphli area, clustered around the Hotel Malaysia and Boston Inn; it's easy to walk between them and compare prices. Others are located along Sukhumvit Road. Some of these agencies have a bad reputation; don't pay more than a deposit until you see the ticket, don't sign any disclaimers, and be sure to read the details carefully (validity and other restrictions).

"Suspect" agencies are often mentioned in travelers' messages on the notice boards in hotel lobbies. In Banglamphu, now the main area for budget travelers, Trad Travel Service is located in the Viengtai Hotel, 42 Tanee Road. The STA Travel in Bangkok is located at the Thai Hotel, 78 Prachatipatai Rd. (tel. 02-281-5314 or 281-5315), close to the Khao San Road travelers' meeting places. This organization is very helpful in gathering information for onward travel.

From Borneo

If you're coming from Indonesia, Singapore, or the Malay Peninsula, consider routing your journey through Borneo. You can fly from this fascinating island to Manila or Davao out of Brunei or Kota Kinabalu (Sabah); no flights currently operate to Zamboanga or Cebu City. Ask for a discount. Some travel agencies in Brunei (e.g., the one next to the Brunei Hotel) will also give small discounts.

From Hong Kong

Bargains can be found on flights out of here. It costs about US$195-200 one-way to Manila. It's always possible to route your North American or other country of origin flight through Hong Kong en route to the Philippines as many flights stop over here anyway. You can also find some excellent fares, via Manila, to Australia, Europe, and other points in Asia. Watch for oddities.

The monthly magazine *Business Traveller*, available at 200 Lockhart Rd., 13th Fl., Hong Kong, is an excellent source of current information. Many discount travel agencies advertise in the classified sections of the *South China Morning Post* and *Hongkong Standard*.

From Indonesia

Some discounts are available. In Jakarta, check Student Travel Australia, Jl. Wahid Hasyim 110; Kaliman Travel in the President Hotel, Jl. Thamrin; Vayatour next door to it; Pacto Ltd., Jl. Cikini Raya 24; Setia Travel, Jl. Biak 45; Travair Buana, in Hotel Sabang, Jl. Haji Agus Salim; and Continental Tours, near Jl. Jaksa 23. Reductions may be given to International Student Card holders and to those paying cash.

Kuta Beach, Bali, has a number of discount agencies; try Carefree Bali Holidays in the Kuta Beach Club; also, travel bargains are sometimes listed on the bulletin board at Agen Post, Jl. Legian. An intriguing idea is to travel up through Borneo and fly from Kota Kinabalu to Manila. Alternative routes are through east Borneo via Tarakan and Tawau, and through west Borneo via Pontianak, Kuching, and Brunei; the latter offers more variety.

From Japan

Tokyo is a better place to buy air tickets than is generally realized, though the bargains are all roundtrip tickets. In addition to the local market, Tokyo has a large population of foreigners, most of whom are required by Japanese immigration policy to leave the country periodically and re-enter, rather than extend their visas in Tokyo. Thus, there's a ready market for cheap excursion fares. The Philippines is one of the most popular destinations, since it costs little more than flying to nearby Korea but has the advantages of warm weather, fine beaches, and low prices. The cheapest fares are on PIA and EgyptAir, and a roundtrip ticket costs only fractionally more than one-way. Many discount travel agencies advertise in the *Japan Times* and *Tokyo Journal*. Tokyo is a big city, so it's best to phone around and compare prices.

From Malaysia

Penang is an excellent place to buy cheap air tickets. Shop around at International Tourist Promotion, 53 Kampong Malabar; King's/Langli Tours and Travel, 340 Leboh Chulia (opposite Swiss Hotel); MSL Travel (in the Hotel Merlin, 25A Leboh Farquhar); Silver Travel Service; and Tropical Tours and Travel (in the New China Hotel). Good discount fares to the U.S., via Manila, are available. In Kuala Lumpur, begin at Student Travel Australia, MSL Travel, 1st Fl., South-East Asia Hotel, 69 Jl. Haji Hussein; and Silver Travel Service, 15 Jl. Alor.

From Singapore

For discounted tickets, check with Airmaster Travel and Airpower Travel, 36 Selegie Rd., just off Bras Basah Rd.; German Asian Travels, 1303/4 Straits Trading Bldg., 9 Battery Rd.; Holiday Tour and Travels, 12 Mezzanine Fl., Ming Court Hotel, Tanglin Rd.; MAS Travel, Ste. 633, Tanglin Shopping Center; Student Travel Australia, Orchard Parade Hotel, on the corner of Orchard and Tanglin Streets. Other agencies advertise in the classified columns of the *Straits Times*.

Discount Tickets
Flights within Southeast Asia are approximately equivalent to flights within Europe and Australia; that is to say, overpriced.

Don't be alarmed. Discount tickets are sold in most major Southeast Asian cities from student and budget travel agencies, though finding the budget outlet in some cities—Manila, for example—can be frustrating. Your best source of information will probably be guesthouses and other travelers. Be sure to check prices with several agencies and carefully examine ticket restrictions before handing over your money.

GETTING AROUND

The archipelago is served by a dense network of land, sea, and air transport, making it an island-hopper's dream. A transportation progression connects Manila to major cities and then to market towns, from which local buses, jeepneys, tricycles, and small boats fan out to almost every village. Only in the most rugged terrain are villages accessible solely by footpaths, and only the inhabitants of the smallest fishing hamlets must rely on their own boats to reach larger communities. Every substantial settlement has public service by land or water, ranging from frequent to erratic, though "last trips" may leave by early afternoon. Modes of transportation are basically modern, interspersed with native elements, and the cost is cheap by international standards. In fact, when faced with irregular service, it's often not too outrageous to charter a boat or tricycle over short distances, especially for a group of travelers.

Within cities, buses and jeepneys are amazingly cheap and taxis are affordable. The idea of queueing hasn't really caught on here; when using the cheaper forms of transport, expect to be jostled. Buses on major routes on Luzon and elsewhere run day and night. Where there's a choice of long-distance land or sea travel, e.g., Manila to Tacloban (Leyte), the boat trip is more relaxing and the cost and duration comparable. For those with limited time, air travel is also very reasonable. The tightly packed island formation ensures that ships are rarely out of sight of land, and flights in clear weather can be spectacularly scenic.

BY AIR

Air departures around the Philippines are listed under each appropriate chapter. For example, all the air departures from Cebu City are described in the Cebu chapter.

Philippine Airlines (PAL) flies to 43 airports throughout the country, using jets between major cities and propeller aircraft for shorter hops. Main routes have frequent departures. Although no in-flight service is provided, other than newspapers and light snacks, flights are dependable and punctual. Check with a PAL office (found in most major cities) for available discount fares. In calculating total costs, add a nominal airport tax for each departure and fares to the airport. Some airports can be reached by local bus, some have a special airport bus, and some necessitate a taxi ride.

If you arrange a multi-leg journey in Manila or elsewhere, be sure to reconfirm reservations for onward travel as soon as you arrive at each interim point. When checking in luggage, make sure that it's locked, and with backpacks, that nothing remotely valuable is near the top or in side pockets. PAL has a round-the-clock information service, tel. (02) 832-3166.

PAL isn't the only airline in the country. Services to both major and minor destinations are also offered by Air Ads, Air Philippines, Asian Spirit, Cebu Pacific, Grand Air, Pacific Airways, SE Air, and Soriano Aviation.

The international departure tax is P500 in Manila, P400 in Cebu City, and P200 in Davao.

BY SEA

Ships
Shipping schedules are listed in each appropriate chapter.

Boat travel in the Philippines will be a necessity for most travelers who spend any

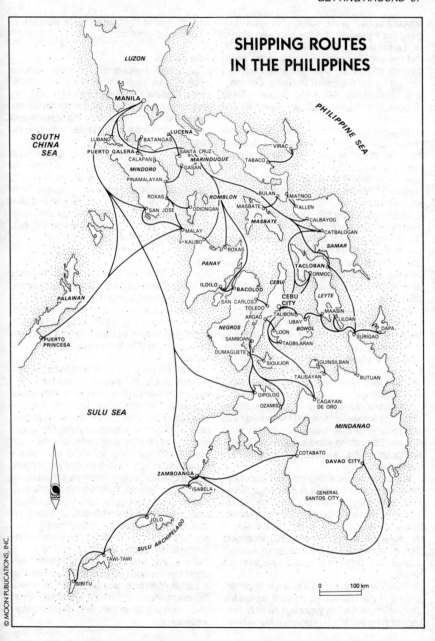

SHIPPING ROUTES IN THE PHILIPPINES

amount of time in the country. Several shipping lines provide service between Manila and most larger cities on a near-daily basis, but the largest company by far is the newly formed WG&A, an amalgamated company formed by the merger of Williams, Gothong, and Aboitiz lines. All of their ships—named Superferry 1, Superferry 2, etc.—are safe and comfortable.

Shipping lines advertise their routes, schedules, and prices in most newspapers. Reservations are difficult to make over the phone, but tickets can be purchased in advance from travel agencies or directly at the pier a few hours before departure. If you're going deck class, arrive early for the best beds.

Sea travel is slow but considerably cheaper than flying. Air-conditioned cabins for two, four, six, or eight persons come equipped with private bathrooms and catered dining. Cabins are about twice as expensive as third-class cots but only half the price of ordinary airfare. First-class air-conditioned dormitories cost 50% more than third class.

By far the cheapest way to travel is on third-class cots spread across the deck or down below the water line. Deck passengers enjoy better air circulation but sometimes get wet during rainstorms. Be advised that third-class "deluxe" ensures a reserved bed, an absolute necessity unless you want to fight for floor space with "ordinary" passengers.

Interisland journeys over 12 hours usually include simple meals of rice and fish in third class and more elaborate meals in first and cabin classes. Bring along some extra food and drink to supplement the basic supplies available from the canteen.

Warning: Be extremely cautious about sea travel during bad weather and holidays. Some Filipino ships are dangerously overloaded, poorly maintained, and lack life vests and lifeboats. Shipping disasters such as the 1987 sinking of the *Dona Paz,* in which over 3,000 passengers died, have cleaned up the industry to a certain degree, but travelers should always exercise caution.

More dangerous than the large ships are smaller crafts and outriggers such as the MV *Jem,* which sank a few years ago en route from Looc to the resort island of Boracay. Never board an outrigger at night, during bad weather, or when it looks overloaded.

Fast Ferries

"Fast ferries" are certainly the most welcome addition to the transportation scene in the Philippines. These are relatively small, high-powered, and very speedy watercraft that quickly zip between most of the islands in the Visayas and cut travel times down by at least 50% from the days of slow ships.

It's amazing the number of connections these ferries can provide, including some very obscure routes such as from Dumaguete on Negros to Siquijor Island. Fast ferries leave several times daily from most towns in the Visayas and Mindanao including Cebu City, Dumaguete, Iloilo, Bacolod, Tagbilaran, Ormoc, Dipolog, Dapitan, Cagayan de Oro, Tubigon, and Surigao.

Bancas

For short distances between adjacent islands or along coastlines, pumpboats or *bancas* are used. They leave from a pier or beach when full and charge a set fare. Figure out the charge beforehand so you pay the same as the locals. In some resorts such as Puerto Galera, however, they insist on different prices for locals and tourists.

With their deep draft and outriggers, *bancas* are very stable, but they do occasionally capsize, so it's wise to carry documents and camera in a waterproof container. Try to sit near the front, away from the motor. Almost all *bancas* have outboard or inboard motors. For longer journeys between minor ports, launches are used. Some maintain a schedule, while others depart when they have sufficient passengers and cargo, often sailing overnight with cramped sleeping conditions. Neighboring islands may also be served by regular ferry service, usually small ships on which passengers sit or sleep on deck chairs for crossings lasting from 30 minutes to overnight. There may be a small surcharge for the upper deck.

If the seas are rough or a typhoon is approaching, use good judgment before embarking in a small open boat onto the South China Sea. Drownings are not uncommon, and small *bancas* rarely have any life jackets, rafts, or other safety precautions.

BY LAND

Railways

Philippine National Railway (PNR) is experiencing a steady decline in railway service. After the eruption of Mt. Pinatubo in July 1991, the railway through the Central Plain on Luzon was shut down and did not reopen. Plans to revitalize the railways throughout the country have been put on hold. It was once possible to travel by train on the island of Panay and north from Manila to San Fernando, but now there is one route open from Manila to the Bicol region near Legaspi.

The train trip to the Bicol is so slow and unreliable that it makes this already long and arduous trip even longer. Typhoon damage often leaves bridges closed and can halt a journey midway, leaving one to find other means of transport. Most travelers don't bother taking the train because of the inconvenience and poor conditions; instead, they opt for buses, which are cheaper and quicker. For more information on train sched-

JEEPNEYS~THE HEART AND SOUL OF FILIPINO TRANSPORTATION

Jeepneys are part of contemporary Philippine culture. At the end of WW II, with public transport virtually nonexistent, the U.S. Army released surplus jeeps, and enterprising Filipinos converted them to passenger vehicles by lengthening the bodies. Filipinos subsequently began making their own jeepneys, and today, these decorated vehicles are scattered throughout the country, about half of them in Metro Manila.

Jeepneys are a form of traveling pop art, some with statues of silver horses on their hoods, myriad mirrors, hand-painted side panels, and humorous or pious sayings. Inside, there's usually a picture of Jesus above the dashboard. You can see jeepneys being built at the Sarao and Francisco factories in Zapote (Cavite).

New vehicles in the provinces are now often the plain, functional Tamaraw, also manufactured domestically. Jeepneys have two passenger seats next to the driver and two rows of inward-facing seats behind. These officially hold 10 passengers, but in practice are crammed beyond full, especially on rural routes. The rear section isn't built for sightseeing, so try to get a front seat.

Jeepneys are used for both urban transport and medium distances on some of the rougher country roads. In provincial towns, they load near the marketplace, leaving when full. Within cities, jeepneys follow established routes along major thoroughfares. Destinations are indicated on the front, with intermediate points and streets marked on the sides. Cities are divided into zones, with set fares according to how many zones are passed through.

In Manila, the basic fare is P2.50 for relatively short distances. Jeepneys stop anywhere to pick up and discharge passengers. Hail a jeepney by flagging one as it passes. Often, they merely slow down, so you must be nimble. Payment is made at any time before you get off and is on the honor system: passengers pay directly or pass money forward to the driver, who simultaneously steers and sorts change. Knock on the roof or say *"para!"* when you want to get off.

CARL PARKES

a calesa in Vigan

CARL PARKES

ules and fares, contact the marketing department of the PNR.

Buses

Air-conditioned and first-class buses with reclining seats, as well as regular buses, operate on the major routes north and south of Manila. Service between major cities on Luzon and beyond to Samar and Leyte is generally frequent and punctual, less so on secondary routes. On some routes, there's only one bus a day; it's wise to board early. Country buses may leave when full, whether early or late.

Other large islands also have frequent departures on main routes, though buses aren't as comfortable as the best on Luzon. Many minibuses operate over medium distances on major highways. To board a bus at an intermediate point on its route, it's best to wait at a town bus station, but when hailing it on an open road, try to stand at a junction. Manila has numerous bus stations, each serving a specific region. Apart from Lawton and the Philippine Rabbit station in Santa Cruz, most are situated in the suburbs so that buses avoid city traffic as much as possible.

Fares, calculated by the kilometer, are very reasonable. Conductors collect fares in three stages. First, they come around and ask where you're going, a little later they return and give you your ticket, and finally they collect the money. Buses are also surrounded by flocks of vendors selling food and drinks at every stop.

Taxis

Taxis are reasonable but rarely seen outside of Manila and Cebu City. Always insist that a driver use the meter, rather than agreeing to a set fare. If he refuses or says it's not working, find another taxi. Unload all your luggage before paying. Taxi drivers often claim to have no change, so obtaining small denominations prior to a trip can save a lot of hassles. Fares are per trip, not per person. It's not necessary to tip, but you might want to if a driver is especially helpful. Small taxis called P.U.'s (public utilities) operate in Cebu and some other cities. They don't have meters, but charge a flat fare around downtown. Longer trips are negotiable.

Tricycles

These motorcycles (or sometimes, bicycles) with sidecars are common in provincial towns and on dirt roads leading out to the *barangays*. Tricycles officially carry two or three passengers. Short rides within town are usually P10 per person. Rides outside town cost a little more, and drivers will want to wait for sufficient passengers or negotiate a "special-trip" price. It's a good idea to ascertain the exact fare beforehand from an independent party, such as a storekeeper or your hotel desk clerk, and obtain change. Then you won't have to ask the driver, who'll rarely quote the local rate. Just get in, state your destination, and upon arrival, hand him the correct fare.

Horse-Drawn Vehicles
Calesas, two-wheeled horse-drawn carriages, are nearly obsolete, but some still operate in Manila's Chinatown, and one or two can be seen on the streets of Intramuros. Some also operate in a few provincial towns like San Fernando (Pampanga) and Vigan. In Cebu, they're called *tartanillas* and in Lubang, *carretelas.* Agree to the fare before riding. *Calesas* ply the route along Roxas Boulevard in Manila, a nice place to trot along at sunset.

INFORMATION AND SERVICES

VISAS

Tourists and businessmen of most Western nationalities are given a 21-day stay upon arrival. Entry requirements vary by nationality. Generally, visitors planning to stay 21-59 days should obtain a visa at a Philippine embassy or consulate prior to arrival, though it's possible to extend the initial 21 days at the Manila Immigration Office. Stateless persons, Indian nationals, Chinese citizens, and nationals of Socialist countries are required to obtain a visa prior to arrival. If in doubt, check with the nearest Philippine embassy or consulate. Visas cost from nothing to US$15, depending on nationality and place of issue. When applying, you'll be asked to show a ticket to and from Manila.

Visa Extensions
The Commission of Immigration and Deportation (CID), Magallanes Dr., Intramuros, Manila (open Mon.-Fri.), is the only place in the Philippines where visitors can extend a visa. This is usually no problem. The first extension should be applied for before your initial 21 or 59 days have expired.

When you extend beyond 59 days, you must pay a series of set fees, and unless you can clear up those fees before departing the country, you will be hit for an additional P500 exit fee to be paid at airport immigration. A stay of more than six months necessitates a Certificate of Temporary Residence and an Emigration Clearance Certificate, obtained before departure. You can't leave the country unless your papers are in order.

INFORMATION

Tourist Information Centers
The Philippine Department of Tourism operates Tourist Information Centers in several countries, plus domestic field offices in numerous cities outside Manila. Within the Philippines, the main information center is on the ground floor, Department of Tourism Bldg., T.M. Kalaw St., Manila, tel. (02) 599-031. It's open Mon.-Sat. 0900-1800. Ask for the free map of Manila and the country.

Reception Units are located at the international airport and the Nayong Pilipino Complex, and Regional Offices in Angeles (Mabalacat, Pampanga), Baguio City, Bauang (La Union), Cagayan de Oro City, Cebu City, Davao City, Iloilo City, Laoag City, Legaspi City, Tacloban City, Tagbilaran, and Zamboanga City.

These regional offices have more complete information on their areas than can be obtained at the Manila office and may provide detailed data sheets.

Ystaphil (Youth and Student Travel Association of the Philippines), 4227 T. Claudio St.,

---

U.S. PASSPORT AGENCIES

Boston, tel. (617) 565-6990
Chicago, tel. (312) 353-7155
Dallas, tel. (214) 653-7691
Honolulu, tel. (808) 522-8283
Los Angeles, tel. (310) 235-7070
Miami, tel. (305) 536-4681
New Orleans, tel. (504) 589-6161
New York, tel. (212) 399-5290
Philadelphia, tel. (215) 597-7480
San Francisco, tel. (415) 744-4010
Seattle, tel. (206) 220-7777
Washington, tel. (202) 647-0518

PHILIPPINE DIPLOMATIC OFFICES

Australia: 1 Moonah Place Yarralumla, Canberra, tel. (06) 273-2535

Canada: 130 Albert St. #606, Ottawa, tel. (613) 233-1121

France: 5 Faubourg Saint Honore, Paris 75009, tel. (01) 4265-0234

Germany: Argelanderstrasse 5300, Bonn, tel. 213-071

Hong Kong: 21F Regent Center, 88 Queen's Rd., tel. (01) 810-0770

Indonesia: 6 Jalan Iman Bonjol, Jakarta, tel. 314-9319

Japan: 11-24 Nampeidai Machi, Shibuya-ku, Tokyo, tel. (03) 3496-6555

Malaysia: 1 Jalan Changkat Kia Peng, Kuala Lumpur, tel. 248-4233

New Zealand: New Hobson St., Wellington, tel. (04) 472-9921

Singapore: 20 Nassim Rd., tel. 737-3977

Thailand: 760 Sukhumvit Rd., Bangkok, tel. 391-0008

United Kingdom: 17 Albemarle St., London WIX 7HA, tel. (0171) 499-5443

U.S.A.: 1617 Massachusetts Ave., Washington, DC 20036, tel. (202) 467-9300; 447 Sutter St., San Francisco, CA 94118, tel. (415) 433-6666

Paranaque, Rizal, Metro Manila, sells an *International Youth Hostel Handbook.* It also issues an International Youth Hostel card to those with proper credentials. (You need two passport-size photos, a photocopy of your passport or ID, and a US$12 registration fee.)

The *Manila Bulletin, Daily Express,* and other newspapers list entertainment, upcoming events, shipping schedules, etc., while "What's happening"-type periodicals such as *Mabuhay Philippines Journal* and the excellent *What's On* in Manila or Visayas and Mindanao are available free or at nominal charge at major hotels. The magazine *Ex-Pat* is also useful. Good unofficial sources of travel information in Manila are the coffee shops of the Santos Pension and Malate Pensionne, which are popular traveler's hangouts; check out the notice boards here.

Books and Bookstores

Manila has numerous bookshops with a wide range of reading matter, including imported English-language fiction and nonfiction. The National Bookstore is the biggest chain, and its branches offer the best all-round selection. Many books on the Philippines, known collectively as Filipiniana, have been published. Also, José Rizal's novels, *Noli Me Tangere* and *El Filibusterismo,* are available in English and make good travel reading. The best selections of Filipiniana are at Casalinda Bookshop (San Antonio Plaza, Forbes Park, Makati) and La Solidaridad Bookstore (on Padre Faura, Ermita).

The Institute of Philippine Culture at Ateneo de Manila University is noted for sociological research and publications; Ateneo de Manila Press has an outlet on the campus in Quezon City. Other Ermita bookstores include Bookmark (Mabini corner Padre Faura) and Alemar's (branches on U.N. Avenue and Taft). Makati's shopping malls have several bookstores: PECO (Philippine Education Co.), Erehwhon, Bookmark, Alemar's. National Bookstore and Alemar's have branches in Harrison Plaza, Malate. In Santa Cruz, National Bookstore, Goodwill Bookstore, and Alemar's are close together on Rizal Avenue.

The major hotels all have bookshops, but prices are substantially higher than regular bookstores. Cebu City, Baguio, Bacolod and other provincial cities also have National Bookstores, and smaller bookstores abound near major universities. There is more selection in Manila, so it's best to buy books before leaving for the provinces. In addition to the National Library (T.M. Kalaw St., Ermita), the British Council, Alliance Française, Goethe Institut, and USIS maintain libraries that are open to the public.

Maps

The patchwork arrangement of the Philippines makes a good map absolutely essential. National maps provided by the Department of Tourism (DOT) are sketchy, although they do have a useful map of Manila and Makati.

Best national map is the 1:1,000,000-scale *Roadmap of the Philippines* published by the National Bookstore and sold in most bookstores in Manila. The Nelles Verlag *Philippines* map is also worthwhile.

Detailed topographic maps of individual provinces can be purchased at the Morbai offices in Manila, Cebu City, Cagayan de Oro, and many other larger towns. Neither the *Petron Map of the Philippines* nor the *Mobil Philippine Travel Map* is worth purchasing.

Newspapers

The Philippine press was long regarded as the liveliest in Southeast Asia, but censorship during the 14 years of martial law dictated a timid approach. Once Cory Aquino came to power, the number of publications rapidly expanded. Today, under Estrada, there are 26 daily newspapers (broadsheets) published mainly in English (with some Chinese dailies included) and six tabloids (mainly in Pilipino) in the National Capital Region (i.e., Metro Manila and suburbs). Prominent publications include the *Manila Bulletin, Philippine Daily Inquirer, Philippine Sun, Business World, Manila Chronicle,* etc. Provincial publications number more than 240. The Sunday papers are bulkier, with a magazine supplement. Up-to-date shipping, air, and bus schedules are often found in the daily newspapers.

International Publications

Domestic newspapers don't provide extensive overseas news coverage but can be supplemented by foreign publications. *Time* and

---

PHILIPPINE TOURIST OFFICES

OVERSEAS OFFICES

Australia: Highmount House, 122 Castlereagh St., Sydney 2000, tel. (02) 9267-2695

France: 3 Faubourg Saint Honrore, Paris 75009, tel. (01) 4265-0134

Germany: Kaissestrasse 15, 60311 Frankfurt am Main, tel. (069) 208-9395

Hong Kong: United Centre, 95 Queensway Rd., Central, tel. (05) 2866-6471

Japan: 11-24 Nampeidai Machi, Shibuya-ku, Tokyo, tel. (03) 3464-3630

Singapore: 20 Nassim Rd., Singapore, tel. (02) 235-2184

United Kingdom: 17 Albemarle St., London WIX 7HA, tel. (0171) 499-5443

U.S.A.: 3660 Wilshire Blvd. #285, Los Angeles, CA 90010, tel. (213) 487-4527; 447 Sutter St., #507, San Francisco, CA 94108, tel. (415) 956-4060; 556 5th Ave., New York, NY 10036, tel. (212) 575-7915

DOMESTIC OFFICES

Bacolod: City Plaza, Bacolod, Negros, tel. (034) 29021

Baguio: Tourism Building, Governor Pack Rd., Baguio, Luzon, tel. (074) 442-7014

Cagayan de Oro: Pelaez Sports Complex, Velez St., Cagayan de Oro, Mindanao, tel. (08822) 723-696

Cebu City: GMC Plaza Building, Plaza Independencia, Cebu City, Cebu, tel. (032) 91503

Cotabato: Elizabeth Tan Building, Cotabato, Mindanao, tel. (064) 211-110

Davao: Magsaysay Park Complex, Davao, Mindanao, tel. (082) 221-6798

Iloilo: Tourism Complex, Bonifacio Drive, Iloilo, Panay, tel. (033) 270-245

Legaspi: Penaranda Park, Albay District, Legaspi, Luzon, tel. (05221) 44492

Manila: Department of Tourism Headquarters, Rizal Park, Manila, Luzon, tel. (02) 523-8411

San Fernando (La Union): Matanag Justice Hall, General Luna St., San Fernando, Luzon, tel. (072) 412098

San Fernando (Pampanga): Paskuhan Village, San Fernando, Luzon, tel. (045) 961-2665

Tacloban: Children's Park, Senator Enage St., Tacloban, Leyte, tel. (053) 321-2048

Tuguegarao: Tuguegarao Supermarket, Tuguegarao, Luzon, tel. (078) 844-1621

Zamboanga: Lantaka Hotel, Valderroza St., Zamboanga, Mindanao, tel. (062) 991-0218

Newsweek are readily available at hotel newsstands and bookstores in major cities, and the *International Herald Tribune* is delivered to Manila's major hotels. In addition, regional publications such as *Asiaweek* and the *Far Eastern Economic Review* provide authoritative economic and political commentary.

Broadcasting

The Philippines has five TV stations, one government-owned, the others independent. TV and radio stations offer programming in English and Pilipino, with frequent commercial interruptions. Most wealthy neighborhoods now have cable television and those that can afford it elsewhere have installed satellites. Radio stations play a lot of Western rock and pop music and the hit songs of the U.S.A. are soon hits in the Philippines and are played constantly. Shortwave radios pick up "Voice of America," the "BBC World Service," and "Radio Australia." If you never watch television in the Philippines, you are not missing a thing.

MONEY

The U.S. dollar is by far the most recognized foreign currency in the Philippines. In calculating how much money you'll need for your trip, the main factors to consider are your traveling style and the amount of time you're on the move. The Philippines is cheap by Western standards, especially after the 40% devaluation that occurred in 1997-98. You can live comfortably in a small town for less than US$10 a day; the longer you stay in such places, the lower your daily average.

In Manila, most budget travelers spend at least US$15-20 a day, depending on where they stay and how much they want to indulge in the city's famous nightlife. For those staying in the city's five-star hotels, allow about US$75-80 a day for expenses. For a typical visit consisting of a few days in Manila, plus a northern loop to see the rice terraces and a southern loop to some beaches, a budget traveler can figure on spending US$20 a day average, including transportation. It's wise to bring more money than you need or a credit card in case of emergency.

Philippine Currency

The unit of currency is the peso (P), which is divided into 100 centavos (c). Banknotes are in denominations of P2, 5, 10, 20, 50, 100, and 500; coins are 1c, 5, 10, 25, and 50, and P1, 2, and 5. Check the official rate of exchange to the U.S. dollar at the time of your trip. Most recently it rated P42 to US$1. Apart from a few upscale hotels, prices in this book are given in pesos. Learning to think in pesos and becoming familiar with handling the coins and notes will save you money.

Exchanging Money

Exchange facilities are located in the airport's arrival area. Those proceeding from Hong Kong or Singapore can get good rates by buying pesos on the money markets there. In Manila, cash and traveler's checks may be changed at commercial banks, authorized foreign exchange dealers, hotels, restaurants, some major department stores and souvenir shops. If you find that traveler's checks are hard to cash, try more than one bank or dealer. Transactions are much faster at exchange dealers, who display a green-and-white authorization sign; many are located along Mabini St. between Padre Faura and Pedro Gil in Manila. Tourist enterprises usually give a lower rate.

While major foreign currencies other than US$ are accepted in Manila, provincial banks are usually reluctant to change them without taking the time to telex their head office in Manila. Since exchange facilities are less common in the provinces than in Manila, it's convenient to carry enough local cash to get by unless you are planning to visit Cebu City, Baguio, or other capital cities. Major department stores, like Shoemart at Harrison Plaza in Manila, have foreign exchange counters and offer good rates, without long lines or hassles.

Traveler's Checks

Carry the bulk of your money in US$ traveler's checks for security, but some low-denomination US$ cash often proves convenient. American Express, Citibank, Bank of America, and Thomas Cook are the most widely accepted in the Philippines. Check that the brand you buy has an instant replacement policy. Make a copy of the receipt and serial numbers in case your traveler's checks are lost or stolen. When cashing them you must show your passport and receipt.

Outside Manila, they can usually be converted only at branches of the Philippine National Bank (PNB) in provincial capitals and other large towns. Reports in the past tell of provincial banks refusing to cash them due to counterfeits (especially American Express) in circulation. Check the situation with the PNB before leaving Manila. It's a good idea to cross-check numbers off your list as you cash them, so that you know which ones are missing in case of loss.

Cash Dollars

It's always a good habit to carry some small-denomination US$ bills, which can be exchanged anywhere, in case you unexpectedly deplete your pesos when banks are closed or distant. They may also be useful for last-minute uses, e.g., paying airport departure tax.

Credit Cards

International credit cards—American Express, BankAmericard, Diner's Club, Carte Blanche, Eurocard, MasterCard, and Visa—are accepted by upscale tourist establishments and are useful for major purchases like airline tickets. An American Express card allows holders to obtain instant cash and traveler's checks. When using a card, be sure to verify the amount charged, and retain the customer copy till you get home to check that the total wasn't altered in any way, e.g., by adding a zero. Keep a separate list of credit card numbers and the phone numbers to call to cancel the cards if you lose them.

A Local Bank Account

If you're staying a few months or more in the Philippines, consider opening a bank account in Manila. It saves you carrying a lot of traveler's checks around and you'll earn interest, though the latter should be weighed against possible loss through devaluation of the peso.

Receiving Funds from Overseas

If you're traveling through Asia and need money transferred from your home bank, it's better to receive it in a major banking center like Singapore or Hong Kong than in Manila. Before leaving home, ask your bank for its telex number and the name of the bank (or banks) with which it has correspondence (an established working relationship) in Manila (or other countries where you'd like to receive funds). Using the head office of that particular bank will greatly facilitate the operation.

Instruct your bank (by phone, cable, telex, or registered letter, depending on the urgency) to wire or telex funds to you at the Manila bank, together with a test cable, which confirms the authenticity of the transfer. Avoid sending or receiving money, especially cash, by mail. It helps to know your home account number. Alternatively, leave savings with family or friends and contact them to send you money through the banks. Receipt of funds should only take a few days, but anticipate your needs; don't wait till you're down to your last US$20. Philippine banks won't normally make the payment in cash dollars—only US$ traveler's checks or pesos.

Reconversion

When you change or receive money at a bank or official exchange facility, retain the Central Bank receipt, which is necessary for reconverting pesos to foreign currency when leaving the Philippines. This may be done at the airport, but the airport banks aren't open for early morning or late-night flights; in these cases reconvert at a downtown bank prior to departure, saving sufficient pesos to last you till departure. While up to P500 may be taken out of the Philippines, it's worthless elsewhere, so unless you're making an imminent return, it's best to exchange or spend your remaining pesos in Manila.

Cash Advances

Running out of money in the Philippines is another tricky problem. There are no ATM machines that gladly spit out money to cash-strapped tourists. Fortunately, cash advances with your Visa or Mastercard can be quickly obtained at any branch of the Equitable Bank. Equitable has branches in almost every town in the country. Cash advances can also be picked up in a limited number of travelers' hotels such as the Swagman chain. Another strategy is to visit any of the casinos in the country and use your Visa or Mastercard for a quick advance.

MEASUREMENTS AND COMMUNICATIONS

Electric Current

In Manila, and elsewhere generally, it's 220 volts AC, 60 cycles, but in some areas, e.g., Baguio, it's 110 volts, 60 cycles like the U.S.; major hotels have both 220 and 110 volt outlets. American-type electrical plugs are suitable for local outlets. Adaptors can also be bought at electrical shops. Electric power failures, called "brown-outs," are not uncommon, and are a big problem these days in Manila and much of northern Luzon.

Measurement

The metric system is used, though traditional measures also survive, e.g., *ganta* (three liters), *cavan* (50 kilograms or 75 liters), *arroba* (11.5 kilograms), and *pulgada* (2.31 centimeters). For help in converting English measure to metric, see the Metric System chart at the back of the book.

Time

In this book all clock times are rendered according to the 24-hour airline timetable system (also known as military time), i.e., 1:00 a.m. is 0100, 1:00 p.m. is 1300, and 11:30 is 2330. For time zones, see the chart **International Clock for the Philippines.**

Business Hours

Government and business offices are generally open Mon.-Fri. 0800-1700, but working hours may be staggered to start between 0730 and 0900 and end between 1630 and 1800. Lunch breaks are spaced between 1130 and 1330. Note that the first floor of buildings is at ground level. Banks are open Mon.-Fri. 0900-1600; airline offices, usually Mon.-Fri. 0830-1230 and 1400-1700, Saturday 0830-1230. Store hours vary slightly within the 0900-2000 range; many are open every day. Hotel restaurants and better establishments typically serve lunch until 1400, and dinner from 1730 till around 2100. Ordinary restaurants remain open from early morning till late at night, and Manila has numerous 24-hour restaurants.

Whatever your business needs are, try to get an early start. Long lines, coffee breaks, lunch breaks, and especially the daily brown-outs can slow things down considerably in Manila and throughout the country.

Mail

Generally, the Philippine mail service isn't bad, but mail is sometimes lost or delayed, so it shouldn't be relied upon. A letter can spend several days in transit between the airport and downtown Manila, or it may arrive a few days after being mailed from Europe or North America. Use the Philippine meter system rather than

INTERNATIONAL CLOCK FOR THE PHILIPPINES

GMT is Greenwich mean time, the time at London, England. The Philippines is at GMT +8 hours, the same as Hong Kong and Taipei. Thus, when it's noon in London, it's 2000 in Manila.

Add or subtract the number of hours indicated below to Philippine time to get the time of day in listed cities.

WORLD TIME ZONES IN RELATION TO PHILIPPINE TIME

Auckland	+4	Delhi	-2.5	Melbourne	+2	San Francisco	-16
Anchorage	-18	Frankfurt	-7	Miami	-13	Singapore	-0.5
Bahrain	-5	Honolulu	-18	Montreal	-13	Sydney	+2
Bangkok	-1	Houston	-14	New Orleans	-14	Toronto	-13
Boston	-13	London	-8	New York	-13	Vancouver	-16
Bombay	-2.5	Los Angeles	-16	Paris	-7	Washington D.C.	-13
Chicago	-14	Jakarta	-1	Phoenix	-15	Zurich	-7
		Kuala Lumpur	-0.5	Rome	-7		

PHILIPPINES AREA CODES

Manila	(2)	Davao	(82)
Angeles	(455)	Iloilo	(33)
Bacolod	(34)	Tarlac	(452)
Baguio	(74)	Zamboanga	(62)
Cebu City	(32)		

Telephone

The Philippines telephone network is operated by the Philippine Long Distance Telephone Company (PLDT) and community telephone systems in the provinces. Overseas and domestic long-distance calls may be placed at a PLDT facility, Philippine Global Communications office, the airport, and major hotels (which add on a substantial service charge).

Connection of international calls is usually quick in Manila but can be slow in some provincial cities. Rates are reduced on Sunday. Public phones are red and require 75c (three 25c coins) for a local call, though in major hotels they may cost up to P2. Dial directory assistance (114) if you have difficulty.

The yellow pages of telephone directories are useful sources of information. Dial 0 then the area code when placing domestic long distance calls, 109 for operator-assisted domestic long distance, and 108 for the international operator. Every provincial city has a PLDT office for making overseas or domestic calls.

stamps as the stamps are sometimes stolen off letters before they leave the country. Tell your family and friends to allow plenty of time for letters to reach you, especially at Christmastime when mail is delayed for weeks.

Don't send or receive documents, financial matter, or other important items unless absolutely necessary. Packages are occasionally stolen. If you must send an important letter or package, it helps to register it; the surcharge is minimal. Parcels must be wrapped in brown paper and string. To receive mail in Manila, the American Express office (c/o Client Mail Service, American Express, Philamlife Bldg., United Nations Ave., Manila, Philippines) is efficient and recommended. The service is free for holders of American Express traveler's checks and credit cards.

Mail can also be collected c/o Poste Restante at the main post office of Manila and all major towns. Unless you plan a lengthy stay in the provinces, it's safer to receive all mail in Manila; you can also make a last-minute check before leaving the country. American Express and the post office keep mail about three months, then return it to sender. You must present your passport to collect mail.

Ask senders to print or underline your surname. If a package or registered letter arrives for you, you're given a notice card designating a postal station where you can claim it, and if necessary, undergo customs inspection. This is usually no problem.

Manila's central post office is on the south bank of the Pasig River. Its philatelic section will be of interest to stamp collectors. Convenient branches are located in various parts of Metro Manila. Hours are Mon.-Fri. 0800-1700 and Saturday 0800-1200.

IMPORTANT TELEPHONE NUMBERS

Operator and Directory Information	114
Direct Dialing Assistance	112
Overseas Long Distance	108
Domestic Long Distance	109
Police	166
Fire (Manila)	(02) 581-1176
(Makati)	816-2553
Emergency	911
Crisis Line	(02) 872-5284

To call the U.S.A. (except Hawaii and Alaska) collect or charge to your AT&T card, dial 105-11. USA Direct phone booths are also available at PLDT offices and other selected areas.

To call:	Dial:
Canada Direct	108-12
Netherlands Direct	105-31
New Zealand Direct	105-64
Japan Direct	105-81

HEALTH AND SAFETY

The Philippines is a healthy place and it's unlikely you will lose even a single day to sickness. The secret to healthy travel is adequate preparation, watching your health during your travels, and understanding how to find adequate medical attention in an emergency.

The following information summarizes the possible risks to help you prepare for your trip.

BEFORE YOU GO

U.S. Government Health Advice

Current health recommendations from the United States government can be checked by calling the **Centers for Disease Control** (CDC) in Atlanta, Georgia, at (404) 332-4559 for general information and a printout of fax services, and (404) 639-1610 for malaria tips. The annual CDC publication *Health Information for International Travel* is available from the U.S. Government Printing Office at (202) 783-3238.

A handy new service is the **CDC Fax Information Service,** which sends country-specific information to your fax machine in a few minutes. Call (404) 332-4565 and follow the voice prompts for instant advice on disease risk and prevention by region, diarrhea, disease outbreak bulletins, prescription drugs recommended for malaria, the biweekly *Blue Sheets,* and updates on AIDS.

Armed with this information, you'll feel reassured about the situation in Thailand and less willing to purchase unnecessary pills and shots from doctors burdened with yacht payments.

Medical Kit

A small medical kit may be useful for simple problems. Most of the following supplies are available from pharmacies in Thailand but may be difficult to locate in remote villages. Which supplies to carry will depend on the length of your vacation, how remote the regions on your itinerary, and the time of year. Travelers generally need only the following:

- bandages, Band-Aid adhesive bandages, scissors, tweezers
- insect repellent, sunscreen, Chap Stick, foot powder
- Pepto-Bismol tablets
- antiseptic for cuts and grazes
- antihistamine for allergies and colds
- antibiotics as prescribed by your doctor
- malaria pills (if necessary)

Vaccinations

Contact a doctor who specializes in travel medicine for a general health checkup, necessary shots, and perhaps the International Certificate of Vaccination, a small yellow booklet that records your immunizations. Occasionally immigration officials demand this card from visitors arriving from an area infected with yellow fever. The CDC does not recommend a yellow fever vaccination, unless you intend to travel to or from a country in Africa or South America.

Cholera and smallpox vaccination requirements for the Philippines have been dropped, though the normal "childhood" vaccinations should be up to date: tetanus, diphtheria, typhoid, measles, mumps, rubella (MMR vaccine), pertussis (DTP vaccine), and polio. Obtain booster shots, if necessary, from your doctor.

A vaccination clinic operated by the Thai Red Cross Society (tel. 02-252-0161) is located in Bangkok at the corner of Rama IV and Henri Dunant Roads.

International Health Certificate

Under the International Health Regulations adopted by the World Health Organization (WHO), a country, under certain conditions, may require from travelers an International Certificate of Vaccination against yellow fever. However, the WHO has recently eliminated the special page for cholera vaccinations, and visitors no longer need an international certificate for entry into Thailand.

INSURANCE

Travel insurance is something many travelers overlook until they face hospitalization abroad or emergency evacuation to medical facilities back home. It may seem unnecessary and over-priced, but a freak accident or serious illness suddenly makes insurance seem like a wise idea.

Finding the right policy at the right price can be tricky. First, review your existing personal insurance policy to find out whether it covers medical treatments and emergency evacuations while traveling overseas. Don't rely on homeowner's insurance, which generally only covers thefts to US$500. Credit cards are limited to flight insurance.

Types of Insurance

Several types of insurance can be purchased from insurance agents, travel agents, student travel agencies, and many tour operators.

Health and Accident Insurance: As mentioned above, check your existing policy for medical coverage overseas. Some policies automatically enroll you with specialized medical-assistance programs described below.

Flight Insurance: Flight insurance sold from machines in airports pays a lump sum to designated beneficiaries if you die on your upcoming flight. Flight insurance is expensive and often unnecessary, and carries worse odds than slot machines in Las Vegas. Flight insurance up to specific limits is automatically provided by all airlines, and tickets purchased with a major credit card also often provide this type of coverage. Save your money for the Philippines.

Baggage Insurance: Airline liability is limited to US$20 per kg for checked baggage and US$400 per passenger for unchecked baggage. Additional insurance can be bought directly from the airline at the airport check-in counter, but many expensive items are excluded by the extensive disclaimer policy on the back of your ticket.

Trip Cancellation Insurance: These policies protect you if you are unable to undertake or complete your trip due to personal or medical problems. Read the fine print carefully, especially the sections on family members and denials for preexisting medical conditions.

Default and Bankruptcy Insurance: This insurance covers you in the event that your tour company or other travel supplier fails to deliver the promised services. To avoid problems, pur-

chase tours packaged from a member of the United States Tour Operators Association (USTOA), which provides an insurance policy of US$1 million to reimburse clients in the case of default or bankruptcy. Call the USTOA at (212) 750-7317 for a member list and its brochure on the pros and cons of independent versus organized travel.

Comprehensive Insurance: Several companies sell comprehensive policies with some or all of the coverages described above.

Exclusions, Exclusions, Exclusions

If none of your existing policies covers medical emergencies abroad, ask your agent for additional coverage or request information from another company. Be sure to carefully read the fine print for exclusions and disclaimers (described below) designed to protect the financial interests of the insurer, not the policyholder.

Destination Coverage: Some policies exclude remote destinations or regions considered high-risk by the U.S. government. The Philippines isn't a problem, but Myanmar, Laos, Cambodia, and Vietnam are excluded by some insurance companies.

Emergency Evacuation: The emergency evacuation described on the policy should include all expenses to a medical facility back home, not just to the nearest adequate hospital.

Family Coverage: Check on coverage for family members and travel partners. Most policies have additional fees for family members, children, relatives, and travel partners not related to the insured.

Preexisting Conditions: This is the most common complaint about medical travel insurance policies. Read the fine print carefully; some policies exclude any condition that has been treated by a doctor during the previous six months.

Time Limitations: Many policies have time limits for medical evaluation and treatment. Travelers sometimes wait several weeks to see a doctor for a condition that appeared harmless at the outset, only to discover later their insurance policy had expired one week after their return.

Medical Ceilings and Deductibles: All policies carry maximum amounts for specific conditions and deductibles. As with automobile or life insurance, unrealistic limitations often make medical insurance hardly worth the cost of the premium.

Payments: Check to see whether you are required to pay for medical conditions on the spot and seek reimbursement, or whether the policy makes direct payments to doctors and hospitals.

Activity Exclusions: Adventurous types should note that some policies exclude any activity considered dangerous by the insurance company, such as hang gliding, mountaineering, scuba diving, motorcycling, rafting, sailing, or even trekking. Avoid these policies unless you intend to spend your vacation inside a hotel room.

Travel Insurance Companies
Comprehensive and specialized policies are sold by insurance agents, travel agents, student travel agencies, and tour operators. Once again, read the fine print carefully. The following companies offer medial assistance policies:
International SOS, tel. (800) 523-8930
Medex, tel. (800) 874-9125
Near Services, tel. (800) 654-6700
Travel Assistance, tel. (800) 821-2828

Try the following for comprehensive insurance policies:
Access America, tel. (800) 284-8300
American Express, tel. (800) 234-0375
ARM/Carefree, tel. (800) 323-3149
Mutual of Omaha, tel. (800) 228-9792
Near, tel. (800) 654-6700
Travel Guard, tel. (800) 826-1300
Travel Insured, tel. (800) 243-3174
Wallach, tel. (800) 237-6615

COMMON HEALTH PROBLEMS

Diarrhea
The U.S. Centers for Disease Control reports that the most frequent problem is common traveler's diarrhea, transmitted by bacteria and parasites found in contaminated food or water. Common sense will minimize the risks: eat only thoroughly cooked food, drink bottled water, wear shoes, resist swimming in fresh waters possibly contaminated with schistomiasis flatworms, and avoid contact with insects, particularly mosquitoes.

Two drugs recommended by the National Institutes of Health for mild diarrhea can be purchased over the counter: Pepto-Bismol Diarrhea Control and Imodium A-D. Both contain loperamide, an antidiarrheal not found in regular Pepto-Bismol.

An alternative to loperamide is three days of a single 500mm dosage of the antibiotic ciprofloxacin, approved by the Food and Drug Administration for traveler's diarrhea.

Hepatitis A
The two main varieties of hepatitis, hepatitis A and B, are highly contagious liver diseases marked by debilitating, long-term symptoms such as jaundice and a feeling of malaise.

Hepatitis A ("infectious hepatitis") is spread by contaminated water and food—conditions common in countries with poor standards of hygiene and sanitation. The disease is transmitted through fecal-oral contact and is often spread by infected food handlers who don't wash their hands. Hepatitis A is a widespread problem in Myanmar, India, Nepal, and Indochina, but is rarely contracted in the Philippines by travelers who exercise caution with their drink and food. On the other hand, hepatitis A is serious. Statistics show each infected adult in the United States spends US$2600 in lost wages, US$700 in medical costs, and an additional US$2800 for hospitalization. About 20% of those infected experience a relapse, and an estimated three percent of adults over 49 years will die from hepatitis A.

Until a few years ago, hepatitis A was regarded as an incurable condition without any effective form of prevention or treatment. A dose of gamma globulin (immune serum globulin) is still the only known antibody that reduces the likelihood of contracting the disease. Gamma globulin's effect wears off after one month, declining to near zero after three months, while also possibly reducing the natural immune systems of the body. Antibiotics administered after infection were useless, and other drugs only increased liver damage. The only treatment remained rest and liquids; travelers were told to "go home and rest."

Fortunately, in early 1995, the U.S. Food and Drug Administration approved a new vaccine called Havrix, the first vaccine proven effective in the prevention of hepatitis A. Developed by SmithKline Beecham, Havrix requires two injections one month apart with a booster after six months; it should be taken at least three weeks prior to departure. The newly approved drug is somewhat expensive—US$50-60 for each of the two injections—but recommended for its long-term immunity, estimated to be up to 10 or 15 years. Obtain more information from SmithKline Beecham, tel. (800) 437-2829.

Hepatitis B

Hepatitis B, formerly called serum hepatitis, also affects the liver but is passed through sexual conduct and the exchange of body fluids such as blood or semen.

Hepatitis B is a more serious disease and is a particular risk for homosexuals, intravenous drug users, and health workers who handle body fluids. The disease can cause irreparable liver damage or even liver cancer.

Hepatitis B can be prevented by a course of three shots of vaccine (Hepvac B) over a five-month period, with a booster shot every four or five years.

Malaria

After a general checkup, discuss malaria with your doctor.

The nine-page CDC regional profile on Southeast Asia recently stated that the risk of malaria in the Philippines throughout the year is low in all parts of the country. Visitors who stick to the standard routes have little risk of exposure and should perhaps avoid powerful antimalarial drugs.

Travelers who plan to get well off the beaten track—explore remote jungles during the rainy season, camp around equatorial lakes—should take malaria pills, remain well covered, wear dark clothing, use mosquito nets, purchase insect repellents which contain DEET (diethylmetatoluamide), and faithfully follow the recommended regimen of antimalarial pills.

Malaria Pills

Prescription drugs recommended by the CDC to treat malaria include chloroquine, mefloquine, doxcycline, proguanil, and primaquine. These drugs resist various strains of malaria with different side effects. About 50% of malaria cases in the Philippines are due to *plasmodium falciparum*, a parasite that causes flulike malaise and high fever with shakes, and which if not treated can lead to organ disease, anemia, and even death.

As a general rule, visitors who've been in risk areas should consider any fever as a sign of malaria and seek early diagnosis and treatment for an uncomplicated and complete cure. Malaria clinics are located throughout the Philippines; free antimalarials are provided to those found blood-smear positive. Medical care in the country is excellent.

1-MINUTE PREGNANCY TEST
BLOODLESS, PAINLESS
- CIRCUMCISION
- EAR-PIERCING
- REMOVAL OF WART/MOLE
VACCINATIONS:
HEPATITIS B, MEASLES, MUMPS

the doctor is in

The CDC currently recommends the use of **doxycycline** for travelers intending to spend significant time in dangerous areas. Doxycycline is a more effective drug than mefloquine (described below), due to mefloquine-resistant malarial mosquitoes found in the border districts.

Common trade names for doxycycline include Vibramycine, Banndoclin, Doxin, Dumoxin, Interdoxin, and Siclidon. The chief disadvantage to doxycycline is that it must be taken every day at an adult dose of 100 milligrams, beginning the day before entering the malarious area and four weeks after departure. One possible side effect is skin photosensitivity, which may result in a sunburn.

Travelers should also ask their doctors about the suitability of **mefloquine,** marketed in the U.S. under the trade name Lariam. The adult dosage is 250 milligrams once a week. Mefloquine has been proven effective against the chloroquine- and Fansidar-resistant strain *P. falciparum,* but is no longer recommended as a malaria prophylaxis due to mefloquine-resistant parasites found in the border areas. Mefloquine in low doses also carries side effects such as gastrointestinal disturbances and dizziness.

Chloroquine is a possible choice for travelers who cannot take mefloquine or doxycycline. The adult dosage is 500 milligrams once a week, starting one week before entering a malarious area, then weekly for four weeks after leaving the area. Chloroquine is marketed in the U.S. under the brand name Aralen and elsewhere as Resochin, Avoclor, Nivaguine, and Kalguin.

Because many mosquitoes in the area have developed an immunity, chloroquine is no longer recommended for visitors to Southeast Asia. It is still effective in the Caribbean, South America, and parts of the Middle East.

The CDC recommends that travelers taking chloroquine should simultaneously take **proguanil.** It's not available in the United States but can be purchased overseas under the brand name Paludrine. The dosage is 200 milligrams daily in combination with a weekly dose of chloroquine.

Fansidar, the trade name for sulfadoxine and pyrimethamine, is a powerful and potentially dangerous drug taken only as temporary self treatment. Fansidar is also sold as Maloprim, the trade name on dapsone and pyrimethamin.

The CDC advises that Fansidar should be taken to treat a fever only if professional medical assistance is not available within 24 hours.

Medical Treatment

Should you require medical care, costs are relatively low. You may be asked to pay in advance. If you have a serious ailment or injury, get to Manila or the nearest city. The bigger the place, the better the facilities and staff. Makati Medical Center in Makati, Manila, is one of the best in the country. A variety of vaccinations are available at the Bureau of Quarantine, off Bonifacio Dr., behind the Manila Hotel (open Mon.-Fri. 0800-1200, 1300-1700). Ermita has several hospitals, including the Manila Doctors Hospital on U.N. Avenue and the Manila Medical Center on General Luna Street. For major problems, go to the Makati Medical Center or Philippine Heart Center for Asia (East Ave., Quezon City).

Most hospitals have 24-hour emergency centers and pharmacies. Deluxe hotels maintain medical and dental services for their guests. The standard of dentistry and optometry is good, and orthodontic work, plastic surgery, eyeglasses, and contact lenses can be obtained at reasonable rates. The Philippine Dental Association (PDA Bldg., Kamagong St., Makati, Metro Manila, tel. 02-832-5413) can recommend a dentist.

Mercury Drug is the largest chain of pharmacies in the country, and they are located in every large town or city throughout the country. Many U.S. drug companies are represented, and most common medicines are available, but bring hard-to-get prescriptions with you.

SAFETY

Awareness of security is a habit that seasoned travelers observe automatically. The great majority of visitors to the Philippines have wonderful experiences and can't wait to return. Taking a few simple precautions will greatly lessen the chance of victimization.

Documents

Treat vital papers like cash. Always carry your passport and other documents, wrapped in plastic, within a money belt or pouch, worn under the clothes. Keep a list of all documents, air tickets, and traveler's check numbers, plus place and date of issue, on a sheet of paper carried in another part of your baggage or by your companion. If possible, leave an envelope containing the same details at a reliable place in Manila. Photocopies of the key pages of your passport (with a photocopy of your birth certificate) and air ticket will facilitate their replacement if lost.

Precautions

Unless you're leading a five-star existence, avoid wearing a fine watch and expensive jewelry. A small pocket calculator with a digital clock is more discreet than a watch. Keep cameras out of sight when not in use. Never leave Walkmans, radios, cassettes, etc., exposed in an unlocked room, even just for a minute.

On crowded streets hold shoulder bags and cameras close to your body. Watch the top of an open bag and feel underneath for razor slits. Snatchers may aim for bags, cameras, watches, jewelry, or items placed on a bar or restaurant table. Never put your bag at your feet as you might do at home, but keep it in your lap. Be especially alert on buses and jeepneys and in crowded market areas. Lock luggage wherever possible, and, if you're carrying a backpack, don't leave anything valuable in side pockets or near the top.

Never leave bags unattended in public places. If you have to deposit them somewhere, ask at a fixed place such as a store or bus station, rather than leaving them in the care of anyone who can move off. If you must ask other travelers to watch your gear, look for another foreigner or a local family or elderly person. On boats and buses, always keep an eye on your possessions. The Manila-Cebu shipping run has a bad reputation for theft. Never get entangled in the rush to disembark from passenger ships; let the crowd thin out first. While sleeping onboard a ship, keep your bags very close at hand or tied to your bunk.

If you swim at a beach where you're not staying, carry valuables in a waterproof pouch. Leave your clothes where you can see them, near the water's edge, and keep close inshore. If snorkeling or swimming far out or along the coast, it's safer for one companion to remain near the gear, and lone travelers should consider forgoing the opportunity. A good snorkeling mask and diving equipment may be hard to replace if stolen.

The following information could leave the impression that the Philippines is an unpleasant and dangerous place to travel. This isn't so. The litany of things that can go wrong should be balanced by the wonderful people and experiences you will enjoy in the Philippines. The trick is to be alert and use common sense: double check hotel rooms and bus seats before leaving. It's most embarrassing to accuse a hotel staffer of thievery, when your spouse may have hold of the camera instead.

Budget Accommodations

Before checking into cheap rooms and hotels, assess their security. Make sure windows and doors shut properly. Where rooms are secured by a padlock, use your own. Unoccupied beach huts are especially vulnerable at night. Don't leave the room unattended and unlocked, even if you're only going to the bathroom. Don't leave valuables in full view through an open door or apparent to the observant eyes of strangers. Tidy things up before going out; if you leave valuables in the room, hide them in a locked bag. The owner or manager will usually look after guests' valuables, but get an itemized receipt to avoid later dispute. Check whether you have access at any time; the night receptionist may not be entrusted with the key. Make sure drying laundry, especially jeans and good shirts, is inaccessible from outside, particularly at night. When checking out, scan your room carefully for anything accidentally left behind: you may not be able to retrieve it later. When in doubt about a hotel's security, move to a more expensive establishment.

Crime

Generally, the smaller the community in which you're staying, the safer it is. It's wise to check the security situation with authorities before embarking on a trip to remote areas. Don't go trekking off the beaten track in such areas.

Avoid showing anger, shouting, insulting, or talking down to people, even if you're provoked. If trouble breaks out in a bar, back away from it, whether you're involved or not. Protagonists may reach for knives, bottles, or any weapon that comes to hand. Avoid dark alleys at night,

TRAVEL ADVISORIES

The Philippines has been devastated by bad press in recent years. Many reports on communist insurgencies, kidnappings, natural disasters, and AIDS have been exaggerated, leaving the country's tourism industry weakened. As you travel throughout the country, you'll find very little to justify the bad press that plagues the Philippines. It remains one of the friendliest nations worldwide, and much of the published reports on dangers in the country seem unfounded.

Travel advisories in the Philippines have been announced by the U.S. State Department in the provinces of Tarlac, Zambales, and Pampanga because of the devastation wrought by Mt. Pinatubo. Daily Manila-based newspapers can offer up-to-date information on travel conditions around the Central Plain. Travelers can also consult the U.S. State Department's Web site http://travel.state.gov/travel_warnings.html.

As far as NPA (New Peoples Army) activity is concerned, the Estrada administration attempted to deal directly with communists, and in early 1993, many of the active groups throughout the country were laying down their arms. At present, the most dangerous places to travel are around the Sulu Archipelago, Basilan Island, and Zamboanga province in southern Mindanao. The dangers have far less to do with the MNLF (Moro National Liberation Front) fighting the Philippine military, than with kidnap-for-ransom activities that have struck prominent Filipinos and some foreign missionaries.

In December 1992, a Filipino family visiting their farm on the island of Basilan, off Zamboanga, was kidnapped, held for a large ransom, and released. An American missionary was kidnapped in September 1992 in Zamboanga City and was taken to Basilan Island where many MNLF have bases in the far hills. He is still missing at the time of publication. The Sulu islands of Jolo and Tawi-Tawi are volatile places and foreigners are not allowed to leave the main cities. In November 1992, two foreign journalists visiting Jolo were confined to their room for the night under guard to prevent them from asking questions. They were sent off by plane back to Zamboanga the following day.

In the Sulu Archipelago, the main problems are piracy, anarchy, lawlessness, and local hostility towards the Philippine military. Bombings and assasinations of military officials and politicians occur in Zamboanga City as well. In February 1993, a bomb exploded at the Zamboanga Airport; fortunately no one was killed. Some foreigners working in Zamboanga City use bodyguards. Local wisdom dictates that foreign travelers who pass through cities, villages, hot spots, or troubled areas are at no risk, particularly because they are moving quickly through an area, may stay only one or two days, and cannot be cause for suspicion or hostility.

The U.S. Peace Corps left the Philippines for a period of time in the late '80s and early '90s, but they have recently returned to the Philippines to work in rural areas of the country. The clearance for the Peace Corps return is a strong indication that the U.S. government does not see the country as a threat to its people. Mindanao, particularly around Davao, Butuan, Camiguin, Surigao, and South Cotabato is very calm and peaceful, although the 1980s were marked by skirmishes among the NPA, MNLF and Philippine Military. Today, there is a great deal more peace in Mindanao. Although Zamboanga City has its risks, it truly is one of the most exotic parts of the entire country, its ocean views are spectacular and the islands of the Sulu Archipelago are enticing. Cotabato City is still a bit hostile so it is advisable not to visit there. Two young American women on a Rotary scholarship were assigned to study in Cotabato City for one year and they were given bodyguards, a sign of prestige. It is not uncommon to see prominent Chinese with bodyguards, as this ethnic group has been targeted in a recent spate of kidnap-for-ransom

especially if you've been drinking. In the unlikely event that you get mugged, or held up on a jeepney, it's best to hand over your valuables.

Con Artists

Like any big city in the world, Manila has its share of confidence tricksters. They also operate in Angeles, Olongapo, and Baguio, but you may also encounter them anywhere. Some men use their girlfriends to make the initial contact. If a complete stranger approaches you and invites you to his or her house, to a party, for a meal or drink, or offers to show you around town or act as a guide, don't accept.

Someone may come up and sit beside you on a bench in Rizal Park and start a casual con-

incidents. Oftentimes, bodyguards are ex-police or army boys who lounge about drinking rum and lean on their rifle butts as they get drunker. Filipino drunks pose the greatest threat to foreigners, as they can be very unpredictable and violent.

Mount Apo, a popular hiking location in Mindanao, has been the scene of hostility between natives opposed to a geo-thermal plant on the slopes of the mountain. Some attacks have been carried out on government workers. The Dept. of Tourism in Davao will have up-to-date information on the situation there.

Kalinga Province in Northern Luzon remains active with the NPA. The Kalingan tribes have always been hostile to central authority, and resent any government intervention in their livelihood. Labeled NPA, the Kalingans may be better described as a hostile minority group resisting the Philippine government. Many backpackers travel around Kalinga Province without incident.

Samar Island in the Central Visayas is one of the least developed and poorest islands in the Visayan region. Poverty, joblessness, and resentment have given this island notoriety for being a hotbed of NPA activity. Central and eastern Samar have been deemed trouble spots, while northern Samar and the west coast are okay. During the crises in the sugar industry that devastated the economy on Negros Island in 1985, many residents were frustrated by the government's inability to help provide land for grain-planting. Some Negrenses who were left jobless after the sugar industry collapsed joined the NPA in the hills, so at one time Negros was not a safe place. Much has changed in recent years as jobs have returned to the Negros and the sugar industry has recovered. Bacolod is slated as a growing convention center for overseas visitors indicating subdued NPA activity and a return to law and order. Manila is a dangerous city for foreigners because of theft, con artists, desperate poverty and overpopulation.

How and When to Travel Safely

Visitors to the Philippines face risks when traveling into the distant hills of Mindanao, Northern Luzon, Samar, and Leyte. However, there has yet to be an incident where foreign backpackers were targeted by either the NPA, the MNLF, or the military. The best way to travel safely in the Philippines is to adhere to local advice. When it comes to security, Filipinos are very straight-forward with foreigners. *Barangay* captains, mayors, local merchants, and housewives will tell a traveling backpacker the truth about their region. The best advice they can give to hikers, trekkers, and adventurists is to bring along an armed local for protection. Guns are ubiquitous in this country, and are a symbol of power and authority. Marching through mountainous country with an armed bodyguard should be ample warning to NPA soldiers who may want to rough things up.

If you are traveling through a troubled area, don't stay long or be very conspicious. Don't ask lots of questions or hang around known rebels. If you look like a rebel yourself, you may become a subject of suspicion among villagers. If you misbehave and belittle authority figures they may turn on you. Misunderstandings and insolence towards locals raises their suspicions. Be nice even if you are irritated with endless questions, but don't offer much information. It is advisable when visiting a small village to go and meet the *barangay* captain or mayor. It shows your respect for them, and they in turn will watch out for your welfare.

Currently, there is no ideal time to travel safely in the Philippines when it comes to unexpected encounters, but the rainy season with typhoons, mudslides, road blocks etc. is certainly a far more unpleasant and hazardous time to come to the country. National election time does not come up again until 1998. In Marcos' time, "guns, goons, and gold" were the order of the day. Today, things are much more subdued in the country, as Filipinos truly are peaceloving people. Remember the People Power movement of 1986 was a bloodless, nonviolent overthrow of their own government.

versation. Four innocuous inquiries tell them almost all they need to know: "Where are you from?" "Is this your first time in the Philippines?" "How long have you been here?" "Where are you staying?" If a visitor replies he's from Texas, it's his first visit, he arrived yesterday, and he's staying at the Sheraton, it connotes rich and naive, the perfect combination! Another common line is "Hi, remember me? I was working at the airport when you arrived recently." Remember, you don't remember! Beware of men claiming to be immigration, customs, or plainclothes police officers. If they are persistent, insist on talking to them only inside a police station, and don't get into a car with them. Don't go with someone who invites you to be massaged (or whatever) by his sister. Be wary of persons looking for an investor in a promising business opportunity. Strangers who approach you too easily and are too hospitable, too quickly, may well have ulterior motives. In the small provincial towns and villages, genuine hospitality and curiosity are still common, and there's usually no problem in accepting invitations.

Gambling

Never be drawn into card games and gambling, however assured winning may seem. The usual ploy is to first make friends by buying drinks, and then invite the "mark" to watch a game being played by two or three co-conspirators. Someone will be winning too easily and another losing heavily. There will be plenty to drink. Then comes "Why don't you try?" or "Can you lend us some money; we'll return it and give you half the winnings."

You may win at first, but you will always lose in the end. The sleight of hand involved can be brilliant, and the acting is good too, creating the atmosphere of a legitimate game. And don't think you can just get up and leave as soon as your "luck" changes. If you want to gamble, go to a casino. But even there, if someone tells you that the croupier is his cousin and invites you to participate in a highly profitable underhand operation—using your money, of course—don't fall for it.

Prostitution

One of the Philippines' main attractions for men is its women. Tourism is cited as a major, though indirect, causal factor in the rise of prostitution and has made the Philippines one of the flesh capitals of Asia, where even children are sold into prostitution. Many rural girls come to the larger cities and towns near former American military bases to escape poverty, seeing the hospitality industry as a practical way to achieve this. The prostitution center of the Philippines is Angeles City, about two hours north of Manila. Prostitution to a lesser degree can also be found in Olongapo (near Subic Bay), Bauang on the northwestern coast of Luzon, and in most larger urban areas such as Manila (mostly in Pasay City) and Cebu City.

In addition, poverty has bred a male parallel to the hospitality scene, with many *bini* boys available for hire. Oftentimes these young men and women are mistreated by pimps, bar owners, or customers, and earn as little as US$1 a day.

For those who choose to partake, be aware that prostitution is illegal in the Philippines and police raids do sometimes occur. Sexually transmitted diseases, including the AIDS virus, are also common among prostitutes. Some Filipinos still believe that one can only catch AIDS from a foreigner. If you are the first foreigner he or she encounters, a sexual history involving fellow Filipinos might not be mentioned.

WHAT TO TAKE

Bags

The best all-around traveling bag is a medium-size, internal-frame, convertible backpack, with shoulder-straps and carrying handle, plus a detachable daypack. Its zippers should be lockable with miniature padlocks. If you're buying a new pack, look for sales but don't economize. A high-quality pack will last for years. As for size, don't start out with a full pack; allow space for handicrafts and other acquisitions.

Many travelers leave bulky backpacks or suitcases at their hotel or guesthouse in Manila and carry short-term requirements in a smaller bag on trips to the provinces. A tubular nylon bag, easily carried, conveniently stowed on public transportation, and fastened with a small padlock is

ideal. Sort and pack the contents in plastic bags (bring plenty) for convenience and protection from moisture. It's also useful to carry a shoulder bag containing items you want accessible.

Clothing

Dress is generally casual, and clothing should be practical, light, loose, and washable. Consider a cotton-synthetic mix. Whites and pastels feel cool, but grime and perspiration will quickly impregnate clothes, necessitating frequent changes and washing. Fortunately, clothes rinsed at night are usually dry by morning. Also, clothes are cheap both to buy and have made. Generally, jeans are worn in town and shorts at resort areas. A basic set of clothing should include several

Need a haircut?

shirts or T-shirts, jeans or light cotton trousers (the latter are cooler), shorts, swimsuit, sun hat, cotton underwear, socks, and handkerchiefs. Bring at least one long-sleeved shirt to shield your arms from sun or mosquitos, and a sweater will be welcome in Baguio and the mountain provinces, especially in December and January, when nights get cold.

For a short stay in northern Luzon, it's more practical to wear layers of T-shirts under a light sweater than to carry bulky clothing. An umbrella, plastic mac, or poncho (can double as a ground-sheet) will be useful during the rainy season (primarily June-Oct.). Take at least one set of "smart casual" clothing for visits to the immigration office, casinos, and better bars and restaurants.

For semiformal occasions, many men have a *barong tagalog* made. Ties and jackets are rarely worn outside the multinational corporations. Women will find a blouse and longish cotton skirt much more comfortable than jeans and a T-shirt in the cities. A shawl is nice for cool evenings and a scarf provides protection against dust and wind. An oversized T-shirt doubles as a nightgown. If you anticipate semiformal occasions, take (or buy) a light, wrinkle-proof dress.

Footwear

Rubber thongs allow the feet to breathe and are easily washable. Treat them as disposable; wear them out and buy a new pair. Running shoes with good traction are fine for hiking and sight-seeing. Most travelers don't spend enough time on rough terrain to justify carrying boots around.

Japanese-style *tabis* are great for safe wading over sharp coral and slippery rocks. A pair of loafers for men and flat-soled, black canvas Chinese shoes for women satisfy the footwear code imposed by casinos and upscale restaurants. Filipinos believe that only the very poor wear sandals and open-toed shoes to a restaurant; it is considered to be in bad taste.

Miscellaneous

Bring sunglasses, a spare pair of eyeglasses or contact lenses, and any personal medication such as contraceptives, antidiarrheal medicine, a motion-sickness remedy, vitamins, and health-food products. Use unbreakable containers. A small pocket calculator with a clock and alarm is invaluable for currency conversions and early morning departures. A flashlight, extra batteries, candles, and matches are always useful. A good penknife, bottle opener, scissors, and tweezers will prove useful. A lightweight sheet sleeping bag of the regulation youth hostel type provides an extra measure of security when sleeping in public places such as boat decks or dormitories.

Unless you have a penchant for climbing volcanoes or staying on uninhabited islands, you won't need a tent, regular sleeping bag (too hot in the lowlands), or cooking equipment. If, however, you like to prepare your own meals (guest-houses usually allow use of facilities), bring eating utensils and a plastic or metal plate and mug. A water bottle is good for hikes and boat trips, though an empty liquor bottle will do. It's worth bringing in the duty-free allowance of two bottles of liquor (except rum, which is good and cheap locally) and 200 cigarettes; they can be sold if you don't use them.

There's no need to bring food from overseas unless you tend to crave particular items. If you travel in remote lowland areas, a mosquito net and/or coils may save you some restless nights; buy them in marketplaces. Other small handy items include a sewing kit, safety pins, length of twine for a clothesline, butane lighter or matches in a waterproof container, a small plastic brush if you do your own laundry. In budget hotels, a small, strong padlock or combination lock to secure your room will bring peace of mind. Likewise, a 60-centimeter length of lightweight chain will enable you to lock your pack to fixed objects in dormitories, ships, buses, etc.

If you travel in the provinces, you'll probably receive hospitality from local people, so consider bringing souvenirs of your home country to give to your hosts or their children. Colorful postage stamps, postcards, or badges are lightweight and appreciated.

If you are trekking into remote areas of the country, bring salt, matches, canned food, or cigarettes as a kind of gift for the villagers. It is not often they can afford any luxuries, and they can always use a few extras to feed the family.

SUGGESTED PACKING LIST

✔ two pairs of long pants, one casual, one formal
✔ one stylish pair of shorts
✔ two short-sleeved shirts with pockets
✔ five pairs of underwear and socks
✔ modest bathing suit
✔ one pair of comfortable walking shoes
✔ sandals or rubber thongs
✔ small towel
✔ small umbrella
✔ medical kit
✔ sewing kit
✔ insect repellent
✔ two small padlocks
✔ Swiss Army knife
✔ photocopies of essential documents
✔ spare passport photos
✔ plastic Ziploc freezer bags
✔ alarm clock
✔ sunglasses
✔ International Drivers License
✔ Philippines Handbook

Some men go skimming over the years of existence to sink gently into a placid grave, ignorant of life to the last, without ever having been made to see all it may contain of perfidy, of violence, and of terror.
—*Joseph Conrad,* Heart of Darkness

To many people holidays are not voyages of discovery, but a ritual of reassurance.
—*Philip Adams,* Australian Age

Countries, like people, are loved for their failings.
—*Yeats,* Bengal Lancer

Pasig River and General Post Office

MANILA

He who travels far will often see things far removed from what he believed was Truth. When he talks about it in the fields at home, he is often accused of lying, for the obdurate people will not believe what they do not see and distinctly feel.

—*Herman Hesse,* Journey to the East

We are all guilty of crime, the great crime of not living life to the full. But we are all potentially free. We can stop thinking of what we have failed to do and do whatever lies within our power.

—*Henry Miller*

Why do people travel? To escape their creditors. To find a warmer or cooler clime. To sell Coca-Cola to the Chinese. To find out what is over the seas, over the hills and far away, round the corner, over the garden wall.

—*Eric Newby,* A Traveller's Life

Manila, the Philippine capital, is the political, social, cultural, religious, educational, industrial, and commercial center of the country. Its population of 11 million hardly compares to the next largest city, Davao (1 million). Manila's streets pulsate with life at all hours. It's a city of contrasts: the difference between spacious, well-maintained elite communities like Forbes Park and overcrowded slum areas like Tondo is immense. As in any major city, sightseeing and shopping are the main tourist activities during the day. Manila's nightlife offers the full spectrum from bawdy to sophisticated. The restaurants, live music, and cultural events provide evenings of pleasure.

Orientation

Manila proper comprises 14 districts, each with

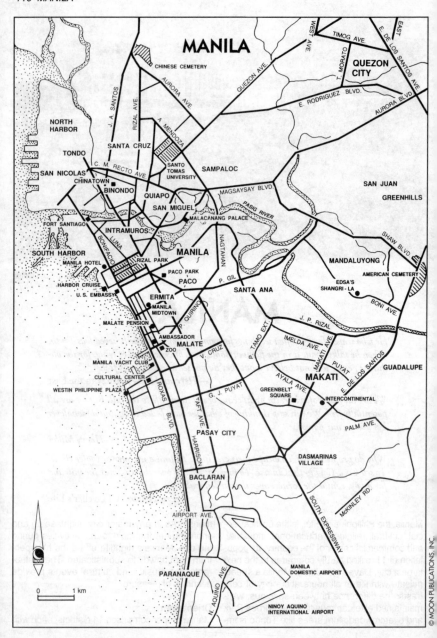

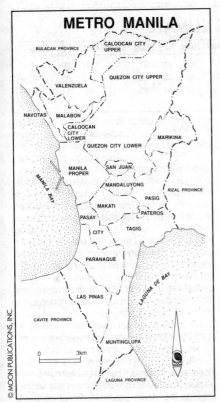

METRO MANILA

BULACAN PROVINCE

CALOOCAN CITY
UPPER

QUEZON CITY UPPER

VALENZUELA

NAVOTAS

MALABON

CALOOCAN
CITY
LOWER

QUEZON CITY LOWER

MARIKINA

MANILA
PROPER

SAN JUAN

MANILA BAY

MANDALUYONG

RIZAL PROVINCE

MAKATI

PASIG

PATEROS

PASAY

CITY

TAGIG

PARANAQUE

LAGUNA DE BAY

LAS PINAS

CAVITE PROVINCE

MUNTINGLUPA

0   3km

LAGUNA PROVINCE

© MOON PUBLICATIONS, INC.

arrive from throughout the archipelago to study or seek work. The large student body imparts a youthful atmosphere, while the substantial Chinese and other foreign communities, busy port, multinational corporations, and constant flow of tourists lend the city a cosmopolitan air.

Manila's streets range from multilane boulevards to maze-like alleys. The main north-south axis is Taft Avenue. William H. Taft was the first American civil governor of the Philippines before becoming U.S. president (1909-13). North of the Pasig, Taft Avenue becomes Rizal Avenue. Together, these avenues, which are paralleled by the Metrorail line, link Caloocan City (Monumento) in the north with Pasay City in the south, which are in turn connected by East de los Santos Avenue (EDSA), a semicircular ring road that traverses the suburbs, including Quezon City and Makati. Quezon Boulevard links the city center with Quezon City, about 12 km northeast, while Roxas Boulevard runs beside the bay.

History

Manila's history closely parallels the nation's. Its native name, Maynilad, is derived from two Tagalog words: *may* (there is) and *nilad* (a kind of waterlily that once grew abundantly along the shores of the bay and can still be seen floating down the Pasig). Manila had been a commercial center for centuries when Miguel Lopez de Legazpi, who was exploring the Visayas, first heard reports of it. In 1571, Legazpi proclaimed Manila capital of the Philippines and began constructing a fortress. In 1574, the year the Chinese warlord Limahong's attack was repulsed, the title of "Distinguished and Ever Loyal City" was conferred on Manila by Spanish royal decree.

The Spanish-style medieval walled city of Intramuros (literally "Between the Walls") was the major Spanish structure in Asia. Soldiers and missionaries fanned out from here to conquer the country. The great Manila galleons arrived and departed, laden with rich cargoes. The ensuing centuries were marked by stable periods interspersed with turbulence. Manila saw uprisings by Chinese immigrants and Filipinos, Dutch blockades, the notorious assassination of Governor-General Bustamente in 1719, and the 20-month British occupation in 1762-64. Strong earthquakes caused substantial damage in 1645, 1754, 1863, and 1880.

its own distinctive character: Binondo, Ermita, Intramuros, Malate, Paco, Pandacan, Port Area, Quiapo, Sampaloc, San Miguel, San Nicolas, Santa Ana, Santa Cruz, and Tondo. In 1975, Manila was integrated with its surrounding cities and municipalities to form Metro Manila, which covers 636 square km and stretches from Manila Bay to Laguna de Bay and the Sierra Madre foothills.

Metro Manila consists of four cities: Manila proper, Caloocan, Pasay, and Quezon City, plus 13 municipalities: Las Pinas, Makati, Malabon, Mandaluyong, Marikina, Muntinlupa, Navotas, Paranaque, Pasig, Pateros, San Juan, Taguig, and Valenzuela. About 11 million people live in this metropolis, and many workers commute from neighboring provinces. The city acts as a magnet for a continual stream of migrants who

MANILA'S CLIMATE

	Jan.	Feb.	March	April	May	June	July	Aug.	Sept.	Oct.	Nov.	Dec.
Avg. Maximum C	29°	31°	33°	34°	33°	33°	31°	31°	31°	31°	30°	29°
Avg. Maximum F	84°	88°	92°	94°	92°	92°	88°	88°	88°	88°	86°	84°
Rainy Days	6	3	4	4	12	17	24	23	22	19	14	11

Manila remained virtually a closed city, an exclusive Spanish domain, until its port was opened to foreign shipping in 1834. The city grew steadily, parish by parish, and by the 19th century, the centers of socioeconomic life had moved outside Intramuros. The contrast between the bustling vitality of the native and Chinese districts and the somnolent community within the walls was a clear indication of the Spanish decline.

Manila was the breeding ground of the revolution, which broke out in 1896 when Andres Bonifacio incited his followers to armed rebellion at Balintawak and led the first attack on the Spanish at San Juan del Monte. Also in 1896, José Rizal was taken from Fort Santiago to be executed in what is now Rizal Park. The rout of the Spanish fleet in Manila Bay by the U.S. Navy in 1898 ended one colonial era and began another. In spite of the Filipino siege of Intramuros, an American takeover from Spain was negotiated.

Manila had a population of about 200,000 at the turn of the century. In marked contrast to the increasingly disinterested Spanish, the period of U.S. government was a time of progress. The Americans installed electricity, gas, and water supplies, sewage and drainage systems. But in 1941, with Japanese troops closing in, they abandoned Manila in an attempt to save it. Three years of repression and hunger ensued.

In 1945, it took the Americans a month to liberate the city completely. Entering from the north, their first objective was the release of Allied prisoners from the University of Santo Tomas internment camp. The Japanese were driven across the Pasig River; after setting fire to Quiapo, Santa Cruz, Binondo, and Tondo, they blew up the bridges behind them. But U.S. troops were also advancing from the south, and the trapped Japanese forces went on an orgy of looting, destruction, rape, torture, and massacre. They resisted desperately, but American bombardment dislodged them and, in the process, reduced the city to rubble. In Intramuros, only San Agustin Church and monastery were left standing. In spite of the city's devastation, the Americans received a rapturous welcome by the Filipinos.

With independence came reconstruction. Postwar development has been hectic and haphazard. The spaciousness of showcase sectors such as the Makati business district contrasts markedly with the congestion of market areas such as Divisoria and Quiapo. The city's postwar population growth has been phenomenal.

ATTRACTIONS

The city sprawls eastward from Manila Bay and is bisected by the Pasig River, which is crossed by seven bridges and plied by barges. On its south banks are Fort Santiago, the immigration office, and the post office. Immediately south of these are Intramuros, Rizal Park (which may be considered the city center), the tourist office, and the Ermita tourist district. North of the river are the densely populated, working-class districts like Quiapo, Binondo, or Chinatown, the slum area of Tondo, and the North Harbor, where interisland ships tie up.

The city's business district was formerly just north of the river, but it has been eclipsed by Makati. Located about six km southeast of the city center, Makati is the corporate and financial district, a major shopping center, and contains the city's wealthiest suburbs, such as Forbes Park and Dasmariñas. At present, Makati has aspirations of becoming a city. The airport is in Manila's southern suburbs.

The outer suburbs, which spread north, south, and east, are mostly residential and industrial areas with new giant shopping malls and high-rises in places like Green Hills and Mandaluyong, where many Manilanos spend their time window shopping. If time is limited when touring Manila, make Intramuros (Fort Santiago, Manila Cathedral, San Agustin Church), Malacanang Palace, and the Chinese cemetery your priorities.

ERMITA AND MALATE

Ermita is the rectangular district bounded by Rizal Park, Taft Avenue, Pedro Gil, and Manila Bay. Blocks are lined with tourist establishments—hotels, restaurants, bars, nightclubs, souvenir and antique shops, airline offices, etc. Ermita is also the center of Manila's famous nightlife. After dark, its parallel main streets, Mabini and M.H. del Pilar, are ablaze with neon, and their sidewalks are bustling with activity.

Malate Church

Malate Church, set back from Roxas Boulevard, was founded by the Augustinians at the end of the 16th century; invading British forces sheltered in it during their attack on Intramuros in 1762. The present structure, with its austere interior, was built following the destruction of its predecessor in 1773 and restored after WW II damage. It's dedicated to Nuestra Señora de Remedios ("Our Lady of Remedies"), the patroness of women in childbirth. Women with newborn babies gather here on her feast day (26 November) to give thanks for a safe delivery. The Virgin's image, brought from Spain in 1624, is at the altar, while a modernistic bronze statue of her and one of Rajah Sulayman stand in the plaza.

Carfel Seashell Museum

The church backs onto Mabini Street, and a half block north is the Carfel Seashell Museum, open Mon.-Sat. 0800-1900, Sunday 0800-1700. Situated above the shell shop, its splendid display includes golden cowries and thousands of other species. From the church, San Andres leads to the San Andres Market—good fruit section.

Manila Zoo

Adriatico goes south from here to the zoo and botanical gardens, open daily 0800-1800. The entrance is across President Quirino Avenue and contains international and indigenous species, such as the *tamaraw* and Philippine crocodile. Many plants are also identified. Follow President Quirino Avenue to Roxas Boulevard and turn south.

Metropolitan Museum

The Manila Yacht Club and Central Bank Complex face each other. The latter contains the Metropolitan Museum—open Tues.-Sat. 0900-1800, Sunday and holidays 0900-1300, free admission—which displays rotating international art exhibitions.

Central Bank Money Museum

This fascinating museum—open Tues.-Sun. 0900-1800, except holidays—features an excellent collection of coins, banknotes, and unusual forms of money from all over the world. Its Philippine collection is the most complete anywhere.

The Cultural Center Complex

This large complex, built on reclaimed land jutting out from Roxas Boulevard into the bay, was the controversial showcase project of former first lady Imelda Marcos.

Cultural Center of the Philippines: Inaugurated in 1969, the CCP complex comprises a fine concert hall seating 2,000 plus an intimate 400-seat theater (both have a/c and excellent acoustics), as well as a library, museum, art gallery, and upscale restaurant. The lobby is opulent, with marble floors, curving staircases, and glass and kapis-shell chandeliers. The art gallery rotates exhibits; the museum has permanent displays of archaeological finds—Stone Age tools, pottery, metalwork, jewelry, Chinese and Indochinese ceramics, and Maranao crafts such as musical instruments, weapons, brassware, and household utensils. The CCP is the home of a symphony orchestra and the Ballet Philippines. A monthly calendar of events is issued, listing the frequent evening performances by national and international artists.

Design Center and Philippine Center for International Trade and Exhibitions: Behind the CCP are two buildings that feature regularly changing exhibits. PHILCITE is also the site of periodic trade fairs.

The **Folk Arts Theater,** open Mon.-Fri. 0930-1700, tel. 832-3660, forms a covered amphitheater that holds 10,000. Built in 70 days

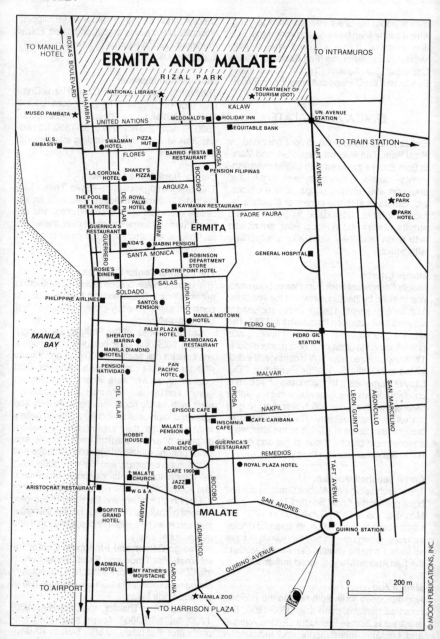

ERMITA AND MALATE

RIZAL PARK

TO MANILA HOTEL

ROXAS BOULEVARD

TO INTRAMUROS

National Library

Department of Tourism (DOT)

Museo Pambata

United Nations

Kalaw

UN Avenue Station

TO TRAIN STATION

U.S. Embassy

Swagman Hotel

Pizza Hut

Flores

McDonald's

Holiday Inn

Equitable Bank

Taft Avenue

Barrio Fiesta Restaurant

La Corona Hotel

Shakey's Pizza

Arquiza

Orosa

Bocobo

Pension Filipinas

The Pool

Iseya Hotel

Royal Palm Hotel

Kaymayan Restaurant

Del Pilar

Mabini

Padre Faura

Paco Park

Park Hotel

Guernica's Restaurant

Aida's

Mabini Pension

ERMITA

Guerrero

Santa Monica

Robinson Department Store

General Hospital

Rosie's Diner

Centre Point Hotel

Salas

Adriatico

Philippine Airlines

Santos Pension

Soldado

Manila Midtown Hotel

Pedro Gil

Pedro Gil Station

MANILA BAY

Sheraton Marina

Palm Plaza Hotel

Zamboanga Restaurant

Manila Diamond Hotel

Pension Natividad

Pan Pacific Hotel

Malvar

Del Pilar

Orosa

Leon Guinto

San Marcelino

Agoncillo

Episode Cafe

Nakpil

Insomnia Cafe

Cafe Caribana

Malate Pension

Guernica's Restaurant

Hobbit House

Cafe Adriatico

Remedios

Royal Plaza Hotel

Malate Church

Cafe 1900

Jazz Box

Taft Avenue

Aristocrat Restaurant

W G & A

San Andres

MALATE

Quirino Station

Sofitel Grand Hotel

Mabini

Adriatico

Bocobo

Carolina

Quirino Avenue

TO AIRPORT

Admiral Hotel

My Father's Moustache

Manila Zoo

0   200 m

TO HARRISON PLAZA

© MOON PUBLICATIONS, INC.

by 2,000 men working around the clock, it was the scene of the 1974 Miss Universe contest and was used as a training camp by Muhammad Ali and Joe Frazier before their fight in 1976. International rock concerts and other events take place regularly.

Philippines International Convention Center: The huge meeting hall was opened in 1976 for the International Monetary Fund-World Bank Group Conference. Its Plenary Hall seats 6,000, with six-channel simultaneous interpreting facilities, and has a history and economy exhibition on the third floor. Note the floors of Romblon marble and paintings by leading contemporary artists.

Manila Film Center: The superb state-of-the-art structure, costing an estimated US$25 million, was built under a very tight deadline for the opening of the 1982 Manila International Film Festival. When about 40 workers were killed here in a construction accident, Imelda Marcos ordered that concrete be poured over the bodies rather than interrupt the schedule to retrieve them. It's said that Imelda subsequently held an exorcism to get rid of the ghosts. The festival was abandoned two years later and the Manila Film Center is now closed, ironically, because of faulty construction.

Coconut Palace: The Coconut Palace is a presidential guesthouse administered by the Department of Tourism. It is a unique showcase of Philippine architecture that uses 100% Philippine materials, 70% of which are coconut-derived. Each of the seven private rooms and function rooms is furnished in choice motifs and indigenous arts and crafts representing a particular region of the Philippines.

Museum of Philippine Art

At the southwest corner of Rizal Park is a minor museum, formerly the Elks Club building, with changing exhibitions of contemporary art. Behind it is the Army-Navy Club. Both buildings were built during the American colonial era. Linked by a walkway during WW II, these buildings used to be a Japanese officers' club and geisha house.

U.S. Embassy

A fine library, the American Historical Collection of Filipiniana, is located in the main building of the Chancery and contains rare books, prints, and artifacts. It's open to the public during business hours.

Paco Park

From Ermita, follow Padre Faura Street across Taft Avenue to the circular Paco Cemetery. Completed in 1820, its first occupants were victims of a cholera epidemic that ravaged the city. The last burials were in 1912, and now it's a national park and a popular lovers' rendezvous. Two concentric walls, whose tops are promenades, surround an oval chapel, fountain, and old acacia trees. The chapel, where a Spanish governor-general is buried, is used for weddings.

A white cross marks the spot where the Spanish, fearful of public unrest, secretly buried José Rizal in a mismarked grave after his execution. His remains, later exhumed, now lie in Rizal Park. The cemetery walls contain burial niches, which were rented on a three-year basis. If the lease was not renewed, or the cemetery became full, the bones were removed and put into a communal *osario* behind the chapel. There are also enclosures with smaller niches where children were buried separately, according to Spanish custom.

For the botanically inclined, many trees and plants here have identification tags. On Fridays at 1800, chamber music, traditional music, and pop are performed at the park.

Just behind the cemetery at 1341 Perez Street is the Paco Hong Giam Taoist Temple. Nearby are the New Swiss Inn, with bar, restaurant, and delicatessen, and the Park Hotel, with lounge, restaurant, and swimming pool.

Walk south on Looban Street, parallel to Perez. A good Indian food stall is opposite the Hindu and Hare Krishna temples. Turn left, then right, and follow Dart to Paco Market. From here, take a jeepney east on Pedro Gil to Santa Ana.

RIZAL PARK

Rizal Park is also known as the Luneta ("Little Moon"), from a half-moon-shaped redoubt that shielded the Puerta Real gate. Earlier, this area was called Bagumbayan ("New Town"), the site of a native settlement that grew outside Intramuros. This well-kept 58-hectare park is popular with locals. It's well lit at night (a favorite lovers' rendezvous), while whole families come on Sundays to enjoy its lawns, flowers, and fountains. Free concerts are held every Sunday afternoon (televised) at the open-air auditorium near the lagoon. Free plays and other presentations are also held here.

Rizal Park is also the site of major national celebrations and parades, including Independence Day on 12 June and Rizal Day on 30 December. In the tumultuous days of early 1986, up to a million people crammed the park, first rallying in support of Corazon Aquino, then in thanksgiving for her victory.

Rizal Monument

Just east of Roxas Boulevard, this monument, with its 24-hour honor guard (changed every six hours), marks the site where national hero José Rizal's remains were interred in 1913. Also in this area are bronze plaques inscribed with his poem, *Mi Ultimo Adios,* a marble slab indicating the spot where he was executed in 1896, the original stone fountain from the village of

RIZAL'S EXECUTION SITE

JOSE RIZAL Y MERCADO, FILIPINO PHYSICIAN, PROPAGANDIST, WRITER, AND PATRIOT WAS EXECUTED WITHIN THESE HALLOWED GROUNDS AT EXACTLY 7:03 IN THE MORNING OF DECEMBER 30, 1896 BY AN EIGHT-MAN SQUAD OF FILIPINO RIFLEMEN FROM THE 70TH INFANTRY REGIMENT, THE 'MAGALLANES', OF THE SPANISH COLONIAL ARMY.

THOSE WHO WITNESSED RIZAL'S PUBLIC EXECUTION INCLUDED LT. LUIS TAVIEL DE ANDRADE, HIS LEGAL DEFENDER DURING HIS TRIAL FOR ALLEGED TREASON AGAINST SPAIN, AND THE TWO JESUIT PRIESTS, FR. JOSE VILLACLARA, S.J. AND FR. ESTANISLAO MARCH, S.J. WHO ACCOMPANIED RIZAL DURING HIS FINAL WALK BEFORE HIS EXECUTION.

RIZAL'S MARTYRDOM FANNED THE FLAMES OF THE FILIPINO REVOLUTION OF 1896 AND INSPIRED THE FILIPINOS IN THEIR RESOLUTE AND EPIC FIGHT FOR FREEDOM.

CARL PARKES

Rizal Monument

Ulm near Heidelberg, Germany (where Rizal stopped to drink during his student days there), an allegorical sculpture entitled *La Madre Filipina,* and a simple obelisk marking the spot where the three Filipino priests, Burgos, Gomez, and Zamora, were garroted in 1872.

North Side

On this side of the park is a manmade cascade and a **Japanese garden,** a gift from Japan to the Filipino people. The nearby **Planetarium** presents audiovisual shows twice a day. Just beyond it is a **Chinese Garden,** with its red-and-gold pavilion, carp-filled pond, and bridge, said to be patterned after the summer pavilion in the Imperial Palace in Beijing. This was a gift of the Filipino-Chinese community.

West Side

The waterfront is reclaimed land. You find here a playground and *sipa* court. *Sipa* (kick) is a Filipino ball game in which players kick a ball over the net to the opposite team. You can promenade along the seawall.

Km 0 Marker: Along the busy road is a modest marker denoting the center of the Filipino universe—all distances in Luzon are measured to the exact centimeter from this very spot.

Manila Hotel: Since opening in 1912, the Manila Hotel, an 18-story, green-roofed landmark, has hosted many celebrities: royalty, statesmen, writers, and Hollywood stars. Its walls have witnessed murder, suicide, and scandal. The penthouse suite housed Gen. Douglas MacArthur prior to WW II, then the Japanese high command. In 1945, the hotel was severely damaged as fighting moved from room to room. Today, the impressive lobbies, the original and a 1976 addition, are worth visiting, while partaking of the fine breakfast buffet is a good way to sample the atmosphere.

Sunset Cruise: For a fine view of the city skyline and anchored ships, take a sunset cruise on Manila Bay. Boats leave from the south end of the park, to the left of the grandstand.

East Side

On the south side of the lagoon, with its dancing fountains, a cafeteria with deaf-mute waiters and waitresses is an unusual place to stop for a snack or refreshment—you write down your order. Warning: The food is lousy and over-priced.

National Library: Claims to have a collection of early Filipiniana, including old maps and newspapers, but the shocking state of this national library will tell you a great deal about the realities of Philippine society.

Rizal Fountain: Across Maria Orosa Street is the globe-shaped fountain, skating rink, and a topographical map of the archipelago, modeled after the one Rizal made during his exile in Dapitan.

NORTH OF RIZAL PARK

National Museum

North across Rizal Park, past the globe-shaped fountain, is the Executive House, which houses the National Museum. Displays feature prehistoric finds, including the Tabon skullcap, pottery and other artifacts, ceramics from China and Indochina, remnants of pre-Hispanic boats that brought Malay immigrants to the Philippines dating to about 1250, and a natural history section with stuffed birds and other exhibits. The museum suffered great losses during WW II and has since had to rebuild its collection almost from scratch.

The building is in shockingly poor condition and the exhibits are nothing short of embarrassing. A National Museum?

North from Rizal Park

Walk north to City Hall and take notice of the massive new wall of sculpture dedicated to a wide variety of Filipino heroes. A mural of the revolutionary Katipunan Society is on second floor of the municipal headquarters. Then continue north through an area once the Parian (silk market), the Chinese ghetto.

Metropolitan Theater: On the right is the Metropolitan Theater, whose predecessor was the biggest theater in the Far East prior to its destruction in 1945. This is a beautiful if completely neglected building with some very fine Art Deco details.

Puerta de Isabel II: Cross between Plaza Bonifacio, with its monument to the revolutionary hero, and the colonnaded post office and bear left along Magallanes Drive outside the walls of Intramuros. Almost opposite the immigration office is one of the seven gates to the walled city. A statue of Queen Isabel stands next to it. Built in 1862 as a storage arsenal, the restored gate contains a small museum displaying religious artifacts. Magallanes leads to the Aduana (Spanish customs building); it later housed the Central Bank.

Behind it is a riverside memorial to the 240-year galleon trade with Acapulco. Chinese junks laden with exotic merchandise once crowded the mouth of the Pasig here.

INTRAMUROS

The walled city was laid out on a grid, with 51 blocks within an uneven pentagon, its massive walls breached by seven gates. Only Spaniards and Spanish mestizos were allowed to live inside; each night, drawbridges across the moat were raised to ensure the colonists' security. The walls contained 12 churches, plus chapels, convents, monasteries, palaces for the governor-general and archbishop, government buildings, schools, a university, printing press, hospital, and barracks.

The elite dwelt in elegant houses with wrought-iron balconies and tiled roofs, though the narrow streets weren't paved until the late 19th century. Not much was left of this medieval European city in the tropics after WW II, but a restoration project by the Intramuros Administration is ongoing. The gates and walls have been restored, along with five period houses.

Yet Intramuros remains a mirror of Filipino society. Along with some finely restored structures are encampments of displaced citizens who cook their meals in the streets and give an almost frightening look to the old historic quarter. Part history, part slum, Intramuros is a study in contrasts.

Fort Santiago

Strategically located overlooking the mouth of the Pasig River, Fort Santiago was the site of Rajah Sulayman's stockade, burned in his retreat from the Spanish, who then replaced it with a stone fort with gun emplacements. Its walls have witnessed many of the major events in Philippine history, and much brutality. From here,

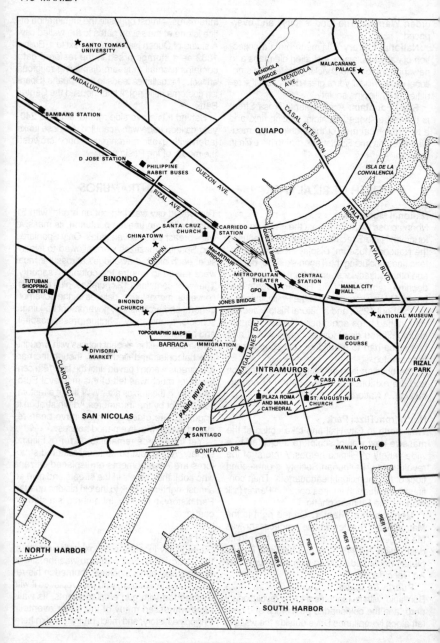

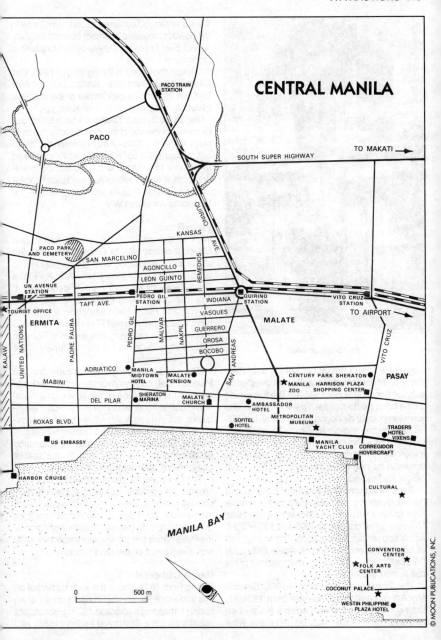

CENTRAL MANILA

PACO TRAIN STATION

PACO

SOUTH SUPER HIGHWAY

TO MAKATI →

QUIRINO AVE.

KANSAS

PACO PARK AND CEMETERY

SAN MARCELINO

AGONCILLO

LEON GUINTO

REMEDIOS

UN AVENUE STATION

TAFT AVE.

PEDRO GIL STATION

INDIANA

QUIRINO STATION

VITO CRUZ STATION

★ TOURIST OFFICE

VASQUES

MALATE

TO AIRPORT →

ERMITA

PADRE FAURA

PEDRO GIL

MALVAR

NAKPIL

GUERRERO

OROSA

BOCOBO

SAN ANDREAS

VITO CRUZ

MABINI

ADRIATICO ● Manila Midtown Hotel

MALATE PENSION

CENTURY PARK SHERATON ●

PASAY

★ Manila Zoo   HARRISON PLAZA SHOPPING CENTER

DEL PILAR

SHERATON MARINA ●

MALATE CHURCH ✝

ROXAS BLVD.

● AMBASSADOR HOTEL

SOFITEL HOTEL ●

METROPOLITAN MUSEUM ★

TRADERS HOTEL VIXENS ●

● US EMBASSY

● MANILA YACHT CLUB

CORREGIDOR HOVERCRAFT

■ HARBOR CRUISE

CULTURAL ★

MANILA BAY

KALAW

UNITED NATIONS

CONVENTION CENTER ★

★ FOLK ARTS CENTER

COCONUT PALACE ★

0   500 m

WESTIN PHILIPPINE PLAZA HOTEL ●

© MOON PUBLICATIONS, INC.

Fort Santiago gate

Legazpi watched the city of Manila rise. Construction of the first stone walls was directed by a Jesuit priest-engineer 1584-90. The fort served as the headquarters of the Spanish military, who were temporarily dislodged by the British in 1762-64, and by the mutinous Filipino Tayabas regiment in 1843. Over the centuries, countless Filipinos were imprisoned, tortured, and left to drown in its notorious dungeons, which were below the high-tide level.

Rizal Museum: The two-story building that held revolutionary hero José Rizal for two months prior to his execution in 1896 is now the Rizal Museum (open daily 0900-1200 and 1300-1700), which houses his memorabilia. The manuscript of his final poem, *Mi Ultimo Adios* ("My Last Farewell"), was supposedly smuggled out of his cell in the base of an oil lamp.

The Americans took it over in 1898; General MacArthur headquartered here from 1936-41. During WW II, the fort was again a place of interrogation and death under the Japanese. After the surrender, 600 charred bodies were found in the powder magazine chamber beneath the Bastion of San Lorenzo; they're buried beneath a cross here.

Almost destroyed in the fighting of 1945, Fort Santiago has since been landscaped and now contains a memorial park known as the Shrine of Freedom, a favorite spot of local people.

Rajah Sulayman Theater: This open-air auditorium on the site of the old barracks presents plays in Pilipino (Dec.-June). Beneath the Western ramparts is a collection of historic cars used to convey MacArthur and past Filipino presidents, plus an old wood-burning steam engine that was General Luna's headquarters in the Philippine-American War.

Plaza Roma

Walk south from Fort Santiago on General Luna Street. It crosses Santa Clara Street, once the site of a convent dating from 1621. Plaza Roma is dominated by Manila Cathedral. As Plaza Real, it was the heart of the old Spanish city. It has also been called Plaza de Armas, Plaza Mayor, and Plaza McKinley under the Americans. It was finally named Plaza Roma in 1956 to reciprocate the renaming of a square in Rome to Piazzale Manila to mark the appointment of the first Filipino cardinal.

The plaza was flanked by the cathedral, the Palacio Real, and the Ayuntamiento. The Palacio was the residence of the governor-general from 1660 to 1863, when it was ruined by earthquake; the building now on this site houses government offices such as the Department of Education, Sports and Culture, and the Intramuros Administration. The Ayuntamiento, the seat of government, was destroyed in 1945.

The plaza was the site of bullfighting and, later, ornamental gardens, fountains, statues, and orchestral concerts. Today, Plaza Roma contains a monument by Filipino modernist sculptor Solomon Saprid to Gomez, Burgos, and Zamora, the three native priests whose execution in 1872 was a key event on the road to revolution.

Manila Cathedral

Dating from 1571, this is the sixth cathedral on this site since the original chapel burned down during Limahong's attack in 1574. Subsequent structures were destroyed by fire (1583) and

CARL PARKES

earthquake (1600, 1645, 1863). The latter had been a magnificent building; its replacement stood from 1879 until the final days of WW II. The cathedral was the only church in Intramuros to be rebuilt after the war.

Completed in 1958, this Romanesque structure follows the contours of the previous building and incorporates some of its remaining walls. Its main features are its octagonal dome and separate bell tower. The facade contains statues of saints and bronze doors; the central door's eight panels depict the building's history. The cathedral is dedicated to the Immaculate Conception of the Virgin Mary; note the Virgin's bronze statue on the high altar. The architect, Fernando Ocampo, was Filipino, but most of the statues, mosaics, and other art were done by Italian artists.

The main thing to see inside is the impressive cycle of stained-glass windows designed by Filipino artist Galo Ocampo. The principal group depicts the Virgin's life in brilliant tropical colors. Other windows portray the Madonna in the different guises she assumes in the various regions of the country. The sun strikes these windows in midafternoon. The cathedral has side chapels, a high altar and archbishop's throne of Italian marble, a fine font in the baptistry, and a Dutch organ, which, with 4,500 pipes, is one of the largest in Asia. Past archbishops of Manila are buried in the mosaic-decorated crypt.

San Agustin Church

From Plaza Roma, General Luna Street leads past the west side of the cathedral to San Agustin Church. On the left is the tiny Plaza Sampalucan, scene of an ill-fated love affair between a Spanish merchant and a governor-general's wife. San Agustin stands at the junction with Calle Real, the old royal road by which new governors and archbishops entered the city to take office. The only structure to survive the bombardment of 1945 (some say it was a miracle), San Agustin was consecrated in 1571 on the same day that Manila was declared capital.

It's the mother church of the Augustinian order in the Philippines. Their symbols, the arrow-pierced heart and bishop's mitre, are carved on numerous parts of the church. The present church was built between 1599 and 1606. It has

withstood five major earthquakes, its survival attributed to its elliptical foundation (like the hull of a ship) and 1.5-meter-thick walls. Its design shows Mexican influence. The courtyard entrance and columned facade are guarded by granite lions given by Chinese converts. The church originally had two towers, but the left one was dismantled after the earthquakes in the 19th century.

Enter through the main door, carved out of native *molave* hardwood. The interior contains a baroque pulpit, near which is a superb wrought-iron door. Fourteen side chapels line the nave; the one to the left of the main altar contains a tomb surmounted by a recumbent effigy of Legazpi. The remains of the great early conquistadores—Legazpi, Martin de Goiti, Juan de Salcedo—and various early governors and archbishops lie here, their bones thrown together in a communal vault since the British plundered the church in 1762.

Note the rose window at the back of the church. The choir loft above the main entrance has 68 seats of *molave* inlaid with ivory, and 16 Parisian chandeliers hang from the ceiling, painted in three-dimensional trompe l'oeil.

The Monastery-Museum

Adjoining the church, this once-great collection of religious art and artifacts is still notable, in spite of having been much depleted through looting and war. It's contained in various rooms, including the vestry, where Spain's surrender to Dewey in 1898 marked the end of the Spanish-American War; the library, which contains rare books and manuscripts; the De Profundis Room, or Pantheon, where members of prominent families were buried; and the refectory. These rooms lie off the cloister, which encloses a garden.

The cloister's galleries are lined with paintings of St. Augustine and his followers. Among them is Father Manuel Blanco, an 18th-century monk who wrote a massive six-volume botanical study, *Flora de Filipinas*. Some 19th-century photos of Manila are also on display. The upper floors comprised the living quarters of the priests and lay brothers. In February 1945, over 7,000 people took shelter within the church's walls as the battle for Manila raged outside. Many were massacred here, and an adjacent 17th-century monastery was destroyed.

Festivals celebrated at San Agustin include the Feast of Our Lady of Consolation on 16 April and the Feast of Santa Rita of Casia on 22 May. Open daily 0800-1700.

Plaza San Luis

Across San Agustin Church, at the corner of General Luna and Calle Real, are reconstructed colonial houses. One of them is **Casa Manila,** which re-creates a rich man's house in the 19th century, with Philippine, Oriental, and European furniture and furnishings. It's open daily except Monday 0900-1200 and 1300-1800. Closing time on Saturday and Sunday is 1900. Casa Blanca features an exhibit of antique jewelry, furniture, and other items from the Intramuros Administration's collection.

Puerta Real

Continue along General Luna to another gate in the walls, the Puerta Real, whose interior holds a collection of church silver. Musical performances take place in the Puerta Real Gardens each Saturday during the summer months at 1800.

Following the Walls

This 4.4-km circuit may begin at Puerta Real. Follow Muralla Street, which runs alongside the eastern walls, past **Baluarte de San Andres** with its original lookout tower. Inside the *baluarte* are military artifacts on display. Farther along is the **Revellin de Recoletos,** which served as defense to Baluarte de San Andres. The next interesting site is **Baluarte de Dilao,** which was part of the original fortification of Intramuros in 1592. Beyond that is the **Puerta del Parian.** The city received many of its supplies through this gate, which linked it with the bustling Chinese ghetto outside the walls. Its defensive bastion stands outside.

Muralla Street continues past the Baluarte de San Gabriel and Puerta de Isabel II. Muralla meets Aduana Street and you can cut across, past Plaza Roma, to **Postigo del Palacio,** once the private gate of the archbishop and the governor-general, on the western side. Outside Intramuros here, on Bonifacio Drive, a traffic circle surrounds the monument to Anda, a distinguished 18th-century governor-general. Beyond it, the South Harbor, with its ware-houses and factories, serves international cargo vessels.

Inside the walls, Arzobispo Street leads to the Santa Lucia gate, with its restored cobbled bridge. Santa Lucia Street passes the **Bastion de San Jose,** MacArthur's headquarters in 1941, and the **Bastion de San Diego,** where the walls were breached by the British for the only time prior to 1945.

Bear left back to Puerta Real. Outside the walls, the old moat, which was crossed by drawbridges and later drained by the Americans for health reasons, is now a municipal golf course. The Spaniards had already ceased using the drawbridges following a series of 19th-century earthquakes. Fortifications protrude beyond the walls at several points, and the Legazpi-Urdaneta monument stands at the southwest corner of the golf links.

NORTH OF THE RIVER

Crossing the Pasig brings you to a poorer and more congested part of Manila. Sightseeing may be divided into east and west of Rizal Avenue, plus the Chinese cemetery a little to the north. The energetic could cover all points of interest in a full day, but most will find it more comfortable to allot two half days. Either way, try to wind up in Chinatown for dinner.

Frequent jeepneys link Mabini Street and Taft Avenue (Ermita) with Santa Cruz, a major shopping area. Here, Rizal Avenue is lined with department stores, bookstores, cinemas, and sidewalk vendors, many specializing in particular products: G. Puyat, music stores; Ronquillo, sporting goods; Carriedo, shoes; R. Hidalgo, photo supplies; Villalobos, hats; Carlos Palanca, textiles and groceries. Just west of Rizal Avenue is Chinatown.

Chinatown

Located in the districts of Binondo, San Nicolas, and Santa Cruz, Chinatown has an unmistakably Oriental flavor and is a fascinating area to wander. Chinese had settled in Binondo as early as 1594; during the 19th century, Binondo became Manila's commercial hub. Today, its importance has waned as banks and big businesses have moved their offices out to Makati and elsewhere. Chinatown is distinguished by Chinese-style arches, a crowded area of narrow streets, small shops, and cramped residences, with horse-drawn *calesas* picking their way through congested traffic.

Chinatown is particularly lively during its observance of the Chinese New Year (falling between 21 January and 19 February) and the Moon Festival (sometime between August and September).

Chinatown's main thoroughfare, Ongpin Street, links Binondo and Santa Cruz Churches. Binondo Church, founded by the Dominicans in 1596 to serve Chinese converts, was repaired after severe WW II damage, though the Western facade and six-story octagonal bell tower are original. Inside, note the ornate pastel-colored reredos behind the main altar. From here, Quintin Paredes Street leads down to Jones Bridge and back toward Ermita, while Ongpin Street traverses Chinatown. Ongpin offers a lot of variety: restaurants, pet shops, bakeries, grocery stores, jewelers, traditional medicine shops, acupuncture clinics, kung-fu schools, and mahjongg parlors.

Ongpin leads to Plaza Santa Cruz, which is where Rizal Avenue curves to meet the MacArthur Bridge. Escolta, now a shadow of its former self, leads off from here. The plaza is dominated by Santa Cruz Church, the Shrine of Our Lady of the Pillar. Founded by the Jesuits in 1608, also serving Chinese converts, its side courtyard was the scene of the formal return of Manila to Spain in 1764, after Britain's 20-month occupation of the city. The current church's predecessor was destroyed during fighting in 1945. From here, frequent jeepneys go to Ermita.

Notable places to visit east of Rizal Avenue are Quiapo, Malacanang Palace, and the University of Santo Tomas.

Quiapo

Quiapo is a short walk from Rizal Avenue and can be reached directly by jeepney from Ermita (Mabini or Taft). (Alight just after crossing the river onto Quezon Boulevard, across from the church.) The Quiapo Church is surrounded by many small stalls selling candles, rosaries, medallions, talismans, and other religious objects, plus herbal medicine, flowers, and food. Founded in 1586, the current structure, built in 1935, is the fourth on this site. It houses the Shrine of the Black Nazarene, a miraculous, life-size statue of Christ bearing the cross that was carved in dark wood by Mexican Indians and brought to Manila by galleon in the 17th century.

Worshippers are particularly numerous on Fridays. Some devotees walk on their knees from the church entrance to the Nazareno. Numbers swell further at the first Friday of the month novenas and during Holy Week, when there's a huge gathering on Palm Sunday and processions on Holy Monday and Good Friday. During the first week of January, concerts and other entertainment occur in Plaza Miranda, in front of the church. These lead up to Quiapo's major Feast of the Black Nazarene, marked by a massive procession on 9 January. Plaza Miranda is often the setting for both entertainment and political speeches. Palm readers frequent its corners.

To the west of the church is a network of crowded narrow shopping streets. Beware of pickpockets here. Walk south beside Quezon Boulevard, beneath the Quezon Bridge—where many small stores offer an incredible variety of handicrafts. To the right is the colorful Quinta Market. On the east side of Quezon Boulevard is Manila's Muslim area with its golden-domed mosque, Muslim restaurants, and coffee shops.

Malacanang Palace

From Quiapo, a lengthy walk or short taxi ride along Arlegui Street brings you to Malacanang, the official residence of Philippine presidents. This ornate Spanish colonial palace, with its arches, grilles, and balconies, was built as a private country house in the late 18th century and purchased by the government in 1825. At first the governor-general's summer residence, it became his permanent residence in 1863, after the Palacio Real in Intramuros was destroyed by an earthquake.

Malacanang, believed to be a shortening of the Tagalog phrase *may lakan diyan* ("a chief lives there"), has been occupied by a succession of Spanish, American, and Filipino chief executives, as well as Japanese commanders. Extensive improvements have been made over the years. The richly furnished State Apartments contain parquet floors, Oriental rugs, crystal chandeliers, and a fine art collection, while the grounds have splendid gardens and a guest-house for visiting dignitaries.

During the Marcos regime, the attractive white colonnaded palace was surrounded by heavy security and could only be glimpsed through its wrought-iron gates. It was from here that on 25 February 1986, helicopters lifted Marcos away from his home of 20 years; two hours later, thousands of jubilant citizens poured through the gates. Manila's poor discovered opulence beyond their dreams. A half-eaten bowl of caviar revealed the haste of the departure.

Among the discoveries were Imelda Marcos's sumptuous bedroom and bathroom, with gallon bottles of custom-made French perfume, and a warehouse-like floor, now known as "Imelda's Department Store," containing racks of designer clothes, electronic equipment, luggage, and furniture, most still bearing price tags. Imelda's 2,700 pairs of shoes symbolized for the world the sheer excess of her vanity. Looting and vandalism were minimal as the crowd displayed remarkable restraint. A blackboard map showed the location and defenses of army rebels, and weapons ready for a desperate last stand that never came. The best-equipped in-home hospital emergency room and operating theater in the country provided evidence of the failing health that Marcos had tried to conceal.

When President Aquino came to power, she declared Malacanang a people's museum. Museo ng Malacanang functions as a Presidential Palace Museum and an official venue of state functions and regular cabinet meetings of the government. The palace museum is a showcase of Philippine art and culture, but all traces of Marcos have been removed.

Of interest is the Presidential Gifts Gallery, which contains official state gifts given to President Aquino, and the room showing old treasures. Guided tours (admission P250) are given several times weekly. General admission (P20) hours are 1200-1500 on Thursday and Friday and 0830-1500 Saturday.

Vicinity of Malacanang

Malacanang Palace is in San Miguel, an area that retains some Spanish flavor. The palace overlooks a stretch of the Pasig between Ayala and Nagtahan Bridges.

Next to Ayala Bridge is the **Isla de la Convalencia,** on which stands the Hospicio de San Jose, a home for orphans and the aged that's been run by nuns since 1782. The island's name was derived from its role as a place of convalescence for Spanish officials and soldiers. It still has a "turn cradle" where unwanted infants can be left. Malacanang Garden, directly across the river from the palace, is closed to the public.

Upstream, beside the Nagtahan Bridge, is the Mabini Shrine, a modest wooden house in which Apolinario Mabini, the revolution's intellectual leader, wrote the Katipunan constitution. The garden contains a replica of the nipa hut in Batangas in which Mabini was born. Visiting the shrine requires a special permit from the military GHQ in Quezon City. During WW II, thousands of refugees crossed the river by ferry at this spot.

From Malacanang, walk up Mendiola. On the right is **San Beda College,** founded in 1901, whose chapel is noted for murals and painted ceilings. The formal gardens used by the monks for meditation may be visited, with permission. **Mendiola Bridge,** which crosses a small canal here, has become a symbol of protest. It has often been the site of barbed wire, barricades, and confrontation between security forces and demonstrators marching on Malacanang.

Across the bridge on the left is **San Sebastian Church** (founded in 1621). Earthquakes destroyed three churches on this site before the Recollect Fathers attempted to make one earthquake-proof. In 1891, they imported 50,000 tons of prefabricated steel from Belgium and built the present neo-Gothic structure. Its design, featuring two openwork towers, is much influenced by the great Gothic cathedral of Burgos, Spain.

Inside, note the steel vaulting and stained-glass windows. Above the altar is an object of pilgrimage, the statue of the Virgin, Nuestra Señora del Carmel. Brought from Mexico in 1617, it survived all the earthquakes, but its valuable ivory head was stolen in 1975. Opposite San Sebastian Church is the **University of the East.** This section of the Sampaloc district is known as the "university belt," since it contains several universities and colleges in close proximity.

University of Santo Tomas

Formerly located in Intramuros (founded by the Dominicans in 1611), the present campus, dom-

CHINESE CEMETERY~ONLY FOR THE WEALTHY

This is one of the most interesting tourist attractions in Manila—it's a town for the dead, complete with streets and houses. Many of these houses are far more ostentatious than those of the majority of living Filipinos. Some are two-story mausoleums, with marble floors, kitchens, bathrooms, furniture, stained-glass windows, running water, electricity, a/c, and mailboxes. Photos of the departed can be seen on the graves through the ornate wrought-iron gates. Many Chinese families make regular visits, especially on Sunday morning, during which a picnic-like atmosphere prevails as they burn metal-coated paper burial money, restock the refrigerator, and play mah-jongg (with empty seats at the table for the deceased).

The cemetery's architecture blends Buddhist and Catholic elements: a temple with green dragons on the roof and an altar featuring both a gold Buddha and the Virgin Mary, for example. The cemetery's exterior walls contain 10,000 burial niches for families that cannot afford lavish tombs. All Saints' Day (1 November) is a busy time to come here; at other times, the streets may be deserted and eerie. Guides are available and can give fascinating insights into the place; agree to a fee beforehand. From Ermita (Mabini or Taft) or Rizal Avenue, Santa Cruz, take a northbound jeepney marked Monumento. Alight at Aurora Avenue and turn right, then left onto Felix Huertas, which leads to the cemetery. Open daily 0800-1700.

CARL PARKES

a town where the living only visit

inated by its clock tower, was inaugurated in 1927. UST, along Espana Street, is open Mon.-Sat. 0800-1200 and 1400-1700 during school terms. The university's famous graduates include the revolutionary heroes José Rizal, M.H. del Pilar, Mabini, and Aguinaldo; the three martyred priests Burgos, Gomez, and Zamora; and presidents Quezon, Osmeña, Laurel, and Macapagal.

When the Japanese entered Manila in 1942, they rounded up all the Allied nationals they could find and used the university campus as an internment camp. Three years later its liberation was the first objective of the U.S. forces that swept into the city. Today, this prestigious private university consists of 12 colleges, includes primary, elementary, and high schools, and has over 30,000 students.

At the main entrance is the "Arch of the Centuries"; despite surviving the destruction of the old university in Intramuros, it was dismantled and reassembled here. The library on the ground floor contains a great collection of Filipiniana: rare, old manuscripts and books (some dating before 1500), coins, medals, and the oldest printing press in the country. The Museum of Natural Science, on the second floor of the main building, has extensive collections in many scientific divisions, plus archaeological, historical, and anthropological sections, and a gallery of religious art. Only a fraction of its 1.5 million objects are exhibited.

PASAY CITY

At Buendia Avenue, Manila proper ends and Pasay City begins. South of the CCP complex, also on reclaimed land off Roxas Boulevard, is the extensive KKK Information and Display Center and the Philippine International Trade & Exhibits (Philtrade) Complex, which promotes Filipino products. Harrison Street runs parallel to Roxas Boulevard, a block inland.

Behind the Hyatt Regency at 10 Lancaster Street off Harrison is the **Lopez Memorial Museum;** open Tues.-Sat. 0800-1200 and 1300-1630, Sunday 0900-1600, closed holidays. It contains a superb collection of Filipiniana, including paintings by Luna and Hidalgo; letters and diaries of José Rizal; early maps, prints, and travel literature, including an account of Magellan's voyage published in 1542; and rare books and periodicals. There's also an original Ptolemy *Geographica* and one of three existing copies of Transylvanus's *De Moluccis Insulis* (1524).

Paranaque

Near the south end of Roxas Boulevard is Paranaque, an old salt-making town noted for embroidery. Within it, the Baclaran district contains the Church of Our Lady of Perpetual Help, better known as Baclaran Church. It was founded in 1931, when Redemptorist Fathers brought a 15th-century image of the Virgin from Europe. The original building was destroyed in WW II; the present Romanesque church was built in 1950.

Nayong Pilipino

Nayong Pilipino ("Philippine Village")—open Mon.-Fri. 0900-1900, Saturday and Sunday 0900-2000—is a 46-hectare park that presents a microcosm of the country and its culture. Located close to the international airport and the Philippine Village Hotel, it contains typical houses and landscapes of six regions: Ilocos, the Cordillera Central, Tagalog, Bicol, the Visayas, and Mindanao.

Philippine Museum of Ethnology: This museum contains informative displays with cos-

tumed models, artifacts, weapons, musical instruments, and photos of various cultural minority groups. It's located in the Mindanao section. In addition, the various regional houses display handicraft and natural history exhibits. Numerous shops sell regional souvenirs and handicrafts.

Other attractions are the **Museum of Philippine and International Dolls,** an aquarium, a garden of Philippine plants (bougainvillea, hibiscus, cactus, and lily collections), an herbal garden, a palmettum (collection of ferns and palms), an aviary of Philippine birds, and a lagoon. There's also a children's playground. Folk dances take place regularly during the weekend, while exhibits, festivals, music, drama, and cultural presentations are shown periodically. Free jeepney rides around the village are available.

Nayong Pilipino is next to the Philippine Village Hotel. To return to Ermita, take a bus going to Taft or change at Baclaran (usually quicker).

MAKATI

Makati is modern, spacious, affluent, and a marked contrast to the congestion and poverty encountered north of the Pasig River. Makati has grown since 1950 and is divided into "villages," whose residents are middle- and upper-class Filipinos or members of Manila's substantial foreign community. Travelers with business at international banks or embassies other than the U.S. will have to go out to Makati, but it's also worth a trip if you want a break from the Third World.

From Taft Avenue take one of the frequent buses marked "Ayala," an avenue lined with high-rise buildings that house the offices of multinational corporations and major Philippine companies. The land on which Makati was built is owned by Jaime Zobel de Ayala, one of the richest men in the Philippines, which explains the frequent use of his name around Makati.

Makati Commercial Center

This large shopping plaza offers Western-style supermarkets, department stores, bookshops, cinemas, restaurants, and fast-food places. Some of Manila's finest hotels are in this area.

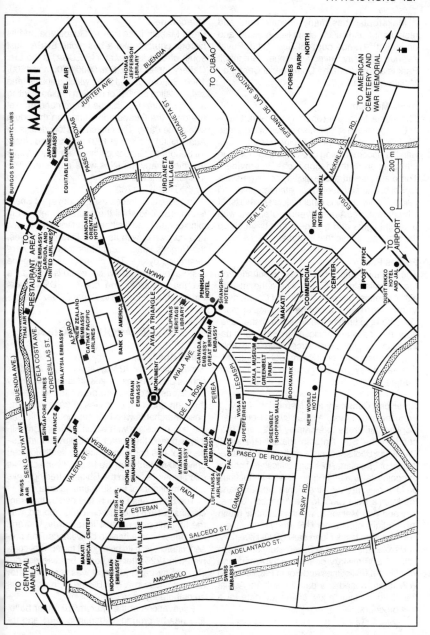

Makati also has many upscale bars and restaurants, particularly along Pasay Road, and on Makati Avenue north of Sen. Gil J. Puyat Avenue (formerly Buendia Avenue). Greenbelt Park is across from the Commercial Center on Makita Avenue.

Ayala Museum

The Ayala Museum (open Tues.-Sun. 0900-1800) contains a remarkable series of dioramas depicting scenes from Philippine history. Along with the accompanying booklet, a good capsule introduction to the nation's past is provided. There are also attractive displays of large-scale model boats, archaeological, ethnographic, and religious artifacts, plus other historical exhibits. At Christmastime, Ayala Avenue is strewn with beautiful lights and greenery that brighten up the concrete jungle that is Makati.

Forbes Park

The Makati Commercial Center is bounded on the opposite side by EDSA, where the "million-aires' ghettos" of Forbes Park and Dasmarinas Village are. There are some spectacular mansions here; to protect this wealth from the have-nots, the roads are enclosed by gates and patrolled by a private police force. There's no problem if tourists walk or drive through during daytime—just say you are going to the American Cemetery.

American Cemetery and Memorial

From the end of Ayala Avenue by the Hotel Inter-Continental, cross to McKinley Road and proceed to the San Antonio Plaza. The small Casalinda Bookshop has a particularly good selection of Filipiniana, including difficult-to-find anthropological and ethnographic works. Continue on McKinley, between the Manila Golf Club and the Manila Polo Club, to the American Cemetery and War Memorial, which is actually within the confines of a former U.S. Army reservation, now Fort Bonifacio. Open daily 0600-1700.

Here, in the largest U.S. cemetery on foreign soil, 17,208 military dead, mostly Americans killed in the Philippines and South Pacific during WW II, are buried in a parklike setting. Ask at the visitor's building just inside the gate for a free brochure.

Guadalupe

From Makati, it isn't far to Guadalupe and its historic church; take a bus along EDSA. Just south of Guadalupe, at 448 EDSA, is the **Luz Gallery** (open Tues.-Sat. 0900-1200 and 1300-1800, Sunday 0900-1300), which displays (and sells) rotating exhibits of modern Filipino painting and sculpture. Guadalupe Church and market are near the Guadalupe Bridge on the south side of the Pasig. The church was founded as an Augustinian mission in 1601 and housed Nuestra Señora de Guadalupe, an image of the Virgin to which many miracles were attributed. The image was saved when the church was sacked by the British in 1762.

In 1899, U.S. forces used a converted Spanish riverboat to shell the church, where a Filipino general had his headquarters. The church and *convento,* with its great library, archives, the Virgin's image, and other treasures, were destroyed by fire. The church has undergone restoration, and a new *convento* is used as a seminary. Across the bridge, EDSA leads through Mandaluyong to Cubao, Quezon City.

SIGHTS AROUND MANILA

Santa Ana

Santa Ana (fiesta: 12 May) is one of the country's richest archaeological sites. In spite of swampy conditions, people were drawn to this area in the 12th and 13th centuries to trade with Chinese merchants who brought metals, silk, and the fine porcelain with which affluent early Filipinos buried their dead. It's believed that residents of this community, conveniently located only 300 meters from the Pasig River, acted as middlemen between the Chinese trading junks and inhabitants of the surrounding area.

The Santa Ana Church, founded by the Franciscans in 1578 and built on a large mound, was the first mission outside Intramuros. Old and sick priests came here to convalesce. The present church, with its hexagonal tower, was completed in 1725 after the earlier building was destroyed by earthquake; it was restored after heavy damage in WW II. Behind the main altar is an elaborately carved reredos.

Excavations of the churchyard, inner patio, and nearby properties began in 1961 and revealed habitation and burial sites estimated to be over 800 years old. More than 200 graves, including some of infants, and skeletons with gold-studded teeth have been uncovered, yielding 1,500-plus pieces of pottery, with unusually large numbers per grave, indicating affluence.

Quezon City

Metro Manila's largest city contains numerous national government offices, large housing projects, and well over a million inhabitants. Quezon City was founded in 1939 by President Manuel L. Quezon. A believer in social justice, his goal was to build a "working-man's paradise," where low-income families would be given a house and lot of their own. In 1948, it was selected as the most suitable site for the national capital, though it hasn't eclipsed Manila's preeminence.

Jeepneys traveling along Taft Avenue and through Quiapo turn northeast along Quezon Avenue, which leads to the Quezon Memorial Circle; the circle is the heart of the city, dominated by the 30-meter-high Quezon monument and mausoleum. Its underground chambers house the Quezon City Museum and Art Gallery. In 1970, the visiting pope celebrated mass here before a vast throng.

Nearby is the city hall and a **Parks and Wildlife Nature Center** (open daily 0600-2100), with a small zoo, picnic area, and lagoon. To the northeast is the main campus of the University of the Philippines at Diliman, reached by buses marked "U.P." A bronze statue, *The Oblation,* marks the entrance to over 500 hectares of peaceful, attractive grounds. The university has a museum of anthropology (open Mon.-Fri. 0800-1700). Check the bulletin boards of the student union for upcoming events, concerts, plays, and films.

At the Central Bank Mint Building on East Avenue is the **Museo ng Buhay Pilipino** ("Museum of Filipino Life"), open Mon.-Fri. 0900-1600; admission is P5. With its polished *narra* floors, *kapis* shell windows, and antique furniture and utensils, this museum evokes the lifestyle of an upper-middle-class family of the late 19th century. Other landmarks of Quezon City include the imposing Batasang Pambansa ("National Assembly") building, the highly regarded Philippine Heart Center for Asia, and the egg-shaped atomic reactor of the Atomic Energy Commission.

South of Quezon Memorial Circle, EDSA leads to Quezon City's commercial district, Cubao, site of a farmers' market, shopping center, and the Araneta Coliseum (which seats 25,000 beneath its dome), site of the 1975 Ali-Frazier world championship fight. Farther south, between Cubao and Makati, EDSA passes between Camp Aguinaldo and Camp Crame, scene of the historic February 1986 standoff in which thousands of civilians stood between military forces supporting Aquino and those loyal to Marcos (now referred to as the "EDSA Revolution").

Caloocan City

On the north side of Manila, Caloocan City was the scene of the "Cry of Balintawak" in 1896, which signaled armed uprising against Spain. This industrial suburb's focal point is Monumento, a monument to revolutionary leader Andres Bonifacio and the northernmost metrorail stop, near some of the northbound bus terminals and, to the south, the Chinese cemetery.

On the coastal side of Caloocan are the neighboring towns of Navotas, the nation's largest fishing port, and Malabon, also a fishing center. Malabon is home of the popular noodle dish, *pancit Malabon,* and site of a Good Friday *senaculo* with masked flagellantes. Each 8 December, a colorful evening fluvial parade takes place on the Malabon-Navotas waterway. Valenzuela, site of a huge San Miguel brewery, is to the north.

Marikina

Metro Manila's eastern suburbs, in addition to Quezon City, comprise Marikina, whose major industry is shoe manufacturing, and San Juan, where the first battle of the Philippine Revolution took place in 1896 and the first shot in the Philippine-American War was fired in 1899. Today it's noted for the **Alto Crafts Doll Museum.** Located at 400 Guevarra Avenue, near Channel 13 TV station, it boasts a collection of over 2,000 dolls depicting Philippine history, costumes, occupations, games, dances, and customs. Dolls are for sale, too.

More Suburbs

Also east of central Manila are Mandaluyong, site of the new Mega Mall and Shangri-La Hotel; Makati; industrial Pasig (church founded in 1574, rebuilt in 18th century); Pateros, a duck and *balut* (fertilized duck egg) center; and the lakeshore municipality of Taguig. The southern suburbs are Paranaque, Pasay City (which contains the airport and southbound bus terminals), Las Pinas, and Muntinlupa, site of a major prison.

SOUTH OF MANILA

Las Pinas and the Bamboo Organ

This old salt-producing town (fiesta: 4 May), 12 km south of Rizal Park on the road to Cavite and Tagaytay, is noted for its bamboo organ, unique in the world. **Las Pinas Church** (open daily 0800-1200 and 1300-1700, except Sunday morning) was built between 1792 and 1819 to replace an earlier structure and rebuilt again in 1888. Father Diego Cerra, a Spaniard, built the organ between 1816 and 1822. Measuring over five meters high and four meters wide, it has 174 bamboo pipes, 122 horizontal reeds of soft metal, a five-octave keyboard, and 22 stops arranged in vertical rows. One tube, if filled with water, imitates bird song. Originally powered by a windmill, an electric blower is now used.

Over the years, it suffered earthquake and typhoon damage, was dismantled, forgotten, rediscovered, partially repaired, and then finally (in 1973-75) restored in Bonn, Germany. There's often someone playing the organ 0900-1100, 1400-1600. The Bamboo Organ Festival, featuring international performers, is held annually. A small adjoining gift shop sells bamboo organ records and cassettes. The church also has stained *kapis* windows, *narra* pews, and carriage lamps on bamboo stands.

To get to Las Pinas, look for a bus with a "Las Pinas/Zapote" sign, or take a jeepney to Baclaran, then any southbound bus or jeepney. Many tourists combine a stop at Las Pinas with a visit to the jeepney factories in Zapote (Cavite) about three km south of Las Pinas Church (take any southbound vehicle) and the Aguinaldo Shrine in Kawit.

Zapote and the Sarao Jeepney Factory

Zapote is three km south of Las Pinas. Tourists are welcome to wander into the Sarao jeepney factory (open Mon.-Sat. 0800-1200, 1300-1700) on the main road. Revolutionary forces fought two bloody battles in Zapote, against the Spanish in 1897 and the U.S. in 1899. The best performers of the *maglalatik,* an old Tagalog war dance, come from here.

During the town fiesta, dancers perform from house to house for gifts or tips, then join the evening religious procession. The highway splits at Zapote, one branch going to Kawit and Cavite City, the other heading south to Tagaytay.

Kawit and the Aguinaldo Museum

This town, 23 km from the center of Manila, has a long-established Chinese presence. During the late 16th century, Chinese merchants exchanged porcelain, silk, and tea here for silver coins brought by galleon from Acapulco. Aguinaldo himself was part Chinese.

Aguinaldo Museum: The mansion (1849), birthplace, and home of this revolutionary hero and president of the short-lived First Philippine Republic is now a shrine and museum. Its balcony, from which independence from Spain was declared, is depicted on the P2 bill. That event was accompanied by the raising of the Philippine flag and playing of the national anthem, each for the first time.

Today, the museum (open daily 0800-1200, 1300-1700) displays Aguinaldo's personal memorabilia, historical relics and weapons, some fine furniture, and decorated ceilings. The dining room ceiling features a map of the Philippines, with Cavite painted red to symbolize war. Aguinaldo's marble tomb is in the garden behind the house. Buses going to Cavite, Tanza, and Naic pass the shrine.

The old municipal building of Kawit was attacked by revolutionary forces led by Aguinaldo in 1896. Kawit is also noted for its Santo Entierro procession, marking Christ's burial, on Good Friday, and Maytinis, a street reenactment of Joseph and Mary's search for shelter, on Christmas Eve.

CORREGIDOR

As the last bastion to fall to the invading Japanese in 1942, this island fortress, nicknamed "the Rock," acquired immense significance as a symbol of the determined resistance of its Filipino and American defenders. Corregidor is

ruins at Corregidor

now a national shrine. Surveying this silent, sea-lapped scene of heroism is a memorable experience, and a visit here is one of the major day excursions from Manila.

The Island

Corregidor lies at the entrance to Manila Bay, six km off the tip of the Bataan Peninsula, 16 km from Cavite to the south, and 45 km across the bay from Manila. Shaped like a tadpole, with the head facing the South China Sea and the tail curving toward Manila, Corregidor is 6.5 km long, 1.5 km at its widest point, and covers about nine square km.

The head, which rises about 200 meters above the sea, flattens into two plateaus called Topside and Middleside. Below them is Bottomside, almost at sea level, and Malinta Hill. The battle-scarred rock, with its poignant memorials presiding over a landscape of concrete ruins and rusty gun batteries, is not without beauty. The summit affords fine views of the rugged coast of Bataan and the surrounding sea, and the island has narrow sandy beaches at its tail end.

History

Corregidor's history is closely associated with its strategic position, since, together with four other small islands, it commands the narrow entrance to Manila Bay, dividing it into north and south channels. Originally called Maribela, it's uncertain whether the name Corregidor ("Cor-rector") derives from its role as a checkpoint where officials corrected the papers of incoming shipping, or from the existence of a former correctional institute. In early times, it was the haunt of Chinese and Moro pirates.

The Dutch used the island as a base for raids on the Bataan coast in 1647. The Spanish subsequently built a dockyard and naval hospital on it, then added a lighthouse and gun emplacements, but its defenses failed to deter Commodore Dewey in 1898. The Americans greatly strengthened the fortifications, building roads, barracks, tunnels, and new gun emplacements, including 23 large batteries. Water, however, had to be brought by barge from Bataan.

1942: After the Japanese invasion and the abandoning of Manila, the cavernous Malinta Tunnel on Corregidor was the seat of government and headquarters for Gen. Douglas MacArthur, U.S. High Commissioner Francis B. Sayre, and President Manuel Quezon of the Philippines, who arrived on 24 December 1941. Quezon left Corregidor by submarine 20 February, MacArthur by PT boat 11 March.

A month later, the Fall of Bataan left Corregidor, which had already suffered intensive bombardment, as the last point of Allied resistance. Against all odds, "the Rock" held out for another month against continuous Japanese bombing raids and artillery barrage. Finally, with the island's guns knocked out by saturation bombing and shelling (it was said to have a bomb crater for every 25 square meters of land), the Japanese landed.

The defenders retreated into the Malinta Tunnel system and defied them for a few more days, but the lack of water, food, medicine, and ammunition left General Wainwright little choice but to surrender on 6 May 1942. He noted in his cable to President Roosevelt that the limit of human endurance was long past. The 13,000 Filipino and American defenders were given no food for a week, then herded in triumph through the streets of Manila, before their internment at Cabanatuan. On 6 May, WW II veterans make an anniversary visit to attend ceremonies commemorating the fall of "the Rock."

1945: In February 1945, it was the Japanese turn for hopeless, stubborn resistance in the Malinta Tunnel. Preferring suicide or suicidal bravery to surrender, fewer than 50 of the 5,200 defenders are believed to have survived. After a savage 11-day battle, Corregidor was retaken at a cost of 210 American lives.

CARL PARKES

the author at Corregidor

Attractions

Since the management and control of Corregidor was turned over to the Department of Tourism (the Corregidor Foundation), the entire historical park has been extremely well renovated and is probably one of the best historical destinations in the country. There are now tourist courtesy centers on the island, sound and light presentations inside Malinta Tunnel, and a pair of very fine places to overnight.

Big Guns: Corregidor's gun emplacements include Battery Hearn, the biggest; Battery Way, the best preserved; Battery Crockett; Battery Morrison; and Battery Geary, which had been the most effective until a direct hit on its magazine made defeat imminent. Cannons brood silently over the landscape, which was once completely denuded by bombardment.

Malinta Tunnel: Malinta Tunnel, since renamed Wainwright Tunnel, is actually a system of bomb-proof tunnels, with three main sections (277 meters by 8 meters) and 24 laterals (49 meters by 4.5 meters). It was bored out of Malinta Hill between 1922 and 1932. During the siege, in addition to being the headquarters, it contained a 1,000-bed hospital, U.S. Navy command unit, and storage areas. MacArthur occupied the third lateral (north side) from the east entrance.

"Mile Long" Barracks: Topside had been the heart of the complex, with the prewar Army headquarters, parade ground, post theater, and "Mile Long" Barracks, which once housed 8,000 men. Middleside contained more barracks and the post hospital. Bottomside, where the gallant allied garrison surrendered, was the site of docks and warehouses.

Caves and Shrine: The island also has limestone caves where Japanese defenders hid during the recapture. A small Buddhist shrine has been set up on Suicide Cliff, from which many Japanese jumped.

Memorial and Museum: Topside is now the site of a marble Pacific War Memorial, a steel sculptured "Eternal Flame," and a museum containing war relics, photos, and descriptive information.

Accommodations

Corregidor accommodations are handled by the Corregidor Foundation in the Department of

Tourism building in Rizal Park. Choices include the 31-room Corregidor Hotel, where rooms cost from P2,200, and the Corregidor Youth Hostel, which costs P250 for a dorm bed. This is a great place to escape the city and enjoy the extreme moodiness of the island.

Transportation

Corregidor tours are somewhat expensive. Escorted tours arranged by Sun Cruises cost P900 and leave daily at 0800 from the ferry terminal adjacent to the Cultural Center of the Philippines. These tours include roundtrip hovercraft transport and a four-hour sightseeing tour by bus. The light and sound show inside the Malinta Tunnel costs an extra P150.

Every Sunday a slower but perhaps more comfortable boat—the *Tennessee Walker*—leaves from the Manila Hotel dock and does a 12-hour Corregidor tour with buffet breakfast and lunch for P850. The *Tennessee Walker,* a converted oil tanker (guaranteed unsinkable), also does dinner cruises nightly at 1930 for P600 per person. Contact the Manila Hotel for reservations.

Other Islands

Near Corregidor are two small islands: Caballo, former site of Fort Hughes and now a Philippine Navy installation, and La Monja. Also associated with Corregidor as a defense unit were El Fraile, site of Fort Drum, and Carabao Island, site of Fort Frank, both near the Cavite coastline.

The heavily fortified Fort Drum, a 100- by 45-meter citadel nicknamed "the concrete battleship" and bristling with guns, was still in operation when Corregidor capitulated in 1942. Though bomb-proof, it was blown up from within in a daring U.S. Army raid in 1945. These islands at the entrance to Manila Bay are visible from interisland ships sailing to and from Manila.

M.G.L. DOMENY DE RIENZI

ACCOMMODATIONS

As in any large city, the prime consideration when choosing accommodations is location. Manila is best known for its nightlife, so most visitors stay in or near Ermita, the tourist/nightlife district. The main action is along the streets of Padre Faura, Mabini, Pedro Gil, and M.H. del Pilar.

A wide range of accommodations, from budget guesthouses to luxury hotels, is found in Ermita and the adjacent districts of Malate and Paco. Room rates drop in price east of Taft Avenue, the boundary between Ermita and Paco, which contains some of the most popular budget lodging. Many travelers find that the savings justifies the 10-minute walk to del Pilar.

Numerous cheap lodging houses are also found north of the Pasig in the congested Santa Cruz area, but they aren't especially good values. If you prefer this area, budget hotels are on both sides of Rizal Avenue north of C.M. Recto. Makati is the business district, and although it has an active and upscale nightlife, accommodations are expensive.

ERMITA AND MALATE

Budget

Budget accommodations under P400 are found in the tourist belt of Ermita and Malate, but most are cramped, dirty, and noisy. You must spend P500-600 to find a decent room with fan and common bath and P750-1,200 for an a/c room. Manila is not cheap, so if you're on a tight budget, it's best to leave the city as soon as possible.

A good starting spot is Malate Pensionne on Adriatico Street. If it's filled, you can drop your bag in the lobby and start your search for another place.

Malate Pensionne: Manila's largest and most popular pension house has the enclosed Portico Café for people-watching, Glasshouse, Sidebar, useful information board, harried but patient employees, and well-maintained rooms in all price ranges—the best budget to midpriced place in Manila. Its business center can help with long-distance phone calls and visa extensions. Bar girls are not allowed inside the rooms. For a discount on your room rate (minimum three days), tell Mila (resident manager) that Carl sent you. 1771 Adriatico St., tel. (02) 523-8304, fax 522-2389, e-mail info@mpensionne.com.ph, P150-200 dorm, P350-990 private rooms.

Shoshana Pension House: Bare-bones but very cheap place just down the alley from Malate Pensionne. 1776 Adriatico St., tel. (02) 524-6512, P250-350.

Pension Natividad: Receives good reviews from travelers and is fairly new, clean, and safe, although it looks intimidating from the outside. 1690 del Pilar, tel. (02) 521-0524, P150-180 dorm, P500-800 private rooms.

Joward's Pension House: Small but acceptable rooms just across from the Midtown Hotel. 1726 Adriatico St., tel. (02) 521-4845, P320-550.

Santos Pension: An old favorite now rundown but with cheap rooms and a completely depressing lobby. This was once the spot for all Peace Corps volunteers? Sad, but true. 1540 Mabini St., tel. (02) 523-4896, P300-600.

Midtown Inn: Just above the Midtown Inn Diner with small but survivable rooms. 551 Padre Faura, tel. (02) 525-1403, P425-800.

Tropical Mansion Hotel: Rough but inexpensive place with discounted monthly rates. 1242 Bocobo St., tel. (02) 521-2639, P550-950.

Moderate

Manila has a wide selection of moderately priced hotels, although many are in fairly rough condition. Note that the best deals are those hotels that quote their prices in pesos rather than dollars—an important consideration after the 40% currency devaluation of 1997-98.

Cherry Lodge Apartelle: Short-time hotel with 10% discount on monthly stays. 550 Jorge Bocobo St., tel. (02) 524-7631, P800-1,200.

Swagman Hotel: This small Australian hotel, which caters to bachelors on holiday, offers good vibes and ice-cold beer plus friendly, helpful personnel. Swagman has daily bus service to Angeles, Subic, La Union, and Baguio. Rooms are barely larger than prison cells, but the friendliness of the staff and weird scene that goes on in the lobby may be compensation, of sorts. 411 Flores St., tel. (02) 523-8541, P1,300-2,000.

Hotel Soriente: A modern, clean, 35-room hotel on a quiet side street with negotiable rates during the low season. 545 Flores St., tel. (02) 523-9480, P900-1,400.

Luxury

After Mayor Alfredo Lim closed down all the bars and nightclubs in Ermita and Malate, most of the budget travelers and solo male visitors abandoned the area and skipped Manila, as it had lost its once-famous reputation for fun and nightlife. After many of the budget hotels closed, a new round of superior hotels started to open to attract businessmen and others with money to burn. Actually, many of them burn their money at the nightclubs down in Pasay and only leave the bare minimum with the hotels in Ermita.

Admiral Hotel: Classic atmosphere in an eight-story former apartment building facing Manila Bay, in an excellent location removed from the dirt and grime of Ermita but within walking distance of many of the nightclubs on Roxas Boulevard and down in Pasay. Rooms are only average but the place retains an old-Manila atmosphere largely lacking from most other modern, luxury hotels in the city. 2138 Roxas Blvd. tel. (02) 521-0905, fax 522-2018, Web site www.philonline.com.ph/~admiral, US$110-155.

Bayview Park Hotel: Fine location near the U.S. Embassy with many rooms facing Manila Bay. This is another older hotel (like the Admiral) that has renovated its rooms and now provides very decent accommodations at very reasonable rates. This hotel is within easy walking distance of Rizal Park, the tourist office, the Manila Hotel, and the remaining bars and nightclubs of Ermita. 1118 Roxas Blvd., tel. (02) 526-1555, fax 521-2674, e-mail bayview@webquest.com, US$120-185.

Century Park Sheraton: Certainly not in the best of locations and quite far from Ermita, but a logical choice for those who need to stay near Ermita but within relatively easy striking range of the business facilities of Makati. Mostly geared to the Japanese visitor and Western businessmen with basic but functional rooms. Adriatico St.

(near Harrison Plaza), tel. (02) 522-8888, fax 521-3413, US$135-180.

Hotel Sofitel Grand Boulevard: Once the Silahis Hotel (with the Playboy Club on the top floor), this old favorite was completely renovated several years ago and now is perhaps the finest hotels in the neighborhood, given the reasonable rates and superb location midway between Ermita and Malate. Rooms really sparkle here. 1990 Roxas Blvd., tel. (02) 526-8588, fax 524-2526, US$150-190.

Diamond Hotel: An exclusive-looking place from the exterior, but rooms are tiny and the management suffers from the hyper-Japanese need to reexamine every facet of the hotel. The result is a very paranoid hotel with security guards lurking in corners and false smiles you can cut with a thick knife. Roxas Blvd., tel. (02) 526-2211, fax 526-2255, Web site www.mindgate.com.ph/diamond, P6,400-9,700.

Holiday Inn Manila: Rooms are acceptable and the location is quite handy to bother the nearby tourist office officials on a daily basis, but the amazingly cramped lobby and lack of recreation amenities is quite remarkable. But never have I seen so many people packed into such tight quarters—must be that fabulous reputation that Holiday Inn seems to have in Asia. Come on folks, HI properties are just north of Motel 6. United Nations Ave., tel. (02) 526-1212, fax 526-5566, US$128-178.

Pan Pacific Hotel: Such an enormous hotel in such a cozy neighborhood, still the place provides first-class amenities and you can also walk across the street for a bowl of *lugaw* from the sidewalk vendor. This monstrous edifice opened in late 1998, and it remains to be seen how successful the concept will be in the old tourist district of Ermita. Adriatico St., tel. (02) 526-6515, fax 526-6503, US$280-420.

Manila Hotel: Not a bad place to crash for a night if you can't get a room at Malate Pensionne. Rooms are pricey, the guards are very uptight (you'll need to show a room key just to visit the lobby), and the place has been in permanent financial turmoil since the days of Marcos, but the rooms have a touch of colonial class. One Rizal Park, tel. (02) 527-0011, fax 527-0022.

FOOD

Those returning from long journeys through the provinces will welcome the tantalizing choice of food available in cosmopolitan Manila. You can find some excellent restaurants offering various specialties in the luxury and first-class hotels. International credit cards are accepted here. Those looking for more reasonably priced restaurants can find them in Ermita, Malate, and Chinatown. Eating native is, of course, the cheapest way to go, and Filipino restaurants are everywhere. Also, many budget lodging houses allow guests to prepare food from the market. Restaurants suggested below are in Ermita, Malate, or Paco, unless otherwise noted.

Filipino

Plenty of Western fast food joints in Manila, but native Filipino cuisine should also be tried. The less expensive ones are often *turo turo* (point point) style, which lets you point to whatever looks best, a convenient way to select something without blindly ordering off the menu. These are plentiful along del Pilar and Mabini Streets. Also worth searching out are *kamayan* restaurants, which serve Filipino fare on banana leafs without the use of silverware. It's hand to mouth in these places!

Barrio Fiesta: The country's largest chain of restaurants specializing in native Filipino cuisine is famous for its *kare kare, inihaw na bangus,* and crispy *pata.* There are two outlets in Ermita, one on Orosa at Arkansas and another on United Nations just west of del Pilar. Moderate.

Aristocrat: Filipino seafood and international specialties served in a large, informal restaurant. Try *alimango* (crabs wrapped in banana leaves), chicken honey, and *maliputo,* a locally raised freshwater fish. Open 24 hours. 432 San Andreas at Roxas Boulevard. Moderate.

Buffets: Luncheon buffets at five-star hotels are one of Manila's best bargains. Although largely a Western smorgasbord, a selection of native dishes will also be included. Prices range P300-500 at the Midtown, Silahis, and Manila Pavilion hotels.

Chinese

Ermita and Malate have several Chinese restaurants. One of the best is the **Empress Garden** (1721 M. Adriatico); try the Special Crab Lomi. The **Wok Inn** and the **New Wok Inn** on Remedios Avenue across from the Malate Church are excellent for fresh seafood, vegetables, and bean curd cooked Cantonese-style.

The **Palo Alto** restaurant on U.N. Avenue serves cheap set meals, while the **China Park Restaurant** (Plaza Nuestra Señora de Guia) offers a good lunchtime smorgasbord. In Chinatown, just walk along Ongpin Street for a wide choice of restaurants. The **Spring Garden Food Palace** is popular with locals, as is the **Oceanic Restaurant** (777 Ongpin, behind the Grand House Restaurant, near the Ongpin N. Bridge), which has very reasonable prices.

A string of small outdoor food stalls is close by along the *estero.* The **Pink Patio** (Uy Suy Bin Bldg., 531 Paredes Street) serves homely Chinese dishes. The **New Carvajal Restaurant** in the Carvajal Alley between Quintin Paredes and Nueva Streets is also a good spot.

Other Asian Food

Numerous restaurants serve Manila's many Japanese tourists. Most offer a set meal—typically miso soup, sashimi, rice, and pickled vegetable—that is good value. Try the **Hakata** (1131 M.H. del Pilar), **Iseya** (del Pilar at Padre Faura), **Fuga** (del Pilar at Pedro Gil), **Mitsuco** (Pedro Gil at J. Bocobo), or the **Fujiyama** (branches at 1410 Mabini and on Adriatico). In Makati, the **Miyako** (Pasay Road at East de los Santos) offers all the tempura you can eat for a set price—outstanding value. **77 Cuisine** (1726 M. Adriatico) serves Singaporean, Taiwanese, and Thai dishes. Those who prefer spicy Asian dishes can try the **Korean Village** restaurant (1783 M. Adriatico, Malate), which serves good food at moderate prices. For Indian food, the **Kashmir Restaurant** on Padre Faura is good but expensive, while **India House** on Adriatico is moderate. An Indian named Ravi runs a small food stall opposite the Hindu and Hare Krishna temples on Looban, Paco. His cheap tasty food is worth a walk!

Several kinds of Middle Eastern food can be found. **Al-Sham's** (1421 Mabini) is primarily Pakistani; it serves excellent breads and yogurt dishes. The cost of a meal can be reasonable, especially if you stick to vegetarian fare. Also try the **Green House Middle Eastern Food** (corner Adriatico and Pedro Gil). A food stand next to the **Savory Restaurant** in the arcade off Padre Faura serves takeout Lebanese-style lamb sandwiches. For variety, try **Howard's Hot Pot & Pension** (formerly Lucky's Guesthouse) on Adriatico Street. Mongolian-style hot pot is cheap and plentiful. The **Vietnamese Food House** on Harrison Street, Pasay City, serves inexpensive lunches and dinners.

Western

Hula Hut: Rosie's Diner on the corner and the Hula Hut behind the Blue Hawaii serve great burgers, steaks, and daily specials from an extensive menu. The place was closed on my last visit but may reopen soon. 1427 del Pilar. Inexpensive.

Aida's: Local specialties and ice-cold beer served at rock-bottom prices to locals, streetwalkers, and the occasional tourist. Del Pilar at Santa Monica Street. Inexpensive.

Iseya Hotel: Escape the belching jeepneys and street hustlers by riding the elevator to this patio restaurant on the sixth floor of the Iseya. Tasty fare, inexpensive beer, and daily specials served around the clock. 457 Padre Faura at del Pilar. Moderate.

Shakey's: The pizza is overpriced and lousy, but the place is air-conditioned and comfortable. Rock bands entertain in the evening at the Mabini branch. Rock 'n' roll in a pizzeria? Only in the Philippines! Mabini at Arquiza Street. Moderate.

Juri's Grand Cafe: Upscale Dutch café and European watering hole popular with Brits and Aussies; look for the giant, comical, wooden waiter figure out front. 1320 del Pilar. Moderate.

Endangered Species: Classy and very hip place with trendy bar and popular restaurant serving steak and seafood specialties. 1834 del Pilar. Moderate.

Remedios Circle Bistros

Manila's trendy neighborhood for espressos, art talk, and nouvelle cuisine is centered around Rotary Circle in Malate. All of the following cafés are somewhat expensive but a refreshing change from pizzas and yet another pot of *adobo*.

Names and locations change with the seasons, but the most popular venues currently are the North American Beef Company, Blue Café, Insomnia Café, Café Iguana, and Café Caribana on Julio Nakpil Street. A block south near Remedios Circle you'll find Café Adriatico, Racks Ribs, Patio Guernica, Camp Gourmet, Dean Street Café, Penguin Café, Café 1900, and Bistro Remedios. Heading down Adriatico Street is Jazzbox, Larry's Café, and Remember Café.

Bistro Remedios offers first-class Filipino dishes including *dinengdeng* from Ilocos, *pancit molo* from Iloilo, and *kamansing bukid* from Pampangna. Patio Guernica serves Spanish specialties like *paella, lengua,* and *callos.*

European

The best value in European food in terms of taste and quantity at moderate prices is provided by several German, Swiss, and Austrian restaurants, which cater primarily to the German/Swiss community and travelers from northern Europe. The **Edelweiss** (1335 M.H. del Pilar, opposite the Fast Food Center) is a local favorite with great pub lunches and dinners serving excellent wienerschnitzel and other dishes. Others include **Munchen Grill Pub** (Mabini corner of Padre Faura), **Fischfang** (1509 M.H. del Pilar), **Swiss Bistro** (494 Soldado, Ermita). The **New Swiss Inn** (General Luna, Paco) and the elegant **Weinstube** (del Pilar, Malate) are good too, though more expensive. Enthusiasts of pasta and other Italian specialties can make their way to **La Taverna** (Adriatico and Pedro Gil); moderate prices. Spanish restaurants include **Guernica's** (del Pilar and Remedios Circle), with music and good food at moderate to high prices, and **El Comedor** (Adriatico and Pedro Gil).

For French-style food, the pleasant **Lafayette Cafe Restaurant** (del Pilar) in the heart of "the strip" serves set, moderately priced "executive" lunches on weekdays; dishes rotate daily and the food is good. More exclusive, **Au Bon Vivant** (1133 L. Guerrero) has an excellent reputation and offers a fine four-course set-price meal. Within the Malate Pensionne building at 1771 Adriatico, try the upscale **Chateau 1771,** a nice French bistro in a garden setting. The Manila Hotel's **Champagne Room** offers formal deluxe dining.

ENTERTAINMENT

Manila is a night city. After the famous and often spectacular Manila Bay sunset, the city comes alive. You can drink and dance till dawn, and cheaply at that. All the ingredients for an exciting night on the town are here in abundance: good food and drink, live music, and gambling. Those who prefer more high-minded entertainment can enjoy frequent cultural presentations, both Filipino and international. Cinemas are also numerous.

Provincial cities offer a much scaled-down version of what's available in Manila. Knowledgeable aficionados of Asian nightlife generally rate Manila and Bangkok as the two great cities to play in. In 1993 Manila began prohibiting prostitution and the licensing of dance clubs, discos, pubs, or any type of establishment that might become a "girlie bar." All of Manila's seamiest bars were boarded up along M.H. del Pilar in 1993.

Nightlife in Manila evolves around several districts, though the area most popular with visitors is the tourist belt, in Ermita and Malate, where accommodations, bars, and restaurants are concentrated. Mabini and M.H. del Pilar Streets have been completely cleaned up. As the Malate/Ermita area begins to change, more trendy or well-to-do Filipinos come to the area for its coffee-houses, live music, discos, and all-night diners.

In Makati, a more sophisticated atmosphere pervades; bars, restaurants, and discos cater to affluent Filipinos, foreign residents, and visiting businesspeople. Buses between Ermita and Makati don't run late, but taxis are plentiful.

Nightclubs in Ermita

Zamboanga Restaurant: Several restaurants put on nightly dinner shows for their guests. Dinner plus show runs P350-600. 1619 Adriatico Street.

Hobbit House: Manila's nightlife includes more than dinner shows and cultural revues. The Hobbit House, one of the most popular small nightclubs in town, features Mexican food and live folk music by some of the country's top performers, such as Freddy Aguilar. Food and drinks are served by dwarf waiters. 1801 Mabini at Remedios Street.

My Father's Moustache: Another small nightclub with folk musicians and modest cover charge. 2144 del Pilar near Quirino.

Guernica's: Spanish guitar and regional dishes like *gambas* and *calamares* served in a peaceful restaurant in operation over 30 years. 1325 del Pilar.

Remedios Circle Clubs: Trendy and chic bistros include all the cafés listed above under Western restaurants. Many have entertainment or drag shows and sometimes collect a modest cover charge on weekends or for special events.

Girlie Bars in Pasay

Manila's nightclubs, bars, and strip joints, once located along del Pilar and Mabini

Pasay nightlife

CARL PARKES

Streets in the heart of the tourist district, were closed down several years ago by the ever-vigilant Mayor Alfredo Lim—a blow that devastated the local tourism industry and almost destroyed the once-famous tourist quarter. Boarded-up doorways, burned-out nightclubs, and scores of homeless squatters are the legacy of Mr. Lim, a puritanical mayor who never bothered to close the prostitution dens in Chinatown, Quezon City, and other districts under his command.

Many of the nightclub owners packed up their bags and headed south a few kilometers to the neighboring town of Pasay where they reopened their clubs along Roxas Boulevard and in the so-called Edsa Entertainment Complex.

Vixens Niteclub: The old spirit of Ermita lives on in this immensely popular nightclub packed with expats and tourists every night of the week. Drinks are P40 during happy hours 1700-1900 and P65 at all other times. Very friendly staff and the Western owners constantly give away free drinks to new clients. This is probably the best bar of its kind in the country. 2102 Roxas Boulevard.

East Asia and Babylon: Just south of Vixens is a pair of Filipino "showgirl" nightclubs. Shows start around 2300. Rather than pay the P300 entrance fee, ask to sit down first to get a feel for the place. After 10 minutes you'll be ready to leave. 2200 Roxas Boulevard.

Pussycat: Great looking frontage and flashy neon signs but a place in perpetual decline. 2265 Roxas Boulevard.

Visions: The former Vagabond Club renamed itself in 1998 to bring in new business. The setting is quite attractive but the place always seems deserted, although it's probably worth a short stop while doing the nightclubs located up and down Roxas Boulevard.

Edsa Entertainment Complex: Somewhat sterile and overpriced but the most concentrated collection of girlie nightclubs in the country. Clubs include the (once) infamous Firehouse, My Fair Club, Esperanza (a hostess club), Pitstop (with car decor), and the Cotton Club (the former Australian Club). My Fair Club seems to be the most popular club in this complex, but it's not as cozy

or friendly as Vixens, while the Firehouse is nothing like its earlier incarnation in Ermita.

Girlie Bars in Makati

A small go-go scene survives on Burgos Street just outside the perimeter of the Makati district. Prices are high and there's little competition between clubs since most venues (Dimples, Papillon, Friday's, Rascals, and Ivory) are owned and operated by a single individual. Go early and take advantage of happy hour.

Jools: One of the best nightclubs in the Philippines isn't cheap but keeps everybody happy with its two floors of dancers and nightly floor shows about the best in the country. Floor shows demand a P150 cover charge, customer drinks are P90, while ladies' drinks are P220—cheap for Makati. This floor show offers no nudity but the costumes and choreography are first-rate. The live rock bands that play here are also quite superb.

Rogues: Right at the bottom of Burgos Street is a small but comfortable club with a pool table and freelance working girls.

Ritzy's: Many visitors would call this the second best nightclub in Makati after Jools. The place has roomy stages for the dancers and an excellent sound system, plus the mamasan doesn't press customers to constantly purchase drinks for the ladies.

Nightwatch: Another traditional Filipino striptease house with a cover charge of P150 and about 20-25 dancers. One of the best clubs of its type in the country and far superior to its sleazy competitors over in Pasay City.

Playhouse: Live rock bands play here five nights a week from 2200-0500. Rather than bands that play cover hits, this place brings in Filipino musicians who actually write and perform original songs—something you rarely find in this country. An excellent place to rock out.

Foxy's: A new club on Kalayaan Street with some of the best design and sound system in Manila, including a two-tiered stage, upstairs sushi bar, and comfortable private lounges. Jool's has finally got some competition in Makati from this new club, which is owned by the same folks from Ritzy's.

GETTING THERE AND GETTING AROUND

Airport Arrival

Manila International Airport (officially, it's the Ninoy Aquino International Airport) is 12 km from city center. After immigration and customs you can pick up tourist information at the Department of Tourism counter and change money at the bank outlets. Rates are good; ask for small change for the cab drivers and don't get freaked out by the enormous crowd of Filipinos waiting for friends and relatives.

Getting from the airport to your hotel without getting ripped off is difficult, but not impossible. Buses leave from the main road some 200 km from the airport terminal, but most visitors take a taxi to avoid getting lost.

Taxis

Metered taxis in Manila are about the cheapest in Southeast Asia when operating properly with well-calibrated meters. Fares average just over P10 per kilometer. There are some problems, however. Cab drivers waiting at the airport and near tourist hotels often claim their meters are broken and then attempt to negotiate flat fees. Always confirm that the meter is operating before getting into any cab.

The airport has a taxi counter where you can purchase taxi coupons to any hotel, but this service is badly overpriced at P300-500 per destination. Ignore all the taxi touts who will pounce on you the moment you enter the airport lobby or exit any door. Instead, walk up the stairs to the departure level, head out the front door, and wait for a taxi to let off passengers. There's also a small taxi halt about 30 meters to the right of the door where the taxis miraculously use their meters. The correct fare to any hotel in Ermita or Makati is P80-100, but you should figure on P100 after including a small tip.

Whether you use the taxi stand or flag down an arriving taxi, confirm with the driver that the meter is working properly and tell him you know the correct fare should be around P100. Do not get inside any taxi that refuses to use the meter or claims the meter is broken—cheating tourists is a major industry among taxi drivers in Manila.

Some drivers will try to renegotiate the fare as they roar down Roxas Boulevard, or illegally attempt to collect individual fares from each passenger. Don't fall for these tricks. If you have a problem, keep quiet until you arrive at your hotel and have unloaded your baggage. Take your gear inside the hotel and explain to the front desk that your taxi driver is attempting to cheat you. Another strategy is to unload your bags, drop them in the lobby, and then return to the taxi and pay the driver a flat fee of P100.

Baggage should be carried inside the cab or carefully watched while it's being loaded in the trunk.

Jeepneys

To take jeepneys around Manila you must learn a few important place-names. Signs above the driver and on the side refer to either a major suburb such as Cubao or Quiapo, an important landmark such as Monumento, or a major street such as Ayala Street in Makati.

Jeepneys going south along del Pilar or Taft Avenues are marked either Libertad, Baclaran, Vito Cruz, or Pasay. These are useful for reaching the Cultural Center, the Philippine Village, and the zoo.

Jeepneys going north along Mabini or Taft are marked Quiapo, Santa Cruz, Divisoria, Blumentritt, or Monumento. All northbound jeepneys pass the Lawton bus terminal and post office before passing over the Pasig River to Quiapo and Chinatown. The fare is P2 for shorter distances and P2-8 for longer journeys. In most cases, you just hand the driver P2.

Front seats are the most highly prized since you can actually see where you are going. Drivers stop on demand when you hiss, rap on the roof, or call out *"para"* or *"bayad."* Blasting disco music was mercifully banned in jeepneys a few years ago, but the flashing Christs and cheeky slogans carry on.

Buses

Buses also display their destinations on the front and sides. Most buses follow a circular route from Taft Avenue in Ermita out to Makati, up EDSA highway to Quezon City, then south to Quaipo before returning to Ermita. Also vice versa.

Light Rail Transit (LRT)

Manila's Metrorail or LRT is a fast and comfortable way to reach Baclaran in south Manila for the Philtranco and Victory Liner bus terminals, and to go north to Victory Liner and Philippine Rabbit bus terminals. The LRT also reaches Quiapo and the Chinese cemetery. When time is important, take the LRT.

GETTING AWAY

BY AIR

International flights leave from the **Ninoy Aquino International Airport** (NAIA), while domestic flights leave from the domestic terminal about two km away.

Philippine Airlines in the PAL building on Legaspi Street in Makati is as perpetually crowded as its branch office on Roxas Boulevard in Ermita. There's also a PAL office inside the Manila Hotel and the Inter-Continental in Makati. Most of the smaller, newer domestic airlines have offices at the domestic terminal.

A metered taxi from Ermita or Makati to NAIA or the domestic terminal should cost P100-120.

Airport departure tax for international flights is P500.

BY BUS

Manila has eight major bus companies and several bus terminals located on the outskirts of town. It's impossible to catch a long-distance bus from Ermita or Makati; you'll need to first take a taxi or bus to one of the outlying bus terminals.

Philippine Rabbit (Santa Cruz): Buses to central and northwestern Luzon including Angeles, Baguio, and the La Union beaches. 819 Oroquieta, Santa Cruz. Take a jeepney on Mabini marked Monumento or Metrorail to D Jose Station.

Philippine Rabbit (Caloocan): Buses to central and northwestern Luzon including Angeles, San Fernando, and Vigan. Rizal Avenue Extension at 2nd Avenue. Take Monumento jeepney or Metrorail to R Papa Station.

Victory Liner (Caloocan): Buses to central Luzon including Olongapo, Alaminos, and Dagupan. 713 Rizal Avenue Extension, Caloocan (near the Bonifacio Monument). Take Monumento jeepney or Metrorail to North Terminal.

BLTB: Buses to southern Luzon including Santa Cruz (for Pagsanjan Falls), Tagaytay, Nasugbu, Batangas, Naga, and Legaspi. EDSA, Pasay City. Take a taxi or Metrorail to EDSA Station and walk east.

Philtranco: Buses to southern Luzon, Samar, and Leyte. It's even possible (though suicidal) to take a direct 44-hour bus to Davao City in southern Mindanao. EDSA, Pasay City. Take a taxi or Metrorail to the EDSA Station.

BY TRAIN

Southbound trains depart **Paco Station** on President Quirino Avenue. To reach the station, take a taxi or tricycle. Trains depart nightly toward Legaspi but terminate at Naga City. The train is rough but memorable, especially as you leave Manila and all the children in the slums wave at you with amazed delight.

First class is very cheap and includes fairly comfortable seats that recline. The bathrooms are disgusting but this might be a superior choice to taking a mad bus ride down the peninsula to Naga or Legaspi.

BY SHIP

Shipping Terminals

Most interisland passenger vessels dock at North Harbor. The area north of the river is particular-

MAJOR SHIPPING LINES IN MANILA

Asuncion Shipping: Pier 2, North Harbor, tel. (02) 204-024; destinations—Lubang/Mindoro, Palawan (Coron and Culion)

MBRS Lines: Pier 8, North Harbor, tel. (02) 921-6716; destinations—Panay and Romblon

Negros Navigation: Pier 2, North Harbor, tel. (02) 251-1103; destinations—Negros and Panay

Sulpicio Lines: Pier 12, North Harbor, tel. (02) 252-6281; destinations—Cebu, Bohol, Leyte, Masbate, Mindanao, Negros, Palawan, and Panay

WG&A (Williams, Gothong, and Aboitiz Lines): destinations—Cebu, Leyte, Mindanao, Negros, Palawan, Panay, Romblon, and Samar. Contact any of the following offices:

Aboitiz Lines; Pier 4, North Harbor, tel. (02) 894-3211

Gothong Lines; Pier 10, North Harbor, tel. (02) 214-121

Williams Lines; Pier 14, North Harbor, tel. (02) 219-821

ly congested, so allow at least an hour from Ermita. Take a northbound jeepney on Taft or Mabini to Divisoria. A few hundred meters before reaching C.M. Recto, it will become embroiled in a horrendous traffic jam, and it's much quicker to get out and walk straight ahead to Recto instead. Watch for pickpockets in this area. On the north side of Recto, jeepneys load for North Harbor. Upon reaching the Port District, they turn right near Pier 4. For Piers 2 and 4 get off here; continue on for Piers 6 to 14.

To avoid the byzantine twists and turns of the jeepney ride, take a taxi. First attempt to find a taxi driver who will use his meter to the port and figure on P40-60 for the journey. Most will refuse. In that case, negotiate a fixed rate of P60-100 for the trip.

Outside Christmas and Easter, it's normally possible to buy a ticket at the pier on the day of departure. To obtain a ticket in advance, some shipping lines have branches or agents in Ermita or Binondo, while others have offices only at North Harbor.

On the north bank of the Pasig, west of Del Pan (or Roxas) Bridge by the San Miguel brewery, is a wharf from which cargo/passenger vessels depart on an unscheduled basis for various small and relatively isolated ports. Islands served include Coron, Cuyo, Lubang, Marinduque, Mindoro, Palawan, and Romblon. The only way to get information on planned sailing times is to go to the wharf and ask.

Major Shipping Lines

Several years ago, three of the largest shipping companies in the Philippines merged to form a super company that now dominates commercial shipping traffic in the country. The merger of William, Gothong, and Aboitiz Lines into WG&A dramatically changed the nature of the industry, though their respective ships continue to leave from their individual ports.

Exact departure times and destinations are listed in most daily Manila newspapers, including the *Manila Bulletin*.

All shipping companies continue to sell advance tickets at their offices at North Harbor and also sell tickets directly on board each ship shortly before and shortly after departure. WG&A has an office on the corner of M.H. del Pilar and San Andreas Streets in Malate. This is the most convenient place to buy tickets in advance and ensure yourself of a sleeping berth prior to departure.

Several travel agencies in Ermita and Malate also sell advance tickets for a modest premium.

To Bohol

The WG&A MV *Superferry 5* leaves Manila for Tagbilaran on Tuesday at 0700, while its *Superferry 7* departs on Saturday at 0700. The trip takes 36 hours and costs P550-650.

Sulpicio Lines' MV *Dipolog Princess* departs Manila for Bohol on Wednesday at 1200 and takes a somewhat shorter 28 hours to reach Tagbilaran.

To Catanduanes

Ships to this island near southern Luzon do not leave from Manila but rather from Tabaco, a small port between Naga City and Legaspi in southern Luzon. The MV *Regina Calixta* of the Regina Shipping Line departs Tabaco daily for San Andres on Catanduanes at 0800 and takes about three hours.

The MV *Eugenia* of the Bicolano Line leaves Tabaco daily for Virac on Catanduanes at 0800 and takes four hours.

To Cebu

This is probably the most popular shipping route from Manila with the possible exception of excursions to Palawan. Ships to Cebu take about 22-26 hours and cost P500-650 depending on the line.

WG&A has three ships to Cebu City. Its MV *Superferry 8* departs Manila on Monday at 0900, Wednesday at 1500, and Friday at 1900, MV *Superferry 6* leaves Saturday at 1500, and MV *Superferry 10* leaves Sunday at 0900, Tuesday at 1500, and Thursday at 1900.

Sulpicio Lines has the MV *Princess of the Orient* on Tuesday at 1000 and Friday at 2000. The same line also provides the MV *Princess of Paradise* on Wednesday at 1000, and the MV *Filipina Princess* on Sunday at 1000.

To Leyte

Most travelers will reach Leyte by bus through southern Luzon and Samar, though direct shipping service is available from several lines.

WG&A's MV *Masbate Uno* leaves Manila on Monday at 1000 and takes 30 hours to Tacloban with a short stop at Catbalogan on Samar. Travelers can also pick up this ship in Catbalogan and enjoy a scenic alternative to the somewhat boring bus trip from Catbalogan to Tacloban. The Manila-Tacloban route with the MV *Masbate Uno* is repeated from Manila on Friday at 1900.

Sulpicio Lines offers the MV *Tacloban Princess*, which leaves Manila for Tacloban on Wednesday at 1000 and Sunday at 0900. The trip takes around 24 hours and costs P450-550.

To Lubang

There are several ways to reach this small island just off the coast from Batangas Province. Asuncion Shipping has the MV *Catalyn B,* which leaves Manila to Tilik on Monday, Thursday, and Saturday at 2100. The trip takes eight hours and drops you at daybreak at the small town harbor.

You can also go with an outrigger from Nasugbu to Tilik on Monday, Wednesday, and Friday. The journey with Montenegro Shipping Line takes just under three hours.

To Marinduque

Marinduque is mostly known for its festivals but also offers some untouched beaches within relatively easy striking distance of Manila. Ships leave from Lucena City, not Manila.

From Lucena, take Viva Shipping's MV *San Agustin Reyes* daily at 0800 and 1400 for the three-hour crossing to Balanacan on Marinduque. This ship leaves from the Dalahican Pier in Lucena.

You can also catch a daily ferry that leaves from the Cotto Pier in Lucena between 0800-1000 and takes about four hours to reach Santa Cruz on Marinduque.

To Masbate

Travelers can reach this island from either Manila, Lucena, or Bulan in the Sorsogon district of southern Luzon.

WG&A provides service from Manila on the MV *Sacred Heart* on Monday at 2100. Figure on about 18 hours for the trip. Sulpicio Lines has the MV *Palawan Princess,* which leaves Manila for Masbate on Wednesday at 2200, and the MV *Cebu Princess,* which departs WG&A's Manila pier on Friday at 1000. These journeys take 20-24 hours to Masbate.

From Lucena, you can take Viva Shipping's MV *Viva Penafrancia V* on Monday, Thursday, and Saturday at 1900 or the MV *Santa Maria* on Tuesday, Friday, and Sunday at the same departure hour.

Travelers hanging out in Bulan can catch the MV *Matea I,* which leaves daily at 1200 and takes less than four hours to reach the cattle island of Masbate.

To Mindanao

Taking a ship from Manila to any port in Mindanao may seem a great deal of trouble, but you'll save some money over the airfare and perhaps have some kind of memorable experience in the process. Ships go from Manila to almost every city and town of any size on Mindanao, but perhaps the best choice is the route to Surigao at the northeastern tip of Mindanao. After exploring the nearby islands (Siargao, etc.), you can take a bus west along the northern coast of Mindanao and visit the immensely attractive island of Camiguin. After that, you can take a fast ferry or slow ship from nearby Cagayan de Oro back to Cebu City or head south to Davao and the tribal areas in southwestern Mindanao (Lake Sebu is recommended).

The following destinations are listed in alphabetical order. You might just go directly to the listing for Surigao or Cagayan de Oro, if your main interest is the island of Camiguin.

To Butuan: WG&A's MV *Superferry 2* leaves Monday at 1600 and takes 40 hours to Butuan via Iloilo City on Panay. The same company also runs the MV *Medjugorje* every Thursday at 2200, a direct service that only takes a quick 32 hours; bring a good book.

To Cagayan de Oro: This is a very popular route since it puts you near Camiguin Island and within striking distance of Surigao and Siargao Island. Plenty of ships make this crossing each week. WG&A has the MV *Superferry 5* on Tuesday at 0700 via Tagbilaran and the MV *Superferry 9* on Wednesday at 2200 via Iloilo City on Panay. Both ships take about 36 hours to reach Cagayan de Oro. The same company also has the MV *Superferry 7*, which departs Manila every Saturday at 0700 and takes 35 hours with a stop at Tagbilaran on Bohol.

Negros Navigation provides the MV *Santa Ana*, which leaves Manila on Friday at 1400 and takes 45 hours via Iloilo City on Panay.

Finally, there's the MV *Princess of Paradise* of Sulpicio Lines, which leaves Saturday at 0800 and makes a direct run to Cagayan de Oro in just under 26 hours. Pretty quick, with no stops.

To Cotabato: Not the most popular of routes, but here goes: WG&A's MV *Superferry 3* sails from Manila to this tourist hotspot on Friday at 2200 with a stop in beautiful Zamboanga; the trip takes just over 45 hours and costs P850-950. The same company also runs the MV *Maynilad*, which leaves Maynilad (Manila) on Sunday at 1900 and takes an amazing 65 hours with excruciating stops at Dumaguete on Ne-

gros and Dipolog on the north coast of Mindanao. Only for masochists.

To Davao: Figure on 46-54 hours with a cost of P950-1,100. WG&A has the MV *Superferry 6* on Tuesday at 0800 with a stop in Surigao, while its MV *Superferry 1* makes the trip on Saturday at 1500 with a stop in Iloilo City on Panay.

Sulpicio provides service on the MV *Filipina Princess* every Sunday at 1000 with stops in Cebu City and Surigao; total travel time of 52-54 hours. Bring patience, a good book, and several bottles of Tanduay rum.

To Dipolog: This isn't a bad destination since you can visit the sights near Dipolog and Dapitan and then head east along the northern coast of Mindanao to Cagayan de Oro, Camiguin Island, and then Surigao for the nearby lovely islands of Siargao and others. WG&A provides the MV *Maynilad*, which leaves Manila every Sunday at 1900 and takes 38 hours via Dumaguete on Negros. It then heads south down to Cotabato.

To General Santos City: Travelers interested in the tribal areas near Lake Sebu may find this connection useful. WG&A has the MV *Dona Virginia*, which leaves Manila on Tuesday at 1200 and takes 44 hours with a stop in Zamboanga. It also has the MV *Superferry 1*, which leaves on Saturday at 1500 and takes 43 hours via Iloilo and then heads on to the big city of Davao.

To Iligan: Not the most popular route, though WG&A sails its MV *Superferry 7* on Tuesday at 0500 via Dumaguete in just about 35 hours. Figure on P600-700 depending on class. The same company also runs the MV *Superferry 5*, which reaches Iligan in 36 hours with a stop in Iloilo on Panay.

To Ozamis: WG&A sails its MV *Medjugorje* on Monday at 0900; the trip takes about 36 hours.

To Surigao: Probably the most logical trip to make from Manila with the possible exception of Cebu City. WG&A has the MV *Superferry 6* on Tuesday at 0800, which takes just 26 hours before continuing down to Davao.

Sulpicio runs the MV *Palawan Princess*, which leaves Manila on Wednesday at 2200 and takes an uncomfortable 54 hours to Surigao with stops at all sorts of places such as Masbate and Maasin on Leyte. The slow boat to China, so to speak. The same company also has the somewhat faster, but still slow, MV *Filipina Princess,* which leaves Manila on Sunday at 1000 and takes 45 hours to Surigao with a stop at Cebu City. The ship then continues down to Davao City.

To Zamboanga: Durian lovers and lovers of the Sulu Archipelago may find these ships an economical way to reach the queen of the south. WG&A has the MV *Dona Virginia* on Tuesday at 1200 and the MV *Superferry 3* on Friday at 2200. Both services take 28-32 hours and continue on to either General Santos City or Cotabato.

Sulpicio provides an alternative with its MV *Cotabato Princess,* which leaves Manila on Saturday at 1500 and takes 45 hours with a stop at Iloilo City on Panay. This ship continues on to Cotabato.

To Mindoro

Most travelers take the public bus, or the charter bus from the Centrepoint Hotel in Ermita, to Batangas and then continue by ferry across to Puerto Galera.

To Puerto Galera: Several small shipping lines have ferries from Batangas City across to Puerto Galera. Santo Domingo Shipping has the MV *Santa Penafrancia VI,* which leaves daily at 0830, 1230, and 1700 and takes about 90 minutes to reach Balatero, three km west of Puerto Galera.

One of the most popular tourist services is the Si-Kat Ferry MV *Si-Kat II,* which leaves Batangas around 1200 and takes just under two hours to reach Puerto Galera. This is the tourist boat that can be booked at the Centrepoint Hotel in Ermita. The ticket includes an a/c bus from Manila to the ferry terminal. Budget travelers can save some money by taking ordinary public transport from Manila, though most visitors heading to Puerto Galera are hardly concerned with saving a few pesos in the process—this is a place for tourists with their Filipina girlfriends or Western scuba divers on a short holiday.

If you miss a larger ferry, and the seas are calm, you might catch one of the big outriggers. Several outriggers make the crossing during calm waters at around 0930, 1030, 1200, and 1330. The MV *Sabang Princess* is probably the largest and safest of the bunch. If you need to charter the entire vessel, figure on a total cost of P650-900.

To Calapan: Most visitors head directly to Puerto Galera, though service is also available to Calapan just south of the beach resorts. From Calapan, you can catch a jeepney to Puerto Galera. This option takes an additional two hours, and service ends daily around 1600.

Aboitiz has the MV *Supercat,* which leaves daily at 0730, 1100, 1430, and 1930 and makes the crossing in less than one hour. Fast ferry choices include the MV *Lourdes* and MV *Fatima,* which cross eight times daily.

More Options: You can also catch boats from Batangas pier to several other towns on Mindoro. Viva Shipping has the MV *Penafrancia* and the MV *Christopher,* which sail from Batangas to Sablayan on Tuesday, Friday, and Sunday. This trip takes just over nine hours and costs P150-200.

You can also go to San Jose with Viva Shipping on its *Marian Queen,* which leaves Batangas at 0700 on Monday, Wednesday, and Saturday. A final option is the MV *Santo Niño* which departs Batangas on Tuesday, Friday, and Sunday at 0700 and takes almost 12 hours to reach San Jose. This is a trip for those heading directly to Boracay who want to skip Puerto Galera.

To Negros

Visitors in a big hurry to reach Bacolod or Dumaguete may want to consider one of the following ship services.

Negros Navigation, as you might expect from the name, provides service from Manila to Bacolod on its MV *Princess of Negros* on Tuesday at 2100 and Friday at 1200. The trip takes around 22 hours and costs P500-620. Negros also operates the MV *San Paolo,* which leaves Manila's North Harbor on Sunday at 1400 and Wednesday at 1600. These services are somewhat quicker at just under 20 hours.

You can also go from Manila direct to Dumaguete. WG&A has the MV *Superferry 7,* which leaves Manila on Tuesday at 1700 and takes 26 hours, and the MV *Maynilad,* which leaves on Sunday at 1900 and does the trip in a slightly lengthier 32 hours.

Sulpicio provides the MV *Philippine Princess,* which leaves Manila on Wednesday at 1200 and takes just over 25 hours to reach Dumaguete.

To Palawan

Flying to Puerto Princesa isn't very expensive, but some travelers may prefer the less expensive shipping options, which also stop at some very unusual islands to the north of Palawan. You might consider hopping off the ship in some remote port to the north of El Nido and then island jumping down to El Nido and onward to Sabang and Puerto Princesa.

To Puerto Princesa: WG&A's MV *Superferry 3* departs Manila for Puerto Princesa on Wednesday at 1000 and takes just under 26 hours to make the direct passage. Sulpicio Lines' MV *Ilolio Princess* heads off from Manila every Thursday at 1000 and Sunday at 1400 and takes the same amount of time to reach the capital city of Palawan.

To Coron: You might want to visit a smaller island before reaching the main destination of Palawan proper. Asuncion Shipping's MV *Catalyn* leaves Manila on Wednesday at 1600 and makes a stop in Coron 22 hours later. The same company also has the MV *Asuncion VII,* which leaves Manila on Thursday at 1600, and MV *Asuncion XI,* which leaves on Saturday at 1600. Both of these ships stop in Coron, from where other ships and outriggers can be found to El Nido and other points in Northern Palawan.

To El Nido: Why go to Puerto Princesa? Asuncion Shipping offers the MV *Asuncion IV,* which leaves Manila on Wednesday at 1900 and takes almost 30 hours to reach El Nido. This service is a reasonable alternative to direct (and expensive) flights to El Nido, or going to Puerto Princesa and then attempting to survive the long and very tiring overland journey.

Batangas to Coron: Viva Shipping provides better conditions with its ships from Batangas. The MV *Viva Santa Ana* departs the port of Batangas every Monday at 1800 for Coron. The ship then continues down to Culion. The same line also runs the MV *Viva Penafrancia IX* from Batangas on Thursday at 1800 and the MV *Maria Socorro* on Saturday at 1800.

To Panay and Boracay

Few travelers bother with shipping connections with Panay, though this route provides a cheaper way to reach Boracay than the somewhat expensive flights to Kalibo or the definitely expensive direct flight to Caticlan near Boracay.

MBRS Line has the MV *Romblon Bay,* which leaves Manila on Tuesday at 1300 and Friday at 1400 and takes about 22 hours to reach Caticlan.

WG&A provides the *Superferry 1,* which sails from Manila once weekly (mostly during the high tourist season) direct to Caticlan. You should call for current information.

Negros Navigation provides a roundabout route to Boracay via the port of Dumaguit, near Kalibo. Not the most convenient of services, but a savings for the truly frugal. The MV *Don Julio* departs Manila on Wednesday at 1500 and takes 16 hours to the port just east of Boracay and Caticlan. WG&A has its MV *Our Lady of Naju,* which leaves Manila on Monday, Wednesday, and Sunday at 1400 for the 15-hour journey to this rarely used port just east of Caticlan.

Another option is to head to Estancia and then continue by bus or minivan to Caticlan. Sulpicio has the MV *Cotabato Princess,* which leaves Manila on Saturday at 1500 and takes 17 hours to Estancia. The ship then continues on to Iloilo City on Panay.

You could also go to Iloilo City and then head north to Kalibo and Caticlan by public bus or private minibus. Negros Navigation has the MV *Saint Francis of Assisi,* which leaves Manila on Monday, Thursday, and Saturday at 1200 and takes 18 hours to reach Iloilo. You can walk to the hotels in city center from the pier.

WG&A has the MV *Superferry 9* on Wednesday at 2000 and the MV *Superferry 1* on Thursday at 1700 and Saturday at 1500. Both take around 18 hours to Iloilo. The same company also runs the MV *Superferry 5* on Friday at 1500.

Sulpicio hangs in there with its MV *Princess of the Pacific,* which sails out of Manila Harbor every Tuesday at 1000 and takes 19 hours to reach Iloilo. Sulpicio also offers the MV *Cotabato Princess,* which splits the North Harbor on Saturday at 1500 and takes 25 hours to Iloilo via Estancia.

Additional services to Iloilo are provided by Negros Navigation's MV *Don Claudio,* which departs Manila on Monday at 1300 and Thursday at 1700, plus the MV *Don Julio,* which sets sail (so to speak) on Saturday at 1700. Figure on 16-20 hours with these services.

To Romblon

Romblon, "Marble Island." Interested in marble?

MBRS Line has its MV *Salve Juliana,* which leaves Manila on Tuesday at 1300 and Friday at 1500 and takes 15 hours to the principal town of Romblon.

You can also get there from Batangas by booking a trip with Viva Shipping, which operates the MV *Viva Penafrancia VIII* on Monday, Thursday, and Saturday at 1900. The trip takes 10 hours, goes from Batangas to San Agustin on Tablas Island, then continues on to Romblon on Romblon Island then finally Magdiwang on Sibuyan Island. Quite the trip.

You can also go from Batangas to Odiongan on Tablas Island with Viva Shipping, which operates the MV *Viva Penafrancia IV* on Tuesday, Thursday, and Saturday at 1800. The trip takes about six hours. The same company also operates the MV *Saint Kristopher,* which leaves Batangas on Wednesday, Friday, and Sunday at 1800 and takes almost eight hours to reach Romblon.

Somewhat faster are the RN Hi-Speed Ferries such as the MV *Florida,* which leaves on Monday and Saturday at 1600 and takes just over four hours to reach Romblon.

To Samar

Visitors just dying to get to Samar can hop several different shipping lines. A singular service heads south from Manila, but overland travelers will need to face the realities of ferries from Matnog to Allen on Northern Samar.

As you might expect, WG&A provides the best service with the MV *Masbate Uno,* leaving Manila on Monday at 1000 and taking almost 24 hours to reach the hip-hop city of Catbalogan.

More useful are the smaller ferries heading from southern dustholes on Luzon (namely Matnog) to northern dustholes on Samar (say, Allen). The MV *Michelangelo* and MV *Northern Samar* provide essential connections from Matnog to Allen. These ferries leave daily around 1000 and perhaps another departure at 1600 (be cautious, as the 1600 departure is subject to cancellation in the event of bad weather or insufficient passengers). However, it's best to leave Legaspi early in the morning and catch the first departure from Matnog; Matnog is not a town in which you want to spend a great deal of time hanging out.

Another ferry, the MV *Marhalika 1* of the famed St. Bernard Shipping Line, leaves Matnog for Isidro daily at 0600 and 1230. The crossing takes about two hours.

The sole cause of man's unhappiness is that he does not know how to stay quietly in his own room.
—*Blaise Pascal,* Pensées

You do not see that the Real is in your own home,
And you wander from forest to forest listlessly.
Here is the truth!
Go where you will,
to Banaras or to Mathura,
If you do not find God in your own soul
The world will be meaningless to you.

—*Kabir*

Peculiar travel suggestions are dancing lessons from God.

—*Kurt Vonnegut*

SOUTH OF MANILA

The area south of Manila, the region between Manila and the Bicol Peninsula, comprises Cavite, Batangas, Laguna, and Rizal Provinces—the latter also wraps around Manila and includes some destinations both east and north of the capital.

The terrain consists of scattered volcanic peaks, rolling uplands, and limited plains, while its dominating feature is Taal Lake and volcano, one of the Philippines's principal tourist sights. In addition to this active cone, a line of dormant volcanoes from Makiling to Banahaw separates the area from Laguna de Bay, while several older, weathered volcanoes rise from the plains, where volcanic deposits have formed fertile soil.

Offshore islands include Maricaban and Verde Island (Batangas), and the Polillo group and Alabat Island (Quezon) on the Pacific side. Quezon—described in the Southern Luzon chapter—is also the gateway to the island province of Marinduque.

Many visitors go to Tagaytay for the spectacular view of Taal Lake, or pass through by bus en route from Manila, via Batangas City, to Puerto Galera, Mindoro. This region, however, has much more to offer the visitor—places like Matabungkay beach, the first-class resorts of Puerto Azul and Calatagan, the dive camps of Anilao, little-visited places like the Polillo and Pagbilao islands, and colorful festivals in Pahiyas and the May harvest celebration of Lucban.

CAVITE PROVINCE

Proximity to Manila means this province can be visited as either a day trip from the capital or an overnight destination. The most popular excursion is to Tagaytay overlooking the Taal volcano. The Aguinaldo Shrine at Kawit, just outside Manila, has a special place in Philippine history

as the home of revolutionary hero Gen. Emilio Aguinaldo.

History
Cavite's proximity to Manila and Manila Bay ensured it a prominent place in the nation's past;

historical markers can be found throughout the province. It's believed that the Chinese were mooring their junks and trading at Sangley Point, on the tip of Cavite Peninsula, by the early 13th century. From there, they crossed to the Pasig River and Laguna de Bay. Sangley is said to be an adaptation of *seng-li* or *xang-li* ("trader" in the Amoy Chinese dialect).

Cavite was sparsely populated when the Spanish arrived. They founded what's now Cavite City in 1571 and fortified it against Moro raiders. *Encomiendas* were granted, and Cavite was designated a politico-military province in 1614. It became a Jesuit stronghold. During the 17th century, Cavite City developed as a center for shipbuilding and naval operations. Giant *molave* trees from the forests around Paete were floated across Laguna de Bay, down the Pasig River, and across Manila Bay to Cavite, where many of the great Manila galleons were built. Cavite City was attacked by the Dutch in 1647, and the British landed here during their 1762 invasion.

Cavite played a crucial role in the struggle for independence. The 1872 mutiny of about 200 native soldiers and workers in Cavite City's ar-

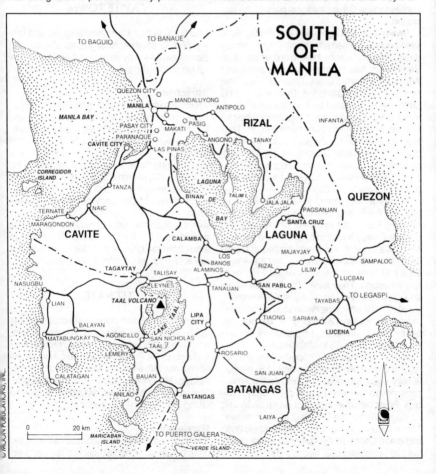

senal, in which they killed their Spanish officers, was swiftly suppressed, but it led to the unjust implication and execution of the Filipino priests Gomez, Burgos, and Zamora. This incident helped focus and inflame the native desire to be rid of the Spanish, and the province was among the first to rise in arms in 1896. Cavite produced many revolutionary leaders and saw much action.

The small, flamboyant general Emilio Aguinaldo (1869-1964) of Kawit came to prominence when he led the Katipuneros in taking Kawit, Binakayan, and several other settlements. His success made Cavite the focal point of the revolution.

Rivalry between Aguinaldo and Andres Bonifacio became intense after a split in revolutionary ranks between factions loyal to one or the other. Bonifacio's headquarters was at Imus and Aguinaldo's at what is now General Trias. After conciliatory attempts failed, Bonifacio and his brother were arrested by the Aguinaldo group, taken to Maragondon, tried, and condemned for sedition by a revolutionary military court. They were executed on Mt. Buntis, outside Maragondon. After this, the revolutionaries' disunity, compounded by a lack of arms and supplies, enabled the Spaniards to recapture town after town and regain control of Cavite.

Aguinaldo was forced to retreat to Bulacan, and after the Pact of Biak-na-Bato he was exiled to Hong Kong, but returned after U.S. Commodore Dewey had destroyed the Spanish fleet off Cavite's coast. Aguinaldo landed at Cavite on 19 May 1898 and, believing that the Americans had come as liberators, urged Filipinos to rise in support. They routed the Spanish forces throughout most of Luzon. Aguinaldo's home in Kawit was the site of the declaration of Philippine Independence on 12 June 1898. Bacoor was briefly the capital of the revolutionary government before it moved to Malalos.

In the same year the Philippines declared independence from Spain, the first U.S. expeditionary force debarked at Cavite as the Americans moved to take control of the country. Sangley Point became the chief naval base and coaling station of the U.S. fleet in Asian waters. These installations and the city's strategic position made Cavite a key Japanese target during the 1941 invasion. U.S. troops parachuted onto Tagaytay Ridge to join others who had landed at Nasugbu (Batangas) before advancing north to liberate Manila.

Transportation
The two main routes, served by frequent transportation, are along the bayshore, where Cavite City is the largest center, or inland to Tagaytay. Minibuses from Baclaran go to most towns in Cavite. Other buses leave from terminals in Manila for Zapote, Cavite City, and Tagaytay.

CAVITE TOWN

This bustling city, a commercial center and fishing port, is situated near the tip of a curving peninsula, 34 km by road from Manila, but only 12 km across the bay.

Attractions
An old Spanish shipbuilding and naval center, Cavite was once like Manila's Intramuros, with fortified walls, narrow cobbled streets, and colonial houses, some with decorated eaves and gables; only a few have survived WW II. The ruins of Porta Vega, a stone fort destroyed by the Dutch in 1647, are still standing, however, among houses behind the city hall.

The Feast of Our Lady of Solitude is celebrated at Porta Vega each 3 October. Other sights include the former provincial capitol and the old church in the San Roque district. A road leads from the city center to the tip of land and naval facilities at Sangley Point.

TERNATE

When the Spanish decided to withdraw from the northern Moluccan islands of Ternate, Tidore, and Siao in 1663, the Jesuit priests brought their converts to the Philippines and built them a new settlement with a familiar name; hence Ternate. Aplayita is a popular beach here; take a tricycle. The area to the southwest, around Mt. Mataas na Gulod (641 meters), is a national park.

Maragondon
A historic Jesuit town, Maragondon has a fine old church with an intricately carved door and or-

nate interior. The great revolutionary Andres Bonifacio and his brother were imprisoned in this church prior to their execution on nearby Mt. Buntis on 11 May 1897.

Accommodations

Two expensive places near Ternate cater to the well-heeled type from Manila in need of a weekend escape.

Novotel Puerto Azul Resort: Beyond Ternate, in a rugged natural setting where the low Dos Picos Ranges descend to Manila Bay, is one of the nation's tourism showcases: an impressive resort and country club complex sprawling along seven coves with black-sand beaches. Opened in 1980, it has a Gary Player championship golf course, where numerous international tournaments have taken place. Other activities include swimming, windsurfing, sailing, water-skiing, tennis, squash, bowling, enjoying the gymnasium and sauna, and hiking on orchid-lined trails. The food is excellent and there's nightly entertainment.

Puerto Azul is a 60-km, 90-minute journey from Manila. Ternate tel. (02) 574-731, fax 536-1584, P3,000-5,000.

Caylabne Bay Resort: Tennis courts, swimming pool, golf course, Hobie Cats, and windsurfing are some of the amenities at this upscale bayside resort just outside town. Ternate tel. (02) 815-8385, Manila tel. (02) 814-8800, P2,000-3,000.

TAGAYTAY CITY~ VIEWS OVER TAAL LAKE

Tagaytay is perched on a ridge, 686 meters above Taal Lake and its active island-volcano. The ridge is believed to be part of the crater of a much larger, long-since-collapsed volcano. Today, the ridge forms part of the outer rim of the Taal caldera as it stretches 32 km from Mt. Batulao to Mt. Sungay.

The overlook at Taal Vista Lodge offers a spectacular view of the volcano (about 15 km distant) and lake, making Tagaytay one of the most popular day trips out of Manila. In clear weather, the South China Sea is visible in the distance, though at other times, fog can come sweeping swiftly across the lake.

Folk dancing sometimes takes place at this viewpoint at midday. Hawks glide above, and during March and April huge black-and-yellow birdwing butterflies frequent the ridge. The elevation results in a pleasantly cool climate, with continual breezes, so that some wealthy Filipinos maintain weekend retreats here.

Tagaytay was, in fact, originally established as a potential alternative summer resort to Baguio. Evenings can be chilly, so if you plan to overnight, bring a sweater. Tagaytay City sprawls over 65 square km; it contains extensive market gardens. Numerous fruit stalls usually line the main road.

Tagaytay is a 60-km, 90-minute journey from Manila. It lies on the road to the beaches of Matabungkay (Batangas) and can easily be combined with a trip there.

Palace in the Sky

One of the more remarkable sights near Tagaytay is this magnificently situated, partially completed, never-occupied home of ex-dictator Ferdinand Marcos. Now called People's Park in the Sky, the rather amazing history of this ill-fated project is related on a signpost erected near the front entrance.

The palace briefly made newspaper headlines in May '89 when a helicopter used in filming a Chuck Norris movie crashed into a nearby ravine, killing four people. Early mornings guarantee limitless views from Manila to Batangas and Corregidor.

The palace is up a winding road five km east of Taal Vista Lodge. It's too far to walk, but jeepneys can be chartered from the Tagaytay road junction.

Accommodations

Nothing cheap up here unless you're willing to scrounge around and perhaps do the homestay routine.

Taal Vista Hotel: Swimming pool, horseback riding, and great views from the front lawn over the lake and volcano. Pricey, but the best place up here on the ridge. Tagaytay tel. (046) 413-1223, fax 413-1225, P2,500-3,000.

Villa Adelaida: Located a few kilometers east of Tagaytay, just beyond the junction with the road that descends to Talisay. The suburb is actually called Foggy Heights. The place has a small swimming pool. Tagaytay tel. (046) 413-1267, P1,200-1,600.

Homestays: About three km before Taal Vista Lodge is a traffic circle, just after which is a "Rooms 4 Rent" sign. The owners of Three Sisters' Store also rent an upstairs room.

To Taal Volcano

A jeepney leaves the Tagaytay rotunda at 1100, and possibly at 0800 and 1500, and descends the ridge to the lakeshore at Talisay (Batangas), from where *bancas* may be hired for the trip to the island. Hotels such as Taal Vista will arrange a half-day trip to the volcano for groups of up to five people for those who want to pay a premium for convenience. Taal volcano can also be visited from other lakeside settlements, such as Caloocan, Agoncillo, San Nicolas, or Balete.

Transportation

From Manila, take a minibus from Baclaran or bus (destination Nasugbu) from the BLTB Terminal, Pasay City, which departs every 20 minutes 0400-1730. To get from Tagaytay to Pagsanjan Falls (Laguna), it's actually quicker to head toward Manila: alight at Zapote, take a jeepney across to Alabang, a southbound bus to Santa Cruz, and a jeepney to Pagsanjan.

To go cross-country, take a jeepney down to Talisay, another to Tanauan, then proceed by bus through Calamba or San Pablo. For Batangas City, you can intercept the Manila-Batangas bus route at Alabang or Tanauan, or make your way via Lemery.

TAAL LAKE AND VOLCANO

One hypothesis holds that Taal Lake occupies the caldera of a massive ancient volcano that was possibly as high as 5,500 meters. A cataclysmic eruption is believed to have caused the slopes to cave in, whereupon water rushed in to form the lake, leaving only the tip of the previous peak exposed as the current Volcano Island. A less dramatic theory suggests the lake occupies a geological depression that formed gradually. If there was, indeed, a huge former volcano, its sloping flanks now rise gently to form ridges overlooking the lake.

The highest point on the lakeshore is Mt. Makulot, or Macolod (947 meters), a volcanic cone on the south side. Tagaytay Ridge (686 meters) forms the north wall, while a lower, almost level ridge surrounds the lake on the other sides. A wide fissure opens at the southwest edge of the crater, enabling the lake, which is only slightly above sea level, to drain via the Pansipit River into Balayan Bay.

The 270-square-km lake is about 27 by 17 km, with an irregular shoreline. It contains two islands: Volcano Island (16 square km, 23 km in circumference), which is a national park, and tiny Napayan Island. Taal volcano (300 meters) on Volcano Island is said to be the world's lowest active volcano.

History

Taal Lake was formerly called Bonbon Lake. It has erupted numerous times, causing much death and destruction. Taal's previous activity is the subject of much local folklore, including tales of lost towns and crocodiles thrown 30 meters into the air. The eruptions of 1716, 1754, and 1911 were particularly destructive. Over 5,000 died during the latter, as an outpouring of smoke and lava preceded a giant explosion that caused boiling water and volcanic ash to devastate 235 square km of surrounding countryside. Before this eruption, the crater floor, which was less than two meters above the lake's level, contained two small pools of hot water—one green and the other almost red. After the explosion, only a hole was left. Lake water seeped back into the crater to form another pool.

The volcano was then quiet for 54 years until observers noted that the temperature of the sulfurous water in the crater pool had risen from 30° to 45° C within a few months, thus indicating an impending eruption. It came without further warning at 0200 on 28 September 1965. The sudden explosion opened a new crater, 1.5 km long by 300 meters wide, on the volcano's southwest slope and devastated the island's south side. Debris-laden clouds moved outward with tremendous velocity, in a manner closely resembling the base surge of a thermonuclear blast. They obliterated all trees within a kilometer of the explosion center and sandblasted objects up to eight km distant.

The explosion continued for hours, sending huge clouds 16-20 km into the atmosphere. An estimated 70 million cubic meters of ash blanketed an area of 60 square km. Nearly 200 people died, and several villages were destroyed. This violent eruption was followed between 1965 and 1970 by six more of mild to moderate intensity, lasting from three to 63 days. Taal volcano last erupted in 1978.

Visiting Taal Volcano

Before 1965, 140 families lived on the island; today, only about 30 families have stayed, attracted by the rich, volcanic soil. They farm, fish, and raise ducks. The main points to visit are the active southwest cone and the dormant northwest cone, whose crater contains an applegreen lake that holds a small crescent-shaped island. It's an island in a crater lake on an island in a crater lake on an island! Be sure to wear strong shoes and gloves if possible (for scrambling over hot rocks).

Boats usually land on the beach beside the 1965 lava flow where two villages were buried. This black rock is sharp; be careful when climbing on it. It's an easy 15-minute climb (signposted) to the rim of the new crater, which is usually emitting sulfurous smoke and steam, and occasionally rumbles. A guide isn't necessary for climbing this southwest cone, but is essential for the two-hour return trek along the ridge and around numerous vents to the old northwest cone, from which the view is superb. Wear long trousers and sleeves for protection from the waist-high grass.

The island's inhabitants will act as guides; agree to a fee before setting off. It's pleasant to end the walk with a swim at the island's beach, where a changing booth and shelter have been set up.

No permit is required to visit the volcano during its quiescent periods, but if you read of increased activity in the newspapers, check with the Volcanology Commission. *Bancas* can be hired to visit the volcano from lakeshore settlements such as Talisay, Caloocan, Agoncillo, San Nicolas, and Balete. The crossing takes about 30 minutes; it's longer and more expensive from Balete. Clarify the exact rate and how much time you wish to spend on the island beforehand.

Allow at least half a day for the trip and set off early to avoid the hot midday sun. Also, winds can come up in the afternoon, making the crossing more difficult.

TALISAY~LAKESIDE AT TAAL

Taal Volcano's constant threat hasn't deterred lakeside residents from farming the fertile soil and fishing for *tawilis, maliputo,* and other species. *Inihaw na tawilis* (broiled *tawilis*) and *pinasingawang maliputo* (steamed *maliputo*) are esteemed local dishes. The lake is also said to contain a sea snake that has adapted to fresh water. Numerous tourist resorts and swimming beaches are located around the lakeshore.

Located beneath Tagaytay Ridge, this town's beaches include Tropical, Lakeside, and Tally Ho (Buko). At night, see the lights of fishing boats sparkling out on the water. The catch is beached at the lakeside market at daybreak. Other places to visit are the **Commission on Volcanology** station in nearby Buko and **Bolbok rock spring.** Some local residents accept overnight boarders in their homes for a nominal amount; ask around.

Accommodations

Rosalina's Place: Simple place at the intersection of the descending and lakeside roads. The owner can help with boat rentals and volcano tours. Banga tel. (0973) 373-6066, P250-400.

Milo's Paradise: Family-run with large rooms, swimming pool, and knowledgeable owners. Balas tel. (0973) 372-0318, P650-950.

Taal Lake Guesthouse: Budget option midway between Tagaytay and Talisay. Leynes tel. (0973) 373-6066, P300-500.

Transportation

Lake Taal can be reached from several directions, but the easiest route is by minitruck down from the road junction on Tagaytay Ridge, a steep and extremely winding journey. What a ride! You can also go direct from Manila with any BLTB bus marked Batangas. Get off in Tanauan and catch another bus or jeepney west down to Talisay.

The lake can also be reached by bus from Pagsanjan via Los Banos, Calamba, and Tanauan.

Other Lakeside Communities
Several other small towns ring the lake though all require some extra time to visit.

Caloocan: One of the shortest crossings to Volcano Island is from the village of Caloocan, six km west of Talisay, near where the road begins to climb up Tagaytay Ridge. Ask at one of the *sari-sari* stores to arrange a *banca*. Excavation of volcanic ash layers in this area has unearthed Chinese Yueh ware shards, dating from the Sung dynasty (960-1126), used for the jar burial of a child.

Agoncillo: On the western shore, Agoncillo, site of **Villa Anna Resort,** is divided by the Pansipit River from San Nicolas, a relatively new town that makes a pleasant side trip from Taal City (seven km) to swim in the lake or hire a *banca* to the volcano; the last jeepney back to Taal City leaves at 1700.

Balete: On the eastern shore, Balete, a village with a good swimming beach, is 11 km off the main Manila-Batangas City Highway; take a jeepney from Lipa City. The established **Taal Volcano Resort** offers water-skiing and fishing.

BATANGAS PROVINCE

Batangas is a city and a province; the city is unremarkable but the province has numerous points of interest. Taal Lake and the volcano are among the sights most viewed by visitors to the Philippines. Though they're usually seen from Tagaytay Ridge in Cavite, it's well worth going across to the island in the center of the lake. Taal City is an important handicraft center and has the biggest church in the Philippines.

Batangas also has excellent dive spots at Matabungkay beach and Anilao. Batangas City is the ferry port for Puerto Galera on Mindoro but is otherwise unremarkable. If you go to one of Manila's better coffee shops, you'll probably be served a cup of flavorful Batangas *barako*.

History
Evidence of human habitation on the shores of Balayan Bay around 250,000 years ago has been recorded. Legend holds that during the 13th century, two or three of the 10 Bornean *datus* who migrated to Panay pushed farther north to Balayan Bay. They made their way up the Pansipit River to the fertile south shores of Taal Lake, where they settled with their families and slaves and subsequently gained control of an extensive part of Luzon and Mindoro. Known as Bonbon, this area attracted Chinese, Arab, and Indian merchants. Before the Spanish arrived, the coastal population was already substantial and included numerous Muslims. Archaeological excavations at Calatagan and Lemery have revealed evidence of a thriving, stratified society.

In 1570, an expedition led by Juan de Salcedo and Martin de Goiti explored Batangas on its way from Panay to Manila. Salcedo was wounded in the foot by a poisoned arrow during a skirmish on the Pansipit River. The Spaniards began settling the coast, mainly through the granting of *encomiendas* to deserving individuals and religious orders. The Augustinians were particularly prominent in the colonization effort and gained control of vast tracts of land. They established cattle ranches in the hills.

The region also suffered attacks by slave-seeking Moros throughout the 17th century; the remains of old stone forts still exist in Batangas City, Bauan, and Lemery. The original province, created in 1581, was much larger, but parts of it were broken off into new provinces over the years. It has been called Bonbon, Balayan, Taal, and Batangas. Batangas City became the capital in 1754. As one of the first eight provinces to rise in arms against Spain in 1896, Batangas saw much action during the revolution.

Prominent native sons include revolutionary hero Apolinario Mabini (1864-1903), regarded as the "Brains of the Revolution" and known as the "Sublime Paralytic" (referring to his crippled legs rather than his drinking habits), who was Aguinaldo's closest adviser and a cabinet member of the First Philippine Republic; Miguel Malvar, the last Filipino general to surrender in the Philippine-American War (in Lipa City in 1902); and Dr. Jose Laurel, president of the Philippines during the Japanese occupation. Japanese forces landed in 1941 at Batangas City, and 8,000 U.S. troops came ashore in 1945 at Nasugbu and advanced on Manila.

Scuba Diving

There are better places to dive in the Philippines than Batangas, but they aren't two hours by road from Manila. This proximity, coupled with its reefs, drop-offs, wrecks, and above-average coral and fishlife, makes Batangas a major year-round dive location. Anilao is the center for on-shore dive camps, but you can also dive from most of the small- to medium-sized resorts scattered along the coast.

Most of the dive-boat companies operate trips out of Batangas for at least part of the year and many offer trips of one to five days out in the Verde Island Passage from November to June. All bets are off during the rainy season. Others sail farther afield to Apo Reef and Busuanga Island in good weather.

Transportation

Three major bus routes connect Manila with the Batangas coast, with Batangas City, Lemery, and Nasugbu as destinations. There are frequent bus departures from the BLTB terminal in Pasay City, while the Sundowner Hotel on Mabini Street in Manila runs a bus to Batangas every day, departing at 0900, to link up with a fast ferry service from Batangas to Puerto Galera that departs at 1200.

Within the province, there's a dense network of roads and transportation, but it's often quicker to take longer routes on main highways than to cut cross-country with several bus/jeepney changes. For example, from Lucena to Batangas City, it's faster to intercept a bus from Manila at Santo Tomas than to go via Tiaong and Lipa City.

Batangas City is the ferry port for Mindoro.

BATULAO

Batulao is a mountain resort 82 km from Manila whose 600-meter elevation ensures an agreeably cool climate. The trail to Mt. Batulao (812 meters) begins here. Its summit, which forms the west end of Tagaytay Ridge, is a six-hour hike (horses also available). Across the

road from the resort is a 30-hectare rainforest and nature reserve with many bird species. Locate guides to the mountain and the forest at the resort.

Another enjoyable walk near here departs from the north side of the highway. A footpath begins about 150 meters east of the Km 84 marker post and descends for about 15 minutes into a ravine with a shallow, fast-flowing stream; its source is Mt. Cariliao (656 meters), which rises straight ahead. The path leads to a beautiful spot with many butterflies and dragonflies, plus a series of rapids and small waterfalls a little upstream.

Accommodations

Batulao Resort: On the south side of the highway, this place offers a range of accommodations, from its campground, Gulod sa Batulao, where tents may be rented, to first-class rooms and cottages, plus there's golf, tennis, a swimming pool, and horse-riding.

Transportation

To get to Batulao, take a bus from Manila or Tagaytay going toward Nasugbu and alight just west of the Cavite-Batangas boundary.

NASUGBU

Nasugbu has a sugar central and is surrounded by cane fields. Buses from Manila (102 km, three hours) stop at the market, from where the shore is a one-km tricycle ride. Nearby are Baybay and Dalampasigan beaches and Wawa Pier, while a series of secluded sandy coves stretches north of town.

Accommodations

Nasugbu has several places, from simple lodgings with no electricity to some surprisingly upscale digs.

White Sands Beach Resort: Simple yet elegant spot with no electricity, but that just adds to the atmosphere. Muntingbuhangin Cove, Manila tel. (02) 833-5608, P750-1,000.

Maryland Resort: Another beachside resort with both fan and a/c rooms plus restaurant and swimming pool. Rooms cost P600-750 with fan and P1,300-1,600 with a/c.

Maya Maya Resort: Very elite resort with pool, tennis courts, all a/c rooms, and professional dive shop. Nasubu, Manila tel. (02) 810-8118, fax 815-9288, P2,000-2,400.

Transportation

You can visit the coves as day trips or overnight at one; most of the resorts are relatively expensive, however. There's no regular transport north of Nasugbu. Some beaches are accessible only by *banca,* while others can be reached by private or hired vehicle. Even if you walk on the road, you must pay an entrance fee. *Bancas* can be hired from Wawa Pier to take snorkelers and sunbathers to these beaches; the boatmen have formed a cartel, so prices are standardized and vary according to the distance of the cove. Try to share the cost with other travelers. For relatively short visits, the boatman will remain with you; for all-day stays, he may leave and return at an agreed time. Don't pay until the end.

The last BLTB bus back to Manila leaves about 1730. The area north of Nasugbu, around the volcanic Picos de Loro on the boundary with Cavite, is a national park. The Spanish defeated the Dutch in a naval battle off Nasugbu in 1600.

FORTUNE ISLAND

This snorkeling and diving spot, about an hour by boat offshore from Nasugbu or Matabungkay, has coral beds and underwater caverns, but it's been decimated by illegal dynamite fishing so that only a few areas are now worthwhile. A knowledgeable local guide is necessary to find these. Visibility is quite good, and there's a blue hole at the northeast corner, with marinelife and coral generally better to the southeast. Trips (good weather only) and equipment can be arranged at Matabungkay Beach Club.

The island remains to some extent a breeding habitat for the endangered giant marine turtles, which nest July-September.

The island also has some famous wrecks for divers such as the remains of the Spanish galleon *San Diego,* which was discovered by a 21-man French underwater archaeological team to hold over 3,500 pieces of important artifacts.

Accommodations

Fortune Island is a privately held estate that caters only to the rich who have acquired either corporate or individual shares in the company. Despite all the hyperbole, resort rooms are surprisingly simple, without the benefits of a/c comfort or hot showers. Rather, the place is a back-to-basics venue with natural materials and solar-generated electricity.

MATABUNGKAY

This is the nearest adequate beach to Manila, about three hours away by public transport. Matabungkay's two-km beach is lined with cottages. *Bancas* can be hired for fishing, snorkeling, and exploring the coast. The beach is fairly good though obviously not to the standards of Boracay or El Nido. Trips can be made out to the above-mentioned Fortune Island for P600-800.

Accommodations

Matabungkay gets crowded at weekends, when accommodation rates may more than double.

Swiss House Hotel: Simple but comfortable place that accepts only Swiss visitors—just kidding, anyone can stay here. Rooms cost P650-750 with fan and P950-1,400 with a/c.

Twins Beach Resort: German-managed resort with swimming pool, windsurfing, and help with local dive conditions, though no dive shop here. Ligtasin, cell tel. 091-2322, P650-750 fan, P850-1,000 a/c.

Coral Beach Resort: Australians go here as the place has a connection with Swagman in Manila, plus rooms are fairly decent and the atmosphere gets almost wild on the weekends when dudes bring down their dates from Manila. Reservations can be made in Manila at Swagman, tel. (02) 523-8541, P1,200-1,800.

Matubungkay Beach Resort: Upscale resort with bamboo rafts on the water for divers (a popular option down here), two swimming pools, tennis courts, and pseudo Thai-Indonesian architecture. Manila tel. (02) 818-0054, P1,800-2,800.

Transportation

Take a Nasugbu-bound bus to Lian, which itself has a beach resort near San Diego Point, then a jeepney from Lian market 12 km south to Matabungkay. From Laguna or the south, it's quicker via Alabang-Zapote-Lian than to cut across central Batangas.

CALATAGAN

This old colonial town south of Matabungkay has a beach and is noted for fighting cocks. It was formerly part of the vast hacienda and forest preserve of the wealthy Zobel-Ayala family that developed Makati.

Calatagan is also one of the Philippines's major archaeological sites. Infant jar-burial was practiced here. Hundreds of pre-Hispanic Tagalog graves dating from the late 14th to the early 16th centuries have been excavated, yielding porcelain and stoneware from China (Ming dynasty), Annam, and Siam; glass beads; coins; bracelets; metal ornaments, including some with gold leaf covering; weapons; native pottery; and statuary. Some earthenware has syllabic inscriptions.

Calatagan's population was probably larger in the 15th century than in 1900.

Accommodations
Punta Baluarte Inter-Continental Resort: A five-star spot perched on a cliff near Calatagan with fresh and saltwater pools and a small manmade beach. *Bancas* take guests to nearby beaches while facilities include sailing, windsurfing, water-skiing, fishing, a glass-bottom boat, scuba diving, an 18-hole golf course, tennis, and horseback riding. Calatagan tel. 892-4202, fax 892-4211, Manila tel. (02) 894-1466, P2,800-4,400.

LEMERY

Ancient gravesites have yielded pre-Hispanic artifacts here. Like neighboring Taal, Lemery is a fishing and agricultural-processing center and also has some two-story colonial houses. Its notable livestock market attracts traders from other provinces. Taal is just one km east of Lemery.

Accommodations
You can stay in Lemery but most travelers head down to the nearby beach at Ligpo Point near the coastal town of San Luis.

Vila Lobos Lodge: The only place in town with fan rooms from P180 and a/c from P350.

Beach Spots: By the beach stay at Leonor Beach Resort, Palmera Beach Resort, or Encarnacion Resthouse. To get there, go about four km northeast around the bay from Lemery (or descend from Tagaytay Ridge on the Diokno Highway through Payapa to the coast road and turn left, continuing for about one km), then follow a 1.5-km winding, sandy lane to the shore; there's a pleasant beach for swimming here.

SAN LUIS AND LIGPO ISLAND

This small fishing town south of Taal City has a gray-sand beach that slopes gently into shallow water. Hiring a *banca* to go snorkeling off Ligpo Point, a little farther south, costs much less than hiring one from Anilao. The main attraction is Ligpo Island, which brings in a fair number of divers from Manila.

Accommodations
Visitors can stay in San Luis and make dive excursions to the island or stay right on Ligpo Island at slightly higher cost.

Ligpo Beach Resort: Despite the name, it's located in San Luis with all fan rooms and private baths for P500-800. But you do have a view of Ligpo Island, so why didn't they name it Ligpo Island View Resort?

Ligpo Island Hotel & Resort: Right on the island with dive facilities and fan-cooled rooms for P600-1,000.

TAAL CITY

Taal and Lemery are twin towns situated between Balayan Bay and Taal Lake, and separated by the Pansipit River. This area had long been settled when Taal was founded by Augustinians in 1572. Provincial capital 1732-54, Taal was originally on the lakeshore, but after enduring a series of volcanic eruptions in the early 18th century, it was finally destroyed in 1754 and rebuilt on its present site.

In 1841, the introduction of Mexican coffee beans, which flourished in the rich volcanic soil, gave rise to an immensely wealthy class of

Taaleño merchants, until a decline in its cultivation due to plant disease in the 1890s diminished the town's role as a commercial center. It was during this period of glory that the biggest church in the Philippines, and probably in the entire Far East, was built.

Taaleños speak one of the purest forms of Tagalog.

Taal Church

Taal's landmark is its huge baroque church, which sits atop a hill overlooking the town plaza and can be seen from afar. Its construction began in 1856 on the site of a previous church (1755) that had been destroyed by earthquake seven years earlier. A broad flight of steps leads up to it from the plaza. The structure is 95 meters high and measures 94 by 45 meters. The massive facade features an array of columns, the lower group Doric in style, the upper level Corinthian. The bell tower provides a spectacular view over the rooftops, the Pansipit River, and the surrounding countryside. Ask at the adjacent convent to have it unlocked; bring a flashlight for the climb, or buy a candle at the church entrance.

Inside the church, note the high ceiling and ornate silver tabernacle. Late afternoon sunlight streams through the central dome's window onto the altar, above which is the 30-cm-high statuette of the Blessed Virgin of Caysasay. She's said to haunt the tiny Caysasay chapel at the foot of the steps below the church. The water of the chapel well is believed to have curative powers. The Virgin's feast is highlighted by the Taal river festival each 8-9 December.

Other Attractions

This small, quiet city's central area was restored in 1976. Its narrow streets hold some 200-year-old colonial houses, many containing antiques. Note the carved wooden eaves and solid stone foundations. From the church steps, bear to the left side of the city hall and continue to the market.

On Taal's main street is the **Leon Apacible Museum and Library** (named for a delegate to the revolutionary Malolos Congress in 1898), which has some fine antique furnishings, old documents, santos, pottery, and other artifacts. The house of Marcela Agoncillo, who sewed the first Philippine flag for the revolutionary generals, is also there.

Handicrafts

Taal is renowned for its fine needlework, which women generally do in their homes. Frames of hand-embroidered, semitransparent *pina* are spread out to sun-dry around the market. Nearby shops sell *barong tagalogs,* tablecloths, blouses, dresses, and cloth, at much lower prices than can be found in Manila. Niogan is particularly noted for its *barongs* and has a street lined with workshops, stores, and display centers.

Carved furniture is produced in Taal; in Balisong on the eastern edge of the city, craftsmen make high-quality folding *balisong* knives, which are excellent for paring fruit. Bamboo mats and peanut brittle are also produced in the area.

Accommodations

An inexpensive room is available above the Taal Volcano Restaurant (the best place to eat), below the church. **Villa Obos Lodge,** P200, on Ilustre Avenue, just across the bridge to Lemery, is basic.

Transportation from Taal

For Manila (two and a half hours), take a jeepney to the bus station at nearby Lemery. Jeepneys also go to Batangas (one hour) and San Nicolas (seven km), where you can swim in Taal Lake and hire a *banca* to the volcano.

ANILAO

Anilao (124 km from Manila) is a fishing village and one of the country's foremost diving and snorkeling centers. It's a *barangay* of Mabini, a small port on Batangas Bay from where supply boats for the oil fields off northwest Palawan sail. The road to Anilao is long and bumpy, and it's almost easier to get to Puerto Galera. But Anilao has long attracted divers and snorkelers as well as weekend yachters.

Located on sheltered Janao Bay, off Balayan Bay at the base of the hilly Calumpan Peninsula, which rises to Mt. Panay (501 meters), Anilao has grown from being the weekend haunt of foreign residents of Manila to an international dive resort. The beach is mediocre, but diving is fairly good and the place remains popular with dive junkies who see no sense in lying on the beach.

Most dive resorts and camps offer inclusive packages that typically include accommodation in cottages, tents, or huts, including simple but ample food and full scuba facilities. They also conduct courses for obtaining a "C" card (International Diving Certificate, popularly called PADI); Anilao is, in fact, a good place to learn to dive. To visit a dive camp, it's recommended that reservations be made at its Manila office.

Accommodations

Anilao is somewhat expensive since it caters to the dive crowd, but it's not unreasonable and facilities are kept up to speed thanks to Western management.

San Jose Lodge: The only truly budget place is on the edge of town with survivable rooms for P150-250.

Anilao Seasport Center: Moving up several notches and moving out of town about two km is this fairly decent place with all sorts of activities from diving to Hobie Cats and windsurfing to sailing. Manila tel. (02) 801-1850, fax 805-4660, P800-1,500.

Aqua Tropical Resort: Swimming pool, dive facilities, and decent rooms either fan or a/c make this among the most popular dive resorts on the south coast near Manila. The resort, with an enormous pool but aging rooms, is a few km from Anilao town and is reached by banca from the pier. Aqua Tropical Resort, Manila Midtown Hotel, Ermita, tel. 521-6407, fax 818-9720, P750-2,500.

Eagle Point Resort: A seaside resort that can help you explore the over 30 dive spots off the shore of Calumpan Peninsula plus finely crafted chalets that stand out from the usual concrete inventions of Philippine dive resorts. The multitiered pools are great plus there's a reef pool and a 30-foot water slide for the kids. Manila tel. (02) 813-3553, fax 813-3560, Web site www.eaglepoint.coml.ph, P1,400-2,800.

Dive Sites

Divers are usually taken to sites off the Calumpan Peninsula and Maricaban Island. They include Ligpo Point and Island; the remains of a sunken fishtrap at Looc; Twin Peaks Coral Head; Cathedral, which is famous for fish-feeding; Bonete Is-

land; Mainit Point, which has a hot spring on the beach; Layag-Layag Point and Reef; Shark Reef; Caban Cove; the hat-shaped Sombrero Island; Devil's Point; Sepok Point; Mapating Rock; Batalan Rock; Merriel's Rock; Papaya Point; Culebra Island; and Malajibongmanok Island. Each spot has its own attractions, whether reefs, walls, caves, wrecks, fine coral, or particularly abundant fishlife, which Anilao's divemasters will be happy to enumerate. Many of these sites offer enjoyable snorkeling as well as diving.

Maricaban Island

This narrow, 11-km-long, densely forested island located off the Calumpan Peninsula is inhabited by farmers and fishermen. *Bancas* cross from Mabini to Tingloy, the main settlement. Inquire at the mayor's office here about accommodations. The island's surrounding waters are popular with divers from the dive camps of nearby Anilao.

On the island itself, Sepok Point at the northwest tip has fine beaches and good snorkeling. Caban Island, separated from Maricaban by a 100-meter channel, also has a good, shallow snorkeling area.

Verde Island

Situated in the Verde Island Passage that separates Batangas from Mindoro, this beautiful eight-km-long island is thickly vegetated, with rugged cliffs and some white-sand beaches. Points of interest include Mahabang Buhangin, an extensive stretch of white sand near Punta and Tinalunan, where a plateau terminates in a rocky, weather-beaten cliff. There's said to be old pottery and artifacts buried on the island. The residents fish and grow rice and coconuts. *Pakaskas* is an unusual local delicacy made by extracting sap from a coconut tree and drying it on a palm leaf.

The presence of many big fish and fine coral makes the surrounding waters popular with visiting divers and anglers, but currents require caution. The island is generally reached by dive boat from Anilao.

Bonito Island

Wedged between the much larger Maricaban and Verde Islands is a tiny speck of a place with superb white sand and acres of palm trees. The privately owned island has the Bonito Residence Inn with simple but elegant cabins, a small café, and plenty of water sports from sailing to scuba. Bonito Island, Manila tel. (02) 899-9595, fax 899-9609, P900-2,400.

Transportation

Anilao can be reached by jeepney from Batangas City. Upon reaching Anilao, you'll find dive camps and resorts to the left and right along the coast from Bagalangit Point to Ligpo Point. Some resorts are in nearby San Jose; take the road to the left after the welcome sign at Anilao.

Several resorts are only accessible by *banca*. If you want to get to one of these, but haven't made arrangements in Manila, or wish to dive or snorkel independently, you can hire a *banca* at the waterfront. Be sure to agree to a price, which will vary with trip time and distance, before setting off. While some of the coast here is lined with dive camps, there are plenty of deserted coves, beaches, and inlets.

BATANGAS CITY

This important commercial center (pop. 158,000), situated on a fine natural deep-water harbor, is a ferry and fishing port and the gateway to Mindoro, especially **Puerto Galera.** Batangas Bay was well settled in pre-Hispanic times. Buses coming from Manila pass the Provincial Capitol and some hotels about two km before the city center.

Most buses from Manila go directly to the pier, two km beyond the center; if the trip terminates downtown, it's easy to get a jeepney to the pier. There's little to detain a traveler here, though the city center contains a baroque-style basilica (1857) and a bustling market with a good handicraft selection.

Accommodations

Stay at **City Hotel,** centrally located near the Viconal Cinema; **J.C's Inn Lodge,** near the Capitol; **Guesthaus,** 224 Silang St., P350-600; **D'Safra Lodging House,** the nearest accommodation to the wharf; **Joseph Lodge,** centrally located; the **Mascor Hotel,** Rizal Ave; or the **Alpa Hotel,** swimming pool, near the Capitol, best in the city, P900-1,800.

Avenue Pension House I: Budget travelers often stay at this fairly clean place just a few blocks from the center of town. 30 Rizal Ave., tel. (043) 725-3720, P300-350.

Transportation

Batangas City is 111 km (two hours by bus) from Manila. The Manila terminals are centrally located in Lawton (used by BLTB and RJM Liner) and Pasay City (BLTB). BLTB has departures for Batangas City every 30 minutes, 0430-2000, including some a/c buses. Beware of pickpockets on this route.

For Tagaytay City from Batangas City, you can go via Taal City/Lemery or Santo Tomas and Talisay, or take a Manila-bound bus to Alabang, jeepney to Zapote, bus to Tagaytay. For Pagsanjan Falls, change at the end of the expressway near Calamba. For southern Luzon, change at Santo Tomas.

TANAUAN AND TALAGA

Tanauan

Tanauan, a market town, was the birthplace of another revolutionary, Apolinario Mabini. The birthplace of Dr. Jose Laurel, Philippine president 1943-45, has been converted into a memorial library museum in Tanauan.

Talaga

The **Mabini Shrine and Mausoleum** (open 0800-1200, 1300-1700) is in Talaga. In contrast to most other revolutionary leaders, Mabini's family was poor. The shrine includes a replica of the hut in which he was born and a small museum containing memorabilia. Take a Talisay-bound jeepney for six km; the shrine is on the right.

Mainit Hot Springs is also in Talaga, which can be reached from Santo Tomas.

LIPA CITY

This city (fiesta: 20 January), pop. 125,000, is located in the midst of a citrus-, coffee-, and coconut-growing area on a rolling plateau between the volcanic Mt. Makulot and Mt. Malarayat (Malepungo).

Lipa is a market center and a major supplier of chickens and eggs to Manila; agricultural processing and clothing manufacturing are important activities. It's also known for the making of *kaing,* fruit, and vegetable containers made of woven bamboo strips, which are a common sight in the markets of Manila and surrounding provinces. Local handicrafts are based on wood and bamboo.

Attractions

Lipa was a Spanish military center; part of it was wiped out by Taal volcano in 1754, and it also suffered heavy damage during the liberation at the end of WW II. A notorious massacre, in which 1,500 men were beheaded, took place during the Japanese occupation.

Cathedral: The domed baroque cathedral was superimposed on a structure destroyed in 1754. It has a barrel-vaulted ceiling painted in trompe-l'oeil style. Note, too, the massive interior or piers and the unusual wooden spiral staircase leading to the choir.

T.M. Kalaw Memorial Museum: This museum displays historical relics of the man (secretary of the interior, 1920-22; director of the National Library) and the region, including a pre-Hispanic boat-shaped child's coffin, a fine collection of ecclesiastical woodcarving, and antique furniture. José Rizal once slept in the Brigido Morada House.

Natural Attractions: Within the municipality are Bulalakaw Falls, the Mt. Malarayat rainforest, and Tagbakin Beach on Lake Taal, believed to be the site of the 13th-century settlement of one of the Bornean *datus.*

Accommodations

Stay at **Family Hotel** (clean, good, and situated near the bus stop), **Lipa Manor Hotel,** or **Pepe's Apartelle.** Eat at the **Batangueno Restaurant** on the main highway facing the Floral Garden Memorial Park.

LAGUNA PROVINCE

Laguna is one of the Tagalogs' cultural homelands. The province is characterized by historic towns, coconut plantations, lakeshores, sheltered valleys, waterfalls, hot springs, and volcanoes. Its proximity to Manila does not detract from the rural beauty of Laguna, especially in small towns like Pangil, Pakil, Majayjay, and Liliw.

You can wander unhurriedly through narrow streets of houses with ornate balustrades and bright flower boxes, admire fine old churches, shop for traditional handicrafts, and stop to share a glass of the potent local brew, *lambanog,* with friendly, hospitable residents. If your time in the Philippines is limited, try to visit Laguna Province, for it is here that the true pulse of tropical life in old, settled communities can be seen and appreciated.

History

The culture of the Laguna Tagalogs was shaped by the presence of Mt. Makiling and Mt. Banahaw. Many myths and legends became associated with these volcanoes, which have magnetic properties and bubbling hot springs. Mount Makiling's summit, for example, is said to be haunted by a beautiful goddess, Mariang Makiling, who guards its forests.

Mount Banahaw is considered the male counterpart of Mt. Makiling. Believers still seek power and knowledge on its misty heights, and its slopes are home to numerous religious sects and practitioners of the occult. These legends and myths form an unbroken link from the Laguna Tagalogs' ancient past to the present.

Laguna also has a history of war. When Manila was secured in 1571, Juan de Salcedo quickly pacified the lakeside settlements, *encomiendas* were granted, and Franciscan friars began their work. In a burst of activity 1578-83, they founded missions at Bay, Caliraya, Majayjay, Nagcarlan, Liliw, Pila, Santa Cruz, Lumban, Pangil, and Siniloan. Many weathered, venerable churches remain to this day. Bay was the first provincial capital, followed by Pagsanjan in 1688, then Santa Cruz in 1858. Spanish influence on native life was great here and is still evident in manners, habits, and architecture.

During Spanish settlement, the friars acquired vast domains of land and power. Around Calamba, for example, they engaged in wholesale evictions and deportations of tenant farmers.

Among them was the family of José Rizal, a native of Laguna, whose later writings sparked the revolution against the Spanish in Laguna in 1896. Spanish troops quickly subdued the insurgents, but the struggle continued. After the U.S. occupied the Philippines, rebels who hadn't surrendered initiated the Laguna-Cavite-Batangas insurrection in 1905. These self-designated "Protectors of the People" and "Defenders of the Country" inflicted a reign of terror on the region and occupying Americans before capitulating.

Even during the 1930s, there was sporadic unrest stemming from land disputes. During WW II, guerrillas were active in the province, which suffered heavily from the Japanese occupation and liberating U.S. bombers.

Transportation

Laguna is served by frequent buses from Manila; Santa Cruz and San Pablo are the main route centers. The Alabang-Calamba Expressway is the major route south out of Manila. At Calamba, the road splits around Mt. Makiling; one branch follows the lakeshore to Santa Cruz and Pagsanjan, while the main highway to southern Luzon curves round via Batangas, then passes through San Pablo and enters Quezon.

Buses start from the Laguna bus station at Lawton and the BLTB terminal in Pasay City, then follow both shores of Laguna de Bay. Pantranco South buses pass through San Pablo on their way to and from southern Luzon. Those who wish to visit the southern suburbs of Manila, the Bamboo Organ at Las Pinas, and jeepney factories at Zapote, and then proceed to Pagsanjan can take a jeepney across from Zapote to Alabang. Pick up a southbound bus from there. From Tagaytay (Taal Lake overlook) to Pagsanjan, it's quicker to go via Zapote and Alabang than to cut directly cross-country.

From Batangas City to Pagsanjan, take a Manila-bound bus. The most rewarding route is to change at Santo Tomas and San Pablo, passing through southern Laguna; the quickest way is to alight at the beginning of the expressway, just before Calamba, and then follow the lakeshore. A rough road links Siniloan with Infanta on the Pacific coast of Quezon.

PAKIL

This town, with its attractive church (built 1732-67) and cool springs, is noted for wood filigree work. Monterrey Gardens rents cottages here in a scenic hillside setting. Homemade cookies are sold in Pakil during Lent. In May and June, boaters collect water hyacinth buds; the flower's white interiors, known as *beno,* are eaten with salt.

Turrumba Festival

The famous Turrumba Festival, which takes place on the second Tuesday and Wednesday after Holy Week and on 19 October, began with the legend in 1778 of a fisherman who found a statue floating in the lake. He tried to carry it ashore at Paete, but it was too heavy, so he rowed to Pakil, where he landed and brought the statue ashore. Upon hearing of this discovery, the parish priest rang the church bell to summon the villagers to the lakeside where they began to dance upon seeing the image.

It was named Nuestra Señora de los Dolores ("Our Lady of Sorrows"), but the townspeople call it the Virgen de Turrumba, and it is their patron saint. Since then, Pakil has celebrated the Virgin's feastday. Some claim that Turrumba derives from *tumumba,* which is Tagalog for tumbling or falling and describes the behavior of participants who jump and skip in the pious procession. It's also possible that *turrumba* is a blend of two words, *turo,* to point, and *umbay,* a dirge sung by invalids.

Originally, the procession was a parade of the sick and dying. At dawn, the town awakes to horns, pipes, and flutes played by men in elfin costumes. The Virgin's image is borne from the church on the shoulders of female devotees. Brass bands play lively marches and women dance, sing, and kneel to kiss the ground. Young men and children join in the frenzied dancing to shouts of "Turrumba!"

PAETE

Founded in 1580, this town, whose name derives from *paet* ("chisel" in Tagalog), is famous for woodcarving. On Holy Monday, wooden images of Christ and the saints are paraded through Paete's streets.

Church and Convent

The stone church and *convento* were built in 1646, rebuilt in 1717, 1840, and 1884, and damaged by earthquakes in 1880 and 1937. Local carving skills are reflected in the ornate stone facade, bell tower, and the main altar, which features an exquisite woodcarving of the Last Supper and a baroque reredos. The bas-relief above the front entrance depicts the town's patron, St. James, on horseback defeating the Moors. The church contains some remarkable paintings, too.

Woodcarving

During Spanish times, the surrounding forests supported boat-building, while santos carved here were carried far afield. Now, a walk around the narrow lanes reveals many workshops with carvers working on chess sets, platters, spoons, religious, animal statuary, with lots of handicraft shops displaying this output. Paete has over 200 workshops and 3,000 carvers. Unlike the Ifugao and other Filipino woodcarvers, several Paetenos may work on one piece. In a typical workshop, tasks are divided between 20-30 people—adults and children who set up a kind of assembly line.

Other Crafts

Paete also produces *bakya,* durable sandals with soles of carved and varnished wood, with leather, suede, vinyl, net, or plastic uppers. Demand for this footwear developed during the Japanese occupation, when conventional shoes were more expensive; at one point it was the only item they produced. Another unusual craft is the making of papier-mâché models of animals.

Kalayaan Festival

On Good Friday, a reenactment of the Longinus legend, simpler than the famous Moriones festival in Marinduque, takes place in a mountain *barangay* above Kalayaan. The converted Roman centurion Longinus, played by an elderly man, runs through the dusty country roads pursued by children dressed as Roman soldiers.

A "fight" ensues between Longinus and the soldiers as they finally seize him in front of the village chapel, near which a stage has been built.

LUMBAN

Just north of Lumban is a hydroelectric complex, utilizing runoff from the Caliraya Reservoir, to which a road ascends. The lakeshore highway bypasses the town, two km north of Pagsanjan.

Attractions

Lumban's original church, built in 1578 and destroyed by fire, was also the initial center of missionary activity in the province. The present building dates from 1600, but was restored after earthquake damage in 1880.

In 1606, a resthouse for sick Franciscan missionaries and a regional boys' school were founded here. Today, the making of embroidered *barong tagalog* shirts is an important cottage industry.

Lumban is a good place for birdwatchers to hire a *banca* and wander into the marshlands of Laguna de Bay to observe many species of waterbirds.

River Festival

In Lumban's River Festival (19 January), the ritual submersion of the image of San Sebastian, the town's patron saint, in the Pagsanjan River precedes a fluvial procession.

PAGSANJAN

A visit to Pagsanjan Falls (pronounced "PAK-saan-han") is one of the major day trips from Manila. The river journey to the falls offers both natural beauty as you pass through a magnificent gorge to reach the impressive 91-meter falls and the excitement of "shooting the rapids" on the return downstream. Pagsanjan (pop. 21,000) is located where two rivers fork, and the name derives from *sanga* (branch).

While the surrounding area contains numerous points of interest, the town itself is not especially absorbing since the Japanese occupa-

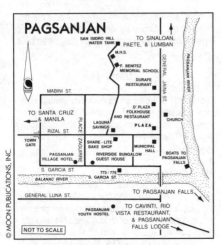

PAGSANJAN

TO SINALOAN,
PAETE, & LUMBAN

SAN ISIDRO HILL
WATER TANK

M.H.S.

F. BENITEZ
MEMORIAL SCHOOL

DURAFE
RESTAURANT

MABINI ST.

D' PLAZA
FOLKHOUSE
AND RESTAURANT

TO SANTA CRUZ
& MANILA

LAGUNA
SAVINGS

CHURCH

PLAZA

RIZAL ST.

TOWN
GATE

SHARE - LITE
BAKE SHOP

MUNICIPAL
HALL

BOATS TO
PAGSANJAN
FALLS

PAGSANJAN
VILLAGE HOTEL

RIVERSIDE BUNGALOW
GUEST HOUSE

S. GARCIA ST.

773 / 775
S. GARCIA ST.

BALANAC RIVER

GENERAL LUNA ST.

TO PAGSANJAN FALLS

PAGSANJAN
YOUTH HOSTEL

TO CAVINTI, RIO
VISTA RESTAURANT,
& PAGSANJAN
FALLS LODGE

NOT TO SCALE

© MOON PUBLICATIONS, INC.

tion led to its destruction by U.S. bombing in 1945. The church remains and was founded in 1687, while the road from Santa Cruz passes through an imposing town gate (1878).

To the Falls
Whichever direction you approach Pagsanjan from, you'll alight at the plaza opposite the church. If you wish to proceed directly to the falls, buy your boat ticket at the Magdapio Lodge, across from the plaza. The seven-km trip upstream takes one hour one-way. There have been cases of tourists being ripped off by boatmen who charged exhorbitant prices for the hire of their boats, asked to be given lunch money, and wait for big tips. To be on the safe side, contact a travel agent or tour operator in Manila to enquire about the Pagsanjan tour and ascertain the cost of a trip there. It may be better to join a group.

You'll get wet, so bring a change of clothing and a plastic bag to protect camera, documents, etc. *Bancas* initially form a convoy to be towed by a motorized boat up to the first set of rapids. A local tourist office now stands on the site of the Indochinese temple constructed for and then dramatically destroyed in Francis Ford Coppola's 1975-76 *Apocalypse Now.*

Other scenes filmed along the riverbanks have appeared in *Platoon* and several of Chuck Norris's war sagas, and here occurred the infamous

helicopter accident that killed Vic Morrow and three children during the filming of *The Twilight Zone.* Vietnamese village film sets, complete with watchtowers and red flags, seem to have become permanent fixtures up here.

Upon entering the gorge, look up at the lush vegetation and the sheer 100-meter cliffsides. Note a lovely, slender waterfall on the left. You'll appreciate the strength and skill that your *banqueros* demonstrate in negotiating the *banca* upstream around numerous boulders and against the powerful current.

After 14 sets of rapids, you disembark and scramble over some rocks to face Pagsanjan Falls, also known as Magdapio Falls. You're given about 20 minutes for photography, swimming, taking a raft trip to the cave behind the falls, or the simple enjoyment of nature. Then comes the thrill of shooting those 14 rapids. Have faith in your *banqueros:* they've done it hundreds of times before.

It's strongly recommended that you stay overnight in Pagsanjan and make this trip early in the morning before the busloads of day-trippers arrive from Manila. Avoid weekend crowds, too; August and September are the most exciting months for descending the rapids. The river, though generally shallow, is at its highest and fastest then, since it's the peak of the rainy season.

Whatever you do, avoid weekends, when the river resembles Disneyland.

Accommodations
Most budget accommodations are on Garcia Street alongside the river.

Willy Flores's Place: A longtime favorite operated by postman Willy, his wife Pacita, and their boatman son, Noli, all of whom can advise on nearby hiking, swimming, dancing, and weekend cockfights. Also on the same street, but somewhat more expensive, is **Pagsanjan Village Hotel and Riverside Bungalows.** 821 Garcia St., no phone, P150-420.

Pagsanjan Youth Hostel: A peaceful but somewhat difficult place to find. Walk across the river, turn right, and look for the AYH sign. 237 General Luna St., tel. (049) 645-2347, P100-200.

Camino Real Hotel: Best choice in the mid-priced range is this modest but very clean hotel on the main street near the bridge. 39 Rizal St., tel. (049) 645-2086, P550-850.

La Corona de Pagsanjan: An upscale lodge with three swimming pools, restaurant, and deck with views over the river. Pansanjan River Rd., tel. (0912) 306-9766, P1,500-2,400.

Food
The **Share-Lite Bake Shop** serves tasty food at reasonable prices. The **Magellan Pub** and the reasonable **D'Plaza Folkhouse and Restaurant** are recommended. The **Durafe Restaurant** on General Jaina Street has very good food. Cross the river at General Jaina Street and try the **Maulawin Bistro,** which has excellent food. On the way out of town past the Pagsanjan Falls Lodge, try the **D & C Luncheonette.** In the evening, check out the D'-Plaza Folkhouse and Restaurant for live music.

Fiestas
May is a busy month in Pagsanjan; it's a good place to observe the monthlong Flores de Mayo and Santacruzan festivals, while on 15 May, San Isidro celebrates the feast day of San Isidro with a harvest festival featuring a carabao race, farmers' procession, and firework display. Pagsanjan's town fiesta (12 December) is a lively affair, noted for the attractive bamboo arches set up along the main streets for the late afternoon procession in honor of Nuestra Señora de Guadalupe, the town's patron saint.

Transportation
From Manila (101 km, three hours), buses depart Laguna bus station at Lawton (near the Manila post office) and the BLTB terminal in Pasay City for Santa Cruz every 30 minutes 0400-1930. From Santa Cruz, take a six-km jeepney ride to Pagsanjan town. To take the longer journey down the east side of the lake, so as to complete a circular route, ask for a bus traveling to Santa Cruz via Pillila (less frequent), which will pass through Pagsanjan, or take a bus to Siniloan and continue by jeepney, perhaps with a stop in Paete.

To return directly from Pagsanjan to Manila, take a jeepney to Santa Cruz, then a bus to Lawton or Pasay City. To Manila via the eastern shore of Laguna de Bay, take a BLTB bus to Pasay, via Pillila; or catch a jeepney to Siniloan, then a bus going to Divisoria (to get to Ermita, alight at Rizal Avenue in Santa Cruz, Manila) and take Metrorail, or a jeepney south to del Pilar or Taft.

To Taal Lake, geography makes it easier to return almost to Manila, then come south again, rather than try to cut cross-country. The latter route is only practical if you want to overnight on the lakeshore and hire a boat to the island volcano. If you wish to view the lake from the main vantage point at Taal Vista Lodge on Tagaytay Ridge, it's best to take a jeepney from Pagsanjan to Santa Cruz, a Manila-bound bus to Alabang, a jeepney to Zapote, then a bus to Tagaytay; connections are quick and easy.

Pagsanjan Falls

For the cross-country route, take a Manila-bound bus from Santa Cruz to Calamba (Rizal's house is worth visiting here), bus to Tanauan, jeepney to Talisay. It's more scenic, however, to alight at the junction three km west of Pagsanjan, wait for a jeepney to Nagcarlan, then hop by jeepneys to San Pablo, Santo Tomas, Tanauan, and Talisay. You must stay overnight at Talisay. The next day, you can charter a boat to the volcano or take a jeepney up to Tagaytay.

To Batangas City and Puerto Galera: Follow directions as above to Calamba (alight at beginning of the expressway) or Santo Tomas, then bus to Batangas City. To southern Luzon, take a bus to Pagsanjan and Lucena City (or jeepneys via Lucban) then a bus or train south. To Majayjay or Liliw, take a jeepney three km west to the junction and wait for one coming from Santa Cruz.

VICINITY OF PAGSANJAN

Enjoy fine views of Pagsanjan's environs—lake, marshes, volcanoes, endless coconut plantations—from San Isidro Hill water tank, about a 15-minute walk from the plaza. Follow Rizal Street to Laguna Savings, turn right into the lane, go straight up the steps past F. Benitez Memorial School and M.H.S. to the water tank; it's nice at sunset. In the parish church of Cubao, an image of its patron saint, St. Jude Thaddeus, has been reported to ooze oil that has miraculous curative powers. On Sundays, there's lots of action at the cockfight arena four km along the road to Santa Cruz.

Santa Cruz and Vicinity

Santa Cruz's status as provincial capital since 1858 is reflected in the town's layout, broader than most lakeside settlements. Note the offshore fish corrals. *Kesong puti,* delicious salty white cheese, made from carabao milk and sold wrapped in square banana-leaf packages, is a local delicacy. Pre-Hispanic Chinese porcelain has been unearthed from graves among the surrounding coconut plantations.

Many stores offer "antiques" here. Examples of the porcelain are displayed in a small museum on the plaza of nearby Pila; request admission at the mayor's office. Pila has a batik factory outlet. Beyond Pila is another old town, Bay.

Caliraya Reservoir

An enjoyable excursion from Pagsanjan is the circular trip that takes in the extensive Caliraya Reservoir (elev. 300 meters) and the upper Pagsanjan waterfall. Take a Siniloan jeepney past Lumban to the junction of the road that zigzags up to Caliraya. Jeepneys on this road are infrequent, so begin walking and try to hitch until one passes; its sign should read Cavinti-Lumot or Caliraya-Lumot.

The lake is cool and deep, with shores of red clay. Several upscale lakeshore resorts offer a variety of sports, including water-skiing in ideal conditions, windsurfing, swimming, horseback riding, and shooting. Fishing is highly rated here, especially for largemouth (black) bass; other species include carp, tilapia, *bangus, dalag,* and an unidentified "monster fish." Birdwatching is good in the area, too.

Development remains light and the landscape uncluttered. The simple **Japanese Memorial Gardens,** commemorating the many soldiers who died here in 1945, are a little past the resorts' boat landings and afford panoramas of the surrounding countryside. Hike for about 30 minutes to secluded waterfalls where you can swim; take the concrete path to the right of the main complex, cross the stile on the right, and follow the track down across a field. It's an area of rock formations, flowers, birds, and butterflies.

To return to Pagsanjan, follow the winding road for several km; turn right at the T-junction just before Cavinti (church founded 1621). After about two km, note a small church on the left.

Luisiana

The road from Pagsanjan to Lucena City (Quezon Province) passes through Cavinti and enters Luisiana through its cemetery. Luisiana is a quiet country town surrounded by swampy groves of pandanus trees, the leaves of which are sun-dried, then woven into mats and bags, which are stocked in sheds at one end of the short main street.

The 12-km road from Majayjay to Luisiana has no public transport; if you hike, ask about the shortcut, via Batohan, to a point where a jeepney can be intercepted.

MAJAYJAY

A visit here is part of the eminently worthwhile journey into Laguna's deep south. Majayjay is located north of Mt. Banahaw amid rolling hills covered by coconut plantations. It has a famous church, some stone colonial houses with tiled roofs, plus a number of waterfalls in the vicinity. Its elevation of 300 meters ensures a pleasant climate.

During the 19th century, Majayjay was a summer tourist resort; dignitaries sailed across the lake from Manila and were then borne uphill to the town on palanquins. Revolutionary general Emilio Jacinto died here of malaria at age 23 in 1899.

Attractions

The town fiesta on 12 March is a particularly good time to visit and sample the potent local *lambanog.*

Church: The first stone church (1606) replaced one made of native materials. The massive present church, built in 1660 following a fire, reflects the history of the town. Its construction and several restorations entailed forced labor that created lasting tension between the friars and their reluctant flock. The parishioners settled just outside the town boundaries to avoid the slave labor, but the priests burned their new huts.

During a major restoration (1711-30), members of the congregation were required to bring sand and stone whenever they attended mass, in addition to providing labor. Failure to do so meant flogging and fining. The animosity eventually caused the partition of Majayjay into three towns and bred local support for the revolution. Majayjay church is a fine example of colonial baroque architecture.

It's an unusually tall stone-and-brick building with six-meter-thick walls, supported by enormous buttresses. The long, high nave has balconies on both sides; note the *kapis* windows in the transept. The altars and *retablos* are impressive, while the adjacent *convento* houses a small museum of old parish documents and ecclesiastical silver. Be sure to climb the bell tower for a panorama of coconut plantations, the lake, and Mt. Banahaw and Mt. San Cristobal.

Bridge of Whims: Also ask directions for the path that leads north to Puente de Capricho ("Bridge of Whims") on the River Olla. The stone central arches are vestiges of what was to be a huge bridge. It was designed in 1850 by Father del Moral, the parish priest, who enforced compulsory labor. His unpopularity led to his transfer before the bridge was finished. In spite of his lack of engineering experience, the structure has withstood many earthquakes. Francis Ford Coppola used the bridge for location shots in *Apocalypse Now.* He blew up the original wooden end sections, and then built a replacement bridge upstream.

Botocan River: Three km out of Majayjay, the road to Botocan Falls and hydroelectric plant crosses a river with clear, inviting pools that locals use to wash laundry. Stones along the riverside are covered with colorful drying clothes. Imelda Falls are a seven-km hike, or ask at the mayor's office or Villa Nogales about hiring a horse.

To climb Mt. Banahaw from Majayjay, you must first walk nine km to Taytay.

Accommodations

Stay at **Villa Nogales,** which has cottages and two swimming pools, also open to nonguests. It's a nice place albeit a little run-down. Bring food or walk one km into town to eat as there is no restaurant here.

Transportation

A direct bus makes a daily roundtrip to Manila (120 km), departing at 0300 and returning from Lawton (Manila) at about 1400. Alternatively, take a bus to Santa Cruz, then a jeepney to Majayjay, or vice versa. From Pagsanjan, take a jeepney three km toward Santa Cruz, then wait at the T-junction for one coming from Santa Cruz. Traveling to or from Liliw or San Pablo, change jeepneys at Sambat (also called Bombat).

Between Sambat and Majayjay, note presses, old ones of rock, newer ones of cement, among the trees. They're used to flatten *buri* leaves, which are then dyed purple, dried, and woven into mats.

LILIW (LILIO)

This riverside town (fiesta: 29 August) in the shadow of Mt. Banahaw is noted for handcrafted footwear and tasty *uraro* (arrowroot) biscuits.

Attractions

Sights include the church, which has survived fire and earthquake; a mural in the post office by De Guzman, a Filipino artist who resided here; and the colorful *labanderas* who wash clothes in the river.

The local *lambanog* is strong, relatively smooth, and cheap. In the coconut plantations beyond Liliw Resort, bamboo scaffolding linking nutless trees facilitates the task of *tuba* gatherers who supply a small *lambanog* still amid the palms.

Accommodations

You can stay at the **Batis ng Liliw, Villa Corcega Resort,** or **Liliw Resort,** which offers campsites and cottages; nonguests can swim for a fee in about 40 naturally terraced pools. Most places charge P350-600 for basic facilities while fancier ones start at P800-1,200.

NAGCARLAN

This historic town is located on a fertile plateau surrounded by volcanoes. The area is Laguna's vegetable garden. Nagcarlan contains some old, narrow three-story houses, surmounted by small watchtowers. Apparently, lot sizes were limited to prevent ostentatious displays of wealth in the home, so residents built upward rather than outward.

Attractions

Nagcarlan is a good place to buy *lanzones,* a sweet tropical fruit, during the harvest season (Sept.-Nov.). All throughout the Laguna region, *lanzones* are harvested and brought to San Pablo or Manila to market.

Church: The church (1752) was badly damaged by fire in 1781 and restored in 1845 in "Laguna baroque" style by Father Vicente Velloc. Blue-and-white tiles impart a Moorish tone to the interior, which features fine woodcarving.

Cemetery and Crypt: Nagcarlan also has a famous chapel, crypt, and cemetery, situated on the main road to San Pablo, opposite a service station. If they're locked, apply at the caretaker's house to the left of the cemetery. The cemetery's octagonal walls contain burial niches and are decorated with scrollwork. In the enclosed garden stand the chapel and crypt. Built in 1845 by Father Velloc, they also display the strange arabesque style and blue-and-white tiles. Stairs lead down to the crypt, which contains tombs and burial plaques. Much mystery surrounds it.

Velloc built an underground passage, now sealed off, that leads to five subterranean chapels where he held solitary masses; it's said

the crypts at Nagcarlan

to continue all the way to Mt. Banahaw. During the 1890s, this crypt was a clandestine meeting place of the Katipuneros as they conspired against Spain. In recent years, the site was cleaned up and restored, and there is a local historian on duty during weekends to answer any questions.

SAN PABLO CITY

This is Laguna's only city (founded 1678), with 155,000 inhabitants. Located 87 km from Manila, it's an important commercial and transportation hub linking three provinces. Frequent buses and jeepneys travel in every direction—Manila (Lawton and Pasay), Batangas (for Puerto Galera), Santa Cruz, Lucena City, and southern Luzon. It's also on the southern rail line.

This is coconut country and San Pablo is a major copra center; the surrounding plantations supply several coconut oil mills and the Franklin Baker dessicated coconut factory, the world's largest.

Attractions
For the traveler, interest lies in the seven lakes, of which only two have some kind of development. San Pablo has an old church, and the circular Sampaloc Lake is centrally located behind the city hall. Lakeside restaurants serve fresh broiled *bangus* and mudfish. There are also many places to eat around the market.

The city celebrates the Feast of San Pablo on 25 January with a colorful fiesta, featuring a parade and carnival. Other events include a music festival during February and March, Flores de Mayo in May, a cultural fair in October, and a cultural show in December.

Accommodations
The cheapest places to stay are near the Mobil gas station, one km west of the city center, where the road forks to Alaminos and Calauan.

Best choice for travelers is the **Sampaloc Lake Youth Hostel** in Efarca Village, which has good rooms for P100-150. A short distance along the road to Calauan is the **Cocoland Hotel, Executive Hotel,** and two km farther the **Bunot Lake Resort.** All are midpriced places with rooms for P450-900.

Many resorts with swimming facilities are scattered throughout the surrounding countryside. At the lower end of the scale are the **Bae-YIW Country Resort** (take a Santa Veronica jeepney five km outside San Pablo) and **San Rafael Swimming Pool Resort** (two km from San Pablo along the Alaminos road).

Hidden Valley and **Villa Escudero** are two of the finest inland resorts near Manila (most are obviously placed near a beach); see details below.

THE SEVEN LAKES OF SAN PABLO

These crater lakes of extinct volcanoes have scenic charm and are worth seeing.

Sampaloc Lake
Sampaloc Lake, roughly one km across and 27 meters deep, is the largest and most accessible; it is best viewed from the small park next to the city hall. A road encircles the lake, serving as a walking path. Local people maintain fishpens and cultivate water hyacinth for sandalweaving.

Bunot Lake
Bunot Lake, 2.5 km along the Nagcarlan Road, is the only lake with resort facilities.

Pandin and Yambo Lakes
Continue by jeepney toward Nagcarlan, and ask the driver to drop you near Pandin and Yambo Lakes, which are close together, north of the road. The trail isn't obvious, but a local kid can get you there for a P3 tip.

Calibato Lake
Return to the road and take another jeepney two km to Calibato Lake, which is south of the road. Although it's unmarked, a guide isn't necessary for the 500-meter walk to this lake, and there's a fine view of Mt. San Cristobal and Mt. Banahaw from here.

Palakpakin Lake
Back in San Pablo, take a jeepney near the market going north to San Buenaventura (six km). After the village, a road turns right and descends to the steep-sided Palakpakin Lake. To

the southeast is Mt. San Cristobal. January through March, coffee beans are dried on the roadside.

Mohicap Lake

Back on the main road turn right toward Santa Catalina. Walk less than a kilometer to a little chapel and a water pump on the left. Follow the trail between them, and when it divides into three trails bear right. Walk for 15 minutes through a coconut and banana plantation to the beautiful and secluded Mohicap Lake, which is bordered by some small rice terraces; Mt. Nagcarlan overlooks it on the northeast side.

ALAMINOS

The gateway to Hidden Valley Springs, Alaminos is a copra town with a coconut by-products factory. Local *lanzones,* harvested in September and October, are highly rated.

Transportation

Alaminos is 10 km west of San Pablo; a few kilometers farther west, on the highway to Santo Tomas, signs indicate the turnoff to **MAKBAN,** the Makiling-Banahaw Geothermal Project. To tour it, apply at least a week in advance to the National Power Corp., BIR Road at Quezon Ave., Quezon City, Metro Manila.

HIDDEN VALLEY SPRINGS RESORT

This resort is located in an ancient 90-meter-deep crater, believed to have been formed by a sudden drop in the earth's crust, on the south side of Mt. Makiling. Locals call it *ilalim* (under)—shades of *Under the Volcano!* The resort is tasteful, consisting of 44 hectares of dense vegetation—old trees, ferns, orchids—interlaced with cement paths linking numerous spring-fed pools (cold, warm, soda, natural massage) and leading to a small gorge and waterfall.

Sadly, the owners of this attractive if somewhat uneventful destination seem determined to kill the golden goose with their absurd entrance fees, which currently stand at over P1,400. Although this includes use of the pool and a buffet lunch, the place is overpriced for most independent travelers and therefore mostly visited by packaged tours.

Accommodations

Rooms are also overpriced here, though the steep tariff includes admission to the park. Singles cost P2,600-3,000 while doubles go for over P5,000. Manila tel. (02) 818-4034.

Transportation

To get there from Manila (77 km), take a bus to Santo Tomas or San Pablo, a jeepney to Alaminos (13 or 10 km, respectively), then a tricycle to the resort in Limbao (4.5 km). You can arrange with the driver to be picked up at a set time or start walking back toward Alaminos and look for a passing tricycle. Major Manila travel agencies offer inclusive day-trips to Hidden Valley.

VILLA ESCUDERO

Another first-class resort in Tiaong is situated about 10 km south of San Pablo on the highway to Lucena City, at the Laguna-Quezon boundary, which is marked by a concrete arch over the road. Pantranco South buses from Manila pass its entrance. The hacienda, 1.5 km off the road, is the focal point of an 800-hectare working coconut plantation that dates from the Spanish era and is tenanted by 300 families.

Admission to the resort costs P550-650 but provides far greater value than Hidden Springs. Included with the fare are rides on carts, admission to the museum, cavorting in the swimming pool, and a boat trip across the very pretty lake surrounded by palms.

Escudero Museum: Apart from swimming and enjoying the resort facilities, guests can explore the Escudero family's fascinating private museum, which features an unusual collection of stuffed wildlife, religious imagery, Chinese porcelain, Spanish carriages, ethnic artifacts and clothing, antique furniture, coins, weapons, and WW II relics.

Accommodations

Overnight accommodations in cottages are available. Charges for day visits include the museum, use of recreational facilities, demonstration of

SACRED MOUNT BANAHAW

This 2,177-meter dormant volcano straddles the boundary between Laguna and Quezon, dominating the skyline. Along with Mt. San Cristobal (1,470 meters), it forms a national park (111 square km). Mount Banahaw is known as Vulcan de Agua due to the many springs that flow from its base. The crater apparently contained a lake prior to an eruption in 1730, when the southern rim burst open. In 1841, the Spanish dealt heavily with the rebellious Cofradia de San Jose movement in nearby Tayabas (now Quezon), and survivors became *remontados* (those who return to the mountains), living on the isolated slopes of Mt. Banahaw and Mt. San Cristobal.

These mountains became religious centers, places of pilgrimage for lowland peasants, and the birthplace of folk Christian religious communities called Colorums. Banahaw is believed to be a powerful center of electromagnetic and energy fields, and many locals consider it sacred. Its slopes are peopled by members of several esoteric and occult sects, and the towns and villages in its shadow have spawned a bevy of soothsayers, faith healers, and amulet makers, who revere the volcano as the source of their mystic power. Myths, legends, superstitions, and tales of strange happenings and rituals abound. Some sects believe it's the site of the Holy Land. On Good Friday, the Colorum procession traces Christ's supposed ascent from Dolores (Quezon) to Banahaw's summit (Calvary).

Climbing Mount Banahaw

Several routes lead up Banahaw, including one from Taytay, nine km from Majayjay, and others from Quezon Province—from Lucban on the east side and Dolores on the west; the latter is generally recommended. In each case, hiring a guide is advisable. Avoid the June-Oct. rainy season, when leeches are plentiful and conditions may be hazardous. The ascent is steep; allow four days.

Day One: Beginning in San Pablo, take a jeepney to Santa Lucia (30 minutes). Here, contact the National Parks and Wildlife Station for a guide. It's then a 90-minute hike to the village of Kinabuhayan. From here, a wide and well-trodden trail leads in 30 minutes to Kristalino Falls (30 meters). Ninety minutes farther is a second waterfall; the surrounding area makes a good campsite.

Day Two: Begin early. The next section is a little difficult, entailing climbing a short, vertical wall leading to a narrow ridge above a small waterfall called Salamin Bubog ("Glass Mirror"); allow one hour. The trail then traverses a treacherous, slippery gully over huge boulders to a cave with a 30-meter-high entrance known as Kuweba ng Dios Ama ("Cave of God the Father"); allow 90 minutes. Climb another steep rock formation, at the top of which are tall grass and trees; allow 30 minutes. Bear right where the trail diverges and, after two more hours, reach a huge boulder called Pintong Lihim ("Hidden Door"). The trail continues over large, moss-covered boulders to Niluhuran ("Place Where Trees Knelt"), a name deriving from the bent, twisted trees lying low to the ground here. After four and a half hours, arrive at the peak, known as Santong Durungawan ("Holy Window"); camp here.

Day Three: To be spent in the crater, which forms a winding canyon whose floor is 25-50 meters wide, with walls soaring up to 900 meters above it. The trail descends steeply into the crater, whose interior is densely forested. Spots along the way include Kuwebang Usa ("Deer Cave") and Katedral ("Cathedral"), a level area surrounded by tall trees. On the east side of the crater stands a wall of vegetation where two springs run down mineral veins. One is white and known as Tubig ng Gatas ("Milk Water"); the other is red and called Tubig ng Dugo ("Blood Water"). A traverse of rough, boulder-strewn terrain leads to the far end of this narrow, twisting corridor, where a 150-meter waterfall plunges down the north wall. Return to the campsite at the rim.

Day Four: Begin the descent early. After five hours reach a series of waterfalls called Tatlong Tangke ("Three Tanks"). Passing through a gully, the trail leads for another two and a half hours between *kaingin* fields to Kinabuhayan. From here, walk back to Santa Lucia and take a jeepney to San Pablo.

coconut harvesting, and a walking tour of the plantation village, available with or without lunch. You can also opt for a two-hour tour of the museum and village, and sightseeing by carabao cart. Camping is allowed. Room prices range P1,200-2,600.

LOS BANOS

This town, 60 km from Manila, sprawls along the south shore of Laguna de Bay, at the foot of Mt. Makiling. Its name is Spanish for "The Baths."

The sulfur springs flowing from the foot of the mountain have a solid reputation for their medicinal qualities, and curative water is piped into the pools and baths of the many hot spring resorts between Los Banos and Calamba.

These thermal waters induced the Franciscans to build a hospital here as early as 1602; this Hospital de Aguas Santas was taken over by the Americans in 1903 and renamed Camp Eldridge. Los Banos was the site of a Japanese concentration camp, and General Yamashita was tried and executed as a war criminal at Camp Eldridge in 1946.

Attractions

Los Banos also contains a church (1790), the Colleges of Agriculture and Forestry of the **University of the Philippines** (UP), the **International Rice Research Institute** (IRRI), and the **National Arts Center.** The lakeshore is lined with fishing villages like Tadlac; talk to the fishermen and they may take you out night-fishing with them.

Local delicacies include *buko* (young coconut) pie and *bibingka cassava* (cassava cake), which is sold everywhere along the road.

Transportation

Los Banos has frequent buses connecting Manila with San Pablo and Santa Cruz; the trip takes 90 minutes.

Accommodations

Hotels and resorts here are not cheap but reasonably priced.

Lakeview Resort Hotel: Simple rooms plus a swimming pool with naturally heated waters. 728 Lopez St., tel. (049) 536-0101, P400-980.

City of Springs Resort: Another place with hot springs doubling as swimming pools and both fan and a/c rooms. 147 North Villegas St., tel. (049) 536-0731, fax 536-0137, P650-1,400.

It may also be possible to overnight in one of the UP dormitories, especially between semesters.

University of the Philippines

The turnoff for this large, attractive campus (three square km), which extends up the slopes of Mt. Makiling, is east of the town center. Take a jeepney from the T-junction on the main highway. You can meet students from all over Asia here,

and eat at the student's union or the **SEARCA** dormitory across the street.

Visit the **Dairy Training and Research Institute's** dairy bar for good ice cream or *kesong puti* (white cheese). Those interested in plants can visit the **Hortorium.** From the UP campus, another short jeepney ride leads to the **International Rice Research Institute** (IRRI).

International Rice Research Institute

The Ford and Rockefeller Foundations established IRRI in 1960 as a nonprofit organization with the objective of advancing the quality and quantity of rice. They selected the Philippines as its location and chose the site adjacent to the UP College of Agriculture in Los Banos primarily for the rich volcanic soil at the foot of Mt. Makiling. The soil is ideal for intensive agricultural experiments, and IRRI researchers have collaborated with scientists throughout the world to improve rice varieties and technology.

In 1966, IRRI released IR8, a rice variety that revolutionized food production in the tropics. When properly fertilized, it produces double—even triple—the yield of native tropical varieties. Its reception worldwide inspired such terms as "miracle rice" and "green revolution." IRRI research is now coordinated with the national rice improvement programs of many countries, which send specialists here for training and to work on their own new rice varieties. Today, about a third of IRRI's staff works outside the Philippines.

MOUNT MAKILING

This dormant volcano (1,090 meters) is the legendary home of the beautiful goddess Mariang Makiling. The lower slopes, on which dry rice, corn, and bananas are grown, give way to dense vegetation on the upper slopes, which are a 40-square-km national park: see huge trees, orchids, birds, butterflies, and flying lizards in the rainforest. March-June, blue-green flowers lying on the trail indicate the presence of the rare and lovely jade vine in the trees above. Wear long pants to guard against leeches.

Allow a full day to climb the volcano; start early, preferably outside the rainy season (June-Oct.). To check trail conditions or hire a guide, inquire at the Office of the Superintendent of the Makiling Experimental and Demonstration Forest, Room 206, Forest Administration Building.

Exploring the Slopes

Roads lead up from the UP campus to a picnic area and hot springs, and to the National Arts Center of the Philippines, but there's no regular transport. Upon entering the campus, turn right, then left at the T-junction. The road goes straight up under the BSP (Boy Scouts of the Philippines) arch to the camping area on the left, and on to the National Arts Center. To visit the 450-hectare **National Botanical Gardens,** containing over 2,000 plant species, turn left onto Narra Street before reaching the BSP arch, cross a small bridge, then turn right onto Waling Waling Street and proceed uphill for about a kilometer to the gardens, which are just past the Arch of Forestry. The picnic area and hot springs are beyond it.

From the gardens, go past the Forest Administration Building and turn right. A short distance along, just past the last building of the university, a path goes right downhill between two tall trees, to nearby Flat Rocks Falls. The road itself brings you, after about 3.5 km, to the picnic area. From here, you can take a pleasant circular hike. Follow the trail for about 25 minutes to a stream and small dam, from which waterfalls are visible. Don't swim—leeches!

A path leads upstream through the forest for another 25 minutes to the hot springs. There's a sulfurous pool, steam rising from vents, and areas of bubbling mud. Keep to the paths, since there may be boiling mud beneath what appears to be firm ground. From the hot springs, a trail leads in 15 minutes to the road; turn left and 300 meters away are the picnic grounds. The road continues toward Makiling's peak, another nine km.

Accommodations

You can camp on Makiling at several sites operated by the local authorities.

National Arts Center of the Philippines

This complex, commissioned by Imelda Marcos and opened in 1976, features an open-sided 2,500-seat pyramidal pavilion/auditorium, plus facilities serving as a retreat and school for artists of all disciplines to live and work. There are fine views over Laguna de Bay and down to Alligator Lake.

To visit the center, you must obtain a pass at the Cultural Center in Manila. Apply at the office of Miss Kasilag at least two days in advance. To get there from the UP campus, pass under the BSP arch, fork left at the first major junction through the Arch of the National Arts Center, turn immediately right, and follow the narrow twisting road for three km to the auditorium.

CALAMBA

This market town on the lakeshore plain of Laguna de Bay is famous in the Philippines as the birthplace in 1861 of José Rizal.

Rizal House

The Rizal House is a national shrine. A reproduction of the original Spanish-style two-story house, it's cool and airy beneath the red-tile roof. The thick stone ground-floor walls have doors wide enough for a carriage to enter. The upper walls and balustrades are of wood, with sliding *kapis*-shell windows. It contains antique furniture and household articles, a library, and Rizal memorabilia; the garden is equally pleasant, with many fruit trees—a revealing example of how elite provincial Filipinos lived in the mid-19th century. It evokes the cultured, comfortable environment, provisioned from family lands and maintained by servants, that gave

---

WORSHIPPING RIZAL

Calamba is the center of the Watawat ng Lahi ("Flag of the Race") sect, whose 250,000 members have deified "Papa" José Rizal, believing he was a reincarnation of Christ and will return to redeem the faithful from their life of suffering. For them, Rizal's novels are the Bible, and his 12 apostles are his former associates and other national heroes—such as Mabini, del Pilar, Blumentritt, and Bonifacio. The sect's main meeting hall outside the town tops a hill locally called Burol Na Ginto ("Hill of Gold"). Other Rizalian cults are also scattered throughout the islands.

rise to the country's first renaissance man. Ceremonies take place here on the anniversary of his birthday (19 June) and execution (30 December).

Across the street is the church, with its typical colonial long-naved layout. Fine views from the bell tower. The plaza opposite contains the giant Calamba Jar, inscribed with the names of the town's *barangays*. It's the town symbol: *calamba* means "jar."

Enchanted Kingdom

Several years ago an almost upscale resort was opened 10 km north of Calamba near the town of Santa Rosa. Rides include all sorts of Western mishmash and Filipinos who have never left their country think this place is the most amazing theme park anywhere. Westerners may enjoy the unique flavor and an opportunity to experience a Disney attempt in struggling Southeast Asia.

Admission is P400 and the park is open daily.

RIZAL PROVINCE

Rizal lies immediately east of Metro Manila, where the eastern part of the province is fast becoming a continuation of Manila's suburban sprawl. The best area in the province is south of this industrial/residential area to the northern shore of Laguna de Bay. This may be conveniently accomplished by incorporating your visit to Pagsanjan Falls into a trip around the Laguna de Bay loop.

History

After the Spaniards took Manila in 1571, this area lay directly in their line of expansion. During the following 50 years, priests and soldiers worked together to found many of the towns situated on or near the lakeshore. A number of old churches have survived from this period. Morong, as capital of a politico-military district, was an early center of influence. In 1762, Pasig (now Metro Manila), Cainta, and Taytay fell to the invading British. The region saw action during the revolution and Philippine-American War. When the Americans created the province in 1901, they attempted to pacify revolutionary sentiment by naming it in honor of the principal Filipino martyr and hero. Through its proximity to Manila, Rizal was in the vanguard of accelerated national progress under the U.S.

After independence, development of Rizal began in earnest. Farmland became subdivisions, factories spawned pollution, while real estate prices multiplied a hundredfold, making a handful of landowners very rich. By 1976, 15 towns adjacent to Manila, containing two-thirds of Rizal's population, had been swallowed up by suburban sprawl and were transferred to the jurisdiction of Metro Manila. One of them, Pasig, ironically remains Rizal's provincial capital.

Today, rapid development of the lakeshore in Rizal Province is once again changing the landscape and livelihood of the residents.

Transportation

Buses from the BLTB terminal in Pasay City pass through Rizal en route to Laguna. Alternatively, from Ermita, take the monorail or a Blumentritt or Monumento jeepney north up Rizal Avenue to Quiricada Street near the San Lazaro Hospital, Santa Cruz.

Regular eastbound buses of Antipolo Highway Line, EMBC, and CERT, coming from Divisoria, cross Rizal Avenue here. The main highway through Rizal follows the lakeshore into Laguna Province. The Manila-Infanta (Quezon Province) road passes just north of Antipolo. From Antipolo or Taytay, jeepneys ply the lesser roads to Angono, Binangonan, and Cardonao.

CAINTA

Numerous residents of Cainta, the first town outside Metro Manila, are referred to as Sepoy. Their distinctive bronze skin and Indian features mark their descent from a company of Indian soldiers under British command who, after the 1762-64 occupation, mutinied and chose to stay with their new Filipina wives rather than leave.

Now an industrial town, Cainta is noted for its Holy Week *senaculo*, which reenacts the Last Supper on Holy Thursday and Crucifixion on Good Friday, during which penitents carry heavy crosses and wear crowns of thorns. The *salubong* (meeting) takes place on Easter Sunday morning.

East of Cainta, the road divides at Taytay, a woodworking town, branching to Antipolo and Angono. Frequent buses and jeepneys serve both towns. The lakeshore route through Angono has more to offer.

ANTIPOLO

This town (founded 1578), situated at 225 meters in the foothills of the Sierra Madre, is cooler than Manila (29 km away). The name of the town derives from the flowering trees that were once common in the area; there's one near the church.

A popular local park is situated beside Hinulugang Taktak Falls, where you can swim. Local products include cashew nuts and clay pots.

May Fiesta

Antipolo is the site of a major pilgrimage in May, when thousands of devotees come from all over the country to pay homage to the miraculous image of Nuestra Señora de la Paz y Buen Viaje ("Our Lady of Peace and Good Voyage"), the patron saint of travelers. The Virgin's statuette was brought from Mexico in 1626 and entrusted to the Jesuits at Antipolo. During a Chinese uprising, it was thrown into a fire but didn't burn.

After being declared patron saint of the Manila galleons, it was sometimes carried aboard them to ensure their safety. It made eight successful roundtrips to Acapulco between 1641 and 1748, despite the blockading efforts of the Dutch and English fleets and the threat of typhoons. Naturally, this was attributed to the miraculous powers of the statuette! Subsequently, the devout believed that no journey should be undertaken without a visit to the shrine. In the old days, pilgrims came from Manila by boat and the wealthy were carried up from the lakeshore in hammocks.

Legend holds that the Virgin was originally enshrined in a makeshift church, but natives used to find her absent from her altar. She was found leaning against the trunk of a *tipolo* tree, and this became the site of the present church, a modern circular structure with a fine marble altar. The icon, which was canonically crowned before 100,000 people in 1926, is taken from its shrine four times daily for the benefit of the faithful, who come year-round to touch and pray to the small statue for safe journeys and the granting of other wishes.

In May, the monthlong pilgrimage, centuries-old and still eagerly anticipated by purveyors of religious paraphernalia, is a combination of spiritual devotion and spirited fiesta. Pilgrims repair from the church for picnics at nearby Taktak Falls. Each afternoon, a hymn-singing procession offers flowers to the Virgin at the church, and for nine evenings, a Santacruzan pageant is held. The Feast of Our Lady of the Immaculate Conception on 8 December is marked by an evening procession.

Accommodations

You can stay at **Las Brisas Resort, Villa Cristina Resort,** or **Antipolo Hotel.** These places cost P300-550.

ANGONO

Angono, 29 km from Manila, is noted for its Carabao Festival on 14-15 May (see **Pulilan,** in Bulacan) and the town fiesta, the Feast of San Clemente, on 23 November, in which fisherfolk carrying paddles, bamboo poles, and fish traps escort the saint's image around town in a lively parade, amidst shouts of "Viva San Clemente!" The entire town then proceeds to the shores of Laguna de Bay, where a huge raft is waiting to take the statue of both the Virgin Mary and San Clemente for a ritual spin on the lake.

As people try to board the huge raft, villagers throw mud and hurl stems from water hyacinth. While the devout on the raft throw crackers and apples, the swimmers and followers throw mud. The raft is dragged farther out into the lake, and while all and sundry swim after it, the somber participants aboard recite the rosary. When finished, the crowd on board begins to throw apples at the people swimming by.

As the crowd returns to shore, covered from head to toe with mud, the rest of the townsfolk line up to dump water on the disheveled. Even the town mayor joins in the merrymaking.

Angono Falls are near town, with jeepneys departing every 10 minutes.

CARDONA

Cardona is the center of a thriving *bangus* (milk-fish) industry, with thousands of hectares of fish corrals stretching out across the lake from the shore. The water area controlled by this municipality is over twice its land area.

Touring the Lake
There are three landings: Cardona Market, Dalig, and Looc. Sample tasty, fresh, broiled *bangus* with a dash of *kalamansi* juice at one of the small restaurants. It's also possible to hire a *banca* for a trip out through the corrals to see the fish harvested and perhaps stop at Cielito Lindo, a small island about two km offshore.

MORONG

This town (founded 1586), four km past Cardona, is noted for its church, considered one of the finest examples of tropical baroque architecture in the Philippines. It was built in 1612-15 by Chinese craftsmen, whose influence is apparent in the stone lions at the entrance to the driveway. The exquisitely carved three-story facade and four-story octagonal bell tower were redesigned in 1850-53. The tower's cross is a prominent landmark. Note the bullet holes in the side walls, where captured Katipunero rebels were shot by the Spanish. The walls of the simple interior are lined with the 14 Stations of the Cross.

The Morong High School building reflects recent Philippine history. It was constructed by forced labor (1881-86), became the capitol of the politico-military district of Morong (1884-96), was taken over by Filipino revolutionaries in 1899, by U.S. forces in 1901, by the Japanese during 1942-44, and has been a high school since 1945.

About one km south of town, a small road leads to Uugong Falls, where you can swim; note the old irrigation system above the falls.

TANAY

Tanay (fiesta: 22-24 January) is an important local trade center 53 km from Manila. Its church was founded in 1606; the current building of lo-cally quarried stone was completed in 1783. It has a four-story octagonal tower, a facade featuring columns topped by carved pineapples, a *convento*, and courtyard. Inside are five ornate altars, plus finely carved 200-year-old Stations of the Cross along the nave. The scenic lakeshore, where fishing *bancas* line the wharf and restaurants serve fresh lakefish, is one km from the church and market.

Subok Festival—A Trial of Faith
During Holy Week, a trial of faith called the *subok* occurs. On Good Friday, when the flower-be-decked *carroza* emerges from the church with the statue of the dead Christ, onlookers scramble to insert an assortment of objects into the hollows of the statue. After the procession, these items, which may include bronze medallions, crucifixes, pebbles, and catfish eyes, are retrieved to become *anting-antings* (talismans).

Francis Ford Coppola
Part of the film *Apocalypse Now* was filmed around Daranak Falls (14 meters) and the smaller Batlag Falls. Get there by traveling eight km by jeepney, going up toward the town of Sampaloc (14 km) in the hills behind Tanay. Ask the driver to drop you at the turnoff, then walk about two km along a dirt road to the falls, where you can swim in forested surroundings.

The hills in this area have been strongholds of Filipino resistance fighters against the Spanish, Americans, and Japanese. They are now favored by hunters, who seek wild pig, deer, monkeys, quail, snipe, and pigeons.

JALAJALA

The lakeshore road out of Tanay continues through the fishing town of Pililla, then zigzags up into Laguna Province. A 14-km branch road stays by the lake, following the peninsula beneath the wooded slopes of Mt. Sembrano (743 meters) to Jalajala. Roxas Island, a private resort, can be seen from this road, and there are good views across the lake to Talim Island.

Paul de la Gironiere Hacienda
Jalajala is a picturesque village containing the ruins of Paul de la Gironiere's hacienda. He was

a French doctor who lived in the Philippines from 1820-40, operating a huge estate and traveling extensively. *Twenty Years in the Philippines* is an entertaining book in which he relates his experiences, including exciting, but exaggerated, accounts of his adventures among the headhunters of northern Luzon.

He is associated with the killing, in 1823, of a giant man-eating crocodile said to have measured over eight meters long and weighed 2,000 kilograms. Its skull, the largest on record excluding fossil remains, is presently in Harvard University's Museum of Comparative Zoology, Massachusetts.

M.G.L. DOMENY DE RIENZI

LUZON~CENTRAL PLAIN

Luzon's Central Plain is the country's most extensive lowland, a fertile region that produces about a third of the country's rice. Roughly 200 by 80 km and covering over 15,000 square km, it comprises the provinces of Bulacan, Pampanga, Tarlac, Nueva Ecija, the eastern part of Pangasinan, and Aurora.

HISTORY

The Central Plain, once rich hinterland, prompted Miguel Lopez de Legazpi to make Manila the national capital. At that time, the population was concentrated within 20 km of the sea around Manila Bay and Lingayen Gulf, while the interior was heavily forested and largely uninhabited. The Spaniards surveyed Bulacan in 1571 and began establishing settlements in 1578. Generally, however, they took relatively little interest in the area, and settlement in the interior remained limited until the 18th century. By the end of the 19th century, most of the land was under cultivation, and the widespread pattern of tenancy and absentee landlords had emerged.

Revolution against Spain

Bulacan, Pampanga, Tarlac, and Nueva Ecija were among the first eight provinces to rise in revolt against Spain in 1896. During the Philippine-American War, Gen. Arthur MacArthur took Aguinaldo's capital, Malolos, and drove him and his followers north across the plain. Several towns were temporary capitals of the First Philippine Republic—San Fernando, San Isidro, Cabanatuan, Tarlac, and Bayombong—where Aguinaldo finally disbanded his army and initiated guerrilla warfare.

World War II and the Huk Rebellion

In 1941, the Japanese swept across the plain from Lingayen Gulf to Manila; just over three years later, liberating U.S. forces took the same route. The Hukbalahap movement had been the country's most effective guerrilla movement; the Americans found the Central Plain largely in Huk hands. But having emerged from the war with a sizable armed force and a mass base spread across the plain, the Huks became a communist-inspired agrarian movement opposed to the feudal land tenancy system.

Regarded as subversives, their rebellion was put down in the '50s, but it had a brief resurgence in 1965. The NPA feeds off the unrest caused by unfulfilled demands for land reform and by perpetual rural poverty.

Mt. Pinatubo

The Central Plain was always a "rice bowl" supplying Manila and other rice-deficient areas of Luzon, until the eruption of Mt. Pinatubo wiped out some of the most fertile land in the Philippines. After four eruptions over five days in June 1991, Mt. Pinatubo gained notoriety for being one of the most devastating active volcanoes in this century.

Soon after the eruptions, Typhoon Yunya hit Luzon, turning volcanic ash and mud into rivers of mud and lahar. The lahar flood wiped out villages, bridges, and farms (causing the premature closure of Clark Air Force Base), particularly devastating Pampanga, Zambales, and Tarlac Provinces. Subic Naval Base was covered with ash, also hastening the U.S. Navy's decision to leave.

The following year, devastation struck again, as Pinatubo erupted once more on 21 September, wiping out another 9,000 homes and killing more people.

In all, more than 1,000 people were killed by the eruptions of Mt. Pinatubo, and over 1.2 million people were displaced from Luzon's rice bowl.

TRANSPORTATION

A good system of transportation operates on the Central Plain's dense network of roads. Two main highways cross the plain, one leading to Baguio and Ilocos, with a branch to Lingayen, the other to Cagayan Valley. The North Luzon Expressway Extension links Balintawak, at the edge of Metro Manila, with Dau, just north of Angeles, where it ends at the old MacArthur Highway.

BULACAN PROVINCE

All routes north out of Manila pass through this densely populated, fertile farming province. The famous festivals of Bocaue, Obando, Plaridel, and Pulilan are fun to attend, while Malolos and Biak-na-Bato National Park are historically significant for their role in the Filipinos' initial quest for independence in 1896-99. The towns of Bulacan can easily be visited as day-trips from Manila but are best seen while on the Manila-Banaue route through the Cagayan Valley.

Bulacan (2,637 square km) has over 1.4 million people. Its name derives from *bulak,* Tagalog for cotton, the former principal product.

Bulacan has produced many notable poets, propagandists, and journalists. Long a hotbed of resistance against Spain, it was the birthplace of Francisco Baltazar (1789-1862), known as Balagtas, whose allegorical verse subtly alludes to Spanish tyranny. His birthday (2 April) is celebrated throughout the province.

Transportation

Baliwag Transit has frequent buses to Bulacan from its Caloocan City terminal. Jeepneys run from the Victory Liner terminal in Metro Manila to Obando and some of the closer communities. Philippine Rabbit serves Malolos; the Metrotren and "Love Tren" serve points in Bulacan. The old MacArthur Highway and railroad link the towns bypassed by the Manila-Angeles expressway. The highway to the Cagayan Valley en route to Ifugao Province and the rice terraces of Banaue branches off the expressway near Plaridel.

NOVALICHES

A road leads northeast off EDSA (East de los Santos Ave.), the Manila ring-road, from a point east of Caloocan to this town, which is noted for Pipigan, a rice harvest festival held in January. *Malagkit* (glutinous rice) is pounded with mortar and pestle into *pinipig,* a popular delicacy that's fried or made into a sweet. The Feast of Our Lady of Lourdes is observed at the Grotto here on 11 February. Though the town of Novaliches is in Rizal Province, it is geographically more convenient to Bulacan.

The Novaliches Reservoir is east of the town and can also be reached by traveling northeast from the Quezon Memorial Circle (Quezon City). Situated about 20 km north of Manila, this large reservoir contained by La Mesa Dam is a major source of the city's water. An archaeological site at Novaliches dates to 300 B.C.

MONTALBAN

Beyond this town is the Wawa, or Montalban Dam, another of Metro Manila's chief water sources, which is surrounded by steep limestone hills and overlooked by Mt. Irid (1,448 meters). Though in Rizal Province, it can be reached through Marikina and San Mateo (founded 1578), making an agreeable day trip from Manila for swimming in the Marikina River, hiking, and picnicking.

Legends of the Dam

In 1945, the dam was the object of a misguided and costly U.S. campaign. The Japanese had prepared a formidable defense system of caves and tunnels in the nearby hills, and it took over three months of intense combat to dislodge them. Late in the battle, it was discovered that the dam had long since ceased to supply Manila with water, so that much time and manpower had been expended in vain.

Treasure hunters are still attracted by talk of gold left buried in the caves. One story relates how a Dumagat who came into town was seen rolling his cigarettes on a gold bar and then sold three more bars to a local resident for a sack of rice. The Puray Settlement of Dumagats is in Montalban municipality.

THE FERTILITY FESTIVAL OF OBANDO

Obando, a fishing town (founded in 1754) 16 km north of Manila, is famous for its three-day religious festival in May deriving from ancient fertility rites. A different saint is honored each day: San Pascual Baylon (17 May), Santa Clara, locally called Clarang Pinongpino (18), and the Virgin of Salambao (19).

The Festival

Legend holds that the image of the Virgin was scooped out of the water by a fisherman from a *salambao,* a raft and net. San Pascual supposedly danced his prayers. Around midmorning, the saints' images are paraded through the streets and colorfully dressed devotees dance the *pandanggo* to lively brass band music.

Childless couples dance in the belief that they will be blessed with offspring; others to find a mate; for a good harvest or catch; for the curing of an ailment; to gain protection from harm; for penance, or piety. Those whose prayers have been granted may continue to participate to thank the saint who interceded for them.

The procession and dancing begin and end at the church altar. Outside the church is a lively market with many food stalls, and handicrafts on sale. Each weekend in June, Pista ng Krus features a fluvial procession in the hope of a bountiful harvest.

This author attended the festival a few years ago and found it to be a minor, yet very interesting event where carnal passion and religious fever made a very odd mixture.

BOCAUE

The MacArthur Highway leads through **Meycauayan** (church: 1668) on the way to Bocaue. The odor of tanneries, which support a leathercraft industry, pervades the town. There are some gold and silver jewelry shops too.

The River Festival

North of Marilao (fiesta: 8 May) is Bocaue, noted for its colorful river festival on the first Sunday of July. Custom holds that 200 years ago, a fisherman found a cross (believed to be miraculous) floating in the Bocaue River. Today, a replica of the original, known as the Holy Cross of Wawa, is brought in a morning procession from the church to the river, where it's enshrined in the bamboo Pagoda Sa Wawa and mounted on an elaborately decorated barge. Crowds line the riverbank as the cross is escorted downstream by a fleet of flower-bedecked *bancas* bearing fishermen, their families, and other devotees.

In the afternoon, the parade returns upriver and the cross is returned to the church. Flagellantes perform penitence in Bocaue on Good Friday.

MALOLOS

This provincial capital and trading center is 45 km north of Manila.

History

For four months in 1898-99, Malolos was the capital of the Republic. After the defeat of Spain and Aguinaldo's declaration of independence, tension between Filipinos and Americans escalated. The revolutionary government moved its capital from Bacoor (Cavite) to Malolos, where Aguinaldo and his cabinet held office in Malolos Cathedral and *convento* (founded 1575, present church built 1817).

Delegates to the Revolutionary Congress met in Barasoain Church (1884), just outside Malolos. The Malolos Congress ratified independence, framed the Malolos Constitution, and inaugurated the short-lived First Philippine Republic, known as the Malolos Republic, with Aguinaldo as president. Twelve days later, the Philippine-American War broke out, and Malolos soon fell to U.S. forces. The inauguration's anniversary is commemorated in the Barasoain Church each 23 January.

Attractions

The **Hiyas ng Bulacan** ("Jewels of Bulacan") is a cultural complex (open Mon.-Sat. 0830-1130 and 1330-1630) located 500 meters from Barasoain Church. One building houses a collection of paintings, antiques, artifacts, and mementos of the revolution; the other displays local handicrafts for sale. On Good Friday, a *senaculo* (passion play) is performed in the complex (another takes place at nearby Ticay).

Casa Real, a large, old Spanish house in the area, is now Malolos's municipal library and museum.

Accommodations

Stay at **Barasoain Hotel, Flying "A" Hotel,** or at **Malolos Youth Hostel.**

Vicinity of Malolos

The town of **Bulacan,** 11 km south of Malolos, is a former provincial capital and site of the shrine of M.H. del Pilar, the revolutionary writer whose work helped instigate rebellion against Spain.

A road leads west from Malolos to the Pampanga River delta region. Note the extensive fishponds. Beyond **Paombong,** where you can see flagellantes on Good Friday, lies **Hagonoy** (church: 1731), a river port 15 km upstream from Manila Bay. Sugar and molasses are shipped from here, and *sinamay,* an abaca cloth, is woven locally. Hagonoy's fiesta (29 April) is noted for attractive street decorations.

Calumpit, north of Malolos, is noted for pottery and has a fine 16th-century church.

EAST OF THE EXPRESSWAY

San Jose del Monte

This town's Gaya-gaya is the site of the Philippine Grotto of Our Lady of Lourdes, built in 1961 by a cancer patient claiming a successful cure in France. Now pilgrims seek miraculous cures here, and crutches left amid the rock formations attest to apparent success.

Pandi

Pandi (church: 1792) is noted for its mineral springs and baths. The Angat River leaves the rugged terrain around the Ipo Dam and flows through Norzagaray (site of an Exotic Deer Farm Project) and Angat (fiesta: 4 May).

In 1945, Japanese troops controlling the dam (one of Manila's major water sources) were forced out of their caves by heavy napalm bombing and overcome by U.S. troops and Filipino guerrillas.

PLARIDEL

Plaridel was formerly called Quingua (Quingwa); Quingua Church dates from 1580. At the Battle of Quingua (1899), Filipino riflemen temporarily checked the U.S. advance, inflicting heavy casualties before falling back.

Calesa Festival

In the Calesa Festival (28 December), horse-drawn *calesas* parade before St. James Parish Church. Many participants are jockeys and horse owners, giving thanks for luck and the good health of their animals. Devotees bring St. James's wooden image in an early morning six-km procession from Sipat to Plaridel. The procession features Ati-Atihan-type street dancing, and the celebration lasts until 30 December.

PULILAN

The Carabao Festival

The popular Carabao Festival (14-15 May) is a harvest festival in honor of San Isidro Labrador, the farmer's patron saint who lived in Spain 1070-1160. Around late morning, local rice farmers ride their carabao, scrubbed and bedecked with ribbons and flowers, to the church, where they urge them to kneel or genuflect as they're blessed by the priest.

The parade also includes brightly decorated carts containing the farmers' families and harvest produce, accompanied by brass bands. Subsequent events may include carabao races, demonstrations of tricks, traditional games, and stage presentations such as *comedias* and *zarzuelas.*

To get here from Manila, take a Baliwag Transit bus to Plaridel, then a jeepney.

Accommodations

Stay at **Calesa Lodge** in Santo Cristo.

BIAK-NA-BATO NATIONAL PARK

The highway leading north to the Cagayan Valley passes through **San Ildefonso,** a town on the eastern side of Pampanga's Candaba Swamp. Maalangaan Cave and Spring are in the vicinity, and a road leads east to Tangue Caves. Farther north is **San Miguel,** noted for its *pastillas de leche* (milk candies). Rattan chairs are made here, and bamboo baskets are woven in nearby Tibagan.

The fiesta of San Miguel de Mayumo (8 May) features attractive street decorations, a religious procession, and the sale of local food and confectionery. Tokod Caves and Tilandong Falls are in the area. San Miguel is the gateway to Biak-na-Bato National Park and Sibul Springs.

History of the Park

For about six months in 1897 during the fighting against the Spanish, General Aguinaldo had his headquarters in the remote caves of Biak-na-Bato. Here, revolutionary leaders approved a constitution and set up the Biak-na-Bato Republic with Aguinaldo as president. Shortly afterward, however, negotiations between the Spanish and Filipinos culminated in a peace agreement—the Pact of Biak-na-Bato—and Aguinaldo and his companions journeyed to Manila to begin their exile in Hong Kong.

Exploring the Park

The park lies northeast of Biak-na-Bato village. Follow the 12-km road from San Miguel, bearing left at the Y-junction after eight km. This hilly area offers good hiking. Upstream on the Baliculing River are limestone formations and the Bahay Paniqui ("Bat House") Caves, one of which contains a natural indoor swimming pool fed by an underground stream. A track leads eight km from Biak-na-Bato to Sibul Springs.

The latter can also be reached from the main highway by a direct all-weather road that begins four km north of San Miguel, at the Km 77 marker, and winds 10 km east through ricefields to the springs. The thermal spring water, piped into swimming pools and an old indoor bathhouse, is said to soothe rheumatism and skin afflictions. Madlum Caves are on the Madlum River, a short distance upstream from the springs.

PAMPANGA PROVINCE

Pampanga sits astride the main highway from Manila to Baguio and was hit very hard both physically and economically by the eruption of Mt. Pinatubo on 12 June 1991. Its focal points are Angeles City and San Fernando.

Angeles was once the site of Clark Air Force Base, until it was abandoned by the U.S. military shortly after the Mt. Pinatubo eruption.

There are still severe volcanic ash slides and seismic activity, but the local economy is still busy with the nightlife trade, as many men still come to this city for its nightlife, camaraderie, and reputation.

San Fernando, the more subdued provincial capital, is noted for its Good Friday crucifixions, flagellantes, and Christmas Eve Lantern Festival.

History

The natives of Pampanga were pacified by Martin de Goiti after fierce battles at Lubao and elsewhere. The *datus* cooperated with the Spanish in exchange for privileges such as retaining their slaves, which they did for decades. They collected taxes in the form of rice, which was sent to feed Manila and the Spanish army. Pampanga was also the province that suffered most from the *bandala,* the compulsory sale of rice and other produce to the government, which the authorities often failed to pay for.

Pampanga's forests, of which little remain, supplied timber to the galleon-building shipyards of Cavite. Pampango soldiers assisted the Spaniards in many campaigns.

But Pampanga also has a long history of rebellion, including early revolts against the Spanish and a notorious Chinese attack on Spanish and Filipino churchgoers in Guagua, known as the Red Christmas of 1762, as well as participation in the revolution. As the province with the highest land-tenancy rate and the greatest agrarian discontent, Pampanga was the cradle of the postwar, left-wing rebellion by the Huks.

The People

The Pampanguenos (or Kapampangan) are a tribe of unknown origin. One theory holds that they came from the shores of Singarak Lake in West Sumatra; another groups them with other lowland Filipinos, having the Malay Peninsula as their ancestral home. Early Kapampangans could write, and their prosperous riverbank settlements were known to Chinese and other traders before the Spanish arrival. Kapampangans retain a distinctive culture and are noted for their clannishness and good cooking. They speak the Pampango language, though Tagalog is widely understood, too.

Transportation

All bus lines linking Manila with Baguio, Pangasinan, and Ilocos pass through Pampanga. Philippine Rabbit, Pantranco North, and Victory Liner have frequent departures. The expressway meets the old MacArthur Highway at Dau, just north of Angeles. Philippine Rabbit serves San Fernando from Manila.

Victory Liner links Angeles and Olongapo (60 km). Baliwag Transit and E. Jose Transport operate cross-country services from Olongapo to Cabanatuan (Nueva Ecija) via San Fernando. **Arayat Express** also serves the San Fernando-Cabanatuan route.

SAN FERNANDO

San Fernando, the provincial capital, 66 km north of Manila, was established in 1775 and named after King Ferdinand III of Spain. There are few reasons to visit this town unless you are coming up here to experience one of their famous festivals.

Tourist Office

The provincial tourist office is located here, and probably gets about 10 Western visitors per year. But then, that's the whole idea . . . put your tourist offices where they will never be visited and your government bureaucrats can spend their days sleeping and eating rather than actually helping to promote tourism in the country.

Festivals

This commercial center has no outstanding sites, but it's worth visiting on Good Friday, and for the town fiesta (30 May) and Lantern Festival (24 December).

Good Friday Flagellantes: On Good Friday morning around 1100, many flagellantes, their backs raw, prostrate themselves in the church courtyard for others to whip them. Don't get too close or you may be splattered with blood. The crowd then walks two km to San Pedro where, at about 1300, fanatical devotees, dressed as Christ, reenact the crucifixion—with nails. A memorable spectacle!

Lantern Festival: The parade and judging of the giant *paroles* (lanterns), with their kaleidoscopic designs, are held late on Christmas Eve, so plan to stay overnight in San Fernando. Eight competing *barangays* each spend about P25,000 to build these huge (5-10 meters across) lanterns out of crepe paper, tin foil, cellophane, bamboo, and hundreds of light bulbs. They're mounted on trucks and powered by generators.

The parade starts around 2100, and the judging by town officials and awarding of cash prizes take place in the town plaza after midnight. The winning lantern is traditionally burned after Christmas to prevent future copies.

TO VIGAN, LAOAG

SAN FERNANDO

SAN FERNANDO BAY

MA CHO TEMPLE

HOTEL MIKKA

GOLD CITY FAST FOOD

NEW SOCIETY RESTAURANT

UNITED CAFE

P. BURGOS ST.

A. BONIFACIO ST.

DUNKIN DONUTS

DON JOAQUIN ST.

GOV. ORTEGA ST.

NEW MARKET

MARKET

OSIAS ST.

MIDTOWN FOOD PALACE

MANDARIN HOUSE HOTEL / RESTAURANT

THE DANISH BAKER

GOV. LUCERO ST.

P. DE TAVERA ST.

SAN FERNANDO BEACH RD.

ADMIRAL FOOD CENTER

MUNICIPAL HALL

POST OFFICE

TO BACSIL RIDGE

HOTEL CASINO ROYALE

JELRA SUPERMARKET

BUSES TO BAGUIO

PNB

RIZAL AVE.

GOMEZ ST.

CHURCH

ZAMORA ST.

GOV. LUNA ST.

PAL

PLAZA

PHILIPPINE RABBIT BUS STOP

JOLLIBEE

GEN. LUNA ST.

GUZMAN ST.

PNR ST.

ANCHETA ST.

TOURIST OFFICE

PLAZA HOTEL

MIDWAY RESTAURANT

BAYVIEW HOTEL

RAILWAY STATION

MABINI ST.

(QUEZON AVE.)

GENERAL HOSPITAL

FRIENDSHIP PAGODA

GAPUZ

ZIGZAG RD.

GOV. AGUILAR RD.

CALTEX

MUSEO DE LA UNION

PROVINCIAL CAPITOL

MANILA NORTH RD.

HIGH SCHOOL RD.

0   100 m

TO MANILA

GIACOMINO'S PIZZA

McDONALD'S

GOV. GUERRERO RD.

PHILIPPINE RABBIT BUS TERMINAL

Accommodations

Stay at the **Pampanga Lodge** (P100 for 12 hours, P200 for 24 hours), which has a Chinese restaurant, plus a balcony overlooking the church courtyard and town plaza. There are other, more expensive, accommodations on the outskirts of town. Horse-drawn *calesas* still provide transportation within San Fernando.

Vicinity of San Fernando

Minalin, to the south, is noted for its "Belles of Minalin" New Year's celebration (1 January), in which men dressed as beauty queens ride through town on festive floats. **Mexico,** to the east, has its fiesta 4 May.

A road leads southwest from San Fernando to Bataan and Olongapo City, skirting the delta region and passing through Bacolor, Guagua, and Lubao. **Bacolor,** the former provincial capital, was also the capital of the Philippines during the British occupation of Manila in 1762-63, when the Spanish under Simon de Anda retreated here.

During the first days of 1942, U.S. and Filipino forces retreating to Bataan dynamited the bridges across the Pampanga River a few hours ahead of the advancing Japanese, then fought a bloody delaying action on the Porac-Guagua line.

APALIT

This town, 11 km south of San Fernando, lies just east of the MacArthur Highway, on the Pampanga River at the southwest corner of the Candaba Swamp. Apalit (church founded 1580, present building 1880) is noted for handicrafts—pottery, *bolos*, and hats, mats, and handbags of *buri* palm fibers.

Festival

Early inhabitants adopted St. Peter, a fisherman, as their patron saint. They call him Apong Iro ("Grandfather Iro"). Apalit's three-day celebration (28-30 June) of the Feast of Saints Peter and Paul is highlighted by a six-km fluvial parade of the saints' images and brightly decorated *bancas*. The life-size images, accompanied by dancing devotees and brass bands, are carried from the home of the *camadera* (fiesta sponsor) in Capalangan, through the streets to the riverbank, where they're transferred to a pagoda mounted on a barge. Dancers and bands also greet the barge upon its arrival.

ANGELES CITY

Angeles was once a jungle clearing that grew to a city of 200,000. It expanded rapidly around the former U.S. Clark Air Force Base, whose presence spawned a thriving hospitality industry with bars, nightclubs, strip clubs, hotels, restaurants, and thousands of available girls. Clark was said to have the highest re-enlistment rate of any U.S. base.

After the eruption of Mt. Pinatubo in June 1991, the abrupt closure of the base caused hundreds of small businesses to fail overnight. Caught off-guard with damages from the volcano and a rapid drop in business, many foreigners and Filipinos simply abandoned Angeles City, taking huge losses.

Today, there is some semblance of recovery, but the city is no longer in the Asian limelight. However, after the hospitality industry died along M.H. del Pilar and Mabini Streets in Manila, due to new laws about "girlie bars," Angeles City has regained some of its former stature as a mecca for girls, girls, girls!

One of the chief draws for male visitors is that the working girls are given 50% of the bar fine by the owners of the establishments and therefore expect little or no tip the following morning.

The town, however, is rough in the roughest sense. No taxis, tons of hustlers, broken sidewalks, destroyed roads, collapsing buildings, and enough heat and dust to choke even the most determined of travelers. Tijuana in the 1950s probably looked better than this hellhole.

The Former U.S. Base

Clark Air Force Base started out as Fort Stotsenburg, with a U.S. Cavalry detachment in 1902; a dirt airstrip was added later. It was renamed in 1919 after Major Harold Clark, an aviator killed in a crash. During WW II, Clark Field was the first Japanese target. It was bombed, evacuated, and taken over by the Japanese until 1945, when they made a major stand here against U.S. forces advancing from Lingayen Gulf. It took a week to recapture the airfield.

Clark served as a key logistical center during the Korean and Vietnam Wars. This 550-square-km complex (the largest U.S. military facility in the world), almost the size of Singapore, was the headquarters of the 13th U.S. Air Force. Virtually a self-contained "state within a state," it had 2,700 buildings, a 3,200-meter runway, and was manned by about 8,000 military personnel, 800 civilians, 12,000 dependents, and 18,000 Filipino employees. The base injected US$115 million annually into the local economy and provided a ready supply of PX goods and other U.S. products.

When it was abandoned in June 1991, widescale looting and destruction occurred, as a way of life disappeared forever for many Filipinos.

Attractions

One doesn't go to Angeles for culture and history, though it has a few old buildings: a church built in 1876-96, post office in 1899, and the City Hall Annex Building also in 1899. The latter was the headquarters of the revolutionary army under Aguinaldo, before being taken over by the pursuing Americans led by Gen. Arthur MacArthur. Angeles City has an excellent infrastructure with modern buildings, banks, fast food outlets, and shops. Its entertainment industry is still alive, and many expats linger on here, rehashing the good old days.

Mabalacat

MacArthur Highway leads north from Angeles and Dau to Mabalacat, where in 1944, the Japanese organized the first kamikaze group, the Shimpu Special Attack Corps. A command post was established on nearby Colacirfa Hill, which still contains multichambered tunnels dug by the Japanese. A **Kamikaze Memorial** is located at the Mabalacat East Airfield, and the **Kameso Museum and Library** houses documents, literature, paintings, and replicas of kamikaze planes.

Accommodations

Angeles has some of the best-priced hotels in the country with dozens of places in the P500-800 price range. Most are located along the road that skirts the former American air base.

New Liberty Hotel: Inexpensive option off MacArthur Highway a short stroll from the go-go bars and nightclubs. Spacious grounds, swimming pool. Coching Alley, tel. (045) 602-5896, P250-600.

Tropicana Resort Hotel: Clean hotel with Mistys Nightclub and reasonably priced a/c rooms. 151 Fields Ave., tel. (045) 785-1822, P500-900.

Phoenix Hotel: Very well maintained hotel with swimming pool, soccer matches on the tube, and friendly managers. All rooms with a/c, telephone, minibar, cable TV, hot showers (who needs it?). 810 Malabanias Rd., tel. (045) 888-2195, fax 204-2074, P600-900.

Sunset Gardens: American-style motel with large swimming pool and breezy restaurant popular with visiting Australians and German travel writers who work for Lonely Planet. Malabanas Rd., tel. (045) 888-2312, P400-700.

Vegas International Hotel: A new place opened in late 1997 with Western management, decent swimming pool, conference hall, restaurant, pool tables, gym, 24-hour security, and clean, spacious rooms with cable TV. Malabanias Rd., tel. (045) 602-6176, fax 888-2564, e-mail wesprent@mozcom.com, P950-1,200.

Woodlands Park Hotel: Somewhat removed from the action but compensates with spacious grounds almost like staying in a tropical park with birds and waterfalls. Rooms are in great condition with cable TV, minifridge, and almost stylish furniture. The place also has an Olympic-size swimming pool and free shuttle up to the nightclubs on Fields Avenue. MacArthur Highway, tel. (045) 892-2100, P700-1,200.

Hotel La Casa: The Hotel La Casa is a family-style hotel/pension house located about 2.5 km west of Margaritaville right off of the Perimeter Road between Angeles and the air base. Good clean rooms with cable TV, decent American food, weekly and monthly discounts, and friendly managers, all at a low price. Perimeter Rd., tel. (045) 602-7984, fax 892-6256, P300-500.

Clarkton Hotel: The Clarkton is conveniently located about 2.5 km west of the entertainment district on the perimeter road between Clark Special Economic Zone and Angeles City. Jeepney service from the front of the hotel to the district is just $0.05 (US), or ride in the hourly Clarkton shuttle service for free. The place has 71 a/c rooms with cable TV, a swimming pool, fitness center, business center, laundry service, gift shop, 24-hour bar and restaurant, 24-hour room service, and game center with pool, table tennis, and darts. 620 Don Juico Ave., tel. (455) 602-3424, fax (973) 440-226, P700-1,200. All rooms rates include government tax and service charge plus one free daily breakfast buffet.

New Fiesta Garden Hotel: Situated about two km from Fields Avenue and one km from the main shopping areas of downtown Angeles City. The place has 30 a/c rooms with cable TV, minifridges, 24-hour poolside bar and restaurant, around-the-clock room service, pool, free bus service to the nightclubs, and services for visa extensions and currency exchange. Angeles Rd., tel. (455) 602-1147, fax 603-4294, P550-750.

Europhil International Hotel: This hotel is located along the Clark Field Perimeter Road only a few meters away from the Fields Avenue tourist district and the Balibago Business District. Stats are 54 a/c rooms with cable TV, hot and cold running water, coffee shop, bar, swimming pool, Filipino restaurant with folk dancing and music shows. Fields Ave., tel. (455) 331-7821, P600-1,200.

Orchid Inn: Right in the midst of all the action with 24 a/c rooms set up with cable TV, minifridge, room service until 0200, swimming pool, restaurant, and nipa bar near the outdoor pool. 109 Ramond St., tel. (455) 602-0370, fax 888-2708, P550-900.

Swagman Narra: This hotel is half a km southeast of the tourist district of Balibago with a large outdoor 24-hour restaurant and bar with live entertainment daily. Popular with older Australian visitors, this hotel has something going on daily from golf trips to live satellite dish American sports, world sports, and Australian telecasts. Decent pool plus 49 almost a/c rooms (some are dismal and dark) plus all the other standard amenities. Balibago Ave., tel. (455) 602-5133, US$25-40.

Premiere Hotel: This hotel is less than a km west of the entertainment/tourist district and is a sister hotel of the Sunset Garden. The place has 32 a/c rooms with cable TV, hot showers, phones, pool, miniature golf course, safety deposit boxes, two pool tables, 24-hour poolside Swiss-Inn Restaurant, money exchange service, and an Internet café, plus it's the home of the Blue Bus (transport from Manila and local tours). Fields Ave., tel. (455) 888-2755, fax 888-2310, P550-800.

Nightclubs

Angeles City probably has well over 100 bars and nightclubs generally found along Fields Avenue, the road that skirts the southern edge of the former American air base.

Rumors: Just across from the Vegas Hotel is a fairly new place that opens early—around 1400 in the afternoon—and kicks off with fine music, video flicks, and some of the friendliest hostesses in this town. San Migs go for P35-40 while ladies' drinks are priced from P95. Malabinias Road.

Lollipop: Cozy joint run by Daddy Dave with two pool tables, dartboards, a large stage for the dancers, and loads of friendly people including many of the local expats who call this wild west town their home-away-from-home. Fields Avenue.

Margaritaville: One of the classic hangouts in Angeles and certainly the best place in town to enjoy happy hour and watch the passing parade as the denizens of the night walk down Fields Avenue to their places of employment. The food is recommended and the nightclub/bar has money changing facilities, several pool tables in the back, and a policy that prohibits bar fines—a popular place for the "last chance" Charlie to find a friend before heading home. 940 Fields Ave., e-mail cts-mv@mozcom.com.

Kokomo's: Another worthy addition to the local nightclub scene is this 24-hour club with an attached Internet café (they call it an Internet bar). Plenty of money was poured into this venue, which certainly has more class and style than most other places in this crazy town. All kinds of rooms: karaoke bar, TV lounge, cafés, disco, and a beauty parlor if you need a manicure. Fields Avenue.

Voodoo: Another Daddy Dave operation just past Margaritaville with a small bar area but quality employees and even a few rooms at bargain prices. Fields Avenue.

Mudbones: An older place that has been renovated with new lighting and a new sound system. Friendly managers make this place a positive stop while doing the rounds in Angeles. Fields Avenue.

Archies: Run by an Australian golf fanatic named Pete, this small but lively joint near the start of Fields Avenue near the Agfa camera shop opens at 1600 and keeps happy hour prices rolling until 1900.

Cleopatra: Another small but happening place near Lollipop, Mudbones, and Blackjacks, with almost professional shows twice weekly. The management seems to be trying something different in a town with too many clubs lacking imagination. Fields Avenue.

Private Dancer Too: Strange name but a well-managed hall with an assortment of friendly employees near the Stingers nightclub on Fields Avenue.

Valentines: Comfortable little nightclub with an unusual bar fine policy: they charge half the going rate but you are expected to tip your hostess the remainder. Fields Avenue.

Thunderstruck: Just past Kokomos is another cozy spot run by Rody with hard rock blasting from the stereo and acceptable food dished out from the kitchen in the back. Best parts are the pool tables and Harley Davidsons on display. Fields Avenue.

Y Not Music Box: Perhaps the premier disco in Angeles and favorite hangout of the nice girls around town, despite the lack of a/c and the horribly heated steam that melts your hairdo. This place is somewhat rough but provides a nice change from the standard nightclubs in this town.

Midnight Rodeo: Another change of pace with live country-and-western music performed by live Filipino bands. Management will let you go inside and sit for a while before they ask for your cover charge. Fields Avenue.

Rick's Cyber Cafe: Will Internet cafés actually survive in Angeles City? This one is the original incarnation and provides Internet connections (use Hotmail, not Compuserve) along with timely video flicks. Fields Avenue.

Events

Sabat, a *moro-moro,* or Muslim, performance, takes place in May. Fil-American Friendship Day is observed 4 July. The city fiesta, second Sunday in October, features an evening religious procession with a brass band and participants carrying lighted candles. **Pista ng Apo** is a procession in honor of Christ and the Virgin Mary on the last Friday in October. Angeles City's *parulan* (lantern festival), 16 December, is a smaller version of San Fernando's.

Money Exchange

Most major currencies can be changed at money changers throughout Angeles City.

Historically, it has been hard to find anyone who will change traveler's checks in Angeles City. Most places only deal with American Express traveler's checks, and only do this at a slightly inferior rate, since banks hold these checks for 30 days. You must have a photocopy of your passport and the purchase receipt for your traveler's checks.

Cash Advances

There are a few places in Angeles to get a cash advance on a credit card, but all will charge you 7.5-10%. Several banks in downtown Angeles have ATM machines. Several customers who have visited on a regular basis have reported no problems getting cash from Angeles ATMs. They all report that cards with a Cirrus logo will work at the Angeles branch of PCI bank. Cards without the Cirrus logo will not work. Additionally, the Regency Casino on Clark is advertising ATMs for Bancnet, Megalink, and Expressnet.

Note: Manila has several banks that will take other cards—Citibank, Bank of America, etc. You can get a local ATM card at PCI banks with a minimum deposit of P2,000. There are hundreds of banks in the Philippines that accept PCI ATM cards. They're nice to have in lieu of carrying cash. Cirrus International ATM cards are also available with a US$500 minimum deposit at PCI Bank.

Mail

If you are planning to be in Angeles City awhile, you can have mail sent to most larger hotels. When regular mail arrives the cashier will post the addressees' names on the notice board. There is no charge for this service.

E-mail

You can use Rick's Cyber Cafe or Checkmark (located in Margaritaville). Rick's Cafe (rickcafe@mail.ang.sequel.net) and Checkmark e-mail service checkmrk@mozcom2.mozcom.com). The Internet has been available in Angeles City tourist district only since September 1996.

There are now several Internet cafés in the Angeles area. The first was in the Datelcom (phone company) building in Angeles proper. In Balibago you can surf the Internet at Rick's Cafe on one of the fastest computers in town. Kokomo's and Swagman also have nice quiet business/Internet centers. Additionally, a large Internet Cafe is located on Clark between the Holiday Inn and the casino.

Activities

There are currently four golf courses and several more under construction. Angeles also has a casino in downtown Angeles and a world-class casino that opened on Clark in October 1996.

Air Flights: Several agencies now offer flights around Angeles City. The Angeles City Flying Club is the oldest flying club in town, with a fleet of ultralight aircraft out of Mabiga, about 10 minutes north of Angeles City. For more information, contact Woodland Park Resort at e-mail woodland@mozcom.com. The resort offers rides over the lahar fields for as low as P600, or full flight lessons.

The newest ultralight outfit in Angeles is the Lite-Flite Club, fax (045) 599-2120. This flying club is operating out of the old aero-club runway on Clark Air Force Base.

Parachuting: The Tropical Asia Parachute Center (TAPC) is located in Margaritaville at 940 Fields Ave., Balibago, Angeles City. Advance and student training are available. Student training includes both tandem and static line parachuting. All parachutes used in student training are "state of the art" square main parachutes with automatic activating devices on the reserve parachutes. Aircraft available for jumping are Cessna 185 and 207, Islander (BN22), and a Dornier.

Cost for student first jump course and equipment rental is reasonable for the Asia area. Tandem and first jump static line course is $240. Additional static line jumps are $80 (including equipment, aircraft, jump master, and parachute repacking). Jump lift fee is dependent upon aircraft available and exit altitude. Parachute equipment rental complete for entire day of jumping is $32.

Drag Racing: Several local and Manila Hot Rod Clubs have drag races at the Cope Thunder Drag Strip on Clark Air Force Base at least every other weekend. Go-carts are available for rent adjacent to the drag strip.

Other Sports: There is currently one miniature golf course at the Premier Hotel, and an Australian lawn bowling center has opened near Josefaville Subdivision. The Chicago Park hotel now has a slot car track in the old Hotsie Totsie Disco.

Billiards: Pool tables can be found in almost every bar and hotel in town. There are very active 8-ball pool leagues and dart leagues in town and many establishments are looking for players. Margaritaville has 9-ball tournaments several days a week, and Shooters bar has a snooker table.

Hash House Harriers: There is a very active Hash House Harrier group with weekly runs from the Birds of Paradise Bar at around 1530 every Sunday. They offer special runs on full moons and other special occasions.

Hiking: The more athletically inclined hikers can explore the slopes of **Mt. Arayat** year-round, and during good weather guides will take you up the slopes of **Mt. Pinatubo**. R&J Pinatubo Trek has guides licensed by the Philippine Department of Tourism that will take you on day treks on the slopes of Pinatubo, or on a three-day, two-night climb to the rim of the crater and back. For more information on Pinatubo trips contact Rusty at R&J Pinatubo Trek, fax (045) 888-2708.

Dirt bikes are also available for rent to individuals that want to explore the river beds and lahar fields without all the physical exertion of a climb.

Medical Facilities

Angeles University Hospital offers good quality medical care. About two hours away, Makati Medical Center—the best hospital in the country—offers a complete regional medical center. Health insurance policies that include basic dental checkup, an annual physical, emergency medical treatment, private room, etc., are available starting at P3,500 per year.

Transportation

Angeles City is about a two-hour ride (80 kilometers) north of Ninoy Aquino International Airport in Manila. There is a wide variety of safe transportation from the airport to Angeles.

Airline Arrival: There are no international flights into Clark at this time. It is doubtful that PAL will resume this operation anytime soon even if it clears up its current strike-related problems. Cathay Pacific has proposed three flights a week, Royal Brunei has discussed one flight a week, and Japan Airlines is talking a flight from Osaka on a charter.

THE FURY OF PINATUBO

Volcanic activity in the Philippines increased in the 1990s with major eruptions at Mt. Pinatubo in central Luzon on 12 June 1991 and again on 21 September 1992 and at the Mayon volcano in southern Luzon on 2 February 1993.

Mt. Pinatubo's initial eruption on 12 June 1991 marked the end of its 600 years of dormancy. In four eruptions over five days, it spewed out seven cubic km of ash and rock, emitting gaseous discharge up to 40 km high. It was the most powerful volcanic explosion of this century so far—on a par with Mt. Katmai, which exploded in 1912 on a desolate peninsula in Alaska. Unlike Mt. Katmai, however, Mt. Pinatubo affected many thousands of people living on the fertile rice lands of the Central Plain.

Despite the warnings and predictions of U.S. volcanologists monitoring the volcano from Clark Air Force Base, the initial eruption and lahar flooding by Mt. Pinatubo killed 900 people and displaced half a million. In the wake of the eruption, much of central Luzon—including Clark Air Force Base, Subic Naval Base, and Manila—was blanketed with gray volcanic ash. Shortly after the eruption, a typhoon struck Luzon, and the heaps of volcanic ash and mud turned to lahar, which sped down the hillsides at gale-force speed, wiping out villages, destroying farmland and fishponds, and killing more people.

Mt. Pinatubo's eruption altered weather patterns worldwide, causing a cooling of the earth's temperature. Things stayed hot around central Luzon, however, as the volcano erupted again on 21 September 1992. This time ash rose 18 km into the sky, and many tons of rock, lava, and debris were ejected. The subsequent lahar flows killed more people and destroyed thousands of homes.

The eventual death toll of the eruptions was over 1,000; 1.2 million were displaced as thousands of hectares of farmland were devastated.

Lahar Destruction

Mudflows, or lahar (an Indonesian word for mudflows), are particularly devastating in Southeast Asia because of the frequent typhoons that meet the "Ring of Fire." The lahar raced down Pintatubo's slopes with gale force when Typhoon Yunya hit Luzon at the time of Pinatubo's first eruption. It spread through six provinces, affecting 87,000 hectares of farmland and fishponds. Roughly 900 people were killed by mudslides and floods; villages were wiped out, bridges destroyed, and farmlands ruined. When the fury subsided, 20% of Pinatubo's ash and rock had reached the once-fertile valleys of the Central Plain.

The following year on 21 September 1992, Pinatubo erupted again, depositing more tons of mud and rock on the slopes of the mountain. The rainy season brought more mudflows, destroying another 9,000 homes, killing 50 people and disrupting the livelihoods of nearly a million people. Each year, the rainy season brings more deadly lahar down the slopes of Pinatubo to the rice lands and rivers of the Central Plain. The silt from the dried lahar has caused flash floods. The dense lahar can engulf houses and lift giant boulders, vehicles, bridges, and buildings.

There are seven rivers that fan out from the base of Mt. Pinatubo reaching populated areas in Pampanga, Tarlac, and Zambales Provinces. The lahar silts up the rivers, causing extreme flooding. As predicted, over one million people in central Luzon have been displaced since the eruption, not to mention the destruction to ricefields, farmlands, and fishponds that sustained the region. Six typhoons in 1992 washed a mere 20% of the volcanic rock and ash down the mountain, much of it settling on the western slopes of Mt. Pinatubo, threatening Zambales Province. The rest settled in a rim stretching 70 km around its slopes. Torrential rains continue to bring much of it flooding down to the valleys below.

The Philippine government has poured millions of dollars into cleaning up the lahar and resettling victims. Yet, lahar from Mt. Pinatubo continues to threaten the Central Plain. Although trucks and tractors push lahar off the roads, and peasants try to plant rice again in this region, typhoons and the annual rains continue to undo their efforts.

The situation remains serious and discourages settlement on areas that could be hit again. Long-time residents of the Central Plain are reluctant to leave their homelands and move elsewhere. Soldiers stand ready to evacuate settlers as soon as the mudflows begin. The torrential rains that come like clockwork every July-Oct. will continue to bring tons of lahar thundering down the river channels to the valleys below for years to come.

Economic Devastation

The eruptions of Mt. Pinatubo in 1991-92 displaced almost a million people from central Luzon and destroyed nearly 87,000 hectares of farmland and fishponds. The government has poured almost US$500 million into cleanup and relief efforts of these once-fertile plains. While many of the 1.2 million farmers and fisherfolk of the Central Plain displaced by Pinatubo have relocated to Manila, neighboring provinces, or the islands of Palawan, Mindanao, and the Visayas, a great many more have stayed put and are now homeless refugees.

Locals earn money taxiing people around the flooded villages by boat. Others scavenge for timber, work with the military to clear lahar, or wait for government assistance.

Angeles City, which was a thriving center for Americans stationed at Clark Air Base, collapsed overnight during the eruption, leaving 18,000 formerly employed Filipinos on the base without jobs. Girlie bars, nightclubs, restaurants, hotels, shops and cinemas were also destroyed in Angeles City, and with the closing of Clark Air Force Base these jobs dried up too.

Each time the residents of the Central Plain begin to rebuild their lives, Pinatubo reminds them of their futile efforts. Because a few farmers have had some success in replanting rice since Pinatubo, they are determined to stay and till the land. There is some hope that the lahar-covered soil is good for growing cassava, which is a tropical plant popular for its starchy edible root. Successful experiments have yielded 25 tons of cassava per hectare of lahar-covered soil. The Department of Agriculture is encouraging farmers of the devastated Central Plain to plant traditional crops in nontraditional ways at nontraditional times to avoid floodings at planting time.

Since the initial eruption on 12 June 1991, the U.S. has donated US$70 million in aid money. International response to the disaster was overwhelmingly helpful, but the U.S. leads in aid and assistance.

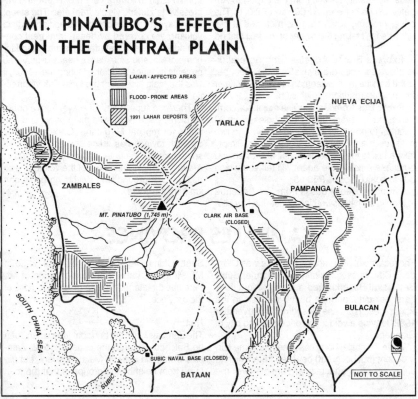

MT. PINATUBO'S EFFECT ON THE CENTRAL PLAIN

LAHAR - AFFECTED AREAS

FLOOD - PRONE AREAS

1991 LAHAR DEPOSITS

NUEVA ECIJA

TARLAC

ZAMBALES

PAMPANGA

MT. PINATUBO (1,745 m)

CLARK AIR BASE (CLOSED)

SOUTH CHINA SEA

BULACAN

SUBIC NAVAL BASE (CLOSED)

SUBIC BAY

BATAAN

NOT TO SCALE

© MOON PUBLICATIONS, INC.

On the good news side, a number of U.S. military flights have transited here in the last several months, and recently they gave their stamp of approval for the airport services at Clark. They say this paves the way for some 30-40 landings per month by U.S. military aircraft at Clark.

There are no longer any domestic flights into Clark.

Private Car from Manila: Several hotels and major nightclubs provide airport pick-up service in Manila direct to Angeles City. You can make reservations via e-mail. The current cost for airport pick-up is P1,800.

Taxi from Manila: The taxis outside the arrival area of the airport are notorious for high prices and not using their meters. It's best to exit the terminal building and climb the stairs one level to the departure entrance. The taxis here are dropping off arriving passengers, versus the "airport taxis" downstairs. A taxi from the airport to Angeles will be between P1,500 and P2,000. The driver probably won't start his meter as at this price he isn't telling the owner of the taxi that he made the trip.

Express Bus to Angeles City: Several direct bus services are available daily. Best bet is the service from Swagman Hotel in Manila or from the Margaritaville nightclub.

Public Bus from Manila: The major bus companies have several buses to Angeles every 30 minutes to one hour, 24 hours a day. The two best buses are Rabbit and Victory Liner. Simply take a taxi to the proper terminal, and when you purchase a ticket, the agent will tell you which bus to board. Cost is P56-65.

Philippine Rabbit buses from Rizal Avenue in Manila stop in downtown Angeles a few kilometers from the hotels and nightclubs. Jeepneys shuttle from the bus terminal to the hotels on MacArthur Highway.

As noted above, direct a/c coaches depart daily from the Swagman Hotel in Ermita—somewhat more expensive than Rabbit buses, but *much* more convenient. There's no obligation to stay at the Swagman hotel (it's a bit of a dump).

Buses back to Manila, up to Baguio, and over to Olongapo can be picked up where MacArthur Highway intersects the road to the Dau Expressway, just beyond McDonald's and the old tourist office on your left.

MOUNT ARAYAT NATIONAL PARK

Mount Arayat, 20 km east of Angeles, rises from the flat plain to form a very prominent and impressive landmark, visible from afar. The steep, nearly symmetrical sides of this ancient extinct volcano are covered by dense rainforest containing springs and waterfalls. It's the legendary home of Mariang Sinukuan, a beautiful fairy who protects its fauna and flora. During the 1950s, it was the main hideout of the local Huk insurrectionists.

There's a superb view of Arayat from a popular picnic place (with swimming pools and cottages for rent) at Magalang. Once a wealthy Spanish town, it has a fine church (1863) and some turn-of-the-century houses. The town of Arayat, at the southern foot of the volcano, also has a picnic ground with swimming pools one km from the plaza.

ZAMBALES PROVINCE

The focal point of Zambales Province was Olongapo City, whose proximity to the former Subic Bay Naval Base kindled a vibrant nightlife—bars, bar girls, and the best live music in the Philippines. The base closed on 24 November 1992, leaving a void in the once bustling city of Olongapo.

While Zambales' long coastline has some fairly decent (but not great) beaches from which to enjoy the often spectacular sunsets over the South China Sea, it is the provincial home of Mt. Pinatubo. Lahar from the eruption of Mt. Pinatubo threatened the rice-growing regions of the province.

History
The Zambals were the principal tribe when Juan de Salcedo explored the coast in 1572. Zambals were held to be of Malay descent, but differed from neighboring groups in that the men

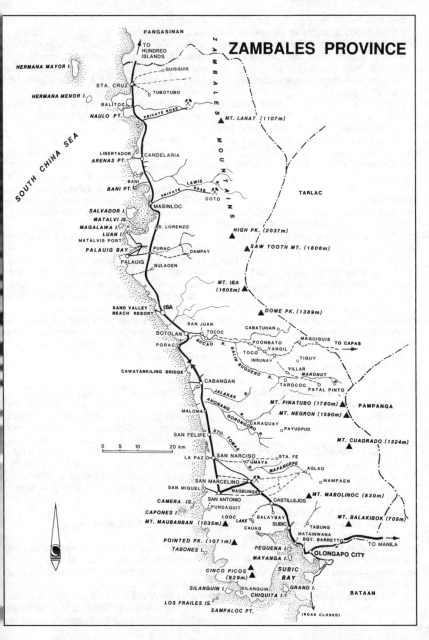

shaved their heads, leaving only a large lock of hair at the back. Zambales was among the first areas of Luzon brought under Spanish control, with early settlements at Iba, Masinloc, and Santa Cruz, but it remained largely outside the mainstream of development and historical events until the 20th century.

The base at Subic Bay was constructed by the Spanish in 1895 and taken over by the U.S. Navy. During WW II, Olongapo and Subic Bay were bombed and occupied by the Japanese. Ramon Magsaysay, president (1953-57), led a wartime guerrilla movement in the Zambales Mountains.

Transportation

The major carrier is Victory Liner, which offers frequent service from Manila to Olongapo, 128 km (three hours), and beyond, plus regular buses from Angeles, Alaminos, Dagupan, and Baguio. Saulog Transit operates from Paranaque (Manila) to Olongapo, while Pantranco North buses leave Quezon City for Santa Cruz, via Pangasinan, three times daily. Baliwag Transport and E. Jose Transport have cross-country services between Olongapo, San Fernando (Pampanga), and Cabanatuan (Nueva Ecija).

Minibuses link Balanga (Bataan) with Olongapo. The Manila-Olongapo Highway crosses ZigZag Pass through the mountains. A single road leads north through the province, with access to the interior limited to tracks and private mine roads.

SAN MARCELINO LAKE

A new attraction has cropped up near Mt. Pinatubo at San Marcelino. When the volcano erupted in 1991, tons of lahar covered a series of river channels in San Marcelino, and in September of the same year, when heavy rains started to pour, two barangays—Aglao and Buhawen—were totally submerged by water, due to heavy siltation along the river channels. As a result, a 30-feet-deep, 300-square-km lake was formed, covering 500 houses, school buildings, and chapels. Meanwhile, families moved to higher ground.

Chinese Artifacts

As the new lake was dredged, local folks found remnants of an old Chinese civilization in the area. They found antique jars, dinner plates, and even a ship anchor. People surmise that 600 years ago, prior to the first eruption of Mt. Pinatubo, a portion of Zambales was a vast ocean where Chinese traders from China traveled en route from Pampanga and Tarlac.

Recreation

San Marcelino Lake is now abundant with fish and attracts other wildlife. The government dispersed about two million fingerlings of tilapia fish to provide the displaced residents with a livelihood. A small pier has been constructed with a fleet of motorized bancas to ferry passengers to the other side of the lake.

The mountaintop lake is 124 meters above sea level. From the lake, there is a 22-km ride along a winding mountain trail that offers a panoramic view of Mt. Pinatubo. Birds, flora, and some wildlife have been spotted in this area.

Along the mountain trail, you will see the Hidden Temple Shrine of Mt. Pinatubo at Sitio, Palan, and Barangay San Rafael. It is said to be an icon of the Blessed Mother that stands amidst a lahar farm and is believed to have warded off further damage from surging lahar.

Transportation

To get there take the Olongapo-Gapan Road that heads toward Pampanga and turn at the Bataan-Olongapo junction. (Travel time is about 30 minutes from Olongapo City.) Jeepneys ply this route between Olongapo and San Marcelino. At the San Marcelino Municipal Hall, take a right toward San Rafael en route to Sition Pili, Buhawen where the lake is located. (Total travel time from Olongapo to the lake is three hours.)

OLONGAPO

Olongapo (pronounced "oh-LONG-guh-poe") is located on Subic Bay, which was a forward operating station of the U.S. Seventh Fleet and its support units.

After the Americans left the 5,000-man Subic Naval Base in 1992, Olongapo and Subic reverted back to very quiet places chiefly known for

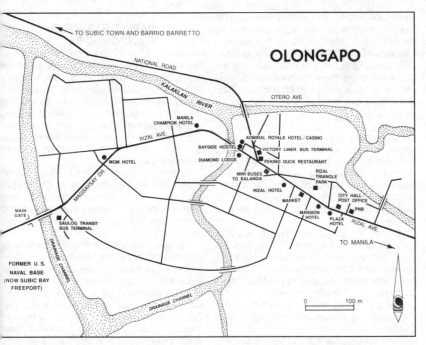

their duty-free shopping, wreck diving, and beach resorts both north and south of town. Most visitors head directly to Barrio Barretto, a beach resort four km north of Olongapo.

Barrio Barretto has almost 20 hotels and a handful of nightclubs that attempt to keep alive the old spirit of Olongapo. But times are tough as local mayors prove their puritanical fortitude and continue to censor or close clubs in their districts.

Olongapo itself has gone through a major renovation since the base closed almost a decade ago. There are no longer any bars or cocktail lounges that cater to single males, and all have been replaced by more sedate restaurants and shops. The city has put in new brick sidewalks on the main street and constant efforts are being made to make this one of the cleanest big Filipino cities in the country.

Accommodations in Subic Bay Freeport

Visitors to the district can stay in Olongapo, directly on the former American naval base of Subic Bay (now called Subic Bay Freeport), or right on the beach at Barrio Barretto. The beachside town is your best bet.

Subic International Hotel: Located on Santa Rita Road on former bachelor officer quarters, this hotel still looks like a military facility but might be acceptable for a few nights. Subic Bay, tel. (045) 888-2288, fax 888-1123, US$70-95.

Zanzibar Hotel: Located on Magsaysay Drive between the gate and the first rotunda with clean rooms at a reasonable rate. Magsaysay Dr., tel. (045) 888-1166, US$25-55.

Accommodations in Olongapo

Rooms have been plentiful since the closure of Subic Naval Base.

Ram's Inn: A budget option two blocks down Rizal Avenue from the Victory bus terminal. 765 Rizal Ave., tel. (047) 222-3481, P150-350.

More Hotels: Diamond Lodge on Rizal Avenue is probably the best of the cheap places with rooms for P150. Across the street is the **Bayside Hostel,** with rooms for P200. **Manila**

Champion Hotel is also on Rizal Avenue in the heart of the former bar area, and many hotels are around the junction of Rizal Avenue and Magsaysay Drive. MGM Hotel on 87 Magsaysay Drive is clean with rooms for P180. At the top end of the scale are the Admiral Royale Hotel (where the casino is), Mansion Hotel, Rizal Hotel, and Plaza Hotel, all on Rizal Ave.; rooms range P250-300.

Entertainment

Olongapo's main industries were beer and prostitution. There were once over 10,000 licensed "hospitality girls" working in the 350 downtown bars and clubs. Ironically, it looks as if Olongapo will become a playground for vacationing Japanese and Taiwanese businesspeople.

However, the enterprising mayor of Olongapo, Richard Gordon, is determined to keep the place lively and prosperous, and there is hope that the area will not become a shadow of its former self. Unfortunately, Gordon may not last long at Olongapo since President Estrada is his sworn enemy and almost immediately after winning the presidency demanded the resignation of Gordon.

The casino in the Admiral Royale Hotel is open Sun.-Thurs. 2000-0400, Friday and Saturday 2000-0500. The city's Mardi Gras Festival (weekend of 14 February) features dancing in the streets around Magsaysay Drive, plus parades and sports events.

Transportation

Bus: Victory Liner buses leave from their terminals in Caloocan and Pasay hourly and take about five hours to reach the terminal in Olongapo. The fare is around P85.

Express Boat: Eagle Ferry Cruises gets you to Subic from the terminal adjacent to the Cultural Center complex. These fast ferries depart daily at 1000 and 1530 and take just over two hours to Subic. The fare is P220-350 depending on the class.

From Angeles: Swagman has a Fly the Bus service from its resort in Angeles daily at 1000. The two-hour trip costs P200. You can also catch an ordinary bus from the terminal in downtown Angeles.

BARRIO BARRETTO AND SUBIC BAY

Subic Bay's strategically located, deep natural harbor once contained the U.S. Navy's largest supply depot outside the United States. This supply, repair, and dry-docking facility was the main logistical support base for the U.S. Seventh Fleet's ships and aircraft, including carrier task forces deployed as far as the Indian Ocean and Persian Gulf. Cubi Point Naval Air Station is part of the complex.

Subic Bay's major asset was the availability of highly skilled workers who could repair any ship in the fleet at one-seventh U.S. labor rates. The base was one of the country's biggest employers and contributed US$200 million annually to the economy.

To avoid wide-scale looting, the Americans departed with everything from faucet fixtures to wall tiles, but the basic infrastructure is there and ready for major investors from overseas to turn Subic Bay into a self-contained city to rival Manila for attractions. Administered by the Subic Bay Metropolitan Authority, the base is now a free port and Special Economic Zone in search of investors to help build it up as a shipping port and convention and recreation center.

The Current Scene

In early 1998 Mayor Kate Gordon made all the bars in the Barrio stop go-go dancing, but a few bars are still hanging in there with "entertainers." The main remaining expat bars in the Barrio are the Rock Lobster (in Mangos), Main Attraction, and Midnight Rambler.

Another cluster of six non-a/c bars in the Barrio are still serving cold beer and conversation. Drink prices in the bars tend to be very cheap when compared with bars in Angeles City and Manila. The VFW is still the best place to eat in the Barrio. Several new hotels have opened with the most expensive being Suzuki at P1,500 for a small room in back and P2,000 on the water.

Accommodations

Barretto—the beach resort area just north of Subic Bay—has over a dozen hotels and resorts in the moderate price range, though the next few years may see some true luxury hotels go up in this beach escape.

Subic Bay Garden Inn: A Barrio Barretto hotel with all a/c rooms. National Highway, tel. (047) 222-4550, P400-750.

Halfmoon Hotel: One of the best in town with pool and landscaped gardens. National Highway, tel. (047) 222-4987, P800-1,500.

Papagayo's: Directly across from Hooters, the rooms are clean and the TV and a/c work—good value at P600-800 per night.

Bart's Hotel: Another reasonable hotel is this place with a small pool and a reasonable restaurant. Barrio Barretto, tel. (047) 223-4148, fax 223-4149, P600-900.

More Barrio Barretto Hotels: You might also try the **Dryden Hotel,** tel. (047) 222-4547, **Subic Mirage,** tel. (047) 223-9245, and **Triple Crown Hotel,** tel. (047) 222-4580.

ZAMBALES COASTLINE

Minibuses and the Victory Liner serve coastal communities between Olongapo and Santa Cruz. Numerous bays, coves, and several offshore islands line the lengthy shoreline. Coral reefs provide good snorkeling, and for those with scuba gear, there are drop-offs too.

Subic Bay to Botolan

Castillejos is the site of the Balaybay Calvary on Good Friday, when penitents drag wooden crosses to a hilltop, accompanied by flagellantes. Looc Lake, 12 km west of town, is the site of a Bureau of Fisheries experimental station. The next municipality on the highway is San Marcelino, site of the BCI-Dizon Copper Ore operation; chromite and gold are also mined.

The highway swings through San Antonio, from where the circular route through Pundaquit and San Miguel makes an enjoyable side-trip. A jeepney serves Pundaquit twice daily; or take a tricycle two km to the river, then walk three km. At this fishing village, hire a *banca* to visit the rocky offshore islands, Camera and Capones. Each has white-sand beaches, coconut and *ipil-ipil* trees, grazing land, and a few inhabitants. Capones has a lighthouse at its western end.

From Pundaquit, it's a pleasant walk along wide beaches and across a shallow river to San Miguel, former site of an important U.S. Naval Communications Station. Jeepneys for San Antonio load at this station; tricycles are also available. Several resthouses line the highway—**Queen Pearl, San Miguel, Highway Resthouse**—and the town of San Antonio has a small lodging house. The La Paz Port Road leads from San Narciso to a beach; **Rosmar Beach Resort** is north of here.

About eight km north of San Felipe, a pottery town, are fine beaches; good swimming spots lie beyond Cawayankiling Bridge, six km north of Cabangan. Salt beds are maintained between San Felipe and Iba. Just before Porac, **Villa Loreto Beach Resort** has cottages.

Inland from Botolan

A crowded truck leaves Botolan, which has a sugar mill-refinery complex, around midday for the inland settlements of Villar or Maguiguis. Aeta settlements are a few hours' walk farther into the mountains. Zambals also live in the Botolan area, and a related group, the Aburlin, inhabits the interior. Villar is close to Mt. Pinatubo.

Iba to Pangasinan

Iba, the provincial capital, is a small market town (fiesta: 28 August) of 26,000, about halfway between Olongapo (83 km) and Pangasinan. Founded in 1611, it was President Magsaysay's birthplace and has good beaches north of town. **V & M Lodging House** is opposite Victory Liner bus station, and nearby are **General Ordonez, Gonzales, Sand Valley,** and other beach resorts.

Sand Valley, two km north of town, is perhaps the best beach resort on this coast—an agreeable place to relax, with tasty food.

Palauig, which has a lighthouse, lies off the main highway on Palauig Bay. Snorkeling is good around Magalawa Island (pop. 200).

Masinloc became the provincial capital in 1607, to be later superseded by Iba. Stay at **Pabilona's Rest House** (P150), north of town, **D'Highway Kubo,** or **Kawayan Grill** (P150), both south of town.

The world's richest refractory chromite deposit is inland at Coto, reached by a 15-km private road. An open-pit mine is operated by Benguet Consolidated Mining, and ore is shipped from the wharf here. Oysters and mussels are raised at the nearby Bamban Sea Farming Complex.

The highest point in Zambales, High Peak (2,037 meters), is in the interior. One km south of Candelaria is a small lake noted for wild duck. The northernmost town in Zambales, Santa Cruz, is a melting pot of different ethnic groups. Important chromite and copper mines are inland. Happy Beach is nearby.

BATAAN PENINSULA

On a clear day, the mountainous backbone of the Bataan Peninsula is visible across the bay from Manila's Roxas Boulevard. A journey down the peninsula will appeal to those who enjoy vistas of sea and hills and the feeling of reaching land's end. Beaches on the South China Sea—around Bagac, for example—are far superior to those on Manila Bay.

It's also a landscape that echoes with the memory of war. The giant cross atop Mt. Samat stands as mute symbol of the bitter fighting that occurred on Bataan.

Early History

The peninsula's strategic position, guarding the entrance to Manila Bay, has ensured it a prominent historical role. Bataan was one of the first areas of Luzon brought under Spanish control. Following exploration in 1572, the Dominicans began to establish mission sites. In 1647, the Dutch, vying with the Spanish for colonial supremacy in the Orient, took Corregidor and plundered the Bataan coast.

But after the massacre of 200 natives in Abucay, Filipinos determinedly fought under Spanish command and drove the Dutch from the Philippines. In spite of subsequent sporadic raids, the Dutch never again seriously threatened Spanish control.

Transportation

Bataan is served by Pantranco, Philippine Rabbit, Victory Liner, and Yabut Transport. Minibuses also operate between Olongapo (Zambales) and Balanga.

DOWN THE PENINSULA

Dinalupihan is the northernmost town on the Manila-Olongapo Highway; stay at **Vianzon Resthouse.** A 58-km expressway to Mariveles leads south from Layac, bypassing the coastal towns, which are connected by the old road with its many Death March markers. The "First Line of Defense" marker is at Hermosa, near which is **Roosevelt National Park,** a game refuge.

The fishing town of **Orani** is the site of a Good Friday "crucifixion" (with nails) and also has a Death March marker. Offshore islets abound in wild duck and other game birds. Stay at **A & D Luncheonette and Resthouse, Bataan Travelodge,** or **Apollo Inland Resort Hotel** (swimming pool). **Samal** (fiesta: 30 April), the site of a pulp and paper mill, is noted for embroidered handicrafts and its fervent Good Friday *senaculo,* a three-hour performance in the town plaza.

Abucay, another fishing port, was a mission center in 1588. The church was badly damaged in the 1852 earthquake, and the area saw heavy fighting in 1942 (battle marker). Sibul Springs and Bangkal Aeta Settlement are in the vicinity.

Balanga

The provincial capital (pop. 45,000) and commercial hub, Balanga is centrally located on the peninsula, 124 km from Manila. Balanga celebrates its fiesta on 25 April, and following the Day of Valor ceremony on nearby Mt. Samat (6 May), it hosts the International Sea Fair (7-8 May), an aquatic Sportsfest with boat races, water-skiing, and other activities.

Stay at **Alitaptap Hotel** on Lerma St.; rooms are P150-200. In the same range, try **El Nido Lodging House.** The **Samat Lodging House** is also good. The **Buenavista Resort** is more upscale with rooms P450-600. In town, try **Glo's Restaurant** or **Fiesta sa Barrio** for Filipino food.

BALANGA TO MARIVELES

Several beach resorts line this stretch of coast. Orion (fiesta: 8 May) has a monument to the 19th-century native poet Balagtas, who lived

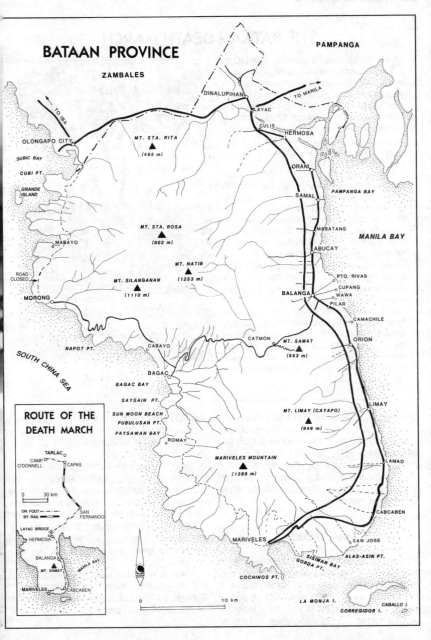

BATAAN PROVINCE

ZAMBALES

PAMPANGA

DINALUPIHAN

LAYAC

TO MANILA

CULIS

HERMOSA

OLONGAPO CITY

TO IBA

MT. STA. RITA
(485 m)

SUBIC BAY

CUBI PT.

ORANI

GRANDE
ISLAND

PAMPANGA BAY

SAMAL

MT. STA. ROSA
(902 m)

MABATANG

MANILA BAY

MABAYO

ABUCAY

ROAD
CLOSED

MT. SILANGANAN
(1110 m)

MT. NATIB
(1253 m)

BALANGA

PTO. RIVAS

CUPANG

WAWA

MORONG

PILAR

CAMACHILE

ORION

NAPOT PT.

CABAYO

CATMON

MT. SAMAT
(553 m)

SOUTH CHINA SEA

BAGAC

BAGAC BAY

SAYSAIN PT.

SUN MOON BEACH

PUBULUSAN PT.

PAYSAWAN BAY

ROMAY

MT. LIMAY (CAYAPO)
(946 m)

LIMAY

MARIVELES MOUNTAIN
(1388 m)

LAMAO

ROUTE OF THE DEATH MARCH

TARLAC

CAMP
O'DONNELL

CAPAS

0   30 km

ON FOOT
BY RAIL

SAN
FERNANDO

LAYAC BRIDGE

HERMOSA

BALANGA

MT. SAMAT

MANILA BAY

MARIVELES

CABCABEN

CABCABEN

MARIVELES

SAN JOSE

SISIMAN BAY

GORDA PT.

ALAS-ASIN PT.

COCHINOS PT.

0   10 km

LA MONJA I.

CABALLO I.

CORREGIDOR I.

THE BATAAN DEATH MARCH

After the Japanese invasion in late 1941, General MacArthur withdrew his forces from Manila to Bataan to await U.S. reinforcements that never arrived. About 15,000 Americans and 65,000 Filipinos dug in along a 30-km line across the upper peninsula. The defenders put up a heroic resistance against the invading Japanese forces. Both sides suffered heavy losses not only through battle but also through sickness and, in the case of the defenders, malnutrition as well.

A revitalized Japanese army ended the stalemate with an unstoppable assault. The forces on Mt. Samat were subjected to an incredible bombardment and surrounded. The fall of Bataan came on 9 April 1942, as 76,000 men surrendered. The Japanese were unprepared for the number of prisoners and their weakened condition; there wasn't nearly enough food, water, or medicine.

Over the next 10 days, the pathetic line of emaciated men inched its way from Mariveles back up the peninsula—the infamous Death March. En route to the concentration camps in Tarlac, 7,000-10,000 men (more than were killed in previous fighting) died from disease and brutal treatment. Many historical markers indicate battle positions, the progress of the 112-km Death March, and other significant sites during the tumultuous events of 1942. U.S. troops landed at Mariveles to recapture Bataan in 1945.

Bataan veterans

CARL PARKES

and died here; **Pulong Bato Beach Resort** rents huts. In Limay, which has an oil refinery, stay at **Sunset Inn** or **Villa Leonor Beach Resort,** two km south of town. At Cabcaben, *bancas* can be hired at the **Villa Carmen** resort or in town for the trip to nearby Corregidor. Another good place to stay at Cabcaben is the **Vista Corregidor** resort hotel.

MARIVELES

An early Spanish settlement, Mariveles lies in the shadow of Mariveles Mountain (1,388 meters) on Mariveles Bay, a fine harbor. Manila is 171 km by road. From a small fishing port, it emerged from the ruins of war into a major industrial center, after its designation in 1969 as

the First Export Processing Zone, a free-trade area where capital equipment, raw materials, and supplies for processing goods for export may be imported duty-free.

This, plus tax incentives and a pool of inexpensive skilled labor, has attracted U.S. and Japanese multinational corporations. The country's largest oil refinery and petrochemical complex is here, as is the National Shipyard and Steel Corp. complex, a pulp and paper mill, copper smelter, electronic and assembly plants, garment factories, and an array of other companies.

Points of interest include the marker indicating the start of the Death March; Balong Anito Springs, with hot sulfurous water; and the Bianan Mariveles Aeta Settlement.

Accommodations

Stay at **White Beach Resort, Bangya Hotel, Kamaya Point (Landoil) Hotel** in Alas-asin (fishing, horse riding, and tennis), or at **Bataan Hilltop Hotel** (swimming pool). Rooms cost more than US$40 a day for singles.

MOUNT SAMAT

Numerous historical markers line the scenic road that winds 49 km across the peninsula from Balanga to Bagac and Morong. A sword-shaped monument stands at the junction in Pilar, just south of Balanga. Minibuses link Balanga and Morong, but the coastal route from Morong to Olongapo is closed for military reasons. On Good Friday, many penitents carrying crosses, either alone or with groups of followers, walk on the Balanga-Bagac road.

Mount Samat

After 4.5 km, the cross-island highway passes Catmon, where a steep road winds 7.5 km to the summit of Mt. Samat, where a giant 95-meter cross, Dambana ng Kagitingan ("Shrine of Valor"), forms a prominent landmark.

It marks the scene of the fierce battle that preceded the surrender of Filipino and U.S. forces in 1942. An account of the battle is inscribed on the monument. Wreath-laying, remembrance of the Death March, and tribute to WW II veterans take place on Bataan Day (9 April). On 6 May, Araw ng Kagitingan (the "Day of Valor"), a wreath-laying ceremony and mass are held. The viewing gallery near the top of the cross gives a spectacular view of the sea and distant Manila. Dunsolan Falls are on the mountain's western slopes.

Bagac

This beautiful place has nice beaches. **Sun Moon Beach,** south of town, is a peaceful stretch of beige sand with shallow water. To rent a cottage or camp, make prior arrangements in Manila, tel. (02) 996-844.

It's a good camping spot, but you must bring food. In the adjacent cove (Pasinay) is the **Montemar Beach Club,** over P450-600 s/d (restaurants, swimming pools, nine-hole pitch-and-putt course, tennis, windsurfing, a picnic area, and a children's playground). For bookings or more information call (02) 888-3919 or (02) 892-5468.

Nearby are the **Chicken Villa,** where fighting cocks are raised, and a pleasant waterfall with a clear pool for swimming. To walk to the latter, follow the road opposite the Montemar gate, bear right through the intersection and uphill; the second road on the right (at a crossroad) leads to steps that descend to the falls. Bagac has a war marker and a Filipino-Japanese Friendship Tower, and a few kilometers northeast are Pasukulan Falls. Flagellantes are active in Bagac on Good Friday.

Morong

Morong has a beach, and it may be possible to stay at the **Ricemill Restaurant** in town. Points of interest include a refugee processing camp for Vietnamese "boat people" and the site of a discontinued nuclear power plant, which has caused much controversy and has finally been scrapped after more than two billion dollars were spent on its construction.

TARLAC PROVINCE

Tarlac is a major agricultural province, but it offers little to detain travelers as they pass through from Manila to Pangasinan, Baguio, or Ilocos. Its focal point is the town of Tarlac, the provincial capital.

History

The province of Tarlac was carved out of parts of Pampanga and Pangasinan in 1874. Its name derives from a tough weed, which the Aetas called *tanlac* or *tarlac,* growing in the wilderness to the north of San Fernando. The Spanish made Tarlac a military *comandancia* or constabulary zone in 1860 to protect the settlers from unfriendly mountain people in the nearby foothills. Later, the towns of Tarlac, Bamban, Capas, Concepcion, Victorias, Anao, Gerona, Camiling, and Paniqui, originally belonging to Pampanga and Pangasian, became part of the province.

Tarlac was one of the eight provinces that revolted against Spain in 1896. In October 1899 Gen. Emilio Aguinaldo transferred the seat of the Philippine revolutionary government from Malolos to Tarlac. A month later, American forces occupied the province and established a civil government in February 1901. Famous native sons and daughters include the revolutionary general Francisco Makabulos, Gen. Carlos P. Romulo, the late Benigno Aquino, and former president Corazon Aquino.

CAPAS~THE DEATH MARCH CAMP

In 1942, survivors of the Death March were brought by rail from San Fernando to Capas, then taken 20 km west to confinement at Camp O'Donnell, near which are thermal springs. Many prisoners died of disease and hunger in the camp's overcrowded conditions. A Death March monument stands at Susuba, three km from Capas town hall. A memorial ceremony is held here on Bataan Day, 9 April.

The Aquino Estate
Concepcion, east of the highway, is the home of former president Corazon Cojuangco Aquino. Outside the town is Hacienda Luisita, the Cojuangco family's vast sugar plantation with its golf course and stable of Arabian horses. Hacienda Luisita has been turned into a corporation, with stocks and bonuses distributed to its tenants and workers.

TARLAC

The provincial capital and commercial center is about halfway between Manila (125 km) and Baguio but has little appeal as a city. Founded in 1686, it was partly destroyed by the Japanese prior to its liberation in 1945. Plaques mark a house in which José Rizal stayed in 1872 and the home of turn-of-the-century resistance leader Francisco Makabulos. Dolores Springs is seven km out of town.

Accommodations
Stay at **Vilmar Hotel** or **Jecson's Hotel,** P150-200.

Northern Tarlac
On the main highway, you can stay at the **Besma Country Club Inn.** Note the old roadside warehouse in Moncada. The Tarlac-Lingayen highway passes through Camiling, a market town with old colonial houses. It was the home of Leonor Rivera, a sweetheart of Rizal, and site of the **Maria Clara Museum.** West of town is Mayantoc, 10 km from which is Magsaysay Dam, a popular local excursion spot.

PANGASINAN PROVINCE AND HUNDRED ISLANDS

Pangasinan is a large, culturally distinctive province. It's associated with many strange legends, and the majority of Filipino faith healers come from here. Why the phenomenon of psychic surgery is focused in this one province remains a mystery (see **Religion** in the Introduction). Urdaneta is a good base for seeking out those who practice here.

The Hundred Islands National Park, Pangasinan's much vaunted main sightseeing spot, is pleasant enough, but overrated by tourist literature.

Bolinao, with its quiet rural charm, is probably the best place for an extended sojourn.

Pangasinan is a renowned basket-weaving center and the home of itinerant traders, whose picturesque ox-drawn wagons, piled high with baskets of all shapes and sizes, are seen on roads throughout the Central Plain.

History
Early inhabitants dwelt in a land of abundance, with bountiful waters and luxuriant forests. Lingayen Gulf became a regional trading center,

as Zambals and Igorots came down from the hills to barter gold for rice, pigs, and carabao, and Ilocanos traded blankets, pots, and *bolos.* Junks also came to trade luxury goods for native products, and Chinese, Japanese, and native artisans cooperated in a boat-building industry.

The Spanish arrived in 1572 to find commerce thriving. Shortly afterward, the Chinese warrior Limahong landed in Sual Bay with 64 war junks, over 3,000 followers, and territorial ambitions. He subjugated the local inhabitants, holding their chiefs hostage so that they supplied him with wood and food as he constructed a fort at the mouth of the Agno River.

But Juan de Salcedo led Spanish and native troops in a surprise attack in which over half of Limahong's fleet was burned and his escape routes blocked. During the ensuing four-month siege, Limahong's men secretly dug a channel to the sea, built new junks, and sailed away on a dark night in 1575. Many Chinese left behind became the ancestors of numerous old mestizo families in Lingayen and Dagupan. It's still possible to see the "Limahong Channel"; it flows from Domalandan, between Labrador and Lingayen, to the sea.

The Spaniards sent missionaries to the area and the province was established in 1611, though rebellions occurred (1660, 1762).

Lingayen Gulf is a natural landing point for an invading army bent on capturing Manila, since it need only cross 180 km of flat terrain with good roads. Hence, the invasion plans of both Lt. General Homma and General MacArthur were remarkably similar. The Japanese struck on 22 December 1941, when 43,000 troops waded ashore and, easily overcoming a defensive line at the Agno River, thrust toward Manila. On 9 January 1945, 68,000 Americans landed on the same coastal stretch to begin the liberation of Luzon.

Transportation

Dagupan City is a transportation hub. Pantranco North buses depart from Manila to Dagupan (216 km) every 15 minutes between 0400 and 1900. The highway from Manila splits at Tarlac.

The main road to Baguio and Ilocos passes through eastern Pangasinan and is served by numerous bus lines. A branch cuts northwest to Lingayen and western Pangasinan. Pantranco North buses leave Quezon City about hourly until midafternoon for Alaminos, gateway to the Hundred Islands, and Bolinao.

Pantranco also has frequent departures from Baguio to Dagupan (81 km) and on the Dagupan-Lingayen-Alaminos-Bolinao route. The Dagupan Bus Co. operates Dagupan-Bolinao, too, and hourly from Cubao (Metro Manila) and Baguio to Dagupan.

Victory Liner buses ply the coastal route from Olongapo (Zambales) to Alaminos and Dagupan. Frequent minibuses link Dagupan with Alaminos and San Fernando (La Union), while Times Transit has a regular Dagupan-Vigan (Ilocos Sur) service.

Buses going to Dagupan from Baguio, San Fernando, and Vigan pass the beaches of San Fabian. Pantranco, Dangwa Tranco, and Greenland Bus pass through Carmen to link Baguio with San Jose (Nueva Ecija), Banaue, and the Cagayan Valley provinces. It's also possible to take the train from Manila or San Fernando (La Union) to Dagupan.

URDANETA

Urdaneta is a bustling market town, 183 km from Manila, 69 km from Baguio. Many faith healers live and work in this area, and Urdaneta is a convenient base from which to seek out healers in and around the nearby towns of Asingan, Binalonan, Rosales, and Villasis. Hotel staffs are often good sources of information. A busy road leads west to Dagupan from here.

Accommodations

The following places are within the P150-250 range. Stay at: **Saben Rosa,** on Alexander St.; **Sunrise Lodging House,** on Belmonte St.; **D'Rose Inn,** next to market, good value, recommended; **Lis Inn,** on main highway; **Nina's Lodging House,** on Alexander St.; **Aires Hotel,** also on Alexander St.; **Reyna de las Flores Inn, Urdaneta Pension,** and **Dama de Noche Hotel,** all on the main highway; **Urduja Hotel,** P250-300, three-star, swimming pool, disco, buffet lunch and dinner, and observation tours of faith healers on Alexander Street.

HUNDRED ISLANDS NATIONAL PARK

This is a cluster of small uninhabited islets (not exactly 100) located a short boat ride from Lucap, five km north of Alaminos. These eroded rocky outcrops have a few small sandy beaches that can get crowded on weekends and holidays.

Snorkeling is often marred by murky conditions and doesn't compare with the country's best. Numerous legends are attached to the islands: they are the tears of a lovelorn giant and mermaids once lived here. A summer Aquasports Festival is held here, 15 April-15 May. Most visitors spend a few hours out among the islands.

Lucap is the main place to overnight, but you can also stay in Alaminos, or with a little organization, on an island. Other possible day trips in the area are to Sabangan Beach and the Umbrella Rocks at Agno, and the Nalsoc Caves and underground river at Bani.

ALAMINOS

Alaminos is the gateway to the Hundred Islands, 254 km (five hours) from Manila, 38 km (one hour) from Dagupan. You can also visit the salt-making plant.

Accommodations
Stay at **d'Plaza Hotel** or the **Alaminos Hotel** (P100 for single, P150 double). Eat at the **Plaza Restaurant,** which often has a folk singer, or at the **Imperial Restaurant.** Evening activities include bowling and a disco.

LUCAP

Lucap has a marine biology museum and fisheries research center, but no beach.

From Alaminos, take a tricycle to Lucap. Drivers try to overcharge foreigners. Go into any store in Alaminos, check the current fare, have the right change, and pay when you arrive.

SOME OF THE HUNDRED ISLANDS

Cathedral has offshore coral and a large cave with rock formations resembling a cathedral.

Children's has a beach, and tents may be rented for an overnight stay.

Clave has good diving offshore.

Devil's—so called because it's surrounded by dark, deep water—is one of the area's best scuba spots.

Governor's—one of the larger islands—has some buildings and, from the highest point, affords a fine view of the surrounding seascape. Extensive coral growth in shallow water offshore.

Lopez has a beach and coral gardens off the eastern side.

Marcos has a beach and caves with bats, and those climbing to the top of the island can peer down a blowhole into Imelda Cave, which is accessible from the sea below.

Milagrosa has a cave.

Padres has a coral garden.

Panacan has nice coral.

Primicias is a good place to watch the sunset.

Quezon—the most visited island—has been developed, with pavilions, a food kiosk, and other tourist facilities. It's surmounted by a monument to President Quezon, from where there's a sweeping view over the other islands. It also has a beach and coral gardens offshore. It may be possible to stay overnight in a tent.

Quinco has a cave and coral reef.

Romulo has a sandy beach and cave.

Scout has a cave and coral gardens.

Shell, with its white-sand beach, is noted for an abundance of shells after the rainy season.

Urduja's twin caves connect both sides of the island.

Accommodations
Lucap has a wide range of accommodations. Try asking for a discount, especially if you're staying more than one night. Many establishments increase their rates substantially at Easter and Christmas. Some of the guesthouses

have restaurants (Gloria's, Maxime's, and Ocean View Lodge are good), and food stalls are near the pier, but for nightlife, go back to Alaminos.

Rodriguez House has cooking facilities and rents tents per day (with cheaper weekly rates). The **Kilometer One Tourist Lodge & Youth Hostel**, P80 s, P95 d, has discount rooms for YH members and students, one km from the pier. **Gloria's Cottages**, P150 d, cottages P450, serves meals and has a motorboat for hire. **Ocean View Lodge**, P150 d, a/c, P300 (family rooms), is a good clean place and also has a restaurant.

Maxime by the Sea, P150, has a restaurant and can arrange transport to islands. The **Last Resort**, P250 s and d, a/c P350 s and d (all rooms have private baths), has arestaurant, souvenir shop, and multipurpose hall. The **New Hotel Lucap**, P100 s and d, a/c P350 s and d (with private bath).

Getting to the Islands
Go to the tourist office on Lucap pier, where you pay an entrance fee to the park before arranging a *banca*, which costs a fixed rate for up to six people to spend about six hours among the islands. Most visitors go directly to Quezon Island, where the boatman waits while they sunbathe and snorkel, then take a brief tour through the other islands on the return to Lucap. The islands are close together, however, and boatmen will usually stop at different spots if asked.

An outrigger from Lucap to the islands costs around P250 for six people, and this should cover some island-hopping. If you just want to go to Quezon, it should cost about P60-90, plus a P5 entry fee. Take some protection from the sun. Guesthouse staff will prepare a picnic lunch if requested.

Quezon Island is the only place with drinking water or drinks for sale. Rent snorkeling gear at the Last Resort or Gloria's, fishing tackle at Maxime's or Gloria's; Maxime's has scuba air. Diving is said to be good off Children's, Clave, Devil's, Lopez, and Quezon Islands. If you know how to sail, you could go to the nearby fishing village and try to rent a sailing *banca*. Make sure you take paddles and an anchor. Conveniently, the breeze is usually offshore in the morning and onshore in the afternoon.

Staying on an Island
Ask the tourist office on Lucap pier about camping on Children's or Quezon Island; you can rent a tent for P60-100. Quezon has a pavilion for camping that rents for P200, while there is a cottage with six rooms on Governor's that rents for P600. It may also be possible to overnight in the Wild Life Office on Quezon Island; it contains two simple beds, pots, pans, and a fireplace.

Bring food from Alaminos market to either island, plus drinking water to Children's Island. Agree with the boatman beforehand about his price and when he'll return for you.

BOLINAO

This small, quiet fishing port near Cape Bolinao, 36 km (one hour) from Alaminos, is a good place to absorb the simple, unspoiled country-town atmosphere.

Bolinao is an important shellcraft center; shells are gathered along the coast and around Santiago and other nearby islands. The townsfolk also catch herring, sardines, shrimp, and squid, gather seaweed, grow maguey to make into rope, and produce *buri* handicrafts. Galleons and junks, perhaps treasure-laden, are said to be lying underwater offshore.

The Bolinao area is associated with unexplained phenomena; tales of strange lights and enigmatic occurrences are recounted in *Faith Healing and Psychic Surgery in the Philippines*, by Jesus B. Lava and Antonio S. Araneta, available in Manila bookstores.

Church
The solid-stone church, built by Augustinian Recollects in 1609, has sheltered local people in the past from pirate attacks and during war. Note the weathered wooden santos in the niches of the facade; in many other churches, such antiques have been taken by collectors in exchange for plaster imitations. Inside, a side altar with sculptured Aztec-like faces and the massive carved wooden door leading to the cloister show strong Mexican influence, reflecting the Philippines's strong former ties with Mexico.

Ask the priest if you may see the adjacent traditional kitchen. The Sunday morning market in the plaza, where people still stop to pray when the Angelus bell rings, is a good place to buy a *buri* sleeping mat made by neighboring islanders.

Bolinao Museum

Some of the most important archaeological finds in the country have been made in this area, indicating a flourishing early culture. They include Tang, Sung, and Ming porcelain, and gold bracelets, earrings, and necklaces.

In Balingasay, six km south of town, excavation of a 13th- or 14th-century burial cave at the mouth of the Balingasay River yielded remarkable skulls with fish-scale patterned gold embedded in the teeth, as well as porcelain and gold jewelry. Some items, including Ming and Sung jars, fossils, and traditional artifacts, are displayed in the Bolinao Museum, about one km south of town, though the most valuable pieces have been carried off to the National Museum in Manila and to private collections.

Accommodations

The **A & E Garden Hotel** has four treehouses for guests to sleep in and serves good food. Rooms are P100 with fan, P200 with private bath, and P300 for a/c and bath. The owner is a useful source of information about the area. **Captain Cascante** is just outside the town by the sea with cottages P100-200. **Celeste Sea Breeze Resort** is also by the ocean and rooms cost P150-200. All three places have restaurants.

Vicinity of Bolinao

Snorkeling possibilities exist off the white-sand beach a little west of town and are better still at nearby Santiago, Silaqui, and Dewey Islands. A regular trip across to Santiago Island (20 square km) costs P2 pp.

You can hike to Bolinao Falls and hire a tricycle to Cape Bolinao (10 km), where a lighthouse guards the entrance to Lingayen Gulf, with a three-km-long white-sand beach nearby. A tricycle to Dendro Beach (16 km) costs about P75 if the driver waits while you swim and relax, and P15 pp if he doesn't, but transportation is irregular, so in the latter case, you may face a long walk back to town.

LINGAYEN

The provincial capital is a sprawling old town of about 85,000, situated on an island in the Agno delta. It has two separate, architecturally distinct districts, built by the Spanish and Americans, respectively. The older, more populous section is clustered around the plaza, with its municipal buildings, and the market. The newer seafront area is more spacious, with a promenade, wide-spreading flame trees, and the imposing capitol with its marble columns and spiral staircase.

Before WW II, Commonwealth President Manuel Quezon hosted elegant receptions and parties on its roof. The west side of the building has been restored after destruction by shelling in 1945. The wide beach, stretching 11.5 km along the gulf's placid waters, was the U.S. landing site, commemorated by a stone marker. Nearby are relics of this period: a Japanese fighter aircraft, two rusty U.S. tanks, the ruins of the old auditorium.

Lingayen holds its town fiesta 4-6 January, and a beach fiesta 1 May.

Accommodations

Stay at **Lingayen Gulf Hotel, Viscount Hotel** (P250, on Maramba Blvd.), **Lingayen Lion's Den Resort, Lingayen Resort Hotel** (P350, swimming pool; on capitol grounds).

Lingayen to Dagupan

This 15-km road passes through Binmaley, an Agno delta town known as the Bangus Queen of the Philippines and also noted for its handicrafts and large old church. It's fun to hike along the *pilapil* (dikes) between the fishponds, where *bangus* and oysters are raised. The town fiesta (2 February) features cultural presentations based on the *bangus* industry.

Stay at **Bangsal Inn,** whose restaurant serves *bangus* delicacies.

DAGUPAN CITY

This city (fiesta: 26-27 December) of bridges and *esteros* (waterways), three km inland on the shallow Dagupan River, is the market center for the province's produce as well as a minor port.

The natives traded with Chinese and Japanese prior to settlement by Augustinian missionaries in 1590; Dominicans took over in 1713. The first church was destroyed in the 1660 rebellion; the present church (1816) stands next to a modern cathedral. Dagupan has a university and was the terminal point of the Philippines's first rail line, inaugurated 1892.

The 120,000 Dagupenos include a long-established, substantial group of Chinese mestizos; the Chinese cemetery is on Perez Boulevard at M.H. del Pilar Street. The Pantranco North terminal is on del Pilar, and Dagupan Bus Co. is on A.B. Fernandez Avenue.

Accommodations

Stay at: **Nel-ar's Travellers Inn** (Arellano St.); **Villa Millagrosa Youth Hostel** (Marama Bldg., Zamora St., P100-150); **YMCA Youth Hostel** (Burgos St.); **Sunshine Lodging House, Caliman Lodge I,** and **Lucky Lodge** (all on del Pilar St. with rooms from P150 and up); **Nipa Lodging House, Avenida Lodging House, Venice Lodge, Caliman Lodge II, Luzon Lodging House,** and **Vicar Hotel** (P150-200, all on Fernandez Ave.); **Car-fel's Travellers Inn** (Arellano St.); **Summerville Lodging House** (Fernandez Ave.); **Boulevard Hotel** (P150, Arellano St.); **Hotel Mil-Excel** (Fernandez Ave.); **Victoria Hotel** (Fernandez Ave.), **Mc-Adore International Palace Hotel** (P350, swimming pool, on Galvan and Zamora).

Restaurants

Dagupan is noted for good seafood, and *bocayo* (coconut candy) is a local delicacy. The many restaurants on A.B. Fernandez Ave. include **De Luxe Panciteria, King's Wanton House** *(sic!),* **Dagupena Restaurant,** and **Shakey's Pizza Parlor.**

VICINITY OF DAGUPAN

Beaches

Pugaro-Suit Island Beach, the "Island Barrio" just north of the city, has more than two km of beach and dunes. A marker commemorates the

U.S. landing (1945) at Blue Beach, Bonuan (three km from Dagupan).

Stay at **Park View Drive-in** or **Tondaligan Marco Polo Restaurant & Cottages.** The 72-hectare **Tondaligan Ferdinand Park** is situated 600 meters off the coast road to San Fabian and has picnic shades and a Tomb of the Unknown Soldier.

San Fabian

A small coastal town with strong faith-healing connections, San Fabian was the home of the great healer Eleuterio Terte, who died in 1979. Take a jeepney from Dagupan to San Fabian (15 km), then a tricycle (1.5 km) to White Beach (it's actually grayish-brown), which stretches from Nibaliw West to Bolasi. Japanese troops landed here (1941); a Filipino-Japanese Friendship Memorial stands on the highway in Bolasi.

Accommodations

Residenz (Patty) Mejia (the family that runs White Sand Beach Resort sometimes accepts guests in their home) is a 15-minute walk and three minutes by tricycle from the beach; reasonably priced meals plus cooking/laundry facilities with rooms for P50-75. **San Fabian Resort** has a long beachfront and restaurant; **Holiday Village Inn & Beach Resort** (restaurant, in Nibaliw West); **Bremen's Resthouse** has rooms for P100 while the **Center Beach Resort** has cottages for P150. Other options are **Lazy Resort** (cottages, also rents tents, restaurant); **Bagong Lipunan Lodge** (restaurant, swimming pool, tennis, in Bolasi); **Windsurf Beach Resort** (cottages, family rooms, restaurant, garden, surfboards for rent).

Manaoag

A Dominican mission was established in 1605 in this town 16 km east of Dagupan. The old church (1720) houses the image of **Nuestra Señora de Manaoag,** revered throughout Pangasinan. Devotees flock to pay homage to it, especially on Saturdays, and at the Feast of Our Lady of the Rosary.

Calasiao

Another old mission center, founded 1609, nine km south of Dagupan, has a hexagonal five-story bell tower, while the Chapel of the Growing

Christ, on the nearby town hall's upper floor, contains a Christ statue said to be growing imperceptibly. The Señor Divino Shrine is here. Local handicrafts include *bolos* and the distinctive *calasiao* hats of woven *buri* palm fibers.

Stay at the **Hotel Cadena de Amor** (on MacArthur Highway); **Inawa Lodge Drive-In** (in Ambunao); **Pangasinan Village Inn** (large rooms with a/c and bath, restaurant, swimming pool, on MacArthur Highway in Bued).

San Carlos City

This is a market center of about 110,000 people. Founded 1587 by Dominican missionaries where San Juan is now, the old town was burned during the 1660 rebellion, then rebuilt (1718) on its present site. Few old buildings remain. Cottage industries include pottery and bamboo craft.

Stay at **Plaza View Hotel.** South of San Carlos on the Agno River is Bayambang.

NUEVA ECIJA PROVINCE

This province is the nation's leading rice producer. Travelers taking the quick route to or from Banaue, or going to the Cagayan Valley, will pass through Nueva Ecija, while its main commercial center, Cabanatuan City, is the gateway to Baler (Aurora), across the Sierra Madre on the Pacific coast.

Transportation

Nueva Ecija sits astride the highway from Manila to the Cagayan Valley; Pantranco North and PNR Bus have frequent buses. Cabanatuan City is the route center, linked to San Fernando (Pampanga) by Arayat Express, Baliwag Transport, and E. Jose Transport; the latter two lines go through to Olongapo.

PNR Bus and Pantranco North pass through from Manila to Baler. From Baguio, Pantranco departs daily for Cabanatuan; Pantranco, Dangwa Tranco, and Greenland Bus pass through San Jose before turning north to Banaue and the Cagayan Valley.

SOUTHERN NUEVA ECIJA

The highway from Manila passes close to Gapan, San Isidro, and Jaen. Locally grown fruit is fermented at a winery in Gapan. The beautiful Minalungao National Park, with caves and facilities for visitors, is 25 km east of Gapan in the foothills of the Sierra Madre.

San Isidro is noted for its Carabao Festival on 14-15 May. San Isidro was the provincial capital 1852-1912, and in 1896, revolutionaries stormed its Spanish garrison, only to be defeated in a counteroffensive the following year.

Woodcraft is a cottage industry in Jaen; the nearby Yuson Orchard has bred over 200 varieties of mangoes, which are canned and preserved.

CABANATUAN CITY

This important commercial center and former provincial capital founded in the 18th century (pop. 155,000) is situated on the left bank of the Pampanga River, 116 km from Manila. In the plaza in front of the cathedral are statues of Antonio Luna, the revolutionary general assassinated by Aguinaldo's guards here in 1899.

Points of interest include **Isag-Bel Ceramics,** which turns out hand-painted items, and *bibingkahan,* where rice cakes are baked over charcoal.

Accommodations

Stay at: **Manrio Hotel** (P250, Diversion Rd., swimming pool), **Mari Jim Inn** (P200, Burgos St.), **Lux Lodge, El Greco Hotel** (P150 on the main highway south of city), **Cabanatuan Travel Lodge** (P150-200, main highway, swimming pool), **Village Inn Resort** (in Mabini Homesite), or **La Parilla Inn** (P200, Zulueta Street).

East of Cabanatuan

Eleven km northeast of Cabanatuan is Palayan City, an administrative center that has been the provincial capital since 1969. Cabu was the site of a large WW II prison camp for U.S. and Filipino troops captured at Bataan and Corregidor; 2,000 Americans died of hunger and disease here during the first two months of captivity.

The road to Baler passes through Bongabon, in a fruit and vegetable growing area, and winds across the Sierra Madre. These hills contain Ilongot villages. Laur, on the road to Dingalan, is noted for bamboo handicrafts.

SAN JOSE CITY

North of Cabanatuan, the highway passes through Munoz, on whose outskirts lies Central Luzon State University, noted for its agricultural school, freshwater aquaculture center, model farm, museum, and the attractive trees and flowers on campus. Its specializations include silk and sunflower culture.

San Jose (pop. 100,000), 45 km north of Cabanatuan, is the province's northern trading and agricultural center. City fiesta: 19 March. City Foundation Day: 10 August.

Accommodations and Food
Stay at: **Mansion Pension** (a two-km tricycle ride from town), **Traveler's Inn,** or **Hotel Tierra** (P200, central), **Aristocrat Hotel, Aquarius Hotel,** or **Olympic Motel** (P150, three km south of city).

Eat cheaply at the food stalls near the market, or better at the **Aquarius Restaurant, Park Lane Cuisine/Food House,** or **Janet and Frankbelle Restaurant,** all along the main road. On the outskirts of town heading north, check out **Sarvali,** a disco pub.

Vicinity of San Jose
Camp Four Park (seven km) is a picnic and campsite with a fine view of the Talavera River and surrounding farmland. Palaspas Falls (eight km) is also a popular picnic spot. Marina Ranch and Dairy Farm (10 km) is noted for its pastures and flowers, including orchids.

To the east, the Upper Pampanga River Project, with its huge Pantabangan Dam complex, provides irrigation, flood control, drinking water, and hydroelectricity. The reservoir behind the dam is a recreation area. Carranglan, 38 km northeast of San Jose, 90 minutes by jeepney, has a colonial church.

M.G.L. DOMENY DE RIENZI

LUZON~THE CORDILLERA

Baguio City lies in a region known as the Cordillera Central—a massive block of high mountains whose rounded summits exceed 2,000 meters—between the Ilocos coastal plain and the Cagayan Valley in north-central Luzon. Baguio City was hit by a major earthquake on 19 July 1990 that killed 800 people and caused massive damage to the city. Repairs were quick, however.

The Cordillera is arguably the most spectacularly scenic area of the Philippines, and the well-preserved highland cultures make it one of the most fascinating. The world-famous rice terraces of the Ifugao and Bontoc Igorot are one of the highlights of a trip to Asia. You have to hike to see the best terraces, which are probably those at Batad, near Banaue, and Maligcong, near Bontoc, but you also get great views from the famous Halsema Highway, linking Baguio to Bontoc.

It's also one of the most spectacular drives in Southeast Asia. Baguio and Banaue are the main gateways to the region, which is divided into four provinces: Benguet, Mountain Prov-

ince, Kalinga-Apayao, and Ifugao. Sagada is the preferred place for an extended sojourn, with its lovely guesthouses built amidst cooling pine trees.

Climate

The Cordillera is markedly cooler than the surrounding lowlands. Temperatures rarely exceed 28° C and are generally pleasantly cool, but drop as low as 5° C during the Nov.-Feb. winter. Frosts occur at higher elevations. Rainfall is very heavy July-Nov., especially on slopes exposed to the southwest monsoon. When a typhoon crosses northern Luzon, rain becomes a deluge and streams raging torrents.

History

Details of the early peopling of the mountains by immigrant tribes are largely a matter of conjecture. The highlanders descended to the surrounding lowlands to barter gold and other upland products for salt, pottery, metal items, beads, jewelry, cloth, pigs, cattle, etc. Development has lagged due to the isolation, inhos-

CORDILLERA

KALINGA - APAYAO

ABRA

○ BANGUED

TABUK ○

MOUNTAIN ⌐ PROVINCE

SAGADA ○ ○ BONTOC
BARLIG ○ ○ MAYOYAO
○ BANAUE
IFUGAO
LAGAWE ○

BENGUET

○ LA TRINIDAD
○ BAGUIO

0   30 km

provinces, each roughly corresponding to an ethnic area. New roads and trails opened up the region.

During WW II, guerrillas operated in the mountains, which were also the scene of the Japanese last stand. The current provinces were formed in 1966. The region came to international attention in the mid-'70s with native opposition to the proposed Chico River Dam project, since suspended. A plebiscite was held in February 1990 to create the Cordillera Autonomous Region. Only one—the Mountain Province—voted "Yes" and is the sole member of the autonomous region.

The People

Survival in the rugged terrain and cool climate has bred tough, hardy people. The Cordillera's inhabitants form several distinct tribal groups—Bontoc, Ibaloi, Ifugao, Isneg, Kalinga, Kankanai, and Tingguian—each with its own culture.

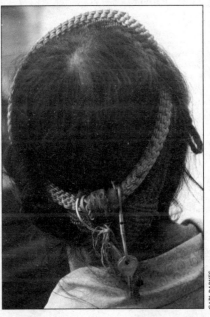

CARL PARKES

pitable terrain, low level of local commerce, and the independent, conservative natives' fierce resistance to colonial subjugation and outside influence.

Spanish incursions were restricted to sporadic exploratory expeditions until late in their era, when they governed loosely through politico-military *comandancias*. The Americans had a much more constructive administrative policy and recognized the tribespeople's unique needs. In 1908, they established the old Mountain Province as a special unit comprising several sub-

snake bones double as a Bontoc key chain

The term "Igorot" is often applied to all the mountain people, but more specifically relates to the Bontoc, Kankanai, and Ibaloi. Head-hunting was, until this century, a common practice, with neighboring tribes constantly warring. Conversion to Christianity has been recent, and many aspects of the traditional religions persist.

Within the region, there is marked diversity of language, social structure, architecture, crafts, dress, beliefs, and customs, though no sharp breaks are discernible from one area to another. Rather, cultural elements tend to flow imperceptibly between adjacent groups. Great social changes have been wrought during this century. With missionaries very active in the region, conversion and education have hastened the inevitable process of assimilation into the national fabric.

Numerous Ilocanos have settled here, also bringing outside ways; Ilocano is the language of commerce in northern Luzon. Today, most mountain people speak their local dialect plus Ilocano English is widely understood.

Transportation

Roads are few, so most travelers follow the same logical route: Baguio-Sagada-Bontoc-Banaue. Travel can be exciting, as buses negotiate winding dirt roads flanked by precipitous drops, but the beautiful landscape makes it an essential part of a trip to the Philippines. Landslides sometimes cause delays during the rainy season, particularly since a devastating earthquake in Baguio City on 19 July 1990 caused extensive damage to Kennon Road, the main route from the Central Plain to Baguio.

PAL also flies Manila-Baguio. Direct buses link Manila with Baguio and Banaue, where local buses serve the area's main towns, while jeepneys operate on secondary roads. Departures are much less frequent than in the lowlands, often only once or twice a day.

BENGUET PROVINCE

Benguet (2,592 square km) is ruggedly mountainous and dissected by numerous valleys. In addition to Mt. Pulog (2,930 meters), several peaks rise above 2,000 meters. Benguet is a major mining center, with gold and copper mines, plus deposits of silver, zinc, and iron. The principal mines are in Tuba and Itogon, south of Baguio, plus the Lepanto copper mines in Mankayan. The mine sites are communities in themselves. Mining here dates from pre-Hispanic times, though the industry has largely been developed during this century.

Commercial vegetable cultivation, by contrast, is a relatively recent activity. Benguet is the country's main producer of temperate vegetables, supplying the Baguio and Manila markets. Prime growing areas include the La Trinidad basin, Tublay, Natubleng, and the Lo-o Valley in Buguias. Natubleng and Atok have vegetable terraces, while Naguey (Atok) and Palina (Kibungan) have rice terraces.

Hot springs are found in almost every municipality. A geothermal plant has been built at Daklan (Bokod). The Agno River has been dammed to form reservoirs at the Ambuklao and Binga hydroelectric projects, which supply electric power to a large area of Luzon; the dams also help irrigate the Central Plain ricelands.

Climate

Benguet is one of the wettest and coolest places in the Philippines. The average annual rainfall is 4,489 mm; the wettest month, August, averages 1,135 millimeters. Benguet holds records for the country's heaviest rainfall in a single month—4,774.7 mm in July 1972; the most rainfall in one year—9,038 mm in 1911; and the greatest rainfall in 24 hours—1215.6 mm on 17-18 October 1967.

The climate is wet May-Oct., dry Nov.-April. Fog is quite common. The high elevation keeps temperatures relatively low, with the monthly mean temperature ranging from 16.6° C in January to 18.8° in May. A warm sweater is necessary during the cold nights Nov.-March.

History

The mountain people panned and mined gold and copper and descended to the lowlands to trade. The Spaniards discovered the Ygolotes, as they called the Igorots, in 1572, during their conquest of Pangasinan and Ilocos. Juan de Salcedo led 45 men into the mountains of southern Benguet, but the natives forced them to withdraw. Resisting Spanish efforts to locate their gold mines, they wisely decided that the gold was safer in the ground than in their huts and mined only what they needed.

Since the mountain people fiercely defended their territory, rejecting all attempts at colonization or Christianization, for more than 200 years, the Spanish could only loosely "govern" them from Agoo (La Union). It wasn't until 1846 that politico-military *comandancias* were established at La Trinidad, Lepanto, and elsewhere.

The Katipunan revolutionaries came to Benguet in 1899 and united the local people; the La Trinidad *comandancia* was burned. In 1945, the Japanese put up a desperate fight against pursuing U.S.-Filipino forces in the Lo-o Valley (Buguias), prior to their capitulation.

Transportation

Benguet's transportation hub is Baguio, from where buses and jeepneys fan out to the province's 13 municipalities. Buses pass through Benguet en route to Baguio from Manila, the Central Plain, La Union, Cervantes (Ilocos Sur), and the north (Banaue, Bontoc, Sagada). The route from Nueva Vizcaya is little used, with irregular transport.

BAGUIO CITY

Baguio sprawls over 49 square km, its winding roads following the contours. Lying within Benguet Province, but administratively separate, Baguio is the main market and transportation hub for the mountain people, an eminent educational center with five universities and the Philippine Military Academy, a major tourist des-

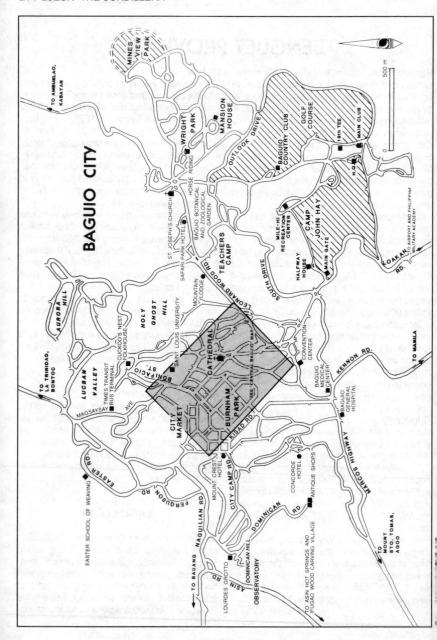

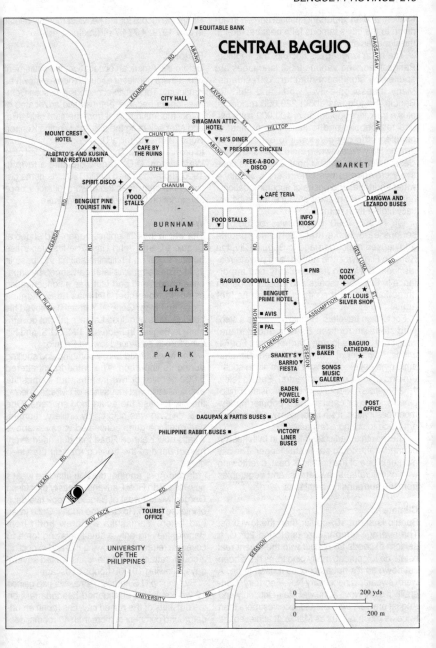

CENTRAL BAGUIO

EQUITABLE BANK

ABANO RD.

LEGARDA RD.

CITY HALL

KAYANG ST.

MAGSAYSAY

ST.

AVE.

HILLTOP

SWAGMAN ATTIC HOTEL

CHUNTUG ST.

MOUNT CREST HOTEL

ALBERTO'S AND KUSINA NI IMA RESTAURANT

CAFE BY THE RUINS

50'S DINER

PRESSBY'S CHICKEN

ABANO ST.

PEEK-A-BOO DISCO

MARKET

OTEK ST.

SPIRIT DISCO

CHANUM ST.

CAFÉ TERIA

FOOD STALLS

BENGUET PINE TOURIST INN

DANGWA AND LEZARDO BUSES

BURNHAM

FOOD STALLS

INFO KIOSK

LEGARDA RD.

KISAD RD.

LAKE DR.

DR.

DR.

RD.

GEN. LUNA RD.

DEL PILAR ST.

Lake

BAGUIO GOODWILL LODGE

PNB

COZY NOOK

ST. LOUIS SILVER SHOP

BENGUET PRIME HOTEL

ASSUMPTION ST.

AVIS

PAL

CALDERON ST.

HARRISON

P A R K

LAKE

LAKE

SWISS BAKER

BAGUIO CATHEDRAL

SHAKEY'S

BARRIO FIESTA

SESSION

SONGS MUSIC GALLERY

GEN. LIM ST.

BADEN POWELL HOUSE

POST OFFICE

DAGUPAN & PARTIS BUSES

PHILIPPINE RABBIT BUSES

VICTORY LINER BUSES

RD.

KISAD RD.

GOV. PACK RD.

TOURIST OFFICE

HARRISON RD.

SESSION RD.

UNIVERSITY OF THE PHILIPPINES

UNIVERSITY RD.

0   200 yds

0   200 m

tination, and an important spiritual center. In addition to the city's famous faith healers, foreign missionaries are much in evidence.

The main language is Ilocano, but Tagalog, Pangasinan, and various tribal languages are spoken by significant numbers of residents. Many tribespeople live, work, and study in Baguio. Baguio has about 220,000 residents, plus a transient population of 100,000 students, businesspeople, and tourists. The number of people in the city can swell to over 400,000 around Holy Week, when the middle and upper classes flee the lowland heat. The city is positively crowded at this time; there's usually a water shortage, and prices of accommodations, handicrafts, and market produce are substantially higher than normal.

On 19 July 1990, Baguio was rocked by a serious earthquake that killed many people and caused major damage to Baguio City, the Kennon Highway, the airport, and private residences. Owing to its popularity and importance to Filipinos, repairs and rebuilding began immediately and the city is back on its feet again.

For foreign travelers, Baguio serves as a stepping stone en route to Sagada and Banaue, which are a day's journey farther north. For Filipinos, however, it's an end in itself. Situated amid pine-covered hills and valleys at the southern end of the Cordillera Central, Baguio (elev. 1,524 meters), with its cool climate, is the Philippines's summer capital and a popular honeymoon destination. It's a nice, mellow city, a pleasant place to spend a few days.

Those with a particular interest in faith healing or handicrafts could easily stay longer. The city market is one of the country's best, overflowing with handicrafts, strawberries, and vegetables from the surrounding highlands.

Climate

Baguio is about 10° cooler than the lowlands. The average temperature is around 20° C. It seldom exceeds 26.5°, but with the recent real estate development, many pine trees have been cut down so it's not as cool as it used to be. A warm sweater is necessary Nov.-February. Generally, it's dry Nov.-April, wet May-Oct.; July and August are *very* wet. Baguio receives more than twice as much rainfall as Manila. It achieved the Philippine record for the heaviest monthly rainfall in July 1972: 4,774.7 millimeters!

History

Before the American occupation, the settlement was a mere hamlet of about 20 homes known as Kafagway. The health-conscious American Commissioners became enthusiastic advocates of a cool mountain retreat from the heat of Manila, and after selecting the site, the winding Kennon Road, named after a U.S. engineer, was built to provide access. The layout was modeled after Washington, D.C. Baguio became a town in 1900 and a chartered city in 1909. Its name derives from *begyiw*, an Igorot word for moss, once abundant on the site of Burnham Lake.

WW II

The war in the Philippines began and ended at Baguio's Camp John Hay. The first Japanese bombs to fall on Philippine soil hit this base in 1941. The camp was later garrisoned by Japanese troops, and part of it was a concentration camp. In November 1944, as heavy fighting raged on Leyte, General Yamashita moved his headquarters and Jose Laurel's puppet government to Baguio. In February 1945, U.S. and Filipino forces advanced toward Baguio.

The city suffered heavy bombing and shelling during its liberation. The cathedral sheltered 5,000 people for two months, but Yamashita eventually allowed thousands of civilians to leave the city to ease the acute food shortage. One U.S. division was held up by artillery, mortars, and machine guns concealed in caves above what's now Kennon Road that defended every hairpin bend of the twisting road up the steep gorge.

In mid-April, another division attacked what's now Naguilian Road, advancing easily until Irisan Gorge, five km west of Baguio. It took five days of intense fighting to clear the ridges. Once Irisan had fallen, Yamashita withdrew north from Baguio, leaving only a small delaying force to cover his retreat. Not knowing this and expecting a counterattack, the Americans waited several days, allowing 10,000 troops to escape.

By tying up U.S. forces, Yamashita had gained 10 weeks. In his abandoned headquarters on the outskirts of the ruined city, GIs found an underground complex of more than 40 rooms, decorated with Oriental rugs and fine furniture taken from the summer homes of the wealthy. On 3 September 1945, Yamashita returned to sign the Japanese surrender at the U.S. ambassador's residence at Camp John Hay.

Orientation

Baguio's scenic location and healthy climate, and its many parks and gardens with Benguet pines and profusion of flowers, make walking around a pleasure. Burnham Park forms the heart of the city, and the commercial district lies to one side of it. The large market sits beneath a dominant downtown landmark—the huge, empty Hilltop Hotel. Many of the budget hotels are in this area, and the Philippine Rabbit and Dangwa Tranco bus terminals are nearby.

Session Road, which climbs from the market to the post office, is the main street. It divides at its southern end. One branch leads to the site of the Pines Hotel, gutted by fire in 1984. The other, Governor Pack Road, leads past the terminals of Pantranco North, Victory Liner, and Dagupan Bus Line, and down to the tourist office and museum. The latter can also be reached by Harrison Road, which runs beside Burnham Park.

The suburbs of Baguio contain several parks and hilltop vantage points, plus the large former

THE PEOPLE OF BENGUET

Benguet's 302,316 inhabitants (not counting Baguio) are mostly Ibaloi and Kankanai, two of the tribes collectively referred to as Igorots. Both peoples are skilled woodcarvers and basket makers, and use back-strap looms to weave colorful cloth. They're generally more developed than other highland groups, but traditions still prevail in the villages, which are governed by a council of elders. Important occasions (marriage, funerals, the harvest) are celebrated with a *cañao*, which involves animal sacrifice and other rituals, plus feasting, drinking, and dancing.

Ibaloi

The Ibaloi (or Inibaloi) are believed to be of Malay descent, landing in Pangasinan centuries before the Spanish arrival. Their dialect is related to that of Pangasinan. They possibly followed the valleys from the plain into the mountains for river gold and refuge. It's believed the first Ibaloi settlement was in the Kabayan area, which remains their cultural center. Today, about 100,000 Ibaloi live in small settlements of 20-50 scattered households in the valleys of southern Benguet and adjacent provinces. Traditional houses are raised about three meters on posts, with a single room topped by a rice storage space under a pyramidal thatched roof.

The Ibaloi, particularly, are noted for their former practice of mummification. Their religion involves the worship of deified ancestral heroes and nature, such as the sun, moon, and thunder. They attach much importance to the souls of the dead, the "spirit relatives," who must be fed and have their needs and desires satisfied, lest they bring illness and misfortune on the living or fail to intercede on the latter's behalf with the gods.

They believe rice wine is a gift from the rice protector goddess. A traditional marriage is by parental arrangement, made even before the children are born. The wedding ceremony is marked by a three-day *cañao*.

Kankanai

Numbering about 130,000, the Kankanai inhabit large, compact communities mostly in northern Benguet. Some also live in Mountain Province. They're renowned miners and also grow wet rice, plant root crops in *kaingin* patches, and hunt. Typical dwellings consist of a single room above a cellar where *tapuey* (rice wine) and tobacco are stored.

The oldest clan member acts as a leader and serves as a rallying point for protection and help. It's customary for couples who are childless after five years of marriage to be ordered to separate and remarry. Rituals are traditionally performed for protection, for a successful harvest, or to pacify spirits.

Kankanai wear a woven headband, known as *changwo*, and traditionally tattoo their bodies in striking patterns. Their speech is closely related to the Lepanto dialect.

The Karaw

In the northern part of Bokod municipality, within the region of the Ibaloi, are eight *sitios* inhabited by the Karaw, a tiny minority group ruled by a council of elders. They speak Ikaraw, a distinct tongue related to Ibaloi. They grow vegetables and produce two rice crops annually.

U.S. military recreation center, Camp John Hay, which is open to the public and run by the Department of Tourism. Get around the city by jeepney, taxi, or on foot.

City Market

This large, crowded market is outstanding. Mountain people, sometimes heavily tattooed and wearing traditional handwoven clothes, come to buy and sell. Sections sell meat, fish (Baguio is only 47 km from the sea), fruit (strawberries are particularly plentiful around Christmas), and fresh vegetables from the nearby La Trinidad Valley. Other sections offer rice, eggs, fresh tobacco, flowers, honey, homemade jam, *kalamay* (a native sweet), shoes, and clothes.

You'll also find handicrafts, textiles, bags, brass, baskets, blankets, brooms, and woodcarving. An upstairs area is full of *carinderias* serving cheap Filipino food, complete with competing jukeboxes. The market area is the site of a huge Christmas tree during the holiday season, when hundreds of Filipinos flock to Baguio.

Burnham Park

Named after the American architect who planned Baguio, this is a pleasant place to observe Filipinos at play. Centrally located, it has a boating lake, orchidarium, and restaurants with terraces. It's dimly lit at night and is full of couples, but you may want to forgo wandering around there alone after dark due to reports of theft.

The Cathedral

This twin-towered structure is now quiet, after the turbulent events of 1945. Its grounds contain the graves of bombing victims. Access is near the post office, the stone steps from Session Road, or the Saint Louis School.

Baguio-Mountain Province Museum

Open daily 0900-1700, on Governor Pack Road next to the Tourist Information Center, the museum has a fine display of minority group artifacts from the Cordillera Central, Mindanao, and elsewhere.

Nearby is the simple Filipino-Japanese Friendship Garden, while Sunshine Park separates the museum from the Convention Center, site of the 1978 Karpov-Korchnoi World Chess Championship series. The University of Baguio

(Bibak Museum) and Saint Louis University also have private museums displaying tribal items.

Parks and Viewpoints

Several recreational areas and vantage points lie on the outskirts of the city.

Mines View Park: Take a jeepney from Mabini Street at C. Carantes to Mines View Park (four km), situated on a promontory where you can enjoy a fine view of the surrounding hills and Benguet's gold and copper mines below. Ask the driver to let you off a few hundred meters before Mines View at the Good Shepherd Convent, which sells delicious homemade cookies, jam, and peanut brittle.

Mansion House: Follow Outlook Drive past the viewpoint. Note the summer houses of wealthy families on the hillsides. Turn right onto Leonard Wood Road, which leads to the Mansion House, the president's palatial official summer residence, parts of which are often open to tourists. Built in 1908 for U.S. governors-general, it was destroyed in 1945, rebuilt, and taken over by Philippine presidents; it has also been the site of international conferences. The main gate is said to be a replica of the one at Buckingham Palace.

Wright Park: Cross the street to Wright Park, with its Pool of Pines, and descend the stone steps to a riding field where enthusiasts can rent a horse and ride around a track, or for a few pesos more, follow established trails for two or three hours.

Imelda Park: Proceed to Imelda Park, which contains examples of Igorot houses, unfortunately now dilapidated. From here, you can take a jeepney three km back to Harrison Road in the city center.

Camp John Hay

The former U.S. military recreation camp, now operated by the Department of Tourism, has accommodations and restaurants available. The camp was returned to the Philippine government in 1991 and closed to the public in 1997 for redevelopment and condominium construction. It's scheduled to reopen in 2001.

To get to the main gate (two km from downtown), take a jeepney going to Scout Barrio from Harrison Road. The camp adjoins the exclusive Baguio Golf and Country Club.

Statue of Liberty in Camp John Hay

ly staff, you may use the warm swimming pool (for a small fee), surrounded by green hills, or luxuriate in a private double sunken hot sulfur bath. Food and drink are available.

The nearby Bosaing's public pool is cheaper, but the surroundings aren't as agreeable. You can swim in the river here, too. A small hydro-electric plant is nearby. Allow at least half a day for this very pleasant excursion from Baguio, or overnight at the Asin Hot Spring Inn.

Jeepneys load outside the R&J Disco at Kayang and Hilltop. The 16-km trip takes nearly an hour, branching left off the Naguilian Road and following a winding road down a steep valley. Note the many woodcarving workshops between Km 2 and Km 6. Check what time the last jeepney goes back to Baguio because they often stop by 1600.

The Naguilian Road

This scenic highway winds down to Bauang (La Union). Numerous vantage points along it, e.g., San Carlos Heights, offer fine views of the coast and of the frequently spectacular sunsets. It passes the Irisan lime kilns, which supply the copper mills, and Sablan (Benguet), 21 km west of Baguio, which produces coffee, pineapples, bananas, and the renowned Baguio brooms, made from a grass called *boyboy*. Just beyond Sablan, a track leads five km south from Palali to Lake Libtong.

Dominican Hill

The best overlook of Baguio is from the Diplomat Hotel, a converted Dominican seminary on this hill. It was previously owned by the late, great faith healer, Tony Agpaoa, who performed countless operations here. There's also a good panorama from the Jesuit Observatory on nearby Mirador Hill.

Take a Dominican Hill jeepney from Kayang Street. It follows the Naguilian Road for about three km to the base of the hill, where 225 steps lead up to Lourdes Grotto, a popular pilgrimage site during Holy Week. Some antique shops are opposite a church about 600 meters before the turnoff, from where the hotel is about one km uphill.

Asin Hot Springs

Asin Hot Springs is a village of 100 families, situated 1,000 meters below Baguio toward the coast. At the resort here, which has a very friend-

The Road to La Trinidad

La Trinidad jeepneys load at Rajah Soliman Street, near the city market, and follow the road leading to Bontoc and Banaue. On the right is the distinctive Bell Church, a cluster of ornate Chinese-style temples and pagodas belonging to Bell Church Inc. (a religious sect). Inside it's an attractive blend of walkways, pools, rock formations, dragons, and yin-yang symbols.

The priests tell fortunes, accompanied by lighting incense and tossing bamboo sticks. Narda's Cottage Industries at Km 5 has a workshop and store displaying fine handwoven tapestries, shawls, ponchos, placemats, baskets, and Igorot antiques.

La Trinidad

This small town, the capital of Benguet Province, is six km north of Baguio and 100 meters lower. It lies in a fertile alluvial basin, known as the "salad bowl of the Philippines." The temperate climate makes it a major vegetable-growing area for the Baguio and Manila markets. Many of the farm families are of Chinese or Japanese ancestry; some of the Japanese laborers who came to help build the Kennon Road from the plains up to Baguio subsequently settled as farmers.

La Trinidad has a market and a cockpit where fights are held each Sunday. The Capitol, located at a T-junction, has some notable photos on the ground floor and a museum (open Mon.-Fri.) with old artifacts, clothing, and displays relating to mining.

Crystal Caves
Off the Marcos Highway, five km from the city center, these caves of crystalline rock are believed to have been an old Igorot burial site. To visit them, in the dry season only, take a Marcos Highway jeepney from Kayang Street. Guides are available near the entrance; agree to a fee in advance. Inside, the caves are cool, damp, and slippery, with most stalactites blackened from torches.

Kennon Road
Although those coming from Manila by bus will take this 38-km road, passing the giant Marcos Bust, it's worth riding out here without luggage once you're settled into Baguio. As you descend the hairpin bends of the steep-sided Bued River gorge, note the sculptured limestone lion above the road.

Colorado Falls are near Camp Six. Some changing rooms are beside the road, from where you can walk and wade for about five minutes to a cool, deep natural pool at the base of the falls. It's a nice place to swim and picnic. About 2.5 km farther down is Bridal Veil Falls. Cross the suspension bridge to reach the lower falls and its pool.

Accommodations
Benguet Pine Tourist Inn: Somewhat isolated with hardly an inspiring lobby, but rooms are fairly clean and it's away from the noise of downtown Baguio. You can book rooms in Manila at the Ermita Tourist Inn on Mabini Street. 82 Chanum St., tel. (074) 442-7325, P275-600.

Baguio Goodwill Lodge: Basic but right in the center of town. 58 Session Rd., tel. (074) 442-6634, P220-500.

Baden Powell House: Moderately priced hotels are plentiful near the top of Session Road, including this old favorite near the Victory, Dagupan, and Pantranco buses. 26 Governor Pack Rd., tel. (074) 442-5836, P210 dorm (free breakfast), P850-1,200 private room.

Swagman Attic Hotel: An Aussie-owned hotel with reasonably priced a/c rooms, 24-hour pub, and international restaurant near Baguio's modest nightlife. 90 Abanao St., tel. (074) 442-5139, P800-1,200.

Mount Crest Hotel: Good spot for midlevel travelers with Café Legarda piano bar on the main floor. Legard St., tel. (074) 442-3324, P1,200-1,800.

Restaurants
Session Road: Most of Baguio's restaurants are located along Session Road. Filipino food is served at Barrio Fiesta, Sizzling Plate, and Tahanang Pilipino. Familiar Western dishes are dished out at Shakey's, Jughead, and Baguio Chicken House. The Mandarin on Assumption Road is a popular Chinese café with well-prepared Cantonese dishes.

Swiss Baker: This clean and comfortable café serves fresh breads, daily specials, and "bottomless" cups of native coffee. Prices are somewhat high, but it's a great place to relax after shopping and sightseeing. Session Road. Moderate.

Cafe by the Ruins: Just across from Baguio City Hall and owned by an anthropologist, two journalists, and a visual artist, this eclectic restaurant features such unusual entrees as fish roe pâté, Ifugao chicken stewed with salted pork, and river eel harvested from rice terraces. Try their homemade *tapuey* (rice wine)—tasty but *very* potent. 25 Chuntug Street. Moderate.

Kusina ni Ima: Filipino and Western dishes served along with Kapampangan specialties. Legarda Road, across the street from the Mount Crest Hotel. Moderate.

Pressby's Chicken: Look for the large, rotating racks of chicken in the front window just a few doors down from Swagman Attic Hotel. 84 Abanao Street. Moderate.

50's Diner: American diner with burgers, shakes, and appropriately dressed waitresses. 88 Abanao Street. Moderate.

Nightlife

Folk and Karaoke Clubs: Baguio's nightlife is evenly divided between karaoke clubs that cater to university students and high-volume nightclubs pumping out disco and rock. Popular folk/karaoke clubs include **Cozy Nook Restaurant** on Assumption and **Songs Music Gallery** on Session Road. **Cafe by the Ruins** has installed an improvised bamboo stage for poetry readings, traditional dance, folk singers, and impromptu theater performances.

Abanao Street: Several of Baguio's low- to medium-quality nightclubs are located along Abanao Street, such as **Peek-a-boo Disco** and an unnamed atrocity across the street. **Café Teria** has live music and plenty of freelancers on the prowl.

Live Music: Much better is **Spirit,** a beautiful nightclub in a converted mansion situated a few blocks from Abanao Street. The modest cover charge includes the first cocktail.

Baguio's most popular spot for live bands is **Alberto's,** which has no cover charge and features two or three bands each night. Alberto's is at the corner of Legarda and Carino streets just across from the Mount Crest Hotel.

Shopping

Baguio has one of the country's broadest selections of handicrafts. The handicraft centers run by church groups feature weavers using traditional methods, who also sell their handiwork at fixed prices. In other stores and market stalls selling handicrafts, it's in order to ask for a discount and *tawad* (bargain).

Antiques are available, too, but beware of fakes. Prices tend to fluctuate considerably, depending on bargaining skills, weekend visitors, or holiday seasons. Holy Week and Christmas bring a great influx from Manila and elsewhere, so prices jump.

Baguio City Market on Magsaysay Avenue has some of the best souvenirs in the city and it's fun to bargain. It specializes in brass items, weavings, jewelry, and purses/briefcases decorated with traditional weaving designs. The quality varies, but the prices are good. **Banaue**

Handicrafts, centrally located at 52 Otek Street, has a workshop and sales room.

The **Easter Weaving Room** (open Mon.-Sat. 0800-1700, Sunday and holidays 1000-1200) has rooms with both Ilocano looms and Igorot backstrap looms. It's on Easter Road in the northwest suburbs; take a Guisad jeepney from the R&J Disco on Kayang Street. **Ifugao Woodcarvers Cooperative,** Km 4, Asin Road, has handcarved items as does **Munsayac Handicrafts,** on Leonard Wood Road. For leather, try **Rim's Leathercraft.**

The **Saint Louis Mission Center** (open Mon.-Sat. 0730-1200 and 1300-1630), reached by a stone stairway from Assumption Road, has a silver filigree shop supplied by an adjoining trade school, where student silversmiths handcraft cutlery and delicate jewelry.

Baguio Bamboo Handicrafts (open Mon.-Sat. 0800-1200 and 1300-1700, Sunday 0900-1200), 10 Laubach Road, behind the cathedral, offers a broad array of baskets, trays, and other bamboo products. **Ceferina's Bamboo & Rattan Crafts Shop** on Outlook Drive has a wide selection of baskets and artifacts, plus some antique furniture.

The **Phoenix Gallery & Coffee Shop** at Rizal Park near City Hall has Cordillera objects and artifacts, photographs, paintings, and prints. For Ikat weavings, try **Narda's Handicrafts,** Km 5, La Trinidad, Benguet. For handmade paper crafts, try **Baguio Paperworks,** No. 7, Ruiz Castro.

Transportation

By Air: PAL flies from Manila (a 50-minute flight) each morning. Baguio airport is at Loakan, about 12 km from downtown. PAL's city office is on Harrison Road, next to the Baguio Park Hotel.

By Road: Baguio is 246 km (five hours by bus) from Manila. The bus no longer goes up Kennon Road but follows the west coast of Luzon and heads east to Baguio just before the town of San Fernando.

The Halsema Highway to Bontoc is spectacular. The road across from Aritao (Nueva Vizcaya) is much less traveled, with irregular transportation. Baguio is a major route center with daily departures to Manila, Vigan, Abra, Bontoc, and Banaue to name a few. Trips into the Cordillera range (Halsema Highway for example) are long and arduous, and you must get an early start as the last bus departs at 0700.

From Manila: Several bus lines link Manila and Baguio. Departures of ordinary buses are very frequent from about 0500 to 1800, with a basic fare of about P75. Most lines also offer some express (about P90) and a/c (about P120) departures.

Bus terminals in both cities are scattered: Philippine Rabbit's are the most convenient to Ermita and most of the budget accommodations in Baguio, and buses leave every 20 minutes. Dangwa Tranco has departures every 45 minutes from Sampaloc; its Baguio terminal is also convenient. Many of the cheaper hotels in Baguio are near the market, so arriving on Pantranco North (every 40 minutes from Quezon City), Dagupan Bus (every 40 minutes from Cubao), or Victory Liner (hourly from Pasay City via Cubao), whose terminals are close together on Governor Pack Road, will necessitate a one-km walk or taxi ride to the market area. Some travel agencies arrange daily direct a/c buses from Ermita; they're more convenient and more expensive (around P180). All buses from Manila pass by the Dau Interchange near Angeles.

To the West Coast: To Laoag (278 km, six hours) and Vigan (196 km, five hours), take Philippine Rabbit to Bangued (197 km, five hours), Times Transit to San Fernando, La Union (60 km, two hours, sit on the left-hand side); buses to Laoag, Vigan, and Bangued pass through, but the best service is that of Marcitas Liner, every 30 minutes.

To Banaue: From Baguio, there are two routes to Banaue. The best way is along the winding mountain route called the Halsema Highway, via Bontoc, and the other is a lowland route to Banaue that backtracks down the road toward the Central Plain. The Halsema Highway is a favorite route for travelers to the Philippines; the rugged, high-elevation ride definitely separates the travelers from the tourists.

To Bontoc and Sagada: From Baguio's Dangwa Tranco station, you can choose to take a direct bus to Bontoc or to Sagada. There is a longer, less dizzying, lowland bus trip to Banaue via Bayombong that leaves at the same hour (0700) as the Bontoc or Sagada bus. From Bontoc, take a jeepney to Banaue in under two hours.

THE HALSEMA MOUNTAIN HIGHWAY

Formerly called "the Mountain Trail," this spectacular highway linking Baguio and Bontoc has played a key role in the region's development. Several buses leave Baguio's Dangwa Tranco terminal daily for Sagada, Bontoc, or Banaue. The highway leads through La Trinidad and winds past vegetable fields and tin-roofed hamlets on steep mountainsides.

The highest point (2,255 meters) on the entire Philippine highway system is at Km 50, near Bayangan, where the road crosses Mt. Paoay. Mount Pulog is visible off to the right in clear weather.

The road is in good condition and is three-quarters paved; however, you may want advice on conditions during heavy rains before setting out.

Timbac Caves
Mount Timbac (or Singakalsa) is east of the Halsema Highway, about 60 km north of Baguio. About 80 old burial caves are said to be in this area. Three have been located at the upper levels of the mountain at around 2,400 meters. Thirteen coffins were found in Cave One, eight in Cave Two, but they had been disturbed.

The nearest village is Bayangan, north of which, at Km 54, a feeder road leads east up the mountain. It's a potato- and cabbage-growing district. Mount Timbac can also be reached from Kabayan. There is a dirt road under construction between the Timbac Caves and Kabayan. You can stay at the **Provincial Restaurant and Lodging House** for P50 per night at Km 62 in Natubleng, a vegetable-growing village.

Bakun
North of Natubleng, a road branches west, through Ampusongan, and deteriorates into a track before reaching this remote municipality on the border with Ilocos Sur; Bakun has virgin forests and offers excellent hiking. Mount Kabunian is a sacred place, named after the Kankanais' supreme god. Its attractions include six waterfalls and the Duligan rock formation. Old coffins with mummies are said to lie on a level shoulder of the mountain.

Abatan

At this junction, a road branches north to Manka-yan, the Lepanto Copper Mines, and Cervantes (Ilocos Sur), reached by bus from Baguio. You can continue down from Cervantes to the Ilo-cos coast, but you must pass through Baguio once again.

Jeepneys depart nightly from Cervantes, but only make daily runs on Monday and Thursday. A secondary road leads south through the fertile Lo-o Valley to Buguias and Kabayan, but trans-port is irregular. The Halsema Highway continues north to Mt. Data and Bontoc. Stay at **Banaue Crossroads Inn,** Km 85, or **Highland Lodging House,** P50-75.

THE ROAD TO KABAYAN

The Dangwa Tranco bus from Baguio to Kabayan (82 km, seven hours) follows a spec-tacular route, traversing mountain crests and crossing the Agno River, on which are two major dams, hydroelectric plants, and reservoirs. After 25 km, a side road descends nine km to Binga Dam and its reservoir, which is visible far below.

At 45 km, the road crosses the 131-meter-high Ambuklao Dam. You can hike along either side of the reservoir. To tour these impressive dams and their power-generating turbines, apply a week in advance for written permission from the National Power Corporation on Bonifacio Street in Baguio, or from its Manila office. The re-quest must be for a specific site, a set date, with the names of all members of the party, and the purpose of the visit, e.g., sightseeing.

Both reservoirs have been stocked with fish. Old burial caves are said to be in the vicinity of Ambuklao. Before reaching Bokod, a road branches east to Nueva Vizcaya. North of Bokod, the Kabayan Road passes close to Daklan ge-othermal project and Mt. Pulog.

KABAYAN

This is one of the oldest towns in Benguet, situ-ated in a wide valley (elev. 1,225 meters) sur-rounded by mountains. The 10,000 inhabitants are predominantly Ibaloi. The town fiesta is held in early December, but the date varies.

THE BENGUET MUMMIES

Mummification was never common among Philippine tribes but was practiced in Ben-guet. Burial caves and niches containing wooden coffins, bones, and mummies are scattered across the province, but are particularly plentiful around Kabayan. Some of the mummies, dis-covered by hunters in 1908, are estimated to be at least 500 years old. The exact method of mum-mification isn't certain, but it was not as sophisti-cated as that of ancient Egypt.

These mummies are naked rather than wrapped in cloth, but are well preserved, never-theless. The mummies are in a fetal position, with the hands on both sides of the head or to-gether on one side of it. The color of the leathery skin ranges from beige to brown, and geometric tattoos are clearly visible. After death, the corpse was tied to a chair in a sitting position, its bodily fluids were drained, and it was treated with herbs and oils.

It was then dried in the sun or smoked. The lat-ter generally lasted 40-60 days, though among well-to-do families it could be for as long as two years. Rituals and animal sacrifice accompanied the curing and burial process, with the *mam-bunong* (native priest) officiating. The corpse was eventually placed in a capsule-shaped cof-fin carved from a hollowed tree trunk and buried in a cave on a date set by the *mambunong,* based on propitious signs.

The art of mummification has largely been lost, but traditional burial practices, including smoking, were accorded to a popular Kankanai man in Kibungan in 1981.

Attractions

Several mountain lakes are in the vicinity: Tabe-yo, Incoles, Bulalacao, Datep-ngapos. Kabayan is noted for its aromatic Arabian coffee and *kin-tuman* (native red rice), but its real claim to fame was its mummies—now removed from public view. But it's a good story.

Formerly, the mummies could be seen in the museum (open daily 0800-1700) in the municipal hall and at several manmade caves outside the town. In 1977, the Kabayan people were stunned when some of the mummies were stolen in thefts that included an overnight helicopter raid attrib-uted to foreign anthropologists.

Now, all of the caves, such as the Banagao Mummy Cave and those of the Tenongchol Burial Rock, are locked. The latter contains five oval caves bored in the rock by ancient people. Some of them require a four-meter ladder to view the coffins inside. The Ordas Cave, about 300 meters from the municipal building, has coffins and a chamber in which about 200 skulls are neatly piled in rows.

Twenty-one burial caves have been mapped, but locals estimate that about 200 caves are located in slopes and cliffs along both sides of the valley.

Transportation

The **Dangwa Tranco** bus departs for Baguio at 0800. Those proceeding to Bontoc may make their way north through Buguias to intercept the Halsema Highway at Abatan, although there is no regular transport along this route. A new route from Kabayan to the Halsema Highway (between the Timbac Caves and Kabayan) has been completed.

MT. PULOG

Mount Pulog (2,930 meters) is the highest peak in Luzon and second highest in the Philippines, after Mt. Apo in Mindanao. Sacred to the Igorots, it has several lakes near its base.

Before attempting a climb here, check with the military authorities to see whether it is safe. A good trail leads to the summit, and, as you ascend, the vegetation changes from pine stands to oak forest to alpine grassland. The weather is relatively dry Nov.-April but is apt to be wet the rest of the year, with extremely heavy rainfall in July and August. Maximum visibility is during March and April.

The trail is slippery when it rains. The area can be cold, especially in January, and there's no shelter near the summit. Take warm and waterproof clothing (rain poncho, windbreaker, sweater), good shoes, a sleeping bag or blanket, and plastic sheets.

To overnight in any of the surrounding villages, ask the *barangay* captain for permission to sleep in the elementary school. Buy food in Baguio for the trek. Water is available at Ellet Bridge, Ellet, Abukot, and a spring on the upper slopes. Allow at least six days out of Baguio for the ascent, a visit to Kabayan, and the return journey.

The Trek

Alight from the 0900 Baguio-Kabayan bus after four hours, at Ellet Bridge (also known as Eddet or Kinayang Bridge) on the road between Bokod and Kabayan. Beginning just before the bridge, walk past rice terraces and fields for 75 minutes to Ellet (elev. 1,100 meters). The *barangay* captain here can arrange a guide for the climb. The trail turns right at Ellet and ascends a pine-covered ridge (no water) to Abukot (elev. 1,900 meters), two and a half hours from Ellet. Sleep under the pines near the sawmill.

Next day, it's a two-hour hike to Lebang Lake, then five more hours to the summit. An old road leads out of Abukot and ends at a pass between two hills, where it becomes a trail leading to the peak and to settlements on the eastern side of the mountain. The pines give way to low oaks, heavily overgrown with ferns, moss, and lichen. Above 2,500 meters, the slopes are frequently covered with clouds, causing this mossy overgrowth to thrive. At 2,625 meters, a spring provides water, and at about 2,700 meters, the trail emerges into rolling, windswept, grassy uplands.

Sleep near the summit; expect a cold night and a beautiful sunrise. On day three, descend and sleep at Ellet, or alternatively, after reaching Lebang Lake, take the trail leading through Palancha to Ambangeg (six and a half hours from the summit) and overnight there. Return to the road on day four to intercept the bus to Kabayan or Baguio or hope for a passing jeepney.

MOUNTAIN PROVINCE

Mountain Province offers outstandingly beautiful scenery and rice terraces that rival those of Ifugao. Bontoc, the provincial capital, is an important market town, cultural center, and junction where the Halsema Highway from Baguio splits into routes to Kalinga-Apayao and Banaue. The relaxed atmosphere of Sagada, which has some of the best guesthouses in the country, great hiking, and old burial caves to explore, induces travelers to enjoy extended stays in the province.

History

The precise origin of the Bontoc Igorots, whether they're of Indonesian or Malay descent, remains a matter of conjecture. Two Spanish missionaries reached the Igorot region in 1641. One lived to tell about the other's unfortunate encounter with the native headhunters. The gold-seeking Spaniards made sporadic expeditions into the region but failed to colonize these fierce highlanders. In 1859, a *comandancia* with a Spanish garrison was finally established in Bontoc.

Meanwhile, the Igorots were trading with their lowland neighbors, and Ilocanos were beginning to migrate into the area. There was much dissatisfaction with Spanish rule, and military expeditions tried to subjugate the rebellious natives. A royal decree of 1881 demanded that the mountain people should all live in Bontoc proper and wear "breeches and coats" when reporting to authorities.

A consequent uprising in Sagada soon spread to Bontoc. The garrison was destroyed, but the Spaniards enlisted the Bontocs' tribal enemies to help ravage the settlement in revenge. Native raids on Spanish positions grew more frequent, and when the revolution broke out in 1896, 300 Bontoc warriors, armed with spears and head-axes, joined lowland Filipinos in the struggle.

In 1899, Aguinaldo retreated into the Cordillera with the Americans in pursuit. The rear-guard action by the "boy general," Gregorio del Pilar, at Tirad Pass enabled Aguinaldo to reach Bontoc from Cervantes, via Sagada. He pressed on toward Ifugao and reached Palanan (Isabela). By the time he was captured in 1901, the Americans occupied the entire Bontoc-Lepanto area.

Schools were established, and missionaries—American Episcopalians and Belgian Catholics—began moving in. In 1908, Bontoc was designated capital of the former Mountain Province territory. Headhunting and constant tribal warfare persisted, however. The track between Baguio and Bontoc was opened to motor vehicles in 1931. Japanese troops occupied Bontoc from 1942 until 1945, when the town was destroyed by American bombs. The people fled to the mountains and the Japanese retreated to join Yamashita at Kiangan (Ifugao).

Transportation

Mountain Province is surrounded by six provinces, but there are road connections with only four of them. The limited highway system consists of winding dirt roads, although the Baguio-Bontoc and Baguio-Sagada route is now two-thirds paved.

The spectacular landscape definitely compensates for any discomfort. The roads from Baguio and Banaue are well used by travelers; those from Ilocos Sur and Kalinga-Apayao much less so. Bontoc is the route center, but direct buses also connect Baguio with Sagada.

BAGUIO TO BONTOC

Mount Data

This mountain is located close to the Halsema Highway, 100 km north of Baguio, just across the provincial boundary, in Bauko municipality. The area is a national park, spreading into Mountain Province, Benguet, and Ifugao. It's the source of some of northern Luzon's major rivers—the Agno, Chico, and Abra. Pines grow at the base of the mountain, while oak forests dominate its heights. Five new genera of small mammals, representing 15 species, have been discovered on a small plateau near the summit.

Stay at **Mt. Data Lodge** (rooms P500-700), nestled among pine forests at 2,256 meters; it offers excellent hiking by day and evenings spent around the fireplace. It's a short distance off the highway where a sign says four km.

THE BONTOC IGOROTS

Numbering about 120,000, these former head-hunters were the most warlike of the mountain tribes. Though characteristically gruff in manner, they're known for their sociability. Today, Igorots adhere to both Christianity and their traditional rituals and beliefs. Their subgroups (Central, Talubin, Barlig, Lias, and Kadaklan) show considerable cultural variation across their range. Like their mountain neighbors, they are industrious, hardy farmers. They, too, have built incredible stone-walled rice terraces.

Headhunting

In the past, the Bontocs were fierce headhunters. The death of a fellow tribesman was avenged by taking the head of a member of the killer's group, thus setting up a vicious circle of revenge. Tribes became bitter enemies; wars sometimes lasted for years before a peace pact was agreed upon.

In addition to being a matter of duty and honor, headhunting was regarded as great sport, and all young warriors aspired to become successful head-hunters. The undertaking of a headhunting expedition involved a great deal of ritual and the observance of omens. Enemy villages were raided at dawn, usually followed by swift withdrawal. A triumphant return was followed by days of feasting and dancing. Sometimes the enemy retaliated during the celebration.

Successful hunters were tattooed. Headhunting is now illegal, but even today, the clan of a murdered Bontoc may observe some of these rites and attempt to kill someone from the offender's clan.

The *Cañao*

A *cañao* is a socio-religious celebration in which a chicken, pig, or carabao is sacrificed and feasted upon. It may be held on occasions such as marriage, death, a cured sickness, and at several stages during the planting and harvesting cycle of the *chinacon* (first rice crop, grown Jan.-July). *Cañaos* may take place at an *ato,* on sacred mountains, or in a home. Mass participation is required, and entire villages attend.

The animal's gall bladder is examined, and an offering is made to the *anito,* accompanied by prayers, and the meat is distributed, or cooked and eaten. Feasting and singing may last till dawn, accompanied by the drinking of *tapuey* (rice wine) or *fayas* (sugarcane wine). Bontocs love to sing and play their metal gongs, and both men and women dance with joyous abandon. Token portions of meat may be sent to faraway kinsmen.

Tengao

Called *tengao* in Bontoc and *obaya* in Sagada, these are days of rest, when no one may leave home to go

The Road to Cervantes, Ilocos Sur

Traveling north from Mt. Data, the highway descends toward Bontoc. It passes through Pingal, where there are old stone coffins, and the first rice terraces can be seen around Sabangan. There's transportation from Sabangan east to Cervantes, where a connection can be made through the historic Bessang Pass to Tagudin on the Ilocos coast.

The road passes through Bauko and Tadian. Bauko is noted for its distinctive, traditional houses whose high, steep roofs contain enough attic space to make them practically three-story buildings.

BONTOC

Bontoc (elev. 1,000 meters) is the Mountain Province's capital and crossroads. Its location in the Chico River Valley is spectacular, but Bontoc itself is not particularly attractive. The cul-

tural center of the Bontoc Igorot, its old social organization remains, with the town subdivided into four sections, each containing three to five *atos* (17 in total). With its surrounding villages, the population is about 30,000. Some older inhabitants are tattooed and wear traditional dress, but young people prefer jeans and T-shirts.

Attractions

The main points of interest can be seen in about two hours, but a side trip to the fantastic Maligcong rice terraces is highly recommended.

The **Masferre Studio** has some excellent 1930s black-and-white photos of the mountain people. Copies are for sale as postcards. The **Bontoc Hotel's** dining room also displays interesting old photos.

At the **All Saints Mission Weaving School,** you can watch backstrap-loom weaving and purchase woven shoulder bags. The market is across the street, but it's not exceptional.

to the fields. They're announced by the council of elders, with penalties such as being fined one chicken for disobeying. *Tengaos* are observed at several points during the growing of the *chinacon* crop, when sacrificial offerings are made on a sacred mountain to ensure the success of the harvest. Other *tengaos* may be held at any time of the year, for a variety of reasons.

The *Chinacon*

Bontoc's *chinacon* rice crop is planted sometime in January and is associated with many socio-religious activities. Planting is followed by a three-day *tengao,* during which a *cañao* called the *lifon* takes place. The fields are then ploughed, watered, and fertilized, after which comes another *tengao,* by which time the seedlings are ready for transplanting.

When transplanting is complete, the first feast of the crop, the *ap-pey* (a three-day *cañao*), takes place. It's preceded by the *enana,* a period of about six days on which pigs and chickens are sacrificed. There are prayers for a good harvest, more feasting, a day of rest, and another *cañao.* For the next month, work continues, night watches over the fields are maintained, and since the weather is dry, noisy rituals are enacted to wake the rain gods. This culminates in *manerwap,* a ritual that may last for days, begging Lumawig for rain.

In May, four months after planting, the Igorot hold the *cañao* known as *kilaw.* They sacrifice a pig and make a *kilaw* (bird-shaped scarecrow), which is taken to the fields to drive birds and rats away from the ripening rice. The *kilaw* ends on the fourth day with another sacrifice and distribution of meat. Family members continue to watch their fields carefully until the harvest in July, which is preceded by three days of ritual known as the *pisit.*

It features the offering of a large pig on Mt. Papattay, washing the rice baskets in the river, and prayers for the harvest. The harvest of the *chinacon* is followed by a four- to five-day *tengao,* after which the fields are prepared for the second rice crop (the *pak-ang*) and *kamote* is planted. The *lesles* is a *cañao* performed in individual homes in thanks for a good rice harvest and plentiful *kamote* crop.

The *Fagfagto*

Simultaneously with the *lesles,* the men of Bontoc and neighboring Samoki engage in the *fagfagto* along the Chico River, which divides the two settlements. This spectacular war game, in which participants throw stones at each other, begins at a signal early in the morning and lasts for several hours. Women, children, and old men stand to the side and cheer for their community.

Though they defend themselves with wooden shields, the warriors inevitably get hit, but it's believed that receiving many cuts portends a good crop, and the bigger the wound the larger the *kamote.* The event ends in friendship.

Turn left at the end of the street; the museum (open daily 0800-1200 and 1300-1700) up the hill is well worth visiting (give a small donation). Established by Belgian missionaries who have been active in the area for decades, it consists of four well-laid-out rooms featuring artifacts and old photos (including some of the Igorot headhunting days), plus a group of traditional houses. The missionaries are very knowledgeable about the Igorot culture.

Nearby is **Zania's store,** which also sells Igorot articles; the post office; PNB (bank); and the Cordillera Peoples Association office, which is another good source of information. For information on transport, ask around at the Chico River Inn.

Accommodations

The isolation of Bontoc has limited accommodations to a few simple inns and one slightly better hotel.

Happy Home Inn: Bontoc's best budget choice is the rudimentary inn just opposite the Dangwa bus terminal. The water supply is sporadic, but owner David Yawan is most helpful with directions and advice.

Other Budget Inns: Mountain Hotel, Chico Terrace, and **Village Inn** are also inexpensive, though the owners aren't as helpful as David at Happy Home.

Pines Kitchenette and Inn: Bontoc's top-end choice has a fairly good restaurant and clean rooms with common bath for P100-350.

Restaurants

Bontoc Hotel and **Happy Home Inn** serve similar fare, both quite good. **Pinikpikan Eatery** is slightly cheaper and good value. **Pines Kitchenette** has a more extensive and expensive menu. Also, several cheap, basic canteens are on and around the main street. The bakery sells good cinnamon rolls. For after-dinner entertain-

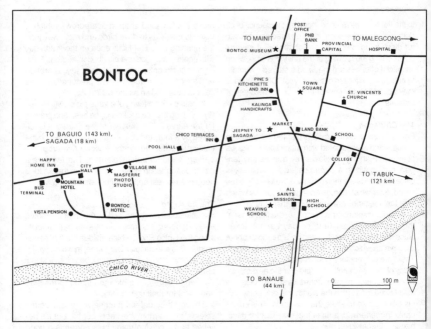

ment, it's drinking and/or a movie. American films are usually shown, since many mountain people speak English better than Tagalog.

Any traveler interested in sampling dog meat can try it here in Bontoc. If trekking to lesser-known villages in the area, bring food for yourself and to share—many highlanders live primarily on *kamote* (sweet potato) and rice. The villagers may not want to kill their best pig or dog just because you showed up hungry. Matches, salt, sugar, and perhaps a ceremonial bottle of *ginebra* or rum as a gift to the leader of the village would be most appreciated.

Transportation

Bontoc is 44 km from Banaue, 143 km from Baguio, and 18 km down the hill from Sagada. Most travelers only overnight in Bontoc en route to Sagada, though the town makes a convenient base from which to explore the surrounding countryside.

Public transportation in spots like Bontoc is subject to delays, cancellations, and early departures depending on the whims of the driver and the capacity of the vehicle. In other words, buses and jeepneys arrive at irregular hours and leave whenever packed to capacity.

Just for the record, the number of travelers along this route between Banaue and Bontoc has made it a popular place for the military to stop local buses and search bags for marijuana, which grows and is harvested around Sagada.

To Sagada: With those caveats in mind, Skyland buses to Sagada leave daily at 0900 and 1500. Jeepneys to Sagada leave in the morning around 0800 and in the early afternoon around 1300.

To Banaue: Dangwa buses to Banaue depart once daily around 0800. A jeepney from Baguio en route to Banaue passes through Bontoc sometime between noon and 1400.

To Baguio: Dangwa buses to Baguio leave hourly 0600-0900 and take a full day to reach Baguio. Seats on the left provide the best views.

To Kalinga: Jeepneys from Manila to Bugnay and the Kalinga region pass through Bontoc between 1300 and 1400.

Vicinity of Bontoc

Samoki is one km from Bontoc across the Chico River. Take the road to Banaue, and it's on the left after the bridge. See backstrap-loom weaving under the houses, and sometimes clay jar-making. The Alab Petroglyphs (figures carved on boulders) are also across the river at Alab, a short distance upstream from Bontoc (Baguio direction).

The road leading north from Bontoc follows the scenic Chico River Valley into the heart of Kalinga country. If the security situation allows, it's well worth venturing into this area. Tucucan, seven km north of Bontoc, is noted for the small-scale production of spears, head-axes, knives, bolos, and *kaleleng,* slender bamboo nose flutes now used to play love songs, but traditionally played during the mourning of headhunting victims.

To visit the unusual high-arched wooden Igorot bridge nearby (see a photo of it in the Masferre Studio), hire a tricycle or take the 1300 Tinglayan-bound jeepney, which will mean walking back to Bontoc. The trail to the bridge descends for one km, from the first curve after Tucucan village (and before the gatehouse). You can also see the bridge from the road, far below on the right about three km past Tucucan. Sadanga (15 km) has medicinal sulfur hot springs, located about 500 meters from the municipal hall, and some rice terraces.

The road enters Kalinga-Apayao, passing the picturesque Kalinga village of Bugnay. It may be visited as a side-trip from Bontoc, but the limited transportation necessitates hiring a vehicle for the return trip or overnighting there.

MALIGCONG RICE TERRACES

The spectacular Maligcong Rice Terraces are a must to visit, unless you are on a tight schedule or don't want to walk 45 minutes uphill. Together with Batad, they're ranked as the region's finest rice terraces. There is, however, no easily reached, all-encompassing vantage point. The stone-walled terraces line two amphitheaters, separated by a ridge on which sit a school and several granaries.

From near the school, enjoy a good view of the second amphitheater and Maligcong village, which, though completely surrounded by terraces, is almost entirely built of galvanized iron, with very few traditional houses left. For the best view of the first amphitheater, proceed from the school to the back of the terraces, then make your way left to where the trees begin. This is also the trail down to Guinaang.

It's possible to overnight in Maligcong at the rice mill, where you can sleep on the floor and share a meal. It's run by Rose Todcor, who speaks English. Donate whatever you think is fair for this boarding and lodging. During celebrations, the Maligcong people may declare *tengao* and close the paths to the terraces and vil-

Bontoc market day

SAGADA-BONTOC REGION

lage: before setting out, check at the Pinikpikan Eatery to find out if the area is accessible.

Getting to Maligcong

The simplest way is to take a jeepney from the Pinikpikan Eatery in Bontoc at 0800 or 1300. (There may be additional trips during the dry season.) They return to Bontoc at around 0930 and 1500 (plus extra trips in dry season). It's a 10-km, 45-minute ride up to the end of the road below the terraces, from where a trail leads two km to the village.

The view from this point isn't special, though en route the road climbs steeply above Bontoc, giving fine views of the town and valleys. Jeepney drivers will make a photo stop on request. Also, if there's more than one traveler, they'll usually wait while you climb up through the rice terraces to the school for a brief view of Maligcong village and its surrounding terraces.

This return hike is about 90 minutes, so the total roundtrip from Bontoc takes at least three hours. It's nevertheless possible to catch the 0600 Sagada-Bontoc bus and continue on the 1230 Bontoc-Banaue bus. Do this if you're in a hurry, but a better alternative is Maligcong via Guinaang and Mainit.

Guinaang and Mainit

Take a jeepney from Bontoc to Guinaang (eight km, 45 minutes) at 0800 or 1400 (they return at 0900 and 1500). Good views of villages and rice terraces en route. The jeepney actually continues about one km past Guinaang to the end of the road, from where it's about a 30-minute walk down to Mainit village. Sulfur hot springs, said to be medicinal, bubble out of the ground on the far side of the village. Guinaang and Mainit are a mixture of galvanized iron and traditional houses.

To Maligcong

A direct, steep, up-and-over trail connects Mainit to Maligcong, taking about 90 minutes, but it isn't very well marked. It starts from the Mainit-Guinaang trail at a small stream spanned by a single-section concrete bridge without sides. It's the first bridge coming from Guinaang, the third coming from Mainit. This climb affords good views of the Mainit rice terraces.

When you reach the top of the ridge, Maligcong lies directly below. The walk from Guinaang to Maligcong also takes about 90 minutes, but it's easier. Start climbing up through the rice terraces at the last small stream before Guinaang village. It's not difficult to navigate, and people working on the terraces will confirm you're on the right path.

Near the top, you'll come to a T-junction. Take the right path, then up above the terraces, where there are grassy slopes between the pine trees, be sure to bear left. This brings you above the first amphitheater of Maligcong terraces to an excellent photo spot. From here, proceed around the back of the terraces to the ridge with the school and granaries, from where you can bear left to Maligcong village, or right, down to the Bontoc road.

Practical possibilities for this trip are to take the 0800 jeepney Bontoc-Guinaang/Mainit, hike to Maligcong, and return to Bontoc by the 1500 vehicle. Or take the 1400 jeepney, overnight in Maligcong, and descend to catch the 0930 vehicle back to Bontoc. Maligcong to Bontoc is a three-hour downhill walk.

BARLIG

Barlig is a noted basket-weaving center with attractive rice terraces and friendly inhabitants, but few traditional houses remain. Find very basic lodging (P25 pp) and food at Ernesto Ingson's house, near the municipal hall at the beginning of the village. Food supplies are available, but scarce, at Ingson's place.

Transportation

To get there, take a jeepney from Bontoc (90 minutes) at 0700 or 1330. The route follows the Banaue road for 12 km, then climbs 24 km on a very rough road—a real bone-shaker. From Banaue, take a Bontoc-bound bus (0500 or 0900) to Talubin gate (two hours), then wait in the gatehouse, which controls traffic on the narrow road, until about 0730 or 1400, when the jeepneys from Bontoc pass.

Jeepneys leave Barlig for Bontoc at 0600 and 1500. For Banaue, take the 0600 jeepney to Talubin and wait at the gatehouse for the bus passing at 0830. The gatehouse has no restaurants nearby, just small *sari-sari* stores and fruitsellers.

Trekking

If you're in shape, you can hike from Barlig to Batad (Ifugao)—a hard seven-hour trek—then proceed to Banaue. Descend from the road, pass through the town, cross two bridges, then ricefields, to a more traditional *sitio* on a hillside. The trail to Pula (three hours) leads up from here; ask the locals. It forks once; bear left. After Pula, take the left side of valley, cross to the right side at Cambulo, and continue to Batad.

The road from Talubin continues 10 km past Barlig to the Lias terminal. Transport is very irregular—not every day, and it may leave at 0400. From the terminal, hike seven km to Lias itself. It's possible to continue on foot for days, following trails into the remote eastern municipalities.

Minority groups in Natonin municipality include the Madukayan, a migrant Kalinga group that occupies the village of Madukayan, and the Balangao. Both cultivate rice terraces and *kaingin* patches. The Gaddang practice *kaingin* farming around Paraceles. It's an area of low mountains and rolling hills, very far from the beaten track!

Kadaclan

On the Barlig-Lias Road, there is the start of a trail (at Lias) to the little-known settlement of Kadaclan. If you want to see this village, with its own beautiful rice terraces, try hiking the trail from Lias. Bring food, salt, and supplies as there are no accommodations or facilities for visitors.

SAGADA

Sagada (elev. 1,480 meters) has become a travelers' meeting place. It's the kind of place where you stay much longer than intended. Some people stay for months, just going down to Manila occasionally to pick up mail, money, and supplies. Sagada's attractions include a beautiful landscape, excellent hiking amid pine trees, stone-walled rice terraces, and cave-studded limestone outcrops, a cool climate, friendly local people, and vestiges of the old Igorot culture, including burial caves and some colorful ceremonies.

Add to this a number of outstanding guesthouses serving good food at very reasonable prices, and you'll begin to understand why everyone likes Sagada.

Enjoying Sagada is as much a matter of appreciating the tranquil highland atmosphere as sightseeing. The guesthouses are convivial places to relax, read, and mingle with other travelers over a pot of superb local coffee or wild mountain tea. Near Masferre Restaurant & Lodging is a small lending library.

Sagada is wet June-Sept., but there may be afternoon rain during nine months of the year, and nights are cold Dec.-Feb., so bring warm and waterproof clothing.

U.S. dollars can be exchanged at the Rural Bank of Sagada.

Celebrations

Sagada is ritually divided into two sections, each with its own grove of sacred trees and several *dap-ay* wards. *Dap-ays* take turns hosting community festivals. It's believed that Sagada's early inhabitants subsisted on *kamote* and ate rice mainly on festive occasions. Hence, fertility rituals are associated with both root crops and rice.

The year's ceremonies begin with the ritual planting of three taro roots, and a crudely carved pig-shaped piece of taro is periodically placed in *kamote* patches. Wange and Begnas are community celebrations performed seasonally throughout the year. Wange is associated with crop growth and involves the carrying of a sacrificial pig between the *dap-ays* to affirm village unity and fertility.

Begnas is a series of communal welfare rites deriving from headhunting days. The spirits of both living and dead Sagadans are called home to achieve protection, fertility, and vengeance. A colorful three-day Begnas featuring ritual, prayer, and dancing to gong music takes place at Sagada around 13-15 June.

Rice-Growing

Since Sagada is 600 meters higher than Bontoc, most fields only get one crop. In addition, the difference in elevation between Sagada's highest and lowest fields is about 400 meters, which, together with other aspects of location, water supply, and fertility, creates considerable variation in their favorability. Ownership of terraces is a major social factor, and the people employ a cooperative system of group labor, supplemented by hiring male or female workers on a daily wage or sharecropping basis.

As in Bontoc, the growing season is accompanied by a full complement of rituals and animal sacrifices to ancestors and spirits, performed either by individual families or the community. All important phases—sowing seedbeds, transplanting, placing scarecrows—are initiated by a "priest" or "priestess" with a record of successful past crops, and village elders conduct the rites that begin the harvest. A second crop is grown in fields below the town to the south, where temperatures are milder, but without the main crop's ceremonies.

Accommodations

Places to stay in Sagada are superb value: recently constructed and still quite clean, crisp linens, wonderful views from the windows, candlelight dinners, fireplaces, buckets of hot water, freshly baked breads, and friendly management. Most charge P75-150 per person.

Masferre's Guesthouse: For over a decade Julia welcomed visitors with her singing, wholesome cooking, and advice on sightseeing. Julia's has now been renamed Masferre's, but it remains a cozy place with great views. A useful map is mounted in the dining room. Masferre's is located in an unmarked tin building just below the

bus stop and Shamrock Cafe. Dinner is served by reservation only.

Mapiyaaw Sagada Pension: Sagada's best homestay is located 15 minutes from the center of town; ask the bus driver to drop you there en route from Bontoc. Two fireplaces, a lounge, and several floors of rooms in various prices. Somewhat isolated but a wonderful place with super vibes.

St. Joseph's Resthouse: Sagada's original pension is often the only place in town serving dinner during the slow season. Bring a flashlight or fall off the narrow stone path. Managed by the Episcopalian sisters.

Olahbinan Resthouse: The only place in town that has rooms with attached baths. P100-500.

Restaurants

The guesthouses generally offer a good, standard meal although **Masferre Restaurant & Lodging** has always been a popular favorite. The **Moonhouse Cafe** is also good and is quite a unique place that is now open seasonally, during the peak months Dec.-May, when it is *the* place to be. An old standby, the **Shamrock Cafe,** is also a traveler's meeting place where lunches are available. Banana cake is a specialty in Sagada and is always available at the guesthouses.

Transportation

Skyland Motors operates direct buses from Banaue to Sagada, leaving around sunrise or whenever filled. Direct buses are much better than attempting a connection in Bontoc. From Sagada, Skyland buses and jeepneys rumble down to Bontoc mornings around 0600 and again at noon.

Dangwa Tranco and Lizardo Motors operate buses to Baguio daily at dawn. Sit on the right side for the best views.

HIKING AROUND SAGADA

Demang

This settlement is about a 15-minute walk from town. Take the Soyu road, which runs downhill from the market, as far as a two-story building on the right, immediately after which is a path. Follow it down across the bridge, go straight, and follow a winding path between houses, fields, and sunken pigpens. The stone circles with low walls and adjoining huts are *dap-ays,* the haunt of old men.

The Soyu Road

Head off downhill from the market. Demang village lies off to the right. After about 15 minutes, an overgrown wreck of a bus sits where the road forks. Look left just before this junction to see hanging coffins on a rock face: a path leads down (five minutes) to some caves. The right branch leads through Ambasing to Mt. Ampucao. Go past Ambasing's elementary school, then ask directions to this mountain from whose summit, two and a half hours from Sagada, it's possible to see the mountains of Abra. The left branch is the Soyu road.

Going down the hill, notice a cave with coffins and skulls close to the road on the right: a path descends to it. Opposite this, across the road, another path bears down to the right, and after a few hundred meters, there's a big cave with piles of coffins. These two caves are the best of several burial caves scattered around Sagada. The oldest *kuongs* (pine coffins) are estimated to be about 400 years old, and traditional funerals at which coffins are placed in caves are still held occasionally.

Follow the road for another kilometer, with rice terraces on the right and passing the cement steps descending to **Balangagon Cave** on the left. Where the road curves right, the landscape changes completely to a rugged, uncultivated valley. From here, it's a 45-minute walk back to Sagada market. The road continues to Soyu village; a bus comes through about 1500 but doesn't return until next morning.

Balangagon Cave

Most people know Balangagon as "the big cave," and it *is* big. It's also deep. Native tradition holds that it leads to the center of the earth. Visitors typically stay two to six hours underground, but you could spend much longer scrambling around in it. There's an underground stream, large chambers, rock formations, and pools where you can swim—no coffins, however.

Be prepared for some steep, slippery, toe-and-finger climbing, and expect to get wet. It's best not to bring your camera. Wear closed-toe

Sagada caves and coffins

shoes. A guide with a very bright lantern is an absolute necessity; your guesthouse can recommend a reliable one. It's common for 10 people to team up with two guides. Groups generally gather at the **Shamrock Cafe** around 0900. Join a group there if you want to see the cave. The going rate is about P50 per person.

The Besao Road

Walk uphill from the market and bear right, past the Sagada Guesthouse. The road winds up above Sagada; good sunset views from here. It passes Danum Lake, actually a small pond. The pine-covered hills and cow pastures opposite and beyond are noted for mushrooms, delicious in soup or fried with eggs and garlic. Some are hallucinogenic, others are toxic, so consult the locals before consuming.

The road forks to Agawa, noted for pipe-making, and Besao, which is 12 km from Sagada. Besao is the site of the Dap-ay Guiday Stone Agricultural Calendar, similar to that at *dap-ay* Bilig in Demang, and has impressive stone-walled rice terraces. Three buses coming from Baguio pass through Sagada between 1530 and 1630, returning from Besao early the next day.

The Bontoc Road

Coming from Sagada market, the path past the Episcopalian church is on the right. Steps lead up to the cemetery; keep right of the graves. There's a spectacular view of the valley and a path leads down to it. The valley has strange limestone rock formations and hanging coffins and caves, but it's overgrown.

Return to the road and turn right past the church to Sagada Weaving. Watch backstrap-loom weaving and shop for fine bags and clothing at reasonable prices. Items can be made to order with a few days' notice. A path leads down through rice terraces and across a small river to a waterfall upstream, beneath which is a *bocong* (natural swimming pool). There's another waterfall nearby on the left. The *bocong* is about 15 minutes off the road.

Return the same way, or climb the hill above the waterfall to emerge on the Banga'an road. Continuing on the Bontoc road a path leads to the right and forks, with each branch leading to small caves with coffins. At the caves on the right, you can hear an underground stream.

Back on the road, pass the turnoff for Banga'an and take the next left, where a sign indicates the Sagada Pension. Opposite the Pension, a path leads up the hill on the right. It's a shortcut to the overlook of the Kiltepan rice terraces. At one spot, the path divides into three; go left. The vantage point provides an unusual bird's-eye view of the terraces far below. Return the same way or follow the road 1.5 km to the Bontoc road, and Sagada is four km to the right.

The Banga'an/Aguid Road and Bomod-ok Waterfall

To get to Banga'an take the first road left that curves past a pink house, a little beyond which, after the second house on the right, a path leads up to a water tank, around which is another noted mushroom-gathering area. Banga'an is about a two-hour walk from Sagada; it is also where you'll find the popular Bomod-ok waterfall. Catch a jeepney to Banga'an; once there, you'll find a grocery store and school with a sports ground.

To reach the Bomod-ok waterfall, take the path on the right side of the road halfway between the sports ground and the store. It de-

scends through a small settlement called Fedlisan and continues for about two to three hours one-way. The swimming hole loses the sunlight quite early, so try to arrive before noon.

If you want to follow the road to Aguid, take the right fork from the school and sports ground at Banga'an and continue past the rice terraces. When you reach a bridge, you can follow the bank upstream for a long way until you reach the Bomod-ok waterfall. The first route is more direct, however.

IFUGAO PROVINCE

If you're only transiting Manila, but have two free days, Banaue, surrounded by terraced mountains, is the place to go. Despite the stupendous scenery and fascinating traditional culture, most visitors to Ifugao stay only a few nights, preferring Sagada for a longer stay in the mountains. This is partly due to the size of Banaue proper, which is really a one-horse town with many trinket shops.

The only other Ifugao settlement with a few facilities for tourists is Batad, which is a very worthwhile side trip from Banaue.

Climate

The elevation accounts for a significantly cooler climate than Luzon's lowlands. November-March is the cool, dry season with January. temperatures averaging about 19° C. Bring a sweater for the evenings. April and May are the dry summer months, with temperatures rising to 23° C. It rains heavily June-October.

History

The Ifugao were feared headhunters who fiercely resisted Spanish colonization. In 1752, a mission was established at Bagabag (Nueva Vizcaya) to serve as a base for the pacification of the "Igorrotes" of Kiangan, who frequently raided Cagayan Valley settlements. But in 1767, the Ifugao routed a large Spanish expeditionary force in the Battle of Kiangan. Part of Ifugao territory was penetrated by Spanish military expeditions between 1829 and 1837, and in 1841, the Spanish set up a politico-military settlement at Kiangan, from which missionaries approached outlying villages.

Resistance continued, however, and an 1868 rebellion needed strong military force to counter it. The Spanish left in 1898, leaving most of the Ifugao region unexplored. Their attempts to control and convert this widely scattered, conservative, and independent people had been in vain.

The Americans arrived in 1901 and immediately began the task of establishing law and order, opening a school, and cutting trails between villages. Their rapid progress was largely due to official effort to develop a friendly relationship with the Ifugao and end tribal conflicts. They held huge *cañaos* (feasts) in Kiangan and Banaue in 1907 and 1908 that unified the natives

Ifugao with ceremonial headdress

END OF THE RICE TERRACES?

Ifugao Province contains the world's finest examples of rice terraces. While great beaches can be found in many lands, the Ifugao rice terraces are unique and should be seen now before they are gone. In recent years, young Ifugao have opted for jobs in towns, cities, or in tourist establishments and would rather ride motorcycles than tend to their ancient, inherited rice terraces.

Other tribesmen who once tilled the fields have been lured by the gold rush in the nearby provinces of Benguet and Nueva Vizcaya, leaving tracts of rice terraces untilled and dried-up. If left dry for a long period of time, the terraces crumble, become overgrown, and erode forever. Another problem is that these terraces have always been naturally irrigated by the flow of countless springs on the mountaintops.

Fast-disappearing forest cover caused by illegal logging has also contributed to the erosion of the rice terraces, as there is an inadequate water supply. At this point, the guardians of the ancient rice terraces feel that they need the help of the government in maintaining this heritage. As the Banaue Rice Terraces have been declared a national park, the people of Banaue feel that the government should help to repair and maintain the terraces, too.

CARL PARKES

Banaue rice terraces

and won their goodwill. Road-building was a major priority, and the Ifugao agreed to give 10 days' free labor a year each. Members of hostile villages were assigned to work side by side, and friendships ensued.

The Bontoc-Kiangan Road and Banaue-Mayoyao trail were completed by 1909. Bus service from Baguio via Bontoc began in 1927, and from Bagabag (Nueva Vizcaya) in 1932, and played a major role in the Ifugao's social and economic development. Steady progress was being made in education, and Belgian missionaries were gaining converts.

In 1942, the Japanese established a garrison in Kiangan. Filipino-American guerrillas operat-

ed in Ifugao throughout the occupation. Within a few months of the U.S. landing on Luzon in January 1945, the Japanese were retreating into Ifugao from both east and west.

General Yamashita established his stronghold on the steep slopes of Mt. Napalauan near Hungduan. Yamashita and his 16,000 troops were subjected to continuous bombing and artillery fire. Although short of food, ammunition, and medical supplies, they fought desperately for every ridge and ravine. Finally, on 3 September he marched to Kiangan to surrender, thus ending WW II in the Pacific theater.

The Ifugao had generally suffered less than lowland Filipinos, but many had died from sickness, starvation, and crossfire. The postwar years have been marked by impressive socioeconomic progress, with a steady stream of tourists passing through Banaue.

BANAUE

Banaue is the focal point of a visit to the Ifugao rice terraces. Its magnificent setting, completely surrounded by terraced mountainsides, is one of breathtaking grandeur. The steady flow of tour groups and budget travelers fol-

lowing the popular circle route from Manila has, however, made the settlement itself rather commercialized.

Banaue also serves as the gateway to more traditional Ifugao areas like Batad and Mayoyao. The town center (elev. 1,300 meters) is a small community at the center of a municipality of about 20,000 people. It consists of a string of relatively new buildings lining the road from the Banaue Hotel down to the hospital. The parking area for buses and jeepneys is the hub of activity and site of a colorful Saturday morning market.

THE PEOPLE OF IFUGAO

Anthropologists debate the origin of the Ifugao. Some believe that migrating people carried the irrigated rice culture and terrace-building techniques from South China or northern Indochina across to southern Japan and Luzon, and southward to the Lesser Sunda Islands and Java—the only regions where true rice terraces exist.

Others contend that the original Ifugao sailed northward from Indonesia to Luzon. Ifugao art forms relating to ancestor worship demonstrate a strong link with the traditional art of Borneo, Sumatra, Leti, Nias, and other Indonesian islands. The Ifugao culture, too, shows strong affinities with Borneo's Dayaks, especially in the rituals.

Even the direction from which they entered the Cordillera is disputed. Some claim they came from the south by way of Kayapa and the Pampanga River Valley; others maintain they ascended from the Cagayan Valley on the east side.

Ancient Clues

It is believed that the Ifugao have occupied their mountain homeland since ancient times (a theory supported by an intriguing archaeological discovery in 1968). In a remote area, about 15 km south of *sitio* Pabalay in Potia municipality, eastern Ifugao, stand huge stone walls, up to two meters thick and five meters high. At first, they were thought to be ruins of the lost Spanish fortress of Isabela, built in the early 1800s. But after studying tools found in the area, scholars claim the walls date from about 2000 B.C. So, like the ruins of Zimbabwe in Africa and Nan Madol on Pohnpei in Micronesia, we are faced with an enigma: massive, archaic stone walls standing incongruously in a place where people still live in small native huts.

While these strange ruins are relatively unknown, every traveler to Ifugao encounters the stunningly spectacular and ancient rice terraces. Thought to have been started about 2,000 years ago, they've been patiently built up to cover whole mountainsides from riverbed to summit. As an ancient man-made wonder, they are compared to the pyramids of Egypt and the Great Wall of China. But whereas those monuments were constructed by slave labor, the rice terraces are assumed to have been a voluntary, cooperative effort.

Appearance

Ifugao are relatively short, well-built, and muscular. Headhunters until relatively recently, the Ifugao wore tattoos to signify that they were successful headhunters; some can still be seen on older people. These tattoos on a man's chest, back, and neck, and on a woman's arms, conferred great prestige.

Both sexes wore earrings, armlets, and leglets of brass wire, plus necklaces of large beads for women and copper earrings with pendants for men. Women part their long hair, twist it around their heads, and hold it in place with strands of beads and colored seeds, while old photos show men sporting a bowl cut. Village people like to chew betel nut, resulting in stained lips and teeth. In more remote settlements, men still wear narrow G-strings and a bolo in a scabbard.

Warriors once carried spears and wooden shields. Women wear handwoven, knee-length wraparound skirts. Formerly, they went topless, but this is rare now. It's possible to see Ifugao ceremonial dress, including hornbill headgear, worn by old men and women who pose for photos at the viewpoint above Banaue.

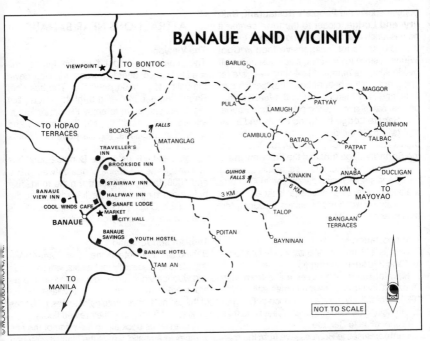

BANAUE AND VICINITY

NOT TO SCALE

The Trade Center contains many handicraft shops. The quality of workmanship can vary greatly, so examine items carefully, especially if looking for genuine antiques. Banaue has one bank; the Banaue Hotel will also cash traveler's checks. Walk up to the hotel for an excellent view of the terraces.

Obtain a free map of the area from the hotel or adjacent youth hostel. The road leading down from the town center passes most of the popular guesthouses. They're all simple, clean, and conveniently located. Some places have rooms with balconies; it's worth asking.

Accommodations

Banaue has a dozen small hotels and pensions and an upscale hotel operated by the Philippine Tourism Authority.

Budget Guesthouses: Pensions at the top of the hill such as Sanafe Lodge, Valgreg Hotel, People's Lodge, Green View Lodge, and Wonder Lodge are slightly more expensive than those at the bottom such as the Cozy Nook Inn, Halfway Lodge, Stairway Lodge, Brookside, and

popular Traveller's Inn, a favorite of veteran traveler and art collector David Howard. Few of these places take advantage of the potential views, but all are perfectly adequate for a night or two. Prices average P75-180.

Banaue Youth Hostel: The hostel adjacent to the Banaue Hotel costs P150 but is clean, and you can use the Banaue Hotel swimming pool.

Banaue View Inn: An excellent choice for a few additional pesos is the clean and friendly lodge about 100 meters up the road toward Bontoc. Banaue-Bontoc Highway, tel. (074) 386-4078, P100 dorm, P400-500 private room.

Banaue Hotel: Top-end choice for group tours and unsuspecting tourists afraid of traveler's hostels. Nonresidents can use the pool for P20. Banaue, tel. (074) 386-4087, P1,400-2,000.

Restaurants

The **Halfway Lodge** is the traveler's meeting place, and backpackers either eat here or make the move over to the **Stairway Lodge** for dinner. These lodge/restaurants serve a similar fare; service is slow but friendly, and the beer flows. A popular spot is the **People's Restaurant, Bakery, and Lodge,** closer to the town center; it serves lunch and dinner, but no alcohol. One of the best spots for inexpensive food is **Cool Winds,** a small rustic eating place built on a bluff overlooking the market. Meals and beer are far cheaper than the better-known traveler's hangouts, and locals tend to join in the fun. Another popular eatery and meeting place is **Cafe Patina.** The **Sanafe Lodge** has good meals and a bar that overlooks the rice terraces. More upscale meals can be found at the **Banaue View Inn,** the **Spring Village Inn,** and the **Fairview Inn.**

The **Banaue Hotel** offers set meals at tourist prices and stages Ifugao dancing at 2030 if there are enough interested guests (at least 20), which is usually on weekend evenings or during the high season Dec.-May.

Transportation
Banaue is 348 km from Manila, 44 km from Bontoc, and 220 km from Baguio.

Manila: Pantranco buses leave from their Quezon City terminal several times daily 0730-1000. Alternatively, take a Pantranco or Dangwa bus to Solano (toward Cagayan Valley) and then the connection to Banaue.

Bontoc: Buses to Bontoc leave from the market daily from 0500-0900. If you miss an early departure, buses passes the historical marker by the main road 1100-1300. The ride is magnificent.

Baguio: Buses to Banaue depart daily 0600-0800 from the Baguio bus terminal and take about eight hours via the less scenic southern route through San Jose and Bayombong.

A better option is the early-morning bus from Baguio to Bontoc, which snakes along the almost unbelievable Halsema Highway, one of the more spectacular roads in Southeast Asia. Direct connections from Baguio to Banaue are possible, though nearly all travelers take a connecting bus from Bontoc up to Sagada.

Bagabag: Bagabag is 61 km or 90 minutes from Banaue. At the junction where the Bontoc-Banaue Road meets the Cagayan Valley Highway, on which frequent transportation goes north or south, take any bus whose destination is Manila, Solano, Tabuk, or Baguio via the lowland route. Alternatively, take a jeepney to Lagawe, then another to Bagabag.

ATTRACTIONS NEAR BANAUE

The Viewpoint
This popular photo spot, three km uphill on the road to Bontoc, affords a wonderful view down the valley to Banaue *poblacion.* The bus from Baguio-Bontoc makes a brief stop here, but many visitors return to enjoy the panorama at leisure. For a small tip, old Ifugao men and women in traditional regalia pose for photos against the rice terrace backdrop.

You could ride up on the Bontoc-bound bus that passes near Adespa Lodge between 0900 and 1000, then walk back down the road. Just before reaching town, a track leads behind the Evangelical Church to Angadal, whose residents practice weaving and woodcarving.

Tam-An and Ambalio
Behind Banaue Hotel is the "new" Tam-An Village, created especially for tourists, where beads and woodcarvings are produced and sold. Several meters away is the original village. Some of the old huts have bundles of ancestral bones sticking out from under their raised floors.

A path leads back along the edge of the rice terraces to Ambalio, where the blanket-wrapped bones of Ponchinlas, a Banaue chieftain, rest. Pass the grave of the famous American anthropologist, Dr. H. Otley Beyer, who took a native wife and studied the Ifugao early this century, and ascend the steps to the Trade Center.

Bocos and Matanglag
You can follow well-marked trails from Banaue on an invigorating two- to three-hour circular hike amid the rice terraces. Take the steps to the left of the Immaculate Conception Mission School, which lead to Bocos. This village is a mixture of both new and traditional houses, some adorned with the skulls of sacrificial pigs and carabao, whose number reflects wealth. *Bulols,* rice god images blackened with sacrificed blood, are stored in the granaries. Customarily, they are only taken out during harvest rituals, but here the owners will allow tourists to see and photograph them year-round for a fee.

A trail ascends from Bocos to a footbridge fronting the waterfall that's visible from Banaue. Some photogenic spots overlooking the terraces lie along this path, which continues to Matanglag, where you can see blacksmiths making jewelry for sale. The trail leads down to steps and the road, from where it's 1.5 km back to town.

Poitan

The road below Bocos and Matanglag leads to Batad. Three km from Banaue, you can take a dip at Guihob natural pools, backed by a small waterfall; a trail (five minutes) leads from the bridge on the road. Farther along the road, enjoy fine views of Poitan. This village is surrounded by protective stone walls, dating from times of tribal war, and has a stone-lined pit where elders gather to discuss village affairs, and a sacred, legendary stone post.

You can also see weavers and woodcarvers, and ask to see *bulols* for a fee. Poitan can be reached by a trail down from the road, or by a 30-minute hike through the terraces from below the Banaue Hotel, crossing the river by footbridge.

BATAD

There's no easy way to see the Batad rice terraces. You must hike two to three hours uphill through mountain trails from the junction at Km 12. But the stupendous amphitheater of terraces, steep, wooded mountains, and relatively unspoiled village life make it a *must*.

Batad can be visited as a day trip from Banaue, but it's definitely worth staying at least one night, or better still, a few days. It's much more traditional than Banaue, and cheaper, too. The trail to Batad emerges at a viewpoint with a breathtaking side vista of the terraces and village, which consist of several small clusters of huts called *sitios*. They're similar, so most travelers find it sufficient to visit two or three of them.

The inhabitants are generally sensitive about being photographed without permission; ask first or use a telephoto lens. By planning to overnight, you can leisurely explore Batad, linger in the *sitios* to feel the rhythm of daily life, and leave early in the morning to intercept vehicles bound for Banaue or Mayoyao.

A Walking Tour of Batad

For those planning a day trip to Batad, the following route enables the village to be seen in about two hours. From the viewpoint, make your way down to the ridge on the right for a face-on view of the amphitheater—a good photo spot. From here, note on your right the *sitio* on a small wooded hill at the foot of the amphitheater. Pass to the left of this hill; a path descends steeply to the river.

Cross the river (no bridge) and walk a short distance upstream along the far bank to an impressive 25-meter waterfall, fronted by a nice pool for swimming. It's directly below the large white scar on the hillside across the Batad—a useful landmark by which to navigate. Return to the rice terraces by the same path and make your way to the largest *sitio,* clustered around the church.

From here, climb up to the *sitio* ahead and to the right, then cross left to the viewpoint and the trail leading up to the saddle. Alternatively, omitting the waterfall allows more time in the *sitios.*

Accommodations

Batad has some guesthouses. The **Hillside Inn,** on the right below the viewpoint, offers a fine view of the terraces and is a good place to spend a few days, since it's peaceful and slightly secluded, and the family makes you feel very welcome. **Romeo's Inn,** good too, is also on a hilltop overlooking the village.

The **Welcome Inn** (or Greenhouse, so called because of its green metal roof) is in the *sitio* to the left of the viewpoint. The red-roofed **Foreigner's Inn** is in the largest *sitio,* down below, close to the church. It's surrounded by traditional houses, giving guests a good feel for village life. Others are **Welcome Inn** and **Simon's Inn.** All charge P50 or less. Depending on the season, you can bargain for less.

A meal consists of whatever's available—usually rice and vegetables, and perhaps *kamote,* pork, or eggs. You can drink beer, soft drinks, native coffee, and rice wine. Everything not produced locally has to be carried from the road on someone's back. The food, in general, is okay, but soon becomes monotonous.

Transportation

Take a jeepney going to Banga'an or Ducligan from the Banaue parking area at about 0900 (also at 1530) or the Mayoyao-bound minibuses that come through between 0900 and 1000. It's possible to begin by visiting Banga'an. Alight at the Banga'an viewpoint (14 km from Banaue), from where steps lead down (20 minutes) to Banga'an village, a cluster of traditional houses surrounded by terraces. Then walk back two km along the road to the Batad turnoff (signposted).

To go directly to Batad, get off after 12 km at the sign. The hike from here is a steep, six-km up-and-over, taking about 90 minutes. The road (no transport) winds up to the saddle. From here (don't follow the road down, since it's incomplete), a narrow trail to the right of the small shelter leads past the viewpoint to the village. You can also hike a hard seven hours to Batad from Barlig (Mountain Province), or approach it from Habbang Bridge or Ducligan on the Banaue-Mayoyao road.

To get to Banaue, hike to the road, then keep walking and hope a vehicle passes. The minibus from Mayoyao comes through around 0800-0830, so to catch it, leave Batad by 0630. Jeepneys are irregular, since they only run when they have enough passengers; the later it is, the smaller the chance.

It's not a difficult walk back to Banaue (about three hours), with good views of Poitan village after seven km. For a day trip to Batad, it's practical to form a group of travelers to share the cost of chartering a jeepney from Banaue to the Batad turnoff. Then you can make an early start, enjoy Batad, and find the jeepney waiting for you when you return to the road; to ensure this, don't pay till the end.

VICINITY OF BATAD

The Batad area offers good hiking, but trails are steep and slippery after rain. The difficulty of the terrain accounts for the isolation of the villages these trails lead to and the relative purity of the Ifugao lifestyle found in them. The hiking is demanding, but rewarding for those in good physical condition. The following can be day hikes or serve as through routes.

Batad to Pula

This hike takes around four hours each way; the trail leads up steeply at the right edge of the rice terrace amphitheater. Cambolo is reached in one hour. Descend through the village and cross the bridge. Then walk between rice terraces, always staying on the right side of the valley to Pula, three hours beyond Cambolo.

At Pula, you can continue for three more hours to Barlig (Mountain Province), overnight, and take transport to Bontoc or Banaue the next morning. It's also possible to overnight in Pula. Bring some canned goods, a bottle, or similar gift as your contribution. Or you may return to Batad to complete a long, strenuous day.

Batad to Habbang Bridge

Descend across the Batad rice terraces to the river, cross the bridge, turn right along the riverbank for 100 meters, then take the stone steps to the left. From here, it's a very steep one-hour climb to the notch at the top. After the steps, cross some small, uncultivated fields, continue up through a forest, then follow a series of switchbacks through fields of tall grass. This notch probably offers photographers the finest view of the Batad amphitheater.

On the other side of the notch, it's 30 minutes down to the village of Patpat. From there, you can return to Batad, making a return trip of four hours plus, or continue to Guitte, an easy 45 minutes—bear left after the school, make a steep descent to the river, cross it, and follow the trail downstream to meet the Banaue-Mayoyao road at Habbang Bridge. All this takes about three and a half hours from Batad. Habbang Bridge is about 24 km from Banaue and 20 km from Mayoyao.

By leaving Batad before 0700, you can catch the bus to Mayoyao, which passes Habbang Bridge at around 1030; this means staying overnight in Mayoyao.

For Banaue, you can't connect with the bus that leaves Mayoyao at 0600, so you must walk at least three km along the road to Ducligan, from where irregular jeepneys return to Banaue. Keep walking, as some jeepneys turn around at Banga'an, seven km before Ducligan. A direct trail also leads from Batad to Ducligan, taking about two and a hal hours. Ducligan has hot springs on the riverbank, adjacent to a deep pool.

To reach Batad from Mayoyao, take the 0600 bus, reaching Habbang Bridge about 0730. Cross the bridge, and the trail to Batad begins immediately to the right; after 45 minutes, cross the river, climb steeply to Guitte, continue through

Patpat and up to the notch, then descend sharply to the river below Batad. You must cross the rice terraces to get to any of the guesthouses, or to the path for Banaue. You could make it back to Banaue the same evening, but you'll find Batad an agreeable place to linger.

MAYOYAO

The Mayoyao rice terraces are broad and relatively flat compared to those of Banaue and Batad, giving a totally different, yet beautiful, impression. Mayoyao is different too. The houses sit alone, surrounded by ricefields, rather than being grouped in clusters as in other Ifugao settlements.

Most houses are traditionally shaped, but the unusually steep roofs are now metal. Not much remains of the old culture here. The *poblacion,* situated beneath 2,702-meter Mt. Amuyao, is a nondescript cluster of buildings, from which trails lead down through the terraces. Enjoy good views of the terraces from the hospital, the fish hatchery above the *poblacion,* and from about 1.5 km along the road to Aguinaldo.

For most travelers, it's enough to spend an afternoon walking around the Mayoyao terraces and to return to Banaue the next morning. Depending on the time of year, if it is festival time in Mayoyao or market day, villagers from Kadaclan may be willing to show you the way to their village. It's a serious nine-hour hike, but the rice terraces in Kadaclan are better than Batad.

From Kadaclan, it's possible to hike out to the small village of Lias and catch a jeepney from there to Barlig in Ifugao Province. You won't reach Kadaclan without a guide because of a secret turnoff through a cave with fast-flowing water. In Kadaclan, there are no accommodations and little food to spare. Go prepared, but if you have a guide, it's a worthwhile experience.

Accommodations
The house of Mr. and Mrs. Montinig, a very friendly couple, is 200 meters from the main square where the bus stops, back along the road to Banaue. **Popular Lodge** is an unmarked canteen on the main square. Mrs. Mary Likiyan's house is on the road to the hospital. The town is dead after 2000.

Transportation
Mayoyao is a scenic 44 km (three hours) from Banaue, with one minibus and one jeepney in each direction daily. Originating in Solano about 0700, it passes Banaue (0900), the Batad turnoff (0930), Banga'an, and Ducligan. It leaves Mayoyao at 0600. Mayoyao is also linked by a daily jeepney with Potia and Aguinaldo.

SOUTH OF BANAUE

Hungduan
Jeepneys go southwest from Banaue through Hapao to Hungduan. Both have impressive rice terraces. Nearby is Mt. Napalauan, which is topped by a small lake, surrounded by dwarf oak and pine. The Japanese Imperial Army made its last stand here. Some believe that General Yamashita's fabulous treasure remains buried on the mountain.

Lagawe
The provincial capital, on the highway between Banaue (26 km) and Bagabag (35 km), is served by buses and jeepneys. Natoban Cave, where the entrance descends to four chambers, is at Boliwong, a four-km hike from the *poblacion.* The smaller Bintacan Cave, which has three chambers of stalactites and stalagmites, is on a mountain slope at Ibulao. Other points of interest include the Buhawit natural pool, where you can swim in a river, and the rock statue of the legendary heroine, Bugan.

Stay at the **Habawel Hotel.**

Burnay
The Burnay area, east of Lagawe, is the territory of the Atifulo, a group of about 2,000 people, culturally related to the Ifugao, who inhabit the rugged upland drained by the tributaries of the Magat, a major branch of the Cagayan River. The Atifulo practice wet-rice farming, plant root crops in *kaingin* patches, raise pigs and chickens, hunt, and fish. Like the Ifugao, they're known for their intricate rituals, intriguing legal system, and fine rice terraces.

Kiangan
This town is 10 km southwest of Lagawe. The residence of the late Don Rafael Bulayungan

contains a celebrated old stone *hagabi* (rich man's bench). The Philippine War Memorial Shrine, a pyramid-shaped concrete building in the *poblacion,* offers a fine view of the surrounding countryside.

The hill overlooking the *poblacion* is nicknamed "Million Dollar Hill," after the vast amount of money the Americans spent on bombs and ammunition to dislodge the Japanese from it in

1945. A memorial in Linda marks where Yamashita and his staff informally surrendered in a home economics building. He was flown from Bagabag to Baguio for the formal surrender. It's possible to swim in Ambuaya Lake on a hilltop about two km from the *poblacio.*

Stay at the **Kiangan Hotel.** Jeepneys link Kiangan and Lagawe, while a Dangwa Tranco bus leaves for Baguio at 0700.

KALINGA-APAYAO PROVINCE

This ruggedly mountainous, underdeveloped province was formed in 1966 by uniting the subprovinces of Kalinga and Apayao, traditional homes of the Kalinga and Isneg peoples, respectively. Poor transportation services and communications have been aggravated by violent disturbances sparked by a government scheme (since suspended) to dam the Chico River.

Due to security reasons, traveling here is somewhat risky. A pity, because these villages retain many aspects of traditional Kalinga culture, and the landscape is beautiful. In spite of such uncertainties, Kalinga-Apayao is worth a visit, but you will be under some suspicion by locals. Before setting out, it is advisable to contact the Cordillera Bodong Administration in Baguio City to coordinate your visit and to be advised on places to see, transport, and accommodations.

Upon arriving in a village or small town, meet the *barangay* captain or the mayor. They can offer protection and insights, and you will quite possibly find the same treatment from the rebels. The Philippine military, who scout these highlands but are unfamiliar with the terrain, are also a bit menacing when you are on your own. Proceed with caution.

There are no hotels or lodging houses in many parts of the province. Homestays can be arranged by contacting a family in town or through the mayor.

The Land
Kalinga-Apayao (704,768 square km) contains about 222,000 people, spread through 15 towns. Since the Cordillera declines in the north and northeast as it nears the coast and Cagayan Valley, the southern half of the province is high-

er than the north. Virgin forest covers much of the territory, and grassland is also extensive. In Kalinga, the 225-km Chico River winds through from Bontoc, turns northeast at Lubuagan, and flows toward the Cagayan River. The ridges on each side of the Chico River rise to 2,000 meters, but most settlements are located on the lower slopes at around 600 meters. Vegetation varies markedly with elevation, coconut palms giving way to pine forest and *cogon* grass on the ridges.

Northern and eastern Kalinga are lower, but nevertheless feature steep-sided sierras and deep canyons. Rainforest remains thick in the narrow valleys, but mountain slopes are being increasingly cleared for upland rice and sugarcane cultivation. The most fertile areas are the wide, flat riverbeds where the Chico's tributaries join it on the Tabuk Plain. Much of Apayao is virgin territory—unexplored mountainous rainforest. Moving north, mountains become lower, with thicker brush and larger trees. A single road crosses the entire region, but one could follow foot trails for days between remote hamlets.

History
The Kalingas and Isnegs are believed to be descended from Indonesian immigrants who reached Luzon thousands of years ago. The region was the last of the mountain provinces to be influenced by Western culture and the last to receive an educational system. For a long time the foothills and plains of the Tabuk/Pinukpuk region were an unoccupied malarial buffer zone between the Spanish missionaries in the Cagayan Valley and the headhunting mountain people who stubbornly resisted subjugation.

DAM THAT CHICO RIVER

The Kalinga region captured international attention in 1975, when the Philippine government initiated the Chico Valley hydroelectric dam project. Originally conceived as a series of four dams, it would have been the largest hydroelectric complex in Southeast Asia. But the project required flooding a number of Kalinga villages, their rice terraces, and sacred burial grounds; some Bontocs would also have been affected.

The government proposed to resettle these villagers at Gubgub, near Tabuk, where they would be given two hectares of riceland—substantially more than most of them have—plus a 150-square-meter residential lot and P10,000 to build a house. Very few families accepted the offer; the majority rejected the project from the start. They argued that they would be betraying a sacred trust by abandoning their ancestral burial grounds and rice terraces, and that the move would also destroy their age-old customs and way of life.

Resistance was firm and marked by the internment of dissenting villagers, a difficult dialogue between the government and Kalinga delegations sent to Manila, bloodshed, and the involvement of outside interest groups.

Successfully completed, the project would have expedited electrification and irrigation programs in northern Luzon, increased rice production, and reduced national energy imports. Alternatives to the dam will eventually be found. It's a question of a delay in the inevitable march of progress versus a permanent, irrevocable cultural loss.

The few Spanish expeditions to enter the region over the centuries had almost no impact. It was only at the end of their era that the Spaniards made Kalinga and Apayao politico-military provinces for administrative purposes, and built a trail from Abra to the Chico Valley to supply military posts established to control the highlanders' periodic raids. The agents of change were not the Spanish but the Ilocano traders who used the trail and brought outside ideas.

During the early 20th century, the Americans began disseminating Western and Christian concepts. They suppressed headhunting and tribal warfare, built roads and trails, and established schools and social services.

Transportation

Kalinga-Apayao can be approached from Bontoc, the Cagayan Valley, and Bangued (Abra). A jeepney leaves Bontoc at 1300, after waiting for the Dangwa Tranco bus from Baguio, and travels down the Chico River Valley. It's usually necessary to overnight in Tinglayan. A daily bus leaves Bontoc for Tabuc, via Banaue.

Buses link Manila and Baguio with Tabuk, via the Cagayan Valley. Regular buses and jeepneys connect Tuguegarao and Tabuk. From the Ilocos coast, you must overnight in Bangued, where jeepneys go to Salegseg (six hours) on Monday and Thursday mornings.

THE CHICO RIVER VALLEY

This lovely valley leads north and downstream from Bontoc into the heart of Kalinga. It is, however, an area of unrest, so before going there, check with the Cordillera Bodong Administration at Cordillera House, across from Mansion House in Baguio City, about the security situation. They will coordinate your visit to remote areas.

Basao is a picturesque settlement, reached by footbridge across the Chico River and a hike up the mountain for one km, which provides a good impression of the Kalinga culture. You can also see waterfalls here and have a view of Mt. Manting-oy, which locals call the "Sleeping Beauty," since its silhouette resembles a reclining woman, whose grief at her husband's death in battle is immortalized in the native ballad "Ullalim."

LUBUAGAN AND VICINITY

Lubuagan is the main town between Bontoc and Tabuk. It's actually a cluster of about 15 hamlets, situated in the most densely populated area of ethnic Kalingas. There are good views of the Chico Valley from the school. Stay at **Acuat's Residence** (P45), attached to the Perpetual Help Pharmacy.

Two km north of Lubuagan, a road branches left and ascends another two km to a T-junction, from where there's a superb view of the

THE PEOPLE OF KALINGA-APAYAO

The Kalingas

The Kalingas comprise several subgroups that display marked variation in physical appearance, dialect, architecture, dress, and ceremonies. These cultural subdivisions are basically geographical. Each group has also absorbed cultural influences from its neighboring non-Kalinga people. Formerly fierce headhunters, Kalingas are a proud people with a taste for decoration and ornaments; the male Kalinga is known as the "peacock of the mountain provinces." They have a strong oral tradition, a talent for oration and debate, and a propensity for social celebration, given the slightest reason.

Appearance: Kalingas are tall and physically well built. Older people bear the tattoos that were the prestigious emblem of the successful headhunter and his family. Generally, the southern Kalingas are more conservative than their northern counterparts. Feuding is more prevalent, traditional dress more in evidence. In the villages off the roads, some men still wear G-strings, while women go topless, with a short wraparound skirt *(tapis)*.

Men wear a small, round pocket-hat to carry matches and tobacco; decorated with a cross and diamond design, it's both attractive and useful and may be worn on the front or back of the head. A woven bamboo and *nito* cap *(aintutun)* is worn on festive nights. Necklaces or chokers of agate, carnelian beads, and silver are worn by both sexes on festive occasions.

The northern group, living around the Sultan River Valley, was formerly the most gaudily attired and heavily ornamented people in the mountain provinces. Both men and women wore short, brightly colored jackets and were adorned with beads, tassels, necklaces, bracelets, feathers, and flowers. Contemporary dress is now the norm, however.

Settlements: The southern Kalingas tend to live in relatively large settlements, while northern Kalingas tend to be in small scattered hamlets. In the past, there was considerable shifting of settlements within an area, due to the nature of dry-rice farming and to safety considerations. Different regions were hostile to one another, and except where ties were occasionally forged through trade or marriage, outsiders were automatically enemies.

Dwellings were located on leveled areas of steep mountain slopes or in isolated pockets in deep canyons. Until relatively recently, villages were stockaded, and approaching trails featured hidden traps, such as pits full of bamboo spikes or tripwires connected to overhanging logs. The *podayan,* a small shrine honoring the village's guardian spirit, may sit at a settlement's entrance.

Modern circumstances and the institution of peace pacts have changed life in Kalinga, but past conditions still influence the way Kalingas think. They're suspicious of strangers and wary of entering areas in which a peace pact doesn't exist, or has been severed, for their group.

The Isneg

The Isneg, also known as the Apayao after the principal river of their territory, are the least known of the mountain people. It's believed they're of Indonesian descent and made their way up rivers from Luzon's northwest coast. Numbering about 25,000, they form several regional subgroups—including Kabugao and Talifugo—living in scattered hamlets along riverbanks in Apayao's mountainous rain-

---

beautiful Pasil Valley. The left road leads to the Batong Buhay gold mine; the right rejoins the main road to Tabuk. Trails lead down to villages in and across the valley. Seven km north of Lubuagan is Cagaluan Junction, where the road forks to Abra and Tabuk.

From Lubuagan

There's no sure same-day connection to Bontoc (68 km). The jeepney returning from Tabuk to Tinglayan passes at 1300. Overnight at Tinglayan. To Tabuk (two hours), a bus leaves at 0630; several jeepneys operate up to 0900, intermittently after that.

THE ROUTE TO ABRA

The entire route from Lubuagan to Abra consists of scenic, twisting roads. An underground river flowing beneath Uguid Mountain can be heard from the roadside at Balbalan, and some exposed sections are visible. Balbalasang, a village surrounded by pine-covered mountains just before the Abra boundary, is particularly attrac-

forests, with a substantial number in Abra and some in Ilocos Norte and Cagayan.

Many communities are named after the rivers and streams from which they obtain much of their food. Today, their isolation is being assaulted by the pressures of civilization, and their lifestyle is increasingly influenced by that of neighboring lowlanders.

Dress: Traditionally, Isneg men wear a plain blue or black G-string; under this or a rattan belt, they carry a small, decorated bag containing tobacco, flint, tinder, betel nut, and lime. They have blackened teeth and long hair, which is coiled and wrapped in a turbanlike cloth. The most heavily tattooed of the mountain people, the Isneg are particularly noted for their boat motif tattoos, which adorn the hands and wrists of men as well as the back of women's hands.

Women sew brightly colored decorations on the dark cloth of their skirts *(tapis)* and long-sleeved blouses, and wear jewelry, such as glass beads fancifully arranged on strings, necklaces of antique stone beads or silver, and carved bone amulets. Their lips are typically stained red from chewing betel nut. Both sexes have a truly elaborate ceremonial costume, which may include feathers for women and a neckband with shell breastplate and headdress topped with scented leaves for men.

Lifestyle: Isneg beliefs and practices are related partly to the animist worship of their other mountain cousins, and partly to the more primitive culture of the Negritos. Their ceremonies play an important role in their lives. A benevolent god, Anglabbang, protects them from ghosts, which may take the form of people, animals, monsters, or giants. Like the Negritos, Isneg are skilled hunters, pursuing wild game in the forests using bow and arrow, spears with leaf-shaped iron tips, snares, and spear pits.

They are also proficient fishermen. When head-hunting and tribal warfare prevailed, they lived in stockaded villages with their granaries between the houses.

Traditional houses are ingenious, complex timber structures with an elongated floor plan and a gabled roof that may protrude to give a ship's-prow profile reminiscent of some Indonesian architecture. Families may also maintain smaller houses at the edge of their *kaingin* fields for seasonal occupancy.

Small, level plots along the rivers are also cultivated. Crops include rice, *kamote,* taro, corn, vegetables, sugarcane, and tobacco. Wet-rice agriculture has spread northward from Kalinga in recent decades, with Bontocs imported for the skilled task of terrace building. Isneg leaders, called *mengal,* are chosen according to wealth, ability, prowess, and charisma.

Arts and Crafts: Both men and women carry axes forged by expert Isneg blacksmiths using stone hammers and anvils. They still prefer their two traditional types of axes to the bolo used elsewhere in the Philippines. Men can hurl an ax with great accuracy from 30 paces. Excellent rattan or bamboo baskets are woven for keeping fish and game.

The women also make small purses, with several compartments, out of pandanus leaves waterproofed with beeswax. Isneg play a bamboo guitar whose strings, made from the outer skin of bamboo, are plucked or struck with a stick. Festivities are marked by fast music and energetic dancing. Since cloth-weaving and pottery-making are unknown to them, the Isneg barter for their needs with Ilocano traders, obtaining clothes, pots, and utensils in exchange for honey, beeswax, coffee, tobacco, rope, mats, and baskets.

---

ive. It's noted for cool climate, sweet oranges, numerous waterfalls, and luxuriant pine and moss forests rich in wildlife. The surrounding area has been designated a national park. Balbalasang's blacksmiths were renowned for their skill at both manufacturing and using the famous Kalinga head-ax.

Take a jeepney from Lubuagan to Cagaluan Junction, where a jeepney from Tabuk passes about 1200 going to Salegseg and sometimes to Balbalasang. From Salegseg, jeepney Tuesday and Friday morning to

Bangued. Inquire about overnight accommodations in Salegseg or Balbalasang before undertaking the journey.

TABUK

The provincial capital and commercial center, Tabuk is located along the Chico River amid a rice-growing area. The town has expanded rapidly in recent decades, so that the district's indigenous Kalinga population has been much diluted by migrants from Ilocos and the Cagayan Valley. Stay at **Traveler's Inn, Tabuk Lodge,** or **Kalinga Pension.**

From Tabuk
To Baguio (536 km, 13 hours), via San Jose (Nueva Ecija), take Pantranco North buses at 0400 and 0600; Greenland Bus Lines at 0430, 0530. To Bontoc (342 km, nine hours), via Banaue (292 km, six and a half hours), catch an Immanuel/Lizardo bus at 0300. To Lubuagan (two hours), take the fairly regular jeepneys or a bus at 1500. To Manila (518 km, 12 hours), catch Pantranco North buses; to Salegseg (six hours) take jeepney at 1000; to Tinglayan (three hours) there's a jeepney at 1100; to Tuguegarao (65 km, two hours) regular buses and jeepneys travel.

APAYAO

Access to much of this virtually unexplored, sparsely populated region of forested moun- tains remains extremely difficult due to the lack of roads. The Isneg use trails and rivers. Whitewater rafting is said to be good on the Apayao River, which is called the Abulug below Kabugao and flows into the Babuyan Channel. At Kabugao, accessible from Tabuk or Tuguegarao, motorized *bancas* can be hired for trips on the river, whose banks are covered by old hardwood forest with abundant wildlife.

The Agamatan National Park and Wildlife Sanctuary has been established in the remote area of mountains and plateaus in the vicinity of Calanasan, along the boundary with Ilocos Norte. It's undeveloped territory, with pine stands and mossy forest.

The Laoag-Kabugao road traverses the area but has no regular transport. Hot springs are found near Conner. Luna, in the northeast corner of the province, is accessible from Abulug (Cagayan); 18 km south of Luna at Pudtol are the ruins of an old church-fortress destroyed by an earthquake.

M.G.L. DOMENY DE RIENZI

CARL PARKES

LUZON~NORTHWEST COAST

Ilocos, also called Ilocandia, is a long, narrow, mountain-backed coastal plain in northwestern Luzon comprising La Union, Ilocos Sur, Abra, and Ilocos Norte. The coast is lined with beaches, while sand dunes are in the north. The typical Ilocos landscape features innumerable tobacco-curing barns-square structures of red brick, corrugated iron, cement, or mud; fields full of squat, round rice haystacks; bamboo stands; and scrub-covered hills.

The region's main attraction is its colonial heritage. Like Iloilo and Laguna, it has the finest colonial architecture remaining in the Philippines. In addition to Vigan, the country's best-preserved Spanish town, Ilocos has several magnificent churches scattered along the plain. Because of the frequency of earthquakes in the region, Ilocano churches are characterized by massive walls and buttresses, with a separate bell tower and exterior staircases, which facilitate roof maintenance. The Augustinian insignia, a transfixed heart and tasseled hat, is carved on inside and outside walls of many churches.

Many visitors also come to enjoy the beaches just south of San Fernando, near the town of Bauang. The sand isn't great but there are few tourists and the atmosphere is pure Filipino-unlike spots such as Boracay and Puerto Galera.

History

Ilocanos are believed to be of Malay descent, with early migrants pushing weaker, less-developed tribes like the Tingguians and Isnegs back into the hills. Long before the Spanish arrival, the Ilocanos, who were literate, traded with the Japanese and Chinese from Amoy, who called the region Liu-kiu. The area was well settled when Juan de Salcedo explored it in 1572. He found the Ilocanos leading a relatively peaceful, comfortable existence on the coast and riverbanks. Laoag and Vigan were already population centers. Like other Filipino peoples, the pre-Hispanic society consisted of kinship groups practicing farming, fishing, hunting, and food gathering.

The Spanish based themselves in Vigan. Augustinian missionaries began building churches and organizing communities, and tobacco, corn, and maguey were introduced from Mexico.

The numerous watchtowers lining the coast testify to the persistent threat of pirate raids.

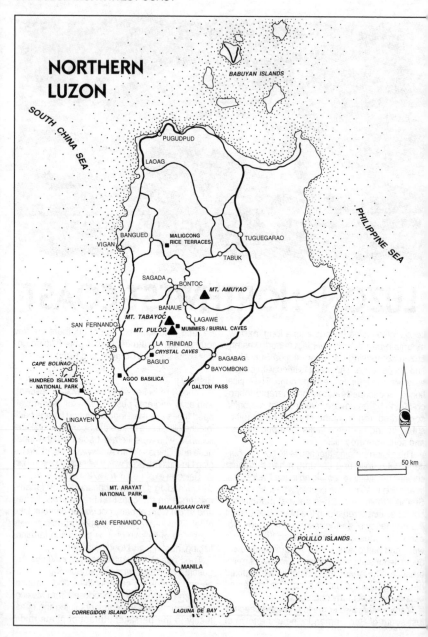

"Ylocos," as the Spaniards called the region, also developed a record of recurring rebellion against the colonial masters, and many Filipino patriots and revolutionaries have been Ilocanos.

Diego Silang led a major revolt in 1762-63. The Basi Revolt (1807) occurred when a new wine monopoly prohibited Ilocanos from making *basi* (homemade sugarcane wine), except with government authorization. Such an unpopular decree, compounded by Spanish abuses, led to open revolt. The rebels took Piddig, Laoag, Sarrat, and Batac before their defeat in a bloody battle on the riverbank at San Ildefonso, north of Vigan; their leaders either died in battle or were hanged.

The Spanish government also imposed a tobacco monopoly (1782-1881), from which it made such huge profits that after 200 years of financial dependence on the Mexican subsidy, the Philippines became self-supporting for the first time and the leading tobacco producer in the Far East. The monopoly resulted in the clearing, irrigation, and cultivation of large tracts and the establishment of a permanent industry for the Ilocanos, but also brought great hardship. Each family was assigned a quota, to be sold entirely to the government, and forbidden to plant other crops. Control was rigid, but the industry was beset with rampant abuses by the government inspectors who graded the leaves, forcing farmers to engage in bribery or smuggling to obtain better prices for their tobacco. King Alfonso eventually abolished the monopoly at the people's request.

Ilocanos

The region is culturally homogeneous. Ilocanos, the Philippines's third major ethnic group (after the Cebuanos and Tagalogs), form the majority of its inhabitants. Shaped by their rigorous environment, they are a hardy, enterprising, austere, thrifty people. Many have been forced to migrate in search of better opportunities, and Ilocanos can be found living throughout the Philippines, in Hawaii, on the U.S. mainland, and elsewhere. The funds they send home to Ilocos are an important source of income to the region.

Ilocano, which has a substantial body of literature, has become the language of commerce throughout northern Luzon, and Ilocanos have had much cultural influence in all the northern provinces. Ilocanos are primarily rice and tobacco farmers, working small holdings by means of extensive irrigation. Ilocos is the country's major Virginia-leaf tobacco producer, supplying cigarette factories locally and in Manila.

It's also a food-deficit area, with rice brought in from the Central Plain and Cagayan Valley. Tobacco is not only profitable, but nicely fills the gap between rice harvesting and planting. Coastal dwellers fish, mostly close to shore, and make salt by solar evaporation. The textile industry is important, on both a factory and cottage basis. *Abel Iloko,* woven cotton cloth or native yarns, was used for sails on the Manila galleons and, it's said, the ships of the Spanish Armada. Weavers traditionally emphasized utility and durability rather than decoration, but in recent years the designs and products have become more varied and colorful.

Transportation

Ilocos can be reached by road, rail, and air. Easy accessibility by land and the lack of good ports make sea travel a negligible factor here. The four provincial capitals-San Fernando, Vigan, Bangued, and Laoag-are the route centers, linked to Manila by numerous bus lines. Smaller companies such as Maria De Leon Transit, Times Transit, and Farinas Transit often have better vehicles than major lines like Philippine Rabbit.

Service on the main coastal highway is frequent. Roads cut down to the Ilocos coast from Baguio, Benguet, Mountain Province, and Kalinga-Apayao. Laoag Airport is served by PAL from Manila and is also the gateway to Basco (Batanes). Laoag is now an international point of entry, though flights only originate from Hong Kong and Taiwan-something for gamblers.

LA UNION PROVINCE

This small province, the gateway to the Ilocos coastal plain, sits astride the main route from Manila to Vigan and Laoag. Its popular beaches are located around Bauang, which is fairly close to Baguio, and makes a nice stopover for a day en route. The beaches are fairly nice but cannot be compared to the white sandy beaches in the southern Philippines. The main highway through the province is extremely busy, and there is little refuge from the noise of traffic, even along the beach.

History

A thriving trade with the Japanese existed before the Spanish arrival; Agoo was known as "Puerto de Japon." Juan de Salcedo subdued the region in 1572, and the Augustinians began their task of conversion. Spanish troops had to put down a serious native uprising in 1661. For more than 200 years, Agoo was the site of the Comandancia Politico General de Igorotes, from which the Spaniards tried to govern the fiercely resistant Igorots of the Benguet mountains.

In 1899, La Union came under revolutionary control, but the following year, U.S. troops occupied the province after a battle at the Aringay River. During WW II, fighting took place in 1941 and 1945, and Damortis, Agoo, Bauang, San Fernando, and Bacnotan saw action. San Fernando was finally liberated after U.S. and Filipino forces had taken a key Japanese bastion at nearby Bacsil Ridge.

Transportation

San Fernando, five hours from Manila, is the focal point. It's 55 km and 45 km from the boundaries of Pangasinan and Ilocos Sur respectively, taking four hours to reach Vigan and two hours to Baguio. Transportation north or south from here is no problem as buses, minibuses, and jeepneys ply this route all day long.

Numerous bus lines linking Manila with Ilocos pass through here. Try to sit on the left for this two-hour scenic trip. From the Hundred Islands, it takes about three hours by minibus, changing in Dagupan. Minibuses and jeepneys also operate along the main north-south highway and serve inland communities.

AGOO

The Spanish built a bamboo-and-nipa church here in 1598. When a later structure was destroyed by earthquake in 1892, the image of

Kids rule on Bauang beach.

Our Lady of Charity survived intact. Today, it's enshrined in the massive Agoo Basilica, which also contains some stone blocks excavated from the old church. The site of the latter's belfry is now marked by the towerlike Santo Niño Pescador de Agoo Wayside Shrine on the main highway; it contains an image of the Holy Infant and the old church's bell.

Many La Union devotees make a pilgrimage to the basilica during Holy Week; the Good Friday procession is the main event. Next to the municipal hall is a replica of the town's former *presidencia,* which houses the Museo Iloko. It displays religious art and artifacts, antique furniture, and porcelain. Imelda Park, in the town center, contains a treehouse in an old acacia tree.

Vicinity of Agoo

From near the church in Agoo, follow Cases Boulevard past the market and 3.5 km to the sea. It turns south along the coast at Agoo Fisherman's Park and passes the luxurious Agoo Playa Hotel at San Nicolas West. This class AAA hotel offers rooms from US$50 per night, with a two-night price of US$80; facilities include swimming pool (nonguests pay for the use of the pool), tennis, bicycles, horse riding, windsurfing, *banca,* sailboats, and a shuttle bus to town.

From the Fisherman's Park, the paved road goes through fishing villages for four km, then becomes a sandy lane that ends 3.5 km farther at an elementary school. The scenic 49-km Marcos Highway links Agoo and Baguio. The highway passes through Tubao, overlooked by the large *Christ on the Mount* hilltop statue, and Pugo, two km east of which are hot springs.

Agoo to Bauang

A signpost 3.5 km north of Agoo at Cubal marks a turnoff that leads to picturesque Santa Rita Beach, backed by trees and picnic shelters. The next town of Aringay has a church with mythical Chinese beasts carved into the beams of its choir loft, and a collection of ecclesiastical silver. Opposite the church, the **Don Lorenzo Diaz Memorial Museum** displays antiques and artifacts.

Enjoy a panoramic view over the town and surrounding countryside from Santo Cristo Park in Eugenio. Caba is a beach area north of Aringay. Stay at **El Caseron Beach Resort,** in Santiago Norte or in San Carlos at **Sun & Sand Beach Resort.** Cottages at these resorts are P600 in the off season and P700 during the high season.

BAUANG

This town at the mouth of the Bauang River, eight km south of San Fernando at the junction where the road from Baguio meets the coastal highway, is La Union's main beach resort. The proper address is Paringao at Bauang in La Union Province.

Bauang (founded 1590) has an old watchtower and is noted for fine sunsets. The beaches between Bauang (to the south) and San Fernando (to the north) are hardly spectacular-the sand is brown and the diving is secondary-but many people love this area for its authentic Filipino atmosphere and near complete lack of Western tourists. The convenient location near Manila and Baguio helps keep this area alive, plus many of the expats who operate resorts here enjoy their distance from more commercialized resorts such as Boracay and Puerto Galera.

Attractions

The long beach here may not be as impressive as elsewhere in the Philippines, but the local flavor perhaps more than compensates. People here are friendly, and the odd Westerner walking down the beach is something almost special. You'll pass fishermen working on their boats, gaggles of kids splashing in the water, and plenty of families who are more than happy to pose for photographs.

After dark, there are several small go-go clubs with dancing girls and happy hours, such as **Tramps** in the Koala Hotel, **Stiletto's** in the Southern Palms Hotel, and **Footlights** across the highway. Strange as it sounds, these might be the three best dance bars in the country.

Poro Point

Poro Point Peninsula contains a lighthouse, presidential rest center, the former Voice of America transmitting station, and the port. The wharf is used for off-loading oil and other imports and for shipping out copper concentrates and gold ore from the Benguet mines.

The dozens of decidedly low-life bars and nightclubs attract a steady stream of Western visitors based down at Bauang. The scene is grungy but quite fun for visitors seeking such thrills. One nightclub has a live show with total nudity, but it's a drag.

White Beach at Poro, five km from the main highway, offers snorkeling possibilities. The remains of a 300-year-old Spanish watchtower adjoin the Carrille resort in Carlatan, 2.5 km north of downtown, then 500 meters to the coast. Coral reefs lie off Carlatan and Lingsat.

Accommodations

Over 20 beach resorts are located between Bauang and San Fernando. Most raise their prices somewhat on weekends, but generally you can find a well-maintained bungalow for P600-1,200.

Bali Hai Beach Resort: Popular resort with small but well-sited pool and open-air restaurant with all the standard fixin's. Be sure to ask about the saga of "Dead Fred." Bauang, tel. (072) 412-504, e-mail balihai@net.com.ph, P750-1,200.

Coconut Grove: Great-looking spot with swimming pool and landscaped grounds plus lawn-bowling venue for all the Brits and Aussies. Bauang, tel. (072) 414-276, P900-1,400.

Cabana Beach Resort: Rooms are just okay but the pool is about the best in this neighborhood. Bauang, tel. (072) 412-824, P900-1,200.

China Sea Beach Resort: Solid cottages plus one of the few dive shops in La Union. Bauang, tel. (072) 414-821, e-mail chinasea@net.com.ph, P900-1,400.

Hideaway: Good budget spot about 20 minutes walk north of the central beach; friendly managers and good vibes. 1312 Baccuit Norte, Bauang, tel. (0912) 311-2421, P350-550.

Koala Motel: Another cheap place in a good location near all the nightclubs and the center of the beach. Bauang, tel. (072) 242-0863, P250-450.

Transportation

Bauang is 260 km north of Manila and 60 km west of Baguio. Philippine Rabbit and several other bus lines take six or seven hours from Manila. You can also catch buses from the Dau interchange in Angeles. Travelers coming from Hundred Islands must change buses in Dagupan.

Philippine Rabbit connects Bauang with Baguio several times daily, a scenic and winding journey down from the mountains.

Naguilian

Naguilian is situated on the scenic Bauang-Baguio Road, which follows the route of an old foot trail from the coast to Benguet. The town has a cellophane factory. The surrounding slopes are planted with bananas, cotton, and bamboo. Lioac is famous for its fine *basi*, the Ilocanos' favorite native wine made from fermented sugarcane juice. It's boiled with pounded *duhat* bark and guava leaves, then put in a jar with dry yeast, and buried. Traditionally, a banana tree is planted over the jar, and when the tree bears fruit, the *basi* is ready. Bad batches are used as vinegar.

SAN FERNANDO

The provincial capital and commercial center (town fiesta: 8-11 February), with about 85,000 inhabitants, is 261 km north of Manila, 218 km south of Laoag, and 60 km west of Baguio. Founded in 1734 and named after King Ferdinand of Spain, it's built on seven hills and situated on a bay formed by Poro Point Peninsula.

The busy northbound highway, called Quezon Avenue here, runs through the town center. Absolutely nobody stays in this town since far superior accommodations are found down at Bauang.

Attractions

The bustling downtown market has some handicraft stalls. The Provincial Capitol complex includes a completely useless tourist office, plus a sad museum that focuses on local culture and archaeological findings. The Chinese Friendship pagoda, which offers a good view of the town, is reached by the Gapuz Zigzag Road or 153 steps leading up from Quezon Avenue. The steps are lined with the statues of Philippine national heroes and presidents and is known as Freedom Park or Heroes Hill.

The highest point in town is Mirador Hill, where the water reservoir is located. San Fernando has a significant Chinese population. The ornate Ma-cho ("Heavenly Mother") Temple is both Taoist and Catholic.

For the Feast of the Virgin (12-16 September), devotees bring the image of the Virgin of Caysasay, patroness of Chinese Filipinos, to the Ma-cho Temple from its permanent shrine in Taal City, Batangas.

Accommodations

San Fernando has a half dozen hotels, all shown on the map, though few Westerners stay in this town but rather hang out at the Bauang beach resorts.

Restaurants

San Fernando's Chinese restaurants include the **Mandarin Restaurant** (at Mandarin House Hotel), the **Midtown Food Palace,** the **Gold City Fastfood,** and the **Bamboo Grill,** all on Quezon Avenue. Also try the **United Food Palace** on P. Burgos Street and the **Hongkong Seafood House** on Governor Luna Street. The downtown area has numerous Filipino and fast-food restaurants, and San Fernando is also noted for seafood. "Jumping shrimp salad" is a local delicacy: a mixture of spiced vinegar and *kalamansi* (lime) is poured onto a bowl of tiny shrimps that "jump" and turn pink as they're marinated alive, a style of preparation called *kilawin.* For fast food, try the **Queen Bee Food Center** on Quezon Avenue and **Big John's Food Emporium** on San Fernando Beach Road. For an inexpensive lunch or dinner try the **Cafe Esperanza,** overlooking the town plaza.

Lunch and dinner specials are *adobo,* pork chops, and barbecued chicken.

NORTH OF SAN FERNANDO

San Juan, whose colonial buildings include a church, the old tribunal, some brick houses, and a ruined watchtower, is known for pottery. *Banga* (containers for *bangus* fry) and other items are produced in Taboc, three km north of the town center. Bacnotan is the site of limestone quarries, the Don Mariano Marcos Memorial State College of Agriculture (with a fine panorama), an old cemetery, and Bata Cave. Old Spanish watchtowers, which served as lookouts against Moro raiders, line this stretch of coast at Bacnotan, Paraoir, Darigayos Point, and Luna. Balaoan (founded 1587), a salt-making town, has a church with a columned facade and an interesting old cemetery.

San Francisco has waterfalls, while religious devotees trek to the shrine of Simmimbaan a Bato in Apatot. The Darigayos-Paraoir Beach is on the shoreline of Balaoan and Luna municipalities. In Luna, Street Catherine's church enshrines the supposedly miraculous image of Our Lady of Namacpacan, patroness of travelers. Bangar, on the plain of the Amburayan River, which irrigates the area's ricelands, is an important weaving center, and many homes contain looms, especially in General Prim. Fine, lightweight, multicolored, seamless blankets are woven by two persons on an extra-wide upright wooden loom. You can watch weaving at the Bangar Weavers' Cooperative (closed Sunday), near the church. Bolos are also handcrafted in Bangar.

ILOCOS SUR PROVINCE

Ilocos Sur's main attraction is the historic Spanish city of Vigan, whose elegant houses, plazas, narrow cobblestone streets, and horse-drawn *calesas* impart a "colonial" atmosphere.

The province also contains some remarkable old churches. But if you've been to Spain, don't expect anything that compares with Avila or Toledo. Spaniards in the Philippines never achieved the degree of architectural excellence

that characterizes their homeland. They did leave a legacy of towns in Ilocos Sur named after their distant Spanish homes, like Sevilla, Burgos, Cervantes, and Santiago.

There are some wonderful examples of Spanish colonial architecture in Ilocos Sur that make a trip here well worthwhile; it's also interesting to note that a tourism brochure advertises the province as the "Cradle of Ilocano

Piety." This may explain why nearly every large settlement has a plaster reproduction of the Ten Commandments written in Ilocano in front of the town square.

History

Trade with Chinese merchants was well established before the Spanish arrival, and over the centuries numerous Chinese settled in Vigan, intermarried, and became wealthy. Many of the big Spanish colonial houses in Vigan were built by Chinese mestizos. The conquistador Juan de Salcedo, who explored the area in 1572, was made lieutenant governor of the Ilocos region and the *encomiendero* of Vigan. Vigan, which he called Ciudad Fernandina, was already a thriving settlement and became the political, commercial, and ecclesiastical capital of northern Luzon. Vigan is the Philippines's third-oldest city, after Cebu and Manila; unlike Intramuros, it was never fortified.

Historically, missionaries were active in the region. Several revolts occurred against the colonial masters over the tributes and forced labor they demanded. The Tagudin tribe rebelled as early as 1581. In 1762, Diego Silang of La Union, after making agreements with the British forces of occupation in Manila, seized Vigan and declared it the capital of free Ilocos. He repulsed Spanish attacks and controlled an area from Cagayan to Pangasinan, before he was assassinated in Vigan; his wife Gabriela continued the revolt. She persuaded tribesmen from the mountains of Abra to join her, but was eventually captured and hung in Vigan.

In the Basi Revolt (1807), the rebels were defeated on the south bank of the Bantay River at San Ildefonso. The Spaniards fostered the cultivation of tobacco, sugar, coffee, and indigo. The indigo trade created great wealth in the 1850s; many of Vigan's fine old houses were built around this time.

Vigan was the birthplace of Father Jose Burgos, a mestizo whose execution along with two other priests in 1872 was a key step on the road to revolution. In 1896, Aguinaldo's supporters captured Vigan and established their headquarters in the Archbishop's Palace, which was seized and occupied by the Americans in 1899. Gregorio del Pilar, the "boy general," made a gallant last stand against superior U.S. forces

in the mountains at Tirad Pass to cover Aguinaldo's escape.

The Japanese landed on the beaches of Ilocos Sur in 1941. In 1945, the Bessang Pass was the scene of a long, fierce battle to breach the western defenses of the Japanese army, which had withdrawn into the Cordillera.

Transportation

Vigan, 92 km from La Union and 40 km from Ilocos Norte, takes 10 hours to reach from Manila. All routes north and south pass through Vigan. The province's major settlements are strung out along the coastal highway. Buses are frequent on this highway, making it easy to get off, explore an old church, and flag down another a few minutes later.

Two routes descend from the Cordillera to the coast road: Kalinga-Apayao across Abra, and from Mountain Province and Benguet through Cervantes. Transportation is much more irregular on these rough roads. Jeepneys serve inland settlements.

TAGUDIN TO CERVANTES

Tagudin, on the north bank of the Amburayan River, has a beach, lighthouse, and old sundials. Five km north, the road to Cervantes branches off the main coastal highway, passing through Suyo, in whose vicinity are Dawara Waterfalls, Ida Mountain Caves, Angalo Footprint Lake, and Lipit Stone Tower. A track leads north from Suyo to the isolated municipality of Sigay, which produces coffee and brooms, and contains Awasen Falls and Banao Lake.

The strategic Bessang Pass lies at an elevation of 1,600 meters along the highest promontory traversed by the road to Cervantes. It was the site of one of the bloodiest battles of the liberation, involving hand-to-hand fighting and thousands of casualties. Filipino infantry, supported by U.S. air and artillery units, finally took the pass on 14 June. It was a major step toward the Japanese surrender. Bessang Pass is now a national shrine.

A wreath-laying ceremony and mass are held here on the **Day of Valor,** 6 May. Cervantes is on the Abra River, 59 km from the coastal highway. Guilong Caves are in the area. From Cervantes, connections are possible to two points on the Baguio-Bontoc highway: to Sabangan, and through Mankayan and the Lepanto copper-mining district to Abatan.

Accommodations

You can stay in Cervantes at the **Municipal Guest House** for P50. A bus leaves for Baguio at 0500 and there is a Bontoc-bound bus at 0600 starting at the east side of the Abra river.

NORTH TO VIGAN

Santa Lucia

An Augustinian mission was established here in 1586. Some old Spanish houses on narrow streets remain. The massive, heavily buttressed church (1808) has a huge dome; a facade featuring a Gothic-style circular stained-glass window, but Romanesque arches over the other windows; an unusual tassel-like frieze around the exterior walls; a fine four-story bell tower; and an ornate interior, with a painted ceiling and an elaborately carved *retablo*. Santa Lucia also has a beach.

Candon

Candon is an agricultural town surrounded by many tobacco-curing barns. Its original church was founded by Augustinians in 1591. The current building has a baroque facade. Candon was the seat of the Ilocos revolutionary government during the Philippine-American War. Darapidap Beach is in the municipality.

Tirad Pass

This historic pass, now a national shrine, is located 25 km southeast of Candon, amid spectacular scenery in the Ilocos Range. To reach it, go inland through the small towns of Salcedo and General G. del Pilar and follow rough trails from there. *Tirad* means "point" in Ilocano, and the pass is at the foot of a sharply pointed peak in the Three Sisters group (1,441 meters). Asin Hot Spring is in the area.

Here, on 2 December 1899, the flamboyant 22-year-old Filipino general, Gregorio del Pilar, was killed by a sniper while covering Aguinaldo's retreat. Del Pilar and 60 men were holding off a U.S. battalion of 300, but an Igorot renegade betrayed them by showing the Americans a path

on the other side of the pass, enabling them to attack from two sides. Only eight of the Filipinos escaped to relate the news to Aguinaldo, whose own escape was made possible by their delaying action.

Santiago to Santa Maria

A sheltered deep-water cove with a beautiful beach lies 1.5 km off the highway at Santiago. San Esteban is well situated on a palm-lined cove, with an old Spanish watchtower on the headland. A marker on Apatot Beach, six km off the main highway, indicates where a U.S. submarine landed supplies for resistance forces in 1944. This is a traditional area for stonecutting, now a dying craft. Stalls sell limestone mortars and pestles, though demand has dwindled as more people use rice mills.

Santa Maria served as an important missionary base for Ilocos and Abra during the second half of the 18th century. According to tradition, the Virgin of Santa Maria Church was washed up on the beach, undamaged, from the wreck of a Spanish galleon.

Resembling a medieval fortress, the church (1769), a revolutionary stronghold in 1896, has massive, heavily buttressed walls and offers a fine view of the surrounding countryside from its position 60 meters above the town. It's approached by climbing a wide stone stairway. Other stairways link it to the abandoned cemetery at the foot of the hill. Wind chimes hang from the lamps inside, and the altar features some fine old tiles. The celebrated tower stands separately and leans significantly.

Pinsal Falls, where cool water fills a natural basin in a scenic setting, is seven km east of the highway. Suso Beach forms a sandy cove and has a restaurant and a small oyster farm. *Susó* (snail) is a local delicacy. Lingsat-Biao Beach is also in the vicinity. You can stay at tranquil Camp Hope, just south of town.

Narvacan

Narvacan Church was founded 1587; the current building is a restoration of an early 17th-century structure. The church has an attractive blue-and-white interior and a small museum of old ecclesiastical items in the sacristy. Narvacan has a large cotton spinning and weaving mill, and salt-making is also important.

The road to Bangued (Abra) branches off the main highway north of Narvacan. Sulvec (or Solvec) is the site of a Spanish watchtower and Northern Luzon Heroes Hill National Park. Paraiso Ni Imelda is a small clifftop park from which Bantay Tower is visible. Stay at **Bagong Lipunan Lodge,** which has a restaurant, swimming pool, and tennis. Santa was the birthplace of the 18th-century revolutionary Gabriela Silang.

South of Santa are the ruins of old watchtowers on both sides of the coastal road, and close offshore, the statue of the Virgin of the Rocks is accessible at low tide. The town is one km off the highway and has a picturesque church standing close to the sea. Barasibis Falls are nearby. Bolo-making and weaving are local cottage industries.

Bantay

A few kilometers southeast of Vigan is the Abra River (or Vigan) Gap. From the highway bridge there's a spectacular view upstream to the Ilocos Mountains. Bantay is just across a river from Vigan (a one-km bike ride). The notable 18th-century baroque-type church has been restored, its facade a combination of neo-Gothic and pseudo-Romanesque styles. Evacuees took refuge here during the Basi Revolt (1807).

Miracles have been attributed to the Virgin of the church, and favor-seekers and grateful recipients gather to pay homage to her image during the Feast of Our Lady of Charity (first Sunday of September). The separate three-story bell tower served as a lookout for approaching enemies and today can be climbed for a fine view of an old nearby cemetery and the surrounding area. Local handicrafts include loom-weaving, jewelry-making, and leathercraft.

VIGAN CITY

The provincial capital, on the Mestizo River, four km from the coast, is a town of about 37,000 with some of the Philippines's best remaining Spanish colonial architecture and many antique shops. It's a pleasant place to spend a couple of days strolling the plazas and streets, where horse-drawn *calesas* still serve residents. Vigan is a perfect location for moviemakers, as the colonial architecture gives the city a Spanish ambience and theatrical setting.

Attractions

In recent years, Vigan has become inundated with motorized bikes with sidecars that disrupt the subtle charm of the place. It's pleasant to get up early before the crunch of traffic or, better yet, roam the old colonial streets at night.

The Old Quarter: Old colonial houses line Mena Crisologo and other streets of what was the Chinese mestizo quarter south of the cathedral. By the 19th century, these nouveau riche mestizos had become Vigan's elite and could afford to build these large homes, which have several distinctive features. The thick lower walls of stone and brick contain wide arched doorways to enable carriages to enter from the street into a stone-flagged space used as a stable and for storage. The living area on the upper story is generally of wood, with polished *narra* wood floors, high ceilings, and sliding *kapis* windows. Balconies, with ornate metal grillwork, overlook the street, and there's sometimes an *azotea* (tiled patio) in the rear. Roofs have overhanging eaves, some of which are decorated, but many of the original red tiles have now been replaced.

Plazas: Vigan has several plazas. Plaza Salcedo, separating the Capitol and cathedral, contains statues of José Rizal and President Quirino. Plaza Singson Encarnacion adjoins the Capitol. Plaza Burgos on the south side of the cathedral contains a monument to the martyred priest after whom it's named. Leona Florentino Plaza, at the corner of Plaza Burgos, contains a memorial to one of the country's first women playwrights and poets, born in the nearby Casa Florentino in 1849.

Cathedral: The cathedral, whose bell tower stands separately in Plaza Burgos, has a main altar with beaten-silver panels. Juan de Salcedo ordered the first church built in 1574; another was built in 1641, and the current baroque-style building was completed in 1800. The Fu dogs carved above the outermost doors of the cream-and-white facade reflect Vigan's strong Chinese heritage. The Archbishop's Palace (1783) is adjacent to the cathedral.

Crisologo Museum: A small but interesting museum with Spanish-era artifacts and memorials to Governor Crisologo, assassinated in

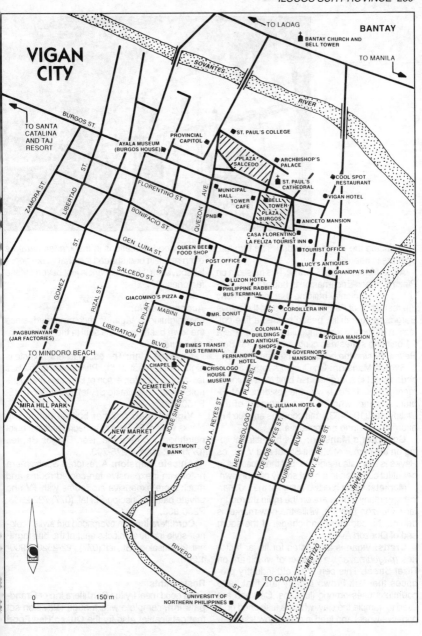

VIGAN CITY

BANTAY

TO LAOAG

BANTAY CHURCH AND
BELL TOWER

TO MANILA

SOVANTES

RIVER

BURGOS ST.

TO SANTA
CATALINA
AND TAJ
RESORT

ST. PAUL'S COLLEGE

AYALA MUSEUM
(BURGOS HOUSE)

PROVINCIAL
CAPITOL

PLAZA
SALCEDO

ARCHBISHOP'S
PALACE

ST. PAUL'S
CATHEDRAL

COOL SPOT
RESTAURANT

ZAMORA ST.

LIBERTAD ST.

FLORENTINO ST.

BONIFACIO ST.

QUEZON AVE.

MUNICIPAL
HALL

TOWER CAFE

PNB

BELL
TOWER

PLAZA
BURGOS

VIGAN HOTEL

ANICETO MANSION

GEN. LUNA ST.

RIZAL ST.

SALCEDO ST.

QUEEN BEE
FOOD SHOP

POST OFFICE

CASA FLORENTINO
LA FELIZA TOURIST INN

TOURIST OFFICE

LUCY'S ANTIQUES

GRANDPA'S INN

GOMEZ ST.

LUZON HOTEL

PHILIPPINE RABBIT
BUS TERMINAL

GIACOMINO'S PIZZA

DEL PILAR ST.

MABINI

PLDT

MR. DONUT

ST.

CORDILLERA INN

LIBERATION

BLVD.

TIMES TRANSIT
BUS TERMINAL

COLONIAL
BUILDINGS
AND ANTIQUE
SHOPS

SYQUIA MANSION

GOVERNOR'S
MANSION

PAGBURNAYAN
(JAR FACTORIES)

TO MINDORO BEACH

CHAPEL

CEMETERY

JOSE SINESON ST.

FERNANDINE
HOTEL

CRISOLOGO
HOUSE
MUSEUM

PLARIDEL

MIRA HILL PARK

NEW MARKET

WESTMONT
BANK

GOV. A. REYES ST.

MENA CRISOLOGO ST.

V. DE LOS REYES ST.

EL JULIANA HOTEL

QUIRINO BLVD.

GOV. E. REYES ST.

RIVER

RIVERO

MESTIZO RIVER

TO CAOAYAN

ST.

0   150 m

UNIVERSITY OF
NORTHERN PHILIPPINES

Vigan Cathedral

1970 inside the Vigan Cathedral. The furniture upstairs is beautiful.

Ayala Museum and Library: This museum on Plaza Singson Encarnacion is housed in a lovely two-story colonial building that was formerly the residence of Father Jose Burgos. It displays Burgos memorabilia, period rooms, a fine collection of Ilocano and Tingguian artifacts, and a 14-painting series depicting events of the Basi Revolt. Behind the house is a pleasant garden.

Syquia Mansion: On Quirino Avenue at Salcedo Street is a large house built for a Chinese merchant in 1830. It was the residence of Elpidio Quirino, who became president of the Philippines (1948-53), and contains antique furniture and Quirino memorabilia.

Governor's Mansion: This beautiful building on the corner of Mabini Street and V. de los Reyes is a private residence, but the facade is in beautiful condition in a quiet shady part of town.

Markets: Vigan has two markets; the old market and many stores are on the main thoroughfare, Quezon Avenue, while the new market is behind the cemetery and chapel at the south end of Quezon Avenue.

Crafts: Vigan is also noted for its jar factories *(pagburnayan),* a number of which are on Rizal Street. This centuries-old industry produces the dark brown *burnay* jars that have countless uses among Ilocanos. Carabao are used to trample the clay, which is fashioned on a primitive wheel and fired in a long, low kiln heat-

ed by wood. Variations in the kiln temperature often result in odd-shaped jars that make popular souvenirs. Mira Hill Park is just beyond these factories

Accommodations

Overnighting in Vigan is recommended, since the town best reveals its soul in the early morning hours.

Grandpa's Inn: The backpackers' favorite is eight blocks east of the Philippine Rabbit bus terminal at the intersection of Bonifacio and Quirino Streets. 1 Bonifacio St., tel. (077) 722-2118, P150-500.

Vigan Hotel: Another budget option two blocks west of St. Paul's Cathedral and in a quiet neighborhood near the river. Burgos St., tel. (077) 722-3001, P275-700.

Aniceto Mansion: A restored Spanish-era hotel with inexpensive fan-cooled rooms and much more expensive a/c rooms with TV and private bath. 1 Crisolog St., tel. (077) 722-2383, P200-800.

Cordillera Inn: An overpriced but stylish colonial-style inn three blocks east of the bus terminal. 29 Crisologo St., tel. (077) 722-2526, P900-1,200.

Restaurants

For a good meal try the **Cordillera Inn** or **Grandpa's Inn,** complete with a huge television set that gets cable! Also try the **Queen Bee Food**

Shop on Quezon Avenue or **Mr. Donut** on Mabini Street. Near the Vigan Hotel, the popular, open-air **Cool Spot Restaurant** near the Vigan Hotel is a nice place to spend an evening.

Fiestas

The Feast of St. Paul, on 25 January, is a colorful fiesta with a parade, native drama performance, and carnival. On Holy Monday and Tuesday is a reenactment in the streets of the journey to Calvary. On Good Friday evening there's a Santo Entierro procession. On 3 May is the Feast of Holy Cross, featuring an evening procession and folkloric events. La Purisima, on 3 December, is a fiesta celebrating the Feast of Our Lady of the Immaculate Conception, with an evening religious parade and fireworks.

Transportation

To Aparri (300 km, 10 hours), take the early morning bus. To Baguio (196 km, five hours), the Philippine Rabbit and Times Transit have regular departures. To Bangued (59 km, 1.5 hours), take the PNP minibus. To Candon (60 km, 90 minutes), buses go to Manila or Baguio, plus frequent minibuses.

To Dagupan (211 km, five hours), the Times Transit has regular service. To Laoag (80 km, two hours), take Philippine Rabbit, Times Transit, plus frequent minibuses.

To Manila (407 km, eight hours), **Inocento Aniceto** (also called St. Joseph Bus Co.), Philippine Rabbit, and Times Transit have regular departures. Farinas Transit, Maria de Leon, and other buses traveling Laoag-Manila stop at Bantay. (Bike from Vigan.) To San Fernando, La Union (139 km, three hours), buses to Manila or Baguio pass by.

MAGSINGAL

Magsingal is 13 km north of Vigan.

Attractions

Church: The original church was built in 1664; the second church, now in ruins, in 1730; the nearby 30-meter bell tower in 1732; and the present church in 1827. The imagery of the three-story cream-and-white facade is echoed by the ornate baroque reredos inside, but two mermaids strike an incongruous note amid the latter's religious imagery. This reredos (which contains no nails), the pulpit, and the pillars supporting the roof are carved out of *molave,* a hardwood once common in the area. Note the stone flight of steps on the church's outside. The church and its *convento,* now a school, are linked by an upper corridor over two arches with *kapis* windows.

Museum of Ilocano Heritage: Well worth a visit. Part of its display is housed within the ruins of the former church and *convento,* which are designated the Ilocaniana Cultural Park. Here, too, are a banyan tree with huge roots and an old statue of Christ, which devotees believe is teething. Other items are exhibited across the street in the house of the curator. They include Neolithic tools, excavated porcelain and earthenware, antique santos, weapons and implements, baskets and headgear, and old parish records.

SAN JUAN

The next town, San Juan (formerly Lapog), is noted for handicrafts, including knives, scissors, bolos, baskets, and *buri* hats and mats. Raois and Sulot-Sulot beaches are here, and inland, Pikkang Falls and Pussuac Spring. At Cabugao, side roads lead from the main highway to Salomague Port and Dardarat Lighthouse.

Three km north of Cabugao town center, another road goes to Pug-os Beach, situated on a large cove with warm, shallow water and offshore coral. Sinait, which was pillaged by the Chinese warlord Limahong on his way south in 1574, has a well-preserved hexagonal Spanish watchtower. Garlic is an important local crop.

Accommodations

There are reasonable rooms available at the **Sabangan Beach Resort** for P150.

ABRA PROVINCE

Mountainous and sparsely populated, Abra is the least explored and developed of the Ilocos provinces. Bangued, the provincial capital, is the only urban center. Abra has no noted tourist spots and entails a side trip off the main Ilocos coastal route. The sole major highway crossing the province, linking Vigan and Kalinga-Apayao via Bangued, is a potentially useful route for travelers, but is currently marred by irregular transportation and Kalinga's uncertain security. Bangued is well worth a visit if time allows, although during the dry months the 160-km Abra River is low and the area becomes windy and very dusty.

History

Bangued was founded in 1598 when a Spanish garrison was established to protect Ilocano converts from Tingguian headhunting raids. Getting there entailed an eight-hour raft journey upstream from the coast. In the early 17th century, a fervent parish priest from Bantay (near Vigan), Father Juan Pareja, made numerous missionary expeditions deep into the mountains and virtually single-handedly converted many natives. The moss-covered ruins of old churches still exist in some remote settlements.

The region was then virtually ignored until the 19th century, when evangelical attention was again bestowed on it. The conservative Tingguians rejected Spanish rule and religion and retreated into the mountains. In 1763, Gabriela Silang, continuing the revolt begun by her slain husband, made her last stand in Abra, resulting in her capture and execution. Guerrilla activity was widespread here during WW II, and Bangued suffered extensive damage.

A Land Dispute

Bangued became a boomtown when a huge pulp mill was constructed in the '70s to process Abra's pines. Strong opposition came from the Tingguians, who saw this as a threat to their livelihood and traditions, since it involved the appropriation of a nearly 2,000-square-km logging concession, which also overlapped into neighboring provinces. The corporation claimed that as there were no legal titles, it was public land. For the Tingguians, however, land ownership is sacred, depending not on title but on the amount of work put into the land. The communally owned land is also the home of their ancestors' spirits. Despite this, the corporation went ahead with the mill complex and cut logging roads into the hills. NPA raids forced the plant to close in 1980, and today it is in ruins, its massive debt borne by the state.

COASTAL HIGHWAY TO BANGUED

From the main coastal highway, the road to Bangued traverses low, barren hills, deforested to fuel the countless tobacco-curing sheds of Ilocos. It passes through the 62.5-meter Tangadan Tunnel before entering the fertile Abra River floodplain, with its rice, corn, and tobacco fields. A side road leads north for a short distance from Barbarit to San Quintin on the riverbank, from where you can see a curious depression in the land called the "Footprint of Angalo," supposedly made by a giant of local folklore.

Pidigan is noted for its shady *kasoy* (cashew) trees, old irrigation wells, and a former church that is now a grocery *bodega* (warehouse). In 1980-81, several archaeological sites were excavated in the Bangued-San Quintin area. Dozens of graves in Palang and elsewhere yielded Chinese ceramics dating to the Ching dynasty.

BANGUED

The provincial capital and market center, situated on the Abra River floodplain, Bangued is an old town whose growth has been limited by the slow productivity of its hinterland.

Attractions

Victory Park on Casamata Hill, close to the center, affords a fine view of the surrounding fields and mountains. The church dates from 1722.

THE TINGGUIANS

The Tingguians (or Itneg) are divided into several regional subgroups. It's believed that they're descended from Indonesian migrants who landed over 2,000 years ago and subsequently moved inland to Abra's foothills and mountain valleys under pressure from later settlers on the Ilocos coast. They kept their traditional customs intact until this century, but are now much assimilated into the prevailing Ilocano culture. During the Spanish era, Ilocanos who rejected Christianity fled into the hills, mingling the two cultures. The Tingguians also have close cultural affinities with the neighboring Kalinga and Isneg.

Tingguian Traditions

Settlements contained the homes of interrelated families and were protected by a double bamboo stockade. Headhunting was closely tied to the ancient religion. Tingguian women wore strings of beads wrapped tightly around their forearms, and among the affluent, around the upper arms too. They took them off only when the beads needed rethreading or when in mourning. A network of fine lines was tattooed beneath where the beads were worn, so that the arms wouldn't appear "naked" when the beads were removed.

Childbirth ceremonies were full of magic and superstition. The woman gave birth in a kneeling position, holding a rope suspended from the ceiling. The umbilical cord was cut with a bamboo knife, and the afterbirth placed for disposal in a small jar containing bamboo leaves, so that the infant would grow like bamboo. For 29 days after birth, the husband maintained a constant fire beside the mother to keep her warm and protect her from evil spirits, a practice related to the custom of "mother roasting" once widespread in Malaysia and India. During this time, the mother was subject to very strict taboos and given many baths a day.

The Tingguians practiced child betrothal, rather than the premarital coupling of the Igorot and Ifugao. But married men were allowed as many concubines as they could obtain. Each concubine lived in her own hut with her children, supported by the man, who lived with his wife. A man's death was followed by a vigil during which his widow spent three nights under a fishnet to shield her from an evil spirit, while old women wailers fanned the corpse.

Burial was under the house in a grave already occupied by one or more of his ancestors; it was believed that the deceased lingered nearby to ascertain that his family had performed the necessary rituals to ensure his place in the spirit world.

Tingguians Today

Tingguians number about 47,000, though many Abra inhabitants now recognized as Ilocanos are actually Christianized Tingguians. Most are farmers, growing rice in both *kaingin* fields and irrigated rice terraces. They weave fine cotton blankets and make bags and baskets from reeds and grasses. Tingguian methods of metalworking and cloth-weaving show clear association with techniques employed in India, Burma, Malaysia, and Indonesia. Tingguians now wear contemporary clothing and live like the neighboring Ilocanos, but the core of their social and cultural world retains its indigenous flavor.

Traditional values manifest themselves in the way they conduct social functions and fulfill social obligations. Acceptance of the supernatural still permeates their outlook, and some reconcile Catholicism with belief in the ancient spirits. Others have been converted to Jehovah's Witnesses, or other Christian sects, depending on which 20th-century missionary group is passing through.

The locals still hold an annual Grand Tingguian Festival, which showcases their sports, dances, songs, and traditions.

Consoliman Cool Spring is just outside town, while at Tayum, five km east of Bangued, is the **Abra Museum** (open daily 0800-1700).

Accommodations

Most accommodations are on or near Taft Street between the Time Transit bus terminal and the cathedral. Stay at **LAF View Inn** (Burgos St., P150, 1.5 km from town center); **Abra**

Diocesan Pastoral Center (part of the cathedral complex) rents rooms for P100, but they prefer to house people who are involved with the church; **Marysol Hotel** is located next to the Allied Bank and serves breakfast. Rooms are P150-200. On the outskirts of town on the road to the river, there's the **Tingguian Lodge** with rooms P150-200.

Restaurants

Eat at **Syd's Cafe** near the municipal hall where steak, chicken, and *pancit canton* are served. Also try **Prince's Restaurant and Bakery** on Taft road. In the evening around the town square, there are plenty of street stalls serving *ihaw ihaw,* fresh donuts, and fruit.

Transportation

The Philippine Rabbit terminal is about one km east of the town center. PNP minibuses for Vigan and Laoag load near the Marysol Hotel.

Bangued is Abra's route center. To Manila (408 km, eight hours), there's at least hourly service by Philippine Rabbit and Times Transit buses; to Baguio (197 km, five hours), Times Transit thrice daily; to Ilocos coastal highway, Km 378 near Narvacan (30 km, one hour), frequent buses and jeepneys; to Vigan (59 km, 90 minutes) and Laoag (139 km, three and a half hours), regular **PNP minibuses,** or quick connection at Km 378 junction. Jeepneys fan out from Bangued to rural municipalities.

FROM BANGUED

To travel north from Bangued, take a tricycle three km to the Abra River ferry crossing; jeepneys start from Muding on the other side. Lagayan (19 km) is the site of the Lusuac Water Spring, which is a natural pool surrounded by boulders and jungle foliage. Mapaso Hot Springs are a one-hour hike beyond Danglas. The road continues north through virgin forest to Nueva Era (Ilocos Norte). When crossing the river at Bangued, you should pay no more than P10 both ways.

To reach the Lusuac Water Spring, take a jeepney to La Paz. The road splits to Danglas or continues on to Lagayan. The Lusuac Water Spring is about a 45-minute walk from here on the road to the friendly village of Pulot. Locals will be glad to show you the way. It's a great place for a cooling swim.

South of Bangued, you'll find caves in Bucay, an underground river in Botot and the ruins of the old Spanish Casa Real. Limbo and Kimkimay are in Villaviciosa, about 20 km from Bangued. About 60 km south is the Bani Hot Spring at Boliney, accessible during the dry season only. The southeastern part of the province contains isolated scenic settlements such as Bucloc, which has rice terraces, and Daguioman.

The Abra River area and surrounding hills are worth exploring. Consult locals if you're continuing through this remote province, and, if possible, introduce yourself to the *barangay* captain when you arrive in a small village. NPA activity in this area is sporadic, so alert the locals of your intentions and destination.

ILOCOS NORTE PROVINCE

Ilocos Norte occupies Luzon's far northwest. Laoag City is the provincial capital and focal point. Most travelers pass through to catch a plane to Batanes or as part of the circular route around northern Luzon. Points of interest include the famous Paoay Church, unusual sand dunes up to 800 meters wide, and spectacular coastal scenery between Cape Bojeador and the Cagayan boundary. Ilocos Norte is the home province of former president Ferdinand Marcos.

History

Laoag was an established settlement when Juan de Salcedo arrived in 1572. Early rebellions took place in Dingras in 1589 and Laoag in 1660. In the latter, Pedro Almazan, a wealthy farmer,

crowned himself king with the jeweled crown of the Virgin's statue from the church and made treaties with the mountain tribes in an effort to rebuff Spanish rule.

The area suffered the abuses of the tobacco monopoly (1782-1881), and the Basi Revolt (1807) began when the townspeople of Piddig rose in revolt when prohibited from making their beloved *basi.* They took Laoag, Sarrat, and Batac before their defeat outside Vigan. Filipino revolutionaries occupied the province in 1896, and local guerrillas were active here during WW II.

Transportation

Ilocos Norte can be reached through the coastal plain in the south, and from the Cagayan Valley via Luzon's northern coast. Laoag City is the hub. Buses and minibuses provide frequent service both north and south on the main coastal highway, while jeepneys serve off-highway communities. A road connects Nueva Era in the south with Danglas and Bangued (Abra).

ILOCOS SUR TO LAOAG CITY

Badoc
The renovated two-story colonial brick house where painter **Juan Luna** was born in 1857 is now a museum containing Luna memorabilia, antique furniture, and reproductions of his paintings. Juan's younger brother, Antonio, was a revolutionary soldier and writer. Badoc also has a notable church, fronted by a walled plaza, to the right of which is a ruined *convento*.

The massively buttressed church has a blue-and-cream facade, a tower, and exterior stone steps. Inside, note the fine old altar table at the left end of the transept (transepts are rare in Ilocos churches). Across the main square from the church are several old ruins. Two km south of town, close to the Ilocos Sur boundary, a rough road traverses farmland for 3.5 km to secluded beaches off which you can snorkel over coral. Salt-making is practiced along the coast. Badoc Island, where goats are kept, is a short distance offshore.

Currimao
This town is located on a wide but unexceptional beach where Juan de Salcedo landed in 1572. The beach is flanked by two wharves, a small one near which are abandoned tobacco warehouses dating from the tobacco monopoly days, and a large one relating to Currimao's designation as an Export Processing Zone.

Stay at **D'Coral Beach Resort,** P450-600, or **Playa Blanca Beach Resort,** P450-700 (with windsurfing, sailing, bicycles, a nightly movie, and free transfer to Laoag airport). Make prior arrangements for Playa Blanca through Swagman Travel in Manila on A. Flores Street in Ermita.

Batac
This important tobacco town was the boyhood home of former president Marcos. **Balay Ti Ili,** a colonial-style former house of the Marcos family, displays Marcos memorabilia (open daily 0800-1200, 1300-1700). "Malacanang del Norte," once Marcos's presidential palace and estate, is closed to the public. Batac is also the site of the Aglipay National Shrine. It was the birthplace of Gregorio Aglipay, founder of the Aglipayan Church, which has a cathedral in the town center. Ilocos Norte is a major center of this church, with a significant number of adherents.

Paoay
To reach this town, 20 km south of Laoag, turn off the main highway at Batac and go four km west. The parish was founded by Augustinians in 1593; construction of the present church began in 1704. This famous fortresslike church is noted for its variety of architectural styles. The massive buttresses, exterior staircases, and facade are "earthquake baroque." Chinese elements are seen in the gable, while the crenellations and niches topping the walls suggest Javanese influence.

The thick walls are of coral rubble faced with brick and sealed with particularly hard lime mortar made by mixing with sugarcane juice instead of water. The separate three-story bell tower, dating from 1793, was used by local guerrillas in WW II and as a lookout by the Katipuneros during the revolution. The ruined *convento* is across the street from the church. Paoay is noted for weaving.

Paoay Lake National Park
The lake covers less than five square km and is 10 meters deep. It's three km from the sea, yet the surface is below sea level; a subterranean source keeps the water fresh. The surrounding countryside, haunt of wild chickens and ducks, is attractive. The lake, several kilometers north of Paoay town, and three km off the main highway, is signposted.

Legend holds that a "lost town," San Juan de Sahagun, once stood where the lake is now, but it was flooded as divine punishment for the inhabitants' materialism. The people became fish, and local fishermen claim to have seen swimming fish wearing earrings and bracelets as well as a church roof and steeple in the middle of the lake. The more probable explanation is that an earthquake swallowed up the settlement and formed the lake.

The **Paoay Lake Resort & Sports Center** is a large complex in Suba on the lake's western shore with an 18-hole golf course, swimming pool, and tennis courts. Rooms run P750-900 but are cheaper in the off season. Suba Beach has good surf and extensive, imposing sand dunes. It's a popular locale for shooting Filipino movies. Jeepneys link Laoag and Suba village.

San Nicolas

Across from Laoag City, on the river's south bank, is San Nicolas. The original church dates from 1584, but the present building is a 19th-century restoration. It has heavily buttressed sides, a three-story bell tower, and a *convento* connected to it by a passageway. Local potters produce traditional Ilocano squat-shaped earthenware *burnay* jars.

LAOAG CITY

The provincial capital and commercial center, Laoag is located on the north bank of the Laoag River, about eight km from the sea. Nearly half its 76,000 inhabitants live in the city proper, the rest in the surrounding *barangays*. The city has a few points of interest and is a good base for exploring the surrounding area.

Coming from the south, the long bridge across the river leads directly to the central plaza, around which sit the city hall, Marcos Hall of Justice, Provincial Capitol, and cathedral. The main shopping thoroughfares, Rizal and Bonifacio Streets, run both east and west of the plaza.

Attractions

St. Williams Cathedral: A wooden chapel dating from 1580 was replaced by the present cathedral, built between 1650 and 1700 in Italian Renaissance style. Occupied by Filipino revolutionaries in 1898 and U.S. forces in 1899, it has suffered damage by hurricane, earthquake, and fire, and been subsequently restored. Note the unusual facade with its urn-motif columns, the *kapis* windows with wrought-iron screens, and the exterior staircases, one of which is converted to a Lourdes-type grotto. Over the main altar is the Augustinian symbol of a transfixed heart and tasseled hat. The Marcoses donated the chandeliers.

Sinking Bell Tower: Across the street, about 85 meters away, is its sinking tower, dating from 1783; the entrance was originally high enough for a man on horseback to pass through, but earth movements have caused it to sink so deeply that you would have to stoop to get inside.

Abolition of Tobacco Monopoly Monument: This monument in the main plaza was erected in 1882 to commemorate the Spanish king's lifting of the hated decree.

Marcos Hall of Justice: Built on the site of the former Carcel Provincial, where the young Marcos was detained when accused of murder.

St. Williams Cathedral

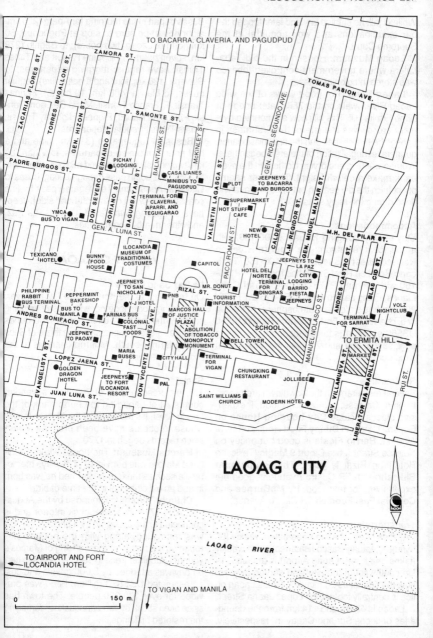

LAOAG CITY

While in jail, he studied law and later topped the bar examinations and won acquittal at the Supreme Court.

Laoag Museum: Housed in the old Tabacalera where government-controlled tobacco was stored in colonial times.

Laoag River: For good views of the wide Laoag River, walk on the 786-meter bridge or climb Ermita Hill. This hill, now surmounted by a giant cross, was the site of the first mass in Laoag, the first chapel, and the first missionaries' quarters; evangelization of the area began here. Women washing and drying clothes on the riverbank make a colorful sight. The river seems peaceful in the dry season but becomes a raging flood during the rainy season.

Accommodations

Stay at **City Lodging House**, P100-150, with an adjacent restaurant; the **Modern Hotel** on Nolasco Street has rooms for P100-150. **Texicano Hotel** on Rizal Street has rooms for P100-150 with fan and P175-200 a/c. **Hotel Casa Llanes,** Primo Lazaro Ave., P150-175 s/d, P175-200 a/c, has a pleasant atmosphere. At the top end, check out the **Fort Ilocandia Resort Hotel,** US$50 s, $55 d (seaside location, swimming pool, sauna, and jacuzzi), near the airport amid sand dunes.

Restaurants

Several restaurants in the downtown area serve Filipino, Chinese, or American food. Inexpensive places include **City Lodging House** on General Luna and **Bunny Food House** on Rizal Avenue. **Barrio Fiesta** is good but pricey on Nolasco Street, while **Cloud 9 Magic** (Texicano Hotel) on Rizal is good. The **Peppermint Bakeshop** on FR Castro Avenue is good but expensive. For fast food, try **McBurgee** and **Colonial Fast Food** on FR Castro Avenue.

Transportation

PAL flies Manila-Laoag three times weekly (85 minutes); Laoag-Basco (Batanes) twice weekly (takes one hour). Laoag Airport is at Gabu, 14 km southwest of the city, and served by jeepney; the ride takes 30 minutes. PAL's Laoag office is centrally located on Lopez Jaena Street.

Laoag is 42 km and 114 km from the boundaries of Ilocos Sur and Cagayan, respectively.

Buses depart in the morning for Aparri (220 km, eight hours)-be sure to stop at Pagudpud, 60 km north of Laoag (two hours); to Baguio (278 km, seven hours), Philippine Rabbit and Times Transit have regular morning departures; to Claveria (126 km, four and a half hours), regular buses; to Manila (488 km, 10 hours), Farinas Transit, F. Franco Transit, Maria De Leon Transit, Philippine Rabbit, Pioneer Highway Transit, Times Transit (regular departures).

Buses to Tuguegarao (316 km, nine and a half hours), morning departures; to Vigan (80 km, two hours), all buses and minibuses to Manila and points south pass through Laoag; buses to Claveria, Aparri, and Tuguegarao pass by fine coastal scenery (sit on the left-hand side). Jeepneys link Laoag with Sarrat, Dingras, La Paz, and other nearby communities.

VICINITY OF LAOAG

La Paz Sand Dunes

On the coast to the north of the Laoag River, these dunes form, together with those stretching south of the river, a 16-km beach. The dunes of La Paz are less impressive than those of Suba Beach farther south. Monroe Island is at the mouth of the river.

Sarrat

This picturesque town of 20,000 is seven km southeast of Laoag on the north bank of the Laoag River. It's the home of the Marcos family, whose forebears have been prominent here since records began in 1770.

Marcos Museum: The house where Ferdinand Marcos was born in 1917 displays memorabilia such as the four-poster bed he was born in and an old clock set to the time of birth.

Church: The church, founded by the Augustinians in 1779, has a redbrick interior and is connected to the *convento* by a brick stairway. It was renovated, along with the houses surrounding the plaza, for the wedding of Marcos's younger daughter Irene in 1983. The lavish ceremony was attended by 5,000 guests and cost an estimated US$10.3 million. Food was provided for over 100,000 people. The town has since been struck by two earthquakes, damaging the restored buildings.

Dingras

Twenty km southeast of Laoag on the south bank of the Laoag River, this town, known as the province's rice granary, sits on the edge of the river's vast sandy floodplain, against a backdrop of the interior mountains. During the 19th century, this area exported rice to China. The main reason to come here is to see the massive ruined church, built in 1598 and destroyed by fire in 1838. The impressive facade and roofless walls are atmospheric and photogenic.

NORTH OF LAOAG CITY

Bacarra

Situated on the Bacarra River floodplain, seven km north of Laoag, Bacarra's famous bell tower dominates the landscape. The church (1783) is one km off the main highway. The massive square belfry, with four-meter-thick brick walls, was damaged by earthquake in 1930. The dome crashed down into the third story and is still poised there! You can climb the belfry for a fine view. The church has a brick facade and stark interior. The roof was lifted by a typhoon in 1934 and has been replaced with one of red corrugated iron. Little remains of the past except for the *kapis*-paned windows with exterior iron grilles, and the old baptistry with its domed roof and original floor of red tiles.

The adjacent *convento,* reached by steps to the right of the nave, is a fine example of the traditional L-shaped building. The upper story still has its original *narra* floor, the wide planks burnished by 250 years of polishing. The ceilings, especially the refectory's, are elegantly painted, though showing signs of deterioration. It also

has a collection of ecclesiastical silver and pewter, plus church records dating back to 1702.

A rare craft, the carving of 17-string wooden harps, is practiced in Bacarra. On the coast are Natba Beach and the Vijia Watchtower. The next municipality, Pasuquin, contains Imelda Garden, Raquisa Cove, and Payupyuan, Texicano, and Seksi beaches. Near the latter, a four-km tricycle ride from town, are salt evaporation beds.

Cape Bojeador to Cagayan

The cape forms Luzon's northwestern tip, 45 km north of Laoag. Enjoy fine views from the windswept lighthouse (1892) situated between the low, scrub-covered Ilocos Mountains and squat coral cliffs onto which the South China Sea's waves break. It's reached by steps from the highway. A pleasant 15-minute walk leads out along the headland, and there's a beach nearby. *Madrecacao* trees flower Jan.-March, and *dap-dap* trees bloom brilliant scarlet Feb.-March.

The highway from here to Cagayan is spectacular, passing deserted gray-sand beaches with exciting surf. It zigzags down from Burgos to Bangui, situated on the wide, beautiful Bangui Bay. Pagudpud has a fine, undeveloped beach where camping is possible. It's the site of a proposed government beach resort complex. You can snorkel off Mairaira Beach, a few kilometers from town. Stay at **Bagong Lipunan Lodge,** where rates start at P400 s, P450 d, in Matarungtong, outside the town. The road passes close to Mabugabog Falls and climaxes in the traverse of the Patapat cliffs, from where you gaze down on beaches, coves, and surf before reaching the Cagayan boundary on Pasaleng Bay.

BATANES ISLANDS

Batanes, a beautiful, rugged, windswept island group, is much closer to Taiwan than to Manila. Often called the Batan Islands, its atmosphere, landscape, and architecture are very different from the rest of the Philippines.

The only practical way to get to Batanes is by air, although weather is a major factor in planning a visit here. The frequency of wet, windy conditions makes landing on Basco's grass airstrip hazardous. With the prevalence of typhoons, which sweep through from the south, the islands can be cut off from Luzon for days at a time. Similarly, rough seas may isolate the main island, Batan, from the other inhabited islands, like Sabtang, and particularily Itbayat, for long intervals during the July-Oct. typhoon season. The best time to visit Batanes is Feb.-May, but anytime Dec.-June is generally okay; outside this period, travelers must have a very flexible schedule and be prepared for lengthy delays.

One goes to Batanes to enjoy hiking and the outdoors rather than nightlife. It's a peaceful place, with almost no crime. Birdwatchers come here during the seasonal migrations of hawks and other birds; the flocks fly farther south to winter in the archipelago or return to nest in Northeast Asia. Batanes is off the tourist trail, but the magnificent scenery and quaint villages, with their distinctive typhoon-proof stone houses, make a visit here well worth the extra expense.

The Land
Batanes is the Philippines's smallest province, both in land area and population. It comprises 10 small islands located in the Luzon Strait about 160 km north of the Luzon mainland and is separated from the Babuyan Islands by the Balintang Channel. The three largest-Batan (where the provincial capital, Basco, is located), Itbayat, and Sabtang-are inhabited. A narrow string of islands stretch north from Itbayat, with Y'Ami being the northernmost island of the Philippines (only 224 km from Taiwan). Radios on Batanes easily pick up Taiwanese stations. The islands are of volcanic or coralline origin, and the terrain is generally hilly, with rocky coastlines.

The landscape is very green, with grassy slopes and short, gnarled trees. The weather is calmest April and May, frequently wet and windy at other times. It's relatively cool Dec.-February. Batanes is struck by a quarter of all typhoons (peak period July-Oct.) passing through the Philippines. This is a major factor in the lifestyle and architecture of the islanders and has hampered economic development. Rainfall is heaviest Aug.-Nov., when agricultural activity is restricted.

The local diet can get very monotonous, consisting mostly of root crops, during the extended periods of bad weather. At such times, the telegraph may be Batanes's only link with the outside world. With few exploitable resources, Batanes is likely to remain isolated and undeveloped.

History
The ancient inhabitants of Batanes, the native Ivatans, are of Malay ancestry, and were divided into small pagan kinship groups inhabiting the mountains near or on the rocky natural fortresses known as *ijangs*. Traces of ancient shelters have been found on top of some of them. Clans were in a more or less constant state of tribal war; defenders threw stones down from the *ijang* onto their attackers. These people traded with the inhabitants of the nearby Babuyan Islands, the north shores of Luzon (Cagayan and Ilocos), and what is now Taiwan. Goods were bartered or gold was used as a medium of exchange. The Ivatans made an alcoholic drink from sugarcane. The wealthy practiced jar burial, and many old earthenware jars have been found.

Since they believed in life after death, they buried their dead with tools, food, pots, and bowls for use in the next world. They held that the souls of the upper classes were taken up to heaven and became stars, but the souls of the poor wandered over the world as *anitos* (spirits). Ivatan huts had been light, since they lacked timber and appropriate tools, and it wasn't until the Spaniards brought logs from Luzon, and introduced new technology and building materials, particularly lime, that the distinctive typhoon-resistant Ivatan house developed.

The colonial era came late to Batanes. The Spanish first surveyed the islands in 1686 out of Calayan (Babuyan Islands). Captain William Dampier of England landed to trade in 1687. He noted that the natives were primitive but not barbarians. From 1686 to 1771, Dominican missionaries made repeated but unsuccessful attempts to convert the Ivatans. In 1782, Governor-General Jose Basco y Vargas, after whom the town is named, asked the Ivatans to become subjects of the king of Spain in return for the benefits of Christianity and the protection of the royal government. They accepted and a Spanish party arrived at Basco in 1783 to formally begin their administration. The Spanish flag and a tall wooden cross were planted, and civil and religious ceremonies were followed by the throwing of coins to the natives, music, dancing, and merriment.

In 1789, the governor ordered the abolition of traditional customs, and Christianization was rapid. The population was greater in 1800 than is today, but in the first decades of the 19th century the people were decimated by a series of plagues. The building of large sailboats greatly improved transportation to Luzon, and Ivatans began migrating to Luzon, a process that continues today.

Katipuneros landed at Ivana in 1898, killed the governor, and put an end to Spanish government in Batanes. At the outbreak of WW II, Batanes was one of the first landing places of the

THE IVATANS OF BATANES

Batanes (209 square km) is sparsely populated, with about 12,000 inhabitants who are almost entirely native Ivatans. The Ivatan tongue is quite distinct from the languages of Luzon, but Ilocano, Tagalog, and English are widely understood. Ivatans have always had to struggle against the elements. The main architectural consideration of their picturesque traditional houses is typhoon resistance. These low, solid cottages are built in a sheltered location with meter-thick stone-and-lime walls, small doors and windows, and heavy thatched roofs, made of several layers of *cogon* grass held together by sticks and rattan. A roof net is used to hold down the roof in typhoons.

Some houses have two stories and a separate kitchen building. There are still many old houses in use, especially outside Basco. The villages, whose clean streets are laid out at right angles, date from 200 years ago when the Ivatans first came down from their hillside settlements to live in coastal communities under Spanish missionaries and officials. Outside today's villages are the high rocky formations, *ijangs,* that once served as fortresses and places of refuge.

The Ivatan Lifestyle

Isolation has induced self-sufficiency and adaptability, and a spirit of close cooperation pervades this society of farmers and fishermen. Even the teachers and government workers are part-time farmers. While arable land is limited, most families own small plots on which they plant storm-resistant root crops: *kamote, gabi, ubi, tugui,* carrots, and onions. Rice and corn are grown only in small quantities; most rice is brought from Luzon. Garlic is the main cash crop. Root crops are supplemented by vegetables and fruit trees. Bananas, oranges, mandarins, pineapple, papaya, jackfruit, coconuts, and watermelon are produced in sheltered spots. The pastures are suitable for cattle-grazing, and carabao, goats, pigs, and chickens are also raised. Livestock is occasionally sold to Luzon.

Both men and women sometimes wear the distinctive traditional cloaks, made of overlapping strips of coconut palm, nipa, *anahaw,* banana, or other leaves, and grass, that protect the head and shoulders from the rain or sun. The Ivatans depend on boats for transportation and fishing. Fishing is good but subject to weather conditions. Huge lobsters inhabit the rocky shorelines. Cottage industries include the weaving of baskets, mats, hats, handbags, slippers, and boat-building, rope- and fishnet-making, and pottery.

Batanes has no private firms or factories, and only government employees receive a regular income. Items not produced locally are much more expensive than on Luzon due to transportation costs. Many islanders leave in search of a better climate and economic opportunity; of 20,000 Ivatans, only 12,000 live in Batanes. The rest are scattered, with concentrations in Metro Manila and Tarlac; some also migrated to the Malinao area of Bukidnon (Mindanao) during the '50s and '60s under a government homestead program.

Japanese, who recognized its strategic location and established an air base here. The occupation lasted almost four years and Basco was heavily damaged. In postwar years, LORAN navigation and communications stations were manned by American military personnel, but their work has now been taken over by Filipinos.

Transportation

Batanes receives only about four irregular supply boats a year out of Manila. In the summer, there is a Philippine Navy boat two or three times a season leaving from Puro Point, La Union, for Basco. There are no bunks or cots, but deck space aboard the boat costs about P100.

PAL is its only weekly link to the outside world, with three flights a week from Manila, two via Tuguegarao, two via Laoag (weather permitting). Sometimes, after an extended period of bad weather, a long passenger waiting list develops. PAL may deposit passengers at Laoag or Tuguegarao and return to Basco to ferry a second load to the mainland before continuing on to Manila. (When flying to Basco, sit on the right-hand side for good views of the Babuyan Islands.)

Batan, Itbayat, and Sabtang Islands are linked by large, open boats, owned and operated on a cooperative basis. Also, many individuals own small *bancas* that may be chartered for the short trip between Batan and Sabtang. The weather may affect interisland trips; even in good conditions, the sea may be fairly rough. Batanes lies between the South China Sea and Pacific Ocean, and when two great bodies of water converge there is considerable current, turbulence, and risk to any sailor.

Be advised not to set out on long crossings in a plywood *banca* or if locals warn of bad weather and rough water. Villages on Batan Island are linked by Tamaraw vehicles operating a jeepneylike service out of Basco. Sabtang and Itbayat have no public transportation.

BATAN ISLAND

Batan is the main island of Batanes, with 7,950 inhabitants. Basco and its nearby airstrip occupy the limited flat land at the island's narrow central part. The highest peaks are the frequently mist-shrouded extinct volcano, Mt. Iraya (1,008 meters) in the north and Mt. Matarem (454 meters) in the center. Basco is the focal point, and the main route follows the west coast through Mahatao and Ivana to Uyugan. Most of the people live in Basco or along this road; the rest of the 70-square-km island remains thinly populated.

Basco

Basco is 483 km from Manila and 222 km from Claveria (Cagayan). The airport is about 1.5 km north of town. Transportation meets the planes, but if you don't have much luggage, it's an easy walk. The town center consists of the Provincial Capitol, the old church, and a grassy plaza leading down to a wharf and beach. This little settlement doesn't even have a market, just small stores.

There are no cinemas, no TV, and battery-operated transistor radios can pick up Taiwan but not Luzon. Until recently, entertainment was virtually limited to cassette tapes. Now, however, video movies are the rage in Basco; several individuals have them flown in and show them at home on their VCRs, charging viewers a few pesos a head. They advertise on boards outside their houses; ironically, travelers have a better choice of good films in remote Basco than in almost any Philippine city outside Manila.

You can stay in Basco at **Casa de Elcano,** P70 pp with meals (rooms are situated above a bakery), or **Mama Lily's,** P120 pp with meals, located next to the Provincial Capitol. Also try the Santo Dominican College Dormitory behind the SDC canteen; rooms are P60.

It's a good idea to write the Ivatan Homestay Association in Basco for advance information on accommodation. There are about 14 members of the association. Try to anticipate these stays and bring gifts or food from Luzon for your hosts. If accommodation at homes is impossible, consider asking if there is a spare room at the hospital. They are always clean, quiet, and more private. For restaurant food, try **Elcano's,** near the hospital.

Around Batan Island

Since Basco has the only lodging in the province, it's the logical base for exploring. There's good hiking all around. It's a pleasant walk up onto the grassy clifftops just north of town. A road leads three km across to Valugan on the island's eastern shore. Fields are often divided by hedges, creating a patchwork-quilt effect reminiscent of Ireland. The coastal road runs down the west side, through Mahatao and Ivana to Uyugan. Each community is worth visiting. Jeepneys depart daily from Basco to Uyugan at 0500 and 0530.

For those who prefer a later start, hitchhiking is easy, though traffic is irregular. In any case, this coastal road is truly beautiful; it's worth walking to savor it slowly, pausing to enjoy a dip in some delightful tiny inlets. Basco to Mahatao is six km, and Mahatao to Ivana eight km. Ivana to Uyugan is four km. If you walk this 18 km, you'll probably have no trouble hitching back to Basco. Alternatively, hitch down and walk back. The road leads beyond Uyugan to the hamlet of Imnajbu, where a LORAN station is located, and completes a circle at Mahatao. It's possible to walk this circular route in a long day, and while vehicles are scarce, it's usually possible to pick up time by hitching at least part of the way. It makes a wonderful day.

There is also bus transportation from Basco to Ivana leaving at 0530, 1430, and 2130. On Sunday, a bus leaves at 0800 to bring the monsignor to church in Itbud, returning to Basco again at 1100.

SABTANG

This beautiful island (32 square km) also has a scenic circular route to hike. The interior is mountainous, and the 1,400 inhabitants live in Sabtang town (also called San Vicente) and four other settlements spread around the shores. Sabtang town is opposite Ivana on Batan, and the channel between them requires skillful boat handling during the 30-minute crossing.

There are scheduled trips from Ivana to Sabtang at 0830 on Monday, Wednesday, and Friday between mid-March and mid-May; the boats return the next morning. Take a jeepney or scheduled bus from Basco to Ivana. At other times of the year, weather determines if a boat is going to the island. A special *banca* trip costs around P200 one-way; contact the mayor to arrange a boatman. A boat also makes a direct Basco-Sabtang return trip about once a week.

Sabtang town has a thatched-roof church and a fishery school.

There's no transport on the 26-km circular route linking the island's coastal communities, but it can be walked in a day. The villages are quaint and unspoiled. The road ascends out of Sabtang town. After two km, it passes close to a beach before cutting across the island. A shortcut branches left. Off the northwest shore are two raised coral terraces: the ranching island of Ivuhus (Ibahos) and, behind it, Dequey Island, used for raising goats. Neither is permanently settled.

From Sumnanga, the trail narrows and climbs inland before descending steeply to Chavayan, which has spectacular jagged pinnacles to the south. From Chavayan to Savidug, the trail hugs a precipitous cliff-side with waves breaking below. There's a beach near Savidug. The Sabtang people have a history of rebellion; the Spanish had to resettle them in Ivana from 1790 to 1841.

ITBAYAT

Itbayat (85 square km) is the largest island in Batanes, and its people are the most isolated. The 2,860 Itbayats have a lighter complexion and more Chinese physical features than the Ivatans of Batan and Sabtang. The Itbayaten dialect is distinct, too. The island is an uplifted coral terrace; its hills are lower than those of Batan and Sabtang. The highest point, Mt. Santa Rosa (278 meters), is at the northern end and offers good views of the small islands stretching northward. Mt. Riposet (231 meters) is on the eastern side of the island. Itbayat is surrounded by steep cliffs, and the land commonly slopes gently downward from the rim to the interior. The terrain is typically coarse grassland.

Itbayat has no bays, beaches, or harbor. Unloading people and goods from boats to the rock that serves as a dock is a tricky operation in the choppy seas. These fairly large boats are then hauled by communal manpower out of the water and up a steep incline for storage in boathouses about 50 meters above the sea.

The crossing from Basco is always irregular and only made in good weather; outside April and May, access or return may be impossible for lengthy periods. The four-hour trip provides fine close-up views of the cliffs lining both Batan and Itbayat, and of dramatic Dinem Island (Diogo Island) in the distance.

From the Chinapoliran boat landing, it's about eight km to the main settlement, Mayan. The trail climbs steeply from the sea and after three km intersects the road that links Mayan with the other community, Raele. There's no transportation, but motorcyclists and drivers of public-works trucks will stop for you if they have room. Mayan is an interesting, sprawling town. From here, you can hike to other boat landings on the coast and to the peak north of town. To visit Raele, 15 km south, arrange to get a ride with the public-works truck that usually goes down in the morning and returns in the afternoon.

Raele is just a small village. Nearby is an airstrip, and trails lead down to boat landings. The main economic activity on Itbayat is growing garlic. Local delicacies include huge lobster and delicious coconut crabs (which *do* eat coconuts).

M.G.L. DOMENY DE RIENZI

NORTHEAST LUZON

Travelers making the circular trip from Manila to Baguio and Banaue will pass through Nueva Vizcaya, partly following the Magat River, a tributary of the Cagayan. It's worthwhile, however, to descend from Banaue to Bagabag, then turn north and travel down the valley, through Isabela, where the Magat joins the Cagayan River, Cagayan Province, and around to Ilocos.

The fertile Cagayan Valley is a major producer of rice, corn, and tobacco and is also pioneer country, with newly opened logging and grazing lands. Its cigar tobacco is famous. The dominating feature is the great Rio Grande de Cagayan, or Cagayan River, the longest river (353 km) in the Philippines, which rises in the Sierra Madre and flows to the Babuyan Channel. The highway from Manila and Central Plain zigzags over the 1,000-meter-high Dalton Pass into Nueva Vizcaya.

The valley is about 380 km long and 60 km wide. The highway to Aparri generally runs close to the Magat and Cagayan Rivers, along which lie a string of market towns, of which Tuguegarao is the largest. Many towns have fine colonial churches, typically built of red brick. In spite of the long Spanish presence, the valley still has a frontier feel, reflected in the many signs of its rapid recent growth.

History

The Cagayan Valley has been inhabited since ancient times. Stone artifacts over 30,000 years old have been found at Solano (Nueva Vizcaya). Archaeological sites nearer the mouth of the river include Cagayan's Musang Cave (8030 B.C.) and Rabel Cave (3000 B.C.), while pottery and jewelry dating from about 2000 B.C. have been found at Magapit and Lal-lo. The Ybanags of the valley were trading with the Chinese, Japanese, and others long before Juan de Salcedo began the Spanish exploration of the region in 1572. He landed near the mouth of the Cagayan River and discovered a fertile land with abundant wildlife and relatively prosperous but belligerent inhabitants.

The Spanish Era: The natives relinquished this land of plenty only with reluctance. It's a tale of rebellion and subjugation from the beginning. In 1581, the Spaniards drove out Japanese pirates who were harassing the shores and established the first colonial settlement and fort at Nueva Segovia, now Lal-lo. They chose a site 13 km upstream for protection from coastal attack; the landscape and climate reminded the Spaniards of their native Segovia. In 1594, the pope created the vast Diocese of Nueva Segovia, which comprised the whole Cagayan Valley, already well populated, and neighboring areas; the seat of the diocese remained here until its transfer to Vigan in 1755.

It was the region's administrative, ecclesiastical, and military center, a European community surrounded by hostile tribes, which they attempted to convert and exploit. The Dominicans built massive, fortresslike churches and tried to eradicate the pagan religions. The land was divided up into *encomiendas,* which were usually awarded to deserving soldiers of fortune who could then demand tribute in gold or produce from the local inhabitants.

Forced labor was another Spanish specialty. Not surprisingly, the natives staged a series of revolts, burning churches and convents, and murdering priests, who tried to pit rival tribes against each other in a determined effort to survive. Native resistance lasted for centuries. They besieged Nueva Segovia up until 1590, and for the next hundred years, the Spaniards made little progress.

A major rebellion occurred in the valley between Tuguegarao and Nueva Segovia in 1718. Even after the valley had been Christianized, the pagan tribes of the adjoining hills continued to be troublesome. Additional revolts were caused by the harsh enforcement of the tobacco monopoly (1782-1881). Its establishment gave rise to tobacco plantations and new settlements in the valley, with product quality upgraded to world-class standard; it brought much hardship as traditional cropping patterns were altered, rice became scarce, and corrupt officials exacerbated the exploitation. Merchants loaded tobacco onto large, flat-bottomed boats from as far south as Echague, to be poled down to Aparri and transferred to Manila-bound ships. The river long remained the only trade and travel route through the region, which remained lightly settled and isolated into this century. The main highway over the Caraballo Mountains, paralleling an old Spanish trail (1768), wasn't constructed until 1924.

World War II: Japanese forces landed at Aparri only three days after Pearl Harbor in 1941. By mid-1945, maintaining access to the fertile valley's crops was a key element in Yamashita's plan to make a protracted last stand in the adjacent Cordillera. He set up strong defenses on the passes guarding the approaches to the valley. While the logical U.S. strategy was an amphibious landing at Aparri, the requisite vessels couldn't be spared from the campaign in the southern islands. The valley had to be taken the hard way!

A three-pronged attack was mounted, with one division attacking Yamashita's headquarters in Baguio, another following the narrow Villa Verde trail, which crosses the Caraballo Mountains to meet the highway at Santa Fe, and a third pushing north on the main highway leading over Balete (now Dalton) Pass into the valley. Fighting on the Villa Verde trail was particularly bitter. It took U.S. forces more than two months to cross a forested eight-km stretch known as Salacsac passes. It also took the other division two months to cover the last eight km to the heavily defended Balete Pass. When Yamashita reached Balete after the fall of Baguio, he decided that he'd sacrificed enough men to hold the pass and ordered a northward withdrawal. But it still took the Americans another three weeks to reach Santa Fe, where the Villa Verde trail group finally linked up with them.

Balete Pass has since been renamed after General Dalton, who died in the battle. U.S. forces then raced down the valley to find much of it already controlled by Filipino guerrillas. Other U.S. forces swept around Luzon's west and north coast to Aparri to meet the northbound contingent. The valley was taken, though Yamashita held out in the mountains for two more months.

The Postwar Years: Since WW II, development of this vast frontier land has accelerated through huge irrigation projects, and the expansion of logging and ranching. Migrants, especially Ilocanos and Tagalogs, are still moving in from other regions, and today they far outnumber the native minorities. Much intermarriage has occurred between migrant and native, so that minorities inhabiting the valley have become increasingly integrated into the homogeneous society-at-large, though some tribes still maintain a fairly traditional lifestyle in the peripheral hills.

Transportation

PAL flies Manila-Cauayan, Manila-Tuguegarao, and Basco-(Batanes) Tuguegarao.

The valley's single main highway is intersected by Pantranco North, which links Manila with valley towns via the Central Plain and Dalton Pass. From Baguio, Pantranco North, Dangwa Tranco, and Greenland Bus all pass through Pangasinan, Nueva Ecija, and over the Dalton Pass en route to Banaue or Tabuk. This is popularly called the lowland route from Baguio to Banaue, as opposed to the highland route along the Halsema Highway.

The more direct (104 km vs. 199 km) but rough road from Baguio to Aritao, via Kayapa, is little used. A daily bus connects Bontoc and Banaue with Tabuk, via Bagabag. The valley can also be approached from Tabuk to Tuguegarao and from Laoag, along the north coast, to Aparri and Tuguegarao. Service along the highway is frequent, while buses, minibuses, and jeepneys fan out from market towns to serve off-highway communities.

It's also possible to make your way along the Pacific coast by launch, paralleling the valley, from Baler (Aurora) via Palanan (Isabela) to San Vicente (Cagayan), but these rocky shores are fully exposed to wind and waves and there are no fixed schedules. Departures depend on demand and the weather, so allow plenty of time.

NUEVA VIZCAYA PROVINCE

Nueva Vizcaya is the southern gateway to the Cagayan Valley. Those taking the lowland route from Manila to the Banaue rice terraces will pass through here. The major towns are on the main highway. Bayombong is the capital, Solano the commercial center, and Bagabag a major junction where the mountain road from Baguio, Bontoc, and Banaue meets the valley highway that leads to and from Manila.

The People

Nueva Vizcaya's population increased sharply in postwar years due to migrants from surrounding provinces, drawn by expanded logging operations and newly opened farmland. In spite of this influx, Nueva Vizcaya remains sparsely populated, with about 330,000 inhabitants. The dominant dialects are Ilocano and Tagalog. Several tribal groups live in the hills, mostly along the provincial boundaries.

The Gaddangs are widely distributed at the upper end of the Cagayan Valley, inhabiting both hills and lowlands. They live mainly in Nueva Vizcaya and Isabela, and on the eastern slopes of Ifugao and Mountain Provinces. Their houses are traditionally built on hilltops in forested areas, each containing a self-sufficient nuclear family.

Ilongots inhabit the remote, semi-explored regions of Nueva Vizcaya, Quirino, Aurora, and Nueva Ecija. They cultivate dry rice, root crops, corn, bananas, and sugarcane, and practice wild pig hunting, fishing, and gathering. Women do most of the farm work, while the men hunt. Settlements are widely scattered. In former times, homes were hidden and barricaded by dense foliage to thwart enemy attacks.

The Ikalahans are found in the area west of Santa Fe, plus some areas of Pangasinan, Benguet, Nueva Ecija, and Ifugao. They're *kaingin* farmers, with *kamote* as their staple food, supplemented by corn, vegetables, cassava, and other root crops. They also raise pigs and chickens, and hunt using spears, dogs, pit traps, and snares.

Iwaks live near Santa Fe and in valleys south of Kayapa. They plant *kamote* and various tubers, and rice.

Isinais, plus some Igorots and Negritos, also inhabit Nueva Vizcaya.

THE HIGHWAY NORTH

Coming from Manila and the Central Plain, you enter Nueva Vizcaya by zigzagging across the Caraballo Range by way of the Dalton Pass (915 meters). A monument recalls the major battle fought here in 1945. Santa Fe, a small town at the foot of the pass, is noted for its pleasant climate and local handicrafts, especially bamboo basketwork. A road leads six km west to the Igorot settlement of Imugan.

Around Salinas
Aritao, founded 1665, is a sawmill town from which a road leads west to Benguet and Baguio, via Kayapa. The latter, situated in a bowl-shaped valley, was an old Spanish politico-military *comandancia*. Bambang, the next town north of Aritao, has an inexpensive guesthouse. Salt springs at Salinas, a 15-km jeepney ride west of Bambang, have created intriguing mounds of petrified white salt in a natural setting; they're not, however, as spectacular as some tourist literature suggests.

Bayombong
The provincial capital (founded 1737) is on the Magat River, 267 km north of Manila and 229 km from Baguio (via Nueva Ecija). The town fiesta, 1-7 August, features a weeklong funfair in front of the church. Events climax on the last weekend with the *sumbali*, a street dance performed by dancers blackened and dressed like Aetas (Negritos). After the main show, the "Aetas" make a round of the houses in town, performing for tips. The final Sunday is highlighted by an all-day *moro-moro* performance.

On Christmas Eve, a noise contest is held, with prizes for whomever produces the loudest bang and most rapid series of explosions; kerosene is the favored fuel. The town is protected from flooding by a nearby boulder dam, while four km out is a waterfall on the edge of a forest where spiritist sects hold rituals.

Solano
Solano, the province's biggest town and main commercial center, is six km north of the capital, along the Magat River. Accommodations are available on the main road at **Banaue Lodge** and **Mountain Lodge,** P150-300. A minibus leaves about 0700 for Banaue and Mayoyao. If you are traveling south from Banaue to Solano, you can catch Manila-bound buses throughout the day from the bus station.

Bagabag
This is an important junction, where the road from Bontoc (111 km) and the one from Banaue (61 km) meet the main valley highway, which winds northwest through hills to Isabela. In 1945, General Yamashita was flown from Bagabag airport to officially surrender in Baguio. Buses to and from Banaue (90 minutes) pass through Bagabag heading to Baguio.

QUIRINO PROVINCE

This province, named after President Quirino (1948-53), is situated to the east of the Cagayan Valley highway between Isabela and Nueva Vizcaya. Stretching into the Sierra Madre, it comprises 3,057 square km carved out of Nueva Vizcaya in 1971. It incorporates only five municipalities—Cabarroguis (the capital), Diffun, Saguday, Aglipay, and Maddela. Diffun and Saguday are in the scenic, fertile Ganano Valley, and both have nearby caves. Maddela is on the upper Cagayan River.

Most of Quirino's 116,000 inhabitants are migrants attracted by its homesteading possibilities and rich natural resources. Logging is the main economic activity. Native minorities include Ikalahans, Ilongots, and Attas (Negritos). Much of Quirino remains wild and undeveloped, a world of densely forested hills and streams. It's accessible through Cordon (Isabela). A proposed road will also link Diffun and Cabarroguis with the Cagayan Valley highway near Bagabag (Nueva Vizcaya).

AURORA PROVINCE

Aurora extends far down the Pacific coast of Luzon, but only two roads lead to the province, ending at Baler and Dingalan. Baler Bay, with some of the archipelago's best surfing conditions, is a prime destination for the small but growing number of surfers exploring the Philippines. The surfing scene in Francis Ford Coppola's *Apocalypse Now* was filmed here.

The Province

Aurora (3,240 square km) comprises a long, narrow strip between the heavily forested Sierra Madre range and the Pacific. The shoreline is rocky, steep, and virtually inaccessible as forests end in cliffs. Waves and heavy surf continually pound the coast. Aurora is exposed to northeast winds off the Pacific, and typhoons are a constant threat. Rainfall is relatively heavy throughout the year, though it's particularly wet Sept.-Dec. when typhoons are most prevalent. The major settlements are situated on bays that provide some shelter from the open ocean—Casiguran, Baler, and Dingalan. The only lowland areas are at the heads of these bays.

In spite of rapid recent growth, Aurora is still largely undeveloped and sparsely populated. Logging is the main industry; rattan and resins are also gathered in the forests. Limited farming (rice, abaca, and coconuts) takes place, so food has to be brought from the Central Plain. Fishing is practiced locally. Substantial numbers of duck and snipe attract hunters and birdwatchers.

History

The conquistador Juan de Salcedo explored this coast in the early 1570s, and missions were established at Baler and Casiguran in 1588. The Spaniards called it the Contra Costa ("Opposite Coast"). Garrisons manned forts and watchtowers to guard against Moro pirates.

Baler was the last Spanish stronghold to surrender to Filipino revolutionaries. Four officers and 50 men were besieged in Baler Church for 337 days during 1898-99. They refused all demands for surrender, until newspapers thrown into the courtyard indicated that Spain had lost the Philippines months before, and theirs was the

only Spanish flag still fluttering. The stubbornly courageous group, broken by starvation and disease, emerged to begin the march to Manila.

Baler is the birthplace of Manuel Quezon (1878-1944), who led the struggle for independence and became the first president of the Philippine Commonwealth. Aurora, named after Quezon's wife, was a subprovince of Quezon until 1979.

Transportation

PNR Bus and Pantranco North serve Baler from Manila, 231 km (seven hours) away. Those coming from or proceeding to northern Luzon can change buses at Cabanatuan City, 116 km (three and a half hours) from Baler. Buses share the rough, winding road through the Sierra Madre with logging trucks, but the views are beautiful; sit on the left. Landslides and washouts sometimes block the way in the rainy season. Buses stop around halfway for a 30-minute break at the entrance to Aurora Memorial Park. The panorama of mountains and ocean is excellent from Dimasingay, the highest point on the highway, 36 km east of Baler. Buses also link Cabanatuan and Dingalan.

The isolated communities along the Pacific shores of Cagayan, Isabela, Aurora, and Quezon are dependent on coastal launches for transportation and supplies. Travelers with a flexible schedule can find a launch in San Vicente (Cagayan), Baler, Dingalan, or Infanta (Quezon) and sail along the coast. Passengers have time to explore remote settlements, while cargo is unloaded and local products like rattan brought aboard. The rugged shoreline and absence of tourists make this an exciting trip.

Baler

Located on the fertile delta lands of the San Luis and Aguang Rivers, and with one of the best harbors on Luzon's northeast coast, this former Franciscan town, with its weather-beaten buildings and old trees, is the provincial capital and trading center. The market is a melting pot where Tagalogs, Ilocanos, and Negritos mingle. A stone marker indicates the site of Manuel Quezon's birth.

The town center is about one km from the sea. Rice and copra are produced on the surrounding plain, and logs are loaded at its outport, Puerto Aurora. Weaving *buntal* hats and mats are local handicrafts. There's not much to do besides enjoy the sea or hike into the hills. The area has undeveloped beaches and fine offshore game fishing for marlin, sailfish, and swordfish.

Cemento

Also known as Puerto Aurora, this fishing village on Cape Encanto is the surfing center of the Philippines. Waves, sometimes reaching 4.5 meters, rise out of the deep offshore waters and crash onto the coral reef fronting the old cement pier. Cemento has a beach and the remains of the Quezon family's resthouse.

Stay at **Cape Encanto Nipa Huts;** the owner is a good source of local information and can recommend competent guides for hiking in the area. Cemento is a 15- to 20-minute *banca* trip across the bay from Baler (inquire at the Hotel Amihan). Alternatively, take a tricycle on the roundabout road, or a tricycle to Sabang, or a ferry across the river, then walk for about an hour, fording two more shallow rivers.

Vicinity of Baler

Dibut Bay was a landing site for U.S. submarines supplying guerrillas during WW II. Get there on foot or by *banca,* 90 minutes around the coast. Dibut has a Dumagat village, a beach, and fine offshore coral; you can also hire a *banca* to go fishing. A good walk is to the radar/weather station at Cape Encanto; the track passes Digisi and several other springs. A circular road leads north from Baler to Dipaculao (14 km) and around through Maria Aurora and back to the main road near San Luis. Numerous rivers flow down to Baler Bay, and trails follow most of their valleys.

Casiguran

Coastal launches and *bancas* sometimes sail from Baler to Casiguran, situated on a stretch of lowland at the head of a narrow bay formed by the coral-fringed San Ildefonso Peninsula. The entrance to the bay is guarded by the crumbled remains of an old Spanish watchtower on the cape. Boats tie up at the muddy confluence of the Casiguran and Casalogan Rivers, from where the town center is a three-km walk. Casiguran consists of about 100 two-story tin-roofed buildings, surrounded by fields and backed by mountains. Logging and milling are major industries.

ISABELA PROVINCE

This large province in the middle of the Cagayan Valley is a major producer of tobacco, rice, corn, and timber, and contains frontier areas of vast economic potential. The massive Magat High Dam across the Magat River, a major hydroelectric and irrigation project, was inaugurated in 1982. Most towns are on or near the main highway, which crosses from the left to the right bank of the Cagayan River south of Ilagan, the provincial capital. Some towns have noteworthy colonial churches. The rugged Pacific coast remains isolated and undeveloped.

NORTH THROUGH THE VALLEY

Buses are frequent on the main highway through Isabela. They serve the province from Manila, Baguio, Bontoc, Banaue, Tabuk, Tuguegarao, and Aparri. The small town of Cordon (stay at Bulakena Lodge) is the gateway to Quirino Province; a road leads south to Diffun.

Santiago

Santiago is the commercial center of southern Isabela. Accommodations include Tahanang Nayon Lodge, Rosario Lodge, Traveler's Lodge, Green View Lodge, Dalagita Lodge, Mary's Lodging House, 13 Karats Lodge, and VICAL Inc. Rates are low compared to more popular areas with prices ranging P100-150.

Ramon

A road leads 14 km off the main highway, passing through riceland, from Santiago to Ramon, where the giant Magat High Dam and reservoir complex has been constructed in Aguinaldo (locally called Bunkian). The four-km-long dam across the Magat River is one of the highest in Asia. This multipurpose project provides irrigation that's expected to double the area's rice yield and enable intensive cropping. The hydroelectric power generated will supply the energy needs of northern and part of central Luzon, save over two million barrels of oil annually, and hasten industrialization of the Cagayan Valley and neighboring areas.

To Cauayan

The valley highway finally meets the Cagayan River at Echague, 15 km north of Santiago. Just south of Echague is Ipil junction, where a road leads southeast up along the Cagayan to Jones, a market town named after an American anthropologist killed nearby, then to San Agustin (28 km), a sawmill town. Echague is the former provincial capital, with a fine old church. Situated in the heart of "tobacco country," it's a center of the cigar-tobacco industry; the headquarters of the famous Compania General de Tabacas Filipinas (Tabacalera) is here. Natural gas has been found near Echague.

The next town, Alicia, is the site of the shrine of Nuestra Señora de Atocha. A Gaddang subgroup lives around Angadanan, an old river town six km east of Alicia.

Cauayan

This town, with an old church and lively market, is in a major rice-growing area; large coal deposits have been discovered nearby. **PAL** flies Manila-Cauayan twice weekly (70 minutes) and has a ticket office on Cento St.; the airport is 1.5 km south of town.

Stay at Cauayan Lodging House, JC Lodge, Grand Hotel, A.C.T. Hotel, Amity Hotel (next to market; roof garden restaurant with live folk music), Cherry Hotel, or Isabela Hotel. Rooms are P150-200.

To Ilagan

The highway bypasses the old town of Reina Mercedes (one km east) and crosses the Cagayan River to Naguilian. Two km north, a road branches east into the hills to the timber town of San Mariano (20 km), situated in a logging area; it continues as a track to Palanan on the coast.

Ilagan

The provincial capital and largest town, Ilagan is 408 km from Manila and 383 km from Baguio.

Located near the confluences of the Cagayan with the Magat, Ilagan, Siffu, and Mallig Rivers, it's the main trading center for the rice, corn, and other produce of these valleys. Ilagan is also, with Echague, the financial and warehousing center for the cigar-tobacco industry. The Capitol is three km southwest of town. Fuyot Spring National Park, noted for birdlife, caves, and springs, is situated on a major watershed about 20 km from Ilagan.

Stay at White Alcove Inn, Ilagan Garden Lodge, Roman's Inn, or San Antonio Hotel. Rooms are P100-150.

North of Ilagan

Tumauini, in timber country, has a notable redbrick church and an adjoining belfry with ornate

---

THE CAPTURE OF AGUINALDO

During the Philippine-American War, U.S. troops drove Gen. Emilio Aguinaldo relentlessly north, but the delaying effect of the Battle of Tirad Pass (1899) enabled him to escape to remote Palanan, after which the Americans lost track of him for over a year. They believed that his capture was a necessary step in persuading Filipino patriots to lay down their arms and accept U.S. sovereignty. Aguinaldo, who was living in a former schoolhouse, sent an order to guerrilla leaders for reinforcements to be sent to Palanan, but the Americans captured the messenger in Nueva Ecija, thus discovering Aguinaldo's whereabouts.

A gunboat brought a party of U.S. officers and Filipino mercenaries led by Brigadier-General Funston to Casiguran Bay (Aurora). These men set out on a nine-day, 160-km jungle march overland to Palanan. They pretended to be the awaited reinforcements, holding five Americans prisoner. Once inside the camp, the guards were overpowered and Aguinaldo arrested. The gunboat returned him to Manila.

Thus ended the First Philippine Republic, though guerrilla resistance continued for some time after. An absorbing account of this episode, culminating in the meeting of Funston and Aguinaldo, is contained in David Haward Bain's *Sitting in Darkness: Americans in the Philippines* (Houghton Mifflin, 1984). Bain retraced Funston's march during his research.

stonework. The Santa Victoria Caves are 19 km east in limestone outcroppings in the Sierra Madre foothills. At Cabagan, a road branches northwest to Enrile (Cagayan) and Tabuk (Kalinga-Apayao), while the highway passes through San Pablo, which has old church ruins, and enters Cagayan Province.

PALANAN

The only significant settlement on Isabela's Pacific coast, Palanan is an isolated, friendly little town with red tin-roofed houses, situated on a floodplain near the mouth of the Palanan River. The local economy is based on subsistence farming and logging. The archaeological site of Dimolit dates from 4000 B.C., while Palanan was a missionary post from the 16th century. A historical marker standing just outside the churchyard on a bluff overlooking the river indicates the site of the house where Aguinaldo was captured in 1901.

In 1972, the seizure by government forces of a ship under North Korean registry, the M.S. *Karagakatan,* which ran aground south of Palanan while unloading Chinese weapons for the NPA, was a key event leading to the declaration of martial law four months later. Palanan can be reached by irregular coastal launch from San Vicente (Cagayan) or Baler (Aurora), by hiking over rough mountain trails from San Mariano (one week), or walking from Casiguran (Aurora).

CAGAYAN PROVINCE

The dominant features of this large province on Luzon's northeast corner are its long coastline and the great Cagayan River Valley. For travelers passing through Cagayan on the circular route of the far north of Luzon, it's well worth detouring to beautiful Cape Engano at the northeastern tip. From here, irregular launches head south down the undeveloped Pacific shores. The coastline around Claveria is scenic, too, while Tuguegarao, the provincial capital, is the gateway to Callao Caves National Park. The remote Babuyan Islands are also part of Cagayan's administrative territory. This group, with its active volcanoes, rewards its few visitors with splendid isolation.

The People

Cagayan had a rapid population growth in postwar years and now has about 860,000 inhabitants. Ilocano migrants outnumber the native Ybanags and Gaddangs. Ilocano and Ybanag are the main dialects. Some Isneg live along the western boundaries, while the province has a substantial Negrito population, variously known as Attas, Agtas, Pugots, and Dumagats. Many have settled, though some nomadic bands still roam the mountains and remote shorelines in the east.

The Ybanag (Ibanag) are Cagayan's major native group. Also found in Isabela, they're considered to be the tallest Filipino tribe. Their name derives from Bannag, the native name for the Cagayan River, along which their huts were clustered after they had moved inland from the Babuyan Channel coast in early times. They traded with neighboring areas, using an unusual type of boat found nowhere else except in Apayao and Melanesia. Today, the Ybanag use irrigation to grow corn, rice, and tobacco. They make *layaw,* a potent corn liquor.

Two related ethnic groups, each with its own subdialect, are also found in Cagayan. The Malaueg (Malaweg) are concentrated around Rizal, while the Itawes (Itawis) are found in Tuao and Piat, and along the Cagayan River from Tuguegarao to Amulung. The Itawes are hardly distinguishable from the Ybanag in appearance or traditional customs and beliefs, but the degree of their acculturation is less marked.

Itawes are also farmers and are noted for pottery and basket-weaving. Many families still have antique household articles. Their houses comprise a living area and a smaller, separate kitchen, connected by a long *batalan,* where a big water jar is kept for washing hands and feet.

TUGUEGARAO

The provincial capital and commercial center is located in the south of the province. Much of the original colonial town's architecture, including the massive redbrick cathedral (1766), was destroyed by heavy U.S. bombing prior to its liberation by Filipino guerrillas in 1945. The cathedral has since been restored, but unfortunately without imagination. Red brick was a major local product, used to build many regional churches, and the ruins of the old horno (kiln) are on the town's edge.

Tuguegarao is situated on the inside of a large bend in the meandering Cagayan River. The commercial area is spread around the large market, while the Provincial Capitol complex is a few kilometers out. This complex contains the excellent Cagayan Provincial Museum, whose distinguished collection covers a vast period of history: fossilized teeth and bones of elephants, rhinoceros, and stegodons that roamed the valley half a million years ago; ancient flaked stone tools; 4,000-year-old pottery and jewelry found near Lal-lo; porcelain tradeware unearthed from Ybanag burial sites; colonial altars, vestments, and other religious artifacts; and antique furnishings.

Accommodations

The lodging houses and hotels are pretty standard here. Stay at **LB Lodging House** on Luna St., **Olympia Hotel** on Washington St., **Georgies Inn** on Aguinaldo St., **Pensione Abraham** on Bonifacio Street. These rooms range in price P150-200. The best hotel in Tuguegarao is the **Hotel Delfino** on Gonzaga St., next to the market. Rooms are P200-300.

For food, try the restaurant at the Hotel Delfino or at Georgie's Inn. There is also a large eatery near the Pantranco Bus Terminal called the **Apollo Restaurant.**

Transportation

PAL flies to Manila daily (75 minutes) and twice weekly to Basco, Batanes (65 minutes). It costs P20 by tricycle to the airport, which is four km out of town. Pantranco North and PNR Bus have several departures daily to and from Manila (483 km, 11 hours), including overnight trips.

To Baguio (471 km, 11 hours, via Nueva Ecija), take Pantranco at 0600 or 0800, or Greenland Bus at 0630 or 0730. To Bontoc (342 km, nine hours) via Banaue (292 km, six and a half hours), take the Immanuel/Lizardo bus at 0500.

Regular buses and jeepneys leave for Tabuk (65 km, two hours).

To Aparri (113 km, two and a half hours), there are frequent buses and minibuses. Regular buses travel to Claveria (190 km, five hours). To Laoag (316 km, nine and a half hours), be ready for morning departures (sit on the right-hand side).

VICINITY OF TUGUEGARAO

Callao Caves National Park

These limestone caves southeast of Tuguegarao are reached via Penablanca, from where a track leads nine km to Callao. The caves are across the Pinakanawan River and are also accessible by boat in season. The cave system, which follows the river for some kilometers, is said to have about 100 chambers, only seven of which have been explored. Each of these has its own distinct character. The name derives from the *kalaw,* a red-billed hornbill whose gaping beak is said to resemble the caves' entrance. The caves were once the haunt of these birds, and some white bats, but tourism has apparently driven them away. Numerous birds still roost here, however.

A steep flight of 206 steps leads from the riverbank, up a cliff face, to the first chamber, which contains an amphitheater. A natural skylight in its domed roof illuminates an underground chapel 30 meters below, where a stone altar, pews, and a replica of the Lourdes grotto have been set up. The other large caverns have stalactites, stalagmites, and different colored and textured walls. They are ventilated by occasional sinkholes in the roof.

Visitors can stay overnight in some cottages close to the caves. The **Callao Cave Youth Hostel** in Penablanca charges P100 pp. Meals are provided. Upstream is thick forest, a lot of butterflies, and a local phenomenon known as *maroran,* a continual spray that's believed to seep up through crevices in the riverbank from a subterranean stream.

West of Tuguegarao

Enrile, a few kilometers southwest, has a notable church. To the northwest is the lower Chico River Valley. Tuao, about 55 km from Tuguegarao, is a 17th-century mission town with an old church and the ruins of a fort. From Tuao, roads lead northwest to Kabugao and south to Tabuk in Kalinga-Apayao.

Nearby is another 17th-century mission town, Piat, whose church contains the Shrine of Nuestra Señora de Visitacion, a notable pilgrimage site. Many miracles have been attributed to the icon, which was brought by Augustinian friars from Macau via Nueva Segovia (Lal-lo) to aid in the conversion of the hostile Itawes tribe. Sugar is grown around Piat. To the northwest, Malaueg has a photogenic church (1617) in a fine setting at the foot of the Cordillera.

NORTH TO APARRI

The highway follows the right bank of the Cagayan River, passing through Iguig (founded 1607), whose church and convent date from 1787. On an 11-hectare site called "Calvary," groups of life-sized concrete statues have been created to depict the stations of the Cross. Farther north at Baybayog, a road leads nine km east to Baggao. Beyond, it's a 10-km hike from San Jose to a hot spring. Back on the highway, Alcala has a massive and distinctive brick church. In the vicinity of Gattaran are Mapaso Hot Springs and the impressive triple Tanlagan Waterfall.

The 76-square-km **Magapit Game Refuge and Bird Sanctuary** will appeal to birdwatchers. Lal-lo, site of former regional capital Nueva Segovia, has an old church, the Tabacalera ruins, and the first suspension bridge over the Cagayan River. Archaeological excavations indicate that this area has been inhabited for thousands of years.

Camalaniugan

Camalaniugan is a small town at the junction of the road to San Vicente. Stay at **Yabes Hotel.** A ruined colonial church and the Santa Maria Bell, reputedly the oldest in the Philippines, are just outside town. You can catch a bus here to San Vicente. Alilino junction, where the road to Ilocos Norte begins at a new suspension bridge across the Cagayan River, is about 2.5 km north of town and eight km south of Aparri.

APARRI

This fishing and trading port and oil depot at the mouth of the Cagayan River is the main settlement on Luzon's north coast. Some of the valley's timber and farm produce are shipped out from here. Small vessels moor close to town on a small tributary off the main river. A ferry crosses the 1.5-km river mouth, and boats go out to Calayan and Camiguin (Babuyan Islands), subject to weather conditions.

Aparri is noted for *bagoong* (shrimp sauce) and has a beach, sand dunes just east of town, and surf.

Accommodations

Stay at: **Dreamland Lodge** (P100-150); **Victoria Hotel,** on De Riviera St. (P150-200); or **Pipo Hotel,** at 37 Macanaya District (P100-150). Dreamland Hotel has a fairly decent restaurant, plus the usual street stalls serving *ihaw ihaw* and other delights.

Transportation

Pantranco North and PNR Bus have several departures daily to and from Manila (596 km, 13 hours), including overnight trips. To Tuguegarao (113 km, two and a half hours) there are frequent buses and minibuses. To San Vicente (78 km, two hours) there is a morning bus.

Regular departures leave for Claveria (96 km, three and a half hours). To Laoag (220 km, eight hours) there are morning departures. An 0500 bus goes to Vigan (300 km, 10 hours). The coast road to Ilocos offers spectacular views; sit on the right-hand side.

TO CAPE ENGAÑO

San Vicente

The 68-km road from Camalaniugan bypasses Buguey. Situated four km off the road, it was the first Spanish settlement on this stretch of coast. Old inhabitants still play 19th-century wooden harps.

San Vicente is a small port at the northeastern tip of the mainland; the crew of the morning bus from Aparri takes lunch here and starts back about 1300. In San Vicente you can charter a *banca* to Cape Engaño or arrange passage on a cargo/passenger launch down Cagayan's Pacific shores. These launches wait here while residents of remote coastal settlements take a bus into Aparri for supplies. Travelers taking this coastal route should have an open-ended timetable, since you may have to wait days for an onward or return trip. It's still an undeveloped, largely unexplored region; a previously unknown tribe, the Jonggo, was discovered in 1978.

There is excellent game-fishing off San Vicente, and the Philippine Game Fishing Association regularly holds fishing expeditions and tournaments here.

Cape Engaño

The name means "Cape of Enchantment," and it's apt. This is an outstandingly beautiful place, with a picturesque old Spanish lighthouse on a windswept headland, high above a gorgeous bay with white sand and coral. The U.S. fleet in 1944 defeated a Japanese force east of here in a major action, part of the Battle for Leyte Gulf. The cape can only be reached in good weather by chartered *banca* (one hour one-way), so it remains undeveloped and seldom visited.

Once here, there's not much to do except enjoy nature, but you can stay in the lighthouse for a few days (take food and drink to share with the keepers) and arrange for the boatman to return to pick you up. The cape is actually on Palaui Island (26 square km). On the east side is a settlement of Dumagats (Negritos), administered by a Filipino church group. It's possible to overnight in the school.

TO CLAVERIA

The road through Cagayan's panhandle heads west across the river from Alilino junction, between Camalaniugan and Aparri. Those seeking a quiet retreat might make for Ballesteros, a coastal town seven km north of the highway or eight km from the ferry landing opposite Aparri.

Stay in the clean, pleasant **Shielda Guest House,** with very good food at P100 per meal; it's opposite the movie theater at the west end of town.

Farther west, the towns of Abulug and Pamplona are surrounded by swampy shorelines where the abundant nipa palm is the basis of mat-weaving and wine- and vinegar-making. The Abulug River is the site of a large irrigation and flood-control project. Pamplona church is noted for its friezes, while bamboo handicrafts and reed baskets are good buys in Sanchez Mira; both of these towns have good swimming beaches.

Claveria

Claveria is surrounded by beautiful coastal scenery, with cliffs, several beaches (including one called Waikiki), plus the offshore islets of Punta Lakay-Lakay and Baket-Baket ("Old Man" and "Old Woman"). *Layaw* (nipa wine) is a popular drink in this area. Boats sail from here to some of the Babuyan Islands, weather permitting. Regular buses link Claveria with Laoag (126 km, four and a half hours), Aparri (96 km, three and a half hours), and Tuguegarao (190 km, five hours).

The cottages at Claveria were destroyed in a typhoon in 1987, but you can still stay at the home of the former owner of Sun Beach Cottages. This family also runs the Grassroots Restaurants in Claveria. You can also try the **Traveller's Inn** between Claveria and Taggat, for P50.

Taggat

This is a "company town," situated around the bay about three km west of Claveria. Taggat Industries is a logging and wood-processing corporation that employs nearly 3,000 people. In addition to the sawmill and timber complex, there's a technical institute, employee housing, hotels, a bar, wharf, landing strip, and a private 100-man security force, complete with armored cars and automatic weapons. Visitors can stay at the **Company House** or the **Public House,** which are next door to each other and cost about P50-75.

THE BABUYAN ISLANDS

This scattered volcanic group, mentioned in the chronicles of early Chinese traders, consists of five main islands—Babuyan (72 square km), Calayan (189 square km), Camiguin (164 square km), Dalupiri (62 square km), and Fuga (92 square km)—and 19 uninhabited islets. They're separated from Luzon by the turbulent 40-km-wide Babuyan Channel.

The Islands

The highest island is Babuyan, which has an active volcano with twin cones: Babuyan Claro (1,088 meters), which last erupted in 1919, and Smith volcano (670 meters), active before 1925. Camiguin volcano, also active, rises to 793 meters; Calayan Island reaches 543 meters; while Dalupiri and Fuga are considerably lower. Didicas Island (244 meters), east of Camiguin, was formerly shown on maps as Didicas Rocks, until, in 1952, a submarine volcano erupted to form the island; it last erupted in 1969. Evidence of a pre-Hispanic jar-burial tradition has been found in the Babuyans. It's believed the custom was introduced from China and Japan. The burial jars discovered here have another jar for a cover, similar to a type found in Japan, and were placed in stone cairns.

Today, these rugged islands remain undeveloped, with a self-sufficiency bred of isolation. Typhoons frequently sweep through, especially July-October. Arable land is limited, and populations are small. Many people have migrated to the Cagayan Valley, and cultural ties to the mainland are strong. The prevalence of strong winds necessitates sturdily built houses and makes root crops like *kamote* the staple, rather than rice or corn. Cattle, pigs, and goats are raised, while offshore, the Babuyan Channel is a rich fishing ground. Most settlements are fishing villages, with racks for drying and preserving the catch.

Transportation

Claveria and Aparri are the gateways to the Babuyans, but there are no fixed schedules and

the weather is always a factor. The islands can be isolated for long periods during bad weather, so it's wise to have a flexible timetable. A boat sails about once weekly from Claveria to Calayan, the main settlement and municipal center (takes five hours). From Calayan, it's another four hours to Babuyan Island, and there are also boats from Camiguin to Babuyan.

The people of Camiguin come into Aparri for supplies and it's possible to return with them. *Bancas* cross frequently March-June. July-Feb., bigger boats are used, but they may make the trip only twice a month or so, depending on the weather.

The trip to Camiguin takes five to six hours. For information on departures, inquire at the Tienda Kailian Supermarket in Aparri. Few travelers come here; on any island, contact the mayor or *barangay* captain to arrange accommodations. Take food and/or a gift for your hosts.

Fuga Island

Situated about two and a half hours by boat from Claveria, Fuga, which is a raised coral terrace, has a cattle ranch, airstrip, an old church, and pink coral beaches. Local delicacies include wild honey and plentiful crayfish. Fuga offers good scuba diving, but prevailing weather limits the season to April and May, and even then, strong currents and heavy swells make it no place for the novice.

It's a place to see big fish—marlin, sailfish, and hammerhead sharks—rather than enjoy coral and reef fish. Needless to say, sportfishing in this area is outstanding. The island is privately owned by Mr. Alfonso Lim, who also owns Taggat Industries near Claveria. Apply to him or his manager at the timber complex to obtain a permit to visit Fuga.

Mt. Mayon and Cagsawa Ruins

SOUTHERN LUZON

Bicol comprises five provinces that make up southern Luzon and its offshore islands: Camarines Norte, Camarines Sur, Albay, Sorsogon, Catanduanes. Also known as Bicolandia or Kabikolan, it's noted for volcanoes and spicy food. Its symbols are Mayon volcano, the world's most perfect volcanic cone, and the Virgin of Penafrancia, whose shrine is in Naga City. Naga is the commercial center while Legaspi City is the prime tourist spot.

Bicol has much to offer the traveler. Mayon volcano is stunning by any standards and is supplemented by beaches, caves, and unique handicrafts. There is also a piquant style of cooking, much loved by many Filipinos. Local dishes, e.g., *pinangat,* are cooked in coconut milk and flavored with a small, fiery chile pepper. A delicious local specialty, *pili* nuts, known as Philippine almonds, and *pili* nut candy are sold in markets and shops throughout the Bicol Peninsula. If you plan to make a return visit to a Filipino family, a jar of this delicacy will be well received.

History

The region has been inhabited since ancient times, as evidenced by archaeological finds, es-

timated to be over 2,000 years old, in a series of caves around Albay Gulf. Known as Ibalon, the region was already well populated when the Spaniards, attracted by reports of gold in Paracale, arrived to find peaceful people whose hospitality they repaid with oppression and extortion. Colonization began early here, and Spanish influence was great, especially on the Bicol Plain. The Spaniards first explored the region in 1569 and returned in 1573 to establish settlements in Libon and Naga.

The Bicolanos

Topographically, economically, culturally, and linguistically, Bicol is a remarkably homogeneous region. The Bicolanos, who, like other lowland Filipinos, are of Malay descent, form a unique ethnolinguistic group whose culture and language form bridges between those of the Tagalogs and the Visayans. The Bicol dialect is the mother tongue of over 90% of the region's inhabitants. The Bicolanos' strong cultural identity has been fostered by Bicol's traditional isolation from its neighboring regions due to the difficulty of traversing the narrow hilly isthmus that connects it to the rest of Luzon, and by the

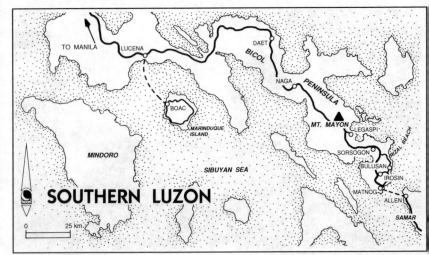

unpredictability of sea travel during the typhoon season.

Transportation

Legaspi City is the focal point for exploring the region. PAL flies to Legaspi from Manila and Cebu, and also Manila-Naga-Virac (Catanduanes). The main highway from Manila to Mindanao passes through the peninsula, ending at Matnog (the ferry terminal for Samar). The entire route from Manila to Matnog takes about 17 hours.

A great majority of Filipinos travel on overnight buses from Manila. It's a long journey south through the Bicol along small, two-lane roads. A road also branches to Bulan, the port for Masbate. Transportation on the only highway in southern Luzon is frequent, with a steady stream of buses traveling to and from Manila.

You might also consider the funky railroad that goes from Manila down to Naga City. Although nothing spectacular, it's perhaps as comfortable as an overnight bus and gives you the chance to experience the only rail service in the country.

While most of the region's offshore islands have daily connections to the mainland, sea links with other parts of the Philippines are minimal.

QUEZON PROVINCE

This long narrow province sits astride the main southern highway linking Manila with Bicol. Most travelers pass through Lucena City en route to Marinduque or Romblon, or go to Lucban, Sariaya, and Tayabas to attend the Pahiyas harvest festival held on 15 May. The province's extremities—the Sierra Madre stretching north through Infanta, the beautiful Polillo Islands, and the Bondoc Peninsula—remain undeveloped and rarely visited.

History

Chinese traders visited Polillo Island in pre-Hispanic times. The shores of Tayabas Bay were well settled when Juan de Salcedo passed through the area in 1571 en route to Paracale (Camarines Norte). The province, created in 1591, was first called Kalilaya, then Tayabas, and was renamed after President Manuel L. Quezon in 1946. Through the centuries, coastal communities suffered heavily at the hands of Muslim raiders. In 1841, Hermano Pule, whose nom de guerre was Apolinario de la Cruz, led the Cofradia de San Jose revolt in Tayabas.

A pious man who embodied native religious aspirations and disappointments, he was among the first Filipino freedom fighters to advocate racial and religious reforms. After being denied entry to a monastic order on racial grounds, he defied authority and founded his own religious society. It rapidly gained adherents throughout the southern Tagalog area and was banned by the suspicious Spanish authorities. Brother Apolinario was proclaimed "King of the Tagalogs" and preached their deliverance from slavery. Several thousand members of the brotherhood, aided by hilltribesmen, rose in armed rebellion around the town of Tayabas, but they were defeated by a force of Spanish and Pampangan soldiers. Brother Apolinario was betrayed, captured, and executed, while survivors fled to the slopes of Mt. Banahaw and Mt. San Cristobal.

Tayabas joined the revolution in 1898; General Malvar was active here against both Spain and the United States. At the outbreak of WW II, the Japanese invaded Lamon Bay, making simultaneous landings at Mauban, Siain, and Atimonan, which, together with the Lingayen Gulf landing, formed a pincer movement that closed in on Manila.

Transportation

The focal point is Lucena City, which is served from Manila by regular BLTB (every 20 minutes 0500-2000) and Pantranco South buses; it takes three to four hours. Pantranco buses also pass on the hour en route from Legaspi City to Manila and vice versa.

Minibuses link Lucena with Daet (Camarines Norte), another eight hours away along rough roads; larger buses tend to be more comfortable and less bumpy. Quezon's only main highway crosses the central part of the province from Laguna to Camarines Norte, off-roads from around Quezon are generally poor. Jeepneys and minibuses fan out from Lucena to the province's towns.

Buses connect Lucena and Pagsanjan, but it's usually quicker to take jeepneys via Lucban. Jeepneys operate on the Batangas City-Tiaong and San Juan-Candelaria roads. The southbound railway from Manila roughly parallels the highway until it cuts off through Tagkawayan into Camarines Sur. Quezon's northern spur has few roads, and coastal boats operate on an irregular basis. Infanta is reached by road from Siniloan (Laguna) and Manila. Cotta, Lucena City's port, has regular boats to Marinduque and Romblon.

LAGUNA TO LUCENA CITY

The main southbound highway from Manila through San Pablo to Lucena is supplemented by country roads through Dolores to Candelaria and from Pagsanjan through Lucban and Tayabas to Lucena. Tiaong, on the main highway, lies in an area noted for its luscious *lanzones,* a sweet tropical fruit, in season in September. North of town, at the boundary with Laguna, is Villa Escudero, a long-established coconut plantation, which also contains a fascinating museum and fine resort.

A road leads north from Tiaong to Dolores. This old country town lies at the foot of Mt. San Cristobal and is also the starting point for climbing Mt. Banahaw by the recommended western route.

The Feast of Our Lady of Sorrows is marked by an evening procession on 28 February, while on Good Friday, devotees participate in the procession that traces Christ's supposed ascent of Mt. Banahaw from Dolores to Calvary at the summit.

Sariaya

The main highway passes through Candelaria, site of a coconut by-products factory, to the old trading town of Sariaya, which has some colonial houses in the narrow streets around the church, originally built 1599; the present structure (1748) contains some fine old santos.

Sariaya is a recognized source of antiques from the homes of Quezon's plantation-owning aristocracy; the **Sina-Una Antique Shop** across from the market has a solid reputation. Sariaya is also a good place to buy rattan items, and traditional local foods such as *pinagong* (turtle-shaped bread), pastries, and fruit candies. Houses and streets are decorated with bamboo, farm produce, and local

CARL PARKES

edible houses at Pahiyas Festival

delicacies for the colorful Pahiyas harvest festival on 15 May.

About five km west of Sariaya, a road leads 10 km off the highway to Guisguis (Guishuis) Beach. Here, you can stay at either the **Paraiso Beach Resort,** where cottages run P300-500, or **Dalampasigan Beach Resort,** where huts cost P250-450.

Lucban

Founded as a Franciscan mission in 1577, Lucban has numerous colonial houses and is noted for its potent local *lambanog.* The current church, fronted by a shady plaza, dates from 1639, but it was damaged by fire in 1733 and U.S. bombs in 1945. Mount Banahaw can be climbed by its northeast side from here.

Pahiyas: Most of the time, Lucban is a quiet old country town, resting in Banahaw's cool, damp shadow, but during its fiestas, it comes alive. Try to be here on 15 May for the Pahiyas. Of the towns that observe this fiesta, Lucban probably offers the most spectacular event. Townsfolk celebrate this harvest festival by decorating their doorways and windows with brilliantly colored *kiping* (dyed, dried rice wafers shaped like cacao leaves), fruit, vegetables, native sweets, straw dummies, coconut fronds, and symbols of family businesses. Walk around town to enjoy the decorations before proceedings get underway. A thanksgiving service to San Isidro Labrador is followed by revelry.

A midafternoon procession winds through the narrow streets, and as soon as the saint's image has passed, homeowners throw the produce decorating their houses to the scrambling crowd. Lucban also holds Gigantes Festivals on the last Friday in June (fiesta in honor of the Sacred Heart of Jesus) and at the 19 August town fiesta. They feature parades of gaily painted papier-mâché giants mounted on bamboo frames. The people inside them may be fulfilling a vow to San Isidro. During Pahiyas, the price for accommodation doubles, so it's necessary to book at least two months ahead.

From Manila, take a bus to Lucena, then a jeepney; there's also direct transportation from Pagsanjan (Laguna).

Mauban

This fishing and market town on the Pacific coast can be reached from Lucban or Lucena (35 km). Its church was founded 1647, rebuilt 1891. Boats go out to offshore islands such as Cabalete and Jomalig.

Tayabas

Once the provincial capital, now a quiet country town with an old church, Tayabas also observes the Pahiyas festival on 15 May. Nearby are Mainit hot springs, open 0700-1700, and May-it mineral springs. You can overnight at the springs by staying at the **Tayabas Spring Resort,** where there are huts and cottages for P175-400. A restaurant and mineral pools available, and it's five minutes from the *poblacion* of Tayabas.

LUCENA CITY

The provincial capital, commercial center, and gateway to Marinduque and Romblon, Lucena (city fiesta: 30 May, pop. 120,000) is situated on the main southbound highway, 136 km and three hours from Manila. It was founded in the late 16th century as Buenavista, renamed Oroquieta, and finally Lucena after an Andalusian town. There isn't much to see here: the domed cathedral (1887) has trompe l'oeil paintings inside; Perez Park, near the Capitol, is a popular local meeting place; and there are copra-processing plants.

Dalahican Beach, five km from downtown, is okay for watching the sunset, but for a day of swimming, it's better to go to the Pagbilao Islands.

Accommodations and Restaurants

The following cost P150-200 pp: **Amparo's Hotel, Suarez Lodge, Marco Polo Inn, Sunrise Lodging House, Traveler's Inn** (all near the BLTB terminal); **Tourist Hotel and Restaurant** (in Iyam); **New Skyview Lodge, Mar-mont City Lodge,** and **Viscount Hotel** (all in central); and **Halina Hotel** on Gomez Street, near the city center. More expensive are: **Lucena Fresh Air Resort,** P250-300 pp, Isabang district with swimming pool, garden, and restaurant (P50-150); and **Travel Lodge,** starting at P250, swimming pool, in Iyam.

Among downtown restaurants, **City Kitchenette** serves tasty noodle dishes; **Casa Arias Garden Restaurant** or the coffee shop at the **Marco Polo Inn** is good.

Cotta

Frequent jeepneys link Lucena (three km) with this river port situated about two km from the sea. Cotta means fort and refers to a former defense against Moro raiders. It's possible to stay here in the house of the Cueto family, near the pier; it's simple, clean, and very convenient when catching an early boat. Boats sail daily 0600-1000 to Balanacan and Buyabod (Santa Cruz), as well as Marinduque (takes four hours). Romblon is an eight- to nine-hour overnight trip. Check current schedules with **Viva Shipping** in Manila.

THE SOUTH COAST

The Pagbilao Islands

Pagbilao Grande and Pagbilao Chico are a lovely pair of islands in Tayabas Bay. They're joined by a sandy isthmus about 500 meters long, 200 meters wide, about three meters above sea level at its highest point. The residents call it Pulo Is-

land. The main settlement, situated at the connecting isthmus is Tulaybuhangin ("Sand Bridge"). These hilly islands are an ancient and still-developing coral rock formation, with numerous coves, caves, and cliffs.

Bansilan Cave is of cathedral-like dimensions. The vegetation is wild, with patches of forest and some giant yucca plants. The islands are surrounded by numerous islets with sparkling white coral sand. You can hire a *banca* to visit some of them; take drinking water. Swimming and snorkeling are excellent.

Estamper Point is a cave and lookout point on the peak of Pagbilao Chico. A **Japanese Memorial Garden** commemorates the hundreds of servicemen who committed suicide by jumping to avoid capture by the Americans at the end of WW II. On 15 May, the Fiesta of San Isidro, the saint's image is carried in a water parade around the islands. Boat races and skin diving and spearfishing contests are also held.

The Pagbilao Islands are generally visited as a day trip but deserve a longer stay. Ask at the mayor's office whether any residents have rooms for rent. The islands are also a great place to camp.

Places to stay on the nearby mainland include a small hotel in **Sitio Basiao** near Padre Burgos and **Cala de Oro Beach Resort,** four km from Pagbilao town; rooms are P150-200. *Bancas* cross regularly from Padre Burgos, a small fishing town in an attractive setting; alight from any southbound bus at Km 59 on the main highway in Malicboy and wait for a jeepney down the rough 11-km road through rice fields to the town. The boat trip takes 15 minutes; on the way, notice the islets of Talabaan Munti ("Little Oyster") and Talabaan Malake ("Big Oyster") with their rock formations and beaches. The crossing from Pagbilao town to the islands isn't recommended since it takes 45 minutes and may be hindered by low tides in the river and strong currents in the bay.

The Bondoc Peninsula

The terrain consists of narrow, discontinuous coastal plains, with wooded hills rising to 413 meters in the interior. Upland rice is the main crop here. A road follows the shore of Mompog Pass, past Padre Burgos and Agdangan, site of Salvacion Beach, General Luna, to Mulanay, then crosses to San Narciso. Beautiful Alibijaban, a tiny, seldom visited island with white-sand beaches in Ragay Gulf can be reached by *banca* from San Andres. Makibaka, a feminist women's leftist guerrilla group founded in 1971, is active in the hills behind General Luna.

QUEZON NATIONAL PARK

The main southbound highway winds across the narrow neck of Luzon between Pagbilao and Atimonan, providing numerous panoramic views. It's worth stopping off at this 10-square-km park, about 30 km east of Lucena, to enjoy a hike through its unspoiled rainforest. Alight from the bus where the road forks, about five km east of the turnoff to Padre Burgos.

Here the old road climbs right into the park, while the highway bypasses it. Walk or try to hitch about four km to where a path begins on the left, about 350 meters before the parking lot. From this point, it takes about 90 minutes to hike to Pinagbanderahan ("Flag Pole") at the summit of Mt. Mirador (366 meters). The trail is easy to follow and not too strenuous, though it may be necessary to scramble over a fallen tree or two, and it can be slippery after rain.

Superb vegetation, teeming with parrots, monkeys, lizards, and other wildlife, surrounds caves, limestone formations, and a waterfall. At the top, it's pleasantly cool, with a spectacular view to both coastlines. Camping is allowed at **Camp Trining** at the park entrance; bring food. The old road continues beyond the parking lot, where a small store sells drinks, meeting the highway again west of Atimonan. To continue a southbound journey toward Legaspi, take a minibus to Atimonan and pick up a larger bus there.

THE PACIFIC COAST

Lamon Bay

The highway descends to the Pacific coast at Atimonan and follows the shores of Lamon Bay amid coconut and rice farms. Copra is shipped from several small ports. The offshore islands boast some classy resorts. Lamon Bay offers good diving. Atimonan is a regional trading center, served by its outport, Siain.

The Dutch burned Atimonan Church in 1640. A restored watchtower, known locally as Iskong Bantay, is the only one remaining of seven built in 1752 to guard against pirate raids.

Accommodations here include **Victoria Beach Resort** on the Maharlika Highway at Atimonan with rooms from P150 with fan and P200-300 with a/c. Beyond Atimonan is Plaridel, where copra is loaded onto oceangoing vessels, and Gumaca, a fishing town, where you can stay at **Rosarian Pension House** or **Pinky's Lodge and Restaurant.**

Lopez is also a trading center with an outport, Hondagua. The highway and railway split after Calauag, a sawmill town. The rail line continues to Tagkawayan, from where anglers can go sportfishing in Ragay Gulf.

Lying just offshore in Lamon Bay is the narrow, 24-km-long Alabat Island. It's well settled, with three towns: Perez, Alabat, and Quezon. The upscale **Ponce's Pacifica Resort** at Perez has scuba facilities and offers both reef- and wall-diving; dive packages are available.

Farther out is **Balesin Island Country Club,** an exclusive beach resort whose facilities include scuba, sailing, water-skiing, a five-hole golf course, tennis, and horseback riding. Most guests arrive by air (45 minutes from Manila), arranged through one of the Manila tour companies. Rates are high, ranging US$60-75 per night.

Infanta

Situated on a small plain on the Pacific coast, this port is the gateway to the Polillo Islands. It's reached by a road from Siniloan (Laguna), the last section of which runs close to the ocean. Infanta's location in the lee of Polillo Island affords some protection from Pacific storms. Some rice is grown around the town, while copra and lumber are shipped from nearby Real. Sportfishers can charter boats from Infanta to chase marlin, sailfish, and swordfish.

Just north of Infanta is General Nakar, which are Dumagat settlements. Infanta's steady postwar expansion is expected to accelerate. Due to its relative proximity to Metro Manila (104 km from suburban Marikina), Infanta and its surrounding area are earmarked to absorb some of the metropolis's overload. The blueprint for development includes designating parks and wildlife preserves, creating fishponds out of the shoreline mangrove swamps, expanding the port to receive international vessels, and reforestation.

Stay at **Sumilang Hotel, Miramonte Hotel, Silangan Hotel,** or **Ionas Hotel,** where rooms run P200-250.

The Polillo Islands

The Polillo Islands are beautiful, with fine beaches. The group consists of Polillo Island (605 square km); Palasan (15 square km); Patnanongan (87 square km), near which is Minasawa Island, a small (four hectares) game refuge and bird sanctuary; Jomalig (52 square km), ringed by white-sand beaches; plus about 16 other islets. Sitting on a submarine platform, the islands are surrounded by shallow waters, with extensive mangrove forests and coral reefs.

Patnanongan's reefs, especially, offer great diving for those who can bring equipment here. Much of the underwater area remains unexplored. Sharks are plentiful, especially white tips and hammerheads, and whale sharks are occasionally seen, too. It's also a good place for shells. Diving is best April-October. Once the typhoon season (June-Oct.) has begun, all visitors to Polillo must keep a wary eye on the weather.

The inhabitants are Tagalogs; some Dumagats live in the north of Polillo Island. Polillo Island has coal deposits, and logs and firewood are shipped from Polillo and Casiguran to Hondagua, then taken by rail to Manila. These lightly populated islands have remained relatively isolated, although regular boats cross the Polillo Strait between Infanta and Polillo Harbor; it takes 90 minutes. Jomalig's main settlement, Casiguran, can be reached by boat from Mauban.

CAMARINES NORTE PROVINCE

Camarines Norte is the gateway from the Tagalog region to the Bicol Peninsula. All bus travelers between Manila and Legaspi pass through this small province, but few stay. It's lush and scenic, with some good beaches, but it lacks the resort facilities and outstanding attractions that induce people to stop over.

Daet, the provincial capital, isn't special. In fact, the best base for exploring the eastern end of the province is Siruma in Camarines Sur. There is limited accommodation there at **Takal Beach Resort,** P200.

History

Camarines Norte has been associated with the dream of gold since historical records began in 1571. Miguel Lopez de Legazpi dispatched Juan de Salcedo, who had just subdued the Laguna de Bay area, to confirm stories of gold deposits. He visited Mambulao (now Jose Panganiban) and Paracale. The Spaniards proceeded to colonize Bicol; this area was called Ambos Camarines (both Camarines) until the 19th century, when it was divided into two provinces.

At the outbreak of WW II, the young Governor Wenceslao Vinzons organized a guerrilla army that valiantly resisted the Japanese and, at one point, briefly recaptured Daet. Vinzons was captured and executed with his wife and children. After WW II, the province's population grew rapidly as people moved in from neighboring areas seeking work.

Transportation

The only main road is the South Highway linking Manila and Legaspi. Daet is the route center (351 km, eight to nine hours from Manila and 185 km, five hours from Legaspi). Philtranco, Inland Trailways, Sunshine, and Sarkies buses have several trips a day from Manila, while minibuses link Daet with nearer cities, such as Lucena and Naga.

Seasoned travelers to Bicol from Manila often take a night bus that cruises straight through Daet, making the long trip in 15 hours. Off-highway roads are generally poor. On most days, *bancas* cross the mouth of San Miguel Bay between Mercedes and Siruma (Camarines Sur) and also connect Mercedes with offshore islands.

QUEZON TO DAET

This 88-km stretch of highway winds through hills devoted to timber, coconuts, and *kaingin* farming. Side roads lead to coastal settlements.

Capalonga, site of the **Shrine of the Black Nazarene,** has waterfalls in Itok. Jose Panganiban has high-grade iron ore deposits; the main mine is at Larap, which has both shaft and open-pit operations only a short distance from the shore. Larap is a company town, with its own hospital and store. The area's small independent mines sell their ore to Larap, from where it's taken by rail to the wharf on nearby Calambayanga Island.

Jose Panganiban is also a lumber town, and you can swim at Pag-asa Beach. The old gold-mining center of Paracale has a youth hostel. The Spaniards worked the gold-bearing gravel in its rivers and streams, while the Americans set up huge dredges and mined primary lode deposits, but a 1952 disaster, in which a tunnel collapsed, killing 56 miners, ended large-scale gold mining here. The mines are, in any case, virtually exhausted, with only small operations persisting. Nevertheless, the dream remains and locals pan for gold around Paracale and Labo. Filipinos still regard Paracale as a good place to buy gold.

The highway descends to Labo, south of which is the Tulay na Lupa Reservoir, and continues through Talisay, which has Pulang Data Beach in San Jose. The Kanapnap Waterfalls are near San Vicente, southwest of Talisay.

DAET AND VICINITY

Daet (pronounced "duh-ET") is the provincial capital and a trading center of about 55,000, situated on a fertile plain. The first Rizal monument in the Philippines was erected here in 1898.

Daet has a lively market, and there's a bank.

Bagasbas Beach, a four-km tricycle ride, is the best mainland beach in the area. Daet is the gateway to Mercedes (seven km); frequent jeepneys load near the Karilagan Hotel. Also in Daet, the booking office for the Swagman Hotel's resort at Apuao Grande is located on J. Lukban Street. While most tourists book through Swagman Hotel Manila, you can get information and reservations at the office in Daet as well.

From the town of Mercedes, 10 km northeast of Daet, you can catch a *banca* for Apuao Island and stay at the resort or just roam the white beach there. PAL flies two times a week on Wednesday and Friday to Daet (40 minutes).

Accommodations
Most travelers only pass through Daet en route to San Miguel Bay or the Australian resort on Apuao Grande Island.

Karilagan Hotel: A clean and popular hotel in the center of Daet. 22 Moreno St., tel. (054) 721-2314, P150-750.

Apuao Grande Island Resort: An Australian-managed resort with clean and comfortable nipa bungalows facing a dazzling beach, a restaurant, a bar, and water sports such as windsurfing, Hobie Cat sailing, and jet-skiing. Rooms cost P250-700.

The island is reached from the town of Mercedes, but most visitors make reservations and transportation arrangements through Swagman Hotel in Ermita.

Restaurants
The **Mandarin Restaurant** serves good Chinese food, as does the **King's Tea and Noodles,** on Lukban Street, where the **New Grandeur Restaurant** is also located.

In the evening, the **Sampaguita Disco and Sing Along** on Pimentel Avenue offers dinner, beer, and live music, or try **Odeum II Disco** on Lukban Street. For cheap eats in a pleasant setting, try **Serrano's Snack House** on Vincents Avenue, near the market. Open 24 hours.

Mercedes
Mercedes is one of the most important and prosperous fishing ports in all Luzon. A lively early morning fish market is supplied by a fleet of large (20-meter-long) fishing boats called *basnig*. It's particularly active March-Sept., when the ocean horizon may be a mass of lights. Much of the catch is transported north to the Manila area.

Check along the wharf for boats returning to the Calaguas Islands, nearby Canimo Island, Canton Island (noted for its sea cave), and across San Miguel Bay to Siruma. Mineral springs at Lanot are a three-hour boat trip down the bay and can also be approached by hiring a boat from Barceloneta (Camarines Sur).

CAMARINES SUR PROVINCE

Camarines Sur's skyline is dominated by dramatic volcanoes. The base of this anvil-shaped province is crossed by the main north-south highway and the rail routes linking Manila with southern Luzon. Naga City is the focal point, but apart from its Penafrancia Festival (mid-September), one of the country's major fiestas, the city has few attractions. Iriga, with nearby Lake Buhi, is a more pleasant spot to break a journey. For most travelers, Takal Beach (Siruma) is the only place to warrant an extended stay. Stopovers at Iriga and Takal offer beaches, a lake, and volcano—the best the province has to offer.

History

The conquistadors arrived to find the Naga-Libmanan area well settled and prosperous. *Camarines* means *bodegas* (food warehouses) and probably derives from the many rice granaries the Spaniards found in the area. In 1573, Captain Pedro de Chavez founded Nueva Caceres, named after Caceres, Spain (later to become Naga City), already a thriving native settlement.

In 1595, a papal bull gave the Franciscans control of a diocese stretching from Masbate and Catanduanes up to what is now Quezon, and Naga became the center of religious activity throughout Bicol. The Penafrancia Festival is over 300 years old, and many early Spanish churches remain in Camarines Sur. During WW II, local Filipinos heroically resisted the Japanese, briefly recapturing Naga.

Transportation

PAL flies to Naga from Manila daily (one hour) and twice on Monday and Thursday. Flights from Manila to Virac depart daily and twice on Wednesday and Saturday, and PAL flies to Catanduanes (30 minutes) thrice weekly.

Camarines Sur lies directly on the main highway and railway linking Manila with the south. Several bus companies serve the province from Manila and also pass through on their way north from Albay, Samar, and Leyte. Frequent minibuses operate between Naga and Lucena, Iriga,

Legaspi, and Tabaco. Jeepneys also leave Tabaco in the morning for Tigaon, taking the scenic, coastal Hanging Road to Joroan; Tigaon-Naga transport is frequent.

Trains from Manila stop at Naga. Boats sail to offshore islands and isolated coastal communities.

There's a daily trip between Pasacao and San Pascual on Burias Island that has regular connections with Masbate. Boats sometimes cross from Cabcab (San Andres) on Catanduanes to Sabang. A pleasant and interesting route between Daet (Camarines Norte) and Naga is to sail across and down San Miguel Bay via Siruma.

FROM CAMARINES NORTE TO NAGA CITY

The provincial boundary lies within the Bicol Forest National Park (52 square km). It's 15 km to the timber town of Sipocot (stay at CMC Hotel), where the railway rejoins the highway after cutting across from Calauag (Quezon). From here, the Ragay Hills, highly eroded and covered with grass and second-growth woodland, stretch northwest to Quezon.

Two routes lead to Naga, one skirting San Miguel Bay, the other swinging south. Both bypass Libmanan, known as "the rice granary of Bicol." Ten km south of Sipocot, a sign indicates the turnoff for Libmanan Caves, also called Culapnitan Caves, a 19-hectare national park.

At the resthouse one km west of the highway, guides are available to show visitors the 19 limestone caves, which contain stalagmites and stalactites. Steps have been built into the hillside, but the caves are slippery during wet weather, so wear sturdy shoes; helmets are provided, and having your own flashlight is useful.

NAGA CITY

This bustling city of 110,000 is situated on the Bicol River a few kilometers inland from San Miguel Bay, in the shadow of Mt. Isarog. Surrounded by the rich ricelands of the Bicol Plain,

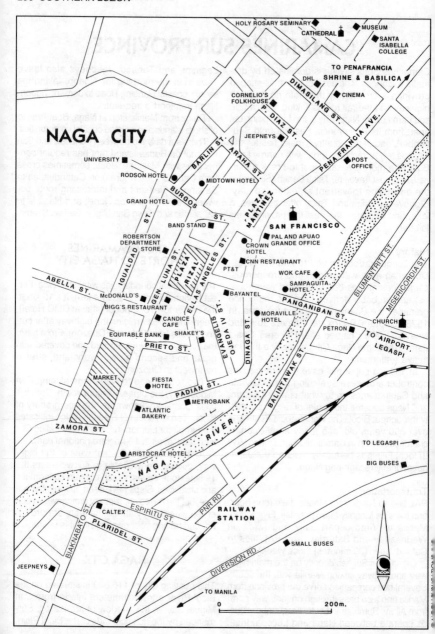

NAGA CITY

HOLY ROSARY SEMINARY
CATHEDRAL
MUSEUM
SANTA ISABELLA COLLEGE

TO PENAFRANCIA
SHRINE & BASILICA

DHL
CINEMA

DIMASILANG ST.

CORNELIO'S FOLKHOUSE

P. DIAZ ST.

JEEPNEYS

PENA FRANCIA AVE.

POST OFFICE

UNIVERSITY

BARLIN ST.

ARAÑA ST.

RODSON HOTEL

BURGOS ST.

MIDTOWN HOTEL

PLAZA MARTINEZ

GRAND HOTEL

BAND STAND

SAN FRANCISCO

IGUALDAD ST.

ROBERTSON DEPARTMENT STORE

GEN. LUNA ST.

PLAZA RIZAL

ELIAS ANGELES ST.

PAL AND APUAO GRANDE OFFICE

CROWN HOTEL

CNN RESTAURANT

PT&T

WOK CAFE

ABELLA ST.

McDONALD'S

BIGG'S RESTAURANT

BAYANTEL

PANGANIBAN ST.

SAMPAGUITA HOTEL

BLUMENTRITT ST.

MISERICORDIA ST.

CHURCH

CANDICE CAFE

SHAKEY'S

EVANGELIS ST.

OJEDA IV ST.

DINAGA ST.

MORAVILLE HOTEL

PETRON

TO AIRPORT, LEGASPI

EQUITABLE BANK

PRIETO ST.

MARKET

FIESTA HOTEL

PADIAN ST.

METROBANK

BALINTAWAK ST.

ATLANTIC BAKERY

ZAMORA ST.

NAGA RIVER

TO LEGASPI →

ARISTOCRAT HOTEL

BIG BUSES

BIAKNABATO ST.

PLARIDEL ST.

CALTEX

ESPIRITU ST.

PNR RD.

RAILWAY STATION

JEEPNEYS

SMALL BUSES

DIVERSION RD.

TO MANILA

0   200m.

MOON

THE PENAFRANCIA FESTIVAL

The Blessed Virgin of Penafrancia was long venerated in Salamanca, Spain, and a priest brought a replica of her image to Naga from Spain over 300 years ago. Miracles were attributed to it, and thousands of the faithful made pilgrimages to the riverside shrine. By 1655, the annual festival celebrated in the Virgin's honor was attracting more devotees than the shrine could handle, so it was decided to take the image to the bigger Naga Cathedral for her feast day.

This Translacion, the ritual transfer of the Virgin, still takes place: from the shrine to the cathedral on the second Saturday of September, and with more pomp and enthusiasm still, from the cathedral back to the shrine on the third Saturday. Both processions comprise, by tradition, all-male retinues; it's believed women would bring bad luck. Nevertheless, the festival has not been without tragedy. In the early '50s, and again in 1973, an overloaded bridge collapsed under the strain of fervent spectators. On the last occasion, 138 died.

Penafrancia features a novena (nine days of devotions). Many Bicolano expatriates make their annual visit home at this time. For a week, Naga is jumping. The cathedral is crowded as people attend masses and vigils, light candles, and line up to kiss the Virgin. Bars are busy. Events include cultural shows in the plaza, cockfights, sports, and a carnival.

The final Saturday, the feast day, begins with a penitential procession from the cathedral at 0330. Later in the morning, boat races take place on the river as the crowds gather on the banks, bridges, and balconies.

Fervor mounts as the grand fluvial procession is about to begin. At around noon, the Virgin's image is borne shoulder-high out of the cathedral. It inches its way through jam-packed streets, preceded by a brass band. Cries of "Viva la Virgen" mingle with the music. The statue eventually reaches Tabuco Bridge next to the market and is carried aboard the gaily decorated *casco* (a large, flat-bottomed barge with an ornate pagoda) that awaits it. The image sways crazily as the masses scramble to touch it, but they say it's never been tipped into the river. It's believed that those falling into the dirty water on this day won't get sick.

The spectacular fluvial procession travels upstream, past densely crowded banks and bridges, to the new Penafrancia Shrine. The barge is towed by dozens of small *bancas* and escorted by a host of other boats, including those carrying officials and newsmen. Only men are allowed on the boats, since it's feared that women would cause them to sink. Upon reaching the Penafrancia Bridge, the Virgin is carried back to her shrine where, following mass, the sacred image is placed for another year.

Naga is the region's principal urban center, transportation focal point, and commercial hub.

From its early colonial foundation, Naga disseminated the Spanish and Catholic influence to the surrounding region, thereby becoming Bicol's cultural, religious, and educational center. It contains the University of Nueva Caceres (UNC), which has a private museum, plus several colleges and seminaries.

The main points of interest are the cathedral, the old and new shrines of Our Lady of Penafrancia, and the huge market, which is a good place to buy *buri* and abaca handicrafts and *pili* nuts. Naga has a small port downriver from the market. During the Penafrancia Festival in September, the city teems with visitors, so it's best to look for a room a few days before the Saturday climax.

Naga is also the access point for Weinert's Guesthouse.

Churches and Shrines

San Francisco Church, originally built in 1578, is Naga's earliest church and one of Bicol's oldest. It became the base of Franciscan missionaries. A 1915 earthquake left only a corner tower standing, however, and the new building is undistinguished. The nearby **Plaza Quince Martires** contains a monument to 15 Bicolano martyrs executed by the Spanish in 1896 for seeking independence. Two years later, a one-day revolt led to the last Spanish provincial governor's surrender in the church. The original building of **Naga Cathedral** was founded in 1595 on the riverbank where the market now stands. It was ravaged by fire and earthquake before being rebuilt in the town center. The present Spanish-Romanesque structure, one of the largest churches in the country, was completed in 1843, suffered more earthquake and typhoon damage, and was restored in 1890.

The austere interior contains a Black Nazarene statue and some fine ecclesiastical silver in the sacristy. Next to the church is a 19th-century *convento*. The original **Shrine of Our Lady** of Penafrancia, known as the *ermita*, is an attractive, simple church constructed around 1753 to replace one built 40 years earlier; it was restored in 1876-77. The statue, which stood on the high altar's *retablo*, was solemnly crowned here in 1924. It's now housed a short distance away across the river in an imposing modern shrine, completed in 1982. Enjoy fine views of Mt. Isarog from the grounds. The devout climb steps behind the shrine's altar to kiss or touch the statue and pray. It's hard to explain the immense significance that this tiny statue of the Virgin, their patron saint, has for Bicolanos, who affectionately call her Ina ("Mother"). It was stolen in 1981, replaced by a replica, then reappeared in Manila in 1982 under mysterious, unexplained circumstances. To Bicolanos, its sudden disappearance was a traumatic event, its recovery an occasion for rejoicing.

Accommodations

Rodson Palace Inn: Budget option two blocks north of the town plaza. Burgos St., tel. (054) 739-828, P100-380.

Fiesta Hotel: Another simple place in the center of town near the central market. Caceres St., tel. (054) 811-1787, P150-400.

Grand Imperial Hotel: Naga's best hotel operated by the local tourist representative. Burgos St., tel. (054) 736-534, P650-900.

Weinert's Guesthouse Pacific: Seaside resort near Sagnay, northeast of Naga. Sagnay, tel. ((054) 454-7001, P400-1,200.

Transportation

Naga is the province's transportation hub, with planes, trains, and buses linking it to Manila and the rest of the Bicol. Bus and jeepney terminals are scattered around the city center. Regular Philtranco buses link Naga with Manila (449 km, 10 hours); a/c and deluxe express service is also available. Prime departure times from Manila are 0800-0900 and 1900-2145.

Frequent buses ply the Naga-Iriga-Legaspi route (98 km, two and a half hours). JB Liner offers express service, while minibuses and jeepneys fan out from Naga to provincial towns.

Northbound and southbound trains stop at the station across the river from downtown.

If you want to skip the chaos at the bus station, you can go to the main north-south road and catch a local Legaspi-bound bus there. Choice seats have to be grabbed at the bus station, however. If you are trying to get back to Manila, it is better to take a large, sturdy a/c bus from the main station.

Vicinity of Naga

Milaor, 3.5 km south of Naga, is noted for its church and *convento*, rebuilt on the site of an earlier structure by the Franciscans in 1740, but unfortunately now in a state of disrepair. The church contains an antique carved wooden confessional, and there are exterior carvings, too. The octagonal stone belfry, added in 1840, is connected to the church by a small archway bridge.

The town of Bombon, a few kilometers north of Naga, is noted for its leaning tower. Access to the 101-square-km Mount Isarog National Park is from Naga to Carolina. The slopes of this 1,976-meter volcano cover a vast base and contain ravines and the 13-meter Panicuasan (or Malabsay) Falls. Nabontolan Springs are in the grounds of the Parks and Wildlife Office.

In Carolina, on Isarog's flanks, visitors can swim at the **Carolina, Kayumanggi,** or **Penafrancia** resorts. Other places to swim near Naga are Inarihan Dam or the beach at Pasacao, 20 km south of Naga. Boats cross daily from this port on Ragay Gulf to San Pascual, Burias Island; you can visit **Caranan Beach Resort** while waiting for a boat. Room prices at the resorts range P250-300.

TAKAL BEACH

Takal beach makes a pleasant stopover between Daet and Naga, with nice views of the islands and villages of San Miguel Bay en route. Takal has one of the most congenial resorts in southern Luzon. Situated on a broad, sandy bay, it consists of a small group of **cottages**, P75-100 pp, clustered around a bar and restaurant. Hanns and Polly, a German/Filipina couple, have created a relaxed, friendly atmosphere with good food and a fascinating library of Filipiniana.

The fishing village of Siruma (fiesta: 12-13 June), a 15-minute walk from the beach, has no special sights, but the area is scenic, with enjoyable hiking, snorkeling, and *banca* excursions. It's fun to sail across the bay to Punta and walk back along the beach, or to visit Old Siruma Island or the hilly Butauanan Island. The latter is noted for its Santacruzan fiesta, 21-29 May, at which residents perform the bolo-fight dance.

To Takal from Manila via Daet

Take a Manila-Daet bus (eight hours), a jeepney to nearby Mercedes (20 minutes), and a *banca* to Siruma (two and a half hours). This scenic crossing of the bay's broad mouth passes close to several islands, though it's prone to rough weather Oct.-December. If you reach Daet in the afternoon, stay over and proceed to Mercedes the next morning, unless you're prepared to charter a boat. Ask at the wharf before noon for fishing *bancas* returning to Siruma.

There are boats every day in good weather. They charge P75-100 pp; you can bargain a little. A charter trip from Mercedes costs P400. From Takal Beach to Mercedes, guests may take a resort boat anytime at set rates. Also from Mercedes, you can take a *banca* to Apuao Grande Island, where the Swagman Resort is located.

To Takal from Naga

Regular jeepneys load near the market for Bagacay (one hour). A launch makes a daily return trip to Siruma (four to five hours one-way), stopping at several coastal villages; departure is between 1030 and 1500, depending on the tide. If you miss it, go back to Naga for the night. The boat stays at Siruma for about an hour, then returns to Bagacay, where you must overnight. The first jeepneys leave very early in the morning for Naga.

EAST OF NAGA CITY

To Iriga City

This scenic 38-km route passes Mt. Isarog and Mt. Iriga, with Mayon volcano coming into view. Fifteen km southeast of Naga, surrounded by sugarcane and ricefields, is Pili (pop. 50,000),

which succeeded Naga as provincial capital in 1948.

Stay at **El Alma Lodging House,** Old San Roque, with rooms P100-150. Pili is noted for handicrafts and *balut,* and nearby are Curry Springs and Boncao Hill, which was the last Japanese stronghold in the Bicol region. A road leads to the slopes of Mt. Isarog.

South of Pili is Bula (founded 1578), whose current church dates from 1706. The highway leads past Lake Baao to the town of Baao, which also has an 18th-century church.

To Lagonoy Gulf

The road to the shores of Lagonoy Gulf cuts northeast from Pili, skirting Mt. Isarog. Sagnay, on the densely populated Lagonoy Plain, has Sibaguan Waterfalls in the vicinity, plus beaches at Nato and Atulayan Island. You can stay around the coast from Sagnay at **Sabang Beach Resort** (P250-300). Beyond Sabang is the beautiful, seldom-visited Caramoan Peninsula, whose isolated communities and offshore islands are served by coastal launch. The Caramoan National Park (3.5 square km) has rugged hills, virgin rainforest, caves, and a subterranean river.

IRIGA CITY

This pleasant city (pop. 90,000), lying in the shadow of Mt. Iriga (or Asog), lacks the congested, bustling atmosphere of Naga. Iriga's main attraction for the traveler is the side trip to beautiful Lake Buhi. In the town center, visit the market and twin-towered cathedral; several churches were destroyed between 1585 and the current building's construction in 1841.

A stay at the **Hotel Ibalon** runs P600-950, but less expensive choices include **Lemar's Lodge** on San Nicolas St. (P140-350) and the **Bay Anihan Hotel** near the train station, with both fan and a/c rooms in the same price range.

Attractions

Even if staying at the **Hotel Ibalon** is beyond your budget, it's worth visiting its small but fascinating **Bicol Folkloric Museum.** Ask at the desk; admission is free. The hotel's owner, attorney Jose C. Reyes, has unearthed and translated an old Bicol Spanish manuscript containing a

LEGENDS OF LAKE BUHI

While it's accepted that Mt. Iriga's 1641 eruption formed Lake Buhi, other theories persist. The Ibalon epic is connected with tales of a lost civilization that vanished, Atlantis-style, into the lake during an eruption. Believers claim the civilization was relatively advanced, based on artifacts found around the lake.

Some hold that the Agtas living on the volcano's slopes are descendants of the lost tribe. Another version describes how the lake was formed by torrential rain on the site of a prosperous town whose people lived sinfully and forgot about God. Shortly after an old beggar was mocked and driven out by townspeople, the town was drowned in a violent storm. Now it's said that sometimes, in clear weather, people can be seen in the depths doing household chores, weaving, and merrymaking.

fragment of the Ibalon legend. This region and its inhabitants were known as Ibalon in pre-Hispanic times. The museum contains carvings and curiosities connected with the Ibalon myth, plus pottery and artifacts found in the area.

In the hotel dining room you can sample the famous "Thousand Fish Omelet," containing *sinarapan,* the tiny fish found in Lake Buhi.

Close to the hotel is Our Lady of Lourdes Emerald Grotto, built on Calvario Hill by Reyes in memory of his father, who was killed during WW II. It's worth the climb for the panorama of Mt. Iriga, the city, and surrounding countryside.

On 11 February, the Tinagba, a traditional harvest festival, is celebrated on the feast day of Our Lady of Lourdes. Bicolanos gather to make offerings of food and handicrafts at the Emerald Grotto, farmers parade in carabao-drawn carts laden with the best local produce, and Agtas come down to the city to dance.

Iriga celebrates its City Fiesta on 13 June and City Foundation Day on 3 September.

Lake Buhi

The town of Buhi, 16 km by jeepney from Iriga, is a former Franciscan settlement, magnificently situated on the shores of 16.5-square-km Lake Buhi (elev. 100 meters). The church tower dates back to 1578, although the present church was completed in 1884 after earlier buildings had been destroyed by fire and earthquake.

Walk through the market to the lakeside. The sweeping view takes in the collapsed crater of Mt. Isarog (half of which fell during a 1641 eruption), ridges around the lake that are the rim of a very ancient volcano, the peaks of Malinao and Masaraga, and the amazing tip of Mayon. Lake boats, heavily laden with people and produce, glide past fish traps as they come in from villages on the far shores to the market. Take a passenger boat or hire a *banca* to cross the lake and then make easy walks to Bye Bye Falls and the Twin Falls of Itbog.

Sinarapan is the local name for the *tabios,* the world's smallest freshwater commercial fish (three to four mm long, about the size of a grain of rice). Until recently, Lake Buhi's fishermen scooped masses of them into their *bancas* with triangular, very fine-meshed nets. Once ashore, these almost transparent fish were pressed together into small, flat, silvery squares and sundried to be cooked later. This is now an increasingly rare activity.

In addition to overfishing, the special nets often destroyed the spawn. Then the lake was imprudently stocked with predatory fish, which (surprise, surprise) ate the little ones. The species is nearly extinct, but it's possible to see some at the Buhi Freshwater Demonstration Fish Farm, located in the village about one km before reaching Buhi town.

Climbing Mount Iriga

The volcano can be climbed from Buhi or from the north side, taking about four hours—great views from the top. Hiring a local guide is recommended. If you start early, it's possible to ascend and descend by different routes.

To begin from the north, take a jeepney (they load about a block from Iriga market) to Our Lady of Perpetual Help (five km along the highway toward Naga; turn right at San Pedro and follow a dirt road for two km). Alight 250 meters after the *barangay* hall and follow the trail to the right. Agtas live in this area, which is known as Hacienda Mamoco. From here, the rim of the half-crater seems tantalizingly close, but it's still a four-hour climb; the Agtas will act as guides.

ALBAY PROVINCE

Albay is less than half the size of Camarines Sur, but Legaspi City, southern Luzon's unofficial "capital," and Mt. Mayon, Bicol's main tourist attraction, give it a much higher profile than its neighboring provinces. Mayon volcano used to be the single overwhelming reason for visiting Albay, worth the arduous overland journey from Manila. Mayon was often said to be the world's most perfect cone.

The Mayon volcano last erupted in February 1993, billowing a five-km-high plume of gritty ash that darkened the sky and sent tons of boulders cascading down the slopes onto farmers in their fields. The death toll was listed at 30 people, and thousands fled their homes. The Mayon volcano has erupted more than a dozen times this century. Its last previous eruption, in September 1984, spewed a cloud of ash 12 miles high. This beautiful, deadly volcano continues to dominate Albay Province, visually, geographically, historically, culturally, and economically.

Apart from the view it affords of Mayon, Legaspi is not a particularly interesting city. The province, however, also offers black-sand beaches, caves, hot springs, and some attractive abaca handicrafts. Albay sits astride the land route to the Visayas and is the gateway to Catanduanes.

History

Archaeological excavations have unearthed prehistoric pottery, including burial jars, beadwork, and stone and shell artifacts from caves around Albay Gulf and in the Hoyop-Hoyopan Caves, near Camalig. Juan de Salcedo, accompanied by 120 soldiers, explored Ibalon, already well populated, in 1573. Conversion of the area followed. The original province of Partido Ibalon was eventually divided into Albay and Sorsogon. Sawangan, a small settlement surrounded by mangrove swamp, became a town called Albaybay in 1616 and has since been renamed Albay, then Legaspi.

Its colorful history includes disturbances of both natural and human origin. In addition to Mayon's frequent eruptions, there were Dutch attacks during the early 17th century and Moro raids throughout the 18th century. The natives rebelled in 1649 to protest being press-ganged into galleon-building in Cavite's shipyards. Disaster struck in 1814 as Mayon's lava killed 1,200 people. During the early 19th century, hemp for shipping rope became an international commodity and the source of old Bicolano wealth. Demand subsequently fell sharply but has recently revived somewhat.

In 1898, the provisional revolutionary government of Albay was formed, and after the peaceful expulsion of the Spanish from the region, the Bicolanos practiced self-rule for 18 months. Then came the Philippine-American War.

By January 1900, American forces had taken Sorsogon Province without opposition and were preparing to occupy Legaspi. Its inhabitants, outgunned and outnumbered, resisted desperately. It took four companies of U.S. troops, supported by a gunboat, to overcome them. In spite of an official surrender in 1901, resistance continued from the hills until September 1903, long after opposition had been suppressed in other regions.

The Bicolanos also heroically defied the Japanese, but overwhelming force led to Legaspi's occupation from 1941 to 1945. Improved communications and facilities have led to rapid postwar growth in commerce and tourism.

Transportation

Legaspi and Tabaco are the route centers. From Manila, Albay can be reached by air, road, and railway. PAL flies from Manila daily and four times a week from Cebu to Legaspi.

Philtranco, Inland Trailways, Sarkies, and Sunshine offer frequent service from Manila to Legaspi, while some buses go to Tabaco and Tiwi and others pass through en route to Bulan (Sorsogon), Samar, and Leyte, connecting with the ferry between Matnog and Allen (Samar). Some departures are a/c or super-express service.

Frequent minibuses ply the main highway linking Legaspi with Naga, Iriga, and Sorsogon

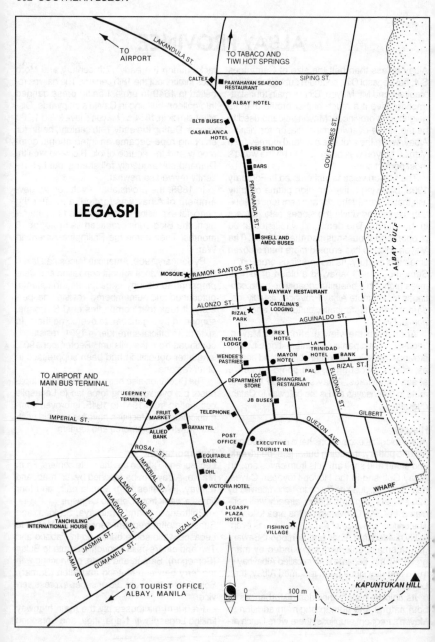

LEGASPI

TO AIRPORT

LAKANDULA ST.

TO TABACO AND
TIWI HOT SPRINGS

SIPING ST.

CALTEX

Paayahayan Seafood
Restaurant

Albay Hotel

GOV. FORBES ST.

BLTB Buses

Casablanca
Hotel

Fire Station

Bars

PENARANDA ST.

ALBAY GULF

Shell and
AMDG Buses

MOSQUE

RAMON SANTOS ST.

Wayway Restaurant

ALONZO ST.

Catalina's
Lodging

RIZAL
PARK

AGUINALDO ST.

Rex
Hotel

Peking
Lodge

LA
TRINIDAD
HOTEL

Wendee's
Pastries

Mayon
Hotel

Bank

RIZAL ST.

PAL

LCC
Department
Store

Shangrila
Restaurant

ELIZONDO ST.

TO AIRPORT AND
MAIN BUS TERMINAL

Jeepney
Terminal

JB Buses

GILBERT

Fruit
Market

Telephone

QUEZON AVE.

IMPERIAL ST.

Allied
Bank

Bayan Tel

Post
Office

ROSAL ST.

Executive
Tourist Inn

IMPERIAL ST.

Equitable
Bank

DHL

Victoria Hotel

WHARF

ILANG ILANG ST.

MAGNOLIA ST.

Legaspi
Plaza
Hotel

TANCHULING
INTERNATIONAL HOUSE

JASMIN ST.

FISHING
VILLAGE

GUMAMELA ST.

CAMIA ST.

RIZAL ST.

TO TOURIST OFFICE,
ALBAY, MANILA

0   100 m

KAPUNTUKAN HILL

as well as hundreds of jeepneys. For Masbate, take a JB Liner bus to the ferry port at Bulan (three and a half hours).

It's possible to travel from Naga to Legaspi via the scenic Lagonoy Gulf coastline, changing vehicles in Tigaon and Tabaco. Transport on the Tigaon-Tabaco section is sporadic, so it's best to travel early. Regular vehicles connect Tabaco with Ligao. Tabaco is the port for Catanduanes and San Miguel Island; Bacacay for Cagraray Island; and Legaspi for Batan and Rapu-Rapu. Irregular boats sail from Legaspi to other ports of Luzon and the Visayas.

LEGASPI CITY

Situated on a small plain between Mt. Mayon and Albay Gulf, Legaspi (pop. about 100,000) is the provincial capital, a seaport, university town, and Albay's commercial and cultural center. It's also southern Luzon's main tourist destination and transportation center.

Legaspi is a sprawling city and none too attractive. For the convenience of visitors, it may be divided into Legaspi Port (downtown) and Albay. The city center contains the port, bus stations, market, a busy shopping district, and most of the hotels, restaurants, and movie theaters. The suburb of Albay, three km from downtown, contains the Department of Tourism office and other government buildings.

The area's main attractions lie outside the city limits, making Legaspi a place to return to at night rather than a city to enjoy for its own sake. The **Great Sibidan Race,** a sea carnival and regatta highlighted by *sibidan* (native canoe) races, takes place 21-24 October.

Attractions

Legaspi is situated on a deep bay that forms a fine natural harbor. The port has a lively atmosphere and is worth a visit. A headless statue near the wharf is said to be a monument to a guerrilla hero beheaded by the Japanese.

The nearby shore is lined with fishermen's huts on stilts. This area is called "Victory Village" (though there is nothing victorious about this slum), and beyond it is the gray-sand Puro Beach. Tankers unload petroleum, and large freighters dock to load copra, abaca, and abaca

products for export. Although there are no scheduled passenger ships, you may sometimes find a vessel going to Cebu and other Philippine ports, while launches serve nearby islands.

Points of interest downtown include the market, which is a good place to shop for handicrafts; St. Raphael Church, whose altar is a large volcanic rock from Mayon; and, at the junction of Rizal and Quezon Streets, a monument commemorating the Bicolano stand against U.S. forces in 1900.

Rizal Street links the city center with Albay district and continues to Locsin (Daraga), Cagsawa ruins, and the north. The tourist office is in dire straits and hardly worth the effort of visiting.

Camalig

Situated 14 km northwest of Legaspi, on the lower slopes of Mayon, Camalig was destroyed in the famous eruption of 1814. Today, its attractions are its church, abaca handicrafts, and nearby caves. Abaca and *caragomoy* fibers and twine can be seen hanging outside houses, and you can visit the abaca wall-covering factory here.

The 19th-century church offers a fine view from its bell tower; note the massive bells. Toward the end of WW II, U.S. troops used the tower as a lookout as they searched for Japanese stragglers hiding in caves in the nearby hills. Inside the church is a memorial to a native who died in 1912 at the age of 115. The adjacent *convento* houses a small museum displaying some of the pottery, beads, and artifacts found in Hoyop-Hoyopan Caves.

Hoyop-Hoyopan Caves

These caves are in Cotmon, eight km from Camalig. Look for a jeepney with a Cotmon sign at Camalig market; if there isn't one, take a tricycle. The caves' name, literally "Blow-Blow," is from the sound of the wind passing through. They are part of an extensive system of limestone caves in the area. In 1972, pottery, bones in burial jars, and beadwork were excavated here. Estimated to date back to 50 B.C., most are now in the National Museum in Manila.

The prehistoric occupants have been superseded in modern times by 100 families who took refuge here from the Japanese during WW II and other locals sheltering from typhoons. Today, children with flashlights show visitors the caves. Three km (a 45-minute walk) beyond Hoyop-Hoyopan are Calabidong Caves, which have fine stalactites, bats, and an underground stream. It's possible to penetrate these large caverns for several hundred meters. Take your own flashlight, and since parts of them are chest-deep in water, wear swimming gear and take plastic bags to keep things dry. A local guide is essential.

Cagsawa Ruins

These much-photographed ruins are situated on the north side of the highway, 3.5 km north-west of Locsin. The church was built in 1587, burned by marauding Dutch in 1636, and rebuilt in 1724. On 1 February 1814, Mayon suddenly erupted with a burst of red-hot boulders. The in-habitants fled, with their belongings, to take shel-ter in the church. A massive lava flow buried the whole town, except the church tower, and also covered Camalig, Budiao, and nearby villages to the height of the coconut palms. Over 200 were buried alive in the church, and about 1,000 per-ished elsewhere.

Church authorities have forbidden excava-tion out of respect for the dead, a decision that disappoints historians and treasure-seekers, since it's believed that some wealthy Spaniards were among the victims. The site is a national park. The stark, blackened church tower, and some remaining walls of the priest's house and municipal building, stand in poignant testimo-ny to the volcano's latent power. The ruins form an evocative foreground for photos of Mt. Mayon.

Survivors of the catastrophe rebuilt their town and church at Daraga (now Locsin). From Legaspi City bus terminal or Locsin, take a Ca-malig jeepney and alight at the Cagsawa. Budiao was the site of the first bullfighting arena in the Philippines. The ruins, less impressive than Cag-sawa, are located about two km northwest, just off the highway.

Locsin

Formerly called Daraga, a name still in common use, this town is five km from the center of Legaspi and now effectively a suburb. The baroque church has a celebrated, ornately carved black exterior whose volcanic rock has been mellowed over time by the elements. A neon cross has been added to the venerable tower. The hilltop setting affords an expansive view of Mayon and the sea. The town shops below the hill offer abaca and other handicrafts, and *pili* nuts. *Sinamay,* an abaca cloth, is hand-woven here.

Jeepneys between Locsin and Legaspi are frequent. A must stop is at **Sherry's Pizza Par-lor** on the hilltop, which serves pizza, beer, and other snacks and offers a great view of the vol-cano. Perhaps if you hang out long enough, the Mayon may blow up again.

Accommodations

Most of Legaspi's cheap and run-down hotels are in the center of town along Penaranda and Rizal Streets. None will inspire you to spend any time relaxing in Legaspi, though you really should try the spicy fried peanuts sold on the sidewalks.

Catalina's Lodging House: A small but friendly hotel with decent rooms. 96 Penaran-da, tel. (05221) 223-593, P100-450.

Hotel Xandra: Another budget option in the center of town. Penaranda St., tel. (05221) 22-688, P100-340.

Tanchuling International House: Large and clean rooms, plus views of Mayon from the rooftop, five minutes south of town. Jasmin St., tel. (05221) 22-747, P300-600.

La Trinidad Hotel: Legaspi's former leading hotel is centrally located and reasonably priced. Rizal St., tel. (05221) 22-951, P800-1,100.

Albay Hotel: Best in town; opened 1996 a few blocks north of city center. 88 Penaranda St., tel. (05221) 243-640, P1,200-1,800.

Restaurants

The choice here is generally between Filipino and Chinese food. The best restaurants in the city are **Wayway Restaurant** on Penaranda Street and the nearby **Hong Kong Dimsum & Tea House.** For good, inexpensive Chinese food, try the **Golden Dragon** on Rizal Street and the **Four Seasons** on Magallenes Street. For Filipino fast food, try the **Quick n' Hearty Fast Food,** 45 Rizal Street, across from the Mayon Hotel. The marketplace has numerous food stalls, both inside the market and around the

MAYON~THE WORLD'S MOST PERFECT VOLCANO

The volcano giveth and the volcano taketh away. Thick layers of volcanic lava, ash, and mud have either flowed down the slopes or been washed down by monsoon rains to give Albay its fertile soil, but the price of this blessing is periodically exacted in lives, crops, and property destroyed by Mayon's fury. Thousands have died during recorded history alone.

Since its first recorded eruption in 1616, Mayon has erupted on nearly 50 occasions. The 19th century's 30 eruptions included the devastating burial of Cagsawa in 1814. In this century, they occurred in 1900, 1928, 1943, 1947, 1968, 1978, 1984, and 1993. Eruptions have generally tended to be to the south; hence the vegetation on the north slope is denser and reaches higher.

During the 1968 eruption, explosions sometimes occurred every few minutes, an ash-laden cloud rose 10 km, and hot ash clouds sped seven km down the southwest flank at velocities of up to 63 meters per second. Eruptions force the temporary evacuation of nearby communities. In 1984, 30,000 left their homes as Mayon spewed lava, ash, and huge flaming boulders. Mayon (2,462 meters), which rises in isolated symmetrical splendor from the surrounding plain, has lost about 100 meters in height since the 19th century due to eruptions.

While volcanologists from the U.S. Geological Survey Department had managed to give Filipinos and residents ample warning of Mt. Pinatubo's increasing volcanic activity in the early '90s, the Mayon volcano erupted on 2 February 1993 without warning.

At the first eruption, the Mayon volcano billowed a five-km-high plume of gritty ash and sent boulders cascading down the slopes onto farmers in their fields. Fifty people were killed minutes after Mayon erupted, and thousands fled. A second eruption followed about two and a half hours later as the ash darkened the sky and blanketed the land as far as 20 km from the blast area. The Philippine Institute of Volcanology and Seismology said the eruption was far weaker than the June 1991 eruption of Mt. Pinatubo.

Volcanologists arrived from bases in the Philippines and the U.S. to monitor the volcano; however, another eruption occurred a week later, killing and injuring a handful of scientists from the U.S.

These eruptions could signal extended activity at Mayon, one of 21 active volcanoes in the Philippines. Be sure to check with the tourism authority before planning any treks up the mountain. Even when it's not erupting, it continually emits a plume of sulfurous smoke.

Mayon's name derives from *magayon,* the Bicol word for beautiful, and the volcano is the subject of local legend. Its slopes, which are part woodland, part grassland, and part desert of rock, cinder, and ash, are a 55-square-km national park.

---

outside. The fancy **South Ocean Villa Chinese Restaurant** across from the market is also good. Legaspi's Chinese community has certainly made its mark here with a number of good Chinese restaurants to choose from. The **La Trinidad Hotel** has a fine restaurant. Find live music in the evenings at **Rore's Eatery and Folkhouse,** the **Xandra's** restaurant, and the **Magic Pan,** an upscale restaurant on Rizal Street near Albay district. *Pili* nut sweets and pastries are a local delicacy.

Transportation

Legaspi is 545 km south of Manila.

Manila: PAL and Air Philippines fly daily between Manila and Legaspi.

Buses to Manila and points south leave from the various bus terminals scattered around town: BLTB at the north end of Penaranda Street, JB Bicol Express in central Penaranda Street, and Philtranco a few blocks west of downtown.

Local Transport: Jeepneys to Tabaco and Tiwi leave north of the public market. Minibuses and jeepneys to Albay, Casagwa, and Camalig leave west of the market.

To Samar: Travelers heading south to Samar should take a very early-morning bus or jeepney to Matnog, since ferry service across to Samar ends around 1300. Allow about four hours to Matnog, including time-consuming changes in Sorsogon or Irosin.

Buses from Manila pass through Legaspi several times daily but tend to be filled with passengers. Philtranco provides direct bus service from Legaspi to Catbalogan and Tacbalogan on a space-available basis, a useful service that saves time and hassle. You might also check with BLTB and JB Bicol Express.

THE COAST:
LEGASPI THROUGH TIWI

The coast road to Tabaco and Tiwi heads out from the Penaranda Street Extension. It passes through Rawis and Arimbay, where some of the better pension houses are located, past the turnoffs for **Kagayonan Resort** on the right, and for Buyuan (starting point for climbing Mayon) on the left. The nearby clubhouse of the Mayon Imperial Golf Course was destroyed in Mayon's 1984 eruption. Buses and jeepneys are plentiful on this route; they depart from city terminal.

Santo Domingo
This town, 11 km from Legaspi, is noted for abaca handicrafts, and has a twin-towered church (1789), some 19th-century houses, and a copra factory. During Mayon's 1968 eruption, the bridge south of the town was swept away, so that the river now flows over new deposits of volcanic debris that the locals use as building materials. The black-sand Kalayukaii Beach is three km east of Santo Domingo; take a jeepney or tricycle.

Stay at **Sirangan Beach Resort** (P150 pp; kitchen, aviary, and wildlife collection) or **Reyes Beach Resort** (P150-200; restaurant, kitchen in cottages).

Buhutan
Buhutan Beach, seven km east of Santo Domingo, can be reached by jeepney or tricycle. A few hundred meters offshore lies the wreck of a Spanish galleon in 10 meters of clear water. It's believed to have sunk during a typhoon. Artifacts from it are in the National Museum in Manila. Local fishermen will take snorkelers over the wreck in their *bancas*.

Bacacay
The main road passes through Misericordia, a village noted for abaca weaving. Beyond it is San Jose junction, where a road leads right, five km, to Bacacay, which is also served by direct jeepneys from Legaspi. This fishing village has a ruined Spanish watchtower, built to warn against pirates.

Stay at **Binitayan Beach Resort** or **Roca Baluarte** (P200-250) on the beach (nothing spe-

cial). The road north from Bacacay stays near the coast for 3.5 km and passes close to the black-sand Sogod Beach before turning inland up to the main road to Tiwi. Sogod has some picnic grounds but no accommodations.

Cagraray Island
Bancas cross from Bacacay to Cagraray (71 square km), which, like its neighboring islands, is undeveloped and seldom visited. The people are superstitious, believing in evil spirits. This low island has no roads, just a network of footpaths. Masibis Beach on the island's southeast corner has fine white sand. It may be possible to stay at the **Sacred Heart Mission** in Cabasan. Nearby are small uninhabited islands such as Guinanayan, where you could be dropped off to camp. (Take food and water.)

Malilipot
The main road passes through Malilipot, whose name means "The Protected One," after the small ridge that shields it from Mayon volcano. The Busay Falls tumble about 250 meters down this ridge in seven tiers, with delightfully cool swimming holes at the foot of each cascade. Take the path to the left of the church and walk about 1.5 km. Confirm directions en route or give a youth P2 to guide you. The trail to the upper tiers begins to the right of the falls. Malilipot is another abaca center—good buys on slippers, bags, and placemats. See twine being made in the side streets. The weaving looms are in the houses. The town is also noted for avocados and pineapples, both in season July and August.

TABACO

Tabaco is a market center situated on a coastal plain adjoining sheltered Tabaco Bay. Abaca and copra are shipped from its port, which is also the gateway to Catanduanes. Entering Tabaco from Legaspi (27 km, 45 minutes), you pass Cubo on the left, a district with a thriving metalcraft cottage industry. Old scrap metal is forged into scissors, shears, bolos, cleavers, razors, cock spurs, and razor blades. Just past Cubo is a Chinese cemetery. Tabaco's crowded two-story central market has many handicraft stalls. Bargain hard! The port is one km from the market.

Accommodations

The cheapest accommodations are close to the market. The **Mabuhay** (P200) is the best of these. Cross to Riosa Street to **Tony's Hotel** (P100-150). In the street behind is the **Seven-Eleven Resthouse.** The **Celebrity Resthouse** is on the small street opposite the Philtranco terminal. **El Mundo Lodging House** is near the port. Inland, next to the Memorial Hospital, **Guillermo's Pension House,** P100-150 with coffee shop, on Karangalan Boulevard, is quite good. Take a tricycle from the market to the latter two places. The **Mayon View Resort** is near the shore, coming in from Legaspi.

Enjoy good Chinese food and free American video movies at the **E.F. Palace Siopao House,** near the market, next to Tony's Hotel. The **Royal Crown Canteen** is opposite the municipal hall and is very clean.

From Tabaco

Buses to Legaspi and jeepneys to Tiwi are frequent. Minibuses and jeepneys head inland to Ligao. For Naga City (Camarines Sur) via the coast, direct transport to Tigaon leaves in the morning, or you can do it in stages, through Tiwi and Maynonong; Tigaon to Naga is no problem. The boat to Catanduanes leaves daily at 0900. The low offshore island of San Miguel has no regular service; cross with residents who come into Tabaco to shop.

To Mayon Rest House

Ligao-bound vehicles pass through San Antonio village, which is noted for wood and rattan furniture. You can stay at **Rocamonte Resort** (with a swimming pool and a children's amusement park). About halfway between Tabaco and Ligao is the turnoff for the Mayon Rest House, located at 762 meters on Mayon's northwest slope. From the junction, it's an eight-km uphill walk unless you're lucky enough to hitch.

The alternative is chartering a jeepney from Tabaco (20 km). The road is paved, with many hairpin bends, and passes through abaca plantations, sugarcane fields, and *kalamansi* groves. Once here, a spectacular panorama takes in Mt. Mayon, Mt. Masaraga, Mt. Isarog, and Mt.

Malinao, plus the Caramoan Peninsula and San Miguel Island.

The Rest House, now abandoned, was built in 1934, renovated in 1948, and subsequently damaged in eruptions. It's possible to stay in it (bring bedding and food), but recent reports of muggings and other incidents discourage this. Also, because of increased volcanic activity, it may not be advisable to stay here. Above the Rest House is a volcanological observatory and a small museum with lava samples and photos of previous eruptions.

TIWI

The coast road from Tabaco passes through Malinao, destroyed in Mayon's 1766 eruption. Palali Falls are inland from here. Tiwi is a small town, 12 km past Tabaco and three km before the famous hot springs. Direct jeepneys link Legaspi and Tiwi, while **Philtranco** has two trips a day to Manila. Just off the main square is a Japanese Garden, built by the Japanese equivalent of Peace Corps volunteers.

The road opposite the market leads to the striking Sinimbahan Ruins, from Tiwi's original church, abandoned due to its vulnerability to typhoon-induced tidal waves. Note a glass case embedded in the wall containing human bones. From the nearby beach, it's possible to hire a *banca* to tiny Coral Island for swimming. The boatmen's initial prices tend to be high, so bargain hard.

Tiwi Hot Springs

Until 1981, the hot springs area consisted of Naglagbong Lake in Naga and the springs in the vicinity of the resort and youth hostel. The volcanic lake, with its boiling sulfurous pools, was declared a national park, then destroyed by geothermal activity. Now there's only crumbled pavement and some strange earth formations to look at. (So much for the legend of the lake being hell, with tormented souls shrieking on moonless nights!) The remaining boiling springs are behind the youth hostel. Local people use them for cooking eggs.

The **youth hostel** and resort both have spring-fed swimming pools and private rooms with hot baths. The youth hostel costs P40 pp for a double cottage, slightly less for those with an international membership or student card. It also has rooms starting at P150; a hot bath is an additional P10. Day visitors pay P2 entrance, P3 to swim, and P10 for a hot bath.

The neighboring **Manantial de Tiwi Resort** rates start at P100 (a/c P125, P5 to swim, and P3 and up pp for the hot baths). Air-conditioned rooms with private pool cost about P350. Both places serve food and are patronized by foreign technicians working on the geothermal project. Take a jeepney from Tiwi nearby, or a tricycle.

Putsan

This picturesque fishing village makes a very worthwhile short side trip from Tiwi. It's about two km off the main road; take a tricycle past what remains of Naglagbong Lake. Putsan is noted for pottery. Watch earthenware water jugs and flowerpots being hand-shaped to perfection. The primitive methods include using a simple wheel without treadle, and open fires without kilns. Follow the road past the beach with fishing boats to a nicer small black-sand beach, but swimming isn't advisable here, since it's said that the geothermal plant dumps sulfuric acid into the sea.

To Camarines Sur

The coastal route from Tiwi includes a scenic section known as the Hanging Road to Joroan. This winding road is cut into the cliffside and gives fine views of the rugged Caramoan Peninsula across Lagonoy Gulf. Past Joroan, at Misibis, steps descend past the narrow Bugsuhan Falls to a tiny black-sand beach. Most jeepneys turn around a little farther on, at Maynonong. After this, only sporadic traffic goes through to Tigaon (Camarines Sur).

SOUTH OF LEGASPI

The main route south from Legaspi returns to Locsin, 18 km from the Sorsogon boundary. The highway passes through Bascaran, a village

where *anahaw* fans are woven from a single leaf; note leaves and fans drying by the roadside. A winding secondary road out of Legaspi follows Poliqui Bay, passing through Cauayan. Near here is **Dalipay Spring and Waterfall,** set in lush vegetation, which powers a small hydroelectric plant.

The road leads to **Manito,** a thermal resort and fishing and copra town, near which is Hologon Beach. Beyond Manito, Balubayon Boiling Lake has an outlet close to the seashore, where each day a geyser erupts periodically from the coral rock and hot sand. It's best seen at low tide.

To the south, the Inangmaharang Mountains straddle the provincial boundary. The **Inangmaharang Hot Springs** are in this area, which is earmarked for a geothermal power project.

RAPU-RAPU AND BATAN ISLANDS

These scenic, seldom visited islands have remained undeveloped. The people believe that they are haunted by malevolent spirits called *malignos.* These include *aswang* (flying vampire witches), *inkantos* (fairies that live in trees, fear of whose retribution has discouraged logging), and *duendes* (mischievous invisible men). Old people walking at night say *"Maki age"* ("May I pass") to avoid offending these spirits.

Such superstition coexists with Christianity. During Holy Week, the people of Rapu-Rapu stage a reenactment of the passion play in Bicol dialect. Rapu-Rapu (64 square km), whose main town is also Rapu-Rapu, is about 65 km (four hours) from Legaspi. Batan (90 square km) is an important coal producer, and Rapu-Rapu also has coal and copper mines.

Batan Island (chief settlement also Batan) is rich in wildlife—monkeys, hornbills, ducks, and large pigeons. The Minaroso Cave is situated near the sea in Villa Hermosa. In calm weather, several launches return daily, around midday, from Legaspi to Rapu-Rapu and Batan, having brought the islanders over for shopping early in the morning.

CATANDUANES ISLAND

Definitely off the tourist trail, this pretty, unde-veloped island province offers the traveler fine beaches, friendly people, attractive, orderly vil-lages, and a scenic hilly landscape. It's easy to get from the Luzon mainland to Virac, the capital and port of entry, but then you face crowded jeepney rides on dusty roads. The south of the is-land has a dense road network, but the three routes leading north don't link up, thus necessi-tating hiking or backtracking. Virac is the center of commerce and transportation. Accommoda-tions are scare.

History

There are two versions of the origin of the name Catanduanes. One holds that it means "Land of Tando," after the formerly common *tando* trees that were used for shipbuilding during the Span-ish era. The other claims that it derives from clicker insects called *tandu* that are found in swarms on the island. Muslims were living on Catanduanes when Juan de Salcedo explored it in 1573. He is believed to have landed near Virac and was welcomed by Datu Lumibao.

The Malayan settlers he found were possibly descendants of the 10 Bornean *datus* who came to the Visayas in the 13th century. In 1576, 10 Augustinians sailing by galleon from Acapulco were shipwrecked off Catanduanes. The Holy Cross of Batalay in the town of Bato is said to mark the grave of their leader, Father Herrera. Catanduanes was allotted to four *en-comienderos* in 1582. Throughout the colonial period, it was a subprovince of Albay. In 1755, it was overrun by Moro raiders who burned and pillaged the settlements. Loyang Cave in Lictin is the site of a mass grave of massacred is-landers.

During the revolution, there was a bloody en-counter between Filipino *insurrectos* and the Spaniards at Sitio Ili in Danicop, Virac. The Span-ish finally sailed from Catanduanes in 1898, shortly before the first revolutionary troops arrived from Luzon. Then came the Philippine-Ameri-can War, and U.S. forces entered Virac in 1900. Catanduanes became a separate province after WW II.

Transportation

PAL flies daily between Manila and Virac (takes 75 minutes), plus three times a week from Mani-la via Naga (takes 30 minutes from Naga). The airport is two km from Virac. A daily ferry leaves Tabaco (Albay) at 0900 for Virac and departs Virac for Tabaco at 0800; the crossing takes four hours. Boats sometimes connect Sabang (Ca-marines Sur) with Cabcab, near San Andres.

VIRAC

The provincial capital and commercial center is situated on the island's largest lowland, the coastal plain bordering Cabugao Bay, which forms a natural harbor. Virac has a small-town at-mosphere, with thatch-roof houses one block off the main street. Virac itself has no sights of particular interest, but fine beaches and nice waterfalls are within easy reach. On Sundays, about five km west of town, the largest cockpit in all of Bicol is packed with enthusiastic patrons.

Accommodations and Food

All lodging houses are within easy walking dis-tance of the ferry dock. Walk 100 meters for-ward to a large traffic circle and bear left. Best of the cheapies is the **L & H Resthouse,** 100 me-ters past the Magnolia ice-cream parlor; rooms are P100. The **Cherry Don Resthouse** is on the circle itself, while 200 meters along the main street is the **Christopher Inn,** and next to it is the **Catanduanes Inn,** above the **Christopher Res-taurant.** Rooms here are P150-200, depending on the season. Behind them, on San Pedro Street, **Sultida's Inn** (no sign) serves very cheap meals to guests.

The only better-class establishment is the **Catanduanes Hotel** located above the PAL of-fice. Next to the staircase leading to the hotel is a good mural map of the island. The **Chicken House,** on the traffic circle, has excellent fried chicken and other dishes and is popular with lo-cals. The **Appetizer** is also centrally located. Find very cheap meals around the market, a tri-cycle ride from the town center.

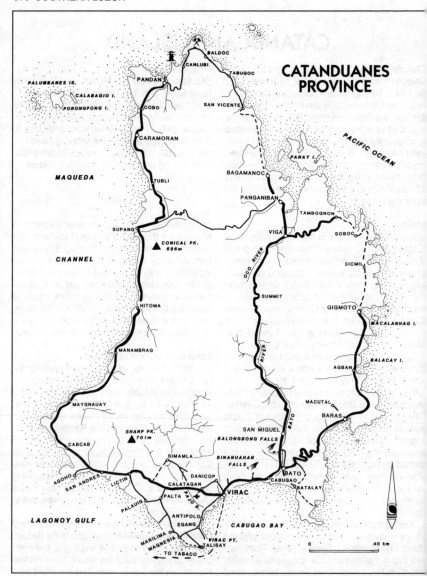

CATANDUANES PROVINCE

PALUMBANES IS.

CALABAGIO I.
PORONGPONG I.

MAQUEDA

CHANNEL

LAGONOY GULF

PACIFIC OCEAN

BALDOC
CANLUBI
TABUGOC
PANDAN
SAN VICENTE
COBO
CARAMORAN
TUBLI
SUPANG
CONICAL PK.
686m
HITOMA
MANAMBRAG
MAYGNAUAY
SHARP PK.
701m
CABCAB
SIMAMLA
AGGHO
SAN ANDRES
LICTIN
DANICOP
CALATAGAN
PALTA
PALAUIG
ANTIPOLO
EGANG
MARILIMA
MAGHESIA
TALISAY
VIRAC PT.
TO TABACO

BAGAMANOC
PANGANIBAN
TAMBOGNON
VIGA
SOBOC
SICMIL
SUMMIT
GIGMOTO
MACALANHAG I.
BALACAY I.
AGBAN
MACUTAL
BARAS
SAN MIGUEL
BALONGBONG FALLS
BINANUAHAN FALLS
BATO
CABUGAO
BATALAY
VIRAC
CABUGAO BAY

PANAY I.

OCO RIVER
RIVER
BATO

0   40 km

From Virac

To see the island, you have basically three choices: short trips to Marilima and its neighboring beaches, and the waterfalls around Bato; full-day roundtrips by jeepney to Pandan, Bagamanoc, and Gigmoto; or circumnavigating the island, which takes about four days. Jeepneys start from the market. It's best to start long trips early, and you can try sitting on the roof if you begin to feel like a sardine. Hold on to something immobile, not the pigs or chickens that are often tied onto the roof.

Jeepneys meet the ferry from Tabaco when it docks at 1300, but they redefine the word crowded. Grab a front seat shortly before the boat arrives. If front seats are already taken, the next best views are from the roof. Most routes have three to seven departures from Virac each day. Routes are as follows: to Antipolo/Talisay; to Bagamanoc via San Miguel, Viga, Panganiban; to Baras; to Bato; to Cabcab; to Gigmoto via Bato, Baras; to Magnesia via Palta, Marilima; to Pandan via San Andres, Caramoran; to San Miguel; to Simamla; to Tambognon via Viga.

Vicinity of Virac

Ferryboat passengers will notice a string of fine beaches between San Andres and Virac Point. The best is at Marilima, from where it's possible to walk to Magnesia, Talisay, and Egang Beach, and then take a tricycle to the river at Antipolo, from where jeepneys return to Virac. Farther along the coast toward San Andres is Isang Beach in Palauig.

The backdrop to these beaches is an intriguing landscape reminiscent of Bohol's Chocolate Hills. East of Virac, a tricycle ride brings you 4.5 km to the turnoff for Binanuahan Falls. Walk 500 meters to this pretty spot, where there's a natural pool for swimming and a picnic site. Continuing on toward Bato and San Miguel, the road passes Cabugao Beach and the turnoff to Balongbong Falls.

AROUND THE ISLAND

Take the 0700 jeepney from Virac to Pandan. It stops for breakfast in San Andres (also called Calolbon), then follows the shores of the Maqueda Channel, crossing promontories and passing through coastal villages, to reach Pandan five hours later. En route, enjoy distant views of the Caramoan Peninsula of Camarines Sur and the glistening beaches of the Palumbanes Islands. To sample these beautiful beaches, stop off in Caramoran and charter a boat or wait until islanders return home after shopping (people stay put in rough weather).

Upon reaching Pandan, it's possible to eat lunch in a house with the jeepney crew. Pandan has a wide beach, with a lighthouse across the bay. The jeepney then returns to Virac. A road follows the coast from Pandan to Bagamanoc, but be prepared to hike, since there's no daily jeepney service. To hike from Pandan to Bagamanoc in less than two days, you should travel light and move steadily. The walking is pleasant and easy. Expect children to stare at you: not too many foreigners pass this way. The coastline is beautiful, with several beaches. Paday Falls are near Bagamanoc.

Panay Island, clearly visible from the shore, is best reached from Panganiban (also called Payo). From Bagamanoc, you can take a jeepney to Virac (four and a half hours) through the interior, or alight at Viga and wait for the Virac-Tambognon jeepney to pass. It's then necessary to walk, overnighting en route, to Gigmoto, from where jeepneys travel the scenic east coast to Virac. Macutal Falls are near Baras. The easy way to see the island is by taking the daily roundtrips to Pandan, Bagamanoc, and Gigmoto, but the hiking sections enable travelers to meet extremely friendly locals and gain insights into the reality of isolated rural living.

SORSOGON PROVINCE

Sorsogon is the name of the province and its capital town. This mountainous, hook-shaped province forms the southern tip of Luzon. The highway from Manila to the Visayas and Mindanao passes through Sorsogon, which is linked by ferry to Masbate and Samar. Sorsogon's landscape is dominated by the active Bulusan volcano. The province's beaches, mountains, and relaxed pace of life make it a pleasant place to spend a few days.

History

Archaeological excavations in 1959 unearthed late Neolithic artifacts at the Bato Limestone Cave. The finds include stone tools and blades, bowls and burial jars, strung shell beads, and spoons made from nautilus shells. Dated to 100 B.C., they're now in the National Museum in Manila. Also, golden crowns believed to date from 91 B.C. to A.D. 79 have been found in Bulan and Juban.

The Spaniards visited the area, then known as Ibalon, early in the 17th century and established a mission at Casiguran. Several galleons were built at Bagatao Island during the 17th century. Galleons sailing from Manila to Acapulco used the San Bernadino Strait, which the Spaniards guarded from Sorsogon's shores. Old *baluartes* (watchtowers) remain at Bacon, Bulusan, Santa Magdalena, Matnog, and Casiguran.

Transportation

The town of Sorsogon is served by regular **Philtranco** buses linking Manila (604 km) with Samar and Leyte. Buses to Manila depart hourly 0830-1900. **JB Liner** minibuses depart every 30 minutes from Legaspi (59 km, 90 minutes). Secondary roads link all settlements with the main highway. On some routes, the last jeepney trip may be about 1630.

Matnog, two hours from Sorsogon by bus or jeepney, is the terminal for ferryboats crossing the San Bernardino Strait to Allen (Samar), with several trips daily. Bulan is the port for Masbate. Philtranco has a Manila-Bulan service, while JB Liner operates hourly from Legaspi until 1500 (takes three and a half

hours). Boats sail twice daily from Masbate town (four hours), and also cross from San Fernando and San Jacinto on Ticao (two hours). Be sure to leave Legaspi before 0900 if you plan to reach Samar or Masbate the same day. Daily boats link Donsol with Claveria, Burias Island.

SORSOGON TOWN

Three km after entering the province from Albay, a road branches west for the towns of Pilar and Donsol. Another side road leads to Castilla, noted for crabs and other seafood. The highway skirts Sorsogon Bay to Sorsogon town. Located at the head of the sheltered bay, it's the provincial capital, cultural, and commercial center, and is also a small port from which abaca is shipped.

The town, almost completely destroyed by an earthquake in 1840, serves as a convenient base for exploring the area. Sorsogon is not a big town, and most accommodations are close to the center.

Sorsogon province at the southern end of Luzon may not be the "Switzerland of the Orient" (an overstatement invented by a former governor), but the district features the impressive Mt. Bulusan and a fairly decent stretch of sand at Rizal Beach.

It's almost impossible to climb Mt. Bulusan without the help of a guide, but a visit to Bulusan Lake just south of the volcanic cone may be worth the effort; a paved trail follows the perimeter of the lake. Rizal Beach is long, broad, has brownish sand, and is almost completely deserted except on weekends.

Accommodations

Dalisay Lodge: Budget hotel in Sorsogon. 182 Peralta St., tel. (056) 211-1330, P100-200.

Fernando's Hideaway: The best in Sorsogon at the north end of town, owned and operated by the mayor's wife, who also serves as the local tourism representative. Pareja St., tel. (056) 211-1573, P600-850.

Rizal Beach Resort: Large two-story motel with an empty pool and rooms from dorms to a/c suites. Rizal Beach, tel. (056) 211-1056, P360-800.

BACON

This town (fiesta: 20-24 May) on Sucot Bay, 10 km by jeepney from Sorsogon, has an old ruined watchtower. Bacon municipality contains Lake Danao at an elevation of 610 meters. Two km past Bacon is **Tulong Gapo Beach;** good swimming and nice views across to Rapu-Rapu Island. You can stay here at **Fisherman's Hut,** a good place run by friendly people, and also at **Dino's Cottages** (P150).

Beyond Tulong Gapo is Long Beach and the Bato Cave archaeological site. Jeepneys from Bacon to Sawanga pass near Bato, which is about 10 km from Tulong Gapo, but access is difficult from the landward side. It's better to hire a *banca,* visiting both Bato Cave and Long Beach. There's no transport between Sawanga and Prieto Diaz, so to continue south, it's easier to return to Sorsogon.

GUBAT AND RIZAL BEACH

Jeepneys go directly from Sorsogon to Gubat, noted for crustaceans. You can stay at **Meliza Lodging House** (P150), although it's really not the kind of town that merits a long stay, and the beach five km south is a far better place to spend the night. Rizal Beach, five km south of Gubat, is an okay beach along a very unspoiled coast.

From Gubat, you must wait for a jeepney or bargain with the tricycle drivers; don't pay more than P20 for a tricycle ride. Rizal Beach gives an impressive feeling of space, with breakers coming in off the Pacific.

Accommodations

Stay at **Rizal Beach Resort** (P250 fan, P350 a/c). The resort is fairly run-down, but it's a nice place to rest after a long bus ride; the rooms have views of the beach. The beach is also backed by many small native-style bathing huts, which are intended for daytime use.

LAKE BULUSAN

Jeepneys continue down the coast from Rizal Beach through Barcelona to Bulusan town, whose church is noted for its old bell. Barcelona is a tiny town, but it's a beautiful spot with one village store and very few tourists stopping by. There's a morning bus to Bulusan from here or Rizal beach, and there are some accommodations in Bulusan, but again, very little available, except for the **Meliza Lodging House.**

South of town, the road begins to climb inland to a junction (11 km) where a paved side road leads right up to Lake Bulusan (two km). You can get a tricycle ride to the lake for P20 roundtrip. A concrete path leads around the small, round crater lake, but it's in a bad state of disrepair and in places completely destroyed by landslides. It's easier to walk halfway around (to the right) then turn back, rather than complete the 1,700-meter circle. The lake is surrounded by lush forest containing orchids, ferns, and flowers. Don't swim, due to the possibility of schistosomiasis.

Lake Bulusan is situated at an elevation of 635 meters on the southeast flank of Bulusan volcano (1,559 meters), which has a double peak. The eastern crest, now a rugged mound, is probably the remains of a vast, high, circular crater. The bell-shaped western summit is still active. It has had about 30 major eruptions since 1852, though none is known to have caused casualties. A mild eruption took place in 1983, and tremors recurred in 1984. The volcano, whose slopes form a 37-square-km national park, serves as a landmark for sailors approaching the San Bernardino Strait, since it's visible from almost 100 km when the weather is clear.

IROSIN

From the Bulusan Lake junction, the main road descends for nine km, passing the turnoff for Masacrot Soda Spring, where you can swim, to rejoin the South Highway at Irosin. This town, noted for its hilltop church, is situated in an ancient sunken crater and is surrounded by fertile fields.

Mateo Hot and Cold Springs Resort is in Sitio San Benon of Monbon; go three km north of Irosin on the main highway to Sorsogon, then one km east. Overnight in the dorm, P100 pp, or a room, P200 pp. A small canteen serves food and drink. Use of the three pools, which have different temperatures, costs P5. Swimming in the warm pool on a moonlit night is memorable. The Mapaso and Bulus springs are also in the vicinity of Irosin.

BULAN

This ferry port, 63 km from Sorsogon, is also a trading center with a lively fish market. Ferries leave for Masbate town (takes four hours) at 1200. Large *bancas* cross (two hours) to San Jacinto and San Fernando on Ticao Island at about 0900.

Accommodations
Three lodging houses are right on the pier, but the best place to stay is in a chalet down at the public park.

MATNOG

Matnog (671 km from Manila, 126 km from Legaspi, 67 km from Sorsogon) is a ferry termi-nal and fishing town on scenic Matnog Bay. Matnog is the departure point for ferries across to Samar. Ferries leave Matnog daily 0900-1300 except during typhoons when all services are cancelled. Matnog has several restaurants and a host of government buildings often used by stranded travelers for an overnight stay.

Transportation
To reach Matnog before the final ferry departure at 1300, it's important to leave Legaspi early in the morning. (There is a later ferry at 1600, but be cautious, as this ferry is subject to cancellation in the event of bad weather or insufficient passengers.) Buses take about four hours from Legaspi to Matnog. You can take a Philtranco bus from Legaspi or attempt to join an express bus coming down from Manila on a space-available basis. Otherwise, take a bus to Irosin (the last major town in Sorsogon Province), then continue south to Matnog by jeepney.

Accommodations
One inexpensive lodge is located in Matnog, though it's best to spend the night in Legaspi or at Rizal Beach and arrive in time to catch an early-morning boat to Samar. If you miss the ferry to Samar, you should backtrack and spend the night in Irosin.

M.G.L. DOMENY DE RIENZI

THE VISAYAS

The Visayas (or Bisayas), the large central group of islands between Luzon and Mindanao, comprise six of the Philippines's 11 major islands, plus many smaller islands. The Visayan Islands are noted for a markedly slower pace of life than that of central Luzon, delectable seafood and fruit, and the attractive lilt of the local dialects.

The Visayas offer the traveler much variety: beaches (the best are on small offshore islands), snorkeling and diving, hiking, important cities like Cebu and Iloilo, plus many exuberant festivals. Short and frequent boat connections make this prime territory for island-hopping, and the loop from Mindoro or Romblon to Legaspi via Boracay, Panay, Negros, Cebu, Bohol, Leyte, and Samar provides a good feel for the region.

Although the Visayas have long been a popular destination for tourists, backpackers, and divers, Palawan has definitely taken over as the number-one destination in the Philippines. Still, you might find it worthwhile to venture from Manila to Boracay via Samar, Leyte, Bohol, Cebu, Negros and Panay.

History

Archaeological excavations indicate that the region has been settled since early times. The name "Visayan" is believed to derive from the Sriwijaya Empire that extended its influence across much of Southeast Asia during the 7th-12th centuries. An extensive trade with other Asian nations flourished before Magellan visited Homonhon (off Samar), Limasawa (off Leyte), and Cebu. The Spaniards called the tattooed Visayans "Pintados" ("Painted Ones").

Early chroniclers refer to the Visayan chiefs' hospitable nature, cleanliness, superstition, polygamy and slavery, heavy gold jewelry, addiction to palm and rice wine, and filed teeth, varnished red or black and inlaid with gold. Since these first, fateful encounters in 1521, the Visayas have been at the forefront of Philippine history. Miguel Lopez de Legazpi moved north from Cebu and Panay to take Manila in 1571. U.S. forces moved north from Leyte to recapture Manila 374 years later.

Spain quickly took control of the region, but the Visayas' exposure to the Sulu Sea left it vul-

VISAYAN HIGHLIGHTS

Mindanao and Palawan are not included in the Visayan group but have been mentioned here to give you additional insight into what's best about the remaining islands beyond Luzon.

Bohol

Sandwiched between Cebu and Leyte is Bohol, among the more attractive islands in the Visayas with its colonial architecture, beautiful beaches on nearby Panglao Island, and eerie geological formations known as the Chocolate Hills. The offshore island of Panglao is a major dive destination with plenty of dive shops and good midlevel accommodations.

Boracay

Boracay, a small island just north of Panay, has long served as the premier beach destination in the Philippines. Once known only to a few backpackers, Boracay today has hundreds of bungalows, dozens of first-class hotels, a championship golf course, condominiums across the north end of the island, raging nightclubs, prostitutes, superb sunsets, decent diving, and cafés and restaurants facing one of the world's most dazzling beaches.

Camiguin

Travelers who dislike crowds and commercialization may enjoy this idyllic little island just off the north coast of Mindanao. Camiguin's isolation and good—but not great—beaches have made it a favored stop for travelers discouraged by the scene at Mindoro and Boracay.

Cebu

The Visayan hub of commerce and transportation has a few good beaches around the island and a handful of historical attractions in the capital of Cebu City, where restaurants, nightlife, and shopping are second only to Manila.

The remainder of the island is a mixed bag. Typhoons have damaged the once-brilliant coral beds on the west coast, but the relatively protected beaches on the southeastern coastline are still in good condition. Mactan Island beaches are mediocre and only recommended for tourists on tight schedules.

One of the upcoming stars of Cebu tourism is Malapascua Island just off the north end of Cebu—a beautiful island with stunning beaches and none of the commercialization that has overtaken many other islands, such as Boracay.

Leyte

Noted for its historical ties to General MacArthur and WW II, Leyte chiefly serves as a transit point for overlanders traveling from Samar to Cebu. The island's handful of natural attractions such as national parks, waterfalls, and offshore islands can be reached with public transportation but only with great difficulty from Ormoc and the principal town of Tacloban.

Mindanao

The Philippines' second largest island is a world of contrasts: modern cities only hours from animist cultures, Christian fundamentalists and traditional Muslims, capitalist warlords battling with communist in-

nerable to Moro pirates, who raided the coasts during the 16th-19th centuries. Most of the major islands have mountainous interiors, with limited arable land on crowded coastal plains, so that during this century there has been heavy out migration, especially to Mindanao and Manila, and overseas to Guam, Hawaii, and the U.S. There have been some problems with NPA activity in places like Samar and Leyte, but most of the region is very peaceful and extremely friendly.

ROUTES AROUND THE VISAYAS

Visitors short on time should take advantage of inexpensive PAL domestic flights and travel directly to the island or beach of their choice. Those with more time and enough patience to deal with irregular boat departures can tour the Visayas on the following circuit. Boat connections between most islands are inexpensive and frequent—except from Boracay to Mindoro where there exists no formal shipping service.

Allow about one month to complete the following route and longer if you plan to explore the national parks or really unwind on the beaches. The Visayan loop can be completed in either a clockwise or a counterclockwise direction, but the clockwise route is perhaps a better choice since it saves Boracay and Mindoro for the final stretches. Palawan and Mindanao could

surgents—a feudal but progressive land with all the strengths and weaknesses of Filipino society. Mindanao also has natural wonders such as the country's highest mountains, thick rainforests, swampy lowlands, and isolated beaches rarely visited by Westerners, plus it's home to dozens of distinct tribes whose traditional lifestyles remain much less affected than those of northern Luzon.

Highlights include the T'boli tribal area at Lake Sebu, a climb to the summit of Mt. Apo, and the beautiful islands around Surigao. Davao and Zamboanga serve as important transit points, although neither has any strong aesthetic appeal.

Mindanao is also, unfortunately, an island troubled by Muslim resistance groups near Cotabato City and the Sulu Islands south of Zamboanga. Otherwise, Mindanao is safe.

Mindoro

A trip to the country's seventh-largest island is synonymous with a sojourn at Puerto Galera, a beach resort five hours distant from Manila. Situated on an outstandingly beautiful harbor beneath soaring green mountains, it's a vision of paradise partially marred by hastily built cottages and other signs of unplanned development.

And yet, Mindoro can still be recommended for its relatively undeveloped beaches to the west and its untouched interior. Mindoro is also an important connection on the overland/oversea route from Manila to Boracay.

Negros

The sugar island of the Philippines is worth visiting for its volcano and beach resorts south of Dumaguete,

and its antique sugar trains near the capital city of Bacolod. Dumaguete is also the departure point for ordinary boats and fast ferries to Siquijor, a small but very beautiful island visible in the distance from Dumaguete.

Palawan

The Philippines' final frontier has the finest beaches, diving, and natural wonders in the country. Transportation is rugged, but inexpensive hotels and restaurants are plentiful. Key attractions include the diving and surrealistic landscapes at El Nido, topographic curiosities such as the underground caves near Port Barton, and the beaches at Sabang, Port Barton, and south of Puerto Princesa.

This is an island where days turn to weeks, weeks to months. In fact, many travelers are now bypassing Boracay and heading directly to Palawan after touring the mountain provinces of northern Luzon.

Panay

Shaped somewhat like a triangular kite fluttering between Negros and Mindoro, Panay's chief draws are the outstanding churches in Iloilo and the January festivals celebrating the original pact between the indigenous Atis and the datus from Borneo. Most travelers rush directly from Negros to Boracay or vice versa, but those with extra time should explore Iloilo and some of the nearby beaches and islands.

Samar

The third-largest island in the Philippines serves as a stepping stone between Luzon and points south. A few surf resorts are located on the rarely visited eastern coast.

be side trips from the Visayas or separate destinations starting from Manila.

Manila to Samar: Transportation is straightforward from Manila to Legaspi, but somewhat problematical from Matnog at the southern end of Luzon to Samar on Leyte, since ferry service ends around 1300. There is a later ferry at 1600, but be cautious, as this ferry is subject to cancellation in the event of bad weather or insufficient passengers. An early start from Legaspi is necessary to avoid getting stranded in Matnog.

Samar to Cebu: Both air-conditioned and ordinary buses wind along the scenic road that skirts the west coast of Samar to Tacloban in Leyte. Fast ferries depart several times daily from Ormoc to Cebu City. Boat service from

Leyte (Bato) to Bohol is undependable, and most travelers go to Cebu and then backtrack to Bohol.

Cebu to Boracay: Cebu City to Bacolod can be completed in a single day with an early start. Alternatively, you could take a fast ferry from Cebu City directly to Dumaguete and then continue around the sugar island by bus. Bacolod is a good place to pause if transportation bogs down.

Fast ferries go several times daily from Bacolod to Iloilo on Panay, from where buses continue north to Kalibo. Outriggers constantly dart from Caticlan, two hours north of Kalibo, over to Boracay. Iloilo to Boracay can be done in a single day of steady travel. Direct flights from

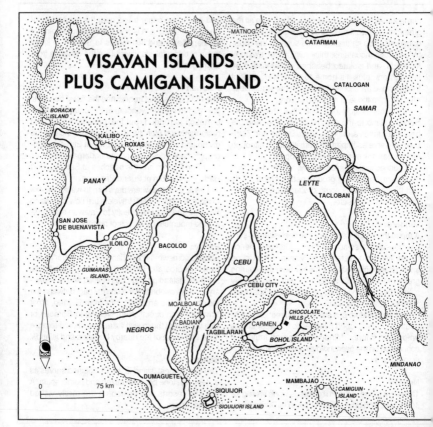

Cebu to Kalibo are useful for those anxious to reach Boracay.

Boracay to Mindoro: Because of high winds and rough waters, this is often the stretch that fouls an otherwise trouble-free journey. Outriggers occasionally leave from Boracay to southern Mindoro, but most travelers sail north to Tablas before continuing west to Mindoro. This crossing should only be attempted on clear days. Alternatives when the weather looks bad are flying from Kalibo to Manila or backtracking to Iloilo. Palawan can be reached by boats from Iloilo.

Mindoro to Manila: Several small boats leave in the mornings from Puerto Galera to Batangas on Luzon. Buses connect from Batangas to Manila.

BOHOL

Bohol's major attractions are the superb churches and the Chocolate Hills, which form a magnificent landscape, especially at dawn and dusk. A quiet, mellow island, Bohol also offers good beaches, excellent scuba diving and snorkeling around the island, and extremely friendly people.

HISTORY

In 1521, Panglao was an international trading center inhabited by tattoo-covered natives. After Magellan's death, his ships sailed across from Cebu to Panglao Island and the village of Bool (near Tagbilaran), from where the name "Bohol" derives. In 1565, Legazpi made a blood compact with Datu Sikatuna, bringing Bohol under Spanish rule, administered from Cebu. The Jesuits founded six parishes in 1595.

Bohol was the scene of two major rebellions against the Spaniards. The Tamblot revolt in 1622, led by a pagan priest, lasted six months. The second started in 1744, when a Spanish priest denied Christian burial to the brother of Francisco Dagohoy, now a local hero. Infuriated, Dagohoy established an independent government in the mountains of Bohol that lasted for 85 years, in spite of many Spanish attempts to overcome it. The longest revolt in Philippine history, it was finally suppressed by an expedition from Manila in 1829, and Bohol was grouped with Siquijor as a politico-military province.

In 1901, Filipino rebels confronted the Americans in a bloody battle at Jagna, and during WW II, Bohol saw widespread guerrilla activity.

TRANSPORTATION

From Manila
Air: PAL flies daily from Manila to Tagbilaran.
Ship: WG&A *Superferry 5* departs Manila's North Harbor for Tagbilaran on Tuesday at 0700, while its *Superferry 7* departs Saturday morning at 0700. The journey takes about 36 hours and costs P550-650.

Sulpicio Lines' *Dipolog Princess* leaves Manila's North Harbor for Tagbilaran on Wednesday at 1200 and takes about 28 hours to reach Tagbilaran.

From Cebu
Air: PAL flies from Cebu City to Tagbilaran on Monday, Wednesday, Thursday, Saturday, and Sunday.

Ship to Tagbilaran: Few people bother to take the large ships around the Visayas since the fast ferries are far more convenient and, well, much faster.

Several large ships continue to make the crossing, however, from Cebu City to Tagbilaran: Cokaliong Shipping's *Filipinas Dumaguete* (daily at 1830), Lite Shipping's *Santiago de Bohol* (daily at 2130), Lite Shipping's *Lite Ferry* (Sunday at 1230), and Trans-Asia Shipping's *Asia-Thailand* at 1200 on Monday, Wednesday, and Friday.

Ship to Talibon: Large ships also reach other ports on Bohol. To Talibon, there's the MV *Andy* daily at noon, the MV *Krishia* daily at 1900, and the MV *Talibon Cruiser* daily at 2100. It takes about four hours to reach Talibon, and passengers on the latter two departures may sleep on the deck until sunrise.

Ship to Tubigon: To Tubigon, Anco Shipping Line's MV *Tubigon* leaves Cebu City daily at 0900, 1200, 1600, and 2200. Charisse Shipping Line's MV *Charisse* departs daily at 1200, while Robie Shipping Line's MV *Betchie* departs daily at 1900. The Cebu City-Tubigon crossing takes two hours.

Ship to Loon: Lite Shipping's MV *LCT Barge St. Mark* departs Argao daily at 1000 and Tuesday and Saturday at 0400 for the three-hour crossing to Loon.

Outrigger to Cabilao Island: An outrigger leaves Argao for Cabilao on Tuesday and Saturday at 1400 and takes two hours to make the crossing.

Fast Ferries: These are the most popular way to make the crossing from Cebu to Bohol. The crossing takes about 90 minutes and costs P150-200 depending on the company. Water Jet Shipping's MV *Water Jet 2* leaves daily at

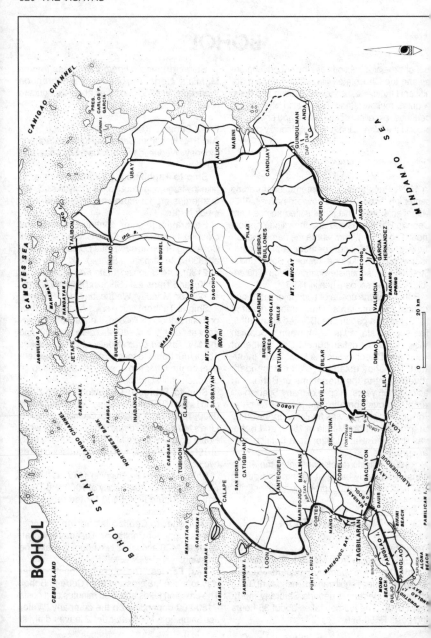

1630, while its MV *Water Jet 1* leaves daily at a more convenient 1030. Other fast ferries to Tagbilaran include the Universal Aboitiz MV *Supercat* daily at 0500 and 1100; Sucor Shipping's MV *Oceanjet 1* daily at 0900; Bullet Xpress's MV *Bullet Xpress* at 1000 and 1500; and the MV *Star Ruby* at 1730.

There's no need to make a reservation in Cebu City; just go down to the ferry terminal and wait for the next departing boat.

The fast ferry takes 90 minutes to Tagbilaran. You then can take a motorized tricycle or jeepney down to Panglao Island. Another option is to hire a taxi at a fixed fare (P200-250) or call one of the metered taxi companies located in Tagbilaran (P180-220).

From Leyte

There are no scheduled big ships or fast ferries from Leyte to Bohol, though several smaller ships make the crossing from smaller towns. A large outrigger goes from Bato to Ubay daily at 1000 and takes three hours to make the crossing. The MV *Star Ruby 1* leaves Bato for Ubay daily at 1300.

Another outrigger goes from Maasin to Ubay daily between 0800 and 1000 and takes four hours for the journey.

From Mindanao

Both large ships and fast ferries make the crossing from various ports on the north coast of Mindanao to Jagna or Tagbilaran.

From Butuan: The MV *Lady of Fatima* leaves Butuan for Jagna on Sunday at noon.

From Cagayan de Oro: From Cagayan de Oro to Jagna, choices include Cebu Ferries' MV *Our Lady of Lourdes* on Monday at 1200, MV *Our Lady of Lipa* on Sunday at 0900, and Sulpicio Lines' MV *Cagayan Princess* on Saturday at noon. The crossing from Butuan or Cagayan de Oro to Jagna takes six hours.

From Cagayan de Oro to Tagbilaran, Water Jet's MV *Water Jet 1* departs daily at 1530, while the WG&A MV *Superferry 5* leaves on Wednesdays at 2300 and the WG&A MV *Superferry 7* departs Sunday at midnight. The Trans-Asia MV *Asia-Thailand* leaves Tuesday and Thursday at 1200 and Saturday at 2000.

The Cagayan de Oro to Tagbilaran crossing by large ship takes seven or eight hours, while fast ferries do the same crossing in three or four hours.

From Dipolog: Folks stuck in Dipolog can catch the Sulpicio Lines' MV *Dipolog Princess* for Tagbilaran on Monday at 0900. Figure on five hours to Bohol.

Negros

Trans-Asia MV *Asia-Japan* makes the crossing from Dumaguete to Tagbilaran twice weekly on Wednesday and Sunday at 1800. The crossing takes three hours.

Getting Around

Buses from Tagbilaran leave hourly for all Bohol destinations, including the Chocolate Hills at Carmen. It's a long but pleasant walk from the highway turnoff to the Chocolate Hills Lodge. Additional service to Carmen is provided by buses and jeepneys departing from the rear of the public marketplace.

Buses from Tagbilaran to Alona Beach on Panglao leave several times daily until 1700. Also note Tagbilaran's tricycles, which have been cheerfully emblazoned with religious slogans.

Leaving

PAL flies twice daily from Bohol to Cebu City. There are also large ships several times weekly from Tagbilaran to Manila.

Fast ferries depart Tagbilaran for Cebu City several times daily and take about 90 minutes in a/c comfort. No need to check schedules or make a reservation; just get yourself to the Tagbilaran port north of town (take a tricycle from city center) and catch the first departing fast ferry to Cebu City.

Ships also leave Talibon and Tubigon for Cebu several times weekly.

SCUBA DIVING

Some superb diving spots surround Bohol's offshore islands, including Pamilacan, with its abundant manta rays; Cabilao; and Balicasag, rated as one of the best dive sites in the Philippines. Diving can be enjoyed year-round. Most divers head to Panglao Island, particularly at Alona Beach where dive tours are relatively inexpensive.

Dive-boat companies sailing out of Cebu also offer cruises to prime sites in the Bohol Strait although these companies are more expensive than the dive operators at Alona Beach. The Cebu-based companies offering tours include **Aquaventure Phils,** Sept.-Dec.; **Carfel Seaventure,** which takes in Cabilao, Panglao, and Balicasag on its 10- and 15-day cruises, Nov.-March; **Gloria Maris Adventures,** Sept.-Nov.; and **Seaquest Ventures,** June-January. Contact their Manila offices for detailed information.

TAGBILARAN CITY

Tagbilaran, a small city of 50,000, is the provincial capital, principal port, and commercial center. Its cathedral, built in 1595 and destroyed by earthquake in 1798, was rebuilt in the second half of the 19th century. The adjacent plaza is a popular local meeting place. You can enjoy the sunset from the nearby K of C Promenade, built on reclaimed land.

Tricycles are the main means of getting around within the city center, out to the pier, and to the nearby airport. Bohol handicrafts can be found in Manila, but not as cheaply as in Tagbilaran's market.

Tagbilaran is simply a stepping-stone to nearby beaches, churches, and other attractions. There is little reason to stay here.

Accommodations

Most of the hotels are grouped together near the city center, though few travelers stay in Tagbilaran unless they miss the last jeepney out to Panglao.

Tagbilaran Vista Lodge: Cheap and centrally located. 12 Lesage St., tel. (038) 411-3072, P80-350.

LTS Lodge: Probably the best budget- to middle-priced choice in town. Garcia Ave., tel. (038) 411-3310, P100-450.

Chriscentville Pension House: New place with spotlessly clean a/c rooms with private baths and cable TV. Gallares St., tel. (038) 411-4029, P550-900.

Restaurants

Tagbilaran is noted for seafood. The **Bistro de Paris** is good and will prepare seafood if or-

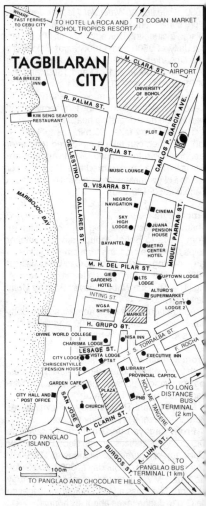

dered in advance. You'll find numerous small, inexpensive restaurants around the market, including **Elena's,** the **Horizon Restaurant,** and the **Harvest Restaurant.** Next to the church and town plaza, try the **Garden Cafe** for pizza.

An excellent spot for lunch is **Ruperto's Bar & Restaurant** on the corner of Torralba Street en route to the bridge leading to Panglao Island. With an excellent view of the bay and good food his is a popular restaurant for local businessmen ut little known by tourists. Recommended. The **Gie Gardens Hotel** restaurant was very bad and unsanitary at the time of writing; food poisoning and rats did not leave a favorable impression, but this does not imply that things have not improved. Check the kitchen if in doubt.

Vicinity of Tagbilaran

Several minor attractions are within easy striking distance of the city.

Blood Compact Marker: One km beyond, in Bool, is the Sikatuna-Legazpi Blood Compact site marker.

Burial Site: Two km east of the city center is Mansasa, where a pre-Hispanic burial site has been excavated.

Tontonon Falls: Swimming is possible in the stream but not underneath the 10-meter falls at the hydroelectric station beyond Loboc.

Punta Cruz Watchtower: The ancient fortress near Maribujoc west of Tagbilaran once served as the island's stronghold against Muslim pirates.

Carlos P. Garcia Memorial Park: This park, two km from downtown, commemorates the native Boholano, born in Talibon, who was Philippine president 1957-60.

Tarsiers: Bohol is also known for its tarsiers, miniature primates with large gogglelike eyes and long tufted nonprehensile tails. Related to lemurs and considered the smallest monkeys in the world, they are said to be so gentle that they cry themselves to death in captivity.

PANGLAO ISLAND

Bohol's finest beaches—and some of the best sand in this section of the Visayas—are on the southeastern coast of Panglao Island, where a wonderful combination of dazzling sand, swaying palms, warm waters, and colorful corals have made the island one of the premier beach destinations in the central Visayas.

All this beauty has not been lost on Manila's tourism officials, who have announced a 20-year blueprint for tourism, in cooperation with the United Nations Development Program and the private sector. The main targets are ecotourism on Palawan, the relatively untouched island of

Panglao, and Samal, another tropical island near Davao.

Panglao has a half-dozen beaches in various states of development but nearby all the bungalows, and dive shops are at Alona Beach on the southwestern corner. Just over the rocky headlands to the east is an immense stretch of dazzling sand that has just one place to stay, the decidedly upscale Bohol Beach Club.

Attractions

This flat, coralline limestone island is connected to the mainland near Tagbilaran by a bridge. Jeepneys link Tagbilaran with the villages of Panglao.

Hinagdanan Cave, 10 km from Tagbilaran, has stalagmites, stalactites, and a spring-fed underground swimming pool; it's illuminated by two natural holes. To visit it, take a jeepney from Tagbilaran going to Panglao via Bingag. The cave is just east of Bingag. Ask the driver to drop you at the nearest point to the cave, from where you must walk about a kilometer; alternatively, you can hire a tricycle from Tagbilaran.

Dauis was well populated even before the Spanish arrived. Like Santa Ana in Manila, its old church is built on the site of an early native cemetery, from which high-quality Chinese tradeware used as grave furniture has been recovered. Dauis church is unusual in that it has a natural well inside, next to the altar; it also has a painted ceiling.

Panglao Island has several attractive beaches, though they tend to be covered in seaweed Dec.-March. They include Bikini Beach, Dauis, 12 km from Tagbilaran; and Momo, Alona, and Duljo Beaches near Panglao, 18 km from the city.

The reefs on Panglao's north and west sides offer good possibilities for snorkelers and divers. The two small islands off the west end of Panglao can be reached by hired *banca*. Panglao Bay's underwater topography varies: from Duljo Point to Pungtud Island, relatively narrow shallows end in sudden drop-offs; between Pungtud and Tapurok Point, the seabed slopes. The coral here has been severely damaged, but the area is still noted for shells, turtles, and plentiful fish.

*the beautiful
white sand beach of
the Bohol Beach Club*

Alona Beach

Alona Beach caters almost exclusively to the scuba diving crowd; few budget travelers can afford the fare for accommodations, and bungalow owners have little interest in catering to low-end visitors.

Accommodations: Most bungalows at Alona charge P600-900 for a fan-cooled room and P1,200-1,500 for a/c suites. Many places now quote rates in U.S. dollars, and you can expect this trend to continue with the devaluation of the peso in 1997.

Lodges include Alona Kew right where the road meets the beach, and then, heading east, Sea Quest, Pyramid Resort, Alonaville, Planet Mars (rooms from P300), and Peter's at the end of the beach. A few hundred meters farther east is Alona Tropicana, the overpriced Crystal Coast, and the superbly isolated and eclectically decorated Bananaland, a great place to escape the scuba frenzy that washes over most of Alona Beach.

Heading west from Alona Kew you'll find Playa Blanca, Swiss Bamboo Bungalows, Casa Nova, and Kalipayan Resort up on the hilltop.

Scuba: Scuba dives can be arranged through several dive shops such as the two largest operations, Atlantis Dive Center (run by Kurt and Thomas) and Sea Quest. Note that snorkeling is possible at Alona but much better on the southwest coast at Cervera Shoal and adjacent islands.

Bohol Beach

A few kilometers east of Alona Beach is an amazing stretch of pure white sand with only one hotel, the expensive and often deserted Bohol Beach Club. Facilities include a swimming pool, a spa, tennis courts, water-sports facilities, and 40 individual bungalows for US$80-140.

The magnificent beach will probably remain sadly abandoned and lifeless until small-scale entrepreneurs are allowed to construct some less expensive bungalows.

Transportation

JG Express buses from the bus terminal on Butalid Street in Tagbilaran leave several times daily until 1700. Late arrivals in Tagbilaran can hire a motorized tricycle or call for a metered taxi.

Buses marked "Panglao" go to Panglao town near Doljo Beach and do not connect directly with Alona Beach. Buses marked "Panglao-Tauala" follow the southern coastline and stop in Alona before continuing on to Panglao town.

BALICASAG ISLAND

Balicasag is a flat, barren island situated four km southwest of Duljo Point, accessible by *banca* from Panglao. Balicasag is a prime spot for rare shells; gatherers fix a spool to the boat's row to facilitate the use of deepwater nets. The island is also a superlative diving spot, offering wonderful coral, caves, big fish, and excellent visibility.

Balicasag is ringed by a sandy beach, which is ringed in turn by a narrow shelf. On the north and northwest sides, the shelf is 10-50 meters wide and about seven meters deep, ending in vertical walls that fall forever. On the south and southeast sides the shelf is covered with large coral patches and slopes to 20 meters before dropping off.

Accommodations

The **Balicasag Island Dive Resort** (P500 s, P600 d) operates dive tours and rents diving equipment. Reservations have to be arranged through the **Philippine Tourist Authority** offices in Manila or Cebu. The tourist authority has exclusive rights to the island, so most divers set out from Alona Beach, dive around Balicasag, and spend the night back at Alona.

Transportation

To get there by car it takes 45 minutes from Tagbilaran, then 40 minutes by boat to Panglao; by boat it takes two hours from Tagbilaran port. The trip must be arranged first with the tourist authority. It takes four to six hours by chartered boat from Cebu City to Balicasag.

Nowadays, quite a few intrepid travelers are arriving at Panglao Island and Bohol from Camiguin Island off Mindanao. It is a four-hour ride on a good day by *banca*. There are no organized trips to and from these islands or set prices as yet, but it's a fast, easy way to get around. Many fishermen would be glad to make some decent money. Camiguin is in view from Panglao Island. Do not attempt this trip in rough weather, particularly during the rainy season.

BACLAYON

Seven km southeast of Tagbilaran, Baclayon's church is one of the oldest in the Philippines, dating from 1595. It's noted for its fine porch and 21-meter-high bell tower, intricately carved altars, and an organ installed in 1824. In the adjacent *convento* is a small museum of antique religious relics and ecclesiastical vestments.

Although currently under restoration and sometimes closed, the painted ceilings, intricately carved altar, and small museum of religious relics can be toured by request.

At least P1 million worth of religious objects were carted away from the church in 1997, the ninth recorded time that the museum had been burglarized over the span of two decades. All of the thefts remain unsolved.

There are a few restaurants that line the attractive road back towards Tagbilaran where you can stop and have lunch.

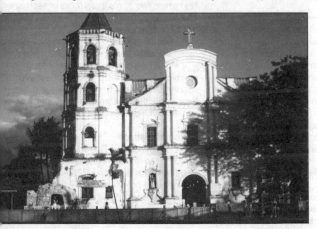

Baclayon Cathedral, one of the oldest in the Philippines

an image of Christ from the Baclayon Cathedral

CARL PARKES

PAMILACAN ISLAND

This lovely island south of Baclayon is developing a growing reputation among divers. Its name means "Nesting Place of Manta Rays," and some fortunate divers get to swim among the local manta population or witness the mating of these huge fish. But other fish species are abundant, too, and corals such as gorgonians are plentiful. The submarine terrain consists of alternating slopes and drop-offs.

Nearby Cervera Shoal is another great diving spot. Pamilacan has a white-sand beach on its north side, off which a wide reef flat offers good snorkeling.

Accommodations

The **Gie Gardens Hotel** operates cottages on the island. It's advisable to bring some food for the first night, since the caretakers may not expect guests, but they will soon get organized.

Transportation

To reach Pamilacan, take a jeepney from Tagbilaran to Baclayon, then charter a *banca* (about P200 roundtrip) for the 45-minute trip. Those on a budget can cross for a few pesos with residents returning on Wednesday from market and Sunday from church, at around 1500. Look for their *bancas* to the right of Baclayon pier.

THE CHOCOLATE HILLS

Clusters of these cone-shaped mounds are scattered over about 50 square km around Sagbayan, Carmen, and Sierra Bullones in central Bohol. Numbering 1,268 in all, the hills are formed of sedimentary limestone, shale, and sandstone; each hill rises 30-120 meters above the surrounding plateau.

The explanation of their formation remains a mystery. Some theories postulate prehistoric submarine volcanic eruptions and the action of sea currents, but most geologists believe that weathering is the main factor. Curiously, although they're regarded as an example of karst topography, none of the hills contain caves.

The hills are also the subject of numerous legends (e.g., they're the teardrops of a grief-stricken giant; or they're strewn across a battlefield where two giants threw rocks at each other). The hills are green during wet weather, but after a dry spell, which is most likely to occur in April and May, the grass turns brown so that they resemble chocolate drops, hence the name.

It's definitely worth staying here for at least one night to watch the sun rise and set over this strange landscape. Early morning and late afternoon are the best times for photography. You can also hike between the hills.

Accommodations

The **Chocolate Hills Resort,** magnificently situated on top of a giant chocolate kiss, charges P100 for dorm beds and P250-480 for private cottages. The hotel restaurant is the only place to eat here. The resort has a swimming pool, but it doesn't always contain water. A flight of steps leads from the hotel to a hilltop observation deck

Because this hotel complex is so run-down, travelers are often disappointed and do not stay overnight at the Chocolate Hills.

It can be done as a day-trip, but the hills are so pretty to watch at dusk it's a shame to miss it. t is a bit grubby at the hotel, but peaceful nonetheless.

Transportation

The main viewing point for the Chocolate Hills is the Resort Hotel/Youth Hostel Complex at Buenos Aires, near Carmen, 55 km, two hours from Tagbilaran. Buses leave regularly from Tagbilaran market; last trip around 1700.

The road from Tagbilaran follows the coast to Loay, then cuts inland. Tell the bus driver you want to go to the Chocolate Hills; the hotel complex is a 500-meter walk uphill from the turnoff, which is about five km before Carmen. If the driver seems useless, and you don't want to miss the stop, look for the Coca-Cola sign that marks the turnoff to the Chocolate Hills Resort. For a great experience, arrive at the junction after sunset, hike in the darkness to the resort, and wake early for one of the world's most surreal sunrises.

From Tubigon, buses for Carmen (43 km, two hours) meet the ferries. Once in Carmen, catch a Tagbilaran-bound bus and alight after five km.

Those making a side trip from Cebu City can take a boat to either Tagbilaran or Tubigon, loop around via the Chocolate Hills to the other port, then sail back to Cebu from there. To catch the 1100 ferry from Tubigon to Cebu, take the 0830 bus from Carmen market. You'll have just enough time to enjoy the sunrise and then be down on the highway by 0730 so you have time to walk into Carmen if a jeepney or other vehicle doesn't pass.

Buses also link Carmen with Ubay (two and a half hours), from where boats cross to Leyte. To reach Jagna (boats to Leyte and Mindanao), change at Loay.

AROUND BOHOL

The 161-km coastal circuit can be completed by bus and jeepney.

Tagbilaran to Loay

The popular Santa Fe Beach is one km east of Albuquerque. The road to Carmen branches inland at Loay. You can stay here at **Paradise Unlimited,** P250 pp, full board; it's run by Bill and Bruna Yost, an American/Filipina couple.

Loay to Jagna

Rosales Beach and **Spring Resort** (P200-250) at Lila have a cool, spring-fed swimming pool; a nearby waterfall descends a cliff into the sea. Dimiao church has two minaret-like hexagonal towers. One km west of Valencia is the Magsaysay Camp, a Boy Scout reserve with a

Chocolate Hills

natural swimming pool and campsite in forested surroundings.

Badiang Spring, located between the highway and beach four km east of Valencia, has a spring-fed swimming pool with facilities for changing. **Roxas Park,** five km inland from Garcia Hernandez in Maambong, is a bathing resort with two natural freshwater swimming pools.

Jagna
This port is an important copra-collecting point and is famous for *kalamay,* a sweet delicacy of rice and coconut milk. If you have to wait for a boat at Jagna, visit Tinugdan Spring, a waterfall located 10 km inland in a beautiful setting.

Anda
A road branches east from Guindulman to Anda, which has a fine beach. There is a resort here called **Dap-Dap Resort,** four cottages with bath, P150-200. To get there take a bus or jeepney from Guindulman to Anda, then walk one km to the beach. Beverages and limited food are sold here.

The Anda Peninsula is mined for manganese. Archaeological excavation of limestone formations in the municipality of Candijay has revealed ancient, intricately carved wooden coffins in small caves and rock shelters.

Ubay
Ubay is a port with boats to Cebu and *bancas* to Leyte. Stay and eat at the clean and friendly **Are Restaurant, Singalong,** and **Pension House,** P150 on Col. Garcias Avenue. The flat, mangrove-covered Lapinio Island is offshore from Ubay. The main road then cuts across the north coast, through a series of fishing towns, to Tubigon.

Tubigon
This small port is the terminal of the shortest ferry crossing from Cebu. Buses go from here to Carmen (two hours) and Tagbilaran (90 minutes).

Stay at **Alexandra Reserva** (P150), near the market, or **Cosare Rice Mill,** a five-minute walk from the market.

Tubigon to Tagbilaran
The church at Calape houses the image of the Virgen sa Calo-oy. Snorkeling is good off nearby Mantatao Island.

Loon is the site of a 19th-century church and Naro Spring, which is situated behind the municipal hall. Cottages are for rent at Lintuan Beach, south of town.

Offshore is Cabilao Island, with a lighthouse. You can cross by *banca* from Loon with island residents. Snorkelers should make for the reef flat on the Cabilao's north side, where conditions are excellent. Scuba divers can concentrate on the north and northwest drop-offs. These walls plunge into the depths, but their upper sections offer good coral, caves, sponges, and plentiful fish, including hammerheads and other large species. Beware of strong currents.

In Maribojoc, the Magsaysay Spring flows from the ground into a concrete catch-basin. Punta Cruz in Maribojoc Municipality has a well-preserved stone watchtower (1615), formerly used as a lookout against Moro pirates; an old wooden cross stands in front of it.

Inland, in Antequera Municipality, Inambacan Falls flow into the Abatan River. The Inambacan Falls are only 15 km north of Tagbilaran just outside of Maribojoc. They are beautiful and well worth visiting.

JAO ISLAND

Jao (pronounced "how") Island is an isolated and relaxing little island situated off the northeast coast of Bohol. Beaches are nonexistent and most of the coral beds have been destroyed by typhoons, but there's an air of tranquility, and fine walks are possible through native villages famous for their nipa weavings.

Accommodations
Laguna Escondido Resort and Yacht Haven, managed by a crusty old German-Canadian sailor who entertains his guests with tales of Pacific crossings, charges P100 for dorm beds and P300-350 for private cottages. Food here is much better than the average Filipino fare.

Transportation
Talibon can be reached by buses from Tagbilaran and the Chocolate Hills. Regular boats from Talibon to Jao Island leave several times daily. Jao Island is a place for quiet conversation and long books.

BORACAY

Beautiful Boracay was an unknown island of farmers and fishermen until it was "discovered" in the mid-'70s. At first its existence was a closely guarded secret, whispered from friend to privileged friend. Now it's a major destination for visitors to the Philippines and has been voted as one of the best beaches in the world by several surveys.

In a mere 10 years, Boracay changed from a traveler's hangout with inexpensive, lantern-lit bungalows and a nearly deserted stretch of the most spectacular beach in Asia to an upscale beach destination known around the world.

Once an isolated island known only to backpackers and world travelers, Boracay today is deservedly the most popular beach resort in the Philippines. The reasons are obvious: sand as fine and white as talcum powder, dazzling aquamarine waters, soaring coconut trees that hang over the beaches like in a scene from *South Pacific,* lonely coves, epic sunsets, plus some of the finest accommodations in the country.

Boracay now has everything an upscale tourist could hope for, and the fabulous White Beach is lined with fancy, a/c bungalows, nightly buffets of fresh seafood, guitar music, and massage. Boracay has also become a mecca for job-seeking Filipinos who work in the restaurants, the shops, and the strip of discos and bars that lines the beach.

Boracay is still relatively inexpensive; the bungalows for backpackers are located behind the beachfront at White Beach, but it's no longer a traveler's hide-out. Everyone has discovered Boracay, and it's not unusual to pass a hundred foreigners a day on the beach.

Boracay (10 square km) is seven km long and only one km across at its narrowest point. It has three main villages—Yapak, Balabag, and Manoc-Manoc—and numerous small *sitios,* all connected by a maze of paths. The spectacular 3.5-km White Beach stretches from Sitio Diniwid to Sitio Angol on the west side, and resorts are strung out along almost its entire length.

ACTIVITIES

The most popular activity on Boracay is simply lazing on the beach and taking an occasional dip in the turquoise water. It's a hard life in the tropics!

There is some windsurfing offered on Boracay, but it is limited to some of the more upscale resorts. Fees are high for all activities on the island, but bargaining is common.

Boracay sunbather

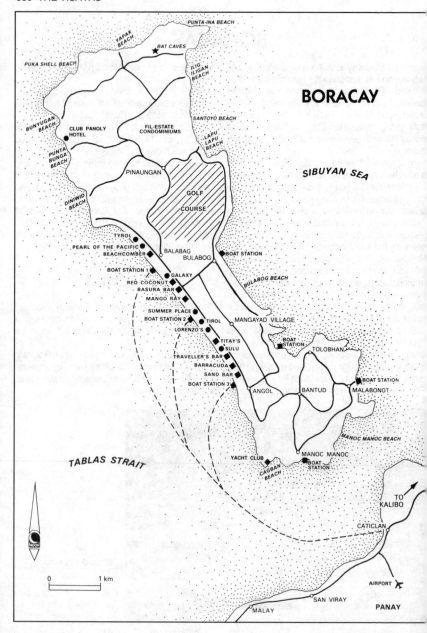

PUNTA-INA BEACH

YAPAK BEACH

★ BAT CAVES

PUKA SHELL BEACH

ILIG ILIGAN BEACH

BUNYUGAN BEACH

CLUB PANOLY HOTEL

FIL-ESTATE CONDOMINIUMS

SANTOYO BEACH

LAPU LAPU BEACH

BORACAY

PUNTA BUNGA BEACH

PINAUNGAN

GOLF COURSE

SIBUYAN SEA

DINIWID BEACH

TYROL
PEARL OF THE PACIFIC
BEACHCOMBER
BALABAG
BULABOG
BOAT STATION

BOAT STATION 1
GALAXY
RED COCONUT
BASURA BAR
MANGO RAY
SUMMER PLACE
BOAT STATION 2
TIROL
LORENZO'S
TITAY'S
SULU
TRAVELLER'S BAR
BARRACUDA
SAND BAR
BOAT STATION 3

BULABOG BEACH

MANGAYAD VILLAGE

BOAT STATION
TOLOBHAN

ANGOL
BANTUD
MALABONOT
BOAT STATION

MANOC MANOC BEACH

TABLAS STRAIT

YACHT CLUB
CAGBAN BEACH
MANOC MANOC
BOAT STATION

TO KALIBO

CATICLAN

NOON

0   1 km

AIRPORT ✈

SAN VIRAY

MALAY

PANAY

Windsurfers can be rented (P300 per hour; instruction P450 an hour). Hiring an outrigger boat for sailing is fun (P450 for a half day, P700 whole day); go on a round-the-island trip by motorized *banca* (P500 per trip for a maximum of eight persons). A sunset cruise, weather permitting, costs P200 pp. Hiring a *banca* for fishing costs P1,000 a day.

Snorkeling is a popular activity; masks can be rented at various places. Snorkeling is better at the south end of White Beach near Angol, but in spite of the clear water, the coral and fishlife are quite mediocre by Philippine standards. Boracay's best snorkeling is off the eastern shore, especially near Lapus Lapus and Sugod, but riptides and currents can be a hazard.

Puka Beach

One of the more unusual beaches on the island is dazzling Puka Shell Beach beyond Yapak at the island's north end. There's a fine view of Carabao Island from the beach and a forest of staghorn coral lies immediately offshore, but be wary of the strong currents that sweep between the islands. Before the advent of tourism, a major source of income for islanders was digging here for *puka* and *heishi* shells. *Puka* shells—small, round, white (sometimes dotted with brown)—are found in only a few other places, e.g., Bali and Hawaii. Boracay's now rare *puka* shells are said to be the world's finest for luster and whiteness.

Diving

Scuba diving has become a major activity on Boracay, and some very good outfits operate along White Beach and at the various resorts. The better resorts have swimming pools where you can get your initial training. Take note that the diving around Boracay is not the best in the Philippines; sites in Cebu, Bohol and Puerto Galera are better, but the PADI certification is interchangeable and no more expensive on Boracay than it is elsewhere.

The dive shops on White Beach and at the better hotels offer full PADI certification for US$250. The course usually takes from three to five days. Some of the established shops include **Inter-Island Dive Center** and **Beach Life Diving Center** at Angol, **Philippine Water Diving School, Calypso Diving School,** and **Victory Divers** at Mangayad, and **Lapu Lapu Div-**

PARADISE LOST?

But all is not well in paradise. Despite the growth of tourism, government agencies—both local and national—failed to construct waste treatment plants or even to pipe in fresh water for human consumption. For over two decades, waste water was pumped into the bay and trash was simply pushed into giant landfills. The result was that the once pristine waters were polluted almost beyond redemption.

Another problem was that the local *barangay* officials sold over 400 tricycle permits to local residents, giving them a wealth of votes-in-pocket but also cursing the island with a ridiculous supply of noisy, polluting machines that buzz incessantly up and down the solitary road that runs from the south to the north end of the island.

Another nail in the coffin was the transformation of the northern third of the island into a wonderland of condominiums and swimming pools surrounding an 18-hole golf course—exactly what most people don't want to find in a tropical resort.

Then, in 1997, the minister of the environment stated in a public address that Boracay was an environmental disaster area. No kidding. After a great deal of soul searching, and a dip in the waters by tourism minister Mina Gabor, Manila finally announced that something would be done to save Boracay. This new plan, approved in late 1997, promises to bring fresh water from a new dam on Panay, a wastewater-treatment plant, and garbage-collection services to the immensely popular island.

If the government fails to take action on the very serious problems facing Boracay, I'd say skip the island and head directly to Palawan.

ing Safari at Balabag. The major resorts also offer PADI instruction; try **Laguna de Bay, Boracay Beach Club Hotel, Fridays Boracay,** and **Paradise Garden Resort-Hotel.**

ACCOMMODATIONS

Boracay's bungalows and resorts are among the finest in Southeast Asia—clean, comfortable, and well priced. At last count, Boracay had over 300 lodging operations with some 4,500 rooms.

Most accommodations are on the west side of the island along White Sand Beach. This four-km stretch of pure-white sand has three villages that serve as general reference points—Balabag in the north (Boat Station One), Manggayad in the middle (Boat Station Two), and Angol in the south (Boat Station Three).

There's little reason to make any specific recommendation, since most places are in good condition and generally charge an appropriate rate for their facilities. A good strategy is to have the boatman drop you somewhere in the center of the beach (ask for Boat Station Two) and then begin your bungalow search. If you're really on a budget, Boat Station Three is the place to be dropped.

Budget

Inexpensive bungalows average P300-600 during the low season from June through October and double that fare during the high months from November to June. Most of the budget places are at the south end of the beach in Angol near Boat Station Three. The place has declined in quality and almost resembles some sort of ghetto, filled with budget travelers and some decidedly seedy types.

The cheapest cottages are back from the beach, but none are far from it, at least 30 meters from the high-tide mark. A typical budget cottage consists of a small room with a double bed or two singles, a mosquito net, and a pleasant veranda with a table and two chairs. Most have their own toilet and shower.

Moderate

Midpriced bungalows cost P600-1,000; the middle of the beach (Manggayad at Boat Station Two) is your best bet for something in this price range. The better midpriced cottages are air-conditioned with nice double beds, bathrooms, and little extras all around. Some resorts offer complimentary breakfast and a few have swimming pools. A discount can be obtained by bargaining during the off season (June-Oct.), or for extended stays.

Luxury

Luxury resorts are mainly found from the middle to the top of the beach (Balabag at Boat Station One) facing some of the best sand on the island.

RESTAURANTS

Restaurants are within easy reach of all cottages. The cluster between Mangayad and Angol is particularly good, and the more upscale restaurants are at Balabag.

Popular places around the crowded Mangayad area from south to north include the **Jolly Sailor,** the **English Teahouse,** the **Sailor's Snack Bar, Mona Lisa, Casa Pilar, The Guitar Bar,** the popular **Tito's Place,** the second **English Tea Room, Nigi Nigi Nu Noos, Sunset Beach Bar,** and **Sharks Bar & Restaurant.**

Farther north up the beach toward Balabag, the excellent **Restaurant Chez de Paris** is recommended; also try the **Red Coconut, La Reserve, Tito Restaurant, Jony's Place,** and the upmarket **Friday's** restaurant and resort.

Many of the bungalows built behind White Beach also have their own small restaurants serving good meals at reasonable prices.

ENTERTAINMENT

Nightlife here tends to begin slowly, as everyone hangs around the beachfront restaurants watching the sunset. With a more upmarket crowd invading Boracay, the party atmosphere has become subdued as many foreigners retire early.

However, as quiet as the beach may seem, the night owls really get going around midnight, meeting at **Bazura** at Mangayad for some dancing. Other popular spots include **Roxy Park, The Beachcomber** (*the* original disco on the island), **Sharks Bar & Disco,** and the newer **Sand Castles** disco at Angol.

The **Guitar Bar** next to **Tito's Place** (another popular hangout) is also fun, as some talented Filipinos play Freddie Aguilar tunes and other songs into the wee hours. There seems to be no defined meeting place for travelers, and more often than not, a bar or resort may be showing a video like *Thelma and Louise* or *Lethal Weapon.*

SERVICES AND INFORMATION

Boracay is a well-developed resort island with all possible facilities. There's a small but helpful

tourist office in the Oro Beach Resort near Boat Station Two.

Money: Cash and traveler's checks can be changed at the Boracay Tourist Center in the middle of White Beach near Red Coconut Resort. The Boracay Tourist Center also has international phone services, both incoming and outgoing faxes, a postal office, a booking agency for all airlines, hotel reservations throughout the Philippines, safety deposit boxes, drugstore, one-hour photo service, and a bulletin board with some very interesting ads posted by local expats (stuff for sale, upcoming events, etc.).

The Boracay Tourist Center will also help with money transfers and will give Visa and Mastercard cash advances with a seven percent service charge.

Cash and traveler's checks can also be exchanged at the three Allied Bank branches scattered around White Sand Beach.

Telephone: International and domestic phone calls can be made from most resorts and from the Boracay Tourist Center, Pantelco Business Center in Balabag, and BayanTel at the south end of the beach.

Post Office: A small post office is in Balabag just behind the basketball court.

Visa Extensions: Visa extensions are handled by Swagman Travel with several offices along the main beach.

Hospital: Emergency medical care is best at the Tirol Hospital on the main road near Green Hill Cottages. Serious problems will require evacuation to Kalibo or Manila.

TRANSPORTATION

Getting There by Air

There are literally dozens of slow ways to reach Boracay but only one fast way: fly. PAL and Air Philippines fly several times daily to Kalibo, from where buses take two hours to Caticlan.

The Department of Tourism offers a Boracay Express minibus from the airport that flies through the small settlements en route to Boracay for about P150-200. Local buses from Kalibo ply the same route in about the same time and cost P25-40. Don't worry—buses and minibuses are waiting for every flight arriving at the Kalibo airport.

Pumpboats shuttle constantly from Caticlan across the narrow straits to White Sand Beach.

Warning: A serious bottleneck exists between Manila and Boracay. Flights between Manila and Kalibo are perpetually filled during the high season Nov.-May. To avoid getting stranded in Boracay (not half bad), you should make roundtrip reservations well in advance.

Here are some useful air connections from Manila, Cebu City, and Puerto Princesa.

Manila to Kalibo: PAL and Air Philippines fly daily from Manila to Kalibo. The fare is P1,400-1,600.

Manila to Caticlan (near Boracay): Caticlan has a small airstrip just 15 minutes from Boracay. Arrivals take a shuttle from the airport down to the Caticlan pier, from where *bancas* head over to Boracay.

Asian Spirit and Pacific Airways fly daily from Manila to Caticlan. Air Ads flies three times weekly, on Monday, Friday, and Saturday. The flight costs P1,600-1,800.

Cebu City to Kalibo: Air Philippines flies daily from Cebu City to Kalibo, while PAL flies this route on Monday, Wednesday, Friday and Saturday.

Palawan to Iloilo: PAL flies from Puerto Princesa to Iloilo City on Thursday and Saturday. The flight continues on to Cebu City.

Ship from Manila

Ships are plentiful to Iloilo, though several lines also provide service to various ports near Boracay, including Caticlan and Dumaguit.

To Caticlan (near Boracay): MBRS Line's MV *Romblon Bay* departs Manila for Caticlan on Tuesday at 1300 and Friday at 1400. The trip takes 22 hours.

WG&A MV *Superferry 1* makes the same trip weekly during the high season months of March and April. This much faster (and more comfortable) ship makes the passage in just under 11 hours. You'll need to check the newspaper or give WG&A a call to confirm the schedule.

To Dumaguit (near Boracay): Negros Navigation's MV *Don Julio* departs Manila on Wednesday at 1500 and reaches Dumaguit in about 16 hours. The fare is P400-450.

WG&A's MV *Our Lady of Naju* does the trip in 15 hours with departures from Manila at 1400 on Monday, Wednesday, and Sunday. This ship sometimes berths at nearby Batan, rather than directly at Dumaguit.

The Tablas Route
Another way is to fly to Tablas Island (Romblon Province) and from there take a boat to Caticlan or Boracay. Flying to Kalibo is more expensive but is more convenient than going to Tablas.

Another way is to take a bus from Manila to Lucena City (three and a half hours), then a boat to Tablas.

Several large outriggers provide connections from Looc on Tablas Island to either Boracay or Caticlan on the north coast of Panay. A large outrigger leaves Looc daily in the morning around 0900 and takes two hours to make the crossing to Boracay. The fare is P100-120.

Another outrigger departs Santa Fe on Tablas Island and heads down to Boracay (or Caticlan) every Tuesday, Thursday, and Saturday. The boat waits for the plane to arrive from Manila (the airport is at Tugdan). After the plane lands, a jeepney takes passengers down to the boat dock in Santa Fe, from where the outrigger loads up and takes off for Boracay.

This outrigger does the crossing in a slightly quicker 90 minutes and costs P80-100.

Getting There from Mindoro
Mindoro also serves as a transit point for visitors going to Boracay.

Roxas to Boracay via Tablas: The most popular route is with a large outrigger from Roxas in southeastern Mindoro across to Looc on Tablas Island, from where *bancas* continue down

to Boracay. The route via Tablas takes about 10 hours and is often cancelled in bad weather.

Roxas Direct to Boracay: There's also a direct boat service from Roxas to Boracay—twice weekly during the low season and almost daily during the busy months from December to June.

Although a somewhat dangerous journey due to unexpected storms, the Roxas-Boracay route allows you to enjoy the beaches at both Puerto Galera and Boracay with a minimum of backtracking. The tourist office in Puerto Galera has the latest schedules for boats from Roxas and other towns on Mindoro.

Mindoro to Panay
Several large outriggers make the crossing from San Jose on Mindoro to various ports on Panay, including Buruanga and Lipata. Both towns are within easy striking range of Boracay.

San Jose to Buruanga: An outrigger leaves on Thursday and Sunday at 0900 and takes at least eight hours to reach Buruanga, about 15 km south of Caticlan (the departure point for Boracay).

San Jose to Lipata: The MV *Princess Melanie Joy* and the MV *Aida* sail weekly to Lipata, a small town on the west coast of Panay, some 70 km south of Caticlan. The trip takes a full 24 hours since stops are made at both Semira and Caluya Islands.

Bus from Panay
Coming from Iloilo or Roxas City, take the bus to Kalibo. From there, regular buses and jeepneys go to Caticlan. From Iloilo, you can wait for an ordinary bus or grab one of the nearby minivans, which will get you to Kalibo or Caticlan in record time. The road is atrocious.

Coming from San Jose de Buenavista, the road branches at Pandan to Libertad and Malay, and to Nabas and Kalibo. For Caticlan, it's quicker to alight at the junction south of Nabas and wait for a vehicle coming from Kalibo rather than follow the coast around through Malay.

Getting Back to Manila
A half dozen airlines depart daily from either Caticlan or Kalibo for Manila. Tickets can be purchased and reservations made at any of the numerous travel agencies on the island. Be sure to reconfirm any return ticket you may have.

You can also travel by boat to Romblon Province, from where several boats a week go directly to Manila or to Cotta (Lucena City). From Cotta, it's only a three-and-a-half-hour bus ride to Manila.

Alternatively, cross to Roxas and make your way up the east coast of Mindoro via Calapan or Puerto Galera.

Banca operators on Boracay also frequently try to form groups of travelers for the trip to Santa Fe (Romblon Province). Ask around. Boats will cross to Santa Fe anytime, subject to calm weather and a minimum number of passengers, or a smaller number willing to share the total cost. Boats also often cross to Santa Fe or Looc from Caticlan.

CEBU

Cebu is a province, an island, and a city. The city's historical and cultural importance makes it a major sightseeing destination; its location in the center of the archipelago also makes it the country's shipping crossroad. The island offers fine beaches and scuba diving. The resorts of Mactan Island and the east coast cater to tourists, while Moalboal is one of the Philippines's most popular travelers' hangouts and Badian has one of the country's best resorts.

Residents of Cebu like to boast about their province and city: oldest university, church, and street in the country; more cathedrals and historical attractions than anywhere else; best beaches and the finest climate; coral reefs and aquamarine waters that rank among the tops in the country; freshest beer and rum (San Miguel and Tanduay are located here); most beautiful women; sweetest mangoes and creamiest *guabanos.*

Shaped somewhat like a giant snake that evenly divides the Visayas in half, Cebu is also an economic miracle that disproves the notion that prosperity never reaches the underdeveloped hinterlands. Credit for growth rates, which have recently far outstripped those in Manila, goes to Chinese-Filipino entrepreneurs, who comprise less than 15% of the population but, as elsewhere throughout Asia, almost completely dominate the local economy.

HISTORY

Cebu was an important trading center, prosperous and well-populated, long before the Spanish "discovered" it. Gold was mined, Chinese traders resided here, and ships bringing merchandise from China, the East Indies, Arabia, and Siam paid tribute to the ruler of Zubu, or Sugbu, as the island was called, upon entering the harbor.

Magellan's expedition was well received by Rajah Humabon in 1521. Fragments of the wooden cross he planted to commemorate the conversion of Humabon and his people still remain in the center of Cebu City, while the basilica houses the statue of the Santo Niño given to Humabon's wife.

A monument on Mactan marks the spot where Magellan died as he made his ill-advised landing to confront Chief Lapu-Lapu, who is now a Filipino hero. When Legazpi reached Cebu in 1565 he was met with hostility, but the Spaniards prevailed. After sealing a blood compact with Rajah Tupas, Legazpi constructed a fortified settlement that would become Cebu City. Early on, it was called San Miguel, then Santissimo Nombre de Jesus.

The accompanying Augustinian priests, inspired by finding the Santo Niño left by Magellan, built the Philippines's first church and began the task of conversion. Cebu served as a base for the exploration and conquest of other islands. For six years, it was the capital of the new colony, but persistent food shortages forced Legazpi to move north to Panay, then Manila.

During the early colonial period, Cebu's coastal settlements suffered frequent raids by Muslim pirates. Cebu, nevertheless, remained an important provincial trading center and military base through the centuries. Spanish cultural influence was great here, with many towns named after places in Spain—Asturias, Santander, San Sebastian, Compostela, and Toledo.

A Spanish royal decree reopened Cebu's port to foreign shipping in 1860. In 1898, Cebuano revolutionaries forced Spanish troops to retreat to Fort San Pedro after a fierce street battle. Insurrection continued for about three years after

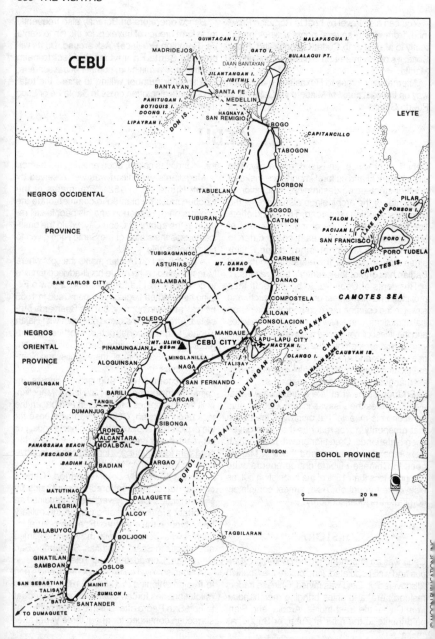

the Americans occupied the island in 1899. They clashed with Filipinos around Toledo's church in 1900.

Cebu suffered heavy bomb damage during WW II. In March 1945, liberating U.S. forces landed on the beaches of Talisay, and fierce battles took place on Antuanga and Babag hills. Among prominent Cebuanos was former president of the Commonwealth of the Philippines Sergio Osmeña, who landed at Leyte with MacArthur in 1944. In 1957, President Ramon Magsaysay's death in a plane crash on Mt. Manunggal in Central Cebu was a traumatic event for Filipinos.

SCUBA DIVING

Cebu is the center for diving throughout the Visayan archipelago. Dive resorts with compressors, divemasters, and fully equipped boats are located throughout the island, but those on

The author prepares for a dive in Cebu.

CARL PARKES

Mactan near Cebu City are the most convenient. Diving at Mactan includes the coral reefs surrounding the Olangos and the double barrier reef at Caubyan Island.

Cebu's second-largest dive site is at Moalboal on the southwestern coastline. Though shoreline corals were wiped out several years ago by a powerful typhoon, excellent reefs remain around the Pescadores and the luxurious Japanese-owned resort island of Badian. Moalboal has inexpensive accommodations.

Other diving is possible north of Cebu City and on Bantayan and Gato islands off the northwestern tip of the island.

All of Cebu's major dive destinations offer shore and boat diving, but Moalboal is substantially cheaper than the resorts, both to stay and to dive. Rates for equipment, two tanks, dive master, and boat vary from about US$30-45 at Moalboal to US$50-85 at Mactan and other upscale east coast places.

At the resorts, you can save money by taking a diving package for a number of days. Many places also offer diving courses leading to the coveted PADI international certification. At present, Moalboal offers the cheapest rates in the Philippines, charging US$200 for the full course.

TRANSPORTATION

Air
Cebu is the transportation hub of the Philippines. PAL, Air Philippines, and most other domestic airlines have daily service from Manila and other Visayan islands. International travelers should inquire about direct charters from America, Europe, Hong Kong, and Japan—a convenient approach that avoids having to mess with Manila.

The airport is on Mactan Island, 13 km from the city center. City center can be reached from the airport on hourly shuttle buses or metered taxis, which cost P100-150 including the bridge toll.

Those wishing to stay at the better beach resorts on Mactan or farther afield (Tambuli, Club Pacific, etc.) can book through any Manila travel agency and prearrange direct transportation from the airport to the resort. It's usually quite easy to simply arrive in Cebu and take transport to the resort, without a reservation.

PAL's ticketing offices are in the Capitol Commercial Complex on Escario St., on Plaridel St., and at the Mactan International Airport.

Other domestic and international airlines with offices in Cebu City include Air France, British Airways, Cathay Pacific, Cebu Pacific, Continental Airlines, Grand Air, Gulf Air, KLM Royal Dutch Airlines, Malaysian Airlines, Northwest Airlines, Pacific Airways, Qantas, Scandinavian Airlines System (SAS), Singapore Airlines, and Thai Airways International.

Air from Bohol
PAL provides direct air connections from Tagbilaran on Monday, Wednesday, Thursday, Saturday, and Sunday.

Air from Camiguin
Flights from this idyllic island were cancelled several years ago due to low demand, but may be resumed sometime in the future. Check with the PAL office in Cebu City or Manila for current details.

Air from Leyte
PAL flies from Tacloban to Cebu City on Monday, Wednesday, and Saturday. Sit on the right side for the best views.

Air from Manila and Luzon
All the major airlines provide air connections from Manila to Cebu City including PAL, Air Philippines, Cebu Pacific, and Grand Air daily. PAL also flies from Legaspi to Cebu City on Monday, Wednesday, Thursday, and Sunday.

Air from Mindanao
Air connections are plentiful from all the major towns and cities on Mindanao.

PAL provides daily flights from Davao, Zamboanga, General Santos City, and Pagadian.

PAL has less than weekly flights from Butuan (daily except Wednesday and Sunday), Cagayan de Oro (Monday, Wednesday, and Saturday), Cotabato (Thursday and Sunday), Dipolog (Monday, Tuesday, Wednesday and Friday), Ozamis (daily except Monday, Wednesday, and Saturday), Surigao (daily except Monday, Wednesday and Sunday), Dipolog (daily except Thursday and Saturday), Tandag (Monday, Wednesday, and Saturday).

Cub Pacific and Grand Air fly daily from Cagayan de Oro and Davao. Air Philiippines provides daily service from Cagayan de Oro, Cotabato, and Zamboanga.

Air from Negros
PAL flies from Bacolod to Cebu City on Monday, Tuesday, Wednesday, Friday, and Saturday. Service from Dumaguete is provided three times weekly.

Air from Palawan
PAL flies on Thursday and Saturday from Puerto Princesa to Cebu City via Iloilo on Panay.

Air from Panay
PAL, as noted above, flies on Thursday and Saturday from Iloilo to Puerto Princesa. This flight connects with the schedule from Cebu City and can be highly booked. Be sure to make reservations well in advance and reconfirm to make sure you have a seat on this popular ticket.

Ships and Fast Ferries
Cebu is served by large passenger ships from Manila and by fast ferries from Tagbilaran on Bohol, Ormoc and Maasin on Leyte, Dumaguete on Negros, and Cagayan de Oro, Iligan, and Ozamis on Mindanao. Fast ferry service is also available from Cebu City to Bantayan Island—a convenient if somewhat expensive option that avoids a long and grinding bus ride.

These fast ferries have revolutionized transportation throughout the Visayan Islands and made the older, larger ships almost completely obsolete—except for connections with Manila. On the other hand, the larger ships are less expensive than the fast ferries and you can often sleep onboard on overnight passages, therefore saving the cost of a hotel room.

All the major shipping lines maintain offices in Cebu City. Most are down at the various piers in the Reclamation Area, though some keep their offices elsewhere in the city. In most cases, you can just go down to the appropriate pier and immediately board a large ship or one of the fast ferries. During holidays, it might be a good idea to purchase your ticket several days in advance as ships are sometimes fully booked out during these periods.

SHIPPING LINES IN CEBU CITY

Aznar Shipping: Padilla Street, tel. (032) 253-5523
Bullet Express: Pier 1, tel. (032) 912-272
Cebu Ferries: Pier 4, tel. (032) 232-0490
Cokaliong Shipping: 46 Jakosalem St., tel. (032) 253-2262
George & Peter Lines: Jakosalem St., tel. (032) 75-914
K&T Shipping: MacArthur Blvd., tel. (032) 62-359
Lite Shipping: Lavillas St., tel. (032) 253-7776
Socor Shipping: MacArthur Blvd., tel. (032) 253-6531
Sulpicio Lines: Reclamation Area, tel. (032) 73-839 or 99-723
Trans-Asia Shipping: Cuenco Ave., tel. (032) 254-6491
Universal Aboitiz: Pier 4, tel. (032) 91-542
Water Jet Shipping: Pier 4, tel. (032) 232-1356
Western Samar Shipping: Sotto St., tel. (032) 255-0930
WG&A: Pier 4, tel. (032) 232-1490

Ship from Biliran

San Juan Shipping's MV *San Juan* leaves Naval on Biliran Island for Cebu City at 2100 on Tuesday, Thursday, and Sunday. Figure on about eight hours for the crossing. The MV *Katarina* or MV *Michael* departs Naval daily at 2000 and takes 12 hours to make the same journey.

Ship from Bohol

You can reach Cebu by ship or fast ferry from Tagbilaran, Tubigon, Talibon, or Loon. Most travelers now take a fast ferry from the Tagbilaran port.

From Tagbilaran: Fast ferries take 90 minutes and cost P150-200. The MV *Star Ruby 1* leaves at 0600, Water Jet Shipping's MV *Water Jet 2* leaves at 0630, Universal Aboitiz MV *Supercat* leaves at 0700 and 1300, Socor Shipping's MV *Oceanjet 1* leaves at 1100, Bullet Xpress's MV *Bullet Xpress* leaves at 1200 and 1700, and Water Jet Shipping's MV *Water Jet 1* leaves daily at 1900.

Several large ships make the four-hour crossing from Tagbilaran to Cebu City. Cokaliong Shipping's MV *Filipinas Dumaguete* leaves daily at 0730, the MV *Santiago de Bohol* of Lite Shipping leaves daily at 1030, and the MV *Lite Ferry I* of the same line leaves every Monday at 1230.

Trans-Asia Shipping has two services, the MV *Asia-Japan,* which leaves Tagbilaran on Monday

and Friday at midnight, and the MV *Asia-Thailand* at midnight on Tuesday, Thursday, and Sunday.

From Tubigon: Ships also leave from smaller ports on Bohol. From Tubigon, there's the MV *Charing* daily at 0900, the MV *Rayjumar* daily at 1100, the MV *Betchie* daily at noon, the MV *Queen Lenora* or MV *Queen Vicki* daily at 1600, and the MV *Harvey* daily at midnight. The Tubigon-Cebu City crossing takes just under three hours.

From Talibon: The MV *Krishnia* departs daily at 0800, the MV *Talibon Cruiser* leaves daily at 0900, while the MV *Andy* does the passage daily at 2200. Allow about four hours for the crossing.

From Loon: You can cross from Loon to Argao with Lite Shipping's MV *LCT Barge St. Mark* at 0700 and 1300 on Monday, Wednesday, and Friday, at 1000 on Tuesday and Thursday, and at 0830 on Sunday. The journey takes just under three hours on this car ferry.

Ship from Camiguin

Departures from Mambajao to Cebu City are limited to the MV *Dona Lili* of Cebu Ferries, which leaves once weekly on Monday at 2000 and takes 10 hours to make the crossing. Most travelers head back to Cagayan de Oro and take a ship or fast ferry from that point.

Ship from Leyte

Plenty of ships and fast ferries make the crossing from various ports in Leyte to Cebu City, but the most popular option is one of the fast ferries from Ormoc. Travelers in Tacloban can take a bus or faster minibus direct to the port and catch any of the departing ferries.

From Ormoc: Fast ferries cost P200-250 and take two quick hours to reach Cebu City. Among your choices are the various incarnations of the MV *Supercat* of Universal Aboitiz, which leaves Ormoc daily at 0600, 0830, 1100, 1345, 1630, and 1845. You can also catch the Bullet Xpress MV *Bullet Xpress* at 0730, Socor Shipping's MV *Oceanjet* at 1530, the MV *Water Jet 1* at 0800, or the *Water Jet 2,* which sails at 1915 on Tuesday, Thursday, Saturday, and Sunday.

Regular ships take six hours to reach Cebu City. Cebu Ferries has the MV *Lady of Rule* on Monday at midnight and the MV *Iligan City* also at midnight on Wednesday and Saturday. The MV *Dona Lili* leaves at midnight on Thursday and Friday, while Sulpicio Lines' MV *Cebu Princess* departs Sunday at 2300. Obviously, you can save a night's lodging by taking one of these overnight ships.

From Baybay: Cokaliong Shipping's MV *Filipinas Siargao* departs nightly at midnight and takes six hours, while Western Samar Shipping's MV *Gregoria May* also leaves at midnight on Tuesday, Thursday, and Saturday and takes a slightly quicker five hours.

From Liloan: The MV *Guiuan* of K&T Shipping departs at 1800 on Thursday and Sunday and takes five or six hours to reach Cebu City.

From Maasin: Both large ships and fast ferries go from Maasin to Cebu City. Universal Aboitiz's MV *Supercat* leaves daily at 1130 and 1600 and takes two hours to reach Cebu. Water Jet Shipping's *Water Jet 2* leaves at 1415 on Tuesday, Thursday, Saturday, and Sunday.

Big ships take almost six hours to reach Cebu City. Cokaliong Shipping's MV *Filipinas Surigao* departs at 1000 on Tuesday, at 0200 on Thursday morning, and on Saturday morning at 0100. The same company also has the MV *Filipinas Dapitan*, which leaves Wednesday at 0200 and Sunday at 2200. Finally, there's the Trans-Asia MV *Asia-Singapore* every Friday at midnight, and the MV *Asia-Taiwan* at midnight on Sunday. Again, you can sleep onboard and save some lodging expenses.

From Palompon: Cebu Ferries' nicely named MV *Lady of Rule* leaves on Monday at 0700 and takes 10 hours with a stop at Ormoc. Faster service includes the Cebu Ferries' MV *Dona Lili* on Saturday at midnight and its MV *Don Calvino* on Sunday at 2300. The latter two ships do the crossing in just under six hours.

From Tacloban: Few travelers use this service since the journey takes 12 or 13 hours. Cebu Ferries' MV *Don Calvino* departs at 1600 on Tuesday and Thursday, while its MV *Dona Lili* leaves Wednesday at 1600. Finally, there's the K&T Shipping MV *Leyte Queen* at 1700 every Wednesday, Friday, and Sunday.

From Isabel: From Isabel on Leyte, you can catch various smaller ships and large outriggers

to either Danao or Carmen. Aznar Shipping's MV *Meltrivic 3* leaves Isabel daily at 1000 and takes three hours to Danao. A large outrigger leaves Isabel daily at 1600 and takes four hours to Carmen.

Ormoc to Camotes Islands: A large outrigger departs Ormoc daily at 1300 and takes three hours to reach Bukog on Camotes Island.

San Isidro to Maya: Travelers heading to Malapascua Island in northern Cebu may want to consider the large outrigger that leaves San Isidro daily at 0800 and takes two hours to reach Maya at the north end of Cebu Island.

Ship from Manila

Several ships go from Manila to Cebu City, and most take 20-24 hours to make the crossing. Figure on P500-600.

WG&A's MV *Superferry 8* departs Monday at 0900, Wednesday at 1500, and Friday at 1900. The same company also has the MV *Superferry 6* on Saturday at 1500 and the MV *Superferry 10* on Sunday at 0900, Tuesday at 1500, and Thursday at 1900.

Not to be outdone, Sulpicio Lines provides the MV *Princess of the Orient* on Tuesday at 1000 and Friday at 2000, the MV *Princess of Paradise,* which leaves on Wednesday at 1000, and the MV *Filipina Princess* every Sunday at 1000.

Ship from Masbate

Trans-Asia has the MV *Asia-Taiwan* at 1800 on Tuesday and Thursday. This service takes 14 hours. Sulpicio runs the MV *Cebu Princess* on Saturday at 1600, but this boat takes almost 36 hours since it makes a stop at Ormoc on Leyte.

Large outriggers cross from Cataingan to Hagnaya on Monday and Thursday, and from Cawayan to Hagnaya on Wednesday and Saturday.

Ship from Mindanao

Dozens of ships and fast ferries make the crossing from various ports on Mindanao to Cebu City

From Butuan: Cebu Ferries' MV *Lady of Fatima* leaves at 1800 on Monday, Wednesday, and Friday, while the MV *Lady of Lourdes* departs Saturday at 1800 and takes 11 hours to reach Cebu City.

Sulpicio Lines' MV *Nasipit Princess* leaves Butuan at 2000 on Tuesday, Thursday, and Sunday and reaches Cebu City in a slightly quicker nine hours.

From Cagayan de Oro: Water Jet Shipping's fast ferry MV *Water Jet 1* leaves daily at 1545 and takes five hours to Cebu City with a stop in Tagbilaran on Bohol. The fare is a pricey P500-550 but it's much quicker than the larger ships, which take about 10 hours to make the crossing.

Trans-Asia Shipping's MV *Asia-China* or MV *Trans-Asia* departs daily at 1900 and takes 10 hours to Cebu City. Sulpicio Lines' MV *Princess of Paradise* departs Monday at noon and takes a quicker eight hours to make the crossing. The same company also has the MV *Cagayan Princess* at 1900 on Tuesday, Thursday, and Sunday.

Additional services are provided by Cebu Ferries' MV *Lady of Lipa* at 2000 every Monday, Wednesday, Friday, and Sunday, and the MV *Lady of Lourdes,* which leaves Cagayan at 2000 on Tuesday and Thursday.

From Dapitan: Cokaliong Shipping's MV *Filipinas Dinagat* departs from Dapitan at 1600 on Tuesday, Thursday, and Saturday and takes 14 hours to reach Cebu City, including a stop at Dumaguete on Negros.

From Davao: Sulpicio Lines' MV *Filipina Princess* leaves every Wednesday at 1900 and takes almost 28 hours to reach Cebu City.

From Iligan: Cebu Ferries has two ships to Cebu City. The MV *Dona Cristina* departs at 1900 on Monday, Wednesday, and Friday, while the MV *Lady of Carmel* sets sail at 1600 on Tuesday, Thursday, and Saturday. The passage takes 11-13 hours.

Sulpicio Lines' MV *Dipolog Princess* leaves at 2100 every Friday and reaches Cebu City in just under nine hours.

From Ozamis: Water Jet Shipping's MV *Water Jet 2* departs at 1415 on Monday, Wednesday, and Friday and reaches Cebu City in just under five hours. This fast ferry costs P500-550.

Slower service is provided by Cebu Ferries' MV *Lady of Carmel,* which leaves at 1900 on Tuesday, Thursday, and Saturday and takes a leisurely 10 hours to Cebu City. The same company also runs the MV *Lady of Rule* at 1900 on Friday and Sunday.

Other options from Ozamis include Lite Shipping's MV *Lite Ferry 1* at 2000 on Tuesday,

Thursday, and Saturday, or Sulpicio Lines' MV *Philippine Princess* every Friday at 2200. The latter is fairly quick at just seven hours for the crossing.

From Surigao: Water Jet Shipping's MV *Water Jet 2* departs Surigao at 1230 on Tuesday, Thursday, Saturday, and Sunday. This very popular service costs P400-450 and takes four hours with a stop at Maasin on Leyte.

Slower but cheaper are the large ships that shuttle between Surigao and Cebu City. Cokaliong Shippings' MV *Filipinas Dapital* departs Surigao at 1900 on Tuesday, Thursday, and Saturday. Allow at least 10 hours for the overnight crossing. The same company also operates the MV *Filipinas Surigao,* which sails at 1900 on Wednesday and Friday. Both of these ships make a stop at Maasin on Leyte.

Finally, there's the Trans-Asia Shipping MV *Asia-Singapore* on Wednesday at 2300 and Sunday at 2200, plus the Sulpicio Lines' MV *Filipina Princess* every Thursday at 1500. The latter ship makes no stops and does the crossing to Cebu City in just seven hours.

Ship from Negros

Most travelers either take the short ferry ride from San Carlos to Toledo or the very convenient fast ferry from Dumaguete direct to Cebu City. There are also several odd connections that may be useful for the traveler somewhat off the beaten track.

Cadiz to Bantayan: A large outrigger leaves Cadiz on the north coast of Negros daily around 1000 and takes just under four hours to reach Bantayan Island at the north end of Cebu. After enjoying a few days around Bantayan, you can take a bus or fast ferry down to Cebu City and continue east to Bohol or Leyte.

From Dumaguete: Universal Aboitiz's MV *Supercat* leaves daily at 0830 and 1745 and takes just over two hours to reach Cebu City. This fast ferry costs P200-250.

One large ship leaves Dumaguete nightly at 2200 and takes eight hours to reach Cebu City. This service is provided by George & Peter Lines with either the MV *Dumaguete Ferry,* the MV *Georich,* or the MV *Palauan Ferry.*

Tampi (near Dumaguete) to Bato (Southwestern Cebu): A ferry runs several times a day from 0700 to 1530 and takes about 45

minutes to make the crossing. To reach the Tampi pier from Dumaguete, take a jeepney or public bus from the corner of Real and Locsin Streets.

Arrivals at Bato are met by ABC Liner buses, which either head to Cebu City via the east coast or go north up the west coast past the dive resorts at Moalboal. Ask before boarding your bus to get going in the right direction!

Sibulan to Liloan: A large outrigger leaves every 30 minutes from 0700 to 1500 and takes just 20 minutes to make the short crossing.

Guihulngan to Tangil: A large outrigger leaves daily at 1100 and takes three hours to Tangil.

San Carlos to Toledo: Ferries shuttle from San Carlos to Toledo several times daily, most likely in the early morning around 0600 and early afternoon around 1330. Additional services are provided on weekends.

This was once the most popular shipping connection between the two islands, but with the advent of fast ferries between Dumaguete and Cebu City, and the very convenient ferries between Tampi and Bato, this particular connection has declined in importance for many travelers. Still, if you're in a big hurry to get between Cebu City and Bacolod, this might be your best option short of springing for a PAL ticket.

Ship from Panay

Shipping service is limited between Panay and Cebu City, though some travelers take the direct ship from Iloilo and skip the island of Negros.

From Dumaguit (near Kalibo): This might be an economical and fairly comfortable way to transit from Boracay to Cebu City and skip the overland hassle of buses, bad roads, and countless ferries. Cebu Ferries' MV *Iligan City* leaves Friday at 1800, while the MV *Tacloban City* leaves Sunday at 1700. The former service takes 11 hours while the latter takes 14 hours including a stop in Roxas City.

From Iloilo: Trans-Asia Shipping's MV *Asia-Brunei* or MV *Trans-Asia* leaves daily at 1800 and takes 12 hours to Cebu City. Cebu Ferries' MV *Iligan City* departs at 1900 on Tuesday and Sunday, while the MV *Tacloban City* sets sail at 1900 on Wednesday and Friday. Both ships take 12 hours.

From Roxas City: Cebu Ferries' MV *Tacloban City* leaves every Sunday at 1900 and takes 12 hours to reach Cebu City.

Ship from Samar

From Catarman: Western Samar Shipping's MV *Elizabeth Lilly* departs Catarman every Sunday at 1700 and takes 14 hours to reach Cebu City.

From Catbalogan: Western Samar Shipping's MV *Elizabeth Lilly* leaves on Wednesday and Friday at 1700 and also takes 14 hours to reach Cebu City.

Ship from Siquijor

Cebu Ferries' MV *Dona Cristina* leaves on Friday at 1900 and takes 24 hours to reach Larena on Siquijor with a stop at Iligan on Mindanao.

Bus

Buses to Negros, Bohol, and southern Cebu destinations such as Moalboal and Argao leave Cebu City from the southern bus terminal on Rizal Avenue. Special direct services include the a/c Ceres Liner buses to Bacolod daily at 0600, Ceres Liner buses to Tagbilaran at 0800 and 1400, and ABC buses to Dumaguete at noon.

Bus touts will direct you, but try to get on a bus that looks almost filled and ready to leave. Otherwise it's a long wait in the sweltering heat.

Buses to Bacolod leave daily from the Rajah Hotel. Buses to northern Cebu leave from the northern bus terminal at Cuenco and Maxilom Streets, and from the closer Rough Rider terminal at Cuenco and Padilla.

CEBU CITY

Cebu, the oldest and third-largest city of the Philippines, with a population of over 650,000, is 587 km south of Manila. In addition to being the provincial capital, it's the commercial, industrial, cultural, religious, and educational center for the central Visayas and northern Mindanao.

It owes its existence to its safe natural harbor, protected by Mactan Island. As a regional distribution and transportation center, the port is constantly bustling with interisland vessels. In fact, it's busier than Manila Harbor. Foreign

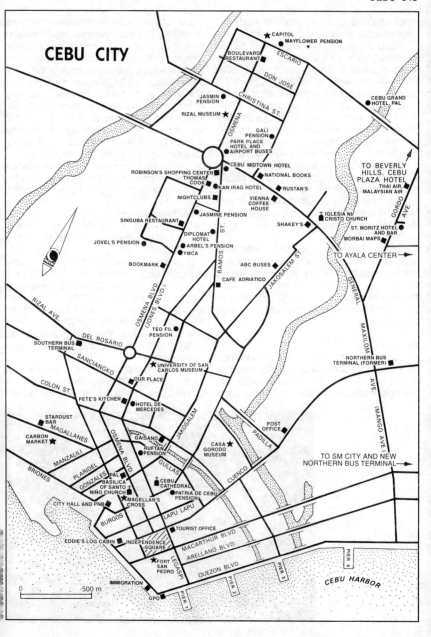

ships also dock to unload imported goods and pick up copra, sugar, and other exports.

The U.S., among other Western and Asian countries, maintains a consulate here. The address is American Consulate, 3rd floor, PCIB Bldg., Gorodo Ave., tel. (032) 311-261. There is also a branch of the Alliance Frannaise.

Cebu has a large Chinese population, primarily engaged in commerce. It has a substantial student population since many young people come from other Visayan islands and northern Mindanao to attend college or university here.

Called the "Queen City of the South," Cebu sprawls north and south along a narrow alluvial plain at the foot of the central mountains. The city is divided between the older and somewhat congested downtown section near Colon Street and the newer uptown neighborhood around Fuenta or Osmeña Circle.

For the Philippines, Cebu City is both lively and livable, and is a far more pleasant place to base oneself than Manila. With increased air travel to places like Kalibo (Boracay) and Puerto Princesa on Palawan, tourists can make an itinerary that cuts down the dreaded return trips to Manila.

Sinulog Festival

Cebu's major fiesta, the Sinulog, coincides with the Feast of the Santo Niño de Cebu. Held during the third Sunday of January, this weeklong celebration features processions, *sinulog* dancing, cultural presentations, fireworks, a carnival, cockfights, and much merrymaking. It reenacts the first conversion of the natives to Christianity. Cebuano believers travel from all over the country to participate and pay homage to the small, historic statue of their patron saint.

Women devotees dance the *sinulog* each day in front of the basilica and Magellan's Cross. The air rings with shouts of *"Pit Senyor!"* ("Hail to the Patron Saint!"). The fiesta culminates on the third Sunday of January with costumed groups participating in a parade. They dance to the accompaniment of drumbeats. A massive religious procession takes place on Saturday featuring the bejeweled Santo Niño. Highly recommended.

Other Happenings

Cebu's City Charter Day, 24 February, begins with High Mass at the city hall Plaza, followed by speeches.

During Holy Week, consider going to nearby Mandaue City; Bantayan and Minglanilla are also good places to be. During May, every city parish celebrates Flores de Mayo. An Independance Day parade is held on 12 June. The birthday of former president Sergio Osmeña, 9 September, is marked by wreath-laying outside his birthplace at the corner of Juan Luna and Lapu-Lapu Streets.

Cebu is a good place to be on 1 November, All Saints Day, when a 24-hour vigil takes place at Caretta Cemetery and the Chinese cemetery op-

snackin' at Sinulog

posite; take a jeepney on Colon Street toward Mabolo Street. On 8 December, the Feast of the Immaculate Conception, a procession takes place from Cebu Metropolitan Cathedral. A parade marks José Rizal's birthday on 30 December.

Magellan's Cross

Magellan planted a cross to mark the spot where Rajah Humabon and about 800 followers were baptized in 1521. Over the centuries, local people took chips from the cross, believing it had miraculous powers. To avoid its total destruction, an octagonal stone kiosk with a red-tiled roof was built in Plaza Santa Cruz to house the remains, which are inside the hollow black *tindalo* wood cross (1845) that's on display. Ceiling paintings depict the events of Magellan's visit.

Basilica Minore del Santo Niño

The former San Agustin Church, the country's oldest, was designated a basilica, the only one in the Far East, in 1965. It contains the image of the Holy Infant given by Magellan to the rajah's wife in 1521 and recovered unscathed from the charred ruins of the settlement by Legazpi's party in 1565. A wooden church built near the discovery site was burned in 1568, as did its stone replacement in 1628.

a stone relief adorning the Basilica Minore del Santo Niño

CARL PARKES

The present structure was completed in 1740. The miraculous 30-cm-high Santo Niño de Cebu image, venerated as the patron saint of Cebuanos, is enshrined in glass in a small chapel to the left of the altar. The statue has a large wardrobe of sumptuous robes, a golden crown, and a jewelry collection, part of which dates to the 16th century.

The basilica also houses a rich collection of religious art and artifacts, and the adjoining *convento* has important archives. Note the Basilica's imposing facade, painted ceiling, and finely carved *retablo* and choir screen. A short block north is another old church, the Cebu Metropolitan Cathedral.

Fort San Pedro

This small tri-bastion fort is situated between the port and Plaza Independencia. The plaza contains an obelisk to Legazpi and a Japanese monument signifying postwar reconciliation. Legazpi founded the fort in 1565, naming it after his flagship, and it formed the heart of the first Spanish settlement in the Philippines. The original wooden palisade was replaced by stone walls six meters high, 2.5 meters thick, with towers 10 meters high. The current structure was completed in 1738.

The Cuerpo de Guardia, the largest building, housed the troops, while the adjacent Viviendo del Tiniente was the living quarters of the fort's lieutenant. The sentry walk is now the haunt of lovers. As a Spanish garrison defended by cannons, it guarded against Moro marauders and later served as a prison for Cebuano rebels. It became an American barracks early in this century, then a school, occupied by Japanese troops during WW II, and used as an emergency hospital during the battle for liberation in 1945.

Today, the interior is landscaped, and it contains beautiful tropical flowers. Entrance is P2 for locals, P7 for tourists. The tourism department left the fort several years ago and is now located just across the street.

Carbon Public Market

Cebu's lively and colorful central market is a good place to buy local produce and handicrafts, plus items from farther afield, such as Bohol basketware. Nearby Lincoln Street has many guitar shops. Beware of pickpockets and bag snatchers.

Colon Street

This is the oldest in the Philippines, dating from 1565 and named after Columbus. It's located in what was formerly the Parian District, the original Chinatown, and remains a busy but somewhat run-down commercial street, with department stores, movie theaters, hotels, restaurants, and shipping agencies.

University of San Carlos

Founded by the Jesuits in 1595, this is the country's oldest university. Its important museum has an extensive collection, comprising pre-Hispanic artifacts, including stone and iron implements, pottery, burial coffins and jars, and body ornaments; Spanish ecclesiastical relics; ethnic items from minority groups of the Visayas and Mindanao; and a natural history section. It's off P. Del Rosario Street.

University of the Southern Philippines

The university's **Rizaliana Museum** contains etchings, writings, letters, and other memorabilia of national hero José Rizal.

Jumalon's Lepido Mosaic Art Gallery

Located at the artist's residence at Basak, Parola, this gallery displays lepido mosaic pictures—landscapes, portraits—made with butterfly wings by Professor Julian Jumalon, head of the University of San Carlos's lepidoptera department. It's fascinating as long as you don't think of how many butterflies died to make each composition. An accompanying exhibit of butterflies from many parts of the world includes the rare Siamese-twin specimen caught on Cebu in 1954. Admission is by appointment with the artist.

Private Collections

Visits to the following private collections can be arranged through the tourist office. Those interested in stamps or coins may view Don Victoriano Reynes's stamp collection on Colon Street. The extensive Medalle Collection of Photos, at the Cebuano Studies Center of the University of San Carlos, dates back to the Spanish era and portrays Cebu when life was more sedate and gracious.

Other collections include the Arcenas collection of ceramics and Spanish colonial art in the Banawa district. Many members of the Cebu Orchid Society have fine collections, and this group also sponsors an annual orchid festival that attracts exhibitors from Singapore, Thailand, and Hawaii.

Beverly Hills

This wealthy residential subdivision in the suburb of Lahug, about six km from downtown, is situated at an elevation of 300 meters and commands a panoramic view of the city, harbor, and Mactan Island. Its architectural landmark is the gaudy red-and-green Taoist shrine (1972), replete with a pagoda-like roof and decorative dragons and lion-dogs. The teaching of Lao-Tze, the ancient Chinese philosopher, is preserved here, and every day, when Taoist ceremonies take place, visitors climb the 99 steps to light joss sticks and have their fortunes read. Don't take photos of the interior.

A taxi from the city center costs P20-30; agree to a fare first. If you are traveling around Southeast Asia, don't fret if you miss this temple; its modern gaudiness depicts the tacky side of Chinese houses of worship, much like remaining temples of Hong Kong. The views from here are real nice, however.

Those on a budget can catch a jeepney to Lahug either on Osmeña Boulevard or Jakosalem Street near Gaisano Department Store. Alight in Lahug, cross the bridge over the creek, turn right, and walk 1.5 km uphill.

The road to Beverly Hills also passes near the Phu-Sian Buddhist Temple on the right and the Heavenly Temple of Charity, for Chinese Catholics, on the left. This temple, whose patron saint is Milagrosa Rosa, is in Peace Valley atop a hill, beneath which flows a curative natural spring. To reach it, go straight ahead from the bridge for 100 meters, pass through the iron gate with its guardian "lions," and follow the trail for 400 meters. Turn right onto a road and continue for 200 meters to the gate of the temple complex. If it's closed, go around the temple to the main gate.

Cebu's small zoo is two km from the Taoist shrine. You can also hike above Beverly Hills to Victoria Peak, named after the hill in Hong Kong. The views are nice and it tends to be cooler and quiet up here.

Brewery

To take a tour of the huge San Miguel brewery in Mandaue City, next to Cebu, apply at the brewery's public relations department. The tours, offered Mon.-Fri., end with free samples in the top-floor reception room, from which there are good views.

Budget Accommodations

Inexpensive places to stay are mainly found in the older downtown neighborhood and just off Oseman Street. Several more are just north of Fuente Circle in a quieter residential area.

Ruftan Pension: Cebu's most popular travelers' center has paper-thin walls, but rooms are clean and the restaurant is a good place to meet other backpackers. Managers Fina and Jose offer advice and give discounts to Peace Corps volunteers. Legaspi St., tel. (032) 79-138, P175-380.

Patria de Cebu: Catholic-run place with simple but clean rooms. Burgos St., tel. (032) 72-084, P150-250.

Arbel's Pension House: Small but adequate rooms in a quiet location off the main road. 57 East Jones (Osmeña) St., tel. (032) 253-5303, P200-500.

Verbena Pension House: Another inexpensive to moderate pension northeast of Osmeña Circle. 584 Garcia St., tel. (032) 253-3430, P390-480.

Jasmin Pension: Upper Cebu is convenient for shopping, dining, and nightlife near Fuenta Circle. The Jasmin and nearby Loreta Pension (once voted the cleanest pension in Cebu) are good choices. 395 Osmeña Blvd., tel. (032) 253-3757, P370-500.

Teo-Fel Pension House: Thirty a/c rooms with private bath plus restaurant, room service, and other perks not found in most budget hotels. 4 Junquera Extension, tel. (032) 253-2482, P350-700.

Century Hotel: An old creaking hotel with countless rooms in a convenient downtown location. Pelaez St., tel. (032) 255-1341, P350-600.

Moderate Accommodations

Hotel de Mercedes: Downtown hotel with reasonably priced if somewhat scruffy rooms. 7 Pelaez St., tel. (032) 253-1105, P600-1,100.

Kan Irag Hotel: An old favorite with funky but acceptable rooms tucked away on a quieter street near Osmeña Circle. Ramos St., tel. (032) 253-6935, P750-1,200.

St. Moritz Hotel: A better name than the hotel itself but popular with visiting Europeans who pack the pub in the evenings. Gorodo Ave., tel. (032) 231-1148, P1,200-1,800.

Luxury Accommodations

Most of the better hotels are somewhat distant from the center of town, but taxis are plentiful here in Cebu City.

Montebello Hotel: Spanish atmosphere, swimming pool, and attractive gardens but a long distance from downtown or Osmeña Circle. Gorodo Avenue, tel. (032) 231-3681, US$40-80.

Cebu Plaza Hotel: Cebu's first five-star hotel has breathtaking views but is inconveniently located about eight km out of town. Lahug, tel. (032) 231-2064, US$120-200.

Restaurants

Cebu offers a wide choice of food—Filipino, Chinese, American/European, and Japanese. Restaurants are spread downtown and along Osmeña Boulevard, around Fuente Osmeña, and Gorodo Avenue.

The sweetest, juiciest mangoes in the Philippines are grown in Cebu, especially in the suburb of Guadalupe. During the March-May harvest season, they're cheap and plentiful.

Eddie's Log Cabin: Cebu's attachment to foreign expats is best experienced in this Western tavern owned by the American Cherokee contractor who made his fortune developing Beverly Hills . . . Cebu, not Los Angeles. Great sizzling steaks, salads, and homemade pies. Briones Street near Plaza Independenzia. Moderate.

Our Place: The most popular expat gathering venue in town with friendly hostesses and American and European grub at moderate prices. Don't be alarmed by the narrow staircase or general dereliction of the neighborhood. Pelaez Street.

Gaisano Cafeteria: Modern and clean downtown restaurant with tasty Filipino specialties. Nearby **Pete's Kitchen** is also recommended; both are inexpensive.

Robinson's Shopping Center: This modern complex near Fuenta Osmeña Circle has three clean and comfortable restaurants: Sizzling Plate on the ground floor, Maxim's Coffee Shop on the second, and the luxurious Lotus Garden for Chinese specialties on the fourth. Good places to cool off from the searing heat. Moderate.

Charlie's: Jazz club and restaurant with delicious *kalamansi* and mango daiquiris. 171 Ramos Street. Somewhat expensive unless you go during happy hour 1700-1900.

Vienna Coffee House: Lousy cappuccino and pricey cakes but well stocked with current newspapers and German publications such as *Der Spiegel.* Mango Avenue. Moderate.

Cafe Adriatico: Upscale and trendy café in an old Cebuano home; excellent coffee and cozy atmosphere. Ramos Street. Moderate.

Chinese Restaurants: The city's best Chinese food is considered to be that of the **Talk of the Town** on 117 Gorodo Avenue. **Great Han Palace** on Osmeña Boulevard also serves good Chinese food. **Golden Cowrie Restaurant** is an established seafood restaurant in Lahug. **Tung Yan** (Chinese) on Archbishop Reyes corner of Kamagong Street is one of the oldest and best-loved restaurants in Cebu, but it's expensive.

Colon Street: There are many places to eat around Colon Street. The **Snow Sheen Restaurant** (two branches) has good Chinese/Filipino food; ask for the delicious *torta cangrejo,* which isn't on the menu. **Pete's Kitchen** on Pelaez Street offers inexpensive Filipino food.

Gorodo Avenue: Some of the best restaurants in the city are along Gorodo Avenue. The excellent **Alavar's Seafood House** is here, as well as **Pistahan Filipino Seafood Restaurant.** Farther down Gorodo Avenue toward the Cebu Plaza Hotel, try **Seafood City** near La Nivel Hotel. Also along Gorodo Avenue is **Kukuk's Nest Garden Restaurant and Pension House,** an outdoor restaurant with clean rooms in an old Cebuano home, run by a friendly German. There is a well-stocked bar here as well. Popular meeting place for travelers.

Angel Arano's: One of Cebu's best kept secrets is this Basque/Spanish restaurant. A former jai alai champion whose lived in the Philippines for 20 years, Angel and his wife run a superb restaurant from their home in the suburbs. There's no sign outside but plenty of customers within as the prices are very reasonable and portions are generous. Specialties are oven-cooked lamb, squid in its ink, exquisite chicken, and plenty of bread and Spanish wine. Recommended; ask the taxi driver to get you there! Fairlane Village, 29 Guadalupe.

Nightlife

Entertainment in Cebu is divided between the low-end bars downtown and the classier places uptown along Osmeña Boulevard and Maxilom Avenue.

Live Music: Charlie's Jazz Club on Ramos Street offers some of the best music in town, plus delicious daiquiris in a Casablanca atmosphere. The **Boulevard** on upper Osmeña Boulevard and **Shakey's** on Maxilom Avenue are popular rock 'n' roll clubs. Raunchy and very loud bands blast away at **Gaw Central Square** on Colon Street. **Hot Gossip Disco** in Robinson's Shopping Center is Cebu's upscale nightclub.

Go-Go Bars: St. Moritz, Cebu's hottest girlie bar, is located near the Magellan Hotel. **The Club** on Mango Avenue is basic but friendly and inexpensive. **Our Place** is modest but the best place in downtown Cebu. The **Stardust** on Magallanes is a wild taxi hall and cabaret that has been entertaining Filipino males for several generations. Only for the brave.

Kentucky Bar: This bar is a popular bar with Cebu's expat community; pub food is also served. This bar is one of those dangerous places where drinking beer at 0900 is the norm, and Kentucky's also draws the men off the ships when foreign fleets come to town. There's plenty of brawling and drinking here and the place is dimly lit with colored lightbulbs. Watch for pickpockets disguised as newspaper boys. Ramos Street.

Cebu Casino: At the other end of the scale is this local casino located in Nivel Hills, Lahug, near the Cebu Plaza Hotel, which offers roulette, baccarat, blackjack, hi-lo, pai kiu, dice, plus rows of slot machines. Overseas visitors must show their passports; a bank exchanges foreign currency. A dress code is observed.

Shopping

Items for which Cebu is particularly noted are guitars and ukeleles, shellcraft, rattan furniture, stonecraft, fashion accessories, and delicious mangoes. The handicraft stalls in **Carbon Market** and near Magellan's Cross are cheaper than souvenir shops.

A good place to buy shellcraft is at **Jewels of the Sea,** operated by the St. Theresa College. Antique hunters can check **Roska's Antique Store** at 24 Pelaez Street, **Likha Antiques and Crafts** at 37 Manga Avenue, and **Inver Treasure House** on F. Ramos Street.

Ursula's Designs on 157 Gorodo Avenue, next to Kukuk's Nest Pension, sells excellent antiques and handicrafts. Next to Ursula's, you'll find the **Duty-Free Shop** of Cebu. Tourists can also buy duty-free items at the Mactan International Airport.

Other shops include **Flora's Antique Shop** on General Maxilom Avenue, **Catalina Antique Shop,** 246 Magallanes Street, and **Cebu Display Center** on Magallenes Street

Gaisano Superbookstore on Colon Street and **National Bookstore** at General Maxilom Avenue have a good selection of reading material. The district of Banawa is a well-known place to buy fruit and flowers, while the suburb of Guadalupe is noted for mangoes.

Although guitars are sold in numerous shops in Cebu City, the best place to buy them is at the guitar factories in the Maribago and Abuno districts of Mactan Island.

Services and Information

Information: The Department of Tourism in the GMC Building on Plaza Independencia near Fort San Pedro is more helpful than most other DOT offices. Its service counter at the Mactan International Airport can help with hotel reservations and transportation into the city.

Money: Traveler's checks and cash can be exchanged at all the usual banks and with money changers outside the post office and around Independence Square. American Express is at the Ayala Center in Cebu Business Park, while Thomas Cook is in the Metrobank Plaza on Osmeña Boulevard.

Cash advances on Visa and Mastercard can be picked up at the Equitable Bank on Port Center Avenue adjacent to SM City in the failed Reclamation Area. City fathers thought this gigantic landfill project would someday be the location of a new supercity, but as you can see, the vast acreage now looks like the city dump.

Mail: The main post office is near Plaza Independencia, and branch offices are on Briones Street, Colon Street, and at the University of San Carlos on Del Rosario Street.

Transportation

PAL has two offices in town and an office out at the Mactan International Airport. Shipping line offices are listed above under Transportation at the beginning of the Cebu section.

Cebu has no city buses. The most convenient means of getting around in the downtown area are the small unmetered taxis that charge a minimum fare of P10. Regular metered taxis are also available and you can get to Mactan Island for P100-150. The fee for longer journeys is negotiable.

Jeepneys charge P1 for the first five km and to nearby cities such as Lapu-Lapu (P2).

Buses to the airport leave hourly from Osmeña Boulevard near Robinsons.

Buses to Negros, Bohol, Panay, and southern Cebu leave from the southern bus terminal on Rizal Avenue. Buses to northern Cebu leave from the northern bus terminal on Cuenco Avenue and from the terminal near the post office.

The traditional mode of city transport was the *tartanilla,* a two-wheeled horse-drawn rig, but this is only seen in the older sections of the city.

MANDAUE CITY

This commercial and industrial city (pop. 156,000) at the north end of Cebu Harbor, seven km from downtown, is effectively a suburb of Cebu City. The Jesuits founded Mandaue in 1600. Mandaue lies at one end of the bridge to Mactan Island. On the shore beneath the bridge is a tower, called Bantayan sa Hari, formerly used to watch for Muslim raiders. Mandaue has been a boomtown in recent decades and is the site of the giant San Miguel brewery complex, plus other factories, plants, and mills.

MACTAN ISLAND

Mactan Island (57 square km), linked to Cebu Island by bridge, is a raised ancient coral reef standing about three meters above sea level. The island, with about 90,000 inhabitants, presents a diverse environment containing an urban center, port, shipyard, oil depot, industrial complexes, an export-processing zone, the fishing town of Cordova, coconut groves, mangrove swamps, cultivated fields, Mactan International Airport, and several beach resorts.

Fishermen catch substantial quantities of shrimp and crab in the shallow offshore waters. Many rare shells have been found around Mactan, especially off Punta Engaño, a great spot for shell seekers. Common species are also gathered for use in shellcraft. Some fishermen have switched to shell-gathering as their main occupation, and a shell-decorated chapel has been erected in thanksgiving for this new source of income.

History
Magellan was felled by Chief Lapu-Lapu in knee-deep water off Mactan in 1521; his body was never recovered. A monument, erected in 1886, marks the spot; it's nine km from the bridge, on the road to Punta Engaño. A large statue of Lapu-Lapu stands in the plaza in front of the city hall. Conflict resumed here in 1565 as Martin de Goiti burned the settlement and the natives retaliated by attacking the Spanish at Cebu. The town of Opon, as it was formerly called, was founded by Augustinians in 1730.

Bahug Bahug Sa Mactan
On 27 April, the Battle of Mactan (1521) is reenacted at this site on the beach at Mactan. Decorated *bancas,* representing Magellan's three ships, lead a water procession to the beach. The planting of the cross and baptism of the natives is followed by the battle, which culminates in Lapu-Lapu's victory. Events begin around 0800, though the exact time may depend on the tide.

Beaches
Marigondon on Mactan has the best public seashore near Cebu City (one hour), but the beach is narrow and gets crowded on weekends. Be careful of strong currents in the channel. You can hire a *banca* to visit offshore islands, but it's relatively expensive here; perhaps, with bargaining, about P400 for half a day.

The upscale resorts charge nonguests an entrance fee for the use of their beach, pool, and showers; in some cases, this fee will be deducted from a meal bill.

Accommodations
Most of Mactan's accommodations are upscale resorts set along the rocky, grayish strip of sand near Maribago and Marigondon Beaches. Most places start at US$120 per night and cater almost exclusively to wealthy Filipinos and Western businessmen.

Transportation
From Cebu City, it's 13 km to the airport and Lapu-Lapu City and about 20 km to the beach resorts across the island. The 864-meter bridge, opened in 1972, has a 75-meter clearance at high tide, and 90 at low tide. A second bridge opened in 1998, taking some of the strain off the older structure.

A road leads south from the foot of the bridge to Lapu-Lapu City center. Use the shuttle bus

---

THE GUITAR FACTORIES OF MACTAN

Guitar factories in the Maribago and Abuno districts, and north of the crossroads at the end of the bridge, are a popular tourist attraction. A wide selection of guitars, mandolins, ukuleles, and other instruments, is offered. Quality and prices vary widely. Some are incredibly cheap, but they don't last long when taken to a nontropical climate.

"Export" guitars of high-quality *kamagong* and *kalantas* wood can cost as much as US$300. The raw materials are generally brought from Mindanao. Avoid instruments with turtleshell backs. Customs officials of some Western countries may confiscate them as a product deriving from a protected species. PAL does not allow guitars as hand luggage; if you don't have a case in which to carry it, a cheap suitcase can be bought in any large marketplace.

from Robinson's Department Store to get to the airport.

For the beach at Marigondon or the Maribago guitar factories, take a jeepney from Manalili Street in Cebu City to Lapu-Lapu City. The locals still use the old name, so listen for the "Opon, Opon" cry. Jeepneys are plentiful, so wait for one with an available front seat for a better view of the island and Cebu Harbor when crossing the bridge.

Alight at Lapu-Lapu City Plaza, from the southeast corner of which, by the FG Enterprises store, tricycles go to all points on the island; ask someone the correct fare. The per person cost of any trip is based on six passengers, so if you take a special trip, it shouldn't cost more than six times the regular fare.

A tricycle tour of the island, e.g., to a guitar factory, Magellan's Monument, then the beach, might cost around P150. Bargain hard! The ride by tricycle will not be extremely comfortable, and that's a point in your bargaining favor.

Taxi drivers will also take passengers all the way to the beaches at Mactan from Cebu City; insist that they use the meter or don't pay more than P150 one-way.

Beach resorts like Tambuli are about 20 minutes from Lapu-Lapu City or the airport. To return to Cebu City, jeepneys load a short distance from the Lapu-Lapu City Plaza.

DIVING AROUND MACTAN

Tambuli Beach Resort, Costabella, Cebu Beach Club, Maribago Bluewater Beach Club, Bahia Beach Resort, and Coral Reef Hotel all offer scuba facilities. Dive shops on Mactan Island offer scuba diving courses and PADI certification.

Be sure to get local advice on currents. The layout of the coasts and seabed can combine with the tide to produce powerful surges of water in the Hilutangan Channel. It's a wise precaution to have a covering *banca,* even when diving fairly close to shore.

Dive Sites

The nearest dive sites are off Mactan, but coral and marinelife improve as you go a little farther and deeper. The seabed between Marigondon and Panguian Point extends out between 12

and 90 meters from shore, then drops off. The reef flat has been severely damaged by coral collectors, fishermen, boat anchors, and the destructive crown of thorns starfish.

The wall off Marigondon and Amboucuan Point has some large caves about 30-40 meters down. Underwater photographers will enjoy the small bay near Punta Engaño. When surfacing, watch carefully for tourist boats in this area.

A series of buttresses near Panguian Point offers good fishlife, but visibility deteriorates around the point. A recompression chamber is located at the Camp Lapu-Lapu Military Hospital.

Olango Island

This narrow 13-square km island, commonly called Santa Rosa, lies across the Hilutangan Channel from Mactan and has white-sand beaches and a fine three-star resort, **Santa Rosa by the Sea,** with scuba facilities and horseback riding. Nonguests are charged an entrance fee. Boats cross to Olango from Maribago on Mactan.

Impressive sightings of big fish, whale sharks, and hammerheads have been made off the northern points of both Mactan and Olango. The north shore of Olango isn't suitable for snorkelers, but it offers exciting drop-offs out from the village of Baring and Mabini Point (also called Tingo Point), with some large caves at about 35 meters. Many divers just stay put and watch the passing fish.

On the west coast of Olango, out from the villages of Santa Rosa and Poo, is a shelf, several hundred meters wide, featuring many small fish, shells, and coral formations. The water gets clearer as you get farther from shore. Good snorkeling here, but it's advisable to have a covering *banca.* The drop-off begins at about 10 meters and falls to 40 meters, and numerous fish inhabit the wall and some small caves at its base.

The eastern side of Olango's fringing reef has better coral and larger fish. The reef extending south of Olango has also suffered much damage, but there are drop-offs around Panganan, Caohagan, and Lassuan Islands. Since the western side of the reef has troublesome currents, it's preferable to make for the eastern wall, which has some nice coral.

Kansantik, southeast of Olango, is the peak of an underwater mountain that rises from great depths to within 30 meters of the surface and offers fine coral, large sponges, and many fish. It should be attempted by experienced divers only, with a knowledgeable dive master and boatman, since it's difficult to find and constant currents necessitate diving on a weighted line.

Danajon Bank

The very best diving out of Mactan is on the Danajon Bank, a maze of reefs, shoals, and islands off northern Bohol. It features one of the world's few double barrier reefs—two distinct reefs separated by a channel.

Danajon comprises a chain of coral reefs up to three km wide, plus seven scattered islets. Much of the reef is exposed at low tide. The most extensive section of the bank is that near the two Caubyan Islands, which are about one km apart. "Caubyan Small" is a densely populated fishing village, and "Caubyan Big" is uninhabited. Near the latter, the seabed is irregular, with a drop-off to about 50 meters and some large fish, including rays and sharks.

Danajon is one to two hours from Mactan and can be reached as a day trip. Resort dive masters are continually exploring new dive sites on this huge bank.

NORTH OF CEBU CITY

The highway north passes numerous beaches en route to Bogo, a port for Masbate Island, Daan Bantayan, and the offshore island of Bantayan. It heads out through Mandaue City to Liloan, named after *lilo,* a treacherous whirlpool found in the sea.

Liloan has a lighthouse dating from 1904, and its sandy beaches are frequented by residents of the nearby cities; beach cottages can be rented. Liloan is also noted for its bakeshops.

Beyond Liloan, the municipality of Compostela also has sandy beaches and produces *chicos,* grapes, and coconuts.

Danao City

This city of 64,000, located 33 km north of Cebu City, has an imposing plaza and city hall. Danao is the site of a heavy industrial complex. Coal from nearby mines is shipped from here. Cottage operations produce pottery, snakeskin bags and shoes, and cottage cheese. The **Sands Recreation and Beach Resort,** Look Beach, and Myrna Beach are popular local swimming spots.

Carmen and Catmon

Carmen is the site of Malbago Beach, oyster farms, and numerous caves with rich guano deposits used by farmers as fertilizer. The town celebrates Ati-Atihan in January. Catmon has a coral garden in the town plaza and beach cottages for rent.

Sogod

Sogod, 60 km, two and a half hours north of Cebu City, has white-sand beaches, caves, and a church dating from 1832. It's best known for the **Cebu Club Pacific Beach Resort,** with rates starting at US$70 s/d; amenities include swimming pool, tennis, and windsurfing. The club also has scuba facilities and offers dive packages.

Dive Sites: Capitancillo Islet, a superb dive site, is a two-hour *banca* trip northeast of Sogod. This flat coralline island is at the center of a reef that extends for two to three km. Other nearby sites include the Nunez Shoal off Calanggaman Islet to the northeast and the submerged (10 meters deep) Ormoc Shoal to the north. All three sites feature shallow ledges leading to drop-offs, with much soft and black coral, caves, and a wide range of fish. Best diving weather is March-November.

Northern Cebu

The road from Sogod to Bogo (101 km from Cebu City) cuts inland, bypassing Borbon, which has caves along Nonoc Beach, and Tabogon, site of sandy beaches and a colonial church (1851). The road continues northwest from Bogo, past the junction for Daan Bantayan, to San Remegio, which has beaches and an old church, and Hagnaya, the ferry port for Bantayan Island.

Daan Bantayan

Daan Bantayan is a raised coral reef connected to Cebu Island by a bridge over the narrow Daijagoan Canal. Nearby is Medellin, whose canefields supply its sugar mill.

The fishing town of Daan Bantayan is 128 km north of Cebu City. It has an old church, and in its vicinity are beaches, caves, and the rich marinelife of the Visayan Sea. Tapilon, five km from town, is noted for its sea snake gatherers.

BANTAYAN ISLAND

Bantayan Island, off the northwestern tip of Cebu, offers excellent diving and some of the best beaches in the region, especially along the southern coastline between Santa Fe and Maricaban. This is an old raised coral island (116 square km) fringed with reefs and shoals, some 15 km offshore from Cebu Island. Fish, crabs, and prawns abound in the offshore waters. It's divided into Bantayan, Santa Fe, and Madridejos municipalities. The first two are important fishing centers supplying Cebu City.

THE POISONOUS SNAKES OF ISLA DE GATO

Poisonous snakes, locally called *balingkasaw,* are gathered for their skins, which are used to make bags and shoes in Danao City, and their meat, which the Chinese value as an aphrodisiac. In 1933, two Japanese fishermen discovered a breeding ground of sea snakes around the tiny Isla de Gato ("Cat Island"), reached by *banca* from Tapilon. They encouraged the locals to set up an industry, teaching them how to catch the snakes, process the skins, and even how to deal with snake bites.

The snakes are found in the caves and crevices of Gato's rocky surrounding seabed year-round, but their breeding season is March-September. The young are born after three months' incubation and then migrate to coral reefs in the open sea, where they prey on reef fish and eels. The "catchman" uses his bare hands to grab each snake by the neck and tail, ties two or three snakes together with a motorcycle inner tube, and places them in a sack.

Overexploitation has greatly reduced their numbers. A diver today will probably take only about a dozen snakes a night, compared to hundreds in the past. Landing on Gato Islet is almost impossible, due to the undercutting of its sides by wave action.

Accommodations

Basic hotels are located in Bantayan, the island's largest town, in Santa Fe, the third largest, and at several beaches near Santa Fe.

Santa Fe Beach Resort: A large and well-developed resort with a café, Windsurfers, outrigger rentals, and boat charters to nearby islands and coral reefs. The resort is in Talisay, a few kilometers north of Santa Fe pier. Santa Fe, tel. (032) 254-4765, P400-1,500.

Kota Beach Resort: Another popular resort, one km south of Santa Fe and three km from the new airport, where the sand and waters are dazzling. Santa Fe, tel. (032) 254-2726, P500-1,200.

Admiral Lodging: Basic accommodation in the town of Bantayan. The Arriola family can advise on other accommodations around the island. 21-23 Rizal Ave., tel. (032) 254-5692, P100-500.

Transportation

Bantayan Island is 138 km northwest of Cebu City and 24 km from Hagnaya port near San Remigio.

Bus and Boat: To reach Bantayan in a single day, take either the 0500 or 0600 bus from the north bus terminal in Cebu City to Hagnaya wharf, from where a regular public ferry departs daily at 0930 and reaches Santa Fe in one hour. Ferries cross from Hagnaya to Santa Fe daily at 0800, 0930, 1800, and 2000.

To Negros: Public ferries also shuttle from Bantayan across to Cadiz on Negros, a convenient route that avoids some backtracking.

Fast ferry: The quickest way to reach Bantayan is with the fast ferry, which departs Cebu City daily at 0530.

MALAPASCUA ISLAND

An even more inviting and certainly more intimate island lies nine km northeast off the tip of northern Cebu. This tiny island—three km long and one km wide—may remind you of a smaller and far less commercialized version of Boracay.

The main beach, Bounty, has the same silky sand as Boracay and the waters are just as dazzlingly blue.

Accommodations

Several simple bungalows are found on Bounty Beach, a one-km stretch of sand on the south side of the island near the principal town of Logon. **BB's Lodging House** and **Nita's Lodging House** in Logon have simple rooms for P100-250.

Directly on the beach you'll find the **Moteluna Beach Resort, Bluewater Beach Resort, Monteruibo Resort,** and **Peter & Hilda's Resort.** All charge P200-450 depending on the season and size of the room. Cocobana Beach Resort is the upscale choice with large cottages plus two meals daily going for P700-950.

Transportation

Malapascua is reached by ferry from Maya on the northeastern tip of Cebu Island. Boats leave Maya several times daily 0900-1200. To arrive in time for the outrigger ferry, take either the 0500 or 0600 Rough Rider bus from the northern bus terminal in Cebu City. The bus trip takes three and a half hours to Maya.

SOUTH OF CEBU CITY

Talisay

The proximity of Talisay to Cebu City (12 km, 30 minutes by jeepney) means that its beaches—Talisay, Pooc, and Cansojong—get very crowded, especially at weekends. They certainly don't compare with what else the province has to offer.

The focal point is the **Tourist Seaside Hotel,** P200-250 s/d, P500 family; swimming pool, scuba facilities. You can also stay on nearby Canezares Beach at the **Canezares Beach Cottages,** P150 for simple cottages. The **Beachcomber Bar** opposite the resort is a popular evening meeting place, as is the *sari-sari* store next to the police station.

To Carcar

Minglanilla is an industrial town where cottage operations produce clothing and embroidered handicrafts. Easter is celebrated with a special fervor here. Naga has a large cement plant based on local limestone and coal; pottery is a local craft.

San Fernando has a colonial church (1858) and a coral stone-manufacturing operation; you can swim at Patalinjug Beach Resort. Carcar is noted for its orchards and colonial houses.

Argao

South of Carcar, the road passes through Sibonga, which has an old wharf and some grape farms. Argao, 66 km, two hours south of Cebu City on Bohol Strait, has several white-sand beaches—Mahayahay, Mahawak, and Kawit.

Argao is an old town, with high limestone walls around its plaza, and remnants of the Spanish era. Bats haunt numerous small caves in Kahiluman.

The once-upscale **Argao Beach Resort** recently closed, and today only a handful of simple homestays carry on in the town of Argao. These spots are actually in Casay of neighboring Dalaguete.

Called the "Summer Capital of Cebu," Dalaguete is noted for its profusion of flowers and has a fine public beach, with shower facilities. Argao, Dalaguete, and Alcoy are noted for their colorful handwoven cloth. Other local handicrafts include shell necklaces and ornaments, and rattan products. Large quantities of vegetables are grown around Dalaguete and Alcoy.

THE SOUTHEAST COAST

To Santander

Alcoy and Boljoon have old churches; Boljoon also has a watchtower. Oslob is a peaceful, picturesque town with a beach of white sand and pebbles, the remains of Spanish buildings, and a hot spring at Mainit to the south.

The **Oslob Reef Club,** P400-450, provides divers with access to sites off the southern tip of Cebu Island, nearby Sumilon Island, and Balicasag and Pamilacan Islands south of Bohol.

Santadar

Santander, at the southern tip of Cebu, 134 km from Cebu City, has an old watchtower. The saltwater Pontong Lake is the haunt of rare bird species.

Cebu's longest white-sand beach is at the southern tip of Cebu near the village of Liloan, two km south of Santandar. The beach is fairly attractive, offshore diving is good, and scuba excursions can be arranged to Sumilon and Apo Islands.

Manureva Beach Resort: Jean Pierre Franck's isolated but lovely resort has a dive center, motorcycle rentals, and sailboards, and organizes big game-fishing expeditions. Pierre cooks great French meals and be sure to ask him about his postcard business. Liloan, P300-1,200.

Transportation: Santandar can be reached in a few hours with hourly ABC bus from the southern bus terminal in Cebu City. It's a spectacular ride on a recently repaved highway.

Sumilon Island

This tiny island off Cebu's southeastern tip is renowned for the wealth of marinelife in its surrounding waters. The western shore forms the Sumilon Marine Park, which is administered by Silliman University in Dumaguete (Negros Oriental). The northwestern and eastern shores have white-sand beaches, while the western, northern, and eastern sides provide fine snorkeling over coral gardens.

The western side offers a drop-off, and the spectacular underwater life includes big *garoupa*. The eastern side slopes. Large schools of jacks, manta rays, sharks, barracuda, sea snakes, turtles, and even an occasional whale shark may be seen off the northern and southern tips. Visibility is excellent.

The island rises to 28 meters and has an old lighthouse, a marine station, and resident guard. It's well worth hiring a *banca* from Mainit or Santander for a few hours' snorkeling, or alternatively, to be dropped off overnight, and be picked up at a prearranged time. Camping is possible, too. Silliman University's Marine Laboratory also has a trimaran that may be chartered out of Dumaguete for diving trips to Sumilon.

THE CAMOTES ISLANDS

These three hilly islands are situated in the Camotes Sea between Cebu and Leyte. **Poro Island** (100 square km), famous for its *kamotes,* has two towns, Poro (the main port)

and Tudela. The Lake Lanao Game Refuge and Bird Sanctuary is on **Pacijan Island** (88 square km), which is very close to Poro. The lake contains an islet. Pacijan's main municipality, San Francisco, is the site of a national school of fisheries.

Both Poro Town and San Francisco have old Spanish churches. **Ponson Island** (38 square km) lies to the northeast; Pilar is the main settlement. Each island has volcanic peaks. The highest is Mt. Three Peaks (366 meters) on Poro.

The Camotes offer a tranquil atmosphere and some good beaches. North of Pacijan is tiny Talong Island, whose white-sand beach leads down to extensive slopes covered in huge growths of table and other hard corals, with many reef fish.

THE WEST COAST

Toledo City

The road winds 50 km across the mountains from Cebu City to Toledo City, a focal point on Cebu's west coast. Toledo (founded 1853) is the ferry port for San Carlos City (Negros), across the Tanon Strait, and a major mining and agricultural center.

Regular buses depart from Cebu City's southern bus terminal on Rizal Avenue; it takes 90 minutes. Buses leave from the terminal about every hour, or when they are full. Ferries leave Toledo for San Carlos on Negros twice daily and once on Sunday.

North of Toledo

The mountains between Toledo, Balamban, and Cebu City form the Central Cebu National Park (119 square km). Balamban has a swimming pool fed by Cambuhawe Spring. In Asturias Municipality, San Roque is the site of the province's biggest reforestation project, and Tubig Manok has seaside hot springs.

Tuburan and Tabuelan have rich offshore fishing grounds. Tabuelan's name derives from *tabugukon,* a kind of octopus that's plentiful here. In the vicinity are Liki Stream, which flows from a cave, and Gumbong Spring, a freshwater spring that's below sea level and is the site of a picnic resort.

COPPER MINES AND ENVIRONMENTAL DESTRUCTION

Outside Toledo, in the *barangays* of Don Andres Soriano, Lutopan, and Biga, the Atlas Consolidated Mining and Development Corporation is one of the largest copper-mining operations in the Far East. Underground block-carving and open-pit methods are used to extract the ore. Gold is a by-product of the copper smelting. Toledo also has coal deposits and a chemical fertilizer factory.

It is a known fact that all the refuse from the mining activities around Toledo is pumped into the sea. Since one by-product of copper is cyanide, one German biologist noted that "it's the same stuff that was used in the gas chambers." However, it's business as usual in Toledo and it's estimated that over half the families here are associated with the mining operations. It is uncertain how much effect the mining has on the reefs and fish around Badian and Moalboal, but it's bound to be bad in years to come.

South of Toledo

The road south of Toledo passes through Pinamungajan, site of Ulbuhan and Anapog Springs and a municipality with many fishponds, and Aloguinsan, which has a pleasant park on a hill overlooking the sea. The views along this road are great and it's a pleasant ride.

At Barili, there is a resort called **Mountain Paradise** (P200-250), which offers all the amenities for tourists.

THE SOUTHWEST COAST

The road from Cebu City to Moalboal and the southwest crosses the island from Carcar to Barili. Points of interest in Barili include the Hospicio de San Jose, an institution for the aged and infirm; the swimming pool at Bolok-Bolok mineral hot spring, whose sulfuric water is said to cure skin ailments; Palalong Cliffs, a place of death for the townspeople during WW II; the Kabolongan and Sayao Beaches; and the Twin Falls of Mantayupan.

Dumanjug has some colonial houses; boats cross from Tangil's wharf to Guihulngan (Ne-

gros). Enjoy fine views across to Negros from atop the forested Libao Hill (145 meters) in Ronda. Alcantara, four km north of Moalboal, has an old church.

MOALBOAL

Panagsama Beach, situated at the edge of a rocky promontory some 90 km southwest of Cebu and five km from Moalboal ("Bubbling Spring"), remains a popular travelers' destination despite the tragic destruction of its beaches and offshore coral gardens by Typhoon Nitong in 1984. Locals say the tides were at their very lowest when the 280-kph winds virtually sandblasted the once-famous coral beds into oblivion.

Fortunately, some of the coral has returned to its natural state near the shore for snorkelers, and the superb coral beds near Pescador Island were spared any damage. The beaches have also improved over the years, but remain somewhat rocky and unpleasant except for a narrow strip of sand just north of the expensive Moalboal Reef Club.

Today, Moalboal's main attraction remains its great snorkeling and diving around the underwater buttresses and coral-studded reefs near Pescador Island. The town also provides some of the least expensive PADI certification in the Philippines. Saavedra Dive Center and other dive shops charge US$25-30 per dive including equipment or US$250-300 for a five-day PADI certification program.

If you're not a diver, you may find that there is little to do as the beaches are not great. Foreigners here are stark raving mad about diving and will talk of nothing else, except possibly where to get the best margarita on the beach.

Moalboal, or Panagsama Beach, also has its fair share of prostitution going on, so be careful about one-night stands. Foreign women are interesting to their fellow man only if they are divers!

Diving

Diving and snorkeling are possible directly from the shore and from a *banca*. Numerous dive shops have sprung up at Panagsama Beach, and while many are run by foreigners, Nelson Abenido has run **Ocean Safari Philippines** for over 10 years and offers full PADI certification for US$200.

Other, newer dive centers offering similar rates are **Visayan Dives, Saavedra Diving Center,** and **Philippine Dive & Tours.**

Pescador Island

The finest diving is found around Pescador, about two km off Panagsama, which rises to 19 meters above sea level. Snorkelers can go out with one of the diving *bancas* for a modest amount. Snorkeling is best on the south side of the island, where a coral-studded reef slopes to a 30-meter drop-off with caves and overhangs.

The north shore has a spectacular drop-off, the northwest corner has several underwater buttresses, and on the west side is the majestic Pescador Cathedral, where divers can drop through a 15-meter-wide funnel to the base at 35 meters, then pass through a series of apertures. It's particularly impressive around noon, when shafts of sunlight pierce the funnel. Beware of stonefish around Pescador; sea snakes and lionfish are also a common sight.

Along the Shore

About 15 meters from Panagsama Beach, the reef drops 35 meters, and the coral-lined edge of this drop-off provides excellent and unusually accessible snorkeling. You can dive directly from the shore here, but if you go north or south along the coast, a *banca* is necessary.

Going north from the Reef Club, there are interesting spots at the north end of Bas Diot Beach, and at Saavedra, just before the tip of the peninsula. The chances of seeing large fish are even better here than at Pescador, and the coral is also good. The drop-off has caves at around 25-30 meters, and currents make drift diving possible.

To the south, there's also good diving and snorkeling around Tapanan and Tongo Point. About 45 meters offshore, the drop-off falls to 40 meters, offering fine wall diving, with plentiful coral and fishlife. The underwater topography is varied by a series of coral arches in four to eight meters of water off Tapanan, and large buttresses off Tongo. The dive sites of Badian, across the bay, are also accessible from Moalboal.

Accommodations

The village at Panagsama is a somewhat scruffy place suffering from a lack of planning, barking dogs, and hustling schoolchildren. But it has dozens of places to stay, mainly in the budget to moderate price range.

Private cottages with fan and private bath cost P150-450 depending on facilities, while a/c lodges cost P500-1,000.

Pacita's Bungalows to the left of the Coke sign is a popular place despite the lack of sand and sad shape of the huts. Norma's, Nanita's, Gabunila's, Eve's Kiosk, Paradise, Calypso, Sunshine Pension, Cora's, and Pacifico Cottages are similarly priced.

The popular **Sumisid Lodge** charges P400-600 (common toilet and bath) with meals; it is run by a Dutch man. Sumsid offers full PADI certification and rents equipment. In the evenings, divers gather here to watch movies or plan the next day's dive. It's not uncommon to meet foreigners who have been living at Panagsama Beach for six months or more, so they know where the good dive spots are.

Moalboal's best lodging options are **Moalboal Reef Club** at the north end of the beach, **Savedra Beach Resort** and **Cabana Beach Club** in the middle, and **Sampaguita Beach Resort** at the southern end of the beach. These places cost P800-2,000.

Restaurants

The best places to eat at Panagsama Beach are **Hannah's Place, Eve's Kiosk,** the expensive **Cafe Europa, Susan's Seaside Restaurant,** and **Pacita's.** Evening fun and partying can be done at **Chief Mau's Station,** a great bar, pool room, and disco combined.

Transportation

Moalboal can be reached in three hours by ABC bus from Cebu's southern bus terminal. Philippine Eagle goes direct at noon. Buses terminate in Moalboal, from where tricycles cost P20-25 out to Panagsama Beach.

If the bus's destination is Moalboal, as opposed to passing through it, the bus may actually go to the beach.

From Moalboal, it's possible to follow the coast road south to Santander. At Talisay, you can catch the ferry to Negros. Some travelers manage to rent motorcycles in Cebu City and tour the whole island by bike. This seems like an ideal way to see the countryside, but travel at your own risk.

Heading to Negros? Good alternatives to the standard ferry from Toledo (Cebu) to San Carlos (Negros) are the hourly boats from San Sebastian and Bato to Tampi near Dumaguete.

SOUTH OF MOALBOAL

Badian Island

Badian has an old church and a beach. Offshore is the new and upscale **Badian Island Beach Hotel,** US$100; scuba facilities, pool, snorkeling, restaurant, and more. For reservations, check at the Magellan Hotel in Cebu City.

At Badian town, on Cebu Island, stay at the **Cebu Green Island Club.** Rooms and bungalows range US$50-65.

Experienced divers will enjoy the area around Badian Point and Badian Island (known locally as Zaragosa Island). Fish and sea snakes are abundant, but currents can be strong, making drift diving inadvisable.

Kawasan Falls

South of Badian is Matutinao, where the fairly scenic Kawasan Falls has two deep, natural pools for a refreshing swim in a lush tropical setting. From Matutinao church, which is 17 km south of Moalboal, follow the trail beside the river for 1.5 km uphill. Some good mountain treks begin from here.

Beyond Matutinao, Alegria has an old church and a *lanzones* plantation, while points of interest in Malabuyoc include its sandy beaches and a hot spring in Montenesa. Ginatilan has an old church and beach. Samboan is an old town from whose center the Escala de Jacob, a 114-step carved stone stairway, rises steeply.

San Sebastian and Bato

Ferries depart approximately every hour to make the one-hour crossing to Tampi near Dumaguete. The San Sebastian-Tampi crossing is as good as any. The ferry wharfs on Cebu are the south terminals of the buses from Cebu City.

If you're going to or from Cebu City, or will stopover en route, check whether the bus follows the east or west coast, according to your wishes. Whichever point on Negros you arrive at, there'll be transportation to nearby Dumaguete.

LEYTE

Leyte is divided into two provinces: Leyte and Southern Leyte. Its densely forested mountains form a beautiful backdrop to fertile plains. Leyte is linked to Samar by bridge and lies astride the overland routes from Manila to Mindanao or Cebu. Tacloban is the major city and transportation center, but several interisland ports line the west and south coasts.

Leyte's best-known tourist spot is Red Beach, Palo, scene of MacArthur's landing in 1944. More recently, Tolosa—a small town slightly south of Tacloban—received international attention and a great deal of economic gain for being the birthplace of Imelda "Shoe Princess" Marcos.

Aside from these historical sidelights, Leyte has a handful of beautiful but rarely visited national parks and some isolated islands perfect for the visitor who wants to get off the beaten track.

HISTORY

In 1521, Magellan proceeded from Homonhon Island, off Samar, to Limasawa Island, off Southern Leyte, which became the site of the first Catholic mass in the Philippines. Leyte and Samar were the original recipients of the name "Felipinas," coined in 1543 by Spanish expedition leader Villalobos and applied later to the whole archipelago. Legazpi visited Abuyog and Limasawa briefly, soon after his arrival at Cebu; Spanish settlement followed. Leyte, already well populated, was known as Tendaya at the time.

The Jesuits founded a mission in Palo in 1596, and in the fishing village of Ormoc in 1597. In 1622, Chief Bankaw of Limasawa, exasperated by Spanish abuses, led a rebellion that ex-

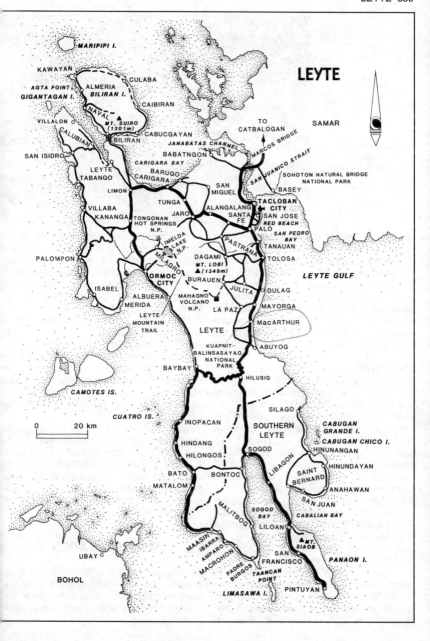

MacArthur, Osmeña, and Romulo storm ashore at Red Beach.

tended up to Carigara, but the Spaniards snuffed it. Bankaw died in battle. The west coast was plagued by Muslim pirates until the 19th century. Leyte became a separate province in 1768. Carigara, Palo, and Tanauan succeeded one another as provincial capital until Tacloban became the capital in 1860; its port was opened to international trade in 1874. Leyte, as a revolutionary stronghold, became a battlefield during the Philippine-American War.

World War II

The Japanese landed in Tacloban in May 1942, fortified the city, improved the airfield, and made San Pedro Bay an Imperial Navy harbor. Two years later, on 20 October 1944, Leyte became the landing site of the U.S. liberation forces. Seven hundred U.S. ships and 174,000 men participated in the invasion. The key objectives: Tacloban and Dulag airfields. About 20,000 Japanese had retreated inland to escape the preinvasion bombardment of the coast. Some hours later, Gen. Douglas MacArthur waded ashore at Red Beach, with Sergio Osmeña and Gen. Carlos P. Romulo. On 23 October, on the steps of Leyte's Capitol, MacArthur formally installed Osmeña as president of the Commonwealth of the Philippines.

From Tacloban, MacArthur led the drive to liberate the Philippines, while Osmeña proceeded to restore the government. A few days after the invasion, the Japanese fleet was devastated in the Battle of Leyte Gulf. Within two weeks, however, the Japanese had landed heavy reinforcements at Ormoc. The toughest battle was at Breakneck Ridge, which the Japanese had turned into a bastion. Here, near Limon, Americans and Japanese fought for three weeks, often hand-to-hand, on slippery, muddy slopes in constant rain.

On 7 December, U.S. troops landed at Ipil, four km south of Ormoc, on the same day that Japanese reinforcements were due to arrive. Each air force attacked its enemy convoys. Most of the Japanese ships were sunk, including an entire convoy in San Isidro Bay, and the loss in Japanese planes was high. The U.S. lost two destroyers, and several vessels were badly damaged.

The U.S. invasion force met little opposition upon landing, but the Japanese defended Ormoc resolutely. Three days later, after heavy bombardment, U.S. troops entered Ormoc effectively ending the Leyte campaign. About 60,000 Japanese died on Leyte's mountains, swampy plains, and surrounding waters. The U.S. Army lost 3,500 men, with 12,000 wounded.

TRANSPORTATION

Traveling across Leyte is rather straightforward. Travelers can reach Tacloban from Legaspi in a single nonstop day, provided they catch the morning ferry from Matnog on Luzon to Allen on Samar.

Tacloban to Ormoc takes two hours by bus. Most travelers then catch a fast ferry from Ormoc to Cebu City.

Other departure options include flying to Tacloban from Manila, daily boats from Tacloban to Surigao in northeastern Mindanao, and fast ferries from Maasin to Surigao. There's also an irregular boat service from Maasin to Ubay on Bohol.

Schedules should be checked with the tourist office in Tacloban.

Air
From Cebu City: PAL flies from Manila to Tacloban three times weekly, on Monday, Wednesday, and Saturday.

From Manila: PAL, Cebu Pacific, and Grand Air fly daily from Manila to Tacloban.

Ship from Bohol
Ubay to Bato: A large outrigger leaves daily at 1000 and takes three or four hours to Bato with a possible stop at Lapinin Island. A quicker alternative is the MV *Star Ruby,* which leaves Ubay daily at 1100 and takes about 90 minutes to reach Bato.

Ubay to Maasin: An outrigger leaves daily at 1000 and takes four hours to Maasin.

Ship from Cebu
Bukog (Camotes Island) to Ormoc: An outrigger leaves daily at 0700 and takes three hours to Ormoc.

Carmen to Isabel: An outrigger leaves daily at 0800 and takes four hours to Isabel.

Cebu City to Baybay: Cokaliong Shipping's MV *Filipinas Siargao* leaves daily at 1200 and takes six hours to Baybay. Western Samar Shipping's MV *Gregorai May* leaves at 2300 on Monday, Wednesday, and Friday and takes five hours to Baybay. You might also try K&T Shipping's MV *Samar Queen,* which departs at 2200 on Tuesday, Thursday, and Saturday and takes six hours to make the passage.

Cebu City to Liloan: K&T shipping's MV *Guiuan* departs at 2000 on Monday and Friday and takes six hours to Liloan, while Water Jet Shipping's MV *Water Jet 2* departs at 1645 on Tuesday, Thursday, Saturday, and Sunday.

Cebu City to Maasin: Universal Aboitiz's MV *Supercat* departs daily at 0900 and 1300 and takes just two hours to Maasin. Water Jet Shipping's MV *Water Jet 2* sets off at 0830 on Tuesday, Thursday, Saturday, and Sunday.

Cebu City to Ormoc: Regular, large ships on this route take six hours, cost around P80, and include Sulpicio Lines' MV *Cebu Princess* on Monday at 2200, Cebu Ferries' MV *Iligan City* at 1300 on Wednesday and Saturday, Sulpicio Lines' MV *Dona Lili* at 1300 on Thursday and Friday, and Sulpicio Lines' MV *Lady of Carmel* every Sunday at 1300.

Fast ferries from Cebu City to Ormoc are somewhat expensive, but they are certainly the quickest and most comfortable way to reach Leyte from Cebu. The trip takes just two hours and costs P200-250. Service is provided by Bullet Xpress's MV *Bullet Xpress* daily at 0500, Water Jet Shipping's MV *Water Jet 1* daily at 0530, and Universal Aboitiz's MV *Supercat* daily at 0600, 0830, 1115, 1400, 1600, and 1830. More runs to Ormoc are made by Socor Shipping's MV *Oceanjet* daily at 1300 and Water Jet Shipping's MV *Water Jet 2* at 1645 on Tuesday, Thursday, Saturday, and Sunday.

Cebu City to Palompon: Cebu Ferries' MV *Lady of Rule* departs Monday at 1200, while the MV *Dona Lili* leaves Saturday at 1200. Both ships take five hours to Palompon.

Cebu City to Tacloban: Several large ships make this trip each week and take 12-13 hours to complete the crossing. Cebu Ferries' MV *Don Calvino* departs at 1800 on Monday, Wednesday, and Friday, while the MV *Dona Lili* leaves at 1800 on Tuesday. K&T Shipping's MV *Leyte Queen* provides additional services with departures at 1800 on Tuesday, Thursday, and Saturday.

Danao to Isabel: Aznar Shipping's MV *Meltrevic 3* sails daily at 1400 and takes about three hours to reach Isabel.

Maya (northern Cebu) to San Isidro: A large outrigger leaves Maya daily at 1030 and takes three hours to reach San Isidro, from where buses continue on to Ormoc and Tacloban.

Ship from Manila
Big ships take 30-35 hours on the average to reach various ports on Leyte. Fares average P450-500.

Manila to Tacloban: WG&A's MV *Masbate Uno* leaves Monday at 1000 and takes 30 hours with a stop at Catbalogan on Samar. The ship also departs Manila at 1900 on Friday and does a quicker, direct route to Tacloban in just 25 hours. Sulpicio Lines offers the MV *Tacloban Princess,* which leaves Manila for Tacloban on Wednesday at 1000 and Sunday at 0900. The trip takes around 24 hours and costs P450-550.

Manila to Ormoc: Sulpicio Lines' MV *Cebu Princess* leaves Manila on Friday at 1000 and takes a heart-stopping 50 hours with a long stop on the island of Masbate. It's probably better to go to Tacloban and continue down to Ormoc by public bus or minibus.

Ship from Masbate
Masbate to Ormoc: Sulpicio Lines' MV *Cebu Princess* leaves every Saturday at 1600 and takes 16 hours to Ormoc. The fare is P200-250.

Masbate to Calubian: Sulpicio Lines' MV *Palawan Princess* heads off every Thursday at 2200 and takes eight hours to Calubian, before continuing down to Baybay and Maasin.

Masbate to Palompon: Service is provided by the WG&A MV *Sacred Heart,* which departs at 2000 on Tuesday and takes 10 hours to Palompon and then onward to Ormoc.

Ship from Mindanao
The fast ferry from Surigao to Maasin is probably your best bet.

Surigao to Liloan: Bernard Service's MV *Maharlika II* leaves daily at 1700 from Lipata, a small port 10 km northwest of Surigao, and takes three hours to Liloan.

Surigao to Maasin: Water Jet Shipping's fast ferry MV *Water Jet 2* blazes off at 1230 every Tuesday, Thursday, Saturday, and Sunday, and takes just two hours to make the crossing. The fare is P200-250. This is a very popular service.

Slower but less expensive large ships include Cokaliong Shipping's MV *Filipinas Dapitan,* which departs Tuesday at 1900 and takes five hours to Maasin. Cokaliong also runs the MV *Filipinas Surigao* every Wednesday and Friday at 1900. Trans-Asia Shipping's MV *Asia-Singapore* sails on Friday at 1700, while Sulpicio Lines' MV *Palawan Princess* does the journey on Saturday at 2000. The latter ship continues on to Baybay and Calubian.

Ship from Samar
The service from Catbalogan to Tacloban has long been a favorite of many travelers, as it provides a welcome change from the long and exhausting road trip.

Catbalogan to Tacloban: WG&A's MV *Masbate Uno* leaves Catbalogan on Tuesday at 1100 and takes four scenic hours to reach Tacloban.

Guiuan to Tacloban: K&T Shipping's MV *Stacey* departs every other day at 2200 and takes just over six hours to reach Tacloban.

TACLOBAN

Tacloban is the provincial capital, as well as the commercial, industrial, cultural, educational, and transportation center of the eastern Visayas region. It's linked to Manila by land, sea, and air.

Its deepwater harbor, strategically located where the San Juanico Strait meets San Pedro Bay, is one of the finest in the Visayas. With an economic hinterland that includes the fertile Leyte Plain and the nearby coast of Samar, Tacloban is the main port of shipment for copra, abaca, fish, and timber from the region.

The 135,000 Taclobanons are mostly Warays. Former First Lady Imelda Romualdez Marcos comes from Tolosa, just south of Tacloban, and the Romualdez family has been prominent in this area.

Tacloban's downtown area is compact. The city is also a good base for excursions to Sohoton Caves and Red Beach at Palo.

Attractions
It's possible to visit the city's points of interest in a half-day circular walk. Beginning at the gate to Tacloban wharf, go two blocks up Justice Romualdez Street, turn left onto Sen. Enage Street, then first right onto T. Claudio Street. About 100 meters down on the right is the Redona residence, which housed President Osmeña and his staff during Leyte's liberation. Return to Sen. Enage Street and Plaza Libertad. On this walking tour, check out the market and the sidewalk vendors on Trece Martires Street for their handicrafts.

The building adjoining Plaza Libertad served as the country's temporary capitol during 1944-45. Bas-reliefs flanking the building depict the

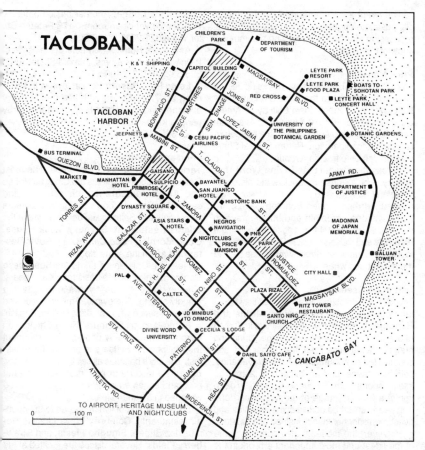

two major events in Leyte's history—the first mass at Limasawa and MacArthur's landing at Red Beach.

Diagonally across from the Capitol is the Children's Park and the useless tourist office.

Turn right onto Magsaysay Boulevard, on which national, regional, and provincial offices are situated. On the left is the **University of the Philippines's Botanical Garden,** which affords a fine view of Samar across the bay. Farther, on the right, is a small park containing the statue of Maria Kannon, the Madonna for Peace, donated by the Japanese people as a peace symbol.

The boulevard curves past city hall, on Kanhuraw Hill (another good view) to reach Plaza Rizal.

Santo Niño Church

Across the plaza is the Santo Niño Church, which enshrines the miraculous ivory image of the Child Jesus, patron saint of Tacloban and Leyte. Affectionately known as the Capitan, it was lost at sea in 1889 and recovered five and a half months later. While the statue was missing, the town suffered from a cholera epidemic, but it's believed that the epidemic ceased upon the reappearance of the statue.

The event is commemorated in the annual city fiesta, celebrated on 30 June with a fluvial procession, dancing, singing, and a communal show of devotion.

Price Mansion

From Plaza Rizal, proceed two blocks up Justice Romualdez Street to the Price Mansion, now the Governor's Guesthouse. Built by an American businessman in 1910, it was used as a Japanese Officers' Club and MacArthur's headquarters during the liberation. Return to Real Street and turn left onto Imelda Avenue.

Across the street is the **Divine Word University,** whose museum depicts the history of Leyte and Samar with 6,000-year-old Stone Age relics unearthed around Sohoton Caves, antique Chinese porcelain and burial jars, and memorabilia of the 1944 landing. After visiting the university and museum, follow Santo Niño Street to Justice Romualdez Street, which leads back to the market and wharf.

Heritage Museum

Top draw to Tacloban and almost certainly the island of Leyte is the **Santo Niño Shrine and Heritage Museum** on Calle Real two km south of downtown. On the site where the young and hungry Imelda once lived, the former first lady constructed a monument to her extravagance, self-importance, and appalling bad taste. The interior sports a baby Jesus surrounded by disco lights, a framed image of the Madonna done with pearls splashed across crimson velvet, and guest rooms for her friends instead of side altars.

However, the museum also contains some of the finest and most important artwork in the country; some of the furniture could almost pay off the national debt. This is the best museum in the Philippines—not the National Museum in Manila.

Accommodations

Most of Tacloban's inexpensive hotels in the P100-250 price range are along Romualdez Street a few blocks from the bus terminal.

San Juanico Travel Lodge: None of the low-end choices in Tacloban are very clean, but for an overnight crash try this spot in the center of town. 104 Justice Romualdez St., tel. (053) 321-3221, P100-200.

Cecilia's Lodge: Another basic homestay with simple yet clean rooms. 178 Paterno St., tel. (053) 321-2815, P100-300.

Asia Stars Hotel: A new hotel in the center of town with spotless rooms. Zamora St., tel. (053) 325-5322, P750-1,400.

Leyte Park Resort: Best in town with swimming pool, food court with live bands every evening, and organized boat tours to nearby parks and beaches. 6500 Magsaysay Blvd., tel. (053) 325-6000, P2,000-3,600.

Food and Nightlife

Tacloban is renowned for seafood. The most famous seafood restaurants are **Sinugba House** and **Agus Restaurant.** You can also find seafood or Chinese food if you go to P. Zamora Street between Salazar and del Pilar, where the **Silahis Restaurant, Savoury Steak House, Good Morning Food Center,** and **Rovic Restaurant** are in the same block.

Near the Childen's Park is the **Seabreeze Canteen,** which serves basic meals and beers, offering one of the best views in the city in a friendly setting. The owner, Ami, is a widowed mother of seven who speaks excellent English.

For chicken, try **Sunburst Fried Chicken** on Burgos Street, a fairly good chain throughout the Philippines. **Felisa's** is popular for breakfast. The city's bakeries all sell the local delicacy, *binagol,* a mixture of *gabi* root, egg, coconut milk, and sugar, whipped together and served wrapped in a banana leaf.

For an evening of live music, go to the open-air restaurants, **Celebrity Plaza** (Justice Romualdez Street), **Sinugbo Fiesta,** and **Strawberry Fields.** Several discos are located at the junction of M.H. del Pilar and Zamora Streets, while **Spacer Disco** on Real Street is somewhat pretentious with a P50 cover charge and semi-imposed dress code.

Transportation

By Air: PAL flies to Manila twice daily (takes 70 minutes) and to Cebu (35 minutes) four times a week. Tacloban airport is a 15-minute ride south of the city. A shuttle bus operates between the airport and downtown.

By Ship: A direct voyage from Manila takes 23 hours, slightly faster than the trip overland. Many buses operate between Tacloban and

Catbalogan in the neighboring province of Samar, but it's worth taking the scenic boat trip through the San Juanico Strait, especially in daylight. Boat service from Tacloban to Catbalogan is sporadic; check schedules with the tourist office.

Fast Ferries: No fast ferries from Tacloban, but you can take a bus down to Ormoc and continue by fast ferry across to Cebu City.

By Bus: Several buses leave daily from Manila to Tacloban. The Luzon-Samar ferry ride breaks up the journey, giving passengers a chance to stretch. Morning and evening departures are timed to connect with the ferry crossings. Philtranco and other buses also go to Maasin, Naval, and Ormoc. PEBL and JD Bus offer nonstop service to Ormoc; it's popular, so buy your ticket early.

From Tacloban, it takes two hours to Ormoc; two and a half to Baybay, three to Naval, and five to Maasin. Frequent minibuses link Tacloban with Catbalogan and Calbayog on Samar, and buses also operate to Guiuan, Borongan, Allen, and Catarman.

VICINITY OF TACLOBAN

The most popular local points of interest are Sohoton Natural Bridge National Park, the San Juanico Bridge, Red Beach, and Palo. Balugo Falls, 10 km north near the San Juanico Bridge, is a developed area with waterfalls and swimming pools. White Beach is conveniently located at the end of the airport runway in San Jose, eight km south of downtown. Apart from Sohoton, these spots are easily reached by jeepney.

Sohoton Natural Bridge National Park

Usually referred to as Sohoton Caves, this park is a must. Unfortunately, it's almost impossible to tour without the help of a chartered boat or a tour organized through the Leyte Park Resort.

The trip to the caves is best done as a two-day trip, at least, from Tacloban, overnighting in Basey. A day trip is possible but very rushed. Take a 0600 jeepney from Tacloban market to Basey, arriving 0700. It will take at least an hour to arrange a boat and petromax lamp (very important). Then it takes two and a half hours each way to the park.

The last jeepney back to Tacloban may leave Basey around 1500. The Tacloban Department of Tourism also organizes weekend guided tours to the caves; ask if one is planned.

See **Samar** for more information on this national park.

San Juanico Bridge

If you travel by bus from Leyte to Samar, you'll cross the narrow, treacherous, scenic San Juanico Strait, with its islets, swift currents, and whirlpools. The impressive S-shaped San Juanico, or Marcos Bridge, is the longest in Southeast Asia. It has 43 spans totaling more than two km long and rising 41 meters above the sea.

Babatngon

The road north of Tacloban divides, one branch crossing the San Juanico Bridge, the other leading to Babatngon on the Janabatas Channel, which leads into the San Juanico Strait. Here, 33 km from Tacloban, is the seven-tiered Busay Falls, with swimming pools, a viewing tower, and a fish hatchery, all amid lush vegetation and orchids.

Red Beach and Palo

Historic Red Beach, scene of the U.S. landing forces in 1944, and Palo, the first town to be liberated by the American forces, may be visited as a day trip from Tacloban, or could be a stopover en route to Ormoc or Southern Leyte. Red Beach is 12 km south of Tacloban and two km north of Palo town center.

Not all vehicles go to Red Beach, so check first before boarding in Tacloban. You can catch a tricycle from Tacloban.

Imelda Park overlooks the beach and contains the bronze statues of MacArthur, President Sergio Osmeña Sr., Gen. Carlos P. Romulo, and four companions wading ashore. The "Liberation Day" anniversary ceremony held at Red Beach each 20 October is a major event.

Palo's notable cathedral served as a refuge for local people during the battle and then as an evacuation hospital for U.S. wounded. Founded in 1596, but completely rebuilt in neo-Gothic style, the cathedral contains an antique gilded altar.

Behind the cathedral is Hill 522 (Guinhangdan Hill), a battlefield now surmounted by a commemorative cross. A path leads to the summit, which affords a superb view of the surrounding area. Japanese bunkers and foxholes still remain on the upper slopes.

The hillside La Purisima Shrine is the scene of a Holy Week pilgrimage.

TACLOBAN TO ORMOC

The highway cuts west at Palo, passing through farmland. This is the site of the Sab-a Basin Development Program, whose objective is to increase food production and rural incomes in the area stretching west from Tacloban to Barugo and Jaro. The road skirts Carigara Bay, then splits for Biliran Island and Ormoc City, respectively, at Limon, 72 km west of Tacloban. Breakneck Ridge near here was the scene of one of the bloodiest battles of the liberation.

Biliran Island

This large (555.4 square km), high island forms a subprovince of Leyte. A bridge across the narrow Biliran Strait links it to Leyte. Structurally an extension of Leyte's Central Cordillera, it has several volcanic peaks around 1,000-1,300 meters high.

Biliran has eight coastal towns. Naval is the transportation center, linked by regular buses to Tacloban (109 km) and Ormoc, and by boat twice weekly to Cebu.

Stay at **LM Lodge** at Naval, **Agta Beach Resort** at Almeria, or **Lodging House** at Caibiran (P100-150 for cottages).

Beaches on Biliran's west coast include Banderrahan Beach, Naval, and Agta Beach Resort near Almeria. Other beaches include Dalutan and Sambawan. Boats leave Naval daily, around 1100, for Maripipi, Higatangan Island, and Villalon on Leyte.

The main town on Biliran's east coast is Caibiran, from which you can make several excursions. The cool, spring-fed San Bernardino swimming pool, which has changing facilities, is located beneath shady trees near a beach. Tumalistis Falls, said to have the sweetest water in the world, is reached by a 20-minute *banca* trip.

Hot sulfur springs near Caibiran include Mainit Spring, 30 minutes by jeepney, which has pools and hot baths; Libtong Spring; and Racquiza Hot Springs. Caucab Falls are inland, and Biliran's volcanoes can be climbed as day trips, with a guide.

Maripipi Island

This 28-square-km island in the Samar Sea north of Biliran (two hours by *banca* from Naval) has secluded beaches and great snorkeling over beautiful coral gardens. A ceramic school here utilizes local white clay.

Gigatangan Island (five square km, one hour by *banca*), west of Naval, also offers fine beaches, coral, and shells. Former President Marcos, then a resistance officer, took refuge here during WW II. Marcos Hill dominates the island, with a spectacular view from the top.

Northwest Leyte

This is corn country. The highway strikes south from Limon and passes through Kananga, which has hot springs. A road branches west to Villaba, which has asphalt deposits, and the port of Palompon, served by shipping lines sailing to Cebu, Roxas City, and New Washington (Panay).

The Bugabuga Hills, near Villaba, were a Japanese Army stronghold where thousands of soldiers died in a desperate last stand. The hills are a natural fortress, with steep cliffs and many caves. The latter are, along with several other places in the Philippines, said to contain hidden Japanese treasure.

North of here, the Larrazabal ranch in Taglawigan is a pastureland resort. Isabel, south of Palompon, is the site of the Leyte Industrial Estate, a major industrial complex with a copper smelter and phosphate fertilizer plant powered by geothermal energy.

ORMOC CITY

Ormoc, the main port and commercial center for western Leyte, chiefly serves as the departure point for fast ferries to Cebu and as a base for exploring the nearby national parks. Ormoc is also a surprisingly attractive town that attracts large numbers of expatriates who retire here with their Filipino wives.

Attractions

Attractions include the wharf and the market, the remains of an old bridge near City Hall, the Zaldibar Museum, a Japanese peace memorial, and Pura Beach, 12 km distant.

Farther afield is Tungonan Hot Springs, with a swimming pool and thermogeyser projects, and Leyte National Park, with its sunken volcanic lake said to be the haunt of giant eels. Hikers might enjoy the 50-km Leyte Nature Trail, which begins near Ormoc.

You can rent motorcycle and cars from Joylyn Trans Rental in the Don Felipe Hotel.

Accommodations

Most of Ormoc's hotels are within walking distance of the bus terminal and the ferry port.

Eddie's Inn: Simple but clean rooms in a small hotel about four blocks from the bus terminal. Rizal Street, tel. (053) 255-2499, P125-200.

Pongos Hotel and Annex: A somewhat more expensive but cleaner choice four blocks from the wharf. Bonifacio St., tel. (053) 255-2482, P200-650.

Ormoc Sky Garden Pension House: New budget place just north of the immense Gaisano shopping center and very near two other cheap options—Ormoc Sugarland Pension House and Ormoc Friendly Inn. Rizal St., tel. (053) 255-5210, P150-550.

Don Felipe Hotel: Ormoc's top-end choice (aside from the new Day's Inn). Bonifacio St., tel. (053) 255-2460, P300-600 in the budget annex, P850-1,500 in the main building.

Transportation

PAL flies twice weekly from Ormoc to Cebu City.

Fast ferries to Cebu City depart five times daily.

Buses leave Ormoc hourly for Tacloban (108 km, two hours); Philtranco, PEBL, and JD Bus Lines have nonstop service. Some buses go directly to Naval (Biliran Island); you can also change at Limon.

Regular buses head south to Baybay and go through to Maasin (four and a half hours). Philtranco a/c buses depart for Manila daily at 0645.

VICINITY OF ORMOC

Tongonan Hot Spring National Park

Located at an elevation of 2,000 meters amid densely forested hills, the park contains a warm, medicinal swimming pool, a geyser that spurts hourly, and formations exuding sulfuric vapors. Wild pigs, deer, monkeys, and birds are also found in the three-square-km park. Tongonan Geothermal Plant provides the area with power. Tongonan can be reached by jeepney from Ormoc.

Lake Danao National Park

Situated at an elevation of 1,600 meters (18 km from Ormoc), the park has Lake Danao (three km long, 200 meters deep), surrounded by forested hills that contain much wildlife. The lake is said to be the haunt of a giant eel. You can camp near the shores.

No regular transportation serves this park, but it can be reached by a secondary road from Milagro, just south of Tongonan. The park is at the west end of the Leyte Mountain Trail. At Albuera, south of Ormoc, is the Villa Ramona Beach Resort, which has a cottage and spring-fed swimming pool.

SOUTH OF TACLOBAN

Tolosa and Dulag

The Pan Philippine (Maharlika) Highway follows the shores of Leyte Gulf from Tacloban through Palo to Abuyog. Nearby Bislig Bay is the site of a beach and fishing village.

Next comes Tolosa, the former first lady Imelda Marcos's hometown, whose retreat, Kalipayan ("Happiness"), sprawls along the beach at Olot. The Tolosa area contains black iron sands that yield iron ore.

Dulag was the site of the Blue Beach landing in the 1944 invasion. A memorial on Hill 120 in San Rafael marks the place where the U.S. flag was raised during the invasion.

A road leads inland from Dulag to Burauen. This was also a major battle site; the Japanese War Memorial Cemetery in San Diego is visited by Japanese tour groups. Daguitan Rapids and Danao Lake are situated near Burauen amid beautiful scenery. It's possible to run the rapids on banana tree rafts or rubber tires and swim in the lake.

Mahagnao Volcano National Park
Located 66 km from Tacloban, between Burauen and La Paz, this six-square-km park contains Mount Mahagnao's volcanic crater, Lake Mahagnao, hot springs, bubbling mud pools, sulfur vents, multicolored rock and mud formations, a lagoon, and forest with giant ferns and orchids. Trails lead to points of interest.

Across the Island
The highway winds across the central mountain ridge from Abuyog and branches near Mahaplag to Sogod and Baybay. Travel on these southern roads may be disrupted by landslides or washed-out bridges after heavy rain. West of this junction is Kuapnit-Balinsasayao National Park, which has a campsite and caves amid mountain scenery.

Baybay
This abaca-exporting port, two and a half hours from Tacloban, 55 km from Abuyog, and 45 km from Ormoc, has an old Spanish church and tower. **Ellan's Lodging House** and **Travellers' Inn,** both near the pier, charge P75 pp. You can also stay seven km north of Baybay at the **Visayan State College of Agriculture,** a modern complex with a beach and small guesthouse, P80 pp.

From Baybay, boats depart once a week to Jagna (Bohol) and thrice a week to Cebu. A boat also makes a weekly trip from Manila via Ormoc to Baybay and Cabalian.

Baybay to Bato
The fishing port of Hindang is the gateway to the Cuatro Islands, a 30-minute *banca* trip out in the Camotes Sea. These four small islands—Daguio, Mahaba, Apit, and Himokilan, the largest—offer sandy beaches and delicious *tatus* (coconut crabs). Nipa huts are available. The bell tower of Hilongos's colonial church is a prominent landmark.

Bato is a small port from where a ship departs for Cebu every other day. A *banca* also leaves daily 0800-1100 for Ubay, Bohol (four hours, P35 pp), and 1500-1700, subject to sufficient passengers and calm weather. Stay at **Green House,** P55 pp.

MAASIN AND VICINITY

The provincial capital, 183 km from Tacloban, is a trading center and port. Its Spanish colonial cathedral contains a notable altar, ceiling, and santos. Places of interest around Maasin include Ibarra, Canturing, and Pugaling Beaches, and Cacao and Busay Falls. Guinsohotan Falls in Kagnitoan are reached after a rugged eight-km hike on mountain trails that are slippery after rain. Cold water emerges from a large limestone cave with stalactites and stalagmites, slides down a 30-meter incline, then drops five meters into a pool where you can swim beneath lush foliage.

Accommodations
Ampil Pensione, on Abugao Street near the pier, with rates starting at P60 pp is the best choice, or try **Skyview Lodging House,** where rates start at P75 pp.

Transportation
To Bohol: Large *bancas* cross from Maasin to Ubay (three and a half hours, P75 pp), subject to sufficient passengers and calm weather. **Escao Lines** sails once a week to Jagna.

To Cebu and Mindanao: Several large ships sail weekly. There is also a daily fast ferry to Surigao on the northeastern tip of Mindanao.

South of Maasin
Amparo and Macrohon have beaches. Kuting Beach has a natural swimming pool and is a popular picnic place. Tubod and Tugayong Springs are in the area. The small port of Padre Burgos is the gateway to Limasawa, visible from Tancaan Point; concrete steps lead to a vantage point. There's good snorkeling off nearby Santa Sofia Beach. Cobcob Beach is also nearby.

Limasawa
A 45-minute *banca* crossing from Padre Burgos brings you to Limasawa, a national shrine, containing Magellan's Cross and a marker commemorating the site of the first Catholic mass in the Philippines in 1521. Magellan planted a cross on a hill at the island's south end. The

grave of Rajah Kolambu, who welcomed Magellan, is also found here. This nine-square km island has two small villages.

Sogod Bay

Limasawa and Panaon Islands form the entrance to the long (56 km), narrow, fish-rich Sogod Bay. From Padre Burgos, the road follows the western shore, passing through Malitbog, near which are Benit Falls, San Vicente grottoes, and Lorenzo Baybay Beach. At the head of the bay lies the port of Sogod.

Stay in town at **Crown Restaurant and Lodging House,** P75 pp.

In the vicinity of Sogod, the forested Magsuhot Park, three km off the main highway, has four 20-meter-high waterfalls falling into a common basin; 12 km from the park are Lum-an and Mahayhay Falls, which have a 60-meter drop. On the east side of the bay is Libagon, site of Biasong Beach.

Liloan

There's good snorkeling around Liloan, and cottages on Bitoon Beach were rebuilt after being destroyed in a typhoon.

Stay at the **Liloan Hillside Lodge** behind the ferry terminal for P75. The **C & S Lodge** also has rooms for P50-75. There is daily bus service from Tacloban to Liloan; three to four hours by combined ferry and bus.

Panaon Island

This long, slender island is structurally an extension of Leyte's Central Cordillera. Panaon (202 square km) is separated from Leyte by the Wawa Strait, which is crossed by Liloan Bridge. Each changing tide creates eddies and whirlpools as it forces water through the narrow channel.

Liloan, the main town, is at the island's north end; the ferry terminal is at the foot of the bridge. Kongkings, a small ethnic group, occasionally come down from the hills on market days. Short, curly haired, and dark-skinned, they are believed to have migrated from Mindanao.

In Liloan, stay at **C & S Lodging House,** P75, near the pier. Outside town at Bitoon Beach are the Swiss-run **Urs and Helena Cottages,** P75 pp, with food. Good snorkeling and scuba facilities are offered here.

M.G.L. DOMENY DE RIENZI

MARINDUQUE

This island province's main claim to fame is the Moriones Festival held during Holy Week in March or April, when thousands of visitors crowd Marinduque for the event. For the rest of the year, the island's towns and beaches are quiet and relaxing places to linger. The beaches aren't exceptional by Philippine standards, but offshore snorkeling is good.

HISTORY

Legend holds that the island rose from the sea simultaneously with the suicidal drowning of two thwarted lovers, Marin and Garduke. Several Spanish galleons were built here in the early 17th century. It's believed the Moriones Festival began

in Mogpog in 1807. The idea of masked soldiers is said to be of Mexican origin, introduced by Spanish sailors who repaired their galleons here. Marinduque saw action during the struggle for independence from Spain and the U.S.

TRANSPORTATION

PAL flies from Manila to Marinduque daily taking 45 minutes. The airport is near Gasan, 13 km from Boac. Boats also sail each morning 0600-1000 from Cotta, near Lucena City (Quezon), to Balanacan and Buyabod (Santa Cruz); they also depart from the Marinduque ports for Cotta about 0600; crossings take four hours. From Mindoro, a boat departs Pinamalayan (three hours) for Gasan and Balanacan twice a week, sometimes three times a week.

AROUND THE ISLAND

Balanacan
This port, situated on a superb natural harbor where Spanish galleons once stopped for repair, is linked by daily boats with Cotta (Lucena). Stay at the **LTB Lodging House** (P150-200). Mogpog has iron and copper mines outside the town, and Paadjao Falls are in the vicinity. From Balanacan port to Boac, it takes 45 minutes by jeepney; to Gasan it's 90 minutes, and to Mogpog 30 minutes.

Boac
The provincial capital and market town is located about three km inland on the Boac River delta; Laylay is its outport. The fortresslike church was built in 1792 as a shrine for the miraculous Lady of Biglang-Awa, to which is attributed deliverance from a Moro attack. The revolution's flag was brought here to be blessed in 1899. Beaches within 12 km of Boac include Sun-Raft, Tabing Dagat, Santo Domingo, Lupac, Balogo, Baliasnin, Laylay, and Ihatub.

Stay at **Cely's Lodging House,** on 10 de Octubre St., P100-150, or the **Boac Hotel** on Nepomuceno St., P150-200 (higher prices during the Moriones Festival). At nearby Caganhao, between Boac and Cawit, try the **Pyramid Beach Resort** (P150-200). Also on the beach are **Aussie Pom Guest House** (P150-200) and

Swing Beach Resort (P200-250), en route to Mogpog just north of Boac. If you wish to use the homestay program in Marinduque, write Mr. Dindo Asuncion, president, Marinduque Homestay Association, Morallon, Boac, or speak with the local mayor or *barangay* captain.

South of Boac
Cawit (10 km) has an unremarkable beach. Stay at **Sun-Raft Beach Resort** (eight km from Boac, P200-250, dining hall, laundry service) or **Sea View Resort** (P300-450). Marinduque's airport is at Masiga, north of Gasan. Stay at **Marigold Kitchenette** (P150-200), near the shore, or **Amigo's Lodge** (P150-200). Banot and Masiga Beaches are two and five km out, respectively. For scuba diving, tennis, a restaurant, and a bit of luxury, try the new **Sunsent Garden Resort and Restaurant,** Pangi, Gasan. Rooms are P300-450. PADI instruction is offered here plus *banca* trips to the islands.

Tres Reyes Islands
These islands are named after the biblical Three Kings: Gaspar, Melchor, and Baltazar. The nearest island, Gaspar, is a 15-minute *banca* ride offshore from the villages of Pingan, Banuyo, or Daykitin. It's inhabited by fishermen and has the group's only beach; take drinking water. The wreck of a 15th-century Chinese trading vessel occurred between Pingan and Gaspar. A large number of ceramic pieces have been recovered, including Shantou porcelain and stoneware jars, and some iron skillets.

The islands have steep cliffs and offer fine snorkeling and diving, especially on the south sides. Baltazar Island has good diving all around it, with reef flats 9-12 meters deep dropping off to 30 meters. The impressive marinelife includes skipjack tuna and big hammerhead sharks. The channels between the islands are subject to strong tides, so be cautious. You can also hire a *banca* in Pingan or its neighboring villages for the one-hour ride to Dos Hermanas Islands. (Romblon), which also provide outstanding diving and snorkeling.

South Marinduque
Caigangan Beach and Malbog Sulfur Springs are 1.5 and three km from Buenavista, respectively. Elefante Island, to the south, can be reached by *banca* from Lipata, in the shadow

THE MORIONES FESTIVAL

This colorful pageant depicts the legend of Longinus, a Roman centurion blind in one eye. When he speared Christ on the cross, blood spurted into his eye and restored his sight; he also witnessed Christ's resurrection while guarding the tomb. He thus attained faith.

The word *morion* relates to the centurion's helmet. Beginning on Holy Monday, *moriones,* dressed in the distinctive masks and colorful homemade costumes of Roman soldiers, roam the streets. Many of them are penitents who are giving thanks for an answered prayer, a good harvest, or cured illness. Longinus's conversion takes place on Good Friday at 1500 as does the reenactment of the crucifixion, which is preceded by the self-inflicted suffering of flagellantes, known as *antipos* here.

The climax is on Easter Sunday during the *habulan* (chase), when Longinus races through fields and streets and is seized thrice by the soldiers but escapes each time, until his final capture when he is brought before Pilate. The trial takes place on an open-air stage in the evening, with the dialogue in Tagalog verse. He refuses to renounce his faith, and the festival ends with the *pugutan* (beheading).

Guests of honor at the festival may be given a floral crown and are seated on a throne while local women sing, dance, and throw flowers in a ceremony called the *putong.*

Practicalities

Moriones is enacted at Boac, Gasan, and Mogpog, with events and times varying slightly by town. Most visitors go to Boac, since a wider range of accommodations is available. Those wishing to stay in the one-star **Boac Hotel** or **Cely's Lodging House** should try to make reservations or arrive early enough to get lodging here. Rooms are generally P200 but will go up during the Moriones Festival. Inclusive tours are offered from Manila, and PAL operates extra flights at this time. *Moriones* masks, hand-carved from local *dapdap* wood, are offered for sale as souvenirs.

Holy Week Events

Marinduque is also a good place to observe many other Holy Week rites, including the reenactment of the "Way of the Cross"; the Santo Sepulkro, a wake by the body of Christ at which older folk exchange riddles based on Scripture; and the *salubong,* when the statues of Mary and the resurrected Christ meet after an Easter morning procession.

Others

The Three Kings' Pageant takes place in Gasan and Santa Cruz on the first Sunday or 6th of January. The Three Kings reenact their journey in search of the Christ child by riding through the community on horseback, accompanied by their "cavalries," giant puppets, townsfolk in native dress, and children clamoring for coins and candies tossed from windows. The folk play ends with a raging King Herod destroying his palace, set up on a stage, upon learning about the birth of the new King.

In May, the Santacruzan and Flores de Mayo festivals are popular events, while Boac's town fiesta is on 8 December. Marinduque also celebrates Niños Inocentes day on 28 December. Here, Jesus' escape from Herod's slaughter of infants is remembered when masked giants and dwarfs roam the towns, reenacting the Roman legions' persistent search for the Holy Infant, highlighted by a merry parade and mock chase.

Moriones Festival

CARL PARKES

of Mt. Marlanga. Torrijos has sandy beaches; stay at **White Beach** cottages, P150, two km from town (take a tricycle). This is probably the best beach on Marinduque. It's possible to hire a *banca* to go snorkeling over the reef drop-off, which is 200-300 meters offshore.

Santa Cruz

A market center and Marinduque's largest town, Santa Cruz's port is at Buyabod, four km from town center, and many jeepneys connect with the boats to and from Cotta (Lucena). Stay at **Park View Lodge** (P150-200) near the town hall or **Rico's Inn** (P150-200) opposite the school. The owner can also arrange a room in a residential house. Eat at **Tita Amie Restaurant,** corner Palomares and Pag-asa Streets. The **Joville Resort Hotel** (P300-350) is four km from town.

Vicinity of Santa Cruz

The northeast coastal plain is largely surfaced with limestone. The Bathala Caves, formed of coral limestone that's been upthrust about 30 meters above sea level, are undeveloped and full of bats. Three caverns have been explored, and there's believed to be another larger one with a

river flowing through it. They're on the property of the Mendoza family; visitors should apply at their house to look at the caves and use the natural swimming pool there. They charge a small entrance fee and guides are available. Bathala is 10 km northwest of Santa Cruz and accessible by regular transportation. It's also possible to visit the huge copper mine operated by Marcopper-Mines at Labo, 18 km from Santa Cruz.

Offshore Islands

The Santa Cruz Islands consist of Polo (or Santa Cruz), Maniuayan, and Mompog. Maniuayan is a peaceful island with long beaches and good snorkeling on its offshore reefs. To reach it, take a tricycle from Santa Cruz to Bitik, then the 0800 boat (takes 45 minutes). Mompog Island, about one hour from Santa Cruz by *banca,* offers good snorkeling, especially on the southern and western corners. A shallow reef, 9-15 meters deep, has superb coral. On the north side, fish are plentiful where the reef flat drops off from about 10 meters. Be careful of currents on the west side. Farther south, on Salomague Island, **Salomague Island Resort** (P250-300) has diving facilities.

MASBATE

Masbate (the name of a province, an island, and a town) occupies a transitional position between Bicol and the Visayas. Since it lies between the main routes south, i.e., the Manila-Tacloban Hwy. and the sea lanes to Cebu and the western Visayas, it's outside the tourist mainstream. But those who do come here can enjoy fine beaches, a scenic, hilly landscape, and friendly locals.

HISTORY

Archaeological excavation of a cave at Kalanay has yielded pottery, some human bones, and a few stone, metal, glass, and shell artifacts. The Kalanay people are believed to have come from Indochina between 400 and 100 B.C. and settled on several islands. Masbate's early inhabitants practiced jar burial. In 1569, Legazpi sent the first of many exploratory expeditions from Cebu to

Masbate, Ticao, and Burias. Spanish settlers followed. They found hardwood forests, and Masbate shipyards built several galleons during the early 17th century. Little economic development, however, took place under the Spanish.

Toward the end of their era, the founding of new settlements accompanied the establishment of cattle ranching and the discovery of rich veins of gold-bearing quartz. Filipinos, Spaniards, and Chinese flocked to Aroroy to dig and pan for gold, but the veins were soon exhausted.

After 1900, the grasslands of interior and southeast Masbate became the object of migrations from the Visayas and Luzon. The American period also saw extensive gold mining south of Aroroy and Masbate town. The ore was of comparatively high grade and employment reached several thousand. But after WW II, the fixed price of gold and the high cost of reopening and maintaining the mines led to the abandonment of operations.

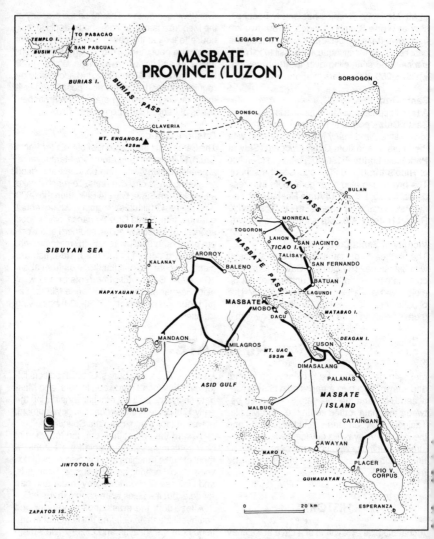

TRANSPORTATION

PAL flies once daily from Manila to Masbate (85 minutes) and three times a week from Masbate to Legaspi City. Masbate's airport is 1.5 km south of town.

Philtranco buses operate Manila to Bulan (Sorsogon) and connect with the ferries to Masbate town, which sail at 0700 and 1300 (four-hour crossing). Boats depart Masbate for Bulan at 0500 and 1300. JB Liner buses link Legaspi and Bulan, via Sorsogon town (three and a half hours). *Bancas* leave Bulan for Ticao Island around 0900 or whenever the boat fills up.

MASBATE TOWN

Masbate, the provincial capital and main port of entry, is an unprepossessing commercial center (pop. 60,000) situated on a picturesque bay. For travelers, it's merely a route center, from where jeepneys fan out to all communities on the island. In addition to regular boats to Manila, Cebu, and neighboring islands, tramping vessels often call at the port, so you might make a convenient connection by checking what's in, and when and where it's sailing.

Accommodations
Masbate is not a big town, and most accommodations are centrally located. All the lodging houses costing under P200 are extremely basic. These are **Crown Hotel** on Zurbilo St., **Sunrise Lodging House, Rodieflor Lodge, C. P. Alburo Lodging House,** and **Rainbow Lodging House.** The more expensive **St. Anthony's Lodge** has rooms for P250-300.

Restaurants
For food, try the **Peking House Restaurant, Paolo's Restaurant, Maxim,** and **Jona's Snackhouse.** The **Petit Restaurant,** across the street from St. Anthony's Lodge, is also good. Masbate is noted for its white *tuba* (potent drink), but not for its water, which should not be ingested unless boiled. Those who want to enjoy nightlife can try the **Hang-out** or **Triple K,** or go disco-dancing at **Nimbus** or **Viewdeck.**

AROUND THE ISLAND

You can make a circuit of the north by taking a boat up the coast from Masbate to Baleno, then return to Masbate by jeepney via Aroroy and Milagros. Aroroy is on a large bay and has a beach. Between Aroroy and Milagros, roads branch off to Mandaon and Balud. Small boats sail up the coast from Mandaon to Napayauan Island, which has a white-sand beach. Inland from Mandaon in Bat-ongan is a 150-meter-high rock. Believed to be a crashed meteor, it has seven openings that lead to an underground river and caves that have revealed traces of ancient inhabitants.

Balud is a commercial fishing port and fish-salting center. On this northwest coast are two of the oldest lighthouses in the country, built by the Spaniards at Bugui Point and on Jintotolo Island in 1800. The latter guards the 32-km-wide Jintotolo Channel, which connects the Sibuyan and Visayan seas. Milagros is situated on rice-growing lowlands at the head of Asid Gulf. Jeepneys link Masbate town with these west-coast ports, thus providing routes to Sibuyan and Panay.

The road south of Masbate passes through Mobo, site of Bitu-on and Dacu Beaches and, inland, Ubo Falls. It follows the eastern shore to Cataingan, in a corn-growing area on the Samar Sea. The road then forks to Placer and Pio V. Corpus. Placer and Cataingan are ports for Bogo on Cebu. Jeepneys depart Masbate market for the dusty ride to Cataingan until about 1330. The boat from Cataingan to Cebu City leaves daily except Saturday at about 1730.

TICAO ISLAND

This is a very pleasant, elongated, hilly island (334 square km), with some good beaches. A low ridge runs the length of the island. The highest point is 405 meters. Hillsides descend directly to the sea on the west side, along which there are only a few small villages. The main road links the four towns along the well-settled east coast. Copra is the main cash crop.

San Fernando
San Fernando town is situated on a scenic palm-fringed bay. Stay at **Delavin Lodging House** (P150-200). Across the island, Talisay has a white-pebble beach. At the north end of the beach, past the village, are some tiny, secluded coves at the foot of cliffs, which are good for sunbathing and offer pleasant swimming in clear water. Boats travel up the coast fairly regularly to Lahon, but to see the Togoron waterfall beyond it, which cascades down cliffs into the sea, you must charter a *banca* from Talisay.

Binitinan Beach is five km north of San Fernando and one km off the road. San Jacinto is an old Spanish galleon port. Manila galleons took on supplies here before heading out across the Pacific. It's older and larger than San Fernando, having been designated a *pueblo* in the mid-18th century. Stay at **Cadag Letada Rest House** (P150-200). Before the main road reaches Monreal, a road branches left from Real; it leads three km to the cool Matangtubig Spring, where you can swim, and at 12 km emerges above the Togoron waterfall.

Transportation

The 20-km-wide Ticao Pass separates Ticao from Luzon. Some large *bancas* leave San Jacinto and San Fernando early in the morning for Bulan (Sorsogon), departing for Ticao at around 0900 (a two-hour crossing). Several *bancas* from Lagundi and a few from Talisay cross Masbate Pass each morning, taking Ticao people to Masbate town for business and shopping; they leave Masbate in the early afternoon. The fare is P30; the boatmen may try to overcharge foreigners. Jeepneys connect with the *bancas* at Lagundi. They travel up to Monreal and to near Talisay. Transport can be scarce in the late afternoon, so it's better to begin trips early.

BURIAS ISLAND

This hilly, copra-producing island (424 square km) has been occupied since pre-Hispanic times, but it is still underdeveloped. The two main settlements of San Pascual and Claveria are linked by boat. The east coast has cliffs and broad promontories; the island's highest point is Mt. Engañosa (428 meters).

Boats sail daily from Masbate town to Claveria and San Pascual. The Burias Pass separates the island from Luzon; there's a daily boat from Pasacao, near Naga City, to San Pascual, while Claveria is served from Pio Duran (Albay). San Pascual (church built in 1563) is as picturesque as Ticao's towns. Claveria has fine white beaches in San Isidro and Halabang Baybay and amazing rock formations in Boca Engaño.

MINDORO

Mindoro has experienced considerable progress in recent decades, especially in the eastern coastal communities. A mountainous spine, with rugged, partly unexplored forests, forms a natural barrier between the island's two provinces: Occidental Mindoro and Oriental Mindoro. The sole highway almost circumnavigates the island. Few roads cross the island, and a network of trails penetrates the interior—preserve of the indigenous Mangyans. Three reserves have been established for the remaining few hundred *tamaraw*, a species of wild water buffalo unique to the island. To many travelers, a trip to Mindoro is synonymous with a sojourn at Puerto Galera (Oriental Mindoro), which has become a travelers' hangout. Occidental Mindoro remains little visited, and the interior much less so. Apo Reef, the world-class scuba spot, lies off the west coast.

HISTORY

Mindoro was part of the land bridge between Palawan and Luzon by which primitive man migrated from mainland Asia and Borneo to the Philippines. Evidence indicates that between 400 and 100 B.C., a group of people called Kalanays came from Annam and Tonkin to settle in Mindoro, the Visayas, and elsewhere. Samples of pottery found in gravesites indicate that they were more advanced than other contemporary inhabitants of the area.

Chinese historians make reference to an extensive trade existing as early as the 10th century between China and Mindoro, called Ma-i. Porcelain, silk, and gilded ornaments were traded for forest products. It's believed, too, that the Bornean *datus* who fled to Panay in the 13th century eventually spread out to other islands, including Mindoro. Thus, the Spaniards found Muslim coastal settlements here.

The Spanish Era

In 1570, Legazpi sent Juan de Salcedo to attack Muslim pirates who were harassing the Panay coast. Salcedo destroyed Moro forts on Ilin and Lubang and captured Mamburao. Some months later, he and Martin de Goiti, passing

Mindoro on their way north from Panay to Manila, attacked two Chinese trading junks in a harbor. Legazpi himself visited Mindoro on his voyage to Manila.

The Spanish began to explore the island. They found some gold and named it "Mindoro," from the Spanish *mina de oro* (gold mine), but no major gold discoveries have ever been made. Missionaries were active around Ilin Island, Mamburao, and Lubang, but recurrent Moro raids forced them to abandon these places. In 1636, Tagal, the Sultan of Maguindanao's brother, led a large fleet along the coast, ravaging settlements, looting churches, and taking captives. Mamburao and Balete (near Sablayan) became Muslim strongholds from which forays were launched against nearby Christian settlements.

Mindoro was a notoriously difficult assignment, as the priests had to contend with murder, piracy, and malaria. Puerto Galera, the island's capital until 1837, regularly received the great galleons on their voyages between Manila and Acapulco. But Muslim attacks, which continued until the mid-19th century, delayed the island's development. After the outbreak of the revolution, rebel forces established a government on Mindoro that lasted until 1901, and during the Philippine-American War the island saw some fierce fighting.

World War II

Mindoro played a key role in MacArthur's drive to recapture Manila. In mid-December 1944, the success of a surprise assault on the thinly defended San Jose area enabled the U.S. to build airfields on Mindoro. U.S fighters and bombers not only protected the Lingayen Gulf invasion convoy, but also attacked Japanese air bases on Luzon and helped close Manila Bay to enemy ships, thereby isolating General Yamashita from his forces in the south and keeping out Japanese reinforcements.

Japanese Stragglers

Mindoro received international attention in 1974 when Lt. Hiroo Onoda, a Japanese straggler who didn't know that WW II had ended, emerged from the hills of Lubang Island after 30 years in the forest. He returned home a hero. His book, *No Surrender: My Thirty-Year War,* is fascinating.

In 1980, Capt. Fumio Nakahura was discovered on the slopes of Mt. Halcon in Mindoro's interior. And in 1983, Philippine newspapers spoke of a search for a former machine gunner said to be mingling with the Mangyans around Mt. Baco. Other stories persist of similarly benighted individuals still wandering around in the hills. One also hears stories of Mangyan children with distinctly Japanese features.

SCUBA DIVING

Mindoro's easy accessibility and well-preserved marine environment have made it one of the top dive locations in the Philippines. Among the highlights are the coral gardens situated off Long Beach; the famous shark cave near Escarceo Point; and the wrecks of a Japanese ship near the Boulders, a Spanish galleon near Verde Island, and another Spanish wreck in the Manila Channel (only discovered in 1983).

Puerto Galera is also the launching point for dives to renowned Apo Reef, a 30-square-km reef off the west coast of Mindoro. Professional dive shops that can help with equipment rentals, boats, guides, and PADI certification include **Capt'n Greggs** on Sabang Beach, **El Galleon** on Small La Laguna Beach, and **Reef Raiders** on Big La Laguna Beach.

TRANSPORTATION

To Puerto Galera

Ferries leave daily around noon from Batangas to Puerto Galera. The easiest way to make the connection is on private a/c buses leaving at 0900 from the Centrepoint Hotel in Manila. The cost is P300-350, and arrival time at the Batangas pier is around 1130.

From the pier, the MV *Si-Kat II* leaves at 1200 and takes about two hours to reach Puerto Galera. It's a beautiful journey at the end as you pass through some stunning landscapes.

A cheaper alternative is an early morning (0700-0800) BLTB bus from Pasay direct to the ferry dock in Batangas. Be sure to get on a bus bound for the Batangas pier rather than just the town of Batangas. This bus costs around P50.

You can then take the MV *Santa Penafrancia VI,* a car ferry operated by Santo Domingo Shipping, over to Puerto Galera for an additional P50. The ship leaves Batangas pier daily at

THE MANGYANS OF MINDORO

Anthropologists have divided the Mangyans into several subgroups: Iraya, Batangan, Buid, Hanuno'o, Alangan, Ratagnon, Tagaydan (or Tadyawan), Bangon, Pula, Buhid, Nauhan, and Furuan. They total about 125,000 and inhabit the remote forest interior. It's believed that some of the groups were coastal dwellers, roaming the island at will, but they retreated into the mountains to avoid religious conversion by the Spaniards, Moro pirates, and the influx of migrants.

Mangyans are simple, submissive people. Their predisposition to retreat rather than confront an enemy has led to their frequent exploitation. Mangyan families, in fact, keep their few valuables within easy reach in case they have to flee without warning from strangers. Mindoro's recent economic expansion hasn't benefitted the Mangyans, whose untitled lands have been taken over by lowlanders who buy their forest products at near-giveaway prices. Since intermarriage is frowned upon by both sides, there's little mixing.

But the Mangyans are emerging from their isolation; steps are being taken to assimilate them into the mainstream of Filipino society, while attempting to preserve their ethnic identity. The Mangyans of northern Mindoro are farther along this route, acquiring permanent dwellings, education, and contemporary clothing.

Traditional Lifestyle

The Mangyans are traditionally nomadic within their own territory and follow the food supply. Their settlements are loose clusters of 10-20 bamboo huts with thatched roofs and raised floors, occupied by related families. They have no formal leaders or social classes, and disputes are handled by elders. Men wear a loincloth of pounded bark and carry a bolo and betel nut container. Women wind a coil of woven nito and rattan around their hips and fasten a piece of pounded bark to it as a breechcloth. Both men and women are commonly addicted to betel nut, their lips permanently stained red.

They grow crops near their huts and cultivate their fields. Corn and kamote are their staples, supplemented by cassava, rice, bananas, papayas, avocados, squash, beans, gabi, and other vegetables. They gather edible forest products and trap wild pigs and chickens, as well as keeping the domestic varieties.

Customs

The Mangyan tribes have generally evolved independently, so in spite of some cultural similarity, individual customs vary by locale. Much remains unknown about Mangyan customs. Animists and polytheists, Mangyans recognize a multitude of spirits in the forest and forces of nature. Marriage takes place without ceremony, and within a family, a 14-year-old bride and her mother may be pregnant at the same time.

Death isn't marked elaborately either. A corpse is buried quickly, and the family soon builds a new hut to escape any lingering spirits. The Hanuno'o, however, practice panludan, a rite involving a ceremonial second burial one year after death in which the bones are exhumed and placed in a shaft or cave.

0830, 1230, and 1700 and arrives at Balatero, three km west of Puerto Galera town.

You could also take the MV Si-Kat II for P150.

Several large outriggers also go from Batangas pier direct to Sabang Beach, at 0930, 1030, 1200, and 1330. These outriggers cost P60 and are somewhat less comfortable than the larger ships.

Late arrivals can charter a private outrigger over to Puerto Galera for about P800.

By using a public bus from Pasay and an ordinary boat across to Puerto Galera, you will spend a combined total of just P100-120 rather than the P300 asked by the folks at Centrepoint Hotel.

Jeepneys waiting in Puerto Galera go in two directions: east to the busy beaches at Sabang and La Laguna or west to the relatively peaceful White Beach. Sabang is best for scuba divers and party animals searching for bars and discos. White Beach is best for long walks, sunsets, and quiet evenings in simple restaurants.

Heading south from town to town by bus from Puerto Galera is scenic but somewhat time consuming: Puerto Galera-Calapan (two hours), Calapan-Roxas (four hours), Roxas-Bulalacao (two hours), Bulalacao-San Jose (four hours), and San Jose-Pandan Island (four hours).

Generally, only sickness is attended by ritual. Medicine men chant night after night facing a dark corner until the invalid has been purged of evil spirits. Only when the native doctor gives up is the sick person taken to a hospital.

The Hanuno'o
These people consider themselves the "true" Mangyans. Numbering about 20,000, they occupy a wide area of the rugged mountains of southeast Mindoro, from San Jose to Bongabon. They are one of the Philippines' few remaining minority groups to use an ancient indigenous script, thought to be Indic in origin and based on a syllabic alphabet with 48 characters. It's carved onto bamboo tubes, limeholders, bolo scabbards, house beams, and musical instruments.

The carvings convey words of wisdom, known as *urukoy*, which are chanted by tribal elders on festive occasions, and record folkloric poems called *ambahan,* a body of riddle-like rhyming love songs recited by teenagers during courtship. This poetic language is quite different from that in everyday use. The Hanuno'o are musically inclined, carving instruments out of wood and using human hair for strings or bow. Musical instruments include the *git-git* (three-stringed violin), the *kudyapi* (six-stringed harp), the *guitara,* the *kalutang* (xylophone), and the *kinaban* (bamboo flute).

The Hanuno'o grow cotton, which they spin and weave on a backloom, then dye with locally grown indigo. On formal occasions, the men wear a white cotton long-sleeved shirt, decorated with red and blue thread. They also wear a white loincloth and a *buri* belt, into which is tucked a bolo in a wooden scabbard. Red scarves are used to tie back their long hair, which provides a constant supply of strings for their musical instruments.

The women wear white or navy blue embroidered blouses, a navy blue *sarong,* and headbands, necklaces, and bracelets of brightly colored beads. In addition to their colorful beadwork, they excel in the making of baskets and mats using bamboo, rattan, vines, and other fibers from the forest. Artifacts are produced in a wide array of striking shapes and decorative designs. Weaving black *nito* into the lighter-colored rattan, for example, creates very pleasing geometric patterns.

The Iraya
If you see Mangyans around Puerto Galera, they are probably Iraya. Well-defined, both culturally and linguistically, the Iraya number about 37,000 and practice *kaingin* farming in the foothills and plateaus of northern Mindoro. They're noted for their fine basketwork.

Visiting Mangyans
Many Mangyans now reside on government reservations. To visit one of these settlements, obtain a permit from the **Office of Muslim Affairs and Cultural Communities** (OMACC) in Manila. Some settlements are run by missionaries who generally don't welcome casual tourists. Mangyans are frequently seen in coastal towns, where they come to trade and shop. But to see anything resembling their traditional lifestyle, you must hike far into the interior with a guide. Even then, a meaningful encounter is hampered by their shyness and the difficulty of communication.

Other Ships from Batangas
Most travelers head directly to Puerto Galera, though boat service is also provided to other destinations on Mindoro.

To Calapan: Universal Aboitiz's MV *Supercat* departs daily at 0730, 1100, 1430, and 1930 and takes 45 minutes to make the crossing to Calapan. Other fast ferries include the MV *Lourdes* and MV *Fatima* which make the crossing hourly from 0600 to 1730. There are also regular slow ferries that cross hourly and take two hours to Calapan.

From Calapan you can head south or take a jeepney until around 1600 for the trip westward back to Puerto Galera. Calapan to Puerto Galera takes around two hours.

To Abra de Ilog: Car ferries operated by either Montenegro Shipping or Viva Shipping leave Batangas daily at 0300, 0900, 1100, and 1500 and take two and a half hours to the port at Wawa. Buses leave Wawa and head south to San Jose via Maburao and Sablayan.

To Sablayan: Departures are provided from Batangas on Tuesday, Friday, and Sunday by either the Viva Shipping Line MV *Penafrancia* or the MV *St. Christopher.* The crossing takes nine hours and costs P150-200.

To San Jose: Viva Shipping's MV *Marian Queen* leaves on Monday, Wednesday, and Saturday at 0700, while the MV *Santo Niño* departs Tuesday, Friday, and Sunday at 0700. Batangas to San Jose takes about 11 hours.

To Boracay
Mindoro also serves as a transit point for visitors going to Boracay.

Roxas to Boracay via Tablas: The most popular route is with a large outrigger from Roxas in southeastern Mindoro across to Looc on Tablas Island, from where *bancas* continue down to Boracay. The route via Tablas takes about 10 hours and is often cancelled in bad weather.

Roxas Direct to Boracay: There's also a direct boat service from Roxas to Boracay—twice weekly during the low season and almost daily during the busy months from December to June.

Although a somewhat dangerous journey due to unexpected storms, the Roxas-Boracay route allows you to enjoy the beaches at both Puerto Galera and Boracay with a minimum of backtracking. The tourist office in Puerto Galera has the latest schedules for boats from Roxas and other towns on Mindoro.

To Panay
Several large outriggers make the crossing from San Jose on Mindoro to various port on Panay.

San Jose to Buruanga: An outrigger leaves on Thursday and Sunday at 0900 and takes at least eight hours to reach Buruanga, about 15 km south of Caticlan (the departure point for Boracay).

San Jose to Lipata: The MV *Princess Melanie Joy* and the MV *Aida* sail weekly to Lipata, a small town on the west coast of Panay, some 70 km south of Caticlan. The trip takes a full 24 hours since stops are made at both Semira and Caluya Islands.

PUERTO GALERA

Situated on an outstandingly beautiful harbor, with numerous fine beaches and sheltered coves beneath a green mountainous backdrop, Puerto Galera spreads out about 10 km around the coast. Its focal point is Puerto Galera town (the Poblacion), where the ferry docks.

This fishing port has changed drastically during the past decade and has become an international travelers' beach resort with both the positive and negative aspects of such status. A few of the beaches are already completely lined with hastily built cottages with inadequate waste

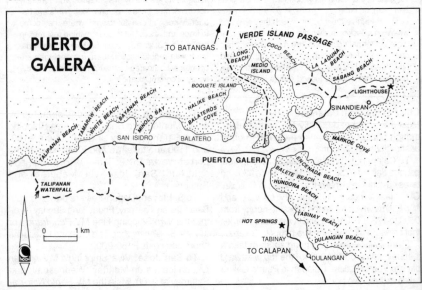

*Sabang Beach,
Puerto Galera*

disposal systems, so that they're in danger of degenerating into a travelers' slum. Others are still beautiful places to stay.

The more developed beaches have gained some of the trappings of internationalism, such as available girls, magic mushrooms, marijuana, and foreigners bathing topless or nude—spurring local resentments.

History
The superb natural harbor was a bustling port as early as the 10th century, hosting Chinese junks and traders from India, Java, and Sumatra, as well as other Philippine islands. Marble, pearls, rare birds, tortoiseshell, and forest products were exchanged for porcelain and other luxury items. The small **Excavation Museum** in the church grounds contains some artifacts and pieces of Chinese pottery found in local pre-Hispanic burial sites.

The Spaniards established the town in 1574, declaring it the capital of Mindoro. San Isidro was the original seat of government, but Moro pirate raids forced a move to the current Poblacion. Puerto Galera means "Galleon Port," and many galleons came here for répairs or to shelter from typhoons. The town is still noted for boatbuilding and repair.

Near the dock, á marble cross commemorates the loss of a Spanish warship, *El Canonero Mariveles,* which sank in a storm in 1879. Puerto Galera's natural beauty has long been recognized.

Opposite the church is a **Marine Biology Station,** established in 1932 for field study by the University of the Philippines. The UNESCO Man and Biosphere Program selected the town as a research center in 1974. But since then tourism has placed a severe strain on the environment.

Puerto Galera Town
The town center is a pleasant place to stroll around, with numerous shops and restaurants catering to visitors. Enjoy an excellent view of the harbor from the government offices behind the town. Over the years, yachts from Manila and elsewhere have found safe harbor year-round here, which adds to the picturesque setting of the harbor community. The Sunday cockfight takes place above Hundora Beach.

The town marks the Feast of our Lady of Fatima on 13 May, and its fiesta on 7-8 December coincides with the Feast of the Immaculate Conception.

Mt. Talipanan (1,185 meters) yields 17 varieties of marble. An old 10-km road leads to a disused quarry, near which stands **Marblecraft Guest House,** built entirely of marble. Rainforest covers the slopes of Mt. Malisimbo (1,228 meters).

Accommodations are found in town, but there's little reason to stay here unless you plan on catching an very early-morning ferry back to Batangas. It's best to immediately take a jeepney east to Sabang or west to White Beach.

Puerto Galera has a small but useful tourist office near the pier and a Swagman travel office near the Puerto Galera Resort Hotel. International phone calls can be made at reasonable prices at the BayanTel office just up from the pier, while traveler's checks can be cashed at the First Allied Savings Bank just opposite BayanTel.

Puerto Galera is only four hours from Manila (two hours to Batangas City, a two-hour crossing) but allow longer. It's safer to leave Manila before 0900 to be sure of getting a good seat on the 1230 ferry. Most buses go directly to the pier; if not, you must change to a jeepney in downtown Batangas.

The entrance to Puerto Galera's scenic harbor is memorable, so it's worth being on the upper deck. The boat is met by *bancas* and jeepneys waiting to take passengers to outlying beaches and villages. If you miss the ferry at Batangas, your choice is to wait there until 1230 next day or take a boat to Calapan (they sail every two hours), then a jeepney to Puerto Galera (40 km, two hours).

More information can be found above under Transportation at the beginning of the Mindoro section.

Sabang and La Laguna Beaches
Once an idyllic beach reached only by chartered *banca,* Sabang and nearby La Laguna Beaches are now fully developed resort areas with hotels, bungalows, restaurants, discos, nightclubs, girlie bars, money changers, a pharmacy, general goods stores, and plenty of dive shops. Most of the visitors here are either scuba divers or bachelors down from Manila with Filipina girlfriends in tow.

Sabang is the main beach where you'll find the nightlife and most of the dive shops. Big La Laguna and Small La Laguna beaches are somewhat quieter and have better sand. It's a 10-15 minute walk from these beaches to Sabang.

Sabang Beach is a midmarket destination with most resorts now in the P500-1,500 price range. A handful of simple bungalows priced P250-500 are in the east side of Sabang, past the Sunset Disco (a girlie dance bar) and a pool hall. **Cathy's Cottages, At-Can's Inn, VIP Lodge, Juling's Place, Seashore Lodge,** and **Sea Breeze Vista Lodge** have rooms for P250-500.

Resorts in the middle of the beach and to the west tend to be more expensive but sometimes have a few budget bungalows tucked away for the budget traveler. Places in the P500-1,500 price range include **Capt'n Gregg Resort, Red Coral Cottages, Atlantic Resort Hotel, Angelyn Beach Resort, Paradise Inn, Kokomo Inn,** and **Lopez Lodge.**

The beach then turns to black sand and rock and ends at the Point Bar where Asia Divers has its headquarters. Heading around the point, you'll arrive at **Small La Laguna,** where midpriced accommodations include **El Galleon Resort, Sunsplash Resort, Havana Moon Resort, Sha Che Inn, Portofino,** and **Carlo's Inn.** Little La Laguna also has outlets for Swagman Travel and Action Divers.

You then climb some steps over a small cliff (visit the viewpoint) and arrive at **Big La Laguna,** which has the best sand at Sabang plus some great swimming in pure-blue waters. Nothing cheap up here but spots in the P500-1,500 price range include **Cataquis, El Oro Resort, La Laguna Beach Club, Fernando's, Lory's Cottages,** and **Millers Corner** at the end of the beach.

Boquete, Medio Island, and San Antonio
These islands form the west side of the harbor. Boquete is where Paniquian Island is joined to the mainland by a sandbar. Accommodations include: **Sandbar Beach Resort and Clubhouse** (P200-300, with restaurant, tennis, surfing, trekking), **Cathy's Inn** (P100 d, P400 cottages; tennis, windsurfing, yacht), **Villa Boquete,** and **Halcon Reef.**

Boquete Beach, on the inside, has riptides and strong currents that can make swimming dangerous. From here it's a 20-minute walk to Haligi Beach on the seaward side, which offers good snorkeling. You must take a *banca* to reach San Antonio, which has several groups of cottages, such as **Ruth's Guesthouse and Nipa Hut** on Medio Island at Long Beach (P150). There's good snorkeling at Long Beach.

Puerto Galera Town to White Beach
Fisherman's Cove Beach House (P150-200) is peaceful and popular, in spite of being a little isolated (it's a 30-minute walk from town) and on a poor beach. It offers good food, hot show-

ers, and free use of a small boat. Owner Caesar Axalan is a good source of local information and has set up a bulletin board with hiking maps.

Beyond Fisherman's Cove is Santo Niño, where you can stay at **Melxa's Greenhills Beach Huts** or the popular **Santo Niño Beach Resort**. **Balatero Beach Huts** is on Balatero Cove. Bungalows are P150-200.

White Beach

White Beach (also called San Isidro Beach) is the quieter and more relaxed alternative to the commercialized frenzy of Sabang Beach. Diving is poor and the water is often too rough for swimming, but the sand is abundant and the sunsets great.

Unfortunately, most of the small bungalows tucked away under the coconut trees were constructed with little imagination, and very few have been maintained over the last decade. And prior to the devaluation of the peso in 1997, all were badly overpriced when compared to similar facilities in Thailand or Indonesia. Prices are more reasonable today (if inflation doesn't wreck the equation), but you'll never really love these concrete cubicles.

You'll need to mention a specific cottage to the jeepney driver or you'll be let out near Jenny's Store at the far western end of the beach.

Cottages, lodges, inns, and huts in the P500-800 price range include (from east to west) **South of the Border Resort, Arco Baleno Cottages, Mylah's Nipa Huts, Delgado's Cottages, Estrella's Resort, Warren's Seaview, Majesty Lodge, Peter's Inn, Traveller's Beach Delight Cottages, Buena Lynn's Lodgin, White Beach Nipa Huts** (all concrete. . . not a nipa palm in sight), **White Beach Lodge, Grace Lodge, Cherry's Inn, Lodger's Nook,** and **Summer Connection.**

Tucked away back from the beach under a wonderful grove of palm trees are **Villa Luisa Lodging, Julie's Store,** and **White Beach Disco.**

Beyond White Beach

Enjoy a beautiful view over White Beach from the road as it winds across the headland out of San Isidro. On the other side, a long, sandy beach stretches three km down the bay with scattered groups of cottages along it. Tamaraw Beach is

the quietest place to stay in Puerto Galera and has its aficionados. **Tamaraw Beach Resort** is good with rooms P150-200. Paradise Beach has several groups of cottages strung out along it. Paradise Beach Lodge is a quiet, well-maintained place with a spacious feeling, eight km from town. Beyond it are **White Sand Beach Cottages** and **El Canonero Mariveles Cabins** with rooms for P150-200.

Aninuan and Talipanan

From these villages at the end of the road, trails lead up to waterfalls with swimming holes, Mangyan settlements, and on to Mt. Talipanan and Mt. Malasimbo. The cottage owners in this area sometimes arrange for their guests to go night fishing with the villagers. It's also possible to hire a *banca* to explore deserted beaches along the coast. A track traverses rugged country to Abra de Ilog. Stay at **Mountain Beach Resort** at the foot of Mt. Malasimbo. Snorkeling and swimming are available. Rooms are P200-250.

CALAPAN

The road southeast from Puerto Galera Town to Calapan is scenic, passing Tabinay Beach, which has a cave and hot springs nearby. At Dulangan, where locals pan for gold in a river, is the Lantuyang Mangyan Reservation. Tamaraw Falls at 14 km has bathing facilities. *Banca* trips here are offered from Sabang Beach. In San Teodoro, the **Saclag Settlements Farm School** has been established for young Mangyans. Older Irayas come here from the mountains, bringing rattan to be made into handicrafts and *tambo* for broom-making.

Calapan, provincial capital since 1837, is the main trading center and primary port of entry. A small museum in the town center is open Mon.-Fri. 0800-1700. The Sanduguan Festival, featuring a reenactment of the original encounter between the Mangyans and Chinese traders, is held around 21 May. *Sanduguan* is a Mangyan word for friendship.

Accommodations

Most hotels within walking distance of the market are: **Traveller's Inn, Riceland Inn, New**

Casablanca Hotel, Eric Hotel Annex, The Casa Blanca Annex, Queen Rose Lodge, Baniway Inn, Garden Hotel, and the **Eric Hotel.** Prices range P150-200. You can also stay with the Dayo family on the black-sand beach of **Agonhao,** about four km from town; the Tiongkeng Trading store, between the market and the main street, will arrange a tricycle there for you.

Transportation
The port is about three km from the market. Ferries cross to Batangas City about every two hours 0730-2130 (takes three hours). A boat comes from Verde Island each morning; it starts back from Calapan at 1100. Buses, minibuses, and jeepneys link Calapan with all the towns of Oriental Mindoro. Buses go to San Jose (Occidental Mindoro) in the dry season, and as far as Bulalacao in the wet. Ramadel Bus has twice-weekly night trips to San Jose, too.

Vicinity of Calapan
Nearby beaches include Balete (three km north), Aganhao (four km east), and Silonay (eight km southeast). Jeepneys go to the Alangan Mangyan settlement of Paitan. Another Mangyan village is Tarogin. To get there, take a jeepney to Barcinaga, tricycle to Apitong (some jeepneys go directly to Apitong), then cross the river and follow the trail.

SOUTH OF CALAPAN

Founded in the early 17th century, **Naujan** is a market town about 20 km southeast of Calapan. In its vicinity are the "church within a church"—a small chapel inside the walls of a massive, roofless, old Augustinian church and priory at nearby Bancurro; the long Estrella-Lagarian Beach two km south of town; and Pungao Hot Springs. **Lake Nauja** with two islets at its south end is a national park. It's a good place for watching ducks and marsh birds, including winter migrants from Siberia. It's also one of the last haunts of the highly endangered Mindoro freshwater crocodile *(Crocodylus mindorensis).* Don't bathe in the lake; there's a high risk of contracting schistosomiasis. The highway skirts the south end of Lake Naujan and passes through Socorro, from

where a road leads to the coast at Pola, site of Bayanan Beach, and Taguan Waterfalls in Tagumpay.

Pinamalayan
This town is in a coconut-growing area 62 km southeast of Calapan. Its name recalls a legend that the settlement was founded by Marinduquenos who sailed toward a rainbow. Marinduque is visible from here. The Upper Sabang Mangyan Settlement is inland. From Marinduque, a boat departs Balanacan via Gasan, another sails from Pinamalayan. Several *bancas* make a daily return trip from Maestre de Ca; they head back from Pinamalayan around 1100. Stay at the **Wortner-Perez House** with rooms for P100-150, where European-style food is served. Also try the **Mindoro Royal Inn** and **Hotel A & J** (P150-200.)

Bongabon
This town has a brown-sand beach and, inland, a settlement of the Batangan Mangyans. The MB *Jan Jan Liner* or MB *Joel* crosses from Romblon via Carmen (Tablas) on Tuesday, Thursday, and Saturday at 0700 (0800 from Carmen) and leaves Bongabon on Wednesday, Friday, and Sunday at 0900. Stay at **Rendezvous Lodging House** (no sign, but near the market), **Atlas Lodging House,** or **Mabuhay Lodging House.** Rooms range in price P150-250.

ROXAS CITY

Roxas is an important connection for travelers going down to Boracay.

A wide variety of boats reach Boracay but only large and safe vessels should be taken. Do not take small outriggers or attempt the crossing during rough weather or after nightfall, since the Tablas Straits are extremely dangerous.

Some boats go directly to Boracay while others go via Tablas. In most cases, you'll need to overnight in Roxas and perhaps the interim island before continuing to Boracay. The tourist office in Puerto Galera has current schedules.

Accommodations
Accommodations in town include the **Hotel Dannarosa** with rooms from P100-200 and the near-

by **Santo Niño Hotel** with both fan-cooled and a/c rooms from P120-500. Some travelers prefer to stay on the beach at **Catalina's Resort** some two km from town, where simple rooms cost P100-250.

SOUTH OF ROXAS CITY

Mansalay

This sleepy coastal town, 110 km south of Calapan and about an hour from Roxas, has no lodging. If you must overnight, ask around for a place to stay, or try the **Municipal Beach Resort.** Panaytayan, a large Hanuno'o settlement, is 11 km from Mansalay. Father Postma, a Dutch priest who has written studies of the Mangyans, lives here. He's known not to appreciate visits by casual tourists, but he is an excellent source of information for researchers and those with a special interest in the problems facing minority tribes. Such individuals should inquire at the mission opposite the Mobil Station before proceeding to the settlement. To get there, either hire a tricycle or share one with Mangyans returning from the market; the track cuts inland from a *sari-sari* store a few kilometers south of Mansalay.

Bulalacao

This town, about 90 minutes by bus from Mansalay, was formerly called San Pedro. Stay at **El Rio Grande Hotel** (P150-200). Nearby Buyallao Island has sandy beaches. To visit the Hanuno'o settlements at Dangkalan and Sitio Bailan, ask the vice mayor to arrange a guide. Boats cross to Semirara Island, between Mindoro and Panay. Exact departure times may depend on the tide.

SAN JOSE

The province's industrial center, San Jose (pop. 95,000), lies at the mouth of the Pandururan River on Mangarin Bay. You can swim at Babog or Aroma Beach, but it's better to go to the offshore islands of White, Ilin, or Ambulong. To visit a Mangyan village, take a jeepney to Bato Ili (one hour), then ask directions and walk for some hours; take food or small gifts to exchange

for overnight board and lodging there. The Buid group has a settlement at Batang.

Daily boats link San Jose with Santa Teresa, south of town; nearby caves have an underground stream. The Inihaw Inn can arrange trips by speedboat to Apo Reef.

Accommodations

Stay at: **Kapit Bahay Mini Hotel** (P150-200), the **Jolo Hotel** (P150-200) on Rizal St., **Travelers Hotel** (P150-200), **Mosquera's Hotel** (P150-175), **San Jose Midtown Pension** on Raja Soliman St. (clean, good, opposite market on Captain Cooper St.), **Big Newk Hotel** on Airport Rd. (clean rooms, near the airport, P100-150), **Red Baron Lodge** (a small, clean hotel about three km out of town near the airport; the owner is a good source of information), or **Sikatuna Hotel** on Sikatuna St. (P100-150).

Food and Entertainment

Restaurants abound in the downtown area: Try **The Shanghai Restaurant** on Rizal St.; the **Mandarin Noodle House,** Kapit Bahay; **Cora's** on the corner of Liboro and Bonifacio Streets; **Chef;** and **Hong Kong** restaurants. Near the airport, the **Red Baron Lodge** has a restaurant, and the **Inihaw Inn,** near the Red Baron Lodge, serves good seafood. The **Mangyan Village** is a popular local nightclub.

Transportation

PAL links Manila and San Jose (40 minutes) four times a week. The airport is five km northwest of town.

Several shipping lines sail Manila-San Jose (17 hours) four times weekly and once a week via Malay (Panay). The San Jose-Malay crossing (seven hours) is a convenient connection for Boracay, which is near Malay. Loreto Shipping has unscheduled voyages to various Visayan ports; ask at its office near the market.

The bus trip from San Jose to Calapan takes nine hours; RCG Liner and Ramadel Express buses depart each morning and some nights Nov.-May. Jeepneys operate between San Jose and Bulalacao 0600-2100. During the rainy season, twice-daily launches from San Jose connect at Bulalacao with buses to Calapan. Similarly, a bus operates daily between San Jose and Mamburao during the dry season; a boat

SEARCHING FOR TAMARAW

Sighting this rare and elusive creature, a species of wild water buffalo unique to the island, is a major thrill for the wildlife enthusiast and provides a great excuse to go hiking in Mindoro's rugged interior. Three reserves have been established for the remaining few hundred *tamaraw*. Arrange a guide through the **Bureau of Forest Development.** Obtain information from the **Philippine Committee for the Conservation of the Tamaraw** (office on Rizal St., San Jose, near the Shanghai Restaurant). Its field stations are at Calintaan, covering Mt. Iglit; Sablayan; and Paluan, covering Mt. Calavite.

The Mt. Iglit-Mt. Baco National Park (750 square km) in the south-central part of the island has two main gateways: Queen's Ranch and nearby Canturoy on the Bugsanga River; and Calintaan. To get to Queen's Ranch, hire a jeepney, or take a regular trip to Bato Ili and walk 10 km. You can overnight at Queen's Ranch.

There's also a guesthouse at Canturoy (eight km from Queen's Ranch). Deer and wild pig inhabit the same areas as *tamaraw*. Attempts are being made to conserve the rare Mindoro imperial pigeon, too.

operates (daily) subject to weather conditions in the wet season. Both depart at 0700. Buses load on the street near the Kapit Bahay Mini Hotel. Boats to Bulalacao, Manila, and Panay use Caminawit Port, four km south of the town center, while launches to Mamburao leave from the north pier across the river.

ISLANDS NEAR SAN JOSE

Ambulong, Ilin, and White Islands

These islands south of San Jose offer good swimming and snorkeling. Several boats depart daily for Ilin and Ambulong from the river mouth near the San Jose market. Hire a *banca* to White Island, which is the closest to San Jose (three km). Turtles lay their eggs on its white-sand beach. Colorful reef fish and lobsters abound. Ilin Island (77 square km), where U.S. forces landed in 1944, has several villages and five beaches, some of which are reef-fringed, making entry to the water difficult at low tide.

Many shell species are found here. Ambulong Island has a fishing village, white-sand beaches, cliffs, rock pillars, underwater caves, plus several coves with fine coral gardens and plenty of reef fish. Stay at **Ambulong Beach Resort** (P600 full board). **Carfel Seaventure** visits Ambulong and Ilin on dive cruises out of San Jose March-May; book in Manila.

SAN JOSE TO ABRA DE ILOG

The village of Calintaan has a good beach and is a gateway to the *tamaraw* grazing grounds of Mt. Iglit. North- and southbound buses and boats stop at Sablayan. **William Lines** sails from Manila to Sablayan (16 hours) every Saturday. Boats from San Jose and Mamburao meet and turn around here, with passengers transferring to the other boat.

You can stay at **Elisas Hotel, Emily Hotel,** or **Executive Inn** (rooms are P150-200) and eat at the restaurant by the pier (closes at 1900).

The **Penal Colony** offers handicrafts for sale. Mangyans frequently come to the market. The nearest Mangyan area is around Malutok, a two-hour walk, and the Kulasisi Settlement of the Alangan group is at San Francisco. *Tamaraw* can be found inland from Sablayan. Snorkeling is good in Sablayan Cove.

APO REEF

This huge, 34-square-km reef beside tiny Apo Island (less than one km long), 37 km west of Mindoro, has been declared a National Marine Park. The reef teems with an estimated 300 species of fish, including hammerhead sharks and manta rays, and is a superlative dive site, with turtles, wrecks, dramatic drop-offs, spectacular coral, plus excellent visibility.

The wooded island has a lighthouse, white-sand beach, its own fringing reef and walls, lots of biting insects, and very little water. Three lighthouse keepers stay here, and you may be able to hitch a ride from Sablayan on their relief boat at the end of each month. In good weather, you could also hire a *banca* for the two-and-a-half-hour trip out to the reef. Ask the boatman to make a couple of snorkeling stops on the reef, and agree on a pick-up time if you plan to spend a few days on the island.

Diving

Numerous spots out on the reef provide good snorkeling, but be careful of strong currents and sharks. Conditions are usually better on the island's lee; check wind direction. Camp at its southeast end and bring food, lots of water (at least four liters per day), and insect repellent. Serious underwater enthusiasts should invest in a dive-boat excursion so they can refill tanks and explore the reef. Most of the established dive-boat companies offer 5- to 15-day trips to Apo. Book in Manila. The number of potential dive sites is vast. The boat's divemaster will make recommendations according to conditions. Diving is possible year-round, but access is easiest March to early June, between the monsoons. Rough seas are common July-February.

MAMBURAO

In this provincial capital (pop. 75,000), boat-building and tending fishponds are local activities. Tayamaan, three km from town, has a beach on an attractive cove.

Accommodations

Stay at **Travelers' Lodge, Easter Hotel,** or **L & E Rest Inn** (rooms are P150). **Mamburao Beach Resort** also has cottages for rent.

Transportation

PAL flies Tuesday and Thursday from Manila (40 minutes). Jeepneys and buses operate between San Jose and Mamburao; boats also make the run during the rainy season—be cautious this time of year.

BEYOND MAMBURAO

Paluan

Jeepneys link Mamburao with this small town to the northwest. United States forces secured anchorage in Paluan Bay and seized the town in January 1945. Paluan has a black-sand beach and good snorkeling. Mount Calavite is a national reserve for *tamaraw*. The foot of the moun-

tain can be reached by *banca*. The Calauagan River Resort (no accommodations) and Mainit Springs are about four km from town.

Abra de Ilog

The Camarang Reservation of Hanuno'o Mangyans is in this municipality. Jeepneys leave Mamburao at 0600 to connect with the 0830 boat to Batangas, which loads from the beach at Wawa. The three-hour crossing gives fine views of Maricaban Island. The boat departs Batangas at 1300 and is met by jeepneys upon its arrival. Since there's no wharf, passengers are carried to and from the boat on men's shoulders (tip P1).

THE LUBANG ISLANDS

Lubang Island and its neighbors—Cabra, Ambil, and Golo—are located north of Mindoro and west of the Batangas coast. Although they belong to Occidental Mindoro, access is easiest through the port of Manila. The waters around Lubang are a good source of shells and a favorite of sportfishermen.

Lubang Island

This elongated island (191 square km, 27 km long) is hilly (reaching about 600 meters), with nice beaches and coves and good offshore coral. The densely settled north side is a plain where most of the 20,000 people live; the south shore, apart from a few small sandy beaches, ends in rugged cliffs. Tilik and Lubang are the chief towns. Garlic is the main cash crop.

Tilik, the port of arrival, has a beach and a campsite. Following the coast north, Kono Beach at Vigo has uninspiring sand but good surf, and numerous coral fish and big lobsters are found offshore.

At Lubang town is the **Mina de Oro Beach Resort,** which has rooms for P200-400. Tour groups of Japanese marksmen stay at the **World Safari Club** on Lubang beach, where they shoot at clay pigeons and other targets, including "wild" pigs that are driven by local beaters into the waiting gunsights.

Tagbac, seven km beyond Lubang, has a beach with white sand but a muddy seabed. Raising *bangus* fry is a local occupation. On the south shore, snorkeling is good off the white-sand beach at Binacas, 18 km from Lubang. A road also leads up to a radar station at a 500-meter elevation from where there's a fine view.

Transportation

For boats to Lubang, ask in Manila's del Pan Bridge. Mindoro Shipping Lines' MV *Superstar* usually departs Wednesday and Friday about 1000 and returns from Tilik Thursday and Saturday also around 1000; the trip takes six hours. The old and slow (nine hours) MV *Mercedes* of Mindoro Navigation Lines leaves unreliably from Pier 6, Manila's North Harbor, on Tuesday at 2200, returning from Tilik on Saturday at 0800.

Connections between Lubang and Mindoro are irregular, but the MV *Mercedes* sometimes continues from Tilik to Mamburao and Sablayan, returning to Manila via Tilik. Jeepneys operate between Tilik and Lubang town, and when a ship arrives, a truck takes passengers south to Looc.

Horse-drawn *carretelas*, still used on Lubang, make regular trips along the main road from Tilik to Lubang town. A jeepney can also be hired per day; a group of travelers could share one and explore much of the island.

The Wreck of the *San Jose*

The *San Jose* was the largest galleon of her day and was said to be carrying incredible wealth when she sank off Lubang in a severe storm after setting sail from Mariveles (Bataan) in 1694. The hull now lies in relatively shallow water, while one of the huge anchors rests in deeper water nearby.

Divers have found pieces of Ming porcelain, earthenware, and wooden and metal fragments among her ballast stones. The wreck of an unknown vessel was also discovered south of the *San Jose*. Since findings consisted of brass sheeting, nails, and spikes, but no porcelain, it's surmised that the ship was not coming from Manila. Galleons carried porcelain, silk, and spices from Manila to Acapulco and returned with silver coins, bullion, and European wares.

Ambil

The waters between Lubang and Ambil were the scene of a Spanish naval victory over the Dutch in 1646. This 28-square-km island is hilly, rising to 755 meters. Ambil Falls are close to a white-sand beach. You can hire a *banca* on Ambil to go snorkeling offshore and at tiny Malavatuan Island, about three km to the northeast. The seabed slopes gradually around Malavatuan, and there are shoals around 12 to 18 meters deep to the east of the island. Here and at Ambil, the coral isn't impressive but the fishlife is, and snorkelers may see big sharks, including tigers, as well as other large fish; crayfish are numerous, too.

Golo

Bulacan is the main settlement on this 18-square-km island south of Lubang.

Cabra

This barren, rocky island north of Lubang has a lighthouse dating from Spanish times. It's the site of a pilgrimage on 25 March to commemorate the Blessed Virgin's miraculous apparition to seven children here in the early 1960s.

NEGROS

Shaped like a boot in the heart of the Visayan archipelago, this elongated island serves as an important stepping-stone for travelers island-hopping between Boracay and Cebu. Negros is a friendly island with some historical sights, a soaring volcano for mountaineers, and wonderful old steam trains that draw rail enthusiasts from all over the world.

This island, the fourth-largest in the archipelago, is divided into three provinces—Negros Occidental (capital: Bacolod), peopled by Ilonggos; Negros Oriental (capital: Dumaguete), culturally oriented toward Cebu; and Negros del Norte, formed in 1985.

Negros's landscape is dominated by the active volcano, Mt. Kanlaon (2,465 meters), which is the highest point in the Visayas and a major attraction for hikers.

Negros also has some good beaches, notably those at Hinoba-an, and pleasant hill resorts such as Hacienda Masulog in La Carlota City.

Trouble in Sugarland

The island is made even more fascinating by the intricate web of political and economic forces that sweep across the land. As the undisputed center of the Filipino sugar industry, Negros has been riding a dangerous roller coaster since the late 19th century. While prices were high during the 1960s and '70s, thousands of migrant workers flooded northern Negros to cut the cane and earn a good living. Everybody seemed to prosper: field workers had plenty to eat, a handful of Chinese-mestizo hacienda owners became fabulously wealthy, and Bacolod was known as the city with the nation's highest number of Mercedes limousines.

But the devastating collapse of sugar prices in the early '80s led to social and economic turmoil, widespread poverty, and malnutrition reminiscent of an African famine. It also brought calls for land reform, the rise of militant Catholic priests who openly supported the demands of the communists, and the emergence of private militias organized by wealthy landowners to protect their financial interests. To the intense embarrassment of local officials, Negros became center stage for television crews and foreign politicians who dubbed it the "Ethiopia of the Philippines." The beleaguered island also became a leading prop in the morality play against Ferdinand Marcos.

Today it's a somewhat better scene here in "Sugarlandia." A small rise in domestic sugar prices has helped keep some of the mills open, although Victoria Mills was forced into bankruptcy several years ago and continues to operate under receivership.

Through all this, the Negrenese have kept their enthusiasm for life and acceptance of *bahala na* . . . what will be, will be.

HISTORY

Negros was discovered when one of Legazpi's vessels, sailing from Bohol in 1565, was forced by a storm to take shelter on the island's east coast. The Spaniards returned to claim it but were discouraged from settling by the sparse population, lack of good harbors, and inadequate food supplies. It's believed that Binalbagan and Ilog were the only native settlements at this time; they became towns in 1572 and 1584, respectively.

The heavily forested interior was inhabited mainly by Negritos. Western Negros was administered from Iloilo until the entire island became a separate military district in 1734, though the southern and eastern sides remained practically uninhabited until the Spaniards founded Dauin in 1787. Frequent Muslim raids along this coast posed a problem that persisted for a century. Negros had one of the slowest population growth rates in the country until the sugar industry began to expand rapidly in the 1850s.

The opening of the Iloilo and Cebu ports to foreign commerce, followed in 1869 by the completion of the Suez Canal, added further impetus. Large haciendas were established and the island's population multiplied as migrants from Panay and Cebu arrived to fill the demand for intensive labor. In 1898, Filipino revolutionaries

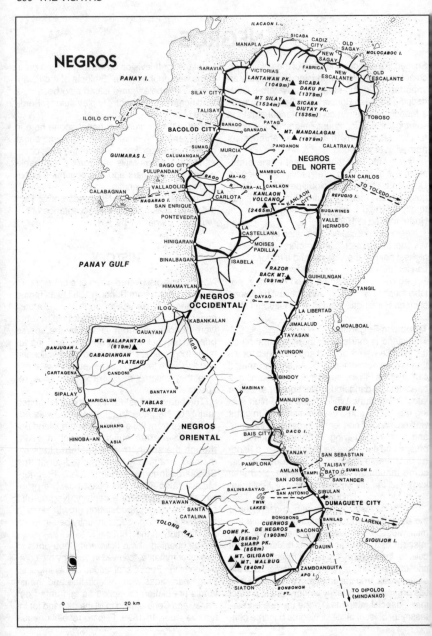

proclaimed the "Republica de Negros" in Bago and pledged allegiance to Aguinaldo's government on Luzon.

The people rose simultaneously in Silay and marched on Bacolod, where the Spanish garrison surrendered bloodlessly. During WW II, Negros was the Japanese Fourth Air Army's most important base south of Luzon, with eight airfields. But by the time liberating U.S. troops landed in 1945, most of the island was under guerrilla control and the Japanese had no functioning aircraft. The sugar industry has been greatly affected by the volatile world-market conditions, causing much unemployment and hardship on Negros.

Sugar

The province's rich volcanic soil is well suited to sugarcane, and 54% of the nation's sugar is produced here. Fifteen sugar centrals are scattered throughout the plains. They operate as company towns, with their own housing, stores, schools, hospitals, churches, and roads. Most contain a rum distillery, while a wide range of other by-products of sugar refining, including fertilizer, acetylene, and building materials, are manufactured. This commercial plantation economy is characterized by high land-tenancy rates and absentee landownership.

Work in the plantations, while labor-intensive, is largely seasonal. During the harvesting season, migrants known as *sacadas* flock to Negros from Panay and other Visayan islands to seek temporary work. The enormously wealthy sugar barons, who are mostly of Spanish mestizo descent, own vast haciendas and palatial homes in Bacolod and in Silay. In past decades, they had a reputation for extravagant lifestyles and political influence, but they, too, have had to weather hard times.

TRANSPORTATION

Air

PAL flies daily from Manila and Cebu City to Bacolod and Dumaguete. Additional services are provided by Cebu Pacific. Pacific Airways flies twice weekly on Monday and Thursday from Siquijor to Dumaguete. The 15-minute hop costs P250-300.

Ship from Manila

Direct ships are available to either Bacolod or Dumaguete.

To Bacolod: Negros Navigation's MV *Princess of Negros* leaves Manila's North Harbor on Tuesday at 2100 and Friday at 1200. The journey to Bacolod takes 22 hours and costs P500-620. The same company also runs the MV *San Paolo,* which departs on Sunday at 1400 and Wednesday at 1600.

To Dumaguete: WG&A's MV *Superferry 7* leaves on Tuesday at 1700 and takes 26 hours to reach its final destination. WG&A also operates the MV *Maynilad,* which leaves Sunday at 1900 and takes a somewhat longer 32 hours. Sulpicio Lines' MV *Philippine Princess* leaves on Wednesday at 1200 and arrives in Dumaguete 25 hours later.

Ship from Cebu

The easiest way to reach Negros from Cebu City is with the daily fast ferry, which zips you across the waters to Dumaguete on the southeastern corner of the island. You can overnight here, look around the next day, and continue by bus around the island to Bacolod.

Another option is the direct a/c bus that departs Cebu City each morning from the central bus terminal and heads directly to Bacolod. Otherwise, take a bus to Toledo City and then a ferry to San Carlos on Negros.

Travelers in Moalboal might take the ferry from San Sebastian to San Jose or Tampi near Dumaguete before continuing around the island.

Cebu to Dumaguete: Universal Aboitiz's MV *Supercat* fast ferry departs daily at 0545 and 1500 and takes just over two hours to reach Dumaguete. The fare is P200-250. Slower but less expensive options include the George & Peter Lines' MV *Dumaguete Ferry,* its MV *Georich,* or MV *Pulauan Ferry,* which leave daily at 2200 and take about eight hours to complete the crossing. Obviously, you sleep on board. Cokaliong Shipping's MV *Filipinas Dinagat* leaves at 1900 on Monday, Wednesday, Friday, and Sunday at 1200. This is a faster service that takes around six hours. Finally, Trans-Asia Shipping's MV *Asia-Japan* leaves at 1800 on Tuesday and Saturday and also takes a relatively short six hours to Dumaguete.

Liloan to Sibulan (near Dumaguete): A large outrigger leaves daily every 30 minutes until around 1500 when service comes to a halt. The crossing takes 20 minutes and jeepneys continue from Sibulan to Dumaguete.

Toledo to San Carlos: Ferries leave daily at 0900 and 1400 daily except Sunday, and every Sunday at 1330. Tickets for the two-hour journey should be purchased from the official kiosk near the entrance to the pier. Buses wait for arriving passengers and immediately head off to Bacolod. Combined boat-and-bus tickets are somewhat cheaper than purchasing separate tickets.

Tuburan to Escalante: Aznar Shipping's MV *Melrivic 2* departs daily at 0800 and 1000 and takes around two hours to make the crossing.

Bantayan to Cadiz: A large outrigger leaves daily around 1000 and takes three and a half hours to reach the small town of Cadiz on the north coast of Negros. The fare is P65-75.

Ship from Bato to Tampi (near Dumaguete): Ferries leave every other hour until around 1630 and take 45 minutes to cross over to Negros. ABC Liner's a/c buses leave daily at 0600, 0700, 0800, 1100, 1330, 1400, and 1500 from the ABC Liner bus terminal in Cebu City for Bato, from where ferries connect and continue over to Tampi on Negros. The bus journey takes around three hours, plus another hour to make the sea crossing, for a total travel time from Cebu City to Dumaguete of four hours.

San Sebastian and Talisay to San Jose (near Dumaguete): Several ferries make the crossing daily from either of these two locations to San Jose, from where jeepneys head off immediately to Dumaguete.

Ship from Guimaras

A small ferry leaves from the town of Cabalagnan in southern Guimaras for Valladolid on Negros, some 30 km south of Bacolod. The boat leaves in the very early morning hours around 0300 or 0400 and stops at several small islands while making the short crossing. Travelers staying on Nagarao Island near Cabalagnan can also take this ferry over to Negros.

Ship from Mindanao

Service is provided from Cagayan de Oro to Bacolod, and to Dumaguete from Cotabato, Dipolog, Ozamis, and Zamboanga.

Cagayan de Oro to Bacolod: Negros Navigation's MV *San Paolo* leaves Friday at 1600 and takes 16 hours to Bacolod.

Cotabato to Dumaguete: WG&A's MV *Maynilad* leaves on Wednesday at 2200 and takes almost 30 hours via Dipolog. The fare is P480-550.

Dapitan to Dumaguete: Cokaliong Shipping's MV *Filipinas Dinagat* departs on Tuesday, Thursday, and Saturday at 1600 and takes just four hours to make the crossing. George & Peter Lines has daily service with either the MV *Dumaguete Ferry*, the MV *Georich*, or the MV *Zamboanga Ferry*.

Dipolog to Dumaguete: Note that the harbor for Dipolog and Dapitan is midway between the two cities but is known as Dapitan Port. Tricycle fare from either town to the port should be around P30-35. Boat fares from the port to Dumaguete are P65-80.

WG&A's MV *Maynilad* leaves on Friday at 0100, while Trans-Asia's *Asia-Japan* departs Friday at 0800. Both ships take four hours to Dumaguete.

Ozamis to Dumaguete: WG&A's MV *Medjugorje* leaves on Tuesday at midnight, while Sulpicio Lines' MV *Philippine Princess* departs on Sunday at 1600. Both ships take six or seven hours, and the fare is P125-150.

Zamboanga to Dumaguete: Trans-Asia Shipping's MV *Asia-Japan* leaves every Sunday at midnight and takes 8-10 hours.

Ship from Panay

Iloilo to Bacolod is the main transport connection, though a minor route is possible from Culasi to Victorias.

Iloilo to Bacolod: Ordinary ferries depart hourly until 1700 and take one or two hours to reach Bacolod. Among the boats operated by Negros Navigation are the MV *St. Rafael*, the MV *Michael*, and the MV *SM/DV*. These ferries cost P55-85. More luxurious service is provided by the a/c catamaran known as the MV *Bacolod Express*, which leaves Iloilo daily at 0715 and 1400. The trip takes one hour and costs P100-120.

Culasi and Malayu-an to Victorias: Culasi and Malayu-an are small towns on the east coast of Panay, while the port for Victorias is located at nearby Da-an Banwa. The MV *Queen* or MV

Princess Jo leaves Culasi daily around 0900 and takes two hours to reach Negros. The MV *Seven Seas* or MV *San Vicente* leaves Malayu-an daily around 0900 and also takes two hours to reach the port at Da-an Banwa.

Ship from Siquijor

Delta Lines' fast ferry departs Larena daily at 0730, 0945, 1415, and 1630 for the 45-minute crossing to Negros. The fare is P60-90.

Marjunnix Shipping's MV *Catherine* leaves daily at 0700 and takes three hours to make the crossing. A large outrigger leaves from Tam-bisan daily at 1300 and 1500 and arrives in Du-maguete two and a half hours later. This outrig-ger—and other outriggers in the Philippines—are not recommended during bad weather.

Getting Around by Bus

Express buses make the 313-km trip around the top, through San Carlos, and down the east coast in about eight hours. There are no direct buses on the spectacular central route, which passes close to Kanleon volcano; you must change at Kanlaon City. Similarly, while direct buses connect with the ferry at San Carlos, four hours from Bacolod, it's more scenic to cut across the center via Kanlaon City.

The long west coast route offers the option of a beach resort stopover at Hinoba-an; to travel through to Dumaguete in one day, you must leave Bacolod before 0800. Minibuses and jeepneys operate over shorter distances on the island.

BACOLOD CITY

This relatively new city is the gateway to the sugar-growing region, and its population has grown to nearly 350,000 Bacolenos. Known as the Sugar City, Bacolod is the nation's "sugar capital" and is surrounded by plantations. Al-though lacking adequate port facilities, it's the commercial, service, and financial center of the island's sugar industry and is a comparatively affluent city—second only to Manila in the num-ber of registered motor vehicles, for example.

Bacolod itself has few points of interest, but it makes a good base for exploring the surrounding area. Bacolod City is growing in importance how-ever, as it is slated to become a convention cen-ter city, where overseas businesspeople and in-vestors will be wined and dined while discussing joint ventures in the Philippines.

Attractions

The Department of Tourism office is centrally located at the seawall complex. At the heart of the city is the plaza, a popular local meeting place and the scene of cultural presentations, especially on Sunday afternoons and during fiestas. It's flanked by the San Sebastian Cathedral, which dates from the end of the 19th century.

Bacolod's business sector has been rebuilt following destruction by a major fire in 1955. The impressive Capitol, on the city's north side, is adjoined by a park and lagoon. Bacolod has some luxurious suburbs.

An indication of the city's wealth is the number of fine antique collections here. These include the **Torres Antique Collection,** in Torres Com-pound, Airport Subdivision, which displays Ming porcelain and wooden and ivory santos; **Vega Antique Collection,** 4 19th St., Mandalagan, which features Chinese and Indo-Chinese pot-tery, wooden and ivory santos, and old furni-ture; **Philippine Arts and Antiques** on Man-dalagan St.; and the **Buglas Collection** on Lizares Avenue.

Those interested in flowers will enjoy visit-ing **Suarez Orchid Collection,** whose rare and exotic blooms are housed in several green-houses at the corner of Lacson and 20th Streets, and **Diola's Rose Garden,** 64 Pag-asa Ave., Villamonte.

The Santa Clara subdivision, in the northern suburbs near Banago Wharf, contains a chapel built of native materials, including a mosaic mural of the *Barangay sang Birhen,* comprising 95,000 pieces of shells ranging from a square inch to about the size of a mung bean.

Fiestas

On 24 June, at nearby Punta Taytay, a fair and fluvial parade are the highlights of a feast in honor of St. John the Baptist. The city's major fi-esta is the weeklong **MassKara Festival,** which coincides with the city's charter day anniversary on 19 October. This festival began in 1980, with a smiling mask as a symbol, adopted to reflect

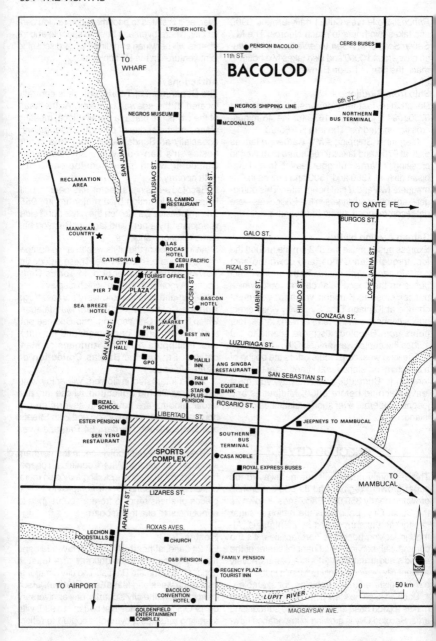

TO WHARF

L'FISHER HOTEL
PENSION BACOLOD
11th ST.
CERES BUSES

BACOLOD

NEGROS SHIPPING LINE
6th ST.
NEGROS MUSEUM
NORTHERN
BUS TERMINAL
MCDONALDS

SAN JUAN STR.
GATUSIAO STR.
LACSON STR.

RECLAMATION
AREA

EL CAMINO
RESTAURANT
TO SANTE FE

BURGOS STR.
GALO STR.

MANOKAN
COUNTRY
LAS
ROCAS
HOTEL
CEBU PACIFIC
AIR
RIZAL STR.

CATHEDRAL

LOCSIN STR.
MABINI STR.
HILADO STR.
LOPEZ JAENA STR.

TITA'S
PIER 7
TOURIST OFFICE
PLAZA
BASCON
HOTEL

SEA BREEZE
HOTEL
MARKET
GONZAGA STR.

PNB
BEST INN
LUZURIAGA STR.

CITY
HALL
GPO
HALILI
INN
ANG SINGBA
RESTAURANT
SAN SEBASTIAN STR.

PALM
INN
STAR
PLUS
PENSION
EQUITABLE
BANK
ROSARIO STR.

RIZAL SCHOOL
LIBERTAD STR.

ESTER PENSION
SEN YENG
RESTAURANT
JEEPNEYS TO MAMBUCAL

SOUTHERN
BUS
TERMINAL

SPORTS
COMPLEX
CASA NOBLE
ROYAL EXPRESS BUSES
TO MAMBUCAL

LIZARES STR.

ARANETA STR.

ROXAS AVES.

LECHON
FOODSTALLS
CHURCH

D&B PENSION
FAMILY PENSION
REGENCY PLAZA
TOURIST INN

TO AIRPORT

BACOLOD
CONVENTION
HOTEL
LUPIT RIVER
0   50 km

GOLDENFIELD
ENTERTAINMENT
COMPLEX
MAGSAYSAY AVE.

THE IRON DINOSAURS OF NEGROS

Perhaps the most intriguing sights on the island of Negros are the antique steam trains which haul sugarcane on the plantations near Bacolod. Originally manufactured in America, Germany, and England shortly after the turn of the century, these extremely rare "Iron Dinosaurs" now attract a steady stream of railway enthusiasts who come to photograph and ride the trains during the cutting season from September to May. Some trains have been retired, but stationmasters can arrange rides whenever the locomotives are in action.

Note: I've received word that many of the old trains have finally been retired. Before setting out to see the dinosaurs, check with the tourist office to verify current conditions and the availability of trains.

Victorias Mills

The world's largest integrated sugar mill and refinery offers more than just old trains. Just as fascinating is a guided tour of the mill, a look at the Filipino company town, and the St. Joseph Chapel where an angry, psychedelic Christ glares down on the huddled masses. Victorias' 400 km of track are worked by modern diesels and about a dozen steams, including German Henschels dating from 1924-30, a Baldwin, and a '24 Bagnall imported from the Fanling railhead in Hong Kong. Visitors are welcome to walk down the tracks and inspect the repair yard. Buses from Bacolod reach the main intersection, from where jeepneys continue to the mill compound.

Hawaiian Mills

Midway between Bacolod and Victoria Mills, and two km north of Silay, stands another mill with a handful of old steam engines operating on sporadic schedules. Apart from a single '29 Henschel, all trains are Baldwins dated 1916-1928.

La Carlotta Mills

Most of the remaining steams from the closed Ma Ao Mill have been transferred to La Carlotta Mills, 50 km south of Bacolod. La Carlotta has 10 Baldwins, a Porter dating from 1912, and two '21 Alcos. Most engines are either dead or in poor condition.

the peoples' happy spirit in spite of the hardships caused by the sugar industry's decline.

Festivities include a variety of competitions (mask-making, brass band, drinking, and eating), games, cultural shows, a beauty contest to crown the MassKara Queen, disco king and queen events, a windsurfing regatta, basketball matches, and other sports events. The climax is a spectacular three-hour street parade on the Saturday and Sunday nearest to the 19th, with revelers wearing colorful costumes and smiling masks in a multitude of designs and shapes dancing to music. Prizes are awarded for ingenuity and creativity in the use of native materials to make costumes.

There's also a monthlong fair held during October at the city's livelihood center showcasing the island's products and handicrafts.

Accommodations

Bacolod has plenty of hotels, but the inexpensive pensions are some of the grungiest in the country.

Ester Pension: Convenient location a few blocks south of city center. Araneta St., tel. (034) 432-3526, P150-300.

Star Plus Pension House: Small, fairly new place with both fan-cooled and a/c rooms three blocks south of the town plaza. Lacson St., tel. (034) 433-2948, P200-400.

Family Pension: Budget spot with minimalistic, rough rooms a few blocks south of town. 123 Lascon St., tel. (034) 438-1211, P150-300.

Regency Plaza Tourist Inn: Good mid-priced hotel in the south of town near Family Pension. Lacson St., tel. (034) 433-1458, P550-700.

Bacolod Pension Plaza: Another new mid-priced option just east of the town plaza. Cuadra St., tel. (034) 433-2203, P600-800.

Sea Breeze Hotel: An old but well-located hotel overlooking the failed reclamation area. San Juna St., tel. (034) 432-4571, P700-950.

Restaurants

Noble's Restaurant on Lacson Street offers a reasonably priced smorgasbord daily except Sunday. The **Mardi Gras Restaurant**'s menu features Filipino, Chinese, American, and Spanish dishes. **Roli's,** near the Sea Breeze Hotel, is a famous coffee shop and meeting place among the city's residents for breakfast and coffee. It serves very good coffee, as well as lunch and dinner. **Mira's Cafe** on Locsin Street serves good native coffee. **Reming's and Sons Restaurant** has good Filipino food and is located in the city plaza.

Gaisano Food Palace on Luzuriaga Street has fast food, and the **Ihaw-Ihaw** restaurant on Gatuslao Street in the Las Rocas Hotel has inexpensive Filipino food. At the Best Inn next door, try the **Kong Kee Diners and Bakery** for cheap Chinese and Filipino food. The **Cactus Room Restaurant** in the Family Pension House has good, inexpensive steaks and other Western food.

The **Las Rocas Hotel** serves good *ihaw ihaw* and other simple meals. Of the chains, **Barrio Fiesta** and **Shakey's Pizza** are represented. A well-respected restaurant that originated in Cebu is **Alavar's Sea Foods House,** featuring great seafood dishes. It's located near the Family Pension House.

Reming's Food Center and **Food Center** are located off the plaza; you can watch the sunset from them. Off the other side of the plaza are the **Manokan Country** chicken barbecue stalls. Centrally located is the **Inaka Japanese Restaurant** at Galo and Gatuslao Streets.

Near the Bacolod Airport, the Goldenfield Commercial Complex has some great restaurants; try the **Old West Steakhouse** for good steak and other Western food. There's a **Shakey's Pizza** at the complex as well as **Carlo Pizza Garden, Foodland,** and the more upscale **Seafood Market Restaurant.** Popular local dishes include *inasal* (barbecued chicken with lemongrass), which you can try at the **Bacolod Chicken House** on Lacson Street, and *batchoy* (noodle soup). You'll find *batchoy* restaurants near the Best Inn. As the nation's sugar capital, Bacolod is appropriately noted for its sweet dishes, e.g., *dulce gatas* (sweetened carabao milk), *pinasugbo* (sticky sugarcoated banana), and *pi-aya* (a flaky, sugar-filled pancake).

Entertainment and Sports

For an after-dinner drink, try the **Music Room** at Gatuslao Street, or the **Camarin** at the Bascon Hotel. The low-life area, which contains several strip joints and go-go bars, is on Gatuslao, north of Burgos Street, while there are some good small bars on Lacson Street. Nearby, the **Peninsula Disco** and the **Macho Disco** offer nightly shows and dancing.

In the Goldenfield Commercial Complex, the popular **Disco 2000** and the **Limelight Pub** have live music nightly. Within the complex, there's the 40-lane **Super Bowling Lanes,** which is the largest in the Visayas. The Commercial Complex is open 1600-0200.

The **Macapara Golf and Country Club,** in the city, has an 18-hole golf course, tennis courts, and swimming pool open to visitors.

Shopping

Bacolod is probably the best place in the country to shop for ceramics, including hand-painted porcelain items and quality household wares. **MDS Ceramics** is conveniently located downtown at 26 Rosario Street, but most workshops are in the suburbs (e.g., **NLS Ceramics,** Lacson St., Mandalagan, and **Anaware Ceramics,** 33 Camia St., Capitolville) or in the nearby *barangays* of Guinhalaran and Pahanocoy.

Other local crafts are the making of colorful artificial flowers from dyed wood shavings at **Samodal Woodshave Flower Shop,** 2nd Rd., Banahaw, Villamonte. *Hablon* is a fabric that originated in Bacolod at GV Handicrafts. Places to shop for handicrafts include **Philippine Antiques and Artwares** on Mandalagan St.; **Recuerdos de Bacolod** on Rizal Street near the center of the city; and **Bacolod Shellcraft and Artwares** in Singcang, near the airport. The Goldenfield Commercial Complex also has a number of shops featuring the lovely ceramics and other handicrafts, but the prices tend to be more expensive.

Transportation

By Air: PAL links Bacolod with Manila by jet three times daily (one hour) and Cebu once a day (takes 40 minutes). The airport is 3.5 km south of downtown; take a cab (costs around P30).

By Sea: Ferries ply between Bacolod and Iloilo (two and a half hours across the Guimaras Strait). Departures from Bacolod's Banago wharf are at 0700, 1000, and 1500, except Friday (0700, 1000, and 1600) and Sunday (0800 and 1600). Frequent jeepneys (P10) link the wharf and city center; allow 30 minutes when going to catch the ferry. Sailings to Manila (19 hours) are three times a week, as well as to Cebu (by ferry and bus).

More information can be found above under Transportation at the beginning of the Negros section.

By Bus: The northern and southern bus terminals are on the same sides of the city as the directions they serve. Jeepneys around Bacolod ply this route all day; catch one labeled "Libertad" or "Shopping" to reach the northern terminal.

Ceres Liner Express Buses to Dumaguete via San Carlos depart from the northern bus terminal at 0400, 0630, 0830, 1030, and 1200; the trip takes eight hours. Buses also make the four-hour trip to San Carlos, leaving in time to connect with the 0530 ferries to Toledo (Cebu); they usually leave at 1330 as well (1030 only on Sunday).

The San Carlos-Toledo ferry costs P45. For buses to Kanlaon City, and Dumaguete via Hinoba-an, use the southern terminal. Ceres now also serves the Bacolod-Cebu route via the Danao-Tuburan ports in Negros Occidental and Cebu, respectively.

VICINITY OF BACOLOD

Beaches

Near Bacolod are a number of beach resorts whose only advantage is proximity to the city. Sum-ag, 12 km south of Bacolod, is the site of **Punta Taytay, Alcala,** and **Villarosa Beach Resorts; Jara Beach Resort,** in Calumangan, 16 km south of Bacolod, rents cottages and has a seafood restaurant. Rooms range P250-300; all come with fans or a/c depending on price. It is also the convention resort of Negros Occidental.

Inland

The **Santa Fe Resort,** P200-250, seven km inland from Bacolod in Granada, has cottages for rent and swimming pools. It's a good choice for those who prefer to stay outside the city. It takes 15 minutes by minicab from the city.

Mambucal Summer Resort is located beyond Murcia, 32 km, one hour southeast of Bacolod. This mountain resort is a popular excursion spot for locals; Sundays are particularly crowded. Situated at an elevation of 900 me-

ters on the northwest slopes of Mt. Kanlaon, its attractions include a cool climate; seven waterfalls, three of them easily reached by footpaths; mountain trails through lush forests; two spring-fed swimming pools; sulfur hot springs; and a canteen.

The resort has a campground, cabins at P100 (P150 on weekends and holidays), and a tourist lodge, P200 and up. A mountain lodge is also available with rooms at P60 a day. Take a jeepney from Libertad St., Bacolod; the last trip back to the city is around 1630. There are also cheaper accommodations at the **Pagoda Inn,** P150. There is good food here as well, and native coffee is available.

BACOLOD TO SAN CARLOS

This highway follows the coastal plain around northern Negros and is served by frequent departures from the northern bus terminal.

Talisay

Sights include the historic mansion of revolutionary general Aniceto Lacson, who led the 1898 revolt in Negros; the **Guinto Antique Collection** of furniture and fixtures in one of the oldest houses in the province; and two sugar centrals.

Silay City

This sugar city (pop. 110,000) is older than Bacolod (14 km away) and was once the area's cultural center. Several colonial houses remain, so the area is well worth exploring. The excellent **Hofilena Art Collection** at 5 de Noviembre Street features works by Goya, Picasso, and the Filipino artists Luna and Hidalgo. Pottery products are on display at **Maninihon Clay Products.** During WW II, Patag, 25 km inland from Silay City and accessible by jeepney, was the last Japanese stronghold in the Visayas and is now the site of a memorial shrine. A day's hike from the Patag settlement brings one to the volcanic vent in the area.

Victorias

The **Victorias Milling Co.** (VICMICO) is said to be the world's largest integrated sugar mill and refinery. Take the **Rainbow** minibus from Ba-

Victorias Mills
steam engine

colod (34 km) to the town of Victorias, then a jeepney to the mill compound, which is a town in itself.

It contains the **St. Joseph the Worker Chapel** (1948), whose famous mural was the subject of a *Life* magazine article. The mosaic made of broken beer and soft-drink bottles was done by Belgian-born American artist Ade de Bethune. It depicts Christ on the Day of Judgment, surrounded by Filipinized saints, in a bold, colorful, psychedelic design. The compound also has a *kapis*-shell handicraft workshop where chandeliers and placemats are made.

Tours of the mill are possible 0900-1330, 1430-1600; a smart casual dress code includes trousers for men, skirts for women.

You can stay in the area at **Ceferina Resort,** which rents cottages for P150-200; it's situated by the sea, north of Victorias.

Manapla
The **Hacienda Rosalia Chapel** is a native church with an agricultural motif; its facade is a stylized wooden *salakot* (a wide-brimmed hat worn by farmers); the walls are discarded carabao-cart wheels; the sliding doors feature 128 panels portraying biblical events; Christ is depicted crucified on a cartwheel. Balulan Beach is off the highway nearby. The area is also where the Gaston house is located. Ives Germaine Gaston, a Frenchman, brought the first sugarcane points to this part of the island.

Ilacaon Island
This nine-hectare island, accessible by hiring a *banca* from a coastal village such as Sicaba or Cadiz Viejo, offers white-sand beaches and good snorkeling on its coral reefs. You could sleep on the beach overnight in tents. A cottage is also available, but prior permission is needed from the Ledesma family in Silay who are landowners here.

Cadiz City
Cadiz (pop. 142,000) is a major fishing port surrounded by sugar plantations, 65 km from Bacolod. It has a pleasant central park and holds its own Ati-Atihan fiesta on the fourth Sunday of January. Like other Ati-Atihans, it's a combination of a riotous street parade, with people painted and dressed as Negritos, and a religious feast in honor of the Santo Niño. **Narra Beach Resort** rents bamboo cottages, while **Stop-Over Village Resort,** located inland, offers upscale accommodations ranging P200-300.

New and Old Sagay
Fabrica, on the Himoga-an River west of New Sagay, was once the site of a huge sawmill and a sugar central. From New Sagay, you can take a jeepney to Pandanan, which has a two-km-long beach and offshore coral; stay at **Pandanan Beach Resort** for P200.

Carbin and Macahalum Reefs and Shoal are about 13 km away, one hour by *banca* north-northeast of the village of Old Sagay. Local fishermen have cooperated with the government in declaring part of the reef a sanctuary for marinelife. Approaching the reef, go beyond the sandspit, which remains above water even at high tide, to the northwest side, where there's a slope, and the northeast side, which has a drop-off. The snorkeling is good, with impressive coral and fishlife, but beware of tricky currents.

The Vito church at Vito is a pilgrimage site for devotees every Friday.

New and Old Escalante

Escalante was the scene of a notorious massacre in 1985, when 21 demonstrators were killed in front of the municipal hall by security forces during the lead-up to the Marcos-Aquino presidential race. Enchanted Isle, off the fishing port of Old Escalante, is a three-hectare white-sand and offshore coral island some 15 minutes away by pumpboat.

SAN CARLOS CITY

This port (pop. 100,000) lies on the main routes linking Bacolod with Dumaguete and Cebu City.

Attractions

A point of interest in the city is the grotto of Our Lady of Lourdes at Hacienda Santa Ana. To visit the grotto, take a tricycle (P5). Other nearby points of interest are Mainit Lake and Spring, and Hacienda Galicia. **Refugio's Island,** also called Sipaway, is just offshore from San Carlos and reached by frequent *bancas*. It has undeveloped beaches in which to swim and relax. Bring food and drink or buy whatever's available (may be limited) in *sari-sari* stores.

Accommodations

Stay at **YMCA,** P70 pp, opposite Coco Grove Hotel; **Van's Lodging House,** P100-150 pp; **La Suerte Pension,** P150 and up pp (price includes breakfast and dinner), good value; or the **Papal Lodge,** P100-150, on V Gustilo Street. **Coco Grove Hotel and Restaurant,** P180-200, on Ylagan St. is quite good. For entertainment, try the **Poor Man's Disco** or the **Centrix Disco.**

Transportation

Frequent buses depart from the northern bus terminals of Bacolod (145 km) and Dumaguete (168 km), taking about four hours from either city.

Buses run to and from Bacolod and Dumaguete until 1600; however, the last bus from Bacolod to Dumaguete via San Carlos leaves at 1200. Some buses are marked "boat service" and go directly to the wharf; others go to the city terminal, from where you must take a tricycle to the port.

Ferries cross to Toledo (Cebu) Mon.-Sat. at 0530 and usually 1330, Sunday at 1030; the trip takes two and a half hours. Buses to Bacolod meet ferries arriving from Toledo, but consider taking the scenic trip across the island via Kanlaon City.

SOUTH OF BACOLOD

The southern bus terminal serves the settlements on the slopes of Mt. Kanlaon and those lining Negros's west coast. Bago City, the first city south of Bacolod, is the site of the **Araneta Museum.** General Araneta led the southern revolutionary forces during the 1898 revolution. The historic Bago Bridge is also found here.

La Carlota City

This city, 45 km south of Bacolod, lies on the slopes of Mt. Kanlaon. Contact the Negros Mountaineering Club to arrange a guide for climbing the volcano; Ara-al is the actual starting point for the climb. The Pasalamat Festival on the last Sunday of April is a labor and harvest thanksgiving fiesta, featuring a parade of farm products and street dancing.

La Castellana

The best views of **Kanleon volcano** are from the highway between La Castellana and Kanlaon City. A route to the summit begins at Biakna-Bato. **Hacienda Luisa,** P150-200, is a small resort 69 km from Bacolod. It has a spring-fed swimming pool and a fine garden with native fruit trees, cactus, bonsai, and other plants, plus a shell collection and menagerie.

The Coastal Road South

This highway leads out of Bacolod, down through Sum-ag, with its beach resorts, and the canefields around Bago City (pop. 100,000). It by-passes the port of Pulupandan and rejoins the coast at Palaka in Valladolid. A *banca* crosses daily between here and Calabagnan on Guimaras Island, via some small islands in the Guimaras Strait. It departs from the northernmost bridge in Valladolid at around 1100. South of here, at Pontevedra, you can stay at **Caingin Beach Resort,** a religious resort that attracts larger groups from Manila, Cebu, and other cities.

Beyond it, at Hinigaran, visitors can swim at Bolobito-on Beach Resort, named after the abundant *bolobito-on* trees here, but there are no accommodations. Binalbagan, 73 km, two hours south of Bacolod, is the site of an old church and the Binalbagan Sugarmill Company (Biscom), which is one of the world's largest sugar mill-plantations.

Inland from Himamaylan, the **Acapulco Spring Resort,** P150-200, located on Hacienda San Juan, offers accommodations, plus spring-fed swimming pools and horse-riding amid forest-ed hills; there's also a subterranean stream here.

The Southwest
Kabankalan holds a Sinulog Festival on the third Sunday of January, with street-dancing parades and horsefighting, while the old town of **Ilog** nearby holds one on 25 March. The long stretch of coast extending from Cauayan to Hi-noba-an has some fine beaches. The Tablas Plateau lies inland.

North of Sipalay is **Danjugan,** a 43-hectare island situated three km offshore; it offers a sandy beach and good snorkeling. Nearby on the mainland is **Tinagong Dagat** ("Hidden Sea"), a lake near the seashore that contains coral and many small fish. An open-pit copper mine operates on the edge of the plateau; the ore is concentrated at the mine and molybdenum is also produced. To the south, Maricalum Bay is noted for its marinelife.

Hinoba-an
This small town, situated on a long stretch of white sand, is five hours from Bacolod (200 km) or Dumaguete (150 km) and is served by regular buses. Its hinterland is a timber area, but in 1981 it was also the site of a feverish gold rush.

Reports of panners taking large amounts of gold out of the Bacuyangan River lured tens of thousands of adventurers and transformed the village of Nauhang into a bustling frontier town. A Wild West atmosphere took hold as claims were violently disputed. To visit the river, take a jeepney seven km inland from Crossing Gold South-bend to Sparill at Sitio Sangke, then follow the trail. Tricycles link Nauhang and Hinoba-an.

There are still plenty of people panning for gold here, and while some have gotten rich, the hopeful continue to pan away their days here.

DUMAGUETE CITY

Dumaguete City (pop. 80,000), provincial capital, port, and commercial center, lies on a fertile plain at the base of the Cuernos de Negros Mountains.

Attractions
Dumaguete attracts a large student population to the prestigious Silliman University, whose facilities are spread through the city and its suburbs. Other sights include the market and a Spanish watchtower, built in 1800 and since restored. Pottery is made at Daro. You'll find beach resorts at Bantayan on the north side of the city and Banilad on the south side, but better beaches are farther afield.

Silliman University
Founded by American missionaries in 1901, this is the only Protestant university in the country. Silliman Hall is built in Southern U.S. architectural style. The attractive 33-hectare campus is dotted with many old acacia trees. The private **anthropology museum** (open Tues.-Sat., 0800-1200, 1400-1700) has a collection of voodoo paraphernalia from Siquijor and also contains locally excavated artifacts, Sung and Ming porcelain, and rare shells such as the Glory of the Sea.

The celebrated **Marine Laboratory** is at Silliman Farm Beach, just outside the city. A short distance offshore lies the country's first artificial reef, built in 1977 using old car tires, and now home to a wide variety of fish. The reef can be reached by swimming from the beach, but it's safer to use a *banca,* due to the strong currents. Contact the Marine Laboratory to hire diving gear and a guide.

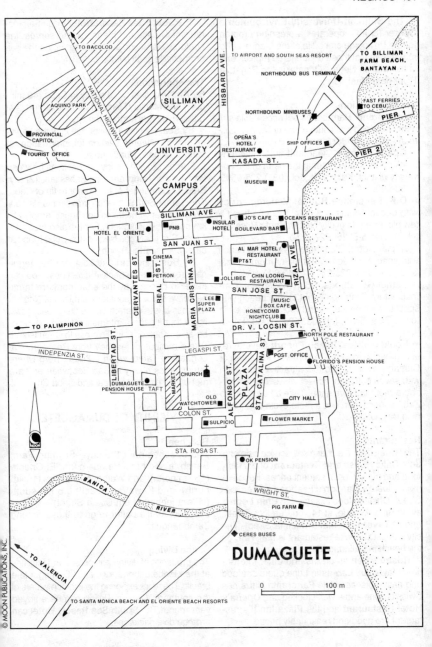

DUMAGUETE

0   100 m

© MOON PUBLICATIONS, INC.

The **Silliman University Environmental Center** (SUEC) operates a breeding program for the Philippine crocodile at the Marine Laboratory. A few of these endangered reptiles exist in the wild on Negros Oriental in the Pagatban River near Maatrop.

Accommodations

Jo's Lodging: Bare-bones but acceptable student crash pad just south of the university. Silliman Ave., tel. (035) 225-4412, P100-220.

Opena's Hotel: Clean and quiet hotel one block north of city center in the heart of the university district. Katada St., tel. (035) 225-0595, P150-500.

O.K. Pensionne House: Modern pension with decent rooms in a quiet neighborhood a few blocks south of city center. Santa Rosa St., tel. (035) 225-5925, P275-650.

Al Mar Hotel: Older hotel right on the beach with spacious if somewhat funky rooms. Rizal Blvd., tel. (035) 225-2567, P240-600.

Bethel Guesthouse: Big, modern, and immaculately clean hotel right on the beach with spotless café on the ground floor; best choice in town. Rizal Blvd., tel. (035) 225-2000, P450-900.

Kookoo's Nest Beach Resort: Several relaxing beach resorts are some 40 km south of Dumaguete, including this attractive operation with seven cottages, sunset views, two-km offshore reef, and dive shop. Take a bus south to Zamboangita then hire a motorcycle taxi. Tambulo Bay, US$4-20.

Restaurants

The university has a cheap self-service cafeteria. **Jo's Cake House and Restaurant** offers tasty food and fruit juices at student prices. For quick meals, there's **Manson's Fastfood** on Perdices Street. Chinese food is served at **Chin Loong,** along Rizal Avenue, at 143 on Perdices Street, and at **Tavern,** on Maria Cristina Street. The city's finest Chinese restaurant is **Mei Yan,** on the beach in Calindagan.

Rosante serves pizzas and other international favorites. **Lab-as** in Looc offers seafood and native dishes, while **Panorama Haus** has Swiss cuisine and a well-stocked bar. **Opeña's Hotel Restaurant** and the **Plaza Inn II's** restaurant are good and reasonably priced.

The **South Sea Resort Hotel's** open-air restaurant is cool and pleasant and serves fine seafood. Barbecue stalls are set up on the sea promenade each evening.

Transportation

By Air: PAL flies twice a day to Cebu (40 minutes) and Manila (75 minutes). The airport is at Sibulan, 3.5 km north of the city.

By Sea: See the Transportation at the beginning of the Negros section for information on various ships to Dumaguete.

Ferries provide hourly connections between San Jose or Tampi and San Sebastian, Talisay, Bato, or Santander at the southern tip of Cebu. The Tampi-San Sebastian crossing is as convenient as any and takes one hour. Tampi is 18 km north of Dumaguete. Ferries also cross the Tanon Strait between Negros and Cebu Island at other points farther north.

By Bus: Northern and southern bus terminals serve their respective directions. You can travel to Bacolod by the east (northern terminal) or west coast (southern terminal) of Negros. Express buses operate on the faster east coast route, but it's more interesting to go via Hinoba-an or Kanlaon City. To cross to Cebu Island, take a minibus or jeepney from Real Street at Legaspi to Tampi wharf (18 km), from where ferries cross hourly to San Sebastian and are met by buses for Moalboal and Cebu City.

VICINITY OF DUMAGUETE

Beaches

The beaches near the city—Silliman Farm Beach, a short tricycle ride north; El Oriente (15 km north); and Wuthering Heights (16 km north); and Kawayan Beach, 8.5 km south (take a jeepney from Colon Street)—are unexceptional. It's better to go to those around Zamboanguita.

Scuba Diving

The presence of diving equipment and facilities at the Marine Laboratory makes Dumaguete a practical base for exploring the fish-rich waters of the southern Visayas. Diving can be enjoyed year-round. The **South Sea Resort Hotel** can arrange dive packages.

In addition to the artificial reef of Silliman Farm Beach, dive sites in the area include Apo and Sumilon Islands, which can be reached by hired *banca*. **Sumilon Island Marine Park** is closer to Cebu Island but is administered from Dumaguete. The Marine Laboratory has a trimaran that may be chartered for diving trips to Sumilon. Apo can also be reached from Zamboanguita.

Twin Lakes

Lakes Balinsasayao and Danao are small adjacent crater lakes to the northwest of Dumaguete, situated at an elevation of 300 meters in a beautiful rainforest setting. Take a San Jose-bound minibus or jeepney from Real at Dr. V. Locsin Street and tell the driver where you're going. The trail is marked by a small sign on the left about two km south of San Jose. From the highway, it's about a 15-km hike.

You can overnight at a small resthouse near the lakes; bring food and water. A trail also leads up from the San Antonio golf course.

Valencia

From Dumaguete, take a jeepney from Colon at Real Street to Valencia, then a tricycle to Camp Lookout, which is 14 km west of Dumaguete in the foothills of Cuernos de Negros (1,903 meters). The name means "Horns of Negros" and derives from the twin peaks, whose summits are usually shrouded in clouds; the mountain is also known as Mt. Talinis. The tricycle trip should cost about P8, but the drivers here are notorious for trying to overcharge foreigners.

Alternatively, it's a one-hour walk from Valencia. The view from Camp Lookout across to Cebu and Siquijor is spectacular, and it's possible to overnight in a cottage for P20 pp; ask for a key at the Silliman University Administration Office in Dumaguete. You can also stay at the **Banica Valley Resort** in Tejero, two km from Valencia; it has guesthouses, a swimming pool, and a shrine from where there's also a good view.

Palimpinon Falls and Hot Springs: These springs are hot enough to boil eggs, and the area has been tapped as a geothermal source. Located 10 km from Dumaguete, it's accessible by bus and tricycle, followed by a short hike.

NORTH OF DUMAGUETE

The coastal road leads north to San Carlos City. It passes San Jose and Tampi, ferry ports for Cebu Island. **Prieto Beach Resort** rents cottages in Amlan, a town surrounded by coconut plantations. Bais City is the province's industrial center but is also noted for fine mangoes. Solar-evaporated salt is produced in large beds around the bay at Manjuyod. The highway continues up through Guihulngan, from where a boat crosses daily to Tangil (Dumanjug) on Cebu. North of Valle Hermoso, the road to Kanlaon City branches inland.

KANLAON (CANLAON) CITY

This newly created city on the eastern slopes of Kanleon volcano is situated on a plateau at an elevation of 914 meters. It's an agricultural community, but owing to its cool climate, it is projected to become a summer resort, "the Baguio of the Visayas." Kanlaon is 103 km from Dumaguete. You can stay at **Mountaineer's Inn.**

Vicinity of Kanlaon

Sights include Quipot Waterfall (30 meters); Iniawan Enchanted Falls (40 meters) on the Iniawan River; the sulfuric Bucalan Springs; Camp Mapot Mountain Park, situated on a high forested plateau; and in Lumapao, a huge Ionok tree estimated to be 1,300 years old.

MOUNT KANLAON

This volcano (2,465 meters), sitting astride the provincial boundary, has two craters, one extinct and the other active. The conical active crater is about 100 meters wide and 250 meters deep. The extinct, older crater, about one km across, is 200 meters wide and 250 meters lower. Its inside slopes descend about 150 meters; they're overgrown and contain a lake during the rainy season.

Kanlaon and its forested flanks form a national park (246 square km) with waterfalls, hot springs, gorges, and rock formations. Flora include orchids, ferns, and mossy forest. Volcanologists observe the mountain's activity from a watchtower on Makawiwili Ridge, a saddle between the two craters. The volcano has erupted several times in recent history—1866, 1893, 1978.

The Climb
The ascent, starting from Kanlaon city, takes two to three days; bring a sleeping bag. The mayor's office will arrange for a guide, who'll cost about P50-70 per day. About halfway up is Margaha Valley, a two-hectare patch of white sand that can serve as a campsite. It's also possible to camp on a shoulder about 600 meters below the summit.

Other possible starting points for the climb include Biak-na-Bato (La Castellana) on the southwest side, Ara-al (La Carlota City), and Mambucal (the longest route). The Bacolod Tourist Office organizes a group ascent during Holy Week.

SOUTH OF DUMAGUETE

The southern bus terminal is on Real Street at Santa Rosa, and from there, buses follow the southern coast of Negros going to Hinoba-an and Bacolod. Jeepneys starting from Real at Colon serve communities closer to Dumaguete.

Around the South Coast
Bacong has an old coral church facing the sea. The village of Malatapay holds a colorful *tabu*

(rendezvous market) beside its black-sand beach each Wednesday. People come down from the hills to auction livestock, buy and sell produce and handicrafts, gamble, and enjoy fresh fish and *tuba*.

Zamboanguita provides the best beach and snorkeling possibilities in the Dumaguete area; it's about 27 km, 45 minutes, south of the city. Stay at the **Salawaki Beach Resort,** P200 per cottage for two persons, with toilet and bathroom.

Lamplighter's Paradise World is a wildlife sanctuary and botanical gardens. There're inexpensive accommodations here. Apo Island, which is accessible by hiring a *banca* from Zamboanguita (about P300 return), offers divers some huge coral mounds, walls, and big fish, including sharks, all with excellent visibility. Strong currents and wave action make the area risky for snorkelers, however. The tiny island has a murky lagoon and a campsite. Snorkelers can find excellent conditions a little farther around the coast, just off Bonbonon Point.

A wide reef flat and slopes feature coral mounds and tables, with a wide variety of fish. Currents are no problem in the area's sheltered coves, but may be strong in exposed water. The main road swings north to the lumber towns of Santa Catalina and Bayawan. The latter contains **La Vista del Mar,** an upscale beach resort noted for fine seafood. It was the site of the International Skin and Scuba Diving competition in 1976.

PANAY

This triangular-shaped island is divided into four provinces: Aklan, Antique, Capiz, and Iloilo, and Iloilo's subprovince of Guimaras Island. Panay's main attractions are the offshore islet of Boracay, the country's foremost tourist beach resort; Iloilo City, which has more elegance than most Philippine cities; and festivals celebrating the original bargain between the indigenous Atis and the Bornean *datus*.

Each of the four provincial capitals holds its own version of this event. Kalibo's Ati-Atihan is the most renowned and impressive, but Iloilo City's Dinagyang, Roxas City's Halaran, and

San Jose de Buenavista's Binirayan are also tremendously exuberant fiestas.

HISTORY

Panay has long been inhabited, as confirmed by the stone tools of an ancient people, found near a fossilized elephant in Cabatuan. When 10 Bornean *datus*, together with their followers, landed near San Joaquin in 1212, they were met by Atis (Negritos). The exchange of gifts and the ensuing feasting and dancing was the origin of today's fiestas. After the Atis had with-

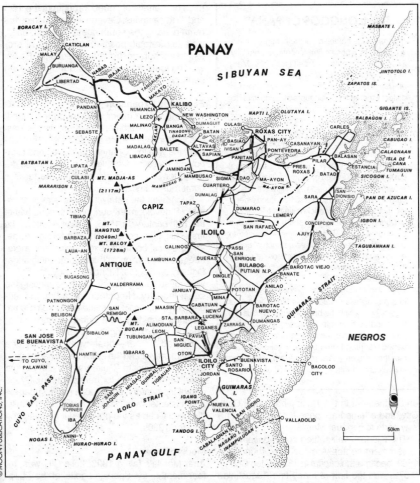

drawn to the hills, the *datus* subdivided Panay into Hamtik (now Antique), Aklan (now Aklan and Capiz), and Irong-irong (now Iloilo), with Hamtik as capital. These districts comprised the Confederation of Madja-as.

Panay was subject to two early legal codes: the Maragtas Code, promulgated around 1225 by Sumakwel, the wisest of the *datus*, in which, for example, indolence was a social crime punishable by banishment or slavery; and the Code of Kalantiaw, written in Aklan in 1433. Chinese and Southeast Asian porcelain found in pre-Hispanic burial sites at Oton and elsewhere indicate an early international trade.

The Coming of Spain
Panay was founded in 1569 by Legazpi, who was forced to move from Cebu due to food shortages there. Panay, said to derive from the Spanish *pan hay* ("there is bread"), was Spain's sec-

THE ILONGGOS OF PANAY

Panay is the homeland of the Ilonggos, or Hili-gaynons, whose cultural center is Iloilo City. They also dominate Negros Occidental. Many have migrated to Romblon, Mindoro, Masbate, and Mindanao. The Ilonggo, or Panay-Hiligaynon, dialect is noted for its languorous, seductive lilt.

The Ilonggos are noted for their hospitality and genial, unharried approach to life, a temperament that can tend toward decadence among the region's free-spending landowners. Visitors are welcomed with "Hapit anay" ("Come in; make yourself at home"). Many traditional customs have survived on Panay. *Dagyao* is the reciprocal assistance given by neighbors, e.g., in building a house. Families also help each other in the fields, collective labor known as *hilo-hilo*.

During the harvest, they share *pang-igma,* a communal picnic. The *to-os* system is used to designate property; if you see a bunch of *cogon* grass tied to a tree it may indicate ownership of the fruit, the path beneath it, and the fishing rights in the stream beside it.

Traditional marriages are preceded by a friend of a prospective bridegroom's family acting as a go-between with the bride's family. Goods are furnished by both families *(pangayo),* and the groom must serve the bride's family for a set period, ranging from several weeks to a few months or even years *(pangagad).* Weddings are celebrated with a joyful meal *(urukay).*

raids on Panay continued throughout the 16th and 17th centuries. Several stone watchtowers remain along the south coast. In 1688, Iloilo, with its strategic position and excellent protected anchorage, became the capital. Panay was divided into provinces during the 18th century.

Economic Expansion

Weaving was a major industry on the island, and in the mid-19th century, there was at least one loom in every home and several in the houses of the wealthy. Changes in fashion and technology, however, have led to decline in the demand for *pina* and *jusi,* so looms are far less numerous today.

Sugar was the catalyst in Iloilo's rapid commercial development during the second half of the 19th century. In 1855, Iloilo was among the first Philippine ports opened to foreign trade, and the local economy expanded swiftly thereafter, in conjunction with the burgeoning sugar industry on Negros. Nicholas Loney, the British vice-consul, played a key role in developing the sugar industry. He cofounded a firm that engaged in importing sugarcane points from Sumatra and machinery from Britain, financing production, and exporting the sugar.

He had *lorchas*—boats with the body of a Brixham trawler and the sails of a Chinese junk—built at Buenavista (Guimaras) to carry sugar from Negros to Iloilo for transshipment. By the end of the century, Iloilo was a major sugar-exporting center with a sizable foreign community. It rivaled Cebu as the preeminent Visayan port until the 1930s.

ond settlement in the Philippines, after Cebu City, and a temporary base for Legazpi on his way north to conquer Manila.

The island's well-settled south became the government center. Arevalo, also founded in 1569, became the capital in 1581. Oton Church (1572) was the first of many fine Augustinian churches on Panay, but it was completely ruined by earthquake in 1948. The Spaniards were harassed by both their colonial rivals and the Muslims. The English buccaneer Sir Thomas Cavendish attacked Arevalo in 1588, and the Dutch made several raids on the area.

A large Muslim force of 70 *vintas* and 8,000 men was repulsed at Arevalo in 1600. In 1616, following a Dutch attack on Arevalo, the Spaniards built Fort San Pedro in Iloilo, where the government was transferred in 1637. Moro

Modern Times

After Manila's fall in 1898, Iloilo City was, for four months, the Spanish capital of the Philippines, but revolutionaries forced the Spaniards to move on to Zamboanga. Almost immediately, a U.S. expedition arrived to take possession of Iloilo. The Ilonggos prepared to fight, and guerrilla warfare against the Americans continued on Panay until the "Peace of Aklan" was signed in Banga in 1901.

A large guerrilla force also operated successfully in WW II. This time, they welcomed the U.S. landing forces at Tigbauan in March 1945.

TRANSPORTATION

Panay can be reached from Cebu, Guimaras, Manila, Mindanao, Mindoro, Negros, Palawan, and Romblon, but probably the most common route is the flight from Manila down to Kalibo (the gateway for Boracay) and the short ferry ride from Bacolod, Negros, to Iloilo.

From the Kalibo airport, a combination of bus and *banca* can get you to Boracay in about three hours. If Manila-Kalibo is fully booked, fly to Roxas and continue by bus.

Return tickets should be booked well in advance and reconfirmed upon arrival in Kalibo.

By Air

PAL flies daily from Manila to Iloilo and Kalibo, and has connections to Roxas; flights from Cebu City leave daily for Iloilo and Monday, Wednesday, Friday, and Saturday for Kalibo. Grand Air flies daily except Sunday from Manila to Iloilo. Air Philippines flies daily from Manila and Cebu City to Kalibo.

PAL also flies every Sunday from General Santos City, Mindanao, to Iloilo, and from Puerto Princesa, Palawan, to Iloilo City on Thursday and Saturday. The flight continues on to Cebu City.

Caticlan has a small airstrip just 15 minutes from Boracay. Arrivals take a shuttle from the airport down to the Caticlan pier, from where *bancas* head over to Boracay. Asian Spirit and Pacific Airways fly daily from Manila to Caticlan. Air Ads flies three times weekly, on Monday, Friday, and Saturday.

Ship from Manila

Ships are plentiful to Iloilo, though several lines also provide service to various ports near Boracay, including Caticlan and Dumaguit.

To Iloilo: Ships from Manila to Iloilo cost P500-600 and take 18-25 hours to make the journey, depending on the number of stops between the two destinations.

Negros Navigation's MV *Saint Francis of Assisi* departs Manila at 1200 on Monday, Thursday, and Saturday and takes 18 hours to reach Iloilo.

WG&A has four ships from Manila to Iloilo: the MV *Superferry 9* departs at 2000 on Wednesday, the MV *Superferry 1* leaves on Thursday at 1700 and Saturday at 1500, the MV *Superferry 5* on Friday at 1500.

Sulpicio Lines' MV *Princess of the Pacific* departs on Tuesday at 1000 and takes 19 hours to reach Iloilo, while its MV *Cotabato Princess* sets off on Saturday at 1500. The latter service requires 25 hours since it makes a stop in Estancia.

To Roxas: Negros Navigation's MV *Don Claudio* departs Manila's North Harbor on Monday at 1300 and Thursday at 1700, while the MV *Don Julio* sets off on Saturday at 1700. Both ships take 16 hours.

To Caticlan (near Boracay): MBRS Line's MV *Romblon Bay* departs Manila for Caticlan on Tuesday at 1300 and Friday at 1400. The trip takes 22 hours.

WG&A's MV *Superferry 1* makes the same trip weekly during the high season months of March and April. This much faster (and more comfortable) ship makes the passage in just under 11 hours. You'll need to check the newspaper or give WG&A a call to confirm the schedule.

To Dumaguit (near Boracay): Negros Navigation's MV *Don Julio* departs Manila on Wednesday at 1500 and reaches Dumaguit in about 16 hours. The fare is P400-450.

WG&A's MV *Our Lady of Naju* does the trip in 15 hours with departures from Manila at 1400 on Monday, Wednesday, and Sunday. This ship sometimes berths at nearby Batan, rather than directly at Dumaguit.

Manila to Estancia: Estancia is a small port town on the northeastern tip of Panay, near the resort island of Sicogon. Sulpicio Lines' MV *Cotabato Princess* departs Manila at 1500 on Sunday and takes 15 hours to reach Estancia. The ship then continues down to Iloilo.

Ship from Cebu

Ships depart Cebu City for Iloilo, Roxas City, or Dumaguit (near Kalibo and Boracay).

To Iloilo City: Trans-Asia Shipping's MV *Asia-Brunei* or MV *Asia-Indonesia* departs daily at 1800 and take 12 hours to reach Iloilo. The fare is P220-260. Cebu Ferries' MV *Iligan City* leaves at 1900 on Monday and Saturday, while the MV *Tacloban City* sets off at 1900 on Tuesday and Thursday. Again, total travel time is 12 hours.

To Roxas and Dumaguit: Both of these ships continue on to Dumaguit after making their first stop in Roxas. Cebu Ferries' MV *Iligan City* leaves Thursday at 1900, while the MV *Tacloban City* departs Saturday at 1900.

Ship from Guimaras

Several small ferries shuttle back and forth between Iloilo and various towns on Guimaras Island. Ferries run hourly from Jordan and Buenavista to Iloilo daily 0500-1730. The 30-minute crossing costs just P5-10.

Most resorts on Guimaras can arrange private transfer service to Iloilo for about P800-1,200.

Ship from Mindanao

All ships from Mindanao go to Iloilo on Panay.

From Butuan: WG&A's MV *Superferry 2* departs this north coast town on Wednesday at 1300 and takes 17 hours to reach Iloilo. The fare is P420-480.

From Cagayan de Oro: WG&A's MV *Superferry 9* leaves every Friday at 1500 and takes 15 hours to make the crossing with a fare of P380-440. Negros Navigation's MV *Santa Ana* does the same route on Sunday at 1600, but is slightly faster at just under 14 hours.

From Cotabato: Sulpicio Lines' MV *Cotabato Princess* departs Tuesday at 2200 and takes 36 hours, including a stop in Zamboanga.

From Davao: WG&A's MV *Superferry 1* goes on Monday at midnight and takes 33 hours via General Santos City. The fare is P650-750.

From General Santos City: WG&A's MV *Superferry 1* leaves every Tuesday at 1100 and reaches Iloilo in about 22 hours. Figure on P600-650. Sulpicio Lines' MV *Princess of the Pacific* sets off on Friday at 1800 and takes 36 hours with a stop in Zamboanga.

From Iligan: WG&A's MV *Superferry 5* departs Sunday at 2100 and does the crossing in just 12 hours. The fare is P350-400.

From Zamboanga: Sulpicio Lines' MV *Cotabato Princess* departs Wednesday at 2000 and requires 14 hours to reach Iloilo, while the MV *Princess of the Pacific* departs Saturday at 1600. Same 14-hour journey.

Ship from Mindoro

Several large outriggers make the crossing from Roxas on Mindoro to Boracay, that small but fa-

bled resort island just north of Panay. Some go direct, while others make a stop at Looc on Tablas Island in Romblon Province. See **Boracay** for more information.

Ship from Negros

Several ferries make the crossing from Bacolod to Iloilo, while service is also provided from Daan Banwa, the port for Victorias.

Bacolod to Iloilo: Negros Navigation operates the MV *St. Rafael,* the MV *St. Michael,* and the MV *SM/DV* between these two cities on a near-hourly basis 0600-1700. The crossing takes 90-120 minutes depending on the boat. The fare is P55-90.

Faster and more comfortable service is provided by the a/c catamaran MV *Bacolod Express,* which leaves daily at 0845 and 1545. The fare is a reasonable P100-120 and the crossing takes just under one hour.

Victorias to Ajuy: Victorias is a small town on the northern coast of Negros, while Ajuy is an equally small town on the east coast of Panay. Da-an Banwa is the port for Victorias. From here, either the MV *Queen Rose* or the MV *Princess Jo* leaves daily at around 0900 for Culasi, near Ajuy. Also, either the MV *Seven Seas* or the MV *San Vicente* leaves daily around 0900 for Malayu-an, another small village near Ajuy. Both crossings take two hours.

Ship from Palawan

One small shipping company operates a pair of fairly funky ships between Puerto Princesa and Iloilo. Milagrosa Shipping's MV *Milagrosa-J-Dos* leaves Puerto Princesa at 1200 on the 1st, 11th, and 21st of each month. Total travel time is 38 hours, including an eight-hour layover on the island of Cuyo.

Travelers hanging out in Cuyo can board this boat on the 2nd, 12th, and 22nd of each month—in other words, one day after the boat has departed Puerto Princesa.

Milagrosa Shipping's MV *Milagrosa-J-Tres* leaves Puerto Princesa at 1600 on the 7th, 17th, and 27th of each month.

Outrigger from Romblon (Tablas Island)

Several large outriggers provide connections from Looc on Tablas Island (Romblon Province) to either Boracay or Caticlan on the north coast of Panay. A large outrigger leaves Looc daily in the morning around 0900 and takes two hours to make the crossing to Boracay. The fare is P100-120.

Another outrigger departs Santa Fe on Tablas Island and heads down to Boracay (or Caticlan) every Tuesday, Thursday, and Saturday. The boat waits for the plane to arrive from Manila (the airport is at Tugdan). After the plane lands, a jeepney takes passengers down to the boat dock in Santa Fe, from where the outrigger loads up and takes off for Boracay.

This outrigger does the crossing in a slightly quicker 90 minutes and costs P80-100.

Getting Around

Ceres Liner operates a comfortable fleet of buses on Panay. Buses from Iloilo to Roxas take about four hours, plus another two to Kalibo. Ceres buses depart Iloilo mornings 0700-1200 direct to Boracay. You can also take faster minibuses to Kalibo and Boracay from the minibus halt just south of the bus terminal in Iloilo. With an early start you'll be on the beach by late afternoon.

ILOILO CITY

Located on the alluvial lowland where the Iloilo River's delta meets the Iloilo Strait, and sheltered by Guimaras Island, Iloilo is the cultural, religious, educational (five universities and several colleges), commercial, manufacturing, and transportation center of the western Visayas.

The city serves a rich agricultural hinterland, and its harbor handles a considerable volume of rice and sugar shipments. Iloilo peaked in influence around the turn of the century but has retained some of the period's genteel charm. Fortunes were made in sugar during the late 19th century, and some fine old mansions still stand in the suburbs. Life is more relaxed here than in Manila or Cebu City.

Orientation

Iloilo (pop. 276,000) is composed of six districts, each with its own plaza, church, and market: the city proper, Arevalo, Jaro, La Paz, Mandurriao, and Molo. A wide range of accommodation is available in the downtown area. Urban transportation is provided by PUs (set-fare minicabs) and the city's decorated jeepneys. The airport is in Mandurriao, six km and 15 minutes from the city center. The wharf is close to downtown. Shipping company offices are near the wharf.

The bus terminals for Kalibo, Roxas City, Molo, and Estancia are on Tanza Street, and for Antique on San Marcos Street. From the central business district, jeepneys run north across Forbes Bridge to La Paz and Jaro, and west to Molo and Arevalo. Each pair of suburbs makes a worthwhile half-day excursion. Villa Beach (Arevalo) is the nearest from town.

The Department of Tourism office (open Mon.-Fri. 0800-1700), located in the Sarabia Building on General Luna Street, tel. (033) 78-701 or 75-411, is helpful. To get there, take a Molo-bound jeepney along General Luna Street.

Festivals

Iloilo City reverberates day and night to drumbeats during the festival of **Dinagyang,** starting in the week preceding the fourth weekend in January and building up to its climax on the Sunday with an afternoon parade. *Dinagyang* is an Ilonggo term for revelry. Costumed "tribes" dance through the streets to commemorate the pact between the Bornean *datus* and Atis, and to honor the Santo Niño. Shouts of *"Viva Señor Santo Niño!"* mix with chants of *"hala bira!"* meaning "hail child!"

The **Feast of Nuestra Señora de Candelaria** is observed in Jaro on 2 February. This festival of candles in honor of Jaro's patron saint features religious processions, masses, a beauty contest, music, a fair, cockfight, and cultural events.

The **Paraw Regatta** in Iloilo Strait is held on the third weekend in February. This 36.5-km race by *paraws* (*bancas* with triangular sails) starts and ends at Villa Beach, Arevalo, or the Anhawan Beach Resort, Oton; boats must round several markers off Buenavista, Guimaras Island.

Each district has its own fiesta: Arevalo, on the third Sunday of January; La Paz, 24 May; Molo, 26 July; Mandurriao, 26 November. On 8 December, Oton's fiesta is highlighted by a parade of *carrozas* (bamboo sleds) decorated with produce and flowers, followed by a carabao-*carroza* race. The Feast of Lanterns takes place in Iloilo City each Christmas Eve.

Attractions

The post office is the hub of downtown activity. Behind it is the riverfront, known as Muelle

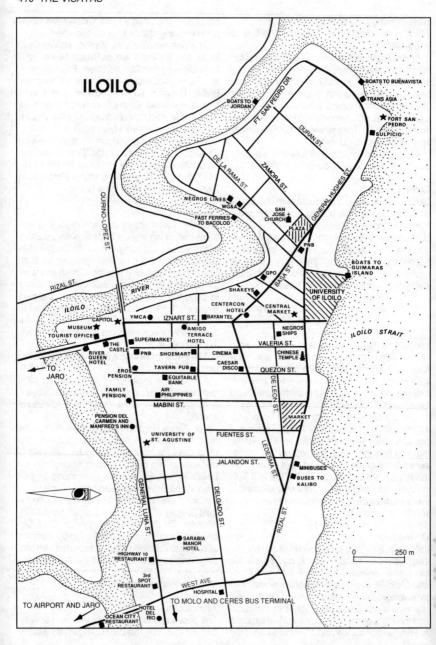

ILOILO

BOATS TO BUENAVISTA
TRANS ASIA
FORT SAN PEDRO
SULPICIO
BOATS TO JORDAN
FT. SAN PEDRO DR.
DURAN ST.
ZAMORA ST.
GENERAL HUGHES ST.
DE LA RAMA ST.
NEGROS LINES
WG&A
FAST FERRIES TO BACOLOD
SAN JOSE CHURCH
PLAZA
PNB
BOATS TO GUIMARAS ISLAND
QUIRINO-LOPEZ ST.
GPO
BASA ST.
RIZAL ST.
RIVER
SHAKEYS
CENTERCON HOTEL
CENTRAL MARKET
UNIVERSITY OF ILOILO
ILOILO
CAPITOL
YMCA
IZNART ST.
BAYAN TEL
ILOILO STRAIT
MUSEUM
TOURIST OFFICE
AMIGO TERRACE HOTEL
NEGROS SHIPS
THE CASTLE
SUPERMARKET
VALERIA ST.
RIVER QUEEN HOTEL
PNB
SHOEMART
CINEMA
CHINESE TEMPLE
TO JARO
EROS PENSION
TAVERN PUB
CAESAR DISCO
QUEZON ST.
FAMILY PENSION
EQUITABLE BANK
AIR PHILIPPINES
DE LEON ST.
PENSION DEL CARMEN AND MANFRED'S INN
MABINI ST.
MARKET
UNIVERSITY OF ST. AGUSTINE
FUENTES ST.
LEDESMA ST.
JALANDON ST.
MINIBUSES
BUSES TO KALIBO
RIZAL ST.
GENERAL LUNA ST.
DELGADO ST.
SARABIA MANOR HOTEL
0   250 m
HIGHWAY 10 RESTAURANT
3rd SPOT RESTAURANT
WEST AVE
TO AIRPORT AND JARO
HOSPITAL
TO MOLO AND CERES BUS TERMINAL
OCEAN CITY RESTAURANT
HOTEL DEL RIO

Loney, with its wharves and warehouses. At the river mouth is a lighthouse and small park. This waterfront, a popular promenade at dusk, was the site of Fort San Pedro, built in 1616 as a defense against enemy raids but almost totally destroyed in WW II.

Following the circular route formed by Fort San Pedro Drive and General Hughes Street, you pass the San Jose Church and Plaza Libertad, formerly Plaza Alfonso XII, where the First Philippine Republic's flag was raised after Spain's surrender in 1898.

J.M. Basa Street leads off from here. It's the city's busy main thoroughfare, lined with shops, restaurants, and movie theaters. Handicraft stores on J.M. Basa include **Iloilo Sinamay Dealer, Avancena Enterprises, Roadson Woodcraft,** and the **NACIDA Handicraft Center.**

A block off J.M. Basa is the central market, which has fascinating fish and fruit sections. J.M. Basa joins Iznart Street, which leads to the Provincial Capitol, behind which is the outstanding Museo Iloilo. Close by is the junction of Bonifacio Drive, which leads to La Paz and Jaro, and General Luna Street, which leads to Molo and Arevalo.

Museo Iloilo: The museum, referred to as the city's "Window on the Past" (open daily 0800-1200, 1300-1700; admission P10), showcases Iloilo's rich cultural heritage. Its well-displayed collection includes Stone Age tools; gold leaf burial masks, ornamented teeth, jewelry, and coffins from pre-Hispanic graves; pottery from China, Annam, and Siam; Spanish ecclesiatical art; relics from the revolution and WW II; and ethnic weapons and artifacts. A section is devoted to articles recovered by divers from the wreck of a 19th-century British steamer lying in seven meters of water on the Oton Shoals; they include Victorian china, port wine, and Glasgow beer.

Accommodations

Most of the better pensions and hotels are a few blocks north of city center.

Family Pension House: A clean place but with small, dark rooms and a treehouse café for breakfast and nighttime entertainment. General Luna St., tel. (033) 270-070, P180-700.

Hotel Centercon: Tucked away in a strange alley is this old hotel with acceptable if some-what worn rooms. Basa St., tel. (033) 73-431, P150-520.

River Queen Hotel: The hotel near the museum looks touristy, but rooms are large and fairly clean plus there's a great patio for dining near the river. Bonifacio Dr., tel. (033) 76-667, P240-550.

Iloilo Midtown Hotel: Good, new midrange hotel just off the main drag in the center of town. 888 Yulo St., tel. (033) 336-8888, P800-1,200.

Amigo Terrace Hotel: Iloilo's top-end choice has recently renovated rooms, a swimming pool, and a cozy café. Iznart St., tel. (033) 335-0908, P1,200-2,400.

Restaurants

Downtown Iloilo offers a wide range of eating places, especially on and near J.M. Basa Street. The **Lee Garden, Jefferson,** and **Grandma's,** among others, offer reasonably priced Chinese and Filipino dishes, including set meals. Sample Iloilo's famous noodle dishes, *pancit molo* and *batchoy;* the latter is served by restaurants on Valeria Street such as **Ted's Oldtimer.** For Western breakfast, try the **Mansion House Restaurant** or the **Summer House,** both on J.M. Basa Street. **St. Angelina** on Iznart Street is also good.

For popular *batchoy,* a western Visayas specialty of beef, pork, or liver in noodle soup, try the **Oak Barrel** on Valeria Street. On the corner of Delgado and Quezon Streets, try the **Tavern Pub** for pub meals in an a/c setting.

The **Tree House Restaurant** is part of the popular Family Pension House and has a good setting. The popular **Fort San Pedro Drive Inn** at the fort is a good place for drinking beer. Barbecues are prepared here, too. Numerous cheap restaurants are around the market area as well, and street stalls serve *ihaw ihaw.*

For baked goods, look for **Panaderia de Iloilo** and **Wewin's** on Iznart Street, and **Panaderia de Molo** on Rizal Street. Upscale possibilities include **Igmaan** at Del Rio and the **Sarabia Manor Hotel,** which has a Japanese restaurant and is renowned for its cuisine. The **Golden Salakot** at the Hotel del Rio offers a fairly cheap lunch and dinner buffet. **Belle Terraze** at Amigo Terrace Hotel offers continental cuisine. For Japanese noodles on the cheap, check out the **King Ramen Restaurant.**

Nightlife

Sugbahan Plaza and **Ihawaw** provide live music, satellite video shows, games, and music in a friendly atmosphere, and the people who frequent these places are excellent sources of local information. The downtown area has many bars: the **Tavern** on Kamalig, near Shoemart, is good, as is the **Open Air Restaurant,** overlooking the water on Fort San Pedro Drive.

The **Treasure Hunt Disco** in the Hotel del Rio is very popular as well as **Tivoli** in the Amigo Terrace Hotel. Other discos include the **Fountain Head, Kuweba,** and **Bayani Super Nightclub.** The **Base Disco** at the Sarabia Manor Hotel is also popular.

Recreation

Some good dive sites lie off Guimaras Island. Contact **Iloilo Scuba Divers Association** (ask for Anto Lee, tel. 033-75-956) for equipment rental and local information. The upscale **Sicogon Island Club** resort on beautiful Sicogon, off northeast Panay, also offers scuba diving. Cockfighting is a popular pastime. The men of Iloilo are renowned for their passionate love of cockfighting, and the city's cockfight galleries, e.g., those in Jaro and Arevalo, are well attended on Sundays and holidays.

Transportation

Air: PAL flies to Manila at least four times daily (takes one hour) and to Cebu at least twice a day (takes 35 minutes). Flights also depart three times a week for Puerto Princesa on Palawan and once a week for General Santos City in Davao.

Ship: By sea, ships sail regularly to Cebu City (19 hours) and to Manila (20-22 hours). Ships to Mindanao call in at Cagayan de Oro, Zamboanga, Dadiangas (General Santos), and Polloc (Cotabato).

Fast ferries from Bacolod (Bullet Express and Sea Angels) dock a few blocks from city center. You can walk to most hotels or flag down a taxi or jeepney on the main road. As the boat sails out between Panay and Guimaras, note the **Roca Encantada** ("Enchanted Rock"), a house perched on a rocky islet overlooking the Strait; it belongs to a prominent local family.

Bus: Buses to Roxas, Kalibo, and Caticlan leave from the intersection of Mabini and Ledesma Streets. Luxury Ceres buses leave from two blocks south on Rizal Avenue. Buses to Estancia are every half hour and to San Jose de Buenavista every hour. The trip to the latter takes two and a half hours. Some buses go up through Antique to Libertad or intermediate towns.

Ferry to Guimaras Island: Ferries to Guimaras Island leave from several different locations along the wharf. A primitive boat leaves for Palawan via Cuyo Island twice weekly on Mondays and Thursdays. Ships to Manila leave from the main wharf near Fort San Pedro.

For more specific information, see Transportation at the beginning of the Panay section.

VICINITY OF ILOILO CITY

La Paz and Jaro

Sample the real La Paz *batchoy* in one of the restaurants around the market before continuing to Jaro, an elite residential center about three km from downtown Iloilo. The streets around the plaza contain several fine mansions that belonged to 19th-century sugar barons, plus some antique collections from which pottery, statues, and coins are for sale.

Look for impressive old buildings on the right as the jeepney from Iloilo approaches Jaro. The plaza features a ruined redbrick belfry standing separate from the Gothic-style cathedral across the street, and a statue of Graciano Lopez Jaena, an orator and journalist who founded the revolutionary newspaper *La Solidaridad* and who died in Barcelona in 1896. His birthplace is noted for woven and hand-embroidered *pina* and *jusi* fabrics.

Molo

This district, three km west of downtown, was formerly called Parian, since it was the Chinese quarter of Arevalo. It's the home of the popular noodle soup, *pancit molo,* introduced by Chinese cooks in the 18th century. **Iloilo Shellcraft Industry** (on M.H. del Pilar Street) sells *kapis*-shell lamps, chandeliers, and mother-of-pearl handicrafts.

Molo's twin-towered Gothic-Renaissance church is a local landmark. Built of coral rock in the 1870s, it has withstood artillery barrage. Note the stained-glass windows and two rows of female saints' statues lining the nave. Across the plaza is the **Timoteo Consing Old House.**

A block north is the Tiongco residence, whose famous antique collection includes burial artifacts, pottery, and sculpture. Objects are only brought out for serious prospective buyers. Antiques are also sold at **Dellota's Gallery** on E. Lopez Street, Jaro.

Walk west from the plaza on Avancena Street to the **Panaderia de Molo,** the oldest bakery in the south, with an assortment of breads and biscuits. Beyond it is the Asilo de Molo orphanage run by the Sisters of Charity, where girls embroider church vestments, *barong* dresses, handkerchiefs, and tablecloths, which are offered for sale.

Arevalo

Arevalo, six km west of downtown Iloilo, is a residential district with some fine 19th-century houses. Locally grown and processed fibers are still woven into *jusi* and *pina* fabrics, which are hand-embroidered and made into clothing and other handicrafts for export to Manila and abroad. You can see looms at **Sinamay Dealer** on Osmeña Street north of the plaza.

This district is also known as the "Flower Village," since its nurseries provide Iloilo City with bouquets, corsages, leis, wreaths, and potted plants. Some restaurants here are noted for *lechon,* while sweet things are sold at **Panaderia de Iloilo** at 150 Osmeña Street.

Villa Beach is located about one km south of the center of Arevalo. Staying at one of the many beach resorts here is a viable alternative to overnighting amid the bustle of downtown, yet with easy access to the city for daytime sightseeing.

Accommodations: Stay at **Punta Villa Beach Resort,** P150 pp; good value and often full; call (033) 77-253 to check for vacancies. **Moonlight Lodge,** P200-250, and **Villa Rosa by the Sea,** P300 and up per cottage, P750 suite (has nice swimming pool), are also good.

Oton

A grave unearthed at this town, 11 km west of Iloilo City, revealed a skeleton with a gold mask, surrounded by 15th-century Chinese, Siamese, and Annamese porcelain. Oton was an important early Spanish mission center. The amphitheater in the town center contains a stone mural depicting local history. Loom- and hat-weaving are local crafts. Oton has a gray-sand beach.

WEST OF ILOILO CITY

The coastal highway between Iloilo City and San Jose de Buenavista passes many points of interest, and since transport is plentiful, it's easy to stop off, visit an old church, for example, then take another vehicle. Numerous beach resorts with cottages for rent line these shores, but the beaches are nothing special. *Kapis* shells are gathered between Oton and Miagao. Even if you're not traveling through to Antique, a day trip from Iloilo City out to Miagao and San Joaquin is worthwhile.

Tigbauan

Tigbauan is a fishing town and the site of the **Southeast Asian Fisheries Development Center,** a multinational aquaculture research facility; its studies include the artificial breeding of prawns and milkfish. The old church, with its baroque facade, was ruined by an earthquake in 1948. Stay at **Ledesma Beach Resort** (P200-250).

North of Tigbauan is **Leon,** site of the impressive ruins of a huge Renaissance-Romanesque-style church (1871), said to be the biggest on Panay; columns, statues, and the coat-of-arms of Leon (Spain), home of the town's founder, remain. Nearby Mt. Bucari was a key guerrilla base during WW II.

Guimbal

A fishing town that's also noted for fine mangoes, Guimbal was founded in 1590 and has a yellow sandstone–coral rock church and three old stone watchtowers. Stay at **Garzon Beach Resort** (P150-200).

A road leads 11 km inland to **Igbaras,** which has a ruined church and is noted for its Santacruzan Festival in May. A 10-km, two-hour hike from Igbaras leads along riverbeds and mountain trails to Passi, site of **Nadsadan Falls** (15 meters), which has two swimming holes and a resthouse. It can also be reached by a one-hour walk from Igtalungon.

Miagao

Situated 40 km west of Iloilo City, this town's unique fortresslike church is one of the finest in the Philippines. It was originally completed in 1797, but has been restored following damage at different times by revolution, fire, and earthquake. Its massive, four-meter-thick walls of honey-colored sandstone were built to withstand earthquakes and Moro pirate raids. The towers are dissimilar because the first priest-foreman died before his work was completed and his successor deviated from the original design.

Note the superbly carved facade, featuring St. Christopher carrying the infant Jesus amid palms, papaya, and guava trees, which symbolize fertility. Nearby is an old stone bridge. *Patadyong* (plaid cotton skirts) and mosquito nets are handwoven in the town's vocational school and surrounding villages. Some looms are over 150 years old.

San Joaquin

This town has a white coral church, dating from 1869, with a fascinating facade. Intricately carved stonework, originally pigmented red, blue, and yellow, depicts the Battle of Tetuan in Morocco (1859), at which Spain defeated the Moors, likened by the Spaniards to the Moros of Mindanao and Sulu. Look for details such as the pained expressions of wounded soldiers. The town also has a noteworthy cemetery.

San Joaquin is cattle country, and on the second Saturday of January, **Pasungay,** the Festival of the Bulls, takes place here, coinciding with the town fiesta. Bulls fight each other in a hillside arena until one tires or flees, the champion being decided by a process of elimination. A horse fight and carabao fight also take place.

The original landing site of the Bornean *datus* in 1212 is believed to have been at the mouth of the Sirawagan River near Sinogbuhan. Near San Joaquin is Cataan Cove, where the Iloilo Scuba Divers Association has rest facilities.

NORTH OF ILOILO CITY

The highway leads north from Iloilo City to Roxas City and Kalibo.

Pavia

In Ungca (Pavia), eight km north of Iloilo, is **RGT Philippine Products,** a center for weaving and handicrafts of shells, bamboo, and native fibers.

Pavia has an unfinished Renaissance-style red-brick church, begun in 1864, with coral rock window frames. As a Japanese garrison during WW II, the church was subject to guerrilla raids, and its walls still bear bullet marks.

Pavia holds carabao-*carroza* racing on 3 May, starting around 0800. The fastest carabao from the surrounding *barangays* pull decorated *carroza* (bamboo sleds), driven by their "jockeys," round a 400-meter course. The town fiesta is the next day.

Santa Barbara's neoclassical church of sandstone and coralline limestone and its adjacent *convento* have a fine inner patio with a wooden gallery, all in a lovely shady setting. Ilonggos first declared revolution against Spain here in 1898.

Cabatuan

Cabatuan Church is also neoclassical and dates from the early 1880s. Note the carved facade. The churchyard contains the graves of the Ilongo poet Flavio Zaragosa y Cano and WW II resistance leader Tomas Confesor. The nearby cemetery has a central chapel and surrounding walls of coral rock.

Cabatuan is noted for its **Sinulog,** or "Dance of Death," performed by hilltribesmen carrying pointed knives. Japanese concrete pillboxes overlook the road from a hill at Cabatuan and at both ends of the bridge north of Janiuay.

Janiuay

In Janiuay plaza, the ruins of the old redbrick church destroyed in WW II stand next to a new white church. Janiuay also has an impressive hilltop cemetery, dating from 1875; the chapel and gates of its three stairways are in Gothic style.

The highway continues through Lambunao, near which is Tinagong Dagat Lake, and Calinog, a sugar-growing area, before reaching the Capiz boundary.

BETWEEN NORTH AND EAST

The towns of Pototan and Dingle are situated 11 km apart between the province's northbound and eastbound main highways. **Pototan,** in the heart of a rice-growing area, has a cemetery

(1894) of red and yellow sandstone with a Mexican cross in the center.

Dingle has a yellow sandstone church dating from the 1880s and a cemetery with a neo-Gothic-style chapel. You can swim in natural spring-fed pools at the nearby Moroboro Springs resort.

The **Bulabog-Putian National Park,** between Dingle and San Enrique, is an 8.5-square km area of caverns, springs, and *tisok* (holes formed by percolating water).

EAST OF ILOILO CITY

This route leads to Estancia, from where you can visit idyllic offshore islands before continuing to Roxas City or Masbate Island. The road passes through Barotac Nuevo, a sugar town with a neoclassical church featuring a mixture of Greek and Roman elements. The Santos-Lopez sugar mill is the home of a famous folk music group, the Sanlop Melodiers.

Barotac Viejo is a fishing port and the site of a Good Friday passion play. About 1.5 km offshore from Ajuy are two islands only 150 meters apart. **Nasidman** has a village and beach at its north end. The wild, treeless **Calabasa** has only a lighthouse.

Estancia

Estancia is a major fishing port on the Visayan Sea and the gateway to the cluster of islands off northeast Panay. Stay at **Family Pension House,** P100-150, which also serves meals. Boats cross from Estancia to Masbate, departing for Balud every second day, and Milagros on Tuesday morning.

GUIMARAS

This large island (579 square km) offers beaches, caves, waterfalls, springs, fishing villages, and offshore islets and makes a pleasant side trip from Iloilo. It's also a place of intriguing spiritual happenings. Guimaras is a subprovince of Iloilo and consists of three municipalities: Jordan, Buenavista, and Nueva Valencia.

Separated from Iloilo by the narrow Iloilo Strait, and from Negros by the shallow Guimaras Strait,

the island is an uplifted coral platform, its surface eroded to a rugged, undulating upland. The highest point is Mt. Bontoc (252 meters) in the center. Numerous coral islets lie off the south and southeast coasts and coral reefs line the eastern shores.

The 80,000 inhabitants engage in growing rice, corn, sugarcane, coconuts, cashew nuts, and fruit, especially mangoes; fishing; charcoal-making; and basket-, hat-, and mat-weaving. A cement plant uses local limestone.

Transportation

The ferry to Jordan departs from near Iloilo's post office every 30 minutes 0500-1700 (takes 25 minutes), while boats to Santo Rosario (Buenavista) load near the lighthouse. Guimaras can also be reached directly from Valladolid, Negros. On Guimaras, jeepneys link the Jordan ferry terminal with Nueva Valencia (20 km, takes one hour).

Some continue to Cabalagnan, but none return to Jordan in the afternoon. Jeepneys serve Jordan and San Isidro, while only tricycles go from Jordan to Buenavista (17 km). The roads on Guimaras are almost entirely situated inland, so they rarely provide views of the coast; generally, you must walk to reach the shore.

Jordan

The main town and ferry port is near Bala-an Bukid ("Holy Mountain"), where a 30-minute climb up a stairway from Punta Bundulan, at the foot of the hill, leads to the huge cross and chapel at the top. Enjoy fine views across to Iloilo from here. Jordan is the site of a sugar refinery and bulk-loading sugar and molasses terminal.

Another plant processes mangoes—for which Guimaras is famous—into juice, jams and preserves.

Two km west of Jordan, halfway to Bondulan Point, you can stay at **Guimaras Hotel and Beach Resort,** P150-200. There's a restaurant and disco here as well. Outside the town is the Philippines's only Trappist monastery; the monks, who grow *kalamansis,* don't particularly welcome the intrusion of casual tourists as they adhere to a vow of silence.

Buenavista

From the wharf, a pleasant, five-minute hike leads to the Daliran Spring and Cave, which has stalactites. Douglas MacArthur survived ambush near here when he was a young lieutenant stationed at Camp Jossman; remains of the camp's target range still exist in Tinadtaran, six km from the wharf. The picturesque Siete Pecados ("Seven Sins") Islands, are situated offshore.

You can stay at **Enrico Beach Resort,** P150-200, in Salag Daku.

Nueva Valencia
Catiliran Cave has yielded Ming pottery, a pre-Hispanic shell bracelet, and huge quantities of bat droppings for use as fertilizer. It's the site of the Good Friday *pangalap* ritual. **Alubihod Bay** has a beach with good swimming; it's 1.5 km off the main road, about 10 minutes by jeepney or a 45-minute walk, south of Nueva Valencia. It can also be reached in 30 minutes by hired *banca* from Iloilo City.

Bancas from Alubihod Bay can bring you to the fine beaches of **Tandog Island** and **Igang Point;** the latter is also accessible by road. **Taklong Island,** off Guimaras's southwest tip, also has beaches and offshore coral and is a noted dive site.

Isla Naburot, a tiny green islet with a sandy beach and good snorkeling, has bungalows with cooking facilities for rent. You can swim in a cave here, and fishing equipment is available. It's 40 minutes by *banca* from Iloilo City and day tours are offered for more than US$50 pp, including meals and use of facilities. Return transfers from Iloilo airport to the island cost US$20 for the first person, US$10 for each additional person. Contact PAL's Iloilo office (tel. 033-73-511 or 78-471) for extended stay rates.

You can also stay at **Guimaras Island Resort** in Santo Domingo; contact Lourdes Dellota (Iloilo, tel. 033-74-084) for rates, which include meals.

The road continues around from Nueva Valencia to Cabalagnan, from where a *banca* leaves daily at 0300 or 0400 and stops at several small islands in Guimaras Strait, including Nagarao, before reaching Valladolid (Negros) two hours later. From Cabalagnan, it's a 15-minute walk to Romagangran, where there's a cave and good snorkeling. Numerous small islands lie offshore.

Nagarao Island
From San Isidro, you can cross by *banca* to Nagarao Island, which is also accessible from Negros. A small resort here offers cottages that may include full board and use of facilities; activities include sailing and scuba diving. Ask, too, about the limited budget accommodations.

Those coming from Iloilo should inquire at the **Casa Plaza Hotel** for a reservation; they can also arrange a transfer from Iloilo (takes three hours). Meals are relatively expensive (breakfast P75, lunch or dinner P150), but it's also possible to arrange cheaper meals with local families on the island. The resort's *banca* is used for the crossing to San Isidro (around P100) and can also be hired for trips to the surrounding islands.

There are also accommodations at **Nagarao Island Resort,** where rooms are P1,500-1,700 including meals. For further information, check with the Nagarao Island Office at 113 Seminario St., Jaro, in Iloilo.

Good Friday on Guimaras
Ang Pagtaltal, a Visayan version of the passion play, is held at Jordan. It climaxes in a one-km-long procession of devotees in biblical attire, accompanied by flagellantes performing penance, and depicts the journey of Christ to Calvary as it winds up nearby Bala-an Bukid ("Holy Mountain") to the large white cross at the summit.

Also on Good Friday, the *pangalap* ritual occurs in Catiliran Cave in Nueva Valencia. Hundreds of believers crawl through the 500-meter cave, chanting Latin prayers, in order to gain supernatural powers, especially protection from evil spirits.

ISLANDS OFF NORTHEAST PANAY

Over 100 small islands are situated off northeast Panay, of which the best known is Sicogon. They offer white-sand beaches, hills covered with virgin forest, simple fishing villages, and rich marinelife.

Sicogon
This beautiful 11-square km island, with its palm-fringed white-sand beaches and clear water, is the former site of the Sicogon Island Club resort, which closed down several years ago. Sicogon's

lush, forested hills contain monkeys, wild pigs, and birds; its surrounding sea has many fish and lobsters. Springs provide abundant fresh water.

The view from its highest point, Mt. Bantili (335 meters), is spectacular. Nearby are the lovely islet of Tumaguin, and Molupulo or Seagull's Point, the haunt of thousands of seabirds. Sicogon is a 30-minute *banca* ride from Estancia. The fishing village of San Fernando is at the island's northwestern trip.

Gigante Norte and Gigante Sur

These rugged islands, reached by *banca* from Estancia or Sicogon, contain many caves where 15th-century coffins have been found and that are also believed to be former pirates' lairs. They're the subject of many strange tales.

On Gigante Norte, Langub Cave is near Piaoa, around which there's a beautiful shoreline and good snorkeling. Gigante Sur has an only partly explored labyrinth that includes Turtle Cave, locally called Pawikan, which has a huge entrance chamber, and Elephante and Tiniphagan Caves. To visit them, seek a guide in Langangan. Wear good shoes and take a flashlight.

There's a natural swimming hole near the caves, and you'll see monkeys in this area. South of Gigante Sur are the Cabugao Islands, each of which has a small village. Cabugao Norte has a small cave and a good bay for swimming, and Cabugao Sur has a nice beach. You'll have to arrange private accommodations on these islands; give your hosts a fair price.

Other Islands

Islands with fine sandy beaches include Balbagon, a flat island near Gigantes Sur; the hilly 22-square km Calagnaan; the small, palm-ringed Isla de Cana; Pan de Azucar off the town of Concepcion (16 square km); Agho, which is noted for shells; Igbon; and Tagubanhan (14 square km).

SAN JOSE DE BUENAVISTA

The provincial capital, 97 km from Iloilo City, is a gateway to the Cuyo Islands and Palawan. It's a small, quiet town noted for its Binirayan festival. When there, check out the cathedral, which has attractive stained-glass windows; the market;

and nearby beaches such as Madrangca, just north of town, Taringting, beyond Madrangca, and Maybato to the south. The Ancores handicrafts factory and San Pedro Cooperatives Handicrafts are places to buy local products, especially bamboo articles.

Binirayan Festival

This exuberant festival is held 27-30 December. Legend holds that the landing of the 10 Bornean *datus* in 1212, the barter of Panay, and founding of the first Malay settlement in Malandog, were followed by a riotous party. This event is reenacted with traditional costumes and decorated boats on the beaches of Malandog (Hamtik). Some participants dress as *datus,* their wives and retinue, while others blacken their faces like the aboriginal Atis.

The event begins at Maybato (San Jose) with the *panguyang,* a ritual in which the *"datus"* pray for a safe crossing. *Budyongs* (giant shells used as trumpets) announce the boarding, and after the picturesque parade of boats, the landing at Malandog, where the *panguyang* again takes place, this time as thanksgiving for a safe voyage. Here, the *"datus"* are met by the "Atis," and the barter and celebration are acted out.

For four days, dancing and revelry fill the streets of San Jose. Real Atis may even come down from the hills to participate. An agro-industrial fair, beauty pageant, and other events are also held.

Accommodations and Food

Stay at **Susana Guest House,** P150 pp; **Autajay Beach Resort,** P300 per cottage; **G&G Lodge,** P150 pp; or **Annavic Plaza Hotel,** P250 s, a/c P300 d, a/c suite P500. A tricycle to Annavic Plaza Hotel costs around P2 pp. San Jose has a **homestay** program; if you wish to have a listing of families included in the program, contact the Antique Homestay Association, c/o its president Mrs. Reylena E. Rodriguez at Cerdena Street. Eat at the **G&G Lodge,** where there is a restaurant, or at the **San Jose Cafe,** near the 76 Lines bus station. The market area, near G&G Lodge, also has plenty of food stalls.

Transportation

To Palawan: Check ferry schedules leaving San Jose for Cuyo, Araceli (Dumaran Island), Roxas

(Palawan), and Puerto Princesa (usually every second Monday), as this is often disrupted and the ferry frequently runs a day or more late. Fortunately, cargo/passenger launches also link San Jose with Palawan about twice a week. It's sometimes necessary to change boats at Cuyo. These crossings are slower than the ferry but allow more time in small island communities.

It takes 28 hours from Manila to Puerto Princesa, Palawan, via Cuyo. If you're on Boracay, it's difficult to get information on which Monday the ferry will leave San Jose unless you happen to meet a traveler who has just arrived from Palawan. It's best just to go to San Jose when you're ready, and if the ferry isn't about to leave, look for a cargo/passenger launch crossing to Cuyo or the Palawan mainland. Check the wharf each day for signs of departure.

By Bus: Buses leave San Jose hourly for Iloilo City (two and a half hours). Buses and jeepneys go up the coast from San Jose; some buses go through to Kalibo. At Pandan, the road branches to Libertad/Malay and to Nabas/Kalibo. For Boracay, it's quicker to cut across to Nabas rather than follow the coast around; wait at the junction south of Nabas for a Kalibo-Caticlan vehicle.

INLAND FROM SAN JOSE

For a pleasant day trip from San Jose, follow the Sibalom Valley into the mountains. Two km beyond Sibalom (fiesta: 22 May) is the Polytechnic State College of Antique, noted for ceramics. The nearby Sibalom Dam irrigates the surrounding ricefields. San Remigio is a mountain town (pop. 9,500) 22 km (45 minutes by jeepney) from San Jose.

The attractions here are scenic. A trail leads two km from town to the red-tinted Pula Waterfalls; Bato Cueva, a hilltop cave near the forest nursery in La Union, provides a sweeping panorama.

THE SOUTHWEST TIP

The old settlement of Hamtik is seven km south of San Jose. Sights here include the marker indicating the landing site of the Bornean *datus* in

1212, now in the grounds of the Malandog Elementary School; the town cemetery's chapel; and the Santo Niño Church. Five km south of Hamtik, the main highway cuts inland toward Iloilo.

Telegrafo Hill, at the provincial boundary, was a WW II Japanese stronghold and offers a commanding view of the surroundings. Another road follows the coast, looping round the southwest tip to rejoin the main highway west of San Joaquin (Iloilo). It passes through Tobias Fornier (formerly Dao), two km south of which is Taguimtim Beach and its nearby hilltop shrine.

Anini-y

This town, 40 km south of San Jose, has a fine white coral church (1875) and an old cemetery. Nogas Island (26 hectares), five km offshore, has a lighthouse, white-sand beach, and good coral. This uninhabited naval reservation is open to visitors and is a 20-minute crossing by hired *banca*. During the dry season, boats carry supplies from Anini-y to Cagayan Island, seven hours out in the Sulu Sea. Homestay types of accommodations, at reasonable rates, are available in Anini-y.

To Iloilo

In Sitio Dapog, Nato, 1.5 km east of Anini-y, the municipal government has constructed some nipa cottages at Sira-an Hot Spring, whose warm, sulfurous water flows into a basin big enough for two people. A swimming pool has been constructed here to accommodate the growing number of visitors.

Beyond Nato is San Roque, where Hurao-Hurao Island, accessible by wading at low tide, is a popular picnic spot. Farther along the road at Iba is Cresta de Gallo, a rocky outcrop resembling a cock's comb. Called Punta Nasog by locals, it has the scenic Rendon and Bantigue beaches at its base. Buses linking Anini-y with Iloilo City use this road.

NORTH OF SAN JOSE DE BUENAVISTA

The highway north follows the coast to Libertad and Aklan Province. The first town is Belison, noted for *salakot* and *sawali* handicrafts. Patnongon has old church ruins. Just south of Buga song, a road goes inland for 10 km, through Bagtason, where *patadyong* (plaid cotton skirts) are woven, to Valderrama, site of a reforestation project.

In the center of Bugasong is Estaca Hill (60 meters), where you can enjoy a fine view. Barbaza has a modern Catholic church. Snorkelers can hire a *banca* to go a kilometer offshore to the Batabat Coral Reef, and to Punta Coral. In Mablad, eight km from town, are Macalbag Falls and many caves.

North of Barbaza, a road turns inland to Capuywan. From here, it's a five-km walk to Cadiao, where there's a cool resort and Lolita Falls. Five km north of Tibiao, in Tiguis, is Manglamon Beach and Cave.

Culasi

This town, 91 km north of San Jose, is a gateway to some offshore islands. Three km northeast of town is the Kipot Falls in Buenavista. To the north is Lipata Bay, where U.S. submarines landed in 1944 to supply local guerrillas. A large *banca* departs every Sunday for San Jose (Mindoro), but be careful of bad weather as it can be a difficult crossing.

Offshore Islands

A *banca* crosses daily (takes 30 minutes) from Culasi to Mararison Island, four km offshore, which has a white-sand beach and caves, and is ringed by coral. Eight km beyond Mararison is Batbatan Island, which offers white-sand beaches, coves, and fine snorkeling. It's inhabited by the Tangays, a cultural minority who speak a distinct dialect. Farther east is Maniguin Island, a naval reservation with a clifftop lighthouse.

Madja-as Mountain

Inland from Culasi is cloud-shrouded Madja-as Mountain (2,117 meters), formerly an active volcano, which has lakes, waterfalls, and rare orchids in its rainforest. The mountain is the legendary home of Bulalakaw, supreme god of the ancient dwellers known as Orang Madja-as.

Penitents make the difficult ascent during Holy Week. Following a long trek to the foot of the mountain, climbers must cross narrow wood and bamboo bridges, clambering up steep slopes. Take precautions against leeches and be prepared for heavy rain.

North of Culasi

Sebaste (fiesta: 2 February) is the site of the Church of St. Blaise, an object of pilgrimage due to miracles attributed to the saint. Bugtong Bukid, 500 meters from town, is a hill topped by a resthouse from which there's a fine view. Three km inland, you'll find a natural swimming pool below Igpasungaw Falls. From Abiera, south of Sebaste, a seven-km trail leads to the beautiful 30-meter Kalamasag Falls.

Sebaste is famous for *mawik,* a native crab delicacy known as *curacha* in southern Philippines. Pandan is 126 km north of San Jose and three km south of where the road forks to Libertad and Kalibo.

Malumpati Health Spring, seven km from Pandan, is a small, cold lake believed to have medicinal qualities. The road to Libertad passes through San Roque, where marble is quarried. An old eight-meter-high Spanish watchtower stands on Osmeña Street. Enjoy a fine view of Libertad from Liberty Park on nearby Mt. Agongon.

You can swim at Idiayan Beach Resort, one km from the town center, and Kaniang Resort, in Cubay, seven km out. The Sunken Garden is a 500-square-meter coral garden off Punta Pucio, nine km from Libertad.

SEMIRARA ISLANDS

This picturesque island group between Mindoro and Panay consists of three large islands—Semirara, Caluya, and Sibay—plus seven smaller ones. Their surrounding waters offer a profusion of underwater life ranging from superb gorgonians and rare shells to sharks; currents can be hazardous. Coal mining is the main activity on Semirara Island (56 square km), which is also noted for birdlife.

Parts of the seabed south of Semirara are nicknamed the "Underwater Cemetery," turned into a wasteland by dynamite fishing. **Caluya** (25 square km) is the island visible on the horizon from White Beach, Boracay. Caluya also has white-sand beaches. The town of Caluya is the main settlement of the Semirara group. Coconut crabs, known locally as *tatus,* are plentiful here.

The Spanish conquistador Martin de Goiti stopped at Sibay on his way north to conquer Manila in 1570.

Transportation

The Semirara Islands can be reached from Panay or Mindoro. A boat sails to Caluya from Culasi, and boats also cross from Libertad. Boats cross from Bulalacao (Mindoro) to Semirara (two and a half hours) twice a week. These islands offer off-the-beaten-track travel at its best.

ROXAS CITY

The provincial capital (pop. 80,000) is a rice-trading city and commercial center at the mouth of the 80-km Panay River. Fishing, poultry-raising, and handicrafts are also significant activities. Roxas, also formerly called Capiz, has been renamed after native son Manuel Roxas, who was president 1946-48. The house where he was born in 1892 is a national shrine; it's just beyond the post office.

Roxas Airport is at Baybay, four km from town, while its harbor is at Culasi, a few kilometers from the city center. The rail and bus terminals are downtown. Ruined watchtowers at the junction of the roads to Culasi and the airport, and on a hill overlooking the sea, attest to former problems with Moro raiders.

Accommodations

Stay at the slightly run-down **Beehive Inn,** with rooms P60-75 s/d and P275 a/c; the **Halaran House,** P150-200 (both are on Roxas St.); **River Inn,** on Lapu Lapu St., P100-150, good value; **Marc's Beach Resort,** P150 d, P200 family, and a/c P250, at Baybay Beach, two km from the city; **Villa Patria,** P350-400, Baybay Beach. **Halaran Plaza Hotel** on Rizal Street opposite city hall has rooms from P150 with fan to P250 a/c (Tabok).

The **Halaran Plaza Hotel** restaurant is the best downtown. **Real Kitchenette** has live folk music at night. **John's Fast Foods** on Roxas Street is pretty good, and **Halaran House Restaurant** serves a good set meal.

Transportation

PAL flies to Manila daily (takes 50 minutes).

Ships sail from Roxas to Cebu City; Palompon, Leyte; Milagros, Masbate; and Romblon at least once a week, and to Manila more frequently. See Transportation at the beginning of the Panay section for more information.

Express buses make 12 trips to Iloilo each day (about two and a half hours), while regular buses and minibuses link Roxas with Kalibo (three hours) and Estancia. R&K Transit and Nandwani's Tourist Transport (a/c) ply the route between Iloilo and Roxas City taking four hours.

Festivals

The **Halaran Festival,** first weekend of October, features Mardi Gras-type festivities based on the purchase of Panay, combined with harvest thanksgiving rites. Halaran is an adaptation of the Hiligaynon word *halad* (gift), which the Bornean *datus* gave to the Atis as goodwill tokens for the purchase of their lowlands.

For the Capizenos, it's a time of feasting, drinking, and a "tribal" parade with street dancing to drumbeats. On 8 December, the Feast of Our Lady of the Immaculate Conception, the city's patroness, is celebrated in Roxas with evening processions, cultural presentations, and beauty pageants.

VICINITY OF ROXAS CITY

Beaches

Baybay Beach is two km from the city; accommodation is available here (see above). Bontod Beach, Pan-ay, is three km of black sand located eight km east of Roxas. **Napti Island,** 20 minutes by *banca* from Roxas, and the larger Olutaya Island, 40 minutes out, have fine beaches and coral reefs, with good snorkeling.

Uninhabited Napti is flat and grassy, its shoreline rocky on one side, sandy on the other; it has a 100-meter-long cave with stalagmites and stalactites and is noted for giant lobsters. The beautiful **Ivisan Coves,** with their fine beaches and swimming, are southwest of Roxas and about 10 km from Ivisan in the *barangays* of Basiao (four coves) and Balaring.

Pan-ay

This town, five km southeast of Roxas, was settled by the Spanish in 1569. The 80-meter-long church has a marble floor and three-meter-thick walls of white coral. Its simple facade belies the ornate interior whose altars have elaborately carved *retablos* of silver and hardwood.

The five-story belfry contains a huge bell, said to be the largest in the country. Over two meters in diameter and weighing 10,400 kilograms, it was made from 76 sacks of coins collected from the townspeople in the 18th century.

The cemetery, 350 meters outside the town, has a surrounding circular wall with wrought-iron gates and a simple chapel built of coral. The **Archdiocesan Museum,** made up largely of liturgical artifacts and considered the best in the province, is located at the church convent of Santa Monica.

THE COAST OF CAPIZ

Sapian Bay is beyond Ivisan, on the road from Roxas to Kalibo. From Sitio Angkin in Sapian municipality, you can travel by *banca* down the Sapian River and out to a 20-hectare mussel farm offshore. Thousands of neatly spaced bamboo poles, to each of which cling hundreds of mussels, make a visually impressive sight.

Pilar
Traveling in the other direction, the eastbound road from Roxas to Estancia passes through Pilar. A rough road leads 1.5 km from the town to the hillside Pilar Caves, whose six entrances lead to interconnected chambers where incised earthen pots have been discovered, indicating that it was a pre-Hispanic burial site. Filipino rebels had an artillery battery here during the revolution; a cannon from it now sits outside Pilar town hall. The nearby fishing village of Casanayan, on a three-km gray-sand beach, contains a strange phenomenon—the exhumed, naturally mummified corpse of a woman who died in 1929.

The making of *patis* (fish sauce) is a home industry here. *Bancas* can be hired at Pilar for the 10-km trip out to Tucad Reef, whose four hectares of colorful corals are exposed at low tide.

INTERIOR CAPIZ

Capiz's interior hills are dotted with caves. **Igang Cave,** in Tapulang, seven km from Ma-ayon, consists of limestone chambers and passages with stalagmites and stalactites. Townspeople gather guano for fertilizer here. Several entrances, at different levels in the hillside, all lead to a large central chamber. Hire a guide and take a bright light.

Mambusao
Quipot Cave is nine km from the old town of Mambusao, on the highway from Iloilo to Kalibo. Starting from the Panay State Polytechnic College campus, a three-km hike up a hillside rich in wildlife leads to the multichambered cave, the biggest nicknamed the Quipot Hilton. Ask someone at the mayor's office in Mambusao to find you a guide.

Dumalag
Dumalag is on the Panay River and the main highway from Iloilo to Roxas and Kalibo. The church (1872) here has thick yellow sandstone walls and a five-story belfry. One km from the town plaza, on opposite sides of the highway, are two coral-walled 19th-century cemeteries, one circular, the other rectangular and disused. The multichambered Suhot Cave is two km from the town and 300 meters off the highway. This site has a natural bridge, and you can swim in the cool river inside the cave or in the swimming hole that it feeds outside the cave's entrance.

On the other side of the same hill, but higher, is Badiang Cave, site of a prewar phosphate mine. Near its mouth are a stream and a sulfurous spring. Cuartero is the next town north of Dumalag, and one km away is the picturesque manmade Agpayao Lake.

The Mundos
In the forested hills west of Tapaz dwell the Mundos, a tiny minority tribe of Indonesian ancestry. They still reproduce ancient Indonesian designs and mythological figures on their ornately carved sword handles and sheaths. The spear, sword, and shield are featured in their social and religious rituals.

Some Mundo weapons can be seen in the Museo Iloilo. The Mundos have a reputation for fighting to the death. They're also noted for the *sinulog*, a dance based on traditional fertility rites, in which the male imitates the erotic body movements of a rooster while the female assumes the languid posture of a hen, to the accompaniment of animal-skin drums and brass gongs.

A public performance of this must be planned weeks in advance, since dancers have to be enticed out of the forest with gifts. The *sinulog* has been adopted by other Visayan communities; Cebu City and Ilog (Negros) hold Sinulog festivals.

KALIBO

Kalibo is the provincial capital (pop. 52,000) and oldest town in Aklan. Sleepy Kalibo comes to life in January, when the Kalibonhons play host to thousands of visitors who descend on them for the Philippines's greatest party, the Ati-Atihan Festival. For the rest of the year, Kalibo has little to detain the traveler.

Attractions
The **Museo It Aklan** displays historical articles and contemporary art, and Busuang Beach is just outside the town.

Accommodations
Gervy's Lodge: Simple but acceptable place in the center of town, one block east of Pastrana Park. Pastrana St., tel. (036) 662-1166, P100-200.

Garcia Legaspi Mansion: Clean midlevel hotel on the main road to Boracay. Roxas Ave., tel. (036) 662-3251, P350-950.

Hibiscus Hotel: Best in town with small pool, café, and landscape gardens some 15 minutes east of city center. 5600 Andagao St., tel. (036) 268-4093, P900-1,400.

Restaurants
Kalibo has some okay restaurants near the plaza. Try the popular **Bistro Kalibo**, S. Martelino Street, on the plaza, where there's good Chinese food and Filipino dishes. Also the **Peking House Restaurant** on 19 Martyrs Street is good, but the restaurant at the **Glowmoon Hotel** is better. Another good restaurant, bar, and entertainment spot is **Dreamland** on 19 Martyrs Street.

ATI-ATIHAN FESTIVAL OF KALIBO

Held on the second week of January, this festival is a mixture of pagan and Christian elements and has its origin in diverse events. Legend holds that after the Bornean *datus* had bartered with the Atis for the lowlands of Panay, they threw a feast at which they blackened their faces with soot to show their oneness with the natives by more closely resembling the Negrito skin color.

Ati-Atihan literally means "To Make Like an Ati." It's claimed that the Atis subsequently came down from the hills at the time of each annual harvest to renew the bond. Centuries later, a miraculous appearance of the Santo Niño, Kalibo's patron saint, is said to have saved the town from Moro marauders. The Spanish friars combined the Ati-Atihan and local harvest rites with the Feast of the Santo Niño into a festival that's now over 300 years old.

Anticipation mounts all through the preceding week, and tension reaches fever-pitch by the time the festival begins on Friday. Three days of parades climax in the main procession on Sunday afternoon that ends at the church. Members of local *barangays* and organizations form "tribes," each with its own striking costume, homemade from local materials, and participants blacken their faces and imitate the Atis.

The Mardi Gras-like atmosphere is a swirl of riotous color, steady drinking, shuffling dancing, reverberating drumbeats, and cries of *"hala, bira!"* Many travelers join in the uninhibited dancing and also get into costume or paint their faces.

Practicalities
The most desirable places to stay are those with balconies overlooking the plaza, where much of the action takes place. Hotel prices increase dramatically (perhaps tenfold) during the festival. Most accommodation is booked far in advance. To be sure of accommodation, write the **Kalibo Ati-Atihan Homestay Association,** c/o KAMB, Municipal Tourism Office, Kalibo, Aklan. (Daily rates during the festival are P450-500 pp.) Another possibility is to go to Kalibo a couple of weeks before Ati-Atihan, make a reservation for the final Friday, Saturday, and Sunday of the festival (pay in advance and get a receipt), then go off to Boracay or Iloilo City and return to enjoy the festivities. Manila and Cebu City newspapers contain advertisements for special Ati-Atihan excursions by ship, and roundtrip passengers can sleep onboard while the vessel's docked.

Transportation

By Air: PAL flies Manila-Kalibo thrice daily (80 minutes). The Kalibo-Cebu connection flies four times a week (55 minutes).

By Ship: Ports near Kalibo are served by several shipping lines. See Transportation at the beginning of the Panay section for more details. Travel time to Manila by sea is approximately 18 hours, to Cebu 14 hours, Palawan 15 hours, and the rest more than 24 hours.

Pumpboats also connect Aklan to Romblon and Mindoro through Caticlan, Boracay, Malay, and Buruanga.

Ships bound for Iloilo leave Manila more regularly, and you can bus it from Iloilo to Kalibo in half a day.

By Bus: Ceres Liner buses go regularly to Iloilo City (four hours), and Obuyes Lines buses ply the Kalibo-Roxas City route (two and a half hours). Some buses go to San Jose de Buenavista via Pandan (Antique). Tricycles serve commuters within Kalibo and other bigger towns while jeepneys travel to other municipalities.

Along with modern transportation to Boracay, good old Third World buses with wooden seats ply the route to Caticlan (where *bancas* leave for Boracay) as well for one-third the price.

SOUTH OF KALIBO

New Washington

Two roads lead south out of Kalibo, one to Iloilo, the other along the coast to the ports of Dumaguit and New Washington. The latter, a fishing town at the midpoint of a 14-km beach, is the site of the **Aklan School of Fisheries.** At the southeast end is a lighthouse near which you can swim at Floripon Point Beach Resort.

Banga

The main highway passes through Banga, eight km south of Kalibo. Banga was founded by pioneers in 1793 and has an attractive plaza. A visit to the **Aklan Agricultural College** near Banga is worthwhile if you're interested. Its ricefields, pastureland, and plantations of fruit trees such as durian, mangosteen, rambutan, and *lanzones* are part of ongoing experimental projects. Within the campus, Manduyog Hill (150

meters), named after a 15th-century *datu,* was once used as a lookout for Moro pirates and now has Stations of the Cross and a chapel at the summit.

Libacao

A road runs south from Banga to Libacao, where the 15-meter Manimpa Falls in Can-awan has several good basins for swimming.

Batan

The main highway leads from Banga to Altavas, where a road branches north to the port of Batan. Batan was an early Spanish settlement and is the site of the **Kalantiaw (Calantiao) National Shrine** (open daily 0800-1700), named after Datu Kalantiaw, who instituted a legal code here in 1433. The shrine houses the province's historical mementos and antiques, including the original manuscript of the code, which the Spaniards obtained from an old chief and translated.

Kapis shells are gathered around Batan, which has a five-km beach with offshore coral.

NORTHWEST OF KALIBO

Buses and jeepneys serve the routes to Caticlan (for Boracay) and to Pandan (Antique). A modern a/c van, the *Boracay Express,* meets the planes from Manila and Cebu and departs from the Kalibo Airport for Caticlan (and the ferry to Boracay).

Just west of Kalibo is Numancia. Its beaches (Camanci and Navitas) are popular weekend spots for the people of Kalibo. A road leads south from Numancia, up the Aklan River Valley, through the pottery-making town of Lezo to Malinao, near which are Mampahon Falls in Tigpalas and Fatima Hill in Bulabod, where steps lead past 14 Stations of the Cross to a marble chapel.

The main road continues west to the old town of Tangalan, site of one of the most beautiful spots between Boracay and Kalibo, the seven-tiered Jawili Falls, with basins for swimming at each wooded tier. Nearby is Agfa Beach and Campo Verde, a reforestation area.

After Tangalan comes Ibajay, a small town that claims to have held the original Ati-Atihan fiesta. It holds its own smaller festival, also in January.

Points of interest around Nabas, the next town, include the multichambered Tulingon Cave, which has an entrance in Libertad and stretches 20 km across to Patria near Pandan, Antique.

Also of note is Laserna, for the weaving of pandanus hats and mats, and site of Basanga Cave, which has two basins where you can swim. The road divides just south of Nabas, with branches going to Pandan, and to Caticlan, Malay, and Buruanga.

ROMBLON AND TABLAS ISLANDS

Romblon (the name of a province, an island, and a town) offers beaches, snorkeling, and hiking amid beautiful landscapes and seascapes. Among Filipinos, it's famous for marble. This mountainous province is fragmented into about 20 islands, with Romblon, Tablas, and Sibuyan as the main islands. Situated southeast of Mindoro, Romblon is growing in popularity as a pleasant stopover between Puerto Galera and Boracay. Romblon, the smallest of the three main islands, contains the provincial capital, and it's near here that beach resorts have sprung up.

HISTORY

Romblon's strategic position made it an important way station on the sailing lanes between Manila and the Visayas. The Spaniards visited Romblon as early as 1582. Recollect missionaries came in 1635. The ruins of Spanish watchtowers and forts testify to the islands' former vulnerability to the raids of slave-seeking Moro pirates. Dutch warships also attacked the islands during the early Spanish era. In 1853, Romblon was made a politico-military *comandancia*. It was linked to Capiz prior to becoming a separate province.

TRANSPORTATION

PAL flies from Manila to Tugdan airport, Tablas (65 minutes) on Tuesday, Thursday, and Saturday. Jeepneys provide transport to and from the west coast of Tablas and up to San Agustin, where ferries link it to Romblon town.

Several lines sail Manila-Romblon town every week. Many ships stop in Odiongan to pick up Manila-bound passengers as part of circular trips. Pumpboats ply between Roxas and Looc

twice a week and between Roxas and Odiongan four times a week.

Pumpboats are the means of transport from island to island, while jeepneys and tricycles link settlements on the major islands. From Romblon, pumpboats go to Sibuyan and Maghali Islands. A mailboat goes from Romblon to Banton Island on Tuesday and Friday, while another boat sails San Agustin (Tablas) to Banton Wednesday and Saturday. From Banton, there's a twice-weekly service to Concepcion on Maestre de Campo Island, from where daily *bancas* cross to Pinamalayan, Mindoro. Ask at Romblon wharf about boats to Corcuera on Simara Island.

ROMBLON

Centrally located in the group, Romblon Island (82 square km) is hilly, rising to 444 meters in the south. Romblon town, the provincial capital (pop. about 30,000), has one of the safest natural harbors in the Philippines. When typhoons pass, it serves as a haven for ships crossing the busy Sibuyan Sea. The town is a quaint mixture of colonial-style architecture and nipa-roofed houses, surrounded by steep bluffs.

Attractions

The cathedral (1726) has a fine interior with a Byzantine altar, stained-glass windows, and old icons, paintings, and other antiquities. The town center also contains a lively market, where *tuba* drinking is a cheap and popular social occasion in the afternoon, and many workshops and stores sell marble handicrafts.

The hilltop Fort San Andres, reached by 250 steps, affords a panoramic view of the town and surroundings. Built in 1640 by a Spanish friar known as Padre Capitan as a watchtower against pirates, it's now a navigational station

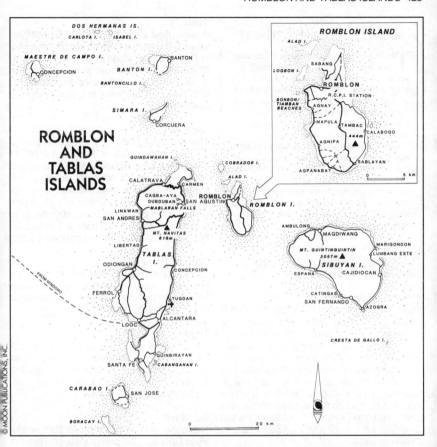

for the Weather Bureau. Fort Santiago also overlooks the town. A road leads 3.5 km north to the lighthouse at Sabang.

Accommodations

Stay at **Kawilihan Mansion House** (dormitory, eight persons to a room); **Seaside Hotel,** overlooking the harbor; or **Feast Inn,** recommended. Room prices range P150-200, depending on the season. The Feast Inn, behind the market, is also a good place to eat. For an extended sojourn, consider staying at one of the beaches a short distance down the west coast. The best beaches in the area are Bonbon and Tiamban, situated on two sides of a point about five km from town. At **Tiamban Beach Cottages** (P200) food is prepared at reasonable prices.

The **Tree House in Agnay,** eight km outside town (inquire at the **Feast Inn**), comprises two adjacent and spacious tree houses. This is one of the most unusual accommodations in the Philippines, and is a good value for a whole house with real privacy, a rare commodity in the Philippines. The friendly caretakers at the beach will prepare food.

The **Tumanon Inn** at Mapula, 1.5 km farther around the same bay, is an eminently social place. Rooms are small and simple-good value, including three tasty meals plus *meriendas.* It's a great place to watch the sun set behind Tablas.

MARBLE? IN THE PHILIPPINES?

The Philippines is the only country in Southeast Asia with commercially viable marble deposits, and most of these are in Romblon, hence its description as "Marble Island." Marble is found on Romblon, Alad, and Cobrador Islands, and at the north end of Tablas. The quarries have been worked since the 18th century, and the marble industry is a major source of employment.

Handicraft stalls selling marble items (marble eggs and chess sets make agreeable gifts) are found near the wharf, while cutters and sculptors are also seen in the town streets and villages. Even the roads are paved with marble chunks in places. Romblon marble is also shipped to other islands for use in gravestones, monuments, and construction.

Tricycles from the town center bring people to Tiamban, Agnay, and Mapula.

Around Romblon Island

Making the 42-km circuit of the island by road is an enjoyable day-trip. Be prepared to hike some distance unless you hire a tricycle for the trip. Start walking early from Romblon or the beach area, and take tricycles as far as they're going. The road passes a lighthouse at Agpanabat on the southwestern tip, and there are many marble workshops in the villages. Transport is scarce from Agnipa through Sablayan where the road climbs inland to Tambac. Here it descends to a level farming area. Finding transport back to town is no problem.

TABLAS

Scenic Tablas (686 square km) is the largest of the province's three major islands. Structurally, it's a long tilted block with its high edge near the east coast. The central range of 500- to 600-meter mountains runs almost its entire 64-km length, flanked by low hills and rolling plains on the western side and a narrow alluvial coastal plain on the east. The main roads follow the coast, where most settlements are located. Cross-island roads are few. Pumpboats coming up from Boracay or Caticlan (Panay) arrive at Santa Fe or Looc after passing close to Carabao Island.

Santa Fe

A minor road leads seven km to Guinbirayan where Cabangahan Island is just offshore. Stay at **Dolly's Place, White House,** or **Tourist Inn** (P150-200). The main road goes from Santa Fe to the T-junction with the Looc-Alcantara road; both towns are a 45-minute jeepney ride from Santa Fe.

Looc

This is a fishing port on a large bay. Stay at **Tirol's Lodging House, Plaza Inn** (P50), or **Tablas Pension House** (P150). Pumpboats cross from Looc to Mindoro, Boracay, and Panay. The trip to Boracay and Malay by pumpboat depends on the number of passengers waiting at the pier. From Looc, jeepneys go to Odiongan and up the east coast to San Agustin. For flights to Manila, PAL has an office in Looc.

Boats to Boracay

There are boats that sail from the airport at Looc to Boracay, at a cost of P80 pp. You can charter a boat from here for P300-400. The trip takes two-three hours.

Tugdan

The provincial airport is located here, north of Alcantara. Stay at **Montecarlo Lodging House** (P150). Transport from Odiongan, Looc, and Romblon town via San Agustin connects with the flights to and from Manila.

Odiongan

The road from Looc cuts inland for the one-hour trip to Odiongan, the province's largest town as well as main port, with connections to Mindoro, Manila, and Masbate. The pier is about three km from the town center. Stay at **Shelbourne Hotel, Fernandez Hotel, Cabrera Lodging House, Gabay's,** or **Haali Beach,** all ranging P150-200.

Odiongan to San Agustin

The last jeepney trip (takes two hours) is at about 1400. **Noche Resort** (P250) is near Libertad, which has a cave with an underground river. At Linawan, north of San Andres, a road leads 3.5 km inland to Mablaran Falls, where you can swim surrounded by towering trees. You can stay at **Traveller's Inn Dormitory** for P55 nearby.

About three km from Calatrava, close to the shore in Kabibitan, are two small lakes, about 80 and 100 meters across respectively, known as Tinagong Dagat ("Hidden Sea"). Hire a *banca* to reach this secluded spot. East of Calatrava, the main road winds across the mountains, making a beautiful descent to the coast. A side road leads to the port of Carmen, on a scenic bay.

San Agustin

Bancas depart Romblon town for San Agustin (Tablas) daily at 0700 and 1300, and make the return trip at 0800 and 1300. Excursions from San Agustin include Bitu Falls near Dubduban (three km), Busai Falls (2.5 km), and Cagba-aya ruins (1.5 km), located in a coconut plantation. From San Agustin, jeepneys go to Odiongan and follow the east coast road to Tugdan, Alcantara, and Looc. In San Agustin, stay at **Madali Lodge House** or **Steve Montessa Lodging House** (P150).

SIBUYAN

Sibuyan (449 square km) is a thickly forested volcanic mountain mass, with a fairly flat terrain. Its center is dominated by Mt. Guintinguintin (2,057 meters), also called Mt. Sibuyan, which rises almost directly from the sea and is the subject of many local myths. Sibuyan is wilder and less developed than Romblon and Tablas. Its forests, some of which are still unexplored, are rich in wildlife and plant species-a world of orchids, ferns, and waterfalls. The inhabitants are engaged in logging, cattle-raising, fishing, and weaving the abundant *nito* vine. They have a reputation for witchcraft.

Boats to Magdiwang dock at Ambulong, less than three km out of town. You can stay at the **Beach House** (P100). Nearby are Cataga and Lambingan Falls. From here, it's possible to make the 93-km circuit of the island by jeepney. Following the north shore to Marigondon, a road branches inland to Lumbang Este, where the three-tiered Kawa-Kawa Waterfall has hollowed out beautiful kettle-shaped pools in the rock. The road loops back to the coast north of Cajidiocan, Sibuyan's largest town and commercial center. San Fernando is a logging town. Catingas Falls are nearby; you can swim in the river.

Cresta de Gallo Island

This sparsely vegetated island, accessible from San Fernando, is known for its outstanding coral. The island's northern tip forms a sandspit. Nearby are Aubarede and Romero reefs. The seabed slopes away from the island and the entire area features broad coral patches and mounds. Fish are plentiful, including schools of small jacks.

OTHER ISLANDS

Simara and Banton

Simara (21 square km), whose main town is Corcuera, can be reached by mailboat from Romblon, as can Banton (28 square km), an island of great archaeological significance.

Early inhabitants practiced secondary burial, placing the bones of the dead in small coffins of hollowed hardwood logs that were left in caves. The **Banton Coffin Burial Cave** was discovered behind an entrance sealed with rocks and yielded 17 coffins dating from the 14th-15th centuries, skulls, two burial jars, and pieces of tradeware from China and Siam. The "Hanging Cemetery" is near a cliff a short distance from Banton town. Pirates frequently raided the island before and during the Spanish era. The Spanish friar known as Padre Capitan fortified the island using local coral and limestone, but little now remains of the fortifications.

Each Holy Week, Banton is the site of a pilgrimage, during which an intensely religious atmosphere is created by the burning candles and chanted psalms.

An interesting possibility is to travel from Romblon to Mindoro via Banton and Maestre de Campo Island (20 square km), whose main town, Concepcion, has daily boats to Pinamalayan.

Dos Hermanas

Although part of Romblon Province, the Dos Hermanas Islands ("Two Sisters," Carlota and Isabel) are only an hour's *banca* ride from Pingan on Marinduque. They're ringed by slopes and drop-offs and offer good coral and fishlife, especially on the western and southwestern sides of Carlota. Porpoises are plentiful in the surrounding sea.

SAMAR

The island of Samar consists of three provinces: Northern Samar, which occupies the entire northern portion of Samar, with a coastline bordering on the Samar Sea, San Bernadino Strait, and the Pacific; Western Samar, the largest of the three provinces; and Eastern Samar, facing the Pacific Ocean, famous for the golden cowrie and other rare shells. The island's major attraction is the Sohoton Natural Bridge National Park, near Basey.

The two main routes follow the northern and western coastlines; there's no east-coast road connection with Eastern Samar. Northern Samar offers the visitor some good beaches, offshore islands, waterfalls, and hot springs.

The second largest island in the Visayas mainly serves as a stepping-stone between Luzon and Leyte. Its outstanding attraction, Sohoton National Park, is most easily reached from Tacloban on Leyte.

TRANSPORTATION

Ferries cross at least twice a day between Matnog and Allen. The most convenient connection is on direct Philtranco buses from Legaspi to Catbalogan and Tacloban. As these buses are often filled with passengers coming down from Manila, independent travelers should get an early start to connect with the ferry from Matnog. It's a spectacular ride through vast coconut plantations along the coast from Allen to Catbalogan.

Travel time from Allen to Tacloban is seven hours with direct Philtranco bus. Add on a few hours by bus from Legaspi, and you can see that this is a very long day. You can break your journey at Catbalogan, though there's virtually nothing to see in this one-horse town.

Air from Manila
PAL flies daily, except Wednesday and Sunday, from Manila to Calbayog. PAL also flies daily, except Monday and Wednesday, from Manila to Catarman.

Asian Spirit flies from Manila to Catarman four times weekly, on Tuesday, Thursday, Friday, and Saturday.

Ship from Manila
Most travelers overland from Manila down to Legaspi in southern Luzon, then continue south to Matnog and take a ferry across to Allen in northern Samar.

Manila to Catbalogan: WG&A serves Catbalogan with the MV *Masbate Uno* departing from Manila on Monday at 1000, with a trip time of almost 24 hours.

Ferry from Matnog: Service from Matnog to Allen is provided by the MV *Michelangelo* and the MV *Northern Samar* which sail daily at 1000 and 1600 and take about 90 minutes to reach Allen. Buses are waiting for each ferry, but it's important to get off the boat quickly and snag a seat on the first departing bus.

St. Bernard Services MV *Marhalika 1* departs Matnog daily at 0600 and 1230 for San Isidro on the northwestern tip of Samar. This is the ferry for travelers heading to the western coast of Samar and the various surfing venues.

Ship from Biliran
Biliran is a small island just off the north coast of Leyte. Just to the north of Biliran is a smaller island known as Maripipi. A large outrigger leaves Danao on Maripipi Island to Calbayog at 0500 on Wednesday and Saturday. The trip takes about three hours.

Ship from Cebu
Western Samar Shipping's MV *Elizabeth Lilly* departs Cebu City at 1800 on Saturday for Catarman, and at 1800 on Tuesday for Catbalogan. Catarman takes 14 hours, while Catbalogan is somewhat quicker at 13 hours.

Ship from Leyte
WG&A's MV *Masbate Uno* departs Tacloban to Catbalogan at 1200 every Wednesday. Sulpicio Lines' MV *Tacloban Princess* leaves Tacloban every Friday at 0500. These four-hour trips cost P80-100 and are probably the most popular sea access used by Western travelers-a nice change from another boring bus ride.

You can also go from Tacloban to Guiuan in Southern Samar with K&T Shipping's MV

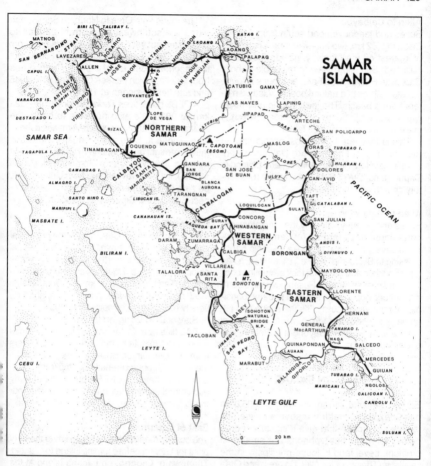

SAMAR ISLAND

Stacey, which leaves every other day at 2300 and takes six hours to make the crossing.

NORTHERN SAMAR

Allen

This small town, the ferry port for Luzon, is 243 km, five hours, from Tacloban (Leyte). Cardinal or San Pablo ferries depart from San Isidro for Matnog (Sorsogon). The crossing takes 75 minutes to two hours and costs P70 plus P1 harbor toll on each side.

The Philtranco bus line has its own ferries, which leave Allen at 0500 and 1200.

Northbound buses arrive in convoys spread over about two hours. By taking one of the earlier buses that connect with the 1200 ferry, you may have time for a swim at the pleasant Buenos Aires Beach.

Ask the bus driver to drop you at the resthouse, where you can change your clothes, swim, then take a tricycle to the ferry dock. But don't time it too tightly, since the ferry sometimes leaves a few minutes early.

Stay at the **Bicolana Lodging House,** P50 pp; it's centrally located. It's also usually possible to sleep on the ferry.

Allen to Calbayog

Buses and jeepneys head south from Allen to Calbayog (62 km, two hours) and beyond. Points of interest off the highway include the Seven Hills near San Isidro, said to resemble Bohol's Chocolate Hills; Victoria Falls; and four km south, Veriata Falls, with a natural pool situated 50 meters from a beach. The jeepney trip only takes two hours, while buses ply this road (which is in excellent condition) a bit faster.

This is truly one of the most scenic rides in the Philippines. Offshore are Dalupiri Island, whose main town is San Antonio, and beyond it, Capul Island, site of Bato Cave and a 16th-century church and watchtower.

Allen to Catarman

Buses and jeepneys also ply the road along the north shore to Catarman (48 km, one hour). From Lavezares, you can make a scenic *banca* crossing to Biri Island, where Talisay Beach has giant boulders and a natural rock swimming pool. The road passes through Rosario, whose steaming, sulfuric hot springs are said to be responsible for miraculous cures. It's the scene of a pilgrimage to honor the Virgin, who's believed to have appeared here. Beyond it is Bobon, site of Calirocan Beach.

EASTERN SAMAR

Eastern Samar (4,340 square km, pop. 325,000) has unexploited natural resources-minerals, forests, the ocean-that give it significant economic potential, but typhoons are an annual problem. Level land is found principally in the valleys and deltas of the Ulut, Dolores, and Oras Rivers, which are separated by mountain spurs. Logging and sawmilling are important in the east coast towns. Eastern Samar, especially around Guiuan, is of major interest to shell collectors as a source of the golden cowrie, *Conus gloriamaris,* and other rare species.

The only road to Eastern Samar is the 70-km cross-island road, winding through forested hills from Buray, on the main west coast highway, to Taft on the east coast, 48 km north of Borongan. It passes through Loquilocon, site of Nasarang Falls, and Bagacay, where copper is mined.

The roads from Oras to Northern Samar, and along the southwest coast from Lauaan to Basey, are not yet complete. A bus leaves from Pier 1 in Catbalogan for Borongan at 0830, but it's recommended to take the Philtranco bus from Manila, which passes Catbalogan at 1045 and reaches Borongan at 1515.

A PEBL bus leaves Tacloban for Guiuan (323 km) at 0630. It's also possible to board the Philtranco bus at Buray, where it makes a lunch stop. Those arriving in Borongan on this bus must overnight and continue to Guiuan the next morning. This bus departs Borongan for Manila at 1500; if you're traveling up from Guiuan for it, be sure to leave there before 0800. Boats connect Guiuan and Giporlos with Tacloban.

Catarman

An old Spanish port, Catarman is the provincial capital, a university town, and the commercial center for Samar's northern plains. Abaca is shipped from here. Beaches around Catarman include Tamburosan (four km out, popular with local students), Calayag, White Beach, and University of Eastern Philippines Beach.

Stay at **DCC Lodging** for P75.

PAL flies from Catarman to Manila five times a week (90 minutes); the airport is 400 meters from the town center. Buses and jeepneys make the 76 km, three-and-a-half-hour trip from Catarman to Calbayog. A PEBL bus departs early each morning from Catarman for the seven-hour trip to Ormoc (Leyte), via Allen and Tacloban.

East of Catarman

The coastal road continues for 35 km to the ferry point for Laoang before turning inland to Catubig. The town of **Laoang,** on Laoang Island at the mouth of the Catubig River, is the trading center for the Catubig Valley, Samar's largest lowland and the rice bowl of Northern Samar. During the '70s, many antiques were found along the riverbanks, including gold chains, silver-plated pitchers, jars, ornaments, and coins dating to 1804.

Farther inland, the scenic Pinipisakan Falls are a three-hour hike from Las Navas. Take a boat from Laoang, site of the beautiful Onay Beach, to Batag Island, which has a lighthouse built by the Americans in 1907 and used as a Japanese lookout in WW II. Old burial jars have been found on Batag.

Palapag, on the mainland east of Laoang, is a former galleon port of call with an old stone watchtower. The coast between here and Gamay is rocky and inaccessible. The **Gomag Cave** in Gamay presents a challenge to serious speleologists.

Borongan

This former Spanish military outpost and trading base is now the provincial capital and commercial center (pop. 40,000). It's surrounded by forests and coconut plantations. Copra is the area's main product. Local handicrafts include those based on fibers-abaca, *buri,* pineapple, coconut husks.

Relics of ancient inhabitants have been found in the nearby **Santa Monica Caves,** which run underground for three km. Also in the vicinity are **Punta Maria Caves,** with sandy-floored chambers, a natural rock staircase, and a human-shaped imprint in one of the walls, which is said to mark where two lovers were struck by lightning.

Divinuvo Island (30 minutes by *banca*) offers swimming, sand, coral, and waves.

Accommodations in Borongan are centrally located. Stay at **Domsower Lodging House** for P100 pp. There's a PNB branch here.

Borongan to Guiuan

Minibuses leave for Guiuan (118 km, five hours) in the morning. Sit on the left-hand side for good views of coastal rock formations and fine beaches on offshore islands. Menasnge Park in Maydolong has a beach with rock formations. Near Naga, a branch road leads partway along the south coast of Samar, passing through Giporlos, from where daily boats go to Tacloban.

Guiuan

This fishing town is situated on a densely settled, long, low, narrow, coralline peninsula on the northeast shore of Leyte Gulf. The area offers a lot to see and do. Guiuan's 16th-century church is considered the finest in the eastern Visayas, with hand-carved doors, altars, and old santos. Two long causeways lined with picturesque huts on stilts lead out from the shore. A boat sails from the western causeway to Tacloban (eight and a half hours) every second night at 2100.

Stay at **Blue Star Lodging House,** P75-100 pp.

Vicinity of Guiuan

Take a tricycle (14 km, P15 roundtrip) to the adjacent Sapao and Dumpao Beaches: they're fine, without being fantastic. The road passes the U.S. Navy-built air base whose three-km runway, now disused, played an important role in the country's liberation. Guiuan has several offshore islands.

White Russian refugees who escaped from China when the communists took power stayed awhile on **Tubabao Island,** 20 minutes by *banca.* **Kantican Island** (45 minutes) has a cultured-pearl farm and laboratory, operated by the Bureau of Fisheries and Aquatic Resources. Kantican has a fine beach and good coral and marinelife for snorkelers. It may be possible to overnight in the pearl farm resthouse.

On **Caliocan,** a low coralline island, the original flagpole of U.S. Navy 3149 Base still stands from WW II at Ngolos, and locals skin-dive from nearby Sulangan Beach in search of the valuable golden cowrie shell. Manicani Island and Homonhon Island have iron ore deposits.

Homonhon Island

This historic island (104 square km) at the entrance to Leyte Gulf is where Magellan first landed in the Philippines in 1521. It's a quiet, pretty island with sandy coconut palm-lined beaches, cliffs, and rocky promontories. The inhabitants farm, fish, and cut wood.

On the beach believed to be where Magellan came ashore is a deep stream called Cantilado. Here, some 100 meters from the shore, the Philippine Historical Committee has erected a marker on a rock bearing inscriptions thought to have been chiseled by Magellan's party. To the west of this spot is a sloping cataract, visible from the sea, that may have been the "Watering Place of Good Signs" that attracted Magellan's thirsty fleet. You can swim in the creek beneath it.

Other noteworthy spots include the spouting rocks at Pigsutan Point and the whistling rock at Cora-coraan Point near Habag, both phenomena due to holes in the rock and the wave action.

It's possible to reach Homonhon by *banca* (two hours) from Guiuan. It may also be possible to find a *banca* for the two-hour ride between

Homonhon and Loreto, Dinagat Island (Surigao del Norte).

Suluan Island

The first Filipinos to make contact with Magellan on Homonhon are thought to have come across from the smaller Suluan Island (five square km), 16 km to the east. Suluan, which has sandy beaches, can be reached by *banca* with natives returning from Guiuan market. Homonhon and Suluan were the sites of the first landings by liberating U.S. forces in 1944.

WESTERN SAMAR

Calbayog City

The name derives from the *bayog* tree from which *cal* (Spanish for "lime") was extracted and used in building churches. Calbayog boomed during the American era. Today, it's a commercial, industrial, and fishing center, and the principal outport for Samar's northern plains. It is at one end of a great Philippine ride; the road between Allen and Calbayog is very pretty.

Copra and abaca are shipped from here. Matmaking is a local handicraft. While the city limits cover a vast 903 square km, the center is merely a medium-sized town, surrounded by fertile lowlands.

Accommodations: Wayside Lodging House, P80 pp, is centrally located; **San Joaquin Inn,** is in town, P100 pp or P200 a/c; the **Calbayog Hotel,** P75-150, by the sea, is one km south of the center, just past the Philtranco terminal. The best hotel in Calbayog is the **Seaside Drive Inn** in nearby Rawis. Rooms are P150-200 pp and P250 with a/c.

Transportation: Minibuses and jeepneys for Catbalogan, Allen, and Catarman leave from near the market. PAL flies from Calbayog to Manila five times a week (one hour, 40 minutes); the airport is northwest of the city at Trinidad. Ships link Calbayog and Masbate about once a week.

Vicinity of Calbayog

The seven-tiered Darosdos Falls are just outside the city. Lo-oc Beach is in Malajog, seven km north. In the district of Oquendo, 20 km north of Calbayog on the road to Catarman, are Pan-

as Falls; Ginogo-An Cave (Longaob), where a pair of fugitives hid for two years; and Mapaso Spring (Rizal).

An oddity of the latter is that the water is hot enough to boil an egg yet it teems with small red crustaceans. Boats cross from Calbayog to islands in the Samar Sea such as Tagapula, Almagro, Camandag, and Santo Niño.

Calbayog to Catbalogan

On this 90-minute trip, the highway cuts inland to the Gandara River Valley. Close to the river and the town of Gandara are Bongahan ruins, which were a settlement at the time of the revolution. After passing the turnoff to the wide, low Blanca Aurora Falls (12 km from the junction), where you can swim, the highway descends to the coast north of Catbalogan.

Catbalogan

Catbalogan is the provincial capital and an important port, fishing town, and Samar's main commercial center, but like Calbayog, it has little to detain the traveler.

Accommodations: Fortune Hotel is a decent place in the north end of town near the Landmark Bank on Del Rosario St., tel. (055) 72-344, P120-500. **Catbalogan Travelers**

CATBALOGAN

© MOON PUBLICATIONS, INC.

Lodge is a simple, friendly new spot two blocks back from the main road on Rizal St., no phone, P80-250. **Kikay's Hotel** is a rough but okay alternative to other budget hotels in town; San Bartolome St., tel. (055) 71-188, P120-250.

Transportation: Buses from Allen take about four hours to Catbalogan, which means you'll probably need to spend the night in this one-horse town. Several small bus halts are scattered around town including the Philtranco terminal on San Bartolome Street in the north of town, Eagle Star buses on San Roque Street three blocks back from Del Rosario Street, and a small bus terminal at the corner of Allen and San Francisco Streets.

Buses arrive and depart in groups, since several vehicles cross between Allen and Matnog on the same ferry. At around 1045, southbound buses leave Catbalogan for Borongan, Guiuan, Ormoc, and Tacloban. Several buses to Manila pass 0630-0800 to connect with the 1200 ferry at San Isidro, reaching Manila next day around 0700. Night buses also pass through Catbalogan 2000-2400 to connect with the 0500 ferry to Matnog. This allows a day trip up through southern Luzon, with views of Mt. Mayon, reaching Manila in the evening.

Frequent buses make the two-hour trip to Tacloban, but it's worth taking the time to sail. The highway south from Catbalogan skirts Maqueda Bay, passes Buray, where the road to Eastern Samar branches left, then cuts across country to emerge at the impressive bridge over the San Juanico Strait to Leyte, 10 km south of which is Tacloban

Ships sail weekly from Catbalogan to Manila (18-21 hours), and from Manila they turn around at, or return through, Tacloban and call at Catbalogan on their way north. A boat sails from Catbalogan to Surigao in Mindanao once a week; departures for Cebu (12 hours by sea) are three times a week.

Catbalogan to Tacloban by sea takes four hours and departures are every second night at 2200. Try to sail through the narrow, scenic San Juanico Strait between Tacloban and Catbalogan (three and a half hours) during daylight.

Vicinity of Catbalogan
Beaches outside the town include Cal-Apog; Ginsorongan (P1 by tricycle), also the site of a

fish cannery; Payao (eight km north, P2 by tricycle); and Buri Beach (take a *banca* from the pier). Commuter launches go to fishing towns such as Daram on Daram Island and Zumarraga on Buad Island out in Maqueda Bay. On the mainland, Guimit Cave at Talalora has stalactites and stalagmites.

Sohoton National Park
Traveling south from Catbalogan, if it's no later than midafternoon, alight at the crossroad to Basey and take a jeepney there. If it's late, it's better to go into Tacloban and return next morning. Jeepneys from Tacloban market make the 27-km journey in about an hour. In **Basey,** ask for help from the mayor, who'll find you a reliable boatman. He can also provide information about staying overnight in the park. Basey is noted for matweaving and its 17th-century church.

The 30-km boat trip upriver to the park takes almost two hours each way. A small group should expect to pay about P400 return for the boat, P30 tip to the boatman, and P25 for hiring a strong Petromax lamp. A lamp is essential: don't leave Basey without one, and bring extra matches.

For those with more money than time, it's possible to charter a boat directly from Tacloban, crossing San Pedro Bay to the mouth of the river. It takes about three hours from Tacloban to the park. Those with more time than money can get close to the park by taking a local passenger boat upriver from Basey for a few pesos, then looking around for someone with a *banca* to take them to the park. Drawbacks of this are that it's impossible to do it as a day trip, and a bright lamp may be hard to find. So chartering a boat from Basey is recommended.

In the park, there are four main features to see in the eight-square-km park, and to do so, an early start is important. The trip up the winding river is engrossing, with small villages, nipa palms, and jungle on the banks, and a motley parade of passing rivercraft. Approaching the park, the banks consist of limestone outcrops and overhangs. **Panhulugan Island** is the first cave reached and the largest. It is part of a series of caves, discovered relatively recently.

The boat moors near the deceptively unprepossessing entrance, behind which is a beautiful, glittering world of exotically shaped stone. Each chamber has a different size, shape, and mood, and is replete with stalactites and stalagmites. Some walls are of sparkling crystal. The silence is remarkable.

Sohoton Cave, a little farther upriver, is less spectacular. Concrete steps lead up to this spacious cave, which contains a balcony overlooking the natural stone bridge. You can descend and swim beneath it. **Bugusan III** cave, a short distance up a tributary, has an underground stream. The caves have yielded prehistoric artifacts, housed Sung and Ming porcelain, and served as a hideout for Filipino *insurrectos* during the Philippine-American War.

This park deserves more than a one-day visit. By arranging to stay overnight, you'll have a better opportunity to observe the monkeys, parrots, and other wildlife. But even as a day trip, Sohoton National Park is definitely worth the money and effort to reach it.

SIQUIJOR

Siquijor lies in the Mindanao Sea, 20 km off the southeast tip of Negros. To many Filipinos, its name conjures up images of voodoo and bizarre rituals. Witchcraft exists in various forms on the island, but the short-term visitor will see few overt signs of it. Siquijor does, however, offer several white-sand beaches, good snorkeling, and an undeveloped rural environment. Larena and Lazi are the ports of entry.

Dive companies stop here since the island is blessed with coral reefs largely undamaged by dynamite fishing.

Larena is the main port and Siquijor town is the provincial capital, but most visitors head directly to the fine beaches at Sandugan, six km northeast of Larena, or Paliton, at the westernmost tip of the island.

WITCHCRAFT ON SIQUIJOR

In spite of the long presence of Christianity, Siquijor is noted for herbal medicine, witchcraft, and magic, with San Antonio as the center of shamanism. There are said to be about 50 *mananambals,* who are classified as "white" or "black" sorcerers according to whether they specialize in healing or harming. You can see a collection of their paraphernalia, including voodoo dolls, potions and concoctions, skulls and candles, at Silliman University's Anthropology Museum in Dumaguete.

San Antonio, named after the patron saint of medicine, is reached by a bad road leading into the interior hills, but don't expect to see much evidence of the dark arts.

Tang-alap

During Holy Week, herbalists and sorcerers come from all over the Visayas and Mindanao to San Antonio to participate in a ritual known as *tang-alap.* They roam the area's forests, caves, and cemeteries to gather medicinal herbs and roots, then sit in a circle, and while a humorous mood prevails, the ingredients are combined in piles. The gathering culminates in an exclusive ritual that takes place in a secluded cave at dawn.

Magbabarang

This is the name given to the "black" sorcerers. These dreaded purveyors of pain and death can be hired as agents of vengeance; they use *barang*—certain bees, beetles, and centipedes that have an extra leg—and magic invocations to achieve their ends. They collect these insects and keep them in a bamboo tube. Always on a Friday, they place several pieces of paper, each bearing someone's name and address, in the tube. They check a short time later, and if the papers have been shredded, it's taken as a sign that the insects will attack the individuals named.

The *magbabarang* ties a white string around the insects' additional legs and releases them. They have been ordered to find their victims, enter their bodies, and cause death by biting the internal organs. Then they return to their master, who examines the strings to see if the magic was successful. If so, the string will be red with blood; if it's clean, it means that the person was innocent and could resist the hex. Those who suspect that a *magbabarang* has been hired against them may employ their own practitioner to counteract the voodoo, which can create a complex power struggle.

HISTORY

The islanders' oral tradition holds that Siquijor rose from the sea amid thunder and lightning, and also describes a legendary King Kihod. Fossilized sea creatures have been found in the interior highlands. Chinese porcelain plowed up by local farmers indicates the prevalence of pre-Hispanic trading. The island's native name was Katugasan, after tugas-the molave trees that covered the hills. The Spanish first called it Isla del Fuego ("Island of Fire"), probably due to the swarms of fireflies they found here, and later renamed it Siquijor.

TRANSPORTATION

Air from Negros
Pacific Airways flies on Monday and Thursday from Dumaguete to Siquijor. The 15-minute flight costs P250-300.

Air from Mindanao
Pacific Airways also flies from Dipolog to Siquijor on Wednesdays, though this service is often cancelled during the low season months. The 30-minute flight costs P550-600.

Ship from Negros
Most travelers reach Siquijor from Dumaguete on the southern side of Negros.

Fast ferry from Dumaguete to Larena: A Delta Line fast ferry leaves Dumaguete daily at 0600, 0830, 1300, and 1515 and takes about 45 minutes to reach Larena on Siquijor. The fare is P60-80.

Outrigger from Dumaguete to Siquijor: Large outriggers-only recommended when the seas are calm-depart Dumaguete daily at 1000 and 1200 and take just over two hours to reach Tambisan at the western tip of Siquijor.

Ship from Dumaguete to Siquijor: Marjunnix Shipping's MV *Catherine* leaves daily at 1400 and takes three hours to reach Siquijor.

A tricycle from Larena or Tambisan to Siquijor Town should only cost P5-10.

Ship from Cebu
The MV *Dona Cristina* of Cebu Ferries departs Cebu City every Saturday at 1900 but takes an uncomfortable 24 hours to reach Siquijor due to its stop on Iligan in northern Mindanao.

AROUND THE ISLAND

The coastal road is a 76-km circuit. The six municipalities are linked by jeepneys and tricycles. Larena has some attractive old houses.

Congbagsa
In the village of Congbagsa, the path to the right, near the large National Food Authority building, leads to a fine white beach with a fresh spring among the rocks.

Lazi
Lazi is an old town with a colonial cathedral. Salang Do-Ong is a small beach at the north end of Maria Bay, reached by a two-km track off the main road. It has coral gardens offshore and is a popular weekend picnic spot for locals.

Accommodations
Larena: A sleepy little port town where you stay at the **Larena Pension House** or **Luisa and Son's Lodge** for P100-250.

Siquijor: Several resorts are within a few km of the provincial capital, such as **Beach Garden Hotel** in Catalinan (one km west of town), **Dondeezco Beach Resort** in Dumanhug (two km west), and **Tikarol Beach Resort** in Candanay (three km east). All charge P250-500 for decent bungalows facing a white sand beach.

Sandugan Beach: Six km northeast of Larena is a long, peaceful beach with decent sand, excellent diving, and almost a dozen resorts priced P300-600, such as **Islander's Paradise Beach, Kiwi Dive Resort, Casa del Playa Beach Resort,** and **Hidden Paradise.**

Paliton Beach: Near San Jose is another fine beach with a few simple bungalows such as **Sunset Beach Resort** and **Paliton Beach Resort.** Both have rooms for P200-350. Two km south of San Juan in Tubod you'll find the **San Juan Coco Grove Beach Resort** with swimming pool, restaurant, jeepney rentals, and a/c rooms with "private marble bath" for P650-1,200.

Journeys, like artists, are born and not made.
A thousand differing circumstances contribute to them,
few of them willed or determined by the will-
whatever we may think.

                    -Lawrence Durrell, Bitter Lemons

Traveling is not just seeing the new;
it is also leaving behind.
Not just opening doors;
also closing them behind you, never to return.
But the place you have left forever,
is always there for you to see whenever you shut your eye.
And the cities you see most clearly at night,
are the cities you have left,
and will never see again.

                    -Jan Myrdal, The Silk Road

I sought trains; I found passengers.

                    -Paul Theroux,
                    The Great Railway Bazaar

M.G.L. DOMENY DE RIENZI

MINDANAO
INTRODUCTION

The second largest island in the Philippines is considered by many Filipinos to be the Wild South—a mysterious and exotic land of high mountains and impenetrable rainforest peopled by intransigent Muslims and pagan hilltribes. In reality, Mindanao is three-quarters Christian and largely developed with towns, roads, and other signs of urban progress. Its role as a meeting ground for Christians and Muslims has brought problems of political assimilation, but the island is also replete with natural wonders, diverse cultures, and dozens of minorities who remain less modernized than those in northern Luzon.

Highlights on Mindanao include the beautiful offshore islands near Surigao in the northeastern corner of the island, Camiguin Island on the north coast near Cagayan de Oro, and a climb to the summit of Mt. Apo near Davao. Visitors interested in cultural minorities should visit Lake Sebu, one of the prettiest and least visited regions in the country. Davao and Zamboanga are nondescript cities with few sights, though both serve as gateways to more exotic destinations.

Most of Mindanao is relatively safe for Western visitors, but travelers should check with local tourist officials or embassies before traveling through the Lake Lanao region and the Sulu Archipelago south of Zamboanga.

HISTORY

Early History
Mindanao was connected by land bridges to Celebes and through Sulu to Borneo and the Asian mainland. This accounts for Mindanao sharing many species of fauna and flora with the islands to its south. Early migrants came via these land bridges, to be followed over the millennia by the sea migrations of Indonesians, from whom many of Mindanao's tribal minorities are descended, and Malays who were the ancestors of contemporary Muslim groups.

The remains of three *balanghais* (boats used for migration) dating from the fourth to the 13th centuries have been unearthed near Butuan

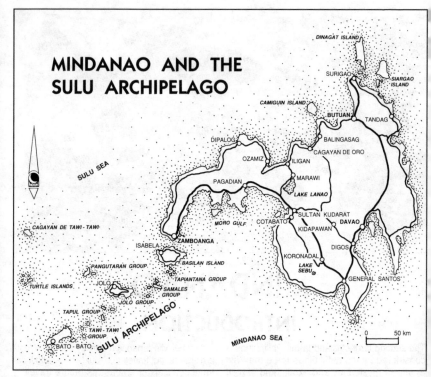

MINDANAO AND THE SULU ARCHIPELAGO

City, and nine more were discovered in the same place later. The center of early development in the region was Jolo. With Sulu's pearls as the magnet, Jolo became a major trading center, receiving ships from throughout Asia. Foreign trade subsequently extended to other ports such as Manila, Cebu, and points such as Butuan on Mindanao's northern coast.

The Coming of Islam

Conversion to Islam began in Sulu in the late 14th century, but it wasn't until after Sharif Kabungsuwan reached Cotabato from Johore in the first quarter of the 16th century that Islam became widespread. After marrying a tribal princess, he established the Maguindanao Sultanate and laid the foundations of Islam, to which various tribes were converted. Islam subsequently spread to other parts of Mindanao, especially the Lake Lanao region, but it hadn't had

time to take hold in northern and eastern Mindanao before the Spaniards began encouraging colonization of the coast by Christianized Filipinos from the Visayas and Luzon.

As the Muslims fought to preserve their sovereignty, Mindanao became effectively isolated, enabling them to solidify and maintain their culture. The first Spanish expeditions to Mindanao and Sulu took place in the 1570s. Following the burning of Jolo in 1578, the Moro Wars continued intermittently right up until a campaign in the Lake Lanao area in 1895. During the 17th and 18th centuries, the only areas where Spain had much influence were along the northern coastal plain and in individual spots such as Zamboanga, Dapitan, and Caraga.

The Fighting Moros

The bravery of the Muslim Filipinos is legendary. Many stories tell of *juramentados,* heads shaven and armed only with a razor-sharp *kris,* who would make frenzied kamikaze-like attacks in a Christian marketplace, killing those within reach until they themselves were cut down. It was a form of ritual suicide by which they believed they'd gain immediate entrance to paradise. Entire villages would oppose foreign invaders.

The fact that all Moros were dangerous affected the way the Spanish fought against them; they had an unofficial policy of *juez de cuchillo*—judgment by the sword. It was a search-and-destroy tactic that involved killing anyone encountered in hostile territory, and it led to many massacres.

The 20th Century

The Muslims resisted the Americans, too, and the years 1899-1914 saw a pacification campaign marked by some fierce battles, especially on Jolo and around Lake Lanao. Civilian government began in 1914, and attempts were made, as elsewhere in the Philippines, to construct schools, hospitals, and public works projects so as to prepare the Moros for modern, "civilized" life. The Americans were certainly more tolerant of Islam than the Spaniards, but U.S. policies still grieved the Moros.

Slavery had to end, taxes were imposed, the status of traditional Muslim leaders was undermined by the new regional governments, customary judicial procedures were bypassed, unused land in their territory was given to migrants, and they feared that education would impart Christian rather than Islamic values to their children. The overall policy of American and Christian Filipino officials was to integrate the Muslims into the mainstream of Filipino society. The Muslims were incorporated into the Philippine nation under a Manila-based government, but animosity continued to simmer.

World War II

The main Japanese base on Mindanao was Davao City. In the wilds of the interior, they could do little to counter an effective guerrilla operation. Macajalar Bay was a possible choice for the initial U.S. landing in 1944, but Leyte was chosen instead. The principal assault on Mindanao didn't begin until April 1945. By this time, the 43,000 Japanese troops on Mindanao were isolated from the progress of the war, and MacArthur

wanted them destroyed and the area liberated. They were concentrated in Davao City and along the main highway south of Macajalar Bay in north-central Mindanao.

After securing the Zamboanga peninsula, U.S. troops swept ashore at Parang and pushed inland along the narrow road parallel to the broad Mindanao River, which they simultaneously sailed up in a makeshift fleet of shallow-draft boats. At the key road junction of Kabacan, a force struck north along the highway to meet another U.S. formation fighting its way south from Macajalar Bay. The two groups met 20 km north of Malaybalay, having driven the Japanese into the mountains. The main body of troops continued across the island to take Davao City.

The Japanese expected the Americans to attack Davao from the sea. Hence, they set up most of their guns pointing outwards, relying on the rugged terrain behind the city to protect the rear. Even U.S. commanders would have preferred a sea-borne attack, but the necessary ships had been diverted to Okinawa. Thus occurred what was to be the longest sustained march by any U.S. unit in the entire Pacific War. It was a remarkable achievement—a race against the coming monsoons across 200 km of steaming jungle. Digos was reached in only 10 days.

Enemy troops delayed the advance on Davao while the entire Japanese force, including 13,000 civilians, abandoned the already heavily bombed city and retired to well-prepared defenses about five km inland. Six days later, the Americans marched unopposed into the city, which had been Japan's last urban stronghold in the Philippines. It took five more weeks to overcome all resistance.

The futile defense of Mindanao cost the Japanese 13,000 men, compared with 820 Americans killed. Today, many Japanese come to Mindanao to visit the graves of their fallen and the memorial erected in their memory. Others come to search for war booty dumped into the seas off Mindanao as the Japanese lost control of the Philippines. The value of this treasure is estimated in the billions of dollars, and during the Marcos era, the president himself had divers uncover some of the loot and pocketed over one billion dollars worth of Japanese war booty. The

Japanese presence was so strong in Mindanao at one time that Davao was referred to as "Little Tokyo." To this day, some locals have distinct Japanese features and can claim part Japanese parentage.

The Postwar Years

Mindanao had remained sparsely populated through the Spanish era, but during the American regime, large numbers of Christian Filipinos, lured by the prospect of land ownership and a brighter future, had migrated from the overcrowded Visayas and also Luzon. This movement continued through the '60s. The government urged pioneers to come to this vast, undeveloped island and start civilizing it. Farmers, loggers, and miners poured into Mindanao, pushing the native minorities into the hills.

The Moros particularly resented the policy of settling Christian migrants on their ancestral land in Cotabato and Lanao, even when the land was virgin forest. The Muslims found themselves a minority, in addition to feeling that their own economic development was being neglected by the Manila government. Religious, political, and economic factors combined, and pent-up passions exploded. Law and order broke down as land-grabbing, cattle-rustling, banditry, and Muslim harrassment of Christian settlers became rife.

Discontent led to rebellion in the '50s, with military-style camps set up to train Muslim youths. The Manila administration attempted to halt this divisive drift by establishing the Commission on National Integration, whose achievements fell far short of expectations, and the Mindanao State University in Marawi City.

The Threat of Secession

Continuing Muslim frustration with government policies led, in 1968, to Datu Udtog Matalam declaring his intention to lead a secessionist movement in Mindanao. The Mindanao Independence Movement proclaimed establishment of the Republic of Mindanao and Sulu, with Muslim leadership and an Islamic constitution and laws. Although merely a local movement based in Cotabato, this struck a chord with the feelings of many Muslims.

The Moro National Liberation Front (MNLF), a coalition of guerrilla groups and dissidents, came to prominence in the early '70s and has been supported by foreign-based Islamic organizations. The outbreak of full-scale civil disturbance in 1971 necessitated mass evacuation of both Muslims and Christians from the most seriously affected areas and resulted in heavy loss of life, crops, and property.

Muslims offered the first armed defiance of martial law a month after its declaration in 1972 with the seizure of Marawi State University. Government troops battled Muslim secessionists in southern Mindanao, 1973-76, including a major conflict in the Sulu Islands in 1974. A Libyan-mediated agreement with the government, based on establishing an "autonomous region" made up of 13 southern provinces, defused some of the tension, but fighting resumed in 1977 after the idea was rejected in a referendum by the region's Christian voters, who greatly outnumbered the Muslims.

The separatists boycotted the referendum. Since the crisis of the '70s, Muslim leaders have been given some degree of local autonomy, to which economic input has been added and concessions to Islamic culture and traditions made. At one time, violence and political strife was so much a part of daily life in areas around Davao that it was dubbed "little Nicaragua." Today, there are far fewer problems in Davao and throughout Mindanao.

A referendum was held at the end of 1989 covering 13 provinces and nine cities in Mindanao. The issue was the creation of a Muslim Mindanao Autonomous Region. Of those polled, however, only four provinces voted "Yes." These were Lanao del Sur, Maguindanao, Sulu, and Tawi-Tawi. The rest, including Cotabato, Maguindanao's capital, and Marawi, Lanao del Sur's capital, voted "No." The four provinces that voted "Yes" now form Muslim Mindanao Autonomous Region.

The Situation Today

The economic development of Mindanao is a major part of government policy in attempting to peacefully integrate the Muslims into the mainstream of the Filipino nation. Muslim society retains many feudal elements, however, and difficulties have arisen between Islamic and national laws and educational systems; polygamy and divorce, for example, are legal under one law and illegal under the other.

Deep alienation between conservative Muslims and the more progressive Christians persists, and the variation in the pace of economic development has only served to widen the gulf between the two societies. The communist NPA has expanded rapidly on Mindanao and joined the separatist MNLF in its active antigovernment role here. The military, in its difficult role of pacifier, remains much in evidence in the south, maintaining an uneasy truce that sometimes flares into skirmish. Muslim traditionalist and liberal-minded leaders are now working to iron out basic differences to make the Muslim Autonomous Region work. At this point, the regions still engaged in guerrilla fighting and hostility are around Cotabato City, Zamboanga Province, Basilan Island, and the Sulu Archipelago.

Many long-term residents of Mindanao, particularly those around Davao, Cagayan de Oro, and Butuan Provinces feel that Mindanao gets a great deal of bad press and hostilities are exaggerated. During this author's visit to Mindanao, the general feeling among the residents was that while hostilities continue in isolated mountain areas and parts of Zamboanga, there is really no reason to skip visiting Mindanao.

THE PEOPLE

Mindanao has an incredibly rich cultural fabric, with a majority composed of Visayans and other Christian lowlanders, a large Muslim population, many indigenous hilltribes, age-old residents with Chinese ancestry, and a large number of Japanese-Filipinos as a result of WW II. Centuries of migration by Visayans have made Cebuano the predominant language everywhere except where Muslims are concentrated, notably Lanao del Sur, Maguindanao, and Sulu. Muslims also form a significant minority in several other provinces.

Culturally, their orientation is toward Indonesia and Malaysia rather than Manila. Muslim Filipinos are fiercely independent and intensely proud of their ties to the broader Malay world. In general, however, economic development and education in the country's Muslim regions lags behind the Christian Philippines. Members of the hilltribes, known as Mindanao Lumads, number almost two million.

Many individual tribes are ethnically part of large "umbrella" groups, such as the Manobos and Atas. Tribespeople vary greatly in their degree of acculturation, from, for example, the Subanon, who have intermarried extensively with their lowland neighbors, to the more isolated T'boli tribes of South Cotabato.

Each group is described in the appropriate section of this chapter.

TRANSPORTATION

Overview

PAL, Air Philippines, and other regional airlines serve major cities in Mindanao from both Manila and Cebu. Visitors who are short on time but would like to see a specific region such as Lake Sebu, Marawi, or Sulu should fly directly to the nearest airport and proceed by bus or jeepney.

Several north-coast ports are served by shipping lines and fast ferries from Visayan cities such as Cebu, Tacloban, and Dumaguete. Cebu City has the most connections, though fast ferries from Leyte, Samar, Negros, and Panay are convenient for travelers coming down from those islands.

On the south coast, Zamboanga, Cotabato (Polloc), General Santos (Dadiangas), and Davao receive regular service from Manila and Visayan ports. Buses are linked with Luzon, and it's possible to journey from Davao to Manila in three days.

Getting Around

Buses link the main cities of the island but usually don't travel at night. Hence, for long journeys, such as Cagayan de Oro to Zamboanga, departures are at the crack of dawn, if not earlier. For medium distances, the last departure may be in the early afternoon.

The day before setting out on a long cross-country journey, it's a good idea to check the departure time at the bus station and to inquire with local authorities about the security situation along your proposed route.

Routes

Buses that link the main cities rarely travel at night, making early-morning departures a necessity for longer journeys. Express buses with nonstop or five-stop signs are the quickest and well worth a few extra pesos.

The easiest and most convenient loop around Mindanao covers the northern coastline with that all-important visit to Camiguin Island near Cagayan de Oro. First, take a ferry from Maasin or Liloan in southern Leyte to Surigao in northeastern Mindanao and spend a few days relaxing on Siagao Island. Then return to Surigao and head west along the coast, passing through Butuan to Balingoan, where boats make the crossing to Camiguin.

After Camiguin, return to Balingoan and continue by bus west to Cagayan de Oro and Iligan before finishing up at Dapitan and Dipolog. From there, you can take a fast ferry back to Cebu, Negros, or Siquijor Island.

A longer circuit involves a bus down to Davao City, then another bus west to General Santos City and Koronadel, from where jeepneys bounce the rough road to Lake Sebu. Then it's north to Marawi and west through Pagadian to Zamboanga. This very long journey can be shortened with flights between larger towns.

Cautions

Some areas of Mindanao are hindered by ongoing skirmishes between the Philippine military and the NPA and MNLF, but their influence varies by region, so inquire about the current situation before making overland trips. While these groups aren't specifically anti-foreigner, they realize that incidents involving tourists may embarrass a government eager for the foreign currency that tourism brings. Kidnappings for ransom have occured, and while no foreigner has been killed or mistreated, it is not a great way to spend a holiday.

The major problems are near Zamboanga, on Basilan Island, and in the Sulu Archipelago. The best way to avoid trouble is to make your visit brief. Where possible, try to avoid public vehicles on which soldiers are traveling, since they are sometimes ambushed to obtain weapons. Always check out the security situation before getting off the main roads of Mindanao, and don't hike forest trails without a guide.

Respect local customs, too; always remove your shoes when entering a mosque or any ground sacred to Islam, and don't photograph Muslim women without prior permission (or a good telephoto lens).

Air

From Manila: PAL has daily flights from Manila to Cagayan de Oro, Cotabato, Davao, and Zamboanga. Cebu Pacific and Grand Air fly daily from Manila to Cagayan de Oro and Davao. Air Philippines flies daily from Manila to Cagayan de Oro, Cotabato, and Zamboanga. PAL flies from Manila to Butuan four times weekly on Monday, Wednesday, Friday, and Sunday. PAL also flies to Dipolog daily except on Thursday and Saturday.

From Cebu City: PAL has daily flights from Cebu City to Davao, General Santos City, Pagadian, and Zamboanga. PAL also flies to Butuan daily except Wednesday and Sunday, four times weekly to Cagayan de Oro, twice weekly to Cotabato, and four times weekly to Dipolog, Ozamis, Surigao, and Tandag.

From Panay: PAL flies every Sunday from Iloilo to General Santos City.

From Siquijor: Pacific Airways flies every Wednesday from Siquijor to Dipolog, though this service is subject to frequent cancellations.

From the Sulu Archipelago: PAL flies daily from Jolo and Tawi-Tawi to Zamboanga. Connecting flights continue on to Davao and Manila.

Ship from Manila

Several large ships make the very long and tiring journey from Manila's North Harbor to various ports in Mindanao. Fares: To Butuan (P700-850), Cagayan de Oro (P600-750), Cotabato (P800-950), Davao (P950-1,100), Dipolog (P550-600), General Santos City (P900-1,000), Iligan (P600-700), Ozamis (P600-700), Surigao (P625-750), and Zamboanga (P650-750).

To Butuan: WG&A's MV *Superferry 2* leaves Monday at 1600 and takes 40 hours to Butuan via Iloilo City on Panay. The same company also runs the MV *Medjugorje* every Thursday at 2200, a direct service that only takes a quick 32 hours; bring a good book.

To Cagayan de Oro: Plenty of ships on this popular route. WG&A's MV *Superferry 5* departs Manila on Tuesday at 0700 and takes 35 hours with a stop at Tagbilaran on Bohol. The MV *Superferry 9* leaves Wednesday at 2000 and Sunday at 1100, while the MV *Superferry 2* departs

Friday at 1200. Finally, WG&A also runs the MV *Superferry 7* from Manila every Saturday at 0700 with a stop at Tagbilaran on Bohol.

Other lines also serve the Manila-Cagayan de Oro corridor. Negros Navigation's MV *Santa Ana* leaves Manila on Friday at 1400 and takes a bone-crushing 45 hours via Iloilo City on Panay, while Sulpicio Lines' MV *Princess of Paradise* leaves Saturday at 0800 and does the trip in a more reasonable 25 hours. The latter is a direct service, something to consider unless you wish to waste a great deal of time staring at the ocean.

To Cotabato: WG&A's MV *Superferry 3* leaves Manila on Friday at 2200 and takes 44 hours with a stop in Zamboanga. The same company also sails the MV *Maynilad* on Sunday at 1900 and requires a very unpleasant 65 hours with stops in Dumaguete on Negros and Dipolog on the north shore of Mindanao. You have been warned.

To Davao: Another long trip no matter which shipping line you go with. WG&A's MV *Superferry 6* leaves on Tuesday at 0800 and takes 46 hours via Surigao. The MV *Superferry 1* leaves Saturday at 1500 and takes 52 hours with a stop at Iloilo City on Panay. Finally, Sulpicio Lines' MV *Filipina Princess* leaves every Sunday at 1000 and takes 52 hours with stops in both Cebu City and Surigao.

To Dipolog: WG&A's MV *Maynilad* departs Manila on Sunday at 1900 and takes 38 hours via Dumaguete on Negros. The ship then continues down to Cotabato.

To General Santos City: Not the most likely of routes, but perhaps useful if your main destination in Mindanao is Lake Sebu. WG&A's MV *Dona Virginia* departs Tuesday at 1200 and takes 44 hours via Zamboanga. Also from WG&A is the MV *Superferry 1* which leaves on Saturday at 1500 and takes 43 hours, before continuing down to Davao.

To Iligan: WG&A's MV *Superferry 7* departs Manila on Tuesday at 0500 via Dumaguete in just about 35 hours. WG&A also offers its MV *Superferry 5,* which reaches Iligan in 36 hours with a stop in Iloilo on Panay.

To Ozamis: WG&A's MV *Medjugorje* leaves on Monday at 0900 and takes a relatively short 36 hours to reach this town on the northern coast of Mindanao.

To Surigao: This is a popular way to get started exploring the attractions of northern Mindanao without overlanding across the Visayas or springing for a PAL ticket.

WG&A's MV *Superferry 6* departs Manila on Tuesday at 0800 and takes 26 hours, before continuing down to Davao. Sulpicio Lines' MV *Palawan Princess* departs every Wednesday at 2200 and takes an uncomfortable 53 hours with stops in Masbate, Baybay, and Maasin. The same company also runs the MV *Filipina Princess* on Sunday at 1000 with a total travel time of 45 hours, including a stop in Cebu City. Once again, the ship continues south to Davao before heading back to Manila.

To Zamboanga: WG&A's MV *Dona Virginia* departs Manila's North Harbor every Tuesday at 1200 and takes just 28 hours on a direct sail to Zamboanga. Not bad. The MV *Superferry 3* sets sail on Friday at 2200 and takes a slightly longer 28-32 hours. Sulpicio Lines' MV *Cotabato Princess* departs Saturday at 1500 and takes an ass-numbing 45 hours due to stops in Estancia and Iloilo City on Panay.

Ship from Bohol
The fast ferry from Tagbilaran to Cagayan de Oro is popular with travelers in a hurry, though slower ships on the same route are somewhat cheaper and don't take a ridiculous amount of time.

Tagbilaran to Cagayan de Oro: Water Jet Shipping's MV *Water Jet* leaves daily at 1200 and takes just three hours to Cagayan de Oro. The fare is P350-400.

WG&A MV *Superferry 7* departs on Sunday at 1100 and takes seven hours at a cost of just P150-200. The MV *Superferry 5* leaves Wednesday at 1100 at the same cost and length of journey.

Another big-ship option is Trans-Asia Shipping's MV *Asia-Thailand,* which departs on Monday and Wednesday at 2000 and again on Friday at 2100. This one takes eight hours.

Tagbilaran to Dipolog: Sulpicio Lines' aptly named MV *Dipolog Princess* leaves on Thursday at midnight and takes five hours to Dipolog. You can then make the long bus journey across the northern coastline of Mindanao, stopping at Cagayan de Oro, Camiguin Island, and Surigao.

Jagna to Butuan: Cebu Ferries' MV *Lady of Fatima* leaves Jagna on Sunday at midnight and takes just under six hours for the crossing.

Jagna to Cagayan de Oro: Cebu Ferries' MV *Lady of Lourdes* departs on Monday at midnight and takes six hours, while the MV *Lady of Lipa* departs on Sunday at 1400. The latter only takes four hours instead of six. Sulpicio Lines' MV *Cagayan Princess* provides another option with a departure on Saturday at 2100. Figure on five hours for this one.

Ship from Camiguin

Several large ferries (or small ships, depending on how you look at it) make the quick 60-90 minute crossing from Camiguin to the mainland at Mindanao.

Benoni to Balingoan: Tamula Shipping's MV *Charles Brown* and MV *Ruperto Jr.* leave Benoni hourly 0600-1400. Corrales Shipping runs the MV *Hijos* during the same time period. Allow 90 minutes for the crossing and an average cost of P15-30.

Guinsiliban to Balingoan: Ferry service is also provided from this small port town at the southern tip of Camiguin. Tamula Shipping's MV *Anita* leaves daily at 0600 and 1100 and takes about 60 minutes to reach Mindanao. Philippine Shipping's MV *Yuhum* sails daily except Sunday at 1400. The Sunday service goes at 1000.

Guinsiliban to Cagayan de Oro: Philippine Shipping's MV *Yuhum* makes this three-hour journey every Wednesday, Friday, and Sunday at 1500.

Ship from Cebu

Ships leave Cebu City and other towns on the island to virtually every possible destination in Mindanao. Fast ferries connect Cebu City with Cagayan de Oro, Iligan, Ozamis, and Surigao.

Cebu City to Butuan: No fast ferries but several large ships make the trip in 8-12 hours. Sulpicio Lines' MV *Nasipit Princess* departs Cebu City on Monday, Wednesday, and Saturday. Sulpicio also runs the MV *Princess of Paradise* on Thursday at 1000, while Cebu Ferries' MV *Lady of Fatima* heads off at 1800 on Tuesday, Thursday, and Saturday. Cebu Ferries' MV *Lady of Lourdes* rounds off the selections with departures on Friday at 1800.

Cebu City to Cagayan de Oro: Speedsters can hop Water Jet Shipping's MV *Water Jet 1* daily at 1030 and reach Cagayan de Oro in just under five hours. All this efficiency will cost you P500-550. More fast services may be added by other companies in the near future and, hopefully, prices will drop due to the new competition.

Trans-Asia Shipping's MV *Asia-China* or MV *Trans-Asia* sails daily at 1900 and takes 10 hours to make the crossing. Cebu Ferries' MV *Lady of Lipa* departs on Monday at 1000 and at 2000 on Tuesday, Thursday, and Saturday. Cebu Ferries' MV *Lady of Lourdes* heads south at 2000 on Wednesday and Sunday.

Sulpicio Lines' MV *Cagayan Princess* leaves Cebu City at 1900 on Monday, Wednesday, and Friday. Another 10-hour crossing.

Cebu City to Dapitan: George & Peter Lines runs either the MV *Dumaguete Ferry,* the MV *Georich,* or the MV *Pulauan Ferry* daily at 2200. The trip takes 12 hours and makes a stop at Dumaguete on Negros. Cokaliong Shipping runs the MV *Filipinas Dinagat* at 1900 on Monday, Wednesday, and Friday. This is a longer journey of 16 hours with a stop at Dumaguete.

Cebu City to Davao: Sulpicio Lines' MV *Filipina Princess* departs Monday at noon and takes 26 hours via Surigao.

Cebu City to Iligan: Water Jet Shipping's fast ferry MV *Water Jet 2* departs Cebu City at 0830 on Monday, Wednesday, and Friday and takes just four hours to reach Iligan. The ferry costs P500-550.

Cebu Ferries' MV *Lady of Carmel* leaves at 1900 on Monday, Wednesday, and Friday and takes 13 hours with a stop in Ozamis. The same shipping line also provides the MV *Dona Cristina* at 1900 on Tuesday, Thursday, and Saturday. Allow nine hours for this journey. Sulpicio Lines' MV *Dipolog Princess* departs Saturday at 2100 and also requires nine hours for the crossing.

Cebu City to Ozamis: Water Jet Shipping's MV *Water Jet 2* fast ferry leaves at 0845 on Monday, Wednesday, and Friday for the four-hour trip over to Mindanao. The fare is P500-550.

Cebu Ferries' MV *Lady of Carmel* leaves on Monday, Wednesday, and Friday at 1900 and takes 10 hours, while the curiously named MV *Lady of Rule* departs Cebu City at 1900 on

Thursday and Saturday. Sulpicio Lines' MV *Philippine Princess* sets sail on Saturday at 2200 and does the crossing in a relatively quick seven hours.

Cebu City to Surigao: Water Jet Shipping's MV *Water Jet 2* departs at 0845 on Tuesday, Thursday, Saturday, and Sunday. The crossing takes three and a half hours and costs P400-450.

Sulpicio Lines' MV *Filipina Princess* leaves Cebu City on Monday at noon and takes nine hours. Cokaliong Shipping's MV *Filipinas Dapitan* departs at 1900 on Monday, Wednesday, and Friday, while the MV *Filipinas Surigao* heads off on Saturday at 1900. Both ships take about 11 hours.

Trans-Asia Shipping's MV *Asia-Singapore* departs Tuesday at 2000 and Saturday at 2200. Figure on 10 hours with this company.

Cebu City to Zamboanga: George & Peter Lines' MV *Zamboanga Ferry* leaves on Monday at 2200 and Friday at 1200. This is a 24-hour journey with a stop in Dumaguete and perhaps Dapitan. Trans-Asia Shipping's MV *Asia-Japan* departs Saturday at 1800 and takes a somewhat quicker 22 hours via Dumaguete.

Ship from Leyte

Several large ships and a single fast ferry connect Leyte with various ports on Mindanao. Maasin is the main departure point from Leyte, while Surigao is the principal arrival area on the big island.

Maasin to Surigao: Water Jet Shipping's MV *Water Jet 2* fast ferry departs at 1045 on Tuesday, Thursday, Saturday, and Sunday. The fare is P200-250 and the journey takes just 90 minutes.

Cokaliong Shipping's MV *Filipinas Surigao* leaves Wednesday at 0600 and Friday at 0300 for the four-hour crossing to Surigao. Trans-Asia Shipping' MV *Asia Singapore* leaves on Friday at 0500, while the MV *Asia-Taiwan* departs Saturday at 0300. Sulpicio Lines' MV *Palawan Princess* sets off every Friday at 2100. All these ships take four hours to reach Surigao.

Liloan to Surigao: Bernard Services' MV *Maharlika II* leaves Liloan daily at 0800 and takes three hours to reach the small port of Lipata, 10 km northwest of Surigao.

Ship from Negros

Most services originate in Negros at Dumaguete rather than the more distant Bacolod.

Bacolod to Cagayan de Oro: Negros Navigation's MV *San Paolo* leaves Bacolod on Thursday at 1600 and takes about 14 hours to Cagayan de Oro.

Dumaguete to Dapitan: Cokaliong Shipping's MV *Filipinas Dinagat* departs at 0700 on Tuesday, Thursday, and Saturday for the four-hour crossing. George & Peter Lines sails either the MV *Dumaguete Ferry*, the MV *Georich*, or the MV *Palauan Ferry* daily at 0800.

Dumaguete to Dipolog: WG&A's MV *Maynilad* leaves Tuesday at 0500 for the four-hour crossing, while the Trans-Asia MV *Asia-Japan* departs Wednesday at 0800. The fare is P60-90.

Dumaguete to Iligan: WG&A's MV *Superferry 7* sets off every Wednesday at 2100 and takes six hours to Iligan. The fare is P140-180.

Dumaguete to Ozamis: Sulpicio Lines' MV *Philippine Princess* leaves Thursday at 2200 and takes seven hours over to Ozamis.

Dumaguete to Zamboanga: Trans-Asia Shipping's MV *Asia-Japan* leaves Sunday at 0200 and takes around 14 hours to reach the southern city.

Ship from Panay

There are no fast ferries from Panay to Mindanao and all the regular ships are fairly slow.

Iloilo City to Butuan: WG&A's MV *Superferry 2* departs on Tuesday at 1500 and requires 17 hours to reach Butuan. The fare is P400-500.

Iloilo City to Cagayan de Oro: WG&A's MV *Superferry 9* leaves at 1900 on Thursday and takes 15 hours, while the MV *Santa Ana* of Negros Navigation leaves Saturday at 1700. Both ships take 14-15 hours, and the fare is P380-440.

Iloilo City to Davao: WG&A's MV *Superferry 1* leaves Sunday at 1400 and takes 32 hours including a stop in General Santos City. The fare is P650-750.

Iloilo City to Iligan: WG&A's MV *Superferry 5* sets off every Saturday at 1400 and arrives in Iligan 13 hours later. The fare is P350-400.

Iloilo City to Zamboanga: Sulpicio Lines' MV *Princess of the Pacific* departs Wednesday at 1500, while the MV *Cotabato Princess* leaves Sunday at 2200. Both services require 14 hours.

Ship from the Sulu Islands

Few travelers wander down to the Sulu Archipelago, though few problems have been reported in recent years.

From Basilan: Basilan Shipping's MV *Dona Lenora* departs Isabela on Basilan Island daily at 0700 and 1300. The crossing up to Zamboanga takes 90 minutes. The MV *Dona Ramona* leaves Lamitan daily at 0730, while the MV *Don Julio* leaves daily at 1000 and 1600. Both passages to Zamboanga take about 90 minutes.

From Jolo and Tawi-Tawi: Most ships in this region are operated by either SKT Shipping Line or Sampaguita Shipping Corporation. Schedules are flexible, but all ships make a continual journey between the various islands of the Sulu chain up to and terminating at Zamboanga.

The principal ships of SKT Shipping are the MV *Lady Ruth,* MV *Lady Helen,* and MV *Dona Isabel II.* Principal ships of Sampaguita Shipping are the MV *Sampaguita Grandeur,* MV *Sampaguita Lei,* and the MV *Sampaguita Blossom.*

NORTHEASTERN MINDANAO

SURIGAO CITY

The provincial capital and trade center is a city of about 180,000 inhabitants, situated on a hook-shaped piece of land at the northern tip of the Mindanao mainland. It was already a thriving settlement when the Spanish arrived.

History

Visayans were already living in the area prior to the Spanish arrivals of 1528 and 1543. Recollect missionaries visited Surigao in 1597 but made little progress. Attempts at subjugation were resisted until an expedition established Spanish authority in 1609. Early settlements were Tandag and Bislig, which became a large mission center. Numancia, now Del Carmen, on Siargao was established in 1621. Muslim raids, however, made settlement difficult, and after Numancia was burned in 1751 by Moros, the Recollect Fathers transferred their residence to Surigao. Visayan migration during the first half of the 20th century increased the pace of settlement.

Attractions

The city's focal point is the plaza, with its popular children's playground.

Adjoining it is the city hall, which contains a tourist office, and a building housing a fine seashell exhibit. The Casa Real (governor's residence) dates from the Spanish era. Be sure to visit the bustling waterfront market. The city celebrates its Charter Day each 31 August with a street parade of floats and evening cultural presentations.

Situated on a hook-shaped peninsula at the northeastern corner of Mindanao, Surigao mainly serves as the launching point for visits to the beautiful group of islands just off the mainland.

Accommodations

It's best to head straight out to Siargao Island, but there are plenty of places if you get stuck in Surigao.

Garcia Hotel: Inexpensive place just south of the town plaza. 311 San Nicolas St., tel. (086) 231-7881, P75-550.

Leomondee Hotel: Newer hotel on the main road a few blocks east of town. Borromeo St., tel. (086) 232-7334, P200-600.

Tavern Hotel: An old favorite with musty rooms but a good location right on the waterfront. Borromeo St., tel. (086) 231-7301, P140-750.

Transportation

PAL flies to Surigao from Manila three times weekly and from Cebu City four times weekly. Waterjet fast ferries leave Cebu City fours times weekly and take three and a half hours to Surigao, including a stop in Maasin in Southern Leyte. You can also catch buses from any north coast town such as Cagayan de Oro or from Davao via Butuan.

Buses from Surigao to Davao and Cagayan de Oro leave from the small bus terminal on the main road a few blocks east of city center.

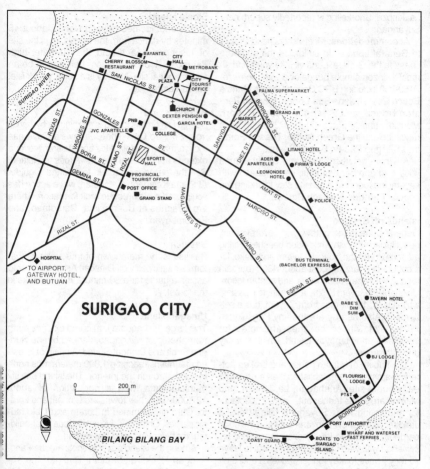

SURIGAO CITY

BILANG BILANG BAY

SIARGAO ISLAND

Siargao Island

Surigao's top draw is the group of islands scattered to the east. Siargao, the largest island, has become a surfers' paradise with large breaks on the eastern side of the island from July to November. The island came of age in 1996 with the inauguration of the Siargao Surfing Cup, an event that placed the Philippines on the international surfing trail.

Dapa is the principal town while General Luna serves as the surfing camp, a short walk from the 10 documented breaks just north of town.

Transportation: Boats to Dapa on Siargao Island leave in the early morning 0800-1100 from the pier at the southern end of Borromeo Street in Surigao. Jeepneys continue 14 km to the town of General Luna, where accommodations are found in beachside nipa huts.

General Luna also serves as gateway to several small islands such as Guyam, Dako, and

La Janoza. Snorkeling is reportedly superb near Suyangan.

Accommodations: Most visitors head straight to General Luna or to Union on the southern coast. In the General Luna vicinity you'll find almost a dozen simple bungalows with rooms for P150-300 including **BRC Beach Resort, Maite's Beach Resort, Jade Star Lodge, Siargao Pension House,** and **Pisangan Beach Resort.** More expensive places in the P300-800 price range include the **Green Room, Tuason Point, and Siargao Pacific Beach Resort.**

At Union between Dapa and General Luna you'll find another beautiful, sandy beach with several inexpensive places to stay including the popular **Latitude 9 Beach Resort.**

Islands off Siargao

General Luna is the gateway to several small, beautiful islands with white-sand beaches. Hiring a *banca* to visit the closest, Guyam and Dako, for a couple of hours will cost about P300 (bargain for a lower price); bring water and suntan lotion. Uninhabited Guyam is only a 10-minute crossing, while Dako, 15 minutes from Guyam, has a settlement. Also nearby are the tiny Pagsukyam White Islet, whose beaches are noted for seashells, and Hanoyoy Island, which is rocky and overgrown.

The finding of human bones and broken pottery in a cave here establishes it as a probable early burial site. Anahauan, La Janoza, and Mamon are a little farther out. There's spectacular snorkeling near Suyangan village on La Janoza, with narrow canyons between the coral gardens. Visitors to La Janoza are traditionally splashed with water when they're about to leave so they'll have to stay longer—at least until their clothes dry. A *banca* for a half-day trip to several islands costs about P400 for three to four people

Nonoc Island

Life on this small fishing island 10 km from Surigao was irrevocably changed in 1974 when the Marinduque Mining & Industrial Corp. began its operations here. Huge mineral deposits support the biggest nickel refinery in Southeast Asia. Cobalt is also mined. Company launches take employees from Surigao City to the mining complex, a 30-minute crossing; Aboitiz makes a weekly return trip from Surigao; there are plans for a Surigao-Nonoc ferry service.

Sibale Island

This island, located beyond Nonoc, about 45 minutes by *banca* from the mainland, is the site of Lisondra Beach and the 10-meter-high Zaragosa Rock Formation, believed to be an ancient burial site. Nearby is a solitary rock islet called Tamulayag.

Hikdop Island

Buenavista on this island is 45 minutes by *banca* from Surigao City. The Buenavista Cave has rock formations, stalactites and stalagmites, and extends hundreds of meters across the island. See the *barangay* captain to arrange a guide. At Punta Kalabera, Catadman, wave action has sculptured a picturesque rock formation. There are beaches at Buenavista, Catadman, and Panomboyon.

Basilisa

Basilisa is the main town of three islands that form a municipality off Dinagat. Ask the mayor to assign a guide for a 30-minute walk to a lake in the forest.

Dinagat Island

This large (801 square km) island extends north from the tip of Mindanao, flanked by the Surigao Strait and Dinagat Sound. A chain of forested mountains reaching 1,000 meters runs north to south through the interior. The island has six municipalities, with a population of about 127,000. The chief towns are Dinagat and Loreto. Chromite is mined in Loreto and Libjo municipalities. Cottage industries include boat-building, mat-weaving, and fish-salting.

Among the island's scenic spots are the Pangpangan Rocks at Cabilan, Dinagat; the 10-hectare, 20-meter-deep Tambongan Lagoon in Tubajon, approached through a narrow, shallow gulf with good coral; and a small island offshore from Loreto where there's good snorkeling. A boat leaves Surigao daily between 0500 and 0700, making numerous stops before reaching Loreto in the afternoon and returning in the evening; boats go to San Jose, too.

Bayagnan Island

Located about an hour by *banca* east of Surigao, this island is the site of the 20-meter-high Buyho Waterfalls in San Jose, and is noted for offshore whirlpools.

Bucas Grande

Socorro, the chief town of this 131-square-km island (pop. 14,000), is a 40-minute *banca* ride from Hayangabon on the mainland and can also be reached by launch from Surigao City. Hire a *banca* in Socorro to visit the island's principal attraction, the **Sohoton Lagoon**, which is approached through a kaleidoscope of rocky islets, hidden channels, coral, lush vegetation, and abundant birdlife. *Bancas* can only enter the tunnel-like Sohoton Cave at low tide; you glide beneath stalactities to emerge into another islet-studded lagoon, an enchanting place known locally as the "City of Sohoton" or "City of the Fairies."

BUTUAN CITY

The provincial capital of Agusan del Norte, this city of about 300,000 sprawls over a flat, marshy area on both sides of the Agusan River. The downtown area is on the left bank, about eight km from the river mouth. Butuan is the commercial hub of the Agusan Valley, both a sea- and river port, and an important center of wood-based industries. Batches of 100-plus logs are towed downriver to supply riverside sawmills and factories.

The name of this region—Agusan Del Norte—relates to the great Agusan River, which rises in the highlands of Davao del Norte and flows about 300 km to Butuan Bay. Butuan City is a crossroads where Mindanao's north-coast highway meets the Agusan Valley highway from Surigao to Davao. Numerous minority tribes live in the interior, which has only recently been opened up due to the impetus of logging. A pioneer atmosphere prevails in the towns of the river valley.

History

In 1976, pottery of the Tang dynasty and the succeeding Five Dynasties was unearthed in the marshy terrain near Butuan. Dating from the 10th century, it's among the earliest-known Chinese ceramics to be discovered in the Philippines. The search for more of this pottery led to a pioneer find—the remains of three *balanghais,* the boats used by early migrants for travel throughout Southeast Asia.

Subsequent excavations unearthed several more, bringing a total of nine boats now known in existence. Carbon-dating of the wood identified one boat as 4th century and another as 13th century; the latter is on display in the National Museum, Manila. The discovery site of the oldest boat is now a museum at Ambangan, Libertad. Fifteenth-century wooden coffins have also been found in the vicinity, along with tradeware and skulls. Some of the pre-Hispanic burial artifacts discovered at Sustan, five km northwest of Butuan, may be seen in Cagayan de Oro's Xavier University Museum.

The province's history is closely connected with the river, long the only means of access to the interior. At the time of the Spanish arrival, foreign merchants were trading with riverbank settlements. Although it's uncertain whether Magellan touched Agusan, records show that early expeditions led by Villalobos and Legazpi explored the coast. Gold was mined around Butuan in the pre-Hispanic era. Legazpi is said to have traded for gold with native chiefs in 1570.

Spanish missionaries were active on the lower Agusan during the 17th and 18th centuries, in spite of the hilltribes' resistance and having to contend with Moro raids. Settlers adapted to the river's regular flooding, Nov.-Jan., by living in houseboats or houses on rafts and farming outside this period of maximum rainfall. Such seasonal flooding or permanent swampiness deterred settlement in the upper valley, which has remained sparsely populated until recent decades, when expansion of the lumber industry has attracted migrants from the Visayas and elsewhere.

Attractions

The main tourist sights here are the market, where you can buy handicrafts and fruit, and the **Northern Mindanao Regional Museum,** located near the city hall in Do-Ongan, two km from downtown, which displays archaeological and ethnological exhibits. The *balanghai* discovery site museum is at Ambangan, Libertad, between the city and the airport.

Festivals

Butuan celebrates the Santacruzan and Balanghai festival during May, and in July, the Kahimonan festival and the Santa Ana Abayan race and procession are held. The fluvial procession in honor of Santa Ana takes place on the Agusan River and is followed by a *banca* race against the current. Adlaw Hong Butuan on 1 August commemorates the anniversary of the city's Charter Day with cultural programs, competitions, a beauty pageant, fluvial parade, and *banca* race.

Accommodations

Butuan is a junction town where the highway coming up from Davao terminates and splits east to Surigao and west to Camiguin Island and Cagayan de Oro. Not much to see here but you might need to overnight if your travel plans include Davao or you miss the final buses heading either east or west.

The bus terminal is outside town and you'll need to catch a jeepney into city center. Otherwise, coming from Surigao, hop off the bus when you see the town plaza or cathedral.

Hensonly Plaza Hotel: An old and somewhat frightening hotel but with acceptable rooms for a single night. San Francisco St., tel. (085) 225-1340, P120-450.

Emerald Villa Hotel: Somewhat better option just around the corner just opposite the Echelon Plaza Hotel. Villanueva St., tel. (085) 225-2141, P350-650.

Hotel Karaga: Modern upscale hotel near La Terazza Cuisine and Weegool's Grill Haus. Montilla Blvd., tel. (085) 242-8387, P600-1,400.

Restaurants

Good food is available at the **Prime Cut Steakhouse** or **New Narra Restaurant.** Also try the **Golden Dragon Restaurant,** on Concepcion Street, the most popular Chinese restaurant in Butuan offering set meals for P50 or less. For good Filipino food there's **Lutong Bahay ni Aling Cora** on R. Calo Street. The food is selected, ready to cook, with an excellent array to choose from.

Alternatives include the **Dragon City Restaurant** and **Jet's Inn Restaurant.** The **Embassy Hotel's** restaurant is better still. **Ramos Lechon and Folk House** is a good place to go in the evening.

Transportation

By Air: PAL flies from Cebu City to Butuan once a day (50 minutes) and from Manila three times a week. The airport is at Bancasi, six km west of Butuan. A taxi ride to the city costs about P30, a jeepney costs P2. Aerolift flies Manila-Butuan City daily; the flight takes one hour and 40 minutes.

By Sea: As an interisland port, Butuan is supplemented by Nasipit, 25 km west along the coast. Several large ships of major lines arrive daily, but as of this writing, Butuan is not served by any fast ferries from Cebu or elsewhere in the Visayas.

By Land: From Cagayan de Oro (207 km, three and a half hours), Bachelor Express leaves every 30 minutes 0400-1930, and also Ceres Liner makes the trip. Buses heading to Cagayan de Oro pass through Balingoan, where the ferry departs for Camiguin Island. There's plenty of traffic along this route.

From Davao City (286 km, six hours), try Bachelor Express (every 30 minutes between 0300-1630), Ceres Liner, or Mintranco. From General Santos City catch Bachelor Express. From Iligan City (300 km, five hours) travel Fortune Lines.

From Surigao City (123 km, two hours), Bachelor has buses every 45 minutes (0430-1730); other companies are Dennis Overland, Nembusco, and Superlines. From Tandag, Bachelor and Superstar Lines buses leave every two hours. Jeepneys ply the coastal routes as well, stopping in the smaller towns en route to Cagayan de Oro or at the ferry for Camiguin Island in Balingoan.

BALINGOAN

Balingoan is the small town between Butuan and Cagayan de Oro from where ferries depart hourly 0800-1400 to Camiguin Island.

Accommodations

If you miss the last ferry to Camiguin, you'll need to overnight in Balingoan at **Lingaya's Pension House, Balingoan Pension House,** or **Balingoan Hotel,** where rooms go for P125-300.

CAMIGUIN ISLAND

All visitors to Camiguin want to "Come again!" It's that kind of place: beautiful, peaceful, with wonderful inhabitants. It's often referred to as an island paradise. Camiguin offers a volcano to climb, tiny offshore islets with white sand and coral, hot and cold springs and waterfalls. Camiguenos are famous for their hospitality.

Typical homes are on stilts built over mangrove swamps decorated with bouganvillea, poinsettias, and orchids. The people will probably greet you with "Hi friends!" rather than "Hi Joe!" The best time to visit is April-June; Camiguin can be very wet mid-December to mid-March. A nice time to visit is at the end of October for the Lanzones Festival in Mambajao, which is well worth seeing.

The Land

Camiguin is a volcanic island (229 square km) situated in the Mindanao Sea, about seven km from the mainland. The rugged, hilly terrain is dominated by seven volcanoes. The island has been devastated by eruptions, such as those of Vulcan Daan ("Old Camiguin Volcano": 838 meters) in 1871 and Hibok-Hibok (1,250 meters) in 1951.

Other volcanos include Mt. Timpoong (1,580 meters), Mt. Mambajao (1,420 meters), Mt. Tres Marias, and Guinsiliban Peak. The coastline alternates between black- or white-sand beaches and volcanic rock.

Camiguin is divided into five municipalities; its more than 64,000 inhabitants are mostly farmers and fishermen. Rich volcanic soil nurtures rice, coconuts, bananas, corn, and root crops. *Lanzones* grown on Hibok-Hibok's slopes are considered to be the sweetest in the Philippines. The island has good fishing grounds offshore. The people are of Visayan descent, hence Cebuano is the main language, though a few people in Sagay and Guinsiliban still speak the old native language.

History

Ancient legends link Camiguin with Surigao's Lake Mainit area. The original inhabitants were Manobos from Surigao. Kinamiguin, the island's old tongue, is similar to tribal languages of Surigao. It's believed that the Manobo retreated to the highlands of Mindanao when Visayan settlers arrived. The people were already trading with foreign merchants before Magellan and Legazpi landed here, in 1521 and 1565, respectively.

The Spanish founded a settlement at Guinsiliban in 1598, but Catarman (where Bonbon is now) was to be their major center on the island until its destruction in the 1871 eruption of Mt. Vulcan Daan, after which they moved the town center to its present site. Mambajao wasn't established until 1855, but it grew rapidly to become the busiest port in northern Mindanao by the beginning of this century, at a time when Cagayan de Oro was only a minor settlement.

In 1901, local resistance to the Americans ended in a short, one-sided battle at Catarman. During WW II, the Japanese burned much of downtown Mambajao in reprisal against guerrilla activity on the island.

Fiestas and Festivals

Easter is a big event on Camiguin, with a passion play and a Good Friday procession of antique, life-size santos in Mambajao. On June 24, Hibok-hibokan is celebrated by the whole island with picnics on the beaches. In Mambajao, for example, there are water processions, games and races, and beauty contests. Events take place at several places, including Cabua-an and Agohay Beaches. Since this is the Feast of St. John the Baptist, visitors just might get "baptized" with water!!

At the end of October, the Lanzones Festival is centered in Mambajao. This exuberant fiesta features a parade with people in costume, games, exhibits, and entertainment. The costumes are particularly colorful as a number of local groups exhibit tribal costumes worn by the many cultural minorities of northern Mindanao. Dancers are judged by a team of local officials and prizes are presented. The whole town takes on a festive atmosphere and plenty of sweet, delicious *lanzones* are sold.

Getting There

Camiguin is reached with a ferry from Balingoan in northern Mindanao (two hours east of Cagayan de Oro) to Benoni on Camiguin. Ferries leave eight times daily and take 90 minutes to make the crossing. Jeepneys continue to the provincial capital of Mambajao.

The fastest way to reach Cagayan de Oro is with a fast ferry from either Cebu City or Dumaguete. Buses leave frequently from the Cagayan de Oro bus terminal for Balingoan.

Also, direct ferries leave Cagayan de Oro several times weekly at 0800.

The port of entry is Benoni (often spelled Binone) wharf, about 17 km, 30 minutes by jeepney from Mambajao, the capital, or at Guinsiliban, where a daily ferry arrives from Cagayan de Oro. The ferry port between Benoni and Mindanao is at Balingoan (Misamis Oriental), which is on the main highway between Butuan and Cagayan de Oro.

The Guinsiliban ferry terminus is in Cagayan de Oro proper. Bachelor Express buses link these two cities every 30 minutes; Balingoan is 90 minutes from Cagayan and two hours from Butuan. The ferry sails Balingoan-Benoni daily; the 10-km crossing takes 75 minutes. There's a direct boat from Cagayan de Oro to Benoni (takes five and a half hours) on Monday and Friday, returning Tuesday and Saturday; departures are scheduled for 2400, but delays are common.

The newer ferry link between Cagayan de Oro and Guinsiliban departs from the city pier at 0800 Tues.-Sun. arriving at Guinsiliban at 1100. Departures from the island leave Wednesday and Friday at 0800 and at 1500 on Saturday and Sunday.

This link between Guinsiliban and Cagayan de Oro is more convenient for travelers, but it's less frequent than the ferry between Benoni and the mainland at Balingoan. From Cebu, Bisaya Shipping sails on Saturday to Benoni (takes 12 hours), then returns to Cebu via Medina and Butuan. Thus, to travel from Camiguin to Cebu, it's more convenient to go via Cagayan de Oro.

There's also a weekly ship from Jagna (Bohol). Adventurous travelers have been chartering *bancas* for the three-hour trip to Panglao Island and Tagbilaran, Bohol. Fishermen and boatmen will gladly make the trip for P700-1,000 one-way. If you can get a group together to cut costs, this makes an interesting and fast way to get to Bohol and the Visayas.

Getting Around

To circumnavigate the island, it's necessary to travel by a combination of bus, jeepney, and *motorella* (tricycle), since public vehicles don't make the complete circuit. Frequent transportation links the two largest towns, Mambajao and Catarman, with the ferry at Benoni and nearby Guinsiliban, for example, while few vehicles operate on the section between Yumbing and Catarman.

The traffic flow coincides with the ferry schedule. Thus, vehicles leave Mambajao early in the morning, taking passengers to the 0600 ferry, then wait in Benoni for the ferry to arrive from Balingoan at 0915. And so on until the last ferry arrives at 1715.

On most days, a sole jeepney goes from Mambajao to Catarman by the back route (takes 40 minutes) at 0400-0430, returning at 0530-0600, after which traffic is sporadic. Only on Sundays is transport frequent all day on this stretch, as islanders travel to attend the market and cockfight.

Motorellas can be hired for short distances, but they're not plentiful outside Mambajao municipality. An alternative is for a group of travelers to share the cost of hiring a jeepney for sightseeing; the local term for this is *pakyaw*.

There's no commercial motorcycle rental on Camiguin, but some individuals in Mambajao will rent their machines. Ask around. Similarly, you may be able to rent a bicycle or easily hitchhike, although private transportation is fairly rare.

MAMBAJAO

The provincial capital and trading center is a small, quiet town. Mambajao makes a good base from which to explore the island. There's a tourist office in the Capitol Building, and a PNB where you can change traveler's checks. The NACIDA handicraft display center offers an array of locally made baskets, and Mambajao's lively market also sells handicrafts.

Mambajao cleverly derives its name from *mamhaw* (let's eat breakfast) and *bajao* (leftover boiled rice).

The town has some old Spanish-style homes and a colonial church, and comes to life in late October during the Lanzones Festival, which is held here. *Motorellas* ply the main road from downtown to about nine km in either direction throughout the day; the regular fare is P2 pp. The electricity supply is cut off at 2300 each night, sometimes earlier.

Accommodations

Inexpensive pensions are located in town and on the beaches a few kilometers west.

Tia's Pension House adjacent to the town hall and RJ Pension House on Neri Street have singles for P80-220. Both rent bikes, motorcycles, and offers tips on sightseeing. Tia also manages some beachside cottages a few minutes outside town. Across from Tia's Cottages is Shoreline Cottages, P200-250.

There's also the run-down Camiguin Travel Lodge for P100 and plenty of locals who will offer a room for the night, particularly during the crowded Lanzones Festival. Southeast of town on Cabua-an Beach, there's Gue's Cottages for P150-200, and a km northwest of Mambajao you can stay in a tree house at Bolokbolok at the Tree House (P150). There is a restaurant nearby, a tennis court, and motorbikes for rent at P400 a day. This is a great way to see the island.

More accommodations are situated in small *barrios* west of Mambajao. First stop is at Turtle's Nest Resort in Kuguita, three km west of town.

Restaurants

Tia's serves good and ample meals. The Camiguin Travel Lodge has a restaurant and serves good cheap meals as do many of the small restaurants along the main street. Have a simple meal at Ligaya Restaurant and Cold Spot near the market or the equally rustic Botica Milagrosa. Grilled fish is also inexpensive when bought at the market. *Sinugba* and *kinilaw* are local specialties as are the sweet *lanzones,* made famous by the Lanzones Festival. For nightlife, there are two small discos, Bidlisiw and Anging's.

INLAND FROM MAMBAJAO

Katibawasan Falls

These 50-meter falls are surrounded by lush vegetation. It's refreshing to swim in the pool below the falls, but the water's cold, so it's best to come here between 1000 and 1400 when the sun's overhead. There's a resthouse where you can change and a cottage in which to overnight, but you must bring food; make a reservation at the tourist office in Mambajao. To get there, take a *motorella* one-half km from Mambajao to the waiting shed at Pandan, walk to the end of the village, then follow the trail to the right for 2.5 km to the falls. Admission to the falls is P5.

Ardent Hot Spring

The best times to visit this small, natural stone swimming pool with 40° C water are in the early morning, on rainy days, and at night. A resthouse provides changing facilities, plus food and cold drinks. Take a *motorella* 3.5 km from Mambajao to Kuguita; the spring is 2.5 km from Kuguita church; walk 1.5 km inland till the road forks; bear right then take the first road left after the school, then the right fork again. Stay at the Ardent-Esperanza Mountain Resort with dorm beds for P50 and cottages for P200. Admission to the spring is P5.

THE COAST WEST OF MAMBAJAO

Baylao

Swiss-operated Turtle's Nest Resort, on the boundary between Kuguita and Baylao, four km from Mambajao, is a pleasant, secluded place to stay. Cottages cost P150 pp, or P250 pp with meals; good food is served in a beachside restaurant with sunset view. To get there, ask the *motorella* driver for Mahayahay Beach.

Follow the road from the highway to the beach. To the left is the sandy Mahayahay Beach, which has no coral, and to the right, Turtle's Nest Beach, where the resort is. There's coral 100-150 meters offshore from here, then a drop-off at about the 200-meter mark. Access can be tricky at low tide, however. The resort rents complete diving equipment for P400 per day, plus P50 for a second tank, P75 for a dive guide, and extra for a *banca,* if necessary. Trips could be arranged, for example, to Hikdop Reef, about four km northeast of Magting, which offers excellent coral and fishlife, or around to the drop-off beneath the lava flows of Old Camiguin Volcano.

WHITE ISLAND

This tiny, dazzlingly white sand bar, also called Medano Island, is about two km offshore from Agoho and Yumbing. It's a good place to sunbathe, with superb views of Hibok-Hibok and enjoyable snorkeling 150-200 meters off the island. There's no shade however, so take suntan lotion. Local fishermen often visit the island; you can buy fresh fish from them, especially in the morning.

Take a *motorella* or jeepney from Mambajao to Agoho (takes 15 minutes) or Yumbing, from where you can hire a *banca;* the boatman will stay with you for two or three hours, which will be enough for most people. It's also possible to be dropped off and picked up later at a prearranged time. One might also overnight here, especially during the full moon; bring a tent, sleeping bag, firewood, food and drink. White Island is often seen on tourist posters and brochures when advertising Mindanao or the Philippines.

SOUTHEAST OF MAMBAJAO

Beaches are rocky on this side of Mambajao. Three km from town, and a few hundred meters inland from the road, are some open pits where old Chinese pottery was unearthed. Anito, five km out, has a beach with coral to the left; it's reached by the first road after the Chinese cemetery. At Magting, seven km out, there's a secluded beach, good coral to the left of the cottages, and cold springs in the sea to the right of them. Ancient skeletons, tools, weapons, and utensils were discovered in caves near here.

Three km beyond Magting, alight from the jeepney at the sign for Macao Cold Spring in Tupsan. Snorkel over good coral then return to the highway and walk inland for one km (take right fork in road) to wash the salt off in the small, natural stone pool of the spring.

HIBOK-HIBOK VOLCANO

This is, at 1,250 meters, the most active of seven volcanoes on the island. Between 1948 and 1951, it smoked and rumbled continually. There

was a minor eruption in 1948 and again in 1949, when 79 individuals perished in landslides. Then in 1951, it erupted without warning, issuing steaming hot gases and absorbing huge amounts of oxygen from the air, so that people were asphyxiated. The death toll was over 2,000, many of whom were found as though asleep.

Lava covered nearly 10 square km behind Mambajao, devastating many villages. You can see these lava flows from the road between Mambajao and Yumbing. The island's population had been 69,000 in 1951, but over 30,000 left Camiguin following the eruption.

DAY TRIP AROUND THE ISLAND

Start early and allow a full day for the 64-km trip around Camiguin. On the open road, it's better to hike until *motorellas* or jeepneys pass rather than wait. Leaving Mambajao, the choice is to go clockwise or counterclockwise. Clockwise, get an early jeepney that connects with the 0600 ferry at Benoni, have breakfast, then take a jeepney that will depart for Catarman after the 0915 ferry.

From here, be prepared to hike about 15 km to Naasag, from where regular *motorellas* go into Mambajao. Traveling counterclockwise, pass by nearby spots such as White Island, which can be visited as day trips, and take a *motorella* directly to Naasag, then begin walking toward Tangub Hot Springs. Start early, since while jeepneys operate all day on the Catarman-Benoni-Mambajao stretch, they become less frequent by midafternoon.

Naasag

Naasag, nine km from Mambajao, is usually the end of the line for *motorellas*. If you continue walking along the road for five minutes, over a hill, look for a small bamboo stairway on the right; it leads down through Downer's Grove to a rocky beach. This is a good picnic spot, with nice coral and a 15-meter drop-off close to shore, a shady grove behind the beach, and a well at the back of the grove.

If you return to the road and walk for another 10 minutes, over the next hill, a path leads down a steep embankment to Fisherman's Landing, a secluded stony beach which also has good coral and a 15-meter drop-off just offshore.

Tangub Hot Springs

About three km, an hour's walk, beyond Naasag, a cement road leads down to these hot springs, which are also called Ocean, Old, or Mainit Hot Springs. To get there by *motorella,* you must pay a special-trip price (about P50). Many volcanic hot springs flow into the sea directly here, and some emerge from rocks directly beside the sea.

There's a small pool to sit in, from which you can spring, so to speak, into the sea at a step. In fact, saltwater and freshwater become mixed at each tide. Thus, the water's cool at high tide, too hot at low tide, and agreeably warm at mid-tide. A delightful place! Just past these springs, the lava flows of Old Camiguin Volcano ("Vulcan Daan") plunge into the sea, and it's fun to snorkel from the springs along this shore.

Where the lava meets the sea, there are rocks on which to sunbathe, and a narrow shelf with excellent coral, followed by a sharp drop-off. Don't leave valuables unattended while snorkeling, however. An alternative is to snorkel from a *banca,* which could be hired for about P60 from Naasag or the first village on the other side of the lava flow.

Bonbon

From Tangub Hot Springs, you can walk along the road for another hour, across the lava flow, high above the sea, to this village, which was the site of the island's old capital. It's 16 km from Mambajao. The story goes that in 1871, an old man appeared and threatened the inhabitants with damnation if they didn't mend their sinful ways. He was ignored, of course, and the next day, May Day, the town was destroyed by Vulcan Daan's eruption.

The ruins of the 17th-century coral church, bell tower, and *convento* still remain. Part of the town, including the cemetery, was submerged. Gravestones were formerly visible at low tide off sandy, secluded Sabang Beach, 200 meters from the ruins, but they can no longer be seen. It's believed that both Magellan and Legazpi landed here in search of fresh water. Snorkel to the right of the beach, where the shallows extend a long way out. There's a spectacular view of the volcano from here.

Catarman

After Bonbon's destruction, the Spanish moved down the coast to Catarman, which is now the is-

land's second-largest town. A small museum in the municipal hall displays antique artifacts. There are no lodging houses here, but local families will accept boarders; ask around. Approaching Catarman from Bonbon, there are several small sandy inlets, some of which have fine coral. The coast is rocky from Catarman town round to Guinsiliban, often with good coral just 30 meters offshore.

Santo Niño Spring and Tuwasan Falls

Santo Niño Spring consists of a large stone pool with a two-meter deep sandy bottom, fed by hundreds of cold springs, in attractive surroundings. There are changing facilities and a small store. To get here, look for a sign saying Kiyab Pool, 500 meters north of Catarman. Walk inland, and after 3.5 km take the left fork to the nearby spring. Ask locals to point out the trail between here and Tuwasan Falls, so that you can make a circular hike.

These beautiful 25-meter falls have a natural pool at their base, but there are plans to build a mini-hydro-plant here. From the falls, follow the road through Mainit to where it meets the main road two km north of Catarman. For those doing this walk in reverse, there's a sign for the falls at this junction.

Guinsiliban

A 300-year-old watchtower, used as a lookout against Moro pirates, is located behind the elementary school. This little town is now the ferry terminus for a large boat from Cagayan de Oro. Boats depart for Cagayan de Oro at 0800 Wednesday and Friday and at 1700 on Saturday and Sunday. Cost is P50. There are no accommodations here as yet but plans to open a guesthouse are in progress.

Kibila Beach

This spot offers 750 meters of coarse white sand, quite good snorkeling, though the seabed slopes steeply, and a well by the beach. To get here, alight from the jeepney at the Cantaan waiting shed, from where it's a pleasant three km walk to the beach. The road forks in the center of Cantaan village; bear right.

Benoni

This is Camiguin's main ferry port. Taguines Lagoon, an artificial lake, is two km south of the wharf; take a *motorella*. You can stay here at the pleasant **Travel Lodge** (P150); a restaurant/bar overlooking the lagoon serves fresh fish raised in its own pond. The bungalows are built on a network of bamboo bridges and stilts so that you can take a cottage over the pond and hear the fish swimming under your bed all night. A unique place and worth staying a night. Food is great and the family is friendly. The lodge is associated with **Camiguin Travel Lodge** in Mambajao, but is in much better condition.

Magsaysay Island
Situated three km offshore, this island, formerly Mantigue Island, is small enough to walk around in 20 minutes. It has shady trees, a white-sand beach, and about 20 resident families. The near side is shallow with little coral, but the far side has a drop-off that provides good diving, with lots of fish. These waters attract many local fishermen, so go to Hubangon and check if any of them are headed out here. If so, they'll drop you on the island for a small tip; if not, you must hire a *banca*.

Mahinog
Mahinog has rocky beaches with good coral offshore. You can stay here at the modern, Western-style **Mychelin Beach Resort** (P150-200), with free coffee and electricity from 1800 to 2100. It's situated three km north of Benoni, facing Magsaysay Island.

NORTH-CENTRAL MINDANAO

The focal point of this progressive coastal province is Cagayan de Oro, the principal city and main transportation center of northern Mindanao.

CAGAYAN DE ORO

The provincial capital and commercial center is a sprawling, relatively clean modern city. The downtown area is on the east bank of the 80-km-long Cagayan River, about five km upstream. The port on Macalajar Bay is a busy interisland stop and the outlet for the pineapples and other products of Misamis Oriental and Bukidnon. Formerly called Cagayan de Misamis, the settlement's name was changed to "de Oro" after the Spanish discovered gold in the river.

Its growth, since the turn of the century, from a small community to a major regional center of about 431,000 inhabitants has imparted a boom-town atmosphere with the first McDonald's (drive-through!) on Mindanao. The Limketkai Center on the outskirts of the city has a brand-new indoor air-conditioned mall as well.

Cagayan de Oro is mainly a transit point for visitors heading west to Camiguin or south toward Marawi and Davao.

Attractions
Sights around town include the Maranao and Bukidnon artifacts at Xavier University on Corrales Avenue in the southeast corner of town. Outside town are the Huluga Caves, where ancient Chinese shards were unearthed; Macahambus Cave, where Filipino revolutionaries defeated American forces in 1900; and the Del Monte pineapple plantation for guided tours. A tourist office is in the Sports Complex on Velez Avenue.

Accommodations
Lodgers Inn: Bare-bones place in the center of town just west of the Excelsior Hotel. Yacapin St., tel. (088) 824-1131, P125-300.

Sampaguita Hotel: Old and basic hotel also in the center of town one block west of Velez Street with both fan-cooled and a/c rooms. Borja St., tel. (088) 872-2640, P250-500.

Excelsior Hotel: Good location plus 56 decent a/c rooms with private baths and color TV. Velez St., tel. (088) P500-950.

Dynasty Court Hotel: Best in town with an a/c lobby for overheated travelers. Hayes St., tel. (088) 872-7908, P850-1,600.

Transportation
Air: PAL flies Manila-Cagayan twice daily (85 minutes); Cebu-Cagayan three times weekly (35 minutes); and Davao-Cagayan three times weekly (30 minutes).

Ship: See the shipping schedules under Transportation in the Mindanao Introduction.

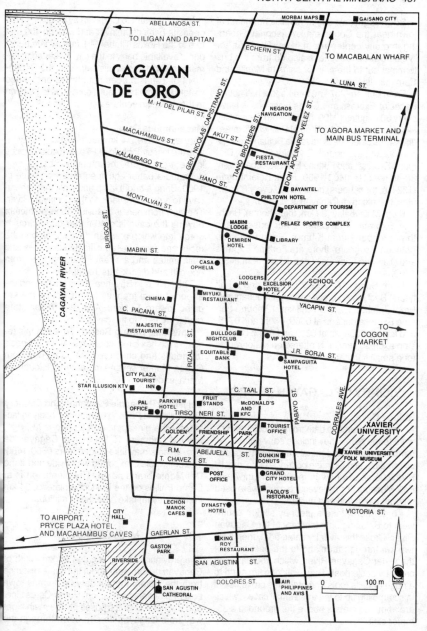

CAGAYAN DE ORO

Bus: Cagayan's bus terminal is northeast of town near the Cogon market; jeepneys heading into city center are marked "Divisoria" or "Velez Street." Jeepneys also go from the bus terminal out to the pier for ships to Manila and Camiguin Island.

From Butuan (207 km, three and a half hours) Bachelor Express and Ceres Liner buses leave every 30 minutes (0400-1930). From Davao City (493 km, nine and a half hours) Bachelor Express and Ceres Liner buses travel via Butuan. From Iligan (92 km, two hours), Bachelor Express, Diamond Express, and Fortune Express depart every 30-45 minutes 0400-1900. From Kolambugan (132 km, three hours) buses leave every 30 minutes; last trip from Cagayan is at 1600.

From Malaybalay (99 km, three hours), Bachelor Express and Ceres Liner buses pass through hourly from Kibawe. From Pagadian (224 km, six hours) there are Fortune Express and Diamond Express buses, hourly from 0430-1300.

From Surigao City (327 km, five and a half hours) Bachelor Express has regular departures. From Zamboanga City (488 km, 12 hours) Fortune Express departs at 0500, 0600, and 0715, and leaves Cagayan at 0300 and 0445. Limited-stop express service is offered on major routes for a small surcharge.

VICINITY OF CAGAYAN DE ORO

Huluga Caves

Artifacts estimated to date from about 2500 B.C. were found here. They include early pottery, ornaments, stone and metal implements, skeletal remains, and Chinese pottery shards, mostly Ming. Some are now in the Xavier University Folk Museum. It's believed the caves were used for both habitation and burial.

To get here, take a jeepney six km southwest to Balulang on a tributary of the Cagayan River. Cross this river by cable boat, then walk two km through farmland to the east bank of the wider Cagayan River, which you can also cross by cable boat. Then walk one km north to a huge tree. Its roots and branches prove useful in scrambling up to the three small caves, which are about 25 meters above the ground in a 33-meter cliff.

You can return to Cagayan by crossing to the opposite bank of the river and walking 400 meters to the Roxas Timber Mill, from where transport's available back to the city. Because of numerous accidents at this cave site, the Department of Tourism does not always encourage visitors to come here, but it continues to be open to the public so venture at your own risk.

Macahambus Cave

This large cave, 14 km southeast of Cagayan, was the last stronghold of Filipino revolutionaries in the area, where, though outnumbered, they defeated a better-equipped American force in 1900. Bring a bright lamp and walk through the cave to a point overlooking the Cagayan River. The view from here is beautiful. About 50 meters beyond the cave is a 40-meter-deep circular gorge into which one can descend among the rocks and ferns to see cliffside stalactites and stalagmites and a stream that emerges from one cliff and disappears into another.

The cave is in Bayanga, three km beyond the airport; take a jeepney from Carmen market going toward Talakag. A small *sari sari* store marks the path to the cave.

Lawndale Spring Resort: To reach this resort, which has large, spring-fed swimming pools for adults and children, take a jeepney from Cogon Market seven km south to Taguanao, Macasandig.

Del Monte Pineapple Plantation and Cannery

The Philippine Packing Corporation canning factory for the pineapple and tomato is at Bugo, beyond Cugman, 15 km east of Cagayan de Oro. Visitors may take guided tours 0800-1400. The pineapple is exported worldwide under the Del Monte brand name. The plantation is at Camp Philips on the Bukidnon plateau, 34 km from Cagayan; take a Bachelor minibus.

MALAYBALAY

The provincial capital, located 99 km south of Cagayan de Oro, and about the same distance from the Cotabato boundary, is a small town built by pioneers from Luzon. Hourly Ceres Liner and Bachelor Express buses ply the main highway from Cagayan de Oro down through the

THE KAAMULAN FESTIVAL OF MALAYBALAY

Kaamulan is a three-day cultural event held in Malaybalay on the first week of September. Its purpose is to unify the eight tribal groups of the area, which have historically been at odds with one another, and to foster understanding between the minorities and the lowlanders who've settled in the region.

In the Binukid highland dialect, *"kaamulan"* means a social gathering for a special purpose. Traditionally, it might be a wedding, harvest festival, or a ritual involving a *datu* or deity. The highlanders trek down from their mountain villages wearing colorful traditional dress, including some spectacular headdresses, to dance, sing, chant, play music, compete in indigenous sports, and perform traditional rituals. Over 30 events are staged at different sites in Malaybalay, with the main activities in Pines View Park, behind the provincial capitol. Key aspects of Kaamulan are Alusod, the offering of native wine and food to visitors. The festival opens with a parade of the tribes, followed by the two-part Pamalas ceremony, conducted by the tribespeople as a sort of cleansing and purification.

Panlisig is a ritual to ward off evil spirits. The tribespeople recognize a traditional god, Magbabaya, but many have also been converted to Christianity. Ecumenical services in Binukid are held in the town plaza. Pangampo (general worship) is featured in between events; its final offering involves the symbolic tasting of food by the *datus*, officials, and dignitaries.

Tagulambong Ho Datu is the first formal hierarchy in the datuship ascendancy. The Panumanod is a ceremony ensuring that a righteous spirit, Mulin-olin, will possess and guide a leader or government official. Pandang-ol is a mass adoption ceremony.

Tribal dances depicting the monkey, frog, and birds are accompanied by gongs and other native instruments are a major feature of the festival. Courtship and mock war dances also enjoy mass participation. Contests in which both males and females try to outdo each other with witty sayings and proverbs, chanting, ethnic sports, and games are popular events.

province toward North Cotabato. The neighboring Matin-ao and Nasuli Springs at Bangcud are

popular picnic spots outside Malaybalay. Also nearby is Camp Kasisang, a WW II POW camp.

Stay at: **Saver's Inn** (P150-200); **Haus Malibu** (P150-200) on Bonifacio St.; **Pamana Inn** (P150) on Fortich St.; **Tiara Lodge** at the public market (P100-150); **Casa Crista** (P100) on Cudal St.; or **Carmen Lodge** and **Canlourd Lodge** (P150-200), both on Fortich Street. There are also cottages for rent at the Kaamulan festival site in Pines View Park, and one could also camp in this park.

ILIGAN CITY

Iligan City, the capital of Lanao del Norte, is an important transportation center on the north coast of Mindanao, and the gateway to the fascinating Muslim area of Marawi and Lake Lanao.

Iligan is the provincial capital, a port, and industrial city of about 178,000 inhabitants, situated on the coastal plain where the Iligan River flows into Iligan Bay. This former Jesuit missionary center and site of a Spanish fort is now a center of heavy industry—steel, tinplate, pulp and paper, with flour mills, fertilizer, plastic, chemical, and cement factories on its outskirts. Job-seeking migrants continue to arrive here.

If you don't plan to visit Marawi, you can still see examples of Muslim crafts at the Maranao Handicrafts store. There's also a NACIDA Display Center, and Iligan's large market has handicraft stalls. The tourism office is at Iligan City Hall, on Buhanginan Hill, a popular place with locals at sundown.

History of Lanao del Norte

Lanao del Norte is the land of the Maranao. In their dialect, *"lanao"* means "lake" and refers to the region's dominant physical feature, Lake Lanao. Lanao is divided into two provinces: Lanao del Norte, which is predominantly Christian, and Lanao del Sur, which is basically Muslim. The region offers great cultural contrast from the Christianized coastal lowlands around Iligan to the intensely Islamic shores of Lake Lanao and Illana Bay.

The region was originally occupied by several highland tribes. The Maranao moved from the coast to the shores of Lake Lanao during pre-Hispanic times and subsequently became or-

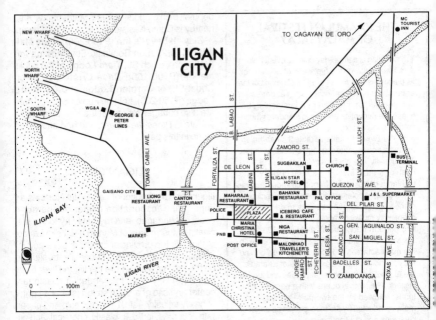

ganized into small sultanates. Iligan, formerly a fishing village called Bayug, has been a Christian settlement since the end of the 16th century. It was taken over by Filipinos who had fled from Panglao (Bohol) to Dapitan and subsequently allied themselves with the Spanish.

Two years after Sultan Kudarat's defeat in 1637, a strong Spanish-led force landed at Bayug and moved to conquer the Muslim shores of Lake Lanao. They reached the lake and started to fortify Dansalan (now Marawi), but the Maranao forced them to withdraw back to Bayug. The Spaniards built a fort here instead, enabling Bayug (Iligan) to remain a Christian outpost settled by Cebuanos, in spite of frequent Muslim raids, while the Lake Lanao region preserved its isolation from Spanish influence. Though the Spaniards mounted sporadic campaigns and occupied Malabang and other south coast towns, they didn't establish even nominal control of the Lanao region until 1895.

The Americans landed at Malabang in 1899, and seven U.S. gunboats anchored off Iligan to take control of the town in 1900. The Maranao, who occupied a series of lakeside *kotas* (forts),

continued to resist until 1913. Religion and its associated political factors were key elements in the division of the old Lanao province in 1959, which resulted in the current concentrations of Christians and Muslims in the provinces where they respectively predominate. At this time, many Visayan settlers in Lanao del Sur moved to the coastal areas of Lanao del Norte. Today, Lanao del Sur is over 90% Muslim, and Lanao del Norte is around 70% Christian.

Ang Sinulog

This fiesta is held on 29 September to honor the city's warrior patron saint, San Miguel the Archangel. The climax of a week of celebration comes in the Pana-ad and the Yawa-yawa. *Pana-ad* refers to the promise made to San Miguel for favors granted. Brightly costumed participants in the main procession dance the *sinulog,* in which they mime a fight with unseen adversaries to cries of "Viva Señor San Miguel!" Other participants march solemnly. These are the "archangels," dressed as warrior-angels.

They also take part in the Yawa-yawa, or Comedia, a *moro-moro*-type miracle play performed in vernacular dialogue, song, and dance. It depicts Lucifer's revolt against God, culminating in the defeat in battle of the bad angels by the good angels led by San Miguel. The songs of the Comedia are very popular with the Iliganons. During the fiesta, the Diyandi, a group of young girls in Bukidnon and Maranao traditional costume, go from house to house to dance and sing in native dialects for the occupants. They're probably reenacting how tribespeople, in spite of missionary efforts to persuade them to stay in Christian settlements, would only come down from the hills for big feasts, when they would pay homage and bring offerings to San Miguel.

Accommodations
Budget accommodations include: **Jiddy Lodge, Molave Lodge, Riva's Lodge, Pagoda Executive Lodge,** and **Fortune Express Resthouse** (P100-150, at the bus terminal). Centrally located, cheap accommodation can be found at the **Maxim Inn,** Quezon Avenue (P150-200). The nearby **Star Inn** (P200) on the same street is also good.

The **Jade Tourist Inn** and **Crystal Inn** (P200-250) on Tibanga Highway are good values. Also try the **Iligan Day Inn** and **Snowland Inn** on Benito Ong Street. The **Iligan Village Hotel** (P200) and the **Maria Cristina Hotel** (P450-500), fanciest in town, are located on Aguinaldo and Mabini Streets.

Restaurants
There are many restaurants in the downtown area. **Canton Restaurant** serves tasty Chinese and Filipino food. **Liong Restaurant** makes good sandwiches. Other places include **Malonhao Traveller's Kitchenette, Niga Restaurant, Iceberg Cafe and Restaurant, Bahayan Restaurant, Sunburst Fried Chicken House,** and the **Corals Restaurant** on Quezon Avenue.

The **Cafe Hermoso,** Badelles St., is considered the best in Iligan, best known for breakfast with papaya and *barako* coffee. Two rooms are also for rent here. Another favorite is **Coconut Palace Lutong,** also on Badelles Street. Traditional Filipino food and soups are served. Also try **Patio Alejandra** on the corner of San Miguel St. and Luna. Watch video movies at the **Snowland** and **Maharaja** restaurants; the latter has a minimum charge.

For some after-dinner beer and music, try the **Sugbakilan** or **Pacific Crossing Beer Gardens,** or the **Ang Kusina Folkhouse.** There are also several bars along Sabayle Street. Find fruit stands on Quezon Avenue and around the port area and barbecue stalls along M.H. del Pilar.

Transportation
By Air: The Iligan airport is closed. All flights go direct to Cotabato City, and trips here must be made overland for the duration of the airport's closure.

By Sea: Several major shipping lines provide passenger service weekly from Manila, Cebu City, and other points in the Visayas. See Transportation in the Introduction of the Mindanao chapter for shipping schedules.

By Land: Fortune Express is the principal bus line, supplemented by Bachelor Express and Diamond Express. From Cagayan de Oro (92 km, 90 minutes), buses depart every 30-45 minutes 0400-1900. From Davao City (585 km, via Butuan, 11 and a half hours) there are early morning departures. From Kolambugan (40 km, one hour), buses leave every 30 minutes. From Pagadian (132 km, three and a half hours), several buses depart daily. From Zamboanga (396 km, 10 and a half hours), departures are at 0500, 0600, 0700, and 0715; buses from Iligan leave at 0330, 0430, and 0615.

At present, some locals advise against the overland route from Iligan to Zamboanga City due to persistent NPA and MNLF activity along this route. Check with the local mayor, *barangay* captain or tourism office if you feel hesitant about making this trip.

VICINITY OF ILIGAN

Maria Cristina Falls
The major trip out of Iligan used to be to these beautiful 98-meter falls on the Agus River, about 8.5 km southeast of the city, until they were harnessed to provide hydroelectric power in 1952, so now there's not much to see except the power station. A road leads from the checkpoint to an observation platform next to the plant. One can also look down from a bridge above the falls. Inquire at the Philippine Constabulary station in Iligan about obtaining a permit to enter.

You may swim in the large, cold swimming pool of Timoga Springs, about one km from Maria Cristina Falls; there's a snack bar and other facilities. Maria Cristina Falls are near the road to Marawi; to get there, take a Marawi-bound jeepney to Agus bridge (seven km), then turn left behind the bridge and walk the remaining 1.5 kilometers.

Kolambugan

This is the ferry port from Ozamis City. Ferries cross from Kolambugan (30 minutes) and depart from Ozamis at the same times. Kolambugan is served by frequent buses from Iligan (40 km, one hour) and Cagayan de Oro (132 km, two and a half hours). The last trip leaves Cagayan at 1600. If you miss the final ferry, stay at **Travelers' Inn** (P75-100) near the bus station, or **Seaside Inn** (P100) near the wharf.

Tubod

Ferries cross from this port on Panguil Bay to Ozamis (30 minutes) and depart from Ozamis at the same times. A ferry also links Ozamis with Baroy, just south of Tubod. George & Peter Lines sails once a week from Cebu, via Lazi, to Tubod. Tubod has a beach, and south of the town, in Kapatagan, are the Cathedral Falls, with a natural swimming pool at their base.

MARAWI CITY

Lanao del Sur, southeast of Lanao del Norte, is a heavily Muslim province, with mosques much in evidence. Iligan City serves as its principal gateway. The dominant physical feature is Lake Lanao, to which the economy is closely related. A visit to Marawi City will give a glimpse of the Maranao culture.

The Muslim Maranao are superb craftspeople, renowned for their fine brassware and *malong*-weaving. Taking a launch across the lake from Marawi's bustling market to the brass-making town of Tugaya is a memorable and fascinating experience, heightened by the perception that one is an alien in these conservative, Islamic communities.

Marawi has a very different atmosphere from that felt in a Christian city like Iligan, even though the two cities are only 37 km apart. The shores of Lake Lanao are a unique area of the Philippines, and a sojourn here will provide insight into the polarity that characterizes Mindanao society. It is one of the few places to observe the Muslim culture as the majority in the Philippines.

Officially, it is the Islamic City of Marawi. If you travel the 37 km from Iligan to Marawi, be prepared for a marked change of culture from standard lowland Catholic Filipino to a Muslim world of mosques and minarets, occasional signs in Arabic script, coffee shops, stores selling brassware, and conservatively dressed but bejewelled women in their brilliant *malongs*. Ask before photographing people here.

The main places to visit are the market and MSU (Mindanao State University) campus. Muslim holidays such as the end of Ramadan are a good time to be here.

The City

Marawi is Lanao del Sur's capital and market center, located at Lake Lanao's northern end. Known as Dansalan until 1956, it's now a city of about 72,000 people. Its elevation gives it a pleasant, healthy climate. Marawi is the spiritual and cultural center for Filipino Muslims. It has several *madrasas,* religious schools whose curriculums include instruction in the basic principles of Islam, performance of rituals, and reading the Koran in Arabic. In addition to observance of the Muslim holidays, which vary according to the Islamic calendar, Marawi holds a city celebration on 15 April.

Attractions

Quezon Boulevard is Marawi's main street. On it is situated a lakeside *torogan* that features carving and painting in traditional *okir* design. Just beyond here, a street leads north to Dansalan College.

Other points of interest in Marawi include the Lanao Islamic Center and Mosque at Pangarungan, the biggest on Mindanao; the Marinaut and Dansalan Mosques; the large, modern RP-Libya Hospital, an example of overseas support for the Moro cause; and the Moncado Colony, or world headquarters of the religious Equifilibricum Society, which claims thousands of members in the Philippines and U.S. The site is now marked by several statues and other remains.

The Route to MSU

Frequent jeepneys link downtown Marawi with the MSU campus, which is three km out. At the western end of Quezon Boulevard, a bridge crosses the Agus River, leading to the 40-meter Signal Hill, from where there's a fine view. U.S. troops sent signals from here during the early part of their regime. A few hundred meters past it, the road forks. The right branch leads one km to the zero-kilometer-stone from which all distances in Mindanao are measured, and the site of Camp Keithley, a former U.S. army base. Two km beyond here is the MSU campus.

MSU Campus

Founded in 1962, and affiliated with the University of the Philippines, the Mindanao State University, with its spacious (10 square km) campus, is considered a showcase of Muslim culture, intellect, and aspirations. It's run by Muslim educators, but students are both Muslim and Christian, since it's intended to be a vehicle for social and cultural integration.

Just inside the campus gate, the modern King Faisal Mosque and Institute of Islamic and Arabic Studies is marked by a tall minaret. Beyond it is the Marawi Tourist Office (housed in Ford Guest House Number 2), the first-class Marawi Resort Hotel, a golf course, and the impressive university buildings.

The **Aga Khan Museum of Islamic Arts,** at the crest of the campus, has two sections: one displays Maranao and other Muslim and tribal artifacts, textiles, and Chinese pottery; the other contains natural history exhibits. There's a fine view across the lake from here.

Sacred Mountain

Just outside Marawi, off the main road to Iligan, is the 150-meter-high Sacred Mountain, a national park surmounted by a pond. Bacolod Chico, on the northeast side of Marawi, has two *torogan* and is a noted *malong*-weaving center. Dayawan

THE PEOPLES OF MARAWI AND LAKE LANAO

The Maranao ("People of the Lake"), together with the Maguindanao and Tausug, are among the three major Muslim groups of the Philippines. Together with the Ilanun, a closely related people who inhabit the shores of Illana Bay, they number over 700,000.

The Maranao dialect is very similar to those of the Ilanun and Maguindanao. *Lanao* means "lake" in the native dialect, and the shores of Lake Lanao are their homeland, though some are found in Bukidnon and the Zamboanga and Cotabato regions. One theory holds that in pre-Hispanic times, the Maranao lived in Tagoloan (Misamis Oriental), but an eruption of Hibok-Hibok volcano on Camiguin, perhaps accompanied by tidal waves, forced them to move inland, and Lake Lanao proved an attractive place in which to settle. Another hypothesis is that they moved up from the Ilanun homeland on the shores of Illana Bay and subsequently became Muslims.

Although they were the last of the Philippine Muslim groups to convert to Islam, they're among the most devout. Of all the Filipino Muslim groups, the Maranao have remained the most isolated from external influences, and the most traditional. Aloof and aesthetic, they resisted the Spaniards and Americans and are still striving to preserve their cultural identity. They are farmers of rice, corn, and *kamote;* skilled artisans; and shrewd merchants.

Maratabat

The Maranao are very sensitive to *maratabat,* a term that derives from Arabic and signifies rank and its due respect. They are status-conscious in the extreme. *Maratabat* is, in fact, the major controlling factor of their social actions, determining not only what they do, but what they avoid doing so as not to offend the *maratabat* of others. It is intricately linked with family honor, and affronts against it that may seem trivial to outsiders can lead a Maranao to demand retribution or exact violent revenge. Its manifestation may range from the extravagant display of wealth in order to gain prestige to killing and generations-long feuds.

In spite of the Maranao's intense Islamic consciousness, they retain some pre-Islamic practices, such as making offerings to a pantheon of spirits during rice-planting and harvesting ceremonies. Farmers customarily give a portion of their harvest as a tithe to the mosque or to the poor. Many Maranao have made the pilgrimage to Mecca, some of them several times.

village also has an ancient *torogan* and *malong*-weavers. Other old, historic buildings are found in towns such as Masiu, Taraka, and Ramain.

Accommodations

There aren't many places to stay in Marawi. The expensive **Marawi Resort Hotel,** P400-500, situated on a hilltop within the MSU campus and offering a swimming pool, tennis, and golf, caters to tourists. Budget travelers may be able to stay in the university dormitory or at the guesthouse of **Dansalan College;** ask at the respective president's office. In a pinch, there's always a chance for a homestay or a night in a clean room at the local clinic, if it happens to be empty.

Be sure to visit the coffee shops of Marawi. Maranao dishes to look for include *kiyoning* (yellow rice), a mixture of rice, coconut milk, and turmeric; *tiyateg* and *dodol* are popular desserts made of rice, coconut, and sugar.

Transportation

From Iligan, take a Pag-asa Express bus, jeepney, or, for a few pesos more, a collective-taxi (holds four to six passengers; takes one hour). There's also direct transport from Cagayan de Oro. Minibuses and jeepneys link Marawi with Malabang on Mindanao's south coast. Minibuses go through from Marawi to Cotabato City daily; alternatively, take an early morning vehicle to Malabang, then a launch to Cotabato.

This route to Cotabato City should be uneventful; however, there is still quite a bit of guerilla activity going on in this region and travelers are advised to be careful.

LAKE LANAO

Lake Lanao is the deepest and second-largest lake in the Philippines. Statistically, it's 35 km long, 26 km across at its widest point, and has a maximum depth of 112 meters. It covers 357 square km and is 700 meters above sea level.

Believed to be the collapsed crater of an ancient volcano, it fills a depression in a plateau that's situated north of a range of active volcanoes. Its outlet, the 30-km Agus River, flows north to Iligan Bay. Lake Lanao is surrounded by lush countryside, with farming hamlets amid their rice and corn fields and lakeside towns dominated by mosques.

Launches link Marawi City with the 25 municipalities around its shores, of which the brass-making center of Tugaya is the best known. The lake contains several endemic species of fish, especially of the carp family. Fishing in the lake has declined in recent decades but continues on a small scale.

There are some islands in the lake, such as Nosa-Nosa Island off B'lindong, and the Southern Islands. A severe series of earthquakes occurred in the Lake Lanao area in 1955.

Tugaya

This municipality of 11,000 inhabitants is situated 23 km from Marawi on the western shore of Lake Lanao.

The abundance of a clay ideal for molding led to it becoming the Maranao brassware center. Virtually every family is involved in the craft, producing a wide variety of items sold all over the Philippines. About a third of the town sank into Lake Lanao during the major earthquake of 1955.

Launches sail from Tugaya to Marawi early in the morning and return to Tugaya between 1200 and 1400. The town can also be reached by minibus or jeepney. Across the lake from Tugaya, there's a particularly fine *torogan* at Kadayonan, Poona Bayabao.

NORTHWESTERN MINDANAO

OZAMIZ CITY

Ozamiz, the province's main port and commercial center, is strategically located at the entrance to the narrow 37-km-long inlet of Panguil Bay that almost bisects Mindanao. An early Spanish fortified settlement, it was known as Misamis and renamed after Jose Ozamiz, a senator and resistance leader who was executed in WW II. Ozamiznons now number about 90,000.

Attractions
The old seafront Spanish Fort Santiago, known as Kota, housed a Japanese garrison during WW II and was damaged by earthquake in 1955. A spiral stairway leads up to a lighthouse, and its western walls now hold the miraculous shrine of the Virgen del Triunfo. Ozamiz Cathedral is noted for its fine German-built pipe organ.

On the 90-meter-high Bukagan Hill, 2.5 km from downtown, are an old lookout and a concrete tower with four large German bells; there's a fine view over the city from here. Regina's Resort, located about four km out, has two natural spring-fed swimming pools.

Ozamis is largely surrounded by coconut plantations. The rugged slopes of Mt. Malindang, 25 km west northwest of Ozamiz, are a national park.

Accommodations
Stay at: **Holiday Tourist Inn,** P200-250; **Country Lodge,** P150-200, near the Lilian Liner bus terminal; the **Grand Hotel,** P100-150, 55 Abanil St.; or **Cebuana Lodge,** P100, on Port Road (basic). Other options are **Hilbon Lodge,** P200; **Minerva Inn,** P200; and **Soriano Tourist Inn,** P150.

Restaurants
Eat at centrally located **Ozamiz New Central Restaurant, Supermix Manukan Country, Sweet Dimsum House,** or **Holiday Mandarin Restaurant.** For evening entertainment, there's the slightly expensive **Inner Motion Disco** as well as **Hines Cocktail Lounge.**

Transportation
By Air: PAL flies Cebu-Ozamiz once a day Thurs.-Sat. (50 minutes). The airport is at Labo, six km from downtown. **Aerolift** also services Ozamiz from Manila.

By Sea: Several lines sail weekly from Manila. See Transportation in the Mindanao Introduction for shipping schedules.

Ferries cross Panguil Bay to link Ozamis with Kolambugan and Tubod in Lanao del Norte. Each trip takes 30 minutes. One leaves Kolambugan at 0730, 0900, 1030, 1200, 1400, 1530, and 1715, while another departs Ozamis simultaneously. Iligan-bound buses meet the ferry at Kolambugan. The ferry from Tubod leaves at 0730, 1000, 1200, 1430, and 1700; likewise, another leaves Ozamis at the same times. A ferry also links Ozamis with Baroy, near Tubod.

By Land: Ozamiz is on the route from Dipolog (four hours) to Pagadian (two and a half hours) and buses pass through regularly. The last bus to Dipolog leaves at 1400. An AMT bus leaves Zamboanga City at 0500; it takes 10 hours with a stop in Cotabato City. Frequent buses link Ozamiz and Oroquieta, 43 km, one hour. To travel along the north coast of Mindanao, one must first take the ferry to Kolambugan, then change to an Iligan- or Cagayan de Oro-bound bus.

OROQUIETA CITY

The provincial capital is a small city of about 50,000 inhabitants, located on an estuary in the coconut-growing northeast. It's an important agricultural center, with coconut-processing the main industry.

Accommodations
Stay at **Rufing's Lodge** (P100 pp), next to the bus station, or **Frelimar's Inn** (P100 pp).

Transportation
Oroquieta port is served by George & Peter Lines, which makes a weekly roundtrip Cebu-Dumaguete-Oroquieta-Cagayan de Oro pas-

sage. Punta Blanca Resort and Sibukal Hot Spring are in the vicinity.

DIPOLOG CITY

A former Subanon settlement, founded as a Spanish settlement in 1834, Dipolog City is the provincial capital and commercial center, inhabited by about 75,000 Dipolognons. There's not much to see in Dipolog, though one could take a dip in the Olympic-size public swimming pool, and Dapitan makes a worthwhile side trip. Get around the city by tricycle.

Dipolog is surrounded by extensive lowlands, made up of rice fields dotted with coconut groves. Galas (four km), Siyacab (four km), Olingan (five km), and Surg Beach resorts are outside the city. Olingan's also the site of a School of Fisheries.

Accommodations
Ranillo's Pension House: Clean rooms and friendly management in Dipolog. Bonifacio St., tel. (065) 415-3536, P100-350.

Ramos Hotel: Another budget place in the center of town. Magsaysay St., tel. (065) 415-3299, P150-500.

CL Inn: Best in town with all a/c rooms. Rizal Ave., tel. (065) 415-3491, P450-900.

Dakak Park Beach Resort: Luxurious resort with a 750-meter white-sand beach, 100 a/c cottages, tennis courts, swimming pool, and dive facilities. Dakak Bay, Manila tel. (02) 721-8164, US$100-240.

Transportation
By Air: PAL flies from the three main cities of Manila, Cebu, and Zamboanga to Dipolog once daily. The airport is three km east of the town.

By Sea: See Transportation in the Mindanao Introduction for shipping schedules.

By Land: From Dapitan (15 km, 30 minutes), jeepneys depart frequently. From Ozamis (136 km, four hours), hourly buses depart until 1400. From Pagadian (234 km, six hours), take regularly departing buses. From Zamboanga City, Lilian Express has six departures between 0430 and 1130, via Ipil and Sindangan; buses depart Dipolog 0230 to 0600. The bus station is downtown. The scenic overland route between Dipolog and Zamboanga City passes through some hostile territory where skirmishes between the MNLF, the NPA and the Philippine military are not uncommon. Proceed with caution and try not to linger in one area for days at a stretch, but keep moving. Kidnappings of foreigners, particularly missionaries, have occurred here.

DAPITAN CITY

This old Spanish town and trading center, which shares a good harbor on Dapitan Bay with Dipolog, is a clean, attractive place.

History
Legend holds that 800 Bohol families settled here, then were joined by 1,000 families and 500 slaves from Panglao. A Jesuit mission was founded here in 1629, and its jurisdiction soon stretched from Iligan to Sindagan Bay. The Spaniards built a fort here. Revolutionary hero José Rizal spent four years in exile in Dapitan, 1892-96.

Attractions
Rizal constructed the town waterworks and a grass-covered relief map of Mindanao, which is still in the plaza. The seaside area at Talisay where he lived, about four km from the city center, is now Rizal National Park. His house is the **Rizal Shrine,** a small museum displaying Rizal memorabilia (open daily 0800-1700).

Nearby is a dam he built to create a swimming pool. Markers connected with Rizal around Dapitan are at his landing spot at Santa Cruz beach; at the site of Casa Real, the official residence and administration building of the politico-military governor of the district, where Rizal lived for several months until his transfer to Talisay; and at the Saint James Church where he attended mass.

Other points of interest in Dapitan include the old city hall, the ruins of the Fort of Ilihan, and a place where fruit bats roost.

Accommodations
Homestay accommodations around Dapitan include those of **Thaddeus Hamoy** and **Paterno Bajamunde,** costing P200 pp, with breakfast and dinner; both are near the beach.

SOUTHERN MINDANAO

The vast Davao region forms Mindanao's southeast corner. Until its partition in 1967, Davao was one huge province. Today it comprises Davao City, the region's commercial and transportation center, whose 244,000 hectares make up the metropolis (much of it is farmland); Davao del Norte; Davao del Sur; and Davao Oriental.

The topography is generally rugged and includes Mt. Apo, the Philippines's highest mountain. The ascent of Apo, with its waterfalls, lakes, and hot springs, is one of the area's main attractions. Davao is noted for orchids and fruit, especially durian, and its fertile plains contain huge banana plantations.

The Davao Provinces are some of the most prosperous and interesting places to visit in Mindanao. Not only does the province have a fast-paced and interesting city, but there are stretches of beach and unspoiled coastline, great diving and snorkeling, and challenging hiking. It was recently approved by the Philippines government that Davao will be slated for development as a major tourist destination, with Samal Island pegged for the construction of an international five-star resort.

History

The first permanent Spanish settlement was established in Caraga (Davao Oriental) in 1591, but the region remained under the Sultanate of Maguindanao until the sultan ceded it to Spain in 1844. An expedition visited the area of mangrove swamps that's now Davao City in 1847 in an attempt to subdue the Muslim inhabitants and to found a settlement. The Manobo and Bagobo were the major tribal groups.

The area developed economically after 1900, when the Japanese established extensive abaca plantations around the shores of Davao Gulf and developed large-scale commercial interests: copra, timber, fishing, and import-export trading. The number of Japanese increased steadily until there were about 25,000 by 1940. The city, with its Japanese embassy, school, newspaper, Shinto shrine, and Buddhist temple, was known as Davao Kuo ("Little Japan").

The Japanese Navy established a strong base here in 1941, and the area saw much action during its liberation. Surviving Japanese nationals were repatriated after the war.

DAVAO CITY

Davao City is the region's hub and gateway to major attractions such as Mt. Apo, the Philippine Eagle Camp, and Lake Sebu. The city itself is unremarkable, but it has all the amenities for tourists. A tour of the city might include the abundant fruit markets; visiting a handicrafts workshop where costumed Mandaya women weave their superlative *dagmay* cloth on traditional backstrap looms; and a meal or snack of *kilawin* (marinated raw fish) or broiled tuna at the food stalls near Santa Ana Wharf.

Covering 2,440 square km, Davao is one of the most extensive cities in the world. Its boundaries contain plantations, swamps, and jungle. Davao, a bustling center of over one million people, basks in something of a boomtown atmosphere. It's the fastest-growing city in the Philippines, after Manila.

The majority of Davaoenos are relatively recent migrants, mainly Cebuano-speaking Visayans. There are also substantial Chinese and Muslim minorities. The Spaniards founded Davao in 1849. The original city was built where the Davao River flows into Davao Gulf, but it now sprawls through the lower half of the Davao Piedmont area.

Attractions

Sights around town include the largest Buddhist temple on Mindanao, handicraft shops with outstanding Mandaya weavings, and the small museum and Dabaw Etnika handicraft shop at the Davao Insular Hotel.

Don't miss the wonderful durian monument erected by the Durian Appreciation Society in Magsaysay Park near the wharf. Durian season runs from March to June; otherwise try the candy or dried preserves sold at the Madrazo Fruit Center.

THE PEOPLE OF THE DAVAO PROVINCES

The Davao natives are the Mandayas, Mansakas, Lamlingans, and Dibabaons of Davao Norte; Mangguangans of Davao Oriental; Manobos, Kalagans, Tagakaolos, and B'laans on Davao Gulf's western shores; and Bagobos on the central plains. Today, the area is an ethnic melting pot, inhabited by people from all over the Philippines: Muslims, Chinese, descendants of pioneer families, and migrants dominated by Visayans. Cebuano is the lingua franca.

The Bagobos

Bagobos number about 80,000, and their homeland extends from Davao del Sur and South Cotabato across the slopes of Mt. Apo and Davao City, to the area between the Davao and Pulangi Rivers, stretching up into North Cotabato and southeast Bukidnon. Bagobos are among the most colorfully dressed of the tribes. Their clothing, woven from abaca fiber, is ornamented with beads, shell and metal disks, embroidery, and colorful appliqué in geometric patterns.

Today, they wear their traditional dress only on festive occasions. Both sexes wear bodily ornaments. Men and women file and blacken their teeth, and shave their eyebrows to a thin line. Bagobo smiths cast bells and hang them on their bags, pouches, anklets, and the tassels of their jackets, so that they jingle when they walk and dance. Their pouches typically contain betel nut and lime.

Bagobo Society: In former times, Bagobo society was divided into *datus,* freemen, and slaves. Young men strived to attain the rank of *magani* (a warrior class whose members had killed more than one enemy and were entitled to wear distinctive red clothing). A communal spirit prevailed, with everyone helping in house-building and cultivation.

The Bagobo religion is a pantheon of innumerable *gimokods* (spirits), knowledge of which resides in old men and women known as *mabalian. Datus* interpret customary law. Marriages are arranged, the groom's parents selecting the bride and negotiating the match. A bride-price is paid according to their wealth, and the bride's parents also give a present equal to about half this amount to dispel the idea that they're selling their daughter. The groom has to serve the bride's family both before and after the wedding. The two- to three-day wedding ceremony takes place in the bride's home and ends with the bride and groom feeding each other a handful of rice.

Gin-em Festival: This major festival displays gratitude to the spirits for success in war or domestic matters, or for warding off sickness, evil spirits, or danger. Two bamboo poles are erected in the house of a *datu,* then offerings are made, and a chicken is sacrificed. In former times, enemy skulls would be attached to the poles, and a slave sacrificed. Each *magani* relates his past exploits, and dancing, chanting of old songs and poems, feasting, and drinking fermented sugarcane wine continue till daybreak.

Arts and Crafts: The Bagobo produce baskets trimmed with beads and fibers, ornate weapons, and inlaid metal boxes finished with bells. They have a rich tradition of music and dance. Instruments include *agong* (gongs) of various sizes and wooden drums.

The Mandaya and Mansaka

These two groups occupy the region northeast of Davao Gulf and are closely related, culturally and linguistically. Mandaya number about 200,000 and inhabit the mountains of Davao Oriental and the eastern areas of Davao del Norte. The Mansaka total about 90,000 and are found in Davao del Norte.

The Chinese are served by the large **Lon Wa Temple,** located four km out toward the airport. The temple, with its gold, bronze, and Italian marble altars, houses the Buddha with the Thousand Hands. A monk will read your fortune from slips of paper, determined by a numbered stick you draw from a container.

Muslim houses on stilts line the waterfront south of Santa Ana Wharf, but Davao's Muslim population is concentrated in the Piapi and Sasa districts, and the city has a predominantly Christian/Visayan atmosphere.

Accommodations

Budget hotels are located downtown on San Pedro, Pelayo, and Pichon Streets.

El Gusto Family Lodge: The travelers' favorite is clean, reasonably quiet, and centrally located. 51 Pichon St., tel. (082) 227-3622 P150-300.

Le Mirage Family Lodge: Another inexpensive place in the center of town. San Pedro St., tel. (082) 221-4334, P150-300.

Downtown Home Inn: Small but inexpensive place tucked away in the downtown shop-

These groups traditionally inhabit remote mountain clearings, hunting wild pig and deer using spears and dogs; fishing with poisonous roots, fish traps, and nets; and gathering forest products. Today, they're *kaingin* farmers, and many have moved to the eastern shores of Davao Gulf.

Society: Traditionally, small groups of several families live together, governed by a headman or *bagani*, usually a warrior who'd killed at least 10 times. These tribespeople occupy high tree houses, situated at the edges of cliffs for defensive reasons. Carved wooden idols placed in their houses and fields reflect their animist beliefs. A *ballyan* (priestess or medium) dances to overcome evil and retain the spirits' favor. She makes offerings to them when someone is sick.

The Mandaya-Mansaka play many instruments, including a five-string bamboo guitar, two-string lute, violin, flute, bamboo Jew's harp, gong, and drum. Today, they sometimes include native songs and dances in the Catholic mass. Marriages are arranged while children are still very young, and the wedding ceremony features feasting and drinking a sugar-cane beer that's seasoned with a gingerlike plant. Death is marked by a two-day vigil, followed by burial of the corpse, wrapped in a mat and accompanied by personal belongings, in the forest. The house of the deceased is then burned.

Weaving: Mandayan cloth is among the finest examples of weaving in the Philippines. Abaca fiber is colored with bark and earth dyes, then woven on a backstrap loom. The art is handed down from mother to daughter. Weavers develop their own designs so that each piece of cloth is unique. Individual pieces require weeks of labor. The end result is a superb coarse-textured cloth, in muted colors such as brown and burgundy, interspersed with white, onto which designs are embroidered with bright red and yellow thread. These may feature geometric patterns and motifs depicting tribal folklore and religion.

Clothing: Women traditionally wear embroidered blue cotton jackets, tube-like handwoven abaca skirts, and ample ornamentation. Men wear a loose shirt and wide blue or white cotton trousers, both of which may be decorated with embroidery and fringes. Both sexes wear large, heavy pendants, often made from coins; necklaces of beads, teeth, herbs, and seeds; bracelets of brass, shell, or vines; and rings of silver or tortoise shell.

The teeth are filed and blackened and the eyebrows shaved to a thin line. Affluent women wear embroidered red blouses with black sleeves, in contrast to the dark abaca blouses of ordinary women. Similarly, only a *bagani* (headman) may wear an embroidered red suit and a red turban.

Silver: Both tribes are renowned silversmiths. Some of the finest examples of their craft are the large silver breastplates worn by men and women. Silver coins are beaten into thin discs with a central hole, around which intricate designs are engraved or stamped. They also produce silver rings and ornaments and fine iron knives and daggers.

The Ata

The Ata, related to the Manobos of the Cotabato region, include subgroups such as the Matigsalug and Talaingod. Totaling about 222,000, their homeland stretches from Davao City up through Davao del Norte and Bukidnon. The Talaingod inhabit the forests around Kapalong, Davao del Norte.

Their colorful tribal clothing features long-sleeved shirts for men, while women supplement their native blouse and *malong* with bead necklaces and brass bracelets and anklets. The men traditionally wield spears. They hunt forest game and grow rice, corn, and root crops in *kaingin* fields. Some of them work as timber cutters, though their homeland is being gradually denuded by logging.

---

ping district across from Smokey's Café. San Pedro St., tel. (082) 226-2180, P350-600.

Aljem's Inn: Good midpriced place in the center of town near the bars and nightclubs along Anda Street. Pichon St., tel. (082) 221-3060, P650-1,050.

Hotel Galleria: Fancy-looking place in the northwestern corner of town behind Gaisano shopping center. Duterte St., tel. (082) 221-2480, P900-1,500.

Apo View Hotel: Best in town with swimming pool, several restaurants, and lively nightclub. Camus St., tel. (082) 221-6430, US$60-120.

Restaurants

Davao is famous for fruit and seafood. Food stalls on Quezon Boulevard near Santa Ana Wharf serve *kilawin* (marinated raw fish), squid, *(bariles)*, broiled tuna, and barbecued chicken. There are also barbecue stands at the corner of Bonifacio and Anda. **Kusina Dabaw** serves set meals that are excellent value, and **Davao Inihaw** and **Davao Famous Restaurant** are also good. **Fish Penn,** on Anda Street, serves fresh fish, picked to order.

Fish Penn is also popular with locals and expats as foreign movies are shown nightly on a large TV screen. Across the street is one of many Chinese restaurants in the city, the **Tai-Pan Palace,** with good prices and nightly entertainment upstairs.

Anda Street has a variety of restaurants, including **Coconut Grove Carinderia, Sunburst Fried Chicken,** and **Tsuru Japanese Sushi Bar.** Other Chinese restaurants in the downtown area include the **Shanghai Restaurant, Famous Restaurant,** and **New China Royale. Dencia's Kitchenette;** the three branches of **Merco Restaurant** are popular Filipino restaurants.

Fast food restaurants are springing up with a **Shakey's Pizza** and **Dunkin' Donuts** on Malvar Street and a **McDonald's** slated to be open soon. **Jollibee's** is on Rizal Street. Upscale places include the **Zugba Restaurant** at the Apo

View Hotel, the **Davao Insular's** dining rooms, and **Sarung Banggi,** Davao's favorite steak house. A popular restaurant with Davaoenos is **Molave** on the corner of Reyes and Rizal Street, famous for its greaseless fried chicken.

Colorful fruit stalls display an incredible variety of tropical fruit: try *marang,* rambutan, and mangosteen! The durian is king here; there's even a statue of one in front of the city hall. In addition to being sold fresh, durian is made into candies and canned preserves. Look for fruit at the Anda-Rizal and Madrazo Fruit Centers and the huge Bankerohan Public Market.

Handicrafts

Davao is a good place to shop for handicrafts. Stores in the Aldevinco Shopping Center on

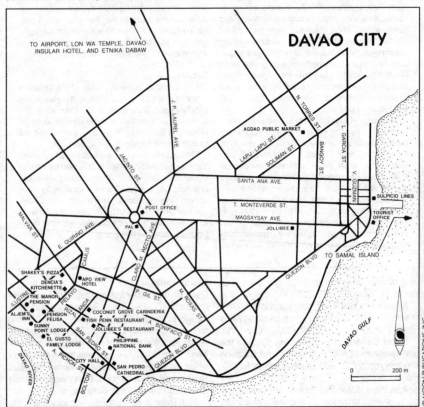

C.M. Recto offer weaving, brassware, shellcraft, antiques, and batik. Bargain! There's a NACI-DA Emporium in the Pelayo Building on Juan Luna Street.

A visit to **Etnika Dabaw** across from the Davao Insular Hotel grounds is a must. It's a Mandaya Weaving Center where women in native dress produce beautiful, unique handicrafts. Bags, briefcases, wallets, wall hangings, floor coverings, belts, and accessories are offered at fixed prices. There's also a selection of traditional Mandayan costumes and beadwork jewelry, plus some antiques and dolls.

Other shops to check are **Precy's Creation** and **Lava Exotika** on J.P. Laurel Avenue, **Nieva's Arts and Crafts** in Lanang, **L'Mars** in Ilustre and **Jay Pee Em** on Magallanes Street, near city hall.

Festivals

Araw Ng Dabaw, held in March, commemorates Davao's creation as a charter city with civic-military parade, carnivals, sports, beauty contests, and cultural events featuring ethnic exhibits. On Good Friday, several of the city's parishes present three-hour passion plays. On 29 June, a fair is held on the feast day of the city's patron saint, San Pedro, featuring a civic-military parade, religious procession, carnival, and cultural exhibits and events.

The weeklong **Kadayawan sa Dabaw Festival** usually takes place in October. Highland tribes come down to the city to perform their traditional dances, songs, and rituals. Highlights include a parade of the ethnic groups in native costume, art and cultural presentations, and indigenous sports, perhaps including a horse-fight. The city also holds an orchid and fruit festival during Kadayawan sa Dabaw.

Nightlife

Find cheap bars on Emilio Jacinto Street, while higher-class nightclubs and girlie bars are located along the MacArthur Highway in Matina. Of note is the inexpensive **Mick Dundee's** on J. Camus, run by a British man and his Filipina wife. Listen to folk music at the **Horizon Folk Theater** or hang out watching movies with a San Miguel at the **Fish Penn.**

Also try **Casa Blanca Bar and Restaurant** on Laurel Ave, Lanang, for good nightlife. In town,

Davao durian monument

try the hot spots **Bodega Disco** on E. Quirino Avenue and **Curves & Faces** and **Electric Dreams,** on San Pedro Street. Major hotels have music bars and/or discos. **Davao Casino** is at the Masters International Hotel (formerly Cuison Hotel); and the Davao Insular Hotel has **Vinta Bar.** Be sure to check out *lambanute,* a local coconut-based liquor that's delicious with lime juice.

Services and Information

The tourist office in Magsaysay Park has information on nearby beaches and islands, plus will advise on treks to Mt. Apo. You can extend visas at the Immigration Office in the Antwel Building near Magsaysay Park and get Visa or Mastercard cash advances from Equitable Bank.

Transportation

Davao's airport is in Lanang about 12 km northeast of city proper. Take a metered taxi into town or take a tricycle to the highway and hail a jeepney marked "San Pedro."

Philtranco, Ceres Liner, and Bachelor Express buses leave from the Ecoland Terminal across the bridge, east of town, toward the Ecoland nightclub complex on MacArthur Highway.

Air: PAL, Air Philippines, and other airlines fly to Davao from Manila twice a day (80 minutes); from Cebu once a day (50 minutes); from Cagayan de Oro four times a week (30 minutes); and from Zamboanga thrice weekly (55 minutes).

Ship: Davao is about 49 hours from Manila, 24 hours from Cebu, and 17 hours from Zamboanga. Weekly sailings depart from Manila and many cities in the Visayas. See Transportation in the Mindanao Introduction for a complete listing of ships heading to Davao.

Bus: From Butuan (286 km, six hours), Bachelor Express leaves every 30 minutes (0300-1630), as do Ceres Liner and St. Benedict Lines. From Cagayan de Oro (493 km, nine and a half hours), Bachelor Express travels via Butuan. From Cotabato City (215 km, five hours), Mintranco buses pass through a few military checkpoints, but there should be no problem for tourists. From General Santos City (149 km, three hours) there are frequent Yellow Bus departures until 1600. From Surigao (409 km, eight hours), take Bachelor Express.

SAMAL ISLAND

Samal is the large island in Davao Gulf, reached by a 15-minute crossing from Davao City. The smaller but equally beautiful Talikud Island is also easily accessible from Davao City. These islands offer a much-needed break from the pace of urban life in the Philippines, so be sure to take a day off to explore here.

Samal island is slated to be developed into a first-class tourist resort particularly along the protected western shore. Check with the Department of Tourism in Davao to see if the big plans for Samal have become a reality.

Samal is divided into three municipalities: Babak, Samal, and Kaputian. Frequent *bancas* cross from Sasa pier, north of the Davao City (take a jeepney from A. Pichon Street), to Babak. Alternatively, ask around at Davao's Santa Ana Wharf for boats crossing to the island. There's a regular day trip every day to Kaputian by launch, leaving Santa Ana Wharf at 1100, returning the following day at 0800.

Bancas also depart from the pier at the Davao Insular Hotel and the adjacent wharf. Crossings cost P10, and frequent service between the pier and the Paradise Island Beach Resort is available. Chartering a *banca* to Samal or neighboring Talikud costs about P300 roundtrip with **Samal Island Adventures,** Bolton Street, Davao. They also operate from the pier next to the Davao Insular Hotel. If you are going to charter a *banca,* it's good to use the boat for touring around instead of merely anchoring. Samal is the home of the Isamal, a Muslim minority group.

Among the resorts on Samal Island are the **Paradise Island Beach Resort,** whose cottages rent for P200 a day, and the **Coral Reef Beach Resort,** whose cottages rent for P250 a day. The most luxurious resort on the island is the **Pearl Farm Resort** at Kaputian. This first-class, innovative resort was built at the site of a former pearl farm, and, although expensive, it is an ideal honeymoon spot or a place to really unwind for a few days during a long trip.

Babak

Visit Babak's Sunday market and the Muslim village of Dunggas, which has huts on stilts and a nearby beach. Local activities include fishing, mat-weaving, and salt-making. Offshore from Babak are the islets of Sanipan, Palma Gil, and the Ligid Islands. These islands contain white-sand beaches, caves, and coconut plantations. Salt-making is practiced on Palma Gil, too.

Archaeological digging on these islands has revealed human skeletons, Chinese porcelain jars and vases, and artifacts of the Kalagan tribe. Upper Caliclic Cave in Caliclic, Babak, is believed to be a Kalagan burial site, since skeletons have been found inside. Its four chambers are infested with snakes and bats. There's also a cave in Kamunod, Bagak.

San Jose

San Jose, in spite of its name, is a Muslim fishing village with huts on stilts. The municipality has a beach and caves, and is the site of Haguimit Waterfall and the Moncadian sect's settlements of Limao, Ma-ag, and Upper Penaplata.

Kaputian

This is the location of the unique **Pearl Farm Beach Resort,** built on the site of a former pearl farm, which used oysters brought from Jolo for making pearls. The farm ceased operation in 1980, but the place has undergone extensive renovation and repairs. Marji Moran, the former Miss Universe, and her husband contracted a talented architect to design the Pearl Farm Resort, which opened in 1992.

The bungalows and private suites are beautifully crafted on a hillside overlooking the Davao gulf. The swimming pool was built right on shore, giving the illusion that the pool water meets the sea. The dining room is exquisite. The food is superb. Rooms are expensive, ranging US$60-100. A full range of sporting events is offered from scuba diving, PADI certification, jet skiing, and snorkeling to tours of the orchid farms, hikes, and other activities around Davao. If you are saving your pesos for a real splurge, this is the place to do it.

Talikud Island

Talikud, which is much smaller than Samal, offers good beaches and snorkeling. A daily boat leaves from the LHS Company dock of Santa Ana Wharf around 0930, though it's often late. The fee for crossing is P10. The boat returns in the late afternoon, but double check that it's not planning to stay on the island until the next day, There is no organized accommodation on this island. The best beach on Talikud is at Dangay with beautiful white sand and turquoise water.

Though there is no accommodation at Dangay beach, you can rent a cottage for the day and picnic for P100. Caves on Talikud are the haunt of snakes (stories of giant pythons) and bats. It's said that one of them passes under Davao Gulf and emerges at Malalag (Davao del Sur).

MOUNT APO

Mt. Apo (2,954 meters, the Philippines's highest mountain) is situated about 40 km west southwest of Davao City. This dormant volcano, whose base covers over 700 square km, has no recorded eruptions, but it is continuously emitting sulfuric vapors.

Its slopes and immediate vicinity form Mt. Apo National Park, which lies partly in the city of Davao, Davao del Sur, and North Cotabato. Naturalists will be in their element around Apo, whose trails pass through several vegetation zones, from virgin rainforest with giant mahogany trees to the shrubs and grass growing above the timberline. These slopes are home to the few remaining Philippine eagles, the tiny falconet, and endemic species such as the Mt. Apo mynah. Butterflies abound.

The exotic flora includes ferns, mosses, carnivorous pitcher plants, and the *waling-waling* and other orchids. There are lakes, waterfalls, hot springs, thermal pools, bubbling mud, and steam vents.

Apo is a sacred mountain to the local natives, who call it Sandawa ("Mountain of Sulfur"), who have literally taken up arms recently to protest against the construction of a geothermal plant on the mountain. Before setting out to hike Mt. Apo, check the current situation with the Department of Tourism in Davao.

The locals believe their Bagobo legend that the gods Apo and Mandarangan dwell on the summit. Mandarangan causes landslides and can only be appeased by blood. In the past, this was provided by their constant deadly feuds, and also by offering human sacrifices when they wanted to collect sulfur. The natives particularly dreaded apparitions called *solfataras* (sulfurous vapors). A halo of vapor shrouding the peak was taken as a sure sign of Mandarangan's presence. When the first European climbed Apo, after the Bagobo had done everything they could to obstruct him, the natives accompanying him swore that they saw Mandarangan ascend from the crater and fly away above the clouds.

Climbing Mount Apo

The strenuous climb takes about four days; those in good shape could do it in three days, and those who desire a relaxed walk should allot five days. There are several possible routes, so it's a good idea to ascend and descend by different trails, e.g., starting from Kidapawan and returning to Digos.

Obtain current information about the ascent from the Davao tourist office, or, in Digos, at the office of the Davao del Sur Pabungan Tek'dag (Mt. Apo Climbers' Association) in the Baryohanon Building. Check the local weather report prior to an ascent. Take good footwear, a windbreaker, sleeping bag, adequate food and water, a flashlight, and a tent or plastic sheet in case it rains. The temperature can go down to 5° C at night near the summit. Guard against leeches by wearing long-sleeved shirts and trousers with tight cuffs, and by rubbing soap on the trouser-legs.

To rent a tent and camping gear for the ascent, contact the **House of Lord Anthony** on San Pedro Street, Davao City. A guide is essential, porters optional. Each man should be paid about P200 per day if he brings his own food, P100 if you provide it. It's a lot easier to let him bring his own! A porter shouldn't be given more than 15 kilograms to carry. If you ascend

and descend by different routes, give guides and porters their bus fare home.

The ascent can be undertaken at any time, since the Davao region doesn't experience a pronounced rainy season, but March to early May offers the best chance of clear, dry weather. The Davao tourist office promotes a "Conquer Mt. Apo" program each Easter weekend and the Octotrek, a semestral break climb, every October. At these events, a large number of climbers may participate. *The First Guide to Climbing Mt. Apo*, by Reynaldo G. Sorongon, Jr., was published in Davao in 1982. Again, because of the geothermal plant construction and the ire of the natives in the region, check the political situation with the Department of Tourism first before setting out.

SOUTHWESTERN MINDANAO

GENERAL SANTOS CITY

Formerly called Dadiangas ("Thorny Shrub"), General Santos City, commonly abbreviated GSC, is an unattractive, modern city situated at the head of Sarangani Bay, a 30-km-long inlet off the Celebes Sea.

Until 1900, the area was occupied by Maguindanao and B'laan. Although some migrants had already arrived, development really began in 1939, when the government encouraged pioneers from Luzon, led by General Paulino Santos, to migrate to the region. The name "General Santos City" was subsequently adopted in his honor. The settlement was built where the Buayan River flows into Sarangani Bay. Crocodiles were plentiful in the area at that time. Newcomers from Luzon and the Visayas moved inland from here to settle the Koronadal and Allah Valleys.

GSC has about 250,000 inhabitants. The city honors its patron saint, Our Lady of Peace and Good Voyage, during the third week of January; commemorates General Santos's landing on 27 February; and celebrates the anniversary of its city charter each 5 September.

Attractions

Tambler, Cabo, and Alunan Beaches are near the city. Rajah Muda Beach Resort is on a sandy

cove, 15 km out; it's operated by the Matutum Hotel. The Olaer Resort, 20 km from the city, is a picnic spot with a natural swimming pool (P10, full of local children) a few kilometers outside the city. It remains a popular weekend spot for locals.

Accommodations and Restaurants

Stay at the **Concrete Lodge,** Pioneer Ave., P75-100; the **Fishermen's Inn,** corner Salazar and Veteran Streets, P100-150; the **South Sea Lodge I,** Pioneer Ave., P200 with fan, P350 a/c; the **Pioneer Hotel,** Pioneer Ave., P250 fan, P350 a/c; the **South Sea Lodge II,** Salazar St., P150-250; the **Mututum Hotel,** P. Acharon Blvd., P600-700. Also try the more expensive **Tierra Verde Hotel,** National Hwy., P550-700; the **Phela Grande Hotel,** Magsaysay Ave., P550-700; and **Pietro's Hotel,** National Hwy., P400-450.

Eat at the **Shanghai Restaurant,** situated below the lodging house. The **Matutum Hotel** and the **Pioneer Hotel** also have good restaurants.

Transportation

By Air: PAL flies Cebu-General Santos two times daily (105 minutes). The airport is at Buayan, eight km northeast of the city.

By Sea: Ships dock at the Makar Wharf (Dadiangas), four km west of the city. See

Transportation in the Mindanao Introduction for information about ships going to General Santos.

By Land: From Davao (149 km, three hours), take the frequent Bachelor Express buses; some come through from Butuan. Yellow Bus also serves this route. The last bus to Davao is at 1600. From Cotabato City (209 km, four hours) there are regular Yellow Bus and JD Express buses. The trip from General Santos City to Davao takes five hours.

GENERAL SANTOS CITY TO LAKE SEBU

The gateway to Lake Sebu is through Koronadal (Marbel) and Surallah. JD Express and Yellow Bus link Koronadal with GSC (58 km, one hour) and Cotabato City (151 km, three hours). Minibuses and jeepneys also operate GSC-Koronadal. From Koronadal, take a Yellow bus, minibus, or jeepney to Surallah and catch another jeepney to Lake Sebu. Jeepneys run between Surallah and Lake Sebu all day long until 1600. It's also possible to reach Koronadal from Kidapawan, via Buluan. Lake Sebu is 34 km, about 90 minutes, from Koronadal.

Koronadal

The provincial capital was formerly called Marbel.
Stay at **Samahong Nayon Home,** Osmeña St., P90-150; **Albado's Home,** corner Alunan and Rizal Streets, P75-100; the **Rosamar Hotel,** Alunan Ave., P75-100; and **Dizon Place,** Alunan and Rizal Streets, P75-100. Of the cheap hotels, Dizon Place is the best. The others are very basic.

Eat at **Breeze Restaurant** or **Capitol Restaurant.**

Surallah

The Allah Valley airport is near here.
Stay at the **Chateau** (P75) or the nearby **Plaza View Restaurant and Lodging.** Both places are new and clean, located on the main road to Koronadal.

Transportation: PAL flies Cebu-Allah Valley thrice weekly (takes 90 minutes).

LAKE SEBU

This picturesque lake is surrounded by rolling hills and is the ancient homeland of the T'boli people. The T'boli market held near its shores on Saturday mornings is one of the most colorful in the Philippines. At harvest time in September, the T'boli hold an important traditional festival, which is highlighted by a nightly procession of torch-carrying T'boli. In November is the Lake Sebu *barangay* festival, which features T'boli dancing and traditions, as well as participation from the many Visayan settlers now living in the region.

The Mission

It's possible to stay at the **Santa Cruz Mission,** which has two small guesthouses; there's no restaurant, but cooking facilities are available, so bring supplies. The mission is a 1.5-km walk past the market. T'boli handicrafts are available in the mission gift shop.

The mission was the long-term residence of a missionary, Father Rex, who was a staunch supporter of the T'boli culture. He was recently deported to the U.S.A., and some of the community spirit at the mission went with him. There's good hiking in the area of Lake Sebu, with several waterfalls to be visited. The mission is the site of the important T'Boli festival, held here on the second weekend of September.

Lake Sebu is well worth visiting, as the region's colorful T'boli offer a unique glimpse into the changing world of a traditional people. Many of the young will no longer wear their colorful, handwoven clothing, and much that is different to the eye of the traveler is fast disappearing.

Hiking the Region

The mayor of Lake Sebu is also a T'boli and offers help and even a guide if you want to go hiking. According to the mayor, many travelers just head for the hills, and it is not always safe due to known NPA activity in the region. If you stay close to Lake Sebu, allow yourself time to hike around the hills and visit some T'boli villages.

The T'boli are accustomed to seeing visiting missionaries and may assume that you are associated with a church. If they have room in their home, they will often put passing foreigners up for the night. They are reluctant to open their homes to outsiders as they consider themselves to be very poor and are somewhat embarrased by their living conditions. This attitude about themselves has been brought on in part by the comparatively high standard of living enjoyed by the settlers, the Visayans. To the T'boli, the Visayans are rich as they own radios, a television, and perhaps a motorbike.

Accommodations

Bao Baay Village Inn: Right on the lakeside is a spot where the hotel owner and "Honorable Vice Mayor," Bao Baay, can help with boat rentals and offer advice on trekking, caves, waterfalls, and forest resorts. P125-350.

Lakeview Tourist Lodge: Good location near the market and lake. P50-150.

Hillside View Park & Tourist Lodge: Another lakeside lodge with simple yet clean rooms.

THE PEOPLE OF SOUTHWESTERN MINDANAO

The Tasaday

The following information about the Tasaday has long been debated among anthropologists, politicians, and resident observers of Philippine politics. Many feel today that the Tasaday discovery was a hoax and was orchestrated by the Marcos government to secure the land of South Cotabato for mining and other interests.

Debate continues, but many intellectuals in the anthropological community do not believe that the Tasaday are a stone-age people, but were simply another remote hill tribe who lived a rather sophisticated, but simple existence. The story goes that deep within South Cotabato's dense rainforest, a world of 60-meter trees and knife-ridged mountains, live a tiny group of Stone Age cave-dwellers.

They were first discovered around 1966 by a hunter named Dafal. Prior to this they were isolated from the outside world. Dafal, who had set out from the isolated settlement of Manubo Blit at the edge of the jungle, communicated with them only with difficulty. As he visited them several times over the next few years, he gave and taught them new things.

The Tasaday came to the notice of the world-at-large in June 1971, when Panamin chief Manuel (Manda) Elizalde Jr. and his companions helicoptered into a clearing at the edge of their territory. The Tasaday, who live near a mountain of the same name, were found to number 24—10 men, five women, nine children. They live as a single family unit, without a formal leader, and without friction. In spite of the two-to-one ratio, they are strictly monogamous. It was established that a few individuals had come from other forest groups, the Tasafeng and Sanduka. Their dialect is related to those of the Blit and other Manubo tribes.

Men and women are scantily dressed in leaf loin coverings and leaf skirts, respectively. The Tasaday live easily from the forest, gathering roots, shoots, palm pith, berries, flowers, bananas and other fruit, and catching small fish, crabs, frogs, tadpoles, and grubs. Fire is made by twirling a stick in a wooden base.

They practice neither hunting nor cultivation, and have no weapons and only primitive tools such as stone scrapers and pounders, a chipped stone bound to a wooden handle with rattan, digging sticks, and knives of sharpened bamboo. Leaves and bamboo sections serve as containers. Items are shared, since they have no sense of personal property. John Nance's detailed account of them, *The Gentle Tasaday*, is fascinating, yet many people believe that it is mostly fiction and was written per request of former president Ferdinand Marcos.

The B'laan

The B'laan, who total about 250,000, occupy the mountain ranges from Davao del Sur westward into Cotabato as far as a line running approximately from Midsayap through Buluan to Kiamba. They're divided into subgroups named after the localities they occupy, e.g., the Tagalakad (inhabitants of forested hinterlands), Tagkogan (inhabitants of *cogon* grasslands), Buluan (dwellers on the fringes of Lake Buluan), and Bira-an (closest neighbors of the Bagobo). They are *kaingin* farmers, growing rice, corn, and millet, and also raise chickens and pigs, hunt, fish, and practice tie-dye weaving.

The Maguindanao

These are the "people of the flood plain," who have had to contend with the regular flooding of their homeland by rain-swollen rivers. Totaling about 765,000, they range from Zamboanga to Davao, but their homeland lies inland along the banks and in the broad valley of the Mindanao River, which traditionally forms a highway connecting their settle-

This is located on a small side road right on the lake. The setting is very picturesque. No restaurant, but a small shop sells the bare essentials. P50-150.

Municipal Guesthouse: Farther down the road, rounding the lake, is a city-run guesthouse, located on a small hill overlooking the lake. Built by funds from the Department of Tourism, the guesthouse was built to ease the accommodation crunch at popular Lake Sebu.

The rooms are nicely designed using all traditional and natural materials. The fee is P350-400, and the guesthouse does cater to officialdom. When the officials aren't visiting, try to stay here as the view of the lake and surrounding hills is beautiful.

Restaurants

Be sure to stop for native coffee at the **Mountain Coffee** restaurant. The friendly Visayan woman

---

ments. Three sultanates are still recognized among them.

The majority of Maguindanao are valley-dwelling tenant rice farmers. Coastal Maguindanao are fishermen and traders. Culturally, the Maguindanao have much in common with the Maranao. Like them, they produce fine handicrafts. Their brassware, though less recognized, is as good as that of the Maranao. Brassworks are particularly concentrated in Datu Piang (formerly Dulawan) and Kapinpilan. Other crafts include hand-weaving textiles to be made into *malong*, mat-weaving, and basketry.

They have a rich tradition of music and dance, their principal instrument being the *kulintang*. The full Maguindanao *kulintang* ensemble requires seven players, compared to five among the Maranao, since there are two additional large gongs. The Maguindanao language and traditional dress are similar to the Maranao. A popular Maguindanao dish is *pizinena*, goat meat fried in coconut oil with spices.

The Tiruray

The Tiruray total about 92,000 and are found in the district of Dinaig, south of the Cotabato River, and in the northern area of the densely forested hills of the Cotabato Cordillera. They also extend down into Sultan Kudarat and North Cotabato. The Tiruray are divided into coastal, river, and mountain groups.

The mountain people have maintained their pagan traditions, while the others have had more contact with their Muslim neighbors and Christian missionaries. They are basically a Malay, horse-riding hill people, whose traditional culture is characterized by communal households, polygamy, and an effective indigenous moral-legal system. Unmarried women wear a special blouse decorated with beads.

Tiruray live in rectangular houses built on posts above the ground and practice *kaingin* farming, supplemented by hunting and gathering. They weave forest fibers such as *nito* and rattan into attractive baskets and handbags.

The Manobo

The Manobo, also called Kulaman, are a widely distributed group divided into several subgroups. Kidapawan is a Manobo cultural center. For them, Mt. Apo is a sacred mountain. Numbering about 250,000, they are concentrated in the mountains north of the Padada River, up through Kidapawan and Magpet, between the Pulangi and Davao River systems. They are spread, however, through a wide area, from South Cotabato and Davao del Sur to Agusan and Surigao del Sur.

The Manobo are closely related linguistically to neighboring groups such as the Bukidnon, Higaonon, Ata, and Dibabawon. They practice *kaingin* farming and also fish, hunt, and trap. Crafts include basketry, pottery, and weaving. Manobo cloth is generally thinner than that of other groups. Their traditional dress is striking. Men wear long, loose trousers or tight breeches, topped by a buttonless jacket.

Women wear a red blouse with black sleeves; an abaca skirt; a girdle of braided human hair or vegetable fiber, from which hangs a bunch of beads, shells, and herbs; plus leglets, a comb, and ear discs. They embroider geometric shapes, or motifs such as the dancing man, onto brown or dark red backgrounds, and sew colored cotton strips on the cuffs and neck. Dress reflects rank. Decorative motifs are reserved for *datus* and the affluent; warriors are entitled to wear certain clothes.

In recent times, many have intermarried with members of neighboring tribes, so that their cultural identity has been somewhat diluted. At present, the Manobo and other minority groups are resisting the Philippine government in their plans to build a geothermal plant on Mt. Apo. Recent skirmishes between the army and the tribes around the mountain have discouraged hikers. Check the situation with the Department of Tourism in Davao or at the branch office in Digos.

THE T'BOLI OF LAKE SEBU

An estimated 200,000 T'boli (pronounced "TEE-bo-lee") inhabit the Tiruray Highlands (Kematu mountain ranges), a 2,000-square-km area within a triangle bounded by Surallah, Kiamba, and Polomolok. The main settlement is Kematu, but it is called simply T'boli. Traditionally, T'boli live in large, elevated houses (about 15 by 10 meters) set well apart from each other on ridges, although three or four houses of a kinship group may form a cluster.

Dress
The T'boli women are among the most colorfully dressed in the Philippines, and while the elderly still dress traditionally, many of the young are discarding the lovely dress in favor of Western clothing. However, on market day (Saturday) the women dress up. They wear a dark blue handwoven jacket embroidered with red, yellow, and white designs.

Their head covering may be a simple cloth, but traditionally it's an abaca turban, or a colorful, broad round hat. This is supplemented by ornamental combs, beaded earrings, necklaces, chokers, chains, bracelets, anklets, finger and toe rings, colorful beadwork, and heavy belts of brass bells. Occasionally, the women carry their beautiful brass betel nut boxes with them, hung around their shoulders. They are magnificent.

When girls are about five or six years old, their earlobes and the entire outer rims of their ears are pierced, so that numerous earrings can be worn simultaneously. The earrings are made of beads and horse hair. Traditionally, teeth are filed and blackened to enhance beauty, and men practice scarification.

Weaving
The ceremonial clothing of both men and women is a dark brown tie-dyed abaca cloth featuring intricate red and beige designs. Natural vegetable dyes are used to stain the fibers before the cloth is woven. The weaving of major pieces, such as a wedding dress, can take several months. Apart from its practical uses as clothing and blankets, the cloth has deep significance for the T'boli.

It's one of the traditional properties exchanged at the time of marriage and is used as a covering during birth to ensure a safe delivery. It also figures in certain sacred feasts. The T'boli believe that cutting the cloth will cause serious illness or death. If it is sold, a brass ring is often attached to the cloth to appease the spirits. Currently, the abaca weavings

CARL PARKES

T'boli woman and child

serves coffee, breads, and lunches and dinners. There is another basic restaurant near the jeepney stop, close to Mountain Coffee.

Transportation
Lake Sebu is in the Alah Valley, south of Koronadel and the nearby village of Surallah. Buses from Davao reach General Santos City and continue on to Koronadel, from where jeepneys head down to Surallah and then up to the lake. The last jeepney leaves around 1500.

Total travel time from Davao is about eight hours.

COTABATO CITY

Cotabato is situated on the northern side of the Rio Grande de Mindanao's swampy delta. It's

are becoming very mainstream in the Philippines, and the style is featured on wallets, briefcases, bags, and as wall hangings. The texture almost looks like leather, but it's all T'boli handiwork and is very unique.

Society

Tribal leaders interpret customary law to settle disputes. Marriages are arranged, sometimes shortly after a child's birth. Most T'boli are monogamous, but prosperous individuals may take several wives. The T'boli love music and dance; their orchestras include gongs, flutes, guitars, a two-stringed lute, one-string violins, Jew's harps, and drums. Their weapons include swords and bows with poisoned arrows. They are farmers, growing upland rice, corn, kamote, and sugarcane.

The T'boli culture is somewhat under siege at present, as Visayan settlers coming to South Cotabato tend to purchase ancestral T'boli land and move into their territory. Their impact has forced the T'boli to re-evaluate their own culture, and many of the young have opted to wear Western styles and listen to disco music rather than hold onto old and, in their eyes, outdated customs.

Another threat to the T'boli is the mining interests on their land. Pressure is on for the T'boli to cede their lands to mining companies as precious minerals, including gold, are thought to be in their mountains. An American missionary, Father Rex, worked to preserve T'boli culture for over 20 years, and to resist the pressure from mining companies. His recent deportation to the U.S. from the Philippines was based on some trumped up charges against him. This has raised fears that the mining companies are ready to coerce the T'boli into selling their lands.

Funerals

The body is placed in a log coffin and allowed to repose for 15 days as a gesture of respect. In a final all-night vigil, the coffin is trotted round and round the house of the deceased, while mourners pay tribute to him with music and song, interspersing gaiety and lament. Finally, at dawn, the coffin is lashed high in a bamboo grove, where it is left to disintegrate. The dead person's house is burned so it can't shelter his soul for malevolent spirits to devour.

Horse-Fighting

The T'boli ride horses, and horse-fighting is a popular tribal betting sport. Two stallions are exposed to a mare in heat, then, held on long leashes by their handlers, the jealous rivals clash until one backs off, usually uninjured, or there's an obvious winner. Contests are usually over in a few minutes and are never allowed to continue to the death. T'boli horse-fighting can only be seen at the September festival and on very special occasions.

The Ubo

The Ubo (or Ubu), who number about 5,000 and live a few hours' hike from Lake Sebu, have much in common with the T'boli. There's a settlement at Datal Tabayong. Like the T'boli, the women are heavily ornamented with brass bracelets from wrist to elbow on both arms, rings on every finger, multiple earrings, necklaces, anklets, beadwork, and bells. Traditional Ubo weapons include swords, spears, and bows with poisoned arrows.

They have a fine handicraft tradition, including cloth- and basket-weaving, metal-casting, and making pottery, horsehair ornaments, and musical instruments. Once an artifact is completed, they believe it has a soul, so they're reluctant to sell it. Ubo smiths, like T'boli metalworkers, fashion bells, bracelets, and other items using the ancient lost-wax process and crude Malay forge.

The desired image is carved in beeswax, covered with clay, then heated so that when the wax is poured out, a mold retaining the pattern is left to receive the molten brass. The Ubo are particularly renowned for the ornate, finely detailed, brass sword hilts they make by this method.

an unfavorable location that has hindered the city's development as a major commercial center. The name means "Stone Fort" and has been extended to the surrounding region. A Spanish fort was built here in 1862.

The city was the capital of the old province of Cotabato, and though Maguindanao has a new provincial capital, Cotabato City remains the regional trading center. It's an ethnic melting pot whose 101,000-plus inhabitants are about 60% Christian and 40% Muslim. An Islamic influence is readily apparent, however. The main languages are Cebuano and Maguindanao.

Cotabato is a minor coastal port; its main interisland port is at Polloc, 26 km north of the city. Currently, Cotabato City has been the site of hostilities between the NPA, the MNLF, and the Philippine Army. Foreigners are generally not subjected to the fighting, but some kidnappings of missionaries have occured. Two American students assigned to a year's exchange program here complained of being constantly accompanied by bodyguards, which may shed some light on the problems in Cotabato City.

The Sultanates
During pre-Hispanic times and through the Spanish era, Cotabato was sparsely settled by highland tribes, Muslims, and some Chinese traders, all coexisting more or less peacefully. The Cotabato Valley was the first area of Mindanao to be converted to Islam. During the first quarter of the 16th century, Sharif Kabungsuwan of Johore was forced by strong winds to anchor at the mouth of the river, where he was received by the pagan inhabitants. He subsequently married a local princess, established the Sultanate of Maguindanao, and converted the area to Islam.

The Maguindanao became the region's dominant group, and Cotabato an Islamic stronghold, with the sultanate remaining, for practical purposes, an independent political state until about 1850. Its influence extended from the Zamboanga peninsula to Sarangani Bay and Davao. There were, in fact, several sultanates among the Maguindanao.

The lower valley formed the heartland of the Sultanate of Maguindanao, which was centered near the present Cotabato City. The upper valley was loosely controlled by the Sultanate of Buayan, based near what's now Datu Piang. For a time, a third state, Kabuntalan (Bagumbayan), located between the larger two, existed. The fortunes of these sultanates rose and fell through the centuries.

Colonists and Migrants
Having visited Polloc briefly in 1525, the Spaniards were to launch sporadic expeditions throughout the colonial era, but they always met with strong resistance. In 1851, they occupied Polloc, which subsequently became a naval base. In 1861, three simultaneous Spanish campaigns against the natives enabled them to gain control of the region. The Spaniards expanded from Polloc into the interior, establishing military posts, but conflict with the Muslims continued unabated right up until the Spanish abandoned the area in 1899.

For the inhabitants of the northern part of Cotabato, their first real contact with foreigners was with Americans, whom they resisted at first. The Americans prevailed, however, and after 1913, extensive tracts of the Cotabato lowlands were opened to settlers from the Visayas and Luzon. Large-scale migration continued into the 1960s, so that today, the Maguindanao are a minority in their homeland.

Many Muslim separatist groups and organizations like the NPA have ceased their guerrilla fighting and are waiting for the Estrada government to improve the quality of life in the Philippines.

Accommodations
Stay at the **New Imperial Hotel,** 51 Don Rufino Alonzo St. (two-star), P350-400; **Hotel Filipino** at city plaza on Sinsuat Ave., P7100-150; **El Corazon Inn** on Makakua St. (first-class inn), P150-200; **Castro's Pension House,** 99 Sinsuat Ave., P250-300; and **Padama Pension House,** Quezon Ave., P100-150.

Restaurants
Dining places include the **VIP Restaurant, Las Hermanas, Red Clover Foodhaus, Metro Garden, Smiley Foods, Jade Garden, Lido, Ang Bagong Hardin,** and **Uptown,** as well as several fast-food centers on Magallanes Street and Sinsuat Avenue. The **Hotel Filipino** has a good dining room and there are also good meals served at **Jay Pee's Restaurant** on Don Rufino Alonzo Street.

Transportation
By Air: PAL flies Manila-Cotabato daily (90 minutes); Cebu-Cotabato five times a week (70 minutes); Malabang-Cotabato five times weekly (25 minutes); Zamboanga-Cotabato daily (50 minutes). The airport is at Awang, 13 km south of Cotabato City.

By Sea: The main port at Polloc receives large interisland ships, while smaller vessels dock closer to the city. See Transportation in the Mindanao Introduction for complete shipping schedules.

By Land: Regular JD Express buses link Cotabato with Koronadal and General Santos City (209 km). From Davao City (227 km) via Kidapawan, there are regular Mintranco buses, including an a/c bus. From Marawi (143 km) there are minibuses. There are buses from Cotabato to Pagadian (180 km), but this is a crisis area and tourists are advised not to travel overland on this route. It's better to go by sea in a rustic old hulk than risk being ambushed by rebels.

WESTERN MINDANAO

ZAMBOANGA

Zamboanga City, strategically located at the tip of the Zamboanga peninsula, is known as the "City of Flowers." Colorful blooms are indeed much in evidence. The population of over 520,000 is about 75% Christian and 25% Muslim. The bustling waterfront reflects its position as an important fishing port, a major regional trading center, and the gateway to Basilan and the Sulu Archipelago. It's a collection point for copra, corn, fish, timber, and other natural products that are then shipped onward.

Southeast Asia is blessed with a handful of place-names so evocative that most tourist offices would kill for them: Mandalay, Borneo, Bandung, and Zamboanga. These destinations sometimes live up to their reputations, which isn't the case with Zamboanga, a hot and congested city filled with ugly concrete buildings, movie posters, tawdry nightclubs, and narrow streets crowded with blasting motorcycles.

Apparently, few travel writers actually come down here to do their research. Some articles have described the city as "the garden of the Philippines" . . . "a provincial town where the pace of life is slow and unhurried" . . . "the heart of the intriguing exotica of Muslim-land."

Hardly. Less than a third of the population is Muslim, and signs of Islam barely extend beyond the fishing slum of Rio Hondo. Colorful *vintas*, primitive sailing crafts that once served as the symbols of exotic Zamboanga, have largely disappeared from local waters.

The main reason to visit Zamboanga is to travel down through the Sulu Archipelago, which, despite reassurances given by local tourism officials, is a risky adventure.

The tourist office is in the Lantaka Hotel, where you can lunch and enjoy cocktails at sunset.

History

The origin of the name is uncertain and may derive from early Malay settlers, who called the area Jambangan ("Land of Flowers"), or 17th-century Spaniards who labelled it Samboangan ("Docking Point"). The Muslims of the area still call it Samboangan. The city was founded in 1635 with the construction of Fort Pilar as a base

the traditional vintas *of Zamboanga*

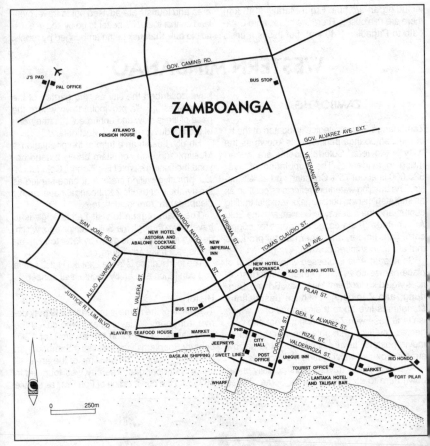

for expeditions against the Moros. The following year, a Spanish fleet sailed out to win an epic naval battle against the Muslims off Punta de Flechas.

Zamboanga was the capital of Mindanao throughout the Spanish era. It was an isolated fort and Christian settlement, surrounded by Muslim territory—Spain's southern outpost, destined to become her last bastion in the Philippines. Spanish influence here is reflected in the prevalence of Catholicism and the number of Spanish words in Chavacano, the local dialect.

The city was built up during the American era and became a Japanese defense headquarters during WW II. The city was pounded by bombers and warships prior to the virtually unopposed U.S. landing in 1945. Following the bombardment, the city has been rebuilt in a nondescript modern style, so that little of its old Spanish atmosphere remains.

Chavacano

The natives, called Zamboanguenos or Chavacanos, speak the distinctive Chavacano dialect, which is a kind of pidgin Spanish, a mixture of 70% Spanish, especially unconjugated verbs, and 30% native tongues. It contains more Spanish than any other Philippine dialect, and those familiar with Spanish will immediately notice the strong Spanish overtones.

Orientation

Tricycles are the standard way of getting around within the city, while jeepneys link the suburbs and outlying points with downtown. The airport and bus station are on the outskirts of the city, while the wharf is centrally located. A tricycle from the airport to downtown (2.5 km) costs P10 pp. Rides within the downtown area cost P2 pp. The Department of Tourism is next to the Lantaka Hotel.

Don't miss the Lantaka Hotel, which has the best views of Zamboanga harbor. It once served the American military as a temporary base of operations; it offers the fortress-like security which is increasingly important in volatile Zamboanga City.

Take note that the city shuts down in the evenings because of continued hostility here. There are still plenty of things to do at night around the hotels, but very few people walk around after dark, and the city streets are deserted. Most foreigners who visit Zamboanga City find themselves spending their evenings at the Lantaka Hotel, where they are safe and comfortable.

Fort Pilar

Located on the waterfront, just east of the city center, this Spanish fort with one-meter-thick coral walls was built in 1635, abandoned in 1663, and rebuilt in 1719. Here, the Spaniards warded off Moro, Dutch, Portuguese, and British attacks. It was occupied by American troops in 1899 and the Japanese in WW II.

Note, on the outside of the east wall, the shrine of Nuestra Señora del Pilar, the city's patron saint. Devotees come here to pray and light candles, especially on Saturday evenings and Sundays. There are some old cannons inside the fort. The walk between the Lantaka Hotel and the fort is pleasant.

Rio Hondo

About 200 meters beyond the fort, a wooden bridge leads to a large Muslim village and public housing project built on piles and platforms over the water. It's actually three villages: Rio Hondo, just across the bridge; Campo Muslim; and Sa-

haya, a Human Settlements project built over a former mangrove swamp. It's fun to wander around the causeways that form the village streets, lined by the houses of Samal, Tausug, and some Badjao.

The arched bridge joining the village to the mainland is a good place to survey the settlement, whose skyline is dominated by Campo Muslim's silver-domed mosque. Be prepared to feel strange and conspicuous as you wander around this Muslim slum. It is definitely not laid out for tourists, but is certainly unique, and exotic compared to the bland city center. Another place to see this kind of Muslim settlement is at the entrance to the harbor at Basilan Island.

Justice R.T. Lim Boulevard

This two-km seafront drive, extending west from the city center, is the Roxas Boulevard of Zamboanga. A late afternoon stroll beneath its acacia trees will lead past restaurants and bars that beckon you to relax over seafood and beer as you watch the sun dip behind the *basnigs* riding at anchor.

Following the shore brings you to Campo Islam, a Samal village on stilts. Farther still, tankers tie up next to factories where copra is processed into coconut oil. After three km, note the small palace built in 1976 for President Marcos. There are some shell and coral shops out in this area.

Festivals

The **Bale Zamboanga Festival,** held each 25-26 February and participated in by Christian and Muslim residents, features cultural events, a regatta, and fair. This is the best time to see those colorful *vinta* sails.

On 10-12 October, thousands of devotees celebrate the **Zamboanga Hermosa Festival** in honor of Our Lady of the Pillar, which commemorates the apparition of the Virgin at Fort Pilar and her miraculous intervention against enemy attacks. This is the biggest fiesta in the City of Flowers and is well worth seeing if you happen to be in the area at this time.

Accommodations

Because of security problems in Zamboanga City, many of the budget hotels have declined as travelers stopped coming to this region. Because of hostilities and uncertainty in Zamboanga City, it may be wise to pay a little extra for a hotel where security is a priority.

Atilano's Pension House: A good escape from the noise, on a small alley just off the former Pasonanca Road. Unfortunately, this place has been downgraded after the death of the original caretaker. His children now run the place and it shows. This is still a viable option for travelers, but it's just not as nice as it used to be. Major Jaldon St., tel. (062) 991-0784, P150-350.

L'Mirage Pension House: Another pension house with both fan-cooled and a/c rooms. Mayor Jaldon St., tel. (062) 991-3962, P180-420.

Paradise Pension House: Bridging the middle gap is this newish spot with clean rooms and friendly management. Barcelona St., tel. (062) 991-3465, P500-750.

Lantaka Hotel: Zamboanga's best hotel with swimming pool and wonderful waterfront location. Valderroza St., tel. (062) 991-2033, P950-2,200.

Restaurants

Sotanghon is a popular noodle dish here, and Zamboanga is renowned for seafood. Be sure to try *curacha,* a local specialty that's a delicious cross between crab and lobster. Many small, inexpensive restaurants are conveniently located in the downtown area. They include **Palmeras, Aldea, Quostaw, Tropical Cuisine, Sunburst,** and **Village.** There are barbecue stands on La Purisima Street and R.T. Lim Boulevard. Moving up in price, **Alavar's Seafoods House** on R.T. Lim Boulevard is the place to sample *curacha.* The hotels often have good restaurants, too. You can eat quite well at the **Lantaka Hotel,** which has a fine, though upscale, restaurant. You can get a good breakfast here for P100.

A nice place for Filipino food is **Antonio's** on Pasonanca Road near the quiet Pasonanca Park. Also try **Puericulture Center Snack House,** P. Brillantes Street on the corner of Barcelona Street. Specialties are barbecued meat—chicken *(tinola)* and goat *(kaldereta).* For upscale dining in a nice location, try the new **La Patissiere** on Pilar Street, a favorite among the business folks of Zamboanga.

Nightlife

At present, the violence in Zamboanga City has driven many local residents into their homes at sunset. The streets are deserted at night and tourists are warned not to roam around after dark. Since foreign travelers aren't much for staying confined to hotels, most visitors meet at the Lantaka Hotel's **Talisay Bar,** a local landmark. Other nighttime options here are the small, cheap bars on Governor Alvarez Ave. near Mayor Climaco Ave., but these are not recommended due to the self-imposed city curfew.

The major hotels have music bars or karaoke. The restaurant at the **Kao Pi Hung Hotel** on Governor Lim Avenue features karaoke and is popular with locals and visiting tourists from Manila, Cebu, and elsewhere. On Camins Road, try **Kiss Me Super Disco** (cover charge) for some dancing or the **Shingjuko Bar** on La Purisima Street. The **King's Palace Disco** (on the corner of La Purisima and Tomas Claudio St.) is still lively as is the **Casa de Oro** on Justice Lim Boulevard. Other late-night spots are near the airport, e.g., **Village, J's Pad,** and **Lutong Pinoy;** the latter has an open-air restaurant.

Shopping

The bustle of the wharf is complemented by the nearby fish market, especially active in the late afternoon, where an incredible array of sea creatures is displayed. The public market beyond sells everything from rice to handicrafts. The selection of fruit is superb. Look for Sulu mats, with their dramatic geometric designs, ethnic cloth and clothing, brassware, shellcraft, and antique coins. This section is known as the flea market.

Zamboanga is also famous for its Barter Trade distribution outlets. These tax-free markets' tiny booths are the cheapest places in the Philippines to buy cassette tapes, and there are many other imported goods available: canned food, toiletries, and batik cloth. Zamboanga is a noted shellcraft and shell-buying center. Badjao and Samal try to sell shells, turtle shells, coral and coral jewelry directly from their *bancas* beside the Lantaka Hotel. The Rocan Shell Shop is about three km west of downtown.

To buy orchids, check out J's Orchids at Tetuan. For Yakan cloth, visit the weaving village seven km to the west on the San Ramon Road. There are seven Yakan families here who make and sell their traditional, colorful handicrafts and weavings. Well worth a visit if you have time.

Transportation

By Air: PAL flies Manila-Zamboanga daily and twice a day on Tuesday, Thursday, and Saturday (90 minutes); Cebu-Zamboanga two times a day (55 minutes); Davao-Zamboanga daily (55 minutes); Cotabato-Zamboanga five times a week (50 minutes); Dipolog-Zamboanga daily (50 minutes); Pagadian-Zamboanga daily (45 minutes); Jolo-Zamboanga twice daily (40 minutes); Tawi-Tawi-Zamboanga is temporarily suspended due to work in progress on the Tawi-Tawi airstrip.

By Sea: See Transportation in the Mindanao Introduction for a complete listing of shipping services to Zamboanga.

Regional Boats: Pagadian is linked to Zamboanga by SKT Shipping thrice weekly and Sampaguita Shipping once a week; the trip takes 13 hours overnight. Sampaguita makes a weekly return trip from Zamboanga to Sirawai/Siocon. In addition to Sulpicio and William Lines, smaller boats operate twice-weekly overnight trips between Cotabato and Zamboanga.

It's also possible to take the overnight boat from Cotabato to Pagadian and continue from there to Zamboanga by bus. There are boat connections between Zamboanga and several towns on both the north and south coasts of the Zamboanga peninsula. Ferries to Basilan operate four times daily to Isabela and once daily to Lamitan (90 minutes). There are almost daily departures to the Sulu Islands, which are served by SKT Shipping Corp. (Rizal St.), Magnolia Shipping Lines (J.S. Alano St.), Sampaguita Shipping and H3R Shipping Lines (both on Valderrosa St.), Ever Lines (Campaner St.), and numerous smaller boats.

By Land: Fortune and Bachelor Express serve the route from Cagayan de Oro (483 km, 12 hours) and Iligan. Buses also leave Zamboanga for Cagayan, Iligan, Pagadian, Buug, and Ipil. Lilian Express has six departures on the Dipolog-Sindangan-Ipil-Zamboanga run; buses leave Zamboanga for Dipolog between 0430 and 1130.

VICINITY OF ZAMBOANGA

The Santa Cruz Islands

Great and Little Santa Cruz Islands, which have been declared a national park, are the most popular picnic, sunbathing, and snorkeling/diving spot near the city. These adjacent islands are both surrounded by beaches. Great Santa Cruz is noted for the pinkish color of its sand, caused by disintegrating coral washing ashore.

Snorkelers will find coral patches just off both islands as the seabed slopes away, and small fish are plentiful, but visibility isn't exceptional. Entry and exit can be difficult at low tide, so snorkeling/diving from a *banca* is recommended. Also, beware of strong tides in the channnel between the islands.

You can hire a *banca* near the Lantaka Hotel for the 25-minute crossing for about P500 return. A local naval vessel also brings tourists out to the island for a predetermined fee. Visiting Pinoys from Manila tend to think of Zamboanga as a war zone, so to play it safe they go with the navy to Santa Cruz. They often have bodyguards and the rest, but don't let this intimidate you. If you care to go along with them, they are usually more than happy to oblige foreigners on whatever outings they have planned for the day.

If you travel with Filipinos, you can be sure to have a meal or two scheduled into the day. You can get to Santa Cruz for less by inquiring at Zamboanga Beach Park in Calauan or by bargaining with the local fishermen near Fort Pilar. Try to find other travelers who will share the trip. The islands' beaches make a nice change from the city, and booths on Great Santa Cruz sell cold drinks. The beach is covered with broken coral so tread carefully as you wander here.

There's a small Samal graveyard in the bush nearby, and on another part of the island, a Samal fishing village by a mangrove lagoon; the latter isn't accessible from the main beach, however. Little Santa Cruz has a lighthouse, Philippine Navy shooting range, and a lovely stretch of sand bar.

West of Zamboanga City

Catch a minibus on Justice Lim Boulevard to go out in this direction. About seven km west of Zamboanga, on the right-hand side of the road, is a cluster of Yakan weaving families, where women use backstrap looms to produce beautiful and very colorful cloth that's sold as placemats and table-runners. It's well worth coming here. There are also beach resorts along this stretch of coast.

The best are the Vista del Mar and the Zamboanga Beach Park. Beyond it are Yellow Beach at nine km, where U.S. forces landed in 1945; Garagasan Beach at 12 km; Ayala Beach at 16.5 km; and Talisayan Beach at 20 km. The San Ramon Prison and Penal Farm, founded by the Spanish in the 19th century, is at 22 km. A souvenir shop outside the prison offers handicrafts made by the inmates.

If there's no direct bus to San Ramon, change at the village of Ayala. Iron ore and manganese are mined in this area. Labuan fishing village is at 35 kilometers. Upcoming attractions are Rancho Frio in Anuling and the Susana Park, some 3,500 feet above sea level.

East of Zamboanga City

Take a minibus from behind the DBP near the market. Taluksangay, 19 km northeast of Zamboanga (45 minutes), is a Samal village consisting of houses on land and on stilts over the water. Some Badjao live here, too. The red-domed mosque is well attended at prayer times. Ask if you can ascend the police tower for an overview of the area, which is mainly brush and swampland. The residents fish and gather firewood.

One km before reaching the village, there's a small Badjao cemetery 100 meters north of the road. You can hire a *banca* at Taluksangay to cross to nearby Sacol Island, which has a wide beach, off which the gently sloping seabed has good coral patches between dynamited areas. Farther along the coast, about 35 km by road from Zamboanga City, is the Bolong Beach Recreation Center, which is on a good beach and serves seafood meals. Off Bolong are the beautiful white-sand Eleven Islands.

PAGADIAN CITY

Pagadian, situated on Illana Bay, was an early Subanon trading center. It's now the provincial capital and the commercial center for the eastern Zamboanga agricultural region.

The first group of Visayan settlers arrived here in 1927. Today, it's an ethnic melting pot. In ad-

dition to migrants from the Visayas and Luzon, and Chinese merchants, numerous Muslim and cultural minority groups are represented—Tiruray, Manobo, Tausug, Maranao, Maguindanao, Samal, Subanon, and Sicubong. Local crafts include the making of wooden shoes and matweaving.

Attractions

Points of interest in the area include Dao-Dao Island, 10 minutes offshore by *banca;* Tukuran Beach Resort, 20 km from Pagadian; Lake Dasay in San Miguel, southwest of the city; Muricay Beach, 10 minutes by pumpboat; and Pulacan Falls, 12 km from the city.

Accommodations and Restaurants

The **Sea View Hotel,** National Hwy. (P100-150), is convenient. In town, there's the **Peninsula Hotel** (P100-150) and the **Zamboanga Hotel,** both on Jamisola Street. **Padadian City Hotel,** Rizal Ave. (P250-300), has a/c and good rooms. The **Roxanne Hotel,** F.S. Pajares Ave. (P100-150), is standard. Eat at **New China Fastfoods,** corner F.S. Pajares Ave.; the **Pagadian City Restaurant,** Rizal Ave.; or the **Roxanne Coffee Shoppe,** F.S. Pajares Avenue.

Transportation

By Air: PAL flies Cebu-Pagadian daily (one hour) and Zamboanga-Pagadian daily (45 minutes). Aerolift flies Manila-Pagadian three times weekly. The airport is five km from downtown, and the PAL office is in the Peninsula Hotel.

By Sea: Pagadian is served by several ships from various locations. See Transportation in the Mindanao Introduction for more details.

By Land: Fortune Sunshine Express and Lilian Express are the principal bus lines. Pagadian is linked by regular buses to Ozamis/Dipolog, Iligan/Cagayan de Oro, Cotabato City, and Zamboanga City. Buses linking Zamboanga City with Ozamis, Iligan, Cagayan de Oro, and Cotabato also pass through the province, while Zamboanga-Dipolog buses cut north from Ipil to Liloy. Pagadian is 259 km from Zamboanga. From Pagadian, it's 98 km to Ozamis, 132 km to Iligan, and 180 km to Cotabato. Again, these overland routes may involve some risk. If the situation is not good here, the best way to get around these provinces is by plane.

THE SULU ARCHIPELAGO

The Sulu Islands form the Philippines's southern extremity. They stretch for about 300 km between Basilan and Sabah (Borneo) and separate the Sulu and Celebes Seas. The archipelago comprises about 400 named islands and at least 500 unnamed islets. It's divided into several subgroups—Jolo, Pangutaran, Samales, Tapul, Tawi-Tawi, and Sibutu. The isolated Cagayan de Tawi-Tawi and Turtle Island groups are also considered part of Sulu.

Historically, the region is a sultanate, but today it consists of two provinces, Sulu and Tawi-Tawi, with Jolo and Bongao as the respective capitals. The Muslim influence in Sulu is unmistakable: mosques, conservatively dressed women, coffee shops rather than bars, and an absence of pork on restaurant menus. The coffee shop, which serves good, strong coffee accompanied by trays of cakes, is one of Sulu's most agreeable institutions.

Sulu has been the haunt of pirates and smugglers for centuries. Often, the pirates prey on the smugglers. Successive Manila governments have maintained only a tenuous control of these islands. The conflict between the Moro National Liberation Front and government forces here in 1974 had a major impact on the entire region, since much of the infrastructure was destroyed and thousands of people were left homeless. Sulu is still recovering from those traumatic events.

While this is a potentially dangerous area for foreign travelers, especially off the main shipping route, it's also one of the most exotic and fascinating parts of the Philippines. The people can be extremely hospitable. A Western traveler is referred to as "Milikan."

Note that while many boats link Sulu with Sabah, this route is closed to foreigners. January-April, when the weather is relatively dry, is the best time to travel.

History

Foreign traders, lured by pearls, began visiting Sulu over a thousand years ago. Ships from throughout Asia, but especially China, moored off the old capital, Buansa, near what is now Jolo. It was an international commercial center when Manila was still a village. It's believed that a colony of foreign Muslims existed in Jolo around 1300, and by the end of the 14th century, Sulu had become the first area of the Philippines to be converted to Islam.

As the faith increasingly took hold over the following century, Sulu was organized as an independent Muslim sultanate. Its traders and raiders made their presence felt from northern Borneo to Luzon. Slavery was an important part of old Sulu society and Moro "pirates" attacked and took slaves from the coastal settlements of Luzon and the Visayas from the 16th to the early 19th centuries.

SULU ARCHIPELAGO

© MOON PUBLICATIONS, INC.

THE PEOPLE OF THE SULU ARCHIPELAGO

The Sulu Archipelago is overwhelmingly Muslim, but there are also a few Catholics, Chinese Buddhists, and traditionally animist Badjao. The main Muslim groups are the Tausug and Samal. The Tausug cultural center is Jolo, while Samal become more numerous as one travels south, as do the nomadic sea gypsies, the Badjao.

To the people of Sulu, the international boundary between the Philippines and Sabah (Malaysia) is an artificial line that separates many families. Literacy is relatively low in the archipelago compared to the rest of the Philippines. This is largely due to the people's conservative nature, indifference to formal education, and ingrained suspicion of government motives, but their resistance is slowly breaking down.

Handicrafts: The crafts of Sulu show marked Islamic and Indonesian influence. Skilled artisans make boats, bladed weapons, jewelry, bronze and brassware, mats, *pis* cloth, embroidered textiles, shellcraft, rattan craft, basketry, traditional housecarvings, and carved wooden gravemarkers. Sulu mats, with their dramatic geometric designs, have been famous for centuries.

Pandanus leaves are dried, stripped, boiled, dyed, dried again, and bundled prior to plaiting. Each mat may take several weeks to produce. A plain, coarse undermat is sewn to it to increase durability. Noted mat-weaving places include Taglibi (Patikul) on Jolo Island, Pata Island, Laminusa Island (Siasi), and Tandubas (Tawi-Tawi). Tausug weapons are also a fine purchase for the collector.

The Tausug

The Tausug, or Tausog, who number around 650,000, dominate the Sulu Archipelago numerically, economically, and politically. Although they're found from Zamboanga to Sabah, and out in Palawan, the Tausug are concentrated in the Jolo Island cluster. They refer to themselves as "People of the Current," reflecting their ties to the sea.

They are loosely classified as Tau Higad, coastal dwellers; Tau Gimba, who inhabit the hinterland, and Tau Pu, who live on offshore islands. The Tau Higad consider themselves more civilized than the others. They also distinguish between Parianon ("People of the Landing"), who live near the coast and trade with Borneo; and Guimbahanon ("People of the Hills"), who are farmers and artisans.

Traditional society was divided into three classes: hereditary aristocracy, freemen, and slaves. The Tausug were the first Filipinos to adopt Islam as a religion and a way of life, and as the elite of the old Sultanate of Jolo, are traditionally the ruling class of Sulu. They're an inordinately proud people who regard themselves as superior even to other Filipino Muslims. Tausug are renowned for their bravery, independence, and love of adventure. They are superb sailors and fighters, as well as shrewd traders. While fishing, farming, and commerce are their ostensible occupations, piracy, slave-trading, and smuggling have been prevalent activities for centuries.

They're very proud of their cultural identity, so that all outside efforts to subdue them have been resisted. A Tausug's family name is vitally important to him, and he would never besmirch it by cowardice. Artistry is the flip side of this aggressiveness. The Tausugs' rich cultural heritage is reflected in their traditional dress, jewelry, weapons, brass artifacts, music, dance, and architecture. They are skillful metalsmiths, woodworkers, and weavers. They are also taller and broader-built than the average Filipino, which may add to their sense of superiority.

The Tausug Home: Coastal fishing communities are compact clusters of houses, while farming homesteads tend to be dispersed through the interior of Jolo and other islands. Settlements are dominated by the mosque. Before constructing a house, the Tausug consult seers, so that the central post is erected on a day considered lucky, and the consultation is repeated when the family is ready to move in.

The typical Tausug house, built of lumber and bamboo, has a *sala,* a large rectangular room, beneath a thatched gable roof. Some houses feature elaborate woodcarving. Houses rest on two-meter-high teak posts, with steps leading to the main door, which faces east if possible to let in early morning light. A porch leads to a separate kitchen. Traditionally, houses had slits rather than windows, for both protection and to keep its young unmarried women from view.

A stockade may surround the whole to confine animals and provide protection. The *sala* is necessary due to their propensity for inviting many guests to their parties. One side of the *sala* has no aperture, and mats and thick mattresses are laid on the floor along its base. These kapok-stuffed mattresses are made on Tapul Island. They're normally covered with colored sheets or mats, but on special occasions such as weddings and baptisms, they're encased in ornately embroidered covers. Large pillows are placed against the walls. Above the mattresses and pillows a canopy, made of colored cloth, forms a ceiling. Red, maroon, green, and pink are common colors. The canopy is replaced by an elaborate one on special occasions.

Guests are invited to rest on mattresses and may be offered a box, which may be of brass, silver, or just basketry and contains the ingredients for chewing betel nut. Food is served on large footed brass trays; these are among the Tausug's most prized possessions and are also used for carrying food during weddings and religious ceremonies.

Dress: Tausug usually reserve their traditional dress for festive occasions. Women's blouses range from the simple, short-sleeved *sambra* and the long-sleeved *sablay*, to the beautiful *biyatawi*, of shiny material and studded with gold buttons, worn on festive occasions. The *patadyong* is the Sulu counterpart of Mindanao's *malong* or the Malay *sarong*. It's worn by both men and women, as are the loose, baggy trousers called *sawal* or *kantyu*.

Sawal kuput are tight-fitting pants with button-edged side slits that are worn by men. There are several types of men's shirts. Men also wear a piece of cloth tied around the waist, or a wide belt with compartments to keep money, documents, and bladed weapons. They wear a kerchief on their heads. This large square cloth may feature multicolored geometric designs and is folded many times. It may also serve other functions, such as a carryall.

Similarly, the *patadyong* can be used as a blanket or hammock. Tausug favor rich materials such as silk, brocade, gold and silver lamé, and film-like fabrics and lace, and traditional costume isn't complete without jewelry.

Gold is the preferred metal. Men and women usually wear at least a ring, and some women may be heavily bedecked, perhaps with matching sets of earrings, bracelets, rings, brooches, and a necklace with a pendant. Blouses are fastened with brooches or *dublum* gold coins, possibly Spanish doubloons, with a safety catch at the back. Parents try to provide their unmarried daughters with a set of jewelry, and a husband is expected to give his wife jewelry from time to time.

Jewelry is also considered a form of saving that can be used as collateral or in pawn shops. Tausug goldsmiths can fashion fine pieces, even with simple tools; gold here is measured by the *sussuk*, which

equals one gram. Pearls, precious stones, mother-of-pearl, black coral, and turtle shell may also be used, and designs can take many forms, e.g., a fish, insect, leaf, or crescent moon. Jewelry, of course, is a measure of wealth, though educated women generally wear fewer pieces of jewelry.

The Yakan of Basilan Island

Basilan is the homeland of this peaceful, industrious Muslim group of farmers and herdsmen. Numbering about 125,000, they grow upland rice, corn, coconuts, *kamote*, cassava, and vegetables, and buy fish from the Samal. Yakan women are famous weavers. They use backstrap looms to blend cotton and silk into cloth featuring intricate geometric patterns. The predominant colors are purple, turquoise, green, and yellow.

They also weave the traditional clothing of the men—the distinctive striped *laup* cloth, *kandit* (a red cotton sash, several meters long), and *pis* (headcloth). The women also weave mats. Yakan traditional dress is extremely colorful. Both men and women wear a close-fitting jacket with long, narrow sleeves, striped trousers that are skin-tight below the knee, and a small metal betel nut box at the waist. The men also wear the sash, headcloth, and helmet.

The women's jackets are usually black with gold buttons, and they wear a short skirt over their trousers, plus rings, bangles, earrings, and a large comb. The Yakan are known for their elaborate weddings and festivals featuring music, games, and horse races. Traditionally, Yakan houses are scattered through their fields, but since the '70s, the security situation has induced them to move into tighter communities.

Houses are rectangular, raised on piles, with a porch and a steep thatched roof. Yakan like to live in the vicinity of a mosque, and the *imam* also functions as a community leader. Nevertheless, their practice of Islam remains somewhat adulterated by animist beliefs.

The Samal

Samal households often form a ward within a larger non-Samal settlement. They typically live in compact communities, with houses built close to the water's edge, or on stilts out over the sea, linked by lumber and bamboo catwalks. Dwellings consist of one or more small, rectangular rooms, with an adjoining kitchen.

The Samal number about 250,000. Their lives
continues on following page

THE PEOPLE OF THE SULU ARCHIPELAGO
(continued)

are closely tied to the sea; they're fishermen, pearl divers, master boat-builders, and sometimes smugglers and pirates. Some are farmers and traders. Samal women weave the renowned Sulu mats. The Samal are also noted for their beautifully carved gravemarkers, which are left on their burial plots on small, sandy islands.

The Badjao

The Badjao (or Bajau) are the "Sea Gypsies" of the Sulu Archipelago. Locally known as Palao, from *paraw* (boat), the Badjao are literally the "Boat People." There are an estimated 35,000 Badjao, about 25,000 of whom live in Philippine waters. The Badjao, who legend holds originated in Johore, Malaysia, were mentioned by Pigafetta, Magellan's chronicler, in 1521. Today, their range extends from Zamboanga to Sabah and Celebes. They're particularly concentrated around Tawi-Tawi and Sibutu, with Sitangkai the best place to see them.

Traditionally, the Badjao are born and live on their distinctive boats, which measure 10 meters long with carved, extended prows, canvas awnings, loose plank flooring, and large water pots. They have a relatively primitive lifestyle, but are superb sailors and fishermen, able to forecast storms by observing the wind and waves and accurately estimating sailing times to their destinations.

It is believed that the Badjao do not come ashore for any reason in their lifetime, except on the day of their burial. They are buried on land, making many of the Sulu islands particularly sacred to the Badjao. The sea is their element, and specific locations in the sea are given names as a mountain or valley would be on land. Sun and salt turn the hair of many Badjao blond.

Fish, caught with nets and spears, are often hung to dry and are cooked in the stern. The Badjao sell fish to buy cassava, their staple, and a stew of seafood and cassava is a common meal. Meek and peaceful, the Badjao are commonly regarded as being socially inferior pagans, and, together with the closely related Samal, they're somewhat oppressed by the dominating Tausug. They are easy prey for pirates, who steal their catch and any valuables they may have. The Badjao rarely testify against their aggressors for fear of reprisal.

For centuries, they've lived on the fringe of stronger societies, trying to avoid conflict. Since the Badjao have always built their boats of the best available wood from the forest, they have recently been unable to get the wood they need due to deforestation and costs of wood. Many Badjao families have been obliged to settle on land, as a family man would not let his offspring live at sea in a plywood boat. This new lifestyle is changing Badjao society, and many sea gypsies are now land-locked.

The Spanish Era: Jolo was the scene of several clashes between Spaniard and Muslim. The Spanish burned the town in 1578. They captured it in 1638 after a three-month struggle, but the Tausugs liberated it seven years later. Spain didn't gain a toehold on Sulu until almost the end of its era. The impetus for this came in the mid-19th century, when Spain's colonial rivals, France and Britain, showed an interest in the area.

The Spaniards took Jolo in 1851 and declared Sulu a Spanish protectorate, but a lack of "cooperation" led to another offensive in 1876. After naval guns had smashed Jolo, the Spanish established a garrison there, though their influence didn't extend far beyond their fort. In spite of a peace treaty with the sultan, who had moved to Maybun, now Maimbung, 20 km away, *juramentados* frequently entered Jolo to kill

Spaniards. Spanish authority over Sulu remained nominal at best.

The American Regime: The Americans, who established garrisons at Jolo, Siasi, and Bongao in 1899, weren't much more successful in colonizing the region. One of the new colonial government's first priorities was to negotiate a treaty with the Sultan of Sulu. The sultan kept Gen. John C. Bates waiting for over a month before they finally met at the sultan's residence in Maybun.

The Bates Agreement in 1899 recognized the sovereignty of the sultan and respect for Islam and its traditions. It was abrogated in 1904, however, because the Americans decided that it implied approval of polygamy and slavery. The Americans launched a campaign to disarm the natives. The Tausugs resisted, and thousands were killed in bloody battles. The massacre of men, women, and children at the Bud Daho Battle in 1906 created adverse American public opinion and led to Gen. Leonard Wood facing a congressional trial.

Following the Battle of Bud Bagsak in 1913, pacification had reached a point where public schooling could be started. In 1915, the sultan abdicated his rights of sovereignty but retained religious leadership, and the sultanate was abolished entirely by a treaty in 1940, in which Sulu became part of the Commonwealth of the Philippines. During WW II, Muslim guerrillas were very active against the Japanese and facilitated the American landings in Tawi-Tawi, Siasi, and Jolo in 1945.

After 1945: The Sulu Moros had never accepted the termination of the sultanate and continued to recognize its existence, though different factions supported rival claims to be sultan. When, however, in the early 1960s, the Philippine government pressed its claim of the region all the way to north Borneo on the basis that it was formerly part of the Sulu sultanate, it became timely to revive the sultanate.

The chosen sultan died in 1973, and his son was enthroned in Jolo in 1974, despite his rivals' challenge to the succession. Meanwhile, the declaration of martial law in 1972 had led to tense confrontation between government forces and the Moro National Liberation Front (MNLF). In 1974, MNLF rebels attacked Jolo and other outlying communities. The government was forced to mount a large-scale operation to reassert its control, and during the ensuing battle, much of Jolo was destroyed, with hundreds killed and thousands left homeless. Many people temporarily left the province for neighboring regions.

Sulu and Tawi-Tawi are now part of the Muslim Autonomous Region. To this day, hostilities continue between the MNLF and the Philippine government and the Sulu Archipelago remains the least politically stable area in the country.

BASILAN ISLAND

Basilan is an island province, situated between Zamboanga and the Sulu Archipelago, and separated from Zamboanga by the 25-km-wide Basi-

lan Strait. Of the 200,000-plus inhabitants, the native Yakans are the biggest ethnic group, with significant minorities of Christians (Chavacanos and Visayans), and other Muslims such as Samal, Tausug, and a few Badjao.

The predominant language varies by region. In Isabela, it's Chavacano, while Lamitan has more of a mixture of Chavacano, Yakan, Visayan, and Tagalog. Basilan has been a trouble spot in recent years, so check the current situation at the Provincial Capitol before venturing out around the island.

One of the best times to visit Basilan is during the Lami-Lamihan Festival, 14-16 April, when the colorfully dressed natives participate in a parade and horse races; Lamitan's a good place to be at this time.

Basilan, at present, is hostile NPA territory where a kidnapping involving a Manila doctor and his family took place. Prior to this kidnapping, an American missionary was abducted and held for ransom on Basilan. The town of Isabela is open to foreigners, but the interior of this beautiful island is dangerous territory indeed.

Transportation

Basilan Shipping Lines ferries depart Zamboanga for and 90-minutes trip to Isabela at 0700, 1000, 1300, and 1600. They stay long enough to load and then return to Zamboanga. There's a boat at 1500 from Zamboanga to Lamitan, returning at 0800 next morning. Connections to Sulu from Basilan are irregular, and it's easier to return to Zamboanga and travel south from there.

The entrance to Basilan harbor is spectacular, with *vinta* boats sailing past the ferry and the small, colorful Muslim settlement across the harbor on Malamawi Island. Sea gypsies, or the Badjao, also live on this island in stilted homes. Although it's an undeveloped area, it's an interesting place to visit with many small Muslim teahouses.

History

Little is known about the early history of Basilan, though it's assumed that it came under the same Muslim influence as Sulu. The island was once called Tagima after a pre-Hispanic *datu*. A *sitio* of this name in Tuburan municipality is today considered holy by the Yakans. Lamitan was the stronghold of the legendary Sultan Kudarat until he was driven out by the Spaniards after a bloody battle in 1637. Some years later, Jesuit missionaries began their work.

The natives repulsed a Dutch attack in 1747. Muslims were also active in the area, and Datu Bantilan of Sulu established a short-lived sultanate here. After building a stone fort, named in honor of Queen Isabela II, and a naval hospital, both of which were destroyed in WW II, the Spaniards established a garrison here in 1848. Earlier, in 1845, France had wanted to establish a free trade zone in Basilan.

Isabela

The entry to the provincial capital's port is a one-km-wide channel lined by mangroves and huts on stilts, between the main island and Malamawi Island. Isabela is a small town, easily explored on foot. Sights include the wharf, market, and Plaza Rizal, which contains a relief map of the province, and a modern cathedral, next to which is Claretcraft, a display center of native handicrafts such as mats and *buri* bags.

Obtain travel information at the tourist office in the Capitol building.

Stay at **Basilan Hotel,** P150-200 pp. Eat in the hotel's dining room or at the excellent **Bistro,** en route to the wharf. Try the calamari!

Another fairly good place is the **Queen Bee,** across from the Basilan Hotel. The market has some okay food and there are Muslim teahouses near the wharf.

Vicinity of Isabela

Four km outside Isabela on the road to Maluso is the Menzi Agricultural Corporation's plant, where you can see latex being processed into rubber (Mon.-Fri.). In addition to rubber trees, it's surrounded by plantations of coffee, black pepper, rubber, and African oil palm. Note the coffee beans laid out on the ground to dry.

You can swim at nearby Sumagdang Beach, which is guarded by armed soldiers—so relax! Other plantations include the B.F. Goodrich rubber plantation, near which is Calabasa Beach, at Latuan, east of Isabela; and the U.P. Land Grant, a government-owned plantation of coconut, rubber, and coffee, with copra- and rubber-processing plants.

Kaum Purnah Mosque and Muslim Village, within Isabela municipality, can be reached by tri-cycle, jeepney, or *banca.* Inland spots, both 15 km from Isabela, are Calvario Peak (400 meters), a photogenic spot and site of a Chapel of Peace, and Kumalarang Falls (14 meters).

Malamawi Island

Bancas cross from Isabela wharf to Malamawi, where there's a ragged Samal village on stilts. Some Badjao live here, too. Swim at White Beach, about four km across the island, though there's no regular transport. Other points of interest include the fishing village of Panigayan, Badjao, Muslim cemeteries, and a small lake that's the haunt of wild duck. This is a crowded, busy community that is very much a slum. If a local offers to take you across by *banca* from Isabela, a half-day tour for P50-100 is reasonable. In this region, its better to travel with locals who know where not to go.

Lamitan

This small town is the best place to see the Yakan. It has a colorful market, especially on Thursday and Sunday mornings, attended by Yakan in traditional dress, Samal and Badjao selling seafood, Chinese, Chavacanos, and Visayans. Shop for textiles and fruit. There's a beach at nearby Balas, and Bulingan Falls are inland.

Two places to stay here are the **Neva Hotel and Restaurant** (P150) or the better **Nalamar Restaurant and Guesthouse** (P175-200). Other choices are with the Lamitan Homestay Association members. You can get here by regular buses from the market in Isabela (28 km), or take a tricycle (P40-50) for the long, bumpy ride.

They take about 90 minutes on a bad road through coconut and citrus plantations. Buses have been ambushed on this route. The last bus back to Isabela is around 1700. The direct daily boat from Zamboanga docks at the wharf on the outskirts of town.

JOLO ISLAND

Pronounced "HO-lo," Jolo is the name of both the island and the main town, situated on its northwest coast. The locals use the name Sug when referring to the island, but Tiyanggi Sug, or simply Tiyanggi, when they mean the town.

Jolo (893 square km, 60 km long, with an average width of 16 km) is of volcanic origin and is crossed by three parallel mountain chains, with several isolated volcanic cones emerging from their rolling hills. The highest of these is Bud Tumantangis (793 meters), whose name means "Crying Mountain" and derives from the clouds that usually surround its peak, or perhaps from the homesickness it arouses in Tausug sailors as it appears and disappears on the horizon.

Bud Dahu (Daho or Dajo, elev. 685 meters), in Patikul, is a national park. There are a number of crater lakes, Seit and Panamao being the largest. The island's interior is rugged and thickly wooded. Parts of Jolo are fertile and support agriculture. Jolo town and Sukuban (Luuk) are important fishing ports.

The municipality of Parang is noted for weaving, especially the square, formal headcloths with multicolored geometric designs, which take three to four weeks to complete. Most of Jolo Island, whose inhabitants are 95% Muslim, is effectively closed to tourists due to the presence of antigovernment forces. At present, the watchful Philippine military will allow tourists to stay only in Jolo town.

Jolo Town

Jolo, the provincial capital, has a population of about 55,000, which makes it the biggest settlement in the Sulu Archipelago. Though it's the historic seat of the sultans of Sulu, the town in its present form dates only from the Spanish garrison established in 1878. A Spanish tower and some remains of the walls they built still stand. In spite of the decline in pearl diving, Jolo remains an important trading center. A large volume of marine and other local products is shipped north from here, while goods and commodities are received from elsewhere in the Philippines. Hence, Jolo has a very active wharf.

There is still extensive trade with Sabah and Singapore, which supplies Jolo's Barter Trade Market. The public market offers a wide assortment of seafood and fruit. Jolo has several mosques, the largest of which is Masjid Jami in the Tulay District, beyond the public market. Behind it, houses on stilts cover the waterfront.

The **Sulu Ethnological Museum,** a private museum at Notre Dame of Jolo College, has displays relating to the local culture and to Jolo's early trade with Indonesia, China, and the Arab world. You can watch mat-weaving and purchase fine handicrafts such as cloth, mats, and bags at the NACIDA shop at Notre Dame College. Jolo is a good place to experience Islamic holidays.

There's a PNB in Jolo.

Accommodations and Food: The most popular place to stay in Jolo is at **Helen Lodge,** P100 pp. Several journalists and casual travelers have been held in their hotel rooms by the Philippine military, to protect them against the Muslim gangs and political factions which now make Jolo a very dangerous destination for most visitors. Other accommodations include **Maharajah Hotel,** P100 pp, and **Unique Hotel,** P100 pp. **Alvar Restaurant** serves seafood and **Plaza Panciteria** offers Chinese dishes. Enjoy a slice of local life in one of Jolo's numerous coffee shops.

Transportation: PAL flies Zamboanga-Jolo twice daily (takes 40 minutes). The airport is 500 meters from downtown, and the wharf is close by, too. Boats depart from Zamboanga for the 12-hour trip virtually daily. The conditions aboard the ship are not great; try to avoid the unsavory passengers who may be involved in some dangerous activities you don't want to be associated with.

Upon arriving in Jolo, check in with the mayor or *barangay* captain. Check in Zamboanga with SKT, Magnolia, Sampaguita, H3R, or Ever Lines, either at the wharf or their downtown offices.

Transportation within the town is by tricycle, while jeepneys ply the two km from the town center to the Provincial Capitol building, which features Moorish-style architecture.

Bud Dato

Bud Dato is a 200-meter-high hill 7.5 km outside Jolo. Here, in a sacred grove, is the revered gravesite of a foreign Muslim, possibly an Arab, that dates from 1310. The coronations of most of the Sulu sultans have taken place here. The nearby Brigade Camp affords a fine view over the town and coast. There's a government agricultural nursery here, too.

Beaches

Patikul, the adjacent municipality to Jolo, has several beaches, including Maubuh Beach at Lambayong, only a short tricycle ride from Jolo town; Tandu Beach (Igasan); and the beautiful Quezon Beach. **Marungas** and **Lahat-Lahat,** fishing islands about 20 minutes from Jolo, offer beaches and good snorkeling. Always check the security situation before venturing out of town, and if you do head out, you may be turned back by the military.

Samales Islands

This group of about 20 islands lies between Jolo and Basilan. The largest is Tongquil and most important is Balanguingui. In the early 19th century, the Samals of Balanguingui were notorious pirates prior to their annihilation by the Spanish Navy in 1848.

Pangutaran Islands

This group, northwest of Jolo, includes Pangutaran Island, Panducan, and about 12 other small islands. Pangutaran is a low, swampy, heavily wooded island, populated mostly by fishermen. It's a source of turtle eggs.

The Siasi-Tapul Islands

Siasi is the largest island of this group, which consists of about 75 islands scattered between Jolo and Tawi-Tawi Islands. Siasi and Tapul Islands have hilly interiors, their highest points being Bud Gomo (483 meters) and Bud Dakut (474 meters), respectively. The group is well populated, with 56,000 people in Siasi and adjacent Lapac, and 25,000 in Tapul and neighboring Lugus.

The town of Siasi is a stop on the main shipping route to the south; it's four hours from Jolo, with ships on most days. The harbor is on the sheltered channel between Siasi and Lapac Islands.

Siasi is an important fishing port with a fascinating wharf, backed by lots of houses on stilts. The market area contains some workshops of jewellers and metalworkers. Pottery and woodcarving are also practiced. Siasi, Tara, and Lugus Islands are all noted for boat-building. Laminusa Island, east of Siasi, is a preeminent mat-weaving center. Kabingaan Island, near Tapul, is a source of the handwoven kerchiefs worn by Tausug men. There are several beaches around Siasi.

From Siasi, launches and *bancas* go regularly to neighboring villages and islands, and it's often possible to go out and return to Siasi the same day. Once in a while, however, these boats are boarded by pirates.

TAWI-TAWI

Tawi-Tawi province, which has few roads, is divided into 10 municipalities, of which Tandubas is the most populated and the Turtle Islands the least. Numerous islands are surrounded by extensive reefs that bar access to all but small boats. Some have sandy beaches. The climate is wet Aug.-Nov. and dry Dec.-July. Wildlife is abundant here and includes monkeys, wild pigs, and many parrots and other birds. The 200,000 people are 90% Muslim, made up of Samal, Badjao, Jama-Mapun, and Tausug. The Samal are the original inhabitants and remain the majority on almost every island.

The name Tawi-Tawi derives from Old Malay and is a corruption of *jaui-jaui* (far away). Tawi-Tawi is the country's southernmost province, only a few hours by boat from Malaysia. Totaling 307 islands and islets, and 1,087 square km, it consists of Tawi-Tawi Island and small neighboring islands, plus the Sibutu group, Cagayan de Tawi-Tawi, and the Turtle Islands. Bongao and Sitangkai are easily reached from Zamboanga, and their exotic local cultures make the journey to these far reaches of the Philippines eminently worthwhile.

The prevailing dialect is that of the Samal, to which those of the Badjao and Jama-Mapun are closely related. Tausug is also spoken, and many people can speak Malay and Indonesian languages, too. Fishing is the main industry, the catch being sold in Zamboanga and other cities. The total catch is relatively low, however, due to the use of traditional methods. The islands have fertile soil but are undeveloped. The people grow cassava and coconuts. Other activities include seaweed-farming, the gathering of seashells, boat-building, logging, cattle-raising, pottery, and mat- and basket-weaving. Proximity to Sabah has led to high hopes of an oil strike in this area.

History

The Sultan of Sulu gave the British East India Company commercial concessions in the southern islands in 1761. The Germans also requested concessions. The Sibutu and Cagayan groups were inadvertently omitted from the 1898 treaty between Spain and the U.S., and they had to be purchased for an additional US$100,000.

Bongao Island

Bongao, like Jolo, is the name of an island and a town that is the provincial capital. Bongao Island is connected by a causeway to Sanga Sanga Island, where the airport's located. Bongao has two harbors, one for the ships coming through from Zamboanga or Sitangkai, another for the launches that go out to neighboring islands such as Simunul, Manuk Manka, and Bilatan.

Points of interest in Bongao include the market and the **Tawi-Tawi Ethnological Museum** at MSU-Sulu College of Technology and Oceanography. The impressive palace-like Capitol building sits on a hillside overlooking Bongao and is worth visiting for the view; take a tricycle to Tubig Bok, from where it's easy to hitch on a government vehicle. Some Badjao live on the outskirts of town near the causeway to Sanga Sanga and close to the hospital and Notre Dame College.

The PAL office and PNB are both on the edge of town, too.

There's good snorkeling around Bongao, and it's even better off the out-islands.

Mt. Bongao (314 meters) forms a backdrop to the town and its ascent is an enjoyable half-day trip. The mountain is a holy place for Muslims and Christians alike, so behave respectfully here. From Bongao, take a jeepney five km to the village of Pasiagan. Ask the driver to drop you at the start of the trail leading uphill from here; bear left. It takes one hour to reach the summit, from where there's a superb view down to the coral-rimmed shores and across to Simunul and Sibutu.

There are two Muslim graves near the summit, including that of Anjaotal, a member of local royalty. Muslims remove their shoes to pray at these graves, which are surrounded by low walls and white sheets. There are many monkeys on the slopes, and local folklore holds that if you touch one of them you'll go insane or die. Birdlife is plentiful and snakes are common, too, so watch where you place your feet and hands. A festival takes place in Bongao during early October, and the hillside gets crowded at this time.

Accommodations and Food: Stay at **Sarah's**, P100 pp, basic, on the main street, near the wharf for larger interisland vessels. **Southern Hotel**, P150 and up pp, has a restaurant and a balcony overlooking the mosque and main street.

Transportation: PAL flies Zamboanga-Tawi-Tawi 10 times weekly (70 minutes); however, the airport at Tawi-Tawi is temporarily closed for repairs. It should be open again soon. Take a jeepney from the airport at Sanga Sanga into town. Bongao is eight hours by ship from Siasi and is served by ships coming through from Zamboanga and Jolo on most days. It is a two-day trip from Zamboanga to Tawi-Tawi, an adventure to tell the grandchildren about.

Simunul

The launch to Simunul leaves Bongao between 1100 and 1400, and the crossing takes a little over an hour. It returns in the morning, so it's necessary to overnight; see the mayor. The small village of Tubig Indangan is the site of the oldest mosque in the Philippines, built around 1380 by Makdum, a scholar and missionary from Mecca who began the conversion of Sulu to Islam.

The original wooden posts are preserved inside a new mosque. Makdum's tomb is behind this mosque. Simunul is noted locally for its beautiful women, some of whom have strong Arabian features. There are tales of visitors having their food laced with a love potion called, literally, "come back, come back," but the catch is that the "victim" must pay a bride-price for the girl's hand to her father.

The Samal of Simunul are noted for fine rattan mats called *boras*. They're used as wall hangings or ceremonial floor mats, and may feature geometric designs or scenes of Mecca.

Other Islands

There are several small islands off Bongao between Bilatan and Simunul. Bunabunaan and Bilatan Poon are Badjao burial islands. There's good snorkeling off Sangasiapu. A trip to the Tiji Tiji Islands may not be a very positive experience, since you'll find a large military contingent and extremely poor people who want everything you have. Since there's no safe place to leave your gear, bring the bare minimum from Bongao.

Manuk Manka, beyond Simunul, is heavily undercut so that it's shaped like an umbrella; Allied submarines avoided enemy depth charges by hiding under it during WW II.

Tawi-Tawi Island

Tawi-Tawi Island (593 square km, about 55 km long) is of volcanic origin, with forested hills rising to 534 meters and some fertile areas suitable for cultivation. The southern and eastern shores have dense mangrove growth that makes navigation difficult. Many islands, such as Baliungan and Tandu Bato, lie just offshore. Most of Tawi-Tawi Island is effectively closed to tourists due to the presence of antigovernment forces. The Philippine Navy has a base at Batu-Batu.

The Kinapusan Group

To the south and parallel to Tawi-Tawi is a chain of low-lying coral islands, stretching from Kinapusan Island to Manok Manka Island. Mangrove is the only thing that thrives on many of these islands. Tahing-Tahing Beach is on South Ubian Island, while the village of Ungus Matata on Tandubas is noted for some of the finest mat-weaving in the Philippines.

The Sibutu Group

This group, which is separated from Tawi-Tawi by the Sibutu Passage, comprises Sibutu, Tunindao, Sitangkai, and other small neighboring islands. Sibutu Island is a low wooded island. There's a natural swimming pool called Kaban-Kaban here. Sibutu is the sole source of the *gayang,* a Samal weapon with long, slender blade and a carved handle and scabbard, similar to the *parang ilang* of the Iban of Sarawak.

Sitangkai

The end of the Philippines is only about 40 km from Borneo and about four degrees north of the equator. Sitangkai is a unique place, one of the most fascinating in the Philippines. It's known as the "Venice of the Far East," since it has no roads and *bancas* are the standard means of transportation. About 10,000 people live around here, mostly in houses on stilts. About a third of them are Badjao, the others Samal and Tausug. If possible, try to be in Sitangkai during the full moon, since this is the time of Badjao weddings, or perhaps the dancing of the shaman.

The main canal is crossed by bridges, and you can walk along its bustling sides, lined with stores and stalls, and gaze down into the dozens of small boats that are crammed into this "street."

Movement around Sitangkai is very much subject to the tide. When it's low, only boats with the shallowest of draft can move. As the tide races in, lines of fishermen and seaweed farmers in their *bancas* and *lipas* pass through the channels leading to the town.

Sitangkai is four hours by ship from Bongao, the end of the line. It's situated in very shallow water on the huge Tumindao Reef, so ships tie up at a wharf out in the Tumindao Channel. Smaller boats then carry passengers and freight the three km, 15 minutes to the town (P10 pp), whose spectacular main street runs along both sides of a crowded canal.

The only accommodations are the **Plaza Hotel** (P100) and the **Yusof Pension House** (P100); the latter is run by Hadji Yusof Abdulganih, who's a very nice guy. It's pleasant to sit on the platform of the house and watch the Badjao float by on their way to market, or bringing their seaweed in to sell.

It can't be reached on foot, however, so ask the boatman to drop you there, or find the vice-mayor's house by the main canal and ask him to send a message for Yusof. Yusof will take you to check in with the military, who will briefly record your passport details. Their camp is beneath the palm trees on the original island, near a 100-year-old Badjao cemetery.

Yusof can arrange for you to hire a *banca* to be poled around Sitangkai to observe the town—where children use stilts to move between houses—and the Badjao *lipas* are moored on the edge of the settlement. Local people gather seaweed and sea cucumbers and lay them out to dry on their house platforms. Agar-agar, a gum made from seaweed and used in the pharmaceutical, dairy, confectionery, textile, and other industries, is an important local product. Shells are collected in the area, too, and there's a sorting warehouse at Sitangkai. In the late afternoon, the stream of boats coming back to the settlement is very photogenic.

Vicinity of Sitangkai

You can also visit the area to the west of Sitangkai, where there are outlying villages on stilts, seaweed farms, and good snorkeling at the edge of the reef. The water here is very shallow until the reef slopes down into the Meridian Channel. Neat rows of seaweed are planted in isolated patches on these shallow banks.

There are several villages on stilts nearby; the largest—Tong Tong—consists of about 50 houses. Hiring a *banca* for a full-day trip to these seaweed-farming villages costs about P200 for two or three persons, plus you should give the guide about P35 per day. You can go by regular boat from Sitangkai to Samal villages on nearby islands such as Sibutu and Tumindao.

The locals buy their basic commodities in Sabah. Boats leave regularly for the four-hour trip to Semporna (P200). It's illegal for foreign tourists to leave the Philippines by this route. Some have taken the risk by chartering a boat and sailing at night. Remember, however, that while crossing that dark, open water, you and your valuables are entirely at the mercy of boatmen whose ancestors were probably pirates. Don't expect them to call the authorities if you sink, either.

Cagayan de Tawi-Tawi

Also called Cagayan de Sulu, this island group sits isolated in the Sulu Sea, about halfway between Palawan and the Sulu Archipelago, and about 110 km northeast of Borneo. The scenic main island (67 square km) has a hilly interior, rising to 337 meters, and is surrounded by 13 islets. The natives are Jama Mapun, a Muslim group of farmers and fishermen numbering about 20,000.

Their practice of Islam overlaps with animist rituals. A spirit house is built in the middle of the field, and both planting and harvesting are initiated by an Islamic official. If your visit coincides with a Jama Mapun social event, such as a wedding, you may witness the Lunsay, an all-night song and dance performance whose key feature is the rhythmic striking of feet on a specially laid bamboo floor. Samal, Tausug, Cebuanos, and Ilonggos also live here. Fish and copra are the main products, and the inhabitants engage in the barter trade.

Moro pirates were very active here as late as the 19th century. Cagayan can be reached by boats from Zamboanga. The main settlement is at the southeast corner of the island. Accommodation is available at the **Yarrada Beach House** (P75) on Long Beach at Ungus Mataha on the north coast. The islands are noted for their unique fauna and flora. Gosong Reef, also known as San Miguel Island, is the nesting place of thou-

sands of seabirds, locally called *tallah-tallah,* and green sea turtles also lay their eggs here.

Turtle Islands

The remote Turtle Islands lie south of Cagayan de Tawi-Tawi only a short distance north of Borneo. The shallow waters around these seven tiny islands are indeed noted for turtles, known as *pawikan* here. Turtles have played an important role in the local culture for centuries. Taganak, the largest island, is just 22 km from Sandakan, Sabah—a mere 45 minutes by speedboat.

From Cagayan, it's an eight-hour *banca* trip. Lihiman Island is just two km from Pulau Selingan, a turtle sanctuary belonging to Sabah. Taganak municipality consists of four *barangays,* and its 600 inhabitants are Jama Mapun, Tausug, and Samal. Turtles come ashore to lay their eggs on the islands' beaches, and 15% of the workforce depends on turtle egg-gathering for its livelihood.

The government's Task Force Pawikan (TFP), which is dedicated to marine turtle conservation, has a two-man research station on Taganak. The field researchers tag the turtles, take body measurements and egg counts, and maintain three experimental hatcheries, one in Taganak, two on Baguan Island, a declared turtle sanctuary (30 minutes from Taganak). Most hatchlings are released into the sea, though a few are taken to Zamboanga City, a 21-hour voyage, to be raised in a nursery pond at the Naval Forces Southern Philippines Compound there.

The Turtle Islands were leased by the Sultan of Sulu to the British North Borneo Company in 1878 and reverted to the Philippines in 1947. The Malay language is widely understood here, and both Philippine and Malaysian currencies are in use. If peace ever comes to this region of the world, some fantastic dive tours could be arranged. At present, it is risky to venture out in these waters without some kind of official or unofficial protection.

As tempting as it may be to explore the Sulu Archipelago in depth, foreigners have been kidnapped and killed, pirates teem through these waters, and anarchy prevails even amongst the military. Someday, this region of the world will be known as one of the best scuba diving areas of Southeast Asia, but it may not be worth the personal risks today.

CARL PARKES

PALAWAN
INTRODUCTION

Situated not far off the northwest tip of Borneo, Palawan is an isolated and mountainous island covered with tropical rainforests inhabited by primitive tribes and some of the last remaining wildlife in the Philippines.

Although many places of interest exist on the main island, the star attraction is undoubtedly El Nido on the northeast coast. Here, cataclysmic geological upheavals have left Bacuit Bay studded with a remarkable collection of limestone pinnacles and dazzling white beaches—scuba diving here is considered about the best in Southeast Asia.

Other natural attractions include the Underground River, Tabon Caves, and pristine beaches at Sabang and Port Barton (northwestern coast), near Roxas and Taytay (northeastern coast), and south of Puerto Princesa.

While Palawan has its drawbacks—such as terrible roads and limited accommodations—these are more than compensated for by the unspoiled beauty of the land and sea.

Palawan is a province (the largest in the country) and an island (the fifth largest). Rich in natural resources and still relatively isolated and undeveloped, it offers a profusion of wildlife, spectacular landscapes and seascapes, fecund jungle, white-sand beaches, world-class snorkeling and scuba diving, and friendly inhabitants. Many travelers declare Palawan their favorite area of the Philippines. Away from the main tourist trail, Palawan requires time to explore and appreciate its wonders.

Climate

Most of Palawan is wet June-Nov., dry Dec.-May, but the east-central coast, stretching north and south of Puerto Princesa, has less-pronounced seasons, with a shorter dry season. Rainfall varies. The wettest month is August in Coron, September in Puerto Princesa, and December in Brooke's Point. The annual rainfall in eastern Palawan and the Balabac group is comparatively low. The entire province suffers a prolonged drought Jan.-April. The southwest monsoon brings gale-force winds June-Sept., but typhoons are relatively infrequent. The Calamian

Group is the most prone to them, while the south is almost typhoon-free.

HISTORY

Early History

Excavations at the Tabon Caves unearthed evidence that inhabitants of Palawan were using crude stone tools perhaps as long ago as 40,000 B.C. The major find was the fossilized skullcap of a woman, carbon-dated to 22,000

B.C. Migrating waves of proto-Malays and Malays first came across the land bridge from Borneo, and then by sea, to settle in Palawan or pass through it on their way to Mindoro and Luzon.

Burial jars and utensils from later eras have been found at several sites in Palawan and the Calamianes. Chinese and Arab merchants traded with the natives as far back as the 9th century. The name Palawan probably originates from the Chinese, Pa-lao-Yu ("Land of Beautiful Safe Harbor").

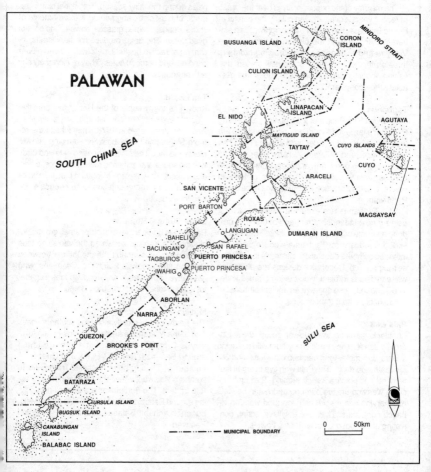

PALAWAN

BUSUANGA ISLAND
CORON ISLAND
MINDORO STRAIT
CULION ISLAND
LINAPACAN ISLAND
EL NIDO
AGUTAYA
MAYTIGUID ISLAND
TAYTAY
CUYO ISLANDS
SOUTH CHINA SEA
CUYO
ARACELI
SAN VICENTE
PORT BARTON
ROXAS
LANGUGAN
MAGSAYSAY
BAHELI
DUMARAN ISLAND
BACUNGAN
SAN RAFAEL
TAGBUROS
PUERTO PRINCESA
IWAHIG
PUERTO PRINCESA
ABORLAN
NARRA
QUEZON
SULU SEA
BROOKE'S POINT
BATARAZA
URSULA ISLAND
BUGSUK ISLAND
CANABUNGAN ISLAND
BALABAC ISLAND

MOON

0   50km

——— · ——— MUNICIPAL BOUNDARY

THE PEOPLE OF PALAWAN

Palawan remains lightly populated. Its inhabitants are of diverse cultural heritage. The native Palaweños are ethnically closer to Borneo than to the Filipino majority. Over 20% of the population belongs to minorities descended from the primitive proto-Malays. Muslims make up about 11% of the population. Palawan also has a sizable group of Chinese ancestry. During this century, many Tagalogs and western Visayans have settled to trade or farm the plains and valleys of the east coast.

The majority of the population lives near the coast. In recent years, Palawan, particularly the capital at Puerto Princesa, has become a boomtown, with settlers moving in from the depleted islands of the Visayas and Mindanao. Their growing numbers threaten the environment, as the new settlers use fishing, logging, and farming techniques that devastate the ecosystem.

Tagbanua

Tagbanua ("The People of the Country") are among Palawan's largest minority groups. Individuals are typically short and slender, with straight hair. The women are fond of jewelry. They wear colorful skirts, with red dominant, and long-sleeved blouses. Their animist beliefs are closely associated with nature, and they practice a thanksgiving ritual called Pagdiwata.

The Tagbanua are excellent basket-weavers, using *buri*, pandanus, rattan, and bamboo to produce a variety of shapes and designs. They're also skilled woodcarvers; Tagbanua woodcarvings are intended as home decoration, children's toys, or just self-expression. Decorative designs are etched as white incisions in black wood using a small knife. The Tagbanua also engrave an ancient alphabet of Hindu origin onto bamboo tubes.

Pala'wan

Another large group, the Pala'wan occupy the southern highlands. They traditionally hunt wild pig using spears, two-meter-long bamboo blowguns, and 30-cm feathered darts. The Pala'wan live in small settlements and practice *kaingin* farming. Their crafts include weaving unique bamboo and rattan baskets and carving items such as decorated wooden tobacco containers. They use a syllabic script, consisting of 13 consonants and three vowels.

Batak

The Batak were once numerous, but now they number about 2,000. They dwell in the hills between the Babuyan and Langogan rivers, north of Puerto Princesa. Their kinky hair and dark skin suggests that they're of Negrito descent. Traditionally nomadic, they're now semisedentary, living in forest settlements and cultivating root crops and fruit.

Small groups may gather to form larger communities during the rainy season. Traditional clothing is made of bark cloth, augmented with ornaments of shells, beads, scented grasses, flowers, and coils of dyed rattan. The Batak produce fine handicrafts, including attractive baskets, delicately carved dipper handles, and bamboo flutes. They're extremely shy with strangers.

Tau't Batu

Known as the "People of the Rock," this primitive tribe of cave dwellers, consisting of only a few families, was discovered in 1978. They inhabit the remote Singnapan Basin, between Ransang and Mt. Mantalingajan. They live by hunting bats and birds with blowguns and gathering roots, fruit, frogs, crabs, and insects. They replace a creature they kill with its wood or stone representation to compensate nature for its death.

Other Cultural Minorities

Palawan is home to several other small groups, including: the Ken-uy, known as the vanishing tribe of Palawan, who inhabit the mountains between Quezon and Brooke's Point; the Kalamians, who are native to the Calamian Group; and the Tagabato, a small tribe found on Coron Island.

Muslim Groups

The Palawani live mostly along the southern coast. The Jama Mapun are seafarers whose main territory is Cagayan de Sulu, but some are found around Bataraza, Brooke's Point, and Quezon. A number of Tausug have migrated from Sulu to southern Palawan, where they are farmers and astute traders. The Panimusan are a small group living around Bataraza. The Molbog, also called Melebuganon, inhabit Balabac Island and southeast Palawan.

During the late 14th century, Muslim Malays settled here and brought the islands under the sultan of Borneo. Another excavation at Issub, Aborlan, yielded porcelain and ornaments, the volume and quality of which suggest that Palawan's rich natural environment enabled its pre-Hispanic inhabitants to develop a defined social stratification and division of labor.

Spanish Era

Survivors of Magellan's expedition replenished supplies here on their way back to Spain. An *encomienda,* based in the Calamianes, was established in 1591, and friars began founding settlements and churches, beginning with Cuyo, Agutaya, and Taytay in 1622. The Spaniards became entrenched during the 17th century. Cuyo was the original capital, followed by Taytay, their first mainland settlement. Spain needed to control this area to help stem Moro raids from the south.

The Muslims failed to take Taytay's fort in 1735, and the sultan of Borneo, who was based in what is now Brunei, was eventually forced to cede the central and southern areas to Spain in 1750. Malaria and native hostility discouraged Spanish development of the south, though Spain gradually extended nominal political control to the entire region. During the 19th century, the Spaniards established a politico-military government in Puerto Princesa.

However, the Spaniards had little impact on Palawan, especially in the south, where they were met by a militant Islamic culture.

Modern Times

The liberation of Palawan in February 1945 was an important step toward ending WW II, since the island's strategic western location enabled U.S. aircraft to extend their range over the South China Sea and the Dutch East Indies.

SCUBA DIVING

Palawan's surrounding waters contain 60% of the Philippines's coral reefs, many of them still uncharted. Although Palawan is becoming a major dive area, much virgin diving remains. Because almost the entire province sits on a shelf in relatively shallow seas, drop-offs are not as plentiful or spectacular as in other areas of the country, but this is more than made up for by the marinelife. Strong currents carry a steady flow of nutrients through the area, supporting an abundance of large fish.

Divers have increasingly interesting choices for diving with ample opportunity to obtain a PADI dive certificate while visiting Palawan. Puerto Princesa is a good base, but El Nido in the far north is favored by divers and travelers alike. The Busuanga Islands north of El Nido are also excellent, as well as the reefs and islands off northeastern Palawan. The best period generally is March-June, but diving is possible year-round at the province's extremes, Calamian and Balabac. The finest diving is found in remote spots like Tubbataha reef, where visibility can be an astounding 60 meters.

Boat Excursions

The sheer number of islands and rudimentary state of land transportation makes boat travel around Palawan an appealing way to explore the island. It's also the perfect way to enjoy scuba diving around northern Palawan and Tubbataha reef.

A typical 10-day excursion from Puerto Princesa heads north to Coco Loco Island, Elephant Island, and Flowers Island before circling around northern Palawan and continuing south to El Nido, Sabang, and the Underground River. Boat operators are also talking about treks into rainforest jungle north of Taytay and spending a few nights sleeping on deserted beaches near Busuanga.

The same boat might also do exclusive dive tours to El Nido, Busuanga, and Tubbataha reef.

Queen Anne Divers and Moonshadow, two Swiss-managed boats, offer these northern Palawan tours and dive excursions each year from December to April. The northern Palawan tours designed for nondivers (or occasional divers) cost US$50 per day and include boat trip, onboard accommodations, all meals, and transfers. Dives are not included on "tours" but cost an additional US$15 per dive.

Dive trips with equipment and two daily dives cost US$500-650 (five days), US$700-900 (seven days), US$1,100 (nine days), and

US1,350 (15 days). You can contact both Queen Anne Divers and Moonshadow at Trattoria Inn, 353 Rizal Ave., Puerto Princesa, e-mail trattori@pal-onl.com.

The success of Queen Anne Divers and Moonshadow has not gone unnoticed on Palawan, and other resorts and travel agencies are now getting into the same business. First off the block is Coco Loco Resort in conjunction with its travel agency in Puerto Princesa. Their 5-10 day tours from Coco Loco Resort near Roxas to Sabang and El Nido are on the 25-meter trimaran *(banca)* the MBC *Serena*. These tours are designed for nondivers and include fishing, snokeling, beach barbecues, and camping on deserted beaches. Contact Palawan Tourist Travel & Tours, Rizal Ave., Puerto Princesa, e-mail cocoloco@pal-onl.com.

Another option is Discovery Cruises, an upscale cruise around the islands of northern Palawan at US$250-300 per night. More information is available from Discovery's office in the Shangri-La Hotel on Ayala Avenue in Manila.

TRANSPORTATION

Puerto Princesa is the principal port of entry, linked by daily air service and regular ships with Manila, and by a ferry service with Panay. In addition, interisland boats sail between Manila and various ports of northern Palawan, such as Cuyo, Coron, and Liminancong, on an irregular basis.

Far fewer boats serve Palawan than other major islands, and the voyage from Manila takes about two days. Many of its outlying communities are very isolated and difficult to reach by public transport. Small, private airlines provide daily service to El Nido airport, Busuanga Island, and an airstrip just north of Taytay.

The road from Puerto Princesa to El Nido is rough but passable during the dry season.

Routes
Most travelers fly to Puerto Princesa then continue overland, and by boat, up to El Nido. Jeepneys and buses are plentiful from Puerto Princesa to Sabang, from where you can visit the Underground River and relax on the fairly attractive beach of Sabang. Boats shuttle up to Port Barton, another fine beach on the west coast of central Palawan.

From Port Barton, the best way to reach El Nido is to charter a private boat (during good weather only) and make an all-day trip up the west coast to El Nido.

After lazing around El Nido for a week or a month, many travelers take the jeepney back to Puerto Princesa, with overnight stops in Taytay and Roxas. Alternatively, boats head north from El Nido to reach Busuanga and other islands off the far northern tip of Palawan.

Air from Manila
Puerto Princesa is the only destination on Palawan served by large, commercial jets. The remainder of the places are reached with small, private aircraft, generally quite more expensive than flights to Puerto Princesa.

To Puerto Princesa: PAL and Air Philippines fly daily from Manila to Puerto Princesa. Grand Air flies daily except Sunday

To Busuanga: Pacific Airways and Air Ads fly daily from Manila to Busuanga.

To El Nido: Soriano Aviation flies daily from Manila to El Nido. Seats are reserved for their customers heading to their offshore resorts near El Nido, but cancellations are fairly frequent. Travelers without reservations at one of their resorts must go to the Manila domestic terminal and sign up on their waiting list. Chances are good you'll get a seat, but only at the last second.

To Cuyo: Pacific Airways flies from Manila to Cuyo on Monday, Wednesday, and Friday.

Air from Cebu City
PAL flies twice weekly on Thursday and Saturday to Puerto Princesa via Iloilo City on Panay. The layover in Iloilo is fairly brief.

Air from Panay
PAL flies twice weekly on Thursday and Saturday from Iloilo to Puerto Princesa. The flight originates in Cebu City, so it's important to make a reservation well in advance.

Ship from Manila
Ships from Manila go to Puerto Princesa and smaller ports such as Coron and El Nido.

To Puerto Princesa: WG&A's MV *Superferry 3* leaves Manila's North Harbor for Puerto Prince-

Pigs ride free in Palawan.

sa on Wednesday at 1000. The trip takes 26 hours and costs P450-500. Sulpicio Lines' MV *Iloilo Princess* departs Thursday at 1000 and Sunday at 1400. This ship also takes 26 hours.

To Coron: Coron could be considered a possible stepping stone on the way to El Nido and points farther south. Asuncion Shipping's MV *Catalyn* leaves on Wednesday at 1600 and takes 22 hours to reach Coron. The same company also operates the MV *Asuncion VII,* which leaves Manila on Thursday at 1600, and the MV *Asuncion XI,* which sails on Saturday at 1600. Again, 22 hours to Coron.

To El Nido: Asuncion Shipping's MV *Asuncion IV* departs Manila every Wednesday at 1900 and takes around 30 hours to reach El Nido.

Ship from Batangas to Coron

As noted above, Asuncion Shipping has several weekly services to either Coron or El Nido. Unfortunately, their ships are somewhat ratty and only the most die-hard traveler will find anything thrilling about a journey on their ships.

For this reason, it's better to take a bus down to Batangas pier and take one of the following ships. Viva Shipping's MV *Santa Ana* departs Batangas every Monday at 1800. The same shipping line also operates the MV *Viva Penafrancia IX* on Thursday at 1800 and the MV *Maria Socorro* on Saturday at 1800. These ships take about 18 hours to reach Coron and then continue down to Culion.

Ship from Panay

Milagrosa Shipping's MV *Milagrosa-J-Tres* leaves Iloilo on the 2nd, 12th, and 22nd of each month at 1800 and takes 12 hours to reach Cuyo. There is an eight-hour stopover in Cuyo, then the ship continues to Puerto Princesa. Total travel time from Iloilo to Puerto Princesa is around 38 hours and the total fare is P360-400. A single journey to Cuyo costs P180-220.

The same shipping company provides transport to Palawan on the MV *Milagrosa-J-Dos,* which departs from Iloilo on the 6th, 16th, and 26th of each month at 1800.

These are rough-looking boats only for the very adventurous. Friendly crew, though. You can walk down to the Iloilo pier and check out their boats before committing yourself to what may be more than you bargained for.

Getting Around

Transportation on Palawan is quite good heading south from Puerto Princesa, but rough going north since the all-weather road from Puerto Princesa to El Nido remains on the drawing boards. At present, it's a fairly easy bus or jeepney ride to Sabang and Port Barton on the west coast, where many travelers continue by public or chartered boat up to El Nido. This is probably the best way to reach El Nido.

From Sabang or Port Barton, you can also return to Roxas and continue north to Taytay and onward to El Nido with a combination of bus, jeepney, and possibly the boat from Liminancong.

Buses and jeepneys from Puerto Princesa to Taytay take eight or nine hours along a very rough and dusty road. From Taytay, you can catch a jeepney in the very early morning for the extremely dangerous ride over mountain ridges to El Nido—not a journey for the faint of heart.

An alternative route from Taytay to El Nido is to take the boat from a dock west of Taytay to the surprisingly prosperous town of Liminancong (superb scenery) and continue to El Nido with a final boat.

Bus journey times from Puerto Princesa heading north are four hours to Roxas, five hours to Sabang, six hours to Port Barton, nine hours to Taytay, and 12-18 hours to El Nido.

CENTRAL PALAWAN

PUERTO PRINCESA

The provincial capital, as well as commercial and transportation center, Puerto Princesa is situated on a deep, sheltered harbor in the middle of Palawan Island's east coast. It was founded in 1872 as Port Asuncion, after the queen of Spain's daughter, but following the princess's untimely death, the name was changed to Puerto de la Princesa and later shortened. The city itself has few points of interest, but several worthwhile day trips are possible, and it serves as the gateway to Palawan's more far-flung wonders.

Orientation
Puerto Princesa occupies the tip of a small peninsula that encloses Puerto Princesa Bay on the north side. The city is thus surrounded by water on three sides. Rizal Street, the main thoroughfare, runs east-west linking the airport and wharf; most of the hotels and restaurants are located on or near it. The airport is about two km from the city center, the wharf 1.5 km.

North- and southbound buses and jeepneys load near the market on Malvar or Valencia Street. Change traveler's checks at the PNB near the Asia World Resort in Puerto Princesa before heading out around the province.

Attractions
The twin-spired cathedral is the dominant landmark. The city has both old-style stone houses and huts built out over the water. Try strolling down to the lively wharf, with its passenger, cargo, and fishing boats, at sunset. You can hire a *banca* for a few hours of fishing in the bay for about P200. The city's public market has an intriguing fish section and sells local handicrafts and cashew nut *(casoy)* sweets.

Puerto Princesa celebrates its Foundation Day on 4 March and its fiesta, in honor of Our Lady of the Immaculate Conception, on 8 December. Various cultural events, e.g., a *caracol* (procession of decorated boats) and concerts in Mendoza Park, take place in the week preceding the fiesta.

Vietnamese Refugee Center
Located out beyond the airport, near Canigaran Beach, this camp, known locally as "Little Saigon," was opened in 1979. Foreign aid workers assist in providing the refugees with orientation and training for eventual resettlement. Since the refugees are allowed to go into the city, there's a constant stream of tricycles going back and forth to the camp. There is an excellent Vietnamese restaurant called **Phoo** at the entrance to the camp. Try the spring rolls!

Services
The city tourist office is at the airport, while the provincial tourist office is in the Capitol building on Rizal Avenue.

Money: Traveler's checks and cash can be exchanged at the Philippine National Bank and at several money changers on Rizal Avenue.

Warning: Exchange facilities elsewhere in Palawan are extremely limited, and it's a wise idea to change plenty of money in Puerto Princesa. Otherwise, you might go broke in some deserted hamlet or find yourself at the mercy of merciless money changers.

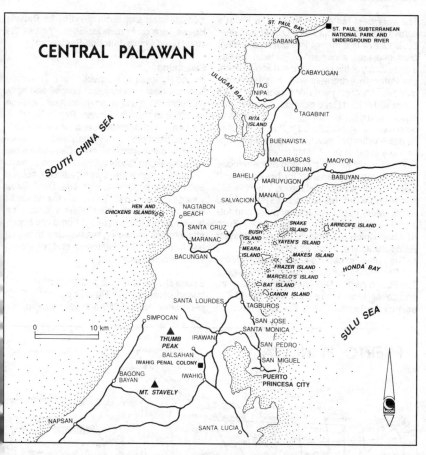

Telephone: International phone calls are best made at the BayanTel office on Rizal Avenue.

Accommodations
Over 20 guesthouses and hotels are located in Puerto Princesa.

Duchess Pension: Popular spot but a bit of a hike from the center of town. 107 Valencia St., tel. (048) 433-2873, P100-250.

Abelardo's Pension: A cozy homestay owned and operated by the very friendly Remedio "Nene" Dizon. 63 Manga St., tel. (048) 433-2049, P150-500.

Puerto Pension: Perhaps the most popular budget place in town with small but comfortable rooms made from natural materials rather than concrete. 35 Malvar St., tel. (048) 433-2969, P175-550.

Trattoria Inn: The best place in town with spotlessly clean rooms, friendly managers, cozy bar, and wildly popular restaurant in the back. 353 Rizal Ave., tel. (048) 433-2719, e-mail trattori@pal-onl.com, P220-750.

Food and Entertainment
Palawan is noted for fine and varied seafood.

The very best restaurant in town is **Kalui's** across from the Badjao Inn. Owner and chef Louis Olieva is a former tour guide, excellent cook, and a real aficionado of Palawan. He has a great library at the restaurant and knows northern Palawan extremely well. Highly recommended. Another great restaurant is at **Casa Linda's,** Trinidad Road behind the Badjao Inn. Built around a garden setting, the restaurant and hotel have been established in Puerto Princesa for many years by Linda Mendoza and her family. They are also very helpful to visitors.

For cheaper meals, try **Phoo** at the refugee camp, **Duchess Pension** for breakfast and lunch, **Edwin's Food Palace** on Valencia St., and **Rumble Bumble Noodle House** on Rizal Street. More upscale places popular with foreigners are **Cafe Puerto** (French food), **Zurn Kleiman Anker** (German food), and **Kamayan Restaurant,** all on Rizal Street.

The Kamayan has live entertainment nightly, and Cafe Puerto has guitar music and folksinging. The **Puerto Airport Hotel** has a fancy restaurant and coffee shop as does the **Asia World Resort** off Fernandez Street. For good Bavarian food and information about diving, try the **Bavaria House,** also on Fernandez Street. Across the street is the simple **Junction Restaurant.**

Swimming

Puerto Princesa has a public pool. The three beaches near the city aren't special and have only convenience to recommend them; you can get close to them by tricycle. Parola Beach is the nearest to downtown, and hence the dirtiest and most crowded. White Beach is farther along the same stretch of shore. Canigaran is beyond the airport, about 3.5 km from downtown.

These beaches are okay for relaxing, but you can really only swim at high tide. Don't leave your gear unattended. To swim in the vicinity of Puerto Princesa, it's better to hire a *banca* for a few hours out in Honda Bay. Some city supermarkets sell snorkeling masks. Day trips can also be made to the river resorts and hot springs within Iwahig Penal Colony.

Scuba Diving and Tourist Information

Island Divers on 371 Rizal Street offers PADI certification for US$250 and daily trips to dive

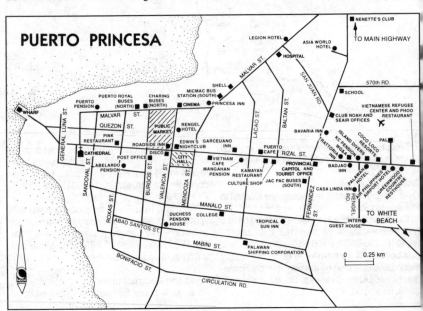

sites around Honda Bay. This is a good place to get your certification for more challenging dives off El Nido and Port Barton. Island Divers is operated by Norman Songco and is recommended. For tourist information, go to the **Department of Tourism** office on Rizal Street where director F. Ami Mendoza can provide helpful and up-to-date information on getting around Palawan. There is also a city information office at the Capitol building on Rizal Street that is useful.

Transportation

Buses heading north to Sabang, Port Barton, Roxas, Taytay, and El Nido leave from the Puerto Royal bus terminal on Malvar Street one block west of the market. A limited number of buses also head south. This must be the filthiest bus halt in the Philippines and the buses aren't much better. You're better off waiting for a departing bus rather than jumping on the first big jeepney that lumbers out of this godforsaken terminal.

Buses south leave from the equally disorganized Mic Mac Trail bus terminal on Malvar Street near the Shell station a few blocks east of the market.

Jeepney and bus trips to Sabang are organized by many of the guesthouses and travel agencies on Rizal Avenue.

HONDA BAY

This broad bay north of Puerto Princesa contains several islands that offer beaches and pleasant snorkeling in shallow water. The presence of mangroves in the area tends to limit underwater visibility, however. An abandoned wharf at Tagburos, about 12 km from Puerto Princesa, is the gateway to Honda Bay. Tagburos is built on the ore tailings of a now-disused mercury mine; don't eat fish from this area.

You can hire a *banca* to visit an island in the bay (most are 15-45 minutes from shore), go island-hopping, or be dropped off for one or more nights. Look for other travelers in town to share the cost. Always explain your wishes to the boatman and agree to a price beforehand. To stay over, check with **Yayen's Pension House** about the cottages they operate on one of the islands, or you can camp in several spots; take food and water.

The Islands

Canon Island isn't far offshore and has a nice beach, and Polding Island nearby it has passable snorkeling. Bat Island is so-named because of the thousands of bats that roost in the mangrove trees during the day and swarm out over the mainland at dusk in search of food. Snake Island has no shade, but the deserted beach on the east side is a possible campsite; the west side offers good snorkeling.

Meara Island and Pandan Island (also called Makesi) are quiet and agreeable. Serious snorkelers and divers can explore the reef between Canon and Pandan Islands, or better still, go about six km west of Pandan, where there's a cluster of submerged reefs whose tops are only about three meters deep. Slopes studded with large coral heads, surrounded by reef fish, descend to about 24 meters. To the north of Honda Bay, Panglima Reef is also a diving destination.

IWAHIG PRISON AND PENAL FARM

This famous "prison without bars" is situated about 25 km southwest of Puerto Princesa, at the foot of Mt. Stavely (1198 meters). Established by U.S. authorities in 1904, it's one of the largest open prisons in the world. Much of its 386 square km is still forested, though large tracts have been cleared and planted with coconuts, rice, corn, vegetables, and orchards. Unfortunately, many of the prisoners at the penal farm have been moved to other locations, so many of the unique qualities of this place no longer apply. It may still be worth visiting, but, if the weather is good, there are far better things to do on Palawan.

Within the Colony

A jeepney leaves for Iwahig at around 0930 (takes 40 minutes) from Puerto Princesa. The colony contains several places of interest. The Balsahan River (22 km from Puerto Princesa) and Montible River (30 km) each have resort areas with swimming pools in pleasant surroundings. A road loops through Balsahan, three km off the main highway. Some jeepney drivers will continue to Balsahan for an extra fare. It's a good picnic place and food is available.

The forest behind Balsahan is a noted butterfly area and contains other wildlife, too; a trail leads about four km up from the dam that forms the swimming pool. To return to Puerto Princesa from Balsahan, either walk back to Central for the 1300 jeepney or, if later in the afternoon, go to the main highway and catch a bus into the city. The last bus passes at about 1700, but to be sure, be there around 1630.

Mainit Sulfur Springs are in Central Sub-Colony, while the hot springs in **Santa Lucia Sub-Colony** are a popular excursion for residents of Puerto Princesa. *Bancas* cross the bay from the city wharf; they leave when full, or you can take a special trip for about P30 one-way. It's then a seven-km walk to the spring (the pool's cleaned each Monday).

On the coast of Santa Lucia is Turtle Cove, at whose entrance is Putol na Ilog, a popular dive site. Reached by a 45-minute *banca* ride from the city wharf, the diving area lies around one km offshore and extends for about eight km parallel to the coast. The sandy bed is dotted with coral patches, whose depth varies from near the surface to 24 meters. Small fish are plentiful, but visibility isn't exceptional. Inagawan Sub-Colony contains **Tagbarungis Swimming Resort,** 48 km from Puerto Princesa; nearby **Antipolo Beach** has a campsite. Jeepneys operate on the road that cuts 26 km across the island from Iwahig to Napsan, where the Salakot Waterfalls are the haunt of rare butterflies.

SOUTHERN PALAWAN

Most travelers head north for El Nido, although a fair number of excellent beaches and tropical islands are also found in the south. Transportation is with either Puerto Royale buses from their terminal one block east of the market or with Mic Mac Trail a/c buses from their terminal two blocks west of the market.

ABORLAN AND TIGMAN

Several beach resorts have opened near the fishing village of Tigman, 10 km south of Aborlan and 75 km south of Puerto Princesa. Take a jeepney or bus from Puerto Princesa past Aborlan to the junction town of Plaridel, and then a tricycle down to the beach.

Accommodations
Villa Christine Beach Resort, operated by an Austrian-Filipino couple and 1.5 km south of Tigman, has windsurfing, water-skiing, snorkeling, and large, natural-material bungalows for P800-1,000 including two meals per day.

Camille Del Sol also offers windsurfing, Hobie Cats, and sea kayaks, and has 12 native-style cottages with private bathrooms for P400-750. It's very close to Tigman.

Princessa Holiday Resort has all the standard water sports and very spacious bungalows under a coconut plantation for P1,800-4,500.

Barona's Holiday Beach Resort can help with boat trips to Sombrero Island and has decent cottages for P450-800.

ISLAND BAY

Island Bay is 100 km south of Puerto Princesa where the island narrows near the town of Aboaba. Almost a dozen small islands are scattered around the bay, and several have been developed as beach resorts.

Accommodations
King's Paradise Islands is an upscale resort with water sports, tennis courts, 25 cottages, and scuba diving provided by Palawan Divers. Bungalows cost P1,000-1,800 and can be booked at the office in Puerto Princesa next to the Airport Hotel.

QUEZON

Quezon, a sleepy west coast town surrounded by coconut plantations, is 157 km, five hours by bus, from Puerto Princesa. Formerly called Alfonso XIII, it's the gateway to the Tabon Caves. Quezon also has a beach, a mini-underground river, and numerous offshore islands.

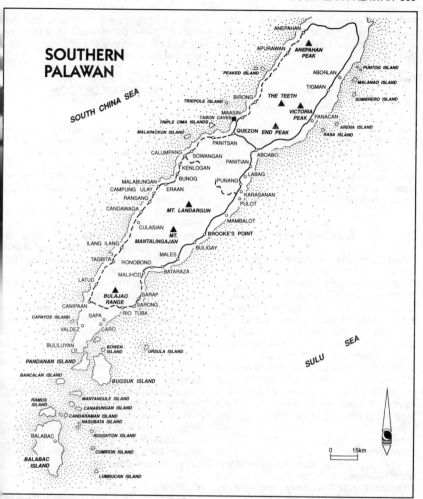

SOUTHERN PALAWAN

SOUTH CHINA SEA

ANEPAHAN
APURAWAN · ANEPAHAN PEAK
PEAKED ISLAND
ABORLAN · PUNTOG ISLAND
TIGMAN · MALANAO ISLAND
THE TEETH
TIDEPOLE ISLAND · BIRONG
MAASIN
TABON CAVES
TRIPLE CIMA ISLANDS
MALAPACKUN ISLAND
QUEZON END PEAK
VICTORIA PEAK · PANACAN
SOMBRERO ISLAND
ARENA ISLAND
RASA ISLAND
PANITSAN
CALUMPANG · SOWANGAN · PANITIAN
KENLOGAN · ABOABO
MALABUNGAN · BUNOG · PUNANG · LABAG
CAMPUNG ULAY · ERAAN
RANSANG · KARASANAN
CANDAWAGA · MT. LANDARGUN · PULOT
MAMBALOT
CULASIAN · MT. MANTALINGAJAN · BROOKE'S POINT
ILANG ILANG · MALES · BULIGAY
TAGBITA · RONOBONO · BATARAZA
LATUD · MALIHOD
BULAJAO RANGE · SARAP
CANIPAAN · SARONG
SAPA · RIO TUBA
CAPAYOS ISLAND · CARO
VALDEZ
BULILUYAN · BOWEN ISLAND · URSULA ISLAND
PANDANAN ISLAND
BANCALAN ISLAND · BUGSUK ISLAND
RAMOS ISLAND · MANTANGULE ISLAND
CANABUNGAN ISLAND
CANDARAMAN ISLAND
NASUBATA ISLAND
BALABAC · ROUGHTON ISLAND
CUMIRON ISLAND
BALABAC ISLAND
LUMBUCAN ISLAND

SULU SEA

0   15km

Accommodations

Right in the small fishing village of Quezon are the **New Bayside Lodging House, Joavech Pension,** and several others with rooms for P100-350. A good place to stay is **Zambrano's Restaurant and Lodging** with simple rooms for P150. There is a karaoke machine that attracts the locals in the evening, meals are pretty good, and the people are friendly.

About two km out of town heading toward Tabon beach, there's **Casa Esperanza,** which has bungalows and a restaurant.

A very interesting place to stay is **Tabon Village Resort,** which has bungalows and a restaurant. Built by Belgian Theo Criel, the restaurant is reached by a bridge, and it sits out in the middle of the small bay. Bungalows are P100-400 complete with bath, mosquito netting, and porch. It's about five km from Quezon; take a tricycle from town. You can also eat in town at **Lita's** or the restaurant at **Zamrano's.**

Tamlagun Island

Situated off Quezon, Tamlagun is a beautiful place with a white-sand beach and offshore coral. Frederick, a friendly German who likes to play chess, lives here and he welcomes visitors, who can stay in a nipa hut for less than P50 pp. Foam mattresses and sheets are provided, but bring all the food and drink you'll require, except fruit, which is available here. Tamlagun is a one-hour boat trip (P70 pp regular trip, around P250 to charter) from Quezon.

TABON CAVES

Tabon Caves, which are a national park, were excavated in 1962 by Dr. Robert Fox, who discovered evidence of human habitation between 40,000 and 800 B.C. In addition to flake tools, he found fossilized bones of bats and birds, and the fossilized skullcap of a woman, carbon-dated to 22,000 B.C. Later relics include burial jars, spoons, and other utensils. The caves thus served as both habitat and burial site.

The entire Tabon complex consists of about 200 caves, only a fraction of which have been explored. They are among a myriad of caves in southern Palawan, some others of which have yielded pre-Hispanic burial jars and wooden coffins.

Transportation

To visit Tabon Caves, go to the **National Museum** in Quezon (open daily 0800-1700), which will provide a guide. The 30-minute pumpboat trip from Quezon costs P160-200. From the boat landing, steps lead 34 meters up the western face of Lipuun Point (Albion Head), a striking limestone promontory.

The entrance, which is 18 meters high and 16 meters across, overlooks an island-studded bay and leads into a domed chamber about 90 meters deep. It's the significance of the place—this home of ancient man—that's important rather than "seeing" anything; there isn't much to see! Of the caves that you can visit, the Tabon

Cave is the largest, and the Diwata Cave the most impressive. On the way back to Quezon, ask the boatman to stop at a white-sand beach on one of the islands.

SOUTH OF QUEZON

Brooke's Point

Named after Sir John Brooke, an Englishman who helped the early settlers, this town is the market center for southern Palawan and is surrounded by farmland. It's served by several buses daily from Puerto Princesa (192 km, seven hours); the day before you go, reserve a seat with Puerto Royale Express.

Brooke's Point is a good place to shop for baskets, musical instruments, and other handicrafts. Points of interest in the area include Sabsaban Waterfalls, eight km from town, and Mainit, 12 km northwest, which has sulfuric hot springs and a small waterfall. Two-day dive trips to Tagalinog Island offshore from here are sometimes offered out of Puerto Princesa.

Accommodations: Places in town include the **Sunset Garden Lodge** and **Silayan Lodge,** where fan-cooled or a/c rooms go for P100-450.

Cristina Beach Resort, seven km northeast of town, costs P100-350.

Bataraza

Bataraza is a predominantly Muslim town about 30 km by jeepney beyond Brooke's Point. Red *bakawan* from local mangrove swamps is shipped to Japan for the manufacture of synthetic textile fibers. A short tricycle ride from town will bring you to a good beach, and Tigwayon Falls are also in the area.

Rio Tuba

A *banca* leaves daily from Brooke's Point at 0800 for this small fishing village, which is also linked by *banca* with Bataraza. Stay and eat around the pier; bargain for the room rate. Boats also proceed south down the coast from here to Bugsuk and Balabac.

Ursula Island

Rio Tuba is the gateway to this uninhabited 20-hectare island, which was formerly an outstanding bird sanctuary. It was the haunt of an estimated 150,000 birds, particularly the *camaso* (nutmeg imperial pigeon), plus some other rare doves, terns, and winter migrants (Nov.-Jan.) from Northeast Asia. From two hours before sunset on, formations of these birds would return to the island to roost, but these flocks have been largely decimated by egg-gathering and shooting.

If you still want to go to Ursula Island, which does have a white-sand beach and good snorkeling, you must hire a *banca* in Rio Tuba, from where it's a 90-minute crossing. Inquire from local sources about the cost of hiring a *banca* and bargain!

Bugsuk Island
Situated between the mainland and Balabac, this 121-square-km limestone island is covered with coconut plantations and is the site of a hybrid coconut seed bank. Bugsuk, which has white-sand beaches, offshore coral gardens teeming with fish, and a campsite, is a two-hour *banca* ride from Balabac.

BALABAC ISLAND

Also a limestone island, Balabac (324 square km) is the home of the Muslim Molbogs. The Balabac group is noted for uncommon plants, animals, and shells. The tiny, nocturnal mouse deer is found in the interiors of Balabac, Ramos, Bancalan, and Bugsuk Islands. Balabac Island is hilly, rising to 569 meters, and has rich mineral deposits: copper, silica, chromite, nickel.

The Spaniards made Balabac, with Bugsuk, a politico-military district in 1858 and used it as a prison for political detainees during the revolution. Today, Balabac town, on the east coast, is an attractive little trading port on a fine harbor.

Exploring Balabac
Places of interest include Morenton Peak Game Refuge, Basay Waterfalls, and the lighthouse at Cape Melville, the southern tip of the island. Balabac Island has some beautiful small offshore islands.

Cadaraman Island, a 30-minute *banca* trip from Balabac, has white-sand beaches, fine coral, and impressive fishlife. The reefs surrounding Roughtan and Nasubata Islands will

also delight snorkelers, while you can find superlative snorkeling on Balabac Great Reefs, which extend 14 km along the island's west coast and come within three km of the shore. They're visible at low tide and offer thriving marinelife, including turtles, sharks, giant clams, and rare cone shells, especially on their seaward side.

Transportation
Balabac is 273 km from Puerto Princesa. Check the wharves at Puerto Princesa, Brooke's Point, or Rio Tuba. One or two boats a week sail down from Brooke's Point. In Balabac, check with the Lims, a Chinese trading family, for boats returning north. The 55-km-wide Balabac Strait links the South China and Sulu Seas and separates Palawan from Borneo. Boats cross regularly between Balabac and nearby Sabah, but as with the Sulu-Sabah connection, this route is closed to foreigners.

ISLANDS OF THE SULU SEA

The Cagayan Group
The Cagayan Islands, or Cagayanes, are a group of seven small islands, located 330 km from Puerto Princesa. They are, in fact, much closer to Panay and Negros. Cagayancillo, the only settlement, has an old Spanish fort, and Monoon and Nipay Caves are nearby.

Fine handicrafts are produced here, including mats, hats, and shellcraft. The men build sailboats with *cubiertas* (covers). The inhabitants are mostly Ilonggos, and during the dry season (Nov.-April), supply boats make the seven-hour trip from Anini-y on Panay to Cagayancillo. These lonely waters, clear and teeming with marinelife, also contain Calusa Island, two hours west of Cagayancillo, and, eight hours to the southwest, the neighboring islands of Cavili (a bird sanctuary) and Arena.

Tubbataha Reefs
These remote reefs, 177 km east of Puerto Princesa, are a world-class diving area. Tubbataha comprises two reefs, separated by a seven-km channel. Landmarks are few, though extensive sand cays are exposed at low tide. The southern reef has a lighthouse on South

Islet, near which the wreck of a log-carrier that ran aground sits high. The northern reef surrounds a large lagoon. The reefs support huge colonies of seabirds, which are the only life on them.

The real wonders of Tubbataha are below the surface—big fish, spectacular coral, superb visibility. Jessie Beazley Reef, 22 km northwest, a much smaller reef with a white-sand cay, is noted for huge table corals. Tubbataha's diving season is April-June, though it's also possible at a limited number of spots during the southwest monsoon (June-October).

Dive Excursions

To dive here, contact, as far in advance as possible, **Island Divers** in Puerto Princesa for a short trip (costs about US$300 for three days), or major dive-boat operators such as **Aquaventure** or **Gloria Maris** in Manila for longer trips. Birdwatchers will be interested in the Haribon Foundation's annual nature study tour.

NORTH-CENTRAL PALAWAN

North-central Palawan has much to offer the traveler: the Underground River, the spectacular Cleopatra Needle (1,592 meters), and the beaches at Sabang and Port Barton, not to mention the fine offshore islands near Roxas and Taytay. Included with the wonders in northern Palawan (El Nido and beyond), these make Palawan the most memorable experience in the country and the perfect place for natural, unspoiled beauty.

BAHELI AND NAGTABON BEACH

A narrow lowland crosses the island, linking Honda Bay and Ulugan Bay. Baheli, a village at the head of Ulugan Bay, is a 48-km, 90-minute jeepney ride from Puerto Princesa. During the dry season, it's a fairly calm, beautiful three-hour trip by *banca* to the Saint Paul Subterranean National Park (Underground River), though most people now use Sabang as their base camp for visits to the national park.

Ulugan Bay

Hire a *banca* in Baheli for the 30-minute trip to Rita Island in the bay. It has white-sand beaches on its southwest side and good snorkeling on the northwest side, where the seabed slopes to nine meters, then drops off to 20 meters. Both shelf and wall have lots of hard and soft coral. Big fish and giant clams are plentiful here. A *banca* could also stop at Oyster Inlet, on the left side of which is a blue pipeline leading up to a waterfall, from where there's a fine view.

Puerto Princesa's dive shops offer day-trips to Rita Island and dive sites outside the mouth of Ulugan Bay such as Kamungyan Island and Tres Marias. The latter is a three-peaked rock formation about two hours by *banca* from Baheli.

Nagtabon Beach

This beach is 25 km north of Puerto Princesa on the west coast. The offshore islands of Hen and Chicken add to the isolated beauty of this small town. There is swimming, snorkeling, and diving in the area. Accommodation is available near the post office at a private home. Ask around upon arrival.

SABANG

The fastest growing traveler's destination in Palawan isn't highly touted El Nido but rather the far more accessible beach at Sabang. Once an isolated stretch of sand occasionally visited by Westerners heading to St. Paul Subterranean National Park, the introduction of direct jeepney service from Puerto Princesa a few years ago dramatically opened up the area to foreign travelers.

Accommodations

Sabang now has over a dozen bungalow operations that charge P150-450 depending on the season and size of the cottage. Starting from the Sabang pier and walking east, you'll come to **Robert's Beach Cottages, Coco Slab Resort, Villa Sabang Guesthouse, Mary's Beach Resort,** and **Bambua Jungle Cottages** past Manlipein Point and just off the so-called Monkey Trail.

Heading north past the park entrance is **Panaguman Beach Resort,** with snorkeling, jungle treks, and cottages for P250-500. Free boat transfers daily at 1300 from the Sabang pier.

Transportation

Sabang is 75 km northwest of Puerto Princesa and can be reached in three or four hours by jeepneys or buses leaving from the bus terminal on Malvar Street west of the public market.

From Sabang, chartered boats for P1,200-1,500 take four hours heading north along the coast to Port Barton.

THE UNDERGROUND RIVER

Saint Paul Subterranean National Park (39 square km) is a superb area, with spectacular mountains and cliffs, sandy beaches, plentiful wildlife, friendly people, plus, of course, the Underground River. Said to be the longest underground river in the world, it flows through limestone for about eight km and emerges from a cave mouth into the South China Sea at St. Paul Bay. It's definitely worth spending a few days around here as one could take at least another trip through the river, hike the Monkey Trail and observe monkeys, snakes, parrots, and lizards.

Permits

Admission to the cave is P150, which includes a 45-minute boat trip inside the cave as far as the 60-meter-high Cathedral. Permits to visit the park should be obtained in advance from the park office at 150 Manalo Street in Puerto Princesa. It's also possible though not guaranteed that you can pick up a permit at the information booth in Sabang or directly at park headquarters near the cave entrance.

Getting There

Visitors can take a 20-minute boat ride from Sabang, but it's far more rewarding to make the two-hour trek through thick jungle inhabited by wild squirrels, bats, and monkeys.

From the ranger station to the river entrance is about an hour's walk. At the end of the beach, you follow the Monkey Trail over the promontory (or around it at low tide) to the next beach.

From here, a trail leads between big rocks and up a steep hill to an area of very jagged gray rocks. A bamboo stairway has been constructed across very dense forest, and it is very common to see wild monkeys along this trail, as well as lizards and wild tropical birds.

Close to the entrance of the river, there is a small ranger station where tours of the Underground River begin. If possible, try to stay at least one night at the ranger station or in the area of St. Paul. This place is one of the last untamed regions of the entire archipelago, and it's worth staying and roughing it a little as no other place in the country is as unsettled.

Inside the Cave

A few meters into the cave of the Underground River, everything's pitch-black. Bats and swifts inhabit the cave mouth, and crabs, freshwater shrimp, and small fish live in the river. You travel upstream through a passageway about 12 meters wide and 15 meters high, its ceiling a continuous fault line, plus several chambers containing fascinating stalagmites and stalactites until, after 4.5 km, the way is blocked and you can land on a small, muddy beach. Bats hang on the cave walls and swoop around the burning lanterns, so keep your head down.

There is a point where the boatmen turn around, but it's possible, with planning, to portage to the upstream section. This extends more than 2.5 km to Pining Cave, where the river begins to flow underground. Do not attempt to explore on your own beyond the point where the guides turn around. As is the case with most local guides, they turn back for a reason. Some guides may be willing to explore farther.

PORT BARTON

Port Barton is situated on a good beach where Pagdanan Creek flows into a bay. This small village has become one of the Philippines's premier travelers' beach hangouts due to a combination of beautiful natural surroundings and the number of dive spots, plus the availability of PADI dive instruction and certification.

You will find that much of the land from the Underground River to Port Barton, including many islands, is unsettled, undeveloped, and unowned.

A large number of foreigners, mostly Europeans, are buying beachfront property and developing resorts (thatched cottages, shared bathrooms, and a dive shop). This has increased the options for travelers who arrive at Port Barton.

Around Port Barton

The bay contains coral gardens and many small islands with white-sand beaches. Hiring a *banca* costs about P400 per day. You can island hop or be dropped off to camp on an island (take food and water), or stay at a new, foreign-owned resort and be picked up at a prearranged time. You can also make longer trips to places including the Underground River and El Nido, although these trips should not be attempted in a small, shallow *banca* if the weather is rough.

A local boatman charges about P100 pp for a snorkeling trip out in the bay; P1,500 pp for a two-day excursion to the Underground River; and P2,500 pp for a three-day journey to El Nido, subject to a minimum of three people. Inland, there's a waterfall, a 30-minute walk behind Port Barton.

Accommodations

At one time, **Elsa's Beach House** was the only accommodation at Port Barton; recently, foreigners have begun building their own beach resorts, so Port Barton has become somewhat overrun with some of the problems that effect Boracay and Puerto Galera. Fishermen sold their beachfront land to these newcomers, and there is a bit of resentment from the locals.

Today, Port Barton has over a half dozen modest resorts that charge P100-200 for basic nipa huts and P250-400 for better bungalows with private baths.

Stay at the friendly **Elsa's Beach House**, P150-200, where there is also a good restaurant. The popular **Swissippini** is good, with a restaurant; cottages are P150-350 for deluxe. The Swiss owner here also offers dive tours, PADI certification, and instruction. Also try the **Shangra La Scandinavian Resort**, P200, for an A-frame bungalow; the **Summer Homes**, P200; and **Allsan's Cottages**, P200.

If you want to try sea kayaking, contact Canadian Toby Clark at **Thelma's Traveler's Store** to see what kind of tours he's organizing. Clark divides his time running sea kayaking tours in the Philippines and living in the Rocky Mountains of Canada.

Also try **Alpine Lodging,** A-frame cottages at P100; **Port Barton Beachside,** P150-200 (four bungalows); and **Flora Satorenas,** P150-200 bungalows.

Islands near Port Barton

Just off Port Barton are several islands blessed with dazzling sand and outstanding diving. **Manta Ray Resort** on Capsalay Island (Three Sisters Island) serves Italian cuisine and has cottages plus three meals daily for P1,800-2,400. Coconut Garden Island Resort on the more distant and much larger Cacnipa Island has rooms and cottages for P175-550.

Some of the other popular nearby islands around Port Barton are Kayoya Island, where **Elsa's Place** has accommodations, and Cone Island, where **Elsa's Paradise Place** has one bungalow for one couple for P350. Water is stored for three days only, so the stay must be brief. Diving is good nearby.

Transportation

Port Barton is 155 km northeast of Puerto Princesa and can be reached in four or five hours with jeepneys departing from the northern terminal on Malvar Street in Puerto Princesa. You can also catch a jeepney from Roxas, or reach Port Barton by chartered boat from either Sabang or El Nido.

The cross-island road passes Matalangao Falls, site of an abandoned tourist resort. *Banca* owners are always willing to take tourists wherever they want to go, often at their own risk and against their better judgment.

SAN VICENTE

San Vicente is located on a spit of land, 20 km north of Port Barton. A 20-minute walk across the spit is White Beach, which extends for 14 km. It's beautiful, but sandflies can be a nuisance. A road leads from the airstrip at nearby Inandeng toward Little Baguio Falls, from where you can follow the stream for some distance through lovely surroundings.

Irregular jeepneys travel up from Port Barton, and *bancas* also make the 90-minute trip between the two villages.

SAN RAFAEL

Back on the east side of Palawan, this small village (two hours from Puerto Princesa and four hours from Roxas) has a beachside government resthouse where you can stay for one or two nights. It's better, however, to stay at San Rafael Beach, just south of the small village, where **Duchess Beachside Cottages** are operated by the **Duchess Pension House** in Puerto Princesa. Very pleasant atmosphere, with good, reasonably priced food available.

It's a nice place to relax, with snorkeling near the beach and around the tiny island off San Rafael, plus excellent jungle hikes to a waterfall, about two hours inland. The proprietors at Duchess cottages will organize hikes from here to visit the Batak tribes. The trip into the tribes takes four hours in and four out. There is also a guide here who will take tourists to the Underground River overland. The trek takes three days and fees run about P300 per day.

ROXAS

Roxas is a fishing village on the east coast of Palawan that provides a nice break from the long bus ride from Puerto Princesa to Taytay. The town has the Palawan Bank and Globe Telecom on Roxas Street and a branch of the First People's Bank on Sandoval Street. The bus and jeepney station, pharmacy, and BayanTel are three blocks back from the ocean on Jacinto Road.

Islands near Roxas

A *banca* can also be hired to visit offshore islands to snorkel and/or camp.

Stanlake Island (30 minutes away) is also called Tabon Island, since it's a nesting site of tabon birds (megapodes), which build mounds with their feet.

Silica sand deposits are mined at Del Pilar, near Roxas on Green Island Bay; they supply the Manila glass industry. Roxas hospital, to which American doctors are sometimes assigned, is well practiced in diagnosing malaria.

Accommodations

Gemalain's Inn down by the fish market and ocean has simple but adequate rooms for P100-150, while **Rover's Pension** adjacent to the jeepney station costs P150-250.

Retac Resort, three km north of Roxas, provides a pleasant escape from the town while waiting for onward transportation or the boat out to Coco Loco Island Resort. Rooms here cost P400-700, and a tricycle ride from town should be about P10.

Coco Loco Island

The main reason to spend any time around Roxas is to escape over to Coco Loco Island, a

traveler's huts at Coco Loco Resort

relaxing resort on a private island that's great for snorkeling, lazing on the beach, or simply waiting for the sunset. Food is quite good and portions are large but prices are somewhat steep, so bring along extra supplies from Roxas. Cottages in various states of repair cost P350-650.

Coco Loco (also known as Green Island) takes about one hour to reach by private *banca;* the island is the site of a former seaweed farm and its reef is 20 km in circumference. The resort itself is run by a Swiss man who runs *banca* trips out here from Roxas two times daily. Coco Loco Island offers full PADI courses of instruction, package tours, and longer trips to dive sites.

You can contact the staff on arrival at the airport or check in at the office in Puerto Princesa on Rizal Avenue. Otherwise, just show up at the office near the pier in Roxas and wait for the departing boat.

Transportation
Roxas is 145 km from Puerto Princesa and can be reached in about five hours by bus or jeepney departing from the northern bus terminal on Malvar Street.

TAYTAY

This small, pleasant fishing port on Taytay Bay, whose name means "Bridge" in Ilonggo, was founded in 1622. Under the Spaniards it was the provincial capital and an important military base. An old church, and the ruins of a stone fort, dating from 1728, remain.

Taytay is a very picturesque town at the northern end of the road from Puerto Princesa. Although a track continues north to El Nido, this is the last town of any size where you can stock up on basic supplies.

Accommodations
Pem's Pension House near the 300-year-old Church of Santa Monica has huts and bungalows for P100-650. You might find better value at **Rainbow Country Lodging** two blocks east or **Publico's International Guesthouse** a bit farther, where decent rooms cost P100-250. Or stay at **Evergreen Cottage.**

Island Resorts
Two very distinct resorts are situated in scenic Taytay Bay. **Club Noah Isabella** is a stunning place with cabanas elevated over a lagoon, priced US$175-250.

Farther out into the bay is **Flowers Island Resort,** where a Frenchman and his Filipino wife have constructed a tropical wonderland. Rooms with three meals daily cost P1,200-1,500; get more information from Pem's Pension in Taytay.

Services and Information
Taytay has an outlet of the Palawan Bank, post office, two pharmacies, a BayanTel office across from the school, and an old Spanish fort worth a quick wander.

Transportation
Taytay is 215 km north of Puerto Princesa and can be reached in nine or 10 grueling hours by bus or jeepney departing from the bus terminal on Malvar Street.

Visitors heading to Club Noah Isabella generally fly from Manila to Sandoval Airport in the north end of Taytay Bay.

Irregular boats sail from Taytay to Manila.

Vicinity of Taytay
You can hire a *banca* in Taytay to visit nearby islands, which offer sandy beaches, caves, rocks, coral reefs, and nesting birds. Paly Island has waterfalls and white-sand beaches where giant turtles come ashore to lay eggs Nov.-December.

Elephant Island, which has large caves, is another possibility. Flower Island, just off Taytay, is the site of a new French-owned dive resort.

Lake Danao (or Manguao) is in the jungle a few kilometers south of Taytay; it takes 30 minutes by jeepney or three hours to walk; ask about the shortcut. In order to stay in the **Government Resthouse** by the lake, contact the forest ranger in Taytay (P100-150). Take food and pay local people a small amount to cook it for you. You can swim and visit the islands in the lake, and the surrounding forest contains much wildlife.

Pinangyarihan Falls are also in the municipality.

South of Taytay, off the coast at Danlig near Dumaran Island, there is an excellent dive area and talk of a new resort being built on a small island here.

Club Noah Isabella

Getting to El Nido

A new Taytay to El Nido road is open during the dry season only. One or two jeepneys depart daily in the early morning hours and take three or four hours to El Nido. This service is cancelled in the rainy months, generally starting in early July until late November or early December, when jeepney service is resumed.

You can also take public boats from Taytay to El Nido. Six km west of Taytay is Agpay boat station (sometimes called Embarcadero), where large outriggers leave several times daily for Liminancong, en route to El Nido. Direct boat service from Agpay to El Nido is provided during the high season Dec.-April.

This route has become an option for those who dread the long road trip to El Nido.

Boats also serve settlements along the northeast coast. From the small village of Ilian, which is accessible by road, you can take an irregular *banca* up the Ilian River and stay in jungle villages; bring food and a mosquito net. It's possible to hike from Ilian to Taytay, between which are many villages.

LIMINANCONG

Liminancong is a surprisingly properous fishing town on the west coast of Palawan midway between Taytay and El Nido. This town, situated at the mouth of Malampaya Sound, is a major fishing center, especially during the northwest monsoon season (Nov.-Feb.). Crabs, shrimp, and other seafood delicacies are plentiful here.

New Guinea Beach is a 20-minute walk from town. Known as the "Fish Bowl of the Philippines" due to the large proportion of the nation's catch it yields, Malampaya Sound is 35 km long by seven km wide

Travelers passing through this town on their way to El Nido may find themselves stranded if the weather turns foul and boatmen refuse to complete the hazardous crossing. A road now connects Liminancong with Taytay, but most traffic continues to move by water.

Accommodations

Accommodations in town include **Puerto Paraiso Inn** and **Ann's Lodging House** at the south end of town, where rooms cost P100-150. **Kaver's Inn** in the center of town has small but clean rooms for P250-500.

Transportation

From Taytay, take a jeepney to Embarcadero, from where *bancas* sail daily (sometimes twice daily) down Malampaya Sound to Liminancong. If you can't wait for a regular departure, a special trip will be relatively expensive.

You can also reach Liminancong by hired *banca* from Port Barton. Passenger *bancas* (two hours) link Liminancong and El Nido, while boats go from Liminancong to Manila about once a week, sometimes stopping at El Nido, and to the islands of northern Palawan irregularly. Ask the storekeepers about boat departures.

NORTHERN PALAWAN

EL NIDO

Talcum-powder beaches fringed with coconut palms, vast coral reefs teeming with an astonishing variety of fish, and spectacular limestone mountains soaring vertically from clear turquoise waters have made El Nido one of the most visually stunning destinations in the Philippines. The area's remote location makes it both expensive and time-consuming to reach, a double-edged sword that also helps preserve the fragile environment.

Attractions

Highlights include the beaches on Inabuyatan Island and coral reefs surrounding Tapituan and Matinloc Islands. Dives and certification programs can be arranged at several dive shops.

Cliffs towering above it are the haunt of the swiftlet that produces the edible bird's nest, so prized by the Chinese. The nesting season is Feb.-May, peaking in March. Daring gatherers, observing certain rigid taboos, ascend the cliffs by means of bamboo scaffolding supported by rattan rope. The nests, which are worth hundreds of pesos a kilo, are destined to be served as *nido* soup in the Chinese restaurants in Manila, Hong Kong, and elsewhere.

Other points of interest in the municipality include Malingay Falls, and Peng and Makalimot hot springs.

Services and Information

Note that El Nido lacks a bank, so bring plenty of pesos or greenback dollars.

Accommodations

El Nido, the picturesque village nestled at the base of sheer limestone cliffs, serves as the main travelerss' center and launching point for dive trips throughout the Bacuit Archipelago. El Nido has a small tourist office, post office, and two jeepney halts for the two companies that provide transportation between El Nido and Taytay.

Over a dozen sets of bungalows are scattered around town, mostly on the beach at the north end of town. Rooms with common bath cost P100-200, while cottages with private bath cost P250-500.

Bungalows include **El Nido Cliffside Cottages** and **Lualhati Cottages** back from the ocean and just under the soaring cliffs, **Austria's Guesthouse** (the original spot), and **Bayview Lodging House, Marina Garden Beach Cottages, Percival Cottages,** and **El Nido Cottages** in the center of town.

North of town you'll find **Lucille's Beach Cottages, L&M Sea Lodge, Marco Polo Cottages, Gloria's Beach Cottages, Dara Fernandez Cottages, Rico Beach Cottages, Tandikan Cottages,** and **Lally & Abet Beach Cottages** where the road curves inland and continues up to the El Nido airport.

A few km south of El Nido at Corong-Corong Bay is **Mago's Beach Cottages** with bungalows for P100-300. Five km south of El Nido is the stylish **Dolarog Beach Resort,** where fully furnished cottages go for P500-850.

Island Resorts

Resorts within Bacuit Bay tend to be elegant but expensive because of higher construction costs and supply problems with water and energy. As of this writing only three islands (Malapacao, Pangalusian, and Miniloc) have been developed, and the remainder are now protected under a World Wildlife Fund "debt for nature swap."

All of the following can be booked at their representative offices in Manila.

Malapacao Island Retreat: An environmentally sensitive resort with lush gardens, sea turtle conservation program, and simple but elegantly designed cottages for US$10-24. You can make bookings at Lucings Eatery next to Bacuit Bay Divers in El Nido.

Marina del Nido: Upscale resort fully attuned to saving the natural environment of El Nido. Modern, circular bungalows cost US$125-175.

Pangalusian Island Resort: Some 15 km southwest of El Nido lies a dazzling island with

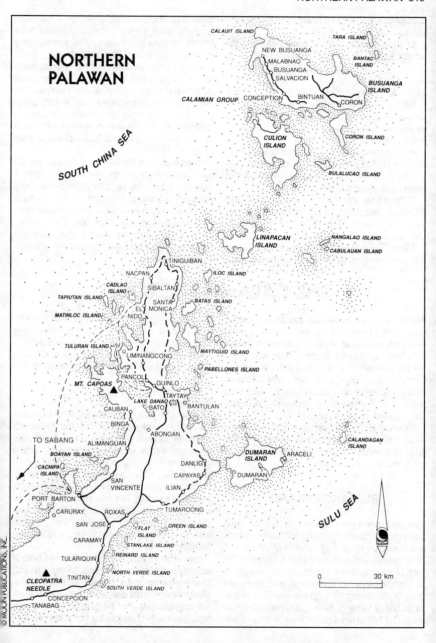

upscale cabanas with full board costing US$145-180 per day.

El Nido Resort: An exclusive hideaway on Miniloc Island, 10 km southwest of El Nido, with rooms suitably priced at US$240-380.

Transportation

El Nido is 271 km from Puerto Princesa and 320 km southwest of Manila. You can reach El Nido by air from Manila, boat from Liminancong, or jeepney from Taytay.

Air: Soriano Air flies daily from Manila to El Nido for US$220 roundtrip. El Nido Airport, four km north of town, is served by jeepneys that meet each arriving flight.

Ship: Along with the regular ships to Puerto Princesa, Asuncion Lines has a weekly service from Manila to El Nido and onwards to Liminancong.

Land: Several Puerto Royale buses depart the northern bus terminal in Puerto Princesa daily from 0500 to 0700 and take about eight hours to reach Taytay. Direct bus service from Puerto Princesa to El Nido may be offered during the high season from December to April.

From Taytay, an early morning jeepney takes two or three hours to El Nido. This service is cancelled during the rainy summer months when the Taytay-El Nido road turns into a muddy quagmire. When service is halted, your only option is to attempt the sea route from Agpay near Taytay to Liminancong and a final boat—perhaps chartered—to El Nido.

Boat from Port Barton: From Port Barton, it's practical for three or more travelers to charter a *banca* for a three-day trip to the El Nido area (Dec.-June only). Travel at your own risk; this is one of the more exciting adventures in the Philippines.

The seascapes make the more famous Hundred Islands pale by comparison. You can sleep on deserted beaches and the snorkeling is wonderful.

THE CALAMIAN GROUP

Also known as Calamianes, this group is separated from Mindoro by the deep Mindoro Strait and comprises three large, mountainous, forested islands: Busuanga, Culion, Coron, and about 95 smaller ones. The main town and port is Coron. The surrounding waters contain dozens of coral islets or barely submerged reefs, plus many WW II shipwrecks, especially in Coron Bay. Big fish are plentiful here.

These islands are hard to reach. You must allow lots of time and check the small shipping lines of Manila or north Palawan ports such as Liminancong.

BUSUANGA ISLAND

This hilly island (890 square km) has two main settlements, Busuanga town and Coron, which are linked by road. Flights from Manila full of dive tourists and enthusiasts have changed the face of this outpost—it's quite popular. Aeroflot is the major carrier to Busuanga, and there are daily flights during the high season. The inhabitants live by farming, fishing, and cottage industries. The island has several manganese mines, producing high-grade ore. Tara Island, northeast of Busuanga, is the site of a Vietnamese refugee camp. Dive boats cruising Busuanga's surrounding waters may visit Nanga Rock, Tara Island, Brown Rocks, and other outstanding dive sites.

Busuanga Town

You can use Busuanga as a base for exploring the western end of the island. At the northwestern tip is Calawit National Park, a game preserve and wildlife sanctuary. It contains a group of the largely nocturnal Calamian deer, which is endemic to Busuanga and Culion Islands. Once common, now only a few inhabit the most inaccessible areas. Pinnacle Rock, off this northwest coast, is an outstanding snorkeling site; the seabed slopes gradually away from its base, which is in five meters of water, and it's surrounded by clouds of fish.

Hire a *banca* in Busuanga town to visit here or another nearby snorkeling spot, Malajon Island. This prominent, barren black rock has white-sand beaches on its eastern side, while the western side plunges into the sea. Much of the island has been undercut by wave action, with the seabed sloping out from about six to nine meters below the surface. Big fish swim around here, including hammerhead sharks. In the vicinity of Busuanga town are caves and Simlayan Waterfalls, while King's Ranch is in the interior.

Concepcion

This settlement between Busuanga and Coron towns is the site of Concepcion Falls and the Lusteveco Co. Pearl Culture Farm. The latter has an air-compressor where visiting divers can refill tanks by prior arrangement. Just offshore from the Pearl Farm, a Japanese cargo ship, torpedoed in 1944, sits on the muddy seabed, with its mast protruding three meters above the surface. The wreck is home to hosts of fish, but exploration should only be undertaken with a local guide and extreme caution, due to strong currents, poor visibility, and live ammunition remaining aboard.

LINAPACAN ISLAND

Linapacan Island (103 square km) and about 47 small islands form a beautiful municipality that's separated from Culion Island by the treacherous Linapacan Strait, which connects the Sulu and South China Seas. Linapacan is a limestone island. The main settlement, also called Linapacan (formerly San Miguel), receives about two passenger boats a month from Manila. Elli Caves are outside the town. The Cabulauan Islands, east of Linapacan, offer great snorkeling, with fine coral on their northern sides and lots of fish and turtles.

CORON ISLAND

Coron Island (71 square km) lies across the Coron Passage from Coron town. It's a high, rocky, and thinly inhabited limestone island of hills, forests, and lakes. The local economy is based on fishing, mining, logging, and shellcraft.

Makinit Hot Springs is one of the best hot spring sites in the Philippines. Here, just a short banca ride from the port of Coron, you can alternately soak in very hot sulfuric water in a pair of waist-deep pools, then run across five me-

ters of beach to cool off in the sea. Also on the island is Lake Abuyok, 110 meters deep and inhabited by a single species of fish: the kalamog.

Seven islands, known as Siete Pecados ("Seven Sins"), lie between Coron and Busuanga Islands. South of Coron Island are two small islands, with excellent snorkeling in their shallows: Guintungauan Island, on the eastern side of which shells and nudibranch are plentiful on the sandy, gently sloping seabed; and Delian Island, which offers coral and big fish at both its northern and southern ends.

CULION ISLAND

Culion, or Kulion (390 square km), is an island of steep hills, but with some fertile soil. It's the site of the large Culion Leper Colony reservation.

The main town, Culion, is on the northeast side; Fort Culion dates from 1740.

Halsey Harbor is a deep indentation in the southwest coast. The Kalamian minority group live around Halsey. Southeast of Culion, between Batabuan Point and Bulalacao Island, is a series of reefs where snorkelers will find fine coral, giant clams, turtles, and many fish. Hire the banca of a local fisherman, to whom the area will be well known.

South of these reefs are the Tres Marias Rocks, whose slopes feature coral, shells, and fish; shark and barracuda come into the shallows here. The Tres Reyes Islands, farther south, also offer outstanding snorkeling amid teeming fishlife; this is believed to be a breeding area for cuttlefish.

THE CUYO ISLANDS

The Cuyo group, situated north of the Sulu Sea amid rich fishing grounds, comprises Cuyo, Agutaya, and about 45 smaller islands, surrounded by reefs, rocks, and shoals. Many of the islets are of coral and inhabited only by seabirds. The Cuyo group offers snorkelers amazing fishlife with superb underwater visibility.

Cuyo Island

Cuyo (58 square km) is volcanic in origin, and Mt. Bombon rises to 260 meters on the northern side. Boats dock at Cuyo town, which is a pleasant and quiet place.

Cuyo Fort, with its square stone walls and four bastions, was built by forced labor under the Spaniards in 1677 as a defense against Moro piracy. A fort was also constructed at Lucbuan on the eastern side of Cuyo around this time. The island's quiet roads are very attractive, with neat villages of distinctive bamboo houses and fences.

Cuyo is noted for cashew nuts *(casoy),* which are positively cheap here. The nuts are made into wine and brittle. Wild monkeys live on Cuyo.

Snorkelers can hire a *banca* to go out to nearby spots such as Gosong Rock, between Cuyo and Canipo Islands, which has coral mounds surrounded by schools of reef fish. The southern and western sides of Canipo are also excellent, as is the southern side of Taganayan Island, a little farther afield.

Agutaya Island

This wooded island (15 square km) north of Cuyo is the site of an old Spanish fort and the Sua Caves and has good offshore coral. An abundance of *buri* palms and pandanus supports local mat-weaving.

Farther north again, Dit Island, site of Baluarte Caves, is 30 minutes by *banca* from Agutaya, while it takes two and a half hours to reach Halog Island Bird Sanctuary, beyond which Quiniluban Island rises to over 300 meters. Agutaya's small out-islands, such as Oco, Manamoc, and Pamalican, offer superlative snorkeling.

Transportation

Cuyo (289 km from Puerto Princesa) is a crossroads. See Transportation in the Palawan Introduction above for tips on reaching Cuyo.

DUMARAN ISLAND

This thickly wooded island (326 square km), separated from the northeastern coast of Palawan by the Dumaran Channel, was originally settled by people from Cuyo and Cagayancillo.

It has two towns, Dumaran and Araceli.

Passenger boats between Puerto Princesa/Roxas and Cuyo stop at Araceli, a fishing port where some of the most beautiful and artistic mats in the country are woven. Araceli's setting is scenic, with beaches nearby, but snorkeling in its vicinity is unexceptional.

Launches traveling between Cuyo and Araceli sometimes stop at Calandagan Island, allowing passengers to stroll onshore or enjoy snorkeling right off the boat. Those staying here could hire a *banca* to reach nearby Maducang Island, which has superb coral in its shallows.

M.G.L. DOMENY DE RIENZI

SUGGESTED READING

PHILIPPINES

Bain, David Haward. *Sitting in Darkness: Americans in the Philippines.* Boston: Houghton Mifflin, 1984. An absorbing account of the U.S. capture of Gen. Emilio Aguinaldo during the Philippine-American War.

Broad, Robin. *Plundering Paradise: The Struggle for the Environment in the Philippines.* Berkeley: University of California Press, 1993. A call to activists and environmentalists in the West to extend their concern to the Philippines in a collection of vivid tales about courageous Filipinos confronting problems of deforestation and pollution.

Karnow, Stanley. *In Our Image: America's Empire in the Philippines.* New York: Random House, 1989. Having covered Asia for 30 years for *Time, Life,* and the *Washington Post,* the gifted author was in a special position to write this copiously detailed yet highly readable political history of the American experience in the Philippines. Karnow also authored *Vietnam: A History,* whose television companion won six Emmys, and a three-part documentary on the Philippines aired on PBS in 1989.

Lava, Jesus B., and Antonio S. Araneta. *Faith Healing and Psychic Surgery in the Philippines.* Manila: Philippine Society for Psychical Research Foundation, 1982. Tales of strange lights and enigmatic occurrences.

Licauco, Jaime T. *The Truth Behind Faith Healing in the Philippines.* Manila: National Bookstore, 1982. Recommended for those who want more information on the faith healing phenomenon. Another of Licauco's titles is *The Magicians of God: The Amazing Stories of Philippine Faith Healers* (1982).

Manchester, William. *American Caesar.* New York: Little, Brown and Company, 1978. An absorbing biography of Gen. Douglas MacArthur, one of America's last epic heroes.

Mayuga, Sylvia. *Insight Guide Philippines.* Singapore: APA Publications, 1998. This is one of a series of guides whose superb photography and lush texts make them the best set of background guides to Southeast Asia. Read before traveling.

Onoda, Hiroo. *No Surrender: My Thirty-Year War.* Translated by Charles S. Terry. London: Deutsch, 1975. Onoda, a Japanese straggler who didn't know that WW II had ended, emerged from the hills of Lubang Island after 30 years in the forest. A fascinating read.

Roces, Alfredo, and Grace Roces. *Culture Shock! Philippines.* Portland, OR: Graphic Arts Center Publishing Co., 1997. This lively and highly amusing guide to Filipino customs will prove indispensable to understanding the country and the people. It is one of a series of practical guides to the rules of Asian etiquette, customs, and recommended behavior for every visitor to Asia. Lightweight and well distributed; excellent books to purchase and read while on the road. Highly recommended.

Simons, Lewis M. *Worth Dying For.* New York: William Morrow, 1987. Simon dissects Aquino's rise and People's Power by analyzing the dynamics of Philippine society including the church, the military, business, and the political left. His sensitive vignettes of the common people give great life to what could have otherwise been another cliché—about the forces of good and evil.

Steinberg, David Joel. *The Philippines: A Singular and Plural Place.* Boulder, CO: Westview Press, 1994. One of America's leading authorities on the Philippines packs a great deal of insight into this outstanding book. His chapters on Filipino society, the religious impulse, and the search for a useable past are a superb introduction to the country.

SOUTHEAST ASIA

Bloodworth, Dennis. *An Eye for the Dragon.* New York: Farrar, Straus and Giroux, 1970. The former Far East correspondent of the *Observer* incisively examines the comedies and tragedies of Asia, from the fanatic wranglings of Sukarno to racial tensions in Malaysia. Bloodworth makes history and politics—often dry and dull subjects—fascinating and memorable.

Buruma, Ian. *God's Dust: A Modern Asian Journey.* New York: Farrar, Straus and Giroux, 1989. Buruma examines a familiar dilemma—can the nations of Southeast Asia modernize without losing their cultural identities?—with great wit, insight, and a sharp sense of humor. His observations on the decline of Burma, the confused Filipino sense of history, and the monstrous contradictions of contemporary Singapore make this an excellent resource for all visitors contemplating travel to Southeast Asia.

Eames, Andrew. *Crossing the Shadow Line.* London: Hodder and Stoughton, 1986. Young and talented Andrew Eames spent two years of his life probing the remote corners of Southeast Asia, from northern Thailand's Golden Triangle to an adventurous sail on Makassar schooners between Bali and Irian Jaya. A great tale spiced with prodigious amounts of humor and pathos. Highly recommended.

Fenton, James. *All the Wrong Places.* New York: Atlantic Monthly Press, 1988. James Fenton, journalist, poet, and critic, is one of the new breed of travel writers: jaundiced, self-indulgent, hard-hitting, and more concerned with personal impressions than scholarly dissertation. The result is a mesmerizing book full of great perception, especially his observations of the Philippines.

Iyer, Pico. *Video Night in Kathmandu.* New York: Vintage, 1988. Iyer's incongruous collection of essays uncovers the Coca-colonization of the Far East in a refreshingly humorous and perceptive style. His heartbreaking accounts of decay in the Philippines, brothels in Bangkok, and cultural collisions in Bali form some of the finest travel writing in recent times. Highly recommended.

Kirch, John. *Music in Every Room: Around the World in a Bad Mood.* New York: McGraw Hill, 1984. An offbeat look at both the pains and the pleasures of contemporary Asian travel. Lively, opinionated, and immensely readable.

Krannich, Ronald L., Jo Reimer, and Caryl Krannich. *Shopping in Exotic Places: Your Passport to Exciting Hong Kong, Korea, Thailand, Indonesia, and Singapore.* Manassas, VA: Impact Publications, 1989. Step-by-step guide to the secrets of shopping in Southeast Asia. Detailed descriptions of shopping centers, arcades, factory outlets, and exclusive boutiques in Hong Kong, Singapore, Thailand, and Indonesia.

Nelson, Theodora, and Andrea Gross. *Good Books for the Curious Traveler—Asia and the South Pacific.* Boulder, CO: Johnson Publishing, 1989. Outstanding in-depth reviews of over 350 books including almost 50 titles to Southeast Asia. Written with sensitivity and great insight. The authors also run a service that matches books with a traveler's itinerary. Contact Travel Source, 20103 La Roda Court, Cupertino, CA 95014, tel. (408) 446-0600.

Richter, Linda K. *The Politics of Tourism in Asia.* Honolulu: University of Hawaii Press, 1989. A scholarly study of the complex political problems that confront the tourist industries in Thailand, the Philippines, and other Asian destinations. Filled with surprising conclusions about the impact of multinational firms and the importance of targeting grass-roots travelers rather than upscale tourists.

Schwartz, Brian. *A World of Villages.* New York: Crown Publishers, 1986. A superbly written journal of a six-year journey to the most remote villages in the world. Filled with tales of unforgettable people and lands of infinite variety and beauty.

Shales, Melissa, ed. *The Traveler's Handbook.* Chester, CT: Globe Pequot Press, 1988. Fifth edition of the award-winning guide, which puts together the contributions of over 80 experienced travelers, all authorities in their particular fields. Practical suggestions on climate, maps, airfares, internal transportation, backpacking, visas, money, health, and theft.

Simon, Ted. *Jupiter's Travels.* New York: Doubleday, 1980. Fascinating account of a 63,000-km motorcycle journey (500cc Triumph Tiger) from Europe, down the continent of Africa, across South America, Australia, and India. And what does Ted do now? Raises organic produce in Northern California!

Theroux, Paul. *The Great Railway Bazaar.* New York: Houghton Mifflin, 1975. One of the world's best travel writers journeys from London to Tokyo and back on a hilarious railway odyssey. Rather than a dry discourse on sights, this masterpiece of observation keeps you riveted with personal encounters of the first order. Highly recommended for everyone!

INTERNET RESOURCES

General Tourism
Philippine Department of Tourism
www.sequel.net/RPinUS/Tourism
Boracay Department of Tourism
www.iloilo.net/dot/bb
Philippine Department of Tourism
(Tokyo Field Office)
www2.gol.com/users/dotjapan/edot.html

U.S. Government Travel Information
U.S. Consular Information
travel.state.gov/philippines.html
C.I.A. Factbook
www.odci.gov/cia/publications/factbook/rp.html

Newspapers and Magazines
Manila Bulletin
www.mb.com.ph
Philippine Star Newspaper
www.philstar.com
Manila Times
www.manilatimes.net
Archipelago magazine
www.archipelago.com.ph
Filipinas magazine
www.filipinasmag.com
The Philippine Diver magazine
www.diver.com.ph

Destinations
Manila Nightlife
www.manilanights.com
Angeles City
geocities.com/Tokyo/Ginza/6656/angeles1.htm
Margaritaville Angeles
www.theville.com

Miscellaneous
Filipino Language Resources
www.filipinolinks.com/travel/travlanguage.html
Philippine-American War
www.boondocksnet.com/centennial/index.html
19th Century Images of the Philippines
www.univie.ac.at/voelkerkunde/apsis/aufi/pop/pop.htm
WG&A Superferries
www.wgasuperferry.com
Haribon Foundation
www.haribon.org.ph/indexa.htm

INDEX

A

Abatan: 223
Aborlan: 508
Abra de Ilog: 387
Abra Museum: 263
Abra Province: 262-264
Abra River Gap: 258
Abucay: 198
accommodations: 72-73; *see also specific destination*
Aga Khan Museum of Islamic Arts: 463
Agawa: 235
Aglipay National Shrine: 265
Agoncillo: 154
Agoo: 252-253
agriculture/agrarian reform: 32-34
Aguinaldo, Emilio: 20-22, 150, 281
Aguinaldo Museum: 130
Agusan del Norte: 449
Agutaya Island: 522
Air Force bases: 28
air travel: 76-86; *see also specific destination*
Aklan Agricultural College: 423
Alaminos (Laguna Province): 170
Alaminos (Pangasinan Province): 204
Albay Province: 301-308
alcoholic beverages: 75
Allen: 429-430
All Saints' Day: 68-69, 344-345
Alona Beach: 323
Alto Crafts Doll Museum: 129
Alubihod Bay: 416
Ambalio: 240
Ambil: 388
Ambulong Island: 386
American Cemetery and War Memorial: 128
amusement parks: Enchanted Kingdom 174
Anda: 328
Angeles City: 185-192
Angono: 175
Ang Sinulog Festival: 460-461
Anilao: 158-160
animals: 10
Anini-y: 418
Aninuan: 383
Antipolo: 175

antique collections: Bacolod City 393; Talisay 397
antique shopping: 71-72; Cebu City 349; Sariaya 289-290
Apalit: 185
Apatot: 255
Apayao: 248
Apocalypse Now: 167, 176
Apo Island: 403
Apo Reef: 386-387
Aparri: 284
Aquino, Benigno: 26
Aquino, Corazon: 26-28
Araneta Museum: 399
Araw Ng Dabaw festival: 471
archaeological sites: 128-129
Archdiocesan Museum: 421
architecture, Spanish: 255-256, 258
Ardent Hot Springs: 453
Arevalo: 413
Argao: 354
Aringay: 253
Aritao: 278
art galleries/musuems: Cebu City 346; Manila 115; Silay City 397
Asin Hot Springs: 219
Ata people: 469
Ati-Atihan Festival: 64, 422
Aurora Province: 279-280
Ayala Museum: 128
Ayala Museum and Library: 260

B

Babak: 472
Babatngon: 365
Babuyan Islands: 285-286
Bacacay: 306
Bacarra: 269
Baclayon: 325
Bacnotan: 255
Bacolod City: 393-397
Bacolor: 185
Bacon: 313
Badian Island: 358
Badjao people: 490
Badoc: 265

Bagabag: 278
Bagac: 201
Bagobo people: 468
Baguio City: 213-222
Baguio-Mountain Province Museum: 218
Baheli: 512
bakaya sandals: 163
Bakun: 222
Balabac Island: 511
Balanacan: 371
Balanga: 198
Balangagon Cave: 234-235
Balaoan: 255
Balay Ti Ili: 265
Balbalasang: 246-247
Baler: 279-280
Balete: 154
Bale Zamboanga Festival: 483
Balicasag Island: 324-325
Balingoan: 450
Balud: 375
bamboo organ: 130
Banaue: 238-240
bancas: 88
Banga: 423
Banga'an: 235-236
Bangar: 255
Bangued: 262-264
Bansilan Cave: 291
Bantay: 258
Bantayan Island: 353
Banton: 427
Banton Coffin Burial Cave: 427
Barlig: 231-232
Barotac Viejo: 415
Barrio Barretto: 196-197
Basco: 272
Basey: 433
Basilan Island: 491-492
Basilica Minore del Santo Niño: 345
Basilisa: 448
Bataan Death March: 23, 200, 202
Bataan Peninsula: 198-201
Batac: 265
Batad: 241-242
Batak people: 500
Batan: 423
Batanes Islands: 270-274
Batangas City: 160
Batangas Province: 154-161
Batan Island (Albay Province): 308

Batan Island (Batanes Islands): 272-273
Bataraza: 510
Bathala Caves: 373
Bato: 368
Battle of Mactan reenactment: 350
Battle of Manila Bay: 21
Batulao: 155
Bauang: 253-254
Bayagnan Island: 448
Baybay: 368
Baylao: 453
Bayombong: 278
beaches: 55-60; Argao 354; Bacolod area
    397; Bauang 253; El Nido 518; Jolo 493-
    494; Mactan Island 350; Panglao Island
    323; Puerto Galera 382-383; Rizal 313;
    Roxas City vicinity 420; Takal 298-299;
    Torrijos 373
bell towers: Bacarra 269; Laoag City 266
Benguet Province: 213-224
Benoni: 455-456
Besao: 235
Beverly Hills subdivision: 346-347
Beyer, H. Otley: 240
Biak-Na-Bato National Park: 182
Bicol: 287-288
Bicolano people: 287-288
Bicol Folkloric Museum: 299-300
Bilatan Poon Island: 495
Biliran Island: 366
Binirayan Festival: 417
bird sanctuaries: 293, 511, 522
B'laan people: 476
Boac: 371, 372
boat travel: 86-88; *see also specific*
    destination
Bocaue: 180
Bocos: 240-241
body language: 52
Bohol Beach: 323
Bohol: 319-328
Bolinao: 205-206
Bombon: 298
Bomod-ok Waterfall: 235-236
Bonbon: 455
Bondoc Peninsula: 291-292
Bongabon (Mindoro): 384
Bongabon (Nueva Ecija Province): 209
Bongao Island: 495
Bonifacio, Andres: 20-21
Bonito Island: 159-160

Bontoc Igorots: 226-227
booklist: 523-525
Boquete: 382
Boracay: 329-335
Borongan: 431
Botocan River: 167
Botolan: 197
breweries: 347
bridges: Bridge of Whims 167; Habbang 242-243; Igorot 229; Mendiola 124; San Juanico/Sohoton Natural Bridge N.P. 365
Brooke's Point: 510
Bucas Grande: 449
Bud Dato: 493
Buddhism: 44
Buenavista: 415-416
Bugabuga Hills: 366
Bugsuk Island: 511
Buhutan: 306
Bulabog-Putian National Park: 415
Bulacan: 181
Bulacan Province: 179-182
Bulalacao: 385
Bulan: 314
Bunabunaan Island: 495
Bunot Lake: 169
burial jars: 286, 301, 499
Burias Island: 376
Burnay: 243
Burnham Park: 218
Busay Falls: 306
business hours: 96
bus travel: 90; *see also specific destination*
Busuanga Island: 520-521
Butuan City: 449-450

C
Cabanatuan City: 208-209
Cabatuan: 414
Cabra: 388
Cadaraman Island: 511
Cadiz City: 398
Cagayan: 269
Cagayan de Oro: 456-458
Cagayan de Tawi-Tawi (Cagayan de Sulu): 497
Cagayan Islands: 511
Cagayan Province: 282-286
Cagraray isalnd: 306
Cagsawa Ruins: 304
Cainta: 174-175

Calabasa: 415
Calamba: 173-174
Calamian Islands: 520-522
Calapan: 383-384
Calasiao: 207-208
Calatagan: 157
Calayan Island: 285-286
Calbayog City: 430, 432
Calesa Festival: 181-182
Calibato Lake: 169
Caliocan Island: 431
Caliraya Reservoir: 166
Callao Caves National Park: 283
Caloocan: 154
Caloocan City: 129
Calumpit: 181
Camalaniugan: 284
Camalig: 303
Camarines Provinces (Norte and Sur): 293-300
Camiguin Island (Luzon): 285-286
Camiguin Island (Mindanao): 451-456
Camotes Islands: 355
Camp John Hay: 218
Candon: 257
Canlaon City: 403
Capas: 202
Cape Bojeador: 269
Cape Engaño: 285
Capiz: 421-422
Carabao Festival: 66
Cardona: 176
Carfel Seashell Museum: 113
Cariboo Festival: 182
Carolina: 298
Carmen: 352
Casa Manila: 122
Casiguran: 280
Cataduanes Island: 309-311
Catarman (Samar): 430
Catarman (Camiguin Island): 455
Catbalogan: 432-433
cathedrals: *see* churches
Catholicism: 41-43
Catiliran Cave: 416
Catmon: 352
Cauayan: 281
caves: Baguio City 220; Balangagon 234-235; Baluarte 522; Bansilan 291; Banton 427; Basanga 424; Bathala 373; Callao Caves National Park 283; Capiz 421; Catiliran

Cave 416; Daliran Spring and Cave 415-416; Gamay 431; Hoyop-Hoyopan 303-304; Huluga 458; Macahambus 458; Panglao Island 323; Saint Paul Subterranean National Park 513; Santa Victoria 282; Siargao Islands 448-449; Sohoton National Park 433-434; Tabon 510; Talalora 433; Timbac 222; Tulingon 424

Cavite Province: 148-154
Cavite Town: 150
Cawit: 371
Cebu: 335-358
Cebu City: 342-349
Cemento: 280
cemeteries: American Cemetery and War Memorial 128; Cemetery town 125Nagcarlan 168-169
Centers for Disease Control (CDC): 98
Central Bank Money Museum: 113
Cervantes: 256-257
Chavacano people: 482-483
Chicken Villa: 201
Chico River Valley: 245
Chinatown (Manila): 122-123
Chinese cemetery: 125
Chinese New Year: 64
Chinese people: 35-36
Chocolate Hills: 326-327
Christmas: 69-70
chromite mines: 197-198
churches: 43-44; Aringay 253; Badoc 265; Batangas Province 158; Bolinao 205-206; Cebu City 345; Dingras 269; Laguna Province 163, 167, 168; Laoag City 266; Magsingal 261; Manapla 398; Manila 120-121, 124; Milaor 298; Naga City 297-298; Narvacan 257; Naujan 384; Palo 365; Puerto Princesa 504; Romblon 424; San Joaquin 414; Santa Lucia 257; Santa Maria 257; Sarrat 268; Sebaste 419; Taal 158; Tacloban 363-364; Victorias 398; Vigan 258
Clark Air Force Base: 185-186
Claveria: 285
climate: 3-8
clothes shopping: 71
cockfighting: 58-59, 201; Iloilo 412
Coco Loco Island: 515-516
Colorado Falls: 220
Compostela: 352
con artists: 104-106
Concepcion: 521

Congbagsa: 435
conservation: 8-9
Consoliman Cool Spring: 263
copper mining: 356
Cordillera: 210-248
Coron Island: 521
Corregidor: 130-133
Cotabato City: 478-481
Cotta: 291
couriers: 81
credit cards: 95
Cresta de Gallo: 418
Cresta de Gallo Island: 427
crime: 103-106
Crisologo Museum: 258-260
Cry of Balintawak: 68
crypts: 168-169
Crystal Caves: 220
Cuatro Islands: 368
cuisine: 73-76
Culasi: 419
Culion Island: 521
Cultural Center Complex: 113-115
cultural issues: 47-53
currency: 94-95
Currimao: 265
Cuyo Islands: 521-522

D
Daan Bantayan: 352-353
Daet: 294
Dagupan City: 206-207
Dalupiri Island: 285-286
Danajon Bank: 352
Danao City: 352
dance: 62
Danjugan: 400
Danum Lake: 235
Dap-ay Guiday Stone Agricultural Center: 235
Dapitan City: 466
Daraga: 304
datus: 15
Dauis: 323
Davao City: 467-472
Day of Valor: 66, 256-257
Death March: 23, 200, 202
Del Monte Pineapple Plantation and Cannery: 458
del Pilar, Gregorio: 257
Demang: 234
diarrhea: 100

DIVING

general information: 59-60
Apo Reef: 386-387
Batangas Province 155, 159
Baylao: 453
Bohol: 321-326, 328
Boracay: 331
Calamian Islands: 520-522
Cebu: 337
Dumaguete: 402-403
El Nido: 518
Iloilo: 412
Lubang Islands: 387-388
Mactan Island area: 351-352
Mindoro: 377
Moalboal: 356-357
Nagtabon Beach: 512
Palawan: 501-502
Polillo Islands: 293
Puerto Princesa: 506-507
Port Barton: 513-514
Sogod area: 352
Tres Reyes Islands: 371
Tubbataha Reefs: 511-512
Zambales Coastline: 197

Dibut Bay: 280
Dinagat Island: 448
Dinagyang festival: 409
Dingle: 415
Dingras: 269
diplomatic offices: 92
Dipolog City: 466
doll museums: 126, 129
Dominican Hill: 219
Don Lorenzo Diaz Memorial Museum: 253
Dos Hermanas: 427
drag racing: 189
Ducligan: 242-243
Dulag: 367-368
Dumaguete City: 400-402
Dumalag: 421
Dumaran Island: 522
durian fruit: 467

E
eagles: 10
Easter Sunday: 65, 451
economy: 32-34
El Fraile: 133
El Nido: 517, 518-520

electricity: 96
embassies, U.S.: Manila 115
Enchanted Isle: 399
Enchanted Kingdom: 174
environmental issues: 8-9, 70; Boracay 331;
   Cebu 356
Ermita: 113-115, 134-139
Escalante: 399
Escudero Museum: 170
ESDA Revolution: 27
Estrada, Joseph: 29
etiquette: 50-53, 75-76
Excavation Museum: 381

F
faith healing: 42-43
fauna: 10
Feast of Nuestra Señora de Candelaria: 409
Feast of Our Lady of the Immaculate
   Conception: 69
Feast of Sts. Peter and Paul: 185
feasts: see festivals
ferries: 88
Fertility Festival: 180
festivals: 62-70; *see also specific destination*
   or festival
fishing: Fuga Island 286; Infanta 292-293
flagellantes: 183
flightseeing: 189
flora: 9-10
Flores de Mayo: 66
food: 73-76; *see specific destination for*
   restaurants
Footprint of Angalo: 262
Forbes Park: 128
Fort Drum: 133
Fort Pilar: 483
Fort San Andres: 424-425
Fort San Pedro: 345
Fort Santiago: 117-120
Fortune Island: 156
Fuga Island: 285-286

G
Gaddang people: 277
gambling: 106
gardens: Bacolod City 393; Japanese
   Memorial Garden (Luzon) 291; Japanese
   Memorial Gardens (Manila) 166;
   Lamplighter's Paradise World 404; National
   Botanical Gardens 173; Tacloban 363
Gasan: 371, 372

General Santos City: 474-475
geography: 2-3
geology: 2-3
Gigante (Norte and Sur): 417
Gigatangan Island: 366
girlie bars: *see specific destination*
Gironiere, Paul de la: 176-177
gold mining: 294, 400
golf: 266
Golo: 388
Gomag Cave: 431
Good Friday: 416
government: 29-32
Guadalupe: 128
Gubat: 313
Guimaras: 415-416
Guimbal: 413
Guinaang: 231
Guinsiliban: 455
guitar factories: 350
Guiuan: 431
guns: 132

H
Habbang Bridge: 242-243
Hagonoy: 181
Halaran Festival: 420
Halog Island Bird Sanctuary: 522
Halsema Mountain Highway: 222
harp carving: 269
headhunting: 226
health problems: 100-102
hepatitis: 100-101
Hibok-Hibok Volcano: 454
Hidden Valley Springs Resort: 170
High Peak: 198
Hikdop Island: 448
hiking: *see* trekking
hilltribes: 37-39
Hinagdanan Cave: 323
Hinoba-an: 400
history: 11-29
Hiyas ng Bulacan: 181
Holy Week: 64-66
Homonhon Island: 431-432
Honda Bay: 507
horseback riding: 253
horse-drawn carriages: 91
Hoyop-Hoyopan Caves: 303-304
Huluga Caves: 458

HOT SPRINGS

Apayao: 248
Ardent: 453
Bacolod area: 397
Baguio: 219
Bangued area: 264
Biliran Island: 366
Bolok-Bolok: 356
Ducligan: 242
Ingangmaharang: 308
Iwahig Prison and Penal Colony: 508
Kananga: 366
Los Banos: 171-172
Mainit: 231
Makinit: 521
Mariveles: 200
Mateo: 314
Palimpinon: 403
Pugo: 253
Sadanga: 229
Talaga: 160
Tangub: 455
Tayabas: 290
Tiwi: 307-308
Tubig Manok: 355
Tungonan: 367

Hundred Islands National Park: 202, 204-205
Hungduan: 243

IJ
Iba: 197
Ibajay: 423-424
Ibaloi people: 217
Ifugao people: 238
Ifugao Province: 236-244
Igang Cave: 421
Igorot bridge: 229
Ikalahan people: 277
Ilacaon island: 398
Ilagan: 281
Iligan City: 459-461
Ilin Island: 386
Ilocano people: 251
Ilocos Norte Province: 264-269
Ilocos Sur Province: 255-261
Ilog: 400
Iloilo City: 409-412

Ilonggo people: 406
Ilongot people: 277
Inambacan Falls: 328
Infanta: 292-293
information centers: 91-92
Ingangmaharang Hot Springs: 308
insurance: 98-100
International Rice Research Institute (IRRI): 172
internet resources: 525
Intramuros: 117-122
Iriga City: 299-300
"Iron Dinosaurs": 395
Irosin: 313-314
Isabela: 492
Isabela Province: 280-282
Isla de Gato: 353
Isla de la Convalencia: 124
Islam: 15, 44, 438
Isla Naburot: 416
Island Bay: 508
Isneg people: 246-247
Itbayat: 273-274
Ivatan people: 271
Iwahig Prison and Penal Farm: 507-508
Iwak people: 277
Jagna: 328
Jalajala: 176-177
Janiuay: 414
Jao Island: 328
Japanese Memorial Gardens: Luzon 291; Manila 166
jar factories: 260
Jaro: 412
Jawili Falls: 423
jeepneys: 89
Jolo Island: 492-494
Jordan: 415

K
Kaamulan Festival: 459
Kabankalan: 400
Kabayan: 223-224
Kadaclan: 232
Kadayawan sa Dabaw Festival: 471
Kalantiaw National Shrine: 423
Kalayaan Festival: 163
Kalibo: 422-423
Kalinga people: 246
Kalinga-Apayao: 229
Kalinga-Apayao Province: 244-248

Kankanai people: 217
Kanlaon City: 403
Kanleon Volcano: 399
Kantican Island: 431
Kaputian: 473
Karaw people: 217
Kawasan Falls: 358
Kawit: 130
Kiangan: 243-244
Kibila Beach: 455
Kinapusan Islands: 496
kite-flying: 64
Kolambugan: 462
Koronadal: 475
Kulaman people: 477

L
La Carlota City: 399
La Castellana: 399
Lagawe: 243
Lagayan: 264
Laguna Province: 161-174
Lake Abuyok: 521
Lake Balinsasayao: 403
Lake Buhi: 300
Lake Bulusan: 313
Lake Danao: 403
Lake Danao National Park: 367
Lake Lanao: 464
Lake Nauja: 384
Lake Sebu: 475-478
La Laguna Beach: 382
Lamitan: 492
Lamon Bay: 292
Lanao del Norte: 459-460
La Naval de Manila: 68
language: 45-47
Lantern Festival: 183
Lanzones Festival: 451
Laoag City: 266-268
Laoag Museum: 268
Laoag River: 268
Laoang: 430
La Paz: 412
La Paz Sand Dunes: 268
Lasema: 424
Las Pinas: 130
La Trinidad: 219-220
La Union Province: 252-255
Lazi: 435
Legaspi City: 303-305

Legazpi, Miguel Lopez de: 15-17
Lemery: 157
Leon: 413
Leon Apacible Museum and Library: 158
Leyte: 358-369
Leyte National Park: 367
Libacao: 423
lighthouses: 375
Ligpo Island: 157
Lilio: 168
Liliw: 168
Liloan: 352, 369
Limasawa: 368-369
Liminancong: 517
Linapacan Island: 521
Lingayen: 206
Lipa City: 160-161
Loay: 327
Locsin: 304
Looc: 426
Los Banos: 171-172
Lubang Islands: 387-388
Lubuagan: 245-246
Lucap: 204-205
Lucban: 290
Lucena City: 290-291
luggage: 106-108
Luisiana: 166
Lumban: 163
Luna: 255
Luna, Juan: 265
Lusuac Water Spring: 264
Luzon: Central Plain 178-209; Cordillera 210-248; Northeast Luzon 275-286; Northwest Coast 249-274; Southern Luzon 287-314

M
Maasin: 368
Mabalacat: 186
Mabini Shrine and Museum: 160
Mablaran Falls: 426
Macahambus Caves: 458
MacArthur, Douglas: 22-24
Mactan Island: 350-351
Madja-as Mountain: 419
magbabarang: 434
Magellan, Ferdinand: 15-16
Magellan's Cross: 345
Magsaysay Island: 456
Magsingal: 261

Maguindanao people: 476-477, 480
Mahagnao Volcano National Park: 368
Mahinog: 456
mail: 96-97
Mainit: 231
Mainit Hot Springs: 160
Majayjay: 167
Makati: 126-128
Makiling-Banahaw Geothermal Project (MAKBAN): 170
Makinit Hot Springs: 521
Malacanang Palace: 123-124
Malamawi Island: 492
Malapascua Island: 353-354
malaria: 101-102
Malatapay: 404
Malate: 113-115, 134-139
Malaybalay: 458-459
Maligcong Rice Terraces: 229-231
Malilipot: 306
Malinta Tunnel: 132
Malolos: 181
Mambajao: 452-453
Mamburao: 387
Mambusao: 421
Manaoag: 207
Manapla: 398
Mandaue City: 349
Mandaya people: 468-469
Mangyan people: 378
Manila: 109-147
Manila Zoo: 113
Manito: 308
Manobo people: 477
Mansaka people: 468-469
Mansalay: 385
Manuk Manka Island: 495
maps: 92-93
Maragondon: 150-151
Maranao people: 462, 463
Marawi City: 462-464
marble: 426
Marcos, Ferdinand: 25-27, 265
Marcos Hall of Justice: 266-268
Marcos Museum: 268
Maria Cristina Falls: 461-462
Maribojoc: 328
Maricaban Island: 159
Marikina: 129
Marinduque: 370-373

Maripipi Island: 366
Mariveles: 200-201
Masbate: 373-376
Masinloc: 197
MassKara Festival: 68, 393-395
Matabungkay: 156-157
Matanglag: 240-241
Mateo Hot and Cold Spring: 314
Matnog: 314
Mauban: 290
Mayan: 274
Mayoyao: 243
Mayon Volcano: 305
Medano Island: 454
Medio Island: 382
Mendiola Bridge: 124
Mercedes: 294
Mestizo people: 40
metric system: 96, inside back cover
Metropolitan Museum (Manila): 113
Mexico: 185
Miagao: 413-414
Milaor: 298
Minalin: 185
Mindanao State University: 463
Mindoro: 376-388
Minglanilla: 354
miniature golf: 189
Moalboal: 356-358
Mohicap Lake: 170
Molo: 412-413
Monastery-Museum: 121-122
money: 94-95
monkey-eating eagle: 10
Montalban: 180
Moriones Festival: 372
Morong (Rizal Province): 176
Morong (Bataan Peninsula): 201
mountain climbing: 54-55; *see also specific
    mountain*
Mountain Province: 225-236
Mount Apo: 473-474
Mount Arayat National Park: 192
Mount Banahaw: 171
Mount Bulusan: 312
Mount Data: 225
Mount Iriga: 300
Mount Kanlaon: 403-404
Mount Makiling: 172-173
Mount Malindang: 465

Mount Pinatubo: 179, 190-191
Mount Pulog: 224
Mount Samat: 201
movies filmed in Philippines: 61
mummies: 223
Mundo people: 421-422
murals: 398
Museo Iloilo: 411
Museo Iloko: 253
Museo It Aklan: 422
Museo ng Buhay Pilipino: 129
Museum of Ilocano Heritage: 261
Museum of Philippine and International Dolls:
    126
Museum of Philippine Art: 115
museums: Abra Museum 263; Aga Khan
    Museum of Islamic Arts 463; Aguinaldo
    Museum 130; Araneta Museum 399;
    Archdiocesan Museum 421; Ayala Museum
    128; Ayala Museum and Library 260;
    Baguio-Mountain Province Museum 218;
    Bicol Folkloric Museum 299-300; Bolinao
    Museum 206; Carfel Seashell Museum 113;
    Central Bank Money Museum 113;
    Corregidor Pacific War museum 132;
    Crisologo Museum 258-260; Don Lorenzo
    Diaz Memorial Museum 253; Escudero
    Museum 170; Excavation Museum 381;
    Laoag Museum 268; Leon Apacible
    Museum and Library 158; Mabini Shrine
    and Museum 160; Marcos Museum 268;
    Metropolitan Museum (Manila) 113;
    Monastery-Museum 121-122; Museo Iloilo
    411; Museo Iloko 253; Museo It Aklan 422;
    Museo ng Buhay Pilipino 129; Museum of
    Ilocano Heritage 261; Museum of Philippine
    and International Dolls 126; Museum of
    Philippine Art 115; National Museum
    (Manila) 117; National Museum (Palawan)
    510; Northern Mindanao Regional Museum
    449; Philippine Museum of Ethnology 126;
    Rizaliana Museum 346; Rizal Museum 120;
    Santo Niño Shrine and Heritage Museum
    364; Silliman University anthropology
    museum 400; Sulu Ethnological Museum
    493; Tawi-Tawi Ethnological Museum 495
mushrooms: 235
music: 61-62
Muslim people: 15, 36-37, 500
mysticism: 44

N

Naasag: 454
Nabas: 424
Naga: 354
Naga City: 295-298
Nagarao Island: 416
Nagcarlan: 168-169
Nagtabon Beach: 512
Naguilian: 254
Naguilian Road: 219
Narvacan: 257-258
Nasidman: 415
Nasugbu: 155-156
National Arts Center of the Philippines: 173
National Botanical Gardens: 173
National Museum (Manila): 117
National Museum (Palawan): 510
natural bridge: 365
Naujan: 384
Nayong Pilipino Park: 126
Negrito people: 39-40
Negros: 389-404
New People's Army (NPA): 25, 32, 104-105, 441
New Washington: 423
nightclubs: *see specific destination*
Nonoc Island: 448
Northern Mindanao Regional Museum: 449
Novaliches: 179-180
Nueva Ecija Province: 208-209
Nueva Valencia: 416
Nueva Vizcaya Province: 277-278
Numancia: 423

O

Obando: 180
Odiongag: 426
Olongapo: 194-196
Olango Island: 351-352
orchids: 393
organ: 130
Ormoc City: 366-367
Oroquieta City: 465-466
Oslob: 354
Oton: 413
Ozamiz City: 465

P

Pacijan Island: 355
packing: 106-108
Paco Park: 115
Paete: 162-163
Pagadian City: 486
Pagbilao Islands: 291
Pagsanjan: 163-166
Pahiyas: 66, 290
Pakil: 162
Palanan: 282
Pala'wan people: 500
Palakpakin Lake: 169-170
Palapag: 431
Palaspas Falls: 209
Palauig: 197
Palawan: 498-522
Palayan City: 208
Palimpinon Falls and Hot Springs: 403
Palo: 365-366
Paluan: 387
Pamilacan Island: 326
Pampanga Province: 182-191
Panaon island: 369
Panay: 404-424
Pan-ay: 420-421
Pandi: 181
Pandin Lake: 169
Pangasinan Province: 202-208
Panglao Island: 323-324
Pangutaran Islands: 494
Panhulugan Island: 433
Paoay: 265
Paoay Lake National Park: 265-266
Paombong: 181
parachuting: 189
Paranaque: 126
Paraw Regatta: 409

NATIONAL PARKS

Biak-Na-Bato: 182
Bulabog Putian: 415
Callao Caves: 283
Lake Danao: 367
Leyte: 367
Mahagnao Volcano: 368
Mount Arayat: 192
Paoay Lake: 265-266
Quezon National Park: 292-293
Saint Paul Subterranean: 513
Sohoton: 433-434
Sohoton Natural Bridge: 365
Tabon Caves: 510
Tongonan Hot Springs: 367

Parks and Wildlife Nature Center: 129
parks: Baguio City 218; Bohol 323
Pasay City: 126
passport agencies: 91
Pasungay Festival: 414
Paul de la Gironiere Hacienda: 176-177
Pavia: 414
Penafrancia Festival: 297
penal colony: 386
Pescador Island: 357
Philippine-American War: 22
Philippine eagle: 10
Philippine Museum of Ethnology: 126
photography: 51
Piat: 284
Pidigan: 262
Pilar: 421
Pili: 299
Pilipino language: 47
Pinamalayan: 384
Pinnacle Rock 520
plantlife: 9-10
Plaridel: 181-182
Plaza Roma: 120
Plaza San Luis: 122
Poitan: 241
Polillo Islands: 293
Ponson Island: 355
population: 34-40
Poro Island: 355
Poro Point Peninsula: 253-254
Port Barton: 513-514
postal service: 96-97
Pototan: 414-415
Price Mansion: 364
prostitution: 106
publications: 92-94
Puerta Real: 122
Puerto Galera: 380-383
Puerto Princesa: 504-507
Pugaro-Suit Island Beach: 207
Puka Shell Beach: 331
Pula: 242
Pulilan: 182
Punta Cruz Watchtower: 323
Punta Nasog: 418
Putsan: 308

QR
Quezon (Palawan): 508-510
Quezon City: 129
Quezon National Park: 292-293

Quezon Province: 288-293
Quiapo: 123
Quipot Cave: 421
Quirino Province: 278
radio stations: 94
Raele: 274
rail travel: 89-90; see also specific destination
rain: 7
rainforests: 70
Ramon: 280-281
Ramos, Fidel: 28-29
Rapu-Rapu Island: 308
recreation: 54-60
Red Beach: 365
Refugio's Island: 399
religion: 41-44
restaurants: see specific destination
rice terraces: 237
Rio Hondo: 483
Rio Tuba: 510
River Festival: 163, 180
Rizal Beach: 313
Rizal House: 173-174
Rizaliana Museum: 346
Rizal, José: 20-21, 173-174
Rizal Museum: 120
Rizal Park: 115-117
Rizal Province: 174-177
Rizal Shrine: 466
Romblon Island: 424-426
round-the-world airfares: 78
Roxas (Palawan): 515-516
Roxas City (Mindoro): 384-385
Roxas City (Panay): 420

S
Sabang: 512-513
Sabang Beach: 382
Sabtang: 273
Saclag Settlements Farm School: 383
Sacred Mountain: 463-464
Sadanga: 229
safety: 102-106
Sagada: 232-234
Sagay: 398-399
St. Joseph the Worker Chapel mural: 398
Saint Paul Subterranean National Park: 513
St. Williams Cathedral: 266
Salinas: 278
Samales Islands: 494
Samal Island: 472-473
Samal people: 489-490

Samar: 428-434
Samoki: 229
Sampaloc Lake: 169
San Agustin: 427
San Antonio: 382
San Beda College: 124
San Carlos City (Luzon): 208
San Carlos City (Visayas): 399
San Fabian: 207
San Fernando (Luzon-Central Plain): 183-185
San Fernando (Northwest Luzon): 254-255
San Fernando (Visayas): 375-376
San Francisco: 255
San Ildefonso: 182
San Isidro Beach: 383
San Joaquin: 414
San Jose (Mindanao): 472
San Jose (Visayas): 385-386
San Jose City (Luzon): 209
San Jose de Buenavista: 417-418
San Jose del Monte: 181
San Jose galleon: 388
San Juan: 255, 261
San Juanico Bridge: 365
San Luis: 157
San Marcelino Lake: 194
San Miguel: 182
San Miguel Brewery: 347
San Nicolas: 266
San Pablo City: 169
San Rafael: 515
San Sebastian Church: 124
Santa Ana: 128-129
Santa Cruz (Laguna Province): 166
Santa Cruz (Visayas): 373
Santacruzan: 66-67
Santa Cruz Islands (Mindanao): 485
Santadar: 354-355
Santa Fe: 426
Santa Lucia: 257
Santa Maria: 257
Santa Victoria Caves: 282
Santiago (Ilocos Sur Province): 257
Santiago (Aurora Province): 280
Santo Domingo: 306
Santo Niño Church: 363
Santo Niño Shrine and Heritage Museum: 364
Santo Niño Spring: 455
San Vicente (Luzon): 284-285
San Vicente (Palawan): 514
Sarao Jeepney Factory: 130
Sariaya: 289-290

Sarrat: 268
scuba diving: *see* diving
seasons: 3-8
Sebaste: 419
Semirara Islands: 419-420
Seven Lakes of San Pablo: 169-170
ship travel: 86-88; *see also specific destination*
shopping: 71-72; *see also specific destination*
Shrine of Nuestra Señora de Visitacion: 284
Shrine of the Black Nazarene: 294
Siargao Island: 447-448
Siasi-Tapul Islands: 494
Sibale Island: 448
Sibuyan: 427
Sicogon: 416-417
Siete Pecados Islands: 521
sightseeing highlights: 56-57; Visayas 316-317
Silay City: 397
Silliman University: 400-402
Simara: 427
Simmimbaan shrine: 255
Simunul: 495
Sinking Bell Tower: 266
Sinulog Festival: 344, 400
Siquijor: 434-436
Sitangkai: 496
snakes: 353
snorkeling: Apo Reef 386-387; Balabac Island and vicininty 511; Bolinao vicinity 205-206; Boracay 331; Calamian Islands 520-522; Honda Bay 507; Liloan 369; Lubang Islands 387-388; Moalboal 356-357; Nagtabon Beach 512; Olango Island 351; Pamilacan Island 326; Panglao Island 323; Sagay 398-399; Sangasiapu 495; Santa Sofia Beach 368; Sumilon Island 355; Tres Reyes Island 371; Zambales Coastline 197; Zamboanguita 404
social conduct: 47-53, 75-76
Socorro: 449
Sogod: 352
Sogod Bay: 369
Sohoton Lagoon: 449
Sohoton National Park: 433-434
Sohoton Natural Bridge National Park: 365
Solano: 278
Sorsogon Province: 312-314
Southeast Asian Fisheries Development Center: 413
Soyu Road: 234

Spanish colonization: 15-21
steam trains: 395
Subic Bay: 194, 196-197
Subok Festival: 176
sugar: 389, 391
Suluan Island: 432
Sulu Archipelago: 487-497
Sulu Ethnological Museum: 493
Sumilon Island (Cebu): 355
Sumilon Island (Negros): 403
Sun Moon Beach: 201
Surallah: 475
surfing: 58-59; Siargao Island 447
Surigao City: 446
swimming: Bacolod area 397; Biliran Island 366; Danao City 352; Dipolog 466; Iwahig Prison and Penal Colony 507-508; Kuting Beach 368; Naga City area 298; Puerto Princesa 506; Sebaste 419; Ticao Island 375-376
swimming pools: Agoo 253; Bohol area 327-328; Paoay Lake 266

T
Taal City: 157-158
Taal Lake: 151-154
Taal Volcano: 152-153
Tabaco: 306-307
Tablas Island: 42424, 426-427
Tabon Caves: 510
Tabuk: 247-248
Tacloban: 362-365
Tagaytay City: 151-152
Tagbanua people: 500
Tagbilaran City: 322-323
Taggat: 285
Tagudin: 256
Takal Beach: 298-299
Talaga: 160
Talikud Island: 473
Talipanan: 383
Talisay (Cavite Province): 153-54
Talisay (Cebu): 354
Talisay (Negros): 397
Taluksangay: 486
Tam-An: 240
tamaraw: 386
Tamlagun Island: 510
Tanauan: 160
Tanay: 176
Tangalan: 423
tang-alap: 434

Tangub Hot Springs: 455
Taoism: 44
Tarlac Province: 201-202
tarsiers: 323
Tasaday people: 476
Tausug people: 488-489
Tau't Batu people: 500
Tawi-Tawi: 494-497
Tawi-Tawi Ethnological Museum: 495
taxis: 90
Tayabas: 290
Taytay: 516-517
T'boli people: 478-479
telephone: 97
television stations: 94
tennis: Agoo 253; Gasan 371; Paoay Lake 266
Ternate: 150-151
theme parks: Enchanted Kingdom 174
Three Kings' Day: 63
Ticao Island: 375-376
Tigbauan: 413
Tigman: 508
Tiji Tiji Islands: 495
Timbac Caves: 222
time: 96
Tinagong Dagat: 427
Tinagong Dagat Lake: 400
Tingguian people: 263
tipping: 51-52
Tirad Pass: 257
Tiruray people: 477
Tiwi: 307-308
Tiwi Hot Springs: 307-308
Toledo City: 355
Tolosa: 367
Tongonan Hot Springs National Park: 367
Tontonon Falls: 323
Torogon Waterfall: 375
tourism: 33-34; information centers 91-93
train travel: 89-90; *see also specific destination*

TREKKING

general information: 54-55
Angeles City: 189
Batad: 242-243
Cordillera: 232, 234-236
Lake Sebu: 475-476
San Rafael: 515

transportation: 76-91; *see also specific destination*
traveler's checks: 94-95
travel insurance: 98-100
Tres Reyes Islands: 371
tricycles: 90
Tuao: 283-284
Tubbataha Reefs: 511-512
Tubigon: 328
Tubod: 462
Tucucan: 229
Tugaya: 464
Tugdan: 426
Tuguegarao: 282-283
Tumauini: 281-282
Turrumba: 66
Turrumba Festival: 162
Turtle Islands: 497
Tuwasan Falls: 455
typhoons: 7

UV
Ubay: 328
Ubo people: 479
Ulugan Bay: 512
Underground River: 513
universities: Cebu City 346; Mindanao State, Marawi City 463; Santo Tomas, Manila 124-126; Silliman 400-402; University of the Philippines 172; Xavier 456
University of Santo Tomas: 124-126
University of the Philippines: 172
Urdaneta: 203-204
Ursula Island: 510-511
vaccinations: 98
Valencia: 403
Verde Island: 159
Victorias: 397-398
Vietnamese Refugee Center: 504
Vigan City: 258-261
Villa Escudero: 170-171
Virac: 309-311
visas: 91
Visayas Islands: 315-436
vocabulary: 45-47
volcanoes: 3; Babuyan Islands 285-286; Camiguin Island 451; Camotes Islands 355; Hibok-Hibok 454; Kanleon 399; Mahagnao 368; Mount Iriga 300; Mount Kanlaon 403-404; Mayon 305

WATERFALLS

Baguio City: 220
Bayagnan Island: 448
Busay Falls: 306
Inambacan: 328
Jawili Falls: 423
Katibawasan: Falls 453
Kawasan: 358
Lila: 327
Linawan: 426
Maria Cristina: 461-462
Pagsanjan: 163-164
Palaspas Falls: 209
Palimpinon: 403
Torogon: 375
Tuwasan: 455

W
water buffalo: 386
water: 75
Wawa dam: 180
weather: 3-8
weaving: 255
what to take: 106-108
White Beach: 383
White Island (Mindanao): 454
White Island (Visayas): 386
wildlife sanctuaries: 404
windsurfing: Agoo 253; Boracay 329-331
witchcraft: 434
women traveling alone: 51
woodcarving: Paete 163
World War II: 22-24, 216-217, 237-238, 276, 360, 377, 439-440

XYZ
Xavier University: 456
Yakan people: 489
Yambo Lake: 169
Ybanag people: 282
Zambales Province: 192-198
Zamboanga: 481-485
Zamboanga Hermosa Festival: 483
Zamboanguita: 404
Zapote: 130
zoos: Cebu City 347; Manila 113; Parks and Wildlife Nature Center (Manila) 129

READER SURVEY

Knowing a bit about you and your travel experiences will help me improve this book for the next edition. Please take a few minutes to complete this form and share your tips with the next traveler. Remember to send along corrected copies of photocopied maps from this book and business cards collected from your favorite hotels and restaurants. All contributors will be acknowledged in the next edition.

The author also appreciates correspondence from expatriates living in Philippines and other local residents with special insight into travel conditions. Research correspondents are also needed to help update several Moon Handbooks to destinations in Southeast Asia. You may write to Moon Publications at the address below or contact the author directly via e-mail: cparkes@moon.com.

Send the following survey to:

Carl Parkes/Reader Survey
Philippines Handbook
Moon Publications
5855 Beaudry St.
Emeryville, CA 94608
USA

Date of Letter:_____

1. Gender: ☐ male ☐ female

2. Age: ☐ under 25 ☐ 25-30 ☐ 31-35 ☐ 36-40
☐ 41-50 ☐ 51+

3. Status: ☐ single ☐ married

4. Income: ☐ $20K ☐ $20-30K ☐ $30-40K ☐ $40-50K
☐ $50K+

5. Occupation: _____

6. Education: ☐ high school ☐ some college ☐ college grad ☐ post grad

7. Travel style: ☐ budget ☐ moderate ☐ luxury

8. Vacations: ☐ once yearly ☐ twice yearly ☐ 3+ yearly

9. Why do you travel? _____

_____

10. What's best about travel? _____

_____

11. What's worst about travel? _____

_____

12. This Journey:

Length of time: _____

   Enough time? _____

Countries visited: _____

Countries planned for next visit: _____

Season: _____

How was the weather? _____

Travel companions? _____

Do you prefer solo travel or with companions? _____

Purpose of Trip?

  a. ☐ Pleasure   b. ☐ Study   c. ☐ Work   d. ☐ Volunteer   e. ☐ Hanging out

Main Activities?

  a. ☐ Sights   b. ☐ Culture   c. ☐ Beaches and outdoor activities

  d. ☐ Meeting people   e. ☐ Nightlife and entertainment

  f. ☐ Food and shopping

Main regions? Please give specific locations:

  a. ☐ Cities _____

  b. ☐ Smaller towns _____

  c. ☐ Beaches and islands _____

  d. ☐ Mountains _____

Primary modes of transportation? _____

Expenses:

  a. Total: _____

  b. Average daily expenses: _____

    c. Average hotel price: _____

    d. Average meal price: _____

    e. Total airfare: _____

    f. Shopping expenses: _____

Unexpected encounters: _____

13. Favorites:

  a. Countries: _____

_____

_____

  b. Hotels and guesthouses (include address, price, description): _____

_____

_____

  c. Restaurants (address, price range, favorite dishes): _____

_____

_____

  d. Airline: _____

_____

_____

  e. Cuisine: _____

_____

_____

  f. Nightspots: _____

_____

_____

  g. Cultural events: _____

_____

_____

  h. Outdoor adventures: _____

_____

_____

  i. Temples or historical sites: _____

_____

_____

  j. Beaches: _____

_____

_____

k. People: _____

_____

14. This Book:

Where did you buy this book? _____

Why did you select Moon Publications? _____

What other Moon Handbooks have you used? _____

What other guidebooks have you used? _____

What is your favorite series of guides? _____

How does this book compare with other guides? _____

Your opinion about the following:

a. Hotel listings (how accurate?) _____

b. Restaurants _____

c. Background information _____

d. Maps _____

e. Charts _____

f. Photography _____

g. Writer's attitude _____

h. Price of this book _____

i. Distribution _____

j. Design and layout _____

How accurate did you find the following information?

a. Hotel prices _____

b. Restaurant recommendations_____

c. Maps _____

d. Charts _____

e. Writer's opinions _____

Favorite introduction section (history, government, etc., none) _____

Did you use the hotel charts? _____

Weakest points of this book: _____

Suggestions for improvements: _____

How does this book compare with the competition?_____

15. Name and Address

_____

_____

_____

Thanks for your help!

ABOUT THE AUTHOR

Carl Parkes, author of *Southeast Asia Handbook, Thailand Handbook,* and *Singapore Handbook,* was born into an American Air Force family and spent his childhood in California, Nebraska, Alabama, and Japan, where his love of Asia first began. After graduating from the University of California at Santa Barbara, Carl traveled throughout Europe and later returned to work in Hawaii, Lake Tahoe, Aspen, Salt Lake City, and finally, San Francisco.

But childhood memories of Asia continued to pull him to the East. After a 12-month journey across Asia, Carl returned to San Francisco to work as a stockbroker and plan his escape from the nine-to-five world. A chance encounter in Singapore with publisher Bill Dalton offered a more intriguing option: to research and write a travel guidebook to Southeast Asia—one that addressed more travel practicalities by exploring the region's rich culture and history.

Carl fervently believes that travel is an immensely rewarding undertaking that affirms the basic truths of life. "Travel is much more than just monuments and ruins. It's an opportunity to reach out and discover what's best about the world. Travel enriches our lives, spreads prosperity, dissolves political barriers, promotes international peace, and brings excitement and change to our lives."

Carl also believes in the importance of political, economic, and environmental issues. "Historical sites and beaches make for wonderful memories, but national agendas such as human rights and rainforest preservation are just as fascinating in their own right. Understanding the contemporary scene enriches travel experiences and opens avenues rarely explored by the visitor."

In addition to his guidebooks from Moon, Carl also writes for Fodor's *Worldview Systems, PATA Travel News America, Weissmann Travel Reports,* and *Pacific Rim News Service.* Carl has also updated portions of *Indonesia Handbook,* appeared on CNN and the Travel Channel with Arthur Frommer, and lectured onboard *Pearl, Princess, Renaissance,* and *Radisson Seven Seas* cruise lines. In 1995, Carl won the Lowell Thomas Award from the Society of American Travel Writers in the travel guidebook category for his *Southeast Asia Handbook.*

Besides travel writing, Carl enjoys straight-ahead jazz, photography, Anchor Steam beer, opera, art openings, poetry readings, and samba nightclubs in his favorite city of San Francisco. Future plans include more books on his favorite destinations in Southeast Asia.

MOON TRAVEL HANDBOOKS

LOSE YOURSELF IN THE EXPERIENCE, NOT THE CROWD

For more than 25 years, Moon Travel Handbooks have been the guidebooks of choice for adventurous travelers. Our award-winning Handbook series provides focused, comprehensive coverage of distinct destinations all over the world. Each Handbook is like an entire bookcase of cultural insight and introductory information in one portable volume. Our goal at Moon is to give travelers all the background and practical information they'll need for an extraordinary travel experience.

The following pages include a complete list of Handbooks, covering North America and Hawaii, Mexico, Latin America and the Caribbean, and Asia and the Pacific. To purchase Moon Travel Handbooks, check your local bookstore or order C/o Publishers Group West, Attn: Order Department, 1700 Fourth St., Berkeley, CA 94710, or fax to (510) 528-3444.

"An in-depth dunk into the land, the people and their history, arts, and politics."
—*Student Travels*

"I consider these books to be superior to Lonely Planet. When Moon produces a book it is more humorous, incisive, and off-beat."
—*Toronto Sun*

"Outdoor enthusiasts gravitate to the well-written Moon Travel Handbooks. In addition to politically correct historic and cultural features, the series focuses on flora, fauna and outdoor recreation. Maps and meticulous directions also are a trademark of Moon guides."
—*Houston Chronicle*

"Moon [Travel Handbooks] . . . bring a healthy respect to the places they investigate. Best of all, they provide a host of odd nuggets that give a place texture and prod the wary traveler from the beaten path. The finest are written with such care and insight they deserve listing as literature."
—*American Geographical Society*

"Moon Travel Handbooks offer in-depth historical essays and useful maps, enhanced by a sense of humor and a neat, compact format."
—*Swing*

"Perfect for the more adventurous, these are long on history, sightseeing and nitty-gritty information and very price-specific."
—*Columbus Dispatch*

"Moon guides manage to be comprehensive and countercultural at the same time . . . Handbooks are packed with maps, photographs, drawings, and sidebars that constitute a college-level introduction to each country's history, culture, people, and crafts."
—*National Geographic Traveler*

"Few travel guides do a better job helping travelers create their own itineraries than the Moon Travel Handbook series. The authors have a knack for homing in on the essentials."
—Colorado Springs *Gazette Telegraph*

MEXICO

"These books will delight the armchair traveler, aid the undecided person in selecting a destination, and guide the seasoned road warrior looking for lesser-known hideaways."

—*Mexican Meanderings* Newsletter

"From tourist traps to off-the-beaten track hideaways, these guides offer consistent, accurate details without pretension."

—*Foreign Service Journal*

Archaeological Mexico	**$19.95**
Andrew Coe	420 pages, 27 maps
Baja Handbook	**$16.95**
Joe Cummings	540 pages, 46 maps
Cabo Handbook	**$14.95**
Joe Cummings	270 pages, 17 maps
Cancún Handbook	**$14.95**
Chicki Mallan	240 pages, 25 maps
Colonial Mexico	**$18.95**
Chicki Mallan	400 pages, 38 maps
Mexico Handbook	**$21.95**
Joe Cummings and Chicki Mallan	1,200 pages, 201 maps
Northern Mexico Handbook	**$17.95**
Joe Cummings	610 pages, 69 maps
Pacific Mexico Handbook	**$17.95**
Bruce Whipperman	580 pages, 68 maps
Puerto Vallarta Handbook	**$14.95**
Bruce Whipperman	330 pages, 36 maps
Yucatán Handbook	**$16.95**
Chicki Mallan	400 pages, 52 maps

"Beyond question, the most comprehensive Mexican resources available for those who prefer deep travel to shallow tourism. But don't worry, the fiesta-fun stuff's all here too."

—*New York Daily News*

LATIN AMERICA
AND THE CARIBBEAN

"Solidly packed with practical information and full of significant cultural asides that will enlighten you on the whys and wherefores of things you might easily see but not easily grasp."

—Boston Globe

Belize Handbook	**$15.95**
Chicki Mallan and Patti Lange	390 pages, 45 maps
Caribbean Vacations	**$18.95**
Karl Luntta	910 pages, 64 maps
Costa Rica Handbook	**$19.95**
Christopher P. Baker	780 pages, 73 maps
Cuba Handbook	**$19.95**
Christopher P. Baker	740 pages, 70 maps
Dominican Republic Handbook	**$15.95**
Gaylord Dold	420 pages, 24 maps
Ecuador Handbook	**$16.95**
Julian Smith	450 pages, 43 maps
Honduras Handbook	**$15.95**
Chris Humphrey	330 pages, 40 maps
Jamaica Handbook	**$15.95**
Karl Luntta	330 pages, 17 maps
Virgin Islands Handbook	**$13.95**
Karl Luntta	220 pages, 19 maps

NORTH AMERICA AND HAWAII

"These domestic guides convey the same sense of exoticism that their foreign counterparts do, making home-country travel seem like far-flung adventure."

—Sierra Magazine

Alaska-Yukon Handbook	**$17.95**
Deke Castleman and Don Pitcher	530 pages, 92 maps
Alberta and the Northwest Territories Handbook	**$18.95**
Andrew Hempstead	520 pages, 79 maps
Arizona Handbook	**$18.95**
Bill Weir	600 pages, 36 maps
Atlantic Canada Handbook	**$18.95**
Mark Morris	490 pages, 60 maps
Big Island of Hawaii Handbook	**$15.95**
J.D. Bisignani	390 pages, 25 maps
Boston Handbook	**$13.95**
Jeff Perk	200 pages, 20 maps
British Columbia Handbook	**$16.95**
Jane King and Andrew Hempstead	430 pages, 69 maps

Canadian Rockies Handbook	**$14.95**
Andrew Hempstead	220 pages, 22 maps
Colorado Handbook	**$17.95**
Stephen Metzger	480 pages, 46 maps
Georgia Handbook	**$17.95**
Kap Stann	380 pages, 44 maps
Grand Canyon Handbook	**$14.95**
Bill Weir	220 pages, 10 maps
Hawaii Handbook	**$19.95**
J.D. Bisignani	1,030 pages, 88 maps
Honolulu-Waikiki Handbook	**$14.95**
J.D. Bisignani	360 pages, 20 maps
Idaho Handbook	**$18.95**
Don Root	610 pages, 42 maps
Kauai Handbook	**$15.95**
J.D. Bisignani	320 pages, 23 maps
Los Angeles Handbook	**$16.95**
Kim Weir	370 pages, 15 maps
Maine Handbook	**$18.95**
Kathleen M. Brandes	660 pages, 27 maps
Massachusetts Handbook	**$18.95**
Jeff Perk	600 pages, 23 maps
Maui Handbook	**$15.95**
J.D. Bisignani	450 pages, 37 maps
Michigan Handbook	**$15.95**
Tina Lassen	360 pages, 32 maps
Montana Handbook	**$17.95**
Judy Jewell and W.C. McRae	490 pages, 52 maps
Nevada Handbook	**$18.95**
Deke Castleman	530 pages, 40 maps
New Hampshire Handbook	**$18.95**
Steve Lantos	500 pages, 18 maps
New Mexico Handbook	**$15.95**
Stephen Metzger	360 pages, 47 maps
New York Handbook	**$19.95**
Christiane Bird	780 pages, 95 maps
New York City Handbook	**$13.95**
Christiane Bird	300 pages, 20 maps
North Carolina Handbook	**$14.95**
Rob Hirtz and Jenny Daughtry Hirtz	320 pages, 27 maps
Northern California Handbook	**$19.95**
Kim Weir	800 pages, 50 maps
Ohio Handbook	**$15.95**
David K. Wright	340 pages, 18 maps
Oregon Handbook	**$17.95**
Stuart Warren and Ted Long Ishikawa	590 pages, 34 maps

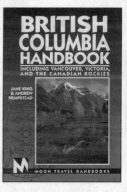

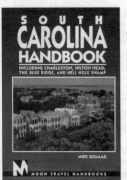

Pennsylvania Handbook	$18.95
Joanne Miller	448 pages, 40 maps
Road Trip USA	**$24.00**
Jamie Jensen	940 pages, 175 maps
Road Trip USA Getaways: Chicago	**$9.95**
	60 pages, 1 map
Road Trip USA Getaways: Seattle	**$9.95**
	60 pages, 1 map
Santa Fe-Taos Handbook	**$13.95**
Stephen Metzger	160 pages, 13 maps
South Carolina Handbook	**$16.95**
Mike Sigalas	400 pages, 20 maps
Southern California Handbook	**$19.95**
Kim Weir	720 pages, 26 maps
Tennessee Handbook	**$17.95**
Jeff Bradley	530 pages, 42 maps
Texas Handbook	**$18.95**
Joe Cummings	690 pages, 70 maps
Utah Handbook	**$17.95**
Bill Weir and W.C. McRae	490 pages, 40 maps
Virginia Handbook	**$15.95**
Julian Smith	410 pages, 37 maps
Washington Handbook	**$19.95**
Don Pitcher	840 pages, 111 maps
Wisconsin Handbook	**$18.95**
Thomas Huhti	590 pages, 69 maps
Wyoming Handbook	**$17.95**
Don Pitcher	610 pages, 80 maps

ASIA AND THE PACIFIC

"Scores of maps, detailed practical info down to business
hours of small-town libraries. You can't beat the Asian titles
for sheer heft. (The) series is sort of an American Lonely
Planet, with better writing but fewer titles. (The) individual
voice of researchers comes through."

—*Travel & Leisure*

Australia Handbook	**$21.95**
Marael Johnson, Andrew Hempstead,	
and Nadina Purdon	940 pages, 141 maps
Bali Handbook	**$19.95**
Bill Dalton	750 pages, 54 maps
Fiji Islands Handbook	**$14.95**
David Stanley	350 pages, 42 maps
Hong Kong Handbook	**$16.95**
Kerry Moran	378 pages, 49 maps

| Indonesia Handbook | $25.00 |
| Bill Dalton | 1,380 pages, 249 maps |

| Micronesia Handbook | $16.95 |
| Neil M. Levy | 340 pages, 70 maps |

| Nepal Handbook | $18.95 |
| Kerry Moran | 490 pages, 51 maps |

| New Zealand Handbook | $19.95 |
| Jane King | 620 pages, 81 maps |

| Outback Australia Handbook | $18.95 |
| Marael Johnson | 450 pages, 57 maps |

| Philippines Handbook | $17.95 |
| Peter Harper and Laurie Fullerton | 670 pages, 116 maps |

| Singapore Handbook | $15.95 |
| Carl Parkes | 350 pages, 29 maps |

| South Korea Handbook | $19.95 |
| Robert Nilsen | 820 pages, 141 maps |

| South Pacific Handbook | $24.00 |
| David Stanley | 920 pages, 147 maps |

| Southeast Asia Handbook | $21.95 |
| Carl Parkes | 1,080 pages, 204 maps |

| Tahiti Handbook | $15.95 |
| David Stanley | 450 pages, 51 maps |

| Thailand Handbook | $19.95 |
| Carl Parkes | 860 pages, 142 maps |

| Vietnam, Cambodia & Laos Handbook | $18.95 |
| Michael Buckley | 760 pages, 116 maps |

OTHER GREAT TITLES FROM MOON

"For hardy wanderers, few guides come more highly
recommended than the Handbooks. They include good
maps, steer clear of fluff and flackery, and offer plenty of
money-saving tips. They also give you the kind of
information that visitors to strange lands—on any budget—
need to survive."

—US News & World Report

| Moon Handbook | $10.00 |
| Carl Koppeschaar | 150 pages, 8 maps |

| The Practical Nomad: How to Travel Around the World | $17.95 |
| Edward Hasbrouck | 580 pages |

| Staying Healthy in Asia, Africa, and Latin America | $11.95 |
| Dirk Schroeder | 230 pages, 4 maps |

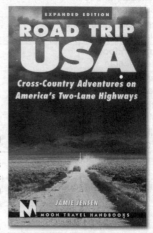

WHERE TO BUY MOON TRAVEL HANDBOOKS

BOOKSTORES AND LIBRARIES: Moon Travel Handbooks are distributed worldwide. Please contact our sales manager at info@moon.com for a list of wholesalers and distributors in your area.

TRAVELERS: We would like to have Moon Travel Handbooks available throughout the world. Please ask your bookstore to contact us for ordering information. If your bookstore will not order our guides for you, please contact us for a free catalog.

> Moon Travel Handbooks
> C/o Publishers Group West
> Attn: Order Department
> 1700 Fourth Street
> Berkeley, CA 94710
> fax: (510) 528-3444

IMPORTANT ORDERING INFORMATION

PRICES: All prices are subject to change. We always ship the most current edition. We will let you know if there is a price increase on the book you order.

SHIPPING AND HANDLING OPTIONS: Domestic UPS or USPS priority mail (allow 10 working days for delivery): $6.00 for the first item, $1.00 for each additional item.

UPS 2nd Day Air or Printed Airmail requires a special quote.

International Surface Bookrate 8-12 weeks delivery: $5.00 for the first item, $1.00 for each additional item. Note: We cannot guarantee international surface bookrate shipping. We recommend sending international orders via air mail, which requires a special quote.

FOREIGN ORDERS: Orders that originate outside the U.S.A. must be paid for with an international money order, a check in U.S. currency drawn on a major U.S. bank based in the U.S.A., or Visa, MasterCard, or American Express.

INTERNET ORDERS: Visit our site at: www.moon.com

ORDER FORM

Prices are subject to change without notice. Please check our Web site
at **www.moon.com** for current prices and editions.
(See important ordering information on preceding page.)

Name: _____ Date: _____

Street: _____

City: _____ Daytime Phone: _____

State or Country: _____ Zip Code: _____

QUANTITY	TITLE	PRICE

Taxable Total _____

Sales Tax in CA and NY _____

Shipping & Handling _____

TOTAL _____

Ship: ☐ UPS (no P.O. Boxes) ☐ Priority mail ☐ International surface mail

Ship to: ☐ address above ☐ other _____

_____

Make checks payable to: **PUBLISHERS GROUP WEST**, Attn: Order Department, 1700 Fourth St.,
Berkeley, CA 94710, or fax to (510) 528-3444. We accept Visa, MasterCard, or American Express.

To Order: Fax in your Visa, MasterCard, or American Express number, or send a written order
with your Visa, MasterCard, or American Express number and expiration date clearly written.

Card Number: ☐ **Visa** ☐ **MasterCard** ☐ **American Express**

☐ ☐ ☐ ☐ ☐ ☐ ☐ ☐ ☐ ☐ ☐ ☐ ☐ ☐ ☐ ☐

Exact Name on Card: _____

Expiration date: _____

Signature: _____

Daytime Phone: _____

U.S.~METRIC CONVERSION

1 inch = 2.54 centimeters (cm)
1 foot = .3048 meters (m)
1 yard = 0.914 meters
1 mile = 1.6093 kilometers (km)
1 km = .6214 miles
1 fathom = 1.8288 m
1 chain = 20.1168 m
1 furlong = 201.168 m
1 acre = .4047 hectares
1 sq km = 100 hectares
1 sq mile = 2.59 square km
1 ounce = 28.35 grams
1 pound = .4536 kilograms
1 short ton = .90718 metric ton
1 short ton = 2000 pounds
1 long ton = 1.016 metric tons
1 long ton = 2240 pounds
1 metric ton = 1000 kilograms
1 quart = .94635 liters
1 US gallon = 3.7854 liters
1 Imperial gallon = 4.5459 liters
1 nautical mile = 1.852 km

To compute celsius temperatures, subtract 32 from Fahrenheit and divide by 1.8. To go the other way, multiply celsius by 1.8 and add 32.

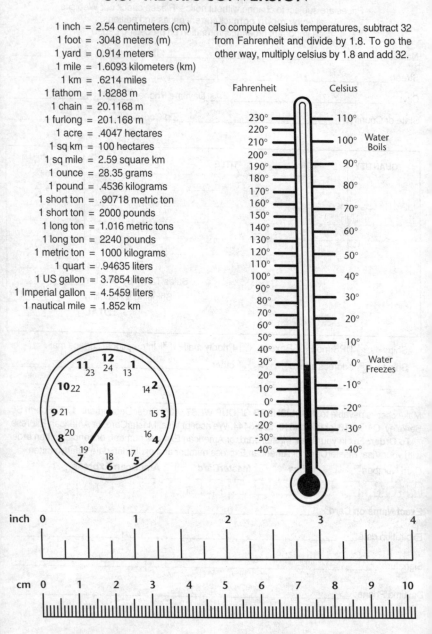

The Philippines is not only for sun, sea and sand lovers.
Discover the numerous attractions in all these places.